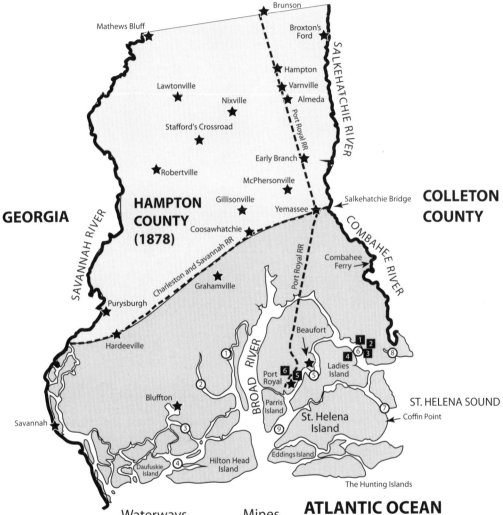

Rebellion, Reconstruction, and Redemption, 1861–1893

Rebellion, Reconstruction, and Redemption, 1861–1893

The History of Beaufort County, South Carolina, Volume 2

Stephen R. Wise and Lawrence S. Rowland
With Gerhard Spieler

Foreword by Alexander Moore

THE UNIVERSITY OF SOUTH CAROLINA PRESS

© 2015 University of South Carolina

Published by the University of South Carolina Press
Columbia, South Carolina 29208

www.sc.edu/uscpress

Manufactured in the United States of America

24 23 22 21 20 19 18 17 16 15   10 9 8 7 6 5 4 3 2 1

Library of Congress Cataloging-in-Publication Data can be found at http://catalog.loc.gov/.

ISBN: 978-1-61117-484-7 (hardcover or cloth)

This book was printed on a recycled paper with 30 percent postconsumer waste content.

Contents

Acknowledgments   vii
Foreword   xi
  Alexander Moore

Chapter 1   The Confederates Evacuate the Sea Islands   1
Chapter 2   Federal Occupation Begins   15
Chapter 3   The Northern Foothold Expands   32
Chapter 4   The Port Royal Experiment Begins   60
Chapter 5   The Confederate Beaufort District   83
Chapter 6   Arming the Slaves and the Battle of Pocotaligo   101
Chapter 7   Emancipation   151
Chapter 8   Initial Tax Sales and the *George Washington*   175
Chapter 9   Revival and the Combahee and Bluffton Raids   200
Chapter 10   The Attack on Charleston, 1863   222
Chapter 11   Tax Sales and Preemption   253
Chapter 12   Sea Island Transformation and Military Stalemate   275
Chapter 13   Battle of Honey Hill   301
Chapter 14   Battles of Tullifinny   340
Chapter 15   Sherman Invades the Beaufort District   367
Chapter 16   The War Ledger   405
Chapter 17   The Beginning of the New South   428
Chapter 18   An Uncertain Future   439
Chapter 19   The District Divided   457
Chapter 20   Decades of Enterprise, 1873–1893   492

Chapter 21   Beaufort County's Maritime Golden Age   520

Chapter 22   The Counterrevolution of 1876 and the Secession of Hampton County   541

Notes   587

Bibliography   639

Index   661

Acknowledgments

When first asked nearly fifteen years ago to participate in producing a second volume for the history of Beaufort County, I was requested by my coauthor—Lawrence Rowland—to contribute three chapters on the region's Civil War history. But soon, the three chapters became eighteen as research soon showed that the area that made up the Beaufort District between 1860 and 1866 was one of the Civil War's most important and critical regions. Not only did the district serve as a location for essential military operations, but it was also a setting for sweeping economic, social, political, educational, and military changes designed to integrate the area's former slaves into the nation's citizenry. The story is fascinating, the personalities exceptional, and the consequences monumental. The Beaufort District hosted all aspects of the war and, at least for a brief moment, became an example to the rest of the country for what the future could be.

Over the years that it took to weave the story together, a number of individuals contributed to the completion of *The History of Beaufort County, volume 2, 1861–1893*. Gerhard Spieler, a colleague and friend, began his work on the history of Beaufort County more than forty years ago. As a title researcher for Beaufort County government, he was in a unique position to appreciate and study the region's local history. With the assistance of his beloved wife, Ruth DeTreville Spieler, he began his own archival collection in the 1960s. His home, the historic DeTreville House in downtown Beaufort, became a great repository of local history. He has shared his vast knowledge of Beaufort County history to the general public through learned articles in local magazines and a weekly column in the *Beaufort Gazette*. He generously contributed his expertise and his huge personal archives to the completion of this volume. Gerhard unfortunately passed away before the work could be finished, but his generosity in sharing his knowledge and archives allowed for the eventual completion of this volume.

Alexander Moore, acquisitions editor of the University of South Carolina Press, has shepherded the manuscript from its inception, assisting in research and outlining the required protocol needed to prepare the manuscript. On his own time, he read, edited, and vastly improved the final publication. Alex also went beyond the call of duty by providing this volume with an excellent and thought-provoking introduction. Also, Mary Katherine Webb provided technical, organizational, and editorial assistance to ready the volume for the press. Thanks to Elizabeth Farry who carried out the tedius but necessary task of properly aligning our endnotes and Barbara Thomas Crow who assisted in preparing the corrections to the manuscript.

Many others contributed directly or indirectly to this book. Special thanks to Henry Mintz, who carried out vital research that added tremendously to the narrative. Dave Smoot assisted with research on specific topics, while William Bragg generously provided information and advice on Georgia militia, state troops, and the Battle of Honey Hill. Antonio de la Cova gave insight into the Elliott/Gonzales family, while his wife Carlina shared her knowledge of Civil War black soldiers. Pat Brennan helped with information on Isaac Stevens, while Robert Browning freely gave assistance on Civil War navies and the South Atlantic Blockading Squadron. Tracy Power assisted with information on South Carolina soldiers and politicians. Willis J. "Skipper" Keith was always handy with needed and insightful information on the war in the lowcounty. Bill Olendorf shared his research on the region, while Cynthia Cole Jenkins was very forthcoming with her knowledge of Beaufort and its history. Ramona Grunden and Colin Brooker also proved to be valuable resources, who never failed to help whenever they could.

Indispensable assistance came from Doyle Clifton who knows the byways and waterwas of the lowcountry and produced drafts of the Honey Hill map. Help also came from Dave Ruth and Rick Hatcher who readily supplied information whenever called upon. Evelene and Peter Stevenson generously shared their knowledge of Beaufort. Neil Baxley provided background on the 11th South Carolina and county sheriffs. Sheila Tombe assisted with Shakespeare referenes and Cecily McMillan imparted her knowledge of Coffin Point. Others who shared their research included Wallace Alcorn, Dana MacBean, Jeff Grigg, and Bill and Fran Marscher. Numerous individuals contributed their knowledge of the region's history people, including Pete Dawson, Claude Dinkins, Jennifer McClung, Donna Elaine Perry, David Lauderdale, George Crist, Brantley Harvey, Daryl Murphy, MaryLou Brewton, and Johnny Bee. The support of everyone was and is greatly appreciated.

Throughout this volume's production, a number of institutions and their professional personnel have assisted in providing archives, photographs, and other essential research data. This includes but is not limited to the staff of the Beaufort County Library, the Beaufort County Historical Society, the South Carolina Battleground Trust, the South Caroliniana Library, and especially the staff of the University of South Carolina Beaufort Library— Ellen Chamberlain, Geni Flowers, Maie Mendoza, Stephanie Grimm, Dudley Stutz, and Kim Handy. At the South Carolina Historical Society, former executive director Eric Emerson, current publications director Matt Lockhart, and archivist Mike Coker were particularly helpful. Former publication director and editor Stephen Hoffius also shared his knowledge on many lowcountry topics. Tracy Power, Roger Stroup, and Alexia Helsley at the South Carolina Department of Archives and History aided in research, along with enthusiastic support. Our colleague Dr. Walter B. Edgar, who has always encouraged publications of local history, was a great aid to the advancement of this project. Dr. Bryan Howard has been a steady friend whose assistance helped fill in gaps in the manuscript. Ian Hill's enthusiastic backing and personal knowledge of South Carolina, its people, and history added greatly to the narrative; he also assisted with the procurement of maps. Others whose suggestions added quality to the volume include John M. McCardell, Allen Stokes, and John "Marty" Davis. Both part-time residents of Beaufort have become tremendous students of the area's history and openly shared their own research and knowledge on southern history and Beaufort and its denizens. Marty Davis was particularly generous in providing access to various drafts on his history of Beaufort.

Acknowledgment must be given to Mike Taylor, whose straightforward advice and good humor were always available whenever needed. A man about everything, Mike loved history and was an accomplished researcher, writer, musician, producer, and manager, who gave all he could to promote and safeguard the lowcountry's history. He is sorely missed.

I also need to thank my parents, Mary and Glenn Wise, who gave me my love for history. Whenever possible they visited Beaufort, and we would travel throughout the area learning about the region's fascinating history. My father reviewed early manuscripts and gave very pertinent suggestions to improve the book.

Special thanks and appreciation go to my wife, Alice Parsons Wise, whom I first met in Beaufort and who shares my love of the region's history and beauty. She worked tirelessly to proof and edit the manuscript, providing suggestions and pointing out sections that needed clarification and modification. Without her love and patience this book could not have been properly completed.

STEPHEN R. WISE

Foreword

Publication of volume 2, *1861–1893,* of *The History of Beaufort County, South Carolina,* is a signal event in the writing of South Carolina and southern history. This is the second of a three-volume history of Beaufort District and County that spans five centuries. Volume 1 was published in 1996. Publication of volume 3 will complete a research and writing project that had its origin in the 1970s. The authors of volumes 2 and 3, Lawrence S. Rowland and Stephen R. Wise, invited me to write forewords to those volumes. I have a small but long-time association with the project. I was a coauthor of volume 1, in company with Lawrence Rowland and the late George C. Rogers Jr. As acquisitions editor for the University of South Carolina Press, I worked with Wise and Rowland to bring volumes 2 and 3 to completion.

Their invitation gives me the liberty to promote appreciation of the volumes and to make some observations on the Beaufort region and on the craft of writing local history. Volume 2 begins in medias res; chapter 1 is continuous with the final chapter of volume 2. This volume begins with the Federal capture and occupation of Port Royal Sound and the Confederate retreat and reentrenchment on Beaufort District's mainland in November 1861 and carries the story through the war and Reconstruction up to the year 1893. Volume 2 offers readers an original, sophisticated study of the famous Port Royal Experiment, in which United States military officers, government officials, civilian northerners, and liberated slaves transformed the Union-occupied sea island corner of the Palmetto State into a laboratory for liberty and a working model of the post–Civil War New South. As the experiment was underway, white South Carolinians on the mainland struggled to preserve their prewar lifestyles. This situation ignited political revolutions in that small corner of South Carolina that changed forever the state's history and the history of the South. Volume 2 dramatically recounts the first revolution that afforded thousands of black South Carolinians the power to raise themselves from chattel slavery to American citizenship and self-determination. It also tells stories of a second revolution, ironically called Redemption, in which whites, defeated in war, sought to take back from black southerners their newly won liberties. Whether they called themselves Red Shirts, taxpayers, Bourbons, or simply Democrats, Beaufort and South Carolina whites sought to impose upon their fellow citizens a post–Civil War racial caste system that differed little from antebellum slavery. The partial success of this reactionary revolution constitutes the post–Civil War chapters of volume 2 and the early chapters of volume 3. Beaufort African Americans, led by Robert Smalls, Thomas E. Miller, and other luminaries, kept Jim Crow at bay longer in their home county than in most other parts of the state. Had the Hurricane of 1893, the first revolution described in volume 3, not struck Port Royal and Beaufort with such fury, the county's "fusion" politics might have become a successful model of biracial democracy in the New South.

Interested readers will wish to know why Beaufort County merits the devotion of three large volumes to a region that today encompasses Beaufort, Jasper, and Hampton Counties in the southernmost corner of a state that ranks twenty-fourth in population and forty-second in per capita income in the nation's fifty states. The population of these counties amounted in 2010 to about 208,000, less than one sixteenth of the state's population.

To answer that big question is the task of this foreword and the one that will accompany volume 3. A simple answer is that the history of Beaufort County from 1861 to 1893 and from 1893 to 2006 is a reflecting (not refracting) mirror of the state's history and of the South's coastal regions since 1861. The mirror reveals the authors' sophisticated knowledge of South Carolina and the Civil War. The Beaufort County mirror also resembles the weird sisters' magic mirror in act 4 of William Shakespeare's *Macbeth*. As Macbeth peered into the mirror held by the illusory child-king, he perceived generations of Scottish history yet to come. Attentive readers of volumes 2 and 3 can look into the work and view South Carolina history and southern history from 1861 to the present age and into the twenty-first century.

An important theme of volume 1 is that Beaufort County had been both a geographical and political frontier from 1514 until November 7, 1861, the day the "big gun shoot" dragged Beaufort and South Carolina into the modern age. For two centuries before the American Revolution, the Beaufort region was a "debatable land" between Spanish, British, and French intrigues to create a North American empire. The region was also an embattled frontier between all Europeans and the indigenous Native Americans. Archaeologists and historians have discovered that even before European discovery the region was the site of complicated intra-Indian struggles between three groups: those who inhabited the region, those who customarily (or conveniently) passed through it, and those outsiders who wished to claim control of it. For all of these groups through the centuries, the Beaufort frontier was sometimes geographical, political, ideological, economic, and cultural. In the long view, those three generic groups—inhabitants, visitors, and immigrants—have changed their identities, but their relationships within the Beaufort region have been remarkably similar through the centuries.

The Yamasee War, European wars of empire, and the founding of Georgia were crises in Beaufort and South Carolina history. Several campaigns of the American Revolution were fought in the terrestrial and maritime Beaufort frontier. Beaufort was an economic frontier centered on rice and sea island cotton that created a cash-crop, slave-sustained empire that created one of the wealthiest communities in the United States. Although sophisticated in wealth and influence, much of the region kept its untamed, marginal character well into the nineteenth century. Beaufort District was a crucible of political extremism. Nullification, state's rights, and secession talk found fertile soil as Rhetts, DeTrevilles, Chaplins, and Seabrooks advocated white superiority and secession to liberate themselves from what they saw as a threatening federal government that their forebears had helped create.

Capture and emancipation by the Union navy and army in November 1861 revolutionized Beaufort more profoundly than the American Revolution and the sea island cotton kingdom. Volume 2 delineates in remarkable detail the character of that revolution. Chattel slavery was destroyed; thousands of enslaved South Carolinians achieved liberty and personhood; and radically new social and economic policies found fertile ground for experiment. Post-1861 Beaufort was another frontier where the modern world supplanted the Old South. Armies clashed in battles and skirmishes, while contrabands, entrepreneurs, "social engineers," and opportunists—all of them representative frontier personalities—fashioned a set of American values that looked to the future centuries. It was up to Beaufortonians, South Carolinians, and American citizens to interpret correctly the images revealed in the weird sisters' mirror.

The rediscovery and modification of Frederick Jackson Turner's frontier thesis in the long history of Beaufort County is one theme of Wise and Rowland's magnum opus. In the 1890s Turner observed that the closing of the western geographical frontier marked an end to American exceptionalism. Frontier settlers through the centuries had been aggressive experimenters in democratic forms, economic innovation, and construction of a unique culture. The authors of *The History of Beaufort County* have demonstrated that the Beaufort region has long been identified as an interior frontier. They have identified the operation of frontier values as the region has moved through centuries of political, economic, and cultural experimentation. Greater Beaufort proves to be one of those locales. Another theme important to Wise and Rowland was well expressed in 1988 by George Calvin Rogers Jr., the dean of twentieth-century South Carolina history. In July 1988 Rogers published "Names, Not Numbers," in the *William and Mary Quarterly* (3rd series, vol. 45, no. 3 [July 1988]: 574–9), an essay in which he extolled history writing that emphasized people and places—all proper nouns—in contrast to history writing based upon grand theories, statistics, and sociological factors. His *History of Georgetown County* (1970) demonstrated rigorous research, but it was also a model of the "names, not numbers" genre. The methodological rigor of *Georgetown County* is found in volumes 2 and 3, coupled with the power of original storytelling. Rogers was Rowland's dissertation supervisor, hence the origin of volume 1 and Rogers's coauthorship. Steve Wise's account of occupied Beaufort District sits squarely in the "names, not numbers" tradition. He is a master of the official records created during the war and of the voluminous secondary literature of the war and Reconstruction. He brings all that knowledge to bear, but he also weaves into his narrative countless first-hand accounts of the occupation of Beaufort District and the skirmishes, battles, and forays by Union and Confederate troops that make for a thick, convincing narrative fabric.

This dense documentation gives volume 2 a powerful, timeless verisimilitude reminiscent of the catalogue of ships in Homer's *Iliad*. Certainly, many historians and novelists have named the Civil War the "American Iliad." Of those works Shelby Foote's *The Civil War: A Narrative* (1958–74) most deliberately linked the Civil War to the ten-year campaign against Troy. The fact that Foote took longer to complete *The Civil War* than the Trojan War lasted in myth and history says something about the convoluted history and the cultural importance of America's war with itself. Charles P. Roland's *An American Iliad: The Story of the Civil War* (2002) and Julia A. Stern's *Mary Chesnut's Civil War Epic* (2010) also discerned ample Trojan War contexts in their monographs. In fact, Steve Wise has been author and historical consultant on one such work, *America's Iliad: The Siege of Charleston*, a television documentary released in 2007, which examined the city's experience from 1861 to 1865 in the light of the Trojan War. Hence, to link volume 2 to the works of Homer is not a literary flourish but a just assessment of the tone and narrative power of the volume.

It is Wise's geologic reconstruction of Union Beaufort and, indeed, of the Port Royal Experiment that ring truest in comparison with the *Iliad*. The heroic activities of many men and women are woven into the narrative. Union officers included Isaac Ingalls Stevens, Rufus Saxton, Quincy Gillmore, John G. Foster, Ormsby MacKnight Mitchel, Thomas West Sherman, and William Tecumseh Sherman. Northern immigrant do-gooders Edward Lille Pierce, Mansfield French, Charlotte Forten, Laura Towne, and Frances Gage found renown as they revolutionized Beaufort. Against them stood white South Carolinians, Beaufortonians, and Confederates fighting to defend the district's prewar society. Thomas Fenwick Drayton, Charles Jones Colcock, Edmund Rhett, Ambrosio Gonzales, and many members of the Barnwell, Heyward, and Cuthbert families rallied to defend their homes and property. Robert E. Lee, Pierre Gustave Toutant Beauregard, John C. Pemberton, Stephen Elliott, and William S. Walker were worthy Confederate opponents who resisted the northern invasion and their former slaves' newfound freedom.

Homer's catalog of ships was a literary device that grounded the *Iliad* in verisimilitude, the most important element in great literature. Wise and Rowland have provided, through their deep research and dedication to "names, not numbers," a verisimilitude born of historical accuracy. It will be a long time before any future historians can write a counternarrative to the Civil War and Reconstruction depicted in volume 2.

Rowland continues the "names, not numbers" method as he narrates stories of Reconstruction and reaction, the so-called "Redemption" in which white South Carolina Democrats battled their former slaves and a new class of African American Republicans for control of their native region. Post–Civil War Beaufort County, especially after the secession of white-dominated Hampton County in 1878, continued in a contrarian manner the political revolution that began the day of the "big gun shoot." Union occupation, the Port Royal Experiment, the Thirteenth and Fourteenth Amendments, and the sales and redistribution of plantation lands transformed Beaufort County into a distinctive New South political entity, one that was multiracial in its government, filled with entrepreneurial spirit and economic prosperity, and an example of the war-defined federalism of the United States.

Volume 3 will carry forward Beaufort's frontier character into unexpected territories: economic, cultural, and even aesthetic histories of the twentieth century. Volume 3 will also present a challenge to the new frontier culture of 1890s Beaufort. The Hurricane of 1893 is the starting point for volume 3, and that storm proved to be another revolution. The social and environmental destruction wrought by that gigantic storm reintroduced—in an awesome manner—the "force of nature" in Beaufort history. Volume 2 narrates the events and influences of political revolution. Volume 3 will narrate the events and impact of environment and human ecology upon that same corner of South Carolina.

ALEXANDER MOORE

Chapter 1

The Confederates Evacuate the Sea Islands

"O Massa, God A'mighty come an de Yankees come wid him"

Ever since the arrival of its first inhabitants, the people of Beaufort County, South Carolina, had been tied to the ocean and the region's internal waterways. It was here that communities flourished, then fell to new invaders. The pattern was repeated many times. The American Indians were forced out by the Europeans—Frenchmen, Spaniards, and Englishmen—who vied with each other to control Port Royal Sound, a body of water said to be finest natural harbor in the New World. When the eighteenth-century wars for empire ended, the English controlled the sound. Soon an economy based upon slavery and cash crops was established. Prosperity was disrupted during the American Revolution when British warships swept into Port Royal Sound and occupied Beaufort, the area's principal community. After the revolution the residents regained their lifestyles and expanded their slave- and cash-crop-based culture. They were not as fortunate in 1861, when another maritime invasion shattered their civilization beyond recovery.

Although Port Royal's value was known for centuries, it was not until the 1850s that the United States Coast Survey intensely investigated the sound. The hydrographers' findings confirmed long-held beliefs about the region's natural qualities. Declared "the finest harbor south of the Chesapeake," Port Royal Sound boasted a two-and-a-half-mile entrance and water deep enough for the nation's largest frigate. Once in the sound, the entire United States Navy could "ride at anchor in the bay which is perfectly healthy and secure."

Despite its distinctive merits, Port Royal never developed into a viable port. Beaufort, the area's largest community, was deemed of "no commercial importance." During the summer months, the area planters inhabited the town. With two large shops and many smaller stores, the town served as the general depot for supplies for the plantations of Port Royal Island. Beaufort's many fine residences were occupied only in the summer, when the population numbered over a thousand white inhabitants. The town also contained sixty-four foreign-born residents and twenty-nine free people of color. Railroad connections from Beaufort to the mainland had been proposed and a right of way mapped but never built. Hence, the town remained isolated except for steamship service on the inland waterway from Charleston to northern Florida.

The closest rail line was the Charleston and Savannah Railroad. The tracks that connected these cities were built on lofty wooden trestles and earthen causeways across the Combahee, Pocotaligo, Tullifinny, and the Coosawhatchie Rivers. The final bridge over the Savannah River was built in the spring of 1861. The railroad was the region's principal transportation and commercial link to the rest of the South and the nation.

The railway did not follow the highway between Charleston and Savannah, bypassing many existing communities. Pocotaligo and Grahamville were missed, while Coosawhatchie and Hardeeville became railroad centers. Train stations created potentially new commercial centers at Gopher Hill, Yemassee Station, Pocotaligo Station, and Salkehatchie. Although there were no dock facilities in the Port Royal region, small vessels could navigate to within a mile of the railroad by navigating up the Broad and into the Pocotaligo and Coosawhatchie Rivers.[1]

The United States government took no steps to defend the Port Royal region, but the local citizens began preparations in the 1850s for a possible war of secession. In 1852 the Beaufort arsenal, home to the Beaufort Volunteer Artillery, was expanded and militia drills increased. In 1858 the sea islands' militia was reorganized into a three-company battalion that was part of the 12th South Carolina Militia Regiment. Once South Carolina seceded, many men from the area participated in the siege and bombardment of Fort Sumter. With the Federals removed from Charleston Harbor, the Confederates turned their attention to Port Royal.[2]

In May 1861 the Confederate commander in South Carolina, General Pierre G. T. Beauregard, surveyed the coast. Colonel George P. Elliott of Beaufort and Elliott's brother-in-law, the Cuban-born revolutionary Ambrosio J. Gonzales, assisted him. Following the survey, the state constructed numerous earthen fortifications strategically placed to deny enemy vessels access to any navigable inlets between Charleston and Savannah.[3]

Forts guarded the mouths of the North and South Edisto Rivers and the entrance to the Ashepoo River. A small work at Sams Point on Lady's Island watched over the Coosaw River, which led to Brickyard Creek and the Beaufort River. At Port Royal two forts guarded the sound's entrance. To the north, at Bay Point on Phillips' Island, was Fort Beauregard. Fort Walker stood across the sound on Hilton Head Island. To watch over Calibogue Sound and the channel that separated Hilton Head from the mainland, a battery was built on the island's western tip. All these forts were built under the direction of state and Confederate engineers, who supervised slave laborers.

Beauregard did not remain in South Carolina to see the completion of his coastal defenses. That responsibility fell to Ohio-born Brigadier General Roswell Sabine Ripley, who took command of South Carolina in August 1861. Though hampered by a lack of supplies and heavy guns, Ripley and his commander at Port Royal, Brigadier General Thomas Fenwick Drayton, believed their fortifications could keep the enemy from capturing the sea islands and reaching the Charleston and Savannah Railroad. Their confidence stemmed from conventional military thought, which held that one gun on land was worth ten aboard a ship. Land-based gunners could easily target slow moving, sail-powered warships. According to one account, Major Francis D. Lee, who oversaw Fort Walker's construction, proudly told his slave laborers that "the Devil couldn't take it—God Almighty himself couldn't take it."

In earlier wars land-based artillery may have been superior to warships, but when the Union squadron under Flag Officer Samuel Francis Du Pont attacked Forts Beauregard and Walker on November 7, 1861, a new era in naval warfare had begun. The Union vessels were steamers that mounted larger and more numerous cannons than the Confederates had in their forts. In less than five hours, the southerners were defeated. As the Confederates fled, a slave who had heard Major Lee's boast called out to him, "O Massa, God A'mighty come an de Yankees come wid him."

The Confederates abandoned their garrisons and fled to the mainland before the Federals could seize the inland waterways. The attempt to stop the northerners at the initial point of attack had been a dismal failure. To prevent the defeat from becoming a catastrophe, a new defensive strategy had to be developed.[4]

The "big gun shoot," as the local blacks called the Battle of Port Royal, shattered Beaufort's prewar society. Though General Ripley had urged the population to leave, the majority of the residents stayed. Some, expecting a southern victory, had gathered to watch the battle. Instead, they witnessed the quick destruction of the antebellum society that had required nearly 150 years to create. Some civilians boarded steamships for Charleston, while others hastily packed a few essentials and fled inland. Some tried to force their slaves to follow, but with few exceptions most of the Africans refused to go. They rightly saw the arrival of the Union military as ending their servitude.

Into this chaotic situation came General Robert E. Lee, the area's new commander. Considered by his peers to be the most talented officer in the regular army, Lee's Confederate career had not yet lived up to this promise. During the summer of 1861, while in charge of forces defending western Virginia, he tangled with quarrelsome, incompetent subordinates. Unable to coordinate an effective campaign, Lee lost the majority of the region to the Federals and received the nickname "Granny Lee" for what was perceived as his reluctance to engage the enemy. Reassigned to Richmond, he was soon ordered to take command of the Departments of South Carolina, Georgia, and East Florida, a vast coastal region threatened by naval assault. While Lee understood the danger, he also perceived the situation as similar to the one he had faced in Virginia. He found his local commanders to be petty and jealous. State governors and other politicians constantly interfered with his decisions. Also, he faced a manpower shortage as the one-year enlistments of his soldiers were nearly over. Before accepting the command, Lee gained assurances from Confederate president Jefferson Davis that his authority would be absolute. However, Lee still had to call upon both his military expertise and his personal diplomatic skills to succeed in his command.[5]

Lee was given charge of the new Department of South Carolina, Georgia, and East Florida on November 5, 1861; the day after, Federal warships began to assemble off Port Royal Sound. When he arrived at Coosawhatchie on the evening of November 7, Lee met General Ripley, who reported the devastating Confederate defeat.[6]

Ripley had brought the soldiers off the sea islands and positioned them to defend the all-important Charleston and Savannah Railroad. But the troops had left behind most of their equipment, clothing, and provisions. They had lost all of their artillery. From Hilton Head, nearly one thousand men under General Thomas F. Drayton had re-formed outside Bluffton near the New River Bridge. Seven hundred troops from Bay Point under Colonel Richard G. M. Donovant had marched through Beaufort to Garden's Corner. Although the Georgia troops who had manned Hilton Head had returned to Savannah, the remaining soldiers were soon joined by two North Carolina and two South Carolina infantry regiments, a South Carolina cavalry regiment, and the South Carolina "Siege Train" artillery. Lee assembled his reinforcements along the headwaters of the Broad River and immediately reported the situation to Judah P. Benjamin, the Confederate secretary of war. Benjamin, who had spent time in Beaufort as a child, received dispatches from Lee informing him that the enemy had secured Port Royal Sound and commanded all the sea islands. Northern warships patrolled the inland waterways as far up the Broad River as the mouth of the Pocotaligo River and even into the Coosawhatchie and Tullifinny Rivers. Lee wrote, "We have no guns that can resist their batteries and have no resource but to prepare to meet them in the field."[7]

Lee hoped he would have time to prepare a proper defense, bring in reinforcements, and organize his men for combat. Aggressive by nature, Lee believed in offensive warfare. He embraced Napoleon Bonaparte's dictum to have a stout defense for his depots, while his field army sallied forth against the enemy. But before he could attack the invaders, he had to prepare the groundwork. Even before he arrived in Beaufort District, Lee knew that the South did not have enough men or cannons to defend every inlet. He faced the fact that strategic withdrawals were necessary. He planned to pull his forces from isolated posts and concentrate them at Savannah, Charleston, and along the Charleston and Savannah Railroad.

Lee may have been implementing his father's theories on coast defense, as well as proposals found in an 1826 army report by Major Joseph G. Totten, which detailed a coastal policy designed to secure the nation's coast from enemy assaults. In his thesis Totten proposed a system of harbor forts manned by regular troops to delay an enemy's advance until local militia could be mustered. Once ready, the militia, with the men in the forts, would defeat the enemy and drive them from the coast. Lee expanded Totten's concept by adding the element of rail transportation. Garrisons at Savannah and Charleston were to be kept strong enough to meet initial attacks. Before the enemy could gain the advantage, reinforcements would arrive via the railroad.[8]

Another plan Lee took into consideration was a recommendation by Colonel Ambrosio Gonzales, the Cuban revolutionary and son-in-law of William Elliott III. A proponent of a Cuba free from Spanish rule but tied to the slave-oriented South, Gonzales had been active in prewar schemes to enlist United States citizens into Cuban filibustering actions, which acquainted him with Jefferson Davis and a number of military officers, including Gustavus Smith and Robert E. Lee.

When the war began, Gonzales readily joined his in-laws and the Confederacy in their bid for freedom. He volunteered and was soon appointed inspector of troops and coastal defenses. Gonzales recognized that the coastline was vulnerable to attack by the Federal navy, which could cut off and capture isolated fortifications. A month before the attack on Port Royal, Gonzales proposed to the War Department a plan that called for the use of "flying batteries." Armed with rifled siege guns, these units could be moved to preconstructed fortifications or behind natural barriers to challenge enemy attacks. Gonzales's suggestion was backed by the Confederate Engineer Bureau, and one day before the "big gun shoot," Gonzales became Lee's unofficial aide-de-camp and commander of South Carolina's "Siege Train."[9]

Lee realized that his defenses were only as strong as their weakest link, and in November and December, his greatest fear was that the Federals would sever the railroad in Beaufort District near the headwaters of the Broad River. If the Yankees cut the railway, they could then send flying columns north and south, taking Savannah and Charleston from the rear. To thwart such a movement, Lee assembled troops in the region stretching from the Savannah River to the Combahee River.

On November 8 Lee established his headquarters in an abandoned house at Coosawhatchie and assembled his staff. Though he referred to the place as a "decrepit and deserted village," its central location afforded him the best position to direct his troops. Lee left Ripley at Coosawhatchie to monitor the headwaters of the Broad River, pressed on to Savannah, and then to Charleston, where he met with Francis W. Pickens, the South Carolina governor. When he returned to Coosawhatchie on November 18, Lee found a report from Ripley that outlined the situation in Beaufort District.[10]

In ten days Ripley had restored order and established a new defensive line stretching from the Combahee River to the Savannah River. Cavalry units watched over potential landing sites, while infantry and artillery stood ready in newly built fortifications. Brigadier General Thomas F. Drayton, the onetime defender of Port Royal Sound, commanded the district's southern region. Lieutenant Colonel Charles J. Colcock's mounted militia patrolled the waterways near Bluffton. Farther inland, Colonels William C. Heyward's 9th and William D. DeSaussure's 15th South Carolina Regiments guarded Hardeeville and manned the new forts built on the road from Hardeeville to Bluffton and the mouth of the New River at Red Bluff. Along the Broad River, Captain James D. Trezevant's cavalry company watched Boyd's and Tenney's Landings, while Colonel Clingman's 25th North Carolina built a strong fortification along the Honeywood Road at a place called Honey Hill to guard the approaches to the Grahamville depot. Near the mouth of Bee's Creek at Huguenin's Landing, Colonel Gonzales oversaw the construction of a massive battery manned by James D. Radcliffe's 8th North Carolina Infantry Regiment. To further impede any waterborne enemy advances, Colonel Gonzales placed obstructions in the Coosawhatchie River while a Mr. Gregory blocked the Tullifinny.

Colonel Oliver E. Edwards's 13th South Carolina regiment was stationed at the Coosawhatchie railhead, while a few miles north at Pocotaligo was Colonel Richard G. M. Dunovant's 12th South Carolina and Colonel James Jones's 14th South Carolina. William E. Martin's state militia cavalry picketed the area from Pocotaligo east to the Port Royal Ferry and north to the Combahee River.[11]

Besides setting up the initial defensive positions, Ripley had ordered raids onto the abandoned sea islands to destroy cotton and to gather up slaves before the Federals seized them, but no raids were carried out before Ripley was ordered to Charleston. Although a competent officer and skilled artilleryman and engineer, Ripley was an irascible, irritating subordinate who had little use for Lee. Some of his expressions may have come from anger at being superseded by the Virginian or from his fondness for alcohol. Whatever the reasons, Ripley's opinion of Lee was well known. Lee did not confront Ripley or remove him from command; instead, he simply moved the troublesome subordinate to Charleston and personally took control of operations in Beaufort District.[12]

Conditions were critical along the headwaters of the Broad River. Lee even received a resolution from the Beaufort District citizens requesting him to declare martial law. In reply to William Elliott III, Edmund Rhett, and Leroy Youmans, Lee explained that he saw no need to suspend civil laws. The citizenry could manage their affairs while Lee took on the task of handling the military situation.[13]

Soon the fifty-four-year-old, gray-bearded commanding officer was seen everywhere overseeing the construction of fortifications. He assembled a skilled staff, which included such specialists as Colonel Joseph Ives, chief engineer, and Armistead Long, chief of artillery. Lee also employed naval officer Lieutenant John N. Maffitt and Captain John R. F. Tattnall of the Confederate Marine Corps. These men and others turned in yeoman service, but the general remained the guiding force behind the fortification of Beaufort District and coastal South Carolina.[14]

At night Lee returned to an abandoned house in Coosawhatchie, reportedly belonging to Mrs. George Chisolm Mackay. From there Lee wrote dispatches, including requests to his superiors for more men and artillery. When he had time, he penned letters to his family. In a note to his daughters Annie and Agnes, Lee told them of seeing Mrs. Mackay, mother of his West Point classmate and friend John Mackay, and her daughters, Margaret, the widow of Dr. Ralph Ems Elliott, and Eliza, now Mrs. Joseph Stiles, all of whom Lee knew in 1829–31, when he was stationed at Savannah's Fort Pulaski. In another letter to Annie, written on December 8, Lee wrote of how warm it was, and to prove it, "I enclose some violets I plucked in the yard of the deserted house I now occupy."[15]

While his thoughts were always with his family, Lee kept a constant eye on the enemy. On occasion he would ride to a vantage point from which to view their fleet. As yet the Yankees seemed loath to leave the protection of their big ships, and Lee used this respite to train his men. His troops, some six thousand men, were a mixture of militia, untrained state units, and regiments newly federalized for Confederate service. For the most part they were raw and, according to Ripley, needed severe discipline and constant vigilance. Lee knew their weaknesses and used them primarily to build new defenses. However, always the aggressor, he also approved expeditions to Beaufort and the sea islands.[16]

The raids had been called for in mid-November, when General Ripley directed Colonel William Martin to lead his militia cavalrymen onto Port Royal and St. Helena islands. The forays were intended to remove citizens, their slaves, and other property and to destroy cotton, food supplies, and other material useful to the enemy. Colonel Martin had been unable to organize the expeditions. Few volunteers came forward and none of the refugee planters could be induced to guide the attack. In early December the idea was revived. This time Martin was to work in conjunction with Captain Stephen Elliott, commander of the Beaufort Artillery. Elliott, a Beaufort native and well-known sportsman, did not wait for Martin. On the night of December 4, he led about twenty-five men into Beaufort. For the men of the Beaufort Artillery, the raid was a homecoming. The muster roll of the unit was a roll call of the Beaufort elite. It contained Fullers, Barnwells, Elliotts, Stuarts, and Fripps. On Bay Street stood the homes of Captain Elliott, his father, and his grandfather. The strike gave them the opportunity to assuage some of the pain of defeat they had suffered a month earlier.

As they entered Beaufort, they noticed only one light, and the only greeting came from a barking dog. The town was clear of enemy and the river empty of warships. They rode on through the town along the shell road to Battery Plantation. Elliott then sent three men to Dr. Thomas Fuller's plantation on Parris Island, where they destroyed seventy bales of cotton and seven hundred bushels of corn. Though the island was crowded with slaves escaping their fugitive masters, the raiders were unable to carry off any slaves, and the men rejoined their comrades at Battery Plantation. Elliott then had his troopers burn cotton and provisions at nearby plantations before returning to the mainland.[17]

Surprised at Elliott's quick move, Colonel Martin requested permission from Lee to carry out his own strike. At midnight on December 5, Martin sent scouts onto Port Royal Island. The men rode into Beaufort and found the town vacant. When this news reached Martin, he immediately organized two columns of horsemen from the Allendale Mounted Guard. He planned to take a screening column of eleven men into Beaufort, while behind them came a stronger force, some fifty men under Major George Washington Oswald. The two units would rendezvous outside Beaufort and then work their way back to the ferry, burning cotton and foodstuffs. To help ensure the raiders' return if they were cut off from Port Royal Ferry, Martin made arrangements with Captain Maffitt, Colonel Jones, and Major Sams to have flats available for a crossing to Page's Point.

At 6:00 P.M. Martin and his men crowded their horses onto a flat at Port Royal Ferry and crossed over to Port Royal Island. Guided by Captain Oscar Barnwell and a Dr. Hasell, Martin and the lead party pressed on to Beaufort. About three quarters of a mile from the town, a discharge of muskets surprised the horsemen. Captain Barnwell was wounded, and the party, all save Martin and his son, fled. Racing back to Port Royal Ferry, the shaken riders mistakenly informed Major Oswald that Colonel Martin was dead. Oswald wanted to press on, but the majority of officers refused to budge. He reluctantly led his men back to the mainland.

When Colonel Martin returned to the ferry shortly before midnight, he ordered Oswald and his men to recross the river. They bivouacked until daylight, when they again moved toward Beaufort. On the outskirts of town, Captain Smart's detachment exchanged fire with enemy pickets, but this time the militiamen did not run. Martin carried out his original plan as he and Major Oswald led separate columns back to Port Royal Ferry burning cotton. By 10:00 P.M. on December 7, with the raid completed, the cavalrymen returned to the mainland.[18]

The raiders had burned large stocks of cotton but found no slaves willing to join their fugitive masters. Indeed, Colonel Martin reported that he had to capture all the blacks he encountered lest they convey information to the enemy. This lack of loyalty, coupled with the fact that slaves were taking every opportunity to escape to the Federals, forced the southerners to realize that their human property saw this war as more than a fight between differing economic and political systems. Indeed, from the first Federal cannon fired at Fort Walker, African Americans saw it as a war to bring them freedom. Their masters and even the invading northerners may not have realized it, but the slaves did.

Initially, gangs of slaves requisitioned from neighboring plantations did much of the fortification work. At first, owners gladly provided laborers. However, as more slaves seized opportunities to flee to northern installations and vessels, slave owners began to withhold their human chattels from military work. Lacking the slaves, Lee and his officers were forced to use their soldiers, who resented doing menial tasks. They soon gave Lee, formerly known as "Granny Lee" in western Virginia, another nickname—the "King of Spades."[19]

To man the fortifications, Lee and Governor Pickens continuously importuned Richmond for additional officers, infantry, light artillery batteries, and cannons. By early December, Secretary of War Benjamin began shifting troops to Lee's department. These reinforcements were essential, as the Federals were finally beginning to show some activity. On December 8, 1861, Union troops came ashore at Cunningham Point near Hall's Island. Lee immediately rushed troops from nearby Page Point and Garden's Corners to the area, but the Federals withdrew before any engagement occurred.[20]

To stop any more thrusts, Lee directed his earliest reinforcements to Beaufort District. South Carolina units arrived as they mustered into Confederate service. Additional help came Brigadier General Daniel Smith Donelson's brigade, which included the 8th and 16th Tennessee and the 60th Virginia Infantry Regiments. Phillips' Legion of Georgia, along with Captain Rowe Thornton's and Walter Leake's batteries of Virginia light artillery, soon followed them.[21]

Brigadier General John C. Pemberton also joined Lee at Coosawhatchie. Pemberton, a skilled artillerist who had been brevetted for bravery in the Mexican War, was, like Ripley, a northern-born West Point graduate who had married a southerner and cast his lot with the Confederacy.[22] The arrival of Pemberton and the new troops allowed Lee to divide his department into districts. The Beaufort area was split into the Fourth and Fifth Districts.

Pemberton was placed in charge of the Fourth District, which stretched from the Ashepoo River to the headwaters of the Broad River, then along the Colleton River and Ocella Creek to Ferebeeville. Although Coosawhatchie, site of Lee's headquarters, was within his command area, Pemberton established his control center at Pocotaligo. The Fifth District, under General Thomas Drayton, made up the region from the Colleton River and Ocella Creek to the Savannah River. By the end of December, General Maxey Gregg of Columbia joined Pemberton at Coosawhatchie.[23]

The reinforcements and new commanders allowed Lee to plan and build new defenses. Works were begun at Red Bank on the New River, at Page Point and Port Royal Ferry along Whale Branch River, and at Tar Bluff on the Combahee. Besides the batteries, Lee ordered more obstructions to be placed in local rivers and creeks. Among these obstructions were torpedoes—canisters filled with powder designed to explode upon contact with a vessel's hull.[24]

Lee also received a valuable addition to his personal entourage, a four-year-old gray horse. The gelding, known as Greenbrier, had arrived in South Carolina with the 60th Virginia Regiment. His owner was Major Thomas L. Broun, but Broun had not come south, and the major's brother Captain Joseph Broun was using Greenbrier. Lee was delighted to see the horse. The commanding general knew the animal well from his time in Virginia, when he had sought to buy Greenbrier, but his owner had already promised him to Major Broun. Though denied ownership, Lee constantly referred to Greenbrier as "my colt." At Coosawhatchie, Lee had a second opportunity to purchase "his colt." After corresponding with his brother, Captain Broun offered to give the horse to Lee, but the general refused the gift and paid $175 for Greenbrier. Lee traveled ceaselessly throughout his command on his new mount, and in time the horse became known as Traveller.[25]

While negotiating for Traveller, Lee spent a lonely Christmas at Coosawhatchie. He spent the day writing his family and working. As he described his routine to his wife, "I am here but little myself. The days I am away, I visit some point exposed to the enemy & after our dinner at early candle light, am engaged in writing till 11 or 12 at night." Lee missed his wife and family, but realized that Mary's condition, rheumatoid arthritis, would make it impossible for her to join him: "But this place is too exposed to attack for the residence of a person as hard to move as yourself." Lee closed by saying that the enemy was increasing in strength, but noted that his command was growing slowly, and like their commander, the men were working hard.[26]

Lee soon realized he had overextended himself. On January 1, 1862, Union troops under the cover of gunboats landed near Port Royal Ferry and forced the Confederates to abandon their new works. Lee did not want this mistake repeated. Soon orders went out and exposed positions such as those at Red Bank were abandoned. Though Lee hoped his defenses would hold, he feared a strong enemy advance against the Charleston and Savannah Railroad. As he wrote Adjutant General Cooper in early January 1862, Lee thought that once his defenses were "completed armed and manned, if properly fought, the enemy's approach ought to be successfully resisted." But his unfinished works required heavy guns, and he had not received the troops expected from Georgia and South Carolina. Without the required men and material Lee feared that the enemy could strike near the head of the Broad River, sever the railroad, and then move on Charleston and Savannah from the land while their fleet attacked from the sea.[27]

Despite his misgivings, the general had done a remarkable job of stabilizing his command and preparing to meet the enemy. Many of his troops were short-term state enlistees or untested and poorly armed volunteers, but he also had a fair proportion of veteran troops. As each day passed, the green units were being disciplined and hardened to army life. Lee continued to call for reinforcements, and he had a masterful way of ingratiating himself. His superiors always gave him a sympathetic ear if not actual help—so that by early 1862 Lee had more than twice as many men in his department as the Federals had at Port Royal. In Beaufort District he could numerically match any strike against the Charleston and Savannah Railroad.

Lee left Coosawhatchie and on February 3, 1862, established his headquarters in Savannah, which was being threatened by enemy expeditions originating from South Carolina. Northern gunboats sailing up the New River had burned the Box and Lawton Plantations. Union scouts had moved from the New River through Wright's Cut to Proctor's Plantation on the Savannah River, where they viewed Fort Jackson and the batteries guarding Savannah. Not only were the raids disturbing, but the Confederates were also alarmed that the slaves in the area were growing insubordinate.[28]

To offset a possible Union strike at Savannah from the north, Lee directed Pemberton to go to Hardeeville and "concert" with Drayton a plan to stop Federal incursions toward the Savannah River. Lee also began abandoning isolated posts on the Georgia coast, bringing the heavy artillery and soldiers to Savannah. He dispatched Major George W. Rains to Augusta to help in defending that city and requested that a railroad be built to link Augusta to the Georgia Central Railroad so that, if the Charleston and Savannah Railroad was cut, communications between Charleston and Savannah could be kept up via Columbia and Augusta.[29]

Although Lee was concentrating his attention on Savannah's defense, he still viewed the headwaters of Port Royal Sound as the citadel from which he and Pemberton could maneuver north against attacks upon Charleston or turn south to support the Confederates at Savannah. However, Lee found his command weakened by circumstances beyond his control. By mid-February, Federal forces in Tennessee had taken Forts Henry and Donelson, the guardians of Tennessee, forcing the Confederates to evacuate much of the state. At the same time Federal forces overran Confederate defenses on Roanoke Island, thereby capturing the North Carolina sounds. The results of these two disasters were orders from the War Department for Lee to send reinforcements to Tennessee and to pull back any forces on the sea islands that might be cut off and captured. Soon four thousand men were on their way west, but Lee did not take them from Pemberton's command in Beaufort District, which he still viewed as the linchpin in his defensive scheme.

The prospect of defending his department with a weakened force did not please Lee. For four months he had struggled to perfect his defenses. While he had felt that he had done an adequate job, he was not entirely satisfied. In a March 2, 1862, letter to his daughter Annie, Lee candidly revealed his frustrations with the southern people and the difficulties of commanding his department:

> Our people have not been earnest enough, have thought too much of themselves & their ease, & instead of turning out to a man, have been content to nurse themselves & their dimes, & leave the protection of themselves & families to others. To satisfy their consciences, they have been clamorous in criticizing what others have done & endeavoured to prove that they ought to do nothing. This is not the way to accomplish our independence. . . . I have been doing all I can, with our small means and slow workmen, to defend the cities & coast here. Against ordinary numbers we are pretty strong, but against the hosts our enemies seem to bring everywhere, there is no calculation. But if our men will stand to their work, we shall give them trouble & damage them yet.[30]

On the same day he wrote to his daughter, Lee received a telegram from Jefferson Davis requesting his presence in Richmond. The telegram was unexpected, but he promptly replied and left Savannah for Richmond the following day. What he found in Richmond was a government in crisis. The disasters at Roanoke Island and in Tennessee had prompted the Confederate Congress to demand a reorganization of Davis's government. Cabinet officials were shuffled, and Davis brought Lee to Richmond to serve as his adviser.

During his four months along the coast, Lee completed defensive works laid out by Ripley, strengthened them, and augmented the line of fortifications to protect the Charleston and Savannah Railroad. Much of his work was done in Beaufort District, where Lee's defenses protected key points and served as staging areas for counterattacks.

Lee understood the value of earthworks, but he saw them as a last resort. He believed in maneuver and attack. By his philosophy the enemy had to be defeated before they reached the final defense lines, where superior numbers and equipment would guarantee victory. Although Lee added to Ripley's line, he held that decisive battles had to be fought away from the fortifications. To this end Lee placed the majority of his field army, the equivalent of three brigades with light artillery, in Beaufort District. This force amounted to one third of his command and was nearly the size of the threatening Federal army. By the time Lee left Coosawhatchie, he had established a strong force ready to react to any enemy movement and took with him a plan that he enacted on a grander scale in Virginia. The genesis of Richmond's elaborate fortifications and Lee's successful counterpunches against the invading northern armies had had its genesis in the South Carolina lowcountry.[31]

Lee's troop deployment was initially kept in place by his successor, Major General John C. Pemberton, who assumed command on March 4 and was officially assigned to the post on March 14. While the Pennsylvania-born general inherited a well-planned defensive scheme, Pemberton had to deal with the same problems that had harried Lee. Besides meddling politicians and insubordinate officers, Pemberton faced a more aggressive enemy and a continuing drain of men and matériel.

By the spring of 1862, the Federals, long dormant at their bases on the sea islands, were beginning to stir. From his headquarters at Pocotaligo, Pemberton carefully watched as northern activity toward Fort Pulaski and Savannah increased. He added to the districts in the southern portion of his department. He placed Brigadier General Maxey Gregg over a smaller Fourth District, which stretched from the Ashepoo River to the East Bank of the Pocotaligo River. A new Fifth District, commanded by Brigadier General Donelson, contained the area from the Pocotaligo to Ocella Creek and Ferebeeville. Brigadier General Drayton's command area, renamed the Sixth District, covered the territory from Ferebeeville to the Savannah River. To support his lowcountry districts, Pemberton ordered into South Carolina three newly organized but as yet unarmed Georgia regiments.[32]

The most sensitive area was Drayton's command. Union activity was increasing along the mouth and northern bank of the Savannah River, suggesting either an attack on Fort Pulaski or a movement inland against Savannah. Yet an assault against the railroad could not be discounted. Besides using the promised Georgia regiments, Drayton began to make arrangements to place additional torpedoes in the New and Wright Rivers. Even so, the Confederates could only react to enemy movements.[33]

Pemberton's first tests came in mid-March when Federal forces left Camp Seabrook on Hilton Head for a reconnaissance into the May River. On March 20 the northerners landed in barges at Bluffton and drove off elements of cavalry from Phillips Legion. The Confederate commander, Major John B. Willcoxon, greatly exaggerated the threat, and Pemberton, fearing an all-out attack, put his troops in motion. Portions of the Tennessee regiments from General Donelson's command moved from their bases at Coosawhatchie and Grahamville toward Bluffton. At the same time, Pemberton directed a portion of the 14th South Carolina to move by railroad from Pocotaligo Station to Coosawhatchie. They then marched to the entrenchments near Bee's Creek, while eight companies of the 12th South Carolina moved from Stony Creek to Pocotaligo Station and proceeded by rail to Grahamville Station and into the evacuated camps at Grahamville.

Although the enemy had long since left the area, the movements of Confederate troops displayed how Lee's defensive scheme worked. Cavalry pickets reported the presence of the enemy. While they skirmished with the attackers, word was relayed to headquarters. In this case the Confederates moved forward men from camps near the rail line. Troops from General Drayton's Sixth District advanced to engage the enemy as units from Donelson's Fifth District and Gregg's Fourth District, sent on railroad cars, occupied the defensive positions vacated by Drayton.

The exercise proved successful, for it showed the responsiveness of the Confederates to any perceived threat. However, unless the Confederates received accurate intelligence, they might end up chasing phantom attacks all along the coast. General Drayton realized this possibility and took corrective measures. Reporting to Pemberton, Drayton wrote that Major Willcoxon no longer held a separate command and that "I trust under a new and severer discipline no such confused reports of the position and numbers of the enemy will again be forwarded like those which have so lately ended in harassing marches and disappointment to the troops."[34]

On April 1, 1862, the Federals again landed at Page Point. The Confederates responded by shifting forces to the threatened area, but the Federals withdrew before any action developed. The Confederates had followed their prescribed plans to meet the enemy, but that was the last time the coastal defenders had such a large force to deploy.

On April 10, the same day that Union siege guns opened up against Fort Pulaski, Pemberton received orders from General Lee, now President Davis's military adviser, to send six regiments to General Beauregard in Tennessee. General Donelson, with the 8th and 16th Tennessee, left Beaufort District. For one day Colonel Peyton H. Colquitt of the 46th Georgia took over the Fifth District. Then on April 11, the district was combined with General Gregg's Fifth District. These troop shifts foreshadowed things to come. Never again would the Confederate districts at the headwaters of the Broad River contain as many soldiers as they did in the winter and spring of 1862. Demands elsewhere continually pulled men away. While the forts and defensive scheme remained in place, the manpower to use them well was greatly reduced. Where once regiments stood to guard the Charleston and Savannah Railroad, there remained only companies.[35]

Chapter 2

Federal Occupation Begins

"A sadder picture of desolation from the desertion of the population cannot be imagined"

While the Confederates fled inland and reorganized their defenses along the Charleston and Savannah Railroad, the United States Navy basked in the afterglow of a spectacular victory that forever changed the face of naval warfare. Powered by steam engines and filled with large-caliber naval artillery, the Union vessels overmatched the Confederate forts and pounded them into submission. The traditional superiority of defensive forts over invading vessels was shattered.

On November 7, 1861, Du Pont, aboard his flagship, the steam frigate *Wabash,* led fifteen warships arranged in two parallel lines northward into Port Royal Sound. The two columns passed midway between Fort Beauregard to the east on Bay Point and Fort Walker to the west on Hilton Head. Once past the forts, the five gunboats in the eastern line steamed into the sound and screened off the makeshift enemy warships. The vessels in the western line, which contained Du Pont's largest ships, circled in front of Walker, moved past the fort and then turned into the sound to form a second circle. By now the overmatched Confederate squadron had retired into Skull Creek, allowing four of the Union gunboats to join the attack against Fort Walker's northern flank. They soon took up a position and began investing Fort Walker from the north, but their movement confused the commander of the *Mohican,* the third vessel behind the *Wabash,* causing him to break formation and join the gunboats bombarding Walker's northern flank. The warships behind the *Mohican* followed suit, leaving the circling *Wabash* and *Susquehanna* and joining the ships inside the sound. Du Pont, realizing that his plan was unraveling, signaled the departing ships to return to formation, but only one of the gunboats—the *Bienville*—joined the now-reduced circle passing in front of Walker.

The attackers ignored Fort Beauregard and concentrated on Fort Walker. Assailed from the front and flanks, the fort's defenders could only put up a token, though spirited defense. The intensity of the bombardment grew when the late-arriving gunboat *Pocahontas,* commanded by Percival Drayton, the brother of Confederate general Thomas F. Drayton, took up a position on Walker's southern flank, completing the crossfire. Overwhelmed by the fleet's superior firepower, the Confederates evacuated Walker and left Hilton Head before Federal vessels entered Skull Creek and cut them off from the mainland.

When word reached Du Pont that enemy troops were abandoning Fort Walker, he ordered Commander Christopher Raymond Perry Rodgers of the *Wabash* to take ashore a force of sailors and marines and occupy the fort. Before Rodgers had organized his landing force, his cousin, Commander John Rodgers, an aide to Du Pont, volunteered to go ashore under a flag of truce to reconnoiter and raise the United States flag. With Du Pont's permission, John Rodgers rowed ashore. No one was found alive in the fort, and Rodgers returned to the *Wabash* with two Confederate swords, one for Du Pont, the other for his son, and a palmetto flag for his cousin Christopher R. P. Rodgers.

To celebrate raising the Union flag, the band on the USS *Susquehanna* played "The Star-Spangled Banner" and the popular tune not yet associated with the South, "Dixie." Soon C. R. P. Rodgers was ashore with the landing party of marines and sailors. Fort Walker was occupied and then the army transports were allowed to enter the harbor.[1]

The first troops ashore were men from Connecticut, the 6th and 7th Infantry Regiments of Brigadier General Horace Gouverneur Wright's brigade. The men of the 6th were carried toward Hilton Head aboard the light-drafted steamer *Winfield Scott,* while the soldiers from the 7th were towed behind in launches. Before they reached the beach, the *Winfield Scott* and the small boats grounded, forcing the men to wade in through cold, armpit-deep water, carrying their rifles and cartridge boxes over their heads. No enemy resisted the landing, but the Federals were "bloodied" by sand burrs and "active fleas with nippers sharpened to perfection." The 7th took possession of Fort Walker while the 6th camped outside. Fires were built to warm the men and dry their clothes. Before nightfall the entire Union army, 12,653 officers and men, was ashore. This would be the largest number of soldiers on Hilton Head at any time during the war.[2]

The arrival of the Federals had not gone unnoticed by the region's slaves, who announced to the newcomers that they had been waiting since March 1861 for the Yankees to come. The refugees, boys and men of all ages, house servants and field hands, came from the neighboring islands to Hilton Head and Bay Point. Though, as one reporter noted, "their jargon" was nearly "unintelligible," they made it clear that many more were coming. An older slave, who remembered President Andrew Jackson and the nullification crisis of 1832, stated that the sea island whites of 1860 were as strong against the Union as they had been in 1832, but in 1832 Jackson had quickly sent warships and, the man explained, "when the frigates came the people all went over again on their side, and I think, Masa, if Masa Lincoln had sent all these ships here last Spring, they'd had made all people change again."

Immediately the masterless slaves celebrated their liberation. On the evening of November 8, just one day after the battle, slaves gathered inside Fort Walker and held a religious service offering thanks to God for their deliverance. A few miles away at Seabrook, some two hundred blacks gathered, many recent escapees from the mainland and Pinckney Island. In front of their quarters, they held a jubilee, dancing and singing around fires.[3]

While the slaves celebrated their freedom, the Federal army commander Brigadier General Thomas West Sherman, whose name would forever be confused with that of William Tecumseh Sherman, organized expeditions to clear Hilton Head Island of any remaining rebels. With men from the 6th Connecticut taking the lead, soldiers followed the enemy's route from Fort Walker to the ferry landings. All along the way, they found abandoned equipment and jubilant slaves selling sweet potatoes. On November 9 three companies from the 7th Connecticut, under its colonel, Alfred Howe Terry, a Yale graduate who eventually achieved the rank of major general and commanded George Armstrong Custer during the 1876 Little Big Horn Campaign, escorted General Wright and the expedition's chief engineer, Captain Quincy A. Gillmore, to the abandoned Confederate fort at Braddock's Point on Hilton Head's southern tip.

From Braddock's Point the Union soldiers could clearly observe Fort Pulaski, the Confederate brick bastion at the mouth of the Savannah River. To let their presence be known, the Federals drilled out a spike hammered into the vent of an abandoned cannon and, using Confederate powder and shot, fired a round at Fort Pulaski. Although the distance was too great to reach Pulaski, the shot awakened "Johnny Reb and brought him up on the walls of the fort in large numbers to see what the Yanks were up to."[4]

While some of the northerners scouted the island, the rest feasted on wine, cakes, jellies, and other delicacies left behind by the Confederates. Quartermaster equipment was unloaded from supply vessels onto scows and surfboats and landed at the growing Union camp around Fort Walker and the Pope Plantation. A soldier from New Hampshire reported that their camp was located in a three-hundred-acre cotton field "surrounded by cotton, sweet potatoes, corn, beans, mules, oranges, palmetto trees, southern pines, niggers, palms, and peanuts." Another New Hampshire soldier wrote, "Aside from the fort I have not seen a hill a foot high nor a rock big enough to throw at a robin. The sun rises from the ocean and goes down in the sand.... The face of nature presents the utmost possible contrast with breezy, sparkling, ever changing New England."[5]

Soon the Union soldiers were making their own mark on Hilton Head. Concerned about a possible counterattack, Sherman immediately put his men to work constructing a massive defensive line one mile from the beach. Designed by Gillmore, the earthworks enclosed not only the expedition's campground but also all of its supporting facilities—ordnance yards, commissary buildings, and warehouses. Work began on a massive pier that stretched 1,277 feet into the sound, where the nation's largest vessels could dock. Rufus Saxton, the expedition's chief quartermaster, wrote to his superior, Quartermaster General Montgomery Meigs, that the sound possessed "unrivaled advantages for a quartermaster's and naval depot, and in the future a great commercial city must grow up here."[6]

Members of the 1st New York Engineer Regiment, commanded by the well-known civil-engineer-turned-soldier Colonel Edward Wellman Serrell, did much of the work on the fortifications and pier. The regiment's officers supervised their own men and working parties provided by the infantry regiments. One soldier reported, "Wheelbarrows, pickaxes and shovels were numerous, and we soon learned their use. . . . we became very proficient with the shovel and the pick, and for a time our rifles became rusty; but the same could not be said of our shovels."[7]

While the soldiers strengthened their hold on Hilton Head, the sailors occupied Fort Beauregard on Bay Point. On the morning of November 8, Lieutenant Daniel Ammen, commander of the gunboat *Seneca,* went ashore with a landing party of sailors and secured the abandoned fort. Although the island was empty of rebel soldiers, danger still lurked around the enemy's camp as the Confederates had left behind numerous explosive devices that could be detonated by trip wires and other ingenious methods. Ammen narrowly missed being blown up in a cottage near the fort by what he called an "essentially mean" device. At noon Ammen turned Bay Point over to Brigadier General Isaac Ingalls Stevens, who came ashore with soldiers from the 79th New York. Company D of the 3rd Rhode Island, an ambidextrous regiment trained to serve as infantrymen and artillerymen, soon joined the New Yorkers. In Fort Beauregard the Rhode Islanders discovered additional booby traps, one so arranged that when the Confederate flag was hauled down it would set fire to a powder train designed to explode the fort's magazine. The traps were defused, but it made the soldiers wary as they explored their new home.[8]

On Hilton Head, General Sherman began preparing his command for possible Confederate counterstrikes. Known by his friends as Tim, Sherman had not quite reached his forty-eighth birthday. He was a career artilleryman who had served at Charleston before the Mexican War. A hero of the conflict, Sherman had received a brevet for gallantry at the Battle of Buena Vista, where his artillery battery, along with that of Braxton Bragg, had stopped the final Mexican charge with a "little more grape."

Sherman had fond memories of his time and friends in South Carolina, but now he represented a government determined to restore constitutional authority in a rebellious state. To assist him, the War Department had given Sherman an impressive array of officers. Prominent among his staff were Quartermaster Captain Rufus Saxton, First Lieutenant James Harrison Wilson of the Topographical Engineers, and Captain Quincy Adams Gillmore, the expedition's chief engineer.

Saxton, a thirty-seven-year-old West Pointer from the class of 1849, was a native of Greenfield, Massachusetts. His family was part of New England's abolitionist movement and staunchly backed the Charles Fourier–inspired Brook Farm experiment. Although Saxton shared his family's views about slavery and Fourierism, his military career kept him from active involvement with his family's abolitionism and zeal for social reform. A trained artilleryman, Saxton spent most of his early army career as a surveyor, first on the route of the transcontinental railroad and later with the Coast Survey. At the start of the war, he returned to the artillery and was stationed in St. Louis, where he aided Captain Nathaniel Lyon in capturing the city's pro-South militia. Saxton served as Lyon's staff quartermaster and later carried out the same duties under General George B. McClellan in western Virginia before his assignment to the Port Royal Expedition.

Gillmore, chief engineer at Port Royal, had been a classmate of Saxton's at West Point, taking top honors in the 1849 class. A quick-speaking, quick-moving man, he was considered a brilliant artilleryman and engineer, an opinion of himself that he shared. Gillmore was a solid six feet tall with a big head, broad shoulders, and a good-humored face. He had a high forehead that was slightly elongated by a suspicion of baldness, curly brown hair, and a full beard that did not hide a frank and open face. The thirty-six-year-old native of Lorain, Ohio, had been a schoolteacher before attending West Point, where he achieved not only a number-one ranking but also the plum assignment of assistant engineer at Fort Monroe, Virginia. He later taught engineering at West Point before being placed in charge of the fortifications around New York Harbor. From that prestigious post Gillmore was named chief engineer of the Port Royal Expedition.

Gillmore's work brought him into close contact with the expedition's topographical engineer, Lieutenant James Wilson. At twenty-four, the Illinois-born Wilson was part of a triumvirate from the 1860 West Point class that had sailed south with Sherman's command. The other members were John A. Tardy, one of Gillmore's assistant engineers, and Horace Porter, the expedition's chief of ordnance and future aide to General Grant. Although Wilson had graduated sixth in his class behind Tardy and Porter, who were second and third, Wilson surpassed them both in wartime achievements. Having served in Oregon before his assignment to the Port Royal Expedition, he was an energetic officer and an expert horseman. His talents for finding solutions to any military problem were first recognized during his brief assignment in South Carolina. Although he never found gossip that he would not repeat, Wilson was an astute soldier who tied his star to such generals as McClellan, William T. Sherman, and Ulysses S. Grant. Before the war ended, Wilson's career with Grant and Sherman would earn him the title of the North's most successful "boy general."

Another promising young officer was Second Lieutenant Patrick H. O'Rorke, the top graduate from West Point's June 1861 class. A veteran of First Bull Run (Manassas), O'Rourke had assisted in the construction of Washington's defenses before being assigned to the Port Royal Expedition. Although he was brevetted a captain for his fine work in mapping and building fortifications around Port Royal, O'Rourke later resigned from the regular army to become colonel of the 140th New York, serving at Fredericksburg and Chancellorsville. He was killed at Gettysburg on July 2, 1863.[9]

Also joining Sherman's staff at this time was Adam Badeau, who accompanied the expedition as a reporter for the *New York Express*. Badeau, a flamboyant, delicate man, joined the army's staff as a civilian volunteer and worked with Lieutenant Wilson, with whom he formed a lasting friendship. Badeau later gained a commission and became General Grant's military secretary. After the war he served in Grant's administration, accompanied the former president on his travels through Europe, wrote the *Military History of Ulysses S. Grant* and *Grant in Peace,* and assisted his former commander to compose his famous memoirs.

Thomas Sherman's small army had a distinct northeastern flavor with seven regiments hailing from New England, four from New York, and two from Pennsylvania. A Michigan regiment and a regular artillery company rounded out the expeditionary force. The infantry regiments were divided into three brigades commanded by Brigadier Generals Horatio G. Wright, Isaac Ingalls Stevens, and Egbert Ludovicus Viele. All three were accomplished engineers. Wright, who hailed from Connecticut, was a forty-one-year-old regular army officer, who had graduated second in his 1841 West Point class and had spent his prewar years building forts in Florida.

Viele, of Dutch extraction, had also attended West Point but had left the army after the Mexican War to pursue a career in civil engineering. For a time Viele served as chief engineer for New York's Central Park but resigned when his landscape plan to develop the park was rejected in favor of one submitted by Frederick Law Olmstead. A well-known civil engineer, Viele kept up his interest in military engineering. His 1861 *Handbook for Active Service* was published both in New York and Richmond and used by Confederates and Yankees alike.

The third member of the triumvirate of brigadiers, Isaac Ingalls Stevens, was a fiery, forty-two-year-old, Massachusetts-born West Pointer, who had graduated first in the 1839 class, which included Henry "Old Brains"

Halleck. Barely five feet tall, swarthy, and bearded, Stevens thought no man his superior. A natural soldier and leader, Stevens was a trained engineer. In Mexico he had been badly wounded and was nursed back to health by nuns. In gratitude, Stevens converted to Roman Catholicism.

In the post–Mexican War army, Stevens found promotion to be too slow. In 1853 he resigned his commission to become governor of the Washington Territory in the Pacific Northwest and director of the northern transcontinental railroad survey. In this capacity he oversaw the work of such officers as Rufus Saxton, George B. McClellan, and Frederick West Lander. Governor Stevens made treaties with the territory's Indian tribes that secured cessions of over one hundred thousand acres of Indian land. He also encouraged the Native Americans to give up their nomadic life to become landowners and farmers. When some dissatisfied Indians joined former British residents to attack American settlers, Stevens raised his own army, defeated his enemies, and summarily arrested suspected Indian or British sympathizers. When challenged by the territorial chief justice, Stevens had him arrested. Rightfully compared to Andrew Jackson, Stevens proved himself a man not to be thwarted.

A staunch Democrat, Stevens served from 1857 to 1860 as Washington's territorial representative to Congress, where he won approval of his high-handed actions as governor. During the 1860 election, Stevens, fearing that a victory for Lincoln or Douglas would bring secession, backed John C. Breckinridge, the Democrat who led the party's southern wing, as the only way to avert disunion. With Lincoln's victory, Stevens denounced disunion and called upon President Buchanan to expel prosecession southerners from his cabinet. Back in the Washington Territory when war broke out, Stevens hastened to the nation's capital, arriving after the Battle of Bull Run. Given command of the mutinous 79th New York Highlanders, Stevens quickly restored order by both appealing to the Highlanders' sense of duty and threatening to order a battery of artillery and infantry regiments to open fire upon the rebellious troops. Knowing that they had met their match, the New Yorkers surrendered to Stevens, who soon made the 79th New York into one of the best-drilled and most disciplined regiments in the Army of the Potomac. When Stevens was promoted to brigade command and assigned to the Port Royal Expedition, the Highlanders requested and (against the wishes of the Army of the Potomac's commander, General George B. McClellan) received permission to join Stevens's brigade for the attack on Port Royal.[10]

While Wright and Viele were cautious, Stevens, once ashore with his command, called upon Sherman to gather up the numerous flatboats scattered around the islands for an immediate push inland against an enemy that he rightly saw as demoralized and unorganized. However, Sherman, backed by the other brigade commanders, refused to move. Instead, the commander continued to improve his defenses and enlarge his quartermaster, commissary, and ordnance facilities.[11]

Although reluctant to begin military operations against the enemy, Sherman did not hesitate to ignite a written salvo in the form of a proclamation to the people of South Carolina. In the brief declaration, Sherman explained that he had been sent south by orders of the president of the United States to suppress an unholy rebellion that was attempting to usurp constitutional authority. Yet Sherman also stated "that we have come amongst you with no feelings of personal animosity; no desire to harm your citizens, destroy your property, or interfere with any of your lawful rights or your social institutions." The proclamation was designed to chastise the southerners, yet assure them that they could retain their property, including their slaves, and their former lifestyle under the benevolent protection of the United States military. Unfortunately there were few whites and even fewer property owners to receive Sherman's proclamation. The only planter who remained was on Parris Island. He stayed for weeks until peer pressure from his absconded neighbors forced him to join them in exile.[12]

In an attempt on November 14 to convince the absent citizens to return to their homes, General Sherman dispatched Surgeon Francis Bacon of the 7th Connecticut and Lieutenant Gus Wagner from his staff to carry a copy of the proclamation and a letter to the mainland requesting that "all loyal citizens should return peaceably to their homes and protect their property from the ravages that the negro population are now committing." Sherman promised that "all loyal and peaceable citizens shall be protected in their persons and property and receive the benefits of all constitutional enactments on their behalf."

Bacon and Wagner were taken to Beaufort aboard the USS *Seneca*, where they procured two "indifferent mules" and, carrying flag of truce, rode toward Port Royal Ferry. They met a number of Negroes who, once realizing they were Yankees, greeted them warmly and warned them that the Confederates still maintained pickets on Port Royal Island. About five miles out they met the Reverend Mr. Joseph R. Walker, rector of St. Helena Episcopal Church, who was returning to the mainland from visiting his home at Retreat Plantation. The Federal officers attempted to give Sherman's letter to Walker, but the minister, not wishing to get caught up in matters of war, refused. Walker did take the opportunity to describe to his companions the terror the inhabitants of Beaufort had experienced over alleged atrocities being committed by U.S. forces in Virginia, though he assured the Union officers that the people had confidence in the officers of the army and navy, commenting that it was the common people of the North whom they feared. Bacon, somewhat tongue in cheek, assured Walker that he and Lieutenant Wagner were "two of these same common people of the north."

The men rode on to Port Royal Ferry, where they were met by Captain Thomas O. Barnwell and Lieutenant Henry McKee of the 12th South Carolina Militia Regiment. The southerners greeted the riders courteously and listened politely while Dr. Bacon read the letter and the proclamation, but the Confederates declined to accept the papers and carry them to the mainland. Captain Barnwell then informed the northerners that he was one of the Barnwells of South Carolina and that the Federals would find it much more difficult when the two sides met on land, beyond the reach of the navy's great guns. The captain also stated that it was a great regret that they had not burned Beaufort. He did state that after its evacuation the southerners had sent slaves to fire the town, but they "did not see fit to do it, preferring to occupy the mansions they were ordered to destroy."[13]

With their mission over, Bacon and Wagner returned to Beaufort and the *Seneca,* which carried them back to Hilton Head. General Sherman never again attempted to communicate to the absent civilians. With his proclamation falling on deaf or unwilling ears, the general had now turned to a more ominous set of instructions from the War Department regarding loyal persons found in the Port Royal area. These directives sprang from a policy begun in Virginia in May 1861 by Major General Benjamin Butler when he refused to return three runaway slaves. Butler's logic was simple. Slaves were vital to the Confederate economy and war effort; therefore, Butler declared slaves to be the equivalent of war matériel or contraband of war. Butler's policy was backed by the War Department and later sanctioned by Congress. It gave refugee slaves legal status in the United States and a new nickname—contrabands.[14]

By the time of the Port Royal Expedition, the War Department, headed by the radical abolitionist Secretary of War Simon Cameron, had expanded the "slaves as contraband" concept. In a directive to Sherman, the War Department authorized the Federal commander, at his discretion, to use the "services of any persons, whether fugitives from labor or not, who may offer them to the National Government." Sherman could also "employ such persons in such service as they may seem fitted for—either as ordinary employees, or, if special circumstances seem to require it, in any other capacity with organization (in squads, companies or otherwise) as you may deem most beneficial to the service; this, however, not being a general arming of them for military service." While his instructions directed Sherman to avoid interfering with local social systems and institutions, he could hire slaves from loyal masters, who would then be compensated for use of their property by Congress. Still, the intent of the order was clear: Sherman could employ fugitive slaves as laborers, and in emergencies he could arm them.[15]

Although Sherman ignored his instructions about arming "such persons," he intended to use African Americans, with or without masters, as laborers.

Available to the Federals were the ex-slaves on Hilton Head. However, while they were happy to be free of "massa," they hesitated to bind themselves to the Yankees. Instead, they took a wait-and-see attitude while consuming the food supplies on their plantations and enjoying the respite from work. Besides the native islanders, slaves arrived from the mainland, hundreds during the first few days of occupation. Some came on their own hook, while others were sent over by their masters to burn cotton and other supplies. Once on Hilton Head, they readily turned themselves over to the Union pickets. These refugees needed shelter and food, which the Federals provided, but like the native islanders, they were reluctant to work for these new masters.[16]

While the slaves were migrating to Hilton Head, Federal soldiers and sailors officially and unofficially began exploring nearby islands and plantations. Some of the initial reconnaissance was done by the soldiers who wandered out beyond their encampments on Hilton Head, while the more adventurous appropriated unguarded launches and boats to inspect the nearby sea islands and mainland. At first the men behaved like visitors viewing museums and left the homes untouched, but soon souvenir hunters began claiming pieces of china and books. Then the soldiers began plundering homes, stripping them of anything useful while destroying or mutilating whatever they left behind. Sherman and Du Pont were outraged by what the general called "gross depredations," including shooting pistols into a piano at Means Plantation on Parris Island. Du Pont felt such behavior disgraced his victory.[17]

To discourage further vandalism, Sherman on November 11 issued orders banning men from entering private homes. He also instructed his soldiers to cease any retaliation against citizens judged to be of an incorrect "political character." At the same time, Du Pont had his command watch all maritime activities in order to head off unauthorized expeditions. During this early stage of the conflict, both Du Pont and Sherman, like most of their peers in the regular service, recoiled at the idea of a war against citizens; but soon the hostilities expanded from a purely military campaign to operations that affected every fiber of the lowcountry's prewar society.[18]

While Sherman tried to keep his men under control, Du Pont began carrying out the next phase of his assignment. With Port Royal taken, the flag officer was able to send some of his larger vessels to stiffen the blockade off Charleston and Savannah. At the same time, the Navy Department placed him in charge of all harbor activities, military and civilian, at Port Royal. Word was sent that two flotillas of whaling vessels, stripped and loaded with granite, would soon arrive to obstruct the channels off Charleston and Savannah. Although this so-called Stone Fleet had been discussed between Du Pont and Assistant Secretary of the Navy Gustavus Fox before the expedition had sailed, Du Pont came to believe the plan useless and referred to the whalers as an "elephant."

While waiting for the Stone Fleet, Du Pont began developing his naval depot. For this he needed navigation aids, supplies, and maintenance facilities. Although the navy used Bay Point, home of the squadron's marine battalion, and part of Land's End on St. Helena Island for shore facilities, the bulk of the naval activities occurred on water. All coaling was done in the sound between contracted colliers and warships. To provide fresh water for his vessels' boilers and drinking water, a schooner was outfitted with a coal-burning condensing apparatus that produced ten thousand gallons of fresh water a day. Du Pont recalled that the French and British had converted ships into repair facilities during the Crimean War and asked Fox to send vessels to be outfitted as floating machine shops.[19]

He requested from the navy's lighthouse board a lightship and a number of buoys to use in and around the sound and the neighboring rivers and creeks, as well as a buoy tender and a pilot boat. Du Pont also hoped to secure some additional equipment, including two light boats that were reported to be at Beaufort.[20]

Beaufort had become virtually an open city upon the evacuation of Forts Walker and Beauregard. By November 8 it had been abandoned by the majority of its citizens. The last Confederates to pass through the town were upcountry soldiers from Company C, 12th South Carolina, the rear guard of the forces retreating from Bay Point. The company, under the command of Captain Henry C. Davis, had begun its withdrawal at sunset on November 7. After floundering through knee- and waist-deep water, the men reached Station Creek, where "full-blooded Gullahs" rowed them on flats to the landing at Dr. William J. Jenkins's plantation on St. Helena Island. Here Dr. Jenkins provided a slave to guide the men to the Beaufort ferry. The slave, mistrusted, was kept at musket point for the entire march. He led the men across St. Helena and Lady's Islands, reaching the Beaufort ferry at sunup. A leaky steamer was commandeered and the company taken to the nearly deserted city. As one soldier wrote, "Where all had been contentment, riches and happiness, was now confusion, sadness, sorrow, desolation and misery; all the loyal citizens had gone."

Not only were the citizens gone, but so also was any semblance of order and authority. Hordes of masterless slaves paid little heed to the retreating Confederates and instead stared down the river anxiously watching for Yankee gunboats. Captain Davis, sensing that his men needed some steadying before continuing the march, directed a detachment to find some whiskey. A store was found where a proprietor named Wilcox was busily preparing his stock for the Yankees. Wilcox refused to take the soldiers' scrip; so, over Wilcox's objections, they took the liquor and returned to their command. Once properly braced, the men moved on. By sunset they reached Port Royal Ferry, where the exhausted soldiers boarded the ferryboat and roped themselves over to the mainland. There the men searched for food. They found some raw beef, grits, and sweet potatoes, but they had nothing to cook with and thus went hungry. After a restless night near the ferry, the marchers started again the next morning. The final leg of the journey was long and discouraging. Wagons, carts, and carriages carrying civilians and what few belongings they had been able to gather up from their homes blocked the road. The flight ended at Pocotaligo, where the men from C Company joined their regiment and finally received proper rations.[21]

As the last of the Confederates gathered near Pocotaligo, the Union gunboats *Seneca, Pembina,* and *Curlew* cautiously moved up the Beaufort River. The small flotilla, commanded by Lieutenant Daniel Ammen, had left anchorage off Hilton Head at about noon on November 9 and steamed into the Beaufort River. Ammen kept his vessels cleared for action, but the only people seen were gangs of slaves lining the bluff along the Beaufort River. Upon reaching the town, Ammen sent Lieutenant J. Glendy Sproston ashore under a flag of truce to communicate with civilian authorities and the light ships. Sproston found no officials, only crowds of slaves celebrating their masters' departure by breaking into buildings and carrying off portable property. Sproston learned from the slaves that many of them had been fired upon when they refused to follow their fleeing masters. The slaves also told Sproston that there were two whites still in the town, Mr. Wilcox and Mr. Allen.

Sproston was taken to Allen's store, where he found the visibly shaken merchant holding a flag of truce. Frightened by the looting slaves, Allen informed Sproston that the light ships had been burned on November 7, immediately after the forts had fallen. As a search for Wilcox proved fruitless, Allen was taken to the *Seneca,* where he met with Lieutenant Ammen. The Union officer thought Allen "overcome with fear or drink" but assured the shaken merchant that the navy would protect the town and the property of any inhabitants who would return to their homes. Allen was sent ashore and Ammen prepared to take his vessels back to the sound. However, both the *Seneca* and *Pembina,* 158-foot regular gunboats with nearly 11-foot drafts, steered out of the channel and ran aground. Ammen managed to free the *Seneca,* but with the tide falling he left behind the *Pembina,* commanded by South Carolina–born John P. Bankhead, and the smaller *Curlew.*

On the way downriver, Ammen came across a boatload of slaves who were brought aboard the *Seneca.* The refugees informed Ammen that their masters too had fired on them and that they were looking for guidance. Ammen, who had no instructions on how to handle the masterless slaves, took the middle road and informed them that the navy had neither come to take them from their masters nor to keep them in slavery. As far as Ammen was concerned, the fugitive slaves were free to go wherever they wished, to Beaufort or to Hilton Head.[22]

When word of affairs in Beaufort reached Du Pont, the flag officer, who could not abide plundering by soldiers or slaves, ordered Lieutenant Napoleon Collins to take the gunboat *Unadilla* to Beaufort to stop looting. By the time Collins arrived, he found that sailors from the *Pembina* and *Curlew* had restored order by threatening to shoot anyone found taking or damaging private property. Collins sent off the *Curlew* and then reconnoitered the town. In Beaufort, slaves told Collins that their owners had fled fearing a slave revolt, which seemed likely since the majority of slaves, under threat of death, had refused to join the flight to the mainland. As many told the lieutenant, "Massa, they more afraid us, than you."

Collins located additional navigational aids at the arsenal, including a Fresnel lens from the Hunting Island Lighthouse. He also posted a notice:

> Every effort has been made by us to prevent the negroes from plundering their masters' houses. Had the owners remained and taken care of their property and negroes, it would not have occurred. I only trust that we will not be accused of the vandalism.
> An American Navy Officer.

An answer to the notice came that night when a volley of musket shots was directed at the gunboats.[23]

On November 12 Du Pont, on a pleasure trip, made an excursion to Beaufort on the *Seneca* with General Sherman. Towed behind the *Seneca,* armed launches carried bronze howitzers and armed sailors. Du Pont described the trip to his wife:

> The day was lovely though warm. General Sherman was with me; my staff, Captains Comstock and Eldridge of the *Baltic* and *Atlantic* I also invited. Ammen, the commander of the *Seneca,* is a kindly and hospitable person as well as a good officer—and had found oysters, boasting he was the only officer who had the purveyance to bring oyster tongs for taking them.
>
> You approach Beaufort on its full seaward facade; the houses are two and three stories, with verandas, large, and have a beautiful effect; the streets are wide, the gardens and shrubbery in the yards show the refinements of educated people but without the order of Northern towns of this description.[24]

At Beaufort, Du Pont and his guests landed under the guns of the gunboats. The bluejackets came ashore with their howitzers, which were placed in the streets to guard against any sudden Confederate attack. While their escorts watched for enemy soldiers, Du Pont and his party toured the town visiting houses, including Edmund Rhett's home. Many of the buildings showed the haste with which the inhabitants had fled. Du Pont wrote:

> A sadder picture of desolation from the desertion of the population cannot be imagined; and the inhabitants fled not from fear of us but from dread of their own Negroes; a few household servants followed their masters, but the field hands they dare not attempt to control, and the overseers had run with the masters. There are fifteen slaves to one white in this part; the latter threatened to shoot if they did not follow them into the interior, but I believe dare not attempt to execute this threat.... Yet these are people whose very slaves were to drive us into the sea, fleeing from the institution with terror in their hearts, not taking a thing with them.

Du Pont was deeply moved by what he saw: "The impression produced by the sight of a city in perfect preservation and bearing all the signs of the most recent inhabitation, yet wanting the animation of ordinary life, was very striking."[25]

Since General Sherman did not consider Beaufort a strategic point worth holding, Du Pont decided it best to withdraw his vessels from their exposed positions. The flag officer felt that he had held the town long enough for the inhabitants to return. He also valued the lives of his sailors over any attempt to protect the property of secessionists from their own slaves. Although appalled by the looting of Beaufort, he understood the motives behind it. He informed his wife, "Negroes are wild with joy and revenge, robbing Beaufort—on the other hand they have been shot down, they say, like dogs because they would not go off with their masters."

After completing their visit, Du Pont and his guests returned to the *Seneca* and with the *Pembina* and *Unadilla* steamed down the river. Stopping at the John Joyner Smith Plantation, they viewed the tabby ruins of old Fort Prince Frederick, a colonial British fort that Du Pont mistakenly described as the 1562 outpost of the Frenchman Jean Ribaut. Up the bluff from the fort stood the Smith Plantation house and outbuildings. The Federal officers visited the slave quarters and cotton houses before returning to the *Seneca* and sailing on to Port Royal Sound.[26]

The short visit to Beaufort and the Smith Plantation had given Du Pont a close up view of slavery. It troubled him. Over the next few months, the old naval aristocrat had numerous opportunities to see the effects of slavery in South Carolina, Georgia, and Florida. Du Pont wrote to his wife, "I have defended the institution all the world over, as patriarchal in the United States, compared with the condition of the race in Africa, But God forgive me—I have seen nothing that has disgusted me more than the wretched physical wants of these poor people." His officers, who became part of an active campaign to assist the former slaves, joined Du Pont in his views. In another letter Du Pont stated, "None of us were prepared for what we have seen of the institution, and the Southern officers, of which this squadron has many, seem more shocked than any others." He later wrote, "I have not been able to ascertain that [a] single officer of this squadron voted for Lincoln, but there is not a proslavery man among them." On the squadron commanders' reading list was Hinton R. Helper's *Impending Crisis,* a book Du Pont and his officers found "so true" in its description of slavery and its effect on people.[27]

Besides beginning their conversion from apologists to opponents of slavery, Du Pont and his officers learned the value of former slaves as crewmen and pilots. On November 19 an expedition piloted by a former slave came to Beaufort to reclaim the Fresnel lens. Sailors and marines landed, seized the lens at the arsenal, and destroyed a quantity of artillery ammunition, gun carriages, and equipment. The leader of the expedition, Commander Jonathan P. Gillis, wrote of Beaufort that "the ravages were commenced by the retreating Confederates ... and the Negroes continued the work. The stores were stripped of their contents and private dwellings are in the greatest disorder, furniture broken, beds ripped open and their feathers scattered ... books, valuable books lying about in the yards and streets, torn, mutilated; in the houses all is disorder."

When first entering Beaufort, Gillis's men found but one slave; the rest were in hiding, as their masters were still attempting to carry them off. The arrival of the warships drove the rebels off but not before they had shot two slaves. With their assailants gone, hundreds of slaves appeared in Beaufort seeking help from the Federals, but Gillis's force only spent the night before returning to Port Royal, leaving the slaves to fend for themselves.[28]

While Gillis had left the slaves in Beaufort to their own devices, other naval commanders were calling on Du Pont to provide protection and care for the refugees. One such officer was Percival Drayton, a native South Carolinian who had commanded the USS *Pocahontas* during the attack against Fort Walker. In that battle he had fired on his own brother, Thomas, the Confederate commanding officer on Hilton Head. A favorite of Du Pont, Drayton was assigned to command the *Pawnee,* a vessel well suited for operations in coastal waters. In late November, Drayton took the USS *Pawnee* and four other vessels on a reconnaissance mission into St. Helena Sound.[29]

Piloting the expedition was Charles O. Boutelle, a top assistant in the U.S. Coast Survey service. Before the war Boutelle had spent six years in the Port Royal area and had lived in Beaufort while surveying the waterways. Assigned to Du Pont's expedition by the survey's director, Alexander Dallas Bache, Boutelle sounded the harbor's entrance before the November 7 attack. Although vilified by his former Beaufort neighbors, Boutelle proved indispensable in assisting the navy and guiding expeditions.[30]

Their first stop was the abandoned Confederate fort on Otter Island, where they found its magazine blown. Drayton then took his squadron into the Coosaw River, past the Morgan River to Barnwell Creek, where they discovered a second, smaller fort called Fort Heyward. It too was abandoned and a shore party, joined by refugee slaves, destroyed the remaining equipment and gun carriages. The Federals then returned to St. Helena Sound and anchored off Coffin Point, where they brought off Lieutenant Patrick H. O'Rorke, an engineer who had been sent by Sherman to reconnoiter St. Helena Island and report on any enemy fortifications. The next day the flotilla, guided by Boutelle, ascended the Ashepoo River, past another abandoned redoubt, and sailed on to Hutchinson Island before returning to the sound. Drayton then took his vessels to Hunting Island, where he visited the remains of the lighthouse, which had recently been destroyed by the Confederates.

Drayton's expedition confirmed that not only the Confederate military but also local civilians had fled the region around St. Helena Sound. Forts were evacuated, cannons destroyed, and plantations, cotton, and slaves abandoned. Drayton was impressed by the willingness of the slaves to voluntarily assist the Federals. He reported that the slaves understood that the military was there to help them, and in turn the slaves believed that they should help the northerners. Drayton called upon Du Pont to occupy Otter Island, which would control the mouth of St. Helena Sound and guard a valuable anchorage.[31]

On this and later expeditions into the Ashepoo, May, and New Rivers, Union gunboats kept up the "panick." At Bluffton and Hutchinson Island, southerners burned their homes, cotton, and outbuildings, but the majority of their slaves remained behind. Soon U.S. warships began transporting the refugees to safer quarters. Some were taken to Hilton Head, while others were placed at a growing colony on Otter Island, where about 140 refugee slaves were gathered and fed.[32]

Though it was only a start, Du Pont was quite satisfied with his and his command's accomplishments. He was amazed at the magical transformation of Port Royal from a little-used harbor to now one of the busiest ports on the coast:

> When we arrived nothing of this existed . . . no business animation of any kind to meet the eye, not a fishing boat. And now great ships of commerce and war cover its waters—14,000 men are on an island where a few blacks resided, houses are going up, wharves building, wagons with six horse teams in all directions, carts, trucks, officers and

men on horseback flying in all directions, boats covering the beach, men up to their waists in water unloading the enormous material of every description which the expedition brought out, 2,000 men with shovels, picks, and barrows at work on the entrenchments, regiments drilling, 250 sailors with their howitzers, and officers from this ship [the *Wabash*] going through the battalion exercise while my gunboats, or their smoke, are seen up the Broad and Beaufort rivers, or at Skull Creek, a pass to Savannah, with tugs and ferryboats plying between Hilton Head and Bay Point, both held by our troops and marines. All this is so wonderful to me.[33]

Chapter 3

The Northern Foothold Expands

"Oh who would inhabit this Beaufort alone?"

While Du Pont basked in the afterglow of the Battle of Port Royal, his army counterpart, General Thomas W. Sherman, never forgot the fact that his soldiers had been mere observers to the navy's great victory. Sherman ought to have been able to overcome his chagrin, but his cautious ways and refusal to take a firm hand on the issues of contrabands and black soldiers worked against him. As commander of the expedition's land forces, Sherman had three major tasks: to protect the naval depot by holding the sea islands around Port Royal, to serve as a military governor, and to organize expeditions against other coastal objectives. Sherman had fortified his camp on Hilton Head, but the base's real protection came from Du Pont's vessels patrolling the waterways between the sea islands and the mainland. The Confederates would not attempt to retake the islands as long as armed gunboats stood in the way.

With virtually no white civilians remaining in the region, Sherman's duty as governor was limited. However, he was directed by the War Department to seize all abandoned cotton and other property "which may be used to our prejudice" and to employ the masterless slaves to pick cotton and build defenses. Sherman had hoped that some of the planters would return, but it soon became obvious that they had not only refused his invitation to live under Yankee rule but were also sending out raiding parties to burn cotton on the sea islands. To remedy the situation and meet his assignment, Sherman appointed William H. Nobles of the 79th New York and James Adrian Suydam collectors of abandoned cotton. So that no one could claim that the general or anyone else was lining his pockets, Sherman ordered Nobles to keep exact records on all cotton and other items appropriated for government use.

For laborers Noble was to use the masterless slaves, now termed contrabands, hired by the Quartermaster Bureau to pick and pack the cotton. Other ex-slaves hired by the army on Hilton Head served as laborers and stevedores, but many refused to serve until they were sure that their new overseers had truly brought them freedom—the long awaited "jubilee." When Sherman received orders to recruit three to four hundred contrabands to work on military projects at Key West, the general feared it might cause a panic among the slaves who would see it as confirmation of prewar stories told by their masters that if Yankees came, they would gather them up for sale to Cuban plantations. Although Sherman managed to outfit the work force in March 1862, some slaves remained suspicious, questioning whether the Yankees were really their saviors.[1]

The governing of nearly ten thousand masterless slaves was an operation unforeseen by Sherman and his superiors. At first the slaves lived off food found on the plantations, but as these stocks dwindled and more escapees arrived from the mainland, a refugee camp was established on Hilton Head. Sherman realized that a system had to be established that would permit them to "sustain themselves."[2] Sherman appealed to the War Department for help, but the northern commander had little time to think through the far-reaching nature of his actions.[3] Instead, the general had to accomplish his expedition's second goal: the capture and occupation of Fernandina, Florida. For this movement Sherman needed naval support, but the navy was too busy exploring the waterways around Port Royal to mount any new expeditions. Besides, Du Pont's warships had fired off so much ammunition against Forts Walker and Beauregard that they could not enter into battle until resupplied. The delay in his Fernandina campaign did not upset Sherman. He believed that even if the navy captured Fernandina, he did not have enough soldiers to guard a second foothold along the southeastern coast.[4]

When first organized as part of General Winfield Scott's grand strategy, popularly termed the Anaconda Plan, the Port Royal Expedition had as its limited objective the establishment of a naval/coaling station at one or two southern sounds. The army's role was to assist in the seizure and to defend the bases while the navy carried out its blockade. Just to hold Port Royal, Sherman requested additional forces. He informed his superiors that for any new offenses he needed substantial reinforcements. He lacked cavalry and transportation and doubted the value of his volunteers. For any new offensive Sherman wanted more regulars. In all, he requested three or four light-drafted steamers, some ferryboats, one hundred rowboats, a siege train, ten thousand infantrymen, and more cavalry, engineers, and artillerymen. Once sufficiently reinforced, Sherman proposed movements against the Charleston and Savannah Railroad and perhaps operations against Savannah and its guardian, Fort Pulaski.

Limited operations may have satisfied Scott, but when George B. McClellan took over as commander-in-chief, the strategic concept expanded. In early December 1861, McClellan informed Sherman that he envisioned strikes from Port Royal against vital Confederate industrial sites and port facilities. High on the list was Charleston, from which forces could be sent against Columbia and Augusta. McClellan viewed such campaigns as a way to destroy the South's ability to wage war, thus shortening the conflict and reducing casualties. Sherman understood the logic behind such moves and directed his chief engineer, Captain Quincy A. Gillmore, to design attack plans against Charleston. When completed, Sherman forwarded them to McClellan, pointing out that the attack would require an additional twenty thousand men, light artillery, and a siege train of thirty guns, pontoon bridges, and munitions.[5]

McClellan did not answer right away. Besides dealing with pressing problems around Washington, the commanding general was stricken with an illness that kept him from reading any dispatches for weeks. When he did respond, he informed Sherman that a siege train and additional surfboats would be sent but not the full complement of troops. Instead, Sherman would have to make do with what he had. McClellan believed that the capture of Charleston was worthy "of our greatest efforts" but understood the need for more men and hoped that Sherman could in the meantime campaign with the navy against Fort Pulaski and Fernandina.[6]

From November 1861 to February 1862, about five thousand reinforcements reached Port Royal. In January 1862 the balloon *Washington,* operated by John B. Starkweather, a Boston aeronaut and member of Thaddeus S. C. Lowe's Corps of Military Aeronauts, came to Hilton Head. New to the military, Lowe's gas-filled balloons had been successfully used to observe enemy movements. McClellan, believing that balloons could be useful along the Georgia and South Carolina coast, had ordered Lowe to send Sherman a fully outfitted balloon, complete with its equipment. Sailing aboard the brig *Empire,* Starkweather and the balloon *Washington* arrived at Hilton Head on January 3, 1862. In eight days he readied his equipment. To the delight of the soldiers, who could see the image of President George Washington on the balloon from a mile away, Starkweather made an ascent on Hilton Head. The next day he took the *Washington* up two more times; but Sherman, seemingly perplexed over the balloon and its use, ignored the aeronaut and gave him no orders, effectively grounding both Starkweather and the *Washington* for months.[7]

But even with the additional eyes and men, Sherman felt his numbers insufficient to undertake the Lincoln administration's desire for quick movements against Charleston and Savannah. Confederate strength was growing. Overall, along the East Florida, Georgia, and South Carolina coast, he was outnumbered. Only in the immediate Port Royal area were the two sides roughly equal. Even so, Sherman felt he had to do something to satisfy his superiors in Washington. Charleston was a greater prize than Savannah, but the navy was unwilling to challenge either city's defenses. In addition, the proposed overland campaign required more men than Sherman had available.

Charleston, with its elaborate array of fortifications and strong garrison, was not a viable choice.[8]

At first glance, Savannah seemed to present the same obstacles as Charleston, but Sherman had certain advantages that might lead to a successful strike on the Georgia city. First was proximity. From the southern tip of Hilton Head Island one could see Fort Pulaski, guardian of the Savannah River. Although it was a formidable work, the massive brick fort could be bypassed using rivers, creeks, and canals that connected the South Carolina waterways to the Savannah River some distance inland from the fort. Sherman hoped that Du Pont would send gunboats through these waterways and move directly on Savannah, but the flag officer viewed the venture with trepidation and refused to take it "by the horns." Instead of moving boldly through the rivers, the navy made timid attempts to maneuver their steamers through the inland passages and into the Savannah River. Disgusted, Sherman changed plans and began preparing for a more direct approach against Pulaski.[9]

A byproduct of the capture of Port Royal Sound was the Confederate evacuation of other island fortifications along the South Carolina and Georgia coast. The new Confederate commander, General Robert E. Lee, feared that these exposed forts and batteries would be easily gobbled up by the Union fleet, thus depriving him of valuable men, supplies, and cannons. Hence, against the protests of coastal planters and state politicians, Lee began a strategic withdrawal to the mainland. Among the first islands abandoned was Tybee Island at the mouth of the Savannah River. Its evacuation was quickly noticed by Union troops on Daufuskie Island and by blockading warships. On November 24, 1861, Union gunboats under the overall command of Commander John S. Missroon, a South Carolina native, bombarded the abandoned Confederate works before landing a shore party. Only lightly challenged by Josiah Tattnall's mosquito fleet two days later, the Federals held onto Tybee. Soon they prepared to turn the island into a gun platform to strike Fort Pulaski.[10]

Being a regular artilleryman, Sherman understood siege warfare and the power of artillery to batter down masonry walls. Unlike Lee, he believed that artillery positioned on Tybee Island could, given enough ammunition and time, crumble Pulaski's walls. Once in Federal hands, the fort would reverse its role. Instead of defending the Savannah River, it would plug it like a cork in a bottle, denying the Confederates use of the city's deep-water route to the Atlantic.

On November 27 Sherman made a personal reconnaissance of Tybee. He viewed the low-lying sandy barrier island with the eye of an experienced cannoneer. A little more than a mile away stood Fort Pulaski, a work considered as impregnable as the Rocky Mountains. Robert E. Lee believed Pulaski to be safe from any bombardment, but the Union commander disagreed.

Sherman thought it "not impossible to reduce Pulaski" from Tybee Island. His curiosity satisfied, Sherman left Tybee and turned the operation over to his chief engineer, Captain Quincy A. Gillmore.[11]

Two days after Sherman's inspection, Gillmore, accompanied by three companies of the 4th New Hampshire, landed on Tybee Island near the island's lighthouse. Abandoned Confederate earthworks were found on the island, including some located around a tabby-built martello tower, a relic of the War of 1812. Gillmore, like Sherman, believed that breaching batteries from Tybee could shatter Pulaski's walls. However, unlike his commanding officer, Gillmore was not planning to use standard smoothbore cannons whose round balls would only chip away at the fort's masonry. Instead, he planned to use new rifled guns that fired bullet-like projectiles that could drill into Pulaski's walls, penetrating feet instead of inches.

While surveying the island's terrain, Gillmore and his party encountered escaped slaves. Eager to prove their loyalty, the ex-slaves provided information and volunteered to burn railroad bridges between Savannah and Charleston. Gillmore considered this a worthy project and forwarded the offer, along with his plans to attack Pulaski, to Sherman. The commanding general did not reply on the subject of slave sabotage but did accept Gillmore's plan for attacking Pulaski. However, Sherman, who was not the true believer in newfangled rifled cannons that Gillmore was, directed that large smoothbore cannons be placed in the batteries in case the rifled guns were "non effective." Gillmore agreed to add smoothbore Columbiad cannons to his arsenal, and on December 6, 1861, the 46th New York moved from Port Royal to occupy Tybee Island.[12]

As Gillmore began his operations, Sherman slowly expanded his foothold around Port Royal Sound. The occupation of Tybee Island was the start of a three-pronged movement designed to place Federals not only on Tybee but also on Otter and Port Royal islands. Naval commander Percival Drayton had long urged the occupation of Otter Island. The low-lying barrier island guarded the entrance of St. Helena Sound and the mouths of the Morgan, Coosaw, Combahee, Ashepoo, and South Edisto Rivers. Drayton also saw the need to protect the island's growing population of refugee slaves, who sometimes burned their masters' homes and plantation outbuildings before taking launches and fleeing to Otter Island. Once there, the ex-slaves established a small village but lived in constant fear of retaliation from their former masters or Confederate soldiers. A South Carolinian, Drayton sympathized with their plight and desire for freedom and directed Lieutenant James W. A. Nicholson, the senior naval officer in charge of St. Helena Sound and the surrounding waters, to guard the island and assist the slaves.

Nicholson took the steamer *Isaac Smith* and the sailing sloop *Dale,* into the Ashepoo, using sailors and marines to raid Confederate positions on

Fenwick Island. Nicholson, who named the abandoned fort on Otter Island Fort Drayton in the commander's honor, then carried confiscated lumber, corn, a corn mill, two horses, and other supplies back to Otter Island. On December 11 the island's population increased when transports landed Colonel Thomas Welsh and five companies of his 45th Pennsylvania Infantry Regiment, some engineers, and Company I of the 3rd Rhode Island.

Once ashore, Welsh and his men renovated Fort Drayton. The Pennsylvanians, along with the engineers and Rhode Islanders, mounted five guns and strengthened the fort's defenses by using a hand-operated pile driver to sink a wooden palisade around its sand embankments. The men placed barrels two to three feet into the ground to tap water. Once collected from the makeshift wells, the water had to be boiled before it was safe to drink. Additional "secesh ponies" were seized from abandoned plantations, along with other booty, including poultry, wine, and lumber. Bricks from the destroyed lighthouse on Hunting Island were used to construct huts throughout the encampment. Wood from Coosaw Island was used to build a wharf, and a cotton house from Fenwick Island was converted into a hospital. In time the Federals constructed on Otter Island a guardhouse, storehouses, stables, a blacksmith shop, and a signal tower that provided communications via towers on St. Helena Island to headquarters on Hilton Head.

The soldiers and sailors got along well with the island community of some four hundred ex-slaves, and the post was comfortable except for the plagues of insects. Smoke from fires helped control the gnats and mosquitoes, but there was little relief from the fleas. Still, the island offered the Federals a post to assist escaped slaves and a jumping-off point for expeditions, including one to nearby Edisto Island, which was first occupied on February 15, 1862, by the 47th New York.[13]

The occupation of Otter, Tybee, and other sea islands extended Sherman's command without straining his resources as the navy stood ready to repel any counterattacks. Port Royal Island was a much different case. Consisting of over twenty-five thousand square acres and containing the abandoned town of Beaufort, the island fronted the mainland, where Confederate pickets watched crossing points along the Coosa and Whale Branch Rivers. Federal occupation would require at least a brigade, some four thousand men, which would deprive Sherman of one third of his effective force. With operations underway to reduce Fort Pulaski and campaigns planned against Fernandina, such an ambitious operation seemed impossible to the cautious general. But Sherman was never the master of his situation. When word reached him that the Confederates were obstructing the Whale Branch River and raiding Port Royal Island to gather up slaves and burn cotton, he was forced into action. To lead the occupation force, Sherman chose Brigadier General Isaac I. Stevens and his brigade. This deployment allowed Sherman to put his most aggressive and vocal commander in closer proximity to the enemy while keeping most of Viele's and Wright's brigades ready for other operations. Stevens's three thousand men were also the expedition's best-drilled and most disciplined troops. The decision to send Stevens also removed from Sherman's immediate presence his harshest critic. Never pleased with static occupation duty, the profane, hard-drinking Stevens had constantly called for strikes against the Charleston and Savannah Railroad and overland expeditions against Savannah and Charleston. Every moment of delay frustrated Stevens because he knew the Confederates used the time to regroup and re-form along the railway. Although Stevens was confident of his ability to defeat Robert E. Lee, an officer he felt was overrated in the prewar army, he knew he had to move quickly and decisively to succeed. To Stevens the occupation of Port Royal Island was only a step toward an attack upon the railroad.

While Sherman agreed in theory with Stevens's plans, he was not a risk taker. To him the occupation of Port Royal Island was dangerous enough, and he wanted no part of an inland advance. Even so, the Confederate raids must be stopped, and on December 5 Sherman asked Du Pont for assistance. Du Pont agreed and the next day the transport *Ben Deford,* under the watchful eyes of gunboats, carried elements of the 50th Pennsylvania, a regiment of Pennsylvania Germans known as the "dirty Dutch," Battery E of the 3rd New York, and Stevens and his staff from Hilton Head to Beaufort. They landed at 7:00 P.M. and the infantrymen quickly advanced through the town along Shell Road and established a picket line. That night they exchanged fire with Confederate cavalry. The next day the rest of the brigade landed and Stevens pushed them on beyond Beaufort to Port Royal Ferry. There they crossed the river, seized the ferry scow, and destroyed the ferry house on the mainland before returning to camp. Within two days Stevens's brigade occupied Beaufort, secured Port Royal Island, and was ready to strike the railroad.[14] Permission to move inland never came, and Stevens's command remained a force of occupation, a duty Stevens detested but carried out efficiently. Instead of using Beaufort as an advanced outpost to attack the railroad, Sherman directed that the town be made a medical center. He rightly considered Beaufort healthier than Hilton Head, which the general declared dangerous because of the "malaria that arises from the swamps and the very sudden changes from hot to frosty cold."

As additional forces arrived, Stevens posted troops on nearby Lady's Island. To watch over the enemy, a long picket line manned by the 79th New York Highlanders was established along the Coosaw River to Whale Branch, with outposts at both Port Royal and Seabrook Ferries. Troops were also posted at the Grays Hill crossroad. The town of Beaufort was placed under strict control. A picket line around the town kept refugee slaves out, while those found in the town were sent back to their plantations. Escaped slaves who had no homes on Port Royal Island were placed in a refugee camp on the edge of town. Stevens also took special care to protect civilian property, including the town library.[15]

While awaiting an opportunity to strike at the enemy, Stevens's men explored their new home. All found Beaufort to be a "delightful town ... wholly exempt from the poorer class." They discovered along the Shell Road to Port Royal Ferry "a large building called 'The Club House,' reported to have been built purposely by a wealthy political club—the leaders in society—for the secret discussion of Southern questions of state." Here, as one Rhode Island artillerymen wrote, "Calhounism developed into rebellion." The soldiers also visited the island's plantation houses, which they found less elegant than they had expected. They also inspected the slaves' quarters, where "the plantation's natural and ornamental beauty over-shadowed misery."[16]

Units were posted in and around the town's largest homes. Many wanted to meet "the last man in Beaufort." Though more than one white man stayed, the honor was bestowed upon Mr. Allen, the frightened merchant the squadron had found. Allen was reportedly a northerner of Massachusetts birth who did quite a tidy business with the occupying forces. As the story of Mr. Allen made its way around the camps, it was suggested that he had stayed because he was too drunk to leave. In time a poem was dedicated to him:

> Tis the last man at Beaufort
> Left sitting alone
> All his valiant companions had "vamoosed"
> No secesh of his kindred
> To comfort is nigh,
> And his liquors expended,
> The bottle is dry!
> We will not have thee, thou lone one
> Or harshly condemned—
> Since your friends have all "mizzled,"
> You can't sleep with them;
> And it's no joking matter
> To sleep with the dead;
> So we take you back with us—
> Jim lifts up his head!
> He muttered some words
> As they bore him away,
> And the breeze thus repeated,
> The words he did say:

> When the liquor's all out,
> And your friends they have flown,
> Oh who would inhabit
> This Beaufort alone?[17]

As Christmas neared, contrabands and the troops from both the North and South observed the holidays. On Hilton Head at Fish Haul, the plantation bell was rung at 11:30 P.M., December 24, and at midnight a fire was started along the slave row in front of a cabin where "a serenade to Jesus" began. Led by three preachers, the former slaves sang hymns and listened to scriptures. A prayer meeting followed. The people called for the blessing of the northern soldiers who had come from their faraway homes to bring them freedom. The prayer concluded, and "a shout went up that sent its notes on the still night air to the distant pickets in the surrounding pines." At 2:00 A.M. coffee was served, after which came the "shouting exercise. It was introduced by the beating of time by three or four with the feet. Soon the whole company formed into a circle and commenced jumping and singing on the time and tune of "Say brothers will you meet me, / Say brothers will you meet me, / Say brothers will you meet me / On Canaan's happy shore."

In Beaufort the men of the 100th Pennsylvania celebrated the holiday by canceling drill and playing baseball. That evening the regiment held a formal review. The unit was camped along Bay Street and its commander, Colonel Daniel Leasure, used the Reverend Charles E. Leverett's house for his headquarters. The regimental chaplain, R. Audley Browne, wrote, "The town is beautiful. The trees nearly all wear their foliage. Roses are in bloom in the gardens and there are pleasant perfumes and songs of the birds to regale the senses."[18]

South of the Coosa River, the Confederates, who had regrouped since their retreat from the sea islands, took up new positions. At their camps around Pocotaligo, soldiers of the upcountry 12th South Carolina came to dislike the local aristocracy. On one occasion, after a Mr. Heyward complained that men from the regiment had stolen some of his ducks, two soldiers were arrested and put on bread and water. After this, whenever Mr. Heyward appeared near the regiment, he was greeted with, "Quack, Quack, Here's your ducks." A member of the regiment wrote, "I am bound to express what is an undeniable fact, and that is he [Heyward] and many of like calibre in the country of the coast treated us with no respect."[19]

By Christmas 1861 the men of the 12th were on duty at Page Point along the Coosa River. Beyond the watchful eye of Mr. Heyward, the men foraged turkeys, chickens, and pigs, which, combined with packages from home, gave the soldiers a fine holiday. At night, as they watched for enemy activity, the men on picket duty could hear dolphins "blowing." In another area Union pickets from the 79th Highlanders held a truce with brethren Confederate Scots on the opposite shore, but both sides knew that the truce would end.[20]

Christmas provided only a brief respite because before the holiday both Sherman and Stevens were preparing to strike the Confederates. Sherman agreed in principle with Stevens's plan to establish a position on the railroad. However, Sherman wanted additional troops and vessels before launching an attack, and securing reinforcements from General McClellan was always difficult. In the meantime Stevens prepared to clear the western bank of the Coosa to make easier a grand assault against the railway. Every rice barge, bateaux, scow, and flatboat on Port Royal Island was seized, and potential oarsmen and pilots from the island's ex-slave population were readied to crew the vessels. The Confederate outposts were carefully watched as the Federals constructed artillery positions at Port Royal and Seabrook ferries. Strikes were carried out, and although the 8th Michigan swept onto nearby Chisholm Island, taking some prisoners, small raiding parties were far short of the full scale rush that Stevens desired.[21]

In the end the Confederates gave Stevens his opportunity. By Christmas 1861 Lee's command was growing in numbers, and he began establishing positions closer to the waterways patrolled by Federal warships. Troops were placed along the mainland opposite Hilton Head Island and a battery located near the mouth of the New River was occupied. Emplacements were built and manned on the mainland side of Coosa River at Port Royal and Seabrook Ferries. The batteries at these ferries were part of the Confederates' layered defense, which was designed to slow any Union movement toward the Charleston and Savannah Railroad. The Confederates also began to obstruct both ends of the waterway to deny its use by deep-drafted warships. Armed with field guns, the works were intended to serve only as an initial barrier to Union attacks. But their presence worried the Federals, who feared the Confederates might launch raids onto Port Royal Island and damage gunboats patrolling the Coosaw and Whale Branch Rivers. One such vessel was the army gunboat *Mayflower,* a small side-wheel steamer operated by the U.S. Army Quartermaster Bureau.[22] She had been outfitted with a 6-pound field gun manned by twenty-five men from Company C, 3rd Rhode Island, and soldiers from the 4th New Hampshire. On December 18 the *Mayflower,* on a mission to sound the depth of the channel and locate enemy obstructions, steamed from the Broad River into Whale Branch. Incomplete pilings were spotted, and while passing Page Point, the vessel was hit by a volley of musketry. The cannoneers on the *Mayflower* returned fire, and the vessel passed by unharmed. As it neared Port Royal Ferry, enemy artillery opened, which was returned in kind. Taking one hit, the *Mayflower* continued, entering the Coosaw River, where more pilings were found. She then ran aground, and the crew had to fight off another infantry attack. Once free, the ship turned around and returned to the Broad River, dueling again with Confederate artillery as she passed Port Royal Ferry.[23]

When word of the attack reached Sherman, the commanding general released his tight reign on Stevens and directed him to "dash" across the river to destroy the enemy batteries and "to punish him for the insult in firing upon the steamer *Mayflower*." At the same time, Sherman emphasized that Stevens was not to advance beyond the batteries or to deviate from instructions. To assist Stevens, Sherman provided two regiments, the 47th and 48th New York, from General Viele's brigade, and called upon Du Pont for naval support. The flag officer quickly agreed. Calling the waterway between Port Royal Island and the mainland "our Potomac," Du Pont realized the importance of controlling the river. On December 29 Stevens came aboard the *Wabash*, where he found the ship's captain, Commander C. R. P. Rodgers, eager to lead the expedition's naval forces. Du Pont was quite happy to turn the venture over to his trusted shipmate. Known as Raymond, Rodgers was one of Du Pont's favorite subordinates. The flag officer remarked to his wife that "I have never yet met such an officer as Raymond Rodgers. One trait about him is very peculiar—the possession of immense energy and force without the slightest apparent effort. I never hear him raise his voice. He is fond of expeditions, has ambition—eminently cool in danger, rather courting it—yet neglecting no precaution to ensure success and safety to those under him." To Du Pont, Rodgers had all the traits needed to cooperate with the army and handle the dangerous task of taking warships into a narrow channel controlled by enemy artillery.[24]

In Stevens, Rodgers found a kindred spirit. The two, with the blessings of their superiors, created an elaborate plan to land men six miles east of Port Royal Ferry and then with naval support sweep the enemy from the banks of the Coosa River. Beginning on the night of December 30, Stevens began to mass some one hundred rice flats, scows, and barges in Brickyard Creek beyond the view of the Confederate pickets. The vessels were manned by contraband oarsmen, masterless slaves who had attached themselves to the Federal forces and were well acquainted with local tides and waterways. On the afternoon of December 31, leaving only a corporal's guard to protect Beaufort, Stevens shifted most of the 100th Pennsylvania to his picket line along the Coosaw and Whale Branch Rivers, where they joined a detachment of the 79th New York and a section of Hamilton's artillery battery Co. E, 3rd New York Artillery. Portions of these troops, stationed at Seabrook and Port Royal ferries, were to await the landing, and once the opportunity presented itself, cross to the mainland and join the main attack. The rest of the 79th New York, along with the 8th Michigan and six companies of the 50th Pennsylvania, pulled back from the picket line and moved to the Grays Hill crossroad. They marched east to a landing on Brickyard Creek to rendezvous with their oar-powered transports. There they awaited the rest of the 50th Pennsylvania and the 47th and 48th New York from Hilton Head.[25]

At noon on December 31, Commander Rodgers arrived off Beaufort aboard the gunboat *Ottawa,* accompanied by the *Pembina* and four armed launches from the *Wabash* commanded by John H. Upshur. In charge of one launch was Lieutenant Stephen B. Luce, who after the war pushed for the placement of a permanent naval base at Port Royal and established the Naval War College at Newport, Rhode Island. Standing off Beaufort were the *Seneca,* commanded by Lieutenant Daniel Ammen, and the smaller sidewheeler *Ellen.* That afternoon Rodgers met with Stevens and finalized the attack plan.

Much like the November 7 assault on Port Royal, this smaller expedition would employ tactics new to conventional warfare. At dark Rodgers, with the *Ottawa, Pembina,* the four armed launches, the gunboat *E. B. Hale,* and two army transports, the *Boston* and *Delaware,* conveying the 47th and 48th New York regiments, steamed down Brickyard Creek about two miles from the Coosaw River to await daylight. Later that night flatboats carrying four companies of the 50th Pennsylvania under Lieutenant Colonel Thomas S. Brenholts left Beaufort for the embarkation point. As the soldiers rowed past Rodgers's warships, they transferred to the gunboats a number of contraband pilots, who were to guide the vessels through the treacherous waters of the Brickyard and Coosaw Rivers. The chief pilot of the expedition was a contraband named Williams, who was stationed on the *Ottawa,* which would lead the flotilla into battle. While Rodgers's squadron waited for dawn, Lieutenant Ammen sailed the *Seneca* and *Ellen* from Beaufort to the Broad River, where he too awaited daylight before entering the Whale Branch River from the west. Stevens, having taken his leave from Rodgers that afternoon, visited his troops at the ferries before riding to the embarkation point on Brickyard Creek.

Because he did not have enough boats to transport his entire amphibious force, Stevens planned two landings along the Coosaw River. The first, by seven companies of the 79th New York, four companies of the 50th Pennsylvania, and the 8th Michigan, was to go ashore at Chisholm Island about a mile south of Brickyard Creek. Once landed, the boats would be sent back to the embarkation point for the six companies of the 50th Pennsylvania, who with the transport-borne 47th and 48th New York were to travel three miles farther up the river and disembark at the Adams House landing. On New Year's morning at 3:30, Stevens directed his men into their crude landing crafts. With his soldiers ready, Stevens, carrying the 79th New York's regimental colors, entered the lead boat, where he was joined by signalman Henry S. Tafft.[26]

To communicate between the ship and shore and help direct naval gunfire, Stevens and Rodgers made use of a system developed by Major Albert J. Myer, who at the beginning of the war was the entire United States Signal Corps. Myer, a medical doctor who had studied visible codes used by the deaf and mute, had joined the army in 1854 as an assistant surgeon. While serving in the American West, he observed how Comanche Indians used their lances to communicate with each other over large distances. Collaborating with a young engineering officer and future Confederate general, Edward P. Alexander, Myer developed a wigwag signal system using flags and torches. Myer tested his system in operations against the Indians and in 1860 was appointed major and named the army's signal officer.

To train men for the signal corps, a school of instruction was established at Fort Monroe, Virginia, where Myer taught handpicked officers and enlisted men. The soldiers learned the signal code and the use of torches and flags to communicate messages. Although Myer's attempt to use his signal system from a balloon failed at the Battle of Bull Run, it worked successfully between ships and forts in Hampton Roads. Its first true battlefield test, however, occurred at Port Royal Ferry.

Seven signal corps officers were assigned to the Port Royal Expedition. On the voyage south and during the battle with Forts Walker and Beauregard, Sherman used the signalmen to pass instructions to his troop commanders aboard the various transports. Once ashore, the area's first signal station was established on top of the Pope House next to Fort Walker, and additional positions were opened on Hilton Head at Spanish Wells and Braddock's Point and across the sound at Fort Beauregard.

When Stevens's brigade occupied Beaufort, it was accompanied by a signal corps unit commanded by first lieutenants Henry S. Tafft and William S. Cogswell. These officers supervised the construction of signal stations that connected a post on top of the Edward Barnwell House in Beaufort to the Pope House on Hilton Head. On January 31, 1862, Stevens informed the lieutenants of the impending attack and instructed them to coordinate the cannon fire from the gunboats with the movement of the landing force. Although notice was short, Tafft quickly made some two dozen distinctive flags having a field with the upper half white and the lower half blue, which could be used to communicate between ship and shore. Tafft and his detachment accompanied Stevens while Cogswell and his men went aboard the *Ottawa*.[27]

At dawn on New Year's Day, black oarsmen rowed the troops from Brickyard Creek to the Coosa River, and soon they were pulling for Chisholm Island. On the way they were joined by the navy's armed launches. Rodgers, like Stevens, was not content to be an observer and had accompanied the launches, joining Stevens at the head of the column. Stevens's boat contained his son, who served as his aide, signal officer Tafft, and eleven other soldiers.

At Chisholm Landing, Stevens's boat ran alongside an overturned flatboat. The general was the first out of the boat, the 79th's regimental colors in his hands; but as Stevens slipped on the slimy wood of the makeshift pier, Lieutenant Tafft clambered ashore. Additional boats approached the improvised dock, and soldiers quickly disembarked and formed a skirmish line that withstood a volley from Confederate pickets. Soon the rest of the 79th came ashore, followed by the four companies of the 50th Pennsylvania along with two naval howitzers manned by sailors who had removed the 750-pound bronze pieces from their bow mounts and placed them on iron field carriages.

With the Highlanders forming up on shore, Stevens sent the flatboats back to pick up the remaining six companies of the 50th Pennsylvania. It was at this time that Stevens realized that the 8th Michigan had not followed but had remained at the debarkation point. Undeterred, Stevens sent back orders for the Michiganders to be transported along with the Pennsylvanians to the landing at the Adams House, about three miles west from Chisholm Island. By now the *Ottawa,* followed by the *Pembina* and *E. B. Hale,* had entered the Coosaw to join Rodgers and the launches. While the tide continued to rise, Rodgers shifted from his launch to the light-drafted *E. B. Hale* and joined the forces moving toward the Adams House Landing. He left the *Ottawa* and the *Pembina* to protect the movement of Stevens's men from Chisholm Island to the Adams place. Soon the big guns of the *Ottawa,* coordinated by signalmen Tafft and Cogswell, were sweeping the shoreline to cover the advance.

The Confederates who had challenged Stevens's landing on Chisholm Island were pickets from Captain Edward Croft's Company H, 14th South Carolina, stationed at a church where a causeway ran from Kean's Neck Road to Chisholm Island. Croft immediately sent word of the landing to his regimental commander, Colonel James Jones, and then withdrew his overmatched company. Shortly after receiving Croft's report, Jones heard from another company commander, who reported that the Federals were also landing in force at the Adams place. Jones quickly sent three companies from his camp at the junction of Garden's Corner and Kean's Neck Road toward the Adams place under his second in command, Lieutenant Colonel Samuel McGowan, as he awaited further developments. Holding three companies in reserve, Jones kept two infantry companies at the ferry, where they supported two pieces, a 12-pound howitzer and a 12-pound gun, inside the earthwork. While Jones readied his men, his department commander, Major General John C. Pemberton, upon hearing the cannonade at his headquarters at Pocotaligo Station, rode toward the engagement, alerting other units along the way.

Although quick to respond and having enough men to match the Yankees, Pemberton could not be sure whether this initial landing was the main Federal attack or a decoy to pull Confederates away from another objective.

To guard against that situation, Pemberton kept Brigadier General Daniel S. Donelson and his troops at Pocotaligo, lest the Federals land at Mackey's Point and dash for the railroad. The same was true with the 12th South Carolina, camped at Garden's Corner. Fearing possible assaults at Page Point and Cunningham Bluff, Pemberton kept three companies of the 12th plus some artillery near the unfinished battery at Page Point. Other portions of the regiment watched Cunningham Bluff. Not until after 1:00 P.M., when the other threats failed to materialize, were the four companies of the 12th South Carolina sent to reinforce those at Port Royal Ferry.[28]

While Pemberton waited for another blow to fall, Stevens consolidated his forces at Chisholm Island, moved them inland, and began a march down the Kean's Neck Road for the Adams House. A few Confederates opposed the advance, but Federal skirmishers backed up by the boat howitzers kept the enemy at bay. By 11:00 the Federals reached the Adams place, where they joined the awaiting regiments. With his column consolidated, Stevens rested his twenty-five hundred soldiers before pressing on to the ferry.

As Stevens massed his men at the Adams House, Captain William St. George Elliott of the 79th New York took a detachment of soldiers and rowed from Seabrook Ferry down the Whale Branch River to meet the gunboats coming from the Broad River. Aboard the *Seneca,* Elliott conferred with Lieutenant Ammen and explained to the naval officer the code of signals needed to coordinate the naval gunfire. As the vessels neared Page Point, shells were fired into the Confederate battery while Elliott signaled his New York Highlanders and Pennsylvania Roundheads to man their boats and cross the river. Elliott then cast off from the *Seneca* and joined his men. Since it was high tide, the soldiers were able to maneuver their boats through the marsh and land at the now-abandoned fort. Built into an Indian mound, the work was unfinished but was nearly ready for a complement of heavy guns. A picket line was established, and the men went about dismantling the fort while signalmen directed fire from the *Seneca* and *Ellen* to keep the enemy from interfering. Captain Elliott then had his boat crew row him to the nearby Stewart House, a Confederate picket post about a half mile toward the Port Royal Ferry. That place was also abandoned, and from it Elliott could see the Confederates evacuating Port Royal Ferry. The young captain was tempted to press forward, but he had no orders. Instead he returned to Page Point with his men. Because the tide was ebbing, they dragged their boats through the mud and back into the river. Once across Whale Branch, the soldiers left their launches and marched to Port Royal Ferry. In the meantime Lieutenant Ammen, coordinating with Rodgers's vessels, attempted to close on Port Royal Ferry. With the tide dropping, the deeper-draft *Seneca* was unable to continue but kept firing shells toward the Confederate fort as the *Ellen* pressed on.[29]

At Port Royal Ferry, Colonel Daniel Leasure, commander of the 100th Pennsylvania, intently watched the growing battle. In command of five companies, Leasure carefully noted the enemy's actions inside their fort at the ferry landing. At 9:00 A.M. the Confederate artillerymen, hearing cannon fire to the east, manned their two guns as the infantry entered their trenches about the earthwork. Half an hour later the Confederates nervously adjusted their guns toward the west when Federal gunboats were spied steaming down Whale Branch. By 10:00 A.M. shells from the *Seneca* and *Ellen* had forced the Confederate infantrymen to seek shelter behind the battery. Then the *E. B. Hale,* with Commander Rodgers aboard, came within range from the east and added her guns to the bombardment. Behind the *E. B. Hale* came the *Pembina.* As the cannonade continued, Colonel Leasure learned that Stevens and his forces were marching from the Adams place toward the ferry. He quickly ordered his men to their boats, ready to cross at his signal once their comrades appeared on the opposite shore.

By now the Confederates were beginning to mass their forces to resist Stevens's advance. Colonel Jones brought up the rest of his regiment and joined Lieutenant Colonel McGowan along the Kean's Neck Road. Jones aligned the regiment from the Kean's Neck Road southwest toward the ferry with his flank near Chaplin House. Seeing the Federals ready to resume their march and that the ferry fort was untenable, Jones ordered its two artillery pieces removed and the work evacuated.

The withdrawal from the fort was accomplished under intense fire. The infantry pulled back with only slight losses. The artillerymen were able to get the light-siege howitzer away but the other, a heavy 12-pounder on a cumbersome siege carriage manned by inexperienced infantrymen, overturned in a ditch. It was spiked and abandoned. Although disappointed at the loss of the gun, Jones, joined by Croft's company, which had circled back from Chisholm Island, had his entire regiment on line and ready for battle.

At about 1:30 P.M. Stevens renewed his advance. With Confederate forces massing across the Kean's Neck Road, Stevens directed his units along the edge of the river where the gunboats, in communication with signalmen ashore, covered the advance. With the Highlanders in the lead followed by the boat howitzers, the 50th Pennsylvania, with the 8th Michigan and the 47th and 48th New York in reserve, the Federals advanced between Keans' Neck Road and the river avoiding the Confederate battle line. All units were accompanied by signalmen carrying the distinctive blue and white flags. Heavy skirmishing occurred, but whenever the Confederates tried to disrupt Stevens's advance, the signalmen coordinated the ship-to-shore fire, driving back the Confederates with 11-inch shells, iron balls filled with powder that exploded, throwing massive iron fragments into enemy ranks. Such indirect fire, with naval gunners shooting at an unseen enemy targeted by signalmen, was the first time such a communication system had been used in battle.

Under intense artillery fire, Colonel Jones tried to arrest the Federal advance. He was soon joined by four companies from the 12th South Carolina and about fifty horsemen under Major G. W. Oswald. With these men Jones extended his line to the Chaplin House. Although outnumbered nearly three to one and under heavy naval bombardment, the Confederates harassed the Yankees. Soon, however, the weight of numbers and the well-directed cannon fire forced the Confederates back. Unwilling to risk his men to the relentless naval gunfire, Jones pulled back to his camp, where he found General Donelson and the 8th and 16th Tennessee. Together the Confederates waited for an enemy strike inland, but none came.

Though tempted to follow the withdrawing enemy, Stevens did not. With his flank free from enemy assaults, he realigned his forces and continued toward the ferry. While Stevens pushed his soldiers forward, Colonel Leasure, on Port Royal Island, saw the Highlanders' skirmishers near the abandoned battery and ordered his men away. Spearheaded by three companies of Roundheads, the men crossed the Whale Branch and joined Stevens's skirmishers in occupying the fort. By 4:30 Stevens arrived at the battery. Although many of his men had been awake for nearly two days, Stevens worked them until dark dismantling the fort and gathering enemy equipment. When they finished, the men were allowed to rest, and cooks from Port Royal Island distributed coffee. Pickets were posted while the rest of the soldiers slept on their arms. Before turning in, a few Highlanders grumbled about the arrival of a New Year without receiving a "wee drop." But near midnight the men were awakened and told to report "all in for your whiskey." Stevens had not forgotten his men and reported to General Sherman, "I hope the general commanding may be gratified with our celebration of the New Year's Day."[30]

While the Confederates waited for the Federals to move inland, Stevens did not press on. Instead, the Union commander followed his orders, and by noon on January 2, his three thousand men had returned to Port Royal Island, Stevens being the last to cross. The battle had cost the Federals two dead, twelve wounded, and one missing. The Confederates lost eight dead and twenty-four wounded. The small number of casualties masked the importance of the battle. Not only did the engagement usher in a new era of warfare based on Myer's signal-directed artillery fire, but it also opened a gateway for further Federal moves against the Charleston and Savannah Railroad. While Stevens had wanted to continue his advance, Sherman held him in check and readied his other brigades for action against Fort Pulaski, the guardian of Savannah, Georgia.[31]

For Sherman, the affair at Port Royal Ferry was a bothersome diversion, something that needed to be taken care of before he could turn his full attention to Fort Pulaski. While that main attack would come from Gillmore's batteries on Tybee Island, the waterways and marsh islands of South Carolina would also play an essential role.

To capture Fort Pulaski, Sherman had to isolate the fort from the city of Savannah. To accomplish this, gunboats could be sent through the labyrinth of shallow rivers and creeks that connected with the Savannah River west of the fort and masked batteries constructed between the fort and the city. Sherman hoped that the navy would take the lead, but Du Pont, fearing that his vessels might run aground and be trapped in the shallow waterways, was cool to the proposal. Still, the flag officer dispatched Captain Charles H. Davis with six gunboats south of the mouth of the Savannah River to Wassaw Sound, Georgia, and ordered Commander John Rodgers to explore the rivers in South Carolina for possible use in the enterprise. Davis and Rodgers probed the waterways but were extremely cautious. While the navy assisted with some of the initial work and guarded the army's positions, the attack would be primarily an army affair.

Sherman, a regular army officer with little faith in volunteers, wanted a fellow West Pointer to oversee the attack on Pulaski. To Sherman the only choice was his staff engineer, Captain Quincy A. Gillmore. In terms of artillery and engineering experience, no one else matched Gillmore's military background. But there was a problem: while Gillmore had the expertise, he was not the expedition's top-ranking engineer. That position was held by Edward Serrell, colonel of the 1st New York Engineers. Although Serrell lacked a West Point diploma and was not a military man, he was a world-renowned civil engineer noted for his construction of tunnels, railroad lines, and suspension bridges.

The problem that Sherman faced, appointing a captain over a colonel, lay in the army's dual-rank system. To fight the Civil War, the United States created a volunteer army and retained the prewar regular army. The two were separate establishments, each with its own rank structure. Because of its size and need for officers to command its large formations, the volunteer army offered men a higher, though not permanent rank. Officers in the regular army were often detached as needed to serve on staffs or in some special service. Others took leave from their assignments to join the volunteer army, where they achieved higher, though temporary rank. Once a conflict was over and the volunteers disbanded, the regulars returned to their commands and reverted to their original, lower ranks. Some regulars immediately joined the volunteer army while others waited before seeking new positions. Some were content to remain captains in the regular army instead of trying for generals' commissions in the volunteers.

Sherman balked at giving nonprofessional volunteers important tasks. Such was the case with the bombardment of Fort Pulaski. With little hesitation, Sherman chose the regular captain Gillmore over the volunteer colonel Serrell, and in late January 1862, to head off difficulties, he unofficially appointed Gillmore a brigadier general in the volunteer army. Sherman then wrote McClellan requesting that he approach President Lincoln, the only authority allowed to verify promotions to the rank of general, to confirm the appointment. Gillmore also pushed his promotion by writing to the army's chief engineer, Brigadier Joseph Totten, pointing out the need to be placed above Serrell. Totten endorsed advancing Gillmore. On Hilton Head, Lieutenant Wilson agreed with the move, but Serrell never forgave the slight. In addition, Captain John Hamilton, a regular officer and Sherman's chief of artillery and Gillmore's senior, mockingly refused to recognize Gillmore's promotion unless he was made a major general. Despite the bitterness over Gillmore's advancement among some of Sherman's regular and volunteer officers, the men from both services joined together for the difficult task ahead.[32]

The Federals first investigated the water route used by the British lieutenant colonel John Maitland to transport his command from Beaufort to Savannah in 1779 in time to defeat the combined French and American attack upon the city. In late December, Sherman's topographical engineer, Lieutenant James H. Wilson, began reconnoitering the South Carolina tidal rivers and creeks between Bloody Point on Daufuskie Island and the Savannah River. Aided by contraband oarsmen familiar with the waters, Wilson found a route from the New River to Wall's Cut, a passage that linked the New River to the Wright and Mud Rivers. The Wright and the Mud connected with the Savannah River west of Fort Pulaski, respectively two and six miles above the fort. Gunboats of fifteen-foot draft could maneuver the Wright, but the Mud was restricted to vessels drawing six feet. At Wall's Cut, Wilson discovered a sunken bark blocking the channel. Beyond the hulk and the Wright River were three rows of square piles driven into the bottom of the cut. The submerged bark was not weighted and swung back and forth underwater with the outgoing and incoming tides. Wilson saw little difficulty in removing the vessel but worried in his report of January 2, 1862, that the piles could prove more difficult. Within two days, however, a solution was found.[33]

The problem posed by the pilings was solved by another of Sherman's staff officers, Provost Marshal Major Oliver T. Beard of the 48th New York. When he learned of the problem, Beard offered to remove the pilings by using a saw suspended under the water between two boats. With a detachment of New York engineers and Rhode Island artillerymen, Beard went to work employing his "peculiarly operating Yankee saw" and began cutting the pilings at the bottom of the channel. On January 14, after four days and nights of work, the task was completed. The hulk was moved aside and the channel cleared for vessels to pass from the New River to the Wright and Mud Rivers.[34]

With Wall's Cut cleared, Lieutenant Wilson, accompanied by Commander John Rodgers, took a small boat to test the water's depth. Where the Wright entered the Savannah stood an uncharted bar, measuring four to five feet at low tide but twelve to fourteen feet at high. Wilson then declared the way clear for gunboats to enter the Savannah west of Pulaski. Rodgers was not so optimistic. Still, he agreed to test the waterways with his vessels before making a final decision. In late January the gunboats *Unadilla* and *Henry Andrew* passed through Wall's Cut, but the *Pembina* grounded, confirming Rodgers's fears. Although the vessel was unharmed, the navy backed away from further creek ventures and concentrated on clearing the upper reaches of the New River, where they found abandoned batteries armed with painted logs at Red Bluff.[35]

With the navy pulling back from joint operations, Sherman went ahead with his own plans and began shifting units to Daufuskie Island. His engineers explored the Beaufort District shore of the Savannah River for favorable locations to locate gun emplacements that would isolate Pulaski from Savannah. The work was dangerous and fatiguing. On one occasion an exhausted Adam Badeau, the civilian aide serving on Sherman's staff, bogged in the salt marsh with the tide coming in. He begged Lieutenant Wilson to leave him to drown, but Wilson, with the aid of soldiers, managed to carry Badeau to safety. On another trip into the marsh, Lieutenant O'Rorke became lost and took refuge in a tree waiting for a thunderstorm to subside. Worried over his friend's fate, Lieutenant Porter went out in the storm and, though the two nearly discharged their pistols on each other in the darkness, retrieved O'Rorke. Porter warned him that the next time the engineer ventured into the South Carolina marsh, Porter would place a bell around his neck.

Gillmore also explored the shorelines and on January 28 scouted the Mud River and the Savannah River shores of Jones Island. There he discovered a suitable battery site and staked out a roadway from the Mud River across Jones Island to Venus Point. The next day Lieutenant O'Rorke and Major Beard took a small boat expedition from Jones Island into the Savannah River, visiting Long and Elba Islands and located on the former another battery site.[36]

While Gillmore and the other "swamp foxes" explored the waterways and shorelines, the Federals turned Daufuskie Island into an engineer and artillery depot. The largest unit sent to Daufuskie was the 48th New York, which broke camp on Hilton Head on January 25 and marched to Seabrook Landing, where the little side-wheel transport *Winfield Scott* waited. Too small to carry the entire regiment, the steamer first transported one wing to Haig Point, where the soldiers marched overland to Dunn Plantation. The second wing's voyage was a bit more eventful. While coming through a passage known as "Pull and be Damned Creek," the *Winfield Scott* hit an oyster bed, and the New Yorkers were forced to take refuge on Long Pine Island until rescued by the steamer *Mayflower*. While waiting for help, the men discovered a goat that shared their misery on the marshy, mosquito-infested island. When they left, the men took the goat with them, and it became an honorary member of Colonel James H. Perry's staff, following him whenever he inspected the regiment. The mascot remained with the 48th until early 1863, when it was taken for a meal by the notorious "Enfans Perdus," a New York infantry battalion comprising hungry Frenchmen.

Daufuskie, like the other sea islands, proved a fascinating, almost mystical locale for the Federals. While exploring the island, they visited the Munger and Stoddard Plantations. A member of the 48th New York described the plantations:

> Both gave evidence of large wealth and cultivated tastes, in character of the houses and beauty of their surroundings, and as we wandered through the shady avenues, and among the shrubs and flowers, in gardens where roses and japonicas grew in tropical luxuriance, where the air was full of sweet odors, and the eye confused with the multitude and variety of brilliant colors, and remembered that these abodes of happiness and beauty had been abandoned to pillage and destruction, and that wherever our armies penetrated, homes would be broken up, and in the place of comfort would come suffering, and in the place of beauty, desolation, we cursed the madness of those who had brought such miseries on the land.[37]

The men had only a short time to enjoy their idleness. During the first days of February while engineers prepared a wharf on the Mud River side of Jones Island, the soldiers on Daufuskie began filling sandbags and cutting down trees to make nearly ten thousand poles five to six inches in diameter. The logs were carried on the soldiers' shoulders to the wharf, where they and the sandbags were placed onto barges. Pulled by rowboats four miles to Jones Island, the barges were unloaded and the poles laid in the jelly-like marsh mud, corduroying the causeway from the Mud River to Venus Point.

On February 7 General Sherman, realizing that the navy was hesitating to send vessels into the Savannah River, ordered Lieutenant O'Rorke to begin constructing the battery at Venus Point. O'Rorke quickly went to work. While the men from Daufuskie continued to build the causeway, the engineers staked out the battery. To spare his men the backbreaking work of pulling cannons across the marsh island, Gillmore made one final appeal to the navy to run warships into the Savannah River, which would protect the landing of guns and matériel at Venus Point. Commander Rodgers agreed to try, and at high tide on the night of February 9, gunboats were readied to steam through Wall's Cut into the Mud River and then on into the Savannah. Once in position the warships would guard the steamer *Mayflower* that would tow the artillery- and ammunition-laden barges to Venus Point. But that night torrential thunderstorms swept over the marshes and waterways. The next day the warships moved into the Mud River to guard the wharf on Jones Island but did not venture into the Savannah River. Tired of waiting, Gillmore had the *Mayflower* unloaded at the wharf and directed his men to haul the guns, munitions, and construction matériel across the marsh.

Under Lieutenant O' Rorke's command, fatigue parties went to work in the midst of thunderstorms and high tides that swept over the island. It took twenty-four hours to build the battery. Standing in water, the soldiers laid planks and sandbags to form the fortification and its magazine. In some places the men shaped the mud into walls and then waited for the sun to bake it into "the hardness of stone." When completed, the parapet stretched nearly one thousand yards along the river and measured six to ten feet thick and four feet high. Behind the battery stood the magazine, with ten-foot-thick walls and a five-foot sandbag and earth roof laid over a wooden ceiling. Manned by artillerymen from Companies E, G, and A from the 3rd Rhode Island, the mud work was named Battery Vulcan in honor of the Roman god of fire and metalworking, but as an artilleryman stated, "it seemed more mythical than real" and that Vulcan would have "desired something more firm than this island for his anvil."[38]

Lieutenants Wilson and Porter and Major Beard were tasked with moving the guns into the battery. The six artillery pieces were split into three sections. Wilson, with thirty-five men, was in charge of moving an 8-inch siege howitzer and a 30-pound Parrott. He was followed by Porter and Beard, who oversaw large work gangs that brought forward two 20-pound and two 30-pound Parrotts. The cannons and their limbers were landed before the corduroy road was completed. For the movement to the battery, the men had to lay planks eighteen feet long and sixteen inches wide in front of the cannon wheels and then carefully guide the pieces and the attached limber along the narrow wooden track. When the end of the board was reached, it was lifted from the mire and the process repeated. All night the soldiers struggled through the marsh pulling the guns, some weighing nearly fifty-four hundred pounds, with drag ropes toward the battery. When the pieces slipped off the slick boards, they sank up to their hubs and had to be raised by levers and repositioned on the boards. To keep mud out of their shoes, men tied empty sandbags around their feet. All night the soldiers worked; some fell asleep standing, held upright by the mud.[39]

By 2:00 A.M., February 11, Lieutenant Wilson had two guns in place. Six hours later Lieutenant Porter and Major Beard positioned their pieces. Gillmore, seeing that the entire position with its magazine, guns, and garrison was in danger of being flooded by the spring tides, ordered a dike thrown up around the fortification. Then he returned to Viele's headquarters on Daufuskie Island, leaving instructions for O'Rorke to finish the work at Venus Point and to build a second mud battery on Long Island in the middle of the Savannah River.

On February 13, before the new work could be started, the Confederate steamer *Ida* was spotted steaming from Savannah toward Fort Pulaski. The *Ida*, a small, wooden side-wheeler, was on its usual run from the city to the fort. Nothing on this day seemed unusual, but as it neared Venus Point, the Union battery opened fire. Nine shots flew at the *Ida*; most fell astern as the vessel sped to Fort Pulaski. The Federals were lucky that the *Ida* was not part of an armed flotilla, for all but one cannon in the battery recoiled off its platform and became stuck in the mud. Immediately the platforms were enlarged and none too soon. The next day Tattnall's mosquito fleet came downriver and engaged the Federals. This time the guns stayed in place and delivered thirty Valentine's Day greetings that forced the Confederate gunboats to withdraw.[40]

The *Ida*, unwilling to make another run past Battery Vulcan, returned to Savannah through connecting creeks on the Georgia side of the river. Over the next few days, Federals moved from their bases in South Carolina to Bird Island, just above Long Island, and established Battery Hamilton, a six-gun mud work facing upriver. Between Batteries Hamilton and Vulcan, the Savannah River was closed to Confederate vessels, and by February 22, Union warships, guarded by the newly built batteries, passed into the Savannah River, effectively isolating Fort Pulaski.[41]

With Pulaski cut off from Savannah, Gillmore now went to work constructing breaching batteries on Tybee Island. The men stationed along the South Carolina shore watched for enemy activity and soon became acquainted with new elements of warfare being developed by the Confederates—torpedoes and ironclads. In February the Federals found in the Wright and Savannah Rivers the war's first torpedoes, floating explosive canisters that could be detonated by friction tubes and electric current. From this point on, the northerners on and around Mud Island viewed all floating objects with suspicion, often firing first on many an innocent alligator.[42]

Also watched for were enemy ironclads, miniature versions of the famed *Virginia* under construction at Norfolk. Two such creatures were being built at Savannah, and their iron-plated sides would be impervious to the Union guns at Batteries Hamilton and Vulcan. Deserters warned the Federals that one of the iron monsters was being prepared to steam downriver, destroy the

North's mud forts, and relieve Fort Pulaski. To protect themselves, the men on Jones Island formed a squadron of ironclad-killers, six rowboats manned by thirteen men each. Armed with grappling hooks, revolvers, hand grenades, sledge hammers, and cold-chisels, the men were to board the ironclads, throw their grenades into any open portholes, and then use their cold chisels to cut a hole in the smokestack. Once the opening was made, they would drop a cannon shell down the stack, blowing the vessel's boiler, scalding the crew, and rendering it powerless. Most felt the whole venture to be foolhardy. Nevertheless, the "forlorn hope" squadron was organized and nicknamed the "Cold-chisel Brigade," which, as one member thanked Providence, never saw any action.[43]

While visions of torpedoes and ironclads played upon the soldiers' imaginations, most slowly adjusted to their home in the South Carolina salt marsh. Tides still flooded Jones Island as the men "in their little Holland" endured mosquitoes, brackish drinking water, and malarial odors. Snakes and alligators were plentiful, and although the men refused to cook the snakes, they found alligator steak a delicacy, especially the more tender flesh of those that measured five or six feet in length.[44]

Besides the troops stationed in the marshes along the Savannah River, Federal forces were also actively trying to clear the Confederate pickets from the islands and mainland bordering Hilton Head. Lieutenant Colonel John H. Jackson took his 3rd New Hampshire regiment on a five-day reconnaissance on the May River. Landing at Dr. James Kirk's Plantation above Bluffton, Jackson moved northeast to Baynard's Plantation near Buckingham Ferry, clearing the area of enemy soldiers. Jackson then took his men to Bull Island in search of more Confederate pickets. Contrabands on the island informed him that there was a strong Confederate force on the mainland near Bluffton. Jackson sent for reinforcements and then moved his amphibious expedition up the May River to Savage Islands. As they passed their previous landing point at Kirk's Plantation, the northerners discovered that the Confederates had burned the plantation and its outbuildings and were using the ruins as firing positions. Braving the musketry, Jackson got his men to Savage Islands and, with another artillery piece, returned the next day, March 22, to Kirk's Plantation. Marching to Bluffton, Jackson found the town deserted with no signs of enemy activity except an old dismounted gun next to the Church of the Cross. By March 24 the raiders were back at Hilton Head, having completed their mission, as Jackson wrote, "in good health and without one accident."[45]

While the army continued to invest Fort Pulaski, Flag Officer Du Pont refitted and resupplied his vessels. He also had to dispose of the Stone Fleet, the squadron of stone-filled sailing vessels sent south by the Navy Department to block the channels off Charleston and Savannah. Though Du Pont had discussed the use of hulks to close enemy ports while serving on the

Blockade Strategy Board, he now believed them to be superfluous and did not want to bother with them. However, the Navy Department insisted, and by early December the initial Stone Fleet, some twenty-five ships destined for watery graves off Savannah, began to arrive. The Confederates, fearing that the ships were part of a new attack force, panicked and sank their own hulks, effectively blocking the Savannah River. This, coupled with the North's occupation of Tybee, ended the need for the Stone Fleet in Georgia waters.

With the Savannah River effectively closed, Du Pont directed his fleet captain, Charles H. Davis, to take the remaining hulks to Charleston. Davis, who shared Du Pont's disdain for the Stone Fleet, sailed the vessels from Port Royal and, starting on December 17, began sinking them in Charleston's main ship channel.

Before Davis had completed disposing of the first set of derelicts, the second Stone Fleet arrived at Port Royal. Though most of these were also sunk in the various channels off Charleston, Du Pont retained some for use at Port Royal as machine shops and storage vessels. Vilified by southerners and Europeans, the Stone Fleets proved to be completely ineffective; and instead of blockading the port's entrance, those hulks placed in Charleston's main ship channel actually caused the tidal flow to scour the passageway to a greater depth of twenty-one feet.[46]

Once the Stone Fleets had been sunk, Du Pont and Sherman, by late March, were finally ready to carry out the long-delayed expedition to Fernandina, Florida. Although the capture of Fernandina was supposed to occur shortly after the fall of Port Royal, delays, mostly on the part of the navy, put the expedition off for months. By late February the flag officer was ready, and the navy, accompanied by elements of Wright's brigade, sailed from Port Royal for Fernandina. When the warships approached the city, the commanders found the Confederates in the midst of a strategic withdrawal, pulling their men, supplies, and guns from not only Fernandina but also St. Augustine and Jacksonville, Florida, and Brunswick, Georgia. Virtually unopposed, the Federals made a clean sweep of the Georgia and east Florida coast, leaving garrisons not only at Fernandina but also at St. Augustine and Jacksonville. Although Du Pont was greatly pleased by his captures, Sherman viewed the occupation of St. Augustine and Jacksonville as unnecessary burdens on his already extended forces. Du Pont offered to use the marine battalion to garrison St. Augustine, but Sherman refused and the battalion eventually returned north. Sherman did place a permanent garrison at St. Augustine and briefly posted men at Jacksonville, where the citizens attempted to organize a new state government loyal to the United States.[47]

On March 2, while Du Pont and his expedition were in Florida, the steamship *Mississippi* limped into Port Royal Sound, barely afloat with a hole in her bow. The wounded transport had been part of a convoy of vessels carrying troops bound for the Gulf of Mexico as part of a joint operation to capture New Orleans. Aboard the transport was the 31st Massachusetts Regiment along with four companies of the 13th Maine and the disgusted commander of the army's portion of the expedition, the North's ranking major general of volunteers, Benjamin F. Butler.

The next day the *Mississippi* was taken into Skull Creek to the army's maritime quartermaster depot at Seabrook Landing, where Butler, his wife, staff, and over one thousand soldiers went ashore. Charles Boutelle immediately took charge of the vessel. Over the next ten days, Boutelle and the marine engineers patched the hole while General Butler and his wife took the opportunity to visit Beaufort, review troops, and pick flowers. On March 9 Boutelle declared the *Mississippi* safe for travel. The next day Butler, his troops, wife, and staff reboarded the vessel. Although Boutelle and others urged the *Mississippi*'s captain, a southerner named Fulton, to have the vessel towed into the sound, Fulton ignored the advice and tried to back his vessel from Skull Creek into deep water. Unable to maneuver in the narrow channel, Fulton grounded the *Mississippi* a half mile from the landing. Some of the troops, as well as Butler and his wife, switched to the transport *Matanzas*, and another day passed before Boutelle could tow the *Mississippi* off the sand bar. Butler, already suspicious of an earlier grounding off Cape Fear, promptly had Fulton relieved of command and placed under house arrest on the *Matanzas*, declaring to the captain that his mind was "in such a state of confusion as to events that the lives of my men are not safe under the guidance of your nautical skill." Finally on March 12, in the company of the *Matanzas,* the *Mississippi* steamed safely out of Port Royal Sound.[48]

Butler's unexpected visit and the Florida expedition did not slow Sherman and Gillmore's preparation for the Pulaski attack. By the end of March, the plan put forward by General Sherman and realized by Gillmore was ready for execution, but the too-much-maligned Sherman was not allowed to see its success. On March 15, 1862, Sherman's command was merged into a regional division known as the Department of the South that encompassed the states of South Carolina, Georgia, and Florida. Authority over the new department was given to Major General David Hunter, one of the highest-ranking and most politically connected officers in the volunteer army.[49]

Sherman was not surprised by his recall. The general knew that the government, blinded by Du Pont's spectacular victory at Port Royal, expected the army to make quick and decisive offensives against Charleston and Savannah. Try as he might, Sherman could not convince his superiors that his command was too small to do much more than occupation duty. Sherman also realized that the radicals in the government expected him to set a more aggressive policy for the use of contrabands. Sherman resisted, believing that contraband management was a political issue outside his purview as a military officer. On the other hand, Hunter had actively lobbied for the new command, promising quick and pleasing results on both the military and contraband fronts.

It might have been possible for Sherman to remain in the department as a subordinate, but when he learned that Hunter was arriving with Brigadier General Henry W. Benham as his second in command, Sherman could not remain. Du Pont, who admired Sherman's soldierly qualities, believed the recall unjust and the work of "extreme" men in the administration who saw Port Royal as a post from which to radically change the South's social, political, and economic status. Sherman agreed with Du Pont and, in a note to the flag officer, reminded him of a previous conversation when Sherman had speculated that certain officials were out to "ruin" him.[50]

On the morning of April 4, 1862, Sherman, under orders to report to the Department of Mississippi, left Port Royal harbor aboard the steamer *Atlantic*. Wishing to give their comrade in arms a fitting farewell, Du Pont and Commander Christopher Raymond P. Rodgers sent the entire crew of the *Wabash* into the rigging and gave Sherman "three hearty cheers." Du Pont wrote his wife that "he was standing alone with his cap off on the wheelhouse of the *Atlantic* and I am sure he was deeply moved.... Poor fellow, a more onerous, difficult, responsible, but thankless piece of work no officer ever had to do, and none ever brought to such a task more complete self-sacrificing devotion—he ploughed, harrowed, sowed, and it does seem hard that when the crop is about being harvested he is not even allowed to participate in a secondary position."[51]

Although their commander was gone, Sherman's former staff continued preparations to bombard Fort Pulaski. Just after sunrise on April 10, 1862, Lieutenant Wilson carried from General Hunter a demand for Fort Pulaski's surrender. Colonel Charles H. Olmstead, the fort's twenty-five-year-old commander, refused. Wilson returned the message to Gillmore, who sent Adam Badeau to Porter, in command of the Tybee batteries. An excited Badeau informed Porter in a high-pitched voice to open fire. Porter, trying not to laugh at his friend's falsetto directive, repeated the order to his gun crews. At 8:15 A.M. a mortar shell arched its way toward the Confederate fort. Soon the firing became general, and the bullet-shaped projectiles from Gillmore's rifled cannons began penetrating Pulaski's brick walls. By the end of the day, a hole had been cut in the eastern wall. Desultory fire continued through the night; then, at daylight on the eleventh, Gillmore's guns began enlarging the breach. Soon, shells were passing through the opening and exploding near Pulaski's main powder magazine located in the work's northwest bastion. Inside the magazine lay forty thousand pounds of black powder. Faced with the destruction of the fort and his garrison, Olmstead surrendered. The day of rifled artillery had arrived, and the day of masonry fortifications had ended.[52]

In his after-action report, Gillmore took special care to commend numerous individuals, including Horace Porter, James H. Wilson, P. H. O'Rorke, Adam Badeau, and O. T. Beard. He also pointed out that the operation had started under General Sherman, "under whose auspices the project for the reduction of Fort Pulaski was pushed to within days of its final accomplishment."[53]

General Hunter also acknowledged Sherman's part in readying the batteries that had isolated and reduced Pulaski. He also recognized the importance of the battle. Not only had it effectively ended Savannah's days as a blockade-running port, but it had also revolutionized warfare. As he wrote, "The result of this bombardment must cause, I am convinced, a change in the construction of fortifications as radical as that foreshadowed by the conflict between the *Monitor* and the *Merrimac*. No works of stone or brick can resist the impact of rifled artillery of heavy caliber."[54]

Besides employing rifled cannons, the Federals attempted another innovation. After the fall of Pulaski, General Benham sent the grounded aeronaut John B. Starkweather and his balloon *Washington* to Fort Pulaski. There Starkweather with a detachment of six men from the 7th Connecticut readied the steamer *Mayflower* to serve as an improvised aircraft carrier. Once outfitted, the *Mayflower* transported the balloonist up the Savannah River along the South Carolina shore. Starkweather made two ascents, the second with Lieutenant O'Rorke. From the balloon's gondola the men could see Savannah, enemy gunboats, an ironclad under construction, and Confederate camps on both sides of the river. Their observations indicated confusion and weakened enemy, but the northern high command did not press their advantage. Instead Hunter turned his energies toward the department's contrabands. Unlike his predecessor, Hunter did not view the masterless slaves as a hindrance to future military operations. Using the groundwork prepared by Sherman, General Hunter planned to mobilize the sea island slaves into a new and decisive tool—not only to win the war but also to destroy forever the South's antebellum economic and social order.[55]

Chapter 4

The Port Royal Experiment Begins

"What is to be done with the contrabands"

Almost as soon as the cannon fire died away on November 7, 1861, private and government agencies realized the potential of Port Royal as a source for cotton and an ideal testing ground to begin Reconstruction. The initial responsibility of managing the abandoned property and slaves first fell upon the shoulders of Brigadier General Thomas West Sherman, but his military superiors expected him to lead military campaigns against Charleston and Savannah. Hence, Sherman viewed the abandoned slaves and plantations as detrimental to the war effort, sapping valuable manpower, energy, and supplies from future military operations. He appealed to the War Department "to decide what is to be done with the contrabands" but received no reply. Instead the general was directed to confiscate all cotton and other abandoned property and ship it to New York, where it would be sold at a public sale with the proceeds going to fund the war.[1]

Authority to collect cotton and other property came from the Treasury Act of July 13, 1861, which allowed the government to confiscate enemy property and sell it to finance the war. To handle that difficult business, Sherman, on December 3, 1861, appointed William H. Nobles as his chief collector. Nobles, a New York friend of General Isaac Stevens, had been appointed lieutenant colonel of the 79th New York, but disliking his duties, he resigned shortly after arriving at Port Royal to accept the collectorship. For his work Nobles received 6 percent of the market value of all collected cotton. The cotton and any other appropriated items were turned over to the expedition's chief quartermaster, Captain Rufus Saxton, who shipped them to Hiram Barney, collector of the Port of New York and Treasury Department agent for all traffic in and out of Port Royal.

Nobles, who took up residence at Dr. William J. Jenkins's plantation on St. Helena Island, appointed his assistant, James A. Suydam, as collector for Beaufort and Port Royal Island while lieutenants Gavin Hamilton and Alexander Graham of the 79th New York temporarily oversaw operations on St. Helena, Lady's, and Cat Islands. Nobles employed contrabands to pick, collect, and pack the cotton. The ex-slaves were given vouchers that were initially redeemed in cash by the expedition's quartermaster. Sherman directed Nobles to keep careful records should the question of remuneration to the absent planters ever arise.

The agents, spurred on by hopes of personal gain, seized not only cotton but also any material that could be sold, including foodstuffs and hardware. Nobles's reign was short lived. On December 20, 1861, William H. Reynolds arrived and took control of Nobles's operation. Reynolds's authority came directly from the secretary of the treasury, Salmon P. Chase, who saw the situation at Port Royal as the perfect spot not only to generate cotton sales but also to establish a reconstruction program that would uplift the former slaves and help fulfill Chase's future presidential aspirations.[2]

One of the founders of the Republican Party, the fifty-three-year-old Chase was a New Hampshire native but was raised in Worthington, Ohio, by his uncle Philander Chase, the Episcopal bishop of Ohio. His uncle, a dogmatic and demanding taskmaster, prepared Salmon for the Episcopalian priesthood. When Philander Chase became president of Cincinnati College, his nephew was accepted into the freshman class at the age of thirteen. Two years later Salmon returned to New Hampshire, where he completed his college education at Dartmouth. Shortly after graduation Chase was caught up in the great revival that swept the nation in the late 1820s. The religious fervor stayed with him throughout his life and helped him survive overwhelming tragedies, including the deaths of three wives and four daughters.

Although an honest and devout Christian, Chase believed that any means short of illegality justified the end, and to achieve his goals he would manipulate any situation as far as possible. First a schoolteacher and then a lawyer, he returned to Cincinnati in 1830 and entered politics. He soon became known for his free-soil, antislavery views. A foe of the Fugitive Slave Law, Chase often tried to stop the return of captured slaves and frequently defended those accused of helping their escape. A friend of the abolitionist newspaperman James Birney, Chase left the Whig Party and joined the Liberty Party. An astute politician, he served in the U.S. Senate and as governor of Ohio. He sought the Republican presidential nominations in 1856 and 1860 but in both cases was perceived as too radical on the slavery issue.

In 1861 Chase accepted the position of secretary of the treasury in Lincoln's cabinet. From this post Chase placed his partisans throughout the department, especially in the nation's customhouses. The most important of these was the collector of customs for the Port of New York, where Chase situated Hiram Barney, an attorney and fellow abolitionist. His close associate Barney oversaw all nonmilitary shipping in and out of Port Royal.

While his principal job was gathering funds to pay for the war, he also advised Lincoln on military matters and was a leading proponent for emancipation. Accomplishing all these duties, Chase never lost sight of his ultimate goal of becoming president. The occupied region of Beaufort District opened a door of opportunity, not only for generating revenue but also to prove to the Republican Party that he, not Lincoln, was best suited to handle issues of emancipation and reconstruction.[3]

As secretary of the treasury, Chase, through Collector Barney, oversaw all nonmilitary traffic in and out of Port Royal. This included both civilians and supplies. Anyone sailing to Port Royal had to receive a Treasury Department pass, and during the weeks following the area's capture, Chase became personally involved in selecting who came to the South Carolina sea islands. Among Chase's first appointments was Lieutenant Colonel William H. Reynolds to be the Treasury Department's chief agent at Port Royal. A well-connected textile merchant from Rhode Island, Reynolds had served as a captain with the 2nd Rhode Island Artillery Battery at the First Battle of Bull Run. Also at Bull Run, accompanying the Rhode Island forces, was the state's governor, William Sprague, who, when his horse was killed, fought alongside his friend and business associate as a volunteer gunner.

Sprague, known as the boy governor, had been elected governor of Rhode Island in 1859 at the age of twenty-nine by a coalition of Republicans and Democrats. He was also the co-owner of A. and W. Sprague Manufacturing Company, one of the nation's largest textile firms. Though a Democrat, Sprague enthusiastically supported Lincoln's war effort and soon became a powerful player within the administration. His marriage to Chase's daughter Katie provided him with direct access to the secretary of the treasury.[4]

Although an ardent supporter of the Union, Sprague ran a business that was dependent on a steady flow of cotton. The majority of the nation's cotton and cotton land was within the borders of the Confederacy and unavailable to Sprague and his partners. The only exception was Beaufort District's sea islands, where Union occupation created a situation that beckoned to textile manufacturers such as Sprague. St. Helena Parish, occupied by the Federals in late 1861, had before the war produced nearly nine hundred thousand pounds of sea island cotton, valued at just under a million dollars.[5]

It may have been the prospect of tapping this cotton source that led Sprague to write Chase on December 1, 1861, recommending William H. Reynolds for the position of collector at Port Royal. Sprague emphasized Reynolds's background in the cotton trade and his strong religious principals. Chase agreed, and before the month was out, Reynolds arrived at Port Royal. Quartermaster Saxton, who had just shipped thirty thousand dollars' worth of cotton north, immediately turned "the whole business" over to Reynolds.[6]

Armed with a directive from General Sherman, Reynolds took over Lieutenant Colonel Nobles's operations and reduced the collector's profit margin from 6 to 5 percent. Reynolds continued to employ contrabands to gather and carry the cotton to collection points but noted that they preferred being paid by the amount of work done—a continuation of the slave-task system—instead of receiving a daily rate. Payment, as established earlier by Sherman, was made with vouchers, but instead of receiving cash as first established, the former slaves had to redeem their vouchers for high-priced supplies at stores operated by the Treasury Department agents. The agents who obtained the goods, mostly clothes and food, without cost from the army, then took the vouchers and exchanged them for cash. Although Reynolds did not personally profit from the system, his agents prospered. They were paying the contrabands only one dollar in four, while the rest went to their stores for the purchase of inflated commodities.[7]

Reynolds's agents' operations swept across the occupied sea islands, gathering up any items that could be sold for the war effort. On St. Helena, Reynolds discovered H. Von Harten, a German immigrant who had operated a general store for eleven years. The refugee planters had owed Von Harten, who remained after the Federal occupation, some two thousand dollars. Not wanting to wait for the planters' return, he had taken cotton from his debtors' plantations to settle their accounts. Although sympathetic to Von Harten's plight, Reynolds seized his cotton. However, since he considered Von Harten a "loyal man," the treasury agent asked Secretary Chase to give the case special consideration.[8]

Reynolds also had to deal with military commanders who were uninterested in or hostile to his work. One in particular was General Stevens, who had earlier challenged Nobles's authority. Conflict between the two was inevitable. Stevens disliked the treasury agents, who not only gathered up items that could have been used by the military but also demanded that the army reimburse the agents for any supplies already appropriated by the army. Stevens reluctantly followed instructions but drew the line when Reynolds's men tried to seize books that Stevens had collected and placed in the Beaufort College building for his soldiers' use.

When first occupying Beaufort, Stevens quickly stopped the looting and destruction carried out by the masterless slaves and returned them to their quarters. Patrols watched over abandoned buildings and enforced strict regulations that governed the conduct of soldiers and civilians alike. Stevens also placed guards over the town's library in Beaufort College on Carteret Street. The general had the books properly arranged and supplemented the collection with books taken from abandoned homes. The library was then reopened for use by Union soldiers.

Reynolds, however, considered the books, many of which were rare and valuable, captured property eligible for confiscation and sale. Stevens refused to hand over the library. The treasury agent appealed to General Sherman, who refused to intervene. In the end Stevens was forced to yield. At Secretary Chase's direction, 3,182 books were crated and bundled and delivered to the New York Port collector Hiram Barney. Chase instructed Barney to hold the collection with the intention to restore the books to the town when a government had been established loyal to the Union. This arrangement remained in place until the fall of 1862, when the Treasury Department gave the War Department authority over Port Royal and confiscated property. General Rufus Saxton, then in charge, directed Barney to sell the library. Arrangements were made to auction off the collection during the week of November 17–24, 1862. A public outcry led by William H. Fry erupted from the citizens of New York. Fry wrote President Lincoln, who asked Chase to intervene. On November 13, 1862, Chase wrote Barney, "I never thought of selling it. We do not war on libraries."

The auction was called off, and in late January 1863 Secretary of War Edwin Stanton enjoined Barney to send the collection to Washington, D.C., where it was housed in the Smithsonian Institution with books and papers taken from the Fairfax Seminary in Virginia for safekeeping, but on January 24, 1865, a fire swept through the Smithsonian Castle's south tower, destroying the books before they could be returned to Beaufort.[9]

Although some considered the treasury agents to be no better than "Ali Baba and his Forty Thieves," General Sherman continued to support the officials. Besides collecting cotton and other items, Reynolds hired the contrabands to cultivate the sea islands' 1862 cotton crop. Growing sea island cotton was involved and tedious, but Reynolds managed to plant several thousand acres. However, he realized that his ability to manage the crop was limited. Possibly hoping to involve Sprague and others in the operations at Port Royal, he urged Chase to lease the abandoned plantations to "loyal citizens" who would employ former slaves to tend the cotton. He also suggested that a steamer be purchased for his work and that a private cotton commission house be employed to broker the sale of the cotton from Port Royal instead of Collector Barney.

Chase agreed to the purchase of a steamer, and by early spring of 1862 the Treasury Department's agents were using the light-draft, 281-ton paddle-wheel steamer *Flora* to gather up cotton and other property from plantations around Port Royal Sound. However, Chase opposed leasing the plantations or hiring a private firm to broker cotton sales. Instead, Chase had formulated his own method for dealing not only with the sea island cotton but also the region's refugee slaves. While Reynolds and his agents may well have wanted their tenure at Port Royal to last for the war's duration, new characters were arriving who would continue the region's social, economic, and political upheaval.[10]

Anyone coming to the sea islands had to gain a pass from the Treasury Department, and Secretary Chase carefully governed all civilian traffic to the area. Among those interested in sending representatives to Port Royal were reform and abolitionist organizations and individuals who saw the place as the perfect setting to begin a new city of God based around the region's masterless slaves. One of the first to be granted permission to venture south was the Reverend Solomon Peck. Born in 1800 at Providence, Rhode Island, Peck was a child prodigy. He graduated from Brown University at the age of sixteen and, after a brief stint as a schoolteacher, attended divinity school at Andover. In 1823 he was ordained as a Baptist minister and the next year accepted a call to a church in Charleston, South Carolina. He traveled to Beaufort and the sea islands, where he formed a deep attachment to the region's slaves. He returned north the following year to teach at Amherst but never forgot his brief experience in Beaufort District. In 1832 Peck began a long association with the American Baptist Board of Foreign Missions. He eventually became the organization's executive secretary, a position he held until his resignation in 1858. Though criticized by his more radical brethren for being too moderate on the slavery issue, no one doubted Peck's zeal to help the outcast and persecuted.

When the war began, Peck volunteered his services as an army chaplain but was turned down for being too old. However, the capture of Port Royal Sound and the occupation of Beaufort rekindled his interest in the region's mostly Baptist slaves, and he applied and received permission from the government to travel to Beaufort. Besides his own missionary zeal, Peck also aided Beaufort native and fellow Baptist preacher Richard Fuller, pastor of the Seventh Baptist Church in Baltimore. Fuller and his family retained extensive land and slave holdings throughout the occupied zone, which Fuller asked Peck to safeguard.

Peck arrived in Beaufort in December 1861. He took up residence in the abandoned Thomas Fuller House on Bay Street and went to work assisting the thousands of ex-slaves who were members of the Beaufort Baptist Church. He organized a school in Beaufort for black children and began preaching on Cat, Cane, and Lady's Islands as well as in the Baptist Church on Charles Street. In time Peck took over the Beaufort Baptist Church as well as its praise house on New Street, the Baptist meeting and lecture hall on Craven Street, and the Brick Baptist Church on St. Helena Island.[11]

A second northern minister, Mansfield French, soon found his way to Port Royal. A fifty-one-year-old native of Manchester, Vermont, French had matriculated at Kenyon College in Gambier, Ohio, which was also an

Episcopal seminary. He married Granville, Ohio, native Austa Melinda Winchell, a kindred soul who shared her husband's passion for education, women's rights, and abolitionism. In Ohio, French helped establish Marietta College and Grenville Female Seminary and was principal of Circleville Female College. During a great religious revival that swept Ohio in 1844, Mansfield and Austa French became evangelicals. The following year Mansfield left the Episcopal Church and became a minister in the Methodist Episcopal Church.

French served as a fundraiser for Ohio Wesleyan College and later president of the Methodist Female College in Xenia, Ohio. At Xenia, French saw the need for a school for the area's large black population and established the Ohio African University, which eventually became Wilberforce University. Governor Salmon P. Chase was one of the college's most active proponents.[12]

A passionate abolitionist, French was noted for his stirring, religious public addresses that demanded an end to slavery and justice for the slaves. He often substituted for William Lloyd Garrison when Garrison was unable to meet a speaking engagement. In 1858, because of ill health, French moved his family to New York City, where they allied themselves with Lewis Tappan's American Missionary Association, founded to assist former slaves in improving their religious, moral, educational, social, and political condition. The association, which traced its history back to an 1839 committee that assisted in the *Amistad* court case, found backing from a number of religious bodies, including the Congregational, Free Will Baptist, Wesleyan Methodist Episcopal, and Reformed Dutch Churches. At the start of the Civil War, the association began establishing educational facilities in areas occupied by the North. Their first school for former slaves opened near Fort Monroe in September 1861 on the grounds of the Chesapeake Female College at Hampton, Virginia.[13]

A month later, after the capture of Port Royal and the occupation of the sea islands, an even greater and larger opportunity beckoned. Tappan selected Mansfield French, who quickly went to Washington, where his friend Secretary Chase arranged a meeting with President Lincoln. Impressed with French's earnestness, Lincoln issued an executive order through the secretary of war on January 6, 1862, giving French permission to visit military installations in the South with the "view of ministering to the spiritual necessities of our troops and other classes." Transported by army vessels, French visited the American Missionary Association's establishments near Hampton, Virginia, before continuing on to Port Royal and Beaufort, South Carolina.[14]

At Port Royal, French met Edward Lille Pierce, who had come south at the behest of Secretary Chase to examine the situation on the sea islands. Of the triumvirate— Pierce, French, and Saxton—who developed the Port Royal program, the thirty-two-year-old Pierce was the organizer who set the project on its course. A Stoughton, Massachusetts, native, Pierce was a graduate of Brown and Harvard Law School. Pierce could be rightly termed a renaissance man. He was a noted expert on railroad law, wrote biographies, and was active in politics and reform movements. Initially a free-soil Democrat, he became an early member of the Republican Party and a protégé of two of its most powerful members, Charles Sumner and Salmon Chase. Pierce worked in Chase's law firm and later became his senatorial secretary in Washington. He was a close friend and confidant to the ambitious Ohio politician, advising Chase on political and social affairs.

At the start of the war, Pierce enlisted as a private in the 3rd Massachusetts Infantry Regiment, a ninety-day unit assigned to Major General Benjamin Butler's command at Fort Monroe, Virginia. Although just an enlisted man, Pierce served as Butler's secretary and assisted the general in writing and issuing his famous directive declaring slaves as contraband. After being mustered out in late July, Pierce returned to Boston. On December 20, 1861, Chase summoned him to the capital. They met on December 27, and Chase pressed Pierce to go to Port Royal as a Treasury Department agent and report back on what could be done for the abandoned slaves. Chase's motives were twofold. The secretary had a genuine concern for the region's Negroes and saw an opportunity to reshape the South by introducing labor and social reforms that would uplift the status of the former slaves by employing them in a free-market economy and preparing them to become citizens. Pierce was to observe and report back on the state of the cotton crop, the traits and capacity of the African Americans, and how best to organize the former slaves into free laborers.[15]

Pierce, who felt that a base for interaction between the contrabands and the government had to be established, suggested to Chase that it "may prove necessary to have a few young men of religious fervor and humanity to aid as teachers and in appealing to the religious element, through which the negroes may be brought in sympathy with us." Chase agreed and Pierce contacted the Reverend Jacob Manning, pastor of Boston's Congregationalist Old South Church, who promised to help recruit missionaries and procure donations for the project.[16]

Pierce left New York on January 13, 1862, on the steamer *Baltic* and arrived at Hilton Head on January 17. He met Colonel Reynolds and informed his fellow Treasury Department official that he was there to observe the situation and report his findings directly to Chase. Pierce also wrote an open letter to the "benevolent people in Boston and vicinity" to contribute articles, especially clothing, for the area's Negroes and to begin recruiting missionaries for service at Port Royal. Pierce carried out a systematic inspection of the region, and on February 3 he wrote a detailed report that amounted to an economic and demographic census.[17]

He found nearly two hundred plantations on Beaufort District's sea islands, divided as follows:

Port Royal	65
St. Helena	50
Lady's	30
Hilton Head	15
Parris and Horse	6
Hutchinson and Fenwick	6
Daufuskie	5
Pinckney	5
Dathaw	4
Coosaw	2
Morgan	2
Bull and Barataria	2
Cat	1
Cane	1

On average, each plantation contained about 40 slaves. The most populated were on St. Helena Island: Coffin Point, home to 260 people, and Dr. W. J. Jenkins's plantation, with 120. Pierce estimated that there were in all about 12,000 contrabands in the Port Royal area, of whom about 8,000 had been prewar residents. The remaining 4,000 were refugees from the mainland. Most of the former slaves stayed in their homes, but on Hilton Head and Port Royal Islands the military established camps to handle the influx of refugees. Each camp had a population of approximately 600 contrabands.

On Hilton Head, Barnard K. Lee Jr. of Boston had been appointed by Rufus Saxton to supervise the refugees. Lee, who had come to Port Royal as the supercargo for the army transport *Ocean Queen,* also established at the camp a school for the contrabands. Lee was assisted by J. D. McNath of Alleghany City, Pennsylvania, and worked closely with the expedition's master carpenter Duncan C. Wilson. Together Lee, McNath, and Wilson organized the refugees into working parties. Men served as laborers while women worked as laundresses. Clothing and blankets were initially provided from captured Confederate supplies. Barracks were built and the laborers were paid from eight to twelve dollars a month for skilled workers and four to twelve dollars a month for manual laborers. Lee also established a school at the camp. A newer camp at Beaufort, initially created by Quartermaster Captains William Lilley and Charles E. Fuller and now under the direction of the Daufuskie Island resident William Harding, contained about six hundred people.

On the sea islands, Pierce reported that Reynolds and his agents expected to gather 2.5 million pounds of sea island cotton, which, using prewar rates, was valued at over two million dollars. In his survey Pierce found that the majority of the ex-slaves had stayed on their former plantations, living in quarters that measured about sixteen feet by twelve feet per family. Occasionally the small huts were divided by a partition and housed two families. The contrabands were very attached to familiar places, especially their homes. Families ate together only on Sundays because their former masters had never permitted their slaves regular meal times. Pierce hoped that in the future, under a new system, they would gather as families for all meals and that better provisions as well as new clothing be provided.

Authority on the plantations still resided in the driver, a privileged slave. The driver, sometimes termed the taskmaster, supervised the field hands, distributed rations, and exercised the discipline of corporal punishment. These privileged slaves had been the actual day-to-day bosses who made the sea island cotton economy work, and initially they retained their authority over the field hands even after the Federal occupation. But Pierce acknowledged that the drivers' authority was eroding as the field hands rightfully saw the driver as a reminder of the master and the old days, but Pierce found that as a group, drivers were open to change and hopeful that they would be retained under any new management system.

Besides the drivers, other important hands included skilled workmen such as carpenters, ploughmen, and—most important—religious leaders known as preachers, watchmen, and their helpers. The preachers held high positions in slave society and were recognized leaders. Besides the Sunday services, there were evening prayer meetings at least once during the week. The majority of ex-slaves were Baptist and on St. Helena Island flocked to the Brick Baptist Church and a chapel on the Eustis Plantation. Pierce was impressed by the lack of profanity among the slaves, especially in contrast to the white soldiers.

Pierce joined in the services, telling the congregants that he had been sent by President Lincoln, a name they knew well, to formulate a plan that would make them part of a new society where all were free and all had to work to succeed. At Hilton Head he spoke to some two hundred refugees from the mainland who found the northern-occupied enclave a convenient station on the Underground Railroad. As noted by a reporter: "To them the north star swung around and now poised over Port Royal. They came to be free." One escaped slave came from St. Peters Parish in upper Beaufort District. He had known the Baptist minister Dr. William Henry Brisbane, Beaufort District's homegrown abolitionist, who had fled the area in 1838 for his own safety. Brisbane eventually settled in Ohio, where he became well known to Chase and other abolitionists.

Pierce was stirred by his first encounter with the Port Royal slaves. He found them anxious to be free but not overly hateful toward their former owners, whom they saw as individuals with their own virtues and vices. On St. Helena the slaves spoke well of William and Clarence Fripp, but not of Alvira Fripp. They had planted acres of corn and sweet potatoes for their own use. While many still watched the occupiers with suspicion, others actively supported the military by serving as guides, spies, and ship pilots. Pierce felt them on the whole to be trustworthy and "as industrious as any race of men are likely to be in this climate."

Besides investigating the condition of the slaves, Pierce studied the cultivation of sea island cotton. He learned the planting schedule, the use of marsh mud and grass to fertilize the fields, the workings of the task system, the use of hoes to create the furrows and maintain the crop, and the ginning process. He believed that growing sea island cotton would provide the slaves with the needed employment and income to sustain their new status as freedmen.

Pierce vigorously opposed Colonel Reynolds's proposal to lease the plantations and the former slaves to northern speculators, pointing out that landlords would only work for their own profit and not respect the interest of the laborers. He saw this as no better than replacing one master with another. Instead Pierce called for the government to appoint farm superintendents to lead the former slaves into a free labor market and prepare them for citizenship.

Pierce lamented that so little was being done to provide education and religious opportunities for the ex-slaves. Besides Lee's school on Hilton Head, the only person active in these areas was the Reverend Solomon Peck, who had opened a ministry for the slaves and taken it upon himself to protect them from depredations by other whites. Peck, aided by three black teachers, including one named John Milton, operated Beaufort's only school, which served sixty students ranging in age from six to fifteen. Pierce spent time in the school teaching the alphabet and watching the other instructors work with the students on spelling and Gospel lessons.

Pierce found a few devisees who laid claim to some of the area's plantations. He viewed most of them with suspicion, believing only two were loyal to the United States. One of these was Frederick A. Eustis, a Massachusetts native who had jointly inherited the property of his stepmother, Patience Izard Eustis, near Pocotaligo and on Lady's Island. The other heirs resided in Charleston and the estate was unsettled. Eustis had come to Port Royal shortly after its occupation and fully embraced Pierce's vision for the region's slaves. Pierce was so impressed that he recommended that Eustis superintend his own plantation on Lady's Island.

Pierce began to conceptualize his views on how to handle the situation at Port Royal. For at least two years, the government should take on the expenses and administration of a system that would begin a great social change resulting in the modern world's first biracial civilization. The plan called for superintendents to receive about fifteen hundred dollars a year to oversee the plantations. These people would serve as guardians over the contrabands with authority to enforce "paternal discipline" and "require a proper amount of labor, cleanliness, sobriety and better habits of life, and generally promote the moral and intellectual culture of the wards." Slave marriages and families were to be recognized. To supervise the program, Pierce suggested that a governor of high character be appointed who would promote and protect the enterprise in close cooperation with the military.

The project was geared toward preparing the former slaves for citizenship. Corporal punishment would be banished. Inducement to work would be based on wages and the desire to better one's self and family. People would be assigned appropriate tasks, and wages would be around forty cents a day or twelve dollars a month, slightly less than an army private's pay of thirteen dollars a month. The government would provide food, clothing, medical care, and housing. Pierce believed that modern agricultural methods combined with wage incentives would result in higher cotton yields. The higher profits would offset the government's cost of running the program.

To complement the superintendents, who would run the business side of the enterprise, Pierce also wanted a corps of Christian missionaries who would establish and staff schools and distribute needed clothing, food, and tobacco. He envisioned the entire operation as filled with a progressive "social gospel" Christianity that promoted and rewarded hard work, fidelity, and adherence to the word of Jesus. Pierce wanted those sent to Port Royal to be of a similar mindset, ready to do God's work of creating a new age in a redeemed South.[18]

While at Port Royal, Pierce discussed his views with Mansfield French, General Sherman, and Flag Officer Du Pont. French wholeheartedly backed Pierce's plan and convinced his fellow visionary that women should be part of the missionary corps. Du Pont approved Pierce's concept, believing too that the former slaves would benefit from a system of government-run plantations and schools to "inculcate industry—all of which a Yankee educated man so well understands." Pierce appreciated Du Pont's support, writing Chase that the naval officer had "the liberal views of a statesman."[19] General Sherman, desperate to be relieved of responsibility for the contrabands, eagerly endorsed the plan. He joined Pierce, French, and Du Pont in opening a four-prong offensive to gain help from the government and private organizations to bring to existence a new South at Port Royal.[20]

As Pierce and French prepared to return north, Sherman completed General Field Orders Number 9, which took Pierce's concept of superintendents and educators and made it a departmental mandate. The directive established on the sea islands a number of districts headed up by government agents charged to secure the plantations' existing cotton and property, organize contraband work forces to grow cotton to support the war effort, and provide wages, food, and clothing for the liberated workers. In his directive Sherman also appealed to philanthropic organizations to provide instructors who would help the blacks "support and govern themselves" and establish a system to instruct the slaves in the rudiments of civilization, Christianity, and the laws of God, man, and society.[21]

Sherman's General Field Orders Number 9 was issued on February 6, 1862, and sent north to the adjutant general on the same vessel that carried Pierce to Washington. On February 14 Pierce reported to Chase, who immediately embraced his agent's concepts and authorized him to begin a program that would permanently remove African Americans from slavery and place them on the road to full citizenship. Slavery in the sea islands was dead; reconstructing a new South had begun.

President Lincoln met Pierce the next day and expressed considerable concern over the situation at Port Royal. The president believed that the contrabands had to be sustained in their new freedom and wrote a note out for Pierce to take back to Chase: "I shall be obliged if the Sec. of the Treasury will in his discretion, give Mr. Pierce such instructions in regard to the Port Royal contrabands as may seem judicious." Chase and Pierce were happy that the president gave them such broad powers. Pierce later wrote that by not acting immediately on emancipation, Lincoln had given the people at Port Royal time to better prepare the former slaves for freedom and citizenship.[22]

With carte blanche from the president, Chase moved quickly. The secretary soon received a letter from Mansfield French promising a supply of clothing and shoes as well as support for schools, teachers, and physicians from New York. Secretary of War Edwin Stanton willingly relinquished his authority over the contrabands and the collection of cotton, rice, and other abandoned property. He directed his quartermasters to support the Treasury Department in the transportation of supplies and personnel and the issuing of food and other necessary commodities. The effect of Stanton's endorsement of the Treasury Department's operation was to cancel Sherman's Field Orders Number 9. The entire cotton and contraband project now rested in the hands of the Treasury Department.[23]

On February 19 Chase named Pierce general superintendent for the cultivation of the abandoned estates at Port Royal and director of "such persons as may be engaged in such cultivation and employment." Pierce was also put in charge of the missionaries who would carry out the religious instruction and ordinary education of the "laboring population." Chase based his authority on section 5 of the Treasury Act of July 13, 1861, which gave the secretary of the treasury sole authorization to prescribe rules and regulations and appoint officials to carry out commercial intercourse with any part of the country declared to be in a state of insurrection.[24]

Even before Pierce and Chase had solidified their plans, donations and recruits were being raised for the Port Royal project. Pierce's associates in Boston, inspired by his letter from Port Royal, formed the Educational Commission for Freedmen and elected Massachusetts governor John A. Andrew as its president. A committee headed up by educators George B. Emerson and Loring Lothrop busily screened applicants. Reverend French returned to New York and reported to the American Missionary Association, which realized that it needed a new, broader-based organization to assist the contrabands at Port Royal. A public meeting was arranged at the Cooper Union Institute on February 20, 1862. Before a packed hall, the editor of the *New York Evening Post,* William Cullen Bryant, called the proposed mission "a noble task" and introduced French. The minister read letters of endorsement from Commodore Du Pont and General Sherman before launching into a moving oration describing the plight of the contrabands. Professor John Lindsay, who had accompanied French to Port Royal, offered remarks. Then came the noted Unitarian minister Dr. Henry Whitney Bellows and the Episcopalian cleric Reverend Dr. Stephen Higginson Tyng, all appealing to support the Port Royal contrabands. A committee was formed consisting of William C. Bryant, Stephen H. Tyng, Charles C. Leigh, Charles Gould, Francis G. Shaw, William Allen Butler, George C. Ward, Mansfield French, Joseph B. Collins, Edgar Ketchum, and John Edmonds, who were directed to "appeal for food, clothing, money, teachers and government aid." Two days later, the New York National Freedmen's Relief Association was organized.[25]

While the final details were being put in place, some prominent reformers called upon Chase to create a bureau within the Treasury Department that would operate the Port Royal project and expand the work to all areas of the occupied South. The noted landscape architect, scientific traveler, social observer, and writer Frederick Law Olmsted was mentioned as a possible director. He was then managing the United States Sanitary Commission, a private organization dedicated to helping the army's medical bureau and aiding soldiers' health and sanitary conditions. Olmsted, a well-known author and a strong opponent of the detrimental economic aspects of slavery, believed that slaves would be more efficient laborers as paid freedmen. He realized that the situation at Port Royal might be the beginning of a new South and wrote to his father, "I shall go to Port Royal, if I can, and work out practically every solution of the slavery question—long advocated in my book."[26] Though he never ventured to the island, Olmsted met with Pierce in February 1862 and later promoted a bill in the U.S. Senate to fund a more comprehensive program to benefit the slaves throughout the South. The bill failed, but Olmsted continued to follow developments at Port Royal.[27]

Pierce, who saw his role as limited to that of an organizer and temporary leader, was placed in charge of organizing the initial cast of characters and beginning the program. To assist his agent in the sea islands, Chase instructed New York agent Hiram Barney to provide travel permits, ploughs, hoes, harnesses, cottonseed, and anything else needed to operate the abandoned plantations. Barney was also to advance funds required to pay laborers. All Treasury Department expenses were to be covered by the eventual sale of cotton and other items grown or confiscated at Port Royal while the War Department was to provide transportation and subsistence.[28]

On March 3 Pierce, French, and their band of religious reformers boarded the steamer *Atlantic* bound for Port Royal. The group consisted of twenty-six men and four women from Boston, sixteen men and five women from New York, and three women from Washington, D.C. The men answered to Pierce, while French was in charge of the women, among whom were his wife and Susan Walker, a native of Wilmington, Massachusetts. A noted mathematician, Walker was one of the nation's leading feminists and abolitionists. Active in the Republican Party, she had accompanied Senator Charles Sumner to Paris to aid in his recovery from the caning inflicted upon him on the Senate floor by South Carolina congressman Preston Brooks. At the start of the war, she established an industrial school in Washington for black women and held meetings to promote schooling for former slave women. The fifty-year-old activist also served as a special adviser to Republican leaders, including Secretary Chase, for whom she agreed to accompany the mission to Port Royal.

Including Pierce, there were fifty-four passengers aboard the *Atlantic*. Sponsored by the New York National Freedmen's Relief Association were Reverend Mansfield French, Nathan R. Johnson, Reverend Isaac W. Brinkerhoff, George B. Peck, Edmund Price, John D. Lathrop, Drury Cooper, Robert N. Smith, Henry A. Cowderry, Dr. James P. Greves, John T. Ashley, George C. Fox, John H. Brown, Lyman Knowlton, Albert Bellamy, Ninian Niven, Miss Hannah Curtis, Miss Mary Nicholson, Mrs. James Harlan, Mrs. Austa M. French, and Miss Ellen H. Peck.

The Boston Educational Commission for Freedmen included Edward W. Hooper, Edward S. Philbrick, William C. Gannet, George H. Blake, John C. Zachos, Dr. A. Judson Wakefield, James F. Sisson, Isaac W. Cole, James W. R. Hill, James H. Palmer, David F. Thorpe, David Mack, T. Edwin Ruffles, James M. F. Howard, Francis E. Barnard, Dr. James Waldock, Richard Soule Sr., Leonard Wesson, Dr. Charles H. Brown, William E. Park, James E. Taylor, Frederick A. Eustis, Daniel Bowe, William S. Clark, Samuel D. Phillips, Mrs. Elizabeth B. Hale, Miss Mena Hale, Miss Mary Waldock, and Miss Ellen Winsor.

Representing Secretary Chase were Susan Walker and her two friends, Mrs. Walter R. Johnson and Mary A. Donaldson. Also on board was the Reverend James Floyd from the New York Association, who was only to remain for three weeks, and William Ellery Channing Eustis, the thirteen-year-old son of Frederick Eustis.

Although united in their mission, the group had divisions, notably in their religious beliefs, which were manifested on the voyage. While there were different denominations represented in each group, those from New York, sometimes termed the French Set, tended to be Methodists and Baptists and were more openly fervent and evangelical in their Christian beliefs, while the Bostonians were mainly Congregationalists, Free Will Christians, Unitarians, and Transcendentalists. On the voyage south, French and his band gathered on deck for religious services and the singing of hymns. The Bostonians kept more to themselves. Susan Walker noted that the two groups had different forms of faith, and though the Unitarians and their religious allies believed that "Work is Worship" she did trust that "one spirit animates our band—one desire to lift up into the glorious light of freedom the oppressed and benighted ones, thrown by this wicked rebellion, so entirely upon their own feeble resources and our humanity." Despite their differences, Walker believed that they all were pilgrims, united in general harmony and spirit.[29]

Also aboard the *Atlantic* was the Massachusetts businessman and U.S. Navy agent John Murray Forbes, who early in the war had served with George D. Morgan to purchase vessels for the Navy Department. Forbes, whose son was stationed in Beaufort with the 1st Massachusetts Cavalry, had started his fortune by trading opium and other goods to China and then expanded into the railroad business and beyond. As manager of a large investment and financial firm, Forbes became a leading national business figure. He also became involved in politics. An opponent of slavery, he joined the Republican Party and worked closely with Massachusetts governor John A. Andrew to ready their state for war. Like Andrew he favored early emancipation and use of black troops.

His trip south had a number of motives. He wanted to visit his son, and Forbes's doctor had urged the businessman to take a sojourn to a warmer climate to relieve a chronic cough. At the same time, Forbes wished to view firsthand the transition of slaves to free laborers and their ability to serve as soldiers, both being concepts promoted by himself and Governor Andrew. Although he was a Massachusetts Unitarian and shared his fellow travelers' social and political beliefs, Forbes remained detached and aloof from the other passengers. He described them to his daughter as consisting of "bearded and mustached and odd-looking men, with odder looking women.... You would have doubted whether it was an adjournment of a John Brown meeting or the fag end of a broken-down philanstery!"[30]

The *Atlantic* docked at Hilton Head on March 7, and Pierce immediately met with General Sherman, who was greatly pleased at their arrival. The next day the missionaries and their belongings were transferred to the steamer *Cosmopolitan,* which carried them to Beaufort, where they found no "joyous welcome." No preparations had been made, and Pierce and the male missionaries stripped off their coats and off-loaded their luggage while bemused soldiers and contrabands looked on. Nor did they have any quarters as the expected housing had been appropriated and the military and treasury agents had seized furniture.[31]

The men found shelter as best they could while temporary lodging was found for the women. Reverend French, his wife, and some of the women joined Dr. Peck in the Thomas Fuller House, while others stayed with General Stevens and his wife at the John J. Smith home. The next day, after a brief snowstorm, Reverend French secured two houses, the Edgar Fripp home for the men and the Paul Hamilton home for the women. Susan Walker reported that the Hamilton house was splendid but worried over the prospect of having twelve strong-willed women together in one house.[32]

The residences were only temporary. Within a few days, Pierce established his headquarters at the Oaks Plantation, the home of John Jeremiah Theus Pope, on St. Helena Island. By April 1, 1862, Pierce had placed his agents throughout the sea islands. Seven, including a physician, gardener, and a teacher, were sent to Edisto Island, where the Federal garrison had been recently reinforced to guard an ever-increasing contraband population. Five were placed on Hilton Head Island, joining two existing agents. Daufuskie received one; two were sent to Pinckney Island; and nine, including a doctor, were situated on Lady's Island. Parris Island was home to John Celivergos Zachos, an educator, theologian, and doctor who had been born in Constantinople to Greek parents and brought to the United States at the age of ten by the reformer and future husband of Julia Ward, Samuel Gridley Howe, who had first gained fame by fighting in the Greek war for independence. A graduate of Kenyon College, Zachos taught before the war in Ohio at Cooper Female Seminary in Dayton, Ohio, and at Antioch College. On Parris Island he carried out both superintendent and teaching duties.

The majority of Pierce's force was placed on St. Helena and Port Royal Islands. The Boston contingent tended to dominate the assignments on St. Helena, where fifteen men and four women took up residence on the abandoned plantations. Twenty-two men and eight women, primarily from New York, worked on Port Royal Island under the supervision of Mansfield French and Solomon Peck.

The average age of the missionaries was thirty. The Massachusetts contingent was made up of people primarily in their twenties and thirties, while the New Yorkers tended to be older. The youngest was twenty-year-old George Wells of Providence, Rhode Island, while the oldest was the sixty-year-old Solomon Peck. Most were well educated, and their number included students from Harvard, Yale, and Brown. Among their ranks were three divinity students and ten clergymen, including three Unitarians, three Methodists, two Presbyterians, a Baptist, and a Congregationalist. There were also five doctors, four medical students, and one apothecary.

Compensation varied. Some took no pay, others only expenses. Mansfield French received $125 a month, while most of the doctors were paid $50 per month. The majority received a monthly salary ranging between $30 and $50. Superintendents received more than teachers, but pay usually depended on one's background. Almost all had experience as instructors, either in public, private, or Sunday schools.

Edward Hooper, a twenty-three-year-old Harvard graduate, served as Pierce's assistant at the Oaks Plantation. One individual of whom Pierce thought highly was Edward Philbrick, a thirty-four-year-old engineer from Brookline, Massachusetts. Philbrick was a trained engineer and architect who served with no compensation. He was assigned to Coffin Point Plantation, the largest under Pierce's jurisdiction. There Philbrick hoped to prove the theory that free labor would be more profitable than slave labor.[33]

In the following weeks, additional personnel from the North and the recruitment of individuals enlarged Price's corps of reformers. On April 13, 1862, eighteen additional missionaries arrived aboard the steamer *Oriental*. Included in this contingent was Miss Laura Towne, the lead pioneer from James Miller McKim's Port Royal Relief Committee, which was heavily backed by the city's Quaker and Unitarian communities. A native of Pittsburgh, Pennsylvania, the thirty-six-year-old activist and Presbyterian minister had been raised and educated in Boston, where she became involved in the antislavery movement. When her family relocated to Philadelphia, she embraced Unitarianism and became an avowed abolitionist. Towne took classes at the Female Medical College of Philadelphia in homeopathic medicine, but the outbreak of the war intervened and she never completed her degree.[34]

Towne had come to the sea islands to distribute clothing and food collected by the Port Royal Relief Committee. Pierce initially sent her to stay with Mr. and Mrs. John M. Forbes at the William Fripp House. Forbes had been given permission by General Stevens to take over the house and was soon joined by his wife and yacht *Azalea*. Towne stayed with the Forbes couple for only a short time before joining Pierce and his contingent at the Oaks Plantation.[35]

Initial impressions of the missionaries varied. Bemused soldiers called them Gideonites or Gids, a nickname the newcomers embraced. Captain Hazard Stevens, whose father supervised Beaufort and Port Royal Island, referred to them as a plague of locusts sent by Moses to ravage Egypt. However, many high-ranking Union officers warmly greeted the missionaries. Du Pont and Sherman were extremely happy at their arrival, believing that they would relieve them of the extraneous duty of caring for the freedmen.

Rufus Saxton, the department quartermaster, was sympathetic, as was General Isaac Stevens, who did not share his son's low opinion of them. Stevens welcomed the missionaries and did all he could to make them comfortable. Such actions initially surprised Pierce and French since Stevens had been a prewar Democrat and campaign manager of John C. Breckinridge, the 1860 southern presidential candidate; but Stevens proved to be, as Pierce wrote, "very courteous" and "a friend of the missionaries."[36]

Pierce gained powerful military backers when in March 1862 two new army officers, Major General David Hunter and Brigadier General Henry W. Benham, disembarked at Port Royal. Their arrival coincided with the creation of a new command, the Department of the South, a division that took in all the territory occupied by General Thomas Sherman's expeditionary corps. Hunter replaced General Sherman, and Benham, Hunter's second in command, took over the department's northern district. Hunter was an avowed abolitionist, while Benham sympathized with the work being done by Pierce and the other missionaries.

While Pierce gained favor with the military, his relations with Reynolds and his agents became worse. Reynolds, who realized that his days as chief Treasury Department agent were numbered, was cordial, though he did write to Chase commenting that Pierce and his band were not fully prepared to handle the situation on the sea islands. Led by Nobles, the cotton agents, whom Reynolds never completely controlled, saw their profiteering days ending and resisted the authority of Pierce and his superintendents.[37]

Confrontations soon broke out between Reynolds's agents and Pierce's missionaries. The agents refused any cooperation. They held back supplies and matériel and refused to evacuate plantations now claimed by Pierce's minions. At the Dr. William J. Jenkins Plantation on Station Creek, Agent Edward Salisbury lived a life of luxury while denying Pierce's superintendents any support. At Coffin Point, St. Helena Island's largest plantation, Alfred Salisbury refused to allow Superintendent Philbrick to take up residence, forcing him to stay at the Oaks with Pierce. Matters came to a head when Pierce and Nobles met outside General Benham's headquarters in Beaufort. Already angry over a dispute involving a horse, bridle, and saddle, Nobles damned Pierce for writing unfavorable reports to Chase, knocked him down, and beat him until soldiers broke up the fight. Pierce reported the incident to General Benham, who quickly ordered Nobles out of the department.[38]

While dealing with the cotton agents, Pierce also worried about the status of the blacks and the rights of the sea island property owners who were in a position to retain their land and possibly their slaves. John Flyer, who had returned to the area, laid claim to his lands on Port Royal Island, and Pierce worried that Flyer might try to reclaim his slaves. Pierce did not worry about Frederick A. Eustis, who owned property on the mainland near

Confederate-occupied Pocotaligo and on Lady's Island. Eustis, who had willingly taken the superintendent's job at his former Lady's Island plantation, had completely embraced Pierce's program. Pierce did have concerns over plantations retained by Reverend Richard Fuller of Beaufort, the current pastor of the Seventh Baptist Church in Baltimore. Fuller, a resident of a loyal state with close connections to Secretary Chase, might try to retain control of his lands and slaves.

Pierce wrote to Chase on March 14, 1862, on these matters. Rumors were rife among the blacks that Fuller had made arrangements to keep his property and slaves. Such tales were causing turmoil among the contrabands at Fuller's property on Cane and Cat Islands and threatened to disrupt the entire operation. Pierce had learned from Dr. Peck, Fuller's agent, that the minister had every intention to retain his property and slaves. In response to that discovery, Pierce instructed Peck to discontinue his representation of Fuller and asked Chase to handle the matter.

Unknown to Pierce, Chase had already dealt with Fuller. The day before Pierce had written the secretary, Fuller had visited Chase, wanting to know "what were his rights" respecting his land and slaves. Chase informed his friend that he still retained his land but that Chase would never consent to the return to slavery of even "one of the Negroes." For all intents and purposes, the African Americans at Port Royal were de facto free. Fuller accepted the judgment but questioned whether the blacks were capable of handling their new status. He quoted Machiavelli: "Next to making Freemen slaves, it was most difficult to make slaves Freedmen." Throughout the war Fuller kept a close watch on the activities at Port Royal.[39]

Besides problems with property owners, relations with the military also varied mightily. Pierce and his band were on good terms with the high command but had problems with some of the northern soldiers. Many resented what they saw as favoritism toward the ex-slaves; others felt that the Port Royal project was taking resources away from military operations against Charleston. Bored soldiers and officers caused trouble. They raided the contrabands' settlements and stole food, chickens, and livestock. They assaulted the contrabands, burned houses, and shot the only bull on Parris Island. The troops made fun of the "Gids." The soldiers would fake enemy attacks to panic missionaries, some of whom fled. Others, such as Laura Towne, armed themselves and contrabands to resist assaults.[40]

At the same time, the missionaries were not united. Problems manifested on the voyage south continued as the settlement grew. Although they all worked toward a common goal, the missionaries split along religious lines. The New England Unitarians considered themselves on a higher ethical plane than the evangelical New Yorkers. However, the New Yorkers' church services were lively and emotional, attracting contrabands more than did

Unitarian services. Susan Walker, a Unitarian, disliked associating with the women recruited by Mansfield French, commenting that they had "no congeniality of taste and sentiment." On the other hand, French declared that the Unitarians "don't get hold of the work in the right way."

The Baptists, under Reverend Peck's leadership, had taken over the Beaufort Baptist Church and its missions. They tried to co-opt the movement, declaring that 70 percent of the blacks were Baptists who preferred emotional over rational religious expression, declaring that the contrabands could not understand a religion not founded on the divinity of Jesus. The Baptist Missionary Society went so far as to blame the U.S. government for sponsoring "scores of Methodists, Congregationalists, Unitarians and Universalists" who came to Port Royal to "disturb their faith and if possible, to destroy their faith, and, to destroy their churches."

Missionaries vied with each other to control the churches, Sunday schools, and religious instructions. Baptists denied communion to Unitarians and attempted to restrict other sects from sending missionaries to Port Royal. The rivalries reached such volume that President Lincoln had to instruct the War Department to make sure that "each church should minister according to its own rules, without interference by others differing from them; and if there still be difficulties about places of worship, a real Christian charity, and forbearance on the part of all might obviate it."[41]

Although beset by external and internal problems, the missionaries were usually able to put aside their differences to meet their common goal of assisting the contrabands, though this did not come easily. The ex-slaves watched carefully to see whether new masters had replaced the old ones. Some believed the tales circulated by their former owners that the Yankees would sell them to Cuba. They wanted land and fair wages and also strong assurance that slavery was gone forever. If some thought freedom meant freedom from work, most realized that their new status gave them new opportunities. Besides working for the government, many had taken possession of nearby plots to plant corn and other food crops. Some planted cotton, though most associated cotton with slavery. A refrain of the slaves as reported by a soldier of the 48th New York accurately described the prewar situation:

> Big Bee sucks de blossom
> Little Bee makes de honey
> Colored people grows de cotton
> White people gets de money

The former slaves, especially after their first experience with the cotton agents, feared the refrain would refer to their new situation. But they soon found the new superintendents to be fair arbiters and sympathetic to the slaves and their desire to establish a new life and society.[42]

Besides working in the fields, male slaves were hired to police the camps, serve in the navy's workshops, and became servants for officers. Females did laundry and sold hoecakes, waffles, pies, sweet potatoes, and oranges to the soldiers. The former slaves knew that a new era had dawned, and with help from the missionaries a new society started.[43]

Most missionaries had had little or no contact with African Americans or slavery before their arrival at Port Royal. Some found the work too demanding; others proved not to be antislavery enough. Such folk were weeded out and replaced. Though paternalistic in many of their values, the missionaries worked hard to assist the former slaves with everything from employment to improving their homes. Patience was required. It took time to learn the local dialect and become used to the climate. Philbrick believed that the plantations on the sea islands should be turned into agricultural factories that employed ex-slaves as laborers. He was convinced that the "blacks will work for other motives than the lash" and was gratified with their industry. He reported that they were planting cotton without any direction. He thought that the West Africans were more energetic than Egyptians and much more so than the Irish.[44]

All were quite happy with their results. Slaves were working for wages and establishing their own family vegetable gardens. Reverend French was busy sanctifying and legalizing monogamous slave marriages. He ended the practice, once encouraged by former masters, of male slaves taking multiple wives on different plantations. By May eight schools were up and running, teaching thousands of ex-slaves, children, and adults. Pierce was very encouraged and reported to Chase, "Be assured that the success of the experiment here is inevitable."[45]

By the spring of 1862, many agreed with James M. McKim, head of the Port Royal Committee, that the old society had been torn down and that it was time to start a building a new one. Frederick Law Olmsted, Reverend Henry Bellows, Alexander D. Bache, and Samuel Gridley Howe were pushing legislation for a government-run bureau to handle not only Port Royal but also all freedmen activities throughout the South. Although some bills were introduced in Congress, the action was premature. The outcome of the war was in doubt, and the War Department was eyeing the ex-slaves at Port Royal as an untapped resource.

The former slaves had adapted to a free market so quickly that some government officials were eager to go the next step to see whether the slaves would fight their ex-masters to preserve their liberty. By April 1862 Secretary Chase was negotiating with Secretary of War Stanton to turn the Port Royal program turned over to the War Department. Stanton saw the region as a fertile recruiting ground for black troops, and Chase correctly believed that the army had more resources to handle the economic program. Chase hoped that Pierce would stay on, but the superintendent would not serve as a subordinate to a military officer. He would have accepted the position of military governor and the accompanying rank of brigadier general but turned down Stanton's offer of a colonelcy as second in command. Rufus Saxton, the former quartermaster who had initiated military employment of the sea island slaves, was commissioned brigadier general with full authority over the Port Royal program. Chase agreed with Stanton's selection but was disappointed that Pierce refused to stay. He was pleased that his department had started the experiment that seemed well on the road to success.[46]

Pierce agreed to stay on until Saxton arrived in June, but campaigns in northern Virginia found Saxton temporarily assigned to Harpers Ferry. With no firm arrival date, Pierce decided it was best to leave. On Sunday, June 1, 1862, after the service at the Brick Baptist Church, Pierce addressed the congregation. Loved and admired by the islanders, Pierce told them that he was leaving and that President Lincoln was sending a new general, a powerful protector who was their friend, and called on them to "love him and obey him." Laura Towne reported, "There was something so self-forgetting and humble in these words, and the manner speaking, that it made my heart swell, and when he thanked them and said good-bye, a good many were much affected." Pierce continued to work for the Treasury Department and on occasion returned to Port Royal to write articles, with satisfaction, on the continued success of the Port Royal Experiment.[47]

Chapter 5

The Confederate Beaufort District

"Flinging away lives and treasures"

As life on the sea islands changed forever, the white population on the unoccupied mainland strove hard to maintain their prewar situation. Court and government business continued at Gillisonville, the Beaufort District seat, and representatives were elected to the state General Assembly and the Confederate Congress in Richmond. Throughout the war Robert Woodward Barnwell served in the Confederate Senate, where he consistently supported Jefferson Davis's wartime policies. Second Congressional District resident Lewis Malone Ayer Jr., who defeated David F. Jamison in the 1862 election, represented the Beaufort District in the Confederate House of Representatives. Robert Barnwell Rhett Sr. revived his political hopes and challenged Ayer in 1864. The incumbent refused to step aside, and in a bitter campaign, he accurately labeled Rhett an anti-Davis demagogue. Handily defeating the Beaufort native, Ayer effectively ended Rhett's last political foray.[1]

St. Helena Parish elected Robert Barnwell Rhett's brother, Edmund Rhett, to the state senate, where he served until his death on February 15, 1863. Joseph Daniel Pope, who had delivered a speech at the July 1850 secession meeting at St. Helenaville and had signed the Ordnance of Secession, took Rhett's seat for the remainder of the war. Other state senators included William George Roberds (1860–63) and Alexander J. Lawton (1864–65) from St. Peters Parish. St. Luke Parish initially elected Hilton Head native Francis Wellman Fickling (1860–63) and then Richard James Davant (1864–65). Prince William Parish senators included James Edward DeLoach (1860–61) and Daniel Hix Ellis (1862–63).[2]

In the state house of representatives, Prince William Parish was served by William J. Gooding (1860–61 and 1864–65) and William Ferguson Hutson (1862–63). Hutson was an author of the Gillisonville Constitution and the reputed author of the Ordnance of Secession. St. Luke's Parish sent John Henry Screven (1860–61) and Leroy Franklin Youmans (1862–65), and St. Peter's Parish was served by Joseph M. Lawton (1860–61), Alfred M. Martin (1862–63), and William McKenzie Tison (1864–65).[3]

Throughout the war Stephen Elliott Jr. represented Union-occupied St. Helena Parish in the General Assembly, although his duties with the Beaufort Volunteer Artillery and later commands in South Carolina and Virginia kept his legislative position a symbolic one. As captain of the Beaufort Volunteer Artillery, Elliott and his men had served the heavy guns at Fort Beauregard during the November 1861 Federal attack. Refitted after the battle as a field artillery unit, Elliott often left his cannons behind and led the oversized company on spectacular raids and reconnaissance missions throughout Beaufort District. On August 21, 1862, he organized an amphibious strike against Federal forces on Pinckney Island that bagged thirty-six soldiers from Company H, 3rd New Hampshire. On other nocturnal scouting operations, Elliott's fluent ability to speak Gullah allowed him to fool local slaves and later black soldiers enlisted from sea island natives who hailed his vessel, thinking that Elliott and his men were escaped slaves.

Elliott was promoted to major and became the region's chief of artillery and ordnance. In this position he experimented with torpedoes, floating canisters containing black powder that were designed to detonate upon contact with enemy vessels. Elliott released a number of torpedoes in the waterways that flowed into Port Royal Sound. While no ships were ever sunk, the appearance of these floating weapons kept Federal mariners on edge.

Besides using torpedoes, Elliott also employed his artillery whenever a potential target presented itself. On April 9, 1863, Elliott directed an artillery bombardment that sank the U.S. Army gunboat *George Washington* in Whale Branch River. His energy, initiative, and ingenuity attracted the attention of General Beauregard, who assigned Elliott to command Fort Sumter in the summer of 1863. By then the fort had been pounded into rubble by Federal cannons, rendering it useless as an artillery position. Taking over at Sumter, Elliott replaced a fellow Beaufortonian, Colonel Alfred Rhett, whose 1st South Carolina Artillery had garrisoned the fort since the start of the war. Elliott, promoted to the rank of lieutenant colonel, was twice wounded while commanding elements of the Charleston Battalion at Sumter against Federal attacks.

In early 1864 Elliott was assigned to the Holcombe Legion, a unit of General Nathan Evans's brigade stationed near Charleston. Evans's "Tramp Brigade" suffered from poor morale and weak leadership and was eventually turned over to Elliott, who was promoted to brigadier general on May 24, 1864, and given the task of restoring the unit's spirit and discipline. Transferred to the Department of North Carolina and Southern Virginia, General Elliott led the brigade in the defense of Petersburg. On July 30, 1864, at the famous Battle of the Crater, Federal attackers exploded a mine under Elliott's position. Immediately, Elliott regrouped his stunned soldiers and, while leading them in a counterattack, suffered a severe wound that crippled his right arm. He remained on the field, not relinquishing command until the breach in the line was sealed.

Before he had fully recovered from his Petersburg wounds, Elliott returned to service as a brigade commander of forces assembled from the Charleston garrison to resist General William Tecumseh Sherman's advance into South Carolina. He led this unit at the Battles of Averasboro and Bentonville, North Carolina. At the latter engagement he suffered another wound. General Elliott returned to South Carolina and participated in local operations until the war ended.[4]

While Stephen Elliott's career gained him tremendous fame, he was not the Beaufort District's senior officer. That honor belonged to Brigadier General Alexander R. Lawton, who had been born near Lawtonville in St. Peter's Parish. He graduated from West Point in 1839, thirteenth in a class that included Isaac Stevens and Henry W. Halleck. Alexander Lawton served in the 1st Artillery along the Canadian border until he resigned from the army in 1840 to attend Harvard Law School. He then made his home in Savannah, where he practiced law, served as the president of the Savannah and Augusta Railroad, and became active in Georgia politics and the state militia.

As colonel of the Savannah-based 1st Volunteer Regiment of Georgia, Lawton, fearing Federal occupation of Fort Pulaski, convinced Georgia governor Joseph Brown to seize Pulaski at the mouth of the Savannah River even before the state had seceded from the Union. After the formation of the Confederacy on April 13, 1861, Lawton was promoted to brigadier general and commanded Georgia's coastal defenses. In June 1862 he led a Georgia brigade during Thomas "Stonewall" Jackson's Valley Campaign, the Seven Days Battles, and the Second Manassas Campaign. At Antietam, Lawton was badly wounded. Once he had recovered, President Jefferson Davis appointed him as the Confederacy's quartermaster general. General Lawton served admirably in that post, providing southern soldiers with adequate clothing, equipment, and transportation throughout the war.[5]

Besides Generals Elliott and Lawton, a number of other Beaufort District men held prominent positions during the war. St. Helena Parish native, politician, and planter Benjamin Jenkins Johnson, left the Beaufort District and moved to St. Thomas and Denis Parish on the Charleston Neck in 1857, where he expanded his fortune and became involved in local military affairs. He commanded the Washington Light Infantry, which later became Company A of the Hampton Legion Infantry. Lieutenant Colonel Johnson was killed on July 21, 1861, leading the legion's infantry at First Manassas.[6]

Beaufort District's oldest and most prominent families supported the war effort. Robert Barnwell Rhett and the families of his five brothers provided the Confederate army with eighteen soldiers. Thomas Smith Rhett, son of Thomas Moore Rhett, was an 1848 graduate of the U.S. Military

Academy and a prewar member of the 2nd U.S. Artillery. He served in the U.S. Army until 1855, when he resigned to become a banker in Baltimore. He joined the Confederacy and served as an ordnance officer. Promoted to colonel, he commanded the artillery defenses of Richmond from August 30, 1862, to April 1, 1863. He supervised all of Richmond's defenses until he was dispatched to Great Britain in October 1863 as a purchasing agent for the ordnance bureau. James Rhett's son, Thomas Grimké Rhett, graduated sixth in the West Point class of 1845 and served with the U.S. Mounted Rifles during the Mexican War. He resigned from the army on April 1, 1861, joined the Confederate army, and spent the war as a staff officer and paymaster. Benjamin Smith Rhett had four sons in Confederate service: Benjamin Smith Rhett Jr., John Grimké Rhett, Julius Moore Rhett, and William Haskell Rhett. John Grimké Rhett was killed at the Battle of Gaines Mill on June 27, 1862.

Four of Robert Barnwell Rhett's sons served in the Confederate army. Alfred Rhett started the war as an officer in the Battalion of South Carolina Artillery, which was expanded in March 1862 into the 1st South Carolina Artillery Regiment. While Rhett was directing a Fort Moultrie battery during the April 1861 bombardment of Fort Sumter, his commanding officer, the West Point–trained William R. Calhoun, bypassed Rhett and gave direct orders to the battery. Rhett never forgave Calhoun for this breach of military etiquette and often referred to his commanding officer as a "damned puppy." During the summer of 1862, Colonel Calhoun went on sick leave, and Rhett took command of the regiment. Rhett never ceased his denunciations, with the result that Calhoun challenged Rhett to a duel. The two met on September 4, 1862, at the Charleston Oak Club, where Rhett killed his commanding officer with a smoothbore pistol. For the offense Rhett was relieved of command, but the charges were dropped and on January 30, 1863, he rejoined his regiment.

From July to September 1862 and January to September 1863, Colonel Rhett commanded Fort Sumter. Thereafter his regiment manned fortifications around Charleston Harbor until the city was evacuated in February 1865. Placed in charge of a makeshift brigade of cannonless artillerymen, Rhett joined the retreat into North Carolina. He was captured on March 16, 1865, at the Battle of Averasboro and sent to a northern prisoner-of-war camp for the last weeks of the war.

Andrew Burnet Rhett began the war as captain of Company K, Brooks Volunteer Guards, 2nd South Carolina Infantry, at First Manassas. He was detached to form the Brooks Artillery Battery and commanded the unit with distinction during the Seven Days Battles. He then returned to the lowcountry as chief of artillery for the region between the Stono and Ashepoo Rivers. Robert B. Rhett's younger sons, Edmund Smith Rhett and Robert

Woodward Rhett, also served. Edmund was a captain in the 1st South Carolina Sharpshooters Battalion, and Robert Woodward, a second lieutenant in the 2nd South Carolina Infantry, was killed during the Seven Days Battles.[7]

The sons of Senator Robert W. Barnwell also saw extensive service. John Gibbs Barnwell was an artillery and ordnance officer with the Army of Northern Virginia while his brother Robert Hayne Barnwell served with the Beaufort Volunteer Artillery before joining the Confederate engineer corps. He was stationed at Battery Wagner during the July 18, 1863, bombardment and attack. When the battery's flag was shot away during that fight, Robert Barnwell coolly mounted the parapet and held a banner in his outstretched arms until the garrison flag was replaced. Later he built fortifications on the path of the Charleston and Savannah Railroad.

Robert W. Barnwell's twin sons, Nathaniel and Stuart, were not quite seventeen in early 1862 when they enlisted into the Rutledge Mounted Rifles. They went to Virginia in 1864 when their unit merged with the Holcombe Legion Cavalry to form the 7th South Carolina Cavalry Regiment. Nathaniel was captured on a scouting mission and after a stay at Point Lookout Federal Prison Camp was exchanged in time to serve in Lieutenant General Richard H. Anderson's artillery battalion. Stuart, who had planned to become a minister after the war, contracted typhoid fever and died in Richmond on July 8, 1864.[8]

Beaufort's DeTreville family traced its martial heritage back to John de La Boularderie de Treville, who was an officer during the French and Indian War and the American Revolution. Richard De Treville graduated from the United States Military Academy in 1823, and after two years with the artillery returned to Beaufort to practice law. He remained active in politics and the militia and was lieutenant governor from 1854 to 1856. During the war the senior DeTreville became colonel of the 17th South Carolina Militia Regiment. He continually applied to President Davis for a brigadier generalship but never secured a Confederate army commission.

All four of his sons served in the army. John La Boularderie and Edward White started the war as members of their father's militia command before going on to further service. Edward joined the 25th South Carolina Infantry, then became a Treasury Department clerk and a steward at Chimborazo Hospital in Richmond, Virginia. John joined the Beaufort Volunteer Artillery and remained on its roster until the end of the war. Richard Jr. also saw some service with the 25th South Carolina before joining the 3rd Virginia Local Defense Regiment.

The most prominent martial DeTreville was Robert, who became lieutenant colonel of the 1st South Carolina Infantry Regiment Regulars, which acted as an artillery unit around Charleston Harbor. The regiment was mainly stationed on Sullivan's Island with Robert DeTreville commanding the Fort

Moultrie garrison. After the evacuation of Charleston, DeTreville and his artillerymen fought as infantrymen. Robert DeTreville was killed in action at the Battle of Averasboro as the Confederates sought vainly to block William Tecumseh Sherman's armies. This loss greatly embittered his brother Richard, who later wrote that the Confederate leaders had kept up the fight too long and wasted "the resources of my country without accomplishing what should have been accomplished, and after . . . they saw ruin inevitable persisted for 6 months flinging away lives and treasures."[9]

Thomas A. Huguenin was a member of the 1st South Carolina Regulars and saw extensive service in the Charleston area. He was born in 1839 at Roseland, his family's plantation near Coosawhatchie in St. Luke's Parish, and was a descendant of original Purrysburg settlers. An 1859 Citadel graduate, he was senior first lieutenant of his regiment and was promoted to major before the war ended. Huguenin participated in the 1863 siege of Battery Wagner on Morris Island and commanded the last Confederate detachment to leave the island in September 1863. Taking a post held earlier by Alfred Rhett and Stephen Elliott, he took command of Fort Sumter on July 20, 1864, and served there until the fort was evacuated on February 17, 1865.[10]

Thomas Osborn Barnwell, son of Captain Edward Barnwell, ranked twenty-third in the 1834 West Point class. He served briefly in the 3rd United States Infantry and then left the army in 1837. When the war began, Barnwell served in a cavalry militia regiment and was wounded in a raid against Beaufort in December 1861. When he recovered, Barnwell served in state reserve units composed of men too young or too old for regular service.[11]

Beaufort District citizens also served the Confederacy as caregivers and ministers. Maria Elliott Habersham aided Reverend Robert W. Barnwell to care for South Carolina soldiers in Virginia hospitals. Her unselfish work was so appreciated by Confederate officials that they gave her authority over the hospital wards located in Charlottesville's Monticello Hotel.[12]

Reverend Stephen Elliott Sr. actively supported the Confederate cause. At the start of the war, he served as unofficial chaplain for the 11th South Carolina and aide to his son Stephen Elliott with the Beaufort Volunteer Artillery. Infirmities forced him to take refuge in Camden, South Carolina, but his sons continued the fight. While the reverend's son Stephen Elliott Jr. became the best known of his family to participate in the war, his other sons also had prominent careers. The youngest, Middleton, started the war as a Citadel cadet before enlisting in the Beaufort Volunteer Artillery and later transferring into the Engineer Corps. Ralph Emms Elliott became a company commander in the 2nd South Carolina Infantry and was mortally wounded in June 1864 at Cold Harbor.[13]

William Elliott, the third son, possibly the most traveled of Beaufort's Confederate veterans, also fought with the 2nd South Carolina, participating at First Manassas as a member of Company K. With Andrew B. Rhett, he formed the Brooks Light Artillery Company, which became part of Colonel Stephen D. Lee's artillery battalion assigned to Lieutenant General James Longstreet's corps in the Army of Northern Virginia. Once Rhett left the battery, Elliott led it at the Battles of Second Manassas, Antietam, and Fredericksburg.

Promoted to captain, Elliott accompanied Stephen D. Lee to Mississippi, where he served during the Vicksburg Campaign. Captured and paroled at Vicksburg, he was released from his parole in August 1863. He was promoted to major and eventually colonel while carrying out duties as assistant adjutant general and inspector general for the Army of Mississippi. Attached to Stephen Lee's command, he participated in the defense of Atlanta and later joined the campaigns in Tennessee. With part of the survivors from the Franklin-Nashville Campaign, Elliott transferred east with the Confederate units sent to North Carolina to resist Sherman's march toward Raleigh. Like his brother Stephen, he was wounded at the Battle of Bentonville. After recuperating at Raleigh and Charlotte, he returned to duty in time to attend the April 26, 1865, surrender of Confederate forces at Greensboro.[14]

Reverend Stephen Elliott's great uncle Stephen Elliott, Episcopal bishop of Georgia, fervently backed the southern cause. Working with Bishop Leonidas Polk of Louisiana, Elliott organized the Episcopal Church of the Confederate States. When Polk joined the Confederate army, Elliott became a spiritual leader of the Confederacy. During the war he organized Georgia parishes into relief groups to provide clothing and bandages to wounded soldiers. When Federal armies invaded Georgia in the spring of 1864, Bishop Elliott conducted battlefield worship services and baptized and confirmed such prominent officers as Generals Joseph Johnston, Braxton Bragg, John B. Hood, William Hardee, and Francis A. Shoup. He also conducted the funeral of his friend and fellow bishop, Lieutenant General Leonidas Polk, killed during the Atlanta Campaign.[15]

While the war touched everyone in the Beaufort District, the conflict was particularly harsh on the Reverend William Hazard Wigg Barnwell's family. Owner of Laurel Bay Plantation and rector of St. Peter's Church in Charleston, Barnwell had gone north to Philadelphia for his health before the war broke out. Unable to return, he died in February 1863, never seeing his family again. Those members of his family remaining in Beaufort at first moved to Bull's Point Plantation, then to Charleston before taking up residence in Columbia on the South Carolina College campus. Five of six Barnwell sons joined the Confederate Army. William, originally a member of the Beaufort Volunteer Artillery, transferred to the 1st South Carolina Infantry. In March 1861, while stationed near Charleston, he was accidentally shot by a friend and died. Edward H. "Teddy" Barnwell was an officer in the Rutledge

Mounted Rifles, then a staff officer to Brigadier General William S. Walker around Pocotaligo. He worked closely with Stephen Elliott, carrying out raids and launching torpedoes in the waterways of Port Royal. In the final months of the war, he became an aide to James Chesnut and served with the South Carolina Reserves.

Stephen Elliott Barnwell started the war in the Beaufort Volunteer Artillery and tied his star to the unit's commander, Stephen Elliott, as an aide for most of the war. When Elliott was wounded at the Battle of the Crater, Stephen Barnwell escorted him back to Charleston. After recovering from a wound suffered at the Battle of Bentonville, Barnwell accompanied Jefferson Davis during the Confederate president's flight across South Carolina and into Georgia. Two of William H. W. Barnwell's youngest sons, Joseph Walker Barnwell and Allard Barnwell, joined the military toward the end of the war. Joseph, a Citadel cadet, campaigned with the Cadet Corps when it was called to active duty in the fall of 1864 and was wounded at the Battle of Tulifinny. Allard joined in the fight at the war's end at the age of sixteen.

Eldest son Robert W. Barnwell, an Episcopal priest and South Carolina College chaplain, suffered the family's worst tragedies. He volunteered to go to Virginia to serve the military's sick and wounded. He then divided his time between the front and Columbia until the college closed for lack of students. Barnwell then took over the South Carolina Hospital Association, directing that organization's efforts to establish hospitals in Virginia for South Carolina soldiers. Aided by Maria Elliott Habersham and accompanied by his wife, Mary, and their youngest children, Barnwell appropriated two hotels in Charlottesville and converted them to hospitals. He also went to the army and assisted the sick in camps and tended the wounded on battlefields. In June 1863 he became ill and succumbed to typhoid fever in an asylum in Staunton, Virginia, on June 23, 1863, his fifth wedding anniversary. Pregnant with the couple's fourth child, his wife gave birth on the same day. On June 25 she received word of her husband's death and quietly passed away. The baby, a daughter named Catherine Osborn, died on the twenty-sixth. The surviving children were sent to Columbia to join their grandmother. The following year the youngest son, Edward, died. The remaining family members stayed at the college until again displaced by the arrival of Sherman's army.[16]

The war brought tragedy and heartbreak to many Beaufort's families. Death took members of Prince William Parish's Cook, Corbin, Crosby, Fennell, Horton, Mixson, Nettles, Gooding, and Harrison families. On the sea islands, a plaque on the side of St Helena Parish Church holds the names of thirty-one deceased soldiers from the region's most prominent families, including the Verdier, Cuthbert, Pinckney, Seabrook, Elliott, Barnwell, Fripp, Edings, Webb, Hamilton, Sams, DeTreville, Chaplin, Johnson, and Hamilton families. After the war the Hamilton family erected in the St. Helena graveyard a monument to Captain Paul Hamilton, who expired on December 29, 1862, from wounds received while fending off General William Tecumseh Sherman's attack against Vicksburg.

Throughout the war the majority of Beaufort District's white population supported the Confederacy. However, as the conflict wore on, war weariness and discontent emerged especially among the subsistence farmers in upper St. Peter's Parish. They echoed the common complaint that the conflict was a rich man's war but a poor man's fight. While that statement may have been true in other parts of the state and the South, it was false in Beaufort District. There the region's richest families and smaller landholders offered up their fortunes and children for a cause they fully supported.

In 1860 Beaufort District's white population numbered 6,714. Such a figure usually translated into approximately 10 percent or 700 men being available for military service. However, because it relied so heavily upon slave labor, the region gave many more soldiers to the Confederacy. Because many Beaufort men enlisted from other districts, service data is incomplete, but state records revealed that at least 135 Beaufort men were killed in the war with the Cook, Fitts, Nix, Rushing, Smith, Rivers, and Tuten families all losing four or more members.[17]

Beaufort District men served primarily in South Carolina organizations, but some enlisted in units raised in Savannah, Georgia. Many joined the Charleston Light Dragoons and Rutledge Mounted Rifles, but most of the district's soldiers were found in the 3rd South Carolina Cavalry and the 11th South Carolina Infantry Regiments. The 3rd South Carolina Cavalry began as the 1st South Carolina Mounted Militia, commanded by Colonel William Edward Martin, a Gillisonville lawyer, who in 1861 was clerk of the South Carolina senate. When he returned to his political position the following year, Martin was succeeded by his second in command, Charles J. Colcock, a native of Boiling Springs in Barnwell District, who owned a plantation at Foot Point and resided at Bonnie Doon Plantation on the Okatie River. Colcock, a Charleston banker and cotton factor, was a director of the Memphis and Charleston Railroad and, with Martin, was an early proponent of the Charleston and Savannah Railroad. When the war began, Colcock joined William Martin in leading mounted militia raised in Beaufort, Barnwell, and Colleton Districts. In May 1862, when the militia unit mustered into Confederate service as the 8th South Carolina Cavalry Battalion, Colcock became its commanding officer with the rank of lieutenant colonel. He was promoted to colonel in July 1862, when the battalion was augmented and became the 3rd South Carolina Cavalry. Major Thomas H. Johnson of the 8th Battalion became the regiment's lieutenant colonel.[18]

The 3rd South Carolina Cavalry contained a number of men from the Beaufort District. Company A, the Marion Men of Combahee, commanded by

Captain A. W. Lowrey, enrolled members from the Bailey, Blocker, Brabham, Bunting, Hudson, Stone, Stokes, Varnadore, Weekley, and Ulmer families of Beaufort and Colleton Districts. Company B was from Colleton District, while Company C, the Beaufort Troop, led by Captains John H. Howard and Thaddeus G. Buckner, was raised primarily from the Pocotaligo and Gillisonville area. The company listed members of the Cleland, Doyle, Farr, Frerebree, Johnson, Oglesby, Sauls, Smart, Tuten, Vaigneur, Youmans, and Tillinghast families. Company D, the Barnwell Dragoons, included men from the upper regions of the Beaufort District and the Barnwell District. Commanded by Captain G. H. Kirkland, they included members of the Brabham, Brunson, Priester, Rowse, Snelling, Strange, Williams, Wilson, and Wise families.

Company E, the Calhoun Mounted Men, took members from around the Savannah River. It was commanded by Captains Alfred M. Martin and Henry C. Raysor, and its rosters held names of the Bostick, Causey, Davis, Goethe, Jaundon, Lowthar, Malphrus, Pope, Tuten, Williams, and Youmans families. Company F, called the Rebel Troop and the St. Peter's Guard, led by Captains Henry C. Smart and J. A. Perritt, contained numerous men from the Bowers, Brunson, Fitts, Harvey, Kinard, Lightsey, Smart, Williams, and Youmans families.

Company G, the German Hussars, primarily hailed from Orangeburg, while Company H, the Ashley Dragoons, led by captains George C. Heyward and Thomas L. Seabrook, came from the Pocotaligo and Salkehatchie area. The Dragoons contained among its members men from the Chisolm, Colcock, Fripp, Heyward, Morrall, Sanders, and Stoney families. The Rebel Troop, Company I, was primarily from Edisto Island. Company K, under Captain William B. Peeples, mustered from Barnwell District and upper Beaufort District, including the Allendale area. Among its members were men from the Allen, Bennett, Brooker, Cockrell, Dunbar, Hardee, Johnson, Killingsworth, and Morris families.[19]

The other major unit from Beaufort District was the 11th South Carolina Infantry, which started the war as the 9th South Carolina Infantry and mustered during the summer of 1861 from extant militia units and new companies. Beaufort District gave the regiment three companies and part of a fourth. The Beaufort Volunteer Artillery made up Company A of the Eleventh Regiment. Commanded by Stephen Elliott Jr. and his brother-in-law Henry "Hal" Middleton Stuart Jr., its roster was a who's who of St. Helena, Lady's, and Port Royal Islands. Barnwell, Chaplin, Elliott, Fripp, Fuller, Stuart, Sams, and Talbird family members filled its ranks. Technically part of the 11th, the Beaufort Volunteer Artillery became an independent light artillery battery after the Battle of Port Royal and was stationed for most of the war between the Combahee and Savannah rivers. Private Milton Maxcy Leverett, son of Reverend Charles Leverett, rector of Sheldon Episcopal Church, referred to his Beaufort Volunteer Artillery as a "gentlemanly company" and reported that Captain Elliott had banned liquor from their camp. Leverett reported that the other companies were considered "crackers" and were referred to as vandals, Visigoths, and Philistines by the soldiers of the Beaufort Volunteer Army.[20]

Among those "Crackers" were the members of Company D, the Whippy Swamp Guards, from Crockettville in upper Prince William Parish. A prewar militia unit, the company had gained a reputation for its activities at militia musters, political rallies, and banquets. Commanded by John J. Harrison, then Daniel H. Ellis and later J. J. Gooding and William J. Gooding, the company counted among its members men from the Brunson, Cliftons, Crews, Harveys, Rivers, Sauls, Standley, and Thomas families. Termed "real muffins" by the Beaufort Volunteer Artillery's drummer boy, they mustered clad in oddly assorted uniforms and unfamiliar, too-large shoes. They paraded out of step, led by a fiddler. A drummer in the rear pounded cadences with his bare hands. While they were hardly picture-perfect soldiers, they trained to use heavy artillery and served beside the Beaufort Volunteer Artillery at old Fort Marion on Spanish Point outside Beaufort and Fort Beauregard.[21]

Company E recruited its combatants from the Bluffton area with a few coming from Barnwell District. Its first commander was Middleton "Minny" Stuart, followed by John H. Mickler. As with Companies A and D, Stuart's soldiers were also trained to use heavy artillery while stationed at Fort Marion. They were later assigned to Fort Beauregard and then Hilton Head. Known as the Hamilton Guards and nicknamed the Goths, the company contained Smiths, Harveys, and Dobsons. Just before the 1861 Federal attack, the company was ordered back to Fort Beauregard. However, their steamer was delayed, and when they embarked on the morning of November 7, they were cut off by the Federal attack. Blocked by Union warships, the transport commander steered his vessel into Skull Creek, where the Hamilton Guards landed and joined their comrades at Fort Walker.[22]

Company F, the Republican Blues, was organized in early August and mustered into service at Braddock's Point on Hilton Head Island. Its initial commander, Captain James White, was succeeded by William Waight Elliott, who had begun the war in the Beaufort Volunteer Artillery. Prominent among its members were men from the Heape, Hutson, Mixson, and Wyman families. The unit too was trained to operate heavy artillery and served both at the Braddock's Point Battery and at Fort Walker during the November 7 attack.[23]

The regiment's first commander was Colonel William Cruger Heyward. Although born in New York, his mother's home state, Heyward's grandfather was William Heyward of Old House in St. Luke's Parish, and his great-uncle was Thomas Heyward, a signer of the Declaration of Independence. Heyward's father, William, married Sarah Cruger of a New York family. The Crugers had been Loyalists during the American Revolution, and some of them had served in South Carolina with the British Provincial Corps. Appointed to the U.S. Military Academy from New York, Heyward graduated twenty-sixth in the Class of 1830. He served briefly with the 3rd Infantry in Missouri, the Indian Territory, and Louisiana before resigning his commission in 1832. Four years later he purchased Cypress Plantation in the Colleton District just east of the Combahee River ferry crossing. By 1849 William C. Heyward was one of the region's largest rice producers.[24]

As commander of the 9th, Heyward had little time to train his regiment before its companies were scattered along the coast from the Edisto River to Hilton Head. During the Battle of Port Royal, Heyward was on Hilton Head with companies C, E, F, and H, while Stephen Elliott and Companies A and D manned the guns at Fort Beauregard. After the retreat from the sea islands, Heyward and his reassembled regiment took up a position near Hardeeville.[25]

During the spring of 1862, as the war promised to be a long, drawn-out affair, the Confederacy lengthened its regiments' terms of service. Men had the choice to reenlist for three years in their present regiments or be subject to the new national draft that might assign them to unknown units far from friends and relatives. The majority of soldiers chose to reenlist, and on May 3, 1862, the old 9th ceased to exist. The newly renamed 11th Regiment voted for new officers. The election removed most of the previous staff officers and company commanders. Distressed by the results, Assistant Surgeon Frederic P. Leverett wrote to his mother that the men had vowed not to have gentlemen over them and "rejected all who had any pretensions to being *gentlemen;* they elected men of their own stamp." William W. Elliott and Middleton Stuart lost their commands, and the popular Whippy Swamp politician Daniel Hix Ellis replaced Heyward as colonel. Leverett declared Ellis to be "a good for nothing drunken, fiddling politician" and that "some of the company commanders can hardly write their own names. . . . One of the best officered and disciplined regiments in the service is virtually *demoralized.*" He concluded that "I never was much of a democrat, and henceforth will be less of one." Only the Beaufort Volunteer Artillery retained its original commanders, and there many displaced officers found like-minded refuge.[26]

Surgeon Leverett's opinions notwithstanding, the 11th, minus the Beaufort Volunteer Artillery, distinguished itself on the South Carolina coast and later in the defense of Petersburg and Richmond. Ellis never commanded the regiment in the field. On November 11, 1862, upon his election to the state General Assembly, he resigned his commission, and Frederick H. Gantt succeeded him as colonel.

For most of the war, the men of the 11th South Carolina Infantry and the 3rd South Carolina Cavalry defended Beaufort District from enemy attack. Until the spring of 1862, they were part of a large force that protected the Charleston and Savannah Railroad, but as Confederate fortunes waned in Virginia and Tennessee, more and more troops were transferred from the coast and sent to these theaters of battle. In April 1862 General Robert E. Lee, who had once commanded the coastal department and was then chief military advisor to President Jefferson Davis, directed his successor in South Carolina, Major General John C. Pemberton, to send regiments to Virginia. The transferred soldiers were among Pemberton's best-trained and best-armed regiments. Lee apologized to Pemberton and sympathized with his plight but insisted that the troops were necessary to defend Richmond. General Lee proposed that Pemberton look to newly enlisted units in Georgia and South Carolina, suggesting that, if necessary, he arm these new troops with pikes.[27] Pemberton had no intention of issuing pikes. Instead, he shifted the majority of his remaining units to garrisons in and around Charleston and Savannah.

In Beaufort District the bulk of the Confederates were stationed near Hardeeville under the command of Brigadier General Thomas Drayton. By April 1862 Pemberton had abandoned positions between the Ashepoo and Okatie Rivers, leaving only cavalry units in place. Onsite protection of the Charleston and Savannah Railroad in the old Fifth District was practically nonexistent. As an alternative strategy, Pemberton pushed the completion of railroad connections through Augusta in case the Federals severed railroad tracks in Beaufort District.[28]

On April 27, 1862, Pemberton moved his headquarters from Pocotaligo to Charleston. About a week later, forty-year-old Colonel William S. Walker of the Confederate inspector general's office was placed in command of a new Third District that encompassed the old Fourth and Fifth Districts. A native of Pittsburgh, Pennsylvania, Walker had been raised in Washington, D.C., by his uncle, Mississippi senator Robert J. Walker. He was a regular army lieutenant in the Mexican War. Mustered out after the conflict, he took a captain's commission in 1855 in the 1st Cavalry. When the Civil War began, he resigned and joined the Confederacy as an infantry captain but was soon promoted to colonel in the inspector general's office for the Department of South Carolina, Georgia, and Florida before being assigned to the region between the Ashepoo and Okatie Rivers. Walker commanded a handful of scattered cavalry companies numbering about a thousand men. Should an enemy column strike at Pocotaligo or Coosawhatchie, his closest help was at Hardeeville, where General Drayton retained a strong force of infantry and light artillery to defend Savannah's northern approaches.[29]

With the massive reduction of military manpower in Beaufort District, the Confederates depended more than ever upon slaves to supplement their operations. Many black men from Beaufort District served the South, not as soldiers but as servants, laborers, and teamsters. They often carried ammunition and other necessary equipment to the battlefronts. A number were impressed into service, while others willingly accompanied their owners to war. Beaufort-born Robert Bee, an Elliott family slave, spent the entire war as a mule driver with Beaufort Volunteer Artillery. As a reward for his service, he received twenty acres in 1865 on Parris Island from the unit commander, Dr. Henry Middleton Stuart. The company's last surviving veteran, Robert Bee died on January 31, 1931.[30]

General Walker also employed slaves as spies, sending some to Beaufort to report on Federal activities. The use of slaves as agents was rare because, among many who professed loyalty, most were only biding their time, waiting for an opportunity to escape servitude. Feigned loyalty often convinced masters that their slaves, even those under Federal occupation, would also maintain their obedience. The true situation was soon revealed when three members of the 11th South Carolina attempted to visit their homes on the sea islands. All three were captured by their former slaves and turned over to the Union army. Edward Barnwell Cuthbert Jr. was discovered on his family's Cuthbert Point Plantation on Lady's Island, and his former slaves sang as they rowed him to imprisonment:

> De Norfmen dey's got massa now
> Hallelujah
> Oh massa a rebel; we row him to prison
> Hallelujah
> Massa no whip us anymore
> Hallelujah
> We have de Yankees, who no run away
> Hallelujah
> Oh! All our massas run away
> Hallelujah
> Oh! Massa going to prison now
> Hallelujah

Coupled with mass desertions from the mainland, such acts unnerved men who had long subscribed to doctrines of racial superiority over a subservient people. In one night all the slaves disappeared from George P. Elliott's plantation near Pocotaligo. They left everything in place, presenting an eerie scene to Confederates who visited the plantation shortly after the slaves' departure. At the same time, southern scouts on Port Royal and St. Helena islands reported to their comrades that tremendous changes were occurring on the sea islands. They noted with disgust that schools had been established for the Negro "contrabands" and that "little wretches" carrying book satchels were happily attending classes. Despite white southerners' attempts to deny reality, there was no doubt that a new society had taken root under the protection of the U.S. Army.[31]

To give the Confederate military tighter control of the restless slave population and to shut down the sale of spirituous liquors, martial law was declared for the lowcountry from the Santee River south to the Savannah River, including the Beaufort District parishes of Prince William, St. Luke, and St. Peter. But even with the new police powers, the military was unable to control the actions of slaves determined to seek their freedom.[32]

In early May 1862, General Pemberton began to realign his defenses near the mouth of the Stono River just south of Charleston harbor. The Stono provided a route to James Island and access to the mainland behind Charleston. Forts on Coles and Battery Islands guarded the mouth of the river. However, depleted manpower and vulnerability to naval assault forced Pemberton to evacuate those forts and to assign his men and cannons to new earthworks overlooking the Stono on James Island. On May 6 orders went out for the removal of artillery. Four of Cole Island's heavy guns were placed on the paddle-wheel steamer *Planter*. Built in 1860 and owned by John Ferguson, the *Planter* was a wood-burning side-wheeler measuring 147 feet by 30 feet by 7 feet, 10 inches, and weighing 300 tons. She had been chartered by the local Confederate Engineer Bureau, and as with other vessels hired by the government, the *Planter* retained her civilian crew, which consisted of three white officers and seven slaves. The ship was armed with a 32-pounder forward and an aft 24-pounder.[33]

Pemberton watched with apprehension numerous incidents of slaves escaping to the nearby Federal forces. One embarrassing incident centered on General Roswell S. Ripley's personal barge, which was rowed out and turned over to the Union squadron by its slave crew. The result of that act was increased scrutiny, as the Confederates began to fear not only escapes but also sabotage. New orders directed supervisors and officers to monitor closely their hired slave hands. Specifically, ships' officers were to remain aboard their vessels to head off trouble. Increased vigilance aimed to stop future incidents, but Confederate authorities did not reckon with the determination of the Beaufort native and *Planter* crewman Robert Smalls.

Smalls was born a slave in Beaufort in the servant quarters behind the McKee family townhouse at 501 Prince Street. His mother, Lydia Smalls, had been born on the McKees' Ashdale Plantation on Lady's Island. Smalls's paternity is uncertain, but most biographers and Smalls descendants have assumed that his father was John McKee, Lydia's owner. Robert Smalls was raised among a privileged class of Beaufort household servants. While he suffered few personal injuries, he never forgot witnessing whippings, confinements, and occasional arbitrary punishments before the war. John McKee died in 1848 and Small's new owner, Henry McKee, son of John McKee and probably Smalls's half-brother, sold the house on Prince Street to Richard DeTreville and purchased the Fuller House, a large tabby home on the corner of Bay and Carteret Streets. A strapping teenager in the 1850s, Smalls was "hired out" in Charleston as a waiter, lamplighter, stevedore, rigger, and sailor. Even as a young man, Smalls was enterprising and ambitious. Although he was still the property of Henry McKee, Smalls had an arrangement whereby he paid his master fifteen dollars per month and kept the rest of his wages. In 1858 Smalls paid Samuel Kingman five dollars per month for the privilege of marrying Kingman's slave, Hannah Jones. When their daughter, Elizabeth Lydia, was born, Smalls contracted with Kingman to purchase his wife's and daughter's freedom for eight hundred dollars. Robert Smalls was only seventeen years old, but before the war he already saw a gradual path to his family's emancipation.[34]

When the Civil War began, Smalls was an experienced helmsman and wheelman (pilot) aboard the *Planter*. He had been part of the crew during numerous voyages between Charleston and Port Royal when the *Planter* carried supplies and equipment to construct Confederate fortifications and lay mines, as well as equip a detachment of soldiers who destroyed the Hunting Island lighthouse. After the Union navy seized Port Royal Sound on November 7, 1861, Smalls and his fellow slave seamen saw a swift, bold path to freedom. On the night of May 12, after the vessel's white crew had disobeyed orders and gone ashore for the night, Smalls and his compatriots began their work of self-liberation. At 4:00 A.M. on May 13, with boilers stoked, steam rising, and the state and Confederate flags flying, the crew cast off. Smalls guided the vessel from her wharf near the Confederate headquarters and into the Cooper River to a neighboring wharf where the steamer *Etowah* lay. Hannah Smalls, their daughter, Elizabeth Lydia, and son, Robert Jr., along with the wife and sister of one of the *Planter*'s crewmen, a slave sailor from the *Etowah*, two other women, and another child, all emerged from that vessel and boarded the *Planter*.[35]

Wearing the captain's coat and straw hat, Smalls steered the *Planter* past the lines of harbor forts. As he neared Fort Sumter, he blew the vessel's steam whistle and was allowed to pass. Once beyond cannon range, Smalls hauled down the southern flags and hoisted a white one. He then steamed the *Planter* toward the Union warships. The closest vessel was the gunboat *Onward*. Her commander, Lieutenant J. Frederick Nickels, readied his cannons and prepared to open fire before he spied the white flag. Seeing that banner of surrender, he had his gunners stand down. As the *Planter* came alongside, her passengers emerged on deck dancing, singing, whistling, and gyrating; some faced Sumter and uttered curses. Smalls removed the straw hat and called to Nickels, "Good morning Sir! I've brought you some of the old United States guns, Sir!"[36]

Nickels's superior officer, Commander Enoch G. Parrott of the *Augusta,* placed a prize crew led by William Watson aboard the *Planter,* and that crew took the steamer down the coast, through St. Helena Sound, and into Brickyard Creek. Toward evening the black-painted *Planter* passed Federal campgrounds on Pigeon Point, panicking northern lookouts who thought she might be an enemy gunboat.[37]

Shortly after 10:00 P.M., the ship reached the Federal squadron's anchorage off Hilton Head, where once again nervous deck officers feared an enemy ram might be approaching. Watson brought the *Planter* alongside the *Wabash,* boarded the flagship, and made his report to Admiral Samuel F. Du Pont. The fleet commander sent for Robert Smalls and met with him. Du Pont later described the meeting in a letter to his wife:

> I sent for the hero, Robert and he soon came, a pleasant-looking darky, not black, neither light, extreme amount of woolly hair, neatly trimmed, fine teeth; a clean and nice linen check coat with a very fine linen shirt having a handsome ruffle on the breast, possibly part of the wardrobe of the Navy officer who commanded the boat, but fitting him very well if they were. I asked him a few questions to check the narrative—when he first took the notion, and what made him think he could be successful, etc. He had been thinking of it a week or two. The boat was taken in the evening to her usual wharf, where General Ripley's house and office are—a steamer was on each side of him. He got his wife on board quietly and the crew were of one accord to try it. Then steam was got up—at four. They let go their fasts and stood down quietly on reaching the forts at daylight with Palmetto and Confederate flags flying; when he came up with the forts successively he blew two long whistles and a short one, the salute customary in passing the forts—this was not only cute but intelligent, instead of trying to sneak by.[38]

Besides being impressed with Smalls and his exploit, Du Pont was especially gratified to learn the escaped slave's thorough information on Charleston's defenses. News that the batteries at the mouth of the Stono River had been abandoned was especially valuable. Within a week Union warships entered the Stono and took up positions to threaten Charleston. Du Pont told Smalls, whom he called Robert, that he would take care of him and his people and that he was a hero. Du Pont immediately employed him as a pilot of inland waters aboard the *Planter*. At the same time Du Pont requested Gideon Welles, the secretary of navy, to award Robert Smalls and his associates prize money, a bounty based on the value of a captured vessel and of her cargo, that was customarily given to captors of enemy ships. Because the contrabands were not members of the military, they had no standing to claim prize money; however, thanks to the request by Du Pont, a special act of Congress awarded them their bounty. With it Smalls started business ventures in Beaufort. The intrepid ex-slave continued to serve the navy and later the army as a pilot and captain of the *Planter* in the quartermaster bureau. As Du Pont predicted, Smalls became a war hero, but he also became a key figure in Beaufort's wartime and postwar development.[39]

Chapter 6

Arming the Slaves and the Battle of Pocotaligo

"There is, however a fine regiment of loyal persons whose late masters are 'fugitive rebels'"

The scene greeting Robert Smalls upon his return to the sea islands was one of unimaginable change. The harbor was filled with warships, transports, supply vessels, dispatch ships, tugs, schooners, and sloops. The Federal forces were busily improving and expanding their bases. From the *Planter*'s deck he could see the great dock on Hilton Head stretching out into the sound. Behind the wharf was a small city where a thousand civilians worked as teamsters, carpenters, machinists, laborers, sutlers, postmasters, and newspaper reporters. Some of the new residents had brought their families. Most worked for the military, but others opened businesses along a road termed Robbers Row, where they sold, among other things, combs, books, newspapers, tobacco, stationary, clothing, dairy products, canned meats, and clothing. They also sold alcohol but, by regulations, only to officers. Known as Port Royal, the town was nestled within the walls of earthen fortifications that arced southward from Fish Haul Creek before turning east and ending at the beach. Besides Robbers Row, the fortified post contained an encampment of nearly twenty-five hundred soldiers and numerous government buildings, including a hospital, stables, storehouses, ordnance, commissary and quartermaster warehouses, a bakery, and quarters for contraband laborers.[1]

A picket line stretched for fifteen miles along the island's western shore. Soldiers manned posts at Seabrook Landing, Spanish Wells, Braddock's Point, and Pope, Fish Haul, and Honey Horn Plantations. Men were also stationed on Pinckney and Jenkins Islands. At Honey Horn the Federals established their picket headquarters. It was a comfortable spot, where they set up fashionable quarters, developed a taste for shark's tail soup, enjoyed the plantation's flower and vegetable gardens, and its fields of sweet potatoes and corn.[2]

The island also boasted a newspaper, entitled the *New South*, published by Joseph H. Sears and edited by Adam Badeau, the former reporter for the *New York Express* and aide to General Thomas W. Sherman. In their inaugural issue, printed March 15, 1862, the newspapermen announced:

> If an occasional copy of a Union paper should find its way to the deluded and unfortunate people with whom we are contending, some idea of the hopelessness of their effort may afford them. When they discover that the Unionists are so firmly established here as to issue and support newspapers, they will admit that we have no idea of returning; they will conclude that our occupation is not purely a military one; they will perhaps see how desperate is their own condition, and submit more readily to the government which has never wished to do more than bring them back to their allegiance, but which is determined to do that at every cost and at every hazard, and if need arises by the employment of every means.[3]

Troops in Beaufort camped just outside the city limits, but the men constantly came into the town exploring the old homes. A favorite activity enjoyed by both the soldiers and slaves was searching the gardens for hidden treasures, valuables hidden in haste by the former residents as they fled inland. Regimental chaplains held services in the abandoned churches. The Episcopal Church also became the home of a debating society with teams from every regiment taking part.[4]

Additional missionaries arrived while others left. Among the new arrivals was Harriet Tubman, the famed Underground Railroad conductor who had led slaves, including members of her family, from Maryland to Pennsylvania. She had been sent south by Massachusetts governor John Andrew, who enrolled her as a member of the New England Freedmen's Aid Society and in May made arrangements for her to sail to Port Royal on the steamship *Atlantic*. By some accounts, Andrew was sending her to collaborate with General Isaac Stevens, but her arrival coincided with the shifting of Stevens's command off Port Royal Island, and there is no evidence she ever worked with the general.

Tubman initially found it difficult to understand the local Gullah dialect, and the island natives viewed all outsiders, no matter what race, with suspicion. Though well known by the other missionaries, her illiteracy limited her usefulness. She eventually found employment with the commissary and medical bureaus and became a nurse in the hospitals that cared for the contrabands.[5]

The *Atlantic*, the ship that had brought Tubman to Port Royal, was part of a maritime system that kept up communications between the sea islands and the North. Fast, New York–based steam vessels, either owned or chartered by the government, transported troops, civilians, and mail and supplies for the missionaries, the army, and the civilian workers. From November 1861 to January 1863, the government chartered the *Atlantic*, which served as the principal vessel operating between New York and Port Royal. Before the war the *Atlantic,* a 2,860-ton, wooden, side-wheel steamer, measuring 282 by 45 by 32 feet, was one of the fastest vessels to traverse the Atlantic Ocean, setting the record for the New York–to–Liverpool run in 1858. Besides her speed, the vessel was a floating palace, containing steam-heated cabins, a two-hundred-seat dining room, a smoking room, and baths with running hot and cold water. Oliver Eldridge, a conscientious and compassionate commander, captained the *Atlantic;* Eldridge was well liked and respected by his passengers. His arrivals and departures from Port Royal were major events, especially for those posting or receiving letters, among them Flag Officer Du Pont, who counted on Eldridge and the *Atlantic* to deliver his personal letters and official dispatches.[6]

At Port Royal, Du Pont oversaw a naval station and forty warships that patrolled the coast from the South Carolina–North Carolina border to the Florida Keys. Numerous colliers, supply vessels, and tugs served the squadron, while workmen in the machine shops aboard the hulks *Edward* and *India,* moored in Station Creek, manufactured brass, copper, and iron fittings and necessary plates and shafts to repair engines and boilers. These floating factories employed and housed nearly a hundred men under the supervision of master mechanics William B. Cogswell and W. S. Kimball.

Carpenter mates aboard the receiving ship *Vermont* initially handled all repairs to hulls, decks, masts, cabins, and anything else made of wood. The sailing ship *Vermont,* a 2,633-ton ship of the line, had arrived at Port Royal on April 12 after surviving a harrowing voyage from Boston during which she encountered a severe gale and driving snowstorm. The ship lost her rudder, sails, and small boats. When her hull broached and berth deck flooded, the *Vermont* received assistance from rescue vessels. Once repaired and provided with new sails, the vessel entered Port Royal under her own power.

Captained by Commander Augustus S. Baldwin, the old sailing ship became the squadron's depot and supply vessel. Unfortunately, Du Pont was unable to work with Baldwin, who believed that the *Vermont* should be outfitted and placed on active duty. Du Pont lamented that the vessel, under Baldwin's command, had become an "elephant" and its commander insufferable. Eventually, in late 1862, Du Pont was able to replace Baldwin with Commander William Reynolds, a native of Lancaster, Pennsylvania, and brother of Major General John F. Reynolds. A well-known officer in the prewar navy, Reynolds had been a prominent member of the John Wilkes 1838–42 Antarctica expedition before being forced to retire in 1849 because of ill health. By the summer of 1862, Reynolds was returned to active duty and, much to Du Pont's pleasure, assigned to the *Vermont.* Reynolds worked so well with Du Pont that he was given command of the entire naval depot. His responsibilities, which expanded as the depot grew, included the day-to-day operations of all naval events in Port Royal Sound. He directed where vessels anchored, handled requisitions, and oversaw all repairs and the receipt and distribution of supplies and sailors.

Under Reynolds's command the *Vermont* served as the depot's store ship, keeping onboard ordnance, fresh water, replacement drafts, contrabands, prisoners of war, and officers awaiting orders. She housed a bakery and a hospital, and her masts became derricks used to hoist cannons, machinery, and other heavy equipment. At times some smaller vessels were also used as warehouses, but the *Vermont* remained the depot's primary supply ship and command center until July 29, 1864, when the ship of the line *New Hampshire* arrived to replace her.[7]

While Du Pont concentrated on enforcing the blockade off Charleston, the navy also provided protection for the army's facilities by patrolling the Broad, Whale Branch, and Coosaw Rivers, Brickyard Creek, and St. Helena Sound. As long as naval guns watched over the waterways, no effective Confederate force could ever threaten the Federals' hold over the sea islands. The same concept held true for offensive operations along the coast. Wherever the Navy could support the army, success usually followed. The two services shared common goals but did not share command; instead, cooperation relied upon the personalities of the commanders and their ability to work out joint operations. Du Pont had found Thomas Sherman to be cautious and often uncommunicative. Sherman's replacement, David Hunter, was also cautious and quiet, but Hunter's initial agenda had little to do with immediate military operations and instead centered on the region's contraband population.

When David Hunter took command of the Department of the South, he inherited the same problems that had so bedeviled his predecessor, but unlike General Sherman, Hunter had an unflappable personality that allowed him to deal with each situation in such a manner so as to please himself and, most of the time, his subordinates and superiors. At age fifty-nine, Hunter was one of the oldest Union generals. To make himself look younger, he dyed his moustache and began wearing a wig, though he seemed not to care if his hair piece was properly positioned or not. Hunter had one of the most varied backgrounds of any officer North or South. Born in Princeton, New Jersey, Hunter's Presbyterian father had been a chaplain in Washington's army, and his maternal grandfather was a signer of the Declaration of Independence. Appointed to West Point by the then secretary of war, John C. Calhoun, he graduated twenty-fifth out of forty-four in the 1822 class. The broad-chested, five-foot eight-inch Hunter had a dark, almost Indian-like complexion, which resulted in his being called Black David. With gray eyes and perfect teeth, he was known to have a volatile temper and never backed down from a fight.

After graduation from West Point, Hunter was assigned to duty with the 5th Infantry Regiment. While stationed at Fort Dearborn, the future site of

Chicago, Illinois, Hunter assisted a young Second Lieutenant Jefferson Davis, who, with a squad of men, had gotten lost while chasing deserters from Fort Winnebago, Wisconsin. To save his men, Davis set out alone to find help. Without food or water for ten days, Davis reached the banks of the Chicago River opposite Fort Dearborn, where he was spotted by Hunter, who quickly took a canoe and rescued the emaciated Davis. Taking Davis back to Fort Dearborn, Hunter assisted in nursing him back to health. Davis's squad was rescued, and Hunter and Davis forged a warm friendship, which grew when the two served together in later campaigns in the West and in Mexico.

Also at Fort Dearborn, Hunter met his future wife, Maria Indiana Kinzie, whose family was among the first to settle the area and helped establish the city of Chicago. After additional service in the infantry, Hunter was promoted to Captain in the 1st Dragoons, serving until July 1836, when he resigned and returned to Chicago to join his wife's family in the hotel and real estate business. Success in the civilian world proved elusive, and in 1842 Hunter rejoined the army as a paymaster with the rank of major. He served in the Mexican War and in 1856 was assigned as the paymaster for army posts in the Kansas Territory. Hunter arrived in the midst of the battles between the free soil and proslavery forces and immediately recognized slavery as a national curse. An avid backer of Lincoln's candidacy, Hunter wrote the president-elect about assassination conspiracies and resignations of pro-South officers. Lincoln thanked Hunter for his concerns, and when the president-elect traveled to Washington, Hunter accompanied Lincoln on a portion of his journey.[8]

After Lincoln's inauguration, Hunter headed up a force that protected the president and the White House before being assigned, in rapid succession, command of a cavalry regiment, an infantry brigade, and finally a division. With the rank of brigadier general, Hunter led his division at the First Battle of Bull Run, where he was badly wounded. Upon recovering, he was promoted to major general and sent to Missouri to become second in command to Major General John Charles Fremont.

The appointment placed Hunter in the midst of a maelstrom. Fremont, who had been the Republican nominee for the presidency in 1856, was a well-connected, powerful politician who owed his rank and command to his many friends in the Republican Party. However, when assigned to the Western Department, the impetuous Fremont, unable to carry out a successful military campaign or control Missouri's pro-South guerrillas, declared martial law, and, without informing Lincoln, emancipated the state's slaves belonging to rebels. Lincoln quickly overturned Fremont's emancipation proclamation but retained him in command, possibly hoping that Hunter's counsel might prove fruitful, especially on the military front.

Hunter, who agreed with Fremont's antislavery stance but disagreed with his commander's military operations, had little opportunity to influence his superior before Fremont was relieved. Hunter took over from Fremont for a week before Fremont's former department was broken up, with Hunter being placed in charge of Kansas while Major General Henry W. Halleck took command of the Department of Missouri. For nearly four months, Hunter languished in Kansas. His new duties were limited. He was away from the war's main theaters, and he did not have enough soldiers to engage the enemy. Chaffing under the inactivity and wanting to be able to strike a direct blow against the Confederacy, Hunter wrote Secretary of War Edwin Stanton a letter stating, "Please let me have my way on the subject of slavery. The administration will not be responsible. I alone will bear the blame; you can censure me, hang me if you will, but permit me to make my mark in such a way as to be remembered by friend and foe." Though Stanton did not reply, he obviously approved Hunter's proposal. The secretary of war, who had served with Cameron in the War Department before the latter was removed, primarily for his views on emancipation and black troops, privately approved the use of black troops and saw in Hunter someone who could promote such an agenda and influence the president.[9]

Over the next two months, Stanton orchestrated a consolidation of the western Departments of Kansas, Missouri, and Ohio into the Department of Mississippi, giving command to Halleck. Since he outranked Halleck, Hunter was ordered to Washington for reassignment. At the capital he conferred with Stanton, who directed on March 15, 1862, that "the States of South Carolina, Georgia and Florida, with the expedition and forces now under Brig. Gen. T. W. Sherman, will constitute a military department to be called the Department of the South, to be commanded by Major General Hunter." Though there are no records of their meetings, the two were both advocates of employing black troops, and the general's subsequent actions suggest that he acted with the approval of the secretary of war.[10]

On March 31, 1862, Hunter arrived at Port Royal aboard the steamer *Adelaide* and relieved General Sherman. Hunter's aides-de-camp included Lieutenant Charles E. Hay, brother to Lincoln's secretary John Hay, and Hunter's nephews, Lieutenants Samuel W. Stockton and Arthur M. Kinzie. Thirty-three-year-old Major Charles G. Halpine served as Hunter's assistant adjutant. Halpine, an Irish-born journalist, had come to the United States in 1851. He wrote for the *Boston Post* and the humor weekly the *Carpet Bag*, and later worked for the *New York Herald,* the *New York Times,* and the *New York Leader* before serving as a private secretary to politician Stephen A. Douglas and joining the Tammany Hall committee. After the firing on Fort Sumter, Halpine enlisted in the 69th New York Militia, a three-month regiment sent to defend Washington. He was elected to the rank of second lieutenant, and when his regiment was attached to Hunter's brigade, Halpine was assigned as an aide to General Hunter. After Hunter received division command,

Halpine remained on the general's staff. Halpine admired Hunter and considered him a father figure. He described Hunter as being courtly, courteous, and a perfect gentlemen and officer. A prolific author, Halpine wrote from Hilton Head under the pen name Miles O'Reilly, a fictional soldier from the 47th New York, a regiment stationed on Hilton Head, and would become the war's leading satirist.[11]

At Port Royal, Hunter organized his department into three districts. The western district, commanded by Brigadier General Lewis G. Arnold, comprised the Federal holdings from Fort Pickens in the Florida panhandle to just north of Cedar Keys. Brigadier General John M. Brannan's southern district, with headquarters at Key West, stretched from Cedar Keys around the Florida peninsula to Cape Canaveral. The occupied areas of South Carolina, Georgia, and east Florida constituted the northern district, headquartered on Hilton Head Island and commanded by Brigadier General Henry Benham.[12]

Du Pont initially viewed Hunter, Benham, and their staffs warily. He called on the generals after their arrival and was not impressed. He thought Benham to be average and initially noted that his impression of Hunter was "n'est pas tres haute." When Hunter and Benham returned the call by visiting the *Wabash,* Du Pont wrote his wife that they appeared in dress uniform followed by "a staff that had no end, like bobs to a kite." The flag officer's view of Benham became worse, but he soon came to like Hunter, a fellow Episcopalian, noting that "General Hunter is a man of fine bearing, tone, and address; silent, but not like most silent men, he is uncommonly gracious and benign in his intercourse. He is easy in his private means, and very independent in thought and action, has no fear of responsibility, yet very devoid of pretension." He later added that "Hunter seems a thorough gentleman; calm and urbane, very reticent, independent in thought and action—a most prepossessing person without being an interesting one."[13]

Hunter left day-to-day operations in the hands of his subordinates and concentrated on larger issues of policy. He allowed Benham to oversee the operations against Fort Pulaski while he planned grand strategy. The Department of the South contained just over thirteen thousand effectives, ten thousand stationed in the department's northern district. However, some four thousand men were required to garrison posts and forts from St. Augustine to Port Royal. To add to his field army, Hunter ordered the evacuation of Jacksonville, but even with its garrison, the general had only a potential mobile command of six thousand men. Hunter had initially asked for reinforcements from the Army of the Potomac. When none were forthcoming, he felt free to pursue the mission he had originally put forward to Stanton: the arming and outfitting of black troops. Hunter knew that negotiations were underway between the secretaries of war and treasury to turn the operation of the plantations over to the army with Saxton, promoted to brigadier general, assigned as military governor. Once the transfer was complete, Hunter, as Saxton's superior, would have the authority to use the contraband population for service in the United States Army.[14]

Three days after his arrival, Hunter, fully expecting approval from the War Department, requested fifty thousand muskets, accoutrements, ten million rounds of ammunition, fifty thousand red pantaloons, and the authority to arm and outfit "such loyal men as I can find in the country, whenever, in my opinion, they can be used advantageously against the enemy." He began sending agents to seek out potential recruits. Abraham Murchison, a black minister, Savannah native, and chief cook for the officer's mess on Hilton Head, addressed a gathering of contraband laborers on Hilton Head and found more than a hundred willing to volunteer. Other agents included contrabands James Cashman and Will Capers, who also found potential soldiers throughout the sea islands. Even Edward Pierce assisted, while Mansfield French went to Washington, where he joined Saxton in meeting with both Secretaries Stanton and Chase to expedite Hunter's program.[15]

Though Hunter found the initial results encouraging, he did not have enough men to fill out one regiment, much less the two he had hoped for. From his agents the general received mixed reports. Some contrabands were eager to volunteer. Others, while happy to be free from their masters, were not willing to fight them. A few feared a possible plot that would see them being sold to Cuba. But the majority did not want to fight in a cause that did not promise them freedom. Hunter listened carefully and made plans accordingly.

While awaiting arms and uniforms, Hunter went forward with his program. He employed the provisions of the First Confiscation Act, passed by Congress on August 6, 1861, which stated that the owners of slaves would forfeit their claim to such property should it be "employed in or upon any fort . . . against the Government and lawful authority of the United States." Based on this, Hunter declared on April 13, 1862, two days after Fort Pulaski's capture, that "all persons of color lately held to involuntary service by enemies of the United States in Fort Pulaski and on Cockspur Island, Georgia, are hereby confiscated and declared free, in conformity with the law, and shall here after receive the fruits of their own labor." Then, on April 25, continuing what he believed to be a logical progression, Hunter declared martial law in South Carolina, Georgia, and Florida, thus giving him greater control over the region's civil affairs.[16]

In early May, Hunter, citing the October 14, 1861, directive issued to General Sherman by the War Department, authorized General Benham on May 6 to begin on Edisto Island to enlist black troops. Two days later Hunter directed General Stevens to raise a company of Negroes at Beaufort under the command of Charles Tyler Trowbridge, a sergeant in the 1st New York

Engineers and an orderly on Hunter's staff who had been appointed the regiment's first officer the day before. The commanding general also instructed Stevens to begin forming "other companies as fast as you can have them organized." On May 9 Hunter directed his subordinates in the department's northern district to send to Hilton Head "all able-bodied Negroes capable of bearing arms within the limits of their command."[17]

Also on May 9, Hunter issued General Orders Number 11:

> The three states of Georgia, Florida, and South Carolina, comprising the Military Department of the South, having deliberately declared themselves no longer under the protection of the United States of America, and having taken up arms against the said United States, it becomes a military necessity to declare them under martial law. This was accordingly done on the 25th day of April 1862. Slavery and martial law in a free country are altogether incompatible, the persons in these states—Georgia, Florida, and South Carolina—heretofore held as slaves are therefore declared forever free.[18]

Hunter's general order emancipating the slaves shocked and surprised everyone at Port Royal, including his subordinates, the missionaries, and Admiral Du Pont. A copy reached Du Pont on May 10. The admiral initially laughed, then realized that it was no joke. Fleet Captain C. R. P. Rodgers went ashore and called on Benham, who also expressed ignorance of the proclamation. When Rodgers met with Hunter, the commanding general only noted that the best way to punish the rebels was to take their Negroes from them.[19]

Though not approved by anyone in the administration, Hunter deemed his emancipation proclamation necessary to give potential contraband recruits a reason to fight. However, if he counted on the proclamation to serve as a recruiting tool, he did not wait for it to take effect. On May 11 orders went out to General Stevens, Edward Pierce, and the plantation superintendents to send to Beaufort on May 12 "every able-bodied negro between the ages of eighteen and forty-five, capable of bearing arms." The next day, using lists compiled by the superintendents, soldiers began gathering up the contrabands. On St. Helena Island, General Stevens's aide and son, Captain Hazard Stevens, went from plantation to plantation with a squad of soldiers from the 79th New York collecting potential recruits. Laura Towne believed that the duty was repugnant to the New Yorkers. She noted that the soldiers were not mean and that Captain Stevens made a short speech at each plantation informing the contrabands that though they had to go with the soldiers, no one would be impressed into service. Where the missionaries had prepared the contrabands, there was little trouble, but where no forewarning had been given, the soldiers were forced to sweep through the fields seizing the workers before they had time to gather up any belongings or say good-bye to their families. Women and children cried, and some worried that they were about to be sold to Cuba. But, for the most part, the men went passively and some willingly, looking forward to service in the army. Known as "the Black Day" by the superintendents, Susan Walker declared it to be the nation's first draft. As she wrote, "A new experience for our country! Never before have free men been compelled to bear arms."[20]

Edward Pierce, outraged by Hunter's action, sent the general a letter plaintively pointing out the irreparable harm the impressments would do to his operations, especially the removal of experienced foremen and plowmen. Pierce lamented that the remaining women, children, and old men could not care for the eight thousand acres, five thousand being sea island cotton, under cultivation. He feared that his enterprise would collapse. The letter reached Hunter on the morning of May 12, and Pierce arrived at headquarters a few hours later. In his discussion with Hunter, Pierce was assured that no one would be forced to join against his will and that all who enlisted would be given papers declaring them free. Hunter was sorry that his actions conflicted with Pierce's operations but believed that the two programs could coexist. Though not fully convinced, Pierce yielded to Hunter's authority, noting that once Saxton arrived, his influence would end.[21]

As it turned out, Pierce and the missionaries had little to fear. The men taken from Port Royal, St, Helena, and Lady's Islands were initially transported to the Union campground along the Beaufort River on the John J. Smith Plantation, and then on May 12 they sailed to Hilton Head aboard the steamer *Mattano*. Here the five hundred men were offered the opportunity to join the army, and a majority eagerly volunteered. A week later, when they returned to their homes before formally enlisting, Laura Towne noted that "nearly all are eager to go" and that they want to "learn to fight."[22]

The volunteers were not Beaufort's first armed slaves. In early January 1862, a squad of ten men under Sergeant John E. Burroughs of Company H, 3rd Rhode Island, occupied Coosaw Island and began gathering up cotton. Burroughs, fearing an attack, took shotguns and ammunition from a nearby plantation and armed a detachment of contrabands to stand guard throughout the night. As one member of the regiment noted, "These, we are sure, were the first colored troops in the Department of the South."

Arguments can be made that Hunter's regiment was the war's first black regiment, but that distinction could also be given to a Creole unit, the 1st Louisiana Native Guard, organized and accepted into Federal service in September 1862 at New Orleans by Major General Benjamin Butler. Hunter's regiment, though not officially mustered until January 1, 1863, can trace its initial recruitment to May 7, 1862, when Charles T. Trowbridge was detailed as the unit's first member.[23]

While Hunter's actions have usually been attributed to the general's radical antislavery feeling and his impetuousness, it is doubtful he would have gone to such lengths without at least the tacit approval of the War Department. Though details from his meeting with Stanton are lacking, the actions of the secretary of war in providing weapons and uniforms and naming Saxton to command demonstrated his backing of black troops. However, events far from Port Royal interrupted any early sanction of Hunter's program.

Up until mid-April 1862, the war had been progressing well for the United States. Great gains had been made in the West, and in the East, Union forces under Major General George B. McClellan stood poised near Fort Monroe, Virginia, less than one hundred miles from Richmond. Other Federal armies in the Shenandoah Valley and outside Washington prepared to support McClellan's operations against the Confederate capital. Then, on May 1, 1862, Thomas J. "Stonewall" Jackson was authorized to strike the Federal forces threatening the Shenandoah Valley. The resulting campaign routed the Union forces and stopped any reinforcements from reaching McClellan. It also caused Stanton to temporarily assign General Saxton to command the defenses of Harpers Ferry. Saxton performed the duty effectively and efficiently, and for his actions he received the Congressional Medal of Honor.[24]

Besides delaying Saxton's return to the sea islands, the movement of Jackson and the following campaigns of Lee against McClellan and later John Pope set back the administration's timetable for the use of black soldiers and emancipation. With the Confederates on the offensive in Virginia, emancipation and the use of black soldiers had to be put on hold.

Complicating the situation was the fact that Hunter had not informed his superiors about his actions. The general had hoped that the government would recognize his deeds as a fait accompli; however, newspapers were soon covering his emancipation proclamation and regiment. All this made for an interesting response from Lincoln. Since he had not been notified, Lincoln, with the military situation unsettled in Virginia and fearing repercussions in the loyal slave states, was not ready to act on emancipation.

On May 19, 1862, Lincoln issued a proclamation stating that "some excitement" had been produced because of various newspapers reporting what purported to be a general order issued by Major General Hunter emancipating the slaves within his department. The president further stated that

> I, Abraham Lincoln, President of the United States, proclaim and declare, that the government of the United States, had no knowledge, information, or belief, of an intention on the part of General Hunter to issue such a proclamation; nor has it yet, any authentic information that the document is genuine—And further, that neither General

Hunter, nor any other commander, or person, has been authorized by the Government of the United States, to make proclamations declaring the slaves of any State free; and that the supposed proclamation, now in question, whether genuine or false, is altogether void, so far as respects such declaration.

I further make known that whether it be competent for me, as Commander-in-Chief of the Army and Navy, to declare the slaves of any State or States, free, and whether at any time, in any case, it shall have become a necessity indispensable to the maintenance of the government, to exercise such supposed power, are questions which, under my responsibility, I reserve to myself, and which I cannot feel justified in leaving to the decision of commanders in the field. These are totally different questions from those of police regulations in armies and camps.

Lincoln then used the opportunity given to him by Hunter's unofficial proclamation to again urge the loyal slave states to accept a congressional resolution that would allow Congress to "co-operate with any State which may adopt a gradual abolishment of slavery, giving to such State pecuniary aid, to be used by such State in its discretion, to compensate for the inconveniences, public and private, produced by such change of system."[25]

While the loyal slave states did not act and ignored Lincoln's proclamation, Hunter could not. Though he later claimed that Lincoln had only repudiated what had been written in newspapers, and not his actual proclamation, the general had to back off. Du Pont felt Lincoln's rebuke to be sharp but marveled at its wording. After meeting with Hunter, Du Pont wrote his wife that the general "smiled at the President's proclamation, said he never received a line on the subject from anyone in the government, had expected to be relieved. He is one of those men who, I fancy, never act from impulse but from conviction, after mature deliberation, and therefore never have any reactionary feeling."[26]

Hunter believed that privately Lincoln rejoiced at his actions, and Lincoln did write two months later that "Gen. Hunter is an honest man. He was, and I hope, still is my friend. I valued him none the less for his agreeing with me in the general wish that all men everywhere, could be free." Lincoln was not yet ready to act on slavery, but Hunter's actions had increased the pressure on the president who realized "that this is not the end of it."[27]

Though he could not emancipate everyone in his department, Hunter continued to promise freedom to the men who enlisted in his regiment. By now his soldiers had been outfitted and were encamped and undergoing training at Fish Haul, the Drayton plantation on Hilton Head Island. Initially known as the 1st Contraband Regiment and later termed the 1st South

Carolina Volunteer Regiment, the unit was the war's first to comprise slaves. The soldiers were outfitted in red pants, blue coats, and black, broad-rimmed hats. The men disliked the red trousers, which had been purchased by the government from France at the start of the war. They rightfully believed that the pants could be seen by the enemy from miles away.[28]

To lead his new regiment, Hunter called for his generals and colonels to locate "active, intelligent, non-commissioned officers even privates" who would be competent to instruct his Negro soldiers. Hunter appointed his aide and nephew, Lieutenant Arthur Kinzie, as its first commander. The first company organized at the Drayton plantation was under Captain James H. Harold, formerly a sergeant in Company I, 1st New York Engineers, First Lieutenant William H. Danielson of the 48th New York, and Second Lieutenant George D. Walker from the 1st New York Engineers. From a list published in 1892, members of Company A were:

Sergeants Sampson, Green, Gabriel; Andrew P. Waring of Co. I, 1st N.Y. Eng., as first sergeant [Warring was a white soldier]; Corporal (Old) Jackson; privates, Julius Goodwin, Abraham, William Brown, Jo Adams, John and Charles Ferguson, Jeffry, Sam Stevens, Henry Singleton, Mingle, Marcus Polite, Esau, Abraham, Harry Pope, Jim Davis (a cousin of Jeff), Profit Bayard, John Davis, Quad, York, Lyman Fisk, Jerry, August and Abraham Pinckney; Isaac, Sawyer, Sam, January Grayson, Henry Graham, Stephen Graham, William Green, Henry Stone, Mayer Bryan, Stephen Bayard, Frank Polite, Jim Grant, Prince Green, Cain, Anthony, Jacob Friday, Joe, Abram Ritter, Prince Seabrook, Paddy Williams, Colonel Prince, Charles Williams, Stephen, Frank and Andre Binyard, George Bryan, Loby Bowles, I. Small, Tom Ismael, Jerry and Sam Williams, Tom Pope, and March.[29]

The men were of all hues and ages. Some were described as being as white as their masters, others as straight from the Congo. There were Uncle Tom varieties and young, jubilant men; the middle aged and eager mixed with the grey-haired and solemn. Some were sea island natives, others refugees from the mainland. And although Hunter also had a small cadre of men willing to serve as officers, he was disappointed that more men did not seek commissions in his regiment. With its status unclear, however, many who were interested held back, awaiting its acceptance by the government. Hunter hoped that Saxton's arrival would also bring official authorization, but Saxton's assignment to Harpers Ferry delayed his return.[30]

While Saxton was still commanding at Harpers Ferry, Reverend Mansfield French returned to Port Royal. An enthusiastic backer of black soldiers, French also wanted to do more to champion the operations at Port Royal.

On May 30 French visited General Hunter at Hilton Head, where he found the general in a meeting with Flag Officer Du Pont. French immediately proposed to the two officers that he be allowed to take Robert Smalls, the *Planter,* and her crew to New York. Once there he would organize meetings at the Cooper Institute and raise funds for the Port Royal operations. Du Pont jokingly suggested that French could make more money if he made an arrangement for Smalls to appear at P. T. Barnum's American Museum. On a serious note, Du Pont stated that he could spare neither Smalls nor the *Planter* at this time, though he did understand that French's true motive was to show to the northern public that slaves were people who had the same feelings and aspirations as anyone else. Du Pont wrote his wife that French "wanted a moral impression produced in favor of the blacks among those people who believe them incapable of any capacity." Since Smalls was unavailable, French quickly associated himself with Hunter's regiment, knowing that an efficient force of soldiers raised from contrabands would also help sway public feelings and government policy concerning the slave population.[31]

Hunter's regiment had a number of advocates, including Secretaries Chase and Stanton and the army's judge advocate general, Joseph Holt. Chase wrote Lincoln asking that he recognize Hunter's actions. Also contacting the president was Massachusetts governor John A. Andrew, who believed it was time for emancipation and black soldiers. He wrote that the conflict was no longer a war for the Union, that it was now a war to conquer the South, and that to win, the nation had to "grapple with slavery" and turn "the guns of that fortress against the power of slavery itself." But Lincoln, who favored eventual use of such units and did not stand in the way of commanders who wished to use black men purely for defensive purposes, held back from mustering the 1st South Carolina.[32]

With a pall hanging over their organization, Hunter and his officers continued to drill the regiment. Acceptance by the white soldiers and sailors came slowly. Men from the 79th New York "bitterly opposed" the use of black soldiers and a few hurled "vile epithets at the poor darkies." Soldiers of the 47th Pennsylvania viewed clothing the contrabands with uniforms an insult, not believing that they would fight "alongside the Yankee boys for the preservation of the Union. Hoarce Greeley and Wendell Phillips notwithstanding." Others expressed little confidence in the former slaves' ability to fight and bitterly denounced the favoritism given to them. But such feelings and verbal abuse did not deter the black soldiers, who continued to train. At the same time, recruiting continued. Prince Rivers, a onetime slave and coachman of the Stuart family, told representatives from the Philadelphia-based Port Royal Relief Committee that he turned down a paying job to fight for the United States since that nation "is now fighting for me."[33]

Initially Du Pont also expressed doubts, but the naval officer soon changed his mind when he and his staff accompanied Reverend French to the regiment's camp at Thomas Drayton's Fish Haul Plantation, where they witnessed the regiment's Sunday service and evening parade. While sitting on the piazza, Du Pont watched as they formed a hollow square and French addressed them from the steps. The men sang hymns, and as Du Pont related when they passed in review: "They march finely, look well in their undress uniforms, drill altogether better than our sailors—who have been at it for fifteen months—and are but little behind the troops, and yet they have not had a drum or fife." Du Pont was impressed that the former slaves could be so proficient after only six weeks of drill and that "there was more civility among white and blacks than I ever before noticed among our troops, and we were all struck with it." He truly believed that "there was another hand but that of man in this work."[34]

As with his emancipation proclamation, Hunter had never officially reported to the War Department the existence of his regiment. However, articles in newspapers resulted in the House of Representatives' passage, on June 9, of a resolution by Kentucky congressman Charles Wickliffe demanding that the War Department report to Congress about Hunter's regiment. Since Stanton had officially received no information, the secretary passed the resolution on to Hunter for action. Hunter, delighted with the opportunity to reply, closeted himself with Halpine and produced a response that Halpine termed a "politico-military champagne-cocktail." Laughing, the two wrote throughout the night in the midst of a raging thunderstorm to finish the reply, which was sent to Stanton the next morning on the steamer *Arago*. After receiving Hunter's letter, Stanton forwarded it to the House on July 2.

The resolution had called for answers on the following: first, whether Hunter had organized a regiment of "fugitive slaves" in his department; second, whether the War Department had authorized such a regiment; and third, whether Hunter had, by order of the War Department, outfitted the regiment with uniforms, arms, and equipment. With the reply in hand, the clerk, finding his decorum severely tested, began to read it. The letter started formally, repeated the inquiries directed to Stanton, and then began a point-by-point rebuttal.

To the charge that he had organized a regiment of fugitive slaves, Hunter informed Congress that

> no regiment of "fugitive slaves" has been, or is being organized in this department. There is, however a fine regiment of loyal persons whose late masters are "fugitive rebels"—men who everywhere fly before the appearance of the National Flag, leaving their loyal and unhappy servants behind to shift, as best they can, for themselves. So far, indeed,

are the loyal persons composing this regiment from seeking to evade the presence of their late owners, that they are now, one and all, endeavoring with commendable zeal to acquire the drill and discipline requisite to place them in a position to go in full and effective pursuit of their fugacious and traitorous proprietors.

On the second point, Hunter referred to the orders given to General T. W. Sherman by Secretary of War Cameron, authorizing him to employ loyal persons in the defense of the nation and the suppression of the rebellion. Hunter stated that such a directive did give him the authority to enlist "fugitive slaves as soldiers" but again pointed out that no such "fugitives" could be found:

No such characters, however, have yet appeared within view of our most advanced pickets—the loyal negroes everywhere remaining on their plantation to welcome us with food, labor and information. It is the masters who have in every instance been the "fugitives," running away from loyal slaves as well as loyal soldiers; and these, as yet, we have only partially been able to see—chiefly their heads over ramparts, or dodging behind trees, rifle in hand, in the extreme distance. In the absence of any "fugitive master law," the deserted slaves would be wholly without remedy, had not the crime of treason given them the right to pursue, capture, and bring back those persons of whose benignant protection they have been thus suddenly and cruelly bereft.

As to the third part, Hunter replied that he had never received any orders to issue clothing, equipment, and arms to the troops in question other than the general direction given by Cameron to Sherman allowing the employment of persons within his department as military exigencies might allow. He also pointed out:

Neither have I had any specific authority for supplying these persons with shovels, spades, and pickaxes, when employing them as laborers; nor with boats and oars, when using them as lighter-men; but these are points not included in Mr. Wickliffe's resolution. To me it seemed that liberty to employ men in any particular capacity implied and carried with it liberty, also to supply them with the necessary tools; and acting upon this faith, I have clothed, equipped, and armed the only loyal regiment yet raised in South Carolina, Georgia, or Florida.

In his conclusion Hunter became serious and informed his listeners that the arming of the blacks had "been a complete and marvelous success. They are sober, docile, attentive, and enthusiastic—displaying great natural capacity in acquiring the duties of the soldier." He noted that owing to the exigencies of the Peninsula Campaign in Virginia, his request for reinforcements had been denied, but he could, if given support, put in the field within a year some forty-eight thousand to fifty thousand "hardy and devoted" soldiers.

Throughout the reading, representatives from both parties were said to be pealing with laughter. Wickliffe, who arrived after the clerk had started, was not amused. His displeasure only added to the merriment, as once the clerk was finished, Congressman Schuyler Colfax of Indiana asked that it be read again since the "honorable gentleman from Kentucky had not heard the whole of it." The clerk repeated his performance with the same result.

Hunter's response had its effect. Three days later the House voted not to further investigate the matter. Also, Congress, over the next few weeks passed the Second Confiscation Act and the Militia Act of 1862. Both authorized the president to begin the enlistment of black soldiers. The Second Confiscation Act also paved the way for emancipation. The two acts awaited the president's action, and though Hunter's regiment and the overall enrollment of black troops were promoted by Stanton and Chase at cabinet meetings in late July, Lincoln, with an eye on the situation in Virginia and on the Border States, held back.[35]

While Congress gave Lincoln the tools to deal with emancipation and black troops, the president continued to resist, and without presidential backing Stanton would not officially support Hunter's regiment. However, the secretary did return Saxton to the sea islands in late June with instructions to take possession of the plantations, set rules and regulations for the cultivation of the land, and provide protection, employment, and government for the inhabitants, who included both the former slaves and the missionaries. When needed, Saxton was authorized to draw upon army rations, medical supplies, and clothing, He answered only to the department commander—Hunter—who was charged with furnishing a military guard for Saxton's operations.[36]

Saxton returned aboard the steamer *McClellan* on June 26 and reported to Hunter on Hilton Head. From there Saxton proceeded to Beaufort, where he established his headquarters in the Lewis Reeves Sams home on Bay Street while his staff took residence in the Fuller-McKee House on the corner of Bay and Carteret. Prominent among Saxton's assistants was Edward W. Hooper, Pierce's former aide and confidant, who was commissioned a captain, headquartered at the Oaks Plantation on St. Helena Island, and charged with managing the region's plantations and laborers.[37]

Though his brother and father were well-known utopian socialists and both would assist him at Port Royal, General Saxton took a practical approach, looking to develop a program among the contrabands that would produce a free-labor, capitalistic system that would allow them to become productive citizens. While charged with growing cotton, Saxton put increased emphasis on education, promoted employment and self-reliance, and backed freedom, military service, and land ownership.

The missionaries welcomed Saxton's arrival. On July 4, 1862, the first true Independence Day celebrated by the contrabands, Saxton and his staff came out to the Oaks Plantation, where Ellen Winsor, known as Nelly, Laura Towne, and Ellen Murray had planted a flagpole, and at 4:00 A.M. raised the American flag. After breakfast they rode to the Chapel of Ease, where a speaker's platform had been raised and a large United States flag hung across the road. Before the ceremony Miss Winsor played on the church organ "John Brown's Body" and "America." Soon other missionaries and contrabands joined them. More songs were sung, and children from Miss Winsor's school sang:

> Now Praise and tank de Lord, he come
> To set de people free;
> Old massa tink it day ob doom,
> But we ob jubilee.

Saxton, Philbrick, and Mr. Winsor addressed the crowd from the platform, with Philbrick concentrating on the virtue of work and cotton. Afterwards the crowd was feted with molasses, gingered water, and "herring and hardtack ... spread on board tables in the woods."[38]

A week after the Fourth of July celebration, Saxton and his staff found themselves facing their first major crisis. Because of the transfer of forces from Port Royal to Virginia, Hunter had been forced to order the evacuation of Edisto Island. Initially the resident slaves and missionaries assigned to the island had asked for arms to defend it, but soon they realized the impossibility of the task. So, by mid-July sixteen hundred men, women, and children, along with their personal belongings, were moved to St. Helenaville, the onetime planters' summer resort on St. Helena Island.[39]

To manage his command and its ever-increasing population, Saxton retained the organization and staffing implemented by Pierce, but to better oversee the operation, Saxton eventually divided the sea islands into four districts, each headed up by a civilian superintendent. Port Royal, Cat, and Cane Islands made up the First District. The Second District consisted of St. Helena, Lady's, Coosaw, Wassaw, Dathaw, and Morgan Islands. The Third District contained Hilton Head and Pinckney Islands, while the Fourth District centered on Parris Island. Saxton also directed that the superintendents stop using gang labor on the plantations and return to a form of the prewar task system, whereby families and individuals were assigned duties to cultivate a particular section of land.[40]

It was thought by some that Hunter would interpret Stanton's orders, which called for the commanding general to provide Saxton with a military guard, to place his black regiment at Saxton's disposal. However, Hunter retained the unit on Hilton Head, where the soldiers continued to drill, although their acting colonel, Arthur Kinzie, had taken ill and command passed to another member of Hunter's staff, Captain James Deering Fessenden, son of William Pitt Fessenden, the powerful Republican senator from Maine and head of the Senate's finance committee. Besides maintaining a rigorous drill routine, Fessenden enlarged the regiment with new recruits and refugees from Georgetown, South Carolina.[41]

While Hunter waited for his government to take decisive action on the use of black soldiers, Jefferson Davis and the Confederacy acted. On August 1, 1862, Davis directed General Lee to contact the United States military to confirm whether reports in newspapers were true that General Hunter had "armed slaves for the murder of their masters and has done all in his power to inaugurate a servile war which is worse than that of the savage." The next day Lee, copying Davis's language, sent a letter to the "General Commanding U.S. Army." No answer came and on August 21, the Confederate War Department issued General Order Number 60, stating that since General Hunter had "organized and armed negro slaves for military service against their masters, citizens of the Confederacy," and since inquiries to the United States government had gone unanswered, the Confederacy ordered that, if captured, General Hunter and any other officer employed with the armed slaves would not be regarded as a prisoner of war but "held in close confinement for execution as a felon at such time and place as the President shall order."[42]

Hunter, proud of his new designation as a felon, may have thought that acknowledgment of his regiment by the Confederacy would bring recognition from his own government. It did not. From early July and into August, Hunter continued to wait for a reply from Stanton about his regiment, but none came. Instead the general was ordered to begin sending regiments to Virginia. Hunter's frustration continued to build, but he did not give up. Plans were made to send Mansfield French and Robert Smalls to Washington to appeal to Stanton and anyone else in the administration to authorize the use of black troops. At the same time, acting under the authority of the First Confiscation Act, Fessenden began issuing "free papers" to the "faithful soldiers" in his regiment. Signed by Hunter, the papers named the soldiers and their families free. Among the first to receive his papers was Prince Rivers.[43]

Then, in an August 10, 1862, dispatch, Hunter suddenly announced to Stanton, "Failing to receive authority to muster the First South Carolina Volunteers into service of the United States, I have disbanded them." Why Hunter ended his quest at this juncture is unknown. It is doubtful that someone of Hunter's determination would give up at this point even with the government's intransigency. However, Hunter may have been attempting to give the French-Smalls mission a better opportunity to succeed by removing any impediment to the use of black troops and open the door to a fresh start.[44]

A number of men from all ranks were happy to see the experiment end. Most in the department were initially against the enlistment of black soldiers. Charles Francis Adams Jr., an officer in the 1st Massachusetts Cavalry and grandson and great-grandson of presidents, wrote his father that that the regiment's dispersal "was hailed with great joy, for our troops have become more anti-Negro than I could imagine. But, for myself, I could not help feeling a strong regret at seeing the red-legged darkies march off." Adams placed the blame on the government and the military's handling of the affair and the influence of "fanatics" who should have waited and "let Providence work for a while. The slaves would have moved when the day came and could have been made useful in a thousand ways. As it is, we are Hamlet's ape, who broke his neck to try conclusions."[45]

While Adams may have correctly summed up the attitude of most soldiers on the sea islands, he was mistaken in thinking that the regiment had marched off into history. Hunter never completely disbanded the regiment. According to Luther G. Riggs, the regiment's adjutant, the men were given extended leave to visit their families. Other reports have the soldiers, still under arms and in uniform, serving as laborers on Hilton Head; and two companies, some one hundred men under Captains William James and Charles T. Trowbridge, were sent to St. Simon's Island, Georgia, to protect a growing colony of refugee slaves. At St. Simon's, Trowbridge and James recruited additional men and carried out an effective defense, keeping southerners from destroying the colony. Trowbridge, the regiment's first designated officer, became a favorite among his troops, causing Susie King, one of the unit's laundresses and teachers, to term him "a man among his soldiers." On a couple of occasions, the soldiers fought off Confederate attackers, and in one skirmish a former slave named John Brown was killed. Brown became known as the first black soldier killed in the war. When the men later learned the marching tune "John Brown's Body," they believed it referred to their comrade and not the famous abolitionist. The song became the regiment's marching song. John Brown's father, Uncle York, would later serve as an unofficial orderly to the regiment's staff.[46]

While he found uses for his black soldiers, Hunter continued to receive instructions to send additional units to Virginia. Hunter, having already evacuated Edisto and Daufuskie Islands, informed Stanton on August 14 that without more men he might be forced to abandon additional islands, including Port Royal and the town of Beaufort. The next day the general asked the secretary of war to reassign him, stating, "You recollect that when you sent me down here, you promised me something to do. I am well aware of the exigencies of the service, which have prevented you from fulfilling your promise. And, as there can be no chance for active service here, I beg you will give me a chance in some other direction."[47]

The day after writing his request for a transfer, Hunter and Saxton composed a letter to be carried by French and Smalls to Washington. Signed by Saxton, the dispatch requested that Saxton be allowed to enroll five thousand contrabands for employment with the Quartermaster Department. The men, depending on their skills, would be paid either five dollars or eight dollars per month. They were to be fed, uniformed, armed, and officered by soldiers detailed from the army. Saxton envisioned them serving as armed pioneers who could double as a local defense force used to protect the sea islands and coastal refugee camps. Saxton even suggested that such a force could reoccupy Edisto Island and reclaim the abandoned 687 acres of cotton, 835 acres of corn, and 300 acres of potatoes that had been left under cultivation when the island was evacuated. Saxton also believed that a successful use of armed laborers would break down prejudice between the white soldiers and the contrabands and increase "the efficiency of our noble Army in its mighty struggles for the integrity of our bleeding country."[48]

The letter was entrusted to French and Smalls, who left Port Royal on August 16, 1862, aboard the steamer *Massachusetts*. Two days later they met with Stanton, followed in quick succession by meetings with Chase and Lincoln. Though Smalls's fame had preceded them and at each stop the pilot of the *Planter* had to retell the story of his escape from Charleston, the two proved to be effective ambassadors, and before the month was out, they returned to Port Royal with two directives for General Saxton.[49]

The first gave Saxton the authority to enlist whites into exiting regiments, while the second went further than Saxton and Hunter had requested. Not only was Saxton allowed to create a five-thousand-man pioneer corps from people of African descent, but in order to guard the plantations, refugee camps, and other settlements and their inhabitants, he was also authorized to "arm, uniform, equip, and receive into the service of the United States such number of volunteers of African descent as you may deem expedient, not exceeding 5,000, and may detail officers to instruct them in military drill, discipline, and duty, and to command them. The persons so received into service and their officers to be entitled to and receive the same pay and rations as are allowed by law to volunteers in the service."[50]

Saxton was directed to, if possible, reoccupy abandoned islands, harass and weaken the enemy, and induce by every means possible the escape of slaves from their masters. He was to cooperate with the navy by turning over black volunteers for duty with Du Pont's squadron. Stanton also declared that by the Second Confiscation Act, all those taken into government service who had been slaves of rebel masters would be "with their wives and children, declared to be forever free."[51]

The instructions must have been bittersweet to Hunter, who had received permission to take a sixty-day leave, pending possible reassignment. He and Halpine planned to solicit reinforcements and, if none were forthcoming, then request reassignment. Hunter temporarily relinquished command to Brigadier General John Brannan, a forty-three-year-old West Point–trained artilleryman.[52]

On September 7 Hunter boarded the steamer *McClellan* and departed Port Royal. As he had done when Sherman left, Du Pont had the *Wabash*'s crew, in their "white 'frocks' and blue trousers," man the yards and salute the general with fifteen guns. Du Pont was sad to see Hunter go. His respect for the general had increased because of his willingness to do everything necessary to end the rebellion. He described his fellow Episcopalian as "manly, brave, cordial, and a Christian man to boot—makes it a point, like a military man, that the Bible and prayer book shall be on his table in his sitting room." The two had worked well together, and they respected each other.[53]

Also aboard the *McClellan* were General Saxton, Mansfield French, and Robert Smalls, who was traveling with his wife, Hannah, and young son, Robert. The three were going north to confer with government officials and other parties about activities in the sea islands. Saxton was especially concerned over the impact of Hunter's replacement on his new command. The acting commander, Brigadier General John Brannan, was known to "hate Gids and Negroes alike," and the newly appointed commander, Major General Ormsby McKnight Mitchel, was thought to be conservative on the contraband and black soldier issues. Saxton hoped to use his influence, especially with Secretary Chase, to guarantee his program's continuance.[54]

While Saxton was on his way to Washington, French was escorting Smalls and his family to New York for an extended tour to raise money and interest in the Port Royal Experiment. Much as he had done in late May, when French first proposed such a venture, Du Pont protested against Smalls's leaving but, believing that Smalls wanted to go, reconciled himself to losing an experienced pilot. Then, much to his surprise, Smalls came to see him. As Du Pont wrote his wife:

> I took for granted that Robert Smalls wanted to go, but he came to know if he was going to lose his place here as pilot in the *Planter*, and confirmed all I thought of this man as being the most superior Negro I had ever known. . . . I told him of course he need not go North unless he wished it—that Mr. F[rench] was a friend of him and his race and saw some advantages to him personally; if he returned in a month

I would take him again as a pilot. He said then he would go to Mr. F[rench] and unless the latter would promise to have him back in three weeks he would not go. I then gave him good advice as to his course of which I said, 'Robert, you have seen how the Navy officers have treated you—they have made no fuss about you, kept you in your place, given you work, and are kind in their feelings, and if you remain as you are now and don't get spoiled by the abolitionists they will always be your friends.' The reply was very striking. 'Admiral, that's the very point— it is because I know this that I have come to see you today; my best friends are in the Navy and on board this ship.'

Though he was quite pleased with Smalls's declaration, privately Du Pont was not so sanguine. He feared the effect of fame and adulation by the abolitionists on his onetime pilot. As he noted to his wife, "They will ruin him, however, it is a pity."[55]

FIRST POCOTALIGO

Hunter's request for reassignment came about from not only his frustration over the raising of black troops but also the lack of support from the government for his military campaigns against Charleston. When Hunter took command in March 1862, the preparations to attack Fort Pulaski were nearly complete, and plans for an expedition against the Charleston and Savannah Railroad were ready to be carried out. As was his custom, Hunter left the active operations in the hands of his subordinates. General Benham oversaw the Pulaski's bombardment, and General Stevens controlled the movement against the railroad.

Ever since his brigade had occupied Port Royal Island, Stevens had been lobbying his superiors to launch an attack against the Charleston and Savannah Railroad. His enthusiasm for the operation only increased after his successful December 1861 strike across Port Royal Ferry. Scouts and patrols, often using slaves as guides, explored the region's waterways and roads, locating Confederate positions. From their reports Stevens developed an elaborate plan to send multiple columns by land and rivers against the railroad between the Pocotaligo and Combahee Rivers. Then, once the railroad was cut, he would move north along the tracks, reinforced by expeditions coming down the Combahee, Ashepoo, and Edisto Rivers until he reached Charleston.

Stevens discussed his plan with Du Pont and Sherman. Du Pont agreed to assist, but Sherman did not want to initiate the operation until after the capture of Fort Pulaski. When Hunter relieved Sherman, Stevens came under the direct command of General Henry Benham, an officer whom Stevens did not respect. Much to Stevens's disgust, Benham rejected any move against the railroad.[56]

Then, when Robert Smalls brought the *Planter* out of Charleston harbor with the information that the Confederates had abandoned their forts at the mouth of the Stono River, opening the back door to Charleston, the Union military at Port Royal went into action. Du Pont sent warships into the Stono River and discovered that the Federals had a clear route to the upper regions of James Island, exposing an avenue of attack that could bypass Charleston's powerful harbor defenses. General Benham made plans to shift the majority of his regiments from Port Royal to James Island, but he miscalculated his timetable and was not able to assemble his forces and transportation and move as quickly as he hoped. Stevens then saw an opportunity to launch his cherished attacked against the railroad, which could complement Benham's landing on James Island.

In the meeting at Hilton Head with Benham, Stevens convinced his superior to approve the sortie against the railroad. Stevens returned to Beaufort and began readying his command. At 6:00 P.M. on May 28, a telegram from Benham reached Stevens, directing him to carry out a brigade-level strike against the railroad at Pocotaligo Station. Then, an hour later Stevens received a letter from Benham altering the movement to a demonstration so as not to affect the embarkation of Stevens's brigade for the Stono River. Accordingly, Stevens modified the operation to a small raid by Colonel Benjamin Christ and his regiment, the 50th Pennsylvania Infantry, along with Company E from the 79th New York Infantry Regiment, Company H from the 8th Michigan Infantry Regiment, a section of artillery from the Connecticut Battery, and eighty troopers from the 1st Massachusetts Cavalry.[57]

Orders went out to gather boats from Port Royal and Lady's Islands. Twelve flats, each manned by a soldier and six contrabands, were assembled at Beaufort and brought down to Port Royal Ferry. By 3:00 P.M. on the twenty-ninth, Christ began crossing his command, and the next morning at 5:00 A.M. the infantry began moving inland, followed by the cavalry at 6:00 A.M. and the artillery at 8:00 A.M. Christ followed a route scouted by Captain William S. Elliott of the 79th New York and a black guide. Two miles from the ferry crossing, the Union troops encountered Confederate pickets, who fell back as the Federals pushed on into Gardens Corners, a small community of a dozen houses, a store, and a blacksmith shop. The day was already hot and the men were suffering from the heat. At Gardens Corner they found a Rhode Island man who said he had been in South Carolina long enough to get all the damned Yankee blood out of him. The men believed him, as he was tall, lean, and walked like a South Carolinian. Even so, he offered the Federals water from his springhouse, but since there were rumors about poisoned wells, the soldiers made him drink first. At Gardens Corner, Colonel Christ detached Company E of the 50th Pennsylvania to guard his rear before taking his command down the Sheldon Church Road.

Though harassed by Confederate skirmishers, the Federals continued on moving across Castle Hill Plantation.[58]

When word of the Federal advance reached Confederate headquarters at Pocotaligo Station, the district commander, Colonel William Walker, was at Grahamville inspecting cavalry units. In Walker's absence, Major Joseph H. Morgan quickly deployed four companies from his 1st South Carolina Cavalry Battalion, Captain William L. Trenholm's Rutledge Mounted Riflemen, and a company from the 2nd South Carolina Cavalry Battalion under Captain Daniel Blake Heyward. Morgan wired for help and dispatched a trooper who met and flagged down Colonel Walker's returning train and informed the commanding officer about the Federal movement.[59]

Walker reached Pocotaligo Station and by 10:30 joined Morgan near Pocotaligo. By this time the Federals were nearing a causeway that led across Screven's rice canal just northeast of Pocotaligo. The causeway, flanked by swamps on either side, stretched eighty yards to a fifteen-foot-wide bridge that crossed the canal. The bridge's flooring had been taken up, leaving only the stringers. Dismounting his troopers, Major Morgan posted to the left of the bridge Lieutenant R. M. Skinner with two undermanned companies, A and D, of the 1st South Carolina Cavalry Battalion, some thirty-eight men, while another thirty-eight men from the Rutledge Mounted Rifles under Captain Trenholm were placed from the right of the bridge to the woods outside Pocotaligo. Morgan kept his remaining three companies in reserve with the troopers serving as horse holders for Skinner and Trenholm's dismounted cavalrymen. Trenholm's men were armed with rifles, but Skinner's had only carbines and shotguns.

Colonel Christ deployed his regiment on both sides of the causeway and for two hours kept up a desultory fire across the canal while awaiting the arrival of his artillery. But the artillery commander, Lieutenant John S. Cannon, fearing the heat would kill his horses, had stopped to water and rest his teams. Captain Charles H. Parker of Company H, 50th Pennsylvania, realizing that the delay would give the Confederates time to bring up reinforcements, volunteered to lead a charge up the causeway and over the bridge. Christ agreed, and Parker and his men rushed forward with bullets "whising and whiring over our heads like hail." The men, using the remaining six-inch-wide stringers as stepping stones, crossed the bridge and dropped down into rice ditches on the right side of the road, where they put down a covering fire as additional Union soldiers came forward. Captain Parker stood up on a floodgate to encourage his men forward and was struck in the head and killed. Still, more and more Federals, now under Lieutenant Colonel Thomas S. Brenholtz, crossed the bridge, and Lieutenant Skinner's position became untenable. In danger of being cut off from the main line of retreat, Skinner began withdrawing his men. During the retreat Lieutenant Skinner and Private Robert Stuart were wounded but made good their escape. At about this time, the guns of the 1st Connecticut Battery under Lieutenant Cannon arrived and began shelling the Confederates. Colonel Walker, his mount wounded and realizing that his entire line was in danger of collapsing, ordered his men to draw back. At about 1:30 p.m., the southerners fell back to their horses, mounted, and withdrew through Pocotaligo to a position just south of Pocotaligo Station, where Walker and Morgan anxiously awaited reinforcements.[60]

With his opponents fleeing, Colonel Christ replanked the bridge and took up the pursuit, but the firefight at Screven's canal had cost him three hours. His men were tired and worn out. They followed the Confederates through Pocotaligo and up the McPhersonville Road as far as Thomas Elliott's plantation, where they rested and drank from the plantation's spring. Others reached Daniel Heyward's home, where they made Heyward's slave Charles "give them liquor" and "stole Mr. H's guns and took a shot at him as he came up towards the house."[61]

While some of his men were exploring the countryside, Colonel Christ occupied Pocotaligo and destroyed the wagon bridge over the Pocotaligo River. He considered pushing on to the railroad, but the day was oppressively hot and his men had already marched twenty-four miles and fought a prolonged engagement. If he moved toward the railroad, he knew there would be another fight, one where he might be outnumbered. Under orders not to bring on a general engagement, Christ by 2:30 p.m. decided to withdraw. On the return march, the tired and hungry Federals drank from mud holes, and some had to be prodded with bayonets to keep up. In contrast to the weary soldiers were the jubilant slaves who fled their masters' plantations, singing as they followed along:

> Wake up, snakes, pelicans, and Sesh'ners!
> Don't yer hear 'um comin'
> Comin' on de run?
> Wake up, I tell yer! Git, up, Jefferson!
> Comin' on de run
> Bob-o-ish-i-on!

Others sang:

> Massa say's it's de day of doom
> And we ob jubilee![62]

Colonel Walker, relieved that the Federals had stopped their advance, kept his dismounted cavalrymen in a rice ditch that ran parallel to the road leading to Pocotaligo Station. At about 4:00 P.M. a train arrived from Hardeeville, bringing with it three pieces of artillery of the Beaufort Volunteer Artillery under Captain Stephen Elliott Jr. and two companies, I and F, of the 11th South Carolina, which Walker placed in line with his dismounted cavalry. When he learned from his vedettes that the enemy was withdrawing, Walker and his men followed, engaging the enemy pickets outside Garden's Corners at about 10:00 P.M. Fearing a trap in the dark night, Walker called off the pursuit while he awaited additional reinforcements.

At Gardens Corner, Colonel Christ found detachments from the 79th New York and the 8th Michigan, who had been sent forward by General Stevens. Christ moved on to Port Royal Ferry, arriving at 11:00 P.M., and by 3:00 A.M. on May 30, crossed over to Port Royal Island. The next morning Colonel Walker, with the recently arrived cavalry companies from the 4th South Carolina under Major William Stokes, the Phillips Georgia Legion, and the 17th South Carolina Infantry, advanced to the ferry. There he ordered Captain Elliott to use his cannons to batter down the ferry house on the opposite side of the Coosaw River and destroy the nearby barges that had been used to carry the Federals to the mainland.[63]

The small engagement had only cost the Federals two killed and nine wounded; the Confederates reported capturing one soldier. The southerners suffered two killed, six wounded, and one missing. While Colonel Walker was justly proud that his small force had slowed the Federal advance and kept them from reaching the railroad, he did not comment on the foray's economic impact. Military results were minimal, but the short incursion had a major impact on the region's slave population. Union officers reported that thousands of slaves from the Prince William plantations, fully aware of Hunter's May 9 emancipation proclamation, fled their masters and accompanied the Federal soldiers to freedom on the sea islands.[64]

General Stevens also commended Colonel Christ and his soldiers. The Federals, in twenty-seven hours, had marched thirty-three miles, fought a two-hour battle, and destroyed an important bridge over the Pocotaligo River. He believed that the reconnaissance had proven the validity of his original program to break the railroad between the Coosawhatchie and Combahee Rivers. He hoped that additional attacks would follow, but one day after the strike, Stevens and his command from Port Royal Island were placed on transports and joined the Federal movement to the Stono River and James Island. By June 2 General Benham had seventy-five hundred men, including most of Stevens's brigade, on the southwestern end of James Island, poised to overrun a weakly held Confederate defense line, turn Charleston's defenses, and capture the southern citadel. But General Hunter, believing his forces outnumbered, directed Benham to avoid combat while he beseeched his superiors for reinforcements.[65]

Left behind on Port Royal Island were the 50th Pennsylvania and a section of the Connecticut artillery. The presence of such a small force emboldened the Confederates. On the night of June 6, Captain Stephen Elliott with twenty men from the Beaufort Volunteer Artillery rowed across the Coosaw River at Port Royal Ferry. Pretending to be escaping slaves, Elliott called out to the Federal pickets in Gullah, the local slave dialect. Fooled, the Union soldiers let down their guard and allowed the boat to land. Elliott and his men sprang forward, scattered the Union pickets, and destroyed the flats used by the Federals in the May 29 raid. The daring strike, covered by artillery fire from the mainland, unnerved many of the missionaries on Port Royal, St. Helena, and Lady's Islands.[66]

Panic quickly spread. Some missionaries, such as Susan Walker, Reverend Peck, and his daughter, hastened their planned departures. Du Pont, responding to requests from the army, dispatched vessels to Beaufort. The gunboat *Ottawa* anchored off the town with the tug *O. M. Pettit,* while the tug *Mercury* steamed into the Coosa River to intercept any invaders. Women on Port Royal Island boarded the army transport *Potomac* and were taken to Hilton Head, while the men went to the arsenal for arms and ammunition. But no enemy attack came, calm was restored, and the women returned.[67]

While the garrison at Beaufort feared phantom Confederates, their comrades under Benham on James Island outside Charleston went against Hunter's orders and attacked a fort near the summer village of Secessionville. In a poorly planned, sharp, and confusing fight, they were defeated. When Hunter learned of the attack, he relieved Benham and eventually withdrew his men.[68]

On July 4 the defeated and disgusted troops from James Island arrived at Port Royal. The men were happy to be back, but many did not stay. By July 17 General Stevens and seven regiments had left for Virginia. Before the month was out, General Wright was sent to a new command, and in August the department's only cavalry, the 1st Massachusetts, was ordered away. With regiments being pulled and his use of black troops in limbo, Hunter informed Washington that he might be forced to abandon St. Helena, Lady's, Port Royal, Parris and Spring Islands, their crops, and population. However the threat was never carried out, and the remaining troops settled down to a garrison routine for the summer, their first in the South Carolina lowcountry.[69]

Life for the Federal troops left at Port Royal revolved around drill and camp duties. The men had time to read and write letters. They caught alligators and tamed mockingbirds. Campsites were improved. Tents were placed on raised wooden floors to keep the sand out. Water was obtained by sinking barrels a few feet into the ground, but it always had a brackish or sulfurous taste. Eventually large condensers were placed at Hilton Head and Beaufort to convert salt water into fresh water. Regimental chaplains vied for use of the Episcopal Church, while the soldiers also attended religious services at black churches and praise houses. Watermelons, sweet potatoes, corn, oranges, and figs were plentiful. The men wallowed in the mud to catch crabs, and from the contrabands the soldiers purchased oysters at twenty-five cents a bushel.[70] Mosquitoes, ticks, fleas, and sand fleas pestered the men, making it nearly impossible to sleep. "Fleas, fleas, fleas, that was the cry everywhere," wrote one soldier. The sand fleas caused men to drink "to insensibility." Another thought that to rid the camps of mosquitoes, the men would "have to form a line of Battle to charge bayonets on them and drive them across the River into Rebeldom."[71]

As the temperatures rose, officers cancelled dress parades. A soldier in the 50th Pennsylvania wrote that it was "almost impossible to breath." The heat also brought sickness. By July the hospitals in Beaufort's great houses were beginning to fill up with patients. Deaths from disease increased, and it was not uncommon to see three burials a day and hear the playing of the "Portuguese Hymn." The deceased were buried in an abandoned cotton field set aside by General Hunter just outside the town limits. As the deaths and fear of yellow fever increased, ceremony was suspended. The dead were put in cheap boxes and taken to the graveyard in a dump cart by contrabands, who slid the coffins into shallow graves. Appalled by such actions and lack of religious ceremony, General Saxton directed that if no one could be found to read the prayers for the dead, he would do so.[72]

Even with heat the Federals continued to improve their camps, build fortifications, and carry out minor expeditions. At Beaufort two new wharves were constructed. Saxton's Dock was placed at the head of Bay Street next to the ferry landing, while a quartermaster pier was built between Scotts and West Streets. Batteries were started outside of Beaufort, protecting the town from attacks along the Shell Road.

On Hilton Head the Federals, fearing a sortie by Confederate ironclads from Savannah, added new batteries and mounted 11-inch cannons in Fort Welles. The work was difficult. Horses collapsed and men became ill and died. Some were taken to the department's general hospital near Fort Walker, while others went to a newly established hospital at the Honey Horn Plantation. Also in July work began on Hilton Head to move the refugee slaves from their makeshift barracks inside the Union lines, which the *New York Times* reported to be "a sort of Five Points, half style, half brothel," to a settlement near the Drayton plantation. With assistance from the military, the contrabands received cut lumber from the army's sawmill and began building individual homes that would eventually become a village known as Mitchelville.[73]

Throughout the summer the Confederates under Colonel Walker watched the growing Federal presence on the sea islands. The Union strike on Pocotaligo had convinced the department commander, General Pemberton, that he could not rely solely on reinforcements from Hardeeville to protect the railroad between the Combahee and Coosawhatchie Rivers. As an alternative, Pemberton proposed placing a force of infantry and artillery at McPhersonville, a healthy locale just north of Pocotaligo Station, and keeping rolling stock at nearby Salkehatchie to transport the troops should an enemy assault occur. However, he was unable to send any troops, and General Lee and President Davis, in turning down pleas for reinforcements, informed Pemberton that the hot and sickly summer months would stop all enemy movements.[74]

While he was heavily outnumbered, Walker did look for opportunities to keep the Federals off balance. On July 4, while Union soldiers and contrabands were celebrating Independence Day, Captain Stephen Elliott, with a section of his battery and some men from Company I, 11th South Carolina, orchestrated crossings along the Coosaw River at Port Royal Ferry and Page Point at Seabrook Ferry. At Port Royal Ferry a barge armed with a small field gun covered a small boat whose crew carried a barrel of turpentine ashore and burned down the ferry house and escaped under enemy artillery fire.[75]

On July 19, Walker had his area of command expanded to include the region from the Ashepoo River south to the Savannah River. To guard this strategic area, Walker was left with a mere 600 infantrymen, 1,000 cavalrymen, and 132 artillerymen. Walker was so strapped for artillerymen that he had to detach two companies—E and G—from his infantry regiment, the 11th South Carolina, for service as artillerymen. The bulk of the force was distributed to protect the railroad bridge over the Savannah River and to guard Savannah's northern approaches.[76]

Walker kept his men busy. Cavalry pickets continued to watch for enemy landings, and whenever possible he sought opportunities to engage the Federals. Besides skirmishes along the Coosaw River, troopers south of the Broad River exchanged fire with the enemy at Buckingham Ferry and captured men from the 3rd New Hampshire, who had left their post on Pinckney Island to do some fishing on nearby Bear Island. The capture of these men convinced Walker that a larger expedition could bag the entire Union force on Pinckney Island. Again Walker turned to Stephen Elliott, who with Captain John H. Mickler of the 11th South Carolina, scouted Pinckney Island and made plans for a dawn assault. Elliott quickly assembled at Bear Island nine boats and 120 men, 50 from the Beaufort Volunteer Artillery under Hal Stuart and the rest from Companies B, C, and E, 11th South Carolina.

At 3:00 A.M. on August 21, Elliott took his small flotilla from Bear Island and landed on Pinckney Island three hundred yards from the dwelling house. Leaving thirty-six men with the boats, Elliott led the remaining soldiers against the camp of Company H, 3rd New Hampshire. A picket shouted an alarm, but before the Federals could respond, the Confederates were on them, killing fifteen, wounding four, and capturing thirty-six. The southerners suffered eight wounded, six by friendly fire. The entire action, from landing to withdrawal, lasted fifteen minutes.[77]

Eight days after the affair on Pinckney Island, General Pierre G. T. Beauregard was named commander of the Department of South Carolina, Georgia, and East Florida, but little was done to supplement Walker's district. In October, Walker wrote Beauregard, pointing out that he had no heavy artillery and only two thousand troops to man defenses designed for ten thousand men. Walker wrote that his infantry and one company of light artillery were needed to protect Savannah's northern approaches, leaving only cavalry and the Beaufort Volunteer Artillery available to guard the area from Ferebeeville to the Ashepoo River. As Walker explained, the horsemen, armed with rifles, were to fight dismounted, using natural defenses to retard an enemy advance, but they were too few to stop any determined attack. Walker prepared for the worst, even going so far as to construct a footbridge five miles north of the Combahee railroad bridge so that the men guarding the Pocotaligo region would have an avenue of retreat to Walterboro. However, Walker's plea did convince Beauregard to send Walker some reinforcements, including the Nelson light artillery battalion.

Later in the month, when Major General Ormsby McKnight Mitchel took over the Union forces, Walker's district received more attention from the high command. Beauregard informed Walker to "keep your pickets alert and spies active—pay latter well. Mitchel more fussy than dangerous."[78]

Though Beauregard's assessment of Mitchel may have been intended to calm Walker's fear of any new attacks, the new Union commander had already obtained a reputation as an aggressive officer. Born in Kentucky and raised in Ohio, Mitchel ranked fifth in the West Point class of 1829. Though assigned to the artillery, he also taught mathematics at West Point and studied law. He remained in the army for three years before resigning. He accepted a teaching position at the University of Cincinnati, where he taught philosophy, mathematics, and astronomy. His great love was astronomy, which he helped popularize throughout the United States. He served as the director of the Cincinnati Observatory and later the Dudley Observatory at Albany, New York, and was largely responsible for the establishment of the observatories at the United States Naval Academy and Harvard University. After the Battle of First Bull Run, Mitchel returned to the army and was appointed a brigadier general. He oversaw the construction of Cincinnati's defenses and later commanded a division in the Department of the Ohio.

While leading his division from Huntsville, Tennessee, east along the Memphis and Charleston Railroad toward Chattanooga, Mitchel allowed his men to live off the land and destroy private property. Such actions, plus accounts in newspapers about the misappropriation of cotton, caused him to run afoul of his commander, Major General Don Carlos Buell, and the army's commander in chief, Major General Henry W. Halleck. Mitchel was relieved and sent to Washington for reassignment. But he still retained friends within the administration. Lincoln liked him, and Chase and Stanton admired his aggressiveness. Though Halleck refused to give him an assignment in a major theater, he did, on September 1, 1862, name Mitchel as commander of the Department of the South. Two days later the War Department designated the forces in the department as the Tenth Army Corps. Mitchel, however, was not pleased with his new position. He thought he was being sent to south "to be buried" in a department whose only function was to protect the naval installation and serve as "a field for Negro Experiments."[79]

On September 15, 1862, amid salutes from the *Wabash* and the harbor forts, the fifty-three-year-old Mitchel arrived at Port Royal aboard the *Arago*. General Brannan visited his successor, and the next day they went to Beaufort to review the town's garrison. While addressing the 47th Pennsylvania, Mitchel promised action, and the soldiers responded with cheers. Over the next few days, the new commander visited every regimental camp on Hilton Head and Port Royal Islands and the garrison at Fort Pulaski. Mitchel met with Du Pont and discussed operations against Charleston, Savannah, and the Charleston and Savannah Railroad; however, Mitchel quickly realized that he had too few men for any major offensive and wrote the War Department that unless reinforcements were provided, it would serve the war effort better if the bulk of his corps was sent to an active theater. His requests found a backer in Secretary Chase, who called on Halleck and Stanton to send additional troops to the department for an expedition against Charleston.[80]

Besides a lack of soldiers, Mitchel also had to deal with the animosity between Brannan and Saxton. Brannan, unlike Benham, had never been a friend of the missionaries and their work. Saxton, who was currently working to resurrect the 1st South Carolina, had refused to acknowledge Brannan's authority over his operations and had complained to Chase, who in turn lobbied Stanton to remove Brannan from the Department of the South. The arrival of Mitchel did nothing to change the situation. The new commander reported to Stanton that "some friction, and even collision, has taken place already between the officers of the two independent commands." Mitchel also found there was "a feeling prevailing among the officers and soldiers of prejudice against the blacks, founded upon the opinion that in some way the negroes have been more favored by the Government and more privileges granted to them than to the volunteer soldier." Mitchel thought these perceptions incorrect, but he did believe that there would always be trouble and misconceptions as long as Saxton had a separate command. Mitchel wanted control over Saxton's operations, but Saxton, refusing to give up his independent status to oversee the plantations and raise black troops, went to Washington to ensure continued backing for his operations.[81]

Though he was against a divided administration, Mitchel was sympathetic to the missionaries and the fate of their protégés. Nor did he oppose the use of black troops or the creation of a new freedman community in the sea islands. He also enthusiastically backed the recently issued Emancipation Proclamation, which had been received with "satisfaction" in the department. Mitchel, in a speech to troops on Hilton Head, declared that he wished that he could live long enough to see the proclamation's "glorious effects upon the coming age." His statement caused the soldiers to fill the air "with cheers and shouts of exultation."[82]

On October 12 Mitchel attended the opening of a church at the refugee slave camp on Hilton Head. Constructed by men from the 1st New York Engineers, the regiment's chaplain, Reverend Henry N. Hudson, dedicated the small building. Mitchel, a staunch Presbyterian, addressed the gathered contrabands, telling them that he believed that God "intends all men to be free." He also told them that the entire nation was watching "the experiment now being tried in your behalf with the deepest interest. This experiment is to give you freedom, position, home, and your own families,—wives, property, your own soil." Mitchel called upon them to work hard and to succeed. He made reference to the nearby homes being built "at a rate of six a week" for their comfort—homes where each family would have a patch of ground to raise their "own garden truck" and "work for the government for good wages." In conclusion Mitchel declared that he expected the experiment to become permanent and that the day of jubilee would come to "God's ransomed people."[83]

Besides the politics of command and lack of troops, Mitchel had other worries. Yellow fever season was approaching. The advent of this killer disease had been expected. General Hunter and Admiral Du Pont had established a quarantine station in St. Helena Sound where troops arriving from posts farther south would be quarantined for twelve days. The department's chief medical officer, Charles H. Crane, took precautions to prevent outbreaks of what was thought to be an airborne sickness. Tents at regimental camps were spaced farther apart and elevated on wooden floors so that air would circulate under and between the tents. Thorough police regulations were observed and every day tents were taken down, turned inside out, and, along with clothing, exposed to the sun. The precautions did not work. In early September the soldiers of the 7th New Hampshire, just in from Key West and the Dry Tortugas, were released from quarantine and allowed onto Hilton Head Island. Within nine days, eight deaths were reported.[84]

Even with yellow fever breaking out, Mitchel made good on his promises for action. Troops from his command assisted the navy in clearing Confederate batteries along the St. John River and briefly occupied Jacksonville, Florida. Mitchel also began launching in the Beaufort District a number of spoiling attacks and reconnaissance missions. On September 30 an expedition consisting of a portion of the 48th New York and the 3rd Rhode Island left Fort Pulaski aboard the armed steamers *Starlight* and *Planter* for Bluffton. The men landed unopposed and carried off furniture, pianos, and all the slaves they could reach. Twelve days later the Federals returned to Bluffton aboard the *George Washington* and the *Planter*. They sailed past the town and destroyed some saltworks along the May River. On their return they again stopped at Bluffton for more furniture and dropped off a contraband spy. On October 18 the Federals on the *Planter* made a third trip to Bluffton. This time Confederate rifle fire kept them from landing, though they were able to retrieve the African American spy who had valuable information on Confederate dispositions.[85]

SECOND POCOTALIGO

The strikes against Bluffton and the dispatching of spies and scouts behind enemy lines were all part of Mitchel's larger plan to break the Charleston and Savannah Railroad. By mid-October Mitchel was readying a force to carry out a reconnaissance between the Tullifinny, Coosawhatchie, and Pocotaligo Rivers to test the ability of his command for rapid deployment, learn the strength of the enemy, and destroy a portion of the Charleston and Savannah Railroad. To prepare for the strike, scouts aided by black guides explored the area, reconnoitered railroad bridges, cut telegraph wires, and mapped fortifications and landing points. The 1st New York Engineers built landing craft and two flatboats with hinged aprons to land troops and cannons.[86]

On October 16 Mitchel gave a patriotic address at Beaufort in St. Helena Episcopal Church to the officers from General Brannan's brigade. Mitchel informed the officers of the coming campaign. He also promised that once a foothold was established on the mainland, he would initiate operations against Chattanooga, Tennessee. The general then concluded his speech by shaking hands with everyone present.[87]

The planned expedition, which Mitchel intended to lead, called for two separate movements designed to break the railroad bridges over the Coosawhatchie and Pocotaligo Rivers. The main assault would land some four thousand men at the southern tip of Mackey's Neck, a peninsula between the Tullifinny and Pocotaligo Rivers, and move overland toward the railroad at Pocotaligo Station. At the same time a smaller amphibious force would ascend the Coosawhatchie River and destroy the railroad trestle at Coosawhatchie.[88]

Though Mitchel's speeches and preparations inspired his soldiers, the increased activity also convinced the Confederates that an attack was imminent. Additional forewarning came on October 19 when Captain Manning J. Kirk and his company of Partisan Rangers captured on Chisholm's Island eight Union soldiers from the 6th Connecticut. The men, whose regiment was preparing for the expedition, had left their post on Lady's Island and crossed the Coosaw River to gather up oranges and shaddocks.[89]

Mitchel originally planned the operation to be primarily an army expedition with minimal naval participation, but lack of transportation forced him to ask the navy for assistance. Since Du Pont had been called to Washington to help plan an attack by the North's ironclads against Charleston, Mitchel contacted Captain Sylvanus W. Godon, the acting squadron commander, for support. Godon, a sixty-three-year-old Pennsylvanian and a forty-three-year naval veteran, readily agreed, and on October 21 he assembled aboard the *Vermont* the commanders of the gunboats that were to accompany the expedition. Commander Charles Steedman, a South Carolina native, was placed in charge of the squadron. The navy provided nine gunboats and three armed launches from the *Wabash*. Each launch mounted in their bow a bronze Dahlgren boat howitzer, which could be placed on an iron field carriage for service ashore. Lieutenant Lloyd Phoenix commanded the launches, whose crews and cannons were to land with the army and provide additional artillery support. Ensigns James Wallace, Frederick Pearson, and LaRue P. James each commanded a launch, its howitzer, and its crew. Once ashore the sailors used draglines to pull the 750-pound cannons, while ammunition was carried either in wheeled chests that sailors pushed or in leather pouches attached to the sailors' belts.

The naval vessels joined eight army steamships. To guide the expedition, signal officers and the region's best African American pilots were placed aboard the vessels. The soldiers carried three days' worth of cooked rations and a hundred rounds of ammunition, while the men of the 3rd New Hampshire carried faggots of fat pine to fire the railroad bridges and trestles.[90]

On October 20 soldiers from Brannan's brigade embarked from Beaufort and sailed for Hilton Head, where they joined elements of Brigadier General Alfred Terry's brigade. At sunset the flotilla sailed to the mouth of the Broad River, where it anchored. Brannan, who had been named commander of the expedition by an ailing Mitchel just hours before its sailing, came aboard the *Paul Jones,* Steedman's flagship, for a consultation. Brannan requested assistance to send 107 men from Terry's brigade to capture Confederate picket posts at Mackay's Landing and Cuthbert's Landing. Steedman agreed and provided Brannan with the three armed launches from the *Wabash,* plus one from the *Paul Jones.* The launches were taken in tow by the army gunboat *Starlight* and preceded the expedition up the Broad River.[91]

Steedman aligned his vessels into a column. The sailing order consisted of:

USS *Paul Jones,* Steedman's flagship.
SS *Ben De Ford,* army transport, Brannan's flagship: 600 men, 47th Pennsylvania; 400 men, 55th Pennsylvania; towing a flat containing 108 men and horses, caissons and guns of Company M, 1st U.S. Artillery under Captain Guy V. Henry.
USS *Conemaugh,* 350 men, 4th New Hampshire.
USS *Wissahickon,* 250 men, 4th New Hampshire.
SS *Boston,* Brigadier General Alfred Terry, commander of the Second Brigade, 500 men, 7th Connecticut; 380 men, 3rd New Hampshire; towing a flat with Lieutenant E. Gettings's section of Company E, 3rd U.S. Artillery horses and caissons.
USS *Patroon,* 50 men, Company F, 3rd New Hampshire.
USS *Uncas,* 50 men, Company F, 3rd New Hampshire.
SS *Darlington,* Colonel John L. Chatfield, commander of the First Brigade, 300 men, 6th Connecticut.
SS *Relief,* towing a small schooner, 200 men, companies D and H, 6th Connecticut.
USS *Marblehead,* 230 men, 3rd Rhode Island.
USS *Vixen,* 70 men, 3rd Rhode Island.
SS *Flora,* 300 men, 76th Pennsylvania.
USS *Water Witch,* 120 men, 76th Pennsylvania.
SS *George Washington,* 250 men, 1st New York Engineers.
SS *Planter,* 300 men, 48th New York.[92]

At 12:30 A.M. on October 22, the expedition got underway. Almost immediately the Federal plan fell apart. The expedition's cavalrymen, 108 horsemen from the 1st Massachusetts Cavalry under Captain Lucius Richmond, who were needed to clear the roadway, missed the debarkation from Beaufort and had been left behind. The night was foggy. Commander Reed Werden, aboard the *Conemaugh,* the third ship in line, missed the signal to proceed, and when Werden got his vessel underway, it grounded, throwing the rest of the line into disorder and delaying its progress. A collision between the *Marblehead* and *Water Witch* added to the confusion and kept the soldiers aboard both vessels from fully participating in the battle. Unaware of the problems with the following vessels, Steedman on the *Paul Jones* and Brannan on the *Ben De Ford* arrived off the end of the peninsula, Mackay's Point, at 4:30 A.M.[93]

While Steedman and Brannan waited for the rest of the squadron, the *Starlight* entered the Pocotaligo River and cast loose the launches. One launch from the *Wabash,* along with the launch from the *Paul Jones,* under the overall direction of Lieutenant Samuel M. Smith of the 3rd New Hampshire, guided by a local black, pulled for Cuthbert's Landing at Bray's Island on the north side of the river. A little after daybreak, Smith and his party disembarked above the landing and were able to gather up seven Confederate prisoners before rejoining the rest of the squadron off Mackey's Point.

The two launches from the *Wabash* launches under Lieutenant Lloyd Phoenix and Ensign Frederick Pearson, each with a black guide, were not as fortunate. Detailed to take the enemy pickets at Mackey's Landing, approximately two miles down the neck from the expedition's debarkation point, the sailors, transporting soldiers from the 7th Connecticut and the 3rd New Hampshire under Captain Sylvester Gray, rowed past the landing. When the guides quickly informed the officer that they had gone too far, Pearson called on Phoenix to turn back, but Phoenix, being senior, refused to listen and ordered them to continue. After rowing farther up the river, Phoenix realized his error and directed Pearson to lead them back to the landing, but by now the sun was up and with all chance of surprise gone, the sailors pulled for Mackey's Point.[94]

While the launches were moving up the Pocotaligo River, Brannan and Steedman anxiously awaited the arrival of the remaining vessels off Mackey's Point. By dawn most of the ships had arrived. Before landing his troops, Brannan directed Colonel William B. Barton, aboard the *Planter,* to take his regiment, the 48th New York, elements of the 3rd Rhode Island and the 1st New York Engineers, and a boat howitzer from the *Paul Jones* to break up the railroad near Coosawhatchie. To support Barton's expedition, Steedman detached the gunboats *Vixen* and *Patroon* to convoy the *Planter* into the Coosawhatchie River while the *Uncas* moved into the Pocotaligo River, where she could provide fire support for the army's advance up Graham's Neck.[95]

As Barton and his force prepared to sail away, beginning at about 6:00 A.M., a portion of the 6th Connecticut came ashore at Abigail Jenkins Mackay's Plantation, followed by the 47th Pennsylvania under Colonel Tilghman Good. The Abigail Jenkins Mackay Plantation was located on a small island separated from the mainland by a tidal creek and salt marsh. From here the Union soldiers marched inland along a sandy road, passing through a strip of woods and then over causeways that connected the island to the George Chisholm Mackay Plantation, where Brannan consolidated his command.

The mix-up in the sailing order had delayed portions of Brannan's division, and he had to send vessels back to Port Royal Island to pick up the missing cavalry. It took time to reorganize and align. It was not until about 11:00 A.M. that the 1st Brigade under Colonel John L. Chatfield was ready to march. Colonel Good deployed four companies of the 47th Pennsylvania, one company from the 55th Pennsylvania, and two companies from the 6th Connecticut as skirmishers and began to march inland. Behind him came the rest of the 1st Brigade, the 47th and 55th Pennsylvania, the 6th Connecticut, a section of Company E, 3rd U.S. Artillery (two 10-pound Parrotts), and the 4th New Hampshire. Following Chatfield's command came General Terry's 2nd Brigade with a section of Company M, 1st U.S. Artillery (two 10-pound Parrotts), with the sailors under Lieutenant Phoenix pulling the three howitzers from the *Wabash*'s launches, supported by men from the 3rd Rhode Island, the 76th Pennsylvania, 7th Connecticut, 3rd New Hampshire, and 1st New York Engineers.[96]

Colonel Walker had long anticipated the Federal advance, but it was not until 9:00 A.M. that he received word that the Federals were landing at Mackay's Point and that Union gunboats had entered the Coosawhatchie River. With his command spread out over a sixty-mile area stretching between the Ashepoo and Savannah Rivers, Walker moved to concentrate troops to meet the Union attack. From Pocotaligo he sent four guns of the Lafayette Artillery Battery under Lieutenant Louis F. LeBenx and a section of the Beaufort Volunteer Artillery under Henry "Hal" Stuart to Coosawhatchie to support Captain B. F. Wyman's Company F, 11th South Carolina. From Hardeeville three companies of the 11th South Carolina were ordered to entrain and move to Coosawhatchie. Three additional companies from the 11th, recently stationed at Bluffton, were called from Hardeeville and directed to take the next train for Coosawhatchie. Colonel Charles Colcock, with five cavalry companies and two companies of sharpshooters, was instructed to take up a position at Bee's Hill and guard the approaches to Coosawhatchie. From Green Pond, Walker ordered three cavalry companies of the 17th South Carolina Cavalry Battalion under Major Robert J. Jeffords to the railroad bridge at Salkehatchie, while Captain Benjamin H. Rutledge's Charleston Light Dragoons were recalled from their position on the Combahee, and Captain William L. Trenholm with his company, the Rutledge Mounted Rifles, and Captain M. J. Kirk's company, the Partisan Rangers, were pulled off picket duty and ordered to join Walker's force, which was marching toward Graham's Neck. Walker also telegraphed General Beauregard in Charleston and commanders in neighboring districts and Savannah, calling for reinforcements.

As his units arrived, Walker began concentrating them behind a tidal stream known as Frampton Creek near the Dr. Thomas W. Hutson's Plantation, now owned by the Frampton Family, about six miles from Mackay's Point. Here, covering a bridge, Walker placed a section of the Beaufort Volunteer Artillery, the Nelson (Virginia) Light Artillery, two companies of the 1st South Carolina Cavalry Battalion, Daniel B. Heyward's company from the 2nd South Carolina Cavalry Battalion, and Company I, 11th South Carolina, under Lieutenant W. L. Campbell. To delay the Federals and give him time to better prepare his defenses, Walker sent Stephen Elliott and a section of the Beaufort Volunteer Artillery, along with Captain Joseph B. Alston's Company B, 1st Battalion South Carolina Sharpshooters, and two companies of the 2nd South Carolina Cavalry Battalion under Major Joseph H. Morgan to delay the Federal advance.[97]

Morgan and his cavalry initially engaged the Union skirmishers under Colonel Good shortly after the Federals left Mackay's Plantation. Forced back, the troopers fled down the road and joined Elliott and the sharpshooters at a new position on the plantation of Elliott's uncle, George P. Elliott. Nearby stood a large, earthen lunette built earlier by the Confederates, but Elliott, carrying out a fighting withdrawal, did not post his guns—two Napoleon cannons—in the lunette. Instead he placed them on the road, where, once the Federals got too close, they could easily limber the guns and extract them from the fight.

A little before noon, with the enemy skirmishers about three quarters of a mile away, Elliott opened with his guns. Colonel Good initially called for help, but when he realized that the Confederate position was not a strong one, he ordered his men to charge. During the fight George Elliott rode along the Confederate line encouraging his nephew's men. Stephen Elliott later wrote: "Uncle George seems to love me very much. He behaved admirably . . . was on horseback in the thickest of the fight. Helped me with my first position. Dashed up to his place and brought off his remaining niggers and wagons and afterwards wanted to pistol whip fellows who were running past who said to him 'Look here old man you had better get behind a tree, I have seen many a better looking man knocked off a horse today'. But the old fellow stuck to his charm and got off unhurt." Elliott kept up a steady fire until the Federals moved within 250 yards and then limbered his pieces and withdrew.[98]

Elliott pulled back about a mile to a new location behind a marsh. The position was covered on the left by an impassable salt marsh, and Elliott's center and right were in woods that gave cover to the dismounted cavalry and sharpshooters. On the road, behind a destroyed bridge, Elliott placed one cannon. When Good saw Elliott's new position, he immediately called for assistance, and Chatfield forwarded the rest of Good's regiment, the 47th Pennsylvania. Good quickly charged his men down the road under heavy fire. Again the Confederates were forced back, retreating half a mile through the woods and across the bridge, where they joined Colonel Walker, who had established a defense on the north side of Frampton Creek. The creek, a deep tidal estuary that bisected Mackey's Neck, had steep banks and was skirted on the south by a wide, muddy marsh. A causeway that crossed the marsh led to a wooden bridge that spanned the creek. Once Morgan and Elliott's men had crossed, the Confederates removed the bridge's flooring, and Walker placed the Beaufort Volunteer Artillery's four guns at the span's northern terminus while the four guns of the Nelson Artillery were positioned in an open field just to the right rear of the South Carolina gunners. Along the creek's northern bank, Walker deployed his dismounted cavalry, Allston's sharpshooters, Campbell's infantrymen, and the recently arrived Charleston Light Dragoons.[99]

Good and his soldiers closely followed the Confederates, advancing into the dense woods, which he described as "a perfect matting of vines and brush" nearly impossible to get through. Behind Good's men came the 6th Connecticut, 55th Pennsylvania, and the recently arrived 4th New Hampshire. Confederate artillery fire raked the woods, cutting down Union soldiers. Southern sharpshooters also took their toll, badly wounding Colonel Chatfield and Lieutenant Colonel John Speidel, who were advancing the 6th Connecticut.[100]

As Good's men emerged from the woods, they came to an open area that stretched one quarter of a mile across sweet potato and cotton fields to Frampton Creek. With little or no cover, but assisted by long-range fire from the gunboat *Uncas,* Good pushed his men forward while Brannan personally positioned the four 10-pound Parrott rifled guns from Lieutenants Henry's and Gettings's batteries and the boat howitzers in the edge of the woods to cover the advancing infantry. Good, with the 47th Pennsylvania, drove to the edge of the creek exchanging volleys at a distance of fifty yards with the Confederates before being forced back. While Good re-formed his regiment in the woods, the Union guns dueled with the Confederate artillery. The boat howitzers, under Lieutenant Phoenix, were pulled into position by their sailor crews, assisted by men from the 3rd Rhode Island, and fired shrapnel into and over the tree tops, taking out Confederate snipers.[101]

The Union artillery fire, however, was not effective, the shells falling short, and Brannan, who upon the wounding of Chatfield, took personal command of the 1st Brigade, ordered Lieutenant Henry to run his guns up to the head of the causeway while the first brigade advanced to the creek bank. Henry had his cannons limbered and led them on horseback to a spot less than a hundred yards from the enemy artillery. Supported by infantry fire, the artillerymen entered into close combat with their counterparts. Henry had his horse shot from under him. An enemy shell disabled half of a gun crew, but the piece was kept in action by the three remaining artillerymen. The Union movement had its effect. Major Morgan, Walker's cavalry commander, received a severe wound. Men and horses in the Nelson Artillery were cut down and one caisson had its wheels shot away. Captain Elliott was grazed in the leg by a shell fragment and his horse wounded. As more and more of the artillerymen fell to enemy fire, Elliott warned Colonel Walker that unless they pulled back, they would be in danger of losing their cannons. Walker agreed. He had accomplished his task of slowing the enemy. His men had done their best. For nearly an hour, by using the terrain to his advantage and deploying just over four hundred effectives, Walker had held up a force of nearly four thousand men.[102]

Orders were passed to pull back, and as the Confederates withdrew, the 4th New Hampshire charged into the marsh on both sides of the causeway and through the creek, crawling up the far bank as the Confederates retreated. Engineers repaired the bridge enough to let infantry cross, and soon General Terry with the 2nd Brigade took up the pursuit, dueling with the Confederate rear guard for nearly three miles. Brannan immediately put his engineers to work strengthening the bridge, allowing his artillery to traverse. Once over the creek, the sailors manning the boat howitzers were able to replenish their ammunition from an abandoned Confederate caisson. Brannan drove his division forward. He was uncertain of reaching the railroad before dark. Much depended upon the ability of the expedition sent to cut the railroad line at Coosawhatchie to complete its mission. If successful, it could stop enemy reinforcements from reaching Pocotaligo Station and allow Brannan to obtain his objective.[103]

While Brannan's division fought its way up Graham's Neck and neared Pocotaligo, the transport *Planter* carried into the Coosawhatchie River Colonel Barton and three hundred men from the 48th New York, fifty men from Company G, 3rd Rhode Island, under Captain John Gould, and one Dahlgren boat howitzer. The little side-wheeler towed one of the specially built lighters, containing a detachment from the 1st New York Engineers commanded by Captain Samuel E. Eaton. The engineers carried implements to break up the railroad and faggots to fire trestles and bridges. Two gunboats, the *Patroon* and the *Vixen,* accompanied the *Planter* into the Coosawhatchie River but ran aground as the *Planter* continued to steam up the river for another half mile. The armed transport *George Washington* also joined the expedition but entered Bee's Creek by mistake, taking her away from supporting distance of the *Planter* but in a position to affect the movement of enemy troops.[104]

Colonel Walker, warned by Confederate pickets about the Union vessels moving from Mackay's Point toward the Coosawhatchie River, had notified Colonel Charles Colcock at Grahamville to intercept any enemy attack on Coosawhatchie. Colcock, who had taken ill, remained in Grahamville and turned field command over to Lieutenant Colonel Thomas H. Johnson. A company of sharpshooters under Captain Robert Chisolm marched to Gopher Hill (today Ridgeland) and continued along the railroad for Coosawhatchie. Johnson, with five companies of the 3rd South Carolina and Captain Henry Buist's company of sharpshooters, moved from Grahamville to the junction of the Grahamville and Coosawhatchie Roads at Bee's Hill, just south of Bee's Creek. The movement of the Union vessels confused the

Confederates, and word soon reached Johnson that Federals were landing in his rear and were menacing Grahamville. To investigate this threat, Johnson sent two cavalry companies. He left Buist's sharpshooters at Bee's Hill and continued north toward Coosawhatchie with his remaining three cavalry companies.[105]

By now the *Planter,* guided by her black pilot, Sam Pope, had nearly reached the steamboat landing in the Coosawhatchie River, but with the receding tide the vessel grounded just below the debarkation point, where Barton off-loaded his infantry. The soldiers came ashore on a miry bank covered with tall sedge grass about a hundred yards from solid ground. The engineers followed, making a path from the landing, some five hundred yards in length, to the main road, which allowed Barton to bring ashore his 750-pound boat howitzer, pulled by twelve men from the 3rd Rhode Island. Confederate forces were spotted to the south, but Barton ignored their presence and hurried his men north along the rode toward the railroad.[106]

When Lieutenant Colonel Johnson spied the Federals coming ashore, he dismounted his cavalry just short of the bridge over Bee's Creek. When the Federals turned north, he remounted his troopers, but because of the presence of the Union gunboats, whose heavy guns could sweep the causeway across Bee's Creek and the adjoining marsh, Johnson took his men off the road and rode cross country to the west, hoping to reach Coosawhatchie before the Federals.[107]

Joined by contrabands who helped guide the way, Barton marched his men along the roadway as it veered to the west, skirmishing with Confederate pickets. As they neared Coosawhatchie, a locomotive whistle was heard. At first the contraband guides thought it was a quartermaster train heading south for Savannah, but as the Union soldiers arrived at the tracks, about a quarter of a mile south of Coosawhatchie, they realized that the train was traveling north toward Charleston. Barton quickly masked his men and the boat howitzer in the trees and brush along the railroad.

The train, consisting of six platform cars and two box or passenger cars, carried from Hardeeville Companies C, D, and K of the 11th South Carolina and two field pieces under Major John J. Harrison, as well as Chisolm's company of sharpshooters, who had been picked up along the way. As the train came into point-blank range, Barton ordered his men to open fire. The locomotive and the cars were swept with rifle fire and canister from the boat howitzer. The train's engineer and Major Grafton Geddes Ruth, on leave from the 3rd South Carolina, were killed in the locomotive's cab. The train's conductor, J. H. Buckhalter, took over and kept the train moving through the ambush toward Coosawhatchie. The Union fire ripped into the following cars, cutting down Major Harrison and killing and wounding his soldiers.

The flag bearer of the Whippy Swamp Guards (Company D, 11th South Carolina) lost control of the company's colors, which tumbled over the side and into the hands of the Union soldiers. Some men jumped off the cars and escaped into the nearby swamps, but most stayed on board, weathered the fire, and made it on through Coosawhatchie.[108]

Once the train had passed, Barton put the engineers to work ripping up the track and cutting telegraph poles. At the same time, he rushed his infantry into Coosawhatchie, where he found the Confederates drawn up on the north bank of the Coosawhatchie River. Four cannons of Lieutenant L. F. LeBleux's Lafayette Artillery guarded the footbridge, while Hal Stuart's two guns of the Beaufort Volunteer Artillery covered the railroad bridge. Infantry from Wyman's company and survivors from the train supported the artillery. A brief firefight ensued but Barton, seeing that he was outnumbered and outgunned, and not wishing to be trapped, decided to return to the *Planter*.[109]

By now Captain Eaton's engineers had managed to tear out two sections of track and partially remove five or six others. They started a fire to warp the rails, cut down two telegraph poles, and severed the wires in numerous places. But as the infantry pulled back, the engineers stopped their work and joined the withdrawal, destroying four bridges on the route back to the *Planter* to slow the Confederate pursuit.

As the Federals retreated, Lieutenant Colonel Johnson and his three cavalry companies completed their circuitous route from Bee's Hill and arrived at Coosawhatchie, where they immediately began pursuing the Union soldiers. By 5:30 P.M. Barton and his command were safely on the *Planter*. As the vessel, now afloat with the incoming tide, pulled away, the southern cavalrymen fired volleys onto her open decks. The Union soldiers responded with musketry and cannon fire from the *Planter*'s pivot gun. During the exchange the Federals suffered their only casualty when Lieutenant Jabez B. Blanding of the 3rd Rhode Island, commanding the Planter's cannons, received severe wounds in his left arm and side. When Blanding went down, a drummer boy from the 48th New York picked up the lieutenant's revolver and emptied it at the enemy.

With supporting fire from the gunboats and the *George Washington*, the *Planter*, minus the lighter, which had been left behind, steamed out of the Coosawhatchie River and rejoined the flotilla off Mackay's Point. The expedition had failed to effectively break the railroad, which was quickly repaired. Before the day was out, it would be carrying Confederate reinforcements from Savannah to Pocotaligo Station. But the Union movement had compelled Walker to split his forces, leaving him with fewer men to oppose Brannan's main attack, which had reached the outskirts of Pocotaligo.[110]

After they had been forced out of their defenses along Frampton Creek, the Confederates retreated toward Pocotaligo. Captain Allston with his sharpshooters and part of Company I, 11th South Carolina, covered the withdrawal. The Confederates made good use of the terrain to harass the Union soldiers, and wherever possible Captain Elliott unlimbered his guns and directed fire down the road at the massed Union columns.

Walker directed his troops to a new position east of the Pocotaligo River. By now Captains Trenholm and Kirk had arrived with their cavalry companies. Walker gave Trenholm command of the cavalry, replacing the wounded Major Morgan. Once across the river, Walker arranged his defenses. He positioned the guns of the Beaufort Artillery and Nelson Artillery to command the bridge and causeway leading across the Pocotaligo, while his infantry and dismounted cavalry took refuge in existing earthworks, nearby houses, and trees. In reserve near the town, he stationed the Charleston Light Dragoons. As the Federals approached the river, Captain John Screven, whose Castle Hill Plantation stood just north of the battlefield, led a party who tore up the bridge but did so before Captain Allston and some of his sharpshooters were able to cross, forcing them to take shelter in the marsh between the two lines for the rest of the fight.[111]

The pursuing Federals closely followed the Confederates. With the 4th New Hampshire in the lead as skirmishers, General Terry's brigade and the artillery pressed forward with the First Brigade, now under Colonel Good, close behind. Upon reaching the Charleston-Savannah Turnpike, Terry left the 3rd New Hampshire and one of the boat howitzers to watch for any enemy coming from the west, while the rest of his command marched to the northeast toward Pocotaligo.

As the Federals advanced, they entered heavy woods that led up to the edge of a marsh. The Confederate infantry, in their earthworks about six hundred yards away, kept up a heavy fire while their artillery swept the roadway and sent shells into the woods, shattering trees and sending splinters into the Union ranks. As they neared the Pocotaligo River, the Union brigades became intermixed. The 4th New Hampshire, which had been deployed as skirmishers in the center with the artillery, depleted most of its ammunition and was sent to the rear. Brought forward and posted in line on the left of the road was the 76th Pennsylvania, followed by the 55th Pennsylvania and the 6th Connecticut. Deployed on the right of the road was the 7th Connecticut, backed up by the 47th Pennsylvania. The troops were kept in the woods while the engineers prepared timbers to repair the bridge. When Gettings's and Henry's batteries and the two boat howitzers arrived, they took up a position in the road and began exchanging fire with the enemy's artillery. Lieutenant Gettings went down with a wound, and Lieutenant Henry took over both sections and their four 10-pound Parrott rifles. Though superior in range and accuracy to the Confederate guns, the Federals were low on ammunition and were forced to slacken their bombardment. When they did so, the Confederates were able to increase their fire.

To make up for his diminished artillery support, Terry directed sharpshooters from the 55th Pennsylvania on the left and the 7th Connecticut on the right to advance to the edge of the marsh and "work upon the enemy's batteries." The fire proved effective, especially from Companies A and B, 7th Connecticut, whose men were armed with breech-loading Sharps rifles. Stephen Elliott wrote that "the bullets were like hail, the infantry would lie in the grass and behind trees and houses but my boys had just to stand up and take it, which they did beautifully." Soon the Confederates were down to only three operating cannons. With the effectiveness of the enemy's artillery reduced, Terry positioned two recently arrived companies from the 76th Pennsylvania with his artillery and ordered the 7th Connecticut to move to the edge of the marsh, where the regiment began firing by file.[112]

The Confederates were in a difficult position. To disrupt the Federal line and to give the appearance of arriving reinforcements, Walker sent one gun from the Beaufort Volunteer Artillery, under the command of Sergeant Major Robert "Rob" B. Fuller, to a position three hundred yards to the right, where it could rake the enemy's line. Walker also ordered up the Charleston Light Dragoons. The troopers were told to rush forward, cheering to fool the Federals into believing that reinforcements had arrived. Led by Lieutenant Richard H. Colcock, who swung his sabre over his head, the dismounted cavalrymen reinforced the Confederate left.[113]

Generals Brannan and Terry, conspicuous under enemy fire, carefully watched the Confederate movements. To reach the railroad, they had to get their men across the river and then march a mile and a half up the McPhersonville Road. Time was running against them, and their men and artillery were nearly out of ammunition. Lieutenant Henry soon found it necessary to withdraw his guns. They were replaced by Lieutenant Phoenix's two boat howitzers. The sailors, using the captured Confederate shells, kept up the bombardment under heavy enemy fire that forced Phoenix to order all men not serving the guns to take cover. Among the sailors working the howitzers was Seaman Oscar Farenholt, who received three wounds, one shattering his left forearm, but he refused to leave the field. After the battle the nineteen-year-old Farenholt talked the surgeons out of amputating his left arm. He would later receive the Congressional Medal of Honor for his actions at Pocotaligo and become the first seaman to achieve the rank of admiral in the United States Navy.

While the boat howitzers took up their position in the road, Terry directed Colonel Hawley of the 7th Connecticut to send scouts forward to see whether a rush could be made across the swamp. Joseph R. Hawley initially dispatched five men, who went into the morass but could not locate the creek. Hawley tried once more, and as he reported, "I called again for volunteers and Lieutenant Edward S. Perry and Private William Crabbe, eagerly offering were accepted, and ordered to keep low and find the creek. Our men were notified and cautioned not to hit them. They went, stooping under the fire of both parties, two-thirds of the way across, and reported a deep creek, of the character common here, with muddy banks and low water. I sent the lieutenant to General Terry."

From Lieutenant Perry's report, Terry realized that there was no possibility of fording the creek, and his only recourse was to continue the firefight in hopes of driving the Confederates to cover long enough for the engineers to repair the bridge and his soldiers to cross. But Terry's men, low on ammunition, were unable to completely suppress the Confederate fire.[114]

Shortly after 4:00 P.M., the Federal soldiers clearly heard locomotive whistles signaling the arrival of Confederate reinforcements. Colonel Walker had been notified earlier in the day that reinforcements were on their way from Savannah and Charleston. The first to arrive were two hundred men from the 7th South Carolina Battalion under Captain William H. Sligh, who had boarded a train at Adams Run Station just south of Charleston. Within thirty minutes of arriving at Pocotaligo Station, the soldiers reached the front. Walker placed one hundred men on his extreme right, where they joined some cavalry in crossing the Pocotaligo River at the Thomas Elliott Plantation and skirmished with the Union left, forcing the commander of the 76th Pennsylvania, Colonel De Witt C. Strawbridge, to refuse his left flank to drive off the attackers. The rest of the reinforcements deployed under heavy fire at Pocotaligo amid cheers from their comrades. By now Terry had relieved the 7th Connecticut, which had nearly exhausted its ammunition, with the 47th Pennsylvania. He brought forward Colonel John H. Jackson's 3rd New Hampshire and the boat howitzer from its position covering roads in the rear to support the 76th Pennsylvania, whose commander had reported a near depletion of cartridges.[115]

The Federals had clearly seen the arrival of Confederate reinforcements, and with darkness falling, Brannan realized he could not reach the railroad. He ordered Terry to begin a withdrawal. Colonel Good's 47th Pennsylvania kept up a steady fire while the rest of the Union troops pulled away from the creek. Men from the 7th Connecticut helped pull Lieutenant Henry's guns to safety. Once the other regiments had passed, Good's men fired one final volley and then retired double quick by the flank one thousand yards to a line held by the 7th Connecticut. The 47th then re-formed a thousand yards behind the 7th Connecticut, a maneuver the two regiments kept up until 8:00 P.M., when they reached Frampton Creek, where they found the 4th New Hampshire drawn up behind the creek. After a brief stop the Federals continued to fall back to their initial landing point at the Abigail Jenkins Mackay Plantation.

On the retreat the Federal soldiers gathered up their wounded from a temporary hospital just south of Frampton Creek. Here surgeons had operated by firelight, amputating limbs and treating wounds. Those unable to walk were placed on blankets tied over saplings for the trip to Mackay's Point. Prominent among those helping the injured was Samuel Cooley, sutler for the 7th Connecticut, who helped move the wounded along the march and later onto the waiting transports. To assist this effort, Colonel Louis Bell, commander of the 4th New Hampshire, which served as the rear guard, detailed half his regiment to serve as stretcher bearers. Just before 4:00 A.M. on the twenty-third, Colonel Bell and his regiment crossed the causeway leading from the mainland to Mackay's Point. Bell proudly reported that no one was left behind and abandoned equipment that could not be salvaged was destroyed.[116]

Once at Mackay's Point, most of the Union soldiers rested while Lieutenant Phoenix and his crews placed their howitzers back in the bow pivots on the launches and rowed out to the gunboat *Paul Jones,* where they secured their boats and fell asleep. On shore General Terry deployed a late-arriving detachment from the 3rd Rhode Island that had been aboard the gunboat *Marblehead,* along with the Massachusetts cavalrymen who had finally turned up to cover the Union position from attack. The soldiers watched over the causeway and were given signal rockets that, if necessary, could be launched to trigger an artillery barrage from the nearby gunboats.[117]

The Union soldiers had been able to pull back with little interference from the Confederates. General Walker dispatched Second Lieutenant L. J. Walker with the Rutledge Mounted Rifles and Kirk's Partisan Rangers after the retreating enemy, but with the bridge over the Pocotaligo destroyed, Lieutenant Walker had to make a wide circuit, north to Pocotaligo Station and then southwest back to the main stage road to follow the retreating enemy. But the cavalrymen were again stymied when they reached Frampton Creek, where they found that bridge destroyed. The pursuit stopped. Colonel Walker, not knowing the outcome of the fight at Coosawhatchie, kept his men under arms while he sent a courier and a locomotive from Pocotaligo Station to reconnoiter. He soon learned that the enemy had been driven off with only minor damage to the railroad, and by eight the next morning a Georgia infantry brigade and artillery company from Savannah reached Coosawhatchie.[118]

While the Georgians were arriving at Coosawhatchie, Colonel Walker was able to forward a detachment of cavalry under Captain Trenholm toward Mackay's Point, but all Trenholm could do was watch the Federals evacuate while he and his men received an occasional shell from the Union warships.

At 8:00 A.M. the Federals began embarking on small boats that carried the soldiers out to the transports and gunboats. The operation took all day. Before leaving, they burned the plantation buildings at Mackay Point. By sunset the last regiment, the 55th Pennsylvania, had been safely removed. The vessels transported the troops back to their camps at Hilton Head, Beaufort, and Fort Pulaski.[119]

The Confederates, unable to interfere, watched the Federals pull away. After nightfall on October 23, Sergeant Robinson of the Rutledge Mounted Riflemen found the enemy gone. Colonel Walker, pleased with his men's tenacity and determination, reported that the damage to the railroad at Coosawhatchie had been quickly repaired. His command had suffered approximately 163 casualties: 21 killed, 124 wounded, and 18 missing. The heaviest toll occurred among his artillerymen, who accounted for nearly a third of the losses. After his successful defense of the railroad, Walker was promoted to brigadier general on October 30, 1862. To honor their commander, Walker's troops gave him a torchlight parade, and the local women had a general's uniform made for him.

General Brannan was also pleased with the conduct of his men. He complimented Captain Steedman and the navy for their support. The battle had been a hard one, nearly continuous from the initial engagement at the Elliott Plantation to the Federal withdrawal from the Pocotaligo River. Out of 4,448 men, Brannan reported 340 casualties: 43 killed, 294 wounded, and 3 missing. The naval contingent suffered 3 wounded.[120]

On the morning of October 23, Rear Admiral Du Pont, who had returned to Port Royal late the previous morning, met with General Mitchel on Hilton Head. There, at the general's headquarters, the initial reports came in confirming a bloody repulse. When Du Pont returned to his flagship, he saw the wounded being off-loaded on the dock. The scene moved the admiral, who for the first time saw the results of a hard-fought land engagement. As he wrote his wife, "I was on the wharf when they were passing those poor fellows out of the transport *Boston* to the ambulances. I asked myself if this was America, so long exempt from such spectacles and now the result of fratricidal hands."[121]

Brannan and Terry met with General Mitchel the next day. Mitchel, in his report to the army's general in chief, Major General Henry W. Halleck, wrote that the expedition had given the Federals complete knowledge of the Pocotaligo and Coosawhatchie Rivers and that success had been thwarted by the numerous delays that kept the men from landing with their full force early in the day. Mitchel also informed Halleck that he planned three more expeditions but needed additional men. He ended by begging Halleck to send him reinforcements so that he could strike his blows with the rapidity needed to ensure success.[122]

Mitchel, though, would never be able to carry out his planned operations. Before the expedition to Mackay's Point had sailed, members of his staff had come down with yellow fever, including his two sons. The origin of the disease was thought to have come from the turning of dirt on Hilton Head for new fortifications. On the twenty-fifth, the general and his staff were moved to Beaufort for a "change of air." They took up residence in the Nathaniel Heyward House on Bay Street. That night Mitchel came down with the fever. As he worsened, he turned command of the department over to Brannan. Surgeon Joseph Davis Mitchell of the 8th Maine and Surgeon Charles H. Crane, chief medical officer for the department, attended the general. The doctors separated Mitchel from his sons. For five days he languished while being nursed by the recently arrived Frances Gage, the renowned abolitionist, woman's rights advocate, and Universalist, who had come to Port Royal to join the great experiment. Mitchel, fearing the worse, requested that the Reverend Dr. William P. Strickland, the chaplain of the 48th New York, come from Fort Pulaski to see to his spiritual needs. Mitchel's aide-de-camp, Captain J. C. Williams died on the twenty-ninth, and on the morning of the thirtieth, Colonel Nathaniel Brown, commander of the 3rd Rhode Island, succumbed to the disease. Mitchel, knowing that he was dying, held an audience with Brannan and Saxton, asking the two to put aside their differences and shake hands. This they did. Then Mitchel dictated his will. He expressed to Chaplain Strickland his unshakeable trust in Jesus Christ, and then, unable to talk, he took the forefinger of each hand, first the left and then the right, and pointed upward before dying. He had been in command for only forty days.[123]

Mitchel's body was taken to a hospital and prepared for burial. The funeral took place the next day. The procession from the hospital to St. Helena Episcopal Church consisted of the 47th Pennsylvania, 3rd Battalion, 1st Massachusetts Cavalry, and a battery of the 1st U.S. Artillery. Mitchel's body, placed in a metallic coffin inside a wooden coffin, was transported in a covered wagon over which stretched an American flag. Following the wagon on horseback came the pallbearers: Rear Admiral Du Pont, Generals Brannan and Saxton, Colonel Richard White of the 55th Pennsylvania, Colonel John D. Rust of the 8th Maine, and Commander C. R. P. Rodgers. Behind them came additional mourners. The streets were filled with people paying their respects, including Robert Smalls, who had recently returned from New York. In St. Helena Episcopal Church, Chaplain Strickland conducted the service, after which the coffin was placed in a holding crypt in the graveyard, where it would remain until sent north once cooler weather arrived.[124]

Had Mitchel lived, he would have been the army's leader in a proposed joint attack on Charleston. While he had been planning and carrying out his initial operations against the railroad, the administration had determined to support a major army-navy campaign against the South Carolina port. Mitchel's death, however, forced the War Department to return General Hunter to Port Royal. For the navy, command in the new venture went to Admiral Du Pont, who had just returned from a briefing with the secretary of the navy. For the assault Du Pont's squadron was to be reinforced with the bulk of the nation's newest ironclads, including the tower ironclad *Keokuk,* the ironclad frigate *New Ironsides,* and seven of the recently completed *Passaic*-class monitors, improved versions of the original *Monitor*.[125]

The new campaign, based out of Port Royal, would result in a massive expansion of the region's military facilities. For the attack Du Pont needed experienced pilots. He was pleased when he spotted Robert Smalls at Mitchel's funeral and even more pleased when he learned that when Commander Rodgers had asked Smalls whether his head had been turned while he was being feted in New York, Smalls replied, "It was turned but one way all the time he was north—towards Port Royal."[126]

Thomas W. Sherman (courtesy of the Library of Congress).

Samuel F. Du Pont (courtesy of the Library of Congress).

Rufus Saxton (courtesy of the Beaufort County Historical Society).

Thomas W. Higginson (courtesy of the Beaufort County Historical Society).

Salmon Chase (courtesy of the Library of Congress).

Solomon Peck (courtesy of the Beaufort County Historical Society).

Mansfield French (courtesy of the Beaufort County Historical Society).

Edward Pierce (courtesy of the Beaufort County Historical Society).

Ellen Murray (courtesy of the Beaufort County Historical Society).

Laura Towne (courtesy of the Beaufort County Historical Society).

Jean Davenport Lander (courtesy of the Beaufort County Historical Society).

Charlotte Forten (courtesy of the Beaufort County Historical Society).

Thomas Drayton (courtesy of the U.S. Army Institute of Military History).

Stephen Elliott Jr. (courtesy of the U.S. Army Institute of Military History).

William S. Walker (courtesy of the Parris Island Museum).

Richard Fuller (courtesy of the Beaufort County Historical Society).

Robert Smalls, 1862 (courtesy of the Beaufort County Historical Society).

David Hunter (courtesy of the Library of Congress).

Ormsby McKnight Mitchel (courtesy of the Library of Congress).

William Tecumseh Sherman (courtesy of the Library of Congress).

William Fripp House, officer's hospital (courtesy of the National Archives).

Nathaniel Heyward House, General Saxton's home (courtesy of the National Archives).

Beaufort City Hall and Contraband Office (courtesy of the U.S. Army Institute of Military History).

Beaufort Methodist Church (courtesy of the Beaufort County Historical Society).

East end of Bay Street from Carteret (courtesy of the U.S. Army Institute of Military History).

Bay Street, looking west from Carteret (courtesy of the U.S. Army Institute of Military History).

USS *Catskill* (courtesy of the Library of Congress).

The pier at Hilton Head: the *Wabash* right of center, *Vermont* far left (courtesy of the National Archives).

Five generations of slaves, now free at Old Fort Plantation (courtesy of the Library of Congress).

Missionaries at Old Fort Plantation in front of the J. J. Smith House (courtesy of the U.S. Army Institute of Military History).

Refugee Quarters Hilton Head (courtesy of the National Archives).

Mitchelville (courtesy of the Beaufort County Historical Society).

Penn School (courtesy of the U.S. Army Institute of Military History).

Elizabeth Botume's school at Old Fort Plantation (courtesy of the Beaufort County Historical Society).

Slave cabin (courtesy of the Beaufort County Historical Society).

Beaufort College building used as a freedmen School.

Thomas E. Miller (from the authors' collection).

Richard H. Gleaves (from the author's collection).

William Whipper (from the author's collection).

Congressman Robert Smalls (from the author's collection).

Beaufort Public School at Carteret and Washington (from the author's collection).

U.S. Atlantic Squadron in Port Royal Sound 1877 (USMC Photo, courtesy of the Parris Island Museum).

Beaufort Waterfront, 1862. Left to right: William Elliott III, Nathaniel Heyward, and Stuart Houses.

Barnwell Castle, Beaufort County Courthouse, 1872–1881 (courtesy of the National Archives).

Freedmen cabin on St. Helena Island, circa 1870 (from the author's collection).

Critter House/freedmen's barn, circa 1880 (from the author's collection).

Beaufort waterfront east, circa 1885 (USMC Photo, courtesy of the Parris Island Museum).

Beaufort waterfront west, circa 1885 (USMC Photo, courtesy of the Parris Island Museum).

Bay Street docks, Beaufort, circa 1885 (USMC Photo, courtesy of the Parris Island Museum).

Coosaw Mining (Phosphate) Company's works (from the author's collection).

Farmer's Mine phosphate loading dock (from the author's collection).

Steam tug at a phosphate loading dock (from the author's collection).

Merchant and civic leaders, left to right: George Waterhouse, Dr. Henry M. Stuart, M.D., Duncan C. Wilson, C. C. Cummings, W. R. Lockwood (from the author's collection).

Chapter 7

Emancipation

*"Let me lib wid de musket in one hand
and de Bible in de oder"*

After General Mitchel's death, the Federals shifted their priorities away from attacks against the Charleston and Savannah Railroad and turned their energies toward capturing Charleston. For the upcoming campaign, both the army and navy began preparations at Port Royal, but it would take months to assemble the required men, matériel, and warships.

The navy acted first. As early as May 1862, Assistant Secretary of the Navy Gustavus Fox suggested that Du Pont use the North's first ironclads, the *Monitor* and *Galena,* to capture Charleston. Not trusting the new ironclads, Du Pont demurred, but a month later Fox informed him that the vessels would be sent to Port Royal once they had completed operations with the army against Wilmington, North Carolina. The prospect of going into Charleston, even with the ironclads, did not sit well with Du Pont, who viewed the Confederate harbor defenses to be nearly impregnable. Du Pont's apprehensions were eased when in May 1862 the *Galena,* cut to pieces in an unsuccessful attack on Richmond's water defenses, was pulled from service and the *Monitor,* on her way to join the assault on Wilmington, sank in a storm on December 29, 1862, off Cape Hatteras.[1]

Du Pont received only a slight reprise. He was soon informed that he would be assigned the ironclad frigate *New Ironsides* and most of the new, improved, monitor-style vessels known as the *Passaic* class. In October 1862, while General Mitchel planned and carried out his attack against Pocotaligo and Coosawhatchie, Du Pont went to Washington to confer with Fox and Secretary of the Navy Gideon Welles and to inspect the new monitors and their ordnance. The admiral was impressed by the destructive power of the 15-inch Dahlgren guns that were to be mounted in the *Passaic*-class monitors and elicited a promise from Fox that as many as possible of the new monitors and other ironclads would be sent to Port Royal. Also, the navy assigned its top officers, Percival Drayton among them, to command the new monitors, but Du Pont remained troubled. His pride in his well-earned reputation from the results of the Battle of

Port Royal would not let him come out officially against the attack, yet his doubts remained.[2]

While Du Pont waited for his ironclads, the northern army made preparations to cooperate with the naval assault. Leaders of the army, like the navy, longed to capture Charleston. With the loss of the *Monitor*, the attack on Wilmington was cancelled, and the army directed Major General John G. Foster to take some ten thousand men from his North Carolina command to Port Royal. Foster, a member of Fort Sumter's 1861 garrison, desired nothing more than to recapture the fort. However, the shifting of troops and the completion of the ironclads would take time. Preparations would drag on into the spring of 1863, and in the meantime major events occurred on the sea islands centered on the region's contraband population.[3]

General Mitchel's death resulted in David Hunter's being reassigned to the Department of the South. Also ordered to Port Royal was Brigadier General Truman Seymour, a veteran officer who, like Foster, had been part of Fort Sumter's garrison in April 1861. It was hoped that Seymour, who replaced Brannan, would provide Hunter with a competent field commander for the coming operations against Charleston. However, Hunter's return was delayed, and for a brief period Generals Brannan and Saxton maintained their uneasy truce, each independently carrying out their assigned duties. A strict disciplinarian, Brannan continued to drill his soldiers, but the general knew that his time at Port Royal was coming to an end. Powerful individuals, including Secretary Chase, knowing Brannan's disdain for black soldiers and the Port Royal Experiment, lobbied for his transfer from the department. A regular officer, Brannan desired duty in a major theater, and though he had close friends at Port Royal, he also had disliked the comments that his broken marriage elicited among the local military personnel and civilians.[4]

While stationed at Beaufort, Brannan associated closely with Dr. Charles H. Crane, the department's chief medical officer and the general's erstwhile brother-in-law. In 1850 Brannan had married Eliza Crane, daughter of Colonel Ichabod Crane. They had one daughter, and then eight years later Eliza disappeared from her mother's Staten Island home. For years Brannan, aided by her brother, Dr. Crane, and her mother, searched for Eliza. Brannan feared that she may have committed suicide or gone insane and was wandering the countryside. Then, in 1860 Dr. Crane received a letter from a former United States Army second lieutenant, Powell T. Wyman, stating that he and Crane's sister had run off to Paris, where they had married. Wyman, a Massachusetts-born, West Point–trained artilleryman, had been on an extended leave of absence before resigning his commission in July 1860 and marrying Eliza Crane.

With Dr. Crane providing an affidavit, Brannan filed for a divorce and full custody of his daughter. The case, which made national headlines, was still unsettled when Brannan was assigned to duty in the Department of the South, but his wife's situation had changed dramatically. While in Paris, Wyman, who had been watching events in the United States, felt it his duty to return once hostilities broke out.

In the summer of 1861, Wyman and Eliza arrived at Boston, where he was appointed colonel of the 16th Massachusetts Infantry. He led his regiment during the Peninsula Campaign until he was shot through the heart on June 30, 1862, while leading a charge at the Battle of Glendale. A year after Wyman's death, Brannan's divorce was granted.[5]

While Brannan awaited word on his divorce and a transfer to a new command, General Saxton on October 18 directed his superintendents to hold frequent meetings to discuss their experiences with the contrabands and report the results to Saxton, who would then inform "the Secretary of War and the country the measure of success which has attended this great experiment of free labor in a district where the friends of slavery have confidently predicted it would utterly fail."

In the same order Saxton also called on his superintendents to "induce the young and able-bodied men, capable of bearing arms, to enroll themselves at once" into a reconstituted "First Regiment of South Carolina Volunteers." The general's task was aided by recent congressional and presidential acts. The Second Confiscation Act, passed on July 17, 1862, allowed the enlistment of black troops with the same conditions and pay—thirteen dollars a month—as white troops. The act also granted freedom to both the soldiers and their families. Five days after the passing of the Second Confiscation Act, President Lincoln presented his cabinet with a preliminary version of an emancipation proclamation. The draft received a mixed response, and on the advice of Secretary of State William Seward, Lincoln postponed issuing the proclamation until the North had achieved a major military victory. Antietam, though not as decisive as Lincoln had hoped, gave him the opportunity to issue his preliminary proclamation on September 22, 1862. Armed with freedom for his black soldiers and their families and a promise of freedom for everyone else in the sea islands on January 1, 1863, Saxton went forward not only with the organization of black regiments but also with preparing his minions for freedom.[6]

The 1st South Carolina had never gone out of existence. Many of the black soldiers remained in the sea islands on extended furlough, while another section guarded a large refugee slave encampment on St. Simons Island, Georgia. Those on leave were directed to report to the regiment's headquarters at the John J. Smith Plantation, now called Camp Saxton, located above the ruins of old Fort Prince Frederick on the Beaufort River. At the same time, one of Saxton's agents, Lieutenant Colonel Oliver T. Beard of the 48th New York, along with Mansfield French, sailed on the steamer *Darlington* from Port Royal to St. Simons Island, where they took on board

Captain Charles T. Trowbridge and sixty-two men from Hunter's regiment. Proceeding to Fernandina, the little expedition began a series of raids along the Florida and Georgia coast, destroying sawmills and saltworks and freeing slaves, many of whom, at Reverend French's urging, volunteered for service in the 1st South Carolina. On November 8 the *Darlington* returned to Beaufort, where Beard disembarked 156 veteran, armed soldiers who marched through the town singing "John Brown's Body" on their way to the Smith Plantation. The next day another 250 recruits arrived from Georgetown on the steamer *Ben De Ford*. General Saxton and the missionaries watched closely the outfitting of the regiment. Frances Gage, writing for the *New York Tribune,* proudly reported that on November 7, the anniversary of the Battle of Port Royal, "the first company of the First South Carolina Regiment was sworn into the service of the United States. Do not say that truth and justice have made no progress in the last twelve months."[7]

Saxton, who understood the importance of his new regiment, realized that he needed as its commander an individual of national prominence who fully supported his Port Royal program. After consulting with friends, Saxton decided to offer command to the radical abolitionist and Unitarian minister Thomas Wentworth Higginson. On November 5, 1862, Saxton sent a letter to Higginson, who at that time was serving as a captain in the 51st Massachusetts, a unit forming at Camp Wool in Worcester, Massachusetts. Intrigued by the offer but not confident that the unit would be more than a mere "plantation-guard," Higginson took leave from his regiment and journeyed to Port Royal. On November 24 he arrived at Beaufort and after meeting with General Saxton, who promised Higginson "Carte blanche," accepted command.

Higginson, who was one month shy of his fortieth birthday when he joined his soldiers, was one of the nation's most accomplished intellectuals, a title with which he readily agreed. He had entered Harvard at fourteen. After graduating in 1841, he went on to attend Harvard Divinity School. Guided by the philosophy and religious tenets of Theodore Parker and Ralph Waldo Emerson, Higginson represented the radical edge of Unitarianism that included transcendentalism and extreme political and social activism. Such views led to his removal as minister of the First Religious Society, Unitarian, in Newburyport, Massachusetts, but he later accepted a call from Worcester's Free Church, where he remained until resigning to join the army. Besides his ministerial duties, Higginson also wrote poetry, published articles in the *Atlantic Monthly,* studied nature, and mentored Emily Dickinson and other aspiring writers and poets. A militant abolitionist, he believed that slaves should rise up and free themselves. He considered John Brown an "enthusiastic fanatic," and as a member of the "Secret Six," a group of abolitionists, financially backed John Brown's planned operations in the Allegany Mountains.

After Brown was captured at Harpers Ferry, Higginson made arrangements with Kansas partisan James Montgomery to free Brown and his followers, but bad weather foiled the attempt.[8]

Higginson considered raising a regiment in late 1861, and when this attempt failed, he eventually resigned his ministry and enlisted in the fall of 1862 as a captain in the 51st Massachusetts. After the call from Saxton and his arrival at Port Royal, Higginson soon realized that he was in a position to confirm his belief in the equality of humanity. The new colonel viewed his work as both military and philanthropic in nature. He felt that the outcome of the war and the destiny of the Negro race might well rest on the performance of African American troops. He immediately requested that his friends, the brothers Dr. Seth Rogers and Captain James Rogers, come to Port Royal, the former to serve as regimental surgeon and the latter as a company commander. Immediately, Higginson went to work drilling his men and readying them for combat. In time he had his soldiers discard what he called the "intolerable" red trousers. At the same time, the missionaries worked closely with Higginson's regiment, setting up a school near their campground. Colonel Higginson was very proud of his unit and called his men natural transcendentalists.[9]

At times Higginson's military duties blended into what seemed an anthropological and sociological study. Both the colonel and Surgeon Rogers carefully recorded their experiences with the black soldiers. Higginson found camp life at the Smith Plantation above the Beaufort River to be a wonderfully strange sensation. All his officers were volunteers, and together they were tasked with suddenly transforming eight hundred former slaves into soldiers. Higginson wrote that the men represented a race that was "affectionate, enthusiastic, grotesque and dramatic beyond all others."[10]

Dr. Seth Rogers wrote about the regiment's top enlisted soldiers, Robert Sutton and Prince Rivers. He described Sutton as "simple, unaffected and dignified without the slightest touch of haughtiness. Voice, low, soft and flooding, as if his thoughts were choking him. He is tall straight and brawny muscled. His face is all of Africa in feeling and in control of expression. By this I do not mean cunning, but manly control. He seems to be knightly. . . . He ought to be a leader, a general, instead of a corporal." About Prince Rivers, Seth Rogers wrote, "He is agile and fleet, like a deer, in his speed and like a panther in his tread. His features are not very African and his eye is so bright that it must 'shine at night, when de moon go away.' His manners are not surpassed on this globe."[11]

The recruits took to drill easily and were eager, serious, and active students, much more so than the soldiers Higginson had trained from the 51st Massachusetts. But when released from duty, the men took on a completely different character. At night they would gather around fires under the live oaks, telling stories and singing hymns and martial songs. One of their favorites, the regiment's marching song, "John Brown's Body," was sung with a verse of "We'll beat Beauregard on de clare battlefield." Men would recite prayers to their comrades, including one that declared: "Let me lib wid de musket in one hand and de Bible in de oder—dat if I die at de muzzle of de musket, die in de water, die in de land, I may know I hab de blessed Jesus in my hand, and hab no fear."

Every night somewhere in camp a religious ceremony would occur known as a "shout," in which every man involved would writhe and shuffle as they "raised something spiritual." Higginson reported that the men were drawn to the singing and dancing as if by "an irresistible necessity," which almost always sounded in the evening air. He wrote that

> men singing at the top of their voices, in one of their quaint, monotonous, endless, negro-Methodist chants, with obscure syllables recurring constantly, and slight variations interwoven, all accompanied with a regular drumming of the feet and clapping of the hands like castanets. Then the excitement spreads:... men begin to quiver and dance, others join, a circle forms, winding monotonously round someone in the center; some 'heel and toe' tumultuously, others merely tremble and stagger on, others stoop and rise, others whirl, others caper sideways, all keep steadily circling like dervishes; spectators applaud special strokes of skill;... the circle enlarges, louder grows the singing, rousing shouts of encouragement come in, half bacchanalian, half devout, 'Wake 'em, brudder!' 'Stan' up to 'em, brudder!'—and still the ceaseless drumming and clapping, in perfect cadence, goes steadily on. Suddenly there comes a sort of snap, and the spell breaks, amid general sighing and laughter.[12]

Higginson referred to his men as "Ethiopians," and "Maroons." Most came from South Carolina, but many hailed from Georgia and Florida. He found them to have virtually no vices and that "scarcely a white regiment in the army shows so little swearing." The men, according to the colonel, loved, besides their shouts, three things: tobacco, sugar, and home. On Sundays the soldiers attended services held by the regimental chaplain, James H. Fowler, a white, Dartmouth College– and Harvard Divinity School–educated Unitarian minister who, armed with pistols and a Ballard rifle, would join the black soldiers on scouts, causing some to question his role as chaplain, calling him the "fightingest more Yankee I eber see in all my days." Yet, as Higginson noted, on Sundays Chaplain Fowler "commanded the respect and attention of all."[13]

On October 20, two days after Saxton issued his general order for the formation of the 1st South Carolina, the steamer *Ericsson* arrived at Port Royal. On board were three individuals— Dr. William Henry Brisbane, Judge Abram D. Smith, and Judge William E. Wording—who would have more influence on the future of the Beaufort District than any other wartime arrivals. The three men were U.S. tax commissioners. They had come to South Carolina to enforce a provision of the Direct Tax of August 5, 1861. The full title of the bill was: "An act to provide increased revenue from imports, to pay interest on the public debt, and for other purposes." It was initiated to provide the United States government with needed money to prosecute the war. Among its sections was one that established the nation's first income tax and, most important for the Beaufort District, a provision for a direct property tax of $20 million to be levied upon lands and houses and apportioned among the states and territories. If states did not wish to burden their citizens, they could assume the tax, paying it from general state revenue. Only Delaware and the Territory of Colorado passed the tax on to their citizens. Initially there was no provision for its collection in the rebellious states, but Congress extended the tax by passing the Statute of June 7, 1862, which allowed tax commissioners to collect it in insurrectionary districts. South Carolina's portion was set at $363,570. The allocated tax for the occupied Beaufort District parishes of St. Helena and St. Luke was $11,911.04.

Though later claimed to be punitive, the act was not. Once the amount of taxes was determined by rates of 4 percent of value on town lots and 2 percent of value on rural property, notification of the amount due would be placed in local newspapers. Landowners had sixty days to pay the tax and had to do so in person. If the tax was not paid within the allotted time, a 50 percent penalty was charged. The landowners were then given two months to pay the tax and the resulting penalties. If still not paid, the government foreclosed upon the property, and it was forfeited to the United States. The land could then be retained for use by the government or sold at auction. If the land was sold, a landowner could still regain his property in the next sixty days by paying the tax, all additional penalties, and swearing allegiance to the United States Constitution. In each case, payment had to be made by the property owner, and here was the rub: in the sea islands the vast majority of property owners had fled inland, and even if they wished to pay their taxes, Confederate regulations threatened seizure of their assets should they enter into any intercourse with the United States. The exiled property owners were damned from any attempt to retain their land and homes.[14]

To enforce the collection in the insurrectionary districts, the secretary of the treasury appointed boards consisting of three tax commissioners. For South Carolina, Secretary Chase named Brisbane, Smith, and Wording. Two of the three had connections to South Carolina. William Henry Brisbane, born in the upper regions of St. Peter's Parish, had been a wealthy slave owner, a medical doctor, and a popular Baptist minister. He initially believed slavery a positive good, but in 1835 he read Dr. Frances Wayland's *Elements of Moral Science* and became convinced that slavery was a sin. His conversion to abolitionism forced him to sell his slaves and flee the Beaufort District. Going to Cincinnati, he became closely associated with antislavery leaders, including Salmon Chase. Brisbane was eventually able to return to the Beaufort District, repurchase and free his slaves, and take them to Ohio, where Chase signed the manumission papers. While in Cincinnati, Brisbane became involved with the Underground Railroad and worked to persuade fellow southerners to give up the institution. He later moved to Wisconsin, where he continued his campaign against slavery. At the start of the war, he became the chaplain of the 2nd Wisconsin Cavalry. Then, in 1862 Secretary Chase appointed the sixty-six-year-old Brisbane chairman of the U.S. Direct Tax Commission for South Carolina.[15]

William E. Wording, a sixty-year-old native of Castine, Maine, and a graduate of Waterville College, taught Greek and Latin at the New Hampton Library and Theological Institution until 1841, when he became the principal of the Cheraw Academy in Cheraw, South Carolina. While there he began reading law in the office of McKee and Inglis and eventually practiced law in Columbia and Charleston. In 1847 he moved to Racine, Wisconsin, where he continued his law practice and served two terms as judge of the Racine County Court before being appointed in July 1862 as a direct tax commissioner for South Carolina.[16]

Abram D. Smith, the third member of the commission, had been born in New York and read law in Sackets Harbor. In 1836 he and his family moved to Cleveland, Ohio. He served on the city's council, became involved with the abolitionist movement, and developed an interest in phrenology. He also joined the Hunter's Lodge, a secret society dedicated to the removal of British rule in Canada. In 1838 the Hunter's Lodge elected Smith as the president of the Republic of Canada; however, he never assumed his post, as invasions failed and the society soon faded into obscurity. Smith, who had a drinking problem, moved to Wisconsin, where he gave lectures on temperance, practiced law, and entered into politics as a Democrat. In 1852 he won election to the state supreme court.

While serving on the court, he ruled on a case centered on Sherman Booth, who had led a mob that freed Joshua Glover, an escaped slave from the Racine jail. Glover, who had been retaken by his master and U.S. marshals acting under the authority of the Fugitive Slave Act, eventually made his way to Canada. His savior, Booth, was placed on trial for aiding a fugitive slave. In the subsequent court case, Smith ruled the Fugitive Slave Act unconstitutional and ordered Booth released. The entire Wisconsin Supreme Court ultimately upheld Smith's ruling; as a result, Wisconsin became the only state to declare the act unconstitutional.

Shortly after this, Smith became embroiled in a scandal when he and other state leaders were accused of accepting bribes to assist the construction of the La Crosse and Milwaukee Railroad. Though Smith maintained his innocence, his political career ended. He did not seek reelection to the court, and though suggested for other statewide offices, he instead joined the Republican Party and operated the antislavery newspaper the *Milwaukee Free Democrat*.

Active in Wisconsin Republican affairs, Smith became a close associate of Senator James R. Doolittle, the state's senior senator. With Doolittle, Smith helped the senator draft the initial legislation for the Direct Tax Act, and when the opportunity arose, Doolittle named him as a South Carolina tax commissioner.[17]

At Port Royal the three commissioners from Wisconsin eventually took up residence in the Edmund Rhett House, where they compiled a tax roll from census lists and old tax ledgers. Army surveyors drew up maps and the commissioners calculated the tax. Notices went out in December 1862. Only a handful of property owners paid their taxes, including six free blacks and Edward Pritchard, David Thompson, Frederick Eustis, John Flyer, and Richard Fuller (by Reverend Peck). Foreclosure proceedings went forward on the remaining property, and the first tax sale was scheduled for February 1863.[18]

Besides the tax commissioners, other important individuals came to Port Royal, among them Dr. Esther Hill Hawks and her husband, Dr. John Milton Hawks. The two were ardent abolitionists, and in April 1862, under the auspices of the New York National Freedman's Relief Association, Dr. John Milton Hawks arrived at Port Royal and was initially assigned to Otter and Edisto islands, serving as a doctor, teacher, and superintendent. In July 1862 he was placed in charge of a contraband hospital in Beaufort; then in October he joined General Saxton's staff as an acting assistant surgeon before being appointed assistant surgeon of the 1st South Carolina.

Esther Hawks, an 1857 graduate of the New England Female Medical College in Boston, had initially remained in Manchester, New Hampshire, with her active medical practice. Kept informed by her husband's detailed and impassioned letters, she also gained an appointment to Port Royal through the National Freedman's Aid Association, arriving at Beaufort on October 16, 1862. She was quartered in the Ledbetter House with Dr. Henry K. Durant, the department's medical director and his family. Though the twenty-nine-year-old Hawks was an experienced doctor, the military did not allowed her to practice her profession, and she was initially assigned to teach in one of Beaufort's schools for contraband children.[19]

Hawks described the school, which was located in a one-room praise house near the Ledbetter House:

There are about 300 pupils, and only two teachers—one at either end of the large room, surrounded by a crowd of children, hearing them read one at a time, while the noise and din of voices made such an uproar that it was impossible to hear oneself think! These teachers are to go to one of the Islands and I am to take charge of this school. For two weeks I struggled with the problem of how to make one teacher do the work of six and was then obliged to give up, not because I had exhausted my resources, but for the time being my stock of articulate speech had become exhausted, and you may try to imagine the effect of a whisper on a class of 300, who were studying aloud![20]

Shortly after Esther Hawks took up residence with Dr. Durant, another teacher, Charlotte "Lottie" Forten, arrived at Beaufort. She was a member of a prominent Philadelphia free black family that had been emancipated for four generations. At the age of sixteen, her father sent her to an integrated high school in Salem, Massachusetts, where she excelled and gained a reputation as a poetess. After graduation she accepted a teaching position at a Salem grammar school. While living in Salem, she became immersed in the region's antislavery movement and met William Lloyd Garrison and Wendell Phillips, as well as becoming a close friend of John Greenleaf Whittier. Between 1856 and 1860, illness forced her four times to give up her teaching position and return to Philadelphia. In one attempt to regain her health, she visited Dr. Seth Rogers's hydropathic clinic in Worcester.

A dedicated abolitionist, Lottie fervently desired to help her race, and in the summer of 1862, while teaching in Salem, John Whittier suggested that she go to Port Royal to teach contraband children. She agreed and applied for a position initially with the Boston Educational Commission; however, with no slots available, she was eventually accepted by the Philadelphia-based Port Royal Relief Association. In late October 1862 she traveled to New York and with her friend Elizabeth "Lizzie" Hunn boarded the steamer *United States,* which on October 28 arrived at Hilton Head. She then transferred to a transport steamer that took her to Beaufort. On board she met General Saxton, whom she found to be "courteous and affable." At Beaufort, Forten was taken to Mansfield French's residence at the Thomas Fuller House. She was introduced to Reuben Tomlinson and Frances Gage. A boat, rowed by contrabands singing "Roll Jordan Roll," ferried her to St. Helena Island, where Laura Towne conveyed her to the Oaks Plantation. Her long day, which she likened to a "strange wild dream," finally ended.

The next day Forten was first taken to the Brick Church, where she would serve as a teacher at the school, now termed Penn School. The institution, whose first instructor had been Ellen "Nelly" Winsor, had started at the Oaks Plantation. Winsor, who had been joined at the Oaks by Laura

Towne and Ellen Murray, had given up her teaching duties to become, at the age of twenty-three, the superintendent of the Eustis Plantation. With Winsor's departure Murray became the school's principal instructor, assisted by Towne and now Forten. In a short time Forten took up residence at Oaklands Plantation. She so loved her new duties and her young students that she requested her friend John Greenleaf Whittier to "write a little Christmas hymn for our children to sing."[21]

Forten's arrival coincided with a shifting of priorities for the Port Royal Experiment. Edward Pierce's initial program had proven that former slaves could readily adapt to a wage-based economy and had an aptitude for learning. Saxton, building on Pierce's premise, continued the operation. Freedom, promised by Lincoln's Emancipation Proclamation, would soon be a reality. It was also decided that on the same day that the Proclamation took effect, the 1st South Carolina would be officially mustered into service. The regiment was to be the first of many organized by Saxton. But the enlistment of black soldiers would severely reduce the number of top field hands required for the growing of cotton on the sea islands and end any chance of the experiment to be self-sustaining, much less profitable. Saxton, however, believed that proficiency as soldiers was the next step in their emergence from slavery.

In the weeks leading up to the New Year, Saxton and his staff proposed numerous activities. A day of Thanksgiving on November 27 would be observed; Christmas celebrations were planned; and a dual ceremony celebrating the Emancipation Proclamation and the mustering in of the 1st South Carolina was scheduled at Camp Saxton at the Smith Plantation.

The days passed slowly for Saxton, the missionaries and the contrabands. To them the preliminary proclamation was a far-from-perfect document. It was a wartime measure and only enforceable while the seceded states remained out of the Union. Throughout the war the Lincoln government operated on a fine line, prosecuting the conflict as both an international and domestic conflict. But other than enforcing a blockade and following certain international protocols, the United States defined the conflict as a "War of Rebellion," the official name given to the nation's greatest conflagration. By declaring the seceded states in rebellion, and therefore outside the protection of the Constitution, Lincoln and Congress were able to advance acts that otherwise would be unconstitutional. The Emancipation Proclamation applied only to states in rebellion, not to slave states still in the Union and not to areas in Tennessee, Louisiana, Arkansas, and Virginia where the president recognized loyal governments.

On the surface, Lincoln's proclamation promised freedom, but it also had caveats. It called upon all slave states, loyal or not, to free their slaves, either immediately or gradually, promising government financial aid and promoting colonization of the former slaves outside the United States. Lincoln had previously floated this project to the loyal slave states only to have it rejected, and there was no reason to expect them to accept it now. There did exist a slight hope that the rebellious states, faced with the immediate loss of their slaves with no compensation, would accept the proposal and return to the Union and the protection of the Constitution. The choice was theirs, and they had a hundred days—from September 22, 1862, to January 1, 1863—to make their decision.[22]

Some radical abolitionists attacked the proclamation as weak, or as a veiled bribe to bring back the seceded states. Many feared Lincoln would alter or rescind the proclamation before it went into effect. The latter possibility worried Saxton and his supporters in the sea islands, where the promise of freedom meant so much to the inhabitants. Though concerned, Saxton went ahead with plans and celebrations that would precede the January 1 ceremony, which would formally proclaim the "Jubilee of Freedom." Any thought that the announcement would induce the South to stop the conflict and seek reconciliation quickly ended when Jefferson Davis damned the proclamation, stating that it showed the "true nature" of the enemy. Davis employed Lincoln's proclamation to rally the South to increase its war effort.[23]

In the weeks leading up to January 1, Saxton carefully orchestrated events, making it perfectly clear to all, in the sea islands and elsewhere, that freedom was at hand. In early November the general issued a proclamation setting aside November 27 as "a day of public thanksgiving and praise," summoning all superintendents, teachers, and freedmen to gather in places of worship and "render praise and thanksgiving to almighty God" for the success that had attended the "great experiment of freedom and the rights of oppressed humanity, inaugurated in the Department of the South." Saxton also called for prayers for those still in bondage.

On the day of Thanksgiving, while the white soldiers were playing baseball, holding mock parades, pitching quoits, and dining on pork, rice pudding, and oyster pie while receiving a whiskey ration, Saxton and his minions gathered in churches and gave thanks. That morning at the Brick Church, most of the superintendents and teachers, along with numerous contrabands, assembled. Reverend Samuel D. Phillips, a man who, according to Laura Towne, was loved more by the freedmen children than any northerner, gave the sermon. Saxton then addressed the congregation, calling on the young men to enlist, relating how Robert Smalls had told the general that he was ready to give up the fifty dollars per week he made tending store in Beaufort to enlist in the new regiment. As he had told Saxton, "How can I expect to keep my freedom if I'm not willing to fight for it?" Frances Gage, who reminded the people how slaves in Saint Croix had risen up against their masters and declared their freedom, followed Saxton. She appealed to the mothers to send forth their sons, as she had done, to fight for freedom. Saxton made a final appeal for recruits before the service closed with the singing, with great spirit, of "Marching Along."[24]

At Camp Saxton, Higginson watched as his men celebrated Thanksgiving, reporting that "my young barbarians are all at play." Over the next few weeks, additional recruits arrived from the neighboring sea islands and scattered points along the South Carolina, Georgia, and Florida coast. The regiment soon numbered six hundred men. Families of the soldiers congregated near Camp Saxton. Among them was Susie Baker, a literate slave who early in the war had escaped to St. Simons Island, Georgia; there the fourteen-year-old established a school for the island's refugee community. Supplies were sent to the school from Port Royal, and on occasion Reverend French came to St. Simons and lectured at Baker's school. She married Edward King, who joined the 1st South Carolina and came to Camp Saxton, where she signed on as a regimental laundress.[25]

While drilling his soldiers, Higginson placed Chaplain Fowler in charge of preparing the January 1 ceremony. As the date neared, activities increased. On the evening before Christmas at the regiment's dress parade, Higginson read Saxton's "New Year's Greeting to the Colored People in the Department of the South":

> In accordance, as I believe, with the will of our Heavenly Father, and by direction of your great and good friend, whose name you are all familiar with, ABRAHAM LINCOLN, President of the United States, and Commander-in-Chief of the Army and Navy, on the 1st day of January, 1863, you will be declared 'forever free.'
>
> When in the course of human events there comes a day which is destined to be an everlasting beacon-light, marking a joyful era in the progress of a nation and the hopes of a people, it seems to be fitting that it should not pass unnoticed by those whose hopes it comes to brighten and to bless. Such a day to you is January 1, 1863. I therefore call upon all the colored people in this Department to assemble on that day at the Head-quarters of the First Regiment of South Carolina Volunteers, there to hear the President's Proclamation read, and to indulge in such manifestations of joy as may be called forth by the occasion. It is your duty to carry this good news to your brethren who are still in slavery. Let all your voices, like merry bells, join loud and clear in the grand chorus of liberty—'We are free,' 'We are free,'—until listening, you shall hear its echoes coming back from every cabin in the land,—'We are free,' 'we are free.'
>
> R. Saxton
Brig.-Gen. and Military Governor.[26]

To prepare for the celebration, Higginson received a directive to roast ten oxen. Tables for a thousand were set up in an oak grove adjacent to the camp. Molasses and tobacco were to be distributed. Higginson did worry about whether anyone could predict the time required to roast an ox, commenting that estimates varied from two to twenty-four hours. He also wondered how one would proffer a rare spare rib to an elegant lady, including Charlotte Forten.[27]

While Higginson prepared his encampment, special arrangements were started for Christmas. On December 21 Charlotte Forten received from Whittier, along with a photograph of the poet, a hymn to be sung to the tune "I Will Believe." Immediately Murray and Forten began teaching the piece to their schoolchildren. The song became the anthem of Penn School and its successor Penn Center.

> Oh, none in all the world before
> Were ever glad as we.
> We're free on Carolina's shore;
> We're all at home and free!
> Thou friend and helper of the poor,
> Who suffered for our sake,
> To open every prison door
> And every yoke to break
> Look down, O Savior, sweet and mild,
> To help us sing and pray;
> The hands that blessed the little child
> Upon our foreheads lay.
> To-day in all our fields of corn,
> No driver's whip we hear,
> The holy day that saw Thee born
> Was never half so dear.
> The very oaks are greener clad,
> The waters brighter smile,
> Oh, never shone a day so glad
> In sweet St. Helen's Isle
> For none in all the world before
> Were ever glad as we.
> We're free on Carolina shore
> We're all at home and free![28]

As their students learned Whittier's hymn, work began on decorating the Brick Church for Christmas. Evergreen letters spelled out, "His people are Free." On Christmas day, after gifts were distributed to the children, a service was held and the tunes "John Brown's Body," "Whittier's Hymn," "Sing oh Graveyard," and "Roll Jordon Roll" were performed. While the ceremony at the Brick Church was directed toward the youth, another service at the Beaufort Baptist Church targeted the older generation. Speaking from the pulpit to an audience of contrabands and soldiers, Reverend Peck read the preliminary Emancipation Proclamation. At its conclusion a call was made for three cheers, but Peck asked that all celebrations be held back for a week until the proclamation went into effect.

On New Year's Eve, Higginson had ten oxen roasted on "vast spits." He worried that there might not be enough meat, stating, "Never was seen such lean kine." He reported that it took three hours to cook one ox well done. Hard bread would be served, and to drink a concoction was made by combining a barrel of water with three gallons of molasses, half a pound of ginger, and a quart of vinegar. Saxton told Higginson to expect five thousand participants, who, combined with the soldiers and their camp followers, would produce a total of over six thousand celebrants.

Throughout the night the fires were kept smoldering and the beeves turned. At about 10:00 A.M. people began congregating, some walking, others coming on steamships to Camp Saxton's pier, a wooden dock built on and over the tabby walls of Fort Prince Frederick into the Beaufort River. Charlotte Forten, with her friend Lizzie Hunn and others, boarded the *Flora* at the Lady's Island ferry landing. The boat then went to Beaufort and picked up more passengers before proceeding up the river. On board with Forten were Reverend and Mrs. Peck and their daughters, as well as General Saxton's father. At the campsite they were taken by rowboat to the dock, where Forten's old friend Dr. Seth Rogers greeted her. With Rogers and others, Forten walked up the gentle riverbank to the camp, where she was introduced to Colonel Higginson. In a beautiful oak grove next to the regiment's camp stood a platform by a single oak tree. Forten was taken to the raised stage, where she joined other white dignitaries and the band from the 8th Maine Regiment. Higginson marched his men, still outfitted in their red trousers, near the platform, where they broke ranks, with some sitting and others standing, waiting for the ceremony to begin. Mixed in with the soldiers were numerous black women with "gay handkerchiefs on their heads & a sprinkling of men." Around them, encircling the group stood a cordon of officers and cavalrymen. Over all the assemblage, live oaks spread their moss-covered limbs, while in the distance one could glimpse the Beaufort River.

At 11:30 Chaplain Fowler opened the ceremony with a prayer. Tax Commissioner William H. Brisbane then came forward to read the proclamation. Brisbane, a Baptist minister and abolitionist who had been born in the Beaufort District and later forced to leave because of his antislavery views, was an appropriate choice.

The celebrants in the sea islands had stolen a march on the president. The proclamation as read by Brisbane was the preliminary proclamation, the one issued in September, which Lincoln had written and Secretary of State William Seward edited. Lincoln would not sign the final version of the proclamation until hours later, and it would not be transmitted over the telegraph until 8:00 P.M. Even so, the message was clear, especially to those to whom it meant the most: freedom had come; the jubilee was officially here. No matter what Lincoln crafted in his final version, which was quite different from the one read at Old Fort Plantation on the banks of the Beaufort River, the trumpet, from which there would be no retreat, had finally sounded.[29]

By the President of the United States of America
A PROCLAMATION

I, Abraham Lincoln, President of the United States of American, and Commander-in-Chief of the Army and Navy thereof, do hereby proclaim and declare that hereafter, as heretofore, the war will be prosecuted for the object of practically restoring the constitutional relation between the United States, and each of the states, and the people thereof, in which states that relation is, or may be suspended or disturbed.

That it is my purpose, upon the next meeting of Congress to again recommend the adoption of a practical measure tendering pecuniary aid to the free acceptance or rejection of all slave-states, so called, the people whereof may not then be in rebellion against the United States, and which states may then have voluntarily adopted, or thereafter may voluntarily adopt, immediate, or gradual abolishment of slavery within their respective limits; and that the effort to colonize persons of African descent with the consent upon this continent, or elsewhere, with the previously obtained consent of the governments existing there, will be continued.

That on the first day of January in the year of our Lord, one thousand eight hundred and sixty-three, all persons held as slaves within any state, or designated part of a state, the people whereof thenceforward, and forever free; and the executive government of the United States including the military and naval authority thereof will, recognize and maintain the freedom of such persons, and will do no act or acts to repress such persons, or any of them, in any efforts they may make for their actual freedom.

That the executive will, on the first day of January aforesaid, by proclamation, designate the States, and parts of states, if any, in which the people thereof respectively, shall then be in rebellion against the

United States; and the fact that any state, or the people thereof shall, on that day be, in good faith represented in the Congress of the United States, by members chosen thereto, at elections wherein a majority of the qualified voters of such state shall have participated, shall, in the absence of strong countervailing testimony, be deemed conclusive evidence that such state, and the people thereof, are not then in rebellion against the United States.

That attention is hereby called to an Act of Congress entitled "An Act to make an additional Article of War" approved March 13, 1862, and which act is in the words and figure following:

"Be it enacted by the Senate and House of Representatives of the United States of America in Congress assembled, That hereafter the following shall be promulgated as an additional article of war for the government of the Army of the United States, and shall be obeyed and observed as such:

Article-. All officers or persons in the military or naval services of the United States are prohibited from employing any of the forces under their respective commands for the purpose of returning fugitive from service or labor, who may have escaped from any persons to whom such service or labor is claimed to be due and any officer who shall be found guilty by a court martial of violating this article shall be dismissed from the service.

SEC.2. And be it further enacted, that this act shall take effect from and after its passage."

Also to the ninth and tenth sections of an act entitled "An Act to suppress Insurrection, to punish Treason and Rebellion, to seize and confiscate property of rebels, and for other purposes," approved July 17, 1862, and which sections are:

"SEC. 9. And be it further enacted, that all slaves of persons who shall hereafter be engaged in rebellion against the government of the United States, or who shall in any way give aid or comfort thereto, escaping from such persons and taking refuge within the lines of the army; and all slaves captured from such persons or deserted by them and coming under the control of the government of the United States; and all slaves of such persons found [or] being within any place occupied by rebel forces and afterwards occupied by the forces of the United States, shall be deemed captives of war, and shall be forever free of their servitude, and not again held as slaves.

"SEC. 10. And be it further enacted, That no slave escaping into any State, Territory, or the District of Columbia, from any other State, shall be delivered up, or in any way impeded or hindered of his liberty, except for crime, or some offence against the laws, unless the person claiming said fugitive shall first make oath that the person to whom the labor or service of such fugitive is alleged to be due is his lawful owner, and has not borne arms against the United States in the present rebellion, nor in any way given aid and comfort thereto; and no person engaged in the military or naval service of the United States shall, under any pretence whatever, assume to decide on the validity of the claim of any person to the service or labor of any other person, or surrender up any such person to the claimant, on pain of being dismissed from the service."

And I do hereby enjoin upon and order all persons engaged in the military and naval service of the United States to observe, obey, and enforce, within their respective spheres of service, the act and sections above recited.

And the executive will in due time recommend that all citizens of the United States who shall have remained loyal thereto throughout the rebellion, shall (upon the restoration of the constitutional relation between the United States, and their respective states, and people, if that relation shall have been suspended or disturbed) be compensated for all losses by acts of the United States, including the loss of slaves.

In witness whereof, I have hereunto set my hand and caused the seal of the United States to be affixed. Done at the City of Washington, this twenty-second day of September, in the year of our Lord, one thousand eight hundred and sixty two, and of the Independence of the United States the eighty seventh.

Abraham Lincoln[30]

Once Brisbane had returned to his seat on the platform, Professor John C. Zachos, the Greek adopted son of Samuel Gridley Howe, an Unitarian minister and superintendent of Parris Island, read an ode he had written for the occasion which was then sung by a choir. Then Colonel Higginson came forward to receive the regimental colors from Reverend French, who had obtained them, without Higginson's knowledge, from Dr. George B. Cheever's New York Church of the Puritans. Much to Higginson's displeasure, French had had his name as presenter "very conspicuously engraved on the standard." After French's short speech, Higginson took one set of the national colors, stepped to the edge of the stage, and waved the flag when "close beside the platform, a strong but rather cracked & elderly male voice, into which two women's voices immediately blended, singing as if by an impulse that can no more be quenched than the morning note of the song sparrow-the Hymn 'My country 'tis of thee Sweet land of Liberty.'"

The spontaneous singing was electric and overwhelming. To Higginson "it made all other words cheap, it seemed the choked voice of a race, at last unloosed; nothing could be more wonderfully unconscious; art could not have dreamed of a tribute to the day of jubilee that should be so affecting; history will not believe it." Higginson went on to add his own comments, and then, taking the national and colors, he handed them to two of his soldiers. Sergeant Prince Rivers received the silk flag while Corporal Robert Sutton accepted one made of bunting. The two color guards—Rivers from Beaufort, and Sutton from the area along the St. Mary's River in Georgia—addressed the gathering. Rivers spoke first, followed by Sutton, who reminded the crowd that most had relatives still in captivity and that if need be, the soldiers would die to free them. He ended by appealing to all to follow "their great Captain Jesus, who was never defeated." Once the color sergeants had finished, the 1st South Carolina sang "Marching Along."

General Saxton, amid loud cheers, gave a short speech. Next came Frances Gage, who spoke directly to the women. Lyman Stickney, the United States tax commissioner for Florida, followed. Stickney spoke to freedmen about their future as entrepreneurs and productive citizens. The final act was a quartet of whites, who sang a hymn composed by Henry G. Judd, superintendent for Port Royal Island. Then all joined the regiment in singing "John Brown's Body."

The crowd dispersed and, as the band continued to play, enjoyed their meal of roasted oxen. Charlotte Forten dined at the camp with Dr. Seth Rogers and other missionaries and officers. During the meal Forten recited Whittier's hymn, after which Higginson and Dr. Rogers escorted her about the camp and introduced her to Doctors John and Esther Hawks. The band, having finished playing, began to pack up their instruments when a member of the 1st South Carolina asked Higginson to have them play "Dixie." The colonel made the request, but the leader of the Maine musicians replied that too many of the bandsmen had left. He promised they would play it the next time, however.

The regiment then performed a dress parade, impressing the crowd with their precision. By nightfall the paddle-wheel steamer *Flora* began transporting the revelers back to Beaufort and the island landings. Forten stayed on in the moonlight amid the campfires and conversed with Chaplain Fowler, Dr. Rogers, and Colonel Higginson. She was invited to stay and witness the soldiers put on a shout and a grand jubilee, but she declined and, with Lizzie Hunn, boarded the now returned *Flora*. On the trip back to the ferry landing, the two women sang "John Brown's Body," "Whittier's Hymn," and "My Country 'Tis of Thee."

While Forten stayed at the campsite, Laura Towne, who had arrived just before the ceremony ended, joined a party at General Saxton's headquarters. At dinner Towne was seated next to the general. Afterwards, while she conversed with Frances Gage, Saxton and other officers decked out Nelly Winsor and Elizabeth "Tilly" Thompson with swords and scarves. Towne noted that Saxton bequeathed his "yellow scarf to Tilly, his red one to Nelly, thus letting Miss Thompson rank Nelly." Though the thirty-six-year-old Saxton would soon be married by Reverend French to the eighteen-year-old Thompson in St. Helena Episcopal Church, on this night the general chose Miss Towne to lead the cotillion, opening the evening's dance that ended the day that permanently altered life in the Beaufort District.[31]

Not everyone in the sea islands had gathered at Camp Saxton on New Year's. Du Pont had spent the day quietly, sharing a case of champagne with his officers, while Federal regiments on Hilton Head and around Beaufort enjoyed special meals and played baseball. Reverend French orchestrated a reduced version of the ceremony on January 4 at the Brick Church, where he, along with Generals Saxton and Seymour, addressed the congregation. Though Saxton was confident that the president had signed the Emancipation Proclamation, others, including Du Pont, watched anxiously for affirmation.[32]

It was not until January 10 that the final version of the Emancipation Proclamation arrived. Its wording was different from the document read at Camp Saxton, as it clearly designated the regions not affected by the proclamation.

> By the President of the United States of America:
> A Proclamation.
>
> Whereas, on the twenty-second day of September, in the year of our Lord one thousand eight hundred and sixty-two, a proclamation was issued by the President of the United States, containing, among other things, the following, to wit:
> "That on the first day of January, in the year of our Lord one thousand eight hundred and sixty-three, all persons held as slaves within any State or designated part of a State, the people whereof shall then be in rebellion against the United States, shall be then, thenceforward, and forever free; and the Executive Government of the United States, including the military and naval authority thereof, will recognize and maintain the freedom of such persons, and will do no act or acts to repress such persons, or any of them, in any efforts they may make for their actual freedom.
> "That the Executive will, on the first day of January aforesaid, by proclamation, designate the States and parts of States, if any, in which the people thereof, respectively, shall then be in rebellion against the United States; and the fact that any State, or the people thereof, shall on that day be, in good faith, represented in the Congress of the United

States by members chosen thereto at elections wherein a majority of the qualified voters of such State shall have participated, shall, in the absence of strong countervailing testimony, be deemed conclusive evidence that such State, and the people thereof, are not then in rebellion against the United States."

Now, therefore I, Abraham Lincoln, President of the United States, by virtue of the power in me vested as Commander-in-Chief, of the Army and Navy of the United States in time of actual armed rebellion against the authority and government of the United States, and as a fit and necessary war measure for suppressing said rebellion, do, on this first day of January, in the year of our Lord one thousand eight hundred and sixty-three, and in accordance with my purpose so to do publicly proclaimed for the full period of one hundred days, from the day first above mentioned, order and designate as the States and parts of States wherein the people thereof respectively, are this day in rebellion against the United States, the following, to wit:

Arkansas, Texas, Louisiana, (except the Parishes of St. Bernard, Plaquemines, Jefferson, St. John, St. Charles, St. James Ascension, Assumption, Terrebonne, Lafourche, St. Mary, St. Martin, and Orleans, including the City of New Orleans) Mississippi, Alabama, Florida, Georgia, South Carolina, North Carolina, and Virginia, (except the forty-eight counties designated as West Virginia, and also the counties of Berkley, Accomac, Northampton, Elizabeth City, York, Princess Ann, and Norfolk, including the cities of Norfolk and Portsmouth, (]) and which excepted parts, are for the present, left precisely as if this proclamation were not issued.

And by virtue of the power, and for the purpose aforesaid, I do order and declare that all persons held as slaves within said designated States, and parts of States, are, and henceforward shall be free; and that the Executive government of the United States, including the military and naval authorities thereof, will recognize and maintain the freedom of said persons.

And I hereby enjoin upon the people so declared to be free to abstain from all violence, unless in necessary self-defence; and I recommend to them that, in all cases when allowed, they labor faithfully for reasonable wages.

And I further declare and make known, that such persons of suitable condition, will be received into the armed service of the United States to garrison forts, positions, stations, and other places, and to man vessels of all sorts in said service.

And upon this act, sincerely believed to be an act of justice, warranted by the Constitution, upon military necessity, I invoke the considerate judgment of mankind, and the gracious favor of Almighty God.

In witness whereof, I have hereunto set my hand and caused the seal of the United States to be affixed.

Done at the City of Washington, this first day of January, in the year of our Lord one thousand eight hundred and sixty three, and of the Independence of the United States of America the eighty-seventh.

By the President: ABRAHAM LINCOLN
WILLIAM H. SEWARD, Secretary of State.[33]

The next day, during Sunday parade at Camp Saxton, the document in its final rendition was read to the soldiers of the 1st South Carolina. As Higginson noted, "The words themselves did not stir them so much, for they had been told so often they were free, especially on Jan. 1." Chaplain Fowler and Colonel Higginson addressed the soldiers, impressing upon them "how great a thing it was." Higginson then called on the men to raise their hands and "pledge themselves to be faithful to those still in bondage," which all but one man did, and he was shoved about and termed a coward by his indignant comrades as they returned to their tents.[34]

A wartime measure, the Emancipation Proclamation could have become moot once the war was over. To head this off, abolitionists, backed by Lincoln and his administration, started a movement in December 1863 to pass a constitutional amendment to end slavery, which eventually became the Thirteenth Amendment. But such machinations in Washington had little immediate effect in the sea islands, where new campaigns were being organized that would continue the march of freedom and expand the use of black soldiers. As Dr. Seth Rogers wrote, "South Carolina is getting a simultaneous doctoring of body and soul."[35]

While the movement to make emancipation permanent began, many at Port Royal believed it was time for the former slaves to take the next step toward social and economic independence. John Zachos, the general superintendent, educator, and doctor on Parris Island, reported in mid-January that his wards had made remarkable progress since his arrival the previous spring. Of the island's 330 inhabitants, Zachos reported that only about 150 were capable for planting crops. With little or no encouragement and only minimum pay from the government, they cultivated 220 acres of cotton, 300 acres of corn, 40 acres of sweet potatoes, and 20 acres of rice and other garden products. The inhabitants attended church regularly and over 100 adults and children attended school. Zachos believed that as the government increased wages in the new year, the system of free labor would take hold with the freedmen, rapidly improving their conditions.[36]

Saxton agreed with Zachos's assessment. He also believed that too much government assistance could undermine the freedmen's progress to self-sufficiency. On January 30 he directed his district superintendents to cease distributing rations from the commissariat to all freedmen. Instead, only the truly destitute and unfortunate would receive food. The superintendents were to make the choice about who would receive help, but if individuals were found to be shirkers, no rations would be given. Freedmen now had a choice to find work or join the navy or army.[37]

While many found employment with the various military bureaus, others enlisted in Higginson's 1st South Carolina. By January 19 the colonel was ready to parade his regiment to Beaufort and back. As Higginson, who had told the men not to be staring about, described the scene: "To look back on twenty broad double ranks of men (for we marched by platoons) every polished musket with a black face at the side of it, every face steady to the front, marching on into the future; it was magnificent." As the regiment marched the three miles from Camp Saxton to Beaufort, they sang "John Brown's Body," "Marching Along," and others "of their own particular songs." One soldier commented that "every step was worth half a dollar." At the edge of the town the band of the 8th Maine joined them and led the regiment through the city. Sergeant Prince Rivers, the regimental color bearer, later declared, "When dat band began to play in front of us Good Heaven, I left dis world altogether." As they moved through the town's streets, crowds gathered to watch. Some of the white soldiers had come to jeer, but most had to admit the regiment performed well. A black recruit commented that the white soldiers were astonished by the unit's precision, and "De buckra soldiers look like a man who done stole a sheep." At the town's parade field, bounded by Bay, Church, Boundary, and Bladen Streets, the regiment formed squares and reduced them and performed other drills. Then they returned to Camp Saxton marching in a column of fours, singing with their weapons at support arms.[38]

Higginson had hoped that General Hunter, who had returned to the department, would be present to view his regiment's parade and drill, but the general had been unable to attend. Hunter and his staff, including his adjutant, Major Charles Halpine, had arrived at Port Royal Sound on January 18, aboard the SS *Arago*. Forts Seward and Welles fired salutes. Once the *Arago* docked at the Hilton Head wharf, Brigadier General Alfred Terry and Fleet Captain John Rodgers came aboard to meet the general, who now sported a dyed moustache and a full dark brown wig, which he never quite properly aligned on his head. Appearances aside, Hunter immediately threw himself into his work. He named Brigadier General Seymour his chief of staff, and his initial general orders enjoined his officers and men to do all possible to ensure the success of the upcoming expedition. Though he had been unable to view Higginson's regiment during its parade through Beaufort, he and his staff, with General Saxton, did come to its camp on the twenty-first, when Hunter viewed battalion drill and addressed the men, promising them pay, better arms, and blue trousers. Higginson, though pleased with the visit, was not overly impressed by Hunter, writing that "he seems like a kindly elderly gentleman in uniform . . . yet I fancy him to be an abstract meditative thinker."[39]

Hunter's arrival also ended Brigadier General Brannan's tenure at Port Royal. On January 23 Brannan left aboard the SS *Osage* to subsequent commands in the Western Theater. His departure coincided with the arrival of Colonel James Montgomery, who came into the sound on the SS *Star of the South* as Brannan sailed away. The exchange of the two officers foreshadowed a dramatic change to the Beaufort District. Brannan, an old-school regular officer, followed established rules of war and did not favor the use of black troops. Montgomery came from a different background and believed in a different type of warfare. Before the conflict, the forty-eight-year-old native of Ashtabula County, Ohio, had led antislavery partisans in Kansas, occasionally cooperating with John Brown. When Brown had been captured at Harpers Ferry, it was Montgomery to whom Higginson had turned to lead a rescue mission, but bad weather terminated the attempt. At the start of the conflict, Montgomery served as the colonel of the 3rd Kansas Infantry Regiment, which he led in ruthless strikes against Missouri slaveholders until given command of the embryonic 2nd South Carolina.

Shortly after Montgomery's arrival, Higginson and his regiment steamed to St. Simons Island, Georgia, for their first operation as an official United States Regiment. Montgomery, whose regimental campsite was next to Higginson's at Camp Saxton, went to Key West to enlist his first soldiers. Hunter had great plans for his black soldiers, but as he and Saxton oversaw their initial recruitment and operations, the department head also had to prepare for combined operations with Rear Admiral Du Pont and Major General Foster against Charleston.[40]

Chapter 8

Initial Tax Sales and the *George Washington*

"The poor negro is fighting for liberty in its truest sense"

While Hunter waited for Foster and his soldiers to arrive from North Carolina, the initial vessels for Du Pont's ironclad attack squadron began arriving at Port Royal. On January 18 the ironclad frigate *New Ironsides* steamed into the harbor, passing the *Wabash* and anchoring in line with the other warships. Du Pont liked the looks of the 230-foot, 4,120-ton, 18-gun *New Ironsides*, an imposing vessel whose lines were similar to those of a wooden warship. The next day the monitor *Montauk*, towed by the *James Adger*, approached the harbor. Captained by John Worden, commander of the original *Monitor* in her fight against the *Virginia*, the *Montauk* came into the sound under her own power. Her passage by the flagship was much different from that of the *New Ironsides*. As described by Du Pont: "Such a sight I never saw. She was literally a' fleur d'eau. In the relatively quiet waters of Port Royal harbor, the spray was flying over her deck; the crew huddled together under the lee of the turret looked like drowned rats."[1]

On the twenty-first Du Pont happily reported that the monitor *Passaic*, captained by his good friend Percival Drayton, arrived at Port Royal having survived the same storm off Cape Hatteras that had sunk the *Monitor*. Drayton, who had made important alterations to the *Passaic* to make her more "nautical," gave Du Pont a full account of his harrowing voyage, causing Du Pont to comment that "iron crew and officers" would have to be invented to man the monitors at sea.[2]

The arrival of the ironclads came none too soon for Du Pont. Though he still fretted over their ability to overcome the Confederate defenses at Charleston, he also had to worry about the Confederate ironclad squadrons at Savannah and Charleston. On January 30, 1863, before he could place any of his iron warships off Charleston, two enemy iron-plated rams attacked his blockaders. Two of Du Pont's gunboats were damaged, but despite Confederate claims to the contrary, the blockade remained in place. To stop any new attacks, Du Pont sent the *New Ironsides* to Charleston, and monitors were stationed in the waterways off Savannah.[3]

While Du Pont moved to counter threats from Confederate warships and anxiously awaited additional ironclads, transports carrying the lead elements of two divisions from Major General Foster's Eighteenth Corps came into Port Royal Sound. As one New York soldier wrote, "We are in the pestilential state of South Carolina—the viper from which has emanated the rank poison of secession that now has been distilled into the veins of every state in the once lovely South."[4]

By early February the waters of the sound resembled a floating city as more and more transports arriving from North Carolina mingled with the ironclads, gunboats, and supply ships. Some units were taken to Beaufort, a town they considered prettier than the Beaufort they had left in North Carolina. Men explored the city, bought peanuts from Mr. Allen, "an elderly looking man of medium height, grayish hair and [who] wears gold spectacles," who was reputed to be the last white man in Beaufort. They inspected the *Planter* and reported that Robert Smalls operated a sailboat in the harbor. The soldiers saw the town as a place of wealth and were amazed that its residents had "exiled themselves from home for the purpose of breaking up a Union that southern Statesmen labored to establish."[5]

While some soldiers were able to explore their new home, the majority of Foster's command remained on their transports in the sound, anchored off St. Helena Island. Foster and staff arrived on February 2 aboard the steamer *S. R. Spaulding*. At first he seemed despondent, not sure of his role, but over the next week, he, along with his staff and Hunter, examined points along the Georgia coast; then, without Hunter, Foster carried out a reconnaissance of Charleston's defenses before going north on the *Arago*. By February 13 Foster was back in his own department at Fort Monroe, Virginia, securing additional cannons and artillerymen. Foster envisioned himself and Hunter as cocommanders, leading their men against Charleston. But Foster had misread the languid Hunter, who, as Foster's senior in rank and the department commander, expected Foster to show respect and deference. As one soldier from the 3rd New Hampshire put it, Foster and Hunter "don't mix worth a cent."[6]

Before leaving Port Royal, Foster had directed his second in command, Brigadier General Henry M. Naglee, to maintain the soldiers from North Carolina as a "distinct command." When Hunter tried to assert authority over Naglee, the latter refused, citing Foster's instructions. Hunter considered this insubordinate, treacherous, and likely to excite mutiny. He informed General Halleck that should Foster return, he would arrest him. Halleck attempted to mediate, but the damage had been done. Foster did not return to Port Royal, and Hunter eventually assumed command of the troops from North Carolina.[7]

With the army in disarray, it fell to Du Pont to take the lead in the movement against Charleston. The responsibility weighed on him as he assayed the ability of his ironclads. On one occasion he took the monitor *Patapsco* up the Broad River, which Du Pont termed "a noble sheet of water," to test the vessel's steering and guns. Among those on board were Generals Hunter and

Seymour as well as naval officers John Rodgers, Christopher Raymond Rodgers, and John Downes, who watched as the gun crews fired their 11-inch Dahlgren and 8-inch Parrott rifle over the river. But even with the monitor's impressive performance, the rear admiral remained troubled. He did not question the ability of his monitors in ship-to-ship combat, but he doubted their ability to take on fortifications. After testing them against the earthen Fort McAllister outside Savannah, he commented to a fellow officer that they were formidable vessels—better than he expected—"but something always breaks." He also worried over reports concerning Charleston's improving defenses. Du Pont described Charleston Harbor as a "porcupine hide with quills turned outside in and sewed up at one end." Others among his command considered Charleston to be the best-defended seaport in the world. Adding to their concerns were rumors about the Confederate explosive devices termed torpedoes.[8]

The monitors had been built to withstand concentrated artillery fire; however, because of their heavy armor and low freeboard, they could become death traps if a torpedo ruptured their hull. An explosion below the waterline would cause immediate flooding, forcing the monitor captain to run his ship aground or risk sinking. If the damage was severe, the top-heavy monitors could easily flip over, trapping and drowning its crew. Such thoughts wore on the minds of the sailors who operated the vessels. Though brave men, they were accustomed to fighting on wooden vessels, not sealed inside an unstable iron container that could quickly become a giant coffin. For months Du Pont held off attacking Charleston.[9]

While Du Pont procrastinated, the soldiers from Foster's corps were landed on St. Helena Island. They established camps at Land's End. The exotic beauty of the island fascinated the men. Some thought their new home a "queenly gem." One wrote, "The beauty and fragrance of the orange and oleander, and the songs of the birds, were full of delightful hints to the soldiers of home and its blessings. The island is an earthly paradise, and we think that the men render a silent and richly deserved homage to all of nature's tropical provisions, so bountifully lavished upon these fruitful islands." Others, not as enamored, camped in old cotton fields and complained about fleas, alligators, rattlesnakes, and copperheads.[10]

The newcomers also caused trouble. The soldiers, once part of the Army of the Potomac and veterans of the Seven Days Battles, were mostly Democrats and had no love for abolitionists or freedmen. The men made no attempt to hide their disdain for blacks. Food was taken from the freedmen, and if met with resistance, the soldiers assaulted them, sometimes burning their homes. One notorious unit was the independent New York battalion known as the "Enfans Perdus," a troop made up of Frenchmen and Germans, who were outfitted in Zouave-type uniforms and marched to "blaring bugles and rolling drums." Nothing was safe from the "ling-swangers," who scoured the countryside for food and valuables. They stole from the blacks, sutlers, and their own commanding officer. They even took regimental mascots and cooked them for their meals.[11]

Some of the soldiers from St. Helena Island crossed the Beaufort River to Parris Island, where they looted freedmen settlements and killed the island's only bull, which caused Lieutenant Colonel Halpine, using his pen name, Miles O'Riley, to compose the "The Butchered Bill: A Ballad of Paris Island":

> Dear General H____, my heart is full,
> Lamenting for my butchered bull:—
> The only bull our Island had,
> And all my widowed cows are sad.
>
> With briny tears and drooping tails,
> With loud boo-hoos and bovine wails,
> My cows lament with wifely zeal
> Their perished hopes of future veal.
>
> Sad is the wail of human wife
> To see her partner snatched from life:
> But he—the husband of a score—
> For him the grief is more and more!
>
> No future hope of golden cream!
> Even milk in tea becomes a dream:—
> Whey, bonny-clabber, curds and cheese
> Are now, ah, me! mere idle words!
>
> The cruel soldiers, fierce and full
> Of reckless wrath, have shot my bull;
> The stateliest bull—let scoffers laugh—
> That e'er was "father" called by calf!
>
> A bull as noble, firm and fair
> As that which aided Jove to bear
> Europa from the flowery glade
> Where she amidst her maidens played.
>
> Dear General H____, accept my vows,
> And oh! take pity on my cows,—
> With whom, bereft of wifely ties,
> All tender hearts must sympathize.

Quick to Van Vliet your order send
(By Smith's congenial spirit penned)
And order him in language full,
At once to send me down a bull:—

If possible, a youthful beast,
With warm affections yet unplaced,
Who to my widowed cows may prove
A husband of enduring love.[12]

To protect Parris Island's inhabitants from further depredations, two companies of the 97th Pennsylvania under Captain Francis M. Guss were sent to the island, where they camped in a cotton house. Their presence stopped the raids and gained them thanks from the island's superintendent, Frances Gage, and her son George.[13]

Hunter believed that many problems stemmed from the proslavery attitudes of the generals who arrived with Foster's command. The two brigade commanders, Brigadier Generals Thomas G. Stevenson and Charles A. Heckman, were placed in confinement for their proslavery sentiments. Stevenson, who publicly declared that he had rather support the rebels than serve "in this nigger department," was told by a smiling Du Pont that "he got hold of the wrong man in Hunter, who would be likely to hang him as well as arrest him." The officers eventually apologized and returned to their commands, but Hunter's point had been made.[14]

To tighten discipline and keep the soldiers occupied, Hunter increased drill, and regimental commanders began calling roll every two hours. Hunter also reviewed the troops. The men eyed their new commander warily, one writing, "Hunter puts on considerable style.... he resembled an Eastern monarch." Another commented, "General Hunter is a very fierce looking officer and his manner would indicate that in his opinion, he is a man of very great importance."[15]

While the men on St. Helena Island were becoming acclimated to their new surroundings and superiors, the soldiers of the Tenth Corps went about their routines as they awaited the coming campaign. On the northern end of Hilton Head, the Federals had "rejuvenated, modernized, painted" the old Pope plantation house and converted it into headquarters for bureau chiefs. The *New York Herald* reported, "Large storehouses—each three or four hundred feet long, ordnance buildings, provost guard barracks, a large magnificent house for the commanding general, and one of the best and largest army hospitals in the country." The new structures sat on either side of Fort Welles, the former Fort Walker. Farther inland were rows of merchant buildings, Patent Adjustable Houses, brought from the north "with doors, glass windows, steps, rafter, floor and everything complete," where they enjoyed "the soubriquet 'Robbers Row,' in compliment to the occupants."[16]

In their camps the soldiers continued to drill, oftentimes with bayonets, which forewarned coming close combat. Rumors that Confederate ironclads from Savannah might attack caused troops to toil in the hot sun to complete Fort Mitchel on Skull Creek. For diversions, officers hunted deer, with Pinckney Island serving as their private game preserve. The troops also put on minstrel shows, the most popular performed by the 3rd New Hampshire's "burnt cork troupe." The performances went on so late that the island's commander, Brigadier General Alfred Terry, had to order the concerts to end fifteen minutes before tattoo. Terry also found it necessary to stop the sale of spirituous liquors by the sutlers at Robbers Row, and no malt liquor or wine could be sold by the bottle or glass. Wine could be sold by the case or basket but only if approved by General Hunter or Terry.[17]

Brass bands also provided a diversion for the soldiers. Initially, nearly every volunteer regiment at Port Royal contained a band that gave concerts and marching music for the soldiers. The bands varied in quality. The 3rd Rhode Island's musicians were not very skilled, and their instruments were reportedly of inferior quality. The regiment's chaplain stated that though music had its charms, "this was hardly true of the kind we had." The band could only play one tune, and after six months the regiment's colonel informed the bandmaster that "if you play it again I will put the whole band in the guardhouse." After this confrontation the musicians did vary their repertoire, but it resulted in "no inspiring improvements."[18]

Musicians who did charm served with the 3rd New Hampshire Regiment. Led by bandmaster and e-flat cornet player Gustavus W. Ingalls, the band landed with the regiment on Hilton Head in early November 1861 and quickly became a popular fixture at serenades and funerals. Their concerts could draw tears and cheers. Its music provided inspiration at dress parades, reviews, and marches. When not performing, the musicians also served in battle as stretcher bearers and hospital attendants. Bandsmen from the 3rd New Hampshire partook in raids on Bluffton, the occupation of Edisto Island, and the Battle of Secessionville. The musicians constantly attracted attention for their fine music. Early in the occupation, the colonel of the 3rd New Hampshire, Enoch Q. Fellows, while serving as post commander of Hilton Head, had the band play at all special occasions, and it soon became one of the most popular institutions on the island.[19]

In July 1862 the War Department decided that the government could no longer afford regimental bands, and their numbers soon dropped from over six hundred to around sixty, which served primarily as brigade bands. At 11:00 A.M. on August 31, 1862, the 3rd New Hampshire band conducted its final ceremony on Hilton Head and was mustered out, but its demise was only temporary. Though shipped north on the *Star of the South,* the band was reorganized as the Second Brigade Band, Tenth Army Corps, and with Ingalls as its conductor, returned to Hilton Head. The band performed for General Hunter and his successors. At night its members often played on the island's great pier and serenaded patients in the general hospital.

The musicians from New Hampshire served throughout the war, seeing service on Morris and Folly islands. They also provided the music for the ceremony that restored the United States flag over Fort Sumter on April 14, 1865. The band's playbook survived the war and has served as the basis for numerous recordings and background music for productions on the Civil War, including Ken Burns's well-known documentary.[20]

Though not as acclaimed as their counterpart on Hilton Head, the band of the 8th Maine gave good service as the brigade or post band in Beaufort, entertaining the troops as they settled into camp life, awaiting the coming campaign against Charleston. Besides attending concerts, the soldiers frequented divine services in the town's churches and organized prayer meetings. They also performed brigade drills, built fortifications, and did picket duty on the "wonderful Beaufort and Charleston shell road, with its bordering wood of magnificent moss-draped live oaks." While most enjoyed the town's beauty, others commented, "on the whole, Beaufort was a 'dull old town.'"[21]

By the beginning of 1863, nearly all the structures in Beaufort had been taken over by the military, merchants, army officers, and their wives. Saxton initially maintained his headquarters in the Lewis Reeves Sams home at the east end of Bay Street. In the neighboring Reverend Stephen Elliott home, James G. Thompson, brother of General Saxton's fiancé, operated a general store and with publisher James M. Latta edited the newspaper the *Free South.* Saxton's staff resided on the corner of Bay and Carteret in Dr. Thomas Fuller's house.

Military offices occupied a number of buildings and homes on Bay Street. The post and brigade quartermasters were in the Cockroft and Porteous houses on Bay Street in front of a pier named for Admiral Du Pont at the foot of Charles Street. The post commissary occupied the Fripp home on the north side of Bay Street opposite Brannan Wharf, while the post treasurer could be found in the Chisholm home at the corner of West and Bay Street. Brigadier General Truman Seymour, commander of Port Royal Island and General Hunter's chief of staff, along with the post adjutant, had offices in the Nathaniel Heyward home at the corner of Bay and Newcastle Streets. Next to Seymour's quarters in the Fuller home was the office of the general superintendent of contrabands and plantations.

Hospitals were scattered throughout the town. Hospital Number 1 was in the Paul Hamilton House at the end of Prince Street; Number 2 in the Edward Means House on Finica (Pinckney) between King and Prince Streets; Number 3 at the corner of Finica (Pinckney) and Hancock Streets in the

John Johnson House. The William Wigg Barnwell House at Scott and Prince Streets was home to Hospital Number 4, while Number 5 was located in Barnwell Castle at Bay and Monson Streets. The Officer's Hospital stood at the corner of North and Hamilton Streets in the home of Senator Robert W. Barnwell, while a hospital dedicated to contrabands occupied the Sams House at Craven and New Streets. As the war continued additional houses and buildings in Beaufort were converted to hospitals.

At the start of 1863, Beaufort was divided into three school districts. For the area east of Craven, students assembled in the Baptist Church Praise House on New Street. The Methodist Church at West and Prince Streets served the district north and west of Craven and Carteret Streets, while the remainder of the town assembled at the Baptist Church Tabernacle and the adjoining building on Craven Street.

On the north side of the Town Square, on Craven Street, west of Carteret, quartermaster and ordnance offices occupied the old arsenal, while the council house furnished quarters for General Saxton's superintendent of contrabands. On the portion of the town square east of Carteret Street stood the city market and town jail.[22]

As the war and occupation continued, uses for buildings and homes would vary. Many of the changes would be accomplished by the work of the U.S. tax commissioners, who had rooms in the Edmund Rhett home on Port Republic Street. The commissioners were well aware of their mission and its impact on the sea islands, the freedmen, and the nation. While all three sympathized with the former slaves' desire for property, they differed on the method. Brisbane and Wording stood against any type of land distribution that might be impractical or challenged as illegal. Smith, however, had no such concerns and instead promoted the use of preemption or a version of "squatters rights" to help the freedmen secure land. Smith's views coincided with those of Saxton, French, and the more radical missionaries, but he was constantly overruled in commission meetings by the more conservative Brisbane and Wording.[23]

With the help of prewar tax lists, the commissioners were able to assess the land and issue tax bills. Notices were published in the local newspapers, and by November 3, 1862, they were ready to receive payments. In the sixty-day period that landowners had to pay their taxes, only a handful paid their bills. By one account, six prewar free-black families paid their taxes on town lots, while two remaining whites, John S. Flyer and David L. Thompson, covered their obligations. Edward Pritchard, John S. Flyer, Reverend Richard Fuller (by Reverend Peck), and Frederick Eustis paid taxes on their rural property. The remaining property, some 153 plantations and the remaining lots in Beaufort, was eligible for auction. On January 17, 1863, notice of foreclosure for all remaining property was listed in the newspapers with the announcement that the first auction would occur on February 11, 1863.

The swiftness of the commissioners in foreclosing property on the sea islands and scheduling the auction caught General Saxton and the Gideonites by surprise. Most hoped that land redistribution, when it came, would favor the region's freedmen. But at this time few freedmen had the means to purchase property, and their supporters feared that northern speculators would buy up most of the land. There was a forewarning of such events, as one of their own band, Edward Philbrick, along with the financier John Forbes, was planning to purchase prime cotton plantations for owners of northern textile mills.

Saxton and French acted quickly. They and many of the missionaries began contacting their supporters in Congress, asking them to amend the tax act to provide the freedmen a better opportunity to obtain land and keep it out of the hands of speculators. Commissioner Smith, with Saxton and French's blessing, went to the capital, where he met with Chase and Senators Doolittle and Sumner. With their support Smith penned an amendment to the tax act.

In the sea islands pressure was also brought to bear on General Hunter. Laura Towne urged General Saxton, who believed the freedmen should be allowed to file preemption claims on the land and was considering using profits from the sale of the sea island cotton to purchase land for the freedmen, to ask Hunter to stop the sale. While people anxiously awaited word from Washington, Hunter acted. On February 7, 1863, he ordered all advertising for the tax sales suspended and all attempts to sell land to cease "until the pleasure of the Government in the premises shall be made known."[24]

A day before Hunter canceled the tax sale, Congress used Smith's amendment to alter the June 7, 1862, tax act. On February 10 President Lincoln wrote to Generals Hunter and Saxton and the commissioners, informing them that Hunter was authorized to select and hold back from sale "such tracts, parcels or lots of land, within the state of South Carolina" for "war, military, naval revenue, charitable, Educational or police purposes." The decision on what property was to be held back from the auction was to be made by a quorum of the generals and the commissioners.[25]

With authority from Congress, the generals, backed by Commissioner Smith, struck off nearly sixty thousand acres, including all of Parris and Hilton Head Islands, half of Port Royal Island, and the majority of Lady's and St. Helena Islands. By severely limiting the amount of available property, Smith and the generals were buying time for the former slaves. Saxton would continue to oversee the superintendents and manage the remaining government land until the next tax sale, when they hoped the implementation of new land regulations would favor the freedmen.

Approximately sixteen thousand acres remained for sale. The auctions opened on March 9, 1863, the one-year anniversary of the arrival of the Gideonites. The sales proceeded slowly. The average price was one dollar an acre. Many former slaves bought land, some individually, while others formed cooperatives or joint ventures or borrowed funds from the Gideonites. Kit Green bought the four-hundred-acre Oakland Plantation on Lady's Island. In all, freedmen managed to obtain some twenty-five hundred acres.

Some Gideonites purchased land that they later sold at cost to freedmen. Government officials, northern speculators, and cotton companies purchased the remaining acreage. Edward Philbrick, partnering with Edward Atkinson, an agent for six Massachusetts textile firms and in part financially backed by John Forbes, obtained eleven plantations, including Coffin Point, on St. Helena Island. Though some of his peers viewed him as a turncoat, Philbrick fully believed that the next step for the former slaves was to serve as free laborers before becoming landowners. Only then, Philbrick proclaimed, would they truly appreciate property. He even stated that the Negroes would be demoralized by obtaining land at $1.25 an acre, which caused a reporter in the *Free South* to ask whether "Mr. Philbrick had been demoralized by obtaining land at that price?"[26]

Undeterred by criticism, Philbrick, who stated that someday, when the freedmen were ready, he would sell his property to his employees, established a working cotton farm. Commissioner Brisbane approved the venture, and other missionaries such as William C. Gannett and Charles P. Ware quit their superintendent positions and hired on as managers for Philbrick's operation. The 950 freedmen who lived on the property became the company's workforce. They were paid with vouchers that could only be used in company stores. Also provided were schools and medical service. Philbrick was confident that free labor would produce more cotton and return a greater profit than slave labor. One abolitionist journal called Philbrick "a second Wilberforce and Astor united into one."[27]

To Hunter and Saxton, the tax sales and Philbrick's operation removed land that potentially could be used as homesteads to induce freedmen to enlist in the army. By now the experiment with black regiments had proven quite successful. On February 1, 1863, the men of the 1st South Carolina returned to their home at the Smith Plantation from successful raids up the St. Marys River and into King's Bay, Georgia. Higginson found an encampment for Colonel Montgomery's 2nd South Carolina laid out next to his. By the middle of the month, Montgomery returned from Key West with about 130 men. At their base overlooking the Beaufort River, the two colonels continued to drill their men while Saxton and Hunter made plans for their use.[28]

Higginson continued to be impressed with his soldiers. He termed them a "gospel army." Saxton referred to the regiment as Higginson's "mamelukes," and Higginson called Saxton the perfect Mohammedan because "his faith is absolute that every thing which occurs in the whole affair is the very finger of God." While in camp Surgeon Rogers, from the veranda of the Smith Plantation, read to the regiment before Sunday service Ralph Waldo Emerson's poem "Boston Hymn," which celebrated the emancipation through the voice of an angry God. Rogers prefaced his presentation by telling the black soldiers that many white people could not understand Emerson's poems, but he felt no apprehension today. The soldiers, drawn up under a Magnolia tree, listened intently. Robert Sutton, the former slave who had planned the raid up the St. Mary, listened with "glistening eyes." Rogers stated that "Mr. Emerson would have trembled with joy to see how much these colored men drank in the religion of the poem."[29]

While awaiting his next assignment, Higginson was visited by a number of missionaries, including Laura Towne. Higginson introduced her to Colonel Montgomery, whom she described as "like a fiery westerner, full of fight and with sufficient confidence in himself."[30]

Saxton had plans for Higginson and Montgomery. After gaining Hunter's approval, who wanted to use former slaves to "fight insurrection with insurrection," Saxton on March 5 ordered the two black regiments to sail to Fernandina, Florida, and from there to proceed to and occupy Jacksonville, where they were "to carry the proclamation of freedom to the enslaved; to call all loyal men into the service of the United States; to occupy as much of the State of Florida as possible . . . to weaken, harass, and annoy those who are in rebellion against the Government of the United States." As the soldiers left Beaufort harbor aboard their steamers, Saxton ordered a salute of thirty-two guns and the playing of a national air while their wives and daughters lined the riverbank waving handkerchiefs.[31]

Higginson commanded the expedition. He oversaw the occupation of Jacksonville, engagements with Confederate forces, and expeditions by Montgomery along the St. John's River that ventured as far as Pilatka. Two white units, the 8th Maine and the 6th Connecticut, soon arrived, giving Higginson the war's first multiracial brigade. Besides filling out Montgomery's regiment, the Federals hoped that Jacksonville would become a permanent base to secure Florida as a refuge for former slaves. Tax commissioners arrived and even Reverend French came from Beaufort to minister to the population. But the occupation was short lived. Hunter, needing additional troops for the Charleston expedition, recalled Higginson's command. As the soldiers evacuated Jacksonville on March 29, many from the city, especially former slaves, left with them. Taken to Beaufort, the civilians were placed in refugee camps. Montgomery's soldiers camped near the town at Pigeon Point, while Higginson's regiment, located at Camp Stevens near the Milne Plantation, picketed the northern end of Port Royal Island along the Whale Branch and Coosaw Rivers.[32]

To speed up the recruitment of black soldiers both in Florida and elsewhere within his department, General Hunter issued General Orders Number 17, which established a draft of all able-bodied male blacks between eighteen and fifty who were not employed in the Quartermaster or Commissary Departments or as private servants to officers. The men were to be enlisted as noncommissioned officers and privates in the regiments and brigades being organized by General Saxton. The plantation superintendents were directed to make up lists of eligible draftees and forward them to Captain Edward W. Hooper, the superintendent of contrabands. Hunter preferred volunteers over draftees and asked the superintendents to appeal to the freedmen's "sense of right, their love of liberty" and "dread of returning to slavery to induce them to come forward." Assisting Hunter's conscription was the arrival of money to pay those black soldiers already under arms.[33]

Payday in the Department of the South found paymasters Majors Dwight Bannister and William J. Wood visiting Camp Stevens near Gray's Hill at the Milne Plantation, where Higginson's men were stationed while on picket duty at Port Royal Ferry. A newspaperman who accompanied the paymasters reported that the black soldiers assembled by company to receive their pay. Then he noted that some of the greatest family names in the nation were called, including George Washington and Abraham Lincoln, followed by the first families of the Beaufort District. As the reporter wrote, "Then the Barnwell family appear. . . . Then the Graysons, the Haywards, the Popes, the Aikins, the Seabrooks, the Elliots, the McPhersons." The pay increased the troops' contentment. They had carried out successful operations, occupied Jacksonville, and now received remuneration for their service.[34]

Hunter hoped to build upon the success of Higginson's Jacksonville operation. A letter from President Lincoln congratulated Hunter and pointed out that the Confederates feared an expansion of Hunter's black phalanx, writing that it was important to the rebels "that such a force shall not take shape and grow and thrive in the South, and in preciously the same proportion it is important to us that it shall. . . . The enemy will make extra efforts to destroy them, and we should do the same to preserve and increase them." A Union soldier, writing his parents, echoed Lincoln's sentiments in a more direct fashion by stating, "The Nigger regts. have done some good fighting down in Florida. bully for the niggers! I tell you it was tough for the Secesh, but they had to stand it!"[35]

As more freedmen joined the ranks of black regiments, recruitment of white officers also expanded. Many noncommissioned officers and field officers saw it as an opportunity to further their careers or escape an unfavorable situation in their own regiments. Officers in the 104th Pennsylvania, a regiment from Bucks County, Pennsylvania, noted as having a demanding colonel who treated his men as little better than serfs, sought transfers to the 2nd South Carolina. One regimental officer wrote that his comrades transferring to a colored regiment were "only going out of a *Nigger* regt. into a *Negro one.*"[36]

Even with their fine showing on the battlefield and their increasing supporters, there still remained a number of doubters who did not believe that the blacks would make good soldiers. Such attitudes caused Hunter's aide, Charles G. Halpine, to pen under his nom de plume Miles O'Reilly the poem "Sambo's Right to be Kilt":

> Some tell us 'tis a burnin' shame
> To make the naygers fight,
> An' that the thrade o' bein' kilt
> Belongs but to the white:
> But as for me, upon my sowl,
> So liberal are we here,
> I'll let Sambo be murthered instead o' meself
> On every day in the year.
> On every day in the year, boys,
> An' every hour of the day,
> The right to be kilt I'll divide wid him,
> An' divil a word I'll say.
>
> In battle's wild commotion
> I shouldn't at all object,
> If Sambo's body should stop a ball
> That was comin' for me direct;
> And the prod of a Southern bagnet,
> So ginerous are we here,
> I'll resign, and let Sambo take it
> On every day in the year.
> On every day in the year, boys,
> And wid none o' your nasty pride,
> All my right in a Southern bagnet-prod
> Wid Sambo I'll divide.
>
> The men who object to Sambo
> Should take his place an' fight,
> And it's betther to have a nayger's hue
> Than a liver that's wake an' white;
> Though Sambo's black as the ace o' spades
> His finger a thrigger can pull,
> An' his eye runs sthraight on the barrel-sights
> From undher its thatch o' wool.
> So hear me all, boys darlins!
> Don't think I'm tippin' you chaff,
> The right to be kilt we'll divide wid him,
> An' give him the largest half![37]

While Halpine's poem helped promote the use of black soldiers throughout the Union, the majority of the white troops in the Department of the South prepared for the expedition against Charleston. The commitment of so many units forced Hunter to make greater use of Higginson's and Montgomery's regiments, along with army and navy gunboats, to defend the sea islands.

Though delayed by Rear Admiral Du Pont's hesitancy to challenge Charleston's powerful defenses with his ironclads and General Hunter's feuding with General Foster over the planned assault, the movement finally got underway nearly one year after it was conceived. By early April over a hundred vessels, including warships, transports, and supply ships, rendezvoused off Hilton Head Island. On Good Friday, April 3, 1863, Du Pont took his ironclad squadron out of Port Royal Sound. His flag was on the ironclad frigate *New Ironsides*. Accompanying the flagship was the tower ironclad *Keokuk*, piloted by Robert Smalls, and seven monitors, the *Weehawken, Passaic, Montauk, Patapsco, Nantucket, Catskill,* and *Nahant*. The army, aboard transports, followed. Neither commander had consulted the other. Hunter viewed his role as merely supportive and wanted to be in a position to occupy Charleston should the attack prove successful.

While the troops waited on their transports, the ironclads moved toward Charleston. Early in the afternoon of April 6, the nine warships crossed the bar and steamed along the main ship channel just off Morris Island. Fog shrouded the squadron, making it too risky to continue, so Du Pont held his vessels off Morris Island until the following day.

In the early afternoon of April 7, the ironclad squadron moved into Charleston Harbor. Turned back by obstructions between Forts Sumter and Moultrie, Du Pont signaled from the *New Ironsides* for the monitors and the *Keokuk* to engage Fort Sumter. It was a very uneven fight. Outgunned and with a much slower rate of fire, the ironclads were battered by enemy shot. The commander of the *Keokuk* had Robert Smalls pilot the vessel to within nine hundred yards of Fort Sumter. For thirty minutes the thinly armored vessel came under intense fire. She was struck ninety times. A 119-pound bolt crashed into the pilothouse, and nineteen shots pieced the vessel at and below the waterline before Smalls received orders to take her out of the battle.

After two and a half hours of dueling with the Confederate forts, Du Pont stopped the attack, and even though the monitors *Nahant* and *Nantucket* had been forced to withdraw along with the *Keokuk,* Du Pont still planned to renew the assault the following day. Then his ship captains began making their reports. The *Keokuk* was sinking and five of the monitors were damaged. Appalled and unnerved by the perceived condition of his squadron, Du Pont refused to risk another attack. The defeat dismayed Robert Smalls, who "cried to think of being so near & yet obliged to give it up." The next day the ironclads remained in the ship channel as the *Keokuk* sank off Morris Island's southern end.[38]

While Du Pont was engaging the harbor works, Hunter allowed Seymour to land a brigade on Folly Island. Though Seymour wanted to press on and capture nearby Morris Island, Hunter refused. The commanding general, fascinated by the naval engagement and under no direct orders to assist the navy, remained immobile. Seymour, frustrated by Hunter's inactivity, contented himself with establishing a base on Folly Island for future operations against Charleston, while Hunter took the rest of his men and sailed back to Port Royal.[39]

Du Pont also returned his monitors to Port Royal, leaving the *New Ironsides* off Charleston. The monitors were closely examined, and though they carried battle scars, none were seriously injured. Their resilience was remarkable. After some quick repairs by the naval workmen at Port Royal, they were returned to fighting trim. Du Pont was impressed by their ability to take a beating, but he firmly believed that the monitors would eventually be destroyed if they ever again ventured against Charleston's defenses.

However, Du Pont's views of the monitors did not match those of his superiors in the Navy Department, who wanted no criticism of their miracle vessels, and when reports began to surface in newspapers criticizing Du Pont's handling of the assault, the rear admiral immediately replied, condemning the monitors. He called on friends with political influence to support him, and soon the matter became a personal vendetta against naval officials and anyone else who backed the turreted ironclads. Du Pont spared no one from his onslaught. He criticized everyone from President Lincoln on down. With such an attitude, Du Pont could not be retained.[40]

The failure at Charleston also exposed the inadequacies of General Hunter as a field commander. His meddling, which drove Foster from the department before the movement began, sabotaged any possibility for a successful joint operation. The campaign for Charleston would continue, but it would take time for the United States government to find and dispatch to the sea islands new senior officers.[41]

General Walker and his troops had closely watched the buildup and activity of the northerners against Charleston. Throughout the early months of 1863, his men ascended in hot air balloons to watch the movement of Federal ships and troops in and around Port Royal Sound. Walker continuously reported to his department commander, General P. G. T. Beauregard, about the enemy's movements. While the Confederates expected an attack on Charleston, they also prepared for a possible strike near Pocotaligo against the Charleston and Savannah Railroad. In February, Beauregard reinforced Walker's district with a few heavy guns and additional light artillery units. These were soon followed by the 24th South Carolina Regiment, the 1st South Carolina Sharpshooter Battalion, and, on February 20, 1863, by

Brigadier General John Rogers Cooke's North Carolina brigade. Four days later Beauregard met with Walker at Pocotaligo and joined in a quick review of the district's troop disposition. At the conference, plans for the region's defense were made that took into account the area's topography of causeways, rice fields, salt marshes, and swamps. The two generals believed that by employing earthworks with the terrain, they could hold off an enemy who could bring to bear a five-to-one advantage.[42]

If the Federals advanced on the railroad at Hardeeville from Red Bluff and/or Bluffton, Walker instructed, Walker's commander in the southern portion of the Beaufort District was to hold at Cheves Battery at the junction of the Screven's Ferry Road and Tunbridge Landing Road and at forts guarding the New River Bridge on the Bluffton-to-Hardeeville road. Should they be forced back from these works, they were to withdraw and defend the railroad bridge over the Savannah River.

In the Coosawhatchie area, Lieutenant Colonel Charles J. Colcock was ordered to hold the works at Bee's Creek and Honey Hill near Grahamville. If forced back to the new works at Coosawhatchie and the railroad bridge over the Coosawhatchie River, Colcock was to make what Walker called "a desperate and determined defense." If forced to retire, Colcock was to retreat to Possum Corner above the point where the Coosawhatchie and Tullifinny branch and with his cavalry and infantry proceed to Walterboro while the artillery and wagons were to cross at Hickory Hill Post-Office.

Walker also gave directives for Pocotaligo's defense. If the enemy landed at Port Royal Ferry, cavalry pickets were to resist at Huspah Creek Bridge and along the Sheldon Church Road. If forced back, a second line of defense would be manned at Pemberton's Battery on Stoney Creek and the works at Dr. Henry Fuller's and Mrs. Eustis's plantations. The final stand would be at the extensive lines around Pocotaligo. Should the enemy land at Mackay's Point and move toward Pocotaligo and the railroad through William Heyward's plantation, Walker planned to meet them by sending forces across the Pocotaligo River at the Tom Elliott and Daniel Heyward Plantations. If forced out of Pocotaligo, the troops from Pocotaligo were to withdraw through Blountville by Izard's Bridge and concentrate either at Salkehatchie Bridge or Walterboro and take up a defense line along the Combahee River.[43]

Walker continued to improve his district's ability to resist an enemy attack. Arrangements were made with the president of the Charleston and Savannah Railroad to keep a train at Pocotaligo capable of carrying a thousand men. The Confederate navy was called upon to provide warships to protect the Savannah River railroad trestle. Work was also pushed forward on the fort at Combahee Ferry, and additional siege guns and field pieces were located in the batteries at Pocotaligo, Coosawhatchie, and Dawson's Bluff. Land mines made from 10-inch artillery shells were planted in the major roadways, and torpedoes were secured in the waterways. In an attempt to destroy unaware enemy vessels, Stephen Elliott designed a torpedo that he successfully tested by floating the explosive devices down the Pocotaligo River, destroying a raft and a flat.[44]

By the end of March 1863, Walker had the following troops distributed throughout the Beaufort District:

COMBAHEE FERRY

Company B. First Battalion South Carolina Sharpshooters, as heavy artillery, Combahee Ferry.
One piece Preston's light battery, Combahee Ferry.

POCOTALIGO.

Forty-seventh and Forty-eighth Regiments North Carolina Volunteers, Cooke's brigade, one-half mile from railroad.
Seven companies Twenty-Fourth South Carolina Volunteers, Colonel Clement H. Stevens, 2 miles from railroad.
Company I, Eleventh Infantry, as light artillery, Salkehatchie.
Nelson Light Artillery (Old Pocotaligo) road, 3 miles from railroad.
Beaufort Volunteer Artillery at Pocotaligo, on railroad.
Preston's light battery (three pieces), Salkehatchie road, 3 miles from railroad.
Nine companies cavalry around and near Pocotaligo Station. Partisan Rangers, Captain Kirk, on Port Royal road, 6 miles from railroad.

COOSAWHATCHIE.

Fifteenth and Twenty-seventh North Carolina Volunteers, Cooke's brigade, at Coosawhatchie, 1 mile from railroad.
Companies A and C, First Battalion South Carolina Sharpshooters, at Coosawhatchie, 1 mile from railroad.
Light Artillery, Captain Raleigh L. Cooper, at Coosawhatchie, 1 mile from railroad.
Lafayette Artillery, Captain Kanapaux, at Coosawhatchie, 1 mile from railroad.
Companies F and H, Eleventh Infantry as heavy artillery, at Bee's Creek Battery, 4 miles from railroad.
Four companies Fifth Regiment Cavalry, on road to Grahamville, 2 miles from Bee's Creek Battery.
Four companies Fifth Regiment Cavalry, at Grahamville.

HARDEEVILLE.

Company G, Eleventh Infantry, at Savannah river trestle.
Company E, Eleventh Infantry, at Bluffton.

Company K, Eleventh Infantry, near New River.
Company B, Eleventh Infantry, at Bluffton.
Company D, Eleventh Infantry, at Hardeeville.
Forty-seventh Georgia (eight companies), near Red Bluff.
Company A, Palmetto Battalion Light Artillery, at Camp Allen, near New River Bridge.
Four companies Rutledge Cavalry, 2 miles south of New River Bridge.
Company F, Fifth Regiment Cavalry, at Camp DeSaussure, 12 miles from railroad, on Screven's Ferry road.[45]

Though Walker prepared primarily for the defensive, he still aggressively carried out reconnaissance and small strikes against the Federals on the sea islands. Scouts were sent to St. Helena Island and a loyal mulatto visited Beaufort, reporting on enemy activity. On March 12 a small boat expedition cast off from Bluffton and landed near Spanish Wells, capturing eight soldiers of the 9th Maine and three signalmen at a nearby signal station. The raiders burned the station and quickly returned to the mainland before the Federals could react.[46]

When not taking part in raids or preparing for an engagement, Confederate soldiers, including those from the Beaufort Volunteer Artillery stationed at Pocotaligo, were able to watch over family property and visit relatives. They also attended a series of live tableaux performed by the young women of Buncombeville and Blountville. With the proceeds going to the sick soldiers at the McPhersonville Hospital, the men paid to view portrayals of the Fatal Secret, the Rivals, Women's Curiosity, Sleeping Beauty, and other scenes. Though one soldier thought them not very dramatic, he did feel he "got his full four dollars worth." The final tableau, Sleeping Beauty, received the most comments, with the men remarking: "Wake her up, Oh God she's dead, Beautiful, B-ea-uti-ful."[47]

Though diversions helped ease the monotony of camp life, the southerners stayed ready to strike at the enemy whenever an opportunity presented itself. Such a situation arose late on the afternoon of April 8, when the men of the Beaufort Volunteer Artillery received word that there were two Federal steamers, one aground, in Whale Branch River near Chisholm Island. General Walker and his chief of artillery, Captain Stephen Elliott, quickly readied their command. Lieutenant Hal Stuart, who had succeeded to command of the Beaufort Volunteer Artillery on Elliott's advancement, immediately had his artillerymen limber up their six cannons and with the four guns of Captain James N. Lamkin's Nelson Artillery, three from Cooper's North Carolina Battery, and two from Captain Campbell's Company I, 11th South Carolina, along with six companies of the 48th North Carolina and five companies of cavalry, began a night march to the causeway connecting Chisholm Island to the mainland.

Their intended quarry was the naval gunboat *E. B. Hale* and the armed quartermaster steamer *George Washington*. The two vessels were familiar sights in the waterways about Port Royal. The *E. B. Hale,* a merchant vessel converted to a naval gunboat, had been built in 1861 at Sleightsburg, New York, and purchased by the navy in July of that year. She was originally christened the *Edmund B. Hale* but abbreviated to *E. B. Hale.* A veteran of the Battle of Port Royal Ferry, the light-drafted, wooden, screw-propelled vessel was a perfect fit for the region's shallow waters. One hundred and fifteen feet long, she carried five guns and was capable of making eight knots. The *George Washington,* an armed side-wheel tug operated by the Quartermaster Bureau, carried three guns, and though about the same size as the *E. B Hale,* she had not, as her consort had, received any strengthening for combat.[48]

The vessels had became more vital in early April after the Federal expedition left Port Royal to attack Charleston. Acting Lieutenant Edgar Brodhead, commander of the *E. B Hale,* had orders to cruise the headwaters of the Broad River, while the *George Washington,* operated by her owner C. H. Campbell and commanded by Captain Thomas B. Briggs of Company A, 3rd Rhode Island, operated in the Whale Branch River, watching for enemy activity near Port Royal Ferry. On April 8 the two ships left Beaufort and sailed along the Beaufort River to Brickyard Creek and into the Coosaw River toward Port Royal Ferry. The deeper-drafted *E. B. Hale,* piloted by William Jenkins, a local black wheelman, followed the *George Washington* through the waterways' narrow channels. The *George Washington* had on board a detachment of two officers and thirty-four men from the 3rd Rhode Island regiment, who manned the ship's two 24-pound bronze howitzers and a 20-pound Parrott gun.

Early in the afternoon, the *E. B. Hale* ran aground off Brickyard Point. Captain Briggs attached a hawser and tried to pull the stranded ship free but was unable to move the vessel. Briggs offered to stand by the stranded warship, but Brodhead refused assistance and cleared for possible action, while Briggs took the *George Washington* to Port Royal Ferry and then returned to a position next to the *E. B. Hale.* As night fell, the two vessels obscured their lights. At 11:00 P.M. the *E. B. Hale* floated free, but Brodhead waited until dawn before steaming toward the Broad River.

By now General Walker and Captain Elliott had massed fifteen cannons on Chisholm Island opposite Brickyard Point. Elliott was ready to fire at dawn but Walker procrastinated, and as Elliott awaited orders, the *E. B. Hale* began to sail away. Walker, wanting to destroy the larger gunboat, instructed Elliott to take ten guns to Port Royal Ferry and intercept the warship.

Brodhead, unaware of the danger, had steamed off without communicating to Briggs. Shortly after the *E. B. Hale* left, the *George Washington* got up steam, but as she began to move up the river, the five Confederate guns left on Chisholm Island opened fire. The second shot crashed into the *George Washington,* exploding the magazine. The vessel was set on fire, her rudder blown off and guns disabled. Captain Briggs hoisted the white flag; however, Campbell, the ship's owner and operator, refused to surrender and backed the stricken vessel until she grounded on the Port Royal Island side of the channel. Those who were able leaped overboard and into the marsh while others crowded into a small rowboat, which they took to shore. Once the passengers had debarked, the oarsmen returned to their ship for other survivors. Four men had remained to care for the injured until the rowboat returned; then they loaded what wounded they could find into the boat and made their way ashore.

Once Captain Elliott heard the cannonade, he rushed his guns back to Chisholm Island. On reaching the river, he found that even though the vessel was flying a white flag, the crew was escaping. Elliott ordered his artillerymen to fire on the fleeing Federals while he took a boat with some companions to the burning wreck. Once on board, the southerners gathered up clothing and rifles. They tried to remove one of he howitzers but were unable to disconnect the tube from its carriage. In the stern they found one dead and two badly wounded men. Elliott had them placed in his boat and along with the scavenged equipment returned to Chisholm Island.[49]

While Elliott scoured the wreck, those Federals who could fled into the marsh. Assisting them were pickets from the 1st South Carolina. Colonel Higginson, at his headquarters in the Milne Plantation at Gray's Hill, had been awakened by the cannon fire at 5:30 A.M. Thirty minutes later a courier arrived, informing Higginson that the *George Washington* had been destroyed. After forwarding the courier on to General Saxton in Beaufort and sending word to the *E. B. Hale,* which had by now entered the Broad River, Higginson mounted his horse Rinaldo and rode toward Brickyard Point. As he approached the picket line, he met "man after man who had escaped from the wreck across almost impassable marsh; poor fellows, some with literally only shirts on, but all with every garment pasted to their bodies with mud." When Higginson reached Brickyard Point, he found the Confederates were throwing shells at the fleeing men. With some crewmen still floundering in the marsh, Higginson sent Chaplain Fowler and a squad of soldiers forward under a white flag. They rescued a number of the survivors, the last being the *George Washington*'s pilot, "an immense black man with a wooden leg."[50]

By the time Elliott had nearly returned to Chisholm Island from the derelict *George Washington,* the *E. B. Hale* appeared. Lieutenant Brodhead, having been informed of the attack by Higginson's messengers, brought his vessel back through Whale Branch River, past Port Royal Ferry and off Brickyard Point, almost in time to capture Elliott and his companions. Lieutenant Brodhead positioned his vessel near the wrecked *George Washington.*

He expected to be fired on, but the Confederates had pulled their cannons inland. Brodhead could see the flag of truce sent into the marsh by Higginson and a second white flag flying on Chisholm Island. One wounded sailor was seen in the marsh, and a small boat was sent to retrieve him. Brodhead also raised a white flag at the fore of the *E. B. Hale* and then dispatched a boat under Acting Ensign George Edwards to communicate with the enemy.

The white flag emanating from Chisholm Island had been put up by Captain Elliott, who had taken the advice from one of his battery commanders, who was "drunk enough to be sentimental," to be benevolent to his enemies and return the wounded prisoners. Ensign Edwards learned that one of the wounded had died and had been buried, but the other two were still alive. Edwards returned to the ship, and Lieutenant Brodhead came ashore and met with Elliott. The two remaining soldiers were returned, and Elliott assured Brodhead that there were no other prisoners and wounded with the Confederates. Elliott found the meeting with Brodhead very cordial, with the two commanders exchanging unimportant conversation. Once back on the *E. B. Hale,* Brodhead lowered the white flag and made haste to take the wounded men to the hospitals in Beaufort. To aid those rescued by the soldiers of the 1st South Carolina, Lieutenant Edward A. Waterhouse, an officer in the 3rd Rhode Island, brought ambulances from Beaufort to Brickyard Point and oversaw their transportation back to the town's hospitals.

The short fight cost the 3rd Rhode Island detachment seven killed and seven wounded. There were also casualties among the civilian crew. The entire contest had lasted less than ten minutes, but its aftermath would go on for nearly two months. During the weeks following the engagement, a cat-and-mouse game went on between the two sides over the *George Washington*'s remains. Both Elliott and Higginson visited the derelict. Elliott managed to remove one howitzer before the Federals brought down artillery whose fire kept the southerners away from the wreck. Eventually the other two cannons settled into the mud.[51]

Though a minor affair, the sinking of the *George Washington* opened a series of recriminations between the Federal army and navy. General Saxton placed the blame on Lieutenant Brodhead, claiming that the naval officer had left the army gunboat exposed to attack when he moved the *E. B. Hale* toward the ferry without notifying Captain Briggs. Brodhead vehemently denied the charges, pointing out that the two vessels were not on the same mission but merely following a joint course out of convenience. The naval officer also declared that Briggs should have known better than to allow his vessel to remain at anchor after sunrise and that the army officer had to be aware of the *E. B. Hale*'s departure since the gunboat passed within ten feet of the *George Washington.* As Brodhead wrote, "I did not leave the *Washington* (the faster boat and drawing much the least water); the *Washington* did not follow me."[52]

An army investigation found that though Captain Briggs acted without proper consideration in surrendering and abandoning his vessel, he was cleared of any responsibility for the destruction of the *George Washington*. Instead the army blamed Brodhead, and Saxton demanded that Du Pont court-martial him. Though Du Pont believed the charges unwarranted, he did convene a court of enquiry, which eventually found "that the conduct of Acting Lieutenant Edgar Brodhead, commanding the USS *E. B. Hale,* in connection with the loss of the army steamer *George Washington,* is irreproachable."[53]

While the two services debated responsibility of the *George Washington*'s loss, Higginson and his men, reinforced by artillery and infantry, continued to picket the waterways between Port Royal Island and the mainland. Some commanders thought the Confederate strike might precipitate an attack on Port Royal Island, but as the Federal regiments returned from the aborted attack on Charleston, the situation soon stabilized. With Higginson along the Coosaw River was the 1st Connecticut Light Artillery, whose men enjoyed their time on the water and, when not shelling Chisholm Island, set up diving boards and swam in the river.[54]

The presence of the 1st South Carolina along the Coosaw and Whale Branch Rivers did not sit well with the Confederates. When white regiments were on picket, the two sides observed informal truces, but once the 1st South Carolina appeared, the southerners kept up a desultory fire on the black soldiers. Higginson informed Hunter of the situation and was told to "give them back as good as they send."[55]

The Confederates also refused to have any official intercourse with the regiment as General Beauregard, following instructions from the War Department, had ordered General Walker to refuse communication "with any officer of the negro regiments," since President Davis had declared them "outlaws and felons." When Walker on April 19 attempted to contact Federal authorities at Port Royal Ferry over the passage of civilians between lines, Colonel Higginson, rowed by a black sergeant to the mainland, met with Captain James Lowndes, Lieutenant George S. Worthington, and Captain M. J. Kirk. The three Confederate officers refused to parley and asked whether there was no other officer with whom they could meet. When Higginson replied that there was not, the Confederates apologized for troubling Higginson for nothing and broke off the meeting.[56]

Higginson considered the incident amusing since the men were acting under orders from General Walker, who had been an acquaintance of Higginson before the war. The two had met at Dr. Seth Rogers's Worcester Hydropathic Institution when Walker, a young army lieutenant, had come for the water cure. Higginson wrote that Walker, though an avowed proslavery man and he an abolitionist, had become friends. Later they crossed paths in Kansas, where Walker declined to arrest Higginson, and now the two faced off across the Port Royal waterways. As Higginson commented, "What an odd little world this is, so constantly the same Dramatis Personae jostle against each other."⁵⁷

Like Higginson, General Hunter also found himself at odds with someone he once called a friend. When in August 1862 Hunter had been declared a felon and outlaw to be executed without trial if captured, the general wore the title as a badge of honor. A month later, following a suggestion from his aide Charles Halpine, Hunter wrote, with Halpine's assistance, a long, scathing letter to Jefferson Davis accepting "the martyrdom you menace." Hunter then went on to lay the blame for the war on Davis and his fellow "treasonous conspirators who had brought about an abominable rebellion," which originated from an "abominable institution." If need be, Hunter declared, he would gladly accept the same fate as that of John Brown, stating, "I am content, if such be the will of Providence, to ascend the scaffold made sacred by the blood of this martyr; and I rejoice at every prospect of making our struggle more earnest and inexorable." Hunter concluded by pointing out that should he or any of his officers be executed, the hands of the North would be "untied" and that they would "treat rebellion as it deserves, and give to the felony of treason a felon's death."⁵⁸

The letter was never sent, probably suppressed by Lincoln, but in April 1863 Hunter wrote a second letter in response to the Confederacy's expansion of their directives, which called for the holding for execution all captured white officers serving with armed slaves. The new orders also stated that captured armed slaves would be returned to their native states to be dealt with according to the laws of those states. In most cases, this meant reenslavement and possibly execution. Again, Hunter was moved to write Jefferson Davis:

HEADQUARTERS DEPARTMENT OF THE SOUTH,
Hilton Head. S.C., April 23, 1863.
JEFFERSON DAVIS, Richmond, Va.:

The United States flag must protect all its defenders white, black, or yellow. Several negroes in the employ of the Government in the Western Department have been cruelly murdered by your authorities and others sold into slavery. Every outrage of this kind against the laws of war and humanity which may take place in this department shall be followed by the immediate execution of the rebel of highest rank in my possession. Man for man, these executions will certainly take place for every one sold into a slavery worse than death. On your authorities will rest the responsibility of having inaugurated this barbarous policy, and you will be held responsible in this world and in the world to come for all the blood thus shed.

In the month of August last you declared all those engaged in arming the negroes to fight for their country to be felons, and directed the immediate execution of all such as should be captured. I have given you long enough to reflect on your folly. I now give you notice that unless this order is immediately revoked I will at once cause the execution of every rebel officer and every rebel slaveholder in my possession. This sad state of things may be kindly ordered by an all-wise Providence to induce the good people of the North to act earnestly and to realize that they are at war. Thousands of lives may thus be saved.

The poor negro is fighting for liberty in its truest sense, and Mr. Jefferson has beautifully said, "In such a war there is no attribute of the Almighty which will induce him to fight on the side of the oppressor"

You say you are fighting for liberty. Yes, you are fighting for liberty—liberty to keep 4,000,000 of your fellow-beings in ignorance and degradation; liberty to separate parents and children, husband and wife, brother and sister; liberty to steal the products of their labor, exacted with many a cruel lash and bitter tear; liberty to seduce their wives and daughters, and to sell your own children into bondage; liberty to kill these children with impunity, when the murder cannot be proven by one of pure white blood. This is the kind of liberty—the liberty to do wrong—which Satan, chief of the fallen angels, was contending for when he was cast into hell.

I have the honor to be, very respectfully, your most obedient servant,

D. HUNTER,

Major-General, Commanding.

As with his initial letter, this correspondence, though forwarded to Secretary of War Stanton, was never sent, but it was extensively printed in northern newspapers.[59]

Undeterred by Confederate threats, Hunter continued recruiting black soldiers. He needed to fill out both regiments for future operations along the coast. Instructions went out from Saxton to the regimental commanders for stricter enforcement of the draft on the sea islands. Higginson did not care for the draft but did admit that the drafted black soldiers, just like white draftees, did just as well as the volunteers. Higginson preferred volunteers and especially admired how Captain James Rogers gained recruits for his company. As Higginson described the method, "James goes with a squad of men & warns them 'If you don't wish to be drafted tomorrow you had better volunteer today.' Then he leaves his sergeant who stretches the point a little farther, 'Dese yer drafted men aint no account. Dey d'ont get no leaves of absence. Dey has to go & stay with Cunnel Montgomery, on a point. We call 'em Bucks & dey stay there while our regiment goes & does all de good tings.' So they come and volunteer for James company."[60]

Higginson and his regiment continued to serve along Whale Branch and Coosaw Rivers, skirmishing with the enemy while the Federals reorganized for a new attack on Charleston. The Confederates took advantage of the lull to withdraw units from Walker's command and send them to join operations around Vicksburg, Mississippi. The 11th South Carolina was slated to go but was never sent. Instead the southern soldiers, like their northern counterparts, began preparing for the coming campaign by taking stock of both their military readiness and their souls.[61]

Chapter 9

Revival and the Combahee and Bluffton Raids

"The hand of Jesus is at work in this town"

The failure to seize Charleston in early April 1863 did not deter the Federals from further operations. Determined to capture the city, the U.S. government called for new plans and leaders. At Port Royal, while Federal soldiers anxiously waited, a religious revival swept through the Union camps as the men wished to prepare their souls before the campaign began. The movement was extremely strong in Beaufort, where it was stated that "the hand of Jesus is at work in this town and many conversions are being made."[1]

In Beaufort catechism soon replaced Casey's book of tactics and all types of "profane recreation were frowned on." Troops frequented churches within easy distance of their encampments. At the Methodist chapel on West Street, white soldiers mingled with black soldiers and freedmen during services conducted by a white minister. At the close of the meetings, they sang a song and joined together in shaking hands in time with the music.[2]

St. Helena Episcopal Church became the site of both soldier prayer meetings and formal services. At the church, revivals found men rising in prayer for their comrades and declaring, "there is no happiness save in Jesus Christ." On Sunday army chaplains conducted services. One soldier noted that the "fine large ancient edifice" was "a beautiful place for worship," writing that when a sermon had "nothing extra in point of merit," he could always look out the window, where "the mocking birds in the yard surrounding the time worn edifice gave us the nearest to heavenly music."[3]

Regimental chaplains vied to preach in St. Helena. Chaplain William R. Gries of the 104th Pennsylvania often conducted services, much to the displeasure of his peers and some of his congregants. One officer complained that Chaplain Gries had made efforts to get exclusive use of the church and often interfered with the soldiers' prayer meetings, writing that Gries "is very much lacking in common prudence, or else it is common honesty; for all he has of the latter article I would not give a great deal."[4]

Many of the troops went to the Beaufort Baptist Church, where black ministers often conducted the services. Revivals at the Baptist Church sometimes ended with a procession from the meetinghouse to the Beaufort River, where black and white people alike were baptized. An officer of the 104th Pennsylvania wrote:

> went to the Baptist church to witness a concert of the Sunday School scholars of Beaufort (all colored children). I should suppose there were several hundred children in all. They sung admirably together and answered questions in the Catechism with a great deal of ease. I never attended a meeting in my life that I was more interested in. General Hunter, General Saxton and wife, Colonel Montgomery and a great many other Army Officers were present. Three Negro preachers made each a few remarks in the intervals of singing, two of them belong to the 2nd South Carolina Regt. And were originally from Florida.[5]

Besides attending services in churches, soldiers held meetings at their regimental camps. Men from the 1st Connecticut Battery formed a Christian Association. They purchased religious tracts and held meetings in the regiment's chapel tent. The members resolved that whereas they had come to the defense of their country, they also wished to profess themselves as followers of Jesus Christ and the reality of his religion through their words and actions. They sought to do all in their power to discontinue and "discourage the use of profane and vulgar language" in their company and encourage the use of the speech of a "refined and virtuous society." Throughout the war the soldiers continued to hold prayer meetings three times a week, read sermons by Henry Ward Beecher, and conduct two to three services every Sunday.[6]

Besides their religious activities, the Federal soldiers also visited photographic studios. In Beaufort soldiers went to Samuel A. Cooley's studio, where they could have their picture "took" for fifty cents. Cooley was one of a number of photographers who set up shop in the Port Royal area. The first, Timothy O'Sullivan, a onetime assistant to Mathew Brady, arrived with Thomas Sherman's expeditionary force as a civilian photographer with the topographical engineers. The twenty-one-year-old O'Sullivan took the first wartime images of the sea islands, including pictures of Forts Walker and Beauregard, the John J. Smith Plantation, and Beaufort. By April 1862 O'Sullivan had left the sea islands to join another former Brady photographer, Alexander Gardner, on Major General George McClellan's staff with the Army of the Potomac.[7]

O'Sullivan's position was filled by Philip Haas, a noted prewar German lithographer who later became a daguerreotypist, known for making both lithographic and daguerreotype portraits of famous people in his studios in New York and Washington, D.C. At the start of the conflict, the fifty-three-year-old enlisted as a second lieutenant in the 1st New York

Engineers. While serving with the regiment, he took photographs recording the bombardment and occupation of Fort Pulaski. By September 1862 Haas had established a studio in Beaufort, where he photographed Rear Admiral Du Pont, a picture that Du Pont's friends believed to be the best likeness taken of the officer, with one commenting after the war that the picture properly captured "the historic Admiral, the man of strength and action and suffering." In the spring of 1863, Haas resigned from the army, citing ill health, but he continued to operate studios in the Department of the South, where he and his partner, Washington Peale, photographed forts, batteries, installations, and units throughout the sea islands.[8]

The first civilian photographer to operate in the Port Royal area was the twenty-seven-year-old Henry P. Moore from Concord, New Hampshire, who arrived at Hilton Head in February 1862 and stayed until early April before returning for a brief visit from late April through May. He primarily took views of the camp of the 3rd New Hampshire, including shots of Bandmaster Ingalls and his musicians. Moore also photographed Federal warships as well as baseball games at Fort Pulaski and scenes on Edisto Island before ending his tenure and returning to Concord.[9]

Though these photographers, plus others such as A. J. Blauvelt and Erastus Hubbard, left valuable visual records of Beaufort, Hilton Head, and the sea islands, the photographer most associated with the region was Samuel A. Cooley. A native of Hartford, Connecticut, Cooley had operated a photographic studio in his drugstore before coming south as a sutler for the 6th Connecticut. Known as Sam, the enterprising entrepreneur gave up his career as a sutler and, with the backing of Generals Hunter and Saxton, opened a first-class photographic gallery in Beaufort in the David L. Thompson House at the northwest corner of Scotts and Craven Streets. Cooley hired three photographers and obtained equipment that included an "instantaneous view camera capable of taking moving objects," a multiplying camera, and a stereoscopic camera. Cooley employed a mobile dark room and announced that he would visit plantations and camps "and take views for a reasonable price." He also sold photograph albums, produced cartes de viste, and packaged pictures for safe delivery by mail.[10]

For two years Cooley operated his business before selling out to one his employees, Edward Sinclair. Cooley and his wife, Emily, continued to operate a general store in the Thompson House; then, in the fall of 1864, he was hired by the Quartermaster Bureau to photograph installations throughout the Department of the South. His photographs of Beaufort and Hilton Head provided an invaluable set of images of the area's structures.[11]

Cooley and other photographers took numerous images of Beaufort's hospitals. Since January 1863 the army, expecting heavy casualties in the planned attack on Charleston, had expanded the number of structures operated by the department's medical bureau. The hospitals, located in the town's largest private residences, were described as spacious and airy. A regimental surgeon supervised each hospital, all under the control of Surgeon Charles H. Crane, the thirty-seven-year-old chief medical officer for the Department of the South.[12]

Jean Davenport Lander, the superintendent of nurses, assisted the surgeons in Beaufort. Lander had little experience in caregiving; instead her fame emanated from a spectacular career as a Shakespearian actress and her marriage to Frederick West Lander, a noted western explorer, surveyor for transcontinental railroads, and brigadier general in the U.S. Army. Colonel Higginson described her as "quite an intelligent & earnest person; English, dignified & rather fine looking," who used "little touches of the stage" to punctuate her conversation.[13]

The thirty-two-year-old celebrity turned nurse had been born in Wolverhampton, England. Her father, a lawyer and theater manager, operated the Richmond Theater, where eight-year-old Jean appeared as Little Pickle in the play *The Manager's Daughter*. A child prodigy, she was said to be Charles Dickens's inspiration for his "youthful phenomenon in Nicholas Nickleby." By the time she was sixteen, she played Shakespeare's Juliet. An accomplished singer, she gave public readings of Shakespeare and intermixed her recitals by singing "the incidental music" from such Shakespeare plays as *A Midsummer Night's Dream, Twelfth Night,* and *Much Ado About Nothing*. Acclaimed in the United Kingdom and Europe, she achieved her greatest success in the United States, which became her adopted home. She met her future husband, Frederick West Lander, while living in Massachusetts. The two maintained contact for seven years before becoming engaged in 1857 and marrying three years later in San Francisco.

The marriage, termed "The Union of Mars and Thespis," was happy but short. Jean retired from the stage, but the national crisis caused her husband to return east, where he assisted the Lincoln administration before being named a brigadier general in May 1861. Later, joined by his wife in the nation's capital, he commanded a brigade along the Virginia and Maryland border, where he was wounded on October 15, 1861, at Edwards Ferry, Virginia. He returned to service before fully recovering and died from an infection on March 2, 1862.[14]

Upon her husband's death, Jean became determined to continue his legacy by supporting the war effort. She served as a nurse in Washington before being assigned by Dorthea Dix, the chief of the nation's nursing corps, to oversee the operations at the Beaufort hospitals. Lander arrived in January 1863 and reported to Surgeon Crane. She immediately requested a carriage, a mounted orderly, three female contrabands, a cook, and twenty washtubs. Crane commented to Admiral Du Pont that she wanted to be the Florence

Nightingale of Beaufort. She also advertised in New York and Boston for qualified nurses who met Miss Dix's requirements of having recommendations from two doctors and two clergymen of good standing and being over thirty years of age, of good moral character, modest in dress, unattractive, and able to cook and write. Dix, who never accepted any compensation for her work, visited Port Royal in March, first inspecting the operations of Ruth Russell, superintendent of nurses at the Hilton Head hospital, before coming to Beaufort to meet with Lander.[15]

While organizing her nursing corps, Lander, still wearing her "widow weeds," visited campsites and arranged picnics and tours of the sea islands. On May 26 she organized a party for John Hay, Lincoln's private secretary, who was in the department to view the ironclad attack on Charleston and to visit his brother at Hilton Head. The repast was held under the great Live Oak at Woodward, the Barnwell place on the Broad River. Mrs. Lander arranged to have musicians present and personally directed the day's activities. Though many were reluctant to exert themselves, she "gave the orders with so much grace" that General Saxton, Colonel Higginson, and their staff "entered the lists manfully." A great sail cloth was laid down for a dance floor, and as Surgeon Seth Rogers noted, "I have rarely seen better dancing and eating." Higginson commented that Hay, who had the duty of representing the president, was a nice fellow but "looks about 17 & is oppressed with the necessity of behaving like 70." All had a grand time and afterwards "they galloped home through the wood paths by the young moon."[16]

Four days later Mrs. Lander accompanied Mrs. Saxton, John Hay, General Saxton, and others aboard the steamer *Flora* for a visit to Parris Island. They were rowed ashore to the Means Plantation on the island's southern tip, where the party visited Frances Gage, who had succeeded John Zachos as the island's superintendent. The party walked the grounds and picked blackberries. Soon the island's freedmen congregated and received greetings from General Saxton and Hay, who reported that President Lincoln "took the greatest interest in their welfare." The chief executive, he said, considered the department's social and educational activities to be extremely important for the future welfare of the former slaves and the nation. After the speeches there followed a general shaking of hands and series of three cheers for the guests, including Mrs. Saxton and Lander. At sunset the visitors returned to the *Flora*, carrying baskets of blackberries for sick soldiers in the Beaufort hospitals.[17]

Lander also provided nurses for a special hospital in Beaufort, Hospital Number 10, the department's first medical facility dedicated to black soldiers. Located in the Barnwell-Gough House on Washington Street, the hospital opened on April 12, 1863, under the direction of Dr. John Milton Hawks, assistant surgeon for the 1st South Carolina and his wife, Esther, who was also a doctor. Mrs. Lander appointed Mrs. Strong, wife of Major John D. Strong of the 1st South Carolina, as the hospital's chief nurse. Once the Doctors Hawks got the hospital up and running, John Milton Hawks was sent by General Hunter to Florida, and Ester took over the facility, serving as its chief surgeon and manager. For a month she not only operated the hospital but also took charge of the surgeon's duties for the 2nd South Carolina. She held the position until the end of May, when Dr. Arthur W. Greenleaf, assistant surgeon of the 2nd South Carolina, took over the hospital and she went back to teaching at a nearby school. But her role as chief of a military hospital and a regimental doctor placed her in a unique position for a woman during the Civil War.[18]

Outside of Mrs. Lander's purview was the local office of the United States Sanitary Commission. At Beaufort the commission, under Dr. Marvin Manville Marsh of Massachusetts, had its headquarters at the end of Federal Street in the James Robert Verdier House. A native of Pompey, New York, Marsh was a trained physician. At the outbreak of the war, he accepted the position of the Sanitary Commission's chief agent and medical inspector for the Department of the South. In February 1863 the fifty-year-old Marsh arrived at Beaufort to take up his duties. The Sanitary Commission carried out numerous activities, including providing the hospitals with needed supplies. Since it was a private organization, free from government bureaucracy, it could obtain and deliver goods in a short and timely matter. As Dr. Marsh informed Seth Rogers, surgeon for the 1st South Carolina, "If you are in want of any hospital or sanitary supplies for your regiment, we shall be most happy to fill out a requisition for you. Send for whatever you need and state in every case the amount wanted. This is all the 'red tape' of our Commission, and there are no knots in it."[19] Besides the activities of Dr. Marsh, Mrs. Lander, and the Hawks couple, another caregiver, Clarissa "Clara" Harlowe Barton, came to the sea islands during 1863. She arrived at Hilton Head aboard the *Arago* with her brother David, a captain in the Quartermaster Bureau, on April 7, 1863. She brought a letter of introduction that stated:

> The bearer Miss Clara H. Barton visits the Tenth Army Corps for the purpose of attending personally to the wants of wounded soldiers. She has rendered great service in all the great battles that have been fought in Virginia for the last six months. She acts under the direction of the Surgeon General, and with the authority of the Secretary of War. The smoke of battle, the roar of artillery and the shrieks of shot & shell do not deter her from administering to those who fall. She will explain all to you and I trust be able to do much good in the coming battles. Here she is highly respected and all bestow upon her much praise.[20]

An independent nurse, operating outside the authority of Dorthea Dix and the Sanitary Commission, Barton received support from women auxiliaries that provided her with supplies to assist needy soldiers. At Hilton Head she escaped direct contact with Dix's operations in the Virginia–Washington, D.C., area and supported her brother, who felt his assignment to the sea islands was akin to banishment to the ends of the earth.

At Hilton Head, Barton quickly made friends. Forty-two years old and unmarried, the five-foot-tall nurse received the attention of numerous officers. She formed a close friendship with Frances "Fanny" Gage and her daughter Mary and spent time with them on Parris Island. She also developed a romantic attachment to Lieutenant John J. Elwell, the department quartermaster. A native of Cleveland, Ohio, and a trained doctor and lawyer, the forty-one-year-old Elwell made an instant connection with Barton. The two read poetry, discussed literature, took rides together, and exchanged passionate notes and letters. Though married with children, Elwell formed an intense relationship with the unmarried Barton, who reciprocated in kind. However, Barton did feel guilty that while heavy fighting was occurring in Virginia, she was enjoying on Hilton Head the beautiful spring weather and Lieutenant Colonel Elwell's company. She considered returning north but did not go, instead staying with Elwell.[21]

Among the activities viewed by Clara Barton was General Hunter's preparation for the campaign against Charleston. For the operation Hunter began forming additional black regiments. In April 1863, to command one of these new formations, Colonel Milton S. Littlefield, a former Illinois lawyer and a prewar friend of President Lincoln, arrived at Port Royal. Littlefield, whom Higginson described as "one of the most prepossessing officers I have seen," had served as a captain in the 14th Illinois Infantry, fought at Shiloh, and served as an assistant provost marshal in Memphis before being appointed lieutenant colonel of the 14th Illinois Cavalry. Littlefield never served with the cavalry regiment. Instead he mustered out and, using his connections with the president, was promoted to colonel and assigned to Port Royal, where he hoped not only to organize a black regiment but ultimately a brigade for service along the coast.

Littlefield, who during his postwar career as a politician in North Carolina gained the sobriquet "Prince of Carpetbaggers," attempted to recruit men for the 3rd South Carolina on Hilton Head, but by May 1863 the freedmen-manpower pool on the sea islands was tapped out. To gain additional troops, Hunter began employing new, somewhat unorthodox methods to solve his manpower needs.[22]

On May 26 Hunter issued a general order, directing that all able-bodied whites not officially employed by the government be drafted into military service. There were to be no exemptions, and the men would be assigned to the department's numerically weakest regiments. To gain additional black recruits, Hunter decided to intensify his policy of raids against coastal plantations and towns. The operations were designed to gain recruits and to "rapidly compel the rebels either to lay down their arms and sue for restoration to the Union or to withdraw their slaves into the interior, thus leaving desolate the most fertile and productive of their counties along the Atlantic sea-board."[23]

Hunter assigned the campaign to Colonel James Montgomery and his 2nd South Carolina Regiment. Montgomery—simple, direct, with no formal military training—trusted his instincts implicitly. Described by a contemporary as "one of the John Brown men of destiny. He is not one of the slow, calculating sort, but being in harmony with the elements around him." A product of the frontier, he made New Englanders "seem puny beside the lusty life born on the frontier." Tall and thin, with grey eyes, a hawk-like nose, and a deeply lined face, he did not look like an army officer. His shoulders sloped and he moved awkwardly, but as a contemporary noted, he "believes that a soldier's use is to fight and is terribly earnest."[24]

Unlike Higginson, whose regiment Hunter declined to use in his burn-and-slash coastal raids, Montgomery had few notions about civilized warfare. He executed men without proper review and led his unit as if it were a feudal host. Higginson, who knew him before the war, considered him a brigand but also admired his daring and courage, commenting that "he is not a harsh or cruel man, but a singular mixture of fanaticism, vanity, and genius."[25]

Before his regiment was mustered into service as a separate command, Montgomery and his soldiers served as a detachment under Higginson. From February through May, recruitment continued, and by May 22, 1863, Montgomery had enough men to form a separate regiment. Four days later Montgomery marched his troops from their camp along the Beaufort River at Battery Plantation to Beaufort, where they passed through the town and drew up in front of General Saxton's headquarters. A large crowd, including Mrs. Lander, Saxton, and Fanny Gage, watched as General Saxton presented the regiment with its colors, a gift from Miss Elizabeth C. Low of Norwich, Connecticut. In addressing the regiment, Saxton told the soldiers that the nation was watching and called upon them to bear the flag proudly, noting that additional black regiments from the North would soon be joining the crusade for liberty. Saxton was followed by the reading of a poem written by Ellen Murray, who in her final stanza compared the movement for the work at Port Royal to that of the colonists of New England:

> We ourselves must pilgrims be! Launch our Mayflower
> And steer boldly through the desperate Winter sea,
> Nor attempt the Future's portals with the past blood-rusted key.[26]

For weeks Montgomery, under orders from Hunter, had kept his regiment ready for action. Normally such directives would have gone through General Saxton, but the overall leader of the black regiments had gone to the nation's capital. A number of rumors swirled about Port Royal concerning Saxton's absence since his departure occurred while the army high command was reviewing candidates to replace General Hunter as the new commander for the Department of the South. By mid-May it was apparent that Brigadier General Quincy A. Gillmore, the former chief engineer of Thomas Sherman's expeditionary force and the conqueror of Fort Pulaski, would replace Hunter. Saxton, who had been Gillmore's classmate at West Point, felt insulted and demeaned by the predicted appointment. He did not care for Gillmore and outranked him. Though Gillmore had graduated first in their West Point class of 1849 and Saxton eighteenth, Saxton had gained promotion more quickly than his illustrious classmate and was Gillmore's senior by nearly four months in the regular army and, more relevant to the situation at Port Royal, thirteen days Gillmore's senior as a brigadier general in the volunteer army.[27]

Saxton, who may have coveted General Hunter's position, threatened to give up his military position as commander of Port Royal Island and serve only as the region's civil governor. Because of Saxton's absence from Port Royal, Colonel William W. H. Davis of the 104th Pennsylvania assumed command in Beaufort, and it was while Saxton was on leave that Hunter launched his first expedition.

It was an opportune time to strike. By the end of May, the Confederate forces in General Walker's Third District, which contained the region between the Ashepoo and Savannah Rivers, had been reduced to an effective force of 527 infantry, 1,463 cavalry, and 596 artillerymen. With the advent of hot weather and on the advice of his surgeons and remonstrations of his subordinates, Walker removed his garrisons and heavy guns from his fortifications and repositioned his soldiers in healthier areas away from the marshy lowlands. Walker knew the dangers of leaving his works on the Combahee and Ashepoo Rivers and at Red Bank and Coosawhatchie undefended, but he counted on his advanced pickets to give early warnings of any enemy movements so that field artillery could be rushed to any threatened area.[28]

Walker especially worried over the defense of the Combahee River. Northern newspapers, obtained through the lines by the Confederates, reported that the Federal forces at Port Royal were being readied for operations along the coast. A number of slaves had escaped from the region's rice plantations, including a skilled Combahee River pilot. Even Walker's superior, General Beauregard, believed an attack eminent and directed his subordinate to advise the planters in his district to remove their slaves to the interior, for otherwise they were "liable to be lost at any moment."[29]

Walker also had concerns about his troops tasked with guarding the area. Stationed at Green Pond were Major William P. Emanuel's battalion of Companies E and F, 4th South Carolina Cavalry, and Captain Thomas Bomar's Chestatee Artillery, a four-gun Georgia battery armed with two six-pound guns and two twelve-pound howitzers. Major Emanuel and his cavalrymen had just recently arrived from Georgetown and were not yet familiar with the region.[30]

Walker's fears were well founded. Escaped slaves from the Combahee had reached the Union lines. Their information caused Hunter to change Montgomery's initial objective and directed him to take his strike force of five companies, about 250 men, into the Combahee River. Montgomery, whose regiment had been reinforced with Captain Charles Brayton's section of light artillery from the 3rd Rhode Island, sailed from Beaufort at 9:00 P.M. on the night of June 1, 1863, aboard the armed quartermaster steamers *John Adams* and *Harriett A. Weed* and the unarmed transport *Sentinel*. Harriet Tubman, the famous former slave and Maryland underground railroad operator, accompanied Montgomery aboard the *John Adams*. The two had been acquainted before the war, and Tubman, who had been working in Beaufort's contraband hospital, was pleased to join her old friend on the expedition. Though later newspaper accounts would give Tubman credit for planning and leading the raid, a letter dictated by her shortly after the expedition gives no such indication. Instead, by her account, she was invited to accompany the expedition by General Hunter.[31]

The expedition sailed from Beaufort River along the Coosaw River into St. Helena Sound, where the *Sentinel* grounded. When the vessel could not be freed, the passengers were transferred to the *Harriet Weed*. By 2:00 A.M. the remaining ships reached the mouth of the Combahee River. The expedition proceeded into the river and at daybreak arrived off Field's Point. To protect his line of withdrawal, Montgomery sent ashore Captain Thomas N. Thompson's company, who quickly occupied an abandoned Confederate earthwork. Two miles farther upriver at Tar Bluff, Captain James M. Carver's company landed to cover the road leading to Ashepoo. The vessels then sailed on to the landing on the river's eastern bank at the Nicholls Plantation, where the *Harriet Weed* stopped.[32]

The unexpected appearance of the Union gunboats in the midst of the Combahee rice plantations surprised overseers, who hastily fled. Slaves, spying the vessels, swiftly gathered what belongings they could carry and rushed to the landing. The companies of Captains William Lee Apthorp and John M. Adams disembarked at the Nicholls place and quickly began breaking up floodgates and set fire to rice barns and the recently deserted mansions. From the woods Joshua Nicholls watched his home burn while hundreds of slaves came through the Federal pickets, blessing the soldiers, and crowding onto the boat. Nicholls later recalled: "My pleasant and comfortable house was in ashes. . . . Every memorial I possessed of my past life, and every material object to which my heart still clung, not for its intrinsic value, but for the unspeakable associations connected with it—vanished, perished in the flames."[33]

While the *Harriet Weed* remained off the Nicholls Plantation, Colonel Montgomery continued on to the Combahee Ferry aboard the *John Adams*. The vessel slowed to pass through a set of enemy torpedoes and then moved on to the pontoon bridge that stretched between the two ferry landings. As the gunboat neared the bridge, mounted Confederate cavalrymen could be seen riding over the structure from east to west toward Green Pond. To hasten their ride, the Rhode Island cannoneers lobbed shells at the fleeing horsemen. No resistance was met, and the *John Adams* reached the pontoon bridge, which work crews destroyed. Montgomery dispatched Captain John Hoyt's company along the eastern causeway toward the Colleton side of the river, while Captain Brayton's Rhode Island troops went ashore on the Beaufort District side.[34]

Though the Federals had met no resistance, their movements had been spotted by Confederate pickets, first at Field's Point and later at Combahee Ferry. At 3:00 A.M. on June 2, the commander of the outpost at Field's Point, Corporal H. H. Newton, spied two enemy vessels in the sound two miles away, steaming toward his position. The corporal and his five troopers mounted and rode a few hundred yards to the rear, where they left their horses and went back to the point to watch the Federals land. Newton dispatched couriers to the picket command post at Chisolmville, where Lieutenant Hewitt relayed the information to Major Emanuel at Green Pond.

By this time Corporal W. D. Wall and his pickets stationed at the unarmed battery on the west of the river at the Combahee Ferry spied an enemy steamer about a mile and a half downriver. Wall immediately sent off a courier to Major Emanuel at Green Pond. A short time later the remaining cavalrymen quickly mounted and, under fire from the gunboat, hurried across the pontoon bridge and over the causeway. Wall sent another courier to Emanuel and another to see whether the enemy had landed at Oakland, the plantation of Charles T. Lowndes. After leaving one soldier at the earthworks at the foot of the causeway on the east side of the river, Wall hurried to warn Colonel William C. Heyward at nearby Cypress Plantation before joining his sentinel at the breastworks. From their vantage point, Wall could see a fire down the river and a force of about fifty to sixty black soldiers with white officers moving up the causeway. Before he could engage the enemy, Wall heard gunfire in his rear, and fearful of being cut off, he and his companion fled toward Green Pond.[35]

At Green Pond, Major Emanuel, having received word from his picket posts that the Federals had landed at both Field's Point and Combahee Ferry, sent a telegram to General Walker and tried to distribute his small force to slow the enemy until help could arrive. Emanuel's main concern was protecting the Charleston and Savannah Railroad. To determine the enemy's movements, he ordered Lieutenant A. E. Gilchrist toward Field's Point while Emanuel, with two pieces of Captain Bomar's artillery and the rest of Company F, 4th South Carolina Cavalry under Captain H. Godbold, took up a position at the junction of Stokes Causeway and the Charleston Highway. Lieutenant Peter L. Breeden with Company I and two of Bomar's cannons moved toward Combahee Ferry, but before Breeden's force reached the ferry, Major Emanuel received word that the enemy gunboat was proceeding past the ferry toward the railroad bridge at Salkehatchie, causing Emanuel to abruptly order the two artillery pieces with Breeden to Salkehatchie some fifteen miles away.[36]

By 9:00 A.M. General Walker at McPhersonville received Major Emanuel's telegram. Walker immediately ordered his command to form and march to Pocotaligo Station while he rode ahead to telegraph for help from Charleston. Once his men arrived from McPhersonville, Walker placed three companies of the 11th South Carolina under Captain J. J. Wescoat and two companies of dismounted cavalrymen and the horse artillery of Captain William L. Trenholm's Rutledge Mounted Riflemen on the troop train that Walker kept at Pocotaligo Station. The force, numbering about 150 infantrymen and 100 cavalry and artillerymen, was placed under Captain Trenholm. At about 2:00 P.M. they arrived at Green Pond, where Trenholm received word that an enemy force was threatening the railroad bridge over the Ashepoo. Trenholm dispatched horsemen to check on the report while he held the rest of his force at the head of Stock's causeway. When he received confirmation that all was quiet on the Ashepoo, Trenholm began marching his soldiers toward Field's Point.[37]

While the Confederates attempted to shift forces to stop the marauding Federals, Montgomery and his officers went about their work gathering up slaves and destroying everything within their reach. At Field's Point, Captain Thompson moved inland, mounted some of his men on captured horses, and sent them out as scouts. He placed the rest of his soldiers in concealed positions covering roadways leading to the point. Farther north Captain Carver pushed his company inland from Tar Bluff beyond a rice mill owned by the Middleton family.[38]

The two companies guarded by the *Harriet Weed* at Nicholls Landing continued their destructive labors. The rice fields became lakes, and all structures belonging to the owners, save the slave quarters, were destroyed. William Kirkland's plantation home, Longbrow, and that of Joshua Nicholls, Rose Hill (with its magnificent library), went up in flames, along with Andrew Burnet's Woodburne and Dalton Plantations and James L. Paul's Paul

Plantation. From each place came hundreds of slaves—men, women, and children. A great number were allowed onto the vessel, but it could not take all of them. Many were left behind, and as the black soldiers embarked, the slaves continued to come. As one Federal officer described the scene:

> We were obliged to go onboard our boat and leave the shore while the crowds of negroes of both sexes and all ages and sizes were still flocking down from the whole neighborhood. Indeed they had begun to pour in from several miles distance. But our boat was loaded and crowded to its utmost capacity and the loss of the Sentinel on the way upriver made it impossible to take the increasing crowds that stretched in every direction as far as the eye could reach.
>
> It was indeed a remarkable scene. Beheld from a [distance] with their large bundles, they reminded many of an army of black ants such as we sometimes see lugging a huge white egg bigger than itself. Remembering the treatment that these poor people would suffer for their attempt to escape to the Yankees it was hard to leave them. But it was impossible to take another one, and sadly we swung away from the landing.[39]

At the ferry landing, after destroying the pontoon bridge and disembarking most of the soldiers, the captain of the *John Adams,* a stout East Boston paddle-wheel ferryboat, steamed his vessel farther upriver, but obstructions blocked his path and he returned her to a position between the ferry landing and the causeway. On the west shore Captain Brayton led his detachment of the 3rd Rhode Island to Newport, a plantation owned by the Middleton brothers Williams, John Izard, and Edward, the last being an officer in the United States Navy. The soldiers destroyed the house and outbuildings, carried off horses, mules, and cattle before returning to the *John Adams.* Watching the Federals were the Confederate horsemen of Captain T. G. Allen's Combahee Rangers under Lieutenant Brunson. Too few to stop the Federals, they instead took up a position and used dogs to stop slaves from escaping from Walter Blake's nearby Bonny Hall Plantation.[40]

On the east side of the ferry, Captain Hoyt's company marched down the causeway past abandoned breastworks and onto William C. Heyward's Cypress Plantation. Colonel Heyward, who, hoping that help would arrive, stayed at his property as long as possible before riding away. On his way to Green Pond, Heyward met Lieutenant Breeden's men slowly moving toward Combahee Ferry. Disgusted with the tardy and inadequate response, Heyward, a West Point graduate and former colonel of the 11th South Carolina, continued on to Green Pond, where he telegraphed General Walker about the situation along the Combahee.

At Cypress Plantation the black soldiers took one of Heyward's horses, his pistols, and sword before burning the house and all outbuildings except the slave quarters. The Federals then moved across the road to the Lowndes Plantation, burning its rice mill and other structures, but turned back before destroying the main house at Oakland Plantation.[41]

While the soldiers continued to plunder and burn, hundreds of slaves fled to the *John Adams,* bringing with them whatever possessions they could carry. Harriet Tubman came ashore along the causeway to assist the refugees. While toting two pigs for a sick woman who was carrying a child, Tubman fell and tore her dress, causing her later to request bloomers from her friends in the North, as such attire would be more practical to wear in the field. Once back on the ship, Colonel Montgomery, reveling in his success, called on Tubman for a song as the slaves crowded on board. By now the Federal troops were returning to their transport. The Confederates, Lieutenant Breeden and his company, followed cautiously. Once he reached the earthworks at the foot of the causeway, Breeden had his men open fire at the fleeing enemy column from about three hundred yards away. The Federals turned and replied with a volley and then continued on to the *John Adams,* whose gun crews began tossing shells into Breeden's position, forcing the southerners back into the woods.[42]

With troops and refugees on board, the *John Adams* cast off and proceeded down the river, leaving behind hundreds of slaves who lined the causeway and the riverbanks, praying and shouting to be taken on the steamer. A member of the 3rd Rhode Island wrote, "This was the saddest sight of the whole expedition—so many souls within sight of freedom, and unable to attain it." At the Nicholls place, the *John Adams* joined the *Harriet Weed,* and the two vessels steamed down the river. As they neared Tar Bluff, Montgomery spotted Captain Carver signaling by waving his hat to show that all was right. The ships sailed past Carver and his men, moving on to ensure that Captain Thompson's company still retained possession of Field's Point. Once Montgomery made contact with Captain Thompson's company and saw that their line of retreat was secure, he sent the *Harriet Weed* back to Tar Bluff for Carver's company while the *John Adams* remained at Field's Point. So far the operation had been a complete success, but the Federals still worried that the Confederates might be able to get field guns to Field's Point and cut off the expedition.[43]

The concerns were well founded, but Major Emanuel had kept the majority of his command, Godbold's company and Captain Bomar with a section of his Chestatee Artillery, at the junction of Stock's Causeway and the Green Pond Road, sending initially only twenty men under Lieutenant Gilchrist toward Field's Point. While en route, Gilchrist learned of the presence of Federals to the right of the road. Turning to the east, he drove the enemy back to Middleton's rice mill on the bank of the Combahee but was unable to dislodge them. The Union soldiers, Captain Carver's company, held on, initially signaling the passing gunboats on their way from Combahee Ferry to Field's Point that all was well, but their position was precarious. However, before additional Confederates could arrive, the *Harriet Weed* returned and under the cover of her guns, Carver and his men were able to burn the mill and safely reembark.

By now the Confederates were finally concentrating their scattered forces. Major Emanuel, after overseeing the gathering up of slaves around the Lowndes Plantation, where some slaves were shot when they refused to return, ordered Lieutenant Breeden to ride along the river, shadowing the gunboats. Lieutenant Gilchrist, having left his position at Middleton's Mill, returned to the Stock's Causeway, where he met Captain Godbold and his men. Together they moved toward Field's Point. Major Emanuel soon arrived, and hoping to trap the Federals, he directed Bomar to take his cannons to Field's Point. As they neared their destination, Emanuel and his staff rode into an ambush set by Captain Thompson and his soldiers. Fired on from all directions, Emanuel and his companions escaped the trap. Hurrying back to his artillery, Emanuel directed Bomar to bring up his cannons and fire into the woods. Uncertain of the enemy's strength and not knowing the effect of his artillery barrage, Emanuel withdrew Bomar's battery men back to Tar Bluff, where he rendezvoused with Lieutenant Breeden.

While Emanuel and the cannoneers were falling back, Captain Godbold, Lieutenant Gilchrist, and their horsemen pressed on to Field's Point, where they engaged Union pickets. But without artillery, there was little the cavalrymen could do. As shells from the *John Adams* exploded in their midst, the Confederate troopers pulled back, allowing Captain Thompson and his men, who had taken refuge in the abandoned Confederate fort, to board the gunboat safely. By now the *Harriet Weed* had rejoined the *John Adams* at Field's Point. A thunderstorm darkened the sky, and the roll of thunder blended with the roar of the Union deck guns while the ships sailed from the Combahee and back to Beaufort.[44]

For the Federals the raid was an unqualified success. Without a single casualty, Montgomery, commanding an understrength and only partially trained regiment of black soldiers, had destroyed one of the South's richest rice production centers and, by Montgomery's report, carried off 727 slaves. The Confederate leaders, chagrined that they had been unable to check the Federals, called for investigations and possible courts-martial, but with a defensive scheme designed primarily to protect the Charleston and Savannah Railroad, coastal areas such as the lower regions of the Combahee River were vulnerable to such raids. Though they suffered the loss of only one wounded soldier, the southerners had been unable to respond properly and as a result lost for the rest of the war vital food crops needed to feed their armies. General Walker did appeal for assistance in case additional forays were launched, but all the high command could do was to suggest the distribution of quinine so that troops could stay closer to the threatened areas throughout the summer.[45]

Montgomery's expedition returned to Beaufort on June 3. The freed slaves were temporarily housed in the Baptist Church, where Montgomery addressed the refugees, who responded by singing, "There is a White Robe for Thee." Harriet Tubman followed with an inspirational speech. The exhortations resulted in nearly 150 men joining the 2nd South Carolina. In a letter dictated later that month, Tubman recounted, "Don't you think we colored people are entitled to some credit for that exploit under the lead of the brave Colonel Montgomery? We weakened the rebels' somewhat on the Combahee river, by taking seven hundred and fifty-six head of their most valuable live stock known up in your region as contrabands, and this too, without the loss of a single life on our part.... Of these seven hundred and fifty six contrabands, nearly or quite all the able-bodied men have joined the colored regiments here."[46] After a few days in the Baptist Church, the refugees were moved to a Freedmen village near Montgomery's camp on Battery Plantation termed Montgomery Hill. Known collectively as the "Combees," they eventually were provided with new homes located in a row of over a dozen buildings, each resembling a huge wooden box divided into four compartments, with a family of five to fifteen in each room. The refugees proved to be resilient and resourceful. They chose one of their own to supervise the village and proudly referred to themselves as "We's Combee" to distinguish themselves from the sea island blacks.[47]

The evening of Montgomery's return to Beaufort found a gathering at Mrs. Lander's quarters. Among those invited were Colonel Higginson, Dr. Seth Rogers, and the *New York Tribune* correspondent Charles A. Page. From Hilton Head came Clara Barton and Colonel Elwell. Dinner was served at 2:00 P.M. Afterward Colonel Higginson and Dr. Rogers called for carriages to take the guests to Camp Saxton, and though the regiment was on picket duty on the northern end of Port Royal Island, they toured their guests on a twilight excursion past old Fort Prince Frederick, the Smith plantation house, and the nearby oak grove. Barton believed the trees with their pendants of Spanish moss to be hauntingly beautiful. That night, while on the veranda of Mrs. Lander's home, Barton, Elwell, and the others were serenaded by the band of the 104th Pennsylvania and discussed with other guests Montgomery's Combahee raid. Over the next few days, Barton visited the 1st South Carolina at their camp near the Milne Plantation and viewed the Combahee refugees at Montgomery Hill before returning with Colonel Elwell to Hilton Head.[48]

Barton and Lander's other guests had been impressed by Montgomery's raid. It had been "quick, decisive, terrible and without loss." It buoyed Hunter, who planned to repeat such expeditions along the coast. He had received word that over a thousand male slaves had taken refuge in the Georgia and Florida swamps, waiting for liberation and a chance to join Hunter's black phalanx. To confirm this intelligence, Hunter sent, in late May, a small expedition consisting of a band of twelve soldiers from Higginson's regiment, including Corporal Robert Sutton, under Captain W. J. Randolph. The regiment's assistant surgeon, John Milton Hawks, accompanied the men. Leading the operation was the "mercurial" and unstable Francis Merriam, a survivor of John Brown's attack on Harpers Ferry, who had come to Port Royal seeking a captaincy in the 3rd South Carolina. The reconnaissance proved a disaster. The three white officers, while scouting the coastline during a night foray, found themselves challenged by one of their men, who considered the expedition a suicide venture. When the soldier refused to continue rowing, the officers ordered Corporal Sutton to disarm the balking man. Sutton, who probably agreed with him, refused, and Merriam and Randolph, at Hawks's urging, opened with their pistols, killing the rebelling soldier and another who was in the line of fire. Sutton was imprisoned, court-martialed, and found guilty of mutiny, though his conviction was later dismissed. Saxton and Higginson were outraged by the incident. Saxton termed the three officers lunatics, and Higginson hoped Hawks would leave his regiment.[49]

Undeterred by this failure, Hunter directed Montgomery to ready his regiment and Brayton's Battery for additional operations along the Georgia and Florida border. Hunter hoped the new campaign would not only gain additional black recruits but also harass the coastal regions, driving the white population inland and forcing Georgia and Florida officials to recall troops to defend their coast. For the new strikes, Hunter planned to add additional units to Montgomery's command.

On the same day that Montgomery forces came back from the Combahee Raid, the 54th Massachusetts, a regiment recruited primarily from free northern blacks, arrived at Beaufort. The soldiers and officers of the 54th were quite different from the black regiments organized at Port Royal. Most of the enlisted men's families had lived in the North for generations, the majority could read and write, and all had volunteered for service. Massachusetts governor John Andrew selected the regiment's officers for their idealism and antislavery views. Properly equipped and armed, the unit constantly received preferential treatment. The trip south brought most of the soldiers and officers into a new environment they had never before experienced. As they sailed aboard the steamer *De Molay* from Hilton Head to Beaufort, scenes along the river fascinated the regiment. As Captain John W. M. Appleton described the voyage, "We saw old plantations with the mansions and the long rows of Negro houses here and there. Also groups of red and yellow dressed mammies and uncles. We ran from side to side of the ship to see the different plantations and were delighted with this part of the voyage. Beaufort, at which place we arrived about half past 7 o'clock, was one of the prettiest and most picturesque places imaginable, but it does not do to rebel if you wish your property respected."[50]

The next day the 54th debarked, marched through Beaufort, and made camp in an old cotton field just outside of town. Colonel Robert Gould Shaw, the regiment's twenty-five-year-old commander, had served previously in the 2nd Massachusetts and participated in the Battles of First Winchester and Antietam, where he was wounded. Asked by Governor Andrew and encouraged by his father, Shaw accepted command of the 54th, a role he knew meant forming, training, and leading a regiment destined to show the nation that black soldiers could and would fight. If the 54th performed heroically, the door would be open to more black regiments; if they failed, the great experiment could collapse.[51]

Shaw met with both Higginson and Montgomery. Higginson and Shaw had dinner and discussed the qualities of black troops. Shaw was worried that his untried men would flinch in combat, but Higginson relieved his anxieties by assuring the young colonel that his soldiers would respond well on the battlefield. The young colonel also sought out Montgomery and requested permission to join the coming expedition into Georgia. As Shaw wrote his father, "Montgomery is a good man to begin under—as he is a guerrilla-man by profession.... He is an Indian in his mode of warfare, and though I am glad to see something of it, I can't say I admire it. It isn't like a fair stand up such as our Potomac Army is accustomed to." Montgomery's expedition initially left Beaufort without Shaw's regiment, and while waiting for their first combat assignment, the 54th worked on constructing forts on the town's perimeter. When not on duty, Shaw and other officers swam in the Beaufort River off one of the town's wharves. Captain Appleton noted that the water was warm and "sparkling with phosphorescent light."[52]

The wait lasted only a few days before Hunter sent the regiment to join Montgomery's force at St. Simons Island, Georgia. Hunter, intensifying his raids, informed Secretary of War Stanton that the 54th would soon have abundant and important employment, as would "all other regiments, white and colored." As he explained, the new raids were a continuation of the Combahee raid, which had been the "initial experiment of a system of incursions which will penetrate up all the inlets, creeks, and rivers of this department."[53]

Besides dispatching Montgomery and his amphibious force to Georgia, Hunter also planned strikes in the Beaufort District. In late May, Hunter requested that Admiral Du Pont provide a gunboat for an expedition against the town of Bluffton, site of a Confederate outpost from which pickets were distributed and raids launched against Hilton Head and Pinckney Islands.

Du Pont was unable to provide a vessel until early June, when he sent the light-drafted side-wheel gunboat *Commodore McDonough* under Lieutenant Commander George Bacon to join the expedition forming at Fort Pulaski.[54]

On June 3 Lieutenant Commander Bacon reported with his warship to Colonel William B. Barton, commander of Fort Pulaski and the 48th New York. Bacon and Barton worked out a plan of attack, and that night Bacon took the *Commodore McDonough* across Calibogue Sound and anchored off the southern end of Hilton Head Island, where he awaited Colonel Barton. The movement was designed to leave at 11:30, but the army gunboat *Mayflower* grounded, and Barton arrived with only the transports *Island City* and *Cossack*. Attempts to free the *Mayflower* failed, and Bacon convinced Barton to continue the operation, assuring the colonel that the *Commodore McDonough*'s guns would be more than adequate to protect the expedition. Shortly after sunrise, the vessels proceeded into the May River. The transports carried about one thousand men: six companies of the 48th New York, two companies from both the 6th and 7th Connecticut, and detachments of the 3rd Rhode Island and the 1st New York Engineers. Three miles downriver from Bluffton at Hunting Island, the soldiers disembarked and marched toward the town. Freed by the rising tide, the *Mayflower* soon joined the *Commodore McDonough*, and the two vessels steamed to within a half mile of Bluffton and readied their batteries.[55]

At about 7:00 A.M. on June 4, Lieutenant Colonel Thomas H. Johnson at Camp Pritchard, eight miles west of Bluffton, received word from his pickets that Federal forces had entered the May River and landed. Johnson, who had just recently taken command of the area, had at Camp Pritchard three companies of his 3rd South Carolina and one company of the 4th South Carolina Cavalry Regiments, a total of just fewer than two hundred men. In Bluffton, camped near the wharf were Captain John H. Mickler's Company E, 11th South Carolina, and a detachment of mounted pickets from the 3rd South Carolina Cavalry.[56]

Since January 1863 Mickler and his company had been using Bluffton as a base to bedevil the Federals on Pinckney and Hilton Head Islands. They also placed torpedoes in Skull Creek to blow up unsuspecting enemy vessels. The Federals considered these devices to be barbaric, uncivilized weapons. On June 4 Mickler was at Hardeeville, and Lieutenant Wilson M. Smith commanded the company at Bluffton, while Captain A. M. Lowrey was in charge of the cavalry pickets. The first picket to spy the approaching Union vessels was Sergeant J. S. Jones, stationed at Baynard's Plantation. Jones immediately sent a courier to Lieutenant Colonel Johnson at Camp Pritchard. When Jones saw the enemy landing at Hunting Island, he dispatched a second courier to Johnson. At Hunting Island, Private A. L. Savage also watched the landing and sent a courier to Bluffton, but the horseman was unable to locate the town and returned. Savage then left the man to watch the Federal movements and, instead of riding to Bluffton, went directly to Johnson at Camp Pritchard.[57]

The first couriers reached Johnson's headquarters at Camp Pritchard at about 7:00 A.M. Johnson quickly mounted his command and put them in motion toward Bluffton. At the same time, he sent messages to nearby units guarding Red Bluff, including Captain H. C. Smart's cavalry company, Captain Thomas D. Ledbetter's infantry company, and Captain William Earle's artillery battery, directing them to Bluffton. Word was also sent to regional headquarters in Hardeeville.

While Johnson coordinated a response to the attack, Lieutenant Smith and Captain Lowry at Bluffton were unaware of the enemy's presence until Federal infantrymen entered the town and the *Commodore McDonough* and *Mayflower* appeared off the bluff. The two officers quickly withdrew their men a mile west to Sandy Bridge, leaving behind some pickets to watch the enemy.

With no opposition Colonel Barton and his soldiers swept into the town, while Lieutenant Commander Bacon brought the vessels near the wharf, where they could quickly reembark the troops. A portion of the Federals took up a position along the road leading into the town from the west, while others began firing buildings to burn down what they considered to be an outpost of vipers who constantly left their nest to kill and maim their comrades. As the flames spread through the town, Johnson and his horsemen reached Lieutenant Smith and his infantrymen at Sandy Bridge. Johnson ordered Smith to take his company forward as skirmishers while Johnson dismounted his men.

When the Union infantrymen spotted the skirmishers, they quickly opened fire. Colonel Barton signaled Bacon, who brought the *Commodore McDonough*'s heavy cannons to bear on the woods where the Confederate horsemen were dismounting. The naval gunfire forced Johnson to pull his men farther back, out of sight of the gunboat, before he could leave his horses and return to assist the infantrymen. With no immediate support, Smith feared that his small command would be overwhelmed and retreated.

By now the Confederates and the Union sailors could see flames and thick smoke billowing over the town. The fire had become so intense that Lieutenant Commander Bacon, who had maneuvered his gunboat to within a few rods of the town, had to back off into the river. Bacon kept the *Mayflower* and the transports off the town wharf to facilitate the withdrawal of Barton's troops, while his gun crews loaded the *Commodore McDonough*'s cannons with shrapnel and shell, ready to stop any renewed enemy attacks.

By now Johnson had returned with his dismounted cavalrymen and joined Smith. Together they advanced toward the town under steady volleys from the Federal soldiers and enfilading naval gunfire. Stopped by the combined barrage, Johnson halted the attack and then went forward with his staff to reconnoiter the enemy's position. While the southern soldiers waited, Captain Mickler arrived from Hardeeville and rode through the Confederate lines to join Lieutenant Colonel Johnson. Seeing that the Federal troops were pulling back, the two decided to renew the attack, hoping to push on rapidly and capture the Federals before they could reach their transports. With Mickler and his men from the 11th South Carolina in the lead, the southerners rushed into the burning town.

In Bluffton, Colonel Barton, with his mission accomplished, began embarking his soldiers while his rear guard dueled with the advancing Confederates along the street leading to the wharf. Aboard the *Commodore McDonough,* Lieutenant Bacon, his vision obscured by the smoke, could hear the southern soldiers cheering and the rolling volleys of musketry. Bacon had his cannoneers fire their guns toward the sound of battle. The shells and shrapnel passed over the heads of the Federals and exploded among the charging Confederates. The *Mayflower* also added its guns, and the Confederates were forced back, allowing the Union soldiers to board the transports, which quickly steamed away.[58]

Captain Mickler attempted to rush sharpshooters to the river bend at Hunting Island but was unable to intercept the Union ships. He returned with his soldiers to Bluffton, where they joined the others putting out the fires. The entire affair cost the southerners only one casualty, Sergeant Samuel K. Mew, of Company E, 11th South Carolina, who had been wounded by shrapnel from the Federal warship. In Bluffton the Confederates extinguished the conflagration, but most of the town had succumbed to the flames. The Methodist church was saved and a heavy growth of trees kept the flames from reaching the Episcopal Church and the western portion of the town. About forty homes burned, including those belonging to Thomas Drayton, J. J. Stoney, Dr. J. W. Kirk, George Allen, Dr. Paul Pritchard, M. J. Kirk, J. McKenzie, A. Crosby, G. Allen, Dr. A. G. Verdier, H. Gerrard, Joseph Baynard, James Seabrook, G. W. Lawton, W. Pope, Dr. Mellichamp, Dr. F. H. Pope, H. R. Pope, J. J. Pope, A. G. Verdier, Henry Verdier, Squire Pope, Mr. Strobhart, Mrs. Hardee, J. Chalmers, J. G. Bullchen, D. and J. Canter, D. Freeman, Crosby, Langballe, Chalmers, W. Winn, J. Bullchen, Mrs. Pinckney, Mrs. Winingham, Wiggins, Estate Norton, H. F. Train, and Martin.[59]

The Confederates were outraged by the destruction. In his after-action report, the department inspector, Captain John F. Lay, wrote: "The ashes of Bluffton, with its withered and scorched remains of noble trees and beautiful shrubbery, present a sad scene of desolation and fiendish vandalism unparalleled in the history of civilized nations." On the other hand, the Federals were quite pleased with the operation, especially the fine cooperation between the army and the navy that resulted in the destruction of a Confederate staging area for raids and deployment of infernal machines against Federal vessels—all accomplished without a single casualty.[60]

As in the raid up the Combahee, the Confederates could not defend fringe areas between them and the Federals. The frustration was clearly evident in their after-action reports, where blame was placed on the ineptness and timid responses of the couriers, pickets, and officers who had not learned the area's geography. The truth of the matter was that the Confederate high command had written off the region as expendable. The majority of the soldiers and artillery were kept guarding the railroad and few or no guns were available to challenge the enemy's gunboats and stop the coastal raids.

General Hunter believed the strikes up the Combahee and against Bluffton to be justified, but protests by both Confederate and northern officials caused him to modify his instructions to his commanders, including Colonel Montgomery, who by now was operating from St. Simons Island with his own command, and Colonel Shaw of the 54th Massachusetts. Hunter's new directives allowed his officers to gather up fugitives, horses, and mules and authorized the destruction of food and other supplies useful to the enemy, but prohibited the devastation of all "household furniture, libraries, churches, and hospitals." The orders, however, did not reach Montgomery in time to soften his expedition against Darien, Georgia, where, much to the disgust of Colonel Shaw, the town was destroyed, with Colonel Montgomery personally setting the torch to the last building.[61]

The Darien expedition ended Hunter's series of destructive coastal incursions. Eventually Montgomery's command returned to Port Royal, where they established camps on St. Helena Island. Though Hunter had been forced to temper his sorties into enemy territory, he never apologized for them. His actions did, however, bring him into conflict with Higginson and Saxton, who loathed the raids, which they felt degraded the black soldiers, but in an offhand way the two subordinates admired Montgomery and Hunter's singularity of purpose. On the other hand, Montgomery considered Higginson and Saxton to be weak, not willing to accept what was needed to create a homeland for settling freed slaves. The controversy revealed a stark contrast between the intellectual, idealistic New Englanders and the realistic, simple frontiersman. Though Higginson and Saxton questioned Montgomery's methods, all the officers wanted a postwar homeland for the freedmen. The creation of any new frontier, however, was put on hold with the arrival of a new department commander who soon renewed the campaign against Charleston.[62]

Chapter 10

The Attack on Charleston, 1863

"Wounded for we"

Missions and operations changed in the sea islands with the arrival of Brigadier General Quincy A. Gillmore as commander of the Department of the South. The onetime chief engineer of the Port Royal Expedition and conqueror of Fort Pulaski had been rewarded for his service with a brigadier general's commission in the volunteer army and a transfer to the Department of the Ohio, where he commanded an infantry division. But even in Kentucky, Gillmore always retained an interest in the Department of the South. In May 1863, while on a leave of absence from his division, Gillmore learned that his name was being mentioned concerning a new attack against Charleston. He quickly let it be known to certain well-placed officers that he was anxious to return to South Carolina to lead the attack. Gillmore probably did not need any help to secure the appointment. His reputation preceded him, and on June 3, 1863, orders were issued relieving General Hunter.[1]

Also on June 3, Secretary of the Navy Gideon Welles wrote orders relieving Du Pont as commander of the South Atlantic Blockading Squadron. The hero of Port Royal was well aware of his professional and national reputation, and the criticism that followed his failure to capture Charleston inflamed his oversensitive nature. Unwilling to accept any rebuke, Du Pont lashed out at his critics, claiming that a national conspiracy existed to cover up, at his expense, the monitors' defects. Though some of the rear admiral's denunciations of the ironclads had merit, he overplayed his hand, and Welles realized that his subordinate's negative attitude would adversely affect any new operation against Charleston.[2]

To replace Du Pont, Welles chose Rear Admiral Andrew H. Foote, an antislavery and antidrink fighter who in 1862 had paired with General Ulysses S. Grant for combined operations against Forts Henry and Donelson. With his vessels Foote captured Fort Henry on the Tennessee River before Grant arrived but was turned back on the Cumberland River at Fort Donelson. During the battle he received a leg wound from wood splinters knocked loose by Confederate shot striking his flagship. Foote repaired his vessels and himself and, while on crutches, directed his flotilla in a more temperate manner. At Island Number 10, he again supported the army in capturing enemy positions. After this victory Foote was forced to relinquish his command to care for his wounds. Ordered to Washington, the fifty-six-year-old, forty-year veteran was placed in charge of the Bureau of Equipment and Recruiting.

In Foote, Welles had the officer he wanted. Not only was Foote experienced in working with the army, but he and Welles were also close friends. His reputation would add prestige to the navy's contingent and give Welles a commander who would ensure the navy an equal voice in the coming campaign. Also, Foote was one of the few officers who could replace Du Pont without creating too much animosity. Welles knew full well that not all the fighting off Charleston would be with the enemy. Du Pont's influence among the officers of the South Atlantic Blockading Squadron was extremely strong, possibly affecting their willingness to cooperate fully with a new commander. Foote, Welles believed, had the character and stature to overcome all problems.[3]

Foote, eager to return to active duty, met with Welles and General Gillmore in Washington to plan the coming campaign. At Foote's request Rear Admiral John A. B. Dahlgren was added to the team as commander of the ironclad squadron. The fifty-three-year-old Dahlgren had spent most of his career at the Washington Naval Yard, where he invented three types of boat howitzers and a class of durable, large-caliber, smoothbore naval ordnance designed for close ship-to-ship combat. A friend of President Lincoln's, Dahlgren had constantly lobbied for a sea command. He had hoped to succeed Du Pont, but at Foote's urging he accepted the role of second in command and captain of the ironclad squadron. An introspective and quiet man, he had few close friends. Many questioned his ambition and lack of sea service, but no one challenged his technical expertise. His tendency toward seasickness would plague him throughout his tenure in South Carolina, but he would prove to be a determined though not foolhardy officer.[4]

In dismissing Du Pont, Welles tried to be as tactful as possible, pointing out that the department could not give up its attempt to take Charleston, and since Du Pont did not concur, the secretary was forced to replace him with Rear Admiral Foote. Du Pont had long expected to be relieved. He and his officers agreed that Foote would attempt to force an entrance into Charleston even if he lost all his ships trying. Du Pont viewed Foote as "a splendid navy officer, sort of a Northern Stonewall Jackson, without his intellect and judgment."[5]

Though impatient to start, Foote, Dahlgren, and Gillmore continued to detail their plans. In early June, Gillmore left for the Department of the South while the naval officers remained in Washington completing final details. Foote flung himself into battle preparations with his characteristic energy, but his wound from Fort Donelson became infected and for a while he languished in bed. He recovered enough to leave for New York, intending to sail for Port Royal, but he suffered a severe relapse. Not wishing to hold up the campaign, Welles on June 21 reluctantly informed Dahlgren that he would have to assume full command. Welles held out hope that Foote would recover, but on June 26, 1863, Foote died.[6]

Rumors concerning the new appointees swirled around the sea islands. On June 9 General Saxton returned to Port Royal aboard the *Arago*. He reported to General Hunter and resumed his command. Then, on June 11 the steamer *Ben Deford* arrived, carrying General Gillmore and orders for Hunter's relief. The next day Gillmore announced the change of command and issued general orders naming his staff. Du Pont planned to give Hunter a formal farewell dinner on the thirteenth, but since the general decided to leave as soon as possible, Du Pont's dinner became a "gouter or lunch," attended by all of Du Pont's army friends, his officers, and visiting French naval officers. The next morning, as the *Arago* left the harbor, Du Pont sent his crew into the *Wabash*'s yards where they loudly cheered Hunter as he, Halpine, and the rest of the general's staff steamed out of Port Royal Sound.[7]

Gillmore arrived with a letter for Du Pont, informing the admiral of Foote's imminent arrival, but Foote's relapse and the time needed for Dahlgren to organize his staff delayed Du Pont's relief. Du Pont knew his time was limited, but circumstances allowed him to leave with one final success.

In early June five Confederate deserters from Savannah arrived at Fort Pulaski. Sent to Hilton Head, the soldiers were interrogated by Major Halpine. They revealed that the ironclad *Atlanta,* built on the hull of the blockade runner *Fingal,* had been completed and was preparing to come out of Wassaw Sound, south of Savannah. With only the wooden warship *Cimarron* stationed at Wassaw, Du Pont quickly dispatched his most trusted officer, Captain John Rodgers, commander of the monitor *Weehawken,* along with Commander John Downes and the monitor *Nahant,* from Port Royal to reinforce the lone gunboat. On the morning of June 17, the *Atlanta* attempted to engage the two monitors but ran aground. Rodgers maneuvered the *Weehawken* to within three hundred yards of the stricken ram, fired five shots, with four striking the *Atlanta,* compelling her commander to surrender before the *Nahant* could engage.

Thanks to a telegraphic system that connected Fort Pulaski to Hilton Head, Beaufort, and Port Royal Ferry. word of the victory reached Du Pont by wire from Colonel Barton at Pulaski. Once a rising tide freed the *Atlanta,* a prize crew brought her to Port Royal Sound. The 204-foot iron, casemated ram anchored next to the *Wabash,* where Du Pont reported her to be "a great curiosity, a great prize, causing great rejoicing ashore and afloat, and everyone, officer and man, is instantly prompted to say, 'I'm so glad for the

Admiral.'" Colonel Higginson echoed these sentiments when he wrote, "It enables Admiral Dupont, the handsome & stately old gentleman, to retire in glory & it really does him credit."[8]

The *Atlanta*'s capture brought Du Pont some solace but could not erase the pain of being replaced. On July 4 the USS *Augusta Dinsmore* carried Rear Admiral Dahlgren into Port Royal Sound. Two days later, in an impressive ceremony aboard the flagship *Wabash,* with neatly attired seamen and full-dress marines, the dignified Du Pont relinquished his command. Du Pont and his staff then boarded the *Augusta Dinsmore,* and when the twin-masted, screw-propelled steamer left the harbor, Du Pont became the recipient of a ceremony that he had so often performed for departing generals, including twice for General Hunter. The *Wabash*'s crew manned the frigate's rigging, lustily cheering their former commander while the sailors on the *Augusta Dinsmore* returned the salutation.[9]

The departure of Du Pont and Hunter ended the tenure of two important personalities whose impact forever changed the Beaufort District. Though Hunter never achieved a great military victory, his overall direction of the contraband situation and recruitment of black soldiers had allowed General Saxton and his civilian associates to alter the sea islands' slave society, giving the freedmen new economic opportunities and military service. There were few, if any, other army commanders who would have so patiently guided such a transformation. While he did not tolerate overt bigotry from his officers or civilian contractors, Hunter understood that the existing racial mindset would handicap the acceptance of the former slaves into the nation's society. He realized that such attitudes would stop any integration of southern society, and therefore he had opened a fierce campaign to create a coastal homeland for the freedmen where they could live until passions cooled. His tool for this was primarily his black regiments, a force that he believed, once enlarged, could win the war.

On the other hand, Du Pont had achieved one of the war's greatest victories, delivering to the North the finest harbor on the southeastern coast. The triumph, which caused the majority of the planters to flee the sea islands, created the environment required for the freedmen associations to take root. Though never as enthusiastic as Hunter, Du Pont became a qualified supporter of the reconstruction movement, lending logistical and moral support whenever possible.

By the summer of 1863, however, the war had changed, and Du Pont and Hunter were expendable. Their past failures against Charleston caused them to be replaced by aggressive, technically astute leaders who could be counted on to press home the attack. Gillmore and Dahlgren were such officers. They were not social reformers. Though they were sympathetic to the plight of the freedmen, it was not their top priority.

At Port Royal, Gillmore counted on General Saxton, who also commanded the military forces at Beaufort and Port Royal Island, to continue his management of the former slaves. But when the new commander arrived, he found Saxton, his former West Point classmate, to be uncooperative. Three days after his arrival on June 14, Gillmore, at Saxton's request, officially removed Saxton as military commander of the post of Beaufort, replacing him with Colonel William W. H. Davis of he 104th Pennsylvania. Higginson reported that Saxton, in high dudgeon, was angling for the departmental command over Gillmore, whom he outranked. For a month Saxton's status remained in limbo as Gillmore prepared his troops for the Charleston campaign.[10]

While Saxton awaited word on his fate, his predecessor, Edward Pierce, came back to the region. Pierce, who had visited the sea islands between March and May 1863, returned in June. Always eager to check on the operation he had initiated, he remained an avid backer and whenever possible participated with his onetime comrades in services and activities. His second trip coincided with the arrival of a War Department commission sent to investigate what was needed to protect the freedmen, improve their situation, and encourage their enlistment into the armed forces.

The commission was an outgrowth of the Boston Emancipation League, which had been founded by leading Massachusetts abolitionists and Republicans in September 1861. By November 1862 the league was calling for the government to form an emancipation bureau. Though heartened by the Emancipation Proclamation, they believed that a "Bureau of Freedom," should have been formed first so as "to make provision for the first necessities of the freedmen, to allot them land out of those forfeited by the rebels, to organize and protect their labor." Antislavery societies backed the program and added a call for "educational instrumentalities."[11]

To bolster their request for a national bureau, the Emancipation League distributed questionnaires to freedmen supervisors throughout the occupied South, inquiring about existing programs. The replies were positive in regard to the capacity of the former slaves to become productive citizens. Further calls by prominent abolitionists such as Governor Andrew of Massachusetts and J. Miller McKim of Philadelphia, both backers of the Port Royal Experiment, resulted in the formation by the War Department of the American Freedmen's Inquiry Commission to seek out additional information on the freedmen's condition. Robert Dale Owen, Samuel Gridley Howe, and James McKaye were named commissioners. The three personally visited freedmen communities, with McKaye coming to Port Royal in June 1863.

McKaye, an organizer of the Wells Fargo Express Company and president of the American Telegraph Company, arrived with a shorthand reporter, whose notations made some of those interviewed nervous since they were not sure whether he was properly recording their statements. McKaye gathered the teachers at superintendent Henry G. Judd's house (the Stuart House) on Bay Street in Beaufort, where he carried out his interviews one at a time. Laura Towne reported that Edward Pierce teased her about the importance of the interrogation. She answered each question in a short and precise manner. In addition to interviewing teachers, McKaye also met with military officers such as General Saxton, Colonel Higginson, Captain Hooper, and other government officials, including Tax Commissioner Abram Smith. What became apparent to McKaye, and was later reflected in the commission's final report, was that the slaves from the sea islands, an isolated region "with the least contact with external civilization," had in less than eighteen months become a model for future reconstruction programs. At Port Royal the former slaves had established family relationships, accepted marital commitments, and formed religious congregations. They attended schools, worked for wages, owned property, and accepted military discipline.

The preliminary report, sent to Secretary of War Stanton on June 30, 1863, emphasized many of the concepts already put in practice at Port Royal that had proven so successful. It also called for the creation of a Bureau of Emancipation within the War Department to oversee freedmen's affairs. The final report, which was not submitted until May 1864, is considered to be the "Blueprint for Radical Reconstruction."[12]

The preliminary report of the American Freedmen's Inquiry Commission emphasized the use of military service to prepare freedmen for citizenship. In the sea islands such activity was already occurring, and in late June, while the commission's report was being prepared, the department's black regiments, as well as their white comrades, readied for a renewed attack against Charleston.

Many of the activities for the coming campaign centered around the troops stationed at Land's End on St. Helena Island. Encampments expanded and quartermaster buildings were constructed. A railroad connected the quartermaster complex's structures to a wharf that stretched out into the Beaufort River. An intense training program began with troops drilling, participating in sham battles, and taking target practice. The men turned in old equipment and received new tents, clothing, and knapsacks. Detachments learned to operate the Billinghurst-Requa battery, a predecessor of the machine gun. It consisted of twenty-five rifle barrels arranged horizontally and attached to a field carriage. The weapon had a range of thirteen hundred yards and could fire 175 shots per minute. The batteries were unveiled on St. Helena Island in late June, and the soldiers who practiced with Requas near their camps at Land's End were impressed with its killing power. But one New Hampshire soldier, who realized what the Requa could do to an enemy formation, worried that the gun crews would have to answer for their use of such an agent of destruction on the Day of Judgment.[13]

Two brigades, approximately five thousand men, camped at Land's End. Brigadier General George C. Strong commanded one brigade consisting of the 3rd New Hampshire, 76th Pennsylvania, 48th New York, 9th Maine, and 127th New York. The thirty-year-old Strong had arrived at Port Royal with General Gillmore. A Massachusetts native and an 1857 graduate of West Point, he had been stationed in arsenals before the war and in 1861 served as an ordnance officer in Virginia before being assigned in early 1862 as Major General Benjamin Butler's chief of staff and chief ordnance officer with the combined expeditionary force that seized New Orleans.[14]

Colonel James Montgomery led the other brigade at Land's End consisting of his own 2nd South Carolina and Colonel Shaw's 54th Massachusetts. Though appalled at Montgomery's actions at Darien, Georgia, Shaw still found Montgomery a man to be admired. In conversations Montgomery informed Shaw that initially he opposed Hunter's destructive policies against civilian targets but had changed his mind and now realized the need to purge the coastal area of Confederate sympathizers. Montgomery also told Shaw that he did not believe that former slaves, held in bondage for two hundred years, could fight as well as freemen and that "all our energies must be devoted to making the most of them." Though Shaw disagreed with his fellow colonel, he did respect Montgomery's direct, unyielding approach; however, he did not want the 54th used in any more raids. In an attempt to remove his regiment from Montgomery's control, Shaw complained to Governor Andrew over its use in the destruction of Darien. And though he did admit in a letter to his wife that there was some justification in burning out the rebels because of their laws declaring black troops and their officers criminals, combined with threats of enslavement and executions, he also viewed such activity as "cruel, barbarous, impolitic and degrading to ourselves and to our men, and I shall rejoice that I expressed myself at the time of the destruction of Darien."[15]

While stationed on St. Helena Island, Shaw worried over his regiment's fate. Stories spread that the unit would be used exclusively as laborers or armed with pikes instead of muskets. Neither rumor had any legitimacy, but Shaw feared his men might be denied their opportunity to prove themselves on a battlefield. The young colonel did strike up a friendship with General Strong. The two discussed the use of black troops, and Strong promised, if the opportunity arose, to employ Shaw's regiment in the coming campaign. A happy Colonel Shaw wrote Governor Andrew that Strong was anxious to do all he could for the regiment and "will no doubt give the black troops a chance to show what stuff they are made of." However, before the new campaign started, directives arrived from Washington that nearly caused the disbanding of the 54th and the ending of the recruitment and use of black soldiers.[16]

On July 17, 1862, to help pave the way for the enlistment of black troops, Congress passed two pieces of legislation, the Militia Act of 1862 and the Second Confiscation Act. The Confiscation Act authorized the president to "employ as many persons of African descent as he may deem necessary and proper for the suppression of this rebellion, and for this purpose he may organize and use them in such manner as he may judge best for the public welfare." The Militia Act overrode the 1792 Militia Act that had barred men of color from serving in the army and militia. Section 15 of the Militia Act stated "that persons of African descent, who under this law shall be employed, shall receive ten dollars per month and one ration, three dollars of which monthly pay may be in clothing."[17]

However, when they initially enlisted, the soldiers of the 54th Massachusetts and the 1st, 2nd, and recently mustered 3rd South Carolina Regiments, as well as other black regiments, had been promised by the War Department the standard pay for enlisted soldiers. Privates received thirteen dollars per month plus a clothing ration, when required, of $3.50 a month. Pay increased accordingly for higher ranks, but in May 1863, when the army established a Bureau of Colored Troops to oversee the recruitment and management of black regiments, Secretary of War Stanton requested that William Whiting, the War Department solicitor general, make a decision setting a consistent level of pay for men of African descent. A Boston patent lawyer and moderate Republican, Whiting examined the Second Confiscation Act and Militia Act, ruling on June 2, 1863, that both black soldiers and black laborers should receive ten dollars a month and that the soldiers could have three dollars of that wage taken out, when necessary, for clothing.

Word of the new regulation reached Port Royal in late June. Reactions to the decrease in pay varied. The paymaster for Higginson's 1st South Carolina ignored the order and continued to give out the thirteen dollars a month until directed to stop, at which time the regiment saw its pay reduced to seven dollars a month to make up for the overpayment. Colonel Shaw, enraged by the injustice, immediately wrote Governor Andrew requesting him to intervene. Shaw reported that the officers and men intended to refuse all pay until they heard from the governor but that if the ruling was not altered, Andrew should remove the regiment from service. The governor asked Shaw to wait, but it was months before Andrew actually went to Washington to meet with President Lincoln, who, though sympathetic, left the matter in the hands of Congress, where War Democrats managed to delay the equalizing of pay until March 1865. In the meantime, the men of the 54th Massachusetts, the South Carolina regiments, and other black units continued to serve and fight while receiving reduced or no pay.[18]

While Higginson and Shaw actively lobbied for redress over the pay issue, Colonel Montgomery found himself directly involved in the controversy when, after returning from Georgia on June 25 and encamping his regiment at Land's End on St. Helena Island, between thirty and seventy men fled the regiment's camp over the pay issue. On June 28 a deserter was brought before Colonel Montgomery, who immediately ordered the man "to be taken away and shot." By the army's general orders, only the department commander, General Gillmore, could authorize an execution, but Montgomery acted on his own hook and was never called to answer for his act. As more deserters were found, Montgomery wanted to carry out additional executions, but Surgeon Seth Rogers from Higginson's regiment convinced Montgomery to cease. However, the single execution had the desired results. Over the next few days, some thirty to forty men returned. While many were shocked by Montgomery's flagrant disobedience, Colonel Shaw defended his fellow commander, telling his wife that "as to the right or wrong of the matter, he only violated a clause of the Regulations, and the result is extremely beneficial."[19]

While Shaw waited for word on the pay issue and the future use of his regiment, he continued to prepare his men for the coming campaign. When not participating in drill, the soldiers from the 54th and neighboring white regiments explored St. Helena Island. They found the island full of luxuriant vegetation that furnished the soldiers with an abundance of plums. They also foraged on the island, finding green cabbage, green peas, new potatoes, string beans, and blackberries. The summer heat varied from 100 to 120 degrees, and all enlisted soldiers were issued straw hats. Besides swimming and fishing, Bandmaster Ingalls brought the 3rd New Hampshire band from Hilton Head to St. Helena for evening concerts. Officers visited the captured ram *Atlanta,* and her captor, Captain John Rodgers, accepted an invitation to dine at Land's End with the officers of the 3rd New Hampshire. Men and officers attended church services at the Brick Baptist Church and the Chapel of Ease, and the soldiers erected a new church on Land's End.[20]

As July 4 neared, the soldiers and the missionaries began preparing to celebrate the nation's birthday. At Beaufort the officers and men of the 52nd Pennsylvania planned a program on the Beaufort Green. The formal ceremony called for an opening prayer by Chaplain William R. Gries of the 104th Pennsylvania, followed by music from the regimental band and the reading of the Declaration of Independence. After the singing of "The Star-Spangled Banner," the exercise would end with a final benediction. Once the formal ceremony was over, the soldiers planned to amuse the gathering with sack races, grease-pole climbing, and a pig race.[21]

However, not everyone was able to follow through with their planned celebrations. During the first days of July, men from Strong's brigade loaded supplies onto quartermaster vessels at the Land's End wharf. Then, to mask the movement from enemy observation balloons and watch towers, the soldiers on the night of July 3 boarded transports and, before sunrise on the fourth, sailed out of Port Royal Sound to join the planned attack against Charleston.[22]

Much to Colonel Shaw's dismay, the 54th Massachusetts did not leave St. Helena Island with General Strong and the white regiments. Shaw wrote to Strong, politely expressing his disappointment in being left behind and pointing out that "I had been given to understand that we were to have our share in the work in the department. I feel convinced too that my men are capable of better service than mere guerilla warfare." The young colonel expressed hope that the regiment would again be placed under Strong and "be associated as much as possible with the white troops, in order that they may have other witnesses besides their own officers to what they are capable of doing."[23]

While Colonel Shaw waited for orders, he and some of his officers continued to explore the area. Many of them had connections to the missionaries and attended dinners and receptions. Colonel Higginson's cousin, Francis "Frank" Higginson, an officer in the 54th Massachusetts, visited his famous relative at his regiment's camp in Beaufort. Shaw accepted an invitation to the Oaks Plantation, where he had tea with Charlotte Forten, Laura Towne, Ellen Murray, and others. Afterward he talked with Forten on the piazza and then attended a shout in the plantation praise house.[24]

On July 4 Colonel Shaw, Lieutenant Colonel Edward Hallowell, and some other regimental officers attended celebrations on St. Helena Island outside the Brick Baptist Church. The ceremony had special significance since it was the former slaves' first Independence Day as freedmen. A national flag hung over the roadway between two live oaks. Under another oak in the grove next to the church on a raised platform sat speakers and other dignitaries such as Laura Towne, Mrs. Lander, the *New York Tribune* reporter Nathaniel Page, Colonel Shaw, and his officers. The schoolchildren assembled in the church, where they received patriotic badges. They marched out and, while standing on the road under the flag, sang "The Star-Spangled Banner." Then Charles F. Folsom read the Declaration of Independence. The Reverend James T. Lynch, a black minister who had been dispatched by the Baltimore African Methodist Episcopal Conference to Port Royal with Reverend James D. S. Hall to organize an A.M.E. Conference in South Carolina, gave the oration. Once Lynch finished, the children sang "Oh, None in All." Edward Pierce then gave an address, after which the children performed "My Country 'Tis of Thee," followed by the assembled crowd who "made the grove resound with the grand tones of *Roll Jordon Roll*." After additional hymns all were treated to molasses and water and hardtack.[25]

Later, Charlotte Forten, who had helped teach the children their songs, was invited by Mrs. Lander to come to Beaufort to attend a dinner party.

Before leaving, while ensconced beneath a live oak, Mrs. Lander entertained Forten and Page by reciting Buchanan Read's poem "Drifting." Once in Beaufort they gathered at Mrs. Lander's, where they were joined by Colonel Higginson and Surgeon Seth Rogers. Higginson, who had been the principal orator at the 52nd Pennsylvania's celebration at the Beaufort green, was asked about his speech. The colonel replied that he did not remember what he had said but did recall receiving a rousing response when he stated that his regiment had no "prejudice against color, and liked white people just as well as black—if they behaved as well!"[26]

General Saxton had been conspicuously absent from all celebrations. Colonel Higginson reported that the general seemed depressed over the command arrangement and rarely visited his camp, which was now located along the Beaufort River just west of Bladen Street, only a few blocks from Saxton's headquarters in the Lewis Reeves Sams home.[27]

Saxton was not the only officer worried about his status. Colonel Shaw anxiously waited for word about the role of the 54th Massachusetts in the coming campaign. To pass the time, Shaw kept his men drilling. On Sunday, July 5, he and other officers attempted to go to church at the Episcopal Chapel of Ease, but finding the service canceled, they continued on to the Brick Baptist Church, where they attended the service and observed a wedding. Shaw commented that the sermon was "full of 'hell and damnation' but administered in such a dull way, that sleep soon overcame most of the congregation."[28]

The following evening Colonel Shaw entertained Charlotte Forten, Lizzie Hunn, and a Mrs. Hitchcock at the regiment's camp on Land's End. The women viewed a dress parade, had tea with the officers, and were serenaded by the soldiers, who sang a rendition of the song "Jubilo." Forten found the young colonel a "wonderfully lovable person" with a "nobleness of soul." She prayed that he would be spared in the coming campaign.[29]

The next day Colonels Shaw and Montgomery received orders to embark for Folly Island, where they would become part of Brigadier General Alfred Terry's division. With their departure the majority of the Federal regiments from Hilton Head, St. Helena, and Port Royal Islands had quit the region. Clara Barton, with an ambulance and riding horses, also departed the area, leaving Hilton Head on July 9, accompanied by Colonel Elwell on the steamer *Canonicus*. Mary Gage, whose mother, Frances, had temporarily left Parris Island to return to Ohio to tend to her dying husband, went along as Barton's assistant. Barton, who had been given a pass by General Gillmore to serve in the campaign, was unsure what might lie ahead and believed she was "going into the wilderness."[30]

The shifting of troops also restored General Saxton to command. When Colonel Davis and his brigade left Beaufort, General Gillmore, who had smoothed out the difficulties with his subordinate, issued General Orders Number 59, which stated that "Brig. Gen. Rufus Saxton, having signified his willingness to resume command of troops, should the exigencies of the service require it, is hereby placed in command of the forces on Port Royal Island and all the outposts supplied therefrom."[31]

Besides being responsible for the defense of Port Royal Island and Beaufort, Saxton also readied the town's hospitals. Port Royal served as the department's logistical center for the campaign. All of the region's medical, quartermaster, commissary, ordnance, engineering, and maritime facilities fed supplies and equipment to the Federal army located on the barrier islands just south of Charleston Harbor. The naval depot also increased its tempo, providing supplies, seamen, and ammunition to the squadron off Charleston. The naval machine shops on St. Helena Island and in Station Creek outfitted and repaired warships, including the all-important monitors, whose presence off Charleston was essential for a successful campaign.

Gillmore, one of the North's best engineers and artillerists, believed that the capture of Charleston came down to superior firepower. To open the harbor for an attack by the ironclads, he planned to use the Union base on Folly Island as a jumping-off point to capture Morris Island, which formed the southern tip of Charleston harbor. Once he captured Morris Island, Gillmore planned to place heavy artillery on the island's northern end—Cumming Point, a mere one-half mile from Fort Sumter—bombard Sumter into submission, occupy the fort, remove the obstructions and torpedoes, and open a passage for the navy to enter the harbor and capture the city.

Gillmore's operation was quick and simple. He also designed a series of diversions to help confuse the Confederates. General Terry's division with the 54th Massachusetts and the 2nd South Carolina landed on James Island on July 9, while that same day Colonel Higginson led an amphibious operation to destroy the Charleston and Savannah Railroad Bridge over the Edisto River at Jacksonboro. For the expedition Higginson proceeded from Beaufort with 250 men from his regiment and a detachment from the 1st Connecticut Light Artillery aboard the army vessels *John Adams, Enoch Dean,* and *Governor Milton*. Sailing up the North Edisto, termed the Pon Pon River by the Federals, the ships, accompanied by the naval sailing gunboat *Kingfisher,* reached Willtown Bluff at 4:00 A.M., where they encountered a Confederate battery and a line of wooden stakes stretching across the river. After the heavy cannons of the *Kingfisher* drove off a section of Confederate field artillery, Higginson posted a company on the bluff under Captain James B. West, while Captain Trowbridge, who had planned and scouted the expedition's route, supervised the cutting of a passage through the obstructions. The sawing took time. The *Kingfisher* returned downriver while Captain West's men moved inland, captured some Confederates, and destroyed the nearby

Morris Rice Mills. The appearance of the Federals also attracted hundreds of slaves, who were taken aboard the *John Adams.*

While waiting for the obstruction to be removed, Higginson transferred a company of soldiers under Major John D. Strong onto the *Governor Milton.* The small, seventy-five-ton, side-wheel steamer, formerly the *George M. Bird,* had been captured in the St. John's River, Florida. She drew only three feet and had rifled, bronze, 6-pound cannons mounted on her bow and stern. The guns were manned by a detachment from the 1st Connecticut Battery. Higginson left the larger *John Adams* at Willtown and joined Trowbridge aboard the *Enoch Dean,* a side-wheel steamer about twice the size of the *Governor Milton.* The *Enoch Dean* was armed with rifled Parrott guns—one on the bow, one on the stern—operated by a detachment of soldiers from the 1st South Carolina trained and commanded by Corporal John F. Bliss of the 1st Connecticut Battery.[32]

By noon the hole through the obstructions had been finished, and the two light-drafted vessels, aided by a rising tide, slipped through the opening and pushed on toward Jacksonboro. But in ascending the river, the *Enoch Dean* kept running aground, and her engine constantly broke down. Higginson directed the *Governor Milton* with Major Strong's forces to continue toward the railroad bridge, but Confederate field artillery, shadowing the Federal ships along the east bank of the river, soon found vantage points to engage the *Governor Milton,* forcing it to return downriver. Higginson abandoned the venture and headed his vessels back toward Willtown. As they neared the obstructions, the following Confederate cannoneers again opened fire on them. During the exchange a Confederate shell passed so close to Higginson that its shock waves caused a severe concussion in the colonel's side. Momentarily disabled, Higginson stayed on deck as the two vessels, still under enemy fire, neared Willtown Bluff. As the ship's captains prepared to negotiate the passage through the obstructions, the *Governor Milton*'s pilot panicked, missed the opening, and ran his vessel onto the remaining wooden stakes. The *Enoch Dean* pulled the vessel free and then passed beyond the barrier, but again the *Governor Milton*'s pilot ran into the obstructions. This time the *John Adams* came up but was unable to free the grounded vessel. After the crew and passengers were transferred to the *John Adams,* the artillerymen threw the *Governor Milton*'s guns overboard and burned the vessel.[33]

While returning down the Edisto, the Federal vessels had another brush with Confederate artillery before they rejoined the *Kingfisher* at the mouth of the river. By July 11 they returned to Beaufort, and Higginson moved into Mrs. Lander's residence to recover from his wound. Dr. Rogers cared for the colonel, as Mrs. Lander had gone to Folly Island, where she assisted army surgeons in caring for the campaign's initial casualties. The little expedition had failed to reach its objective, though it did force the Confederates to keep some units guarding the approaches to the railroad. Both sides reported a few soldiers wounded, and the Federal casualty list also included the civilian engineer of the *Governor Milton,* who was killed along with at least one black refugee. As one Connecticut artilleryman summed up the raid: "We destroyed a few hundred bushels of rice, burned the mill, captured a lieutenant and two men, brought off some two hundred contrabands with their baggage, lost two men and several wounded. I got a hundred pound note of 1776 and other Continental money from the Morris house."[34]

On July 10, the day after Higginson's operation on the Edisto, Gillmore opened his attack, sending General Strong's brigade from Folly Island onto Morris Island. By the end of the day, the Federals had captured three-fourths of the island, driving the Confederates back to a fortification known as Battery Wagner. The next morning Strong's brigade attacked Wagner. Turned back, Gillmore began constructing breaching batteries to cover his next attack. The wounded from the initial assaults were placed on steamers and sent to Beaufort. Colonel Higginson, still recovering from his injury at Mrs. Lander's, reported, "Boat loads of wounded are coming in from Folly Island & every hour brings some new rumor."[35]

By July 17 Gillmore had finished his preparations. Terry's brigade, with the 54th Massachusetts and 2nd South Carolina, having completed its demonstration on James Island had rejoined the rest of the Gillmore's army on Folly and Morris islands, ready to support the next assault on Wagner. With his batteries completed, Gillmore on July 18 opened a heavy bombardment on Battery Wagner. That night he drew up a division of nearly seven thousand men under General Truman Seymour. General Strong's brigade again led the way. Strong, remembering his promise to Colonel Shaw, requested and received from Terry's brigade the 54th Massachusetts, which was assigned the honor of leading the assault. Before joining his men at the head of the column, Shaw took time to have supper with Strong and Edward Pierce, who had accompanied the expedition as a reporter.

At nightfall the bombardment ended and the troops went forward. Though some, including elements of the 54th Massachusetts entered the battery, the Confederates held it, inflicting over fifteen hundred casualties on the assaulting column. Colonel Shaw was killed, General Strong mortally wounded, and General Seymour wounded. Throughout the night Union soldiers and stretcher bearers from the Sanitary Commission, directed by Dr. M. M. Marsh, carried wounded back to the field hospital on the southern end of Morris Island, where surgeons tended the Union casualties. Clara Barton and Mary Gage assisted the army doctors. Among Barton's patients were many officers she had known on Hilton Head, including the badly injured Lieutenant Colonel Elwell. Once treated, the wounded were carried onto the steamer *Alice Price,* which transported them to hospitals on Folly

Island. From there, those who could be moved were placed on the hospital ship *Cosmopolitan* and taken to Beaufort and Hilton Head.[36]

For over a week, the people on the sea islands listened to cannon fire "day and night." The sound reached its crescendo on July 18. Beginning the next day, wounded began to arrive. Mrs. Lander and Edward Pierce returned to Beaufort to help prepare the hospitals. The entire town turned out, black and white civilians, officers and enlisted men. On the twentieth, as the flow of wounded increased, Pierce summoned the missionaries and freedmen on the neighboring islands for help. Laura Towne, Charlotte Forten, and others hurried to Beaufort, where they joined the townspeople, including Harriet Tubman, in caring for the casualties. The freedmen brought chickens, melons, and potatoes to the hospitals, stating that the "wounded for we."[37]

The injured, arriving on transports, were quickly distributed among the town's hospitals. The soldiers from the nine white regiments that followed the 54th were placed in Hospitals 1 (Paul Hamilton House), 2 (Berners B. Sams Number 2 House), 3 (John Johnson House), 4 (William W. Barnwell House), 5 (Barnwell Castle), 8 (Edward Means House), and 9 (John Joyner Smith House).[38]

The men of the 54th were taken to Hospital 10, the Barnwell-Gough House, and Hospital 6 (the Joseph Johnson House). At Hospital 10 Esther Hawks reported that 150 men from the 54th Massachusetts were "laid on the floor all mangled and ghastly.... We had no beds, and no means even of building a fire, but the colored people came promptly to our aid and almost before we knew what we needed they brought us buckets full of nice broth and gruels, pitchers of lemonade, fruits, cakes, vegetables indeed everything needed for the immediate wants of the men was furnished—not for one day but for many."[39]

Though Saxton directed all citizens in Beaufort to serve in the hospitals three days a week, most readily volunteered. With aid from the freedmen, the Sanitary Commission, the post quartermaster, and local citizens, the wounded soon had clean clothes and beds. In Hospital 10 Hawks and the hospital's two surgeons kept up an exhausting schedule for twenty-four hours, cleaning and dressing wounds, performing amputations, and comforting the dying. A few of the men had been slaves, but the majority were freemen, some Canadians. A number of them were students educated at Oberlin College. Hawks also learned from the soldiers about Colonel Shaw's death while leading his regiment against Battery Wagner. One, Sergeant Morgan, told her that "I suppose his friends will consider it a great disgrace for him to lie buried with a lot of niggers but if they know how all his men loved him, they would never wish to take him to any other resting place."[40]

At Hospital 6 Charlotte Forten worked with Mrs. Lander and Saxton in assisting the wounded. Also joining them was Frances Gage, recently returned from Ohio, where she had stayed with her husband until his death. Forten, who repaired clothing and wrote letters for the soldiers, stated that the wounded, all from the 54th Massachusetts, endured their wounds bravely: "Many, indeed, have only flesh wounds. But there are others—and they among the most uncomplaining—who are severely wounded;—some dangerously so. Brave fellows! I feel it a happiness, an honor, to do the slightest service for them."[41]

On the same day that Colonel Shaw's death was confirmed, Forten accompanied Edward Pierce to the officer's hospital located in Hospital 7, the Edgar Fripp House, where Pierce had been assisting the wounded. Forten visited with a number of the 54th's officers including the regiment's badly wounded lieutenant colonel, Edward Hallowell. Many of the officers, including Colonel Higginson, went north as soon as they were able. General Strong, leaving too early, never recovered from his wound and died after reaching New York.

Once the situation with the wounded had stabilized and the summer heat increased, others left Beaufort. On July 31 Forten, Edward Pierce, and Dr. Rogers left aboard the SS *Fulton*. As the vessel steamed north, she passed close to Charleston and the passengers could see the city's church steeples, Fort Sumter, Morris Island, and Battery Wagner, causing Forten to shudder as she thought of Colonel Shaw and his regiment's forlorn attack.[42]

Others also remembered Shaw and wanted to memorialize him. Saxton appealed to the region's freedmen and black soldiers to raise money to erect an "enduring monument" to Colonel Shaw. Mansfield French repeated the plea on August 6, the day President Lincoln set aside as a "Thanksgiving to God for northern victories on land and sea," at a great assembly held at the Beaufort Baptist Church. Collections continued into the fall, with Laura Towne and others joining the blacks in giving money, but the memorial was never erected. Instead the funds were given to a black orphanage in Charleston named for Colonel Shaw.[43]

Throughout the summer the hospitals at Beaufort and Hilton Head continued to serve the wounded, sick, and injured from the Charleston campaign. Besides serving as a medical center, the area also functioned as a massive logistical base. Union warships, especially the monitors, which were shuttled from Charleston to Port Royal two at a time, received repairs in Station Creek and Port Royal Sound. Dahlgren also increased his use of sea island freedmen, who enlisted in the navy as landsmen and were assigned to his squadron's warships.

The engineer depot on Hilton Head Island provided finished products, including items made of iron and cut boards manufactured at steam-powered lumber mills. Beaufort workshops manufactured siege material, turning saplings, trees, and bushes into gabions, fascines, and fagots. The completed products were placed on quartermaster steamers that kept up a constant shuttle between Port Royal Sound and Folly and Morris Islands.[44]

Troops were also transported. After the failed attack on Battery Wagner, Gillmore, fearing a strike against his base at Port Royal, dispatched the survivors of the 6th Connecticut to Port Royal, where they replaced regiments being discharged at Hilton Head. At Beaufort the soldiers from the 1st South Carolina joined their comrades in performing picket duty and labored intensely to improve Beaufort's fortifications and turn out siege materials required for the Morris Island operations. On Hilton Head Island the men of the newly mustered 3rd South Carolina found their military instructions cut short and were assigned arduous and menial work loading quartermaster vessels with supplies and coal and policing the camps of white soldiers.[45]

Though Gillmore worried over the security of the sea islands, there was little the Confederates could do. When the Federals launched their strike against Morris Island, five companies of the 11th South Carolina, and Earle's company of artillery were immediately removed from General Walker's district and sent to Charleston. With his reduced command, Walker could do little except watch over the Federals at Port Royal and inform his superiors of any enemy movements. By this point in the war, Walker had established a system of signal towers throughout his district, stretching from Foot Point on the Broad River to Pocotaligo, where couriers were stationed to carry the information to Hardeeville, McPhersonville, and Pocotaligo Station. Walker also occupied the "very tall house" known as Whitehall near Euhaw Creek to observe Federal vessels in Port Royal Sound.[46]

The ships sailing in and out of Port Royal transported not only supplies and troops but also civilians. The summer, exceedingly hot and humid, forced even more individuals, including Jean Lander, to leave the sea islands and seek respite in the north. While civilians left for "a change of air," reinforcements arrived to support Gillmore's operations, including five regiments of black troops from North Carolina and New York. The long and arduous campaign off Charleston continued into September 1863, when Gillmore's army finally captured Battery Wagner and Morris Island. During the siege Federal cannons had smashed Fort Sumter to pieces, but the Confederate citadel resisted capture and the deadly torpedoes remained. And as long as infernal machines populated the ship channel, Dahlgren refused to send his ironclads into the harbor. The operation that had cost so much blood and matériel ended in stalemate.[47]

While the campaign raged outside Charleston, the freedmen who were not in or working for the military continued to toil in the cotton fields around Port Royal. By now most no longer considered sea island cotton a "slave crop," and instead viewed it as a means to gain prosperity. In 1863 only a few freedmen, who had purchased property at the tax sales, grew their own crop. Most still worked for the government or labored for Edward Philbrick's operation, but all took pride in the 1863 harvest, which exceeded expectations and, by some accounts, surpassed any grown under slavery.

Philbrick was particularly pleased. His consortium alone exceeded the entire previous crop produced by the occupying forces by ginning 287,790 pounds of sea island cotton versus the 1862 mark of 265,000 pounds. By prevailing rates in Liverpool, Philbrick's harvest was worth one hundred thousand dollars (two million in current dollars). The results, Philbrick believed, proved his concept that free labor would produce more cotton than slave labor. He also wanted an expansion of his system, where the freedmen toiled on cotton plantations for wages instead of remaining under the "philanthropic benevolence" of working directly for the government or as landowners growing their own crops. Philbrick believed that it was essential to prove that "Negro labor," employed by enterprising entrepreneurs, could be used to turn a profit in a free market. Only then, he stated, would the freedmen be welcomed as equals into a self-sustaining, capitalistic society.[48]

The freedmen also wanted to see a change, but unlike Philbrick, they did not see their future as laborers working for northern capitalists. Instead they wanted to be their own entrepreneurs, working their own farms. As Edward Pierce wrote, "The instinct for land—to have one spot on earth where a man may stand, and whence no human being can drive him—is one of the most conservative elements of our nature; and a people who have it in any fair degree will never be nomads or vagabonds."[49]

Pierce saw great changes in the experiment he had created. In a September 1863 article published in the *Atlantic Monthly,* he reported that the freedmen at Port Royal had made remarkable advances. He noted that the former slaves "during their first year under the system, have acquired the idea of ownership, and of the security of wages, and have come to see that labor and slavery are not the same thing." Whenever possible, the freedmen planted cotton on two- to four-acre plots; cotton gins they had destroyed when their owners fled were rebuilt and used to gin the new crop. Refugee camps became towns. For the displaced Edisto Island natives at St. Helenaville, the government contracted with a black foreman, Frank Barnwell, to oversee freedmen work gangs in the construction of over twenty two-room, eighteen-by-fourteen-foot houses. Villages expanded around Beaufort and Camp Saxton and on Hilton Head, where refugees cultivated gardens growing corn, peanuts, and other vegetables. Women took in laundry and, with most of the men serving in the military, ably tended not only the gardens but also the cotton crop.

Pierce commented on the eagerness of freedmen of all ages to gain education and the great success of the schools. He believed that the enterprise started in the spring of 1862 had become a consummation. As he wrote, "The Negroes will work for a living. They will fight for their freedom. They are adapted to civil society." He did point out that they were not exempt from "frailties" and "vices," stating that "one who expects to find in emancipated slaves perfect men and women will meet disappointment"; but he believed that they had proven their capacity for "knowledge, for free industry, for subordination to law and discipline, for soldierly fortitude, for social and family relations, for religious culture and aspirations" and would, with blessing from God, become a "progressive race" ready to be part of the nation's growing civilization. However, Pierce did sound a forewarning when he finished his article by writing that all should be well as long as the freedmen never suffered "another enslavement, and ourselves from the worse calamity of being again their oppressors."[50]

Also in his article Pierce lavished praise on the black soldiers enlisted from the sea islands and Colonel Higginson. They had opened the door for other black regiments who were now serving in all theaters, including the Department of the South. During Gillmore's operations against Charleston, black regiments from North Carolina and Massachusetts, along with government-raised United States Colored Troops organized in New York and Pennsylvania, arrived at Port Royal. By the fall of 1863, black regiments made up 16 percent of the department's overall operating force. The influx of black troops caused the medical department to expand the number of hospitals in Beaufort reserved for black soldiers. In September, to create a new medical facility, Reverend Solomon Peck moved his congregation from the Baptist Church on Charles Street to the Baptist Tabernacle meeting house on Craven. In early 1864, as the number of black soldiers increased, St. Helena Episcopal Church would be converted into a hospital for black soldiers, and by the end of 1864, Hospital Number 10 expanded to take in the Beaufort College Building and the nearby H. M. Fuller House.[51]

Though the government made some accommodations for the comfort and care of wounded black soldiers, the pay issue was not immediately resolved. In late August, when Colonel Higginson returned to Beaufort, he discovered to his dismay that during his absence, when his men mustered for their pay in early August and received only ten dollars instead of the promised thirteen, desertions began. Though disillusioned, Higginson understood and pronounced his men "intensely human," a term meaning no different from whites. Higginson was able to handle the matter through the use of squads headed up by black noncommissioned officers, who used their knowledge of the sea islands to sweep through the plantations and gather up the missing soldiers.[52]

Higginson realized that if the soldiers continued to receive no redress over the pay issue, desertions would continue. He and others tried to convince the administration to change its policy. While Higginson contacted influential friends and wrote letters to the New York papers, Massachusetts governor John Andrew took the cause directly to Washington, where he lobbied President Lincoln, Attorney General Edward Bates, and Secretary of War Edwin Stanton. Governor Andrew hoped to gain a ruling from Attorney General Bates by asking him to make a decision about the pay authorized for Samuel Harrison, the black chaplain of the 54th Massachusetts. Harrison, who was a frequent visitor to the churches and hospitals in Beaufort, held the rank and pay scale of a major, and while the enlisted soldiers had had their pay reduced, Harrison remained eligible for full pay. Bates investigated the case, and soon Harrison became the center of a ruling that found Attorney General Bates informing the president that constitutional obligations dictated that the War Department equalize pay among all enlisted soldiers. But Lincoln, not wishing to upset the Republican Party's delicate alliance with the War Democrats, decided to let Congress handle the matter.[53]

While northern politicians tried to resolve the pay issue, black soldiers on Hilton Head from the 3rd South Carolina continued to work as common laborers. The recently mustered regiment had never received proper military training. Its officers, primarily former enlisted men, had not yet been fully schooled in their duties. Used exclusively as laborers and stevedores, the men had no respite from fatigue duty. Their colonel, Milton S. Littlefield, rarely served with the regiment and temporarily took over the 54th Massachusetts after Colonel Shaw's death. In his stead Lieutenant Colonel Augustus G. Bennett, a former captain from the 81st New York Infantry who had been with the unit since inception, commanded the regiment. The intense fatigue duty quickly wore out the men's uniforms, resulting in an additional three dollars being removed from their pay to cover the standard clothing allowance. Complaints from the soldiers increased. Among those protesting was Sergeant William Walker.

A twenty-three-year-old Hilton Head native, Walker was a trained boat pilot who enlisted in the 3rd South Carolina during the spring of 1863. As a pilot, Walker was exempt from the draft and was eligible to work for the military for a substantial salary, but instead he willingly volunteered for military service. A natural leader, he soon became a sergeant in Company A.

But instead of combat, Walker and his comrades were assigned fatigue duty. Treated with little respect, the soldiers were given menial, degrading tasks around the campsites and received insults from white soldiers. Their officers were often absent and some stole their men's rations. Many soldiers physically collapsed while others deserted. In early August, Walker's captain complained to Lieutenant Colonel Bennett that his men were giving out under the constant fatigue duty. Some relief came the following month when General Gillmore issued a general order prohibiting the use of black soldiers to police the camps of white regiments. While this removed some of the more odious work, the soldiers continued to toil as common laborers with no respite on the pay issue.

On the morning of November 19, Sergeant Walker and his company marched to Lieutenant Colonel Bennett's tent, stacked their arms, and placed their accoutrements on their weapons. When Bennett demanded to know what the action meant, Walker replied that they "would not do duty any longer for seven dollars a month." When Bennett ordered the men to return to assigned work under threat of being shot, Walker directed the soldiers to leave their equipment and return to their tents.

Colonel Bennett placed Walker under arrest, ordering him to remain in his tent, but when Walker left his quarters, unescorted, to visit the latrine, Bennett had him placed in the guardhouse. In January 1864 Walker came before a general court-martial, charged with mutinous conduct for his protests against pay in August and October, conduct prejudicial to good order and discipline, mutiny for his actions on November 19, and breach of arrest for leaving his tent when he visited the regimental sink. After being found guilty on all counts, Walker was sentenced to be executed. General Gillmore approved the court's ruling, and on March 3, 1864, a squad of his fellow comrades in Jacksonville, Florida, where his regiment was then stationed, shot him to death.

Sergeant Walker's case and execution had a direct impact on the black soldiers serving in the Beaufort District sea islands. On the same day that Walker was arrested, a sympathetic Lieutenant Colonel Bennett and other regimental officers wrote the army's adjutant general to protest the pay inequality. Though Bennett's appeal brought no relief, he did attempt to provide rations for his soldiers' families. Colonel Higginson used Walker's execution to promote equal pay, pointing out in his letters to politicians and newspapers that his soldiers feared the possibility of executing one of their own over the pay inequality. As he noted, "The fear of such tragedies spread a cloud of solicitude over every camp of colored soldiers."[54]

Governor Andrew also employed Walker's execution to reopen his campaign for equal pay, and with support from President Lincoln and Attorney General Bates, Congress in June 1864 passed a bill that equalized pay and reimbursed black soldiers who had been freemen on April 19, 1861. The bill did not apply to men enslaved on or before that date. It was not until March 1865 that Congress finally passed legislation that provided equal and back pay to the former slaves who had enlisted in the army, including the freedmen from the sea islands. As a postscript, when Walker's case was reviewed by Joseph Holt, the army's judge advocate general, Holt ruled that since Walker had been convicted on charges other than desertion, spying, mutiny, and murder, the case needed to be reviewed by the president before a death sentence could be carried out. Holt returned the file to General Gillmore, directing that it be forwarded to the president, but by now Sergeant Walker had been dead for a year. The Hilton Head native, who faced his execution without flinching, became one of the nation's first martyrs for racial equality.⁵⁵

Though he had approved Sergeant Walker's execution, General Gillmore advocated better treatment and identical pay for all of his department's black soldiers. While Gillmore put most of his energy into his military operations, he understood the need for the same treatment within a military command, especially one that was gaining additional regiments of African descent every month. By December 1863 black regiments made up 25 percent of his overall force. Gillmore believed that his Charleston campaign, where white and black formations had served side by side, had ended all vestiges of prejudice and ill feeling in his multiracial command. Gillmore overstated the situation: racism had not died in his department, but prejudice was down.

To further improve conditions for his regiments of African descent, Gillmore urged that the South Carolina regiments be placed under the Bureau of Colored Troops. He also asked permission to consolidate the 3rd, the 4th, and the unmustered 5th South Carolina regiments into one unit: the 3rd South Carolina under Colonel Milton Littlefield. The general requested that all South Carolina regiments be given designations as United States Colored Troops (USCT), and eventually the War Department complied. On February 8, 1864, the 1st and 2nd South Carolina were redesignated as the 33rd and 34th United States Colored Troops and on March 14, 1864, the 3rd South Carolina, which contained the embryonic 4th and 5th South Carolina, became the 21st United States Colored Troops.

Gillmore recognized the need to create a freedmen community in the Port Royal area and requested that the families of his black soldiers be allowed to preempt and purchase government-owned land in the sea islands. He and Saxton believed that this would give the soldiers greater incentive to fight and help remove the sting of reduced pay. As Gillmore noted, "This is important as a military measure by making the soldier content with his lot, by securing to him a home for his family during the war and for himself when the war is over."⁵⁶

Besides dealing with his black regiments, Gillmore also had to contend with a number of visitors coming to his department to study both his military and social operations. Reporters continued to arrive to cover the activities of the missionaries and the freedmen while military observers studied engineering and artillery operations off Charleston. Among those arriving at Port Royal were the inventor and producer of the North's primary rifled cannon, Robert Parrott, and, representing the King of Würtemberg, the future designer of military airships, Count Ferdinand Adolf Heinrich August Graf von Zeppelin.⁵⁷

While dignitaries inspected General Gillmore's batteries and fortifications near Charleston, small-unit actions continued around Port Royal. Such operations suited the Confederates. Though some troops had returned to

General William Walker's district after the Federals had ceased their attacks on Charleston, the majority of the 11th South Carolina remained near Charleston. On October 1, 1863, Walker reported ready for duty only 2,168 effectives and eighteen pieces of artillery. This force was too small to defend the area properly, and Walker proposed that a more "retired" line be established to protect the railroad between the Ashepoo and Combahee Rivers. The high command realized the dire circumstances and sent orders for Walker to remove property exposed to enemy attacks, "especially able-bodied Negroes who are apt to be made soldiers by the enemy."[58]

Much to Walker's relief, the Federals made no major moves against the railroad, but the two sides sparred with each other. In late September men from Higginson's regiment, including Sergeant Sutton and Chaplain Fowler, accompanied John E. Bryan, formerly of the 8th Maine and now a captain in the 4th South Carolina, on an expedition up the Combahee River. They reached the railroad and tapped into the nearby telegraph line, reading Confederate messages. Their position, however, was given away when a northbound train passed by, and Conductor J. H. Burkhalter, one of the heroes of the Battle of Pocotaligo, spotted the attached wire and informed Lieutenant Colonel William Stokes once the train reached Green Pond. Stokes immediately pursued with horsemen from his 4th South Carolina Cavalry. Among those captured were Chaplain Fowler and a black soldier. The enlisted man immediately took on the persona of a subservient slave, lulling his captors until he found an opportunity to escape while Chaplain Fowler, the regiment's white Unitarian minister, remained defiant, berating his guards at every opportunity. Though chaplains were not supposed to be held as prisoners of war, Fowler's presence on the raid resulted in a year-long imprisonment. While the men of the 1st South Carolina worried about their chaplain's fate, they were also fully aware of Fowler's bellicose nature, and as Higginson noted, they also had a "feeling that the rebels must have the worst of it."[59]

The Confederates retaliated with their own strikes. On October 10 forty men from the Beaufort Volunteer Artillery under Sergeant Stephen Barnwell raided Big (Barnwell) Island. While one party gathered up poultry, rice, corn, and pumpkins, another laid an ambush for Federal soldiers whom they expected to visit the island, but instead only a group of freedmen with one soldier appeared. In a quick firefight, the Union soldier was killed, two freedmen were captured, and the rest returned to their boats and fled to Little (Barnwell) Island.[60]

On November 2 the southerners took a brief respite from their active military duties to welcome President Jefferson Davis to the Beaufort District. The Confederate president, returning from a visit to the Army of Tennessee, came by rail to Savannah and then took the Charleston and Savannah Railroad to Charleston. From Hardeeville to Green Pond, women dressed in their finest clothes and carrying flowers waited to greet Davis. At Gopher Hill the president gave a brief oration to Colonel Charles Colcock and men from the 3rd South Carolina Cavalry. At Pocotaligo Station, General Walker drew up a portion of his command and listened to a brief address. Farther down the line at Green Pond, Lieutenant Colonel Stokes had Captain William Earle's Furman Artillery fire a thirteen-gun salute, and the tired president accepted bouquets from the adoring women waiting for him.[61]

After Davis passed through the area, the two sides resumed their cat-and-mouse games. On the night of November 22, Captain John E. Bryant again led soldiers from the 1st South Carolina behind enemy lines. This time Bryant took with him thirty men each from companies E and K under Captains Alexander Heasley and Henry A. Whitney. Bryant guided them up the Pocotaligo River, where they captured two Confederate pickets at Cunningham Bluff, opposite Hall's Island. Bryant then scouted the Confederate position at Pocotaligo, while Sergeant Harry Williams of Company K led a party around Pocotaligo and freed twenty-seven slaves from Daniel Heyward's plantation. Once detected, the Federals retreated toward their boats. Throughout the night, cavalrymen from Colonel Rutledge's 4th South Carolina Cavalry kept up a pursuit, described by General Walker as "resembling a fox hunt." As the Federals neared their embarkation point, the Confederates released a pack of bloodhounds used to track down escaped slaves and prisoners. Captain Heasley, commanding the Federals' rear guard, waited until the hounds were nearly upon them before opening fire. One dog was shot while four others were skewed on the soldiers' bayonets. Elsewhere in the foggy morning the Federals ambushed another group of Confederate horsemen, and the southerners ceased their pursuit.[62]

The raid embarrassed the Confederates and caused elation in the Union camps. The Federal soldiers brought one of the carcasses of the bloodhounds back to Beaufort where it was skinned. Captain James Rogers planned to send the hide to New York to be mounted, and Dr. M. M. Marsh of the sanitary commission asked that it be exhibited in Boston at the commission's fair, where money would be raised to aid wounded Union soldiers. However, Colonel Higginson later noted that the dog's hide "spoiled on passage."[63]

The Federal raids caused General Beauregard, the Confederate Department commander, to take a greater interest in the Third District. On December 2 Beauregard reorganized the area and placed the region between the Ashepoo and the Combahee into an expanded Second District under Brigadier General Beverly Robertson, with instructions to properly fortify the northern bank of the Combahee at Field's Point. To assist General Walker in defending the reduced Third District, Beauregard sent Major General Jeremy Gilmer, chief engineer of the Confederacy and Beauregard's acting second in command, to inspect the area. During his tour Gilmer suggested a number of improvements, including the combining of the Third District with the District of Georgia. Beauregard concurred, and on December 24 Gilmer was given temporary command of the combined districts.[64]

To aid in the region's defense, Gilmer directed the construction of new works at Red Bluff, the New River Bridge, and Morgen's and Tunbridge Landings on the Wright's River and Cook's Landing on the New River. Gilmer also requested that Brigadier General Gabriel J. Rains be sent from Charleston to place additional torpedoes in the district's waterways. To assist Walker, Gilmer dispatched additional troops from Georgia into South Carolina. By the end of the year Walker's command, supplemented by men from the Savannah defenses, numbered about forty-one hundred effectives, distributed around the district's three main depots of Pocotaligo, Grahamville, and Hardeeville.[65] Included were:

Pocotaligo Subdistrict—Brigadier General Walker
12th Georgia Infantry Battalion
32nd Georgia Infantry Regiment
54th Georgia Infantry Regiment
2nd South Carolina State Troops (nine companies)
4th South Carolina Cavalry Regiment (eight companies)
Company D, 5th South Carolina Cavalry Regiment
Company G, 11th South Carolina Infantry Regiment
Kirk's Partisan Rangers (cavalry company)
German Artillery Company
Lafayette Artillery Company
Rutledge Mounted Rifles (horse artillery)

Grahamville Subdistrict—Colonel Charles Colcock
3rd South Carolina Cavalry regiment (five companies)
Colcock Light Artillery

Hardeeville Subdistrict—Lieutenant Colonel T. H. Johnson
Company D, 2nd South Carolina State Troops
Companies A, B, F, G, 3rd South Carolina Cavalry Regiment
Company B, 4th South Carolina Cavalry Regiment
Company E, 11th South Carolina Infantry Regiment
DePass Artillery Company[66]

While the Confederates added to their troop strength, the Federal army and navy at Port Royal maintained routine operations. Though not undertaking any new offensive movements, Rear Admiral Dahlgren strengthened the blockade off Charleston and Savannah. At Charleston he deployed monitors in the harbor channels, but the extended duty caused mechanical breakdowns and fouled bottoms, resulting in the monitors being shifted continuously between Charleston and Port Royal for needed maintenance. Mechanics and blacksmiths repaired the vessels, and in Station Creek a diver, clad in a 185-pound diving suit fed by an air hose, cleaned their bottoms. From the *Montauk* alone, he removed 250 bushels of oysters, shells, and seaweed. While the removal of the oysters increased the vessel's speed, it also drew complaints from the ship's crew, who were deprived of an easily accessible food source.[67]

The army also reduced its activity around Charleston, and by the end of the year, it returned a number of regiments to Port Royal. Units were refitted and a number of them received seven-shot Spencer rifles. On St. Helena Island, Colonel Joseph Hawley's 7th Connecticut began training in the sound with small flatboats called "dinkies," practicing for a landing on Fort Sumter. In November the men and their boats were sent to Folly Island, where they constructed scaling ladders, but much to the soldiers' relief, the "dinkie plan" was abandoned and the regiment returned to St. Helena Island.[68]

At Hilton Head soldiers performed picket and provost marshal duty. Some of the men guarded Confederate prisoners, including Captain John R. Macbeth, son of the mayor of Charleston, whom Gillmore detained on Hilton Head in case he needed to retaliate in kind to any Confederate actions against captured black soldiers and their officers. Gillmore never had to use his hostages, for despite its threats, the Confederacy never officially executed, put to hard labor, or returned to slavery any of its captives. The Confederates grudgingly accepted the North's use of black soldiers.[69]

While stationed on Hilton Head, Union regiments, depleted from the arduous campaign off Charleston, recuperated and received replacements. A smallpox scare resulted in mass vaccinations, which headed off a possible epidemic. Though soldiers continued to drill and participate in target practice and brigade maneuvers, discipline was lax, and most of the men considered their time at Port Royal a vacation. Whenever possible, they formed foraging parties that often crossed over to Pinckney Island, where they hunted wild hogs and dug up sweet potatoes and peanuts. Such conditions encouraged the soldiers to reenlist, which provided them with cash bonuses and thirty-day furloughs for signing on for an additional three years.[70]

At Beaufort the 56th New York, the infantry portion of a combined arms legion raised in the area of Newburgh, New York, found relief from heavy fighting, hard labor, bad water, poor food, fever, ague, and other diseases, The regiment that camped in an oak grove in the town's suburbs lived well, "with comfortable, clean quarters, cool evenings and sea breezes." The soldiers often provided pickets along the Coosaw River, where they gathered oysters, fished, and got sweet potatoes and peanuts. Along the picket line and at Port Royal Ferry, the New Yorkers maintained a truce with the southern pickets on the mainland. At night men from both sides advanced to their respective ends of the causeway. Separated by 150 feet of water, they built fires and conversed over the river. Some from the 56th New York took a canoe over to the southern guards, and around the fire they traded coffee for tobacco and exchanged newspapers.[71]

The regiment's colonel, Charles H. Van Wyck, a prominent Republican lawyer and politician who split his time between his regiment and the U.S. Congress, where he was a member of the infamous Joint Committee for the Conduct of the War, found Beaufort a congenial station. Van Wyck became an eager backer of the Port Royal Experiment and assisted the missionaries, participating in a number of their ceremonies and events. He also supported their goal of providing land for the freedmen.

Van Wyck soon became a close associate of Colonel Higginson and General Saxton. He often served with Higginson on courts-martial boards at Beaufort, reviewing charges for everything from accusations of incompetence in combat to drunkenness and theft of government property. In Beaufort the courts-martial took on added importance when freedmen, including Harriet Tubman, were called on to be witnesses testifying against white defendants. At Port Royal, such activity seemed only logical, considering the status of the region's freedmen, but elsewhere it was seen as another important step of integrating the former slaves into a colorblind society.[72]

Besides serving on courts-martial boards, Von Wyck also backed the development of a major port on St. Helena Island. The first step for establishing a port and normal maritime activities began in December 1863, when the Treasury Department reduced restrictions on vessels carrying goods to Beaufort and created a special trade district that allowed merchants, other than sutlers or those who operated stores for the freedmen, to open and stock businesses at Hilton Head and Beaufort. To oversee the maritime trade, Albert G. Browne Jr. of Massachusetts was appointed as the Treasury Department's special agent. In Beaufort the increased commercial activity spurred the town's citizens to form a volunteer fire department. Among those expanding their trade was photographer Sam Cooley, who in December visited New York and returned with an assortment of photographic material and new cameras. Cooley announced that he was ready to supply his customers with "large portraits, carte devisettes, ambrotypes, mellainotypes" and place pictures in "lockets, pins and seals."[73]

While some northerners were expanding their businesses, others began leaving the area. On Hilton Head Island, Clara Barton evaluated her situation. Like Mrs. Lander, she had incurred the jealousy of army doctors. In mid-September, just as the campaign for Charleston ended, General Gillmore sent her a letter, thanking her for her valuable work with the wounded and sick on Morris Island, but with operations over and upon the recommendation of the island's military medical director, he ordered her to Beaufort, where suitable quarters would be provided.

Though enraged, Barton had little choice but to acquiesce. In Beaufort, however, she found the hospitals closed to her. Dorothea Dix, the Union's superintendent of female nurses, directed her staff to rebuff Barton. The superintendent of nurses had little use for the independent caregiver, who worked on her own outside Dix's realm. Even her acquaintance Mrs. Lander, who had entertained her just three months earlier, obeyed Dix's orders and eventually denied Barton work in the town's hospitals. During her brief stay in Beaufort, Barton was able to briefly enter the black soldiers' Hospital Number 10, where she met Susie Baker King, who often came from the 1st South Carolina's bivouac at nearby Camp Shaw to visit the sick and wounded. King, a regimental laundress and teacher whose husband, Edward, was now a sergeant in the regiment, found Barton very cordial and devoted to helping the soldiers.

Unable to find work in Beaufort, Barton departed for Hilton Head. Though Colonel Elwell rejoiced in her return, she curtailed their relationship. Her supporters in the North continued to send supplies, which she distributed to both soldiers and freedmen. She also gathered up war trophies, many from Morris Island, which were shipped north and sold at fairs to help fund her operations.

Barton found solace and support from Fanny Gage, who having completed her work in the Beaufort hospitals, had returned to Parris Island with her daughter to resume her superintendent's duties. The two became fast friends, with Gage mentoring Barton on civil rights for women and freedmen. On Parris Island the women took long walks, memorized poems, and wrote poetry to each another. In November, Fanny Gage left Parris Island to go north to lecture on the plight of the freedmen. Barton remained and celebrated Thanksgiving on St. Helena Island with Colonel Hawley and his activist wife, Harriet Foote Hawley, who worked in freedmen schools and assisted in hospitals. In mid-December, Barton was able to return briefly to Morris Island before spending a quiet Christmas day, her forty-second birthday, on Hilton Head. By now she was ready to leave the department, and on December 27, after sending three hundred shirts to freedmen on St. Helena Island and a similar supply to the destitute at Mitchelville on Hilton Head Island, she said her farewells and sailed north on the steamer *Fulton*.[74]

While Clara Barton was preparing to leave Port Royal, others were looking forward to Christmas and New Year's celebrations. General Saxton intended to hold a grand event to celebrate the first anniversary of the Emancipation Proclamation. As he announced in the newspapers:

On the anniversary of this, the birthday of your liberties, on the 1st of January, 1864, I therefore recommend you all to assemble at "Camp Shaw," there to join in such exercises as are suited to the occasion.

Come together with grateful hearts and pay a tribute to the memory of those who have laid down their lives for your cause. Come as "little children," with prayerful hearts for your friends who are yet in bondage. Come with brave hearts pledging your own lives, if necessary, for their redemption, and be strong in good resolutions for the future. Then make merry and be glad, for the day of your deliverance has come.[75]

On the outskirts of Beaufort, at Camp Shaw, Higginson's men prepared their campsite for the celebration and constructed a structure to serve as a praise house and school. Saxton asked Higginson to invite Wendell Phillips to speak to the freedmen. Higginson hoped Phillips would attend but was not surprised when the noted abolitionist declined. For the ceremony Higginson learned that black businessmen from Beaufort had raised money to buy both him and General Saxton a sword that would be picked out and delivered to Beaufort by Francis Shaw, Colonel Robert Shaw's father.[76]

While Higginson and his regiment readied to host the coming event, General Gillmore on December 23 held a ball for five hundred people at his headquarters on Hilton Head. Though Higginson did not attend, General and Mrs. Saxton, Mrs. Lander, and others took a steamer to Hilton Head, where they found a temporary building framed in wood and covered with canvas. Bunting and regimental flags draped the candle-lit interior, and the woodwork was strewn with Spanish moss and cedar. Gillmore invited most of his field officers and nearly all of the department's white women. Colonel Voris of the 67th Ohio wrote his wife that there were 150 officers and sixty women present. He commented, "They danced, the music played, the wine flowed and I *flowed* about eleven o'clock P.M. for my lonely tent."[77]

Saxton and the contingent from Beaufort returned the next day in time to participate in Christmas Eve celebrations. At Camp Shaw, Higginson's men held a "voluminous Prayer Meeting" to dedicate their praise house. A ball was held in town for all troops, black and white. The integrated dance was a great success, and Higginson noted that when an argument occurred between a black soldier from the 54th Massachusetts and men from his regiment, each had their backers among the whites, with the regular artillerymen siding with the troops from the 1st South Carolina, while the Massachusetts infantrymen found backing from white New England soldiers. The affair did not lead to a fight and was quickly quieted, but Higginson felt the situation showed "how far the feeling of color may be ignored": the episode was "particolored," with the taking of sides based on states and not race.[78]

On Christmas Day, Higginson reported that his regiment received the present they "have enjoyed the most"—the assignment in Beaufort to provost guard duty. The significance of the event was not lost on the colonel or his soldiers, as during the placement of sentinels, a black squad leader would drop off men from the 1st South Carolina while relieving white soldiers. To complete the task, the white soldiers had to follow directives from a black sergeant to "support arms" and "forward march." The maneuver went off without a hitch, pleasing Higginson, who wrote that it "is rather dramatic, but what pleases the men is that it is the only military duty hitherto withheld from them, and then it is sort of self government, guarding the peace of their own town." The black soldiers took their duty seriously and soon had the guardhouse filled with offenders.[79]

That night Higginson joined Mrs. Lander, Charlotte Forten, and others at General Saxton's, where the attendees entertained each other by performing music, juggling, playing charades, and acting out role reversals. Higginson, ever the astute observer of people, noted that General Saxton, "the mildest & timidest of men was more free & easy in assumed parts than he ever was in his own, while Mrs. Lander who never before saw a charade, but bred to the stage from childhood, was seriously embarrassed by timidity" in attempting the new game.[80]

With the Christmas activities over, preparations continued for the New Year's celebration at Camp Shaw, the 1st South Carolina's bivouac on the bluff overlooking the Beaufort River just west of the intersection of Bladen and Bay Street. On New Year's Day 1864, in the midst of a bitterly cold southwesterly wind, the grand celebration, orchestrated by Colonel Higginson and Jacob Robinson, a black resident of Beaufort, was carried out. It opened with a procession of over a thousand people led by the 1st South Carolina, followed by quartermaster employees, women, and children. The parade ended at Camp Shaw, where a large platform had been erected. The Reverend Abram Hutchinson, a black minister from Savannah who had been an active supporter of the Federal operations since their arrival and the spiritual leader of the freedmen on Hilton Head, opened the ceremony. Schoolchildren sang, the bands of the 8th Maine and 48th New York provided music, and salutes were fired from the town's fortifications and the vessel *John Adams* anchored in the Beaufort River.

Mr. Gilbert Pillsbury, a fifty-year-old superintendent and activist from Ludlow, Massachusetts, read the Emancipation Proclamation. Pillsbury, brother to abolitionist and women's rights advocate Parker Pillsbury, had come south to join General Saxton on Hilton Head, where his wife, Ann, taught school. Once Pillsbury, who would later become the mayor of Charleston, South Carolina, had finished reading, Reuben Tomlinson, superintendent for St. Helena Island, read a New Year's greeting from General Saxton. Then the black A.M.E. minister, Reverend James T. Lynch, presented the general with a ceremonial engraved sword. In his remarks Lynch declared that the condition of the freedmen was rapidly improving, with the freedmen becoming self-sustaining and educated. For proof he pointed to the more than seventy-five schools operating in the sea islands.

In accepting the gift, Saxton proclaimed that he would wear the sword "until every slave in this land is as free as you are today." He also called on the black soldiers to "stand by the old flag whether they received $10 a month or nothing." After the presentation Colonel Van Wyck addressed the crowd, proclaiming that the Negroes, like the Jews of old, should be allowed to possess their land as "an inheritance forever." Colonel Elwell, the department quartermaster, followed and, after alluding to the cold day as Yankee weather, predicted that northerners, who had come to stay with their guns and steamships, would soon bring a railroad that would open up the finest harbor on the southern coast to vast commercial ventures.

Dr. William H. Brisbane, who had read the proclamation the previous year, came next with a short speech, followed by a poem by Henry G. Judd. Then Reverend Mr. James D. S. Hall, a black A.M.E. minister, presented a ceremonial sword to Colonel Higginson on behalf of "prominent colored residents in Beaufort and vicinity." In accepting the sword, Higginson stated that he took it not for himself but for his regiment, which had paved the way for all other black regiments. A benediction ended the ceremony, followed by cheers for Generals Saxton and Gillmore and President Lincoln. The crowd then moved to tables arranged in the rear of the camp for a barbecue of eight roasted oxen, hardtack, and molasses.[81]

Though a number of participants were the same as at the 1863 ceremony, the 1864 celebration showed more participation in its planning and execution by the region's black population, who took a leading role in organizing and orchestrating the event. Slowly but surely the freedmen at Port Royal were taking on more responsibility in planning their future. Their influence would continue to grow in 1864, as early in the year many of the freedmen's initial supporters and mentors, including Harriet Tubman, Charlotte Forten, Colonel Higginson, Mrs. Lander, and others, permanently left the region. The year 1863 had set the stage for dramatic changes, and 1864 promised to provide even greater gains that would forever transform the face of the Beaufort District.

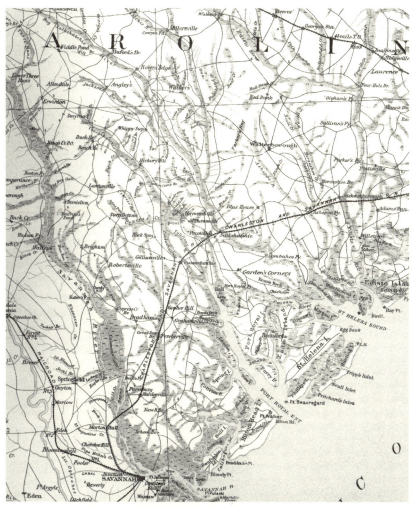

The Beaufort District and Adjoining Territory (*Official Atlas of the Civil War*, plate CXLIV).

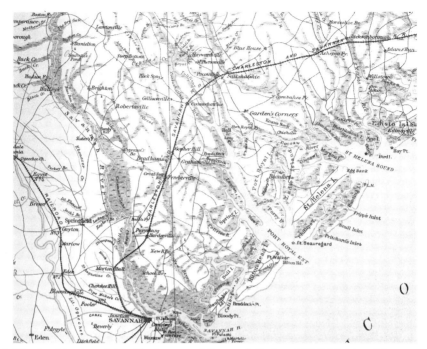

The Sea Islands and the Charleston and Savannah Railroad (*Official Atlas of the Civil War*, plate CXLIV).

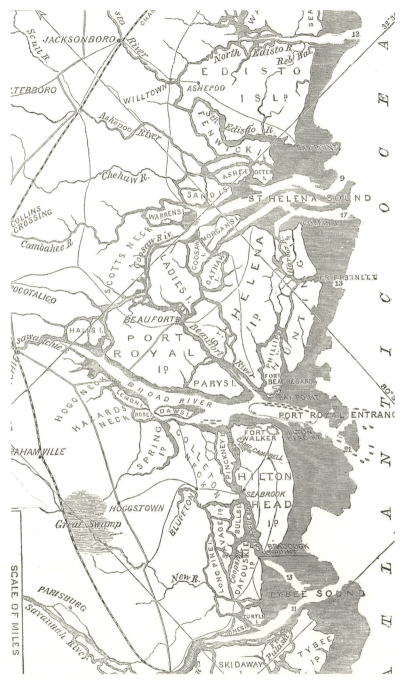

South Carolina Coast, Edisto to Savannah River, 1861 (McCracken and McCracken, *The Forgotten History*).

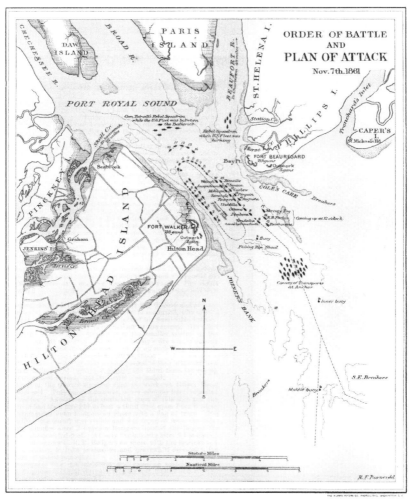

The Battle of Port Royal (*Official Records of the Union and Confederate Navies in the War of the Rebellion*, Volume 6).

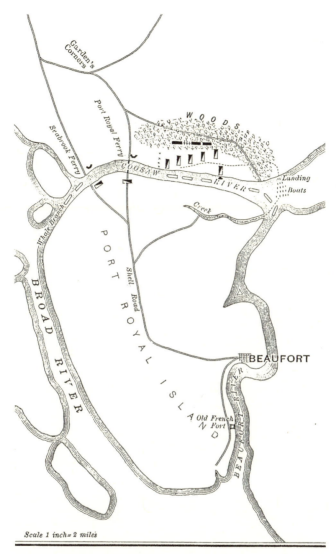

ACTION AT PORT ROYAL FERRY, JANUARY 1, 1862

The Battle of Port Royal Ferry (Palmer, *History of the Forty-eighth Regiment New York State Volunteers*).

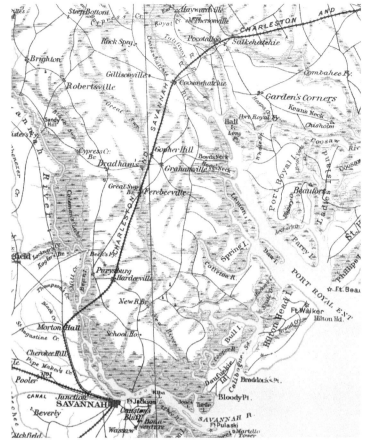

Approaches to Fort Pulaski (*Official Atlas of the Civil War*, plate CXLIV).

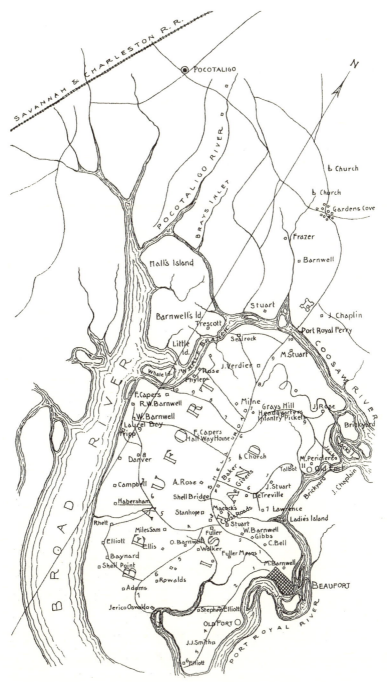

Port Royal Island to Pocotaligo (Crowninshield, *History of the 1st Massachusetts Cavalry*).

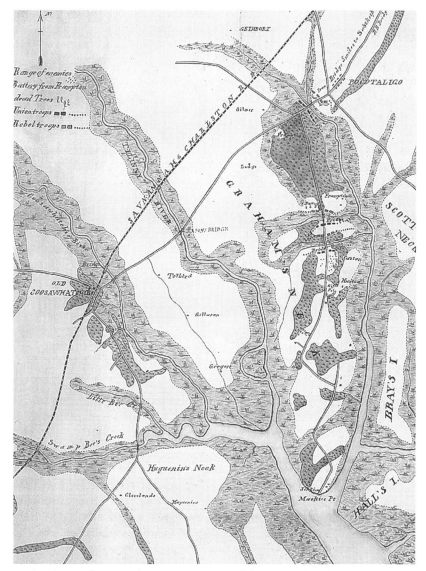

Battle of Pocotaligo, October 1862 (courtesy of the National Archives).

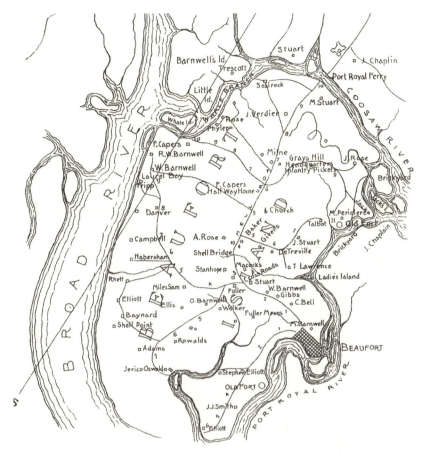

Port Royal Island (Crowninshield, *History of the 1st Massachusetts Cavalry*).

Coast Between Savannah and Charleston 1863 (Walkley, *History of the Seventh Connecticut Volunteer Infantry*).

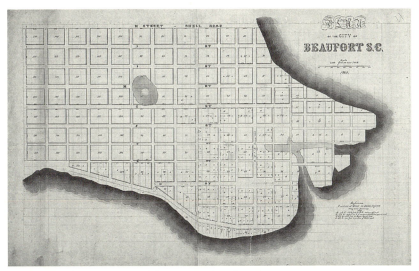
City of Beaufort (courtesy of the National Archives).

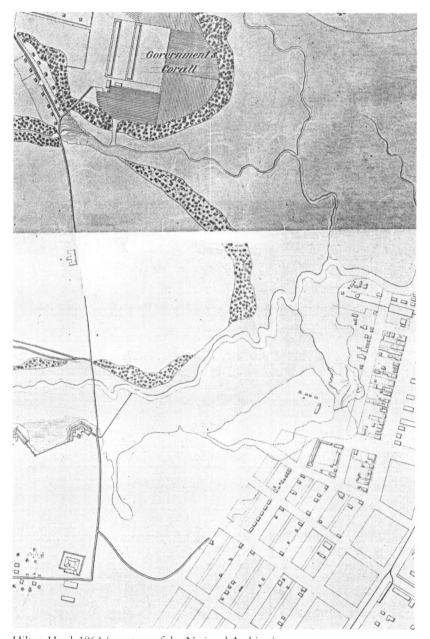

Hilton Head, 1864 (courtesy of the National Archives).

Beaufort Defenses, Spring 1864 (courtesy of the National Archives).

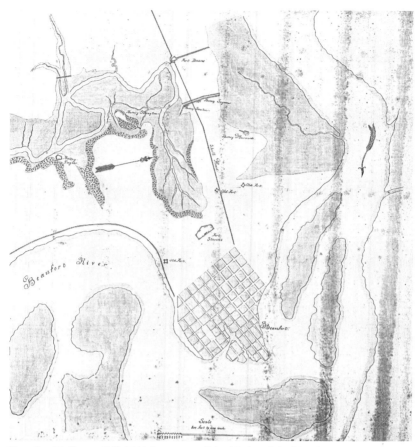

Beaufort Defenses, Fall 1864 (courtesy of the National Archives).

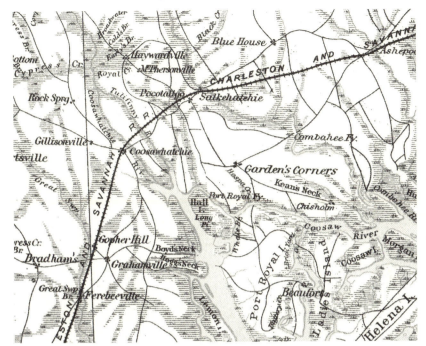

Area of the Broad River Campaign, 1864–1865 (*Official Atlas of the Civil War*, plate CXLIV).

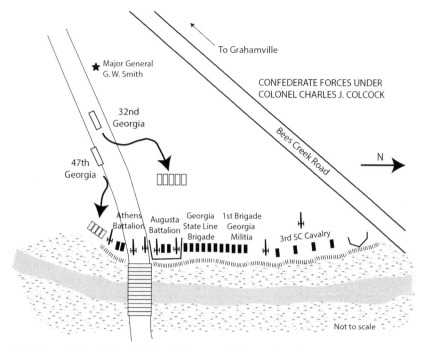

CSA Troop Dispositions Battle of Honey Hill (from the authors' collection).

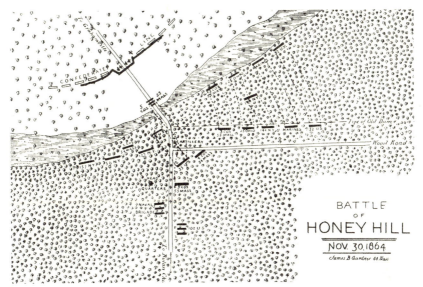

USA Troop Dispositions Battle of Honey Hill (Emilio, *A Brave Black Regiment*).

DeVeaux and Graham Necks (courtesy of the National Archives).

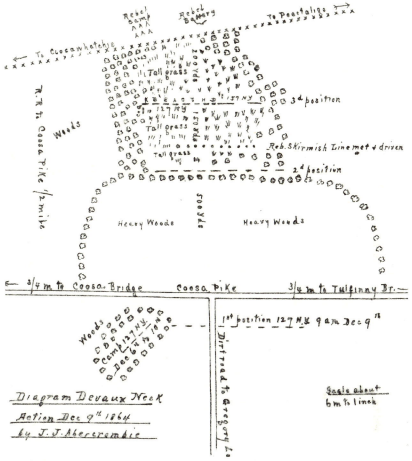

December 9 Engagement, Tuliffinny (McGrath, *The History of the 127th New York "Monitors."*).

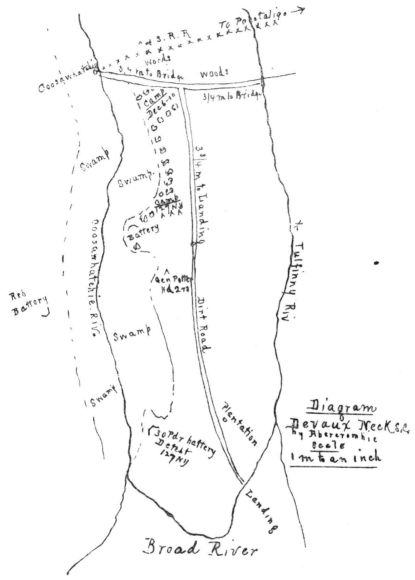

USA Dispositions, DeVeaux Neck Mid-December 1864 (McGrath, *History of the 127th New York "Monitors."*).

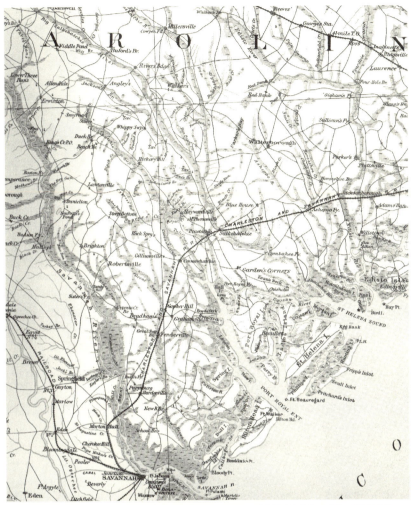

Beaufort District at Time of Sherman's Movement (*Official Atlas of the Civil War*, plate CXLIV).

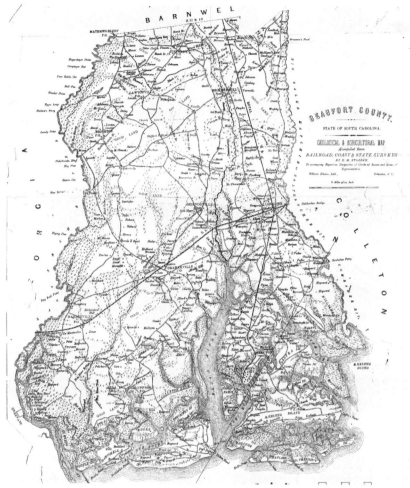

Beaufort District, circa 1873 (courtesy of the South Caroliniana Library).

Beaufort and Hampton Counties (from the authors' collection).

Chapter 11

Tax Sales and Preemption

*"We are nothing now but speculators,
and the righteous rail against us"*

The abbreviated tax sales of early 1863 had pleased no one. Of the approximately sixteen thousand acres sold, most went to a northern consortium of businessmen fronted by Edward Philbrick, leaving only a few thousand acres to freedmen. The next round of sales, with hundreds of lots in Beaufort and tens of thousands of rural acres available, were to be more sweeping and would ultimately alter the Beaufort District sea islands forever.

At the first sale Abram Smith, breaking with his fellow tax commissioners, convinced President Lincoln to appoint Generals Saxton and Hunter to serve as equals on the tax commission board. Smith, Saxton, and Hunter managed to restrict the sales, holding back property with the hope that later auctions would provide the freedmen an opportunity to gain homesteads. However, the generals were no longer in the mix for the second round scheduled in late 1863, and all authority would be in the hands of the tax commissioners.

The coming sales found businessmen, politicians, military officers, missionaries, and freedmen pushing various concepts for the foreclosed property's division and ultimate fate. Most wanted the land sales to benefit the freedmen. The question was how and how many privileges would be allotted the former slaves. No land was to be given away, but questions remained about to whom the distribution would go and how it would occur. A line had been drawn in the sand with General Saxton, Reverend Mansfield French, and Commissioner Abram Smith at odds with Commissioners William Wording and William Brisbane.

The division among the commissioners became personal, with Smith, who had assisted Senator James R. Doolittle of Wisconsin in drafting the Direct Tax Act, becoming an outcast from his fellow commissioners. During the summer of 1863, Wording and Brisbane replaced the commission's clerk, who was sympathetic to Smith, with their own man. The factions constantly argued, and by the fall of 1863, Brisbane and Wording lobbied Secretary Chase to remove Smith, whom they claimed had resumed drinking.[1]

Chase declined to act and both sides readied for the next round of tax sales. Saxton, French, and Smith sought to give the freedmen exclusive rights to bid in on any available property before the tax sales opened. To do this, they wanted to employ a mechanism known as preemption, which the tax act allowed. By preemption, freedmen could petition the tax commissioners for specific lots, which for a down payment would be stricken from the sales list and held for the preemptor. In this fashion the freedmen could select individual plots that allowed them to retain the land where as slaves they had lived and worked for generations.

Commissioners Wording and Brisbane were sympathetic to the freedmen and favored some concessions to help them gain land but opposed any preemption. They questioned the legality of preemption and believed it could not be done in an equitable manner. They also feared that too many favors would spoil the recently freed slaves and restrict their development into productive citizens. They wanted the freedmen to bid against other possible landowners and, if successful, follow the set pattern of any citizen farmers.

While they differed over preemption, both the Wording-Brisbane and the Saxton-French-Smith factions wanted to establish a farming community for the freedmen. Edward Philbrick, however, believed that the freedmen needed to work as wage-earning farmhands before being allowed to become landowners. He felt the future lay in a corporate agricultural industry with the freedmen providing the necessary workforce. Though Philbrick's concept mirrored the changing pattern from farming to factories in New England, the majority of the missionaries backed the plan forwarded by Saxton, French, and Smith, hoping that preemption would create a new community of small farms that would resemble preindustrial New England.

The freedmen viewed the maneuvering between the various factions with amazement and apprehension. Those who had the required money viewed preemption as a possible way of obtaining land, but most feared the property they inhabited would be gobbled up by northerners. One freedman, known as "Uncle Smart," asked a missionary to tell President Lincoln that "we wants land—dis bery land dat is rich wid de sweat ob we face and de blood ob we back. We born here; we parents grave here; we done oder country; dis yere our home." Uncle Smart and others questioned why northerners left their homes to come to the sea islands. "What a pity dat dey don't love der home like we love we home, for den dey would never come here for buy all way from we."[2]

Uncle Smart was correct about appealing to President Lincoln. No matter what others put forward, ultimate authority lay with Lincoln. The president personally oversaw the major aspects of reconstruction, including the implementation of the tax and tax sales at Port Royal.

On September 16, 1863, Lincoln sent instructions to the tax commissioners directing them to survey and subdivide certain foreclosed property in St Helena Parish. Hilton Head Island in St. Luke's Parish did not come under the president's decree. Lincoln instructed that land be sold in parcels not to exceed 320 acres to any one purchaser.

Lincoln also proposed that members of the army, navy, and Marine Corps be allowed to purchase land by paying one fourth of the purchase price with the remainder due within three years by the buyers or their heirs. If payment was not received in the allotted time, the commissioners could seize the property and sell it for the money due the government.

To facilitate the establishment of a port at Land's End on St. Helena Island, Lincoln directed that the Benjamin Chaplin and Land's End Plantations be "laid off and divided into town lots of such size as you may judge proper, not exceeding five acres each, and you will proceed to sell all said lots not needed or selected for Government purposes at public sale, for cash." Or, as with other land sales, the land could be sold to members of the military for one quarter of the purchase price with three years to pay the remainder.

Though all property in St. Helena Parish, except that set aside for the port city, was surveyed, plotted, and mapped into twenty-acre lots, not all was made available. Excepted from the president's instructions were tracts reserved for use by the government. This included the following land:

On St. Helena Island, Eddings Point, St. Helenaville, St. Helenaville Co., pine land, Lands End, and the Ben Chaplin place.
On Coosaw Island, Coosaw.
On Ladies [Lady's] Island, White Hall and Laurel Bay.
On Port Royal Island, the Hermitage, the Cottage, the Old Fort, The Farm, Pigeon Point, the Campbell place, the Bell place, Magnolia, and the Middleton Steward place.
On Parrys [Parris] Island, the Means place.
On Hunting Island, and on Phillips woodland tracts deemed necessary for the use of the United States.

Also set aside for educational purposes was property, not exceeding 160 acres and containing structures, known as school farms. These tracts were to be leased for no more than five years with the proceeds being applied to the establishment of schools and "to the education of colored youths, and of such poor white persons, being minors, as may by themselves, parents, guardians, or next friends, apply for the benefit thereof." The tracts were to be taken from:

On St. Helena Island—The Oaks, Indian Hill, The Thomas James Tripp [Fripp] place, Cedar Grove, the McTurens lands, Frogmore, the Frank Prichard place, the Oliver Tripp [Fripp] place, the Wallace place, and Eddings Point, and the whole of the Thomas B. Chaplin place, the Grove, and the Baker place.
On Coosaw Island, Coosaw.

> On Ladies [Lady's] Island—Orange Grove, White Hall, the James Chaplin place, including the Saxby Chaplin lot, Pleasant Point, the John Johnson place, Springfield, the Williams place and the Capers place.
> On Port Royal Island—the Cottage, the Old Fort, Swamp Place, Halfway House, Gray Hill, the [sic] Middleton Stuart place, Oak Mulligan, Little Baynard, the Rhett Place, Laurel Bay and the Thompson place.
> On Parry's [Parris] Island—the Fuller place and the Means place.

Lincoln also instructed the commissioners to set aside tracts not being used by the government for sale "to heads of families of the African race." The sections appropriated were:

> On St. Helena Island, the Oaks, Oakland, Indian Hill, Eddings Point, The Thomas James Tripp [Fripp] place, Cedar Grove, The Hamilton Tripp [Fripp] place, the McTurens lands, Hope place, Woodstock, Frogmore, the Frank Prichard place, the Jane Prichard place, the Scott place, the Oliver Tripp [Fripp] place[,] the Wallace place, the Fendon place.
> On Coosaw Island, Coosaw and Corn Island;
> On Ladies [Lady's] Island, Orange Grove, the Hazel Farm, White Hall, the James Chaplin place, Pleasant Point, the John Johnson place, Springfield, Laurel Bay, the Williams place, and the Capers place.
> On Port Royal Island—the Farm, the Old Fort, Polly's Grove, the Bell place, the Campbell place, the Swamp place, Halfway House, Grays Hill, Magnolia, the Middleton Stuart place, Oak Mulligan, the John F Chaplin place, Oakland, Little Baynard, Jericho, the Oswald place, the Ellis place, the Rhett place, and Laurel Bay, and
> On Parry's [Parris] Island, the Fuller place, the Elliott place No.1. The Elliott place No. 2[,] the El[l]iott place No. 3, and the Means place.

Once the plantations set aside for the freedmen were surveyed and divided into twenty-acre plots, the commissioners were

> to issue certificates for the said lots and parcels of land to the heads of families of the African race, one only to each, preferring such as by their good conduct, meritorious services or exemplary character, will be examples of moral propriety and industry to those of the same race, for the charitable purpose of providing homes for such heads of families and their families respectively, so as to give them an interest in the soil, and to form an industrial settlement of worthy persons of said race, they the said heads of families paying to the commissioners

such sum not less than $1.25 per acre as the said commissioners shall designate and determine as proper to be charged for the said lands, in view of the charitable purposes aforesaid.

On tracts that contained structures, the commissioners were instructed to appraise the buildings and add one third of their value to the asking price. If the lots failed to sell, they would be readvertised and offered for sale a second time. If the property still remained unpurchased, then the commissioners could sell them to the highest bidder.

Lincoln also directed his agents to appraise all the lots and buildings in the town of Beaufort except those being used by the government or not yet redeemed. The available property then would be put up for sale, with opening bids matching one third of the appraised value. If not initially sold, the property would be withdrawn and then offered a second time. If still unpurchased, the asking price could be reduced to one fifth of its appraisal, and if still unsold, the commissioners could sell to the highest bidder. The commissioners could also reserve bids on any property in Beaufort should they believe the property to be useful to the government.[3]

The president's instructions struck a compromise between those wanting the right of preemption for freedmen on all available property and those wanting an open auction with no restrictions on the amount or to whom the property could be sold. It also opened up land to military personnel and educational purposes. Available for general bids were an estimated 20,000–24,000 acres: 6,081 reserved for School farms, 13,370 held for military personnel, and 16,529 for "the heads of families of the African race."[4]

But there were concerns. Though over 16,000 acres had been set aside for sale to the freedmen, the tracts were located on particular plantations, forcing many to decide whether they should move and take advantage of the reduced rates or, in order to remain in their homes, to bid in against other potential purchasers at open auctions. And here was the rub: most freedmen did not have the resources to compete in an open auction against outside speculators. Such a situation did not sit well with the freedmen or the majority of the missionaries. But it would take time to complete the required survey that would divide St. Helena Parish into neatly organized twenty-acre plots. This gave Saxton, Commissioner Smith, Reverend French, and other supporters the opportunity to muster their allies in Washington to lobby the president to alter his initial proclamation. Commissioner Smith went north and met with Secretary Chase and Judge Joseph Jackson Lewis, the nation's commissioner of internal revenue.

While Smith was in Washington, Saxton and French organized a meeting to rally the freedmen to the cause of preemption and create a fait accompli they hoped the government would not undo. On November 1, 1863, a mass meeting was held outside the Brick Church on St. Helena Island. The gathering opened with the singing of "Children of the Heavenly King, As we journey let us sing." The Reverend Mr. J. D. S. Hall, an A.M.E. minister, then gave an opening prayer before Reverend Mansfield French delivered a message comparing the freedmen to the Israelites, declaring that God would sustain them as they took possession of land, constructed homes, and gathered their families. General Saxton followed, describing the importance of establishing permanent homes and communities with governing regulations. Saxton then went on to present a written set of "Laws to Govern the Claimants in Securing Their Lands."

The laws outlined a course of action that allowed any head of a freedmen family (male or female) to claim after November 1 on St. Helena Island any available tract of no more than twenty acres and no less than ten. Once the current cotton crop had been harvested, the claimed land could be marked off and a description of the desired property filed. Within thirty days of making the claim, the claimant had to erect a residence. When the tax sale occurred, potential purchasers would be discouraged from competing against the freedmen, who could secure their claims by bidding $1.25 per acre.

The rules also applied to members of the military and those employed by the government, but for them the requirement of constructing a dwelling was waived. Arbitration was also available should two or more freedmen claim the same property. A model house designed by the department's chief contractor, Duncan C. Wilson, and first used at Mitchelville on Hilton Head, was displayed. Mass produced on Hilton Head, the sixteen-by-twenty-four-foot dwellings, constructed with poles instead of nails, were being made available to the freedmen at cost for twenty-five dollars.

> After the presentation of the "Laws," Colonel Charles Van Wyck of the 56th New York addressed the crowd, praising black troops and predicting that their presence would bring about an end to the war. Sergeant Prince Rivers followed and made a stirring speech commending Generals Saxton and Hunter and called for more freedmen to join the army, criticizing any women who kept their husbands and sons out of the military. He informed the crowdNow we sogers are men—men the first time in our lives. Now we can look our old masters in the face. They used to sell and whip u, and we did not dare say one word. Now we ain't afraid if they meet us, to run the bayonet through them. Now we help the Government. The white soldiers used to say, the niggars fight! Oh no, dem black niggars don't fight. I won't fight if they be sogers. Now they done cursing—they say, come on brother soldier, we will whip out the Rebels. My brethren, I don't intend to lay down my

gun till the war is done, and our brethen all get their freedom—and then if I be alive, I will come home and enjoy my family an my land

Rivers went on to announce that members of the 1st South Carolina had formed a co-op and raised a thousand dollars to buy land in the coming auctions. He completed his speech by stating: "For my part, I mean to stand by the agreement. Gen. Saxby our friend, and I mean to stand by him an work for the Lord."[5]

In the days after the meeting, freedmen began making down payments on lots and staking out land. Others wrote the tax commissioners requesting that land be set aside for their purchase. General Saxton followed up the meeting by releasing a circular to the superintendents, teachers, and freedmen outlining the plan for preemption. He directed all heads of households to mark out their twenty acres, construct a prefabricated Wilson house, and deposit a down payment of just over twenty-five dollars with his staff member, Alexander P. Ketchum, who would give out receipts. Ketchum would then turn the money over to Saxton's aide-de-camp, Captain Hooper, treasurer of the preemption fund, with a description of the claimed land. Upon implementation of the tax sales, the tax commissioners would bid in the deposited money on the requested property. Saxton believed that outsiders would not interfere with the freedmen's preemptions and called upon the superintendents and teachers to do all in their power to assist the freedmen in their claims, declaring "that this system, if properly carried out, will work great advantages to the freedom, the Union cause, and to humanity."[6]

By opening all the available land to preemption, Saxton was violating the president's intent. But the general realized that if the land sales went on as originally stated, the freedmen could be heavily handicapped in their quest to become property owners and productive citizens. He feared that without total preemption white civilians and military officers in Port Royal would outbid the freedmen in a general auction and purchase the majority of the land, driving many freedmen from property they had lived on for generations. Saxton, using his position as governor and his authority to issue proclamations, general orders, and circulars concerning the Port Royal freedmen, hoped his local ordinance would be recognized by the authorities in Washington.

Saxton had good reason to believe his circular would be accepted. Mansfield French had gone to Washington to promote preemption. In the capital French found a number of supporters. The president was sympathetic and Secretary Chase had always been an ally of Saxton's operations. Radical Republicans in Congress promoted the concept, and in the House, Indiana congressman George W. Julian, chairman of the Committee of Public Land, proposed extending the Homestead Act of 1862 to include all confiscated and abandoned land in the rebelling states.[7]

Initially Saxton, French, and Smith had taken the lead over Commissioners Brisbane and Wording, who opposed unrestricted preemption; however, Smith's opponents did not surrender. Instead the two opened their own campaign to lobby the president, Commissioner Lewis, Secretary Chase, and others. The two, backed by Edward Philbrick, did not object to the special conditions setting aside property for the freedmen as set forth in Lincoln's instructions. They did, however, oppose any unrestricted preemption as being against the basic American concept of equal opportunity for all.

Brisbane and Wording also questioned the capacity of the freedmen to become functioning citizens immediately. They doubted the legality of the tax sales and the confiscation of abandoned property. Though passed by Congress, the acts had been instituted after the southern states had seceded, and they debated whether the sales would stand once the rebellious states were back in the Union and their citizens again protected by the Constitution. The commissioners doubted the wisdom of creating a segregated community and thought whites, especially northern immigrants, were needed to form a viable society.

Edward Philbrick also was an opponent of preemption. He thought it too soon to allow the freedmen to become independent farmers. His views, undoubtedly colored by his business interests, mirrored that of his employers and other capitalists in the North, who believed that the freedmen needed to go through a period of apprenticeship as laborers before becoming landowners. Like others, he thought the nation was turning away from small, family-operated agricultural pursuits, and he enthusiastically promoted factory-style farms worked by the freedmen as the way of the future for the sea islands.

While his employees harvested cotton, Philbrick watched carefully as the pro- and antipreemption factions squared off. He declared that Smith fought like "cat and dog" with Wording and Brisbane and did not believe much would be accomplished. Two sets of surveyors slowly marked off the twenty-acre plots following the method used in the territories, except that in the sea islands the geography did not conform as neatly as it did in the West. The surveyors, sailing boats in the tidal creeks and struggling through the underbrush, mapped out lots with geometric precision using lines of latitude and longitude. But many of the lots contained only slivers of usable land or extended over salt marsh and water.[8]

Uncertainty over the coming land sales continued until early January 1864 when Mansfield French returned from Washington with revised instructions. Arriving on the steamship *Arago,* French delivered the new directive to Saxton and Smith and then waited until the *Arago* had sailed before sharing the order with Brisbane and Wording. Immediately Brisbane cried foul. Denied any opportunity to send an immediate response on the *Arago,* he confided to his diary:

> Oh! That man French does mean mischief by his meddlesome spirit than his head is worth; and General Saxton seems to be a crazy man about the division of these lands.
>
> Much, more trouble is ahead, and I fear my colleague Judge Wording will resign and if he does I could not long remain with any satisfaction here.⁹

The new instructions to the commissioners backed full preemption and were prefaced by Secretary Chase:

> Treasury Department, Dec. 30, 1863
>
> Gentlemen: By direction of the President I transmit the following instructions, which you will observe in disposing of lands struck off to the United States. You will consider them as applying to all lands in your district which are now, or may be hereafter owned by the United States, except such as are or may be set apart for military, naval, school, or revenue purposes, and the plantations on St. Helena Island known as "Land's End," and the "Ben Chaplin Place," and the City of Beaufort on Port Royal Island.
>
> All previous instructions or parts thereof which conflict with those now given, are hereby rescinded.
>
> Yours respectfully
S. R. CHASE

> To U.S. Direct Tax Commissioners.
> December 31, 1863
> Additional instructions to the Direct tax Commissioners for the District of South Carolina in relation to the disposition of lands:
>
> 1. You will allow any loyal person of twenty one years of age, or upwards, who has at any time since the occupation by the national forces resided for six months, or now resides upon, or is engaged in cultivating any lands in your district owned by the United States to enter the same for preemption to the extent of one, or at the option of the preemptor, two tracts of twenty acres each, paying therefore one dollar and twenty five cents per acre. You will give preference in all cases to heads of families, and married women whose husbands are engaged in the service of the United States, or are necessarily absent.
>
> 2. You will permit each soldier, sailor or marine actually engaged in the service of the United States, or any who may have been, or

hereafter shall be honorably discharged to preempt and purchase in person, or by authorized agents, at the rate of one dollar, twenty five cents per acre, one tract of twenty acres of land, if single and, if married, two tracts of twenty acres each, in addition to the amount, a head of family, or married woman in the absence of her husband, is allowed to preempt and purchase under the general privilege to loyal persons.

3. Each preemptor on filing his claim and receiving a certificate of preemption must pay in United States notes, two fifths of the price, and the residue on receiving a deed for the parcels of land preempted, and a failure to make complete payment on receipt of the Deed will forfeit all rights under the preemption, as well as all partial payments for the land.

4. When persons authorized to purchase by preemption desire to enter upon, and cultivate lands not yet surveyed, they may do so, but they will be required to conform in their selection, as nearly as possible, to the probable lines of the surveys, and to take and occupy them subject to correction of title and occupation by actual surveys when made.

5. In making surveys, such reservations for paths and roadways will be made as will allow easy and convenient access to the several subdivisions entered for sale and occupancy by preemption or otherwise. Approved December 31. 1863.

A. LINCOLN.[10]

The preemptionists hailed the alteration of the original instructions as a great victory. Commissioner Smith wrote his chief, Judge Lewis, the commissioner of internal revenue, that the people of the sea islands met the new orders with great happiness. They considered it "a second deliverance" that awakened great ambitions. Smith met with Wording and Brisbane on January 15, asking them to accept the new orders, but he was rebuffed. In his diary Brisbane declared Smith drunk and the new instructions illegal.[11]

Upset and angry, Brisbane demanded and received an audience with General Saxton, in which he asked the governor to delay implementing the proclamation until Brisbane and Wording could confer with officials in Washington. Saxton refused. Brisbane, trying to stall, asked for a week to think about the instructions. Again Saxton refused but did agree to give Brisbane twenty-four hours before putting the orders in effect. Brisbane used the time to vent his spleen. In writing to Judge Lewis, he suggested that Saxton, either drunk or in a fit of anger, had refused to listen to Brisbane and that the general had readied orders directing his subordinates "to go immediately and divide up the lands."[12]

The day after meeting with Brisbane, an exuberant Saxton issued another circular that overrode his previous one. By the new presidential instructions, certain land was no longer set aside for the freedmen. Instead all property was opened up to preemption. To give the former slaves an advantage in claiming land, Saxton called upon all superintendents and teachers to give their entire attention "to assist the people to the extent of their power in locating, staking out their claims and securing their title deeds under this order of the President, which, in its beneficent results is second only to the Emancipation Proclamation." Saxton called for people "to lose no time in pre-empting their claims and preparing their grounds for the coming harvest." He also requested that the freedmen plant corn and vegetables and to "remember that cotton is the great staple here. I advise you to plant all you can of it. So profitable was its culture in the old days of Slavery, that your former masters said 'Cotton is King.' It is expected that you will show in a Free South that cotton is more of a king than ever."[13]

Though there was some fear that nonfreedmen, who had been in the sea islands for six months, would take advantage of the preemption directive to stake out property, most believed that the new instructions would prove very beneficial to the former slaves. For the forty-three thousand acres available on the sea islands for preemption, it was estimated that there were eighteen thousand freedmen in the department of whom thirty-six hundred as heads of households were eligible to preempt. There was even hope that Wording and Brisbane would resign. The *New York Tribune* hailed Commissioner Smith and General Saxton as heroes whose names would be ever associated with "the good work of planting civilization in a moral and intellectual wilderness, and saving the land from becoming a desert."[14]

On Sunday, January 17, Saxton orchestrated a meeting at the Brick Baptist Church on St. Helena Island to encourage the freedmen to begin preempting property immediately. Both blacks and whites attended the ceremony, which was run much like a church service. After an opening prayer by Reverend W. S. Phillips, Reverend French addressed the congregation from the pulpit, urging them to go and locate their lots. General Saxton came next and in a short address told the people to go at once and "not to sleep till they had staked out their claims."

The department quartermaster, Colonel John Elwell, warned that if action was not quickly taken, the old masters might return and reclaim their property. Reverend French then brought Commissioner Smith forward. By one account, a seemingly inebriated Smith, chewing tobacco with tears of joy running down his cheeks, cajoled the crowd on what he declared a joyful occasion. However, Edward Philbrick, who had made a special point of attending the ceremony and was no friend of preemption, had no adverse comment about Smith's appearance, reporting that the commissioner merely explained "to the Negroes the meaning of preemption" and its Latin roots. While Philbrick found the whole "fandango" rather long and tiresome, numerous freedmen did begin claiming land, and by the end of

January, petitions for some six thousand acres had been recorded with the military.[15]

However, the directive from the president soon hit a roadblock. Brisbane and Wording controlled the board, and though Smith urged them to implement immediately the new instructions, they refused to act. Brisbane and Wording believed the new instructions, which allowed preemption, were illegal and violated the Direct Tax Act. They refused to accept preemption petitions and any deposits that had been taken by General Saxton's aides.[16]

In a letter written immediately after his meeting with Saxton to his direct superior Joseph Lewis, Brisbane pointed out that the twenty thousand acres originally set aside for the former slaves were now open to anyone. He warned that the "adroit, skillful and ready witted and educated white man" would outmaneuver the freedmen in the race to claim property. Brisbane insisted that if the government's purpose was to place land in the hands of the freedmen, then the most beneficial method was to return to the original instructions. He also attacked the legality of the new order, stating, "Under the law there is no authority whatsoever for the preemption of improved lands." Since the new instructions were "inconsistent" with the law, Brisbane did not believe a valid title could be given. He and Wording would only support the directive if Congress made "these new instructions law."[17]

While Brisbane pleaded his case to Lewis, Saxton wrote directly to Secretary Chase, expressing extreme gratification for the wise and humane measures. He informed Chase about the meeting with the freedmen at the Brick Baptist Church and how he had advised "them to lose no time in availing themselves of the beneficial provisions of these instructions." Saxton praised Commissioner Smith but expressed great surprise and disappointment in the opposition of Wording and Brisbane, especially the latter, who he felt had proven "false to the record of his whole life." Saxton urged Chase to replace either Wording or Brisbane with someone whose "heart and head are more in sympathy with your enlightened policy."[18]

Chase did not act on Saxton's suggestion. Though Wording seemed to consider leaving, neither he nor Brisbane offered their resignations. They held fast to their refusal to accept land claims and continued to delay in hopes that officials in Washington would agree that preemption was a flagrant misrepresentation of established property law and revoke the new instructions.[19]

Newspaper accounts detailing the sea islands land sales and preemption soon reached the North, sparking the Reverend Richard Fuller to again contact Secretary Chase. Fuller, concerned over the fate of both the native whites and freedmen, continued to keep a close eye on affairs in Beaufort. In his letter Fuller appealed to Chase as a friend and a "true Christian" to use his influence to assist the white "women & children-widows & orphans" who would lose their lands to freedmen should the sales at Port Royal go forward. Fuller did not believe the freedmen ready for land ownership, declaring that "this idea of investing these ignorant, improvident, indolent people with landed estates, & expecting them to improve or cultivate them, is a most Utopian & fanatical delusion." He believed them to be a virtuous and decent people but felt they still needed discipline, control, and regulation before they could become independent farmers. Fuller feared they would be easily duped by the selfish and rapacious. He prayed for the freedmen to be delivered from doom and asked that God "direct & overrule all things for his glory & the advancement of the Redeemers Kingdom & the peace & prosperity of the country!"[20]

Ten days later Chase replied to Fuller, telling his friend that he would not backtrack on the freedmen's program. Chase did express sympathy for the families of white southerners caught up in the war and hoped that Christian patriots would help alleviate their suffering; however, he also believed that those who supported the rebellion had to accept the consequences of their actions, pointing out that the calamities affecting the absentee land owners had been caused by those who had brought on and supported the rebellion. He summed up the situation by stating, "But what can human power do when earthquakes shake the world?"[21]

Nearly lost in the debates over the preemption of farmland was the sale of blocks and lots in Beaufort. For the auction the tax commissioners had renamed the town's streets. From south to north, streets were designated A (Bay Street) through K (Boundary Street), while those running east to west became 1 (Short) through 16 (Hamar).

On January 18 the auction for foreclosed town lots began. Though numerous buildings, especially those homes being used as hospitals, were held back from the proceedings, large sections of the town went up for bid. Of Beaufort's 137 blocks, 74 were auctioned off. Most of the property sold lay between Charles and Monson Streets, an area with few or no dwellings. As described by a *New York Times* reporter:

> At 10 A.M., the hour appointed, the apartment in which the Commissioners convened, was densely crowded with officers, soldiers and contrabands—the latter class in the preponderance. Unfortunately the weather was inclement, in consequence of which the sale was postponed till the following day. At the hour announced, the Commissioners, accompanied by a crowd of expectant possessors, proceeded to the eastern portion of the town, and commenced the sale by offering lot No. 1. The bidding was spirited throughout the sale, and, as a general thing, the property was disposed of at rates considered high for this district at this time. The contrabands were foremost in the bids. How

in the world these fellows manage to exhibit so much money is a mystery to many sharpers among white officers. One sable son pulled from his pocket a roll of "greenbacks," amounting to $2,000. Of course the "white sogers" had to back out until the contraband had selected his lot and expended his capital. The desirable lots brought prices varying from $800 to $1,200. The sale was continued on Wednesday, and is in progress to-day. Ten days or two weeks will probably be occupied in disposing of the entire lands. By the terms of the instructions the Commissioners are empowered to reserve such buildings as may be required for use by the military authorities. I learn some dissatisfaction has been expressed on account of the Commissioners offering for sale premises actually occupied by the military, and found to be indispensable for the need of the service. This is a point that certainly claims the serious attention of the Commissioners. Nothing should be done to impede the military operations of the department.[22]

Prominent among the buyers were Prince Rivers, and Lieutenant Colonel John D. Strong of the 1st South Carolina, most likely part of the regiment's consortium established to purchase town property for their comrades. The area would eventually develop into a predominately freedman neighborhood. No lots west of Monson, the site of camps and a parade ground, were sold.

Among the more prominent structures sold included:

House or Property Location	Purchaser	Appraised Va	Sale Price
Elizabeth Hext Sams 207 Hancock	Samuel Cohen	$600	$620
Block 6 The Green	Merritt A. Sizer	$150	$220
William Fripp House 302 Federal	William B. Reed	$1000	$650
John Bell House 315 Federal	Mary Bell	$700	$250
Thomas Hazel House 509 North	Prince Rivers	$600	$925
John F. Chaplin House 507 Washington	Israel Cohen	$800	$950
Rev. Stephen Elliott House 607 Bay	Wilkes & Thompson	$1500	$1200
Rev. Thomas Ledbetter 411 Bayard	T. W. Lewis	$1025	$900
The Baker House 701 Green	American Freedmen Association	$1800	$850

(continued)

House or Property Location	Purchaser	Appraised Va	Sale Price
Thomas Fuller 1211 Bay	Rev. Mansfield French	$1000	$1700
Nathaniel Heyward 1015 Bay	Gen. Rufus Saxton	$1800	$2000
McKee/R. DeTreville House 511 Prince	Robert Smalls	$700	$605
Stuart House 1011 Bay	Sgt. A. G. Henry	$900	$4055

Beaufort Free South, January 30, 1864

In the eastern portion of the town, Merritt A. Sizer purchased the lot known today as the "Green." Samuel Cohen bought the Elizabeth Hext Sams House, and William B. Reed obtained the William Fripp House. The former slave Mary Bell bought the home of her master, John Bell. Prince Rivers of the 1st South Carolina obtained the Thomas Hazel House, while Saxton's brother-in-law John G. Thompson procured with his business partner John Wilkes the Reverend Stephen Elliott's house on Bay Street, site of their general store and their jointly operated newspaper the *Free South.*

Of special note were purchases by General Saxton, Reverend French, and Robert Smalls. Saxton secured one of the town's largest structures, the Nathaniel Heyward home, which he maintained as his home and district headquarters. The property had been appraised at $1,800 and Saxton obtained it with a bid of $2,000. The Heyward House eventually became the Sea Island Hotel. Reverend French bought his quarters, the Thomas Fuller home, valued at $1,000, for $1,700. Robert Smalls made the winning bid of $605 on his former master's home, now owned by Richard DeTreville, which had been appraised at $700.

Lots downtown also sold to merchants, among them Sylvanus Mayo and Stephen Caldwell Millett Jr., who would become prominent in postwar Beaufort. Among the properties purchased by Mayo, a merchant from Yonkers, New York, was the former Daniel DeSaussure Store, a three-story tabby structure at 719 Bay Street, owned before occupation by the merchant Charles Bold of the firm Rhodes and Bold.

Another New Yorker, Stephen C. Millett also invested in Beaufort. Born in Jamestown, New York, the twenty-three-year-old Millett was the son of the Episcopal priest Reverend Stephen C. Millett and Sarah Fuller Appleton. His wife's father was James Appleton, a staunch Massachusetts abolitionist and temperance advocate. His uncle, Daniel Fuller Appleton, was the cofounder of the Robbins and Appleton Company, importers of watches. In 1857 the firm purchased a small watch company in Waltham, Massachusetts, that eventually became the American Waltham Watch Company.

Stephen C. Millett served in the 71st New York, a National Guard regiment that had been activated for ninety days early in the war and saw service at the Battle of First Bull Run. Though appointed a lieutenant in the 31st New York volunteer regiment, illness kept him from joining the unit, and in 1863 he came to Beaufort. Millett purchased a number of lots in Beaufort, including a large store/house owned before occupation by Henry McKee that fronted Bay Street at the northwestern corner of Carteret and Bay Streets, as well as a residence once owned by John Morgandollar Baker at the northwestern corner of East and Craven Streets.[23]

While new owners bought up lots in Beaufort, the argument continued to rage over preemption for the district's rural property. Saxton insisted that Brisbane follow the president's directive and approve preemption. Brisbane refused, declaring that he would not soil Lincoln's name for honesty by putting forward an illegal plan.

Brisbane received support from the department commander, Major General Quincy A. Gillmore. Though not as intensely involved with the affairs of the freedmen as his predecessors, Gillmore did watch over activities that affected his command, especially those that might impact the morale of a community he counted on for laborers and recruits. Gillmore saw the new instructions as undermining the freedmen. On January 31 a concerned Gillmore wrote Chase to express his fears that the new instructions would hurt the freedmen since, he believed, they could not compete against white speculators. He urged a return to the original directive.[24]

In early February, Commissioner Lewis received two contradictory reports from Brisbane and Smith. In his statement Brisbane informed Lewis that he and Wording were awaiting further instructions before proceeding. Brisbane also noted that wet weather and lack of equipment had slowed the surveyors. On the other hand, Smith filed a brief informing Lewis that weather and lack of transportation were not an issue and that the entire delay was the result of Wording and Brisbane's refusal to comply with the new directive.

Arguments continued to flow back and forth. Claims, true or not, of Smith's drinking and drug use reached high-ranking officials, including his old comrade Senator Doolittle, causing the senator to lose confidence in his friend. In writing Chase, Doolittle expressed greater faith in Brisbane's proposals over the "utopian ideas" of French. Lewis also contacted Chase, reporting that he saw no hope of cooperation between Smith, Wording, and Brisbane. Favoring Wording and Brisbane, Lewis informed Chase, "I assume the responsibility of recommending that Judge Smith be removed," saying he should be replaced with someone who could act in harmony with the other commissioners.[25]

On February 6 Chase "suspended" the "recent instructions touching preemption" and instructed the commissioners to proceed under the previous directive. The secretary gave no reasons for the change. The legal question would not have concerned Chase or the president. So far in the conflict, the Congress, the president, and cabinet members had issued decrees and proclamations that stretched the government's powers. Most likely it was believed that under the original instructions the freedmen had the best opportunity to secure land, instead of taking their chances at an open auction, where both blacks and whites could employ preemption to their advantage.[26]

The directive suspending the preemption orders reached the sea islands on February 12, 1864. While a blow to the preemptionists, the revised instructions did not end the melodrama. On February 13 Reverend Phillips, the rector of the Brick Baptist Church, died unexpectedly. The next day Solomon Peck conducted the funeral services at the church, where a month earlier Phillips had opened a ceremony promoting preemption. After Peck's sermon Reverend French followed and addressed the congregation. He lamented the suspension of preemption but urged the freedmen to hold on to the lands they had staked out at "every hazard" in hopes that the government would eventually recognize their claims. If that did not happen, the freedmen should give the government "all the trouble they could."[27]

French's performance at the funeral outraged and frightened many. Brisbane asked Lewis to remove French from the department for instigating resistance to the government. Though not advocating violence, French's actions worried Brisbane and others. Rumors of threats and riots surfaced, prompting General Gillmore to promise protection to anyone taking part in the land sales.[28]

While French and Commissioner Smith protested, hoping that the suspension of the preemption instructions would be lifted, the initial sales went ahead as planned. On February 18 the commissioners began their work. Brisbane described the first day: "We opened the sales today of the plantations; but in consequence of the factious opposition & hindrances by Judge Smith we sold only one small piece of 33 acres. Really it is too bad that the administration will keep such a man in office." The next day, when several plantations were sold, Saxton's aide Alexander Ketchum, backed by Smith, made an effort to recognize some preemption claims but failed to stop the sale.[29]

Ketchum reported that freedmen, bidding against whites, managed to purchase land on Wassaw Island and Bolus Point but lost in their attempts to buy Ashdale and Bluff Farm Plantations. Ketchum, who had collected $7,354.80 from petitioners returned $4,204.80. But the remaining preemptors maintained their deposits in hopes that their petitions would eventually be honored.[30]

Initially only property on St. Helena and Lady's Islands, where the survey had been completed, was offered for auction. For sixty days the auction continued. At its conclusion 10,022 acres were sold in 91 tracts of about 112 acres each for a total of $87,669. Seven thousand one hundred forty-seven acres were sold under the provisions setting aside land at a special rate for military personnel or those with previous service, while another 2,875 acres went to civilians. Because of the confusion over preemption, the majority of the acreage sold to whites. However, as the sales continued and expanded, freedmen obtained homestead titles and purchased property in open auctions. Some even secured property through their original preemption petitions.[31]

Besides land and structures, the commissioners also auctioned furniture and livestock. As government property was sold off and superintendents left their abodes, special sales were held. Individuals who bought homes also had to bid on livestock and furniture. Offered up were beds, tables, and chairs as well as farm animals. At the Oaks Plantation two mules sold for $130.

While sales of household goods, animals, and property continued, the conflict between Brisbane and Wording and Saxton, French, and Smith persisted. Three days after receiving the revised instructions, Brisbane thanked Chase for saving him and Wording from the "utter confusion into which General Saxton, Mr. French & Judge Smith were precipitating us." He reiterated his opposition to preemption, which he called a "wild scheme" that "out radicals all the radicalism I ever heard of in agrarian history."[32]

French and Smith, realizing they had lost their preemption bid, appealed to Lewis. The two expressed concerns over the fate of freedmen who, believing that preemption would be implemented, had followed General Saxton's instructions by planting crops and building homes. French feared the freedmen would fall victims to white speculators who would destroy any hope for a productive, active agrarian society, while Smith worried that the freedmen would be deprived "of the fruits of their toil."[33]

Brisbane, pleased that his and Wording's stance on preemption had been confirmed, opened a campaign to remove Smith from the tax commission. In late February, Brisbane wrote Commissioner Lewis, accusing Smith of annoying the other two commissioners, not being on time for meetings, and encouraging violence by freedmen against whites who purchased land occupied by preemptors. He also complained that Smith held a position on Saxton's staff that interfered with Smith's commissioner duties. Brisbane stated that if Smith was not removed, he would happily return to his farm in Wisconsin rather than "have official association with such a man as he is." In concluding, Brisbane asked that Lewis place the issue before Secretary Chase for a final judgment.[34]

The treasury secretary put the matter before President Lincoln. On March 1, 1864, in writing Brisbane, an exasperated Chase expressed his amazement that Brisbane and Wording could not work with Smith, Saxton, and French for the betterment of the freedmen. The secretary still believed that "the plan of preemptions by which the colored man will be enabled to obtain a home in the shortest possible time is the best plan." But Chase, though he regretted relieving Smith, informed Brisbane that the president had decided it best to appoint Judge Dennis N. Cooley, a thirty-nine-year-old lawyer from Iowa, to replace Judge Smith.[35]

On March 5 Brisbane received word that Smith was to be removed. In his diary he stated, "This is truly agreeable news. God be thanked for it." Willard Saxton, General Saxton's brother and staff member, recorded a different reaction. In reference to Brisbane and Wording, he noted, "The last mail brought the news of the relief of Judge Smith from the Board of Tax Commissioners. The 'Jesuit and Jackass' are triumphant."[36]

Saxton, knowing that Brisbane had maligned him, contacted Chase to defend his position. The general also wrote to Smith, assuring his friend and confidant that he greatly appreciated the commissioner's work and his consideration for the freedmen. Saxton promised Smith that his memory would be "cherished" by the freedmen "long after those who slandered you shall have been forgotten." Smith remained in Port Royal and became part of Saxton's staff and later worked before the war's end to create a biracial Republican Party in the sea islands.[37]

Though Brisbane and Wording seemed to have triumphed over their adversaries, Saxton, Smith, French, and their allies managed to delay full possession of the sold property to its new owners. While Generals Saxton and Gillmore acknowledged the property sales, they did request that technical questions about titles be reviewed. Saxton went so far as to ask that the matter be placed before both the attorney general and the Supreme Court. In the meantime, land not yet surveyed remained under control of the government and leased to individuals, or it remained under the supervision of government agents until surveyed and sold. Arrangements were also made to protect the freedmen who had followed Saxton's preemption instructions and built homes and planted crops on land now in the hands of new owners or renters.[38]

Saxton, who had been temporarily assigned to court-martial duty, was momentarily removed from the controversy, but his successor as military governor and commander of Beaufort and Port Royal Island, Brigadier General William Birney, proved an able replacement. Birney, son of the renowned Alabama abolitionist James G. Birney and older brother to Major General David D. Birney, had served as an officer in the 4th New Jersey Infantry Regiment in the Army of the Potomac until named colonel of the forming 22nd USCT Regiment. Before he could assume command, Birney was promoted to general and placed in charge of recruiting black troops in Maryland. In early 1864 Birney and some of the USCT regiments he helped organize arrived in the Department of the South and were assigned to duty in Florida.[39]

After service in Florida, the forty-five-year-old Birney briefly replaced Saxton in overseeing military operations on Port Royal Island and civil affairs for the area's freedmen. Colonel Higginson described Birney as a superior, cultivated volunteer officer, both "a martinet & a moralist." Birney also cared deeply for the region's freedmen and took steps to protect their interests. On March 30, 1864, Birney issued an order that allowed the freedmen to "for the present be left in undisputed possession of all lands occupied and planted by them." This had the immediate affect of stopping the purchasers of land occupied by preemptors until the harvest at the end of the year.[40]

Birney and Saxton also reviewed contracts between the purchasers. They discovered a number of callous labor agreements that placed the freedmen in a position of accepting low wages and surrendering up to three-fourths of their cotton crop to the new property owners or face eviction. An outraged Birney threatened the base contractors with a military tribunal and sentences that would force the offenders to make full restitution and perform hard labor in their own cotton fields. Though such draconian measures were not carried out, the military officials and tax commissioners carefully oversaw contracts between both landowners and lessees and the freedmen.[41]

The preemptionists also had the satisfaction of seeing parts of their program implemented. At least forty petitions, filed before the initial sales, were honored. Other claims were accepted throughout the year. In March 1865 Congress passed legislation directing the acceptance of preemption claims, and approximately one thousand freedmen petitions were approved.[42]

However, the confusion over the tax sales and freedmen preemption petitions had a chilling effect on the new property owners. Many were hindered and in some cases barred from independently operating their land. In some instances the restrictions proved too much, and individuals abandoned their ventures. Even Edward Philbrick's operations were affected. Philbrick and his superintendents found their employees becoming disgruntled, with some workers demanding that Philbrick sell them his property. There were questions over the legitimacy of his purchase and ownership of Coffin Point and Cherry Hill Plantations and many, including Saxton and the tax commissioners, believed Philbrick had promised to sell to the land of these estates to the freedmen within a year. Philbrick managed to deflect criticism and continued to work the company's holdings until 1866 when he and his associates began selling off their property.[43]

The new situation was not lost upon the missionaries, especially those who had abandoned their philanthropic crusade and joined the ranks of businessmen or had become foremen for private landowners. William C. Gannett, a onetime missionary turned Philbrick employee commented to his father, "Did you know we had long ceased to be philanthropists or even Gideonites? We are nothing now but speculators, and the righteous rail against us."[44]

Among those who began viewing the Gideonites with suspicion and railing against the and speculators were the freedmen. Throughout the preemption controversy, the sea island freedmen watched the "immense mischief" being brought about by the commissioners and became dismayed when whites purchased property they believed to be rightfully theirs. Befuddled and angry, many complained directly to President Lincoln. The former slaves wanted land and disliked the usurpation of what they believed was their God-given inheritance. While Brisbane and Wording dueled with the Smith-French-Saxton faction over their vision for the sea islands, the freedmen, amazed and confused by the actions of their liberators, began to take matters into their own hands and commence the formation of their own community, free from the petty squabbles and directives of their government masters.

From the tax sales a new community took root in the sea islands. The new order had started with the 1863 auctions and continued with the 1864 land sales. In a report compiled by Commissioner Wording on March 21, 1864, it was stated that in St. Helena Parish:

> 2469 acres on St. Helena Island had been redeemed by its owners
> 599 acres set aside for a city on St. Helena Island.
> 3368 acres reserved for military purposes
> 5090 acres for Educational purposes.
> 20430 acres reserved for sale to head of Freedmen families
> 21342 acres sold in March 1863 tax sale
> 18689 acres available for sale to military personnel and other bidders.

Wording wrote that the 1864 sales so far had brought in $73,794, of which $62,101 was paid for or secured to be paid for by military personnel, both black and white. Property not yet sold, primarily on Port Royal Island, was leased though sales that could be made to "responsible persons," freedmen and whites, as opportunities arose.[45]

The land sales continued for years. By the end of the war, 650 African families on the sea islands had been issued homestead titles. By 1872 the number increased to 2,269. These sales, coupled with land purchased at auctions and the 1863 sales, netted the sea island freedmen between 25,000 to 30,000 acres. Another 30,000 were sold to whites, leaving 40,000 to be eventually redeemed by prewar owners. The records of the U.S. Direct Tax Commission also reveal that of the total 101,930 acres that were foreclosed upon during the war, 47,841 acres, or 46.93 percent of the land, were retained or bought by the federal government; 21,011 acres, or 20.6 percent, were bought by outside, mostly northern investors; and 31,016 acres, or 30.4 percent, were redeemed by the original owners or their heirs within ten years following the war. Two thousand sixty-two acres, or 2 percent of the total, were of uncertain distribution. The last plantation successfully redeemed by its former owners was Lands End Plantation, with 434 acres. It was redeemed by Mary Farmer, surviving heir of Dr. Joseph Jenkins, for $124.37 in taxes and penalties on June 28, 1876.[46]

In a bit of irony, the three original commissioners left the sea islands on June 2, 1865, on the steamship *Arago*. While boarding the vessel, Brisbane noted that Smith was "broken down and will probably even pass away." On the voyage north, Smith's condition worsened. Brisbane did all he could for his onetime foe. He had Smith moved into a neighboring stateroom and, with the vessel's physician and a waiter, cared for the dying Smith. At 6:00 A.M. on June 4, Smith died, five days short of his fifty-fourth birthday. As Brisbane noted, "I was with him in his last moments & closed his eyes."[47]

While he did not survive to see the results of his work, Smith, along with Wording and Brisbane, had commenced a tremendous transformation. They oversaw the sea islands' greatest real estate transaction since Charles II deeded the area to the Lord Proprietors. Though the sales did not go the way any of them expected, they did begin the creation of a new community. William Gannett, who had observed their work, aptly summed up the situation in the sea islands when he wrote, "Still it is a beginning of a great thing,—negroes become land-owners and the door is thrown open to Northern immigration. Years hence it will be a satisfaction to look back on these beginnings."[48]

Chapter 12

Sea Island Transformation and Military Stalemate

*"Immense crowds would assemble
and make the place ring with God's praise"*

While debates raged over the sale of foreclosed land, other aspects of the Port Royal Experiment continued to evolve. By 1864 there were just under one hundred schools operated by about one hundred teachers on the sea islands. Most were still supported by freedmen associations, though Edward Philbrick maintained schools on his property while the Catholic Church supported two schools on Hilton Head Island, including one at Mitchelville. The military also provided a facility for the children of soldiers on Hilton Head and a school for destitute white children in Beaufort, many of them the offspring of refugees from Florida.[1]

Sunday schools supplemented the educational centers. On the Sabbath, students reinforced their coursework by reading the Bible and other religious tracts. In Beaufort, at the Methodist Church on West Street, an observer noted that eighty to a hundred children attended Sunday school and that "most of whom can read very well, particularly the younger ones, as they have the privilege of attending day schools while the older ones are at work."[2]

Quality and instruction time varied among the schools and depended upon the teachers' dedication. Some instructors only sporadically held classes, while others maintained set schedules. Ellen Murray and Laura Towne's Penn School, located in the Brick Baptist Church on St. Helena Island since September 1862, was among the best, attracting students from neighboring institutions. But in October 1863, Murray and Towne found their tenures being challenged by the church's acting minister, Reverend W. S. Phillips, who wanted the teachers and their school removed from the church. Phillips, a white man from the Baptist Home Mission Society, informed the two teachers that the building was property of the Baptist Church and not the government. The minister also complained that the school's activities disrupted his ability to fully utilize the structure, and he made it clear that he intended to turn them out.[3]

When General Saxton learned of Phillips's threats, he summoned the minister to Beaufort and informed him that the school would stay. A chastised Phillips reversed his stance but still complained about desks intruding on the sanctuary and the teachers decorating the church. Saxton later sent a note to Towne informing her that their use of the building was safe as long as he was in charge and that he would throw out "2 ministers in order to keep it a school."[4]

Despite this reprieve, Towne and Murray continued to feel threatened by Phillips. Towne also feared that the Baptists, under direction from tax commissioner and Baptist minister Brisbane, were scheming to take over the government schools. On February 8, 1864, the black members of the Brick Church voted to name Phillips as their minister. Then, four days later Reverend Phillips died of smallpox, which was raging across the sea islands. His successor, Reverend J. W. Parker of the Baptist Home Mission Society, assured Towne that he would not disturb the school. Parker later confided to Towne that he had come to the islands in hopes of "finding peace + zeal" with everyone working in harmony, but only discovered "friction—friction—in every quarter military, religious + political."[5]

Though Reverend Parker had informed Laura Towne that he would return to talk her "out of Unitarianism," she thought him to be "kind." Still, she and Ellen Murray worried over the fate of their school, and when General Saxton sent them a note asking whether they would be interested in a new facility provided by the Pennsylvania Freedmen's Relief Commission, they quickly accepted.[6]

The new building, a prefabricated structure shipped from Philadelphia, arrived by the end of the year. The army's chief contractor, Duncan Wilson, oversaw its construction by his team of freedmen carpenters; work was slow, however, and the building was not ready for classes until mid-January 1865. The new schoolhouse not only afforded a better environment for learning but also security from eviction. Besides providing the building, the Pennsylvania Freedmen's Relief Commission continued to support the school financially long after the war ended.[7]

While Murray and Towne worked with the Pennsylvania Commission to operate their school as an independent facility, the region's other education centers eventually merged into a government system financed by the leasing of property known as school farms. By the president's directive, thirty-five school farms were to be established: thirteen on St. Helena Island, one on Coosaw, eight on Lady's, eleven on Port Royal, and two on Parris Island. The tracts contained buildings and were no larger than 160 acres. They were to be leased for periods up to five years, with a portion of the proceeds being applied to the establishment of schools and "to the education of colored youths, and of such poor white persons, being minors, as may by themselves, parents, guardians, or next friends, apply for the benefit thereof."[8]

The tax commissioners were charged with overseeing the leased school farms, applying the money they generated to maintaining educational facilities. Commissioner Dennis Cooley was appointed school superintendent, though all of the commissioners handled the appointment of teachers. Some farms were leased in 1864, but evidence indicates that the commissioners did not operate any schools until early 1865. School farms were leased to speculators, including teachers and superintendents, who saw an opportunity to combine their philanthropic work with a moneymaking enterprise. This included Josiah Fairfield and his wife, Nelly Winsor Fairfield, who sought to take over the Oaks Plantation school farm, which included the plantation house, for their use. Laura Towne looked suspiciously on the Fairfields' venture, believing it part of Commissioner Brisbane's attempt to place the school farms and the region's educational system in the hands of his fellow Baptists.[9]

Brisbane's Baptist education plot, if indeed there was one, never came to fruition, but the mere fact that Towne suspected such a scheme merely emphasized the growing friction among the various sea island groups. The Baptists continued to dominate the religious activities on the sea islands. The American Home Baptist Society provided clergy who set up congregations in Beaufort and the neighboring sea islands. Reverend Solomon Peck continued to serve as the area's senior minister. Peck ordained several black ministers, including Abraham Murchison. Before the war Murchison had officiated to black congregations in Savannah and, after his escape to Federal lines, formed a congregation on Hilton Head.

While the Baptist Home Mission controlled much of the area's religious activities, their independent brethren of the Freewill Baptists Home Mission also brought their theology to the sea islands. In March 1864, with backing from churches in Maine, Massachusetts, and New Hampshire, the Reverend Ebenezer Knowlton of Montville, Maine, an ordained minister who had served in both the Maine legislature and the U.S. Congress and as a trustee of Colby University and Bates College, came to Beaufort and organized what was proclaimed to be the first Freewill Baptist Church "ever formed of colored people, formerly slaves." Placed in the charge of the Reverend William F. Eaton, the congregation initially counted 177 members. By the summer, funds were raised for a sanctuary, and with money provided by Rufus Deering of Portland, Maine, a church building was constructed. Its frame was shipped to Hilton Head and eventually erected in Beaufort.[10]

Also active in the sea islands were pastors from the African Methodist Episcopal Convention. In the spring of 1863, the New York–based National Freedmen's Relief Association requested that the A.M.E. Church send two ministers to Port Royal. Reverends James Lynch of the Baltimore Conference and James D. S. Hall of the New York Conference volunteered. They arrived in May 1863 aboard the *Arago*. At Hilton Head, Lynch and Hall attended a service led by Abraham Murchison in the Baptist church constructed early in the war by the direction of General David Hunter. They then continued on to Beaufort, where they took up residence in the Mission

House—the former home of Thomas Fuller now used by Reverends Peck and French. At Beaufort they found a large freedmen congregation at St. Helena Episcopal Church led by two local black ministers, William Seward and Vincent Cruz. Hall took charge in Beaufort while Lynch carried his ministry to St. Helena Island.

At St. Helenaville, the prewar planter's resort on St. Helena Sound, Lynch "found a snug church," an Episcopal chapel where a large Sunday school operated but no organized congregation. He quickly united freedmen Methodists, Presbyterians, and Episcopalians into a single congregation of 260 members and licensed three preachers: Smart Campbell, Caesar Miller, and James Townsend. An excellent proselytizer, Lynch preached on Parris and St. Helena Islands and at the St. Helenaville Episcopal and Brick Baptist Churches. He supported preemption, Freedmen schools, and the outfitting of black regiments. Frances Gage wrote that he "preached to us yesterday one of the most eloquent, and at the same time plain, common-sense discourses that I ever heard." Gage declared him a "marvel" and compared him to Henry Ward Beecher and Wendell Phillips.[11]

Laura Towne was also impressed with Reverend Lynch and his sister, who came to teach on St. Helena Island. Lynch and his sister lived in St. Helenaville and often visited Towne and Ellen Murray at their St. Helenaville home. During one of their conversations, Towne asked Lynch whether she should attend communion. Taken aback, Lynch replied that he could not understand why she would want to since "Unitarians did not acknowledge Christ." A long discussion followed, and when he left, Lynch told Towne that he hoped that Ellen Murray, a Baptist, would convert her. Towne appreciated his concern but also wrote that "he is really wonderfully liberal, and, as he will probably fall in with the right kind of people by reason of his eloquence and genius, he will perhaps be a Unitarian himself."[12]

Once he had solidified his congregation on St. Helena Island, Lynch carried his ministry to Hilton Head, where he organized over a thousand parishioners. Services were initially held under "the Big Elm Tree" at Mitchelville, where "immense crowds would assemble and make the place ring with God's praise." Lynch happily reported that soon a church for four hundred people was constructed in Mitchelville for "the dispensation of God's word."[13]

While Lynch labored on the outlying islands, Reverend Hall, in Beaufort, attempted to place a permanent African Methodist Episcopal congregation in St. Helena Episcopal Church. In December 1863 he participated in a "Festival and Fair" held by the women of Beaufort at the Methodist Church on West Street. Proceeds from the fair went to assist the poor and support Hall's ministry. But Hall found his calling unsuccessful and was unable to bring the various factions together; eventually the Reverend T. W. Lewis of the Methodist Episcopal North Eastern Conference came to dominate the black congregants in Beaufort. Upon learning of his partner's failure, Lynch quickly came to Beaufort and informed Lewis and others that he considered the African Methodist Episcopal Church to have jurisdiction. He organized a congregation and applied to General Saxton for St. Helena Episcopal Church. Saxton agreed, but Lynch never had the opportunity to move in. In early 1864 the sanctuary, which had been briefly used as a government storehouse, was turned into a hospital for black soldiers a few months later. It remained one for the rest of the war.[14]

Though Reverend Lynch worked with white missionaries, he was adamant that the new churches have black leadership. By early 1864 many freedmen were forming independent congregations headed up by black ministers and deacons. Even such icons as Towne and Murray were urged by the freedmen to leave the now-segregated churches. Towne believed such feelings derived from the confusion and disappointment over the preemption issue and the resulting land sales. Many freedmen felt they had been misled while others thought they had been purposely betrayed. To protect themselves, the former slaves found comfort and solidarity in segregated activities.

Besides forming their own religious bodies, the freedmen also began expanding their political strength. Obvious leaders included Prince Rivers, Abraham Murchison, and Robert Smalls. Northern freemen also saw opportunity in Beaufort. Loudon S. Langley, a twenty-eight-year-old, freeborn Vermont native, arrived at Port Royal in February 1864 as a replacement soldier for the 54th Massachusetts. Langley, whose grandfather had fought in the Revolution and whose parents conducted runaway slaves to freedom, had written antislavery letters to Vermont newspapers before the war, and once in the military, he continued to report on his activities in the Department of the South. Langley remained with his regiment for only two months before transferring to the 1st South Carolina, now designated the 33rd USCT, where he eventually became the sergeant major of Company K. Langley, whose military records list his first name as Landon, remained in the sea islands after the war, purchased the green in Beaufort's point area, which was briefly known as Langley Square, and became a noted regional leader and politician.[15]

The most prominent black leader was Robert Smalls. Since escaping with his fellow mates on the *Planter*, he had served as a pilot on vessels for both the navy and the army. As a contractor, hired by the department's quartermaster, Smalls became the pilot of the *Planter*, having the unique experience of serving as wheelman of the same vessel in both the Confederate and Federal armed forces. In November 1863 the *Planter* was operating outside Charleston Harbor off Folly Island near the mouth of the Stono River, when the department's chief quartermaster, Lieutenant Colonel Elwell, directed her captain to take his vessel into an area where she could come under enemy fire. The captain refused the order, so Elwell immediately removed him from command and sent directions to his chief assistant at Folly and Morris Island, stating:

> Sir:—You will please place Robert Small [sic] in charge of the United States transport Planter, as captain. He brought her out of Charleston harbor more than a year ago, running under the guns of Sumter, Moultrie, and the other defenses of that stronghold. He is an excellent pilot, of undoubted bravery, and in every respect worthy of the position. This is due him as a proper recognition of his heroism and services. The present captain is a coward, though a white man. Dismiss him therefore, and give the steamer to this brave black Saxton.

General Gillmore immediately approved Elwell's order. The advancement added luster to Smalls's reputation. Though his duties often kept him away from the sea islands, his status as a principal leader among the freedmen grew.[16]

Evidence of increasing black political power became evident when the leading citizens of the occupied sea islands proclaimed in the Beaufort newspaper, the *Free South,* a call for a state convention to elect delegates to represent the "Union people of South Carolina in the National Convention" of the Union party on June 7, 1864, in Baltimore, Maryland. The announcement called for all male inhabitants, twenty-one or older, who had resided in the area for six months "with the intention of making it their home" to come and vote. The meeting was to occur without "distinction of party or color," and the local assembly was open to all "who believed in the supremacy of the constitution and the complete suppression of the rebellion."[17]

The local convention met on May 17 at the Saxton House, a recently opened hotel operated by Gorman Dennis and James G. Richardson and located in the W. J. Jenkins House at the corner of Eighth and C Streets (West and Craven). The former tax commissioner Abram D. Smith was named chairman. The convention adopted a set of resolutions that called for the complete ending of slavery, greater use of "colored troops," the equality of pay between black and white soldiers, the removal of all restrictions from commercial vessels employing the Port of Port Royal, the encouragement by the government of northern emigration to the South, and the reserving of lands as homesteads for soldiers and freedmen. The representatives also praised General Saxton for his work as chief magistrate and military governor in preparing the way for civil government.

The convention backed no candidate for president and asked that the sea islands be used as an example for a reconstructed South Carolina. After some raucous debate between white and black attendees, the convention selected sixteen delegates, twelve of them white and four black.

The white representatives were Brigadier General Rufus Saxton, Honorable Abram D. Smith, Major Edmund J. Porter, E. G. Dudley, B. K. Lee Jr., James G. Thompson, Henry G. Judd, Jno. C. Alexander, S. W. Ely, Stephen C. Millett, Smauel A. Cooley, and Colonel P. Dunbar. The black delegates were S. W. Bennett, Robert Smalls, Prince Rivers, and Henry Haynes.[18]

While Robert Smalls, assigned by the army to take the *Planter* to Philadelphia for repairs, was unable to attend, the rest of the deputation—the first integrated delegation sent to a national party convention—arrived at Baltimore and were seated. However, since they only represented an occupied area and not a federally recognized state government, they were not allowed to vote. Still, the fact that an integrated slate had been elected foretold coming political events in the Beaufort District.[19]

As the freedmen expanded their political, economic, and religious roles, they also continued their service with the military. Since 1862, the Federal government had viewed Port Royal as a reservoir of potential black soldiers. Initially the 1st South Carolina was filled out with volunteers, but the 2nd and 3rd South Carolina found recruiting more difficult, and in January 1863 Generals Hunter and Saxton had initiated a draft of all able-bodied blacks aged fifteen to fifty in Union enclaves at Fernandina, Key West, and St. Augustine, Florida. In March 1863 they expanded the draft to the entire department. Freedmen serving as officer servants, army laborers, navy landsmen, and employees of contractors received exemptions, but all other physically fit men were expected to serve.[20]

Throughout 1863 press gangs led by black noncommissioned officers swept over the region, sometimes interrupting church services and school classes. Numerous freedmen were gathered up, even those with exemptions. Taken to regimental camps, officers inspected the men and determined whether they were eligible for duty. The troops carried out their duties so zealously that on one occasion a group of black women attacked a detachment of soldiers with hoes to keep them from impressing their husbands. The startled squad reacted by discharging their weapons, scattering the women.[21]

Though disruptive and occasionally causing injuries and wounds to those who fled the press gangs, the 1863 draft was mitigated by General Saxton's judicious and sympathetic review. Those with exemptions, or who were too young or old to serve, returned to their families and employment; but in 1864, as the war entered its final and most deadly stage, Union officials expanded the draft. In December 1863 the War Department directed General Quincy Gillmore to "enlist and organize all the colored troops that can be recruited within his Department." In January, Gillmore implemented the instructions by establishing a Board of Examination and appointing Colonel Milton S. Littlefield of the 3rd South Carolina, now termed the 21st USCT, as the general superintendent of recruiting.[22]

Littlefield oversaw not only the raising of USCT units but also supervised recruiters who had come south to enlist men for black regiments being organized in northern states. The various state recruiters, who received payment for men enrolled, created an interesting competition between state and U.S. agents. Freedmen enrolled into northern regiments went toward the levy of soldiers placed upon the state by the U.S. government. Every freedman recruited reduced the number of white citizens needed to meet the state's quota. State recruiters had an advantage. They could offer both a Federal and a state bounty, while Littlefield could only offer a limited Federal bounty not to exceed ten dollars.

The department's veteran white troops, who were embarrassed that eligible white recruits could avoid service by their states' enrolling sea island freedmen, did not appreciate the work of state recruiting agents. A member of the 144th New York compared the recruiters to slave drivers and reported that the soldiers greeted them by saying, "Here he comes boys—the negro driver—the slave hunter—don't know much about it—green in the business—hasn't got his outfit. Say mister where's you dogs? Can't hunt niggers without dogs."[23]

Under Gillmore the draft included not only freedmen but also eligible whites residing in the department. Gillmore carefully watched over the enforcement of the draft, keeping it controlled and well regulated; however, when he was transferred with a large portion of his army to Virginia and the Army of the James in May 1864, his successor, Major General John G. Foster, greatly intensified the local draft.

A tough, hardened, regular army officer, Foster had been Fort Sumter's chief engineer in 1861, when the Confederates captured the fort. Appointed brigadier general on October 23, 1861, he participated in Major General Ambrose Burnside's North Carolina Expedition and assumed command of the Department of North Carolina in July 1862, when Burnside was transferred to Virginia. He briefly served in the Department of the South in 1863, when he brought a detachment from North Carolina in a failed attempt to work with General Hunter for an attack against Charleston. He returned to North Carolina and later was assigned to the Department of the Ohio, where, injured in a fall from his horse, he was forced to relinquish his position and take convalescence leave. Though not yet recovered from his injury and on crutches, the forty-one-year-old Foster was appointed on May 26, 1864, to take over the Department of the South. He had little regard for assisting the region's blacks and the Port Royal Experiment. What he did care about was recapturing Fort Sumter and occupying Charleston.[24]

Since most of the department's veteran troops and seasoned officers had been sent to Virginia, Foster required additional men for his operations against Charleston. He received untested black regiments from the North and augmented his command by removing any exemptions from the local draft. In August all civilians and "idlers," black and white, ages eighteen to fifty, were liable to conscription. The threat of being drafted increased enlistments since volunteers received a government bounty, and amnesty was offered to any deserters who returned to service. Field hands and men in refugee camps were swept up, and military-age freedmen fleeing to Union lines were immediately reviewed for service.[25]

Foster's impressments, enforced by the department's superintendent of recruiting, Colonel Littlefield, enraged General Saxton, who protested the removal of needed laborers from the plantations and the means by which they were impressed. Freedmen were carried away at night from cabins, seized in the fields, and even taken while fishing. Some were shot and killed or wounded by press gangs. As Saxton noted, "The order spread universal confusion and terror.... Men have been seized and forced to enlist who had large families of young children dependent upon them for support, and fine crops of cotton and corn nearly ready for harvest, without an opportunity of making provision for one, or securing the other." Saxton believed that Foster's orders had implemented an atmosphere that created "prejudice of color and race here in full force" and manifested in "forms of personal insult and abuse" reminiscent of the "old plantation life."[26]

The sea island freedmen taken into the army by General Gillmore and later General Foster were used to fill out existing formations and create new regiments. Along with African American units from the North they supplemented a greatly reduced fighting force. The long, strenuous 1863 summer and fall campaigns against Charleston had taken a heavy toll on the department's effective troops. Casualties, disease, and expiring enlistments found regiments being reduced in strength and in some cases mustered out of service. Any future campaigns would have to rely heavily on draftees and untested formations.

When the campaign against Charleston ended in September 1863, General Gillmore began withdrawing the majority of his units from the crowded, pestilent islands off Charleston and returned them to healthier camps around Port Royal Sound. Recently recruited black regiments soon joined them. By December, after providing his soldiers with needed rest, relaxation, and refitting, Gillmore applied for and received permission to begin a new campaign against either Savannah or Jacksonville, Florida.[27]

The massing of Federal forces at Port Royal caused the Confederates to send reinforcements to Brigadier General William S. Walker's Third Military District. In January 1864 Walker's command expanded by twenty-two hundred infantry and artillerymen, giving him approximately five thousand men to defend the area between the Combahee and Savannah Rivers. To help slow an anticipated enemy advance, Walker placed additional torpedoes in the Combahee on Andrew Burnet's Plantation. But the enlarged command, the largest ever directed by Walker in South Carolina, only lasted a few weeks. On January 14 Confederate pickets at Foot Point reported the sailing of thirty-five vessels from Port Royal Sound. When he learned of the enemy's movement, General Beauregard, the department commander, immediately began shifting units. At first he suspected an attack against Savannah, but by early February, Federal gunboats and transports had entered the St. Johns River destined for Jacksonville.[28]

The movement into Florida had received the blessing of President Lincoln, who saw it as an opportunity "to reconstruct a loyal State government in Florida." Lincoln sent his secretary John Hay, commissioned a major and named an assistant adjutant to General Gillmore, to assist with the reconstruction. Gillmore, who saw the campaign achieving important military goals, including the cutting off of the state's cattle herds from the rest of the Confederacy and the recruitment of additional freedmen, formed a division under Brigadier General Truman Seymour. On February 7, 1864, with assistance from Rear Admiral Dahlgren, Seymour occupied Jacksonville and began marching his men inland.[29]

At Port Royal, Colonel Higginson and his soldiers of the 1st South Carolina anxiously awaited transportation to join the Federal expedition. On February 18 the soldiers broke camp and marched to the main wharf in Beaufort, but before they could board the transport, General Saxton, not wishing to risk his favorite regiment to possible destruction in battle, had the order countermanded by suggesting to his superiors that the unit was infected with smallpox. Returning to camp, a disgusted Higginson noted that "every man seemed crushed." While the 1st South Carolina reestablished their bivouac just outside Beaufort, the northern forces in Florida continued their movement toward Tallahassee. The initial Federal success soothed Higginson and his soldiers, who believed, if transferred to Florida, they would be given garrison duty. And they preferred to remain in camp at Beaufort rather than in Jacksonville.[30]

On the evening of February 22, Saxton orchestrated at Beaufort a Washington's Birthday celebration in a recently completed government forage building outfitted with flags from the garrison's regiments. General Saxton, Mrs. Saxton, Major John Hay, Colonel Higginson and the post's officers, and civilians and their ladies attended the ball, where Higginson reported that the sound of revelry reverberated throughout the hall.[31]

General Gillmore arrived, but Higginson noted that the commanding general, though accompanied by "an impressive female in blue silk," seemed distracted. Soon Gillmore and Saxton left, and though the dance continued, the attendees began to murmur among themselves about vague rumors concerning a battle lost in Florida.[32]

Before leaving Hilton Head for the ball, Gillmore had learned that General Seymour's column had been defeated at the Battle of Olustee, just east of Lake City. Seymour retreated to Baldwin, and his wounded were sent to Jacksonville for transportation to Beaufort's hospitals. On February 22 the hospital ship *Cosmopolitan,* carrying hundreds of wounded, arrived at Hilton Head.

Surgeon Meredith Clymer, the department's chief of hospitals, immediately telegraphed his subordinates in Beaufort to be ready for incoming wounded. Clymer, with General Gillmore, sailed for Beaufort ahead of the *Cosmopolitan.* Gillmore made a perfunctory appearance at the ball and with Saxton left to meet the hospital ship. The *Cosmopolitan* arrived at about 8:30 P.M. Saxton, after seeing the condition of the wounded, returned to the hall, pale and "almost sick with anxiety." Higginson reported that the mistimed "revel" was immediately ended, and many from the ball joined Generals Gillmore and Saxton on the hospital ship. Some of the wounded were brought ashore, but Surgeon Clymer kept most on board to rest until morning, when they were transported to the hospitals.[33]

Unlike earlier occupations of Jacksonville, the Federals did not evacuate after their setback at Olustee. Though unable to place a loyal government in Tallahassee, the northerners brought in reinforcements and continued operations along the St. John's River. The Confederates countered by sending additional units to Florida, including the 11th South Carolina. While moving by rail through the Beaufort District on their way from Charleston to Valdosta, Georgia, a number of soldiers took the opportunity to leave their comrades for a quick, unauthorized trip home to family and friends. Most returned but some deserted. Gathering up the absentee men were members of the Beaufort Volunteer Artillery, who, for capturing their former comrades, received a twenty-day furlough.[34]

While the two sides dueled in Florida, General Walker, with a reduced command, harassed the remaining Federal forces. To imitate troop movements, the southerners fired rockets and beat drums. On February 15 a squad of Confederates brazenly landed near the Smith Plantation and moved toward a Federal battery at the "Dudley Place," accosting freedmen and demanding information on Federal positions before escaping back to the mainland. Other raiders boldly landed near Beaufort. Walker continued to authorize additional sorties, and plans were made to launch a small boat attack against the *Kingfisher,* a Union blockader that guarded St. Helena Sound.

The attack on the *Kingfisher,* deemed too risky, never occurred. The warship, a bark-rigged sailing vessel of 451 tons mounting five guns, had long been a fixture in St. Helena Sound, watching the mouths of the Combahee, Ashepoo, and Edisto Rivers. Commanded by Acting Master John C. Dutch, the vessel, her captain, and crew were a comforting sight to the Union military and civilians on the neighboring sea islands. An aggressive and vigilant officer, Dutch carried out small-boat raids against the Confederates, even scooping up on Bailey's Island a number of native southern soldiers, termed "big bugs of Edisto," including some Seabrooks, near their Edisto Island homes. Besides furnishing protection and carrying out counterstrikes, Dutch also provided excursions on the *Kingfisher* for the missionaries, even carrying Ellen Murray, Laura Towne, Nelly Winsor, and others on a pleasure cruise to view the great homes and gardens on Edisto Island.[35]

While the *Kingfisher* still stood guard in St. Helena Sound, Walker went forward with an expedition against Port Royal Island. On the evening of March 11, Confederate forces carried out a diversion on Pinckney Island, while at midnight Captain William K. Bachman's German Artillery Battery bracketed northern Federal pickets at Port Royal Ferry. Both actions covered a landing party of 120 men under Captain J. J. Magee, sent against Port Royal Island's western shoreline. Magee, commander of a battery in the South Carolina Rutledge Mounted Rifles, planned to capture a company of black soldiers at Laurel Bay. But "owing to the rawness of some of the oarsmen and some other contretemps," the expedition did not reach its landing point until 4:30 A.M. With the tide receding and daylight near, Magee had to call off the operation. The following night Union gunboats retaliated by sailing around Port Royal Island, shelling enemy outposts.[36]

Undiscouraged, Walker authorized additional demonstrations. On the night of March 19, an attempt was made with two launches to cross fifty men and a cannon near Port Royal Ferry, but an alarm was given and the boats put back. The next evening the Confederates tried to land on Hilton Head at Jenkins Island and Spanish Wells. But Federal pickets, alerted by previous attacks, spotted the approaching boats and fired off signal rockets. The navy gunboat *Chippewa* and the armed quartermaster steamers *Croton* and *Thomas Foulkes* quickly responded and drove off the attackers.[37]

To assist his diversions, Walker suggested that *David*-style torpedo boats be sent from Charleston through "intermediate streams" to Bennett's Point and into St. Helena Sound for a strike against Federal warships. Though eventually the movement of three of the fifty-foot, cigar-shaped torpedo boats was approved, none were ever sent.[38]

While unable to take direct action against the enemy vessels in St. Helena Sound, the Confederates did find the odds somewhat reduced when their nemesis, the *Kingfisher,* went down. Though Acting Master Dutch had warned his superiors that his vessel needed refitting, the sailing ship remained on station until March 30, when she grounded on the Combahee Bank in St. Helena Sound and took on water. Unable to save his vessel, Dutch made arrangements to remove her armament and nearly all her equipment. Once done the bark settled into the sand.

With the *Kingfisher* wrecked and the watchful Acting Master Dutch gone, the Confederates were able to mount successful raids along the eastern rim of St. Helena Sound, including a May 21 landing on Morgan Island, where they carried off foodstuffs and freedmen and harangued the island's teacher, Mrs. George M. Wells. The following day at the church in St. Helenaville, Mrs. Wells reported that

> eleven people, men and women, had been carried off by fifteen Secesh—three of Hamilton Fripp's sons were among them. They took all the clothes, money, and eatables they could find, and told the people that they were living well and earning forty cents a day while their old mistress was starving and had no one to work for her, and they thought it was time they went to take care of her. One man escaped after his hands were tied, and one woman refused to get into the boat, and they knocked her down and left her."[39]

The Federals reacted to the stepped-up enemy activity by increasing maritime patrols by both navy and army gunboats. Colonel Joshua Howell, the forty-seven-year-old Hilton Head post commander and colonel of the 85th Pennsylvania, organized raids against Daufuskie Island and into the May River. Howell also sent reconnaissance expeditions to test Confederate strength south of the Broad River. On March 31 the lawyer turned soldier took a hundred men from his regiment aboard the naval gunboat *Chippewa* and, with the army gunboat *Thomas Foulkes,* sailed into the Chechessee and Colleton Rivers. After landing at the Seabrook Plantation on Foot Point, the Federals continued on, with the *Chippewa* providing cover fire against Confederate sentinels until they reached Spring Island before returning.

A week later, with the armed steamers *Thomas Foulkes* and *Croton* and the warship *Chippewa,* Howell launched an operation into the May River. Men from the 76th and 85th Pennsylvania landed on Hunting Island at the James Kirk Plantation. They skirmished with southern pickets while the *Chippewa* continued up the May River and shelled Bluffton. Both movements confirmed that the May and Colleton rivers were not obstructed and that the region was not held in force by the Confederates.[40]

Before Howell could open any thrusts against the mainland, the entire strategic situation in the Beaufort District changed. After the Battle of Olustee, active operations in Florida ended, and the Federal high command began preparations to move the bulk of General Gillmore's field army to a new theater. By the end of April, the Tenth Corps, including Gillmore and the majority of his experienced regiments and commanders had been sent to Fort Monroe, Virginia, to join Major General Benjamin Butler's Army of the James for an advance on Petersburg and Richmond, Virginia. Many of the regiments removed from the Department of the South were formations that had been part of the expeditionary force that seized Port Royal Sound. Now these units were returning to Hampton Roads, Virginia, completing a round trip they had started in October 1861. As his regiment sailed out of Port Royal Sound, one member of the 48th New York wrote, "Tears came to many as the low shores of South Carolina faded away in the sea, and we realized that we had left behind us places with which we had grown familiar, and associations never to be forgotten."[41]

While the Federals began shifting units northward, the southern military found their affairs in the Beaufort District deteriorating. The region's commander, Major General Jeremy Gilmer, who had jurisdiction over General Walker's district and the neighboring Georgia District, reported that cartridges were short and soldiers were raiding private property for food and supplies. Then in March the War Department ordered to Virginia the majority of the department's horsemen as replacements for decimated South Carolina cavalry units serving with Lee's army. Removed from Walker's district was the 4th South Carolina Cavalry and William Trenholm's Rutledge Mounted Rifles.[42]

In April, when Confederate officials realized that Federal troops from the Department of the South were being shifted for campaigns in Virginia, they quickly directed that officers and additional formations be sent north. General Beauregard was transferred to the Department of North Carolina and Southern Virginia to protect Richmond and Petersburg from attacks. General Gilmer was sent to Atlanta, and General Walker took command of General Nathan S. Evans's brigade, which was one of the units being dispatched from Charleston to Virginia. The Eleventh South Carolina, with its many Beaufort District denizens, was attached to a newly formed brigade commanded by Johnson Hagood and by June was stationed near Petersburg, Virginia.[43]

By early May 1864, the forces stationed in the region between the Combahee and Savannah rivers had been reduced to one cavalry regiment, Colonel Charles J. Colcock's 3rd South Carolina, Captain M. J. Kirk's cavalry squadron, and four artillery companies. Colcock, the new district commander, had fewer than two thousand effectives and seventeen pieces of artillery to defend the area. The Beaufort Volunteer Artillery was among the units that remained. The formation had become one of General Walker's favorites; he told the unit's commander, Captain Henry "Hal" Stuart, that he had considered taking the battery with him to Virginia but thought it more important to keep the company in their native region. Before leaving, a tearful Walker sent Stuart a note stating that "during my continuance with their command they have been linked to me by *ties* which I hope may never be *broken* and connected with me by associations which I *trust* will never be *forgotten*."[44]

The transferring of units to Virginia also coincided with the annual withdrawal of troops from the lowcountry to healthier summer quarters. Before moving to their new station, the men of the Beaufort Volunteer Artillery's "Thespian Corps" presented the play "Lady of Lyons" at their camp in Pocotaligo. Men from the company took on the roles of both actors and actresses with Privates John L. DeTreville, Henry Elliott, and Robert M. Gibbes taking the female leads. It was noted that "Johnny DeTreville represented Pauline so well that a great many men said she was the prettiest girl there that night (thirty-six ladies were present, the general public generally had been invited . . .)." Two weeks later, after a successful theater run, the artillerymen relocated their bivouac to McPhersonville, establishing their summer quarters in the rear of Ferguson Hutson's house.[45]

Besides the shifting of troops, new commanders arrived in the Department of South Carolina, Georgia, and East Florida. Major General Samuel Jones replaced General Beauregard, while Major General Lafayette McLaws took over Gilmer's position as commander of the combined Third District and the District of Georgia. Though technically answerable to McLaws in Savannah, Colonel Charles Colcock, the Third District commander, also cooperated with Brigadier General Beverly Robertson's Second District, which provided the garrison of the Combahee fort, located in Colcock's district.[46]

In late May 1864, Colcock and Robertson's districts contained the following emplaced artillery and field batteries:

ARTILLERY IN FIXED POSITIONS

SECOND MILITARY DISTRICT.

Work on the Ashepoo, at Barnwell Rhett's: One 24-pounder, rifled and banded, barrette, one 18-pounder, rifled.

Work at Mr. Thomas Rhett's, on the lower Ashepoo: One 12-pounder rifle, siege.

Work at Stock's Causeway: One 12-pounder rifle, siege.

Work at Bennett's: Assigned not yet in position, one 32-pounder, rifled and banded, barbette, one 32-pounder, barbette, one 4.62-inch, rifled and banded, siege.

Glover's Causeway: One 24-pounder Austrian howitzer.

THIRD MILITARY DISTRICT.

Work at Combahee Ferry: One 6-pounder.

Old Pocotaligo: One 24-pounder iron howitzer, two 24-pounder Austrian howitzers.

Dawson's Bluff: One 24-pounder siege, one 3-inch rifle.

Bee's Creek Causeway: Two 6-pounders.

New River bridge-work. Two 12-pounder bronze rifle guns, to be used as smooth-bores.

Red Bluff: One 8-inch Columbiad (pivot), two 24-pounders, rifled and banded, barrette.

FIELD ARTILLERY

SECOND MILITARY DISTRICT.

Washington Light Artillery, Captain G. H. Walter: Two Napoleons, two 10-pounder Parrotts.

Company A, Palmetto Battalion Light Artillery, Captain W. E. Earle: Two 12-pounder howitzers, two 6-pounders.

THIRD MILITARY DISTRICT.

Beaufort Light Artillery, Captain H. M. Stuart: two 12-pounder howitzers, one 10-pounder Parrott.

German Light Artillery, Captain W. K. Bachman: Blakely, two 12-pounder howitzers.

Lafayette Light Artillery, Captain J. T. Kanapaux: Two 3.5-inch Blakely, two 12-pounder howitzers.

Company G, Palmetto Battalion Light Artillery, Captain W. L. De Pass: Two Napoleons, two 12-pounder howitzers.

SECTIONS OF HORSE ARTILLERY

Trenholm's, Lieutenant L. J. Walker: Two 12-pounder howitzers.

Colcock's, Captain R. Johnson: two Wiard rifle guns.[47]

Throughout the summer and early fall of 1864, the diminished Confederate troops watched for enemy activity. Rumors of a possible cavalry raid from Port Royal to Augusta and Andersonville resulted in reinforcements being dispatched to the Third District in June. When the raid failed to materialize, the reinforcements remained behind while some companies from the 3rd South Carolina, were sent into Georgia to guard the coast south of Savannah. Though fort construction slowed in the Third District, Robertson planned to expand the works in the Second District on the Ashepoo at Chapman's Fort and Field's Point.[48]

While the district commanders continued to show energy in preparing their reduced commands for combat, questions arose over the ability of General Jones to direct the department, and President Davis superseded Jones by assigning Lieutenant General William J. Hardee to command the department. Hardee, who had been made a scapegoat by General John B. Hood for the loss of Atlanta, arrived in Charleston on October 5, 1864. With Jones in charge of the Charleston District and McLaws in Savannah, Hardee began making the best of a deteriorating situation. Work crews were sent out to repair the rail line. The building of additional torpedo boats in Charleston and Savannah was ordered, and fortifications were strengthened.[49]

Changes also occurred in the northern high command. Major General John Porter Hatch replaced General Gillmore as commander of the Department of the South. The forty-two-year-old Hatch, a West Point–trained career soldier, had twice been cited for bravery in the Mexican War and served on the frontier before being named in September 1861 a brigadier general in the volunteer army. Hatch went on to command a cavalry and infantry brigade in Virginia while serving with the Fifth Corps in the Shenandoah Valley. He was wounded at Second Bull Run but stayed in the field and fought at Chantilly. Placed in command of a division in the First Corps, Army of the Potomac, during the Antietam Campaign, he led his unit against Confederate positions located at Turner's Gap, Maryland. An aggressive officer who led from the front, Hatch had two horses shot from under him and received a severe leg wound. Brevetted a major general, Hatch eventually received the Medal of Honor for gallantry under fire for his actions at Turner Gap.

Five months after his wounding, Hatch returned to light duty before being ordered on March 24, 1864, to the Department of the South, where he was assigned to Florida as General Seymour's replacement. When Gillmore left, Hatch, as the senior officer, was in line to take over the department, causing General Halleck, the army's chief of staff, to write that Hatch was "hardly the man for the place, but he is the best that can now be spared from the field." On May 1 Halleck appointed him to command the Department of the South.[50]

Hatch's tenure as the department leader was a short one. Four days after appointing Hatch, General Halleck directed Major General John G. Foster to leave his headquarters at Knoxville, Tennessee, trading his position as commander of the Department of the Ohio for a similar posting at Hilton Head. It took Foster nearly a month to reach Hilton Head, and in the interim Hatch, in conjunction with the navy, organized a strike against the Charleston and Savannah Railroad. The plan called for Brigadier General William Birney, now commanding the troops on Hilton Head, to take an expedition up the Ashepoo River, landing on Bennett's Point at the junction of the Ashepoo and Mosquito Creek. From there Birney would march inland and destroy the railroad trestle over the Ashepoo River east of Green Pond. To support the movement and create a diversion, Admiral Dahlgren agreed to send warships with a landing force up the Edisto River against the Confederate works at Willtown Bluff.[51]

The operation began to unravel as soon as it left Hilton Head. On May 25 steamers carrying elements of Birney's detachment from Hilton Head, including portions of Colonel Thomas Bayley's brigade and a troop of cavalry from Company B, 4th Massachusetts, rendezvoused at about 6:30 P.M. in St. Helena Sound with the gunboat *Dai Ching*. But the screw steamer *Mary A. Boardman*, with Colonel Bayley and the 9th USCT, ran aground on the Combahee bar, and the side-wheeler *Boston,* carrying Colonel James Montgomery's 34th USCT (2nd South Carolina) as well as men and horses from the 4th Massachusetts, had not yet arrived. Unable to free the *Mary A. Boardman* and not wishing to delay his expedition, Birney directed his transports into the Ashepoo and onto Bennett's Point. Before he left aboard his flagship, the armed side-wheeler *Plato,* Birney conferred with Lieutenant Commander James C. Chaplin of the *Dai Ching,* who informed Birney that he was awaiting a pilot and would proceed into the Ashepoo come morning. In the meantime Chaplin sent Acting Ensign William Nelson to the grounded *Mary A. Boardman*. Once the vessel was freed, Nelson was to assist the vessel's captain in reaching Bennett's Point.[52]

Once near Bennett's Point, Birney removed the soldiers aboard the transport *Edwin Lewis* and distributed them among the other vessels, which sailed on and landed the soldiers. Birney, who stayed on the *Plato,* sent the *Edwin Lewis,* along with his chief pilot from the *Plato,* William C. Mandel, back to the grounded *Mary A. Boardman*. Once the *Edwin Lewis* reached the stranded ship, the soldiers from the *Mary A. Boardman* were placed on the *Edwin Lewis,* which then pulled the *Mary A. Boardman* off the bar and into deep water. Pilot Mandel, having boarded the *Mary A. Boardman,* stayed with the vessel while Colonel Bayley, aboard the *Edwin Lewis,* waited for the *Boston* and Colonel Montgomery

When the *Boston* arrived, it was dark. Acting Ensign Nelson, no longer needed on the *Mary A. Boardman,* transferred to the *Boston,* where he joined her captain, F. M. Faircloth, and Colonel Montgomery in the pilothouse. Fairfield was ordered to follow the lighter-drafted *Edwin Lewis* to the landing point. While the *Edwin Lewis,* followed by the *Boston,* sailed off into the night, the *Mary A. Boardman* stayed in the sound. The *Edwin Lewis* and the *Boston* sailed past the rendezvous and continued up the Ashepoo. With Mandel remaining on the *Mary A. Boardman,* only Colonel Bayley knew the location of the landing point, and he did not share the information with the *Edwin Lewis*'s captain or pilot. The *Edwin Lewis* missed the turnoff at Mosquito Creek and sailed farther up the river, and though Nelson, piloting the *Boston,* informed Colonel Montgomery that they had passed the turnoff, Montgomery, under orders to follow the *Edwin Lewis,* kept on.[53]

Light-drafted, the *Edwin Lewis* glided over obstructions and passed an unmanned earthwork at Chapman's Bluff on a plantation owned by Philip Smith Price known as Chapman's Fort. Hailed by Confederate pickets, Colonel Bayley finally realized his mistake and ordered his vessel turned around. Again passing the fort and the obstructions, Bayley discovered the much larger *Boston* hard aground on a sand bar. All attempts to free the stranded ship failed. After a conference with Montgomery and the *Boston*'s captain, Bayley took the *Edwin Lewis* to Bennett's Point and reported the situation to General Birney. If the *Boston* was not freed by daylight, it would be an easy target for enemy artillery.[54]

Word that an enemy ship had entered the Ashepoo River and was off Chapman's Fort reached the Confederate Combahee Subdistrict at Chisolmville at about 1:00 A.M. on May 24. Immediately the area commander, Lieutenant Colonel John D. Twiggs of the 1st South Carolina Cavalry, moved to protect both the overland and water approaches to the railroad. Twiggs sent a section of Captain William Earle's battery, Company A, Palmetto Artillery Battalion, to Chapman's Fort. Earle arrived before dawn. The fortification was not an enclosed fort but rather "a simple line of parapet for infantry defense, about 300 yards long," flanked on each end by rounded bastions. Earle placed his guns behind the earthen curtain between the fort's two bastions. At dawn, when Twiggs and some cavalrymen joined the artillerymen, he discovered the derelict *Boston* hard aground, bow on, one thousand yards from the battery. Captain Earle quickly had his gunners open a raking fire with their two 6-pound guns.[55]

Aboard the *Boston,* while enemy shot slammed into the vessel, Colonel Montgomery tried to keep panic from engulfing his detachment. Though nearly a hundred shots struck the *Boston,* only a few soldiers were hurt, but numerous horses were killed or wounded. Many men, stripping off their equipment and in some cases their clothes, jumped into the water and bogged down in the marsh as they made for the river's eastern shore. The *Boston*'s crew tossed spars, boxes, and other equipment into the water to assist the floundering men. Those who could swim helped their comrades. Sergeant Gabriel Turner of the 34th USCT, one of the slaves who with Robert Smalls had taken the *Planter* out of Charleston, constantly rescued men who sank into the water. Privates William Downey, John Duffy, David L. Gifford, and Patrick Scanlan of the 4th Massachusetts Cavalry were also conspicuous in their efforts to help their fellow soldiers. First Lieutenant George Washington Brush of the 34th USCT volunteered to command one of the *Boston*'s small boats and, while under enemy fire, carried a large number of men from the vessel to the nearby shore. For their actions Downey, Duffy, Gifford, Scanlan, and Brush would later be awarded the Congressional Medal of Honor.[56]

The *Edwin Lewis* and *Boston*'s errant voyage past Bennett's Point and the subsequent grounding of the *Boston* completely undermined General Birney's plans. Once Colonel Bayley reported the disaster on the Ashepoo, Birney immediately called off the campaign and returned his soldiers to Bennett's Point. The element of surprise was gone, Confederate forces had been alerted, and an entire regiment was in danger of being lost. Birney, aboard the *Plato,* sailed up the Ashepoo, followed by the *Edwin Lewis,* and arrived off Chapman's Fort at about 8:30 A.M. Though the *Plato* ran aground, her gun crews from the 3rd Rhode Island directed their cannons against the Confederates, but the range was too far. Helpless, the Federals watched while Captain Earle's artillerymen continued to pummel the *Boston,* a stout prewar oceangoing vessel. Though hit many times by Confederate guns throwing 6-pound shot, the ship was damaged but did not break up. By now many of the men from the *Boston* had reached high ground on the eastern shore and made their way toward the *Plato* and *Edwin Lewis.* Sailors manning the *Plato*'s small boats soon began shuttling the soldiers back to the flagship. The captain of the *Edwin Lewis* tried to reach the *Boston,* but his vessel ran aground. After backing off, he returned her downstream.

By now the gunboat *Dai Ching* had arrived, and Lieutenant Commander Chaplin quickly directed his heavy guns against the Confederates. In a short time the southerners ceased fire. However, it was not the barrage from the *Dai Ching*'s guns that silenced Earle's battery; rather, Lieutenant Colonel Twiggs had ordered Earle to conserve his ammunition in case the Federals should land the soldiers and march on Chapman's Fort.[57]

General Birney had no intention of moving against the fort; instead he sought to extract his troops still on the *Boston* and in the marsh. Once the Confederate battery had ceased firing and under covering fire from the *Dai Ching,* the captain of the *Plato,* freed by the rising tide, took his vessel up to the *Boston,* where Birney, after meeting with Colonel Montgomery, decided to burn the stranded vessel. With his men ashore, but the horses, alive and dead, still aboard, Montgomery set the ship on fire. At 11:00 A.M. the little flotilla returned to Bennett's Point, where the remaining soldiers embarked, and by 2:00 P.M. the transports started their journey back to Hilton Head.[58]

While Birney's expedition was falling apart, the naval portion of the operation, led by Lieutenant Commander Edward E. Stone and consisting of the *Commodore McDonough, E. B. Hale,* and the coast survey vessel *Vixen,* sailed up the Edisto River. Guided by hydrographer Charles O. Boutelle aboard the *Vixen,* the vessels arrived at Governor William Aiken's plantation on Jehossee Island on May 25, and Stone sent ashore a small force of marines and sailors manning two boat howitzers. The shore party moved across the plantation and took up a position overlooking Willtown. The next day Stone advanced his ships toward an enemy battery near Willtown and opened a long-range bombardment. No reply came from the seemingly unmanned work, and after a few hours, Stone ceased fire, withdrew his ships, and pulled his marines and howitzers back to their landing site. While maneuvering in the Edisto, Stone noticed "a large fire" to the west. He quickly dispatched an armed cutter through Mosquito Creek to investigate the cause of the smoke and locate General Birney. The boat returned at 3:00 A.M. on the twenty-seventh, reporting the destruction of the *Boston* and the canceling of the army's operation. Stone, realizing that his mission was no longer necessary, reembarked his shore party and returned to Port Royal.[59]

On May 26, the day Birney ordered the destruction of the *Boston,* Major General John G. Foster arrived at Hilton Head and assumed command of the Department of the South. The next day he announced his staff appointments and named General Hatch as head of the District of Hilton Head, Fort Pulaski, St. Helena, and Tybee Islands. On May 28 Foster reported to the War Department that the expedition to destroy the railroad had failed. Besides the destruction of the *Boston,* Foster wrote that "our loss is 13 killed, drowned, or missing. Seventy-five cavalry horses and 8 team horses that were on the *Boston* were burnt with the vessel." In conclusion, the new commanding general reported that he had ordered a court of investigation to review the operation and "fix responsibilities for the losses."[60]

The court concluded that though he did not take all the required precautions to ensure the safe arrival of the *Boston,* General Birney was not charged with any wrongdoing; however, the court did place the blame for the steamer's loss on Colonel Bayley. General Foster convened a court-martial, charging the officer with four counts of neglect of duty. Bayley pleaded not guilty to each specification, and the court eventually ruled in his favor, declaring that the colonel was not guilty of "neglect of duty, to the prejudice of good order and military discipline" in the loss of the *Boston.*[61]

The debacle at Chapman's Fort provided General Foster with an early and sobering example of affairs in his department. Orders from Washington directed Foster to stay on the defensive, but Foster, an aggressive and feisty officer, refused to remain passive. His greatest ambition was to redeem the 1861 loss of Fort Sumter (a defeat that, as Sumter's former chief engineer, he took quite personally). To do so, he had to train and outfit a competent attack force. Though he had some experienced formations, nearly 50 percent of his regiments were raw black units with little or no combat experience.

To prepare his untried regiments, Foster established a school of instruction at Beaufort. He reported that "at the end of two or three months, at the farthest, I will have these colored regiments so set up that they can be taken into battle with confidence." He also had the soldiers of the 26th USCT trained as artillerists and charged them with defending the numerous forts and batteries guarding the Shell Road leading into Beaufort (listed below).[62]

ARMAMENTS OF THE DEFENSES OF BEAUFORT[63]

Fort Duane and rifle-pit: one 8-inch gun, one 32-pounder, four 18-pounders, one 12-pounder howitzer, two 24-pounder howitzers.

Battery Burnside: two 8-inch guns, one 30-pounder Parrott, one 24-pounder.

Battery Seymour: two carronades.
Battery Saxton: three 8-inch siege howitzers.
Battery Brayton: one 10-pounder Parrott, one 24-pounder howitzer.
Battery Taylor: two 30-pounder Parrotts, one 10-pounder Parrott, one 24-pounder.[64]

On Hilton Head, Foster had the 102nd USCT (the former 1st Michigan Colored Volunteer Infantry, a regiment formed in Detroit) instructed "in artillery with a view to have them serve such works in Hilton Head District which cannot be manned by the artillery." The general also directed improvements to the defense lines guarding the base on the island's northeastern tip. Because of the lack of trained cannoneers, Foster felt it necessary that "every available man should be on duty" and recalled those soldiers who had been assigned as clerks, orderlies, teamsters, boatmen, bakers, and attendants in hospitals back to their parent organization.[65]

By the end of June 1864, Foster felt confident enough to test his army against Charleston's defenses. On July 1 his expedition, including a brigade led by General Saxton, made demonstrations in the North Edisto River and on John's and James Islands. For over a week, the Federals attempted to breach the Confederate defenses, but unable to gain any advantage, Foster called off the campaign. Undeterred, Foster turned his efforts against Fort Sumter, opening a new bombardment that he hoped would bring down the fortress's walls and open a breach for a small-boat attack. To prepare for the amphibious operation, Foster commenced building at Hilton Head two "assaulting arks." The oar-driven vessels were to be sheaved with three-eighths-inch iron and carry a thousand men each. To protect his arks, the general also proposed constructing at Hilton Head a light-draft ironclad, requisitioning iron and other equipment from Major General Montgomery Meigs, the army quartermaster general.[66]

How far along Foster got with his special assault galleys is unknown, but his ironclad construction was quickly nipped by the high command. His requisition for iron was forwarded to the army's chief of staff, Major General Henry H. Halleck, who replied on August 26: "By direction of General Grant, General Foster has been repeatedly ordered to confine himself to the defensive, and to send north all troops not required for holding his present position without offensive operations. Requisition disapproved."[67] Not only did Halleck nix Foster's plans to seize Fort Sumter, but he also directed the department commander to send another five thousand men north for service in Virginia, effectively removing any excess troops that would have allowed Foster to form a field army. Foster soon found himself in the role of a caretaker, leaving him with little to do except manage the recruitment of additional black soldiers and protect his camps and installations from enemy assaults.[68]

To keep his men occupied, Foster authorized his chief engineer, Lieutenant Charles R. Suter, to begin the construction of new fortifications. In June, Suter commenced remodeling on Hilton Head a portion of the existing perimeter around the department headquarters for an enclosed work mounting twenty-nine guns. It was eventually named Fort Sherman for the island's first Federal commander. Since the Union base had outgrown the existing earthworks, Suter also started that month a new fort for eighteen guns. Eventually named Fort Howell, it was part of a proposed perimeter extension that would provide protection to government corrals, stables, encampments, and the refugee camp at Mitchelville.[69]

In August, to push forward the construction of Fort Howell, Brigadier General Edward A. Potter, commander of the post of Hilton Head, directed Colonel George W. Baird of the 32nd USCT, to "furnish daily as large a detail for this purpose as the strength of the Regiment will permit." The regiment established a campground named Camp Baird near the fort and provided fatigue parties to work with men from the 1st New York Engineers. The black soldiers remained on duty at Fort Howell into September, when they were assigned guard duties at Seabrook, Jenkins Island, Fort Mitchel, and Braddock Point, replacing the 144th New York, which, with the 25th Ohio, took over fatigue duties at Fort Howell.[70]

By September both Forts Sherman and Howell had their parapets thrown up and revetted and magazines completed. To keep the wind from blowing the sand off the walls, the men "were principally engaged in trimming and manuring the slopes." Also in August, Suter began building two batteries, Holbrook at Spanish Wells and Williams on the sound east of Fort Howell. Battery Holbrook, built by details from the 32nd USCT, received its armament from the navy, but Williams was never finished.[71]

At Beaufort additional regiments were added to the town's garrison, including the 102nd USCT. The black Michigan soldiers took up picket duties to guard against Confederate raids, while the regimental musicians became the post band. Engineers oversaw the strengthening of the existing fortifications. In August they started an enclosed citadel northwest of town, just south of the Shell Road. Named Fort Stevens in honor of Isaac Stevens, Beaufort's first Federal commander, it was designed for eighteen guns.[72] Though work was slowed by sickness among the troops constructing the fort, Suter reported by October that "the parapet was all thrown up and partially revetted."[73]

While the Federals carried out routine duties and the construction of fortifications, Foster's command also policed the region's expanding towns and freedmen refugee camps.[74] By the summer of 1864, both Beaufort and the hamlet of Port Royal on Hilton Head Island had shaken off their status as military cantonments and become blossoming communities. Beaufort boasted three hotels that promised first-class accommodations for the traveling public. In August 1864 General Saxton established a soldiers' bank. Numerous commercial businesses lined Bay Street to serve the military and its civilian employees, freedmen, and those who had migrated, planning to make it their home and develop Beaufort into a thriving town. Located in the city was a bakery that promised its customers the "manufacture of Ornamental Pieces, Fancy Confectionary, and elegant Pastry." The town also contained a first-class ice cream saloon that featured cream and sherbet ices.[75]

On Hilton Head the town of Port Royal had outgrown its original military establishment. A reporter for the *New York Daily Tribune* stated that the wharf was the busiest he had ever seen, "surpassing any of the thronged piers of New York City." The ships off-loaded military equipment and goods for the island's commercial establishments located in an area known as Robbers Row, where sutlers took delight in overcharging soldiers for cheese, milk, butter, pickles, canned meats, tobacco, clothing, Bibles, soap, candles, razors, and medicines. The street also contained "saloons invariably dirty, hot and greasy; which no one but a starving wretch could ever be induced to enter with a view of satisfying the cravings of hunger."[76]

Photographic studios, a post office, a printing shop for the newspapers *New South* and *Palmetto Post,* a druggist and physician's office, a shoe store, a business that sold safes and coffins, and a firm that brought in lake ice from Rockland, New York, lined the town's commercial district. There was also a theater where plays were produced and a baseball field. The Port Royal House served as the town's only hotel, and in 1864 the main building received a third story. Though an active settlement, Port Royal was a crude community made up of prefabricated buildings or rough-cut structures. It was primarily a wartime settlement, dependent completely on the military for survival. One visitor who came to the island during the summer was quite happy when it came time to leave Port Royal "with its fleas, its rats and its fiddlers," stating that he "left it with a sense of relief such as I have seldom felt in leaving any place."[77]

Though the civilian population was growing, the military still governed day-to-day operations in Beaufort and Port Royal. Foster's provost marshal kept order and enforced regulations against illegal trade, alcohol sales to enlisted soldiers, and gambling establishments. The provost marshal also provided protection to freedmen refugee camps.[78]

There were a number of camps throughout the sea islands. The houses and government quarters at St. Helenaville gave shelter for refugees from Edisto Island, while government barracks at Montgomery Hill, next to the Federal bivouac at Camp Saxton, provided a home for the "Combees," the slaves freed by Montgomery's June 1863 raid up the Combahee River. Large refugee communities were located on Hilton Head at the village commonly termed Mitchelville and at a camp northwest of Beaufort that eventually came to be called Higginsonville. Throughout 1864 more and more escaped slaves came "not only daily, but hourly," into the sea islands, which had been named, "Nigger's Heaven and the Black Country." As described by Elizabeth Hyde Botume, the forty-year-old teacher who ran the school at Camp Saxton: "They came alone and in families and in gangs, slaves who had been hiding, and were only now able to reach safety. Different members of scattered families following after freedom, as surely and safely guided as were the Wise Men by the Star of the East."[79]

While additional refugees arrived, their management and protection became more difficult. At the Mitchelville camp, Union personnel harassed the freedmen, and on one occasion three drunken soldiers raped the wife of a man they claimed was avoiding the draft. Reverend Abraham Murchison reported the rape to General Foster and asked that men from Battery G, 2nd USCT Artillery, be assigned to protect the village. Foster passed the matter on to his provost marshal, and Murchison was eventually named chief magistrate for Mitchelville and assigned black soldiers to arrest persons for "riotous or disorderly conduct."[80]

Foster and his provost guard also found it tricky to control the actions of the freedmen. Unauthorized excursions by freedmen operating small boats and dugouts resulted in goods being smuggled to the enemy and the carrying of deserters from camps to their home islands. The Federals also had a difficult time handling the freedmen women who flocked "back & forth by scores to Hilton Head, to Beaufort, to the country simply to while away their time, or constantly to seek new excitement, or what is worse to live by lasciviousness." To control the freedmen population, the military authorities increased the workload for both men and women and set up regulations concerning the use of small boats. Though all were necessary for the betterment and good order of his department, such nonmilitary proceedings rankled Foster, who, stripped of troops, could no longer take the field and had become an administrator.[81]

While Foster dealt with his problems, Admiral Dahlgren also tried to continue operations out of Port Royal Sound with a diminishing command. The first ten months of 1864 had been difficult. Gunboats had been dispatched to support the army's activities in Florida, and operations around Charleston and Port Royal stretched Dahlgren's already overtaxed squadron. In February, Dahlgren suffered the loss of the screw sloop *Housatonic,* which, while on blockade duty off Charleston, was sunk by the *H. L. Hunley,* becoming the first vessel to be destroyed by an enemy submarine. By June he reported a deficiency of thirteen hundred sailors and that for "six months I have detained men whose terms had expired," but he noted that it could no longer be done, as "murmurs" of discontent had arisen. The Navy Department promised relief and dispatched the ship of the line *New Hampshire* with a thousand men, but her arrival coincided with the outbreak of smallpox at Port Royal. Dahlgren was forced to quarantine the sailing vessel and her crew.[82]

Dahlgren also worried about the condition of his warships, which constantly required repairs. Numerous ships, including the ironclad frigate *New Ironsides,* went north for needed overhauls, while others received maintenance at the facilities in Port Royal Sound. Throughout 1864 at least two of Dahlgren's monitors per month underwent rehabilitation in the yards off Bay Point. While workshops were moved ashore, the navy continued to use the floating machine shops in Station Creek, but in August high tides carried the floating blacksmith shop *India* off her pilings and she had to be abandoned. The *Edward* was also swamped, and though righted, her equipment and repair facilities were moved onto land. The carpentry boat *Ellen* survived the tides, but fearing that she could break up at any time, Dahlgren directed a new shop built on shore. Most of the land-based operations were placed on Bay Point, while a large foundry was located on the spit of land protruding southward into Station Creek from Land's End. Also on St. Helena Island just north of Station Creek, the navy established a naval hospital. On Bay Point a large T-wharf was built, and a rail line ran inland to the army's quartermaster shops and storage facilities.[83]

Like Foster, Dahlgren found himself and his command losing their position of importance in the North's grand strategy. While Foster saw a continual drain of soldiers to different theaters, Dahlgren realized that the Navy Department had turned its attention away from the Southeast and to campaigns against Mobile, Alabama, and Wilmington, North Carolina. Still, the two Federal commanders continued to work with the resources at hand. Foster kept up the training of his green regiments, while Dahlgren provided the army with additional powder and heavy guns for the general's bombardment of Fort Sumter. The admiral even gave the army 9-inch guns for a battery at Spanish Wells on Hilton Head to guard against any movements by Confederate naval forces from Savannah.[84]

Always hoping for some future activity, Dahlgren directed his ship captains to begin drilling their crews for service on land. The sailors were given the hard-hitting Plymouth Rifle, a .69-caliber weapon with a unique bayonet. Both the rifle and its bayonet had been designed by Dahlgren, who proudly described the qualities of the bayonet as a "short, broad, and stout knife, of the well-known Bowie pattern, the principal use of which I designed to be in the hand in close conflict, such as boarding. In campaigning it would also serve many wants; but it may be fixed and used as a bayonet."[85]

However Dahlgren, fearing his star was diminishing, wondered whether he would ever be able to use his shore parties in conjunction with Foster's weakened command. Both officers desired glory. Both feared they would never have an opportunity to achieve it. The war in the Beaufort District seemed to be winding down with little chance for them to gain any further fame.

Chapter 13

Battle of Honey Hill

A place so "sweetly named" as Honey Hill

Behind us lay Atlanta, smoldering and in ruins, the black smoke rising high in air, and hanging like a pall over the ruined city... before us the Fourteenth Corps, marching steadily and rapidly with a cheery look and swinging pace, that made light of the thousand miles that lay between us and Richmond. Some band, by accident, struck up the anthem of "John Brown's soul goes marching on;" the men caught up the strain, and never before or since have I heard the chorus of "Glory, glory, hallelujah!" done with more spirit, or in better harmony of time and place.... I had no purpose to march direct for Richmond by way of Augusta and Charlotte, but always designed to reach the sea-coast first at Savannah or Port Royal.[1]

The Beaufort District may have escaped any final campaigning had not Major General William Tecumseh Sherman, the author of the above words, decided to challenge the standard rules of war and proceed with an operation designed to destroy the South's infrastructure and will to fight. The resulting expedition forever seared into the national psyche an image of Federal troops devastating a prostrate, helpless Confederacy. The movement was seen as both a brutal, unnecessary exercise in terror and a brilliant strategy that quickly ended the conflict and minimized battlefield casualties. While the operation did and still does cause fervent debate over its results, the Beaufort District fully felt the consequences of Sherman's great march.

By November 11, 1864, Sherman had made his final preparations, and he telegraphed General Halleck:

My arrangements are now all complete, and the railroad cars are being sent to the rear. Last night we burned all foundries, mills, and shops of every kind in Rome, and to-morrow I leave Kingston with the rear guard for Atlanta, which I propose to dispose of in a similar manner, and to start on the 10th on the projected grand raid. All appearances still indicate that Beauregard has got back to his old hole at Corinth, and I hope he will enjoy it. My army prefers to enjoy the fresh sweet-potato fields of the Ocmulgee.... Tomorrow our wires will be broken, and this is probably my last dispatch. I would like to have General Foster to break the Savannah and Charleston road about Pocotaligo about December 1. All other preparations are to my entire satisfaction."[2]

General Grant, who as commander-in-chief had approved Sherman's campaign, also weighed in, writing Halleck on November 12: "I presume you have sent instructions to General Foster in accordance with General Sherman's request. I think it will have a good effect to make the attempt to get into Pocotaligo even if it should not succeed entirely. If the troops cannot get through, they can keep the enemy off General Sherman a little."[3]

The following day Halleck wrote Foster, informing him of Sherman's proposed movement. Though Halleck left open the possibility that Sherman might advance to Pensacola, he directed supplies gathered at Hilton Head to refit the western armies should they arrive on the southeastern coast. Halleck also passed on Sherman's request for action against the railroad and ordered that Foster, in the early part of December, organize a strike force and "if possible, to cut the Charleston and Savannah Railroad near Pocotaligo about that time. At all events a demonstration on that road will be of advantage. You will be able undoubtedly to learn his movements through rebel sources much earlier than from these headquarters, and will shape your action accordingly."[4]

On November 16, 1864, Sherman's armies of sixty-five thousand effectives left Atlanta on their march toward Savannah. The general trusted that his request for assistance from Foster's command had been forwarded and that appropriate preparations had been made. At best, the movement by Foster could trap the Confederates in Savannah; at the very least, it could make the southerners spread their meager forces even thinner as they attempted to fend off attacks from the east and west.

Foster received Halleck's message on November 22. The opportunity to strike at the enemy thrilled Foster, who immediately replied, "I am preparing to carry out your instructions. Although my disposable force is very small, I think I can do what is required. I shall move out the night of the 28th, and make my attack on the next day. I shall continue to attack whether I succeed in the first attempt or not, and do the enemy as much damage as I can until I see General Sherman." Foster quickly contacted Admiral Dahlgren, who gladly offered to render all aid. The war had returned to the Beaufort District, presenting the Union commanders with a new opportunity for glory.[5]

Most of November had been quiet for the Union troops stationed around Port Royal. Replacements had arrived and men returned from furlough. Early in the month, the soldiers had voted in the presidential election that returned Lincoln to the White House for four more years. On Hilton Head the Walton Cornet Band of the 144th New York gave "tonic influences in continuing and preserving morale," while in Beaufort the black musicians from the 102nd USCT provided entertainment.[6]

November 24, the last Thursday of the month, found the soldiers celebrating the nation's second Thanksgiving, a national holiday proclaimed by Lincoln a year earlier to render "as a day of thanksgiving and praise to our beneficent Father who dwelleth in the heavens," asking that the nation be restored "to the full enjoyment of peace, harmony, tranquility, and union." In Beaufort the day was clear and warm. At the camp of the 127th New York, religious services were held at 10:00 A.M. with the regimental chaplain, Samuel B. Willis, using the text from Psalms, chapter 4, verses 8 and 9, for his sermon:

> In peace I will both lie down and sleep;
> for thou alone, O Lord, makest me dwell in safety.

At noon General Saxton reviewed the post troops; then the soldiers spent the afternoon in sporting contests consisting of five-hundred-yard foot races, sack races, and wheelbarrow races. For dinner one company consumed stewed chicken, sweet potatoes, white potatoes, turnips, boiled onions, and pumpkin pie.[7]

At Coffin Point Plantation, two officers, Captains Charles C. Soule and William D. Crane of the 55th Massachusetts, came from their regimental camp on Folly Island to celebrate Thanksgiving Day with fellow Bay State natives, including Harriet and Charles Ware, William C. Gannett, Edward Philbrick, and others. Also attending was Laura Towne. Captain Crane entertained the group by playing the piano and singing. William Gannett wrote,

> we gathered together all our friends,—all our 'set,' at least,—and sat down, twenty-six of us, together, to eat turkeys and pies. It was a rather formidable thing to attempt, with negro servants and St. Helena supplies, but we had quite a good time, and have done our duty in giving the party. It is probably the last time that we'll all meet together.... War, in the person of the triumphant Sherman, was again drawing near, and the two young officers of the Fifty-fifth had barely celebrated Thanksgiving with the people from home when they were summoned to take their part.[8]

Throughout the Thanksgiving celebrations, murmurs of a coming campaign filtered throughout the camps. The men realized that something was afoot, and the following day their apprehensions were confirmed when orders came to be ready to move "at short notice." General Foster had allowed his men, unaware of his plans, to enjoy the holiday, the partying helping mask the proposed movement from the Confederates. Though his resources were slender and he had to draw his formations from his entire department, Foster planned to organize a "Coast Division" of approximately fifty-five hundred men and with assistance from the navy proceed up the Broad River, come ashore at Boyd's Landing, and make a quick strike against the Charleston and Savannah Railroad at the Gopher Hill station near Grahamville. Foster believed this route would provide him with success as it bypassed the enemy's main defenses known to exist at Pocotaligo and Coosawhatchie.[9]

Troop movements began on November 28. Sent on transports from Jacksonville, Florida, came the 34th and 35th USCT Infantry Regiments, Captain George R. Hurlbut's 2nd Battalion detachment of the 4th Massachusetts Cavalry, and Captain Edgar H. Titus's Battery F, 3rd New York Artillery. Colonel James C. Beecher, youngest son of the Congregational minister Lyman Beecher and half brother to Harriet Beecher Stowe and the Reverend Henry Ward Beecher, commanded the 35th USCT, a regiment organized originally as the 1st North Carolina at New Berne, North Carolina, from North Carolina and Virginia freedmen. Though the unit had seen combat at Olustee, Beecher had been on leave and had yet to lead his command in battle. The 34th USCT, the former 2nd South Carolina, was no longer under Colonel James Montgomery, who had resigned from Federal service in September 1864 and returned to Kansas, where he took over the 6th Kansas Militia Regiment. Command passed from Montgomery to Lieutenant Colonel William W. Marple, onetime captain in the 104th Pennsylvania. While the USCT regiments had limited experience, Titus's artillery company, organized in Syracuse, New York, had been in service since March 1862. Armed with four 12-pound Napoleon cannons, the battery had seen extensive duty along the coast, especially on Morris Island during the 1863 campaign against Battery Wagner.[10]

Shipped from Morris and Folly Islands off Charleston came Colonel Van Wyck's 56th New York, an experienced regiment that had fought with the Army of the Potomac and in operations off Charleston and eight companies each from two black regiments, the 54th and 55th Massachusetts. Accompanying the infantry were the Auburn, New York, veterans of Battery B, 3rd New York, and its four Napoleon cannons, commanded by Captain Thomas J. Mersereau.[11]

From Fort Pulaski came five companies of Colonel James C. Carmichael's 157th New York, a regiment organized at Hamilton, New York, which had fought at Chancellorsville and Gettysburg before being transferred south in the summer of 1863. Brought from Hilton Head Island was the 32nd USCT, an untested regiment that had been organized primarily from Pennsylvania blacks in March 1864 and commanded by Colonel George W. Baird. The 32nd had initially been assigned to building fortifications, picket duty, and grand guard duty on Hilton Head and Morris Island. Other Hilton Head units joining the campaign included the 25th Ohio, a regiment raised from across the state and led by Toledo native Lieutenant Colonel Nathaniel Houghton. The unit had been formed early in the conflict and had seen action during the Valley Campaign, Second Bull Run, Chancellorsville, and Gettysburg before being transferred to the Department of the South. On Hilton Head the Ohio regiment provided details for fatigue and guard duty and assisted in constructing Fort Howell.

Also from Hilton Head came eight companies of the 144th New York, a unit raised in Delaware County, New York, and commanded by Lieutenant Colonel James Lewis. The regiment had been stationed in southeast Virginia before being transferred to the Department of the South in the summer of 1863 in time for operations against Battery Wagner. The New Yorkers remained off Charleston for the rest of the year and then were sent in February 1864 to Jacksonville, Florida. Later assignments included action on James and Johns Islands during the summer of 1864. They then joined the Hilton Head garrison, where they rotated with the other garrison regiments doing picket and prison guard duty on the island and fatigue duty at Fort Howell.[12]

Breaking camp and boarding vessels in Beaufort were the 127th New York, the 26th and 102nd USCT, and Company A, 3rd Rhode Island. The 127th, known as the "Monitors," had been raised in New York City and Long Island. The regiment had defended Suffolk, Virginia, during the spring of 1863 before coming south for operations off Charleston. The 26th USCT, commanded by Colonel William Silliman, had been organized primarily from New York freemen and trained at Rikers Island. The regiment had been bloodied in fighting outside Charleston on John's Island in July 1864 before being stationed on Port Royal Island.[13]

The 102nd Regiment sent a wing of soldiers, some three hundred men, to the expedition. The regiment's colonel, Detroit resident Henry Laurens Chipman, had entered the army as the lieutenant colonel of the 2nd Michigan before transferring to 11th U.S. Infantry as a captain in June 1861. He fought at the Battles of Chancellorsville and Gettysburg and then in April 1864 took command of the 102nd. In May 1864 Chipman brought the regiment from its first duty station at Annapolis to Hilton Head. Here the black Michigan soldiers were primarily used to construct and man fortifications on Hilton Head and Port Royal Islands. Later they saw limited action in August 1864, when they were briefly stationed in Florida before returning to duty at Beaufort.[14]

Company A, 3rd Rhode Island, under twenty-six-year-old Captain William Henry Hamner, also embarked at Beaufort. A regular artilleryman,

Hamner had been the quartermaster sergeant in Fort Sumter's garrison in April 1861 and personally lowered the United States flag upon its surrender. While stationed at Fort Hamilton, New York, he helped train the soldiers of the 3rd Rhode Island in handling heavy artillery before joining the regiment as a second lieutenant. In South Carolina, Hamner and the men of Company A served cannons aboard army transports and in entrenchments at Beaufort, Hilton Head, and Jacksonville and manned artillery positions on Morris Island that bombarded Fort Sumter. Adept at operating everything from field pieces to siege guns and heavy artillery, the company in the fall of 1864 was placed under Hamner, by now a captain, and outfitted with three 10-pound Parrott rifles and assigned to Foster's Coast Division.[15]

The Federal soldiers had less than two days to prepare. They were issued 60–140 cartridges and five days' rations for what was termed "a short trip." Every effort was made to mask their passage from the enemy. As one soldier put it, "The movement was conducted after the usual and well-established methods popular in the Department. It was the 'wait–till-tis-dark-and-don't-say-a-word-about-it' plan." Transports rendezvoused off Hilton Head on November 28. Troops were placed on light-drafted ships for movement up the Broad River. The vessels took on coal from supply centers on Parris and Hilton Head Islands before rendezvousing in the sound.[16]

Since his injury kept him from taking the field, Foster placed the Coast Division in the hands of Brigadier General John Hatch. The division was divided into three brigades, two infantry and one artillery. The first brigade consisted of the 56th, 127th, 144th, and 157th New York, the 25th Ohio, and the 32nd, 34th, and 35th USCT Infantry Regiments. Many of the units were missing companies and all were understrength. Control of the first brigade went to one of Foster's favorite subordinates, Brigadier General Edward E. Potter, a forty-one-year-old Columbia College graduate and New York City lawyer. Potter had served as a commissary officer in General Ambrose Burnside's expedition that seized the eastern North Carolina coast in the spring of 1862. He later became a lieutenant colonel in the 1st North Carolina, a regiment raised from white loyalists in the Washington, North Carolina, area. Promoted to brigadier general, Potter served loyally under Burnside's successor, General Foster, who gave Potter numerous special assignments. When Foster was placed in charge of the Department of the Ohio, Potter accompanied him to his new command. After Foster took disability leave, Potter remained in the department until his former chief took over the Department of the South, when he transferred and was reunited with Foster and resumed his role as his chief's primary troubleshooter.[17]

Massachusetts native Colonel Alfred S. Hartwell led the division's Second Brigade. At the start of the war, the twenty-eight-year-old Harvard graduate had been in St. Louis, and after a brief tenure with a militia unit, he came east and accepted a commission as a lieutenant in the 44th Massachusetts. When Massachusetts governor John Andrew began enlisting black soldiers for the 54th Massachusetts, Hartwell joined the regiment as a company commander. His stay was brief, as he soon transferred to the state's second black regiment, the 55th Massachusetts, becoming its lieutenant colonel. Initially assigned to service in Foster's Department of North Carolina, Hartwell's regiment came to the Department of the South in August 1863, joining the campaign against Charleston. In November 1863 Hartwell was promoted to colonel, taking over the regiment and leading it in further operations off Charleston and in Florida.

In October 1864 Hartwell took leave but returned in time to join the expedition against the Charleston and Savannah Railroad. When his regiment arrived at Port Royal Sound, Hartwell was waiting, having been named brigade commander with authority over the 54th and 55th Massachusetts and the 102nd and 26th USCT. Among Hartwell's staff was Captain William Crane, the young officer who had spent Thanksgiving at Coffin Point. Crane, whose company had been left on Folly Island, requested permission to join the expedition, and Hartwell agreed, naming Crane his brigade chief of staff.[18]

Lieutenant Colonel William Ames commanded the division's artillery brigade, which consisted of three batteries: Mersereau's Battery B and Titus's Battery F, 3rd New York Artillery, and Hamner's Battery A, 3rd Rhode Island Artillery. Ames, a veteran of the 2nd Rhode Island Infantry Regiment, had transferred to the 3rd Rhode Island Artillery in January 1863 as a major. By March 1864 he had become the regiment's lieutenant colonel, and in October, when part of the unit was transferred to Virginia, he took over the companies remaining in the Department of the South. Ames held numerous positions, including commander of Fort Pulaski, chief of artillery on Morris Island, and eventually the department's chief of artillery.[19]

For the campaign Hatch assembled a staff with William True Bennett as his chief. Bennett, the 102nd USCT's lieutenant colonel, oversaw the hastily organized officers drawn from various formations. Hatch's staff reflected the makeup of his division, whose brigade commanders and units had never served together. With no time to develop any familiarity or cohesion, the division's units made final preparations to sail up the Broad River.[20]

To supplement the Union expedition, Rear Admiral Dahlgren provided a brigade of sailors, marines, and boat artillery. The navy's contribution was also a hodgepodge of formations drawn from the entire squadron. Like Foster, Dahlgren enthusiastically backed the operation. Instructed by Secretary of the Navy Gideon Welles to cooperate with Sherman's movement against Savannah, Dahlgren quickly agreed to Foster's proposal for a joint campaign against the Charleston and Savannah Railroad. On Thanksgiving Day, in celebration of the holiday and the coming movement, and in remembrance of his son, who had recently been killed in a controversial cavalry operation against Richmond, Dahlgren ordered an illumination of the naval buildings and vessels and the firing of rockets from his warships. To Dahlgren, with "Sherman coming like a thunderbolt," the day of "retribution seemed nigh."[21]

Orders went out to assemble a corps of howitzers, seamen, and marines at Bay Point. Men were detailed from the squadron's warships and shore detachments. The naval brigade consisted of 493 men divided into three battalions: sailor infantry, marines, and boat artillery. The sailor battalion, commanded by Lieutenant James O'Kane consisted of 164 men and officers and was divided into four companies. The men received Dahlgren's hard-hitting .69-caliber Plymouth rifled muskets with their intimidating Bowie knife–style bayonet.

The 160 marines were assembled from ten warships and placed under First Lieutenant George G. Stoddard, who was assisted by Acting Ensign Woodward Carter. The marines were divided into three companies, each commanded by a sergeant. With the sailors, the marines were taught battalion drill at Bay Point. Dahlgren believed his officers "clever" and his men "zealous" but feared that two days of instruction were too short to ready them for combat, commenting that "it is very difficult to get the officers into the idea of light drill and open order. They will mass the men."[22]

Though he carefully oversaw the organization of the sailor and marine battalions, Dahlgren's gave special attention to the disposition of the boat artillery. Placed under Lieutenant Commander E. Orville Matthews, the section consisted of eight bronze Dahlgren boat howitzers, six smoothbores, and two rifles, all mounted on iron field carriages. Twelve men manned each howitzer. Once ashore, the sailors were expected to pull the cannons using drag and guide ropes, though for this expedition General Foster had promised to provide horses and teamsters to transport the cannons as well as rations for the seamen and marines.[23]

The howitzers fired 12-pound shells. The fixed ammunition was carried in two portable, wheeled chests per piece, while each crewman also carried an individual leather pouch containing one fixed round. Besides the twelve-man crews and gun captain, Dahlgren assigned to each cannon seven sailors armed with Plymouth rifles. Also allotted to the brigade were fifers and drummers, eleven freedmen who served as hospital stewards and nurses, and a fatigue party of black landsmen, who were charged with cooking, preparing campsites, pioneering, and constructing breastworks. Among the officers detailed to the battery was a young, twenty-four-year-old lieutenant and future naval historian and theorist Alfred Thayer Mahan, whose writing on naval operations would change nations' global military strategy.

Dahlgren named Commander George Henry Preble as the brigade leader. A career naval officer, the forty-eight-year-old, Portland, Maine, native had started his career in 1835 as a midshipman. At the start of the war, Preble served with Flag Officer David Farragut's squadron, commanding the gunboat *Katahdin* during the New Orleans campaign. While in charge of the blockade off Mobile, Alabama, his career nearly ended when he was unable to stop the Confederate commerce raider *Florida* from escaping. An outraged secretary of navy dismissed Preble from the service, but he was later reinstated and given command of the sailing sloop *St. Louis* and dispatched to seek out Confederate warships in the Atlantic before joining Dahlgren's squadron on November 2, 1864. The *St. Louis* had only limited value as a blockader, but Dahlgren viewed the crew as a reservoir for possible naval land operations against the Charleston and Savannah Railroad. Though he was unable to organize any inland strikes, Dahlgren was quite happy to assign Preble and a number of the vessel's crew and marines to Foster's expedition.[24]

From their temporary training site on Bay Point, Preble's landing force embarked on November 28. Dahlgren created from his squadron a flotilla of light-drafted vessels capable of traversing the shallow waters of the Broad River and consisting of paddle-wheel and screw-propelled steamers. While Preble would take over once ashore, Dahlgren planned to sail with the expedition. He directed a sailing order in a single line led by the side-wheeler *Mingoe*, followed by the *Pontiac, Sonoma, Harvest Moon* (Dahlgren's flagship), *Pawnee, Winona*, and *Wissahickon*. The tugs *O. M. Pettit* and *Daffodil* were to guide the flotilla or serve as flankers keeping the warships in the channel. The *Pontiac*, commanded by the future founder and first president of the Naval War College, Stephen B. Luce, carried the naval cannoneers, including his future history professor, Lieutenant Alfred Thayer Mahan. The *Mingoe* took on board the naval infantry, and the *Sonoma* carried the marines, while the howitzers were carried in launches pulled behind the steamers.[25]

A freedman named Jenks, who knew the channel, piloted the naval expedition. A heavy fog kept the warships from leaving until 4:00 A.M. The squadron was to sail before sunrise on the morning of the twenty-ninth. Each ship showed a light "below her rail to her second astern," careful to keep it from being seen from any direction except directly astern. Dahlgren ordered the vessels' speed to be kept slow, no more than four or five knots, as they steamed from the sound and through the shoals at the head of the Broad River. When they cast off, the squadron groped along the river with the tugs on either side of the line, keeping the warships from wandering into shallow water. For twenty miles, in waters "where not an officer or man of us had been before save the pilot," the steamers inched along until they reached and entered Boyd's Creek. At about 8:00 A.M., as they approached the landing, Confederate pickets hailed the warships, which soon anchored. Dahlgren was quite pleased, noting that "I had the satisfaction of finding myself, with five of my six steamers at the landing designated." The *Wissahickon*, having run aground, had not arrived at the landing point. Also missing were the army's transports, and for a moment Dahlgren "feared that some mistake may have been made."[26]

The army's maritime operation did not go as smoothly. As a soldier from the 25th Ohio wrote, "Fortune seemed improprietous." Throughout November, twenty-eight transports came into Port Royal Sound. Coal was taken on and regiments distributed among the vessels. To mask their departure, Foster, who accompanied the expedition aboard the *Nemaha*, planned to sail before sunrise on the twenty-ninth. At about 2:00 A.M. the army's transports set out, but a heavy fog and a dark night, coupled with poor organization and inept pilots, scattered the boats. Many ran aground. Others missed the channel and entered Skull Creek or the Chechessee River. Some vessels stopped and awaited daylight while others pushed on. All sailing order was lost. Lead vessels carrying the engineers required to build wharves and cavalry to scout roadways, along with the headquarter ships, fell out of line and instead of being the first became the last.[27]

At about 8:00 A.M. General Hatch, aboard the transport *Fraser* with Companies G and H of the 54th Massachusetts, joined a relieved Dahlgren at Boyd's Landing. Lieutenant Colonel Henry N. Hooper took the two companies of black soldiers ashore, secured the landing site, and established a picket line. They debarked at the Boyd Plantation, a house with large piazzas and outbuildings nestled in a grove of live oaks. Enemy cavalrymen were seen but no opposition was met. Preble's naval brigade followed. Though the fog had thrown off the army's landing order, Hatch did not want to wait, and while the promised horses for the naval cannons had not yet arrived, he directed Preble to take his howitzers, sailors, and marines inland to seize the junction of Boyd's Landing and Coosawhatchie Roads, where Federal maps showed the Boyd's Landing Road crossing the Coosawhatchie Road and continuing on directly to Grahamville and the railroad.[28]

By 9:00 A.M. Preble, with Dahlgren accompanying, had his sailors and marines marching along an oak-lined, sandy roadway that led through a series of cotton fields. Two companies of marines were thrown out as skirmishers with one company in reserve. Behind them came the sailor infantry and the boat howitzers, pulled by their crews. The day was warm and the march arduous for men not used to shore duty. The brigade advanced two miles to where the road dead-ended into the Coosawhatchie Highway. Preble, who by his chart expected a crossroads, halted his command and set up a defensive perimeter, while Dahlgren, satisfied with the brigade's progress, returned to Boyd's Landing.

Though confused by the faulty map and without a guide, Preble did not want to give up the initiative. With his aide Lieutenant Commander Alexander Crossman and fifteen sailors, Preble scouted north toward Coosawhatchie, skirmishing with enemy pickets. Returning to his command, Preble discovered that Colonel Baird, with most of his regiment, the 32nd USCT, had arrived. Preble and Baird then determined that the enemy presence to the north probably indicated the most direct route to the railroad, and the two advanced their commands two miles farther north until stopping at an abandoned enemy entrenchment.

While Preble attempted to ascertain the proper line of march, the rest of the Union expedition dribbled ashore in no apparent order at Boyd's Landing. By the time Dahlgren returned, Hatch was trying to sort out the various regimental components. Foster arrived at about 2:00 P.M. in the midst of troop debarkation. While waiting for orders, the soldiers rested in the nearby cotton fields. Foster stayed until 4:00 P.M.; then he returned to Hilton Head, leaving Hatch in charge. Dahlgren remained until early evening, when he also left with his flagship, the tugs, and the screw gunboat *Winona,* leaving behind to cover Boyd's Landing the lighter-draft screw sloop *Pawnee,* and the double-ender side-wheelers, *Mingoe, Pontiac,* and *Sonoma* under Commander J. Blakeley Creighton. The vessels laid in close to the bank, anchored at each end, head and stern, with their combined broadsides mounting one 11-inch and twelve 9-inch Dahlgren guns, six 100-pound Parrott rifles, and sixteen howitzers—ready, if necessary, to sweep away any enemy attack against the landing.[29]

Throughout the afternoon, under the protection of the warships, the majority of Potter's brigade landed. Hatch, still hoping to reach his objective, kept the regiments under arms and ready to move. At 3:30 General Potter arrived and energetically took over his available regiments, the 144th, 127th, and 157th New York, the 25th Ohio, the 35th USCT, and cavalrymen from the 4th Massachusetts. Hatch left Colonel Hartwell in charge of the landing site and accompanied Potter's forces as they marched inland. At the road junction, Potter followed the route taken by the naval brigade and the 32nd USCT, which were overtaken around 5:00 P.M. The sailors and the men of Baird's regiment had entrenched and were cooking supper when their comrades arrived. It was also at this time that Potter learned he had taken the wrong road. The entire force returned to the Boyd's Landing road, where the naval brigade was left, much to the relief of the cannoneers, who were allowed to "refresh" themselves after dragging their 750-pound howitzers for six miles.[30]

Though it was nearly dark, Hatch still pushed on with the available regiments of Potter's brigade, hoping to close on his destination. The command continued south to Bethel Episcopal Chapel, commonly known as Bolan Church in honor of its benefactor, the local planter James Bolan. A small white frame structure, it sat where a road led to the west toward Grahamville and the Federal objective, but instead of turning west, the Federal commanders, either by "some mistakes in maps or blunder of guide, or both," kept heading south for four miles before realizing their mistake. The entire force then countermarched, but it was so dark "that the sense of hearing and feeling were the only guides." Companies and regiments became mixed while the soldiers stumbled through the darkness. At some time between 2:00 and 3:00 A.M. the Federals returned to Bolan Church. The men had been up for twenty-four hours and few had rested the day before. They had marched fifteen miles and were exhausted. Hatch called a stop and his soldiers went into bivouac. No fires were allowed and the men slept on their arms. If the Federals had not taken wrong turns, or continued following the route initially taken by Preble, they would have found only a scattering of cavalry and some artillery pieces to resist their advance, but given a twenty-four hour reprieve, the Confederates were able to create a formidable defense.[31]

Since the fall of Atlanta, the Confederacy had reorganized its command system to deal with Sherman's campaign. General Beauregard was recalled from Virginia and placed in charge of the newly formed Division of the West, which encompassed the area from Georgia to the Mississippi River, with supervisory duties over General John B. Hood's Army of Tennessee and General Richard Taylor's forces in Alabama. Beauregard's job was to advise and coordinate operations designed to draw Sherman's army away from central Georgia and defeat it. His command did not extend to Lieutenant General William J. Hardee's Department of South Carolina, Georgia, and East Florida. Hardee, who carefully watched Sherman's initial movements, could not make out the Union general's ultimate destination. Augusta, Port Royal, or Savannah all seemed likely objectives. To oversee resistance to Sherman's movement through Georgia, President Davis ordered General Braxton Bragg, his military advisor and troubleshooter, from Wilmington, North Carolina, to Augusta, where he took charge of opposing the Federal advance. Bragg brought with him a large portion of Wilmington's garrison. His presence caused a change in the area's administration. Since Bragg outranked Hardee, he also assumed control of the Department of South Carolina, Georgia, and East Florida.

Hardee remained in charge of the department's coastal region. He left Major General Sam Jones at Charleston and shifted his headquarters to Savannah, where he began feverish preparations to ready the city's landward defenses. Hardee brought units from the Beaufort District into Georgia and combined them with troops into a mixed-arms division of cavalry, artillery, and infantry under Major General Lafayette McLaws.[32]

Though stripped of men, the defensive scheme for the area between the Savannah and Combahee Rivers had changed little since its inception in 1861. Cavalrymen still watched over potential landing sites ready to give early warning of Federal movements. Once pickets reported the presence of the enemy, the district's garrison was to man existing fortifications and delay the enemy's advance until reinforcements arrived on the railroad.

Two sets of fortifications guarded the approaches to Grahamville and the railroad depot at Gopher Hill. Located two miles east of Grahamville on a sand ridge known as Honey Hill and overlooking a marshy creek were two earthen lunettes and some trench lines that had been started in late 1861 by Thomas L. Clingman's North Carolina Brigade. One lunette was situated along the road between Bolan Church and Grahamville, while the other sat a half mile to the north. The area directly in front of the lunette on the road and its adjoining trenches had been cleared of trees from the entrenchments to the creek.[33]

The other set of fortifications, positioned south of Bee's Creek near the junction of the Bee's Creek and Grahamville Roads, guarded the approaches to Coosawhatchie and Grahamville. Located in an area more vulnerable to enemy attack, the Bee's Hill Battery had been maintained, but those at Honey Hill had been neglected and fallen into disrepair.

Charles J. Colcock, the forty-four-year-old colonel of the 3rd South Carolina, commanded the district between the Combahee and Savannah rivers, but he, with three companies and his regiment's horse artillery, was not on the coast. Instead, he and his men were inland building defenses at crossing points on the Savannah River should Sherman decide to bypass Savannah and enter South Carolina to head for Port Royal through the Beaufort District's upper regions. Colcock situated himself at Matthew's Bluff in the northwestern corner of St. Peter's Parish. While there, the colonel, who had outlived two wives, planned to marry his third bride, Robertville native Agnes M. Bostick.

Further distribution weakened the district's coastal area. Besides the units stationed along the Savannah River, two companies of Colcock's regiment had been sent to Savannah and placed in McLaws's combined division. A third company, Captain William B. Peeples's Company K, had also been ordered from Pocotaligo to Georgia, and Captain Archibald Campbell's Company B was stationed near Charleston on Johns Island.[34]

Sherman's grand movement forced the Confederates to focus their attention inland with little thought given to the defense of the Beaufort District's coastline. Though vigilant, the southerners were too few to stop a determined attack. Along the coast were only four cavalry companies, approximately 250 troopers, and four artillery batteries, about 200 artillerymen, to guard the approaches to the Charleston and Savannah Railroad. Three cavalry units, Captain James Gregorie's Company C, Captain John L. Seabrook's Company I, and Captain Henry C. Raysor's Company E were stationed at Pocotaligo. In late November troopers from Companies C and I picketed landing sites watching for possible Federal incursions.[35]

Four artillery companies remained in the district. The experienced and locally raised Beaufort Volunteer Artillery under Captain Henry Middleton Stuart was stationed at McPhersonville, positioned to rush its guns to any threatened spot within the district. At nearby Pocotaligo was Bachman's Battery, a veteran unit that had started the war as part of the Hampton Legion. It was separated and became an independent artillery company, seeing combat with the Army of Northern Virginia from the Seven Days Battles through the Gettysburg Campaign before coming back to South Carolina. Commanded by Captain William K. Bachman, the formation, also termed the German Light Artillery, boasted four Napoleon cannons.

Captain John T. Kanapaux's Lafayette Artillery, a Charleston militia unit originally formed by men of French descent, guarded the fieldworks at the junction of the Coosawhatchie and Grahamville Roads at the fortifications near Bee's Creek, while Captain William Earle's Furman Artillery was located along the May River between Bluffton and the fortifications on the Savannah Road over the New River.[36]

When the enemy's naval vessels arrived at Boyd's Landing, they interrupted the Confederate vedettes' sweet potato breakfast. While his comrades left their cooking fires and cautiously watched the shadowy warships anchor in the creek, William A. Miller rode to outpost headquarters and reported the enemy's presence to Lieutenant Thomas Heyward Howard, who quickly dispatched a rider to the district headquarters at Grahamville. Howard's men from Company C, 3rd South Carolina Cavalry, shadowed the Federals as they marched along the Boyd's Landing Road and then withdrew north down the Coosawhatchie Road toward the works at Bee's Creek. By now local mounted militia, including Captain John H. Howard, the sixty-four-year-old owner of nearby Whitehall Plantation, had joined the running fight with Preble's sailors and marines. Howard, who had organized Company C, 3rd South Carolina, at the start of the war before resigning his commission because of age, later joined a home guard unit. Infuriated at the presence of the Yankees, Howard often rode out in advance of his fellow cavalrymen, discharging his double-barreled shotgun at the enemy.[37]

In Colcock's absence Major John Jenkins of the 3rd South Carolina Cavalry commanded the troops in the district's coastal area. A native of Edisto Island, Jenkins had raised the Rebel Troop, a cavalry unit that became Company I, 3rd South Carolina Cavalry. While his younger brother, Micah Jenkins, went on to fame with the Army of Northern Virginia before his death in May 1864 at the Battle of the Wilderness, John Jenkins, promoted to major, remained with his regiment throughout the war.

When the Federals began landing at Boyd's Landing, Jenkins was in Charleston. At Grahamville, Captain Edward W. Fraser, the regiment's assistant adjutant general, received Howard's dispatch at about 10:00 A.M. Fraser immediately sent telegrams reporting the enemy's presence to Generals Beverly Roberson at Adams Run, William Hardee at Savannah, and Samuel Jones at Charleston. Word was also sent to Colonel Colcock via relays of couriers that Colcock had established along the fifty-mile route between Grahamville and Matthew's Bluff. Once notified, Major Jenkins, along with Lieutenant William N. Heyward, quickly boarded a locomotive at Charleston and rode in the cab for Pocotaligo.

Besides notifying his superiors, Lieutenant Fraser also called on Captain Earle to send a section of artillery from his company currently camped along the May River to help delay the enemy's advance. While waiting for Jenkins or Colcock to arrive, Fraser dispatched Captain Louis D. DeSaussure to observe the enemy's movements.

Fraser had available at Grahamville Captain Peeples's Company K, 3rd South Carolina Cavalry, who were on their way to Savannah, but the arrival of the Union troops stopped the movement to Georgia, and soon Captain Peeples's resounding "clarion" voice was heard calling his troopers to action. Once mounted, Peeples put his men in motion up Bolan Causeway toward Boyd's Landing.[38]

Major Jenkins arrived at Pocotaligo Station in the early afternoon on the twenty-ninth and received reports about the Federal movements along the road toward Coosawhatchie. He quickly ordered Captain Raysor and his company to join the pickets skirmishing with the Federals and forwarded the Beaufort Artillery from Pocotaligo to the Bee's Hill entrenchments. Jenkins also called for the rest of Earle's Battery to come to Grahamville.

From Charleston, General Jones directed Captain Campbell's cavalry company to make a forced march from Johns Island to Pocotaligo. While Jenkins waited for help to arrive, he proceeded to Grahamville, arriving at about 4:00 P.M. Jenkins was faced with trying to deduce the enemy's route and objective, which, thanks to the erratic Federal movements, was difficult to ascertain. From the junction of the Boyd's Landing and Coosawhatchie Roads, three routes led to Grahamville. The Federals, as their initial movements seemed to indicate, could march north towards Bee's Creek, seize the junction of the Coosawhatchie and Grahamville Roads, and then march south, passing in rear of the Honey Hill line into Grahamville.

When the Union forces reversed their march and moved north, it opened the possibility of their moving onto Bolan Causeway at Bolan Church and on toward Grahamville. If they passed Bolan Causeway and continued north, they could still reach Grahamville and the railroad by taking the Bellfield Causeway into Grahamville. Jenkins also considered the possibility that the Union landing might be an elaborate hoax, with the actual operation directed against Mackey's Neck and Pocotaligo.[39]

Though heavily outnumbered, Jenkins had certain advantages. Fixed works at Pocotaligo, Bee's Creek, and Honey Hill guarded the approaches to the railroad. The Confederates also had the use of interior lines, allowing them to shift forces on good roads between Grahamville–Bee's Creek and Pocotaligo, while the Federals had to operate on a longer exterior arc. Still, without reinforcements Jenkins would be hard pressed to protect the railroad.

Since receipt of the telegrams calling for help, Jenkins's superiors had been working to forward troops to Grahamville. From Savannah, General Hardee planned to send thirty-two hundred Georgia forces that included militia, state troops, and reserves once they arrived from Thomasville, Georgia. Hardee also ordered General Jones at Charleston to send two regiments (about seven hundred men), while General Bragg put one thousand South Carolina reserves and a two-thousand-man North Carolina brigade onto trains at Augusta. With seven thousand men on their way to Grahamville, the Confederates would have more than enough forces to check the Federals if the southern railroads could get them to their destination in time.[40]

While adjusting his defenses to handle all contingencies, Jenkins wired both Generals Jones and Hardee: "Ten gunboats, with transports and barges at Boyd's landing, troops near Grahamville. Four gunboats coming up Broad River to Mackay's Point, which is the approach to Pocotaligo and Coosawhatchie. Reinforcements needed." Both officers replied. Jones promised help by the morning of the thirtieth. From Hardee's headquarters came a communication also informing Jenkins to expect the arrival of troops from Savannah the following morning. Colonel Ambrosio Gonzales, the Cuban revolutionary who had married Beaufortonian William Elliott III's daughter Harriett, signed Hardee's dispatch. Gonzales, the department's ordnance chief and a staff officer whom Hardee employed when needed as a troubleshooter, informed Jenkins to expect help from Major General Gustavus Smith's Georgia State Army, which was anticipated to arrive that night at Savannah from Thomasville, Georgia. Jenkins was directed to have horses available for General Smith and his staff. In the meantime Gonzales admonished Jenkins to do all in his power to keep the enemy away from the railroad until help arrived.[41]

The final warning was hardly necessary. Jenkins had already ordered his subordinates to resist the enemy's advance and to hold them in check at all hazards. On the evening of the twenty-ninth, Jenkins returned to Pocotaligo. Because he was unsure of his enemy's final route, Jenkins had to maintain his pickets to watch other possible landing sites along the Whale Branch, Pocotaligo, and Tulifinney Rivers. At Pocotaligo, Jenkins had Bachman's artillery company and the recently arrived cavalrymen of Company B, 3rd South Carolina Cavalry, who were resting after completing a seventy-mile march from Johns Island. Located at the Bee's Hill fortification were the Beaufort and Lafayette artillery batteries. Company E of the 3rd South Carolina Cavalry, along with elements of Companies I and C and mounted militia, watched the Coosawhatchie Road north of Bee's Creek. Captain

Peeples's troopers from Company K, 3rd South Carolina Cavalry, patrolled the roadway between Grahamville and Bolan Church, while Captain Earle and his entire company of the Furman artillery bivouacked at Grahamville after a thirty-five-mile march from the May River.

Later that evening Jenkins directed one gun from the Lafayette Artillery under Lieutenant C.J. "Kit" Zealy shifted to Grahamville. Jenkins planned additional adjustments in the morning once the Federals renewed their advance, but he realized that no matter what direction they took, he had far too few resources to stop them. He needed help, especially infantry, and anxiously awaited their arrival.

Jenkins's anxiety would have been greatly heightened had he known about the drama that had played out on the night of the twenty-ninth in Savannah. The dispatch from Colonel Gonzales promising assistance had been sent prematurely and had not taken into account Georgia state laws and the prickly nature of the officer in charge of the Georgia troops.

While Generals Bragg, Jones, and Hardee promised reinforcements from their respective commands, only the men from Savannah held any prospect of reaching Gopher Hill in time to stop the Federal advance. A breakdown on the South Carolina Railroad 112 miles from Charleston delayed the soldiers from Augusta, while at Charleston, Jones was having difficulty dispatching the 32nd and 47th Georgia Infantry Regiments. The steamer carrying the 32nd to the city ran aground, and though the 47th arrived that afternoon at the St. Andrews Depot, a train coming from Savannah delayed its debarkation.

Transportation problems also plagued the troops from Savannah. A lack of locomotives had slowed the movement of General Smith's Georgians from Thomasville, forcing the Confederates to relay their troops in two sections. However, once the initial elements of Smith's Division reached Savannah, Hardee planned to quickly shift their troop cars to the Charleston and Savannah Railroad tracks and send them to Gopher Hill. Hardee had already prepared his order for Smith, but until the general and his men arrived, there was little the department commander could do except wait. Throughout the evening Hardee harangued Jones with telegrams urging him to hurry the 32nd and 47th Georgia and Captain Manning J. Kirk's cavalry squadron from Charleston to Grahamville. Hardee also ordered Jones to proceed to Grahamville and take over the troops in the 3rd District, but the Charleston commander was also receiving telegrams from a concerned Bragg in Augusta, directing him to coordinate the reinforcements being sent to Grahamville. Since Bragg outranked Hardee, Jones remained at his headquarters handling the movement of forces through Charleston.[42]

Finally, after midnight, trains carrying about fourteen hundred men of the 1st Brigade Georgia Militia, the Georgia State Line, and the Athens and Augusta Georgia Reserve Battalions arrived at the Savannah Depot. The soldiers came from a mixed force commanded by Major General Gustavus Smith. The militia brigade was part of the First Division Georgia Militia, a unit formed by Georgia governor Joseph E. Brown, consisting of men either too old or too young for the Confederate draft or exempt because of occupation. The division referred to as "Joe Brown's Pets" was mocked in the song "Goober Peas," but in the right circumstances the soldiers could be effective. A separate organization, the Georgia State Line was composed of two regiments initially formed to protect Georgia railroads. The formation had seen some service earlier in the war at both Charleston and Savannah, when Federal forces threatened the cities. The Augusta and Athens Battalions were units made up of men exempt from the draft, primarily factory workers, who could be called out in times of emergency.

Smith's soldiers had seen service during the Atlanta Campaign and had been part of the forces resisting Sherman's march through Georgia. Roughly handled at the Battle of Griswoldville, the division garrisoned Macon, and when the Federals bypassed that city, the formation was ordered to Savannah. The trip to the coast was long and exhausting. The units were transported to Albany by rail and then marched overland to Thomasville, where they were supposed to meet five trains for the trip to Savannah. When the soldiers arrived, they found only two trains to carry them the final two hundred miles. There was room only for the men of the 1st Brigade, the State Line, and the Augusta and Athens Reserve Battalions under General Gustavus Smith, who boarded an assortment of railroad cars for the first relay to Savannah.[43]

The forty-two-year-old Smith, a Kentucky native, who had graduated eighth in the U.S. Military Academy class of 1842 and served with distinction in the Mexican War, had been a highly respected engineer before leaving the army in 1854 to join a Cuban filibuster adventure. When the planned operation failed to materialize, he began a prosperous career as a civil engineer and in 1858 became the street commissioner for the City of New York. During the Fort Sumter crisis, Smith, who opposed the Lincoln government and its stance on slavery, suffered a brief paralysis attack, and while traveling to Hot Springs, Arkansas, for recuperation, he learned that the U.S. government, thinking he was joining the seceding states, had issued an arrest warrant for him. Outraged, Smith immediately resigned as New York's street commissioner and offered his services to the Confederacy.

Appointed a major general, he was part of the Confederate army in Virginia, and when General Joseph Johnston was wounded outside Richmond in May 1862, Smith briefly commanded the southern army until again afflicted by an onset of paralysis, forcing him to relinquish the post to General Robert E. Lee. After a brief tenure as acting secretary of war, Smith resigned his commission when denied promotion to lieutenant general. He moved to Georgia and became president of a mining company before becoming

Georgia governor Joseph Brown's military aide-de-camp and commander of Georgian state forces. Smith served well as commander of the Georgia militia and other state formations during the Atlanta Campaign and continued to lead the militiamen and state troops in resisting Sherman's march to Savannah.[44]

An exhausted, tired, and irritable Smith, along with fourteen hundred men, arrived in Savannah after midnight. At the railroad depot an aide to General Hardee delivered two orders to Smith. The first, originally composed at 10:00 A.M., read, "Lieutenant-General Hardee directs that you proceed at once with the first two trains of your troops which may arrive at Savannah to-night, and in the same cars to Grahamville and Coosawhatchie, on the Charleston and Savannah Railroad, which places are being threatened by raiding parties of the enemy; and, if you find yourself the ranking officer present, that you command, and drive the enemy back to their gun-boats."[45] The second, composed before the Confederates had determined the Federals' objective, stated, "Lieutenant-General Hardee directs me to say that, from information received, he thinks it best that the first train of your troops which arrives should go to Coosawhatchie, the farthest point, and the second to Grahamville."

Smith believed the orders to be a burden on his fatigued soldiers, who had had little rest over the last five days. He also considered them illegal. Though the Georgia State Line and the Athens and Augusta Battalions could serve in other states, the majority of his force was made up of Georgia militia, which by state law were banned from serving outside Georgia. Outraged, Smith went directly to Hardee's headquarters, where he awoke the department commander, demanding that "if you can satisfy me that it is absolutely necessary that my command shall go into South Carolina, I will endeavor to carry out your orders. If you do not satisfy me, and persist in your orders, I will be under the disagreeable necessity of withdrawing the State forces from your control."[46]

Hardee, one of the officers promoted over Smith in 1862, used maps and dispatches to demonstrate the critical state of affairs. Even though it violated Georgia law, Smith agreed that the situation necessitated the movement of his entire command into South Carolina, though he made it clear that his men should be promptly withdrawn once the emergency was over.[47]

Smith, accompanied by Hardee's staff officer, Colonel Gonzales, a compatriot from the Smith's filibuster days, returned to the trains. His officers were willing, but many of the enlisted men argued against the proposed movements since South Carolina authorities had refused earlier in the month to send their militia to assist in the defense of Augusta. But Smith overruled the objections and promised they would be back in Georgia within forty-eight hours. In a few minutes, the railroad cars were being transferred to the Charleston and Savannah tracks. With the delays of the reinforcements from Charleston and Augusta, the arrival of Smith's forces was extremely fortuitous. At 1:00 A.M. Hardee wired Jones that Smith was on his way.[48]

While his superiors scrambled to reinforce his command, Jenkins spent a short night at Pocotaligo. Though he believed that the enemy's primary advance would be down Bolan Causeway against Gopher Hill, Jenkins still prepared for other contingencies. He left Bachman's artillery company at Pocotaligo and kept his cavalry pickets watching potential landing sites between Bee's Creek and the Combahee River. Before dawn Jenkins ordered Campbell's cavalry company to Grahamville and sent orders for Lieutenant Zealy to join Captain Peeples's troopers before Bolan Church. As Zealy recalled, the instructions were "to go and find the enemy and shoot at them."[49]

At dawn Jenkins rode to Grahamville, and while passing through the works at Bee's Creek, he ordered a second gun of Kanapaux's battery and three guns from the Beaufort Volunteer Artillery to Grahamville. Once at Grahamville, Jenkins ordered his available cavalrymen and artillerymen to begin clearing off the brush from the lunette along Bolan Causeway and directed a gun under Lieutenant E. H. Graham from Earle's Battery to join Zealy's cannons and Captain Peeples's company in resisting the Federal advance. He then rode to the railroad depot at Gopher Hill, where he joined the recently arrived Colonel Colcock.[50]

With only a brief stop in Robertville to meet with his fiancée and her family to postpone the wedding, the 3rd South Carolina's colonel had ridden all night, reaching Gopher Hill just after sunrise at about 7:00 A.M. Twenty minutes later the lead train carrying General Smith, Colonel Gonzales, and the initial elements of the units from Savannah pulled into the depot. After a brief conference, Colcock and part of his staff rode off to locate a defensive position for Smith's men. Major Jenkins and Lieutenant Thomas H. Colcock remained behind to guide the Georgians from the following train to the front. Jenkins also provided General Smith with a mount, but the first proved too spirited and the general commented that since he had "once had a stroke of paralysis," he preferred a "quiet horse." Jenkins then gave Smith his mount, "Old Rebel."

While Jenkins waited at Gopher Hill and Smith got his men in column, Colonel Colcock rode into Grahamville, where he found Captain Hal Stuart with three guns of the Beaufort Volunteer Artillery. Colcock ordered Stuart to take his guns along the Bellfield Causeway, a roadway west and parallel to Bolan Causeway. By posting Stuart on the Bellfield Causeway, Colcock could protect his southern flank and have men in a position to threaten the enemy's rear.[51]

The northerners had spent an uneasy night in their camps around Bolan Church. Few could sleep, including General Hatch, who was seen by a soldier of the 144th New York in his nightshirt, "mixing a whiskey toddy." Hatch faced a difficult decision. He knew that the lost day had given the southerners time to consolidate. No word had been received from Sherman's forces. His division, scattered between Bolan Church and Boyd's Landing, was exposed to enemy attacks from three directions and every step inland increased the distance between his soldiers and their naval support. Still, no matter what the dangers, Hatch was determined to press on. Though throughout his career superiors had questioned Hatch's administrative and tactical abilities, no one doubted his bravery and determination. Complications had denied him from reaching the railroad on the twenty-ninth, but Hatch was determined to do all he could to reach his objective on the thirtieth.[52]

But to achieve his goal, Hatch had to quickly put his force in motion at daylight. The previous day's delays haunted Hatch, who had not yet been able to consolidate his division. Only a portion of Potter's brigade at Bolan's Church was available for the immediate advance. The naval brigade spent the night at the junction of the Boyd's Landing and Coosawhatchie Roads, while the remaining units of Potter's brigade, those regiments of Hartwell's brigade that had arrived and the artillery batteries from the 3rd New York, camped at Boyd's Landing. Still missing were the 34th, 26th, and 102nd USCT Regiments and the artillery battery from the 3rd Rhode Island.

Before dawn the Federals began consolidating their forces. The naval brigade began the short march to Bolan Church. From Boyd's Landing, Colonel Hartwell forwarded the remaining portion of Potter's brigade—the 35th USCT, the remaining elements of the 32nd USCT, and the 56th New York. Once the sun rose, Hartwell followed with the two eight-company regiments, the 54th and 55th Massachusetts, and the two 3rd New York batteries to Bolan Church.

It took hours for the units to close up. When the naval brigade arrived, Hatch discovered that all but the two rifled howitzers had been furnished horses. Not wishing to be slowed by the hand-pulled guns, he sent the two horseless pieces with their crews back to the road junction, where they joined four companies of the 54th Massachusetts that Hartwell had left under Captain George Pope. By about 8:00 A.M., the two New York batteries and Hartwell, with elements from the 54th and 55th Massachusetts, arrived. Though additional formations were still absent, Hatch prepared to march down the Bolan Causeway toward Gopher Hill.[53]

After posting two companies of the 54th Massachusetts at Bolan Church, Hatch placed his men in motion. The forty horsemen from the 4th Massachusetts led the way, riding along a narrow dirt road that ran through dense woods broken by low marsh and some fields of corn and cotton. Behind the cavalrymen, in column, came Potter's brigade, led by the 127th New York, a section of Battery F, 3rd New York Artillery, the 25th Ohio, and the 157th and 144th New York Regiments. Behind them came the rest of the brigade, followed by the remaining artillery, the naval brigade, and what formations were available from Hartwell's brigade. Hatch had assigned start times for each formation. Just before 8:00 A.M., the cavalry moved out, but the tail of Hatch's column did not step off until nearly 10:00 A.M.[54]

Almost immediately the Massachusetts cavalrymen came in contact with Captain Peeples's skirmishers and Lieutenant Zealy's Napoleon. After firing three rounds into the tightly packed Federal column, Zealy pulled his gun back to the northwestern end of a causeway that traversed marshy terrain about a half mile from Bolan Church. While his forward pickets dueled with the Federals, Peeples dismounted the rest of his cavalrymen and placed them across the road in support of Zealy's cannons. Soon Lieutenant Graham and his artillerymen arrived and placed their artillery piece in the roadway to the right of Zealy's artillery piece.

Too few to drive back the enemy, the Union cavalrymen at the head of Hatch's column gave way as the 127th New York, which shifted from column to line, formed a skirmish line across the road and advanced through the woods and fields. At the head of the causeway, the solders found it bordered on the left by a swamp and on the right by an old cotton field cut by deep ditches covered with heavy grass. To support the 127th, Potter directed the 25th Ohio, still in column, to form on either side of the road behind the skirmishers and ordered the 144th New York to the right while Lieutenant Edward A. Wildt's section of two Napoleon cannons supported by the 32nd USCT took position at the causeway's northeastern end. As Wildt's guns dueled with those of Zealy and Graham, the Federal infantry deployed, taking valuable time to form into line and maneuver toward the enemy.[55]

While the Federals prepared to attack, an additional sixty Confederate cavalrymen from Companies I and B, 3rd South Carolina, joined Captain Peeples, but even with the reinforcements, the outnumbered Confederates were in danger of being overrun. Still, they kept up a spirited defense. The southern artillerymen sent solid shot into the Federal formations, slamming into bodies and ripping off limbs. Zealy concentrated his cannons against the Federals forming on the left, while Graham directed his gunners to shoot down the causeway.

The Confederates could see, behind the skirmishers of the 127th New York, the 32nd USCT forming in their front around Lieutenant Wildt's rapidly firing cannons, while the 25th Ohio stood behind the battery in column along both sides of the road. On their far left, the southerners spotted the soldiers from the 144th New York, who were crossing the ditches near the cotton field. The New Yorkers were seen leaping down into the deep furrows and then pushing their comrades up the other side. Those atop the steep slopes then reached back and pulled up their remaining companions.

Wildt's artillery, about six hundred yards from the Confederates, fired approximately seventy-five rounds while the infantry prepared to advance. At about this time, Colonel Colcock and his staff arrived. Seeing that the enemy was in force, Colcock, determining that this was their main effort, sent a courier, Owen Riley, to Captain Stuart on the Bellfield Causeway, ordering Stuart to leave one gun on the causeway and rush his remaining two pieces to the Honey Hill works. Colcock then joined Lieutenant Zealy, calling for a status report. The lieutenant, who had been concentrating his artillery piece against the 144th New York forming off to the left, anxiously answered, "Colonel, if something is not quickly done to drive back those Yankees yonder they will capture our guns." Colcock, surmising the situation, quickly gave orders to his staff to get matches and light the dried-out cotton broom and grass in the field separating the Confederate left from the advancing Federals. Soon flames, fed by a prevailing breeze, swirled toward the Yankees. Most of the New Yorkers double-quicked to the right and then, as the fire swept down a swale, hurried through the flames.[56]

While the 144th had to extend its line, the 32nd USCT charged up the causeway. Confederate shells from Lieutenant Graham's cannon overshot the advancing Federals, landing their shells in the center and rear of the attacking column, severely wounding the regiment's lieutenant colonel, Edward C. Geary. With the time he bought from firing the field, Colcock was able to retire his cannons and men before contact and, leaving behind a skirmish line to delay the Federals, repositioned his guns and cavalrymen a mile to the rear.

The Federals followed. Potter organized a heavier skirmish line under Colonel William Gurney, with Gurney's 127th New York on the left of the road, the 56th New York in the center, and the 144th on the right. Behind them on the causeway in column came the 25th Ohio and the 32nd USCT, followed by the rest of the brigade and the artillery. The reinforced skirmish line gave better protection to the following column, but it also slowed the advance.

While the Federals plodded forward, General Smith and the initial elements of his command reached the entrenchments at Honey Hill. Smith, seemingly wanting to engage the enemy in front of the works, directed his lead unit beyond the fortifications, down a gentle slope and across a wooden causeway that spanned a swollen creek, over twenty feet wide, which had flooded the area along the base of the hill. A short distance from the creek, the road took a turn to the right and continued about a quarter of a mile to the position now held by Colcock and his delaying force.

Smith rode ahead of his men and joined Colcock at the latter's second position, where the general could see the advancing enemy. Like Colcock, Smith quickly realized that this was more than a diversion and rapidly turned his soldiers around and back to the Honey Hill defenses. Before returning to his troops, Smith conferred with Colcock, informing the colonel that once the breastworks were fully manned, he would send forward infantry skirmishers to relieve the colonel and his cavalrymen. The general also told Colcock that when the time came, he would give the colonel command of the Honey Hill battle line.[57]

At the lunette next to the road, Smith arranged his formations. On the far left, behind a trench line that ran off the lunette to the north, stood the First Georgia Militia Brigade under Colonel James Willis. To their right came two regiments of Lieutenant Colonel James Wilson's Georgia State Line. Major George T. Jackson's Augusta Reserve Battalion manned the lunette, with Major F. W. C. Cook's Athens Battalion to the right of the lunette behind breastworks south of the road. The fourteen hundred Georgians quickly went to work cleaning and improving the line. They removed bushes and other growth that had come up since early 1862. Trees came down and were placed as headlogs along the top of the earthworks.[58]

While Smith's soldiers readied their fighting line, about three-quarters of a mile away, the Federals had reached Colcock's second position. The Confederate artillery again shot down the road into the advancing enemy, and again Lieutenant Wildt's artillery section deployed on the road and returned fire. At a distance of about eight hundred yards, Wildt's gunners expended twenty rounds before the southerners withdrew. During the exchange a Confederate shot struck Lieutenant Wildt in the groin, nearly severing his leg. The shot that mortally wounded Wildt continued on, killing a horse and a private. Taken to the rear, Wildt was immediately cared for by Surgeon Henry Orlando Marcy of the 35th USCT, who, with assistant medical officers from the naval brigade and the 55th Massachusetts, had established a crude triage station. Using a pocketknife, Marcy removed the fragment of flesh that still held Wildt's leg to his thigh, bound up the stump, and sent "the brave fellow to the rear where he died a few hours later."[59]

By now Confederate infantry skirmishers were coming forward, and Colcock began pulling back his cavalrymen. Colcock soon joined Colonel Gonzales, Major Jenkins, Captain Stuart, and General Smith on Honey Hill. Together the officers completed their final defensive arrangements. The cavalry under Major Jenkins was posted on the far left beyond the Georgia militia, with Captain Campbell's Company B placed at the extreme northern end of the line. Next came Captain Raysor's Company E, recently arrived from the Bee's Creek Battery, and then Captain Peeples's company. Also mixed in were elements of Companies I and C: a total of just over two hundred troopers.

South of Peeples's command came the fourteen hundred Georgia troops. Along the line were at least seven pieces of artillery. In the lunette were two cannons from the Beaufort Artillery. To the right of the road were two guns from Earle's Furman artillery. When lieutenants Zealy and Graham withdrew their pieces from the skirmish line, they joined Earle's guns at the head of the road. To bolster the far left, one of Earle's guns was placed with Campbell's troopers. The Confederate artillery consisted of hard-hitting Napoleons, whose shells could devastate enemy attacks. An eighth piece, a 6-pound gun from Earle's Battery, was present and may have been employed on the Confederate left late in the battle.

Command of the mixed battery in the immediate vicinity of the lunette went to Captain Stuart. The area in front of the lunette, cleared of trees and underbrush from the fortification to the creek, gave the cannoneers a clear field of fire. While his gunners readied their pieces, Stuart carefully paced off the distance from his cannons to the creek and then to where Bolan Causeway curved to the right before running straight toward Honey Hill. With this information, Stuart's gunners could accurately cut their fuses so their rounds of shrapnel (case shot) would explode in the enemy's ranks.[60]

By 11:00 A.M. all was ready and General Smith turned command of the battle line over to Colonel Colcock and, with some staff, including Captain Louis D. DeSaussure, took up a position along the road about seventy yards behind the lunette to direct reinforcements forward. Why Smith turned field command over to Colcock has always been a matter of conjecture. He may have felt that Colcock, knowing the territory, would prove a better field commander. Also, as a State of Georgia officer, Smith held no authority in South Carolina or over Confederate troops. But most likely the general may have feared an onset of paralysis while directing the battle and, following the example he had set at the engagement at Griswoldville, turned the battle line over to a subordinate.

Unaware of the waiting reception, Potter's brigade pressed forward, the heavy line of Federal skirmishers sweeping over the now-vacated Confederate artillery position. As they neared the point where the road curved to the left, the Federals encountered enemy infantrymen. The fighting was confused. The dense woods limited visibility from fifteen to twenty yards. On both sides of the road, resistance slowed the lead Union regiments. The terrain was described as "such a dense growth of underbrush and interlacing vines that it prevented a connected movement by the front and compelled frequent resort to an 'Indian file' movement on the part of companies." The 144th New York found itself dueling with an unseen enemy. Fighting tree to tree, the New Yorkers lost a number of officers and noncommissioned officers. The southerners concentrated heavy fire on the regiment's color guard, wounding four of the seven-man detachment but were unable to capture the 144th's flag.[61]

The colonel of the 25th Ohio directed his regiment to the right of the 144th New York. The Ohioans pressed on, seizing a road junction where a lumber trail meandered to the northeast through the woods. Next they overran an embankment being used by the enemy as a trench line. As the Federals followed the retreating southerners, the axis of their advance turned west, where they suddenly discovered the Confederates' main defense line, which one soldier described as being on top of a rise so "sweetly named" as Honey Hill.[62]

General Potter quickly deployed his lead regiments in the woods to the south, east of the swollen creek in the woods that ran along the marsh, about two hundred yards from the Confederate defense line. The five companies of the 157th New York held the extreme left, their southern flank covered by the creek and marsh that curved back toward the east. On their right came the 56th and 127th New York Regiments. Across the road were arrayed, from left to right, the 144th New York, 25th Ohio, and 32nd USCT On this compact battlefield, the Federal lines extended only a few hundred yards on either side of the road. The dense woods made it difficult for the regiments to form in line and maintain contact. As the Federal units on the right deployed in the heavy woods, their battle line bent back to the northeast, with each unit barely linking, if at all, to its neighbor.[63]

By now it was about noon. To reach their objective, the Federals had to breach the rebel line, secure the roadway, move through Grahamville, watch for enemy forces arriving from Bee's Creek, and drive on to the railroad at Gopher Hill. There was little room to maneuver, and there were no readily available routes to carry out an effective flanking movement. Potter, doing what he could, organized his brigade in front of the Confederate works. He ordered forward Captain Thomas J. Mesereau's Battery B, 3rd New York Artillery. All four guns were deployed, but only Wildt's section, now commanded by Lieutenant George H. Crocker, could be effectively employed. Crocker positioned his section in the road, just beyond the bend, a mere two to three hundred yards from the enemy. It was the only spot where they could see and fire on the Confederate entrenchments. The narrow road allowed the placement of only two guns, bronze Napoleons, hub to hub, which Crocker and his men worked furiously under concentrated enemy artillery and sharpshooter fire. For their shells to reach the Confederate position, the Federals had to elevate their guns and send their rounds through branches and tree limbs. In the midst of the exchange one of the Napoleon guns recoiled off the road into a ditch. Confederate fire exploded two ammunition chests. Lieutenant Crocker, shot in the right eye, tied a handkerchief around his head and kept up the uneven duel.[64]

While Potter hoped his regiments on the north side of the road could turn the Confederates out of their works, he brought forward the 35th USCT, directing their commander, Colonel Beecher, to fill the gap between the 127th New York on the left and the 144th on the right. Their assigned position was the most exposed on the battlefield. The Confederates, perched on Honey Hill in and around the lunette, could see the Federals forming and were ready when Colonel Beecher led his black soldiers forward. The unit, in column, advanced around the bend in the road, filling the gap between the 127th and 144th New York.

Next to the lunette, Major George T. Jackson, commander of the Augusta Reserve Battalion, watched as the cannoneers sighted and fired their guns. On the first round fired at the enemy, he commented, "If the gun had been aimed at a painted target and the shot had struck the 'bull's-eye' it would not have been any better." Soon small arms fire joined the artillery barrage, cutting down the black soldiers. Colonel Beecher, "his fine gray horse killed under him," was struck in the thigh, hand, and right groin, the last wound nearly cutting his femoral artery. The regiment surgeon treating him, Dr. Marcy, advised Beecher to leave the field, but the colonel refused. Unable to advance, the shattered regiment retired behind the artillery, where the injured Beecher and his soldiers stayed for the remainder of the battle.[65]

After the repulse of the 35th USCT, Potter kept his brigade in line, encouraging his men to keep up a steady fire on the enemy works. His options were limited. He had committed his entire brigade, along with a section of Battery F, 3rd New York Artillery. Potter still hoped his regiments on the right could find a vantage point to overrun the Confederate defenses, but the thick woods separated the regiments and broke up their cohesion.

Immediately to the right of the road, Confederate fire kept the 144th New York pinned down, but part of the regiment was able to use an old dam embankment for cover. On their right Lieutenant Colonel Haughton, with no opposition in his immediate front, moved the 25th Ohio forward through the woods toward the swamp. After sending forward a scouting party, Haughton learned that the enemy flank might be pressed. Orders went out for the regiment to make a half-change of front, pivoting to the left. The movement carried the Ohioans out of the woods and beyond the 144th New York and forward about a hundred yards to the edge of the swamp. Unable to cross the quagmire, the Federals engaged the southerners in a severe firefight. To the right of the 25th Ohio, the 32nd USCT deployed, and when Haughton shifted to the left, Colonel Baird directed his regiment to follow. As they swung to the southwest, the black soldiers advanced to the edge of the wide, marshy morass. Across the bog the soldiers saw, through heavy undergrowth, "an abrupt rise of ground crowned with an earthwork." Separated from their enemy by only a short distance, the 32nd USCT kept up a rapid fire but could not advance.[66]

By now General Hatch had established his headquarters just east of the bend in the road. From here Hatch and his staff directed arriving units to the front and oversaw the distribution of ammunition and evacuation of the wounded. Posted nearby was Preble's naval brigade. Though Preble and his men wanted to join the battle, they remained in reserve, with the sailor infantry turning back stragglers. At about noon Hatch dispatched the marines to reinforce the right. Lieutenant Stoddard led his men behind Crocker's rapid-firing battery along the wood road, initially taking up a position behind the 25th Ohio. When that regiment advanced and shifted to the left, the marines filed to the right, beyond the 32nd USCT, and formed in battle line at the extreme right of the Union line.[67]

From their vantage point atop Honey Hill, the southerners could easily view the enemy units as they deployed. When Federal units came forward, the Confederates directed their artillery, rifle, and carbine fire against the attackers, sometimes enfilading the Union line. General Smith, a short distance behind the line, controlled the distribution of reinforcements. Colonel Colcock initially remained in the lunette, overseeing the defense of the roadway. On the left Major Jenkins maneuvered his dismounted cavalry along the breastworks, occasionally relocating his men to meet enemy strikes. Captain Stuart controlled the artillery in the center, his cannons sweeping the area along the roadway, while Colonel Gonzales rode along the battle line, giving advice as needed.

On the extreme northern end of the Confederate line, Jenkins's cavalrymen, firing both to the left and right, discharged their weapons so rapidly that they often had to cease fire to let the barrels cool. However, early in the battle, the gun crew serving the single artillery piece supporting the dismounted troopers accidentally jammed a projectile in the gun's barrel, rendering it useless. Though his forces were able to turn back all threats, Jenkins constantly worried that should the Federals overrun his line, they could roll up the Confederate position north to south. Early in the fight, Jenkins sent two couriers to General Smith requesting help and more ammunition. Smith replied that Jenkins could have one more field piece, but he had no men to spare. Still worried that his line would be breached, Jenkins turned command over to Captain Campbell and rode to see General Smith. Arriving at the lunette, Jenkins met with Colonel Colcock, who advised the major to dismount so as not to attract the fire of enemy sharpshooters. Jenkins declined but quickly realized the danger when a bullet passed between him and his horse's neck. Soon the Union sharpshooter responsible for the mayhem was shot from his perch in a tree, and Jenkins rode on to meet General Smith, who again informed Jenkins that he had no troops to spare. His only reserves were the recently arrived 47th Georgia, whom he kept ready to plug any gaps in case the militia should break under enemy pressure.[68]

As Jenkins headed back to his troopers, the Federals again pressed forward against the Confederate center. In the early afternoon, Colonel Alfred Hartwell brought forward elements of his brigade—eight companies of the 55th Massachusetts under Lieutenant Colonel Charles B. Fox and two companies of the 54th Massachusetts led by Lieutenant Colonel Henry N. Hooper. Left behind were six companies of the 54th guarding road junctions, and yet to arrive were the 102nd, 34th, and 26th USCT Regiments. Hartwell found the roadway congested. As he neared the front, he was directed to deploy his brigade in support of the 35th USCT behind the artillery.

While forming his men, orders arrived for a portion of Hartwell's brigade to support Lieutenant Colonel Stewart L. Woodford's 127th New York. Lieutenant Colonel Hooper filed his two companies to the left and placed them on the left front of the 127th. Hooper ordered the soldiers to lie down, conserve their ammunition, and await developments. Though the Federal high command worried about their left flank, Woodford, who had assumed leadership of the 127th when Colonel Gurney took charge of the skirmishers, believed his regiment had an opportunity to break the Confederate line in his front where the enemy's trench line curved down from the lunette close to the marsh. Woodford sent word to Potter stating that his New Yorkers could sweep up the hill and flank the lunette if a regiment on his right could support the attack.

The suggestion was accepted and instructions came to Hartwell from Captain George E. Gouraud, an aide to General Foster serving on Hatch's staff. Hartwell initially moved his eight companies forward in line, but enemy fire drove them back. The initial advance had gone in without support from Crocker's artillery. Casualties, overheated guns, and lack of ammunition had silenced the battery, and with their horses killed or wounded, the cannoneers could not withdraw guns. Lieutenant Edgar H. Titus had been directed to bring forward his company, Battery F, 3rd New York Artillery, but as yet they had not arrived, and any renewed assault would have to go in without artillery support.

Undaunted, Hartwell re-formed the 55th Massachusetts into column, but during the previous advance, three companies under Lieutenant Colonel Fox had veered off to the north behind the 144th New York, mingling with that regiment's right flank and the left of the 25th Ohio, resulting in black and white soldiers fighting side by side, a rarity for the times. The departure of Fox's detachment left Hartwell with only five companies, some three hundred men, to support the 127th New York. In his first attempt to charge up the road, concentrated enemy fire drove Hartwell's column back. Though wounded in the hand, Hartwell, with the help of Captain Gouraud, rallied his men. Gouraud, who would receive the Medal of Honor for his actions on the battlefield that day, helped Hartwell re-form the companies into a double column for a second charge. The regiment's color guard was placed at the head of the column, and Hartwell with his aides, Captain William Crane and Lieutenant Edwin R. Hill, conspicuously mounted on their horses, took positions at the front.[69]

Inside the lunette Captain Stuart had kept his cannoneers busy flinging shells into the Federal formations. At about 2:00 p.m., Major Ferdinand Cook of the Athens Battalion, stationed in the lunette, informed Stuart that he could see the Federals forming for an attack up the road. Stuart quickly readied his guns. He initially had them loaded with shrapnel, with fuses cut to explode the case shot at the bend in the road. Once fired, his artillerymen were then to load with double canister and fire their cannons as quickly as possible.[70]

With the five companies of the 55th Massachusetts re-formed, Hartwell led them forward. He later wrote that the men "cheerfully" followed. As they rounded the bend with Hartwell, Crane, and Hill riding in front, Captain Crane cried out, "Come on boys, they are only Georgia militia!" The soldiers came on cheering and yelling. Immediately cannon and rifle fire ripped into the column. Captain Crane was killed, and Lieutenant Hill was knocked to the ground. Artillery fragments hit Colonel Harwell and his horse was killed. Major Jenkins later wrote that Hartwell's mount was shot by one of his troopers, Thomas J. Giradeau, using a telescopic rifle and detailed as a sharpshooter. Hartwell, wounded and pinned under his horse, lost consciousness, but his soldiers, cheering madly, continued on. Lieutenant Winthrop Boynton, commander of the lead company, was wounded and knocked down; he stood up, waved his sword, and urged his men forward before being struck again and killed. Unknown to Boynton, he had been promoted to captain just a few days earlier. He fell near his close friend Captain Crane. The two had been nearly inseparable in life and now shared the same site in death.

Somehow a portion of the attackers crossed the bridge and moved up the slope toward the enemy works. The Confederate fire intensified. An artillery shell mangled the foot of Sergeant Charles L. Mitchel. While being carried to the rear, he encouraged his comrades to fight on. Sergeant Major James M. Trotter and Sergeant John F. Shorter, both nominated to become officers, were wounded, as was Captain Soule, who had spent Thanksgiving at Coffin Point on St. Helena Island with his friend Captain Crane. The color guard had somehow managed to escape the initial fuselage, but now, as they crossed the creek and neared the southern defense line, enemy fire began taking its toll. Color Sergeant Robert King, only eighteen years old, bore the national colors forward until he was torn apart by an artillery shell. Corporal Andrew Smith immediately seized the flag and maintained it throughout the charge. For his actions Smith was promoted to color sergeant and eventually awarded the Medal of Honor.

The charge lasted less than ten minutes. It was reported that some of the black soldiers had come to within twenty yards of the enemy fortifications before being driven back. Two-thirds of the attackers were killed or wounded. Forced to retreat, the men gathered up their wounded. Under heavy enemy fire, Private Elijah Thomas and Lieutenant Thomas F. Ellsworth of Company B managed to extract Colonel Hartwell from under his dead horse. Thomas fell mortally wounded, but Ellsworth dragged his colonel to safety, an act that would gain him the Medal of Honor. As the soldiers from the 55th retreated, the Confederates emerged from their defense line and charged down the road until driven back. The remnants of Hartwell's column re-formed beyond the bend in the road, rallying on Corporal Smith and the national colors. Still under enemy fire, the regiment continued to take casualties. Among those wounded was Private John H. Patterson, a member of the color guard who carried the state flag. Smith, who stood next to Patterson, quickly seized the state colors and with both standards maintained a prominent position on the field.[71]

Though the attack failed, it had kept the attention of the Confederates in and around the lunette concentrated on the roadway. This gave Lieutenant Colonel Woodford and the soldiers of the 127th New York the opportunity to move forward, through the swamp and across the stream breaching the Confederate line. Swinging to the right, the New Yorkers worked their way through the bog, using roots and brush to pull themselves up the slope, where a portion of the regiment gained a foothold near the top of the hill.

The appearance of the Federals cresting Honey Hill on the Confederate right threatened to dissolve the Confederate line. The Georgia militia and reserves, steady behind breastworks, might panic and break once flanked. General Smith, worried that such a scenario might occur, had kept Colonel Aaron C. Edwards's 47th Georgia in reserve to stop any breakthroughs. Smith quickly gave orders for Edwards to counterattack. The Georgians scrambled off to the right and, in a series of advances, drove the New Yorkers back, regained the lost parapet, and forced the enemy across the creek. The battered New Yorkers re-formed and Colonel Gurney, who had commanded the skirmish line, returned to his regiment and had his men take up a position lying down in front of the artillery and to the south side of the road.[72]

After the failure of the 55th Massachusetts and 127th New York to break the enemy line, the Federals settled down to exchanging fire with the entrenched Confederates. While action continued along the approaches to Honey Hill, smaller engagements occurred in the Federal rear at the junction of the Boyd's Landing and Coosawhatchie Roads. Earlier in the day, while elements of the 2nd Brigade advanced toward the front, Colonel Hartwell, finding the junction unguarded, left behind four companies of the 54th Massachusetts under Captain George Pope. After sending out skirmishers, Pope had his men build a breastwork facing north across the Coosawhatchie Road. Pope was soon joined by Lieutenant Colonel William W. Marple's 34th USCT (the former 2nd South Carolina), which had finally come ashore at Boyd's Landing, and by the two naval boat howitzers returning from Bolan

Church. The cannons, under Acting Ensign John A. Edgren, had not been provided with horse transportation and had been sent back by Hatch from Bolan Church. Dragged by their gun crews, the howitzers silently came forward. At about 10:00 A.M., the Federal pickets reported that Confederate cavalry was approaching. The skirmishers pulled back, and as enemy sharpshooters began to pepper the entrenchment, Edgren discharged his cannons. Shrapnel ripped into the cavalrymen, who immediately retreated. After this skirmish Captain Pope, leaving Colonel Marple's command at the road junction, moved his companies to Bolan Church, where he joined two other companies of the 54th Massachusetts and then broke for lunch.[73]

At about noon General Foster, still exercising command over units in the area around his headquarters at Boyd's Landing, sent orders to Lieutenant Colonel Marple to advance north along the Coosawhatchie Road and seize the junction of the Grahamville and Coosawhatchie Roads. Marple, accompanied by Ensign Edgren and one of the boat howitzers, marched his regiment north about two miles, where they encountered dismounted cavalry and two pieces of artillery located behind earthworks. As the black soldiers advanced, the southerners fell back but continued to skirmish with Marple's regiment for another three miles. Marple, fearing that he might be moving too deeply into enemy territory, stationed the majority of his regiment with the boat howitzer along the road and continued on with his skirmishers until they engaged the Confederates stationed in the Bee's Hill Battery. Coming under heavy enemy fire, Marple pulled his skirmishers back to his main line and remained in position until ten o'clock that night, when he received an order from General Foster to withdraw to Boyd's Landing Road.[74]

While Lieutenant Colonel Marple advanced toward Bee's Creek, Colonel Chipman marched his regiment, the 102nd USCT, from Boyd's Landing past Lieutenant Colonel Pope's men at Bolan Church and on toward Honey Hill. Arriving at about 1:30 P.M., Chipman was ordered to hold his Michigan soldiers in reserve near the sailor infantry and boat howitzers. Chipman, who had become the 2nd Brigade's senior officer upon Hartwell's wounding, was not informed that he was in charge of the brigade for more than two more hours.

At Bolan Church, before Captain Pope and his men from the 54th Massachusetts could finish their lunch, they heard intense fire originating from the west. Pope quickly put his men on the road at the double quick. As they neared Hatch's headquarters, they received orders to move up to the artillery and join the attack. Pope continued on but found ambulances, caissons, and wagons blocking the way, making it impossible for the column to maintain its cohesion.[75]

As the men from the 54th came forward, they saw black soldiers from the 102nd USCT retrieving the cannons of Crocker's Battery B, 3rd New York. Because of heavy casualties among the cannoneers and the loss of most of their horses, the artillerymen had managed to remove only one gun, leaving three on the field exposed to enemy fire. The division's artillery commander, Lieutenant Colonel Ames, requested that Colonel Chipman provide soldiers to haul off the guns. Initially Captain Arod E. Lindsay and men from his company were detailed, but before they could reach the cannons, Lindsay was killed and his subordinate Lieutenant Henry H. Alvord severely wounded. The soldiers, unaware of their task, filed past the guns and took a position in the woods out of the enemy's direct fire on the right side of the road. Before another attempt was made to remove the cannons, Colonel Chipman formed his regiment in line of battle, its left across the road behind and to the right of the abandoned guns. He then sent forward First Lieutenant Orson W. Bennett, brother of Hatch's chief of staff, and his company to bring in the artillery pieces. Bennett and thirty men advanced a hundred yards under intense enemy fire and manhandled the cannons back to safety, where they were hooked to horse-drawn limbers and taken to the rear. For his actions Lieutenant Bennett received the Congressional Medal of Honor.[76]

While the black soldiers pulled off the abandoned guns, Lieutenant Titus's Battery F, 3rd New York Artillery, came forward at the gallop to replace the now-secured guns of Battery B. Titus's limbers, caissons, and four Napoleons sliced past Pope's command, separating the captain from the majority of his men. Pope, with only nine soldiers, came up by Titus's battery. From here he could see the dead of the 55th from the unsuccessful charge littering the roadway. Enemy fire soon cut down two of his comrades, including Lieutenant David Reid. Pope and his remaining men joined Colonel Beecher's 35th USCT to the left and rear of Titus's battery.[77]

The rest of Pope's column, now commanded by Captain William H. Homans, took a position in the woods on the right of the 35th USCT. Nearby, Titus's battery frantically engaged the enemy, "but the gunners had a hard time of it." The first shot from the battery immediately "drew down such a storm that nearly everyman serving it was wounded." One observer saw two cannons disabled, horses struck down, and an officer using his sword to pitch powder charges from a burning caisson just before it exploded.[78]

Though he still had reserves, Hatch fed no more units into combat. By mid-afternoon regiment after regiment began running out of cartridges. On the far left, the 157th New York had to be pulled from the battle line and brought back to the road to receive more ammunition. A wing of the 56th New York shifted to the south to man the vacated area. The Confederates watching the maneuvering came out of their trenches to pressure the Federal flank, but they were driven off when the 157th New York, with their ammunition replenished, hurried back to their old position.[79]

Hatch's right flank also required additional ammunition. The 25th Ohio had to cease its attempt to breach the Confederate defenses when they ran low on cartridges. At the far end of the line, the marine battalion also expended their rounds but managed to keep up the fight when their acting quartermaster sergeant, Sergeant Jeremiah Cogley, braved enemy fire to retrieve and bring forward ammunition.[80]

While Hatch did not commit any of his reserves, some his subordinates felt there still might be an opportunity to break the enemy line. On the northern flank, marines scouting to the right found no enemy. Closer to the road, to the left, Lieutenant Colonel Hooper scouted the ground in his front and sent two messages to General Hatch urging an attack against the Confederate right, but Hatch refused.[81]

Though the Federals had ceased their attempts to break through the Confederate position, they kept up a steady fire on their opponents, forcing the Southerners to maintain vigilance all along their line. Major Jenkins, still worried that the enemy would sweep around the northern flank, directed a portion of Captain Campbell's Company B to shift farther to the left. The cavalrymen manned detached earthworks and rifle pits, from which they continued to pour fire down upon the Federals. When Campbell warned Jenkins that the extreme left might be in danger, he received instructions to spread his men out along the line and occupy the lunette at the far end of the line. Campbell sent Sergeant Malichi P. Hiott to secure the lunette, but no enemy ever threatened the northern tip of the Confederate defense line.[82]

By now the Federals were worried about whether they could maintain their positions until nightfall. The inability to resupply front-line formations with cartridges had become critical. Lieutenant Colonel Haughton, his regiment's ammunition nearly expended, pulled the 25th Ohio from the battle line. Believing his left unsupported, about-faced his men and moved slowly back to the junction of the wood road and the Bolan Church Causeway, taking up a position near the artillery. Before withdrawing, Haughton notified Colonel Baird on his right of his intention, and Baird had no choice but also to retire his regiment. With the 25th Ohio and the 32nd USCT pulling back, the marines also had to move farther to the rear and eventually rejoin the naval brigade. By about 3:30 Hatch had received and issued six thousand cartridges, but he planned no more advances. He ordered Titus's battery, which was down to twenty rounds per gun, to be replaced in the road by two howitzers from the naval brigade.[83]

Each passing hour meant more time for Confederate reinforcements to reach the field. By 4:30 an additional train arrived from the north with Brigadier General Beverley Robertson, the 32nd Georgia, two companies of Bluffton native Captain Manning J. Kirk's cavalry squadron, and Company D, 2nd South Carolina Artillery, a battery of light artillery under Captain William E. Charles also known as the Inglis Artillery. Because of his rank, Robertson assumed command of the Confederate forces, but other than sending Kirk's men to join Jenkins on the Confederate left, Robertson took no offensive action and held the reinforcements in reserve.[84]

At dusk Hatch ordered Potter to commence a withdrawal. A heavy fog came over the battlefield. Potter kept the 127th New York on the left of the naval howitzers while the 102nd USCT stood on the right. The sailor cannoneers maintained a slow fire on the Confederate defenses. Half a mile to the rear Potter positioned a second rear guard across the road consisting of a section of Titus's battery with the 144th and 56th New York in support. While the preparations for retreat were underway, the Union soldiers gathered up the wounded, placing some in ambulances, while others were carried away on makeshift litters composed of blankets tied between two muskets. Once the rear guards were in place, the remaining regiments began withdrawing, first those on the left and then those on the right. As they filed to the rear, Potter prepared a third position held by the 25th Ohio and 157th New York a mile east of the 144th and 56th New York. Once the soldiers had passed the third defense line at about 7:30, word was sent for the 127th New York, the 102nd USCT, and the naval howitzers to leave the battlefield. Thirty minutes after they cleared, the second line of soldiers from the 144th and 56th New York withdrew. As they moved away, a member of the 144th recalled that a rebel band began playing Beethoven's "Funeral March."[85]

While most of the Federals continued on to the road junction of the Coosawhatchie and Boyd's Landing Roads, Potter remained at Bolen Church with the 144th New York, the 32nd USCT, and Mersereau's battery as the rest of the troops marched by. The church, converted into a hospital, presented an eerie site. Nestled "among the moss-hung oaks," the structure was surrounded by large fires of fence rails and brush. The church's pews, taken out of the structure, lay scattered about the yard mixed in with abandoned supplies. Around the church, in full view of the retreating soldiers, were surgeons performing amputations on makeshift operating tables. As described by a member of the 127th New York: "On passing the church which had been used as a hospital during the engagement we saw a large pile of arms and legs which had been sawed off by practicing surgeons."

The church was full, and outside hundreds of wounded were packed "as thick as they could lie." No ambulances were available and the black soldiers of the 26th USCT, who had not arrived in time to participate in the fight but did come up in time to serve as stretcher bearers, were divided into squads of four men each, who "tenderly" carried the injured on to Boyd's Landing. It was described as "a fearful journey for both. Six miles in the dark."[86]

Once back to the makeshift wharf, the men were placed on the hospital vessel *Cosmopolitan*. The ship shuttled the casualties to the hospital on Hilton Head and the medical facilities at Beaufort. Wounded white soldiers were debarked at Hilton Head, while the injured blacks were sent to Beaufort.

Laura Towne reported that the people on the islands saw "a great column of smoke" used to announce the arrival in Beaufort of "hundreds of wounded." Officers were placed in the Edgar Fripp House in Beaufort. Civilians, officer's wives, and freedmen rushed to the hospitals to aid the wounded, including Colonel Beecher's wife, Frances, known as "Frankie," who came up from Jacksonville to tend to her husband and other wounded soldiers.[87]

By the morning of December 1, the Federals started entrenching around the junction of Boyd's Landing and Coosawhatchie Roads with the naval guns arranged to cover the approaches from Bolan Church. Joined by the 26th and 34th USCT and Hamner's Battery, Hatch finally had his entire division together. Before noon the Massachusetts cavalrymen and two companies of the 127th New York returned to Bolan Church, where they buried the amputated limbs, destroyed any abandoned military gear, and then on their return gathered up livestock and burned the bridges between Bolan Church and Boyd's Landing Road.[88]

Even though they had received reinforcements, the southerners did not pursue the retreating Federals. Captain John H. Howard, the volunteer militiaman and master of Whitehall, went forward and brought back a prisoner, who informed his captors that the Federals had been badly cut up. But even with this information, the southerners did not follow. Content with their tidy tactical victory, they waited until morning before venturing beyond their lines. Losses were minimal. General Smith listed them at 8 killed and 42 wounded; later reports reduced this to 4 killed and 40 wounded. Others placed the casualties between 80 and 100, though both sets of numbers seemed too few and may only reflect the casualties from Smith's Georgia units. One officer, Captain Benjamin S. Williams, who commanded a portion of the 47th Georgia in its counterattack against the 127th New York, reported losses of 30 men. A more accurate count for Confederate casualties would be approximately 200 of just over 2,200 engaged.[89]

The Federals, who sent into battle just under 4,000 men, suffered between 700 and 760 casualties. General Foster reported 88 killed, 623 wounded, and 43 missing, a total of 754, while Hatch listed the same number killed but reported 629 wounded and only 28 missing for a total of 745. A number of valuable and experienced officers were among the casualties. Foster, however, was quick to point out that 140 of his wounded were so lightly injured that they never left their regiment's ranks. A newspaper listing of regimental losses reported:

Unit	Killed	Wounded	Missing	Total
25th Ohio	20	118	0	138
56th NY	6	14	0	20
127th NY	5	41	0	46

(continued)

Unit	Killed	Wounded	Missing	Total
144th NY	17	50	0	67
157th NY	0	30	0	30
32nd USCT	8	56	0	64
35th USCT	7	107	0	114
54th Mass	2	37	4	43
55th Mass	29	108	0	137
102nd USCT	3	20	0	23
Artillery	2	12	0	14
Naval Brigade	1	11	0	12
34th USCT	0	5	0	5
Cavalry	0	1	0	1
Total	100	610	4	714

ORA, 44: 420, 425; Trudeau, *Voices of the Fifty-fifth,* 220; Soule, "Honey Hill," *Philadelphia Weekly Times,* May 10, 1884; *New York Tribune,* December 9, 1864.

That evening additional Confederate forces arrived under the command of Brigadier General James Chesnut. A former U.S. senator and signer of the South Carolina ordnance of secession, Chesnut had helped write the Confederate constitution. Early in the war he served as an aide to General Beauregard and Jefferson Davis before joining the ruling executive council of South Carolina and heading up the state's military department. Better known as the husband of the Civil War diarist Mary Boykin Chesnut, the forty-nine-year-old politician and statesman accepted a commission in the fall of 1862 as a colonel and special representative of the president. Promoted to brigadier general in April 1864, Chesnut took command of the South Carolina Reserves, a force of men either too old or exempt from the draft who could be mustered to bolster the state's defenses. When the Federal forces initially landed at Boyd's Landing, Chesnut and his 1,000 reservists were sent by rail from Augusta to Grahamville to protect the Charleston and Savannah Railroad. After delays Chesnut, with a vanguard of 350 men, arrived at midnight on December 1.[90]

Other Confederate reinforcements who began arriving by train before dawn the next morning at Gopher Hill consisted of the lead elements of Brigadier General Laurence S. Baker's brigade of North Carolina Reserves. The thirty-four-year-old Baker, who graduated last in the U.S. Military Academy class of 1851, had had a successful career serving in the Army of Northern Virginia's cavalry forces with the 1st North Carolina Cavalry until a severe wound during the Gettysburg Campaign forced him to take medical leave for nearly a year. He was then assigned to an administrative position in North Carolina. Given command of a brigade of North Carolina Reserves,

Baker and his men had been sent to Augusta from Wilmington, where they joined Chesnut's South Carolinians in guarding the city against a possible strike by Sherman's forces. Once the Federal threat failed to materialize, the two commands were dispatched to Grahamville.[91]

Though the reinforcements secured the railroad, General Bragg in Augusta directed General Jones in Charleston to "send everything you can to Grahamville, so as to crush out the enemy in our front there," and then be ready to meet Sherman's advancing forces. But General Hardee, who arrived at Grahamville on December 1, saw the situation differently. Elated with the victory at Honey Hill, Hardee allowed Smith to take his Georgia militia back to Savannah, and since he expected the Federals to evacuate and return to the sea islands, he made plans to shift the majority of the troops around Grahamville to Georgia. Hardee instructed Colonel Colcock to take a company of cavalry and some artillery and return to watching the Savannah River crossings. The assignment also gave Colcock the opportunity on December 3 to complete his nuptials at Robertville to Agnes M. Bostick.[92]

The day after the fight, the southerners inspected the battlefield. The effect of the mass artillery fire was evident in front of the lunette. General Baker commented that he "never in any previous battle seen such evidence of terrible havoc from artillery." Another observer believed that the cannon fire would have stopped a rabbit from crossing the road. In one place the bodies of six black soldiers were piled one on top of the other. Dead floated in the creek, and the road leading to the lunette was strewn with bodies that had been horribly mutilated, many missing heads or disemboweled. Lieutenant Zealy simply wrote, "They lay five deep dead as a mackerel."[93]

The Confederates swarmed over the battlefield. They found evidence of the northerners pulling off their wounded and dead. One officer wrote, "Many traces were left where they were dragged from the woods to the road, and thrown into ambulances or carts." The southerners gathered up badly needed goods and stripped the dead of equipment, accoutrements, shoes, and uniforms. Among the items gleaned from the battlefield was Colonel Hartwell's saddle, which was presented to Captain Stuart.[94]

The victory raised spirits but also troubled the southerners. Time was running out on the old ways of the Beaufort District. Numerous ominous signs were apparent. Over half their opponents had been black soldiers, many former slaves and some former South Carolina slaves. Confederate officers tried to dismiss the bravery of the black soldiers by suggesting that they were drunk or driven into battle at the point of bayonets. While the white Federals killed on the field were buried in shallow graves, the southerners, after stripping the dead black soldiers of their clothing, left the bodies to rot. Planters, some from a great distance, brought their slaves to the battlefield to show them the exposed dead, emphasizing the folly of running away and joining the Federal army. Also, though in contradiction of government orders, two of three prisoners from the 54th Massachusetts were executed; the one spared was a former slave from South Carolina, who expressed a desire to return to his home state. By this point in the war, such actions were uncalled for, but old attitudes and racial views died hard. A way of life was ending, and a noose was tightening around the Confederacy, the state of South Carolina, and the Beaufort District. In a matter of months, it would close.[95]

Chapter 14

Battles of Tulifinney

"In that New Jerusalem"

The South's euphoria after the victory at Honey Hill was short lived. The same day that the Federals were defeated at Honey Hill, General John Bell Hood wrecked the Army of Tennessee at Franklin, Tennessee. Local victories such as Honey Hill could do little to relieve the Confederacy's desperate situation. To coordinate the defense against both Sherman's marauding army and the forces operating along the southeastern seaboard, Jefferson Davis expanded General Beauregard's command to include the Georgia and South Carolina coast, placing him over Hardee and Bragg. Upon receiving the order, Beauregard immediately left Macon for Charleston. Before the new commander could arrive, General Hardee realized that the Federals at Boyd's Landing were not following their usual pattern after a defeat of withdrawing to Beaufort and Hilton Head; instead they were improving their defenses and preparing to continue the campaign.

Charged with protecting Savannah, Hardee had to contest Sherman's march and guard his communications via the Charleston and Savannah Railroad. To assist Colcock in the upper regions of the Savannah River, Hardee dispatched the warship *Macon,* a 150-foot-long, six-gun, twin-screw gunboat built at Savannah during the war to Two Sisters Ferry. On December 3 Hardee directed General Jones to send the battalion of the South Carolina Military Academy cadets from Charleston to Grahamville. The battalion, under the school's headmaster, Major James B. White, comprised two companies: B, made up of first-year cadets from the arsenal in Columbia, and A, the upper classmen from the Citadel in Charleston. The next day Hardee ordered General Jones to leave Charleston and take command of the troops guarding the railroad.[1]

Jones arrived from Charleston on the evening of December 5, 1864, and was not pleased with what he found, complaining to Hardee,

> I was not informed as to the number, description, or location of the troops in that vicinity, and immediately endeavored to obtain information on

those points. I ascertained that the troops, with the exception of the Fifth and Forty-seventh Georgia regiments, a battalion of the Thirty-second Georgia regiment, the artillery, a part of the Third South Carolina Cavalry, and Kirk's squadron, were composed of Georgia and South Carolina reserves and South Carolina militia, and occupied positions extending from Pocotaligo to the Savannah River, and up that river beyond Sister's Ferry. Those at and near Grahamville were commanded by Brigadier General Chesnut; those at and near Coosawhatchie, by Brigadier General Gartrell. They had arrived but a few days previously, and until my arrival were under the immediate orders of the Lt. General commanding [Hardee], or other officers under him. The reserves were very imperfectly organized, and the militia without organization, and many of the men were without arms.[2]

Jones's ranking subordinates, Generals James Chesnut Jr. and Lucius J. Gartrell, had similar backgrounds. Like Chesnut, Gartrell had limited combat experience. A forty-three-year-old Georgia lawyer, he had raised the 7th Georgia Infantry Regiment and served as its colonel at First Manassas before being elected to the Confederate House of Representatives, where he was a consistent backer of Jefferson Davis's policies. In August 1864 he was commissioned a brigadier general and given command of a brigade of Georgia reserves before being assigned to duty at Coosawhatchie. Jones prepared his defenses by placing a troop train at Coosawhatchie and ordering Brigadier General Chesnut to keep the 47th Georgia Regiment and a section of artillery at Coosawhatchie, ready to board at any moment and be thrown to any threatened point.[3]

To assist Jones, Bragg sent from Augusta the Georgia cavalry brigade of Brigadier General Pierce Manning Butler Young. The commander of the depleted brigade, which consisted of 250 mounted and 550 dismounted troopers, was born in Spartanburg, South Carolina, grew up in Georgia, and attended the Georgia Military Institute. He briefly studied law before being appointed to the U.S. Military Academy. When Georgia seceded, he resigned before graduating and served with the Army of Northern Virginia's cavalry, rising from the rank of second lieutenant to brigadier general. In late November the twenty-eight-year-old general and his brigade had arrived in Georgia from Virginia for remounting, refitting, and service against Sherman's armies. Once the initial threat to Augusta had passed, Bragg sent Young and his troopers to Pocotaligo, where Jones reassigned them to Hardeeville and positions guarding the crossings of the Savannah River above Savannah.[4]

While the Confederates anxiously watched as Sherman's armies approached Savannah, they also kept a close eye on the Federal troops at Boyd's

Landing, where General Hatch showed no signs of withdrawing. On December 2, while his skirmishers dueled with the enemy and the two sides exchanged artillery fire, Hatch had his men improve the defensive line at the junction of the Boyd's Landing and Coosawhatchie Roads. The soldiers felled trees and in low areas brought additional dirt to build more substantial trenches. Still hoping to attract the attention of the Federal forces in Georgia, which he thought might be close, Hatch launched rockets and balloons and burned calcium lights in futile attempts to attract the attention of Sherman's columns.[5]

Over the next few days, Foster and Hatch kept their forces in motion while they contemplated their next move. On the third, while the defensive works were extended beyond the Coosawhatchie Road, the 32nd and 102nd USCT, and part of the 55th Massachusetts with two 10-pound Parrots from Battery A, 3rd Rhode Island, challenged the Confederates near Bolan Church. The next day an expedition consisting of the 34th and 35th USCT, 144th New York, and artillery advanced south along the Coosawhatchie Road to the enemy battery at Euhaw Church. The gunboats *Pawnee* and *Sonoma* supported the movements by sailing up the Coosawhatchie River. General Foster outfitted his infantry with rockets so that they could communicate with the warships. In one of the few cases recorded during the Civil War of indirect fire, the vessels ranged their guns against the battery by direction of artillery spotters located in tall pine trees. The observers relayed messages to the men on the ground who signaled the ships. One rocket meant, "Enemy in front; do not fire to the left of this." Two rockets fired together indicated, "You are firing too far to the left." Three simultaneous rockets: "Shots fall too short." And four rockets together: "Shots too far over." Shallow water limited the vessel's ability to shadow the troops and the effectiveness of the indirect bombardment was unreported, but the Federals did secure the battery before withdrawing to their entrenchments at the Boyd's Landing Road.[6]

On the same day that the expedition moved against the Euhaw Church battery, the 25th Ohio embarked on the transports *Nemaha* (Foster's flagship) and the *Plato,* and accompanied by the navy's armed tug *Daffodil,* the troops were carried into the Pocotaligo River, coming ashore at 11:00 A.M. at a landing just north of Bray's Island. The Ohioans quickly marched inland and seized from the rear a Confederate work at Church Bridge on the west side of Huspah Creek. The approximately forty southerners manning the garrison fled into the woods, leaving behind two 24-pound howitzers. The Federals spiked one and dragged the other to Port Royal Ferry, where the regiment reembarked on their transports and returned to Boyd's Landing.[7]

On December 5, while naval launches operated in the creeks around Boyd's Landing, Foster and Hatch sent the 55th Massachusetts with two naval howitzers on a diversion to Bolen Church, while General Potter led a portion of his brigade with Battery F, 3rd New York Artillery, toward Bee's Creek. As the Massachusetts soldiers drove in Confederate pickets near Bolan Church, Potter moved his brigade south along the Coosawhatchie Road past Euhaw Church. As they neared the Confederate defenses at the junction of Coosawhatchie and Grahamville Roads, Potter had his lead regiment, Colonel James C. Carmichael's 157th New York, deploy as skirmishers.

The New Yorkers worked their way through a tangled forest before coming to an open field in front of what seemed to be an abandoned battery. Potter ordered Carmichael to push on, but the colonel suspected a ruse and halted his men about a hundred yards from the work and then rode out with three cavalrymen to investigate. A few enemy horsemen were seen, and as the colonel and his companions neared the fortification, "the redoubt suddenly was alive with Johnnies, who poured a heavy volley into the colonel and his escorts." The colonel and his escort turned and "spurred to rear," one mortally wounded. Carmichael's horse was struck and reared, throwing him over his horse's head on to the ground. The Federal skirmishers laid down a covering fire on the battery. Two men were detailed to go out and bring the colonel to safety. Carmichael, untouched by the enemy fire, had been badly hurt when his sabre, swinging under him, cut into his spine, an injury from which he never fully recovered.[8]

With Carmichael carried to safety, Potter quickly brought up his artillery and fired into the Confederate works but did not advance. During the exchange a southern soldier managed to come into the Federal lines. He turned out to be a "galvanized Yankee," a former Union soldier who with others had volunteered to serve in the Confederate army to escape the ravages of the Andersonville prisoner-of-war camp. The man, who claimed to be one of many northerners serving in the 47th Georgia, warned the Federals that the Confederates had prepared an ambush. Armed with this information, Potter withdrew his men back to Boyd's Landing.[9]

In actuality, the advance toward Coosawhatchie was merely an elaborate diversion. As Potter led his men south, Foster and Dahlgren, not wishing to abandon the campaign, explored the Tullifinny River, which with the Coosawhatchie formed a peninsula known as DeVeaux's Neck, over which the railroad passed on bridges spanning both rivers. Dahlgren had always looked favorably on an attack up the neck, where a small force could have its flanks covered by the two streams. General Foster readily agreed, and upon returning to Boyd's Landing the two officers began making preparations to continue their operations.[10]

At about 1:00 A.M. on December 6, regiments from Potter's brigade, along with the naval brigade, began withdrawing from the fortifications at the junction of the Boyd's Landing and Coosawhatchie Roads. The second brigade, under Colonel Silliman, held the position until the next morning, when Silliman withdrew his soldiers half a mile to a line of unfinished entrenchments recently laid out by engineers; it consisted of three field batteries connected by rifle pits. Silliman's brigade, supported by artillery and cavalry, guarded the debarkation from Boyd's Landing of the naval brigade, the 127th, 56th 144th, 157th New York and 25th Ohio Infantry Regiments, and Battery F, 3rd New York. Directed to leave behind their knapsacks, the men believed they were going on a quick raid. The soldiers boarded the transports while the sailors and marines climbed onto tugs and the howitzers were placed on scows and launches provided by the army. At daybreak, while Lieutenant Commander Stephen B. Luce's gunners on the warship *Pontiac* shelled the Bee's Creek Battery to mask the movement, the gunboats *Mingoe* and *Sonoma* escorted the Federal forces into the Tullifinny River and to the designated landing sites on the river's western bank.

Fog obscured the Federal expedition as it sailed out of Boyd's Creek, up the Broad River, and into the Tullifinny. The naval infantry and the men from Potter's brigade came ashore at the upper landing near the James Gregory House. The marines and the Naval Artillery debarked near the tip of Deveaux's Neck at the lower landing, but low tide hindered the off-loading, causing the marines and sailors to wade in through the mud. The howitzers sank into the ooze, and nearby structures had to be taken down and the boards used to construct a crude roadway through the salt marsh.[11]

Potter did not consolidate his forces before moving inland but instead dispatched an advance force under the commander of the 127th New York, Colonel William Gurney. With portions of the 127th, 157th, and 56th New York, the 25th Ohio, and the sailor infantry, Gurney pushed inland, brushing aside southern pickets. When General Jones learned of the Federal movement, he directed units from Pocotaligo, including Major John Jenkins's elements of the 3rd South Carolina Cavalry and the battalion of state cadets, to DeVeaux's Neck while infantry and artillery batteries were sent to Graham's Neck on the east side of the Tulifinney opposite Deveaux's Neck to thwart any movements farther up the river. Jones also ordered General Gartrell at Coosawhatchie to counterattack in force, but Gartrell sent only the 5th Georgia, an understrength unit under Colonel Charles P. Daniel, which met Gurney's advance guard about a mile from the highway that connected Charleston and Savannah.

The Georgians, coming through the woods that ran along the southern side of the pike, drove in the enemy skirmishers and then took up a position behind a hedge, from where they opened on the Federals with a heavy musketry barrage. Gurney reacted by deploying the four companies from the 127th New York under Lieutenant Colonel Stewart L. Woodford in the center across the DeVeaux's Neck Road with the naval infantry on the 127th's right. To the left, where Gurney's line bent back at a 45 degree angle, were the 56th and 157th New York and the 25th Ohio. The Union infantry held firm, but the sailors, unused to fighting in the open, began to give ground, exposing the 127th New York's right flank.

A rifle ball struck Colonel Gurney in the arm, forcing him to leave the field and turn over command to Lieutenant Colonel Woodford. Things, as Dahlgren later wrote, seemed "squally," but soon Union reinforcements reached the field. The marines joined the sailors on the right, and the boat howitzers were placed in the center on the road, while the 144th New York arrived and began forming on the far right. Woodford, sensing the critical moment had come, ordered a bayonet charge by the four companies of the 127th New York. On the right the 144th and the naval brigade, with the sailors shouting, "come on my hearties," swung forward, straightening the line and joined the advance. A rifle shot, either from a sailor or a member of the 127th New York, brought down the color bearer of the 5th Georgia. As the 144th New York swept over the field, a member of the regiment picked up the southern battle flag. General Potter, having arrived and taken personal control of the engagement, took the flag and rode in front waving the captured banner, encouraging his cheering men to follow the enemy, who were fleeing from the field.[12]

The Georgians, carrying out a fighting withdrawal, fled back to Coosawhatchie. The Federals followed. At the highway the 144th New York moved east, driving enemy cavalry over the Tullifinny bridge. A portion of Company G crossed the bridge while their comrades began preparing the structure for demolition. Confederate artillery deployed on Tullifinny Hill opened on the Federals, but the New Yorkers were able to finish their work, withdraw their detachment from the river's eastern bank, and destroy the bridge.[13]

While the 144th New York dealt with the bridge over the Tullifinny, the rest of Potter's units pushed toward Coosawhatchie. The advance ceased at nightfall. The Federals, many of whom had been up for over forty-eight hours, fell exhausted along the Charleston Road, a mere half mile from the railroad. While he allowed most of his men to sleep, Potter made some minor adjustments. Two marine companies, A and B under Lieutenant Stoddard, were placed at the road junction, while Company C under Acting Ensign Woodward Carter, was posted on the far left.[14]

Throughout the night additional elements of Potter's brigade came ashore on DeVeaux's Neck, along with a fresh supply of ammunition. A cold rain fell on the men as they marched to the front. Standing under a protective tree, Potter directed his arriving units into line. When Lieutenant Titus and his Battery F, 3rd New York Artillery, came forward, Potter placed them in a field on the right, behind the sleeping 56th New York. During the evening, while their comrades rested, skirmishers patrolled across the road ranging toward the railroad. Throughout the night those who managed to stay awake could hear locomotives running by nearly every hour.[15]

While the Federals waited for daybreak before pushing on to their objective, the Confederates prepared to counterattack. General Jones, outraged by Gartrell's failure to send only an understrength regiment against a much more powerful enemy, began massing about seven to eight hundred men under Colonel Aaron C. Edwards near the Tullifinny railroad trestle. Edwards's command was divided into two battalions. One wing consisted of some two hundred men from Edwards's 47th Georgia, under Captain J. C. Thompson, while the other wing, led by Lieutenant Colonel Edwin H. Bacon Jr. of the 32nd Georgia, was made up of two companies of the 32nd Georgia, the Georgia Augusta Reserve Battalion, Captain Mitchell King Jr.'s Company A of the 3rd South Carolina Artillery, and a detachment of South Carolina militia. Also attached to Edwards's attack force was Major J. B. White's South Carolina Cadets. By General Jones's plan, Edwards would open the fight by probing the Union right. Once the Federals turned to engage Edwards, Jones planned to send in Gartrell from Coosawhatchie with 5th Georgia troops and Georgia reservists against the enemy's left.[16]

At dawn on December 7, Edwards began his advance. Leading were four companies of skirmishers, including Major White's South Carolina Cadets. Behind them came Captain Thompson's and Lieutenant Colonel Bacon's wings. Covered by a dense fog, the Confederates came out from their position near the railroad through an open field and into a dense wood. North of the Charleston pike, the southerners struck and scattered pickets from the 32nd USCT. Edwards then aligned his forces at a right angle to the road and pushed onward. Lieutenant Colonel Miles Nesbitt with elements of the 1st South Carolina Cavalry arrived and joined the assault on the far left of Edward's line. Not only were the Confederates in place to enfilade the Union line east to west, but they also could strike into the enemy's rear, cutting the Federals off from their landing zones.

In danger of being rolled up, Potter quickly began shifting units. The sailors, after pulling their howitzers out of harm's way, repositioned their cannons to fire on the Confederates coming from the direction of the Tullifinny River, while other units also aligned themselves to protect the exposed right flank. As the southerners neared the main Federal line, the Confederates came under heavy fire from Titus's battery of four Napoleon cannons. As one artilleryman described the action, "The Battery was once left without infantry support and had to skirmish for itself, which it did with excellent success, its canister clearing out every rebel from its front."[17]

Under the accurate bombardment provided by Titus's guns and the naval howitzers, the Union line held firm. Stopped by the artillery fire, Edwards maintained his position, awaiting Gartrell's detachment to carry out the next phase of Jones's plan, but the attack from Coosawhatchie never fully materialized. It started well, with Colonel Daniels leading his 5th Georgia and the 1st and 3rd Georgia Reserves out of Coosawhatchie, scattering Federal pickets and engaging Ensign Carter's marines, who found themselves nearly cut off; but the marines held, and then, when an artillery shell wounded Gartrell, the Confederates retreated. With the movement from Coosawhatchie suddenly abandoned, Edwards found his small force alone facing superior numbers. Unsupported and with his left flank in danger of being overlapped by the re-forming Federals, Edwards reluctantly withdrew his men back into the woods that had covered his initial assault.[18]

For three hours the two sides continued to exchange fire. The South Carolina Cadets, in their neatly tailored clothes, provided a stark contrast to the worn uniforms of the 47th Georgia and the mixed costumes of the reservists. The interaction between cadets and their officers bemused the Georgians. As described by the 47th Georgia's adjutant, Ben Williams, a future resident of Brunson, South Carolina:

> With all their training and discipline it was impossible for their officers to prevent their popping up along the line regardless of the whizzing bullets to a look at 'the Yankees,' in lines of blue, wreathed in battle smoke, advancing and firing down on us. Continuous were the commands of their officers, 'Down Mr ——, down Mr ——,' calling the names of the rash offenders, but prefixing the title 'Mr.' This amused some of the old 47th, who hadn't been called 'Mr' in about four years, one of whom said, 'Them Charleston people is the damndest politiest officers to their men I ever struck up with in the army.'[19]

By noon the fighting ended. Though they had fended off the attack, the Federal flanks remained exposed to artillery barrages from Coosawhatchie to the west and Tullifinny Hill to the east. To secure his position and remove his army's flanks from enfilading fire, Hatch decided to construct a fortified line a few hundred yards down the peninsula, near the Talbird House, close to the area where the December 6 battle had taken place. Here the flanks would be anchored on the Tullifinny and Coosawhatchie Rivers and the men safe from any end-on cannonades. As the battle ended on December 7, various regiments, including the 54th Massachusetts, began constructing the new entrenchments.[20]

The action on DeVeaux Neck resulted in minimal casualties. Neither side produced a complete list. Federal casualties for the December 6 action, sometimes called the Battle of Gregory's Landing, numbered approximately twelve killed and one hundred wounded; Confederate casualties were unreported. The December 7 battle for Tullifinny Crossroads cost the Federals about eighty killed, wounded, and missing, and the Confederates approximately ten killed and sixty wounded. The South Carolina Cadets, who saw their first field action of the war, suffered eight wounded, including the mortally wounded William Bailey Patterson. Receiving a severe leg wound was Beaufort native Joseph Walker Barnwell, the eighteen-year-old son of William Hazard Wigg Barnwell.[21]

Also on December 7, while Potter's brigade repelled the Confederate counterattack at Tullifinny Crossroads, the Federals remaining at the junction of the Boyd's Landing and Coosawhatchie Roads began withdrawing to the new defense line built by engineers days earlier. The fortifications, nearly a half mile in length, required a full brigade. But Foster had no intention of leaving that many men at Boyd's Landing. Throughout the day additional Federal regiments, accompanied by General Hatch and Colonel Silliman, embarked from Boyd's Landing for Deveaux Neck.

By that evening most of Silliman's brigade had joined Potter's forces on DeVeaux's Neck. One of Silliman's regiments, the 26th USCT, was sent across the Tullifinny River to Graham's Neck, where they took up a position around Michael Jenkins's plantation opposite the Federals' main landing and primary supply center at the Gregory Plantation. Their presence also denied the Confederates a position to place artillery on Graham's Neck, where they could interfere with Federal vessels sailing up the Tullifinny and the depot at Gregory's.

Besides the troops at Graham's Neck, Foster continued to maintain a presence at Boyd's Landing, forcing the Confederates to retain soldiers in a line stretching from Grahamville to Bee's Creek and on to Coosawhatchie and Pocotaligo. Though he continued to pressure the enemy along the railroad, Foster remained uneasy. He worried that with the majority of his troops stationed at the front, the Confederates might strike at Beaufort and Hilton Head. To be safe, Foster directed that arms be distributed to civilians at those two locations.[22]

Dahlgren also kept his naval and marine units in the field. Proud of the naval brigade's actions at Honey Hill and the recent fighting at DeVeaux Neck, the rear admiral felt obliged to honor Preble and his command by issuing them "distinguishing pennants." A red pennant went to the boat howitzer unit, while the sailor infantry was awarded a blue one and the marines a white and blue one, each marked with an anchor. Though pleased with his sailors and marines, Dahlgren did worry that close association with the army might weaken their discipline. As he admonished Preble, "It will be well not to let our sailors and marines forget the habits to which they have been accustomed, for they may lose this without acquiring those of the soldiers, and I must confess to a preference for the more exact and respectful training of the Navy."[23]

Dahlgren's pennants did not reach the naval brigade until after the next engagement. While most of the unit was reunited on DeVeaux Neck, a sailor detachment with two boat howitzers remained at Boyd's Landing along with the Massachusetts cavalrymen and Battery B, 3rd New York artillery, supporting the depleted 55th Massachusetts Infantry Regiment under Lieutenant Colonel Charles Fox. Too few to man the second defense line laid out by the engineers, the Union soldiers withdrew another quarter of a mile closer to the landing, where the cannons of Lieutenant Commander Luce's gunboat *Pontiac* provided protection. Another rifle pit was constructed, and the men settled down into garrison duty. The Boyd mansion became a makeshift hospital and quarters for some of the officers, but Lieutenant Colonel Fox joined his black soldiers bivouacked in a nearby field. Fox occupied a little "A" tent under a tree "by a fireplace of earth and brick built in front so as to throw the heat into it." Though he had only one regiment, the position was strong and supported by artillery and the *Pontiac*'s heavy guns. Fox had little to fear and believed that if attacked, the enemy would "go back quicker than they came."[24]

Other than some skirmishing, the Confederates did not oblige Fox with an assault but instead readied their forces to defend the line from Pocotaligo to Savannah. General Jones, worried about the rail line between Coosawhatchie and Tullifinny, recalled Brigadier General Beverly Robertson from his position as commander of the Second Military District at Adams' Run to Pocotaligo. Jones, who never trusted the competency of either General Gartrell or Chesnut, desired an experienced officer to coordinate the railroad's defense. Robertson, who had commanded the Confederates during the later stages of the fight at Honey Hill, arrived at Pocotaligo on December 8, just in time to meet a new Federal assault.[25]

Early on the morning of December 9, with Sherman's columns nearing Savannah's outer defenses, General Beauregard, risking possible capture by Federal troops at Tullifinny, came by rail through the Beaufort District and arrived in the threatened city. The situation was serious. Beauregard, realizing that Hardee, with Sherman in his front and Foster threatening his rear, was caught between two fires, gave his subordinate specific instructions: "You should hold this city so long as in your judgment it may be advisable to do so, bearing in mind that should you have to decide between a sacrifice of the garrison or city, you will preserve the garrison for operations elsewhere."[26] Beauregard left Savannah the next day, but he was unable to take the same route that had brought him to the city. Sherman's men, now approaching the Georgia portion of the Charleston and Savannah Railroad, forced the general to take a steamer to the railroad bridge over the Savannah River, where he boarded a train on the South Carolina shore. His trip through the Beaufort District was also different, for by now, thanks to an unusual maneuver on the part of the enemy while he was visiting Hardee, Federal guns were in a position to take his train under direct artillery fire.[27]

While Beauregard and Hardee planned their delaying actions and a withdrawal from Savannah, Generals Hatch and Foster were continuing their campaign to cut the Charleston and Savannah Railroad. Even with the majority of the Coast Division deployed between the Coosawhatchie and Tullifinny Rivers, they had no intention of launching any more direct assaults against fixed enemy positions. Instead they decided to spread out the Confederates, open up fields of fire, and employ their artillery to shut down the railroad while waiting for the arrival of General Sherman's armies. The new tactic suited Foster, a career engineer who saw an opportunity to establish siege guns in batteries along the southern side of DeVeaux's Neck that could shoot up the river to the railroad trestle at Coosawhatchie. Foster also approved a unique plan to bring his field batteries into play against the passing trains.

From their fortifications being constructed across DeVeaux's Neck the Federals were in easy cannon range of the railroad, but a belt of heavy timber, five hundred feet wide and just west of the roadway, blocked their field of fire. Skirmishers, who had advanced through the woods during the December 6 engagement, reported that on the far side of the woods there was an open field leading up to the railroad. If a passageway could be cut through the forest, field guns could join in firing on any trains that attempted to pass between the Coosawhatchie and Tullifinny Rivers.

On December 9, to open a line of sight for the cannoneers, Hatch organized a special attack force. In the lead was a six-hundred-man skirmish line under Colonel William C. Silliman that consisted from south to north of the 127th, 157th New York, and the marine battalion. Silliman, the twenty-seven-year-old son of the abolitionist Presbyterian minister Reverend Jonathan Silliman and his wife, Anna, of the Canterbury Presbyterian Church in Cornwall, New York, had been trained as a lawyer at the Albany Law School. At the start of the war, the younger Silliman joined the 7th New York Cavalry Regiment as a lieutenant and in July 1862 became a captain in the 124th New York Infantry, serving briefly as the regimental adjutant before taking over Company C and seeing service at Fredericksburg, Chancellorsville, and Gettysburg. On February 1, 1864, Silliman accepted the colonelcy of the 26th USCT at Rikers Island, New York.[28]

Silliman, whose regiment had arrived after the engagement at Honey Hill, had by seniority become the ranking officer in the 2nd Brigade. Given command of the heavy skirmish line, Silliman was to screen the main Federal line of eleven hundred men made up of the 144th, 56th New York, and 102nd USCT Regiments and the sailor infantry under General Potter. Behind them came the soldiers of the 25th Ohio, carrying axes, with instructions to cut a one-hundred-foot-wide path through the woods. Hatch assigned Commander George Preble to command the reserve consisting of the 32nd, 34th, and 35th USCT Regiments.

At 9:00 A.M. ten artillery pieces, including the naval brigade's howitzers, Napoleons from Battery F, 3rd New York, and Parrott guns from Battery A, 3rd Rhode Island, opened a rapid bombardment into the forest. After ten minutes, to protect the flanks of the attackers, the artillery directed their fire to the left and right, while Colonel Silliman led the skirmishers forward. Just before 10:00 A.M., the Federal troops encountered enemy pickets, who were driven back through the woods toward the railroad. While leading his men, Colonel Silliman was shot in the right leg above the knee. The bullet nearly ripped his leg off. A normal minié ball would have caused a bad wound, not a mortal one, but Silliman was struck by an explosive bullet, a projectile that contained a chamber filled with fulminate that was detonated by a short fuse seconds after being fired. The fuse, ignited by the weapons discharge, would burst the bullet, sending jagged fragments whizzing toward the enemy. Though rarely employed by either side, the explosive bullet, should it enter a body and then burst, would have catastrophic results. The exploding projectile forced the surgeons to amputate Colonel Silliman's leg "short," after which he was placed on a steamer and sent to Beaufort.[29]

With Silliman's wounding, Lieutenant Colonel Stewart Woodford of the 127th New York took over the skirmish line. Woodford had the skirmishers push on until, in the center, they advanced to within two hundred yards of the railroad, where he had the men lie down in the tall grass. Behind them came the main Federal line, which took up a position on the western edge of the woods, firing volleys over the prone skirmishers, while in their rear the Ohioans began felling trees. At about 11:30 Preble ordered in the 34th USCT to assist the tree cutters. In the center the Federals maintained their position for four hours, while the axmen completed clearing a passageway before withdrawing, but on both flanks the advance encountered heavy resistance and counterattacks.[30]

Brigadier General Beverly Robertson, orchestrating the Confederate defense, directed strikes against the Federals from Coosawhatchie and Pocotaligo. Robertson's command had changed little since the December 7 engagement. At the works near the Tullifinny trestle, Colonel Edwards deployed the 32nd and 47th Georgia, the 7th North Carolina Reserves, the State Cadets, Bachman's artillery company, and some cavalrymen from the 3rd South Carolina Cavalry, while at Coosawhatchie, General Gartrell brought forward the 5th Georgia and the 1st and 3rd Georgia Reserves under Colonel Daniel.[31]

Near the Tullifinny River, Edwards's soldiers engaged Lieutenant Stoddard's marines, who had advanced through a dense, wooded swamp that reduced visibility to a few feet. The marines had worked their way through knee- to waist-deep water dueling with their adversaries and coming under artillery fire. Once clear of the morass, Stoddard and his men found themselves near the railroad. A Confederate battery raked the marines, and Stoddard readied his men for an attack against the offending artillery when suddenly the regiment on his left, the 157th New York, withdrew. Stoddard quickly faced his men about and pulled them back, heading southeast until they struck the Tullifinny River, where they worked their way along the bank, eluding the pursuing Confederates.[32]

The Federals on the southern end of the line also came under severe pressure from the Confederates advancing from Coosawhatchie. Though Gartrell went down early with a wound, his men kept up the fight, striking the Union line nearly end on. The left of 127th New York, prone in the grass with Federal artillery firing over their heads, held the skirmish line and dueled with southern pickets hidden in thick pinewoods. One southerner, hidden behind a large tree, would stick "out his hat to draw fire," and when the Union soldiers "raised up to fire, he would fire at them." A small, local skirmish ensued until the Federals dropped the rifleman.

The 127th held until the 144th New York came forward to support them. The 144th was divided into two wings. The right wing under Lieutenant Colonel Calvin A. Rice came in behind the 127th, while the left wing under Major William Plaskett veered off to the southwest and came under a heavy fusillade from enemy sharpshooters, a number of them located in a large live oak tree. The southerners concentrated their musketry on the New Yorkers' regimental color guard, wounding some and killing the color bearer, Corporal Cyrus C. Hotchkiss. Men from Companies H and I eventually drove off the enemy sharpshooters and recovered Corporal Hotchkiss's body. A shallow grave was dug in the woods using bayonets and once the body was interred, the regiment's colonel, James Lewis, conducted a brief service, reading chapter 15 of 1st Corinthians and making a short prayer.[33]

At 2:30 orders came for the Federals to fall back. As they did so, the Confederates from Coosawhatchie increased their pressure against the Union left. The 144th held the southerners in check. At about 4:15 P.M., Preble ordered up from the reserve the 32nd USCT. While the black soldiers came forward, the men of the 144th, their ammunition nearly exhausted, were relieved by the 25th Ohio, whose soldiers, happy to exchange their axes for rifles, opened volleys on the following Confederates. The sharp firefight continued until nightfall, when darkness ended the fight and both sides withdrew.[34]

The action did accomplish the Federal goal of opening up a line of fire against the railroad for their artillery in the Tullifinny fortifications, but it had not been done without loss. Though no official tally was made, Federal casualties were about two hundred while Robertson reported eight killed and forty-four wounded, though Federals placed the Confederate count higher.[35]

The next day the Union soldiers pulled back about five hundred yards from the Charleston Highway down DeVeaux's Neck to the now-finished defense line. The fortifications, running from the Coosawhatchie to the Tullifinny, not only provided emplacements for cannons to shell the rail line through the recently cleared path to the railroad but also removed their flanks from enfilading artillery bombardments from Tullifinny Hill and Coosawhatchie. The Federals also began constructing batteries along the Coosawhatchie River side of DeVeaux Neck for cannons that could range down the river against the Coosawhatchie railroad trestle. On December 11 a 30-pound Parrott, located in a battery on the neck's southwestern tip, opened on the bridge. Five days later two more 30-pound Parrotts, located in an earthwork termed the "Swamp Battery" one thousand yards from the trestle on a small island separated by marsh from DeVeaux Neck, joined the fray.

The Parrotts, siege guns capable of firing a 30-pound shot or 25-pound shell over six thousand yards, kept up a bombardment of the trestle whenever any trains that ventured across the span. The locomotives heading west to Savannah were allowed to proceed unmolested, the logic being that their cargo and passengers would soon be gobbled up once Sherman arrived and seized the city, but those running east received a short, furious six-minute barrage. The southern engineers made the run from the Coosawhatchie to Tullifinny River at full throttle while enemy shot crashed around them. Though track, cross ties, trees, cars, and locomotives received damage, only one train, the *Isundiga,* was put out of commission with a shot to her boiler. For operators and most passengers, running the "gauntlet" was a harrowing experience, though one set of travelers, Union prisoners being sent to the prisoner-of-war camp in Florence, South Carolina, actually hoped their train would be hit. As one later wrote,

> About noon we were put on a train for Charleston which had to run the gauntlet.... The train was to pass in the daytime and would be the first for three days to make the attempt. We were in the rear car. They ran the train as fast as possible in passing places exposed to the fire.... One solid shot struck about twenty yards from the rear car of the train in the centre of track. Two rifle balls, fired by our sharp shooters, struck the train. I was never on a train before when I wished for an accident, but we were carried safely through to Charleston.[36]

While Sherman's forces approached Savannah, General Hatch's division continued to threaten the city's line of communication through the Beaufort District. On the evening of December 9, after the engagement at Tullifinny ended, the 33rd USCT (the former 1st South Carolina) and the 54th New York Infantry Regiments joined Hatch on DeVeaux's Neck. Colonel Edward N. Hallowell of the 54th Massachusetts, who had remained on Morris Island off Charleston when the majority of his regiment joined Hatch's Coast Division at the start of the campaign, accompanied the units to DeVeaux's Neck, where he replaced the mortally wounded Colonel Silliman as the commander of the 2nd Brigade. Two days later the 75th and 107th Ohio also arrived from Jacksonville, Florida.[37]

Hatch continued to probe the Confederate lines and improve his defenses and siege batteries. Additional artillery was brought from Boyd's Landing, including the rifled Dahlgren howitzers that were placed in a new battery along the Tullifinny River nine hundred yards from the railroad trestle. For the first time in the campaign, the Federal soldiers received hot food and mail, but the unseasonably warm weather soon ended. Cold rain swept down on the men. To warm themselves, the soldiers of the 107th Ohio dug pits fourteen feet square and about nine feet deep. During the day they built in the hollows "big fires" that would burn down and provide a "large pile of hot coals" over which they warmed themselves throughout the night. Many men were without overcoats and blankets. A soldier of the 127th New York wrote, "I let my woolen blanket do what it would toward covering three men besides myself at night. Some of the men are still short of clothing. It is a hard place."[38]

Morale rose on December 10 when the soldiers heard cannon fire coming from the direction of Savannah. On December 14 word arrived that Sherman's right wing had captured Fort McAllister and that Sherman and Foster had met aboard Foster's flagship in Ossabaw Sound south of Savannah. The news sparked cheers all along the Tullifinny line, and a band struck up "The Star-Spangled Banner."[39]

Sherman's armies had reached Savannah's outer defense lines on December 9. Approaching the southern portion of the city's fortifications came General Oliver O. Howard's Army of the Tennessee, while to the north advanced General Henry W. Slocum's Army of Georgia. On December 10 elements of Slocum's army seized Monteith Railroad Station and began ripping up the tracks of the Charleston and Savannah Railroad; however, by now the company's rolling stock had been removed to South Carolina, where operations continued between Hardeeville and Charleston. A Federal forage party from the 150th New York, working its way down to the Savannah River south of the trestle, encountered the little side-wheel steamer *Ida,* which had once operated between Savannah and Fort Pulaski. The vessel was coming up the river with dispatches for the Confederate naval officer Captain William W. Hunter, the commander of the Savannah Naval Squadron, who with the gunboat *Sampson* and the tender *Resolute,* had steamed upriver to protect the railroad bridge.

The *Ida*, a frail, unarmed vessel, was surrendered to the Federals, who removed her crew and Colonel Duncan Lamont Clinch Jr., who carried messages for Captain Hunter. The New Yorkers, fearing that Confederate warships would arrive and recapture the *Ida*, burned their prize. Two days later Hunter, his flotilla increased by the gunboat *Macon*, which had sailed down from Two Sisters Ferry, burned the railroad trestle over the Savannah River.[40]

On December 12, the same day the Confederates destroyed the trestle over the Savannah River, the commander of the Twentieth Corps, Brigadier General Alpheus S. Williams, a fifty-four-year-old, Connecticut-born, Yale-educated politician from Detroit, saw the opportunity to gain a position to threaten Hardee's line of retreat and ordered Colonel Ezra A. Carman, commanding the Second Brigade, First Division, to send a regiment across the south channel of the Savannah River and occupy Argyle Island. Once he secured the island, Williams planned to use it as a jumping-off point to launch a strike into South Carolina and threaten the Union Causeway, the only road connection between Savannah and Hardeeville. Carman selected Colonel William Hawley's 3rd Wisconsin Infantry, which crossed over in small boats. Once on the island, the Federals spotted Captain Hunter's three gunboats, which, after destroying the trestle, were attempting to reach Savannah. A battery of Federal field guns located on the Georgia shore opened on the wooden warships, and while the gunboats *Sampson* and *Macon* maneuvered to escape the artillery fire, they ran into the *Resolute*, damaging her paddle wheels. Caught in the current, the *Resolute*, a veteran of the fighting in early November 1861 at Port Royal Sound, ran aground on Argyle Island and was captured by the Wisconsin soldiers. The vessel was taken to the Georgia shore, where the crew was removed. Repaired by northern engineers, the *Resolute* was turned over to the Twentieth Corps quartermaster.[41]

On the same day that the Federals occupied Argyle Island and seized the *Resolute*, troops from Sherman's right wing south of Savannah captured Fort McAllister on the Ogeechee River, allowing Sherman to meet with General Foster and Admiral Dahlgren. After briefing Sherman on the situation north of the Savannah River and promising all possible aid, Foster returned to Port Royal, where he immediately directed the department's quartermaster vessels, including the *Planter* captained by Robert Smalls, to transport supplies, siege artillery, and six hundred thousand rations to Sherman's forces. Over the next few days, Sherman, who had been placed over the Department of the South, joined Dahlgren and Foster in planning operations to capture Savannah and trap Hardee's command. Different schemes were proposed, and thought was given to transferring Hatch's Coast Division into Georgia; but instead a dual movement employing Hatch's Division and the Federals on Argyle Island was started to sever Hardee's line of retreat through the Beaufort District.[42]

On December 15 the 2nd Massachusetts joined Hawley's regiment on Argyle Island and the next day Colonel Carmen brought over the remainder of his brigade and two pieces of artillery. The Federals took up a position on the island's eastern tip, where they came under fire from a Confederate battery on the South Carolina shore and the gunboat *Isondiga* steaming up from Savannah. That night orders came to Carman to take his brigade into South Carolina, but the lack of boats and the presence of Confederate cavalry and artillery delayed the movement until daybreak, December 19, when Colonel Hawley landed the 3rd Wisconsin, 2nd Massachusetts, and 13th New Jersey at the former Ralph Izard rice plantation and advanced inland, driving enemy skirmishers past the plantation's rice mill and occupying the Beech Hill House on the neighboring Joseph Allen Smith rice plantation. Carmen then joined Hawley on the South Carolina shore with the 115th New York. Defenses were built, and that night the two field pieces were brought over from Argyle Island. Carman, making his headquarters in the mill, established a strong entrenched position, with his left on the Savannah River and his right on an inlet near Clydesdale Creek. The next day Carman extended his line to Clydesdale Creek and attempted to advance on the Savannah-Hardeeville Road, but the terrain, comprising rice fields cut by dikes and canals, with bridges burned and the enemy drawn up in strength, made a further advance impossible.[43]

On December 17 Sherman demanded the surrender of Savannah. Hardee refused and the next day Sherman suggested to Foster that he shift as many men as he could spare east of the Tullifinny River to Graham's Neck for a bold rush against the railroad near Pocotaligo. After receiving Sherman's dispatch, Foster wrote Hatch, "I think you can best destroy the road by crossing the Tullifinny with a portion of your force and striking the road near the Pocotaligo River." While the preparations in the Beaufort District were going on, Sherman, ever hyperactive and rarely satisfied, decided that it might be best to send Hatch's division to Bluffton and then on to Hardee's line of retreat. Leaving his subordinates, Generals Oliver O. Howard and Henry W. Slocum, in charge of the operations around Savannah, Sherman sailed with Dahlgren to Hilton Head to confer with Foster.[44]

While Sherman, Dahlgren, and Foster met on Hilton Head, Hatch, on the evening of December 19, dispatched Colonel Hallowell with the 54th Massachusetts and the 33rd USCT across the Tullifinny, where they joined the 26th USCT at the Mike Jenkins Plantation. The following afternoon Hallowell ordered a probe by the 33rd USCT and two companies of the 54th Massachusetts under the 33rd's commander, Lieutenant Colonel Charles T. Trowbridge. The soldiers moved along the Tullifinny River before turning inland toward the Mackay Point Road. As they neared the Stuart Plantation, Trowbridge and his men encountered Confederate cavalry pickets, whom they drove back until they discovered a strong line of dismounted cavalry posted in heavy woods. Trowbridge formed his men into line and sent them across an open field and into the woods. The southerners fled, leaving behind haversacks, blankets, and forage. Returning to the Jenkins Plantation, Trowbridge reported that the only way for Hallowell's brigade to reach the railroad was to follow the route taken two years earlier by General Brannan's division, a movement that meant assaulting a line of well-prepared Confederate works built on the north side of Frampton Creek.[45]

The Confederates carefully monitored the Federal operations in the Beaufort District, both along the Savannah River and between the Coosawhatchie and Tullifinny Rivers. Between December 10 and 20, units and commanders were shifted between Charleston, Savannah, and the Beaufort District. South Carolina governor Milledge L. Bonham dispatched additional militia, and unsuccessful appeals were made to President Jefferson Davis for reinforcements from Virginia.

General Beauregard still hoped that General Jones could drive the Federals away from the railroad, but he also realized the necessity for Jones to send help to Savannah. Brigadier General William B. Taliaferro was brought from Charleston to supersede General Robertson, who was assigned to replace the wounded Gartrell as commander at Coosawhatchie. Beauregard also called General Bragg to come from Augusta to Charleston, but with no position equal to Bragg's rank available, Bragg left the department and returned to Wilmington. When the new officers arrived in the Beaufort District, they found mixed, understrength formations made up of militia, reserves, and a sprinkling of regulars.[46]

With Sherman's forces investing Savannah, Hardee asked that the majority of Lieutenant General Joseph Wheeler's cavalry corps be shifted from Georgia into South Carolina. Wheeler, a dapper, twenty-eight-year-old Georgia cavalryman and an 1859 U.S. Military Academy graduate, had led the resistance against Sherman's movement across Georgia. The cavalry leader had tried to carry out a scorched-earth policy in front of the advancing Federals, but his attempts at destroying food and forage failed to slow the march and only incurred the wrath of the Georgians, who found Wheelers's undisciplined cavalrymen to be little better than brigands and thieves. Their actions caused Robert Toombs, a Georgia politician, former U.S. senator, and Confederate general to remark, "I hope to God he will never get back to Georgia." And Major General Daniel H. Hill stated that "the whole of Georgia is full of bitter complaints of Wheeler's cavalry."[47]

To facilitate the transfer of Wheeler's troopers, Confederate warships and auxiliary vessels steamed up to Two Sisters Ferry and carried two of Wheeler's three divisions to the South Carolina shore. Wheeler took command of all the cavalry in the Beaufort District and was directed to watch the region from the crossings of the New River to Hardeeville. To help cover possible lines of evacuation, Beauregard ordered Tunbridge and Morgan Landings fortified. Colonel Colcock and his regiment, minus three companies serving dismounted in the Savannah defense lines, were assigned the important duty of guarding the forts at the New River Bridge from any possible attack from Bluffton and keeping open the line of retreat that led north from Savannah to the New River and then northwest to Hardeeville.[48]

Initially Beauregard directed operations from Charleston, but on December 16, while Federal forces were preparing to shift from Argyle Island into South Carolina, he left Charleston by rail for Hardeeville. That evening Beauregard arrived at Dr. Charles Cheves's house on the Upper Delta Plantation across from Savannah. On the seventeenth Beauregard held conferences at the Cheves home with Hardee and other officers. An evacuation strategy was discussed, and the next day Beauregard shifted his headquarters to Pocotaligo, where he finalized the plan. The appearance of Union troops at the Izard Plantation caused Hardee to act. As he wrote Jefferson Davis, "On the 19th the enemy forced a landing on the South Carolina side, so near my communications that to save the garrison it became necessary to give up the city."[49]

While Wheeler skirmished with the Federals at Izard's, Hardee had a pontoon bridge laid from Savannah to Hutchinson Island, where a second bridge ran to Pennyworth Island. A final span crossed the Black River to the South Carolina shore, where rice dikes had to be used as roadways to reach the Union Causeway, the principal road that connected Savannah to Charleston. On the evening of December 20, the Confederates began leaving Savannah. The march, as described by Beaufort native John Barnwell Elliott, son of the Episcopal bishop of Georgia, Stephen Elliott, resembled "an immense funeral procession stealing out of the city in the dead of night." The Federals on the Izard Plantation reported that "the noise of the retreating enemy could be plainly heard as they crossed the bridges from Savannah to the South Carolina shore." Forty miles away at DeVeaux's Neck, the Federals noted that trains from Hardeeville had stopped at Coosawhatchie, waiting for night to run the gauntlet. They also could see long columns of Confederate soldiers "with their colors" marching along the railroad.[50]

Beauregard remained at Pocotaligo until December 22, when he returned to Charleston. He directed Hardee to defend Charleston as long as possible but not to allow himself and his garrison to be captured. To guard the city against an advance from the south, Beauregard directed an initial defense line established along the eastern bank of the Combahee and Salkehatchie Rivers to Barnwell, where it was to turn west and continue on to Augusta. To create the required fortifications, Hardee dispatched engineers, including his chief engineer, Major John A. Johnson. Unable to construct a continuous line, the southerners placed works at all the primary river crossings. The duty of arming the batteries was placed in the hands of the department's chief ordnance officer, Colonel Ambrosio Gonzales. One strong battery mounting five guns was positioned at Andrew Burnet's Plantation, where its cannons could range downriver, covering the approaches to the Combahee Ferry. Another battery was built to guard the railroad trestle at Salkehatchie. Work progressed slowly. Slaves ran away. Residents from the Beaufort and Colleton Districts sent off food and supplies and fled inland. One officer wrote that his superiors seemed "bewildered by the enemy, they know not what to do." Still, by early January fortifications had been completed at all major crossings of the Combahee and Salkehatchie Rivers.[51]

While work on the new fortifications was underway, the Confederates maintained their positions from the Savannah River to the Combahee River. The forces guarding the region consisted of:

BRIGADIER GENERAL JAMES CHESNUT, GRAHAMVILLE

Honey Hill, Infantry: 2nd South Carolina Militia, Lieutenant Colonel William H. Duncan, 76 men; 3rd South Carolina Militia, Lieutenant Colonel John W. Harrington, 412 men; 4th South Carolina Militia, Colonel Robert B. Ligon, 249 men. Artillery: section of the DeSaussure Artillery (Company G, 3rd South Carolina Artillery Battalion); Furman Artillery.

Bee's Creek and Dawson Bluff: 1st, 2nd, 3rd South Carolina Reserves, Brigadier General Albert G. Blanchard, 583 men. Artillery: Lafayette Artillery, section of the Beaufort Artillery.

Cavalry: Companies C and E, 3rd South Carolina Cavalry, 114 men.

Cannon: Beaufort Volunteer Artillery at Bee's Creek, one 12-pound howitzer, at Honey Hill, one 12-pound howitzer; Furman Artillery at Honey Hill, one 10-pound Parrott, two 6-pounders, one Napoleon; Lafayette Artillery at Honey Hill, one 12-pound howitzer at Bee's Creek two 6-pounders.

Total for Chesnut's command: 553 reservists, 737 militia, 294 artillerymen, 114 cavalry, total: 1,728

BRIGADIER GENERAL WILLIAM B. TALIAFERRO COOSAWHATCHIE TO POCOTALIGO

Coosawhatchie to Tullifinny Trestle

Colonel John L. Moore's Command, Infantry: 3rd Georgia Reserves, Colonel John L. Moore, 465 men; one company 1st South Carolina Militia, 24 men; Artillery: One section Beaufort Volunteer Artillery, one section DePass artillery, one section Johnson's Horse Artillery, Lieutenant Richard Johnson, one gun, Furman Artillery.

Captain Archibald L. Campbell's Command, Infantry: Company C, South Carolina State Reserves, 40 men; Company H, South Carolina

State Reserves, 37 men; Cavalry: Company B, 3rd South Carolina, 32 men; Company H, 3rd South Carolina Cavalry, 66 men; Company D, 3rd South Carolina, 10 men.

Colonel Aaron C. Edwards' Command: 47th Georgia, Colonel Aaron C. Edwards, 304 men; 32nd Georgia, Lieutenant Colonel Edwin H. Bacon, 291 men; 1st North Carolina Reserves, 301 men; 1st South Carolina Militia, 612 men; South Carolina Cadets, 125 men; Young Dismounted Cavalry Brigade, 387 men. Artillery: German Light Artillery; section Girardey's Battery.

Colonel Charles P. Daniel's Command, Infantry: 5th Georgia, Colonel Charles P. Daniel, 231 men; 1st Georgia Reserves, Lt Col James J. Neely, 170 men. Artillery: section Girardey's Battery.

Pocotaligo

Major John Jenkins Command, Cavalry: Detachment 1st South Carolina Cavalry, Captain James D. Trezevant, 130 men; Detachment 1st South Carolina Cavalry, Captain Angus P. Brown, 32 men; Kirk's Squadron, Captain Manning J. Kirk, 107 men; Artillery: Company A, Siege Train, Captain Benjamin C. Webb.

Cannon: Section Beaufort Volunteer Artillery, two Napoleons at Coosawhatchie; Section DePass (DeSaussure) Artillery, two Napoleons at Coosawhatchie; Section Lafayette Artillery at Coosawhatchie, one 12-pound howitzer; German (Bachman) Artillery, four 12-pound howitzers at Tullifinny Trestle; Girardey's Artillery, three Napoleons and two 12-pound Blakelys at Tullifinny Trestle, one Napoleon at Pocotaligo; Johnson's Horse Artillery, two Napoleons at Tullifinny Trestle; Company A, Siege Train, two 20-pound Parrotts at Pocotaligo.

Total for Talliaferro's command: 1338 regular infantry, 1013 reservists, 636 militia, 474 artillerymen, 377 cavalry.

Fixed Artillery: one 24-pound iron howitzers and two 12-pound Blakelys at Pocotaligo; two 12-pound iron howitzers at Honey Hill.[52]

Over time additional units reinforced the region, and by the end of December, General Jones was reassigned to the District of Florida. Replacing Jones was Major General Lafayette McLaws. A Georgia-born 1842 graduate of the U.S. Military Academy and Mexican War veteran, McLaws had resigned from the army in 1861 to join the Confederacy. Initially assigned to duty in Virginia, he served with the Army of Northern Virginia from the Seven Days Battles through Gettysburg, advancing from regimental to division commander. In the fall of 1863, he and his division were part of the units under General James Longstreet sent to reinforce the Confederate forces in north Georgia. During operations at Chickamauga, he incurred Longstreet's wrath for what Longstreet believed to be a lack of aggressiveness to pursue the enemy, and after a failed assault against Fort Sanders at Knoxville, Tennessee, McLaws was accused of failing to prepare his soldiers properly for the attack. Longstreet relieved him from duty.

McLaws demanded and received a court-martial, which, with intervention from the Confederacy's adjutant general, resulted in his return to service and assignment to the defenses of Savannah. The forty-three-year-old officer had approximately seven thousand men in the Beaufort District. Also stationed in the region, though not directly under McLaws, were two divisions of Joseph Wheeler's cavalry, which manned the forts at the New River Bridge and watched the Savannah River crossings from Savannah north to Matthews Bluff.[53]

On December 26, 1864, Confederate returns for McLaws's division listed:

- At Grahamville: Brigadier General James Chesnut's brigade (1st, 2nd, 6th Battalions of South Carolina Reserves, Company B, 8th South Carolina Reserves, 2nd, 3rd, 4th Regiments South Carolina Militia); Captain William E. Charles' battery of artillery and sections of the Lafayette and Earle's artillery batteries and companies C and E, 3rd South Carolina Cavalry. A total of 1,233 infantry, 174 artillery, and 110 cavalry.

- From Coosawhatchie to the Tullifinny River: Colonel George P. Harrison's Brigade (5th, 32nd, 47th Georgia, 1st, 3rd Georgia Reserves, 7th North Carolina Reserves, 1st South Carolina Cavalry, and a detachment South Carolina Cavalry Reserves); Artillery: Ruel W. Anderson's battery, Captain Camille E. Girardey's battery, Henry M. Stuart's Beaufort Volunteer Artillery and a section of William E. DePass' artillery battery; Cavalry: Company H and detachments from companies F, D, and G, 3rd South Carolina Cavalry. Some 2,169 infantry, 391 artillery, and 110 cavalry.

- At Pocotaligo: 817 men of Colonel John C. Fiser's Brigade (1st Georgia Regiment, 27th Georgia Battalion, and Symons's Regiment of Reserves). As a mobile reserve kept near the Pocotaligo railroad station was John B. Cumming's Brigade (5th Georgia regiment Reserves, 2nd Georgia Battalion Reserves, Detachment Athens Battalion); Colonel Washington M. Hardy's Brigade (50th North Carolina Regiment, 10th North Carolina Battalion); Artillery: Brooks's, Barnwell's, Abell's, Kanapaux's Artillery batteries, sections of Wagener's and Earle's artillery batteries; Cavalry: Companies I, K, and D, 3rd South Carolina Cavalry, and Kirk's Cavalry Company. A total of 1,323 infantry, 385 artillery, and 352 cavalry.[54]

The presence of so many hungry and undersupplied soldiers did not bode well for the Beaufort District. The Confederates stripped the area of provisions, livestock, and fodder. Wheeler's troopers continued to live up to their reputation by ravaging the countryside. One officer reported that the cavalrymen were worse than the enemy in this pursuit. Wheeler tried to increase discipline by quarantining one brigade commanded by Colonel John W. Caldwell at Robertville to "see if it is this brigade that is committing all the depredations reported to him through the country or not."[55]

By late December information had reached Beauregard of the catastrophic defeat suffered by General John B. Hood's army outside Nashville, Tennessee. The remnants of Hood's command had regrouped at Tupelo, Mississippi. On December 31, 1864, Beauregard, believing his presence was necessary in Mississippi, turned direct command of the Department of South Carolina, Georgia, and Florida over to Hardee. Before leaving, Beauregard directed Hardee to maintain his defensive position along the Combahee and Salkehatchie Rivers and guard the approached to Augusta. McLaws's division maintained the river line while Wheeler's cavalry watched over the region between Barnwell and Augusta. Beauregard hoped for success, but he warned Hardee, "The fall of Charleston would necessarily be a terrible blow to the Confederacy, but its fall with the loss of its brave garrison would be still more fatal to our cause." He directed his subordinate to make preparations for the city's possible evacuation.[56]

The Confederates' departure from Savannah and their subsequent retreat through the Beaufort District occurred while Sherman was at Hilton Head; the Union general did not learn of the evacuation until December 21, when he returned to Georgia. Immediately he recalled Carmen's brigade from Izard's Plantation. Savannah was occupied and arrangements made to refit his army. Initially orders were received from Lieutenant General Ulysses S. Grant, commanding officer of the United States Armies, to transport the western troops to Virginia, but Sherman proposed a continuation of his march through the Carolinas and if need be to Virginia. On December 27 Grant gave Sherman the go-ahead. The path forward led directly through the Beaufort District.[57]

Sherman wasted little time in preparing his campaign. He refitted his army and rearranged his command structure. Returning to his armies at Savannah were a number of officers who had been furloughed after the fall of Atlanta to campaign for Lincoln's reelection and other Republican candidates. Among those who had missed the march through Georgia and hurried back to rejoin their units were corps commanders John A. Logan and Francis P. Blair Jr. and brigade commander Benjamin Harrison. On January 2, 1865, with his forces and officers ready, Sherman wrote to Grant, enclosing "a copy of a project" for the next phase of his campaign:

[Entirely confidential]
PROJECT FOR JANUARY.

Right wing to move men and artillery by transports to head of Broad River and Beaufort; reestablish Port Royal Ferry, and mass the wing at or in the neighborhood of Pocotaligo. Left wing and cavalry to work slowly across the causeway toward Hardeeville, to open a road by which wagons can reach their corps about Broad River; also, by a rapid movement of the left, to secure Sister's Ferry, and Augusta road out to Robertsville. In the mean time, all guns, shot, shell, cotton, etc., to be moved to a safe place, easy to guard, and provisions and wagons got ready for another swath, aiming to have our army in hand about the head of Broad River, say Pocotaligo, Robertsville, and Coosawhatchie, by the 15th January.

The whole army to move with loaded wagons by the roads leading in the direction of Columbia, which afford the best chance of forage and provisions. Howard to be at Pocotaligo by the 15th January, and Slocum to be at Robertsville, and Kilpatrick at or near Coosawhatchie about the same date. General Fosters troops to occupy Savannah, and gunboats to protect the rivers as soon as Howard gets Pocotaligo.

W. T. SHERMAN, Major-General.[58]

While Sherman prepared his troops, Hatch's division maintained its position between the Coosawhatchie and Pocotaligo rivers. All offensive movements were called off, and some formations were withdrawn to Hilton Head and Beaufort. But even with the lull in active operations and a reduced force, Hatch continued to launch probes and carry out artillery bombardments. At night numerous Confederate deserters, some "galvanized Yankees," men who had joined the southern army to escape the ravages of prison camp, came into the Union lines. Few festivities were held for Christmas, and the cold weather caused the men to "burrow like foxes" into miserable hovels covered with branches.[59]

From a battery of siege guns located at Dawson Bluff on the Coosawhatchie River, the Confederates enfiladed the Union line on DeVeaux Neck, disrupting the Union artillerists from ranging their cannons against the railroad. One shot, directed at the Swamp Battery, took off the head of Joseph Stadelbauer, a member of the 107th Ohio, while he was pouring coffee from a canteen for his comrades who were serving as pickets. The Federals called the Confederate work Battery Damnation and their own Battery Hell. To silence the annoying work, Commander Preble made plans to launch an amphibious assault on December 26 by 120 sailors and marines under Lieutenant O'Kane, but "the morning proved very rainy" and the intervening "marsh was found to be impassable and the enterprise was reluctantly abandoned."[60]

Two days after the aborted attack on the Dawson Bluff Battery, Preble received orders from Dahlgren to withdraw his naval brigade. Preble left behind two howitzers with their crews and embarked the rest of his sailors and marines on the *Geranium*. They returned to Port Royal, where the marines encamped at Bay Point and the sailors joined their vessels.[61]

While the soldiers of both sides awaited their next assignments, the region's remaining civilians also took stock of their situations. Along the Combahee the southern planters were described as "very gloomy." Their slaves, impressed to build fortifications, ran away. The Confederate government continued to collect taxes and confiscate rice to feed soldiers. Those who could sent their slaves, farm implements, and provisions inland. Stephen H. Boineau, property manager for Charles Heyward's Combahee rice plantations wrote,

> Deserters from our ranks, yankee raiders & negroes who have left their owners will be prowling and plundering all over the Country, twenty miles from the seaboard. I can see no hope whatever for us. Misery and starvation will necessarily be the consequence. It is not despondency that causes me to write thus. Truly I am distressed, but not alarmed. With hundreds of others I shall patiently wait the dreadful calamity which I believe is in store for us, and bow to the will of providence.[62]

Though the situation for the Federals on the sea islands was not as dire, their Christmas was somber due to the large number of casualties off-loaded at Hilton Head and Beaufort. Injured soldiers arrived daily, forcing the medical directors in Beaufort to open additional hospitals. Officers were brought to the Edgar Fripp home. Among those convalescing in the house were Colonels Silliman, Hartwell, Beecher, and Guerney, the latter three sharing a room. It was thought that Colonel Silliman, tended by his wife, might survive, but he took a turn for the worse and died on December 17. The other officers, once stable, were sent north.[63]

The numerous casualties caused the civilians, black and white, to temper their Christmas celebrations. Christmas Eve at Old Fort Plantation found the freedmen coming to the schoolhouse, which had been dressed up with evergreens, gray moss, and rows of candles for a praise meeting. Elizabeth Hyde Botume, the school's principal teacher, wrote that as she came to the building she could see "the bright lights, which cast a glow over the trees and far out upon the water." The shouting of songs could be heard, along with the clapping of hands and the stomping of feet. Botume made out the familiar words of Whittier's "Song of the Negro Boatmen," which began:

> Oh praise an' tanks! De Lord he come
> To set de people free
> An' massa t'ink it day ob doom,
> An' we ob jubilee

Botume read the Sermon on the Mount and then explained the schoolhouses decorations of the "evergreens and wreaths, the cross and illuminations, typical of Christ's life and teachings." The service went on throughout the evening and concluded with everyone shaking hands.[64]

Laura Towne described Christmas Day as cold and dull, with rain that kept her and Ellen Murray from attending church. The next day the teachers gave presents to their students. Since the new schoolhouse was unfinished, they met in the Brick Baptist Church. Towne gave the students ginger cakes and pocketbooks while Murray presented the girls with workboxes containing needle books, pincushions, thread, buttons, scissors, and thimbles; the boys received knives and combs.[65]

Two days after Christmas, General Rufus Saxton left for Savannah to meet with General Sherman to discuss the freedmen situation. He returned on the thirtieth. He told his brother Willard that it was a pleasant visit but that many in the high command "don't care much about humanitarian labors; so the rebellion is crushed & the rebels killed or conquered, they are content to leave the more important & more perplexing work for others."[66]

Rufus Saxton had returned in time for the festivities commemorating the second anniversary of the issuing of the Emancipation Proclamation. Since the anniversary fell on a Sunday, the celebration was postponed one day, allowing people to attend church and Sunday school.

January 2, 1865, a bright and mild day, began with a parade of freedmen led by the post band from the 102nd USCT through Beaufort. Tillie and Mary Saxton, the wives of General Saxton and his aide and brother Captain Willard Saxton, dressed a black woman as the "Goddess of Liberty," who rode in a cart pulled by six white horses. The parade ended at the College Building. Among the dignitaries were Reverend Mansfield French, the Port Royal Experiment's acknowledged spiritual leader; John "Father" Hunn, a Delaware abolitionist and Quaker minister, who served as the superintendent for Seaside Plantation; Reuben Tomlinson, a Philadelphia activist and superintendent; and George Newcomb, a Dedham, Massachusetts, school teacher, who had arrived at Port Royal in 1864 to become a teacher and was later named head of the area's freedmen schools. They joined General Saxton and his staff on the college steps in front of thousands of freedmen. Speeches were made, and the "Goddess of Liberty" sang "In the New Jerusalem," which Lizzie Botume described as the "Marseillaise" of the freed slaves, who joined in singing the chorus:

> In that New Jerusalem,
> I am not afraid to die;
> We must fight for liberty,
> In that New Jerusalem[67]

The celebration took on new significance, as the arrival and expected movement of General Sherman's forces seemed to open an opportunity that would spread the Port Royal Experiment from the sea islands and create a "New Jerusalem" throughout the Beaufort District and possibly the entire South.

Chapter 15

Sherman Invades the Beaufort District

*"South Carolina don't intend to be conquered—
She intends to fight"*

On the same day that the celebrants in Beaufort commemorated the anniversary of emancipation and celebrated their new Jerusalem, elements of Sherman's Twentieth Corps pressed forward from Savannah into the Beaufort District. The initial movement started on December 31, when Brigadier General William T. Ward began moving his division into South Carolina. Ward, a fifty-six-year-old, Virginia-born, Kentucky-raised lawyer and former U.S. congressman, had served as a volunteer officer in the Mexican War. A loyalist from a border state, he received a commission in September 1861 as a brigadier general. After a series of assignments behind the lines in Kentucky, he joined Sherman's forces in early 1864 for the attack on Atlanta, where he eventually took over the Third Division, Twentieth Corps. Wounded twice at Resaca, Ward had declined to leave the field and remained with his unit throughout the Atlanta Campaign and the March through Georgia.[1]

His corps commander, Major General Alpheus Williams, had chosen Ward to take his division and establish a bridgehead on the South Carolina shore across from Savannah. On the last day of December 1864, Ward attempted to negotiate the Savannah River, but conditions thwarted his initial operation. Battling a severe wind, chilling rain, Confederate vedettes, and unstable pontoon bridges that ran from Savannah to Hutchinson Island and then to South Carolina, only a portion of Colonel Henry Case's First Brigade managed to reach the opposite shore by nightfall. Their stay was short. That evening Ward, worried that his undermanned bridgehead would be overrun, withdrew his men to Hutchinson Island. The next day Colonel Case, using small boats, began shifting his troops from Hutchinson Island to Screven's Ferry Landing at the head of the Union Causeway. By sunset Case had his entire brigade on South Carolina soil, and by 9:00 P.M. his men were driving inland, scattering Confederate pickets before them, not stopping until they reached Dr. Charles Cheves's Upper Delta plantation house, where they bivouacked for the night.

While Case's soldiers proceeded toward Cheves's plantation, the 19th Michigan of Colonel Daniel Dustin's Second Brigade, "in two or three small boats after a tedious effort," crossed the river. Before any additional units could be sent over, Dustin received word that the quartermaster vessel *Planter*, captained by Robert Smalls, was coming to assist his beleaguered soldiers. Dustin held back his remaining regiments, and the next day the *Planter* carried them and Colonel Samuel Ross's brigade from Hutchinson Island to Screven Ferry's Landing. By January 4 the Case and Dustin brigades were united at Dr. Cheves's house, and Ward led his division to the Hardee Plantation, where they "made a fine encampment" around an abandoned Confederate fort that the Federals called Fort Hardee. While awaiting the campaign's next stage in the midst of thunderstorms, Ward drilled his men and scouted toward Confederate positions at the New River Bridge and Red Bluff.[2]

Back in Savannah, while Ward's men hunkered down in their waterlogged camps, Sherman laid before Major General Oliver Otis Howard the plans for the coming operation By Sherman's initial design, Howard, who commanded Sherman's right wing—the Army of the Tennessee—would take his Fifteenth and Seventeenth Corps to Beaufort by boat and be ready to march inland to Pocotaligo by mid-January. At the same time, Sherman planned for his left wing—the Army of Georgia under Major General Henry Slocum—to enter South Carolina from Georgia. Slocum's soldiers would cross at two points. The remainder of the Twentieth Corps would follow Ward's division across the pontoon bridges at Savannah and occupy Hardeeville and Purrysburg while the Fourteenth Corps, with the armies' cavalry, proceeded northwest along the Georgia shore some twenty-five miles to Two Sisters Ferry. Slocum was to concentrate at Robertville and, in conjunction with Howard's force at Pocotaligo, move northeast toward the South Carolina Railroad and on to Columbia.[3]

Beginning on January 3, Brigadier General Joseph A. Mower's First Division of Major General Francis "Frank" Preston Blair Jr.'s Seventeenth Corps began arriving at Beaufort. Embarking from Thunderbolt on the Savannah River, the soldiers came ashore at the town's main wharf at the foot of Carteret Street and marched to their camps just beyond the city's defense lines. The western men trooped through the town, loudly singing, making jokes, and yelling at civilians. They resembled "coal heavers" and were described as strange, rough-looking, misshaven, and badly dressed. Full of merriment and good nature, they wore patched uniforms and wide-brimmed army hats, many with ripped brims and battered crowns. The officers were clad similarly to their men, wearing only shoulder straps and carrying swords to distinguish them from the enlisted soldiers. The men impressed the Beaufort onlookers with their individual hardiness.[4]

Used to having their own way, the soldiers raided gardens, appropriated fence rails for fires, and chased down chickens. To the stolid civilians, it seemed a riot might occur but soon the senior officers arrived and took control. The troops gathered up whatever caught their fancy, horrifying the white northerners. The freedmen, however, often eagerly gave the soldiers anything they desired.

The racial attitudes of the western soldiers varied, but most behaved well toward the freedmen. At Beaufort they found a unique situation—thousands of refugees, black soldiers, property-owning freedmen, and a society and military command that actively promoted racial advancement. Most accepted the situation, but others railed at seeing black noncommissioned officers who outranked them. Some complained bitterly about a situation that gave former slaves privileges not available to white soldiers and their families. As one described the situation at Beaufort, "There is a great many niggers here, nigger Regiments nigger schools and churches, the eternal nigger is everywhere and the only place that I care about seeing him is with a musket in his hand." Though a number of Sherman's men felt the blacks at Beaufort to be "pampered, petted and spoiled," many realized that the war had turned them into emancipators and that the black community at Beaufort surpassed anything they had seen elsewhere in the South.[5]

Captain Samuel Willard Saxton, who served as an assistant aide-de-camp to his brother Rufus, described Sherman's soldiers as being "a rough looking set, as if they had seen service, as if marching & fighting was their business, instead of drilling & guard duty." He later wrote, "The troops continue to come by the thousands, & the town is full. The merchants & all who have anything to sell are reaping a harvest & raising their prices."[6]

The arriving troops were encamped four miles outside Beaufort along the Shell Road. Though plundering against the loyal citizens and freedmen was kept to a minimum, General Saxton, not wishing to endanger his minions to further depredations, sealed Beaufort off from Sherman's soldiers. Allowed in were headquarters and provost guard units. Among those establishing residence in the town were Generals Blair and Howard. The forty-three-year-old Blair took quarters in the John Joyner Smith House. Blair, whose headquarters was always known for its convivial parties, was a former Democratic congressman from Missouri. Son and namesake of a onetime speaker of the house, General Blair's older brother, Montgomery Blair, had been Lincoln's first postmaster general.[7]

Major General Oliver O. Howard, accompanying the lead elements of Blair's corps, arrived in Beaufort on January 3. The thirty-four-year-old commander of the Army of the Tennessee, known as the "Christian general" thanks to a prewar evangelical conversion and his habit of praying before making any major decisions, was a graduate of both Bowdoin College and the United States Military Academy. On June 1, 1862, during the Peninsula Campaign at the Battle of Fair Oaks, Howard was twice struck in the right arm, which was subsequently amputated. He recovered in time to lead a division at the Battle of Antietam and later commanded the Eleventh Corps at Chancellorsville and

Gettysburg. Howard, with a portion of his corps and other troops from the Army of the Potomac, had been transferred west in late September 1863, when he participated in the Chattanooga and Atlanta Campaigns. Upon the death of Major General James B. McPherson outside Atlanta on July 22, 1864, Howard succeeded to the command of the Army of the Tennessee, which he led for the rest of the campaign and the march through Georgia.[8]

At Beaufort, Howard placed his army headquarters at the Stevens House Hotel, the former H. S. Gibbes House at the southwest corner of Bay and Carteret Streets. It took nine days for the entire Seventeenth Corps, with its horses, wagons, and artillery, to reach Beaufort. Beginning on January 9, before all of Blair's formations had arrived, the first troops from John A. "Black Jack" Logan's Fifteenth Corps began arriving at Beaufort. While awaiting his wing's consolidation, Howard constantly socialized with Rufus and Willard Saxton and their families, often visiting them at their quarters in the former Nathanial Heyward home on Bay Street. Howard came to admire General Saxton and wrote that the military governor had been become "quite domesticated amid a new Northern community and multitudes of negroes that were peopling that part of the seacoast which came into our possession."[9]

Mrs. Saxton and Willard Saxton escorted Howard throughout the sea islands, visiting schools and churches with the general occasionally speaking to freedmen and leading Sunday school services. On St. Helena Island, he toured the new Penn School and met with Laura Towne, Ellen Murray, and Ellen's mother. Howard also went to Elizabeth Botume's school at Old Fort Plantation. He found the children to be as well advanced as white children of the same age. During his time in Beaufort, the weather was cool and delightful and the Saxton dinner table filled with "luxuries." General Howard enjoyed his time in the sea islands, but official duties soon interrupted his pleasant sojourn when, on January 9, word reached Beaufort that Secretary of War Edwin Stanton, aboard the steamer *Nevada* while journeying to Savannah, had touched at Hilton Head. Generals Howard and Saxton rushed to Hilton Head hoping to meet Stanton; but the secretary had continued on, and the two officers left that evening for Savannah.[10]

Secretary of War Stanton was accompanied by an entourage that included the army's chief quartermaster general, Montgomery Meigs, Assistant Adjutant General Edward D. Townsend, and Collector Simon Draper. General Meigs had come to oversee the refitting of Sherman's armies, while Draper, who had replaced Hiram Barney as the collector for the port of New York, the office that controlled all maritime activity in and out of Port Royal Sound, was there to reopen the custom house at Savannah. The main reason for Stanton and Townsend's trip was to investigate troubling reports about abuses between the army and the freedmen, occurring both in the sea islands and during Sherman's march through Georgia.

Sherman had been warned in a private letter from General Halleck, the army's former commander-in-chief and current chief of staff, that "certain influential parties" well placed near the administration, had questioned Sherman's "fidelity" on the national Negro policy. Halleck informed Sherman that these individuals would use the western commander's attitude toward the "inevitable Sambo" against him. Sherman appreciated the warning. A realist, he blamed the war on slavery and the issues surrounding the institution. He also believed that unless the government was careful about how freedmen were integrated into the military and society, the same issues that helped bring on the conflict could wrack the postwar nation.[11]

During the grand procession through Georgia, so many slaves had followed Sherman's formations that they slowed the Union troops. Whenever possible, army officers tried to free themselves of the refugees. At Ebenezer Creek one of Sherman's corps commanders, Brigadier General Jefferson C. Davis, took up a pontoon bridge while a crowd of escaped slaves slept. Worried that Confederate cavalry would soon arrive, some of the blacks drowned as they tried to swim across the creek, while others may have been shot or sabered when Confederate horsemen arrived and swept up the refugees. This incident, coupled with Sherman's reluctance to employ black troops and reports that sea island freedmen were being abused and even shot by General Foster's recruiters, caused the secretary of war, a champion of freedmen rights and soldiers, to visit Sherman's and Foster's commands to personally investigate the treatment of the former slaves by the two generals.[12]

Even before Stanton arrived, Sherman began to address the issues of recruiting abuses and establishing a haven for the refugee slaves. At Savannah, Sherman and his officers challenged the authority of state recruiters who attempted to entice black laborers from the western armies. They also challenged the recruiters who had begun gathering up eligible blacks among the city's former slaves and the arriving refugees. Sherman was appalled by the high-handed abuses employed by the recruiters, who held potential recruits in warehouses against their will. The general quickly ordered an end to the involuntary draft. He did not stop any freedmen from freely joining the army but would not abide forced conscription.[13]

The refugee problem also bedeviled Sherman. Though no accurate numbers were available, at least ten thousand escaped slaves followed the Federal forces to Savannah. Thought was given to transporting these refugees from Georgia to Port Royal, South Carolina, but General Saxton informed Sherman that he could not care for them on the sea islands, writing, "I very much regret, general, that my power to relieve you of the burden of these people is not equal to my inclination, but I have no means at all under my control." He added, "Every cabin and house on these islands is filled to overflowing—I have some 15,000." As an alternative Saxton suggested that the refugees in Savannah be resettled on Edisto and St. Simons Islands.[14]

While Sherman and his subordinates attempted to deal with the influx of refugees and the recruitment of freedmen, Secretary of War Stanton arrived in Savannah. Though wracked by stomach pains, the fifty-one-year-old Stanton never allowed his condition to slow his activity. He immediately met with Sherman and toured the city. The secretary also received Generals Saxton and Howard. Saxton had a productive meeting with Stanton, who sent him back to Beaufort for reports documenting his work and incidents between Foster, the recruiters, and the freedmen. Stanton told Saxton that he would make things right and that Saxton, because of his experience and ability to work with the missionaries and freedmen, was needed on the sea islands and not in the field leading troops.[15]

Stanton also conferred with Sherman, and the two met in the general's headquarters, the Charles Green house, with a delegation of twenty black churchmen, including Reverend James Lynch, the A.M.E. minister who had organized congregations at Port Royal. With General Townsend recording the responses, Stanton queried the pastors, who assured the secretary that they admired and trusted Sherman and asked that he be placed in charge of any future enlistments. Among the inquiries posed to the ministers included questions about how and where the former slaves should live. The church leaders answered that they preferred to be placed "on land until we are able to buy it and make it our own." They also wished to be separated from whites. Only the freeborn Baltimore minister Reverend Lynch expressed a desire for the establishment of integrated settlements. The rest thought it best for the freedmen to be located away from whites until racial prejudices had waned. Before he posed his final question, Stanton asked Sherman to leave the room. He then queried the assembled leaders about how they regarded General Sherman. They replied unanimously that they had full confidence in the general and that their concerns could not be in better hands.[16]

Though quite pleased with the ministers' responses, Sherman continued to maintain his belief that the freed slaves were not yet ready for complete equality, much less the vote. Sherman allowed former slaves to enlist voluntarily and employed freedmen in his army as pioneers but warned that problems would arise after the war when the victorious freedmen soldiers would find themselves living among their defeated masters. Stanton, taking into account the opinions of Sherman, the black ministers, and Saxton, asked Sherman to write out a directive that would help alleviate a dangerous postwar situation and address the recruitment of blacks.

On January 16, 1865, Sherman, under his authority as the commander of the Military Division of the Mississippi, which included the occupied areas of Georgia and South Carolina, issued Special Field Orders Number 15:

Order by the Commander of the Military Division of the Mississippi
IN THE FIELD, SAVANNAH, GA., January 16th, 1865.

I. The islands from Charleston, south, the abandoned rice fields along the rivers for thirty miles back from the sea, and the country bordering the St. Johns river, Florida, are reserved and set apart for the settlement of the negroes now made free by the acts of war and the proclamation of the President of the United States.

II. At Beaufort, Hilton Head, Savannah, Fernandina, St. Augustine and Jacksonville, the blacks may remain in their chosen or accustomed vocations—but on the islands, and in the settlements hereafter to be established, no white person whatever, unless military officers and soldiers detailed for duty, will be permitted to reside; and the sole and exclusive management of affairs will be left to the freed people themselves, subject only to the United States military authority and the acts of Congress. By the laws of war, and orders of the President of the United States, the negro is free and must be dealt with as such. He cannot be subjected to conscription or forced military service, save by the written orders of the highest military authority of the Department, under such regulations as the President or Congress may prescribe. Domestic servants, blacksmiths, carpenters and other mechanics, will be free to select their own work and residence, but the young and able-bodied negroes must be encouraged to enlist as soldiers in the service of the United States, to contribute their share towards maintaining their own freedom, and securing their rights as citizens of the United States.

Negroes so enlisted will be organized into companies, battalions and regiments, under the orders of the United States military authorities, and will be paid, fed and clothed according to law. The bounties paid on enlistment may, with the consent of the recruit, go to assist his family and settlement in procuring agricultural implements, seed, tools, boots, clothing, and other articles necessary for their livelihood.

III. Whenever three respectable negroes, heads of families, shall desire to settle on land, and shall have selected for that purpose an island or a locality clearly defined, within the limits above designated, the Inspector of Settlements and Plantations will himself, or by such subordinate officer as he may appoint, give them a license to settle such island or district, and afford them such assistance as he can to enable them to establish a peaceable agricultural settlement. The three parties named will subdivide the land, under the supervision of the Inspector, among themselves and such others as may choose to settle near them, so that each family shall have a plot of not more than (40) forty acres of tillable ground, and when it borders on some water channel, with not more than 800 feet water front, in the possession of which land the military authorities will afford them protection, until such time as they can protect themselves, or until Congress shall regulate their title. The Quartermaster may, on the requisition of the Inspector of Settlements and Plantations, place at the disposal of the Inspector, one or more of the captured steamers, to ply between the settlements and one or more of the commercial points heretofore named in orders, to afford the settlers the opportunity to supply their necessary wants, and to sell the products of their land and labor.

IV. Whenever a negro has enlisted in the military service of the United States, he may locate his family in any one of the settlements at pleasure, and acquire a homestead, and all other rights and privileges of a settler, as though present in person. In like manner, negroes may settle their families and engage on board the gunboats, or in fishing, or in the navigation of the inland waters, without losing any claim to land or other advantages derived from this system. But no one, unless an actual settler as above defined, or unless absent on Government service, will be entitled to claim any right to land or property in any settlement by virtue of these orders.

V. In order to carry out this system of settlement, a general officer will be detailed as Inspector of Settlements and Plantations, whose duty it shall be to visit the settlements, to regulate their police and general management, and who will furnish personally to each head of a family, subject to the approval of the President of the United States, a possessory title in writing, giving as near as possible the description of boundaries; and who shall adjust all claims or conflicts that may arise under the same, subject to the like approval, treating such titles altogether as possessory. The same general officer will also be charged with the enlistment and organization of the negro recruits, and protecting their interests while absent from their settlements; and will be governed by the rules and regulations prescribed by the War Department for such purposes.

VI. Brigadier General R. SAXTON is hereby appointed Inspector of Settlements and Plantations, and will at once enter on the performance of his duties. No change is intended or desired in the settlement now on Beaufort Island, nor will any rights to property heretofore acquired be affected thereby.

BY ORDER OF MAJOR GENERAL W. T. SHERMAN[17]

By keeping it simple, direct, and to the point, Sherman hoped the order would at least initially provide a temporary refuge for the thousands of slaves that so encumbered his forces as they marched across the South. The property to be appropriated was land taken under the Captured and Abandoned Property Act, which allowed the government, as a wartime measure, to use the territory for the war effort. However, the directive, a military order, would be in effect only while the seceded states remained outside the Constitution. Once the conflict ended and the rebellious states returned to the Union, Congress would then need to decide whether the order should become law. If law, then the possessory titles would be converted to land deeds or homesteads. Sherman, however, would leave that to the politicians; he had a new campaign to plan and execute.[18]

Sherman's Special Field Orders Number 15 did not apply directly to the Beaufort District, where land redistribution had been handled by foreclosure proceedings and tax auctions. The order did, however, cause repercussions in the region's administration and black and white population. General Saxton, his command expanded to take in the area described in the order, had an estimated forty thousand refugees to settle on approximately four hundred thousand acres. Saxton found the task daunting. From St. Augustine, Florida, to Port Royal, South Carolina, there were tens of thousands of refugees. They lived in quartermaster villages, makeshift camps, and independent dwelling sites along the coast. Some owned property. Others had abodes in established hamlets. The most pressing need was to find a haven for those who had followed Sherman to Savannah and to prepare for additional refugees that would be gathered up on the planned march through the Carolinas.

The orders also, as Stanton had promised, put things right for Rufus Saxton. His duties were clearly defined. He was named inspector of freedmen, put in charge of resettlement, and made recruiting agent for the Department of the South. He was given complete control over the freedmen "now in, or who may hereafter come into the Dept., & power to establish colonies." Saxton encouraged former slaves to begin settling abandoned coastal property. He planned his first community for Edisto Island. This would allow the island's natives, who had come to St. Helena Island when Edisto had been abandoned in the summer of 1862, to go home and also provide space for some of the Georgia refugees. For this and future freedmen colonies, the islands around Port Royal would serve as the major staging point for all resettlement activities.[19]

Soon thousands of destitute freedmen arrived from Georgia with little more than the clothing on their backs. On St. Helena Island, Laura Towne described the newcomers brought to St. Helenaville by steamboat as "utterly wretched in circumstances—clothes all torn to rags; in some cases children naked." The island's residents, many of them refugees themselves, took the Georgians into their houses. Towne and Ellen Murray distributed tea to the sick, who were "broken down with fatigue, privation of food and bad air at night."[20]

At Montgomery Hill on Port Royal Island, Elizabeth Botume reported that "between three and about four hundred poor, ragged, destitute people" were helped. Clothing, soap, needles, and thread were distributed. Many of the camp's previous inhabitants had left for work or land elsewhere, and space was available in the barracks. Since the hamlet was no longer associated with Colonel Montgomery and his regiment, General Saxton directed that the cantonment be renamed in honor of the recently deceased Colonel Silliman. At what became known as Silliman or Sillimanville, the forlorn and destitute Georgia refugees soon received assistance, and the children began attending Botume's school at Old Fort Plantation.[21]

The former slaves from Georgia transferred to the sea islands were the first among thousands who would eventually be sent to the enclave. As Sherman's forces moved across South Carolina and into North Carolina, large numbers of freed slaves joined the march, and in time many were shipped back to Port Royal, where they joined a large melting pot of freedmen from throughout the Southeast. Though some would leave to return home or go to new locations, many stayed, creating on the sea islands a large population numbering between twenty and forty thousand, an increase of over three to five times the region's prewar numbers.

While additional refugees were being sent to the sea islands and General Sherman was writing the final version of Special Field Order Number 15, Secretary of War Stanton left Savannah aboard the *Nevada* and came to Hilton Head, where he transferred to the smaller side-wheel steamer *Namaha,* the former *Flora,* and sailed to Beaufort, arriving on January 14. The post band, stationed at the city's main wharf, greeted him with music and the USCT soldiers from the 26th Infantry Regiment and Battery G, 2nd Light Artillery, lined Bay Street. Stanton walked up the avenue arm in arm with General Saxton, followed by the secretary's entourage, to the general's home, where they were joined by General Foster for a reception.

Early in the evening, Stanton and the other dignities were serenaded by both the post band and, as Willard Saxton wrote, "the much finer band from Hilton Head." Stanton stayed with the Saxtons and the evening was spent socially, allowing the secretary to show a side of his personality rarely seen: that of a genial and affable guest. In the house he discovered a volume of poetry by the Englishman Thomas Babbington Macaulay. Referring to Macaulay's poems as "old friends," Stanton relaxed. Rufus Saxton read aloud "Horatius," and Stanton followed with "The Battle of Ivry." Stanton spent the evening and the next day with the Saxtons, and for the first time during his sojourn, he was at ease.[22]

The next day after a hearty breakfast of beefsteak, mutton chops, cold turkey, coffee, and other "fixins," General Saxton escorted Stanton to the Smith Plantation and introduced the secretary to Elizabeth Botume and her two nieces Frances "Fanny" Sophia Langford and Elizabeth "Lizzie" Botume Langford, who taught at the Old Fort Schoolhouse. Willard Saxton accompanied Assistant Adjutant General Townsend to a Sunday school while other members of the official party took rides around the town and Port Royal Island. After lunch Stanton left. Willard Saxton reported the secretary's farewell to Tillie Saxton, the general's wife, as "quite affecting," writing that "he seemed to have enjoyed his visit & had what is for him, a day's rest; business was not mentioned while he was here."[23]

General Saxton accompanied Stanton on the *Nemaha* to Hilton Head, where the secretary boarded the *Nevada* for his trip north. Before the vessel cast off, Stanton sent General Townsend ashore to give Saxton a document promoting both Rufus and his brother Willard to the brevet ranks of major general and major. Through brevets the War Department honored the recipients for exceptional service and gave them deserved recognition among their peers. Brevets, however did not confirm any advancement in rank. Still, the fact that the secretary of war had personally honored the Saxtons gave them increased status, especially for Rufus, who often had to deal with superiors, such as General Foster, who opposed his work with freedmen.[24]

While Stanton visited the Saxtons, General Howard readied elements of his army for an advance on Pocotaligo. The presence of Sherman's forces at Savannah and Beaufort sparked a response from South Carolinians. Governor Andrew Gordon Magrath wrote Jefferson Davis asking that reinforcements, specifically the South Carolina regiments of Kershaw's Brigade, now under Colonel John Doby Kennedy, be sent from Lee's army to South Carolina. Magrath pointedly informed the president that if Charleston fell, so would Richmond. A delegation of prominent South Carolinians petitioned the Confederate War Department asking that an army corps be sent from Virginia to defend the state. In both cases President Davis, agreeing with General Robert E. Lee, initially refused to weaken the forces in Virginia for South Carolina. Lee did, however, point out that elements of the Army of Tennessee had been ordered to the Carolinas, but the South Carolinians knew only too well that the time required for these western units to arrive from Mississippi through a destitute region with little or no rail service, could not compare with reinforcements that could be readily sent from Virginia on functioning railroads.[25]

Beaufort native Robert Barnwell Rhett Sr., in his editorials in the *Charleston Mercury,* also called for help to defend his native state. Direct and unyielding, he railed against President Jefferson Davis for sacrificing South Carolina for Virginia. Rhett believed the time of crisis had arrived, that the majority of the soldiers defending South Carolina were nothing more than "a herd of stragglers and outlaws." Rhett proclaimed that nerve was needed. Men had to stand and not be afraid of dying. To inspire privates, he declared that cowardly captains might need to be shot, and to inspire captains, Rhett called for the shooting of colonels. In an editorial he declared:

> What is a man's life to the institutions and liberty of the country? Nothing. Let old things pass away—let us have a new condition of things. We want no more Jefferson Davis foolery; we want one atom of brains, one spark of nerve—we want no more Burnhamism—we want no more mermaids with heads of monkeys and fishy attachments at the nether extremities—we want men, real men, earnest men—North Carolina, Georgia and South Carolina are in no mood for trifling. They have had enough of this sort of thing. They don't intend to have much more. South Carolina don't intend to be conquered—She intends to fight. She don't intend to be hampered or turned over to the enemy. When she is thus dealt there will be a reckoning—a reckoning where there will be no respectors of person. We want implicit order and calm forecast. South Carolina is a Commonwealth of order; we expect order, and we demand order. We are accustomed to order. We are not use to lawless triflinism; we don't intend to suffer it.[26]

Rhett asserted that South Carolinians stood as gladiators, "stripped to the fight," trained and prepared to battle for "life and death," and the state was "ready to stand or fall where she is." In the coming struggle, Rhett called for "all humanitarianism to be buried." He also derided the Confederacy's and Virginia's attempts to enlist slaves, on the promise of freedom, into the southern army, declaring that Robert E. Lee, who backed the proposal, to be a "Federalist" akin to Daniel Webster. Rhett flatly stated that South Carolina soldiers would never "fight beside a nigger" and that emancipation would lead to "mobocracy on one hand—nigger equality and gradual miscegenation on the other." Instead he called for South Carolina to defend the platform laid down in 1860. He declared that South Carolinians wanted no slaves to fight for them, and with disciplined and capable commanders, fighting creek to creek, they could defeat a dozen Shermans.[27]

Rhett's editorials may have raised the spirits of some in his native state for the coming Armageddon, but it also inspired their enemies. General Sherman made use of the threatening declarations. He wrote, "Taunting messages had also come to us, when in Georgia, to the effect that, when we should reach South Carolina, we would find a people less passive, who would fight us to the bitter end, daring us to come over, etc." Sherman realized that he would not be able to restrain his men, nor would he try for fear it would impair his soldiers' vigor and energy. He noted that "somehow, our men had got the idea that South Carolina was the cause of all our troubles; her people were the first to fire on Fort Sumter, had been in a great hurry to precipitate the country into civil war; and therefore on them should fall the scourge of war in its worse form." Nor were the feelings confined to the Federals. While traversing Georgia, Major General William B. Hazen, a division commander in the Fifteenth Corps, reported that he "heard Georgians say: 'Why don't you go over to South Carolina, and serve them this way? They started it.'"[28]

By mid-January Sherman was ready to serve South Carolina. In conjunction with General Foster and Admiral Dahlgren, he orchestrated a multifaceted campaign, with the Beaufort District serving as his army's gateway. While Sherman readied his columns, Foster realigned his forces. On January 11, the 55th Massachusetts abandoned Boyd's Landing and for a short while occupied the Confederate works at Thunderbolt outside Savannah before joining Federal forces off Charleston. Foster also removed some regiments from Hatch's Coastal Division and formed them into an amphibious unit for a landing north of Charleston at Bull's Bay. At the same time Foster directed his northern district commander on the islands off Charleston, Prussian-born Brigadier General Alexander Schimmelfennig, to carry out demonstrations against the city.[29]

To assist both Foster and Sherman, Admiral Dahlgren sent warships into the rivers to facilitate the movement of troops and threaten southern communications. Gunboats entered the Stono River while ironclads demonstrated off Charleston harbor. Dahlgren and Foster's maneuvering, though sideshows, kept the southerners off balance and their attention riveted on Charleston while Sherman's armies prepared to head for Columbia, cutting the railroads to Charleston as they went. The plan was simple: as Sherman shook the tree, Foster and Dahlgren would pick up the fallen fruit.[30]

By mid-January Sherman was ready to send his armies into the "pinewoods again." On the thirteenth Howard moved Frank Blair's Seventeenth Corps and one brigade of John Logan's Fifteenth Corps out of Beaufort to Port Royal Ferry. A small party of soldiers, led by twenty-seven-year-old Lieutenant Colonel Dennis T. Kirby of General Blair's staff, crossed the Whale Branch River in small boats. Kirby, a New York–born Missouri officer who would eventually be awarded the Medal of Honor for his actions during the May 22, 1863, attack on Vicksburg, quickly established a fortified post. Throughout the night a six-hundred-foot pontoon bridge was constructed, connecting Port Royal Island to the mainland. The next morning Blair's soldiers began gingerly crossing the wobbling bridge, which Howard described as poor because of rotten canvas covering the pontoons. Once on the mainland, the Federals quickly pushed on to Garden Corners, where the Fifteenth Corps brigade was detached, while the rest of the formation turned west toward Pocotaligo.[31]

Drawn up in fortifications behind Huspah Creek resisting Blair's 12,800 men were about 150 dismounted troopers from the 3rd South Carolina

Cavalry and three cannons commanded by Colonel Charles J. Colcock. The Confederates' position was strong, but their numbers were few. At 9:30 A.M. Colcock reported the enemy in his front, but the commander of the lead Federal division, the forty-four-year-old, New York–born Ohio lawyer, Brigadier General Mortimer Dormer Leggett, did not launch a frontal attack. Instead he dispatched part of his command down the Sheldon Church Road until they reached a spot beyond Colcock's defense line and then moved across rice dikes, turning the Confederates out of their defenses.[32]

Colcock, closely followed by the Federals, retreated to the fortification at Stony Creek. Again Leggett refused to attack head on and personally directed one of his brigades on a march three miles below the enemy battery, where again he found a passage across the rice fields. Turned out of his second position, Colcock at about 3:15 P.M. led his troopers to Pocotaligo, where they found refuge in a fortification, the largest and strongest southern work in the Beaufort District. Leggett's soldiers, wading through swamps and flooded rice fields, braving heavy artillery and musketry fire, closed on the enemy inside the Pocotaligo defenses, but soon darkness ended active operations.[33]

The next morning, January 15, the Federals found Pocotaligo evacuated. They quickly pushed on to Pocotaligo Station and the railroad, where Howard happily placed his foot on the track. The Union soldiers quickly went to work building entrenchments north of the train depot. Sherman, who later inspected the Confederate works around Pocotaligo, was surprised that they had been abandoned without a fight. He wrote, "All the country between Beaufort and Pocotaligo was easily defended by a small force; and why the enemy had allowed us to make a lodgment at Pocotaligo so easily I did not understand, unless it resulted from fear or ignorance.... It was to me manifest that the soldiers and people of the South entertained an undue fear of our western men, and, like children, they had invented such ghost-like stories of our prowess in Georgia, that they were scared by their own inventions." General Hardee agreed with his opponent's assessment, stating that Colcock "did not win any laurels," and directed McLaws to place the South Carolina cavalry directly under Wheeler, who should "see that it fights."[34]

In reality the Confederates had few resources with which to defend Pocotaligo or any of their fixed defenses in the Beaufort District. Colcock's delaying action had bought time for the southerners to withdraw the majority of their forces at Grahamville, Coosawhatchie, and Pocotaligo across the Combahee River; the evacuation left elements of Wheeler's cavalry corps and Colcock's regiment as the only forces operating between the Combahee and Savannah Rivers. Colcock, headquartered at Kadesh Church near McTier's Mill on the Salkehatchie Road, kept close watch on the growing Federal forces around Pocotaligo.[35]

The withdrawal of the southern defenders also released the remains of Hatch's division stationed at DeVeaux's and Graham's Necks. On the morning of January 15, soldiers at Mike Jenkins's plantation on Graham's Neck heard drums and fifes from the north along with bugles playing reveille. Colonel Hallowell marched the 54th Massachusetts and 33rd USCT, the former 1st South Carolina, out of their encampment to Frampton Creek, where they found the formidable Confederate entrenchments abandoned. Advancing to Pocotaligo, the Massachusetts and South Carolina black soldiers made contact with the Seventeenth Corps before returning to their camps.

While Hallowell was meeting Blair's men, Federals from DeVeaux's Neck began a tentative probe toward the railroad. Units occupied Coosawhatchie and the fortifications at Bee's Creek and Tullifinny Trestle. The 25th Ohio began destroying the track between the Coosawhatchie and Tullifinny Rivers, while the 127th New York joined in burning ties and twisting rails from Gopher Hill to Coosawhatchie. The soldiers also foraged liberally, gathering up cattle, horses, and chickens, with the 56th New York seizing a hoard of a thousand plugs of tobacco. The men reveled at the end of the combat and campaigning that had been going on for forty-eight days since the start of the Honey Hill expedition. As Captain Luis Emilio of the 54th Massachusetts noted, "It was a welcome change to be freed from the anxiety of the enemy's proximity and thus enabled us to sleep until daylight, and relieved from all picket duty."[36]

The advance of Howard's troops and their linking up with Hatch's division at Pocotaligo pleased Sherman, who hoped to continue a fluid movement that would culminate in an advance inland. However, the lack of transports had slowed the transfer of Logan's Fifteenth Corps to Beaufort. Only a portion of Charles R. Woods's division had arrived, while Hazen's division had yet to embark. To hurry things along, Sherman decided to march the corps' remaining two divisions overland from Savannah to Pocotaligo.

While the right wing consolidated at Pocotaligo, Slocum directed his left wing to begin its movement toward Robertville. The Fourteenth Corps was to march from Savannah to Two Sisters Ferry, cross the river into South Carolina and seize Robertville while the Twentieth Corps was to occupy Hardeeville and Purrysburg and then continue on to the rendezvous at Robertville.

On January 17 the remaining units from Sherman's field armies at Savannah began their excursion. The Twentieth Corps started first. Initially the weather was clear. From the Hardee Plantation, General Ward advanced his division to Hardeeville, while the forty-six-year-old Massachusetts native and former machinist and mill operator Brigadier General Nathaniel James Jackson led his division of the Twentieth Corps across the Savannah River. The men filed over rickety pontoon bridges, one connecting Savannah to

Hutchinson Island and then another taking them to the South Carolina shore. Once in the Palmetto State, the Union soldiers weaved their way over rice dikes until they reached the Union Causeway, which led to the New River Bridge, where the road forked, one going northwest to Hardeeville, the other northeast to Coosawhatchie.

To facilitate Jackson's division, Federal pioneers, both white infantrymen and former slaves enlisted in Georgia into labor detachments by Sherman's commanders, placed logs, fence rails, and tree limbs across the top of the earthen rice-field embankments. A technique known as corduroying, this created a stable roadway for wagons and caissons. Once over the river, across the rice fields, and on the causeway, Jackson's division followed Ward's men to Hardeeville, and then on the nineteenth, Jackson's soldiers continued on and secured the old steamboat landing at Purrysburg, where Jackson established his headquarters in the midst of the town's cemetery.

Williams's third division, commanded by Brigadier General John W. Geary, was supposed to follow Jackson's soldiers, but Geary's unit had been assigned guard duty in Savannah and could not leave until relieved by Brigadier General Cuvier Grover's division, which had been dispatched from Virginia to take over as the city's garrison. Grover's force, made up of white troops, had been sent in response to pleas from the city's white population, who asked to be spared from occupation by black troops—a request that Sherman, who wanted to avoid incidents between the white southerners and black troops, happily granted. Grover did not arrive until January 19, delaying Geary from immediately following Jackson's soldiers out of Savannah and joining the rest of the Twentieth Corps around Hardeeville and Purrysburg.[37]

Because of the time required to exchange duties with Grover, Geary's forces lost their place behind Jackson's division and had to wait while two divisions of Logan's Fifteenth Corps prepared to traverse the unsteady pontoon bridges. Ordered to cross first was the corps' Third Division, commanded by General John E. Smith. His division had two brigades, and the first ordered into South Carolina was Colonel Clark R. Wever's Second Brigade. By 9:30 A.M. elements of Wever's command had maneuvered their way across the narrow, corduroyed rice dikes. Then it began to rain, and soon the soldiers found themselves in the midst of a deluge. The heavy downpour worried General Smith, who feared the rest of his division might not be able to continue into South Carolina.

The forty-eight-year-old Smith had been born in Switzerland and grew up in Philadelphia. Trained as a jeweler, he settled in Galena, Illinois, a town that provided the Federal army with nine generals, including Ulysses S. Grant. A veteran of every campaign of the Army of the Tennessee, he had gone from commanding a regiment to leading a division. Smith accompanied Wever's brigade. Among the last to cross the river, he discovered the roads on Hutchinson Island badly gutted and had to assign detachments to reposition the pontoons. Shortly after noon, Wever's soldiers occupied the abandoned Confederate camps and forts at the New River Bridge, where Smith closed up his column and had a working party rebuild the bridge over the New River.

A hard rain continued to fall, and by nightfall the following day, six inches to a foot of water covered the encampment along the New River. The flood masked the presence of deep wells, which caused a number of men to contribute "to the merriment of their comrades by suddenly disappearing from view." Smith also fell victim when his "major domo" plunged into a well, losing the headquarters mess kit and leaving the servant with only a pig's foot and some hardtack to feed General Smith. As the aide explained, "Dere was no plate, knife and fork, left; dey was all clean done gone."[38]

Smith soon learned that his division's other brigade and all following formations, except some supply trains, had been unable to negotiate the flooded rice fields and had returned to Savannah. Undaunted amid heavy downpours and flooding, Smith resumed his march on the twenty-first, and over the next three days, he and Wever's soldiers slowly traversed the roadway from the New River to Hazzard's Creek near Whitehall Plantation, then past the Federal entrenched camps near Boyd's Landing and on to Roseland, the Huguenin plantation at the head of the Broad River. After building bridges over Bee's and Little Bee's Creeks, the rain-soaked brigade finally reached Pocotaligo at 3:00 P.M. on January 23, corduroying nearly five hundred yards of road on the expedition's final day.[39]

While the men of Wever's brigade struggled across the Beaufort's District's lower regions, the commander of the Twentieth Corps, Major General Alpheus Williams, was also experiencing difficulties reaching his destination. Williams, accompanied by his staff, had crossed the Savannah River with General Smith's supply and ammunition wagons. They expected an easy ride to join their comrades near Hardeeville, but soon the rain began to fall. Williams and his aides hoped to find shelter at Dr. Cheves's plantation house, but they found the place "a heap, a mass, of smouldering ruins," which Williams claimed "hissed and laughed" at them. The house's destruction, the result of the men from Wever's brigade losing their "equanimity of temper," forced Williams and his companions, over twenty men, to take refuge in a small slave hut, where Williams was "honored with the structure's only bunk."[40]

The next morning, after a breakfast of cigars and water, part of Williams's staff pushed on to Hardeeville while the general and some aides went in search of his wagon trains, which the general feared may have bogged down in the rice fields. Riding down the Union Causeway toward Savannah, Williams learned that his trains had successfully reached Hardeeville, but having gone twenty-four hours without food, he decided to continue searching for something to eat. As he rode on, Williams reminisced about home, commenting that the swamps reminded him of the Grand Marsh near Hamtramck, Michigan. But soon the general discovered that his route, which led over rice dikes, had disappeared under a sheet of water, causing the logs from the corduroyed passageway to bob up to the surface.

Across the flooded landscape Williams could see the white canvas tops of supply wagons moving toward Savannah. Driven by a desire to eat and to drink coffee, the general, mounted on "Billy," a "tough Canadian-looking racker," tried to negotiate the submerged levees. Williams, a "full, fat man," wore high riding boots, a brigadier's coat, corduroy pants, and a private's army hat with the brim turned down fore and aft. His face, which reminded a soldier of a dull old doctor who loved good whiskey and had a disposition to gout, "was covered by a full luxurious beard, liberally mixed with grey." As he directed Billy forward, the horse slid into a hole so deep that water ran into Williams's riding boots. Williams sat still. Billy quickly regained his balance and sprang back onto the dike. With his boots full of water, the general rode away.[41]

Rejoining his aides, Williams looked unsuccessfully for another route to the pontoon bridge and the coveted supply wagons, but with the rain continuing and the water rising, the men rode back toward the ruins of Dr. Cheves's house, where they found a handful of older blacks at the plantation's slave quarters. While drying his feet by a fire, Williams learned that most of the plantation's slaves, some two hundred, had been carried off to Abbeville, South Carolina. He asked those left behind whether they had heard about the Confederacy's proposal to arm slaves. One older man replied that they had but that if it happened "dey'll turn the guns on the rebs." Once reshod with dry socks and boots, Williams remounted. After checking on some stalled wagons, where he found a feast of hardtack and pork, he continued on to Hardeeville, arriving at General Ward's headquarters. Here the fifty-four-year-old corps commander reported that he "found a good supper waiting, spread my blankets on the floor of a shell of a house, and I don't think I rolled over until daylight." He also made sure that his horses, unfed and in the rain for thirty-six hours, got a "good feed."[42]

While the Federals struggled on the roads in the Beaufort District, General Sherman made changes to his original plans. General John Smith's First Brigade, stopped from crossing the Savannah River by the high water, followed Hazen's division by boat to Beaufort, while the Fifteenth Corps' Fourth Division under Brigadier Generals John M. Corse and John W. Geary's Second Division of the Twentieth Corps were temporarily added to Brigadier General Jefferson C. Davis's Fourteenth Corps and Brigadier General Judson Kilpatrick's cavalry division, which Slocum was to march to Two Sisters Ferry along the Savannah River's western bank.

On January 20 General Slocum commenced his foray. Slocum, a thirty-seven-year-old West Point graduate born in Delphi, New York, was a trained artilleryman. After service in the Seminole War, he was briefly stationed at Fort Moultrie in Charleston Harbor. Resigning from the army in 1856, Slocum became a lawyer and was elected to the New York legislature before being appointed at the start of the war as colonel of the 27th New York. After being wounded at First Bull Run, he participated in all of the Army of the Potomac's campaigns from the Peninsula through Gettysburg, becoming the second youngest major general in the U.S. Army and commander of the Twelfth Corps. A cautious, yet inspiring leader, he was nicknamed "Slow Come," a reference to his actions on July 1, 1863, when he vacillated in pushing his troops on to Gettysburg. After the Gettysburg Campaign, Slocum and a portion of his corps were transferred to the Western Theater. He led a corps during Sherman's Atlanta Campaign and was later assigned to lead the Army of Georgia during the march to the sea.[43]

While taking his forces from Savannah to Two Sisters Ferry, Slocum again appeared to be slow in coming, though this time he had both manmade and natural conditions to contend with. The march began and continued through a heavy downpour. The roads became quagmires as "the bottom fell out," with mules, horses, wagons, and artillery pieces sinking into quicksand. Soldiers, who had started the day full of enthusiasm, waded waist deep into the mud and after two days became silent and spiritless. East of the road, the Savannah River continued to flow well over flood stage, while to the west a sheet of water covered the countryside. Ahead, the highway dissolved into a sliver of "fathomless mud" and soon "General Georgia Mud" stopped Slocum's attempt to reach Two Sisters Ferry.[44]

On the twenty-second the Federals encamped. To warm themselves, the men used pine knots to build roaring bonfires "that transformed the grim trees into burnished columns supporting a canopy of dark green foliage whereon the raindrops sparkled like strings of pearls." For five rain-filled days, the troops gathered around their blazes while work crews struggled to fill in deep holes and corduroy the roads.[45]

The deluge set back Sherman's plans. The red-headed general had hoped to begin his campaign on about January 18, but by the twenty-first he admitted in a letter to Grant that it would be some days before he could "cast off." He wrote his fellow Ohioan that "the rains are villainous, and all the country is underwater, and retards us much.... The roads are underwater and my men are not exactly amphibious yet, nor the mules either."[46]

While waiting for Slocum to come, Sherman, "having accomplished all that seemed necessary," prepared to take his armies into South Carolina. On January 22, 1865, he embarked aboard the steamer *W. W. Coit* from Savannah for Beaufort with his entire headquarters, officers, clerks, orderlies, wagons, and horses. The *W. W. Coit* touched at Hilton Head, where Sherman conferred with General Foster and Admiral Dahlgren about the coming campaign.[47]

Once the western armies and their commander left the Beaufort District, Foster would resume full charge of the Department of the South. This position included responsibility for not only recently acquired Savannah but also the Federal positions in coastal North Carolina, where he was expected to lay up supplies for Sherman's armies when they emerged from their march through South Carolina.

Sherman also directed Foster to implement Field Orders Number 15, and in a dispatch sent that same day, Foster enclosed a copy of the order to General Saxton, informing his subordinate of his appointment as "inspector of negro settlements and plantations in this department." Saxton was also told that he had been relieved as the military commander of the Beaufort District and replaced by Brigadier General Edward Potter. The message went on to state that Sherman had left within the department "a large number of animals, partially broken down, that will be loaned to the negroes to be used by them on the plantations until they are sufficiently recuperated for active service, when they will be called for." Should Saxton require these horses and mules for the freedmen, he only needed to apply to Foster's headquarters. Though not an outright gift, the proposed use of army livestock was the closest the government ever came to providing the so-called "mule" to the freedmen to go with the reputed "forty acres."[48]

While Sherman remained at Hilton Head, some of his staff went on to Beaufort, arriving during the evening of January 22. The officers were not impressed, with one writing, "It is not a pretty place, nor even has a fine sea-view like Hilton Head." While in town some of the men visited the Edmund Rhett mansion, where they dined with Tax Commissioner William E. Wording, who resided there. Major Henry Hitchcock, Sherman's assistant adjutant general, noted that it was said, "but tis doubtful," that in the house "the South Carolina ordinance of Secession was got up and drafted." Still the irony made an impression on Hitchcock, who wrote, "It is odd that this house, if its local celebrity is deserved, should now be occupied by one of the 3 U.S. Direct Tax Commissioners' whose business it is to carry out the law which is stripping those conspirators of their property."[49]

The officers of Sherman's staff, like their commander, looked upon those involved in the great freedmen experiment with a skeptical eye. They referred to General Saxton as "Moses" and questioned whether he had gotten into the "nigger business in order to get advancement," though they did note that General Howard, whom they admired, held Saxton in high esteem, and in time the officers came to respect General Saxton. They also initially doubted the sincerity of Reverend Mansfield French, whom they termed the "Aaron" of the enterprise. The staff had been present in Savannah when French, whom Major Hitchcock described as having a "face far more sanctimonious than sanctified," lectured Sherman about the freedmen's future. The officers called French "Holy Joe" and were quick to believe the rumor that the minister had made a tidy sum in charging the freedmen "a dollar apiece" to perform marriage ceremonies.[50]

On January 23 at about 2:00 P.M., Sherman arrived in Beaufort. He lodged with the Saxtons at their home in the former Nathaniel Heyward House. The Saxton wives, Tillie and Mary, pronounced Sherman "horrid looking," while Willard Saxton admitted that the general was not handsome and had no great humanitarian feelings. He described Sherman as "sharp looking, nervous & restless & anxious to start again on his campaign." After dining with the Saxtons, Sherman met with General Howard, who had returned to Beaufort and had been staying with the Saxtons since his army had occupied Pocotaligo. Together Sherman and Howard worked out the logistics for the coming movement, sending out a series of dispatches from the Saxton home. While the generals busily issued directives, Tax Commissioner Brisbane came by, and in the evening a number of the house guests joined in some games of backgammon.[51]

The next morning Sherman, Howard, and some staff rode on toward Pocotaligo. The rain had ended, and an energized Sherman wrote Slocum, "Weather is now magnificent and we must take all advantage possible of it." That night Sherman and his aides stayed at General Blair's headquarters in a house at the end of a majestic avenue of live oaks. As it was a cold night, Sherman slept on the floor by a fireplace. When the flames burned low, he rekindled the fire with fragments of a mantle clock and a bedstead, which he claimed was the only act of vandalism that he committed during the war. The next day he established his headquarters at John White Gregorie's Richfield Plantation along the Combahee River.[52]

The five days of rain had slowed Sherman's campaign. Only Blair's and part of Williams's corps had been able to take up their assigned jumping-off points. Logan was still transferring Hazen's division and the marooned brigade from Smith's division to Beaufort, while Slocum and his forces, including Judson Kilpatrick's cavalry division and a division each from Logan's and Williams's corps west of the Savannah River, had not reached Two Sisters Ferry. However, with the weather clearing, Sherman believed that his movement across the Beaufort District would begin soon.

A man of tremendous nervous energy, the mercurial Sherman looked older than his forty-four years. Nearly six feet in height, wiry, and muscular with a deeply furrowed face, he had a broad forehead with thick, reddish hair and a close-cut beard and moustache. He possessed an iron constitution and preferred serving outside in all types of weather. Sherman slept in spurts. He often retired early, only to be up before midnight, wandering through the camps, smoking a cigar, and conversing with anyone present. Unpretentious, he judged individuals quickly. Though believing Africans to be inferior, he treated them individually with respect, never refusing an audience and often interrupting his work or conversations to greet and shake their hands. Determined, honest, unyielding, and earnest, he acted with no regrets once he had made a decision.

Though a tough, hardened soldier, Sherman was sensitive to criticism, especially from journalists and politicians whose denigration of his policies early in the war caused him to take a leave of absence, nearly derailing his career. He reappeared as a subordinate to General Grant and served with him from Shiloh to Chattanooga. When Grant became the North's commander-in-chief, Sherman succeeded to overall commander in the West.

Sherman knew the coming campaign would be a terrible one. His soldiers were eager to visit upon South Carolina, the progenitor of secession, destruction in its worse kind. As one soldier observed, "Here is where treason began, and by God here is where it shall end." There were forewarnings. Sherman's primary mount for the coming march was "Old Sam," known to be "a horribly fast-walking horse." The men took this as an omen and readied themselves for a new, furious campaign. In a larger picture Sherman saw what would happen as he marched inland toward Virginia. As he commented to an officer, "I shall have to go up there and do that job myself. Eat 'em up as I go, and take 'em backside."[53]

Poised to resist Sherman was a ragtag force of Confederate cavalry, regulars, militia, and reserves. Some reinforcements had arrived. President Davis and General Lee, having relented from their earlier convictions not to send help, had dispatched from the Army of Northern Virginia the remains of Kershaw's Brigade, now commanded by Colonel John D. Kennedy. The decimated South Carolina unit had arrived in mid-January and was assigned to guard the crossings of the Combahee River at Salkehatchie. Also sent south were the remnants of Brigadier General Matthew Butler's cavalry division, along with Major General Wade Hampton, who was assigned to command the area's cavalry. Lee directed that Butler's troopers be sent without their horses and that they be returned to Virginia for the spring campaign; however, neither Hampton's nor Butler's men arrived in time to join the fight in the Beaufort District.[54]

When the Federals occupied Hardeeville, Purrysburg, and Pocotaligo, the area's southern commander, General Hardee, quickly removed his infantry and artillery from the Beaufort District and drew them up, along with other formations, along the Combahee-Salkehatchie River line. All along the rivers, under the direction of engineers and the department's ordnance chief, Colonel Ambrosio Gonzales, the Confederates hurriedly constructed, armed, and garrisoned fortifications at river crossings. Hardee divided the defense line between two experienced officers, Major Generals Lafayette McLaws and Ambrose R. Wright, both veterans of the Army of Northern Virginia. General McLaws's division, withdrawn from the line between Coosawhatchie and Pocotaligo, had deployed on the east side of the Salkehatchie River running from just north of the railroad bridge at Salkehatchie to the crossing at Rivers Bridge. McLaws had approximately six thousand effectives, half of whom were reservists, to guard a line that in theory ran from Salkehatchie to Barnwell and on to Augusta, Georgia.

From the railroad to the mouth of the Combahee River stood Major General Ambrose R. Wright's division. Wright, a thirty-eight-year-old lawyer and politician turned soldier, had been born in Louisville, Georgia. A militia commander at the start of the war, he eventually compiled a distinguished career with the Army of Northern Virginia, serving as a brigade commander in nearly all the army's major battles, including Gettysburg, where on July 2 he led his men on the deepest penetration of the Federal line on Cemetery Ridge before being forced to withdraw. He served throughout the Overland Campaign and at the Battle of the Crater before being selected as a major general and ordered to the Army of Tennessee. However, because of illness and political duties with the Georgia State Senate, Wright never reported, but by January 2, 1865, he returned to the military and joined Hardee's forces in South Carolina. To defend his portion of the river line along the Combahee, Wright had about three thousand men, mostly artillerymen serving in fifteen field batteries, including the Beaufort Volunteer Artillery, plus some South Carolina reservists and militia who covered not only river crossings but also coastal waterways open to incursions by Federal warships.

The southerners, unable to ascertain Sherman's intentions, initially distributed General Wheeler's cavalry corps on both sides of the Savannah River. In Georgia, Brigadier General Alfred Iverson Jr.'s division guarded the approaches to Augusta, while across the river in South Carolina, Wheeler's other two divisions, along with Colonel Colcock's 3rd South Carolina Cavalry, some four thousand horsemen, were posted in a wide arc across the Beaufort District. From his headquarters at Lawtonville, Wheeler kept a close watch on the Federals. Brigadier General William W. Allen, a twenty-nine-year-old Alabamian and a Princeton College graduate, placed his division headquarters at the Maner House near the junction of the Orangeburg and Augusta Roads. His troopers patrolled the area around the Savannah River and the roadways leading from Purrysburg to Augusta. General William Y. C. Humes, a Virginia-born, thirty-four-year-old Virginia Military Institute graduate posted at Hickory Hill, positioned his troopers to resist enemy advances along the roads leading north from Gillisonville and

McPhersonville, while Colonel Colcock kept his men on the Salkehatchie Road near McTier's Mill.

The horsemen could do little to stop the Federals. Besides being too few in number, there was little cooperation or communication between the commands. Wheeler rarely responded to dispatches from McLaws. Colcock complained that men from Humes's division were stripping the countryside of food and refusing to do picket duty. Wheeler's cavalry exasperated General Hardee, who alternated between praising the horsemen and referring to them as thieves and robbers.[55]

While Sherman waited for his formations to reach their assigned jumping-off points, Admiral Dahlgren continued to maneuver his warships along the South Carolina coast. Arrangements were made with General Foster to transfer troops to Bull's Bay, north of Charleston, where a landing could threaten Mount Pleasant. In the region between Savannah and Charleston, Dahlgren dispatched Lieutenant Commander Stephen B. Luce with the warship *Pontiac* into the Savannah River to assist Slocum's soldiers as they advanced along both sides of the waterway toward Two Sisters Ferry. To threaten the enemy's lines of communications between the Beaufort District and Charleston, Dahlgren sent the gunboat *Dai Ching* and the tug *Clover* into the Combahee River, while the *Pawnee* and the tug *Daffodil* patrolled the Ashepoo River and the *Sonoma* entered the North Edisto River.[56]

At about 4:00 P.M. on January 25, Confederate pickets spotted the *Dai Ching* and the *Clover* entering the Combahee River. The *Dai Ching*, a 170-foot long, screw-propelled merchantman turned warship was armed with four 24-pound smoothbore howitzers, two 20-pound Parrott Rifles, and one 100-Parrott Rifle. She was commanded by Lieutenant Commander James C. Chaplin, while the *Clover*, a 90-foot screw-propelled tugboat carrying one 12-pound rifle and one 12-pound smoothbore was captained by Acting Ensign Franklin S. Leach. At nightfall the makeshift gunboats anchored off Tar Bluff. The next morning the two vessels got underway. A couple of miles farther up the river they captured the schooner *Coquette*, laden with seventy-four bales of cotton. Ensign Leach took the *Coquette* in tow behind the *Clover*. As they continued up the Combahee, the Federals could see Confederate fortifications at Burnet's Point, and at about 8:00 A.M. three shots rang out from the battery, one falling short and two passing over the *Dai Ching*'s deck.

Chapin quickly ordered the engines on the *Dai Ching* reversed and turned his ship downriver, where he wanted to place the vessel in a less exposed spot and in a better position to return fire. While navigating a sharp bend in the river, a strong wind coupled with an ebb tide drove the *Dai Ching* toward the western bank. On the bridge Chaplin discovered that the pilot, Stephen Small, had abandoned his post, and he was unable to stop the vessel from running aground. Though stranded, the *Dai Ching*'s crew immediately took up the challenge and returned fire with their howitzers and a 20-pound Parrott. The sailors also tore down the ship's railing so that they could bring to bear the pivot gun, a 100-pound Parrott, a weapon most capable of dueling with the enemy battery.

Signals were made to Ensign Leach, who brought the *Clover* near the *Dai Ching* in an attempt to pull the larger gunboat off the bank. A line was passed but it parted, and before a hawser could be connected, Leach, without explanation, took the *Clover* downriver out of range of the enemy guns. Chaplin quickly sent off two cutters, one to communicate with the *Pawnee* in the Ashepoo or the *Stettin* in St. Helena Sound and the other to recall the *Clover*. While waiting for assistance, Chaplin and his crew kept up a vigorous artillery exchange with the Confederate battery. The southerners in Battery Burnet, employing three of the work's five guns—a rifled 32-pounder, a 4.6-inch rifled siege gun, and a 30-pound Parrott—fired 180 rounds at the stricken vessel. During the fight the *Dai Ching* was struck over thirty times. Her decks were riddled, smokestack and masts struck repeatedly, and the hull penetrated. Once the ammunition for the lighter guns had been expended, Chapin ordered his crew, "except enough to work the 100-pounder and pass the ammunition," into the marsh and to "keep close to the bow, clear of the enemy fire."[57]

Projectiles from the vessel struck near the Confederate battery but caused only minor damage, which was easily repaired with only a few spades of earth. At 2:30 a shot disabled the *Dai Ching*'s 100-pounder. Unable to respond and with the tide going out, Chapin, after seven hours of constant combat, decided with his remaining officers, to evacuate the ship and set her afire. The wounded were placed on the remaining small boat, while the rest of the crew made their way through the marsh until they were able to hail and board the *Clover*, whose commander had ignored all pleas to assist his comrades on the *Dai Ching*.

That evening Commander George Balch, captain of the *Pawnee*, having been reached by the sailors of the *Dai Ching*'s cutter, brought his vessel and the *Daffodil* into the Combahee River, where he made arrangements for the surviving members of the *Dai Ching*'s crew to be taken to Port Royal. The resulting Court of Inquiry cleared Lieutenant Commander Chapin and commended him and his men for their brave actions. The black civilian pilot, Stephen Small, was punished for deserting his post, and the commander of the *Clover*, Acting Ensign Leach, charged with disobedience and deserting his post, was court-martialed, dismissed from service, and sentenced to confinement and hard labor for five years.[58]

While the *Dai Ching* was being riddled by Confederate shot and shell, Lieutenant Commander Stephen Luce, commanding the 205-foot side-wheel gunboat *Pontiac,* patrolled the Savannah River off Two Sisters Ferry, waiting for the arrival of General Slocum's army. Landing a detachment from the *Pontiac,* Luce established an entrenched picket post on the Georgia bluff opposite the ferry and dispatched a party of sailors to search for the lead elements of Slocum's force, but the blue jackets were captured by Confederate cavalry. Undeterred, Luce on January 28 again tried to communicate with Slocum by sending inland Marine Sergeant Christopher Stewart and two privates. The marines managed to avoid enemy cavalry, and at 10:00 A.M. met up with soldiers from Brigadier General Jefferson Columbus Davis's Fourteenth Corps.[59]

Later that day General Davis reached Luce's picket post at Two Sisters Ferry and made arrangements to join the naval officer on the *Pontiac* to search for sites along the South Carolina shore to connect a pontoon bridge. One of the most controversial of Civil War generals, the Indiana-born Davis had initially served in the United States Army during the Mexican War as an enlisted man in the 3rd Indiana Volunteers. Cited for gallantry at the Battle of Buena Vista, he received a commission as an officer in the 1st U.S. Artillery Regiment and had been a member in April 1861 of Fort Sumter's garrison. A protégé of Indiana governor Oliver P. Morton, Davis was appointed colonel of the 22nd Indiana and later a brigadier general of volunteers. He led a division at Pea Ridge, the Siege of Corinth, and the Kentucky Campaign, during which, after a heated argument, he shot and killed his former commanding officer William Nelson at the Galt House Hotel in Louisville. Though accused of murder, no official action was taken, and with Morton's influence Davis continued to lead his division in subsequent campaigns until assigned to the Fourteenth Corps for the march to Savannah.

It was during the advance across Georgia that the aforementioned Ebenezer Creek incident occurred. After crossing the creek east of Springfield, Davis ordered his pontoon bridge taken up before the refugee slaves following his corps could cross. As Confederate cavalry approached, many of the slaves panicked and tried to swim the river, some of them drowning. Witnesses later reported that the southern cavalry cut down many of the runaway slaves. Though Sherman dismissed the incident and placed no blame on Davis, word of the episode reached the War Department and helped give rise to Secretary of War Stanton's visit to Savannah. As with the shooting of Nelson, Davis escaped any charges and remained with the army.[60]

Aboard the *Pontiac,* Davis, with Luce, carried out a fruitless search for a spot on the South Carolina to anchor the pontoon bridge. The high water had submerged the river's low banks, and the officers could not locate a point where a bridge could be constructed without the South Carolina end of the bridge terminating in an overflowing, dense cypress swamp. That night

General Slocum arrived, and the next morning, after examining the banks, he decided to establish the pontoon bridge at the old ferry crossing, even though it meant building additional bridges over the flooded landscape on the South Carolina shore to reach the Robertville Road.[61]

While waiting for his pontoon train to arrive, Slocum attempted to contact his other corps, Williams's Twentieth, which he expected to be on the South Carolina shore above Two Sisters Ferry. Williams had arrived but not at the anticipated spot. Contending with rain and a flooded countryside, William, who briefly had to establish his headquarters in the limbs of a great tree, directed his two divisions, Ward's and Jackson's, to march out of Purrysburg to the hamlet of Bradham's, where the highway from Purrysburg forked. Williams planned to take the route running northwest, which led to a series of high sand hills above Two Sisters Ferry, but the recent rains had submerged the road. Unable to reach the ferry by the direct route, the Union troops turned to the northeast, and by the evening of the twenty-ninth, Williams's divisions had occupied Robertville. Richard T. Van Wyck, a member of the 150th New York attached to General Jackson's division, described his impressions of the area: "The country as we advance up the river becomes more fertile, large plantations handsomely arranged, and houses luxuriously furnished. No poor class of people are met with. The slaveholders and the slaves only have been occupants, but the former have deserted, scarcely two or three whites I have seen upon the twenty or thirty farm houses I have visited. They have taken all except their furniture, all provisions except a little corn, and all live stock."[62]

Van Wyck described Robertville as having a fine church and residences but that "not a *soul* could we find upon entering." Confederate cavalry challenged the Federals northwest of town, but soldiers from Brigadier General Nathaniel J. Jackson's division quickly drove the horsemen across the Black Swamp. With Robertville, the hometown of Federal officer Henry Martyn Robert, the future author of *Robert's Rules of Order*, secured, Williams detailed Brigadier General James L. Selfridge's brigade from Jackson's division to begin rebuilding the bridges and causeway leading to Two Sisters Ferry. The following day Slocum and Williams, using rowboats, met and began planning their movement through the Beaufort District.[63]

While waiting for the pontooniers to arrive, army transports carrying vast amounts of ammunition and rations came up the river from Savannah and, under the protection of the USS *Pontiac*, a depot was established above the site, selected for the bridge where quartermaster employees off-loaded vital supplies required to outfit Slocum's soldiers for their initial entry into South Carolina. Lieutenant Commander Luce kept the *Pontiac* in a position to guard the depot and intercept any enemy gunboats that might venture down the river from Augusta and threaten the pontoon bridge.[64]

Beginning on the night of January 29, Lieutenant Colonel Joseph Moore began running the pontoon bridge across the Savannah River. Moore's pontooniers, 650 men from his regiment, the 58th Indiana, managed a train of eighty-five wagons that carried enough equipment to create a 1,000-foot bridge. The crossing of the river went smoothly, but once in South Carolina, the men, with help from Selfridge's soldiers, had to place an additional 250 feet of pontoons and construct 750 feet of wooden bridges to connect the South Carolina terminus to the Robertville Road. From the ferry to the sand hills, a distance of over two miles, the road was covered by one to six feet of water. The Confederates had blocked the road by felling large trees that were laced with torpedoes, which, when detonated by the unsuspecting laborers, killed and maimed Union soldiers. The use of these infernal machines outraged the Federals, increasing their wrath against South Carolina. General Davis, referring to the use of the explosive devices, later wrote that "South Carolina has since paid the penalty of a resort to this low and mean spirit of warfare."[65]

While Slocum's wing struggled to reach and cross Two Sisters Ferry, Howard kept his soldiers busy preparing for the coming campaign. To supply his men, Howard ordered General Blair to construct a wharf at the head of navigation for steamships on the Pocotaligo River. Located just north of Bray's Island, the site became an important supply depot, and since it initially served the Seventeenth Corps, it was termed Blair's Landing, in honor of the commander.[66]

Troops were also kept busy breaking up the Charleston and Savannah Railroad. The Confederates who had taken up the railroad from the Savannah River as far as Great Swamp Bridge had already accomplished part of the task. Men from General Hatch's division had also destroyed the track between Coosawhatchie and Pocotaligo, while Colonel Wager Swayne was directed to take his regiment, the 43rd Ohio, and destroy the remaining line from Pocotaligo to the Combahee River "in the most perfect manner, every tie burned and every rail warped and bent." In four days "the work of destroying the railroad" was completed.[67]

General Howard also had Blair keep up pressure on Confederate positions, especially against their lines at the Combahee Ferry and the bridges at Salkehatchie. Efforts were made to cross the Salkehatchie, but high water thwarted the soldiers. Still, the feints had the desired effect, as the Confederate high command kept shifting part of their cavalry forces from one side of the Salkehatchie to the other. In the meantime Logan's Fifteenth Corps, save Corse's division, which was with Slocum, had moved through Pocotaligo and consolidated at McPhersonville while Blair's Seventeenth Corps was positioned along the Salkehatchie River Road, both waiting for the Army of Georgia to take their jumping-off point at Robertville before advancing.[68]

For a week Sherman waited impatiently for word that Slocum had crossed the Savannah River. Anxious and ready to be in the field, Sherman moved his headquarters to Dr. Ficklin's home just north of Pocotaligo Station on the McPhersonville Road near the Federal entrenchments. Then, on January 31 information arrived from freedmen "that our troops engaged the enemy over about Lawtonville." Though not official, it was enough for Sherman, who immediately told Howard, "We will start tomorrow."[69]

The great excursion across the Beaufort District began on February 1 with Logan's and Blair's corps leading the way. Along the Beaufort District's eastern boundary, paralleling the Salkehatchie River, came the three divisions of General Blair's Seventeenth Corps. The column stretched six miles from head to tail. Starting at 7:00 A.M., the 9th Illinois, a regiment of mounted infantry, led the way, followed by Major General Joseph A. Mower's First Division, the headquarters wagons for General Howard, Brigadier General Manning Ferguson Force's Third Division, Major General Giles Alexander Smith's Fourth Division, and the corps' pontoon bridge train.[70]

Blair's procession up the River Road toward River's Bridge, just north of the Beaufort District line, placed his corps in a precarious position. As the corps advanced, Confederate forces could sweep across the Salkehatchie River from fortified crossings and strike at the Federal column, slicing it into sections, or strike the rear of the line as it passed by. But the southerners remained passive and stayed on their side of the river, leaving only elements of Humes's cavalry division and Colcock's cavalry regiment to resist the Federal advance.

General Mower, a Vermont native who grew up in Lowell, Massachusetts, had fought in the Mexican War as a private and later was appointed an officer in the regular army. Colonel of the 11th Missouri, he amassed an impressive record as he rose from colonel to major general, causing General Sherman to refer to the thirty-six-year-old Mower as the "boldest young soldier we have." Nicknamed "Fighting Joe," Mower led from the front. On February 1 he pushed his division, led by the Illinois horsemen, along the Salkehatchie's western bank, driving Confederate troopers before them. About eleven miles from their starting point, Mower's men reached a fork in the highway. Most of the Confederate cavalry withdrew to the northwest toward Whippy Swamp Crossroads, followed closely by the Illinois mounted infantry.[71]

While the 9th Illinois drove on and secured Whippy Swamp Crossroads, Mower kept his division on the river road and shortly after noon, two miles farther on, his soldiers came to Whippy Swamp Creek, described as "ten parts swamp to one part creek." The overflowing stream covered an area three-quarters of a mile wide with a depth of six to twelve inches, laced with timber ranging from immense cypress trees to brush and vines. A causeway broken by the remains of five destroyed sixty-foot bridges ran through the flooded morass. Confederate skirmishers picketed the causeway, and a larger force held the opposite side of the quagmire behind a rail barrier. Orders went out to clear the swamp using an infantry regiment, and the task fell to the 18th Missouri from Mower's First Brigade. The soldiers dropped into the cold water, engaged the enemy, and drove them through the flooded terrain and out of their breastworks.[72]

While the Missourians forced the Confederate skirmishers out of Whippy Swamp, General Howard and his staff dismounted and took up a position to view the action on high ground overlooking the marsh. During the firefight a bullet hit one of the general's aides, Lieutenant William N. Taylor. The projectile struck Taylor in the throat, cutting his windpipe and an artery. Standing next to Taylor, Howard quickly placed his hand over the wound and stopped the bleeding until a surgeon arrived. Taylor survived and returned to Beaufort for treatment with the other wounded from the first few days of the campaign.[73]

With Whippy Swamp cleared, Mower moved his division across the rebuilt bridges and camped for the night at the Harrison Plantation. The next morning while Mower continued along the Salkehatchie Road, the following division under Brigadier General Manning F. Force took the road that led to Whippy Swamp Crossroads. Force, a forty-year-old Harvard-educated Cincinnati lawyer had served with the Army of the Tennessee since the Fort Donelson Campaign. For actions at the Battle of Atlanta, where he received a disfiguring facial wound, he eventually was awarded the Medal of Honor. He recovered from his wound and led a brigade during the march through Georgia. Promoted to command the Third Division in the Seventeenth Corps, Force was given the duty of seizing Angley's Post Office, a location on the eastern side of Jackson Creek in the Barnwell District, where the Fifteenth Corps was expected to move through on its way toward the crossings of the Salkehatchie River.[74]

Preceded by the 20th Illinois Mounted Infantry, Force's division reached Whippy Swamp Crossroads, which had been occupied the previous day by the 9th Illinois. That morning before Force's soldiers arrived, the 9th had left, taking the highway leading to the east and Broxton Bridge. Force did not linger at Whippy Swamp but continued on across Caw Caw Creek and out of the Beaufort District. By nightfall the Federals arrived at Barker's Mill, where they drove off the Confederate defenders and seized the bridge over Jackson Creek. Force never did locate Angley's Post Office, which he later learned had been discontinued "thirty or forty year ago and the name forgotten." That evening Force received a message from Howard, directing him to leave a small detachment near Barker's Mill to await the arrival of the Fifteenth Corps and to bring the bulk of his division to Rivers Bridge, where Mower's division had secured a crossing over the Salkehatchie River.[75]

On the same day that Force's soldiers seized Barker's Mill, General Mower's division met stiff resistance along the Salkehatchie Road. The Federals, with Colonel John Tillson's brigade leading the way, had broken camp at daylight on February 2. About a mile out, the four companies from the 25th Indiana, deployed as skirmishers, engaged Colonel Colcock's 3rd South Carolina Cavalry, which had formed a line of battle and even charged the Indiana soldiers, but were unable to slow the Federal advance. When the northerners reached the junction of the Salkehatchie and Broxton Bridge Roads, Tillson's men met the troopers from the 9th Illinois, who that morning had ridden in from the Whippy Swamp Crossroads.

General Blair had no intention of attacking the fortified Confederate position at Broxton Bridge, where the roads did not provide a direct, unencumbered route to the South Carolina Railroad between Williston and Midway, the Federals' initial objective. To confuse the enemy, Blair ordered Mower to demonstrate toward Broxton Bridge. The task of holding the Confederates in place fell to the 25th Indiana from Tillson's brigade. The Indiana soldiers drove the southerners across the Salkehatchie and into their fortifications. As they approached the crossing, the Hoosiers came under enemy artillery fire that covered two men from the 10th North Carolina Battalion, who coolly walked out from their entrenchments onto the bridge and set it on fire.[76]

While skirmishing continued in front of Broxton Bridge, the 9th Illinois resumed the lead of Blair's column, spearheading the movement north toward the next Salkehatchie River crossing at Rivers Bridge. The mounted soldiers of the 9th Illinois, carrying seven-shot Spencer rifles, were followed closely by the 32nd Wisconsin. In charge of the advance was Lieutenant Colonel Kirby of Blair's staff, the general's chief troubleshooter. Near the Beaufort District border with the Barnwell District, the northerners discovered a force of Confederates drawn up across the road behind a rail barricade with both flanks anchored on a swamp and an open field in the front. Kirby deployed his mounted infantrymen for an assault with the foot soldiers formed close behind. Moving within easy range of the enemy, Kirby, riding a "magnificent" horse, led his men on a charge across the field into the enemy works. A ball struck Kirby in the calf, passing through his leg and killing his mount, but his men pressed on, using their Spencer rifles to good advantage, scattering the Confederates.[77]

The infantrymen followed and passed into the Barnwell District to a crossroads where the highway from now-forgotten Angley's Post Office to Rivers Bridge crossed the Salkehatchie River Road. Tillson, a thirty-nine-year-old Illinois-born lawyer, placed his brigade at the road junction, while Mower pushed his remaining two brigades, commanded by Colonel Milton Montgomery and Brigadier General John W. Fuller, toward Rivers Bridge, seizing without opposition a portion of the elevated causeway that carried the road through the Salkehatchie River's flooded bottomland. But when the roadway turned to the right toward the river's main channel, the lead Federal units came under severe fire from fortified batteries on the river's eastern bank, located on a rise eight hundred yards away.

Positioned in a series of earthworks were Confederate detachments from the 32nd and 47th Georgia under Lieutenant Colonel Edwin H. Bacon Jr. and dismounted horsemen from Companies B, H, and I of the 3rd South Carolina Cavalry. Captain William Earle's Furman Battery provided artillery support. The southerners, perched on top of a ridge overlooking the flooded terrain and the destroyed bridge, had a fine field of fire on any enemy who dared to venture along the causeway.[78]

When the Federals came into sight, the Confederates immediately opened an intense fusillade on the leading regiment, the 25th Wisconsin, forcing the soldiers to scramble into the icy waters on either side of the causeway. Braving the enemy fire, Mower brought forward additional regiments from Montgomery's brigade. As Colonel Wager Swayne, commander of the 43rd Ohio, was being shown where to place his unit, a shell fragment struck Swayne just below the knee. Swayne, a Columbus, Ohio, lawyer and son of U.S. Supreme Court Justice Noah Haynes Swayne, was placed on a litter and hurriedly carried to the rear. General Howard saw Swayne being taken off the field and, realizing that the colonel was in pain, took the time to straighten the colonel's leg, using a pinecone to support it. Howard recalled that Swayne looked at him and with a smile exclaimed, "The Lord Sustains Me!" Swayne was taken by ambulance to Blair's Landing, where he received treatment from Dr. Henry Orlando Marcy, who later accompanied Swayne and the other wounded aboard a transport to the hospitals at Beaufort.[79]

Mower joined his soldiers wading through the frigid, waist-deep waters, leading by example and encouraging them forward. His actions earned him the sobriquet "the swamp lizard," but his exposure to the icy water may have contributed to his early demise after the war from pulmonary complications. Finding the Confederates too strong and unwilling to launch a direct attack, Mower waited until darkness before pulling the majority of his men out of the swamp. Throughout the night Mower maintained a skirmish line in front of the enemy works, while he detailed his pioneers to begin constructing a roadway north of the causeway beyond the enemy works.[80]

While the Federals kept up a desultory fire throughout the night and started their roadway in the swamp, the Confederates improved their position and received reinforcements. Joining Lieutenant Colonel Bacon's command were the 5th Georgia Reserves and elements of Colonel Thomas Harrison's cavalry brigade. The reservists and cavalrymen brought the total number of defenders to over twelve hundred men, enough to properly man the earthworks but too few to guard either flank.[81]

That evening Mower met with Blair and Howard and was instructed to effect a crossing. By now General Force's division, which had made a night march from Barker's Mill, had relieved Tillson's brigade at the crossroads, allowing Tillson's soldiers to rejoin their comrades at Rivers Bridge. The next morning Mower ordered Tillson to take his regiments into the Salkehatchie Swamp in front of the Confederate defenses, while Fuller and Montgomery started their men cutting two more pathways through the swamp farther to the north of the road begun earlier by the pioneers.

At 2:00 P.M. Mower learned that some soldiers from Tillson's brigade had managed to cross the Salkehatchie on a downed cypress tree about eight hundred yards north of the Confederate defenses. Mower quickly ordered Tillson to cross with additional men and for Fuller and Montgomery to cease their roadwork and follow with their brigades. More cypress trees were cut over the river, and soon the Federals were forming, poised to enfilade the Confederate right flank.[82]

To support Mower, General Blair ordered Brigadier General Giles A. Smith, whose division was positioned between Rivers and Broxton Bridges, to cross the Salkehatchie River. Smith, a handsome, polite individual, nearly six feet in height and thirty-five years old, was an Illinois businessman and hotel proprietor. He had risen from captain to brigadier general while serving in all of the Army of the Tennessee's campaigns. He was brave, cool, and resourceful, well liked and popular with his soldiers.[83]

Though the Confederates believed the mile-and-a-half-wide Salkehatchie to be an impenetrable swamp, the Federals discovered a route three to four feet deep across the flooded river. Entering from the Beaufort District at 2:00 P.M., Smith managed to get his division over the river and consolidated on the Colleton District's side by 5:00 P.M. Once across, Smith's soldiers engaged in "brisk skirmishing" with the Confederates to the south in the direction of Broxton Bridge.

Though unable to move north immediately against Rivers Bridge, the presence of Smith's division on the east bank of the Salkehatchie, coupled with Mower's men enfilading the Confederate line, forced the southerners, after suffering and inflicting about a hundred casualties, to evacuate their defenses at Rivers Bridge, a position that General Howard later described as "the strongest position I ever saw in my life."[84]

While Blair's corps passed through the Beaufort District and secured the crossing of the Salkehatchie at Rivers Bridge, Logan's Fifteenth Corps marched steadily northwest from their camps between Pocotaligo and McPhersonville. Preceded by the 7th Illinois and 29th Missouri Mounted Infantry Regiments, Logan pressed his men up the McPhersonville Road toward the important crossroad at Hickory Hill. They proceeded along a highway that crossed numerous swampy streams and was blocked with felled timber and rail barricades.

Sherman accompanied Logan's corps, which served as the linchpin connecting the two wings. As the three divisions of the Fifteenth Corps advanced, they seized important road junctions from which, if needed, they could turn west to assist Slocum's army or east to bolster Blair's forces along the Salkehatchie River.[85]

A small force of enemy cavalry challenged the Fifteenth Corps, but they were easily pushed aside. By the end of the first day's march, the Federals reached Hickory Hill, the home of a Mrs. McBride who had fled her homestead before the arrival of the Yankees. On February 2, still contested by enemy troopers, Logan's men advanced out of the Beaufort District, seized Loper's Crossroads, and crossed Duck Creek. By February 3 Logan had arranged his divisions just across the district line in the Barnwell District, holding a position running from Jackson Creek Bridge along the road from Duck Branch Post Office to Barker's Mill, where they relieved the regiments left behind by General Force. With no information as to Slocum's whereabouts, Sherman had Logan make camp while they awaited developments. During the one-day lull, Sherman, on his own hook, rode over and met with Howard while foragers scoured the countryside, bringing back to camp large amounts of peanuts. That evening word was received that the Seventeenth Corps had crossed the Salkehatchie River at Rivers Bridge, and Sherman instructed Logan to move his corps rapidly toward a crossing point of the Salkehatchie at Buford Bridge, north of Rivers Bridge. The next day a brigade from General Woods's division reached Buford Bridge, which had been destroyed, and discovered the "works of the enemy deserted."[86]

While General Howard's army achieved its initial objectives, Sherman pensively waited for word from Slocum, his slow-coming subordinate. High water and enemy torpedoes had detained the commander of the Army of Georgia, causing him to fall behind schedule. On the same day that Mower made his initial assault at Rivers Bridge, General Williams pushed Ward's division and two brigades of Jackson's division from their camps around Robertville northeast into the flooded Cypress Swamp. The men built roads through the high water before reaching the Gillisonville Road and taking it past Steep Bottom toward Lawtonville.

Enemy cavalry skirmished with the Federals, and about a mile from Lawtonville the Confederates took up a strong position behind Black Creek. Ward deployed his division in a double line and attacked. With the loss of two killed and twelve wounded, he drove the enemy through Lawtonville. The next day the northerners continued on and secured Beach Branch Post Office. General Williams, who had accompanied Ward, then rode on to Duck Branch Post Office, where he met a relieved General Sherman. With his two wings now in contact, Sherman authorized a general advance. On February 4, while Logan's men advanced to Buford Bridge, Williams had his Twentieth Corps skirt west of the Coosawhatchie Swamp and forge out of the Beaufort District and on to Smyrna Post Office, Allendale, and the Barnwell Pike.[87]

On February 3, while the Twentieth Corps was securing Lawtonville, General Slocum finally began shifting the portion of his army still in Georgia over the Savannah River and into the Beaufort District. Slocum, his uniform spattered with mud, "scarcely distinguishable from the wagon drivers," knowing that tales of slowness were again being spread throughout the armies, stood by the bridge encouraging his men as they hurried over. Brigadier General Judson Kilpatrick's cavalrymen were the first to cross. The small division, "indifferently mounted, badly armed," consisted of 5,068 men in three mounted and one demi-brigade of dismounted troopers. The horsemen rattled over the pontoon bridge, along the newly built roadway and encamped near Robertville. Nicknamed Kill-Cavalry, both for their propensity to use up their horses and for their flamboyant leader, the force was known for its hard riding, numerous fights, and the free hand General Sherman gave to them to destroy enemy property, military and civilian. Attached to the division for the invasion of South Carolina was the 1st Alabama, a regiment composed of Deep South white men primarily from Unionist areas in northern Alabama and Georgia with a sprinkling of South Carolinians. The troopers, whose families had been targeted by Confederate officials, took pleasure in gaining what they believed to be just retribution for their loyalty to the United States government.[88]

General Kilpatrick, a twenty-nine-year-old U.S. Military Academy graduate, had been chosen by Sherman to lead his horsemen in the marches across Georgia and the Carolinas, during which he dueled with his former West Point classmate Joseph Wheeler, with neither admitting that he was ever bested by the other. A teetotaler, Kilpatrick disdained gambling and drinking, but he had a fondness for women and was accompanied by at least one female companion on his initial journey into South Carolina.[89]

Kilpatrick was expected to cover Sherman's left flank and feint toward Augusta. To do this, his troopers had to make up for lost time. On February 4, after driving off Confederate cavalrymen around Robertville, the Federal horsemen followed the route taken initially by Williams's Twentieth Corps over well-worn, rutted roads where the horses and men "floundered through literal oceans of mud." Streams became torrents and the countryside a vast quagmire. The cavalrymen rode northwest to Brighton and then through Lawtonville and Allendale before turning toward Barnwell and the South Carolina Railroad near Williston.[90]

Behind Kilpatrick came the two displaced divisions of Generals Geary and Corse. John White Geary's division of the Twentieth Corps crossed the Savannah River on the morning of February 4. Geary, an antislavery, forty-six-year-old Pennsylvania-born lawyer, had fought in the Mexican War before moving to California and becoming mayor of San Francisco. Later, as the territorial governor of Kansas, he supported those wishing to make Kansas a free state, which resulted in his removal by the pro-South Buchanan administration. Geary joined the army at the start of the war and served in the Eastern Theater. He was a division commander at Chancellorsville and Gettysburg before being transferred with his unit west for the Chattanooga campaign. A prompt and efficient officer, Geary, because of his previous civic duties, had been selected with his division as governor and occupation force of Savannah, a duty that kept him and his men from joining their comrades of the Twentieth Corps at the start of the Carolina Campaign.[91]

Once the 250 wagons of the cavalry division had crossed the pontoon bridge at Two Sisters Ferry, Geary began moving his 5,322 soldiers, 159 wagons, 33 ambulances, and 234 pack mules into South Carolina. Trying to make up for lost time, Geary, who had Selfridge's brigade of Jackson's division attached to his command, moved his men through Robertville and followed the track of the Twentieth Corps. They entered the inundated Cypress Swamp before stopping for the night. The next day Geary put his soldiers to work improving the rutted and water-covered roads through the swamp and on the sixth advanced past Steep Bottom Church through Lawtonville to Beech Branch Post Office and out of the Beaufort District.[92]

On the evening of February 4, after Geary's division had plodded across the pontoon bridge, Brigadier General Corse proceeded with his Fifteenth Corps division over the Savannah River and encamped on the sand hills above the ferry crossing. Corse, a thirty-year-old Pennsylvania-born Burlington, Iowa, lawyer and politician who had briefly attended the U.S. Military Academy, was well known for his bravery and fearlessness. At the Battle of Altoona Pass on October 5, 1864, he was badly wounded while defending his position against a superior Confederate force. Corse became nationally known after the battle when he telegraphed Sherman, "I am short of a cheekbone, and one ear, but am able to whip all hell yet."[93]

Corse's division, which had been separated from Logan's Fifteenth Corps by high waters that kept it in Savannah while the rest of the corps concentrated around Pocotaligo, began an east-to-west march through the center of the Beaufort District to rejoin its parent organization. On February 5, with twenty-two days' rations of hard bread and eighteen days' rations of sugar and coffee, Corse's men set off, carrying fence rails on their shoulders to corduroy roads. They left Robertville and pushed through a three-mile-wide portion of the Black Swamp to Spafford Crossroads, Nixville, and Hickory Hill, where they met the 9th Illinois Mounted Infantry, which had just returned from convoying the wounded from the fight at Rivers Bridge to Blair's Landing.

On February 8 Corse and his soldiers left Hickory Hill, crossed Whippy Swamp, and exited the Beaufort District by crossing the Salkehatchie at Rivers Bridge.[94]

The last formation to come over the pontoon bridge at Two Sisters Ferry and the final unit to pass through the Beaufort District was Major General Jefferson C. Davis's Fourteenth Corps. By the night of February 5, the entire corps had encamped in South Carolina on the sand hills above the ferry landing. On the sixth Davis's soldiers began spinning a web across the northwestern corner of St. Peter's Parish. Brigadier General William P. Carlin's division was the first to advance, marching from Robertville to Brighton. On February 7 a heavy rain started. Carlin, a thirty-five-year-old U.S. Military Academy graduate and veteran of the campaigns of the Army of the Cumberland, found the roads that had been recently improved by previous Federal troops flooded out. Because of the weather, it took Carlin an additional day to reach Lawtonville, but by the ninth his soldiers passed by Beech Branch Church and beyond the Beaufort District.[95]

Behind Carlin came Brigadier General Absalom Baird's division. Five years older than Carlin and also a veteran of the Army of the Cumberland and a U.S. Military Academy graduate, Baird on February 8 took his soldiers from their camps between Robertville and Brighton and followed Carlin's track through Brighton before taking the Augusta Road over Pipe Creek and camping at the Bostick Plantation. The next day his men continued north, marching for sixteen miles across Dry Gall Creek and into the Barnwell District.[96]

The last Federal division from Sherman's armies to enter and depart the Beaufort District was Brigadier General James Dada Morgan's Third Division. Morgan, a fifty-year-old Quincy, Illinois, merchant, had served in his town's militia and as a captain in the 1st Illinois during the Mexican War. An officer in the 10th Illinois at the start of the war, he rose to command of a division during the Atlanta Campaign. At Two Sisters Ferry, Morgan's division guarded the Georgia side of the pontoon bridge from enemy attack and simultaneously provided fatigue parties in South Carolina, who struggled in ankle- to waist-deep water to maintain the road leading from the bridge's eastern terminus to the sand hills above.[97]

At 4:00 P.M. on February 5, Morgan moved the bulk of his division across the Savannah River, leaving the 34th Illinois Infantry on the Georgia shore to guard the pontooniers as they dismantled their bridge. Once over, Morgan camped his division in the sand hills outside Robertville, where they remained for two days. While waiting, Morgan, like the previous formations of Slocum's army, loaded his train with rations and ammunition from the supply depot above the ferry. Once Morgan's men had been outfitted, the quartermasters closed down their operation. The excess equipment was loaded onto the army transports and with the USS *Pontiac* steamed down the river to the site of the now-removed pontoon bridge, where the vessels picked up the rear guard from the Georgia shore and delivered them to the South Carolina side before returning to Savannah.[98]

On February 8 Morgan's division followed Baird's troops to Brighton. The next day Morgan continued along the Augusta Road toward King's Creek Post Office and out of the Beaufort District. With the passage of Morgan's division, the last formations of Sherman's field armies left the Beaufort District. Though the movement from its beginning on February 1 lasted only eight days, the impact of the march had a serious effect, both in terms of the immediate destruction of property and its indelible impression on the district's and state's cultural memory.[99]

Chapter 16

The War Ledger

"War is no respector of property"

When Sherman's armies entered the Beaufort District, they supposedly followed the same instructions issued by their commanding general before they left Atlanta for Savannah. Known as Special Field Orders Number 120, Sherman's mandate included specific instructions governing the conduct of foraging parties:

> The army will forage liberally on the country during the march. To this end, each brigade commander will organize a good and sufficient foraging party, under the command of one or more discreet officers, who will gather, near the route traveled, corn or forage of any kind, meat of any kind, vegetables, corn-meal, or whatever is needed by the command, aiming at all times to keep in the wagons at least ten days' provisions for his command, and three days' forage. Soldiers must not enter the dwellings of the inhabitants, or commit any trespass; but, during a halt or camp, they may be permitted to gather turnips, potatoes, and other vegetables, and to drive in stock in sight of their camp. To regular foraging-parties must be intrusted the gathering of provisions and forage, at any distance from the road traveled.
>
> To corps commanders alone is intrusted the power to destroy mills, houses, cotton-gins, etc.; and for them this general principle is laid down: In districts and neighborhoods where the army is unmolested, no destruction of such property should be permitted; but should guerrillas or bushwhackers molest our march, or should the inhabitants burn bridges, obstruct roads, or other-wise manifest local hostility, then army commanders should order and enforce a devastation more or less relentless, according to the measure of such hostility.[1]

While on the march, upwards of five thousand soldiers formed into foraging parties that spread out across the countryside ahead of the Union armies. The men were termed "bummers," from the German word for loafer—*bummler*.

Besides appropriating supplies, the men served as trip wires, warning the main columns of impending enemy attacks. The bummers were also the first to make contact with civilians and slaves, foraging and jubilating as they went. In Georgia, barns, cotton gins, and other outbuildings were destroyed. Abandoned homes were often burned, but in Georgia, unlike in South Carolina, inhabitants stayed in their houses, and while they suffered harassments and indignities, they were able to keep their residences from being razed.[2]

In the Beaufort District, few people stayed in their homes. Sherman's hopes that the tales of his western soldiers in Georgia would frighten the South Carolinians and cause them to panic came true. Terror reigned in South Carolina before his men ever trod into the Palmetto State. John W. Kirk, writing his daughter from Black Swamp near Robertville in December, reported that folks were abandoning the area: "DuPonts to Georgia with carriages and wagons. The Gregories—I know not where. Mrs. Strobhan to St. John's—Mrs. Glover returned to Marietta." Other members of the Kirk family, along with the Ferebees, went to Columbia and on to Chester while the McKenzies fled to the river swamp. Kirk reported that residents of Lawtonville had packed and abandoned the town, commenting, "They were the most awfully frightened set you can imagine." Slaves, who had been positioned along the roads to warn their masters and mistresses of the Yankee approach, "increased the terror by disseminating any reports that a passing wag might stuff them with."[3]

Upon entering the Beaufort District, Lieutenant Colonel George Ward Nichols, a prewar journalist serving on Sherman's staff, wrote, "The well-known sight of columns of black smoke meets our gaze again; this time houses are burning, and South Carolina has commenced to pay an installment, long overdue, on her debt to justice and humanity. With the help of God, we will have principal and interest before we leave her borders." Though Sherman had not altered his orders against the destruction of dwellings, he expected a difficult campaign and "would not restrain the army lest its vigor and energy should be impaired."[4]

However, some of the Federal commanders tried to minimize the devastation to civilian property. Before the movement inland, General Oliver O. Howard issued an order to the Army of the Tennessee directing that the officer in charge of the foraging parties be "held strictly accountable for all abuses of his authority or improper conduct of the men under his command." Though proud of his bummers' ability to bring in "horses, mules, cattle, and all kinds of food for men and animals," Howard was distressed that his orders for their comportment were not obeyed. He wrote, "In spite of every precaution to check the taking of private property, including watches, money and jewelry, the system of foraging operated to loosen restraints of discipline, and many acts were committed that every right officer deprecates." Howard noted that the troops became experts in discovering and seizing valuables they considered legitimate prizes of war. The soldiers used their ramrods to probe recently disturbed ground. They "ripped open featherbeds, the wardrobes ransacked, chests stripped of contents, looking glasses taken from the walls, cooking utensils gone, and all corn meal and bacon missing, bed quilts stripped from beds, the last jar of pickles gone, was no incommon sight."[5]

Howard's subordinates also found it difficult to control their soldiers' activities. General John A. Logan, who like Sherman was not one to show sympathy to the enemy, reported to Howard, "Before the rear of our column passed through McPhersonville, I regret to inform you that the village was in flames." But then he explained the incident by stating, "This was doubtlessly induced by the desertion of their houses by the entire population, for on our entrance into the village not a human being was found."[6]

The commander of Logan's Second Division, General William B. Hazen, bitterly complained about the waste and ruin applied to the countryside. Born in Vermont but an Ohio resident since the age of three, the thirty-four-year-old Hazen was held in high esteem by his peers. A U.S. Military Academy graduate, he was known as a stern disciplinarian, and had gained a superb reputation rising from the rank of colonel of the 41st Ohio to that of division commander. When the march from Pocotaligo began, Hazen commented that "the demon of destruction seized possession of everyone," that even "the smallest drummer boy seemed to get even" on South Carolina, causing "a carnival of destruction that ended with the burning of Columbia." He noted that as his soldiers moved inland, "black columns of smoke began to ascend." Hazen tried to save homes, but once his guards had been recalled, he believed that loiterers or stragglers set them on fire. Almost apologetic, he later wrote, "Thus we soldiered in South Carolina. An order prohibiting the destruction of property in any particular case was of no effect beyond one's immediate presence and power to enforce it."[7]

While Howard's wing trekked through the eastern portion of the Beaufort District, General Slocum's Army of Georgia swept into the district's western region. General Williams, responding to actions of his corps in the march from Hardeeville to Robertville, issued a circular to his officers stating, "The indiscriminate pillage of houses is disgraceful and demoralizing to this army. The houses of this vicinity, of free negroes even, have been stripped of the necessary bedclothes and of family apparel." Williams ordered that all foraging or other parties be prohibited from leaving camp without a commissioned officer, who would be held responsible for the good conduct of the men in his charge. Williams expected the "hearty cooperation" of all officers to "put a stop to practices disgraceful to our arms and shocking to humanity." The circular was communicated to all men, soldiers and civilians, accompanying the Twentieth Corps, but when Williams was able to post a letter to his wife, he admitted, "Orders to respect houses and private property . . . were not greatly heeded. Indeed not heeded at all. Our 'bummers,' the dare-devils and reckless of the army, put the flames to everything and we marched with thousands of columns of smoke marking the line of each corps."[8]

While much of the destruction was motivated by a desire to chastise South Carolina, the state the soldiers held responsible for starting the war, some came from direct actions perpetrated by the Confederates. The men of General Davis's Fourteenth Corps and Kilpatrick's cavalry responded with vengeance to the Confederate use of torpedoes, the land mines planted at Two Sisters Ferry that ripped off the legs of their comrades as they entered South Carolina.

Also fueling the Federals' outrage was the slaying of three men from Company H, 33rd Indiana, a regiment in the Second Brigade of General Ward's division. The soldiers, who had marched with their unit out of Robertville eight miles to the junction of the Robertville and Gillisonville Roads had, with the consent of their commander, left the highway and ventured to Thomas Trowell's farm, where they were killed by a squadron of Wheeler's cavalry. A few days later, when Geary's division passed through the area, the bodies were discovered and slaves testified that Trowell had "pointed out" the men to the Confederate horsemen, who "shot them in cold blood." Geary had the soldiers buried, arrested Trowell for accessory to murder, and ordered the destruction of his home and property.[9]

A final tally or even an estimate of the destruction inflicted on the Beaufort District is impossible to determine. Much of the upper portions of St. Peters and Prince William parishes were devastated, though there was no pattern as to how it was done or by whom. A man in the 34th Illinois, bringing up the rear guard of the Fourteenth Corps along the Orangeburg Road in the district's northwest corner reported, "Our brigade marching in the rear, witnessed the destructive work of the column ahead. Amid the ruins of many houses we saw but two standing." The first soldiers marching through Robertville reported no damage, yet the town disappeared, either by burning or dismantling for use in corduroying roads and building bridges. Usually churches were spared, though even a few houses of worship were taken down and the wood employed for construction material. By local lore the Stoney Creek Presbyterian Church was dismantled, its boards and beams taken for roads and erecting bridges. The church's chapel at McPhersonville was spared, though the nearby Episcopal Chapel of Ease disappeared.[10]

Members of Howard's army, advancing amid the swamps of the Salkehatchie and Coosawhatchie Rivers, described the region as having some plantations and "a few poor houses." The disparity of wealth was starkly evident, causing some northerners to question why the poor whites were furnishing the rank and file of the southern armies. As they pressed on, a member of

Howard's staff wrote, "The houses are mostly abandoned. A great share of the abandoned houses are being burned by the soldiers, while those with families are not molested further than to take the forage and provisions for the army." In years after the war, descendants of the people who had lived through the invasion in the upper portions of the district referred to times when they had large numbers of folks to dinner as "visits from Sherman's army."[11]

Though the movement by the Federals through the Beaufort District lasted only until February 8, they were blamed for any plundering or destruction that occurred for weeks or in one case, years after their departure. The destruction of Prince William Parish Church, commonly referred to as Sheldon Church, burned by the British and Loyalists during the Revolution and rebuilt in 1826 has, in popular lore been blamed on Sherman's forces, but a year after the soldiers had left the area, Milton Maxey Leverett, son of the church's last rector, wrote his mother, "Sheldon Church is not burned down. It has been torn up inside somewhat but it could be repaired." In a letter written four days later on February 7, 1866, Leverett told his mother that the freedmen were taking down structures throughout the Pocotaligo-Sheldon area, including the cannibalization of the church for building material, stating, "I see fragments of Sheldon Church all about."[12]

Sherman's soldiers received condemnation for nearly all the destruction in the Beaufort District inflicted by other culprits, including former slaves, criminals, Confederate deserters, and the troops from General John G. Foster's units, who occupied the region after Sherman's formations had left. Foster's soldiers, veterans of the Department of the South, swarmed over the area, visiting abandoned Confederate fortifications and nearby towns and churches, often taking items and destroying property. It was most likely soldiers from General John Hatch's Coast Division of Foster's command who removed souvenirs from the Holy Trinity Episcopal Church at Grahamville and defaced the communion silver at Gillisonville Baptist Church. Freed slaves, with their masters gone, eagerly gathered up property and either destroyed or encouraged soldiers to burn the homes of their owners, carrying out effectively a strategy proposed by General David Hunter two years earlier of using slaves and soldiers to cleanse the territory of any remnant of slavery and create a new homeland for the freedmen.[13]

While active fighting in the Beaufort District between regular formations ended, bushwhacking continued as Confederate soldiers, irregulars, and diehard civilians caught in the vacuum between the armies, refused to accept the revised situation. Gillisonville, the district's county seat, stood in an area frequented by the Federals and remnants of regular Confederate units and home guards. Skirmishes occurred in and around the community, initially with little damage to the town's structures. Major Henry O. Marcy, surgeon of the 35th USCT, now serving with the department's medical staff, described Gillisonville as "a small village made up of the few houses and little businesses which the county business would necessitate, to which are added a few county residents of the neighboring planters." Marcy found the courthouse to be "a large, well-built structure covered with mastic" and filled with records.[14]

But Gillisonville did not survive. A former slave once belonging to a town resident, now serving with a black regiment, was captured, beaten, and hanged by the district sheriff Thaddeus G. Buckner, a Confederate veteran who had returned to the area after being wounded. In retaliation, troopers from the 4th Massachusetts Cavalry burned the courthouse, jail, and other public buildings. As Marcy wrote, "War is no respector of property."[15]

The cavalrymen who burned much of Gillisonville were part of General Hatch's Coastal Division, which, once Sherman's men left their camps, had occupied the region between the Salkehatchie and Coosawhatchie Rivers. The division consisted of two brigades commanded by Colonels Edward N. Hallowell and Charles H. Von Wyck. The soldiers occupied the fortifications at Pocotaligo and Pocotaligo Station; General Hatch moved into Sherman's vacated headquarters in the Gregory House at Richfield Plantation. Colonel Hallowell took up residence in General Blair's onetime headquarters in the John A. Cuthbert home near Pocotaligo while his former regiment, the 54th Massachusetts, bivouacked around the Daniel Heyward House outside Pocotaligo Station.[16]

While the officers settled into their new quarters, Sherman, who needed to tend to some final details before setting out, went in search of General Hatch. He came to the Cuthbert House and surprised a group of officers who were playing cards. Asking for Hatch, the card players, not looking up from their game, informed the middle-aged officer that Hatch was absent. The visitor then quietly replied, "Please say to him that General Sherman called." The startled officers immediately apologized but Sherman "departed as he came."[17]

Once Sherman and his armies had vacated the area, General Hatch put his forces around Pocotaligo in motion toward Charleston. On February 3 Hatch directed the 25th Ohio to move from Pocotaligo to Garden Corners. The next day the Ohioans advanced to the Combahee River. The Confederates, having evacuated the fort on the west side of the river, had taken up a strong fortified line, bristling with field pieces, on firm ground overlooking rice fields about a mile east of the ferry crossing. Under intense artillery fire, some of the Ohioans crossed the river, securing the eastern end of the causeway, but while trying to flank the enemy, the Federals became bogged down in the flooded rice fields, forcing Hatch to recall his men.[18]

On February 5 the 107th Ohio also marched from Pocotaligo to Garden Corners and on to join their fellow Buckeyes near the Combahee River.

On the way the regiment stopped at Christ Church on the Combahee, the large chapel built by the Reverend Stephen Elliott before the war as a place of worship for slaves. The soldiers received orders to tear down the structure, sort the lumber, and "pile it up on nice ricks." That night, while the majority of the soldiers continued to dismantle the church, a detachment carrying picks and spades went down to the river and began digging rifle pits. The men were told to work as quietly as possible, as enemy pickets had reoccupied the western end of the causeway.[19]

The next morning General Hatch directed his soldiers to occupy the rifle pits and, with supporting artillery fire, cleared the head of the causeway of enemy troops. The southerners retreated to their defense line beyond the rice fields and opened an artillery barrage that stopped the Federals from advancing. Unable to continue, Hatch decided it would be best to shift his efforts to the south and bridge the Combahee at Salkehatchie.[20]

On February 7 Hatch had the 34th USCT (the former 2nd South Carolina) replace the Ohio regiments at the Combahee Ferry, while the 54th Massachusetts and the 102nd USCT under Colonel Hallowell crossed the Combahee River on footbridges next to the charred remains of the Salkehatchie railroad trestle. On the far side Hallowell discovered that the enemy had abandoned extensive works, including a strong seven-gun battery that had guarded the now-destroyed trestle and wagon bridge. Hatch, hoping for a rapid movement that might trap the Confederates at the Combahee Ferry crossing, sent additional units to Hallowell's command, but the Federals in the Colleton District, noting that the enemy in their front was Kennedy's brigade, veterans from the Army of Northern Virginia, proceeded cautiously along the railroad toward Blue House.[21]

Hatch wanted his troops to follow the railroad through Blue House to Green Pond and Ashepoo. He transferred additional regiments, artillery units, and companies of the 4th Massachusetts Cavalry over the Combahee River at Salkehatchie, but mud, rain, enemy soldiers, and guerrillas slowed the advance. Besides ripping up railroad tracks and destroying trestles, Federal soldiers, described by one officer as "the hand of the destroyer," gathered up provisions and livestock and burned plantations, barns, and rice mills. The troops took particular relish in putting the torch to plantation jails. Liberated slaves welcomed them, especially the black soldiers as they fanned out throughout the area. At Rose Hill, Charles Heyward's handsome plantation on the eastern bank of the Combahee River, Surgeon Orlando Marcy reported that "the slaves are overjoyed at our coming. They thank God, and say they have long prayed for our coming." When informed that the great house would be destroyed, Marcy said they responded by declaring that they "don't want Massa anymore" and were glad that the structure was to be burned. An old man told Marcy that "my work help build dis house. We make Massa rich." Then, while pointing at the mansion, he declared, "Now burn him, burn him. I'se want to see him burn."[22]

Though thwarted by the flooded terrain to the east, including the overflowing waters of Cuckold Creek, the maneuvering of Hatch's forces pressured the Confederates to withdraw from their fortifications guarding the Combahee Ferry before they were cut off. On February 12 Hatch learned that the 34th USCT, with the southerners to their front gone, had crossed the river at the Combahee Ferry, passed over the rice fields and occupied the enemy's abandoned works. Immediately Hatch pulled his men back from their advance along the railroad, recrossed the river at Salkehatchie, and sent them to the Combahee Ferry. To facilitate the movement, the Federals took the lumber from the dismantled Christ Church and some nearby slave huts to build a new bridge over the Combahee River. As one Union soldier, believing the chapel to have been a Baptist house of worship, wrote, "While the good Baptists who worshipped in that church believed in going down into the water, we believed that it would make a good passage way for us to go over the water on." The same soldier did hope that a new and more commodious house of God would be located on the site. Today the Bethel United Methodist Church is located near the site.[23]

On February 19, as the marchers proceeded from the Combahee to Charleston, word was received that the city had been abandoned on the night of February 17. As described by an officer of the 54th Massachusetts: "Cheer after cheer rang out; bonfires were lighted; and the soldiers yelled long and frantically." The advance slowed and on February 23 reached the Ashley River. One soldier noted, "There, across the river, we saw Charleston, long the Mecca of our hopes."[24]

The march of Hatch's division north to Charleston did not remove the Federal presence from Prince William Parish. Shortly after Sherman's armies moved inland, Foster established a supply and personnel depot known as Camp Sherman near Blair's Landing under the command of Brigadier General Henry Prince. A fifty-three-year-old West Point graduate and career army officer, Prince had been assigned to the Department of the South in early February. His task was to forward supplies, soldiers, and officers to Sherman's armies before all lines of communications between the invading force and Port Royal were cut.[25]

Many of the soldiers reporting to General Prince were veterans who had been detached, ill, or delayed in rejoining their commands at Savannah and Port Royal. Among those arriving at Blair's Landing was the thirty-two-year-old, Ohio-born Indiana lawyer and politician Colonel Benjamin Harrison. Named colonel of the 70th Indiana, a regiment he helped recruit, Harrison showed promise as a military commander and eventually took over the First Brigade of the First Division, Twentieth Corps, during the Atlanta Campaign. After Atlanta's capture Harrison and other prominent Republicans were sent to their home states to campaign for President Lincoln's reelection and for other Republican candidates. Afterwards Harrison attempted to rejoin his brigade but was unable to reach Sherman's armies before they had begun their march from Atlanta to Savannah. Assigned to a brigade at Chattanooga, Harrison and his unit joined General George Thomas's army, which had routed the Confederates at the Battle of Nashville. Harrison, who had distinguished himself in the fight, was released by General Thomas to rejoin Sherman at Savannah.[26]

Harrison hurried to New York to catch a steamer to Port Royal, but a bout with scarlet fever delayed his departure. Traveling on the steamer *Fulton,* Harrison arrived at Hilton Head on March 2, 1865. He stayed only two hours before boarding a vessel for Blair's Landing, but fog engulfed the ship, forcing the captain to drop anchor. While waiting for the weather to clear, Harrison joined in an outing to gather oysters. A small boat took the future president to an oyster bed. He described the adventure to his wife: "I have never seen an oyster bed before and they were quite a curiosity to me. The shells grow together in great bunches, the larger shells being inside, and great clusters of smaller ones grown fast around them. The shells are very sharp, hands and boots suffered a good deal in the expedition."

Once back to transport, the oysters were placed in buckets and steamed. Harrison wrote, "I soon got to be expert in opening them and took two or three dozen with great relish; which was perhaps not to wondered at, as we had no supper or breakfast. The oysters are not large, but have a very good flavor."[27]

When he finally arrived at Blair's Landing, Harrison immediately hurried on to Camp Sherman, located between Pocotaligo and Pocotaligo Station, where he applied to General Prince for permission to go into the interior, alone if necessary, and rejoin Sherman's forces. Prince, who had not heard anything about Sherman's whereabouts, refused Harrison's demand, citing the dangers of such an impetuous act. Disappointed, Harrison remained and took on the duties of a training officer, drilling the various units that came into the camp and fighting mosquitoes and sand fleas. As he told his wife, "I fit and blid for my country every day."[28]

Finally, by the end of March, word reached Port Royal that Sherman had opened communications with Federal enclaves in North Carolina, and immediately the men at Camp Sherman prepared to rejoin their old commander. Before leaving on April 15, Harrison took a final ride in the countryside near Blair's Landing to the ruins of a once splendid plantation house, where he took two rose petals, which he sent to his wife, Carrie, asking her to "retain one of the buds yourself and imagine my whispering in your ear with the simple gift that could be delicate and affectionate in a lover, in his first declarations."[29]

While the removal of the men from Camp Sherman and the departure of Hatch's Coastal Division to Charleston ended active military operations in the Beaufort District, political battles continued between the department's most prominent officers: Generals Foster and Saxton.

The first salvo in the fight occurred on January 30 when Foster ordered the Beaufort College Building, long the home of a school for black children, be taken for use as a hospital. Willard Saxton declared it an outrage that the "flourishing & superior school turned into the street." He immediately protested in the name of his brother to General Foster, but the building soon became part of Hospital Number 10.[30]

Larger problems flared between the generals over the implementation of Field Orders Number 15, which named General Saxton as the officer responsible for settling freedmen on abandoned property and charged him with enlisting Negro recruits and forming them into regiments. The combination of duties brought together two important aspects of the orders because any freedman enlisting in the army was "eligible to locate his family in any one of the settlements at pleasure, and acquire a homestead, and all other rights and privileges of a settler, as though present in person." The promise of land was seen as a strong inducement for enlistment, and Saxton used this portion of the orders to encourage blacks to join the army. In the latter part of January, Saxton traveled with Reverend Mansfield French to Savannah and at mass meetings with the freedmen called on them to sign up.[31]

Foster railed against Saxton's serving as the department's chief of recruiting. The commanding officer had once before relieved Saxton of such duties. In August 1864 Foster, who felt that Saxton's philanthropic work and sympathy for the former slaves interfered with his recruiting duties, had replaced him with Colonel Milton B. Littlefield. Under Littlefield a rendezvous and training camp was established at Hilton Head, and the enlistment of freedmen became more vigorous, leading to incidents that prompted Secretary of War Stanton's visit to Port Royal and the reinstatement of Saxton as the general superintendent of volunteer recruiting services. Loath to have Saxton returned as chief recruiter, Foster wrote to Sherman on January 31, 1865, requesting that he alter "paragraph 5 of his Special Field Orders, No. 15" so as to leave in Foster's hands the "duties of enlistments and organization of negro troops."[32]

In his letter to Sherman, Foster asked that Littlefield be retained as chief of recruiting, pointing out that Saxton and French's efforts to enlist blacks were not having much success and only confusing the eligible recruits in Savannah, who were more likely to await developments than to volunteer.

Sherman received Foster's letter "In the Field, Four Miles south of Hickory Hill" on the first day of his march. Dashing off a note, Sherman replied to Foster that "I think the impression at Washington is that both you and

I are inimical to the policy of arming negroes, and all know that Saxton is not, and his appointment reconciles that difficulty." Sherman suggested that should anything serious occur, Foster should contact Secretary Stanton. Sherman, most likely happy to be in the pine woods again and away from politics and politicians, finished by asking Foster to let General Grant know that he was in motion and to keep pressure on the Confederate line along the Combahee River.[33]

Foster did write Stanton, as well as General Halleck, requesting that the last sentence of paragraph 5 of Special Field Orders Number 15 be annulled and Colonel Littlefield retained as the recruiter and organizer of black men in the Department of the South. Foster argued that change would "disorganize the machinery" now in place to establish new black regiments and disrupt the formation of the 103rd, 104th, 105th, and the 128th USCT Regiments currently outfitting on Hilton Head and at Beaufort. Foster also tried to alleviate any doubts about his interest in arming freedmen, pointing out that he had put in the field some of the war's first black regiments—the 1st and 2nd North Carolina—while commanding the Department of North Carolina. Foster closed, "As a soldier, I wish to see our armies strengthened; as a citizen, to that which will most benefit this unfortunate race, and fit them to rightly use that liberty with which the war has blessed them."[34]

To Halleck, Foster was more blunt, declaring that blacks in Savannah were slow in joining the army and that their idea of freedom was "exemption alike from work and care." Foster asked that he be allowed to begin conscription "under such restrictions and exemptions as may be deemed most wise" by the War Department. Foster declared that military service would be most beneficial for the freedmen: "The camp is to-day the school-house of this race; it may be that in the future the soldierly training of these people will be their protection against injustice, while the habits of care and economy will make them self-supporting."[35]

The same day that Foster wrote his letters to Halleck and Stanton, he received a second note from Sherman, this one written from a spot two and a half miles north of Duck Branch Post Office. Sherman counseled Foster that should Saxton do anything that produced disorder or committed some breach of military propriety, then, as his superior, Foster could take action. But Sherman also noted that "were I in your place," he would allow Saxton to recruit and organize the black formations, a tedious and dull duty, and that once mustered into service, the units could then be used in any manner that Foster wished. As to Littlefield, Sherman suggested that Foster assign him to new duties as necessary.[36]

While Foster awaited a reply from Halleck, the animosity between him and Saxton grew. Saxton did not cease his activities in Savannah. After establishing a headquarters in the city, he and Mansfield French addressed a crowd of freedmen in the Second Baptist Church. The general gave an inspiring speech explaining Field Orders Number 15, while French fashioned "one of his best talks, that carried the people as if he held them in his hand." Overcome with emotion, a former slave rushed up to Saxton, telling him that for thirty-five years he had been a slave and now he thanked the Lord that he had lived to see this day. The meeting closed with the singing of the first verse of "Old Hundred." Willard Saxton declared that the effect was thrilling and that "it seemed as if the angels were present, & the spirit of God had entered into each one of the two thousand hearts present filling it with a joy never experienced before, & opening their eyes to a clearer view of the glorious day of freedom just dawning upon them."[37]

The ceremony thrilled the freedmen but was unpalatable to the city's white citizens and to General Foster, who met with Saxton the following day. Willard Saxton reported that during their "war talk," Foster "grossly" insulted his brother and demanded that all requests concerning the implementation of Field Orders Number 15 be submitted in writing. It was evident that General Saxton could expect no favors from Foster, but he also knew that the final disposition would come from Washington. As Willard Saxton noted, "We will see which will go under first."[38]

Over the next few days, Foster sent another message to the War Department, requesting that Brigadier General William Birney, onetime superintendent in enlisting United States Colored Troops and brigade commander in the Department of the South, be detailed to replace General Saxton and enforce a draft upon the freedmen. Foster also denied Saxton's application that Littlefield be placed under him and that his recruiters be allowed into Savannah. Instead Foster had Littlefield continue the enforcement of conscription within the city. But Foster's days were numbered. Still suffering from an injured leg that required medical attention, Foster announced on February 7 that he had to "relinquish for the present command of the department." Before leaving, he thanked Generals Hatch and Potter and their gallant officers and men for their service in the recent campaign.[39]

General Foster's replacement was Major General Gillmore, the former commander of the Department of the South. In writing to his successor, Foster described the military situation and the movements toward Charleston. He also detailed his request to have General Saxton replaced by General Birney. The same day that he wrote to Gillmore, Foster also told Saxton of his imminent departure and that all requests concerning freedmen activity had been forwarded to General Gillmore.[40]

His departure from the department must have been a bitter blow to Foster. He had long hoped to restore the national flag over Fort Sumter, the post he had defended in April 1861, when it fell to the Confederacy. Equally disheartening was the answer to his appeal to sustain Colonel Littlefield as the department's chief recruiter. On February 9, the day Foster officially turned command over to Gillmore, a dispatch from Assistant Adjutant General Edward D. Townsend, who had been part of the official party that had accompanied Secretary Stanton to Savannah and Beaufort, denied the request and, in a short, terse special order, relieved Littlefield from duty in the Department of the South and ordered him to the Military Division of West Mississippi.[41]

General Gillmore, well acquainted with departmental affairs from his previous service, renewed his amiable relationship with General Saxton. On February 14, ending any doubts that might be lingering from Foster's administration, Gillmore named Saxton as the superintendent of volunteer recruiting service for the Department of the South, to be "obeyed and respected accordingly." Gillmore also retained Colonel Littlefield, placing him under Saxton as the department's mustering and disbursing officer.[42]

Though Saxton was happy to see Gillmore return, Rear Admiral John Dahlgren, commander of the South Atlantic Blockade Squadron, was not. Dahlgren, who had detested Gillmore ever since the general had blamed the admiral for the failure to capture Charleston during the summer of 1863, initially asked to be relieved, but with final victory and the capture of Charleston in sight, Dahlgren swallowed his pride and stayed on.[43]

Throughout February events at Port Royal moved at a rapid pace. With military operations ending, the region's atmosphere changed. Both soldiers and civilians prepared for the next transition that would take the area from a military encampment to a thriving community of small farms and mercantile centers. Businessmen looked to expand their operations at Hilton Head and Beaufort, while others hoped for the consummation of the great city and port at Land's End on St. Helena Island.

The fledgling community, however, suffered a severe jolt when word reached Beaufort of the sinking of the passenger ship *Melville*. The vessel, the former screw-propelled blockade runner *Ann*, had been captured off Mobile, Alabama, in 1862 and sold to private owners. The refurbished steamer, renamed *Melville*, operated out of New York on runs south. During a voyage for Port Royal in January 1865, the vessel sank. Among those lost were businessmen M. A. Bellows and E. P. Bellows of Vanderveer, Thorn and Bellows, who had recently initiated operations in Beaufort and Hilton Head. Bernard K. Lee, who had been instrumental in setting up the freedmen camp on Hilton Head, and his wife also perished, along with Lieutenant Colonel James D. Strong of the 1st South Carolina, who was coming back to Beaufort with his son.[44]

The terrible, sad news, as Willard Saxton described the foundering of the *Melville*, was deeply felt on the sea islands but did not stop the merchants at Port Royal from continuing to develop their businesses and plans for the future. On Hilton Head dealers increased their inventory and expanded their shops. Hoes, stoves, cooking wares, hats, caps, boots, and dry goods were advertised. In Beaufort, Sam Cooley expanded his enterprises by adding to his photographic studio on the corner of West and Craven Streets a bakery and confectionary establishment, which produced "Ornamental Pieces, Fancy Confectionary and Elegant Pastry for holiday or festive tables." Watches became a popular commodity, with salesmen for Robbins and Appleton, agents for the New York–based American Watch Company, promoting their solid-plate, substantial, reliable, and economical watches, which came in four patterns: a soldier's watch, a high-quality watch, a lady's watch, and a three-quarter-plate watch, which was thinner and lighter than the others.[45]

To help spur development on Hilton Head, a 1 percent sales tax was added to all invoices of goods arriving at Port Royal. Revenue from the tax went to purchase fire engines and construct footbridges and sidewalks. Port Royal Sound was seen as a "new Chicago," with Beaufort, Hilton Head, and Land's End all in competition to become the region's commercial center. Plans were put forward to connect the area by railroad to Hardeeville and Branchville. Merchants envisioned a line to Hilton Head with a spur running to Foot Point, where a naval station was proposed.

Many saw a great future based around shipping. The largest craft in the world could enter Port Royal Sound. To assist maritime commerce, Charles Boutelle, the coast survey hydrographer, who had served the military at Port Royal since November 1861, was placed in charge of reopening the coast's lighthouses. To protect the sound, new forts were projected, replacing Forts Welles and Seward on Hilton Head and Bay Point with modern fortifications supplemented by a Fort Sumter–style work in the middle of the harbor. It was thought that the proposed community would become the South's new "Point Comfort" and that Charleston and Savannah would be nothing more than subsidiaries of Port Royal. Such concepts thrilled the populace and "everybody seemed possessed with a mania for speculation."[46]

Elsewhere the Tax Commissioners began expanding their operations to Prince William Parish, implementing the property tax on land previously outside their domain. General Saxton, worried that returning southern whites might interfere with land acquired or set aside for freedmen, issued circulars that the superintendents were to post "in conspicuous positions, and to take every opportunity to inform those concerned of its existence." The documents called for citizens to immediately report to headquarters any interlopers who might impede the former slaves from retaining or gaining property and promised that military action, if necessary, would be taken to remove any suspicious characters.[47]

Changes also occurred with the operations of the refugee centers. Though all the camps, such as Saxtonville and St. Helenaville on St. Helena Island and Higginsonville and Sillimanville on Port Royal Island, most likely had charters, only limited information on the establishment and organization of Mitchelville on Hilton Head Island has come to light. On February 13, 1865, Colonel Littlefield formally established Mitchelville as a semi-independent community. Though many of the day-to-day operations were handled by its residents, the village remained under the control of a superintendent employed by the army. Whitelaw Reid, a *New York Tribune* journalist visiting the area in 1865, left a description of the village and its regulations: "The population is made up entirely of freedmen, and is regularly organized, with a Mayor and Common Council, Marshal, Recorder and Treasurer—all black, and all, except the Mayor and Treasurer, elected by the negroes themselves. The Common Council requires every child, between the ages of six and fifteen, to attend school regularly, except in cases where their services are absolutely necessary for the support of their parents, of which the teacher is made the judge!" Reid then went on to list some, but not all of the articles in the village's charter:

> The following are the main points of the military order under which Mitchelville is organized:
>
> I. All lands now set apart for the colored population, near Hilton Head, are declared to constitute a village, to be known as the village of Mitchelville. Only freedmen and colored persons residing or sojourning within the territorial limits of said village, shall be deemed and considered inhabitants thereof.
>
> II. The village of Mitchelville shall be organized and governed as follows: Said village shall be divided into districts, as nearly equal in population as practicable, for the election of Councilmen, sanitary and police regulations, and the general government of the people residing therein.
>
> III. The government shall consist of a Supervisor and Treasurer, to be appointed by, and hold office during the pleasure of the Military Commander of the District, assisted by a Councilman from each council district, to be elected by the people, who shall also, at the same time, choose a Recorder and Marshal. The duties of the Marshal and Recorder shall be defined by the Council of Administration.
>
> IV. The Supervisor and Councilmen shall constitute the Council of Administration, with the Recorder as Secretary.
>
> V. The Council of Administration shall have power:
>
> To pass such ordinances as it shall deem best, in relation to the following subjects: To establish schools for the education of children and other persons.
>
> To prevent and punish vagrancy, idleness and crime. To punish licentiousness, drunkenness, offenses against public decency and good order, and petty violation of the rights of proper and person.

To require due observance of the Lord's Day. To collect fines and penalties. To punish offenses against village ordinances. To settle and determine disputes concerning claims for wages, personal property, and controversies between debtor and creditor. To levy and collect taxes to defray the expenses of the village government, and for the support of schools. To lay out, regulate, and clean the streets. To establish wholesome sanitary regulations for the prevention of disease. To appoint officers, places and times for the holding of elections. To compensate municipal officers, and to regulate all other matters affecting the well-being of citizens, and good order of society.

VI. Hilton Head Island will be divided into School Districts, conform, as nearly as practicable, to the schools as established by the Freedmen's Association. In each District there shall be elected one School Commissioner, who will be charged with supplying the wants of the schools, under the direction of the teacher thereof. Every child, between the ages of six and fifteen years, residing within the limits of such School Districts, shall attend school daily, while they are in session, excepting only in case of sickness.

Where children are of a suitable age to earn a livelihood, and their services are required by their parents or guardians, and on the written order of the teacher in such School District, may be exempt from attendance, for such time as said order shall specify. And the parents and guardians will be held responsible that said children so attend school, under the penalty of being punished at the discretion of the Council of Administration.[48]

While Littlefield labored to make Mitchelville an example for the creation of a new civilization on the sea islands, men from his regiment, the 3rd South Carolina, now designated the 21st USCT, became the first Union troops to set foot in Charleston upon its evacuation by the Confederates. Great rejoicing swept through the sea islands when news of Charleston's occupation arrived. General Gillmore quickly left Hilton Head for Charleston, and General Saxton made plans to follow. Gathering up a party that included his brother Willard, Dr. Henry K. Durant, Duncan Wilson, and Colonel Charles H. Howard, the brother of General Oliver O. Howard, who had gone north with dispatches and returned too late to assume his spot on the general's staff for the march into the Carolinas. Saxton and his entourage went down to the main wharf in Beaufort at about noon on February 26 and boarded the steamer *Planter*, captained by Robert Smalls.

The vessel made good time, with Smalls following in reverse the same track he had taken when he absconded with the *Planter* from Charleston and Confederate control nearly three years earlier. The party steamed along the

Beaufort River to the Coosaw River and St. Helena Sound, where fog and rough seas slowed the journey and Smalls was forced to anchor for the night just short of Charleston harbor at Lighthouse Inlet. The next morning, fog delayed their departure; then, before it fully lifted, Smalls cautiously crept his vessel along the coast. As they passed Fort Sumter, the weather cleared. As Willard Saxton stated, "T'was worth something to go up on the *Planter*, with a black captain."[49]

At about noon Smalls docked the *Planter*, and her passengers disembarked. The Saxton brothers toured the beleaguered city and met with General Alexander Schimmelfennig and General Hatch, along with other officers and civilians who had come from the sea islands. General Saxton, ready to begin recruiting in the city and resettling freedmen on nearby islands, decided to take a house on the Battery. The next day around noon, the party left Charleston and returned to Beaufort on the *Planter*, with Captain Smalls delivering them to the town's wharf at about 8:00 p.m.[50]

While Saxton prepared to move his operations to Charleston, recruiting continued at Port Royal. Over the next few weeks, additional enlistees arrived for the new black regiments organizing on the islands. White officers were named for the units, among them Colonel Howard, who gave up his position on his brother's staff to accept command of the 128th USCT Regiment being formed at Beaufort. While recruits arrived, freedmen families, with their livestock and household goods, left the area aboard the steamers *Enoch Dean* and *Planter* for Edisto Island. Most were former slaves who had been evacuated from the island in 1862 and were now returning to claim land in accordance with Special Field Orders Number 15. Auctions continued on the sea islands with lots at Land's End and homes in Beaufort sold to the highest bidders. Among those purchasing houses in Beaufort were Duncan Wilson and Rufus Saxton.[51]

The fall of Charleston brought visitors from the North to Port Royal, where they had to obtain passes from the military before continuing to the captured city. Some were northern missionaries, who opened freedmen schools and other establishments, including an orphan house named for Colonel Robert G. Shaw in a mansion on the Battery. Merchants appeared, eager to initiate new businesses. Politicians, wanting to view firsthand the beleaguered city and the freedmen activities, also arrived.

On March 18 a group that included Senators Lyman Trumbull of Illinois, Benjamin Wade of Ohio, James W. Grimes of Iowa, James R. Doolittle of Wisconsin, Alexander Ramsey of Minnesota, and John Sherman of Ohio (General William T. Sherman's brother), as well as former senator Simon Cameron of Pennsylvania and Representative Justin S. Morrill of Vermont, arrived at Hilton Head aboard the *Fulton*. The next day the party, escorted by Colonel Littlefield, came to Beaufort. They visited General Potter's headquarters and toured the town, stopping at the Saxtons' home, where Willard Saxton took them to see the view from the mansion's piazza. The region and its potential impressed the dignitaries and senators Cameron, Wade, and Doolittle eventually purchased at a foreclosure auction Bull Island, located northwest of Hilton Head Island.[52]

After visiting Beaufort, the dignitaries continued on to Charleston, where on March 21 a grand jubilee of freedom was held by the city's freedmen. The 21st USCT, the former 3rd South Carolina, which was organized on Hilton Head and counted many former Charleston slaves among its numbers, led the parade. Behind them came the black ministers of Charleston, "carrying open Bibles," followed by a cart on which were fifteen black women in white dresses representing the slave states. Next in line some eighteen hundred black children marched, singing, "John Brown's body lies a-moldering in the grave, We go marching on!" Though their teachers had been asked to keep them from singing the verse "We'll Hang Jeff Davis from a Sour Apple Tree," the children sang it nevertheless.

At the conclusion of the procession, a mass rally was held on the Citadel Green, where speakers, including General Saxton, addressed a crowd estimated at over ten thousand. At its conclusion the fifteen black women who had symbolized the fifteen slave states presented General and Mrs. Saxton with bouquets. Numerous hurrahs were given for General Saxton, the Yankees, the United States flag, and three long tumultuous cheers for Abraham Lincoln. Reverend French ended the ceremony by leading the singing of a doxology.[53]

General Saxton returned to Beaufort on March 24 but frequently visited Charleston to continue settling freedmen and enlisting them into regiments. To assist Saxton, the Federal government sent Major Martin Delany to Charleston. Born to a free mother and an enslaved father, the fifty-two-year-old Delany was a descendant of an African prince. In his hometown of Charlestown, Virginia, he had been taught to read and write at an early age. A remarkable individual, Delany became a college professor, medical doctor, journalist, novelist, and reformer. Before the war, because of the nation's racial attitudes, he promoted the removal of blacks from the United States and the formation of a new national homeland. In 1859 Delany traveled to Africa but returned at the start of the Civil War to support the Union war effort and emancipation.

Beginning in 1863, Delany started recruiting blacks for military service. Then in February 1865, he requested permission from President Lincoln and Secretary of War Stanton to form an army of black soldiers that would march into the Deep South, liberating and enlisting slaves as they went. The concept, reminiscent of one put forward by General Hunter earlier in the war, was well received, and Delany was commissioned a major, becoming the first black field officer in the United States Army. He was assigned to duty in South Carolina with General Saxton. Delany arrived at Hilton Head in early April 1865 and, after visiting Beaufort, continued on to Charleston, where he met with Saxton and commenced his recruiting duties.[54]

While Saxton expanded his operations, he and General Gillmore began preparing for a celebration commemorating the anniversary of the April 1861 capture of Fort Sumter. The directive coordinating the event from the War Department read:

> That at the hour of noon on the 14th day of April, 1865, Brevet Major General Anderson will raise and plant upon the ruins of Fort Sumter the same United States flag which floated over the battlements of that fort during the rebel assault, and which was lowered and saluted by him and the small force of his command when the works were evacuated on the 14th day of April, 1861. After the flag raising a salute was to be fired from Fort Sumter and the surrounding forts and batteries followed by an address by the famed abolitionist the Reverend Henry Ward Beecher.[55]

In early April, to organize the celebration, Generals Saxton and Gillmore went to Charleston. On the sea islands, both black and white people requested permission to go to the city. Many school teachers and superintendents, among them Laura Towne, received passes and left for Charleston during the days leading up to the celebration. In early April participants for the flag-raising ceremony began arriving at Hilton Head. On April 12 a group including General Robert H. Anderson, U.S. Military Academy professor Dennis Hart Mahan, and Major General John A. Dix came to Beaufort. General Dix and his daughter visited Willard Saxton, spending some time on the great piazza of the Saxtons' home. That night Willard Saxton, his wife, and others took a vessel to Hilton Head, where they attended a grand ball. Present were Senator Henry Wilson of Massachusetts and the abolitionist and newspaper editor William Lloyd Garrison, who before the war had been burned in effigy in the streets of Charleston. The next day ships began leaving Port Royal carrying passengers for an event about which Willard Saxton wrote: "The pen falters & language fails when they come to tell of the great & glorious doings of this day, one of the most eventful of the war & one that will be recorded on the page of history as one of the brightest."[56]

The morning of April 14 found the vessels from Port Royal standing off the Charleston bar. Rough seas and high winds kept some ships from entering the harbor and necessitated the transfer of their passengers onto smaller packets for transportation to Fort Sumter. While the shifting progressed, the steamer *Diamond* ran out from the city carrying word that General Lee had surrendered the Army of Northern Virginia. Immediately cheers reverberated across the waters, while bands on board the liners struck up national airs.

Throughout the morning boats of all sizes exited from Charleston's wharves, mixing with those in the harbor. The waterways were so congested that vessels became entangled and occasionally crashed into one another. Among the steamboats vying to reach Sumter was the *Planter*, captained by Robert Smalls. A participant reported that the paddle-wheeler was "crowded almost to suffocation upon her three decks" with freedmen who hung "over the gunwales, mounted on the posts, doubled up in the furtive corners, peering through the gangways, darkening the wheel-house, upon the top of which stood Robert Small [sic], a prince among them, self-possessed, prompt and proud, giving his orders to the helmsman in ringing tones of command." As Smalls maneuvered the vessel toward Sumter's wharf, the vessel ran aground, and the passengers, which included Major Martin Delany, were unable to land but did observe the flag as it rose over the fort's walls.[57]

Nearly four thousand people crowded into the battered fortification. Detachments of black and white soldiers, including a contingent of the 54th Massachusetts, sailors, and marines, formed an honor guard in the fort. At about 11:30 General Gillmore, accompanied by General Anderson and Anderson's daughter, entered the parade ground, followed by members of the official party that included the Reverend Henry W. Beecher; Theodore Tilton, editor of the *New York Independent* newspaper; William Lloyd Garrison; Senator Wilson; British abolitionist George Thompson; Supreme Court Justice Noah Swayne, whose son had been wounded and lost his leg at the Battle of Rivers Bridge; and the reformer Reverend Joshua Leavitt. Among those representing the army were Generals Saxton, Hatch, Abner Doubleday, and John Dix, Assistant Adjutant General Edward D. Townsend, and Adjutant General Joseph Holt. Assistant Secretary of the Navy Gustavus Fox headed up a navy delegation that included Commodore Stephen Rowan, Admiral Dahlgren, and members from Dahlgren's staff consisting of Fleet Captain Lieutenant Commander Joseph M. Bradford, Chief Engineer Robert Danby, Squadron Judge-Advocate Charles Cowley, and Lieutenant Commander E. Orville Matthews.

Once the official party took their places on the raised platform built over the fort's parade ground, the ceremony commenced with the singing of a song and chorus entitled "Victory at Last." An opening prayer and Psalm reading followed; then General Anderson made a few remarks, ending with, "I thank God I have lived to see this day, to be here to perform this perhaps the last act of duty to my country in this life. My heart is filled with gratitude to Almighty God for the signal blessings which he has given us—blessings beyond number. May all the world proclaim glory to God in the highest, on earth peace and good will toward men." Once finished, he raised the tattered flag that he had lowered four years earlier. When it cleared the walls, the wind blew it straight out above the celebrants, and every soldier and sailor instinctively saluted. Then began the prescribed salute of one hundred guns fired from Sumter, followed by rounds from every fort and battery that had bombarded the fort in 1861. When the forts were done, the naval vessels began to fire one after the other until the air was thick with smoke. National airs were played, ending with everyone singing "The Star-Spangled Banner."[58]

Reverend Beecher followed with an impassioned speech thanking God for the ending of the rebellion and slavery. For the good of the nation, he called for educating the former slaves and gave solemn congratulations to God for sustaining President Lincoln, the administration, and the military. He concluded with these words of thanks: "God of our fathers! We render thanksgiving and praise for that wondrous providence that has brought forth from such a harvest of war the seed of so much liberty and peace. We invoke peace upon the North; peace be to the West; peace be upon the South. In the name of God, we lift up our banner and dedicate it to Peace, Union and Liberty, now and forever more. Amen!"[59]

At the conclusion visitors (including Laura Towne) explored the fort, bought photographs, and gathered up souvenirs before returning to Charleston. The wharf at Sumter was so congested that the embarking passengers had to walk across the decks of ships moored side by side to reach their vessels. The *Planter* was pulled free from the mud bank, but as Smalls tried to guide her away from the fort, she smashed into the steamer *Golden Gate*'s wheelhouse. No major damage was done, and both vessels returned to Charleston. That evening Smalls was an honored guest aboard the steamer *Oceanus*, where he recounted his escape from Charleston nearly three years earlier. The day's festivities concluded with a banquet at the Charleston Hotel and a magnificent fireworks display provided by the fleet. As the citizens of Charleston had done four years before, the northern visitors watched the fireworks from the rooftops of homes along the Battery.[60]

The next day many of the visiting sea islanders, both black and white, participated at mass meetings at the Citadel Green and the nearby Zion Presbyterian Church, a slave mission church that ministered to the city's black population. Laura Towne believed that this day was the actual "grand day," and Esther Hawks called it "the most jubilant and the longest to be remembered by us!" Senator Wilson, William Lloyd Garrison, George Thompson, and others addressed large crowds, who enthusiastically embraced the new vision for the freedmen and felt that "it was their day & that they had a right to hold up their heads & rejoice with exceeding great joy." A large ovation greeted Major Martin Delany, and when General Saxton got up to speak, he received cheer after cheer, with only the mention of President Lincoln's name eliciting a greater response.[61]

Over the next few days, many of the celebrants returned to the sea islands. On April 17 a number of the dignitaries came to Beaufort, including Senator Wilson, William Lloyd Garrison, Henry Ward Beecher, and Theodore Tilton. The next morning the whole party crossed the ferry to Lady's Island and rode in ambulances escorted by Rufus, Tilly, and Willard Saxton to the freedmen village Saxtonville on St. Helena Island. After the visit, plans had been made for speeches in Beaufort, but news unexpectedly arrived that President Lincoln and Secretary of State Seward had been targeted by assassins and that the president, who had been shot in a theater on the same day as the celebration at Fort Sumter, was dead. Immediately the visitors hurried to Hilton Head to return north and a "gloom" was thrown over the sea islands.[62]

In remembrance of the president, the district commander, Colonel Littlefield, ordered a cannon fired from Fort Welles on Hilton Head every half hour from sunup to sunset. All businesses were closed, flags hung at half-mast, and officers were directed to wear black crepe around the left arm above the elbow and on their sword hilts for thirty days. That evening, in the theater on Hilton Head, Littlefield, who had known Lincoln, addressed a meeting of civilians and soldiers about the president's life. A Lincoln Monument committee made up of army and naval officers was formed and a proposal made to erect a fitting memorial in the sea islands honoring martyred president.[63]

Lincoln's death greatly affected former Beaufort resident Dr. Richard Fuller. On Easter Sunday, Fuller addressed his congregation at the Seventh Baptist Church in Baltimore, Maryland, denouncing "the horrible crime." With tears in his eyes, Fuller recounted his last meeting with Lincoln, after which he told an acquaintance, "If that is not an honest man, and a man with a kind heart, my judgment of human character is worth nothing." Fuller called for people to seek humiliation for their sins, which were still bringing sorrow to the country, and to realize that in crisis God allowed true human nature to come out boldly and openly and that "this sad calamity might rebuke and alter the bitterness of political feeling."[64]

On St. Helena Island, Laura Towne reported that the new Penn School building was dressed in black and that the teachers "gave a shred of crepe to some of our children, who wear it sacredly." The Sunday after Lincoln's assassination, the black minister at Frogmore said he could not mourn for Lincoln because he refused to believe he was dead. The people on St. Helena Island agreed with the preacher. As Laura Towne wrote on April 23, "on the island here, they are inconsolable and will not believe he is dead."[65]

The following week, after the news had sunk in, Laura Towne's domestic helper, Rina, said she couldn't sleep, "thinking how sorry she was to lose 'PaLinkum.'" Another man asked Towne quietly if it were true that "the government was dead." A third man declared, "Lincoln died for we, Christ died for we and me believe him de same mans."[66]

At the Smith Plantation, Elizabeth Botume found that the freedmen were "filled with consternation and despair." Women asked for black cloth to sew on their gowns. The schoolroom was draped in black, and a solemn shout was held, where prayers were woven into supplications that became a rhythmical chant, continuing until the leader ended with "Massa Lincoln! Our 'dored Redeemer an' Saviour an' Frien'! Amen!"[67]

Botume also noted that Lincoln's death worried the freedmen, who felt they had lost their greatest ally and benefactor. They watched suspiciously as more and more northerners arrived. Even the Hilton Head–based newspaper, the *New South*, warned against trusting New Englanders who were now coming to the area for commercial gain, commenting that they were the "meanest beings that ever stood on two legs—cunning, rapacious, hypocritical, ever ready to skin a flint with a borrowed knife and make (for others) a soup out of the peelings." The paper called on the freedmen to "Trust thyself," pointing out that a Yankee was not necessarily a friend.[68]

Many of the newcomers were merchants and speculators with little regard for the former slaves, who believed that in some cases the new immigrants were mimicking the airs of their former masters. On Hilton Head a restaurant advertised that their waiters and cooks were white, while other businesses refused to hire blacks. Even some of the missionaries, entering into commercial activities, took advantage of their former minions, causing one freedman to remark about his abuser: "He don't deserve to be a white man. He'll shuck han's wid his right han', an fling a brick-bat at you wid his lef."[69]

Also worrying the freedmen was the potential return of their former masters. With Lincoln the freedmen had received special consideration, but his successor, Andrew Johnson, a southerner and former slaveholder, was an unknown entity. Much had been accomplished, but more was expected as their quest for equality and acceptance continued. Only five months into the New Year, considerable changes had occurred, and more was yet to come. As Willard Saxton noted, "What strange times we live in, & how full of great events seems every hour. History makes itself fast."[70]

Chapter 17

The Beginning of the New South

"Give him more light!"

History was hurtling fast—for the nation, South Carolina, and the Beaufort District. By the spring of 1865, troop strength on the sea islands was reduced and the draft ended. Most of the units stationed at Beaufort and Hilton Head were transferred to Charleston. Some of the northerners who had come to the area during the conflict, their tasks completed, began leaving, while new immigrants, black and white, arrived. From the interior of the state came freedmen, aware of the region's promised safety, employment, and land. White northern businessmen appeared with hopes of developing lucrative commercial activities at Beaufort and Hilton Head, while white southerners, coming home from exile or military service, sought to reestablish their residence and reclaim their homes and property. Among the latter were Confederate soldiers from the 11th South Carolina Infantry Regiment, the 3rd South Carolina Cavalry, and the Beaufort Volunteer Artillery, all part of the Confederate forces surrendered on April 26, 1865, by General Joseph E. Johnston to General Sherman. The surrender not only included those formations in Johnston's immediate army but also those within his departmental command. The capitulation applied to the men of the 11th South Carolina and the Beaufort Artillery, who were among those surrendered at Bennett's Place near Durham Station, North Carolina, and the troopers of the 3rd South Carolina Cavalry, whose companies were scattered throughout the upper regions of South Carolina.[1]

During his armies' month-long march across South Carolina, General Sherman had left behind no garrisons to occupy the state's interior, thus creating a void where little to no authority, civil or military, existed. It fell to General Quincy A. Gillmore to secure the region and protect the freedmen. Gillmore directed that all Negroes be "treated like white men, subject to special instructions touching their education, support, and colonization as have been given by the War Department to Brevet Major General Saxton." Shortly after this, General Sherman, aboard the *Russia,* the former blockade runner *Mary Ann,* returned to Hilton Head and Savannah, touching at Charleston on his way south. He met with Gillmore and Saxton, confirming the end of hostilities throughout the region and directed Gillmore to reestablish Federal authority.[2]

Though General Johnston had directed all forces under his authority east of the Chattahoochee River to lay down their arms and cease hostilities, civil officials refused to capitulate. In South Carolina, Governor Andrew G. Magrath issued a call on April 25, 1865, for the convening of a special session of the state's legislature in Columbia. Few responded, and when Gillmore learned that Magrath had directed that all Confederate stores and property be turned over to the state, he quickly sent word to Magrath informing the governor that by the agreement between Sherman and Johnston all Confederate assets were now the property of the United States. When the governor refused to acquiesce, Gillmore on May 14 declared Magrath disloyal for committing treasonous acts. The general also made it clear that the war had changed the status of the South's slaves, stating that "the people of the black race are free citizens of the United States; that it is the fixed intention of a wise and beneficial Government to protect them in the enjoyment of their freedom and the fruits of their industry." Eight days later Gillmore ordered Magrath's arrest, and when Federal troops occupied Columbia, the governor surrendered and was briefly confined at Fort Pulaski.[3]

While Gillmore dealt with the chaos in South Carolina, the U.S. government acted to remove from the region's military commanders the extraordinary duties centered on the freedmen's care and protection. Early in the war, reformers and abolitionists had called for the creation of a bureau to protect and educate slaves freed by the military. Senator Charles Sumner, Congressman Thaddeus Stevens, Secretary of the Treasury Salmon Chase, and Secretary of War Stanton received the concept favorably but debated over whether the new bureau should be under the treasury or war department. The wrangling between the cabinet members set back the section's creation until March 1865. With the bureau placed under the War Department, further delays ensued while a search was initiated to locate a suitable leader. Though General Saxton was considered, the post eventually went to General Oliver O. Howard, who on May 16, 1865, was appointed commissioner of the Bureau of Refugees, Freedmen, and Abandoned Lands, commonly referred to as the Freedmen's Bureau. Two days later Rufus Saxton became the bureau's assistant commissioner for South Carolina and Georgia.[4]

Before Saxton received word of his appointment, a special delegation of two individuals who had had a profound effect on the Beaufort District arrived in the sea islands: Reverend Richard Fuller and the former secretary of the treasury and now the chief justice of the supreme court, Salmon Chase. Throughout the war the two had maintained a strained friendship, with Chase never wavering from his conviction that former slaves should be awarded all the privileges of citizenship, including full voting rights for adult male freedmen. Fuller, on the other hand, went through a long conversion from a paternalistic view of blacks as a race who had to be controlled and cared for via slavery to an opinion that the freedmen deserved an opportunity to succeed or fail in the postwar society by their own merits.

In early April, Chase attended two dinner parties at Reverend Fuller's Baltimore home, where Fuller expressed his great joy over emancipation. At the second gathering, Chase stated his opinion that "the only solid foundation of social order & political prosperity was universal suffrage." When the other guests demurred from Chase's view, the chief justice went on to declare that the nation would be condemned by all impartial men if it did not reward the fidelity of the blacks who had been "eminently loyal" with a "voice in the affairs of the country they had helped save."[5]

Dr. Fuller then related his own experience with slavery, stating, "Formerly I felt bound to sustain the burden of the institution, but was never easy under it. My slaves were my continual anxiety. How could I die & leave them? To what? To whom? I thank God for emancipation—it has taken a great burden off my mind. My friends tell me 'You have lost a hundred & fifty thousand dollars!' I tell them 'Say rather that I have had one hundred & fifty thousand weight of iron taken from my conscience.'" Chase was very pleased to hear this and hoped that Fuller's epiphany would continue.[6]

With the rebellion winding down and hostilities ending, Chase planned an extended excursion throughout the South, primarily to gather data on the freedmen and promote his reconstruction policy. Lincoln's assassination momentarily disrupted his plans, but President Johnson, whom Chase had sworn into office, approved the trip, and on May 1, 1865, the chief justice and his official party, which included his daughter Nettie, Reverend Fuller, and the journalist Whitelaw Reid, embarked from the Washington Navy Yard. They initially sailed south aboard the revenue cutter *Northerner*, a small paddle-wheel steamer. Then at Fort Monroe, Virginia, they transferred to another revenue cutter, the sleeker, screw-propelled *Wayanda,* for the rest of the trip.

Numerous stops were made. At Morehead City, North Carolina, they unexpectedly rendezvoused with General Sherman, who was returning north from his visit to Charleston, Savannah, and Hilton Head. Sherman heartily welcomed the travelers aboard his headquarters vessel, the *Russia,* and later exchanged correspondence with Chase over the future of freedmen in the reconstructed South. Chase, the adopted Ohioan, again stated his belief that the former slaves should be fully integrated into society with complete voting rights. Sherman, the native Ohioan, believed the nation, both the North and the South, was not ready to accept Negroes as equals, and that if such policies were forced upon the South, it could rekindle a war that would be "more bloody and destructive than the last." The general did not believe that the government could combat the existing racial views with force and hoped that over time practical statesmanship could work out a solution.

Chase agreed that a conservative approach should be followed, but he refused to waver from his conviction that the Union was "safest with universal suffrage" and that all loyal men, black and white, must be allowed to maintain the government through the right to vote. Chase did tell Sherman, "Our ends are the same, permanent Union & permanent peace."[7]

After meeting with Sherman, the party sailed on, stopping at Wilmington, North Carolina, and then Charleston, where Admiral Dahlgren greeted them and Generals Gillmore, Hatch, and Saxton served as guides about the ruined city. While Fuller met with destitute relatives and Reid interviewed former Confederates, Chase accompanied Saxton to a meeting at Zion Presbyterian Church, where Saxton, Gillmore, Major Martin Delany, and Chase addressed an enthusiastic throng of freedmen, who burst into thunderous applause when Chase came to the podium. The chief justice gave a "simple, straightforward and weighty talk" advising the former slaves that they deserved the vote, but should it be denied, they needed to educate themselves and through hard work and industry prove that they deserved the right of suffrage. He counseled the freedmen that God would render each their due, "diffusing happiness to the extent of His power through the sphere of which He is the center." He declared that "there reigns one God and one Father, before whom all his children are equal." Prolonged cheers followed, and Whitelaw Reid heard a freedman behind him tell his neighbor: "T'isn't only what he says, but it's de man what says it. He don't talk for nuffin, and his words hab weight."[8]

On the evening of May 12, the *Wayanda* carried Chase and his party from Charleston to Port Royal. The next morning Chase rose early to view Forts Beauregard and Walker and reminisce about Du Pont and the great naval victory that had forever changed the Beaufort District. Soon the sailors aboard the warships anchored in the sound manned the yards and salutes were fired, rendering honors to the chief justice. Generals Saxton and Gillmore, who had reached Port Royal in advance of the official party along with Mansfield French, greeted the new arrivals and took them on a carriage tour of Mitchelville.

The next day Chase, his daughter Nettie, Reverend French, and Whitelaw Reid, along with General Gillmore, came to Beaufort aboard the *Nemaha*. General Saxton met them with carriages at the town's wharf. A short ride took them to the camp of the 128th USCT, where Colonel Charles Howard had his raw soldiers perform a dress parade that impressed the spectators. Reid noted, "They were all coal black, and seemed larger and more muscular than the negro troops raised farther north." Reverend Fuller, greeted enthusiastically by some of his former slaves, was astonished at the changes from his last visit to Beaufort eighteen years earlier. He told Reid that "he never saw the slaves of Beaufort so well clad, or seemingly so comfortable."[9]

Taken by ferry to Lady's Island, General Saxton escorted the party to a gathering on St. Helena Island at the Brick Church. The crowd of freedmen was so large that the meeting was held outside in an adjacent oak grove. The dignitaries took their seats on a small raised platform. The appearance of Gillmore, Saxton, and Chase caused a sensation, but the presence of Fuller, a Beaufort native, former pastor of the Baptist Church of Beaufort, and antebellum "apostle" to the sea island slaves, caused the greatest stir. All the freedmen seemed to know him and greeted him almost like a returning messiah.[10]

An African preacher opened the meeting. Then the assembled sang, "Roll Jordon Roll," first singing "Massa Fuller sitting on the tree of life," a tribute to a man who had given up a lucrative law practice to join the ministry and expand the Baptist faith to the region's slaves. Then, to recognize their new benefactors, the freedmen sang next a verse to "General Saxby sitting on the tree of life" and "Mister Chase sitting on the tree of life."[11]

While Saxton and Chase made impassioned speeches, it was Fuller who captured the freedmen's attention. He warned them that they would have to prove to their doubters that they could and would succeed. He told the assembled freedmen, "If a man who has been shut up for a long time in a dark room, is suddenly brought into the light, it dazzles his eyes, and he is apt to stumble. Well then what will you do? Put him back in the dark again?" The crowd responded, "No! No!" "What then?" Fuller asked. Some of the crowd suggested, "Tell him what to do." Others proposed, "Lead him a little while." Then preacher Fuller exclaimed, "Give him more light!" All nodded and murmured in assent. Fuller's words carried great weight and telling the freedmen that they would proceed into the light of freedom and not back into the darkness of slavery. It was the greatest reassurance they could imagine.[12]

There were other speakers and the service ended with a benediction by Reverend Fuller. After the ceremony the former slaves mobbed Fuller. They pressed against him, clasped his hands as in the antebellum ceremony of the "quarterly seasons." They touched his coat and stroked his hair, all asking whether he remembered them. This was witnessed by one of the officers of the *Wayanda,* the revenue cutter that had brought the chief justice's party to South Carolina. The officer had not liked Fuller on the voyage south because the old preacher had rebuked him for using foul language aboard ship, but witnessing the freedman's reaction on St. Helena Island, the rugged sailor said, "I'd give all I'm worth, or ever hope to be worth, to be loved by as many people as love him."[13]

While the crowd continued to throng around Fuller, Saxton took Chase and the others to the freedmen village of Saxtonville, a half mile south of the

Brick Church. The community stretched along a single road for a mile and a half. Each house along the highway had its own garden of potatoes and corn, and poultry swarmed around the homesteads. Behind each cabin stretched individual cotton fields owned by the residents.[14]

After retrieving Reverend Fuller, the visitors returned to Beaufort, where they dined at the Saxtons' home. At 5:00 P.M. a second meeting was held in Beaufort. The crowd was too large for any building, so they gathered in an ancient live oak grove on the town's edge. The ranks of two regiments of black soldiers joined the throng of freedmen. Saxton, Fuller, and Chase again addressed the assembly. Fuller's sermon had the audience "swaying to and fro, now weeping, then laughing, in agitation of a common passion the orator evoked." Fuller told them that "I have been in the habit of addressing all sorts of people, but never felt so intensely the inspiration of a deeply sympathizing audience." Chase was profoundly moved when Fuller stated that former slaves who could read a chapter of the Bible should immediately be given the right to vote and that the privilege would eventually be extended to all. Chase later wrote a friend, "Was not this something strange to be said in South Carolina, by an ex-planter to his ex-slaves?" After Fuller spoke, the crowd clamored for Chase, their cheers swaying "the Spanish moss that hung in pendant streamers above our heads and made the leaves of the live-oaks quiver as if a gale were blowing through the branches."[15]

At the conclusion of the prayers and formalities, the crowd of freedmen surged forward to touch old "Massa Richard." One of the older women started a ring dance, or "shout," around Richard Fuller. The shout was the unique expression of the sea island Gullah people, and Fuller understood that it was their highest spiritual compliment. The circle became bigger and bigger while others engaged Fuller in conversation. Eventually the party had to leave, and they pushed their way through the crowd while long lines of black soldiers marched away, "their glistening bayonets setting the red rays of the sinking sun to flickering in grotesque lights and shades over the shouting and dancing slaves."[16]

Chase and his daughter went to the Saxton's, where they spent the night. Fuller and Reid and the rest of the party went to the town wharf on Bay Street for the trip back to Hilton Head. There on the pier was Captain Robert Smalls, again standing at the gangplank of history, with his "lead colored little steamer," the *Planter*, waiting to take them down to Hilton Head Island. Fuller and Smalls, representing the old and new of the Beaufort District, set sail together. On the moonlight passage to Hilton Head, the natural beauty of the sea islands worked its magic on Whitelaw Reid: "The breeze over the island was delicious; not a film of mist flecked the sky; and down to the very meeting of sky and water, we caught the sparkle of the stars, brilliant with all the effulgence of a tropic night."[17]

The next day General Saxton and his wife escorted Chief Justice Chase and his daughter to the Smith Plantation, where they visited the school operated by Elizabeth Botume and her nieces Lizzie and Fanny Langford. After returning to Beaufort, the Chases went to the town's college building, which had been returned to its use as a school, and viewed students performing arithmetic exercises. Before returning to Hilton Head, Chase met with the tax commissioners, who he reported were busy issuing sale certificates to freedmen who had purchased property at recent tax sales.[18]

That evening Chase and his entourage embarked on the *Wayanda* for Savannah. The *Wayanda*'s captain, unwilling at night to enter the Savannah River, which was still laced with Confederate obstructions, anchored off Fort Pulaski. The next morning Chase awoke to find a steamer, the quartermaster side-wheeler *Emilie,* tied up next to the *Wayanda*. Word quickly passed throughout the *Wayanda* that aboard the *Emilie* was the Confederate president, Jefferson Davis. Before Chase could dress, General Gillmore rapped on the chief justice's cabin door, asking whether he or anyone in his party wished to see Davis. Chase responded, "I don't want to see him, unless he expresses a wish to see me." Chase also refused to let anyone in his group see Davis, as he "would not make a show of a fallen enemy."[19]

By the time Chase had dressed, the two vessels had parted. The *Wayanda* continued on to Savannah. After a day visiting the Georgia city, the dignitaries returned to Hilton Head, where on May 17 Reverend Fuller took leave of his friends and boarded the *Arago* for a trip north. Chase, knowing he would miss Fuller's company, watched forlornly as the steamer carrying his friend passed out of Port Royal Sound and receded over the horizon.[20]

While Chase continued his grand tour, the *Emilie,* carrying Jefferson Davis and other prisoners, anchored in Port Royal Sound. Davis, his family, and his traveling companions had been captured at Irwinville, Georgia, on May 10, 1865, by Union cavalry. They were sent to Augusta, where other Confederate prisoners, including Vice President Alexander Stephens and Lieutenant General Joseph Wheeler, were placed on the old side-wheel packet *Emilie* and sent downriver to Savannah. On May 16, after the brief encounter with Chase's transport, the prisoners arrived at Port Royal Sound. The next day they were confined aboard an ocean steamer that had been recently employed in carrying former Union prisoners, once inmates of Andersonville, north for passage to Fort Monroe, Virginia. In one of the ironies of the war's end, Davis's military aide-de-camp and fellow prisoner was Colonel Francis Richard Lubbock, the former governor of Texas, who had been raised in Beaufort fifty years before while his father was captain of a paddle-wheel steamer that plied the waters between Charleston and Savannah. And in a double irony, the famous prisoners were carried to Virginia aboard the new screw-propelled steamer SS *William P. Clyde,* whose owner,

William P. Clyde, was to assemble a whole fleet of steamships called the "Clyde Line" and become one of the captains of the transportation industry in the so-called Gilded Age. In the 1890s William P. Clyde returned to Port Royal Sound and bought up twenty thousand acres of Hilton Head Island's old plantation lands to use as his private hunting preserve.[21]

Among the Davis's household that arrived off Hilton Head was a young, free-born mulatto boy named James Henry Brooks, who became known to the Davises as Jim Limber. An orphan rescued by Varina Davis from an abusive guardian, he became a ward of the first family and a playmate to their children. Before the *William P. Clyde* sailed, Mrs. Davis sent a note to General Saxton. As Willard Saxton recorded the event:

> The Gen. received from Mrs. Davis in the steamer from the Head, a small yellow boy, wishing him to take care of him, & have oversight over his education & general bringing up. She says he is bright & brave & he has that appearance. Says his name is "James Henry Brooks," & that he loves Jeff Davis, & hates Lincoln & was not sorry he was killed. He was free born & "a waif, taken from the street," Mrs. D. says, & eight years old. He is a little rebel & shows the influence he has been under. He has the smartness in him that will make a smart man, if he lives & is rightly trained & educated.[22]

Initially General Saxton and his wife, Tilly, took the child and cared for him, but "Jim Limber" remained loyal to the Davises and fought with freedmen children in Beaufort, especially when they sang the popular wartime tune "We'll Hang Jeff Davis from a Sour Apple Tree." General Saxton consoled Jim, praising his loyalty to his former friend but suggested that for the moment he cease mentioning the Confederate president. The boy soon became friends with Eddie, the young son of Willard Saxton, playing with him on the piazza of the Saxton home. He stayed with the Saxtons for about a year, accompanying them to Charleston, but the Saxtons could not properly care for him and placed him with Elizabeth Botume and her nieces at the Smith Plantation. Elizabeth Botume eventually took him north and enrolled him in a school where he received "a good practical education, until he was old enough to support himself." And then he drifted out of the pages of history.[23]

Shortly after Chief Justice Chase left Hilton Head to continue his journey throughout the South, General Saxton received notification that General Howard had appointed him as assistant commissioner for South Carolina and Georgia. Much of his previous work had prepared him well for his new role since the bureau focused primarily on providing the freedmen with food and medical care and reuniting families. It also oversaw contracts between freedmen and whites, established independent courts, and maintained schools.

Among Saxton's first acts was to appoint George Newcomb superintendent of his district's freedmen schools. Newcomb, a native of Quincy, Massachusetts, was an abolitionist and temperance leader. A schoolteacher and principal of a school in Dedham, Massachusetts, Newcomb had been sent by the citizens of Dedham to Port Royal to teach the freedmen. He arrived in Beaufort on May 1, 1864, and the following year Saxton named him head of the freedmen schools in South Carolina. Newcomb later assisted James Redpath in establishing education facilities in Charleston.[24]

Besides schools, the Freedmen's Bureau also managed abandoned and confiscated property, including the making available to loyal, white refugees and freedmen "not more than forty acres of such land" from the territory set aside under Sherman's Field Orders Number 15. The Saxton home in Beaufort became the bureau's first headquarters, and the general continued his resettlement of freedmen on abandoned property outside the Beaufort District, primarily on Edisto Island. In a conversation with Whitelaw Reid, Saxton informed the journalist that he had provided for nearly forty thousand freedmen on the sea islands around Port Royal, and now, with his area of operations expanded, he had the opportunity to carry his work into the interior of Georgia and South Carolina.[25]

The day after General Saxton received news of his appointment to the Freedmen's Bureau, a surprise visitor arrived in Beaufort. After the surrender of the principal Confederate armies in Virginia and North Carolina, President Lincoln had proposed to Secretary of the Navy Gideon Welles a journey to see his friend Admiral Dahlgren. Such a trip would have inevitably brought the president to Charleston, Savannah, Hilton Head, and Beaufort had not the assassination intervened. Welles, however, did make the sojourn, stopping first at Charleston to see Dahlgren.

Welles intended to visit Beaufort after touring Savannah, but threatening weather caused the captain of his vessel, the brigantine-rigged, side-wheel gunboat *Santiago de Cuba*, on May 30, 1865, to seek shelter at Port Royal. After being saluted by the harbor batteries, including those on warships stationed in the sound and at the fort named in his honor on Hilton Head, Welles, along with his wife, Mary Jane Hale Welles, and Post Master General William Dennison Jr., came to Beaufort, where Willard Saxton escorted them around the town, visiting the Saxton home and the freedmen school in the College Building. The group returned to Hilton Head for a short meeting with General Gillmore before continuing on to Savannah, where Welles met Sam Cooley, a friend from Welles's home state of Connecticut who was expanding his Beaufort-based photographic business to Savannah.[26]

What Welles observed in Beaufort was only a small portion of the operations of the Freedmen's Bureau. By May 1865 Saxton had expanded his undertakings deeper into Georgia and South Carolina. But the bureau had a limited staff and no troops to enforce its authority. Saxton had to rely on General Gillmore to provide the needed protection for his employees throughout the region. Gillmore tried to oblige. By late May the department commander had directed that telegraph connections be extended from his headquarters on Hilton Head to Savannah, Augusta, and Charleston. Gillmore also planned to reopen the Charleston and Savannah Railroad. But he too had limited assets. With recruitment over and units mustering out, only the Port Royal sea islands, Charleston, Savannah, and Augusta could be considered safe for U.S. officials, northern soldiers, and their southern allies. In the Beaufort District, orders went out to increase vigilance against guerillas who might launch attacks against the sea islands' inhabitants. The army commander at Pocotaligo received instructions to patrol the countryside and police affairs between the freedmen and their former masters.[27]

The enforcement of U.S. law was usually delegated to black regiments, but they were too few to produce any lasting effect, and their presence often caused a backlash from the white southerners. Major Martin Delany's scheme to enlist an expeditionary force of former slaves to carry word of emancipation across the Deep South had been dropped, and Delany was sent to assist Saxton's Freedmen's Bureau activities in the sea islands. Delany handled affairs on Hilton Head and St. Helena islands and eventually came to supervise the freedmen village of Mitchelville.[28]

The Beaufort District, split between the sea islands and the mainland throughout the war, was also divided during Reconstruction. The Federals had maintained full control on the islands, where foreclosure proceedings and resulting tax auctions had established a new society and created a black, land-owning yeoman class. The mainland, devastated by Sherman's troops, still retained its prewar society and land-ownership patterns. It seemed unlikely that the new culture of the sea islands could ever be transferred to the district's upper regions, but many who had doubted the experiment started by the great naval victory in 1861 had now become believers.

Among those who had witnessed the transformation of the sea islands and hoped that it could spread throughout the South was Samuel Francis Du Pont, one the individuals who had helped initiate the great experiment. After being relieved of duty in July 1863, Du Pont had retired to his home, Upper Louviers, near Wilmington, Delaware. His success at Port Royal had been the highlight of his long career, and he maintained an interest in the region's affairs throughout the war. On June 22, 1865, the admiral penned a letter to his friend and fellow Port Royal veteran Percival Drayton to describe a recent meeting he had with Charles Follen Folsom, one of the original members of Edward Pierce's operation. An enthusiastic Folsom related to an interested Du Pont stories about activities on the sea islands. As the admiral wrote Drayton,

> One thing I think will please you. He [Folsom] was on the plantation of your brother [Confederate general Thomas Drayton] when the latter returned, or found all his servants at the large town on Hilton Head. So soon as he was recognized there was a rush of enthusiasm to greet him, this young man said. Quite indescribable—they followed him all day and showed in every way the deepest affection.
>
> Another item is also worth mentioning as it fits into your repeated declarations that the blacks would work. This population at Hilton Head have saved and invested $60,000! This he knew to be a fact—another computation put it higher.[29]

This was the last letter written by Du Pont. He died that night from a bronchial attack. Percival Drayton died five weeks later, but their participation at the Battle of Port Royal put in motion events that forever changed the Beaufort District.[30]

Chapter 18

An Uncertain Future

"Do we pray thee tuck care o' we"

The Civil War split the Beaufort District. On the sea islands, Union occupation provided a laboratory for emancipation, education, land redistribution, and free labor economics built around a burgeoning freedmen population. On the mainland, white southerners, who had managed to preserve control over their real and human property until the final months of the war, even in defeat, were unwilling to surrender their perceived rights.

The collective opinion of the sea islanders, whose population far exceeded that of the district's mainland, was well expressed in a May 1865 editorial in the Hilton Head newspaper the *New South*. Responding to commentary in the Democratic newspaper the *Charleston Courier* regarding the proposed "Reconstruction" of South Carolina, the editorialist stated, "Being in South Carolina ourselves, we have a word to say on the subject.... The people of South Carolina either are or are not conquered. If conquered they are in a position to receive terms, not dictate them.... It strikes us very forcibly that these citizens should come up with an unwritten sheet—all their prejudices and predilections cast aside—and ask that they should have the liberty of instituting a civil government such as any community in the North is living under and be thankful that the road is open towards the eventual withdrawal of military rule." The commentator then reflected on the posture of innocent victims adopted by many South Carolina politicians in 1865: "On the contrary, South Carolina, as the hot-bed of rebellion, had she suffered a thousand fold more, would not have been adequately punished for her complicity in the great crime of precipitating a happy country into a bloody and hideous civil war." As to who should lead the new civil government of South Carolina, the editorialist wrote,

> If there are no Union men among the influential and solid citizens, then the wheels of government must first be started by another class of men who have a deep interest in this thing of re-construction.... It must be recollected that a great many men of the North are seriously

considering the propriety of making their homes in the South, especially soldiers, and their motives may be of the very best character.... Begin right and the result will be all that the most ardent lover of free institutions could desire. Begin wrong and the work of reconstruction will be going on for years amid bickerings and heart-burnings and semi-military interventions.

The prediction of the *New South*'s editorialist was remarkably accurate.[1]

Throughout the war President Lincoln and Republican radicals in Congress had dueled over what reconstruction plan should be employed in the rebellious South. Lincoln favored conciliation and quick restoration with some protection for the freedmen. Radical congressional leaders wanted to punish the white southerners and restrict their voting rights while enfranchising the blacks and providing them with land confiscated from the former rebels.

Shortly after Lincoln's death, President Andrew Johnson began his version of Reconstruction. Though somewhat harsher than what Lincoln had proposed, Johnson's plan, similar to that of his predecessor, was designed to bring the rebellious states back into the Union as quickly as possible. In May 1865 Johnson issued a general amnesty proclamation. He pardoned all except those who fell into fourteen categories that included the Confederacy's primary civil and military leaders, those who had left United States civil and military positions, and all persons who had voluntarily participated in the rebellion who had taxable property estimated at over twenty thousand dollars. Besides restoring constitutional rights to the majority of the former Confederates, the amnesty allowed the recovery of confiscated and abandoned land. Those not pardoned by the proclamation could retrieve their civil liberties and regain their property by personally requesting absolution from President Johnson. Many did and Johnson, enjoying the power and potential patronage, obliged nearly all who applied.[2]

In South Carolina, General Gillmore interpreted President Johnson's amnesty program as allowing the restoration of land seized under wartime abandoned and confiscated property acts. Gillmore's action, however, threatened the newly established ability of the Freedmen's Bureau to distribute property to former slaves and loyal white refugees.

The president's and Gillmore's actions caused J. H. Sears, publisher of the *New South* to write an editorial on May 13, 1865, in which Sears lamented Sherman's issuing of Special Field Orders Number 15: "We admit that we are sorry that the General ever signed the now renowned Memorandum: We admit he should have placed himself on the basis of negotiation indicated by the President ... that of taking into consideration military matters alone, leaving those of a civilian character to the government."[3]

However, when General Howard, whose enabling legislation for the Freedmen's Bureau had superseded Special Field Orders Number 15, learned of Gillmore's actions, he immediately overrode any property restoration and called General Saxton to Washington for consultation. While in the capital, Saxton pressed Howard to move aggressively and begin distributing land as quickly as possible. Howard, after gaining an affirmative ruling from the nation's attorney general, agreed and boldly implemented the land agenda of the Freedmen's Bureau. On July 28 he issued Circular 13, which directed the setting aside of plots of land of up to forty acres to freedmen and loyal white refugees from the pool of abandoned estates. Howard also stated, "The pardon of the President will not be understood to extend to the surrender of abandoned or confiscated property."[4]

The land policy of the Freedmen's Bureau applied only to a portion of the Beaufort District in St. Luke and St. Peter's Parishes where Federal officials claimed abandoned property. Some freedmen gained possessory titles, while others merely squatted on land they expected to be awarded. General Saxton, determined to carry out the mandate started with Special Field Orders Number 15 and continued by the Freedmen's Bureau legislation and circular, directed his brother Willard in Beaufort to begin informing freedmen in South Carolina, Georgia, and Florida of their rights to settle on abandoned land.[5]

In St. Helena Parish questions arose over property seized and auctioned under tax foreclosure proceedings. When William Gabriel "Young Gabe" Capers returned in June 1865, he warned freedmen, many of whom had been enslaved by his family, not to buy any more of his land "as he shall soon have possession of it, again." Capers, a former member of the 3rd South Carolina cavalry, then contacted his former slaves and asked them to take him in as "he had no money and nothing to eat." Laura Towne's housekeeper, "Old Rina," let him stay with her, but he soon began behaving like the old planters in "putting on airs." The whole episode was unsettling to Rina and her husband, Hastings, as it must have been to many freedmen on St. Helena Island. As Laura Towne recorded, "Hastings and Rina are greatly exercised upon this question of the return of the old Masters."[6]

Many of the reappearing planters attempted to ingratiate themselves to their conquerors, among them Joseph Daniel Pope, who was invited by some Federal military officers to survey and comment on the situation in the sea islands. The forty-five-year-old Beaufort native seemed an odd choice to review the freedmen situation. An ally of the Rhetts, Pope had been instrumental in organizing the 1850 Beaufort District Southern Rights meeting at Gillisonville and the state's secession movement. A signer of the Ordnance of Secession from St. Helena Parish, he succeeded Edmund Rhett as the district's state senator in 1863. Still, he received the task and, upon its completion in June 1865, sent his report to General Gillmore.

Pope began his account by praising the United States military and how, with their installations on Bay Point, Hilton Head, Land's End, and St. Helena Island and the coaling station on Parris Island, they had so transformed Port Royal Sound that it was hardly recognizable from its appearance five years earlier. He reported that Beaufort was dilapidated and neglected but believed that some "general repairs would soon renovate and restore its former neatness and comfort." He stated that the plantations and cotton fields were neglected, poorly cultivated, and "miserable beyond description." Pope also noted with alarm that "the Negroes are armed, the whites are unarmed. May God protect the people in this extremity."

To bring back order and prosperity to the region, Pope believed it essential to allow the white population to regain their lands and homes and take over the growing of prized sea island cotton. Pope noted that "the abolition of slavery has worked the most gigantic practical confiscating of property that has ever been enforced in the history of the world. It is too a confiscation not for life but for all time. It is so much property that can never be returned again to one or to one's prosperity. If we are to expect any kind of prosperity the lands at least must be returned."

Besides the return of foreclosed and sold property, Pope also called for the sending back of all freedmen who had come to the coast during the war, stating, "In and around Port Royal are Negroes from every state in the South." Neither the land nor the community, Pope declared, could support them. Once the recent immigrants had been evacuated, Pope wanted to institute a system of passes and permits to keep the blacks from "running all over the county vagabondizing from city to city" and "idling from one place in the country to another." In addition to controlling the movement of the former slaves, Pope believed that a system of punishment to compel the freedmen to work had to be implemented, without which he believed "there can be no success."

He also asked that negro troops be removed from the area, believing that in peacetime the quartering of black soldiers in a community of black laborers was always "attended with evil consequences." Without the rigors of war to keep them busy, Pope felt that the soldiers' discipline would erode and they would set "an example of idleness that is injurious." The soldiers, he said, would "encourage habits of immorality and dissipation which must destroy the usefulness of the laborer."

Though Pope admitted that times change and that people must change with them, his conclusion called for a return to a slightly altered prewar system. Pope summed up his report by telling Gillmore that if the free negro laborer could not be made industrious, then it would become necessary to replace him with free white laborers. He concluded by stating, "No one can look upon the future without fearful misgivings but now that the war is over we should look forward with a hopeful trust in the Providence of God and our assurance of returning prosperity to the country if we discharge our duty."[7]

By the time Gillmore received Pope's report, the general had had his area of control and number of troops reduced. On June 27, 1865, the Department of the South was discontinued, and Gillmore became the military commander of South Carolina. Though he initially retained his headquarters at Hilton Head, the majority of his thirteen thousand soldiers were stationed at Charleston. In the District of Port Royal, commanded by Colonel James Durell Greene, the 6th United States, 9th Connecticut, and the 21st and 32nd USCT Infantry Regiments garrisoned Hilton Head, while the 128th USCT and Battery C, 2nd USCT Artillery, were posted at Beaufort. Just outside Beaufort the 104th USCT manned Fort Duane, while on the mainland the 26th USCT occupied the camp at Pocotaligo. By July further reductions cut Gillmore's numbers to around fifty-eight hundred, nearly evenly split between white and black soldiers. As the War Department continued to disband the volunteer army, President Johnson, eager to restore the former rebellious states, announced on August 20 the ending of hostilities. With peace declared, military operations over, and martial law ending, Johnson began returning the insurgent states to the Union.[8]

The reduction of Federal forces in South Carolina greatly concerned the freedmen and their supporters. Also adding to the uncertainty was the quickness with which President Johnson recognized a new civil administration in South Carolina. On June 30, 1865, Johnson appointed Benjamin Franklin Perry as the state's provisional governor with authority to form a government that would restore South Carolina to the Union. Perry quickly established a temporary regime filled with former, pardoned Confederates and called an election in July for delegates to a constitutional convention. Chosen from the Beaufort District were three representatives: Leroy F. Youmans of Gillisonville, Henry C. Smart of Beech Branch Post Office, and James G. Thompson of Beaufort. Youmans and Smart, both former officers in the 3rd South Carolina Cavalry, represented the district's old planter class, while Thompson, a Yankee from Philadelphia and General Saxton's brother-in-law, stood for the reconstructed sea islands. Thompson, who had come to Beaufort from Philadelphia in 1862 to be a superintendent under Edward Pierce, had purchased the Reverend Stephen Elliott House on Bay Street and converted it to a general store and home to his newspaper, the *Free South*.[9]

Thompson, however, was an exception among the representatives who gathered in mid-September 1865 at the Columbia First Baptist Church. The vast majority of the constitutional convention was made up of former Confederates. To rejoin the Union under President Johnson's guidelines, the South Carolina delegates merely needed to declare null and void the Ordinance of Secession, end slavery, and repudiate the Confederate debt. The members of the convention did their best to avoid the presidential mandate. Instead of stating the Ordinance of Secession invalid, they merely repealed it. Slavery was declared over not by state legislation but by "action of the United States authorities," and no mention was made of the Confederate debt. A reporter covering the convention noted that there were still "two or three delegates who will not so much as admit that slavery is overthrown.... There are two or three more who think the whole matter ought to be referred to the legislature." Ultimately, eight delegates, including the Beaufort District's Leroy Youmans from St. Luke's Parish, voted against the repeal of slavery. Though defiant, the actions of the convention had met President Johnson's requirement for readmission, and South Carolina returned, at least in the eyes of the president, to the Union that it had left nearly five years earlier.

While the convention had garnered national attention for its bellicose attitude, its members did pass a number of progressive features to the new Constitution of 1865, including the popular election of the governor and the removal of property qualifications to hold office. Directly affecting the Beaufort District was the abolishment of the old colonial parish system, and in its place Beaufort County was established. The county retained the same boundaries as the old Beaufort Judicial District (1769–1865) and was placed in the Second Congressional District along with Charleston, Colleton, and Barnwell Counties.[10]

The vast majority of the delegates to the constitutional convention were the state's surviving prewar leaders, who desired the restoration of the old social, economic, and political order. To regain control of South Carolina, they needed to remove Federal authority, reassert state sovereignty, and disarm the freedmen. The question of civil order also weighed heavily on the minds of freedmen. In areas outside the sea islands, there occurred numerous acts of violence, primarily by whites against former slaves but also some incidents of freedmen attacking their former masters. Reports of these events circulated throughout the state and profoundly unsettled those living in the new Beaufort County. As Elizabeth Hyde Botume reported from Port Royal Island, "Of course the freed people around us watched every movement with trembling interest and wondered what would come next. It is not strange that they became faint-hearted." The "colored leaders" on Port Royal Island called a mass meeting at the schoolhouse at the Smith Plantation. Without any certain support from the U.S. government, the elders on Port Royal Island turned to prayer. It was simple and direct: "Oh Lord, if it so please thee, do we pray thee tuck care o' we."[11]

Though prayer had power, many freedmen realized that they needed to supplement it with something their former masters would respect. During the war many of the freedmen at Port Royal had obtained weapons for protection against marauding Confederates, and with the war ending, discharged black soldiers, well versed in combat and military tactics, came back to their sea island homes. To the returning Confederates, the specter of former slaves armed and trained to fight revived the fear of slave revolt, and appeals were made to military authorities to disarm the freedmen before a race war broke out.

The incessant clamor for the military to head off possible riots against whites reached such a crescendo that in July 1865 U.S. authorities investigated freedmen affairs on St. Helena Island and were directed to "take away all their guns" if necessary. This caused great resentment among the former slaves. As Laura Towne noted, "They all are very indignant at the supposition of their taking up arms against the Yankees and they say it is a 'secesh' trick to spread such a report and bring reproach on them." Laura Towne pointed out that the freedmen had purchased weapons for their own protection: "These guns the people had bought themselves, and they never have done any serious mischief with them." Colonel Charles Howard and Major Martin Delany investigated and both found no evidence of any plots against whites. Ultimately, Colonel Howard thought better of seizing the freedmen's personal weapons, believing that the best "way to make them rebel was to do this." The presence of a large number of personal weapons and army rifles among the freedmen of the sea islands would be a significant political factor in Reconstruction-era Beaufort County.[12]

Besides retaining their weapons, the sea island freedmen also had some allies who continued to promote their interests. In Beaufort County the tax commissioners—Brisbane, Wording, and Cooley—maintained control over the pool of foreclosed lands and continued the auctioning of houses and lots as they became available. The commissioners also published "Notices of Assessment" to property owners on the mainland in Prince William and St. Luke's Parishes to pay their back taxes. Most landowners complied, avoided foreclosure, and retained their land.[13]

Outside Beaufort County, along the South Carolina, Georgia, and Florida coast, the Freedmen's Bureau claimed authority over 485,000 acres where Saxton intended to settle loyal white and black refugees. Prime candidates for the possessory titles of this land were the thousands of displaced freedmen now living on the sea islands. Already Saxton had placed numerous families on Edisto Island, many of whom had been prewar natives but had been relocated to St. Helena Island in 1862 upon the abandonment of Edisto by the Union military.

General Saxton, who, after meeting with General Howard, had taken leave to restore his health at Saratoga, New York, returned to Beaufort with his wife on August 6 and immediately took charge. The next day he was up early, dictating dispatches to his subordinates at Augusta and Tallahassee, directing them to send status reports about their activities with the freedmen. Colonel

Howard, detached from his regiment, became Saxton's inspector general and chief of staff. Saxton knew the fickle atmosphere in Washington and the pressure being brought to bear on General Howard by the president and influential former Confederates to return confiscated lands, so he moved swiftly to issue preliminary titles and relocate freedmen. Saxton later reported that he issued forty thousand possessory titles, a figure challenged by some historians, but one not unlikely considering the portions of Florida, Georgia, and South Carolina administerd by Saxon's employees. Also, possession of a title did not mean occupation of property. Indeed, only a small number of individuals were ever placed on land, most on Edisto Island and only a few in Beaufort County.[14]

But soon Generals Howard and Saxton found their mission challenged by President Johnson and his political allies. The president never allowed Howard to implement Circular 13 and eventually denied compromises on the land issue offered by both the general and Congress. Other changes also altered General Saxton's influence. In September, General Howard, moving to align his bureau's operations with the army's occupation zones, removed the states of Florida and Georgia from Saxton's area of control, leaving him authority only in South Carolina.

Though dismayed by events in Washington and the contraction of his domain, Saxton continued his work. On September 26 the general and his brother moved with their families from their home in Beaufort and relocated the headquarters for the South Carolina Freedman's Bureau to Charleston, where they could concentrate on the distribution of land on the nearby sea islands.[15]

About the same time that the Saxtons moved, General Gillmore also transferred his headquarters from Hilton Head to Charleston, reducing the posts around Port Royal Sound to minor stations that were discontinued by January 14, 1868. Gillmore retained command until November 17, 1865, when he was assigned to the Engineer Bureau in Washington and replaced by Major General Daniel E. Sickles. The forty-six-year-old New Yorker had had a long and colorful career. A prewar Tammany Hall politician and noted womanizer, Sickles first gained national notoriety when he shot his wife's lover, Philip Barton Key II, son of Francis Scott Key, and was later acquitted when his lawyers, among them Edwin Stanton, successfully employed the first use of the temporary insanity defense. After the case Sickles reconciled with his wife, some eighteen years his junior, and they remained married until her death in 1867 from tuberculosis.

An early backer of the war effort, Sickles recruited and commanded the New Yorker Excelsior Brigade. A veteran of the Army of the Potomac, Sickles proved an unruly subordinate but was fearless in battle. He rose to the rank of major general and chief of the Third Corps, which he led at

Gettysburg. On the second day of the battle, he disobeyed orders and placed his men in an exposed position, where they were crushed by a Confederate assault during which Sickles received a wound that resulted in the amputation of his right leg. He avoided court-martial and for his actions eventually received the Congressional Medal of Honor for conspicuous gallantry on the field at Gettysburg.

Once recovered, Sickles performed services for the War Department before being assigned to command the Department of South Carolina. He took up residence in Charleston at about the same time that the Saxtons arrived at their new headquarters at 4 Meeting Street. The Saxtons were pleased with Sickles, with Willard commenting, "There is a different tone in the Dept. since he assumed command, & the wheels of the Bureau move smoother."[16]

Shortly after arriving at Charleston, General Sickles received a visit from the army's commander-in-chief, Ulysses S. Grant. Dispatched by President Johnson to tour the South, Grant was to report on affairs in the former Confederate states. After stops in Richmond, Raleigh, and Wilmington, Grant arrived by train at Charleston around 11:00 A.M. on December 1, 1865, accompanied by Brigadier General Cyrus B. Comstock, Colonel Orville E. Babcock, and Adam Badeau, all attired in civilian clothes. At the train station, Sickles, Rufus, and Willard Saxton, with Colonel William True Bennett, the city's garrison commander, and Major General Charles Devens, the district commander, greeted Grant, along with an honor guard and band from the 47th Pennsylvania. Willard Saxton described Grant as a "plain, unpretentious, farmer-like looking man."

After spending a day in Charleston meeting with civilians and military personnel, Grant, his aides, and General Sickles and staff boarded the steamer *Cosmopolitan* on the morning of the eleventh for Savannah. While leaving the harbor, the vessel stopped at Fort Sumter, now garrisoned by black soldiers. A reporter later wrote, "The group dispersed over the ruins, each wrapt in somber thoughts of the past. Gen. Grant, leaning against the lookout, was truly meditative and sad. The scene was impressive."

After returning to the boat, they continued south on the *Cosmopolitan*, touching at Hilton Head at about 6:00 P.M. A salute of fourteen guns was fired from Fort Welles, and an honor guard of black and white soldiers received the visitors, who inspected the post and attended a reception before sailing on to Savannah.

Grant's tour ultimately took the general to Augusta, Atlanta, Knoxville, and Lynchburg before returning to Washington. In his report to the president, Grant expressed his belief that most southerners had accepted the decision brought about by the North's military victory. He did, however, call for the continued occupation of the South by Federal troops for the security of both the white and black population. He noted that there was a "belief widely spread among the freed men of the Southern states, that the lands of their former owners will at least in part be divided among them." Grant feared that this conviction, planted by agents of the Freedmen's Bureau, was keeping the former slaves from entering into labor contracts. The general also commented that the racial attitudes of the former Confederates could not be "changed in a day" and that the freedmen would require protection and care from the Freedmen's Bureau agents "for a few years."

Though Grant hoped that reconciliation between the North and South, white and black, former master and slave, could be accomplished, the tide was turning against the reformers and the freedmen. The new South Carolina Constitution of 1865 was not put to a vote by the people but was ratified by the convention's delegates. Elections for the permanent state government quickly followed. Chosen to the house of representatives from Beaufort County to the state's Forty-Seventh General Assembly were Alfred Maner Martin, William Ferguson Hutson, Stephen Elliott, Jr., and Leroy Franklin Youmans. Richard J. Davant represented the district in the state senate.[17]

The election of Richard James Davant (1805–1873) of Gillisonville as their state senator must have been extremely alarming to the freedmen and the missionaries of the Port Royal Experiment because Davant was an old secessionist. He was instrumental in the formation of the Beaufort District Southern Rights Association in 1850, was a Beaufort District delegate to the state Southern Rights Convention in 1852, and a delegate from St. Luke's Parish to the 1860 Secession Convention. On December 20, 1860, he signed the fateful Ordinance of Secession.

The representatives elected to the South Carolina House were equally alarming. Leroy Franklin Youmans was a former Confederate cavalry officer and planter. William Ferguson Hutson was the U.S. congressman who followed Robert Barnwell Rhett into the House of Representatives, the keynote speaker at the Beaufort District Southern Rights Association meeting of 1850, and a signer of the Ordinance of Secession, a document he helped compose.

Alfred Maner Martin was the eldest son of Judge Edmund Martin, one of the wealthiest men (with an estimated worth of $445,000 in 1860), largest landowners (approximately 8,000 acres), and largest slaveholders (306 slaves) in the antebellum Beaufort District. Martin had served in the state legislature from St. Peter's Parish before the war, was a captain in the 3rd South Carolina Cavalry in charge of Company E until 1863, when he was elected to the South Carolina legislature from St. Peter's Parish. His property, in the upper region of the parish, was devastated by Sherman's troops as they passed through on their march to Columbia.

Stephen Elliott Jr., a former Confederate brigadier general, had seen more action defending the Confederate cause than any other Beaufort resident.

Having suffered numerous debilitating wounds, including one that paralyzed his left arm, Elliott returned to the sea islands to find his family's plantation on Parris Island foreclosed upon and sold to freedmen. Though treated well by his former slaves, who provided him with "beautiful breakfasts and splendid dinners," he was "firmly and respectfully" told, "We own this land now. Put it out of your head that it will ever be yours again."[18]

The entire Beaufort County delegation of 1865 was made up of archsecessionists and Confederates. These were decidedly not the men that most of the sea islanders wanted to reconstruct the civil government in South Carolina. The reforming of the state government under the same leadership that had brought about secession was deeply disturbing to the sea island freedmen. Laura Towne commented on the freedmen's attitude toward the returning planters, writing that "they believe [President] Johnson is going to put them in their old masters' power again and they feel that they must conciliate or be crushed.... They keep an ominous silence and are very sad and troubled."[19]

Returning planters also found the situation in the Beaufort District ominous. Many of the occupying troops in South Carolina were African American veterans, and it was too shocking for many white South Carolinians to accept their authority. Former Beaufort planter Robert W. Habersham, in exile in Sumter, South Carolina, complained to General Oliver O. Howard that "Negro meetings plotting, insurrection, murder and conflagration ... young women who are reserved for a worse fate" were threatening to ignite a "war of the races."

These may have been alarmist sentiments, but they were widespread and not without factual justification. Habersham stated that an acquaintance, living on the county's mainland, was beaten by his black workers, and many lowcountry planters were afraid to return to their farms. As the *Charleston Courier* reported, "the owners of the lands are regarded as intruders and feel so insecure that they consider it unsafe to return with their families to their homes."[20]

The mainland sections of Beaufort County became dangerous for blacks and whites. African American soldiers, rather than being symbols of civil order, became targets for troublemakers. As Laura Towne reported from St. Helena Island on October 15, 1865: "On the mainland it is so dangerous for a negro to go about, especially with the United States Uniform on, that orders are out that no more will be allowed to go to recover their families and bring them here." As to white complaints about black troops, Towne countered, "It is not true that the Negro soldiers do not behave well.... These stories about them are manufactured for a purpose."[21]

Anxiety increased among the freedmen and their allies as Federal troops left Beaufort County. From her schoolhouse on the Smith Plantation outside Beaufort, Elizabeth Hyde Botume worried that a race war was brewing on the mainland and declared, "If the military was entirely removed, as announced, bloodshed and insurrection were predicted before New Year's. In the country great bitterness arose between the whites and blacks.... The blacks had armed themselves and were drilling. It was resistance against force. I mention these things to show the spirit of the times."[22]

The lawlessness and rumors of insurrection, rampant in South Carolina, caused the new merchants and new property owners of Beaufort and Hilton Head to petition the president of the United States to establish a U.S. District Court. "With the new interests that have been created by the change of property and revival of trade," the *New South* reported, "it is eminently desirable that a tribunal should be established to adjudicate matters which may come into dispute." The civilian federal court was not established, however, and matters of basic civil law and order continued to be brought before military provost marshal courts for another year.[23]

One entity that potentially could challenge the authority of the military courts was a reestablished South Carolina state government. In October 1865 the state's General Assembly, authorized by the recent constitutional convention, first met in October on the University of South Carolina campus. In a brief meeting they organized their bodies—senate and house—and ratified the Thirteenth Amendment that abolished slavery throughout the United States. Two months later, in December, they reconvened and passed the infamous "Black Codes," which established a separate set of laws for black South Carolinians. Whites were given nearly complete control over the freedmen. Strict racial segregation both in society and under the law was their version of civil order. Edmund Smith Rhett, son of Robert Barnwell Rhett Sr., wrote the Black Codes, which in effect re-created slavery under a renamed legal system. Though warned by Edmund Smith Rhett and others not to implement the codes immediately for fear of a U.S. government backlash, the assembly quickly put them in place. The reaction of the U.S. authorities was immediate, and on January 1, 1866, General Sickles declared the "Black Codes" invalid ten days after their passage.[24]

Sickles's action gave comfort to the South Carolina freedmen and also coincided with a gigantic "Jubilee" in Charleston on January 1, 1866, at the city's Washington Race Track, the site of a Union prisoner-of-war compound and graveyard of Federal soldiers who died at the camp during the war. This "Emancipation Day" was held exactly three years after the seminal "Jubilee" on Port Royal Island, and many sea islanders from Beaufort County attended the Charleston Jubilee.

Rufus Saxton and Reverend Mansfield French, leaders of the Port Royal Experiment, were featured speakers. The military escort was provided by the 33rd USCT. Many of the soldiers had been attendees of the first Jubilee on Port Royal Island, where the regiment was officially mustered into service. More than ten thousand people attended the celebration, and with the recent ratification of the Thirteenth Amendment ending slavery on December 6, 1865, the celebration took on special meaning. As Gideonite teacher Elizabeth Hyde Botume noted, "The streets were filled with happy, freed people."[25]

The joy was short lived for some. General Saxton, who with Mansfield French had participated in the festivities, had seen the freedmen's position deteriorate since September, when President Johnson refused to allow General Howard to implement Circular 13, stopping the distribution of land to Freemen and loyal whites, including the 485,000 acres set aside by Sherman's Field Orders Number 15. To replace Circular 13, Howard proposed a compromise wherein plantation owners, in order to gain a pardon and restoration of their estates, would grant lots to their former slaves.[26]

But Johnson, who had initially favored some understanding, was under intense lobbying from former Confederates, among them Charleston lawyers William Whaley and Julian Mitchell. Whaley, whose primary holdings were on Edisto Island, made "repeated and anxious interviews with the President and Secretary of War." Also influencing Johnson was William Henry Trescott, South Carolina's executive agent for land restoration. Trescott, who through his marriage to Eliza Natalia Cuthbert had acquired Barnwell Island, became an advisor to Johnson on affairs in South Carolina.

The pressure from the Whaleys and Trescott soon swayed the president. Howard fell out of favor and later reported that Johnson seemed "amused" by his recommendations and "gave no heed" to the general's proposals. The only concession that Howard did gain was the recognition of the validity of the titles issued for property foreclosed upon and sold at tax sales, which legitimized the majority of the land transactions in Beaufort County.[27]

Though Saxton was pleased that the work on the sea islands by the tax commissioners had been sustained, he realized that the larger effort to distribute land was coming to an end. In direct opposition to General Howard and the president, he refused to be part of the restoration of estates to individuals whom he viewed as rebels and enemies of the newly freed slaves. He declined to accompany Howard when the general came to Charleston and met with the freedmen on Edisto Island to initiate the reversal of the settlement policies started by Saxton.

While Howard still hoped that a compromise could be implemented between the pardoned landowners and former slaves, Saxton knew that the planters would never accept any agreement that would benefit the freedmen. Howard tried to convince his subordinate to accept a new assignment within the Freedmen's Bureau. President Johnson offered Saxton a promotion and transfer "to any post he wanted," but Saxton remained adamant. He would not voluntarily leave those whose fortunes he had so long advocated. On January 9, 1866, General Howard, believing him a hindrance to any possible negotiations, removed Saxton from his position as the assistant commissioner of the Freedmen's Bureau for South Carolina.

Howard's hope for even the smallest compromise was never realized. Legislative attempts by Congress to allow the Freedmen's Bureau to sell or rent public land were vetoed by the president. There also was no relief for the Edisto Island settlers. The Freedmen's Bureau order countermanding the settlement plan was issued on March 7, 1866, by Saxton's replacement, Brigadier General Robert K. Scott, who later became the first Reconstruction governor of South Carolina. Those on Edisto Island were not removed until they had harvested their crops and received compensation for any improvements they had made to their homesteads. Then the freedmen, refugees again, were given the opportunity to purchase, at $1.50 an acre, plots of twenty acres in the Port Royal area still controlled by the tax commissioners.[28]

Shortly after Saxton's removal, one of his greatest accomplishments also completed its service. The 1st South Carolina, raised primarily from sea island slaves, was mustered out of service. The unit, now known as the 33rd USCT, ended the war on Morris Island, its campground near the site of Battery Wagner where the 54th Massachusetts had made its bloody charge during the summer of 1863. The regiment had been conceived by General David Hunter, re-formed and sworn in by Saxton, and commanded and nurtured by Colonel Thomas W. Higginson. Lieutenant Colonel Charles T. Trowbridge, who had been with the unit since its inception, led the black soldiers through their final campaigns. In his farewell address, Trowbridge announced,

> COMRADES: The hour is at hand when we must separate forever, and nothing can take from us the pride we feel, when we look upon the history of the "First South Carolina Volunteers," the first black regiment that ever bore arms in the defense of freedom on the continent of America.
>
> On the 9th day of May, 1862, at which time there were nearly four million of your race in bondage, sanctioned by the laws of the land and protected by our flag,—on that day, in the face of the floods of prejudice that well-nigh deluged every avenue to manhood and true liberty, you came forth to do battle for country and kindred.

Trowbridge reminded his men of how they had soldiered without pay, been furloughed, and then re-formed, and how their service had inspired the formation of an army of black men numbering over 140,000—a fighting force that helped "remove forever the possibility of human slavery being established within the borders of redeemed America." He asked his comrades to "harbor no feelings of hatred toward your former masters" and to "grow up to the full stature of American citizens. The church, the school-house, and the right forever to be free are now secured to you, and every prospect before you is full of hope and encouragement." Trowbridge concluded by thanking the regiment's officers for fulfilling their mission, declaring that the cause they had promoted had "been crowned with abundant success."[29]

The 1st South Carolina was one of Saxton's glorious achievements, and its success should have eased his bitterness over the government's abandonment of the freedmen and his work to create independent black communities. In Charleston tributes were held for him at Zion Presbyterian Church, but he did not attend them. He and his wife briefly returned to Beaufort, where he visited Laura Towne and Ellen Murray before returning north.[30]

While assigned to bureaucratic duties in Washington, D.C., at the Freedmen's Bureau headquarters, Saxton was called to testify before Congress's Joint Committee on Reconstruction. His deposition summarized the situation in South Carolina, his views, hopes, and fears of the future, and his pride in his accomplishments and those of the sea island freedmen. Saxton began by stating that the freedmen wanted to purchase land, but that southern whites desired to keep them landless and in a condition as similar to that of slavery as possible: "The freedman has no faith in his former master, nor has his former owner any faith in the capacity of the freedman. A mutual distrust exists between them. But the freedman is ready and willing to contract to work for any northern man." Saxton believed that if the "Negro is put in possession of all his rights as a citizen and as a man, he will be peaceful, orderly, and self-sustaining as any other man or class of men, and that he will rapidly advance."

Saxton dismissed any fears that the freed slaves would ever politically support their former masters. To protect the freedmen, Saxton told the committee that it was "vital to the safety and prosperity of the two races in the south that the Negro should immediately be put in possession of all his rights as a man; and that the word 'color' should be left out of all laws, constitutions, and regulations for the people; I think it vital to the safety of the Union that this should be done."

Saxton testified that a general hostility still prevailed in South Carolina against the United States government, freedmen, and loyal southern whites, and that northerners were "treated with entire neglect, and, so far as my experience goes, with discourtesy. My wife has seldom walked the streets of Charleston without being insulted. I, myself, have seldom passed through the streets without receiving, from man or woman, indignities."

Saxton feared that without U.S. government protection, the freedmen would either be returned to a form of slavery, or a race war would break out. The new state leaders, onetime Confederates allowed back into power by President Johnson, could now implement state-sanctioned actions against the former slaves that Saxton believed would "lead to insurrection and a war of races, in which the United States troops will be called upon to aid in the extermination of the black race. I think it is the belief of a great majority of the former masters that the freedom of the black race is a failure, and that slavery is his best condition, and that they desire to pursue such a policy as to prove that they are correct in that belief. I can see no hope for the freedmen except through the care of the United States government."

In describing the character of freedmen, Saxton told the committee that under slavery their lives had "been one of concealment, and they had to lie to avoid punishment. I do not consider them any more untruthful than any other people, or any more truthful. I think they share all the vices and all the virtues of our common humanity. Perhaps under the condition of slavery they are not so truthful. But I think they are as truthful as any other people in the same circumstances. I am aware of all their vices and all their faults, but I think they have no more vices or faults than are shared by any other race."

Saxton related that the freedmen desired education, feeling that it "is one of the means by which they are going to be elevated; and they have a particular avidity and desire to learn. All the schools established there by northern benevolence are crowded by children, and the teachers have assured me that their progress is as great as that which they have seen among white people at the north, owing, probably, to their great desire to learn. I have been surprised at the progress of the colored people at the schools."

Proud of his work in the sea islands, Saxton told the committee that his operations had proven the ability of the freedmen to sustain themselves in a free-market society:

> I established regulations for the cultivation of two or three of the abandoned sea islands in South Carolina (St. Helena, Lady's, and Port Royal), and appointed local superintendents to oversee and direct their labors. By the payment of moderate wages, and just and fair dealing with them, I produced for the government over half a million dollars' worth of cotton, besides a large amount of food beyond the needs of the laborers. These island lands were cultivated in this way for two years, 1862 and 1863, under my supervision, and during that time I had about 15,000 colored freedmen of all ages in my charge. About 9,000 of these were engaged on productive labor, which relieved the government of the support of all except newly-arrived refugees from the enemy's lines and old and infirm who had no relations to depend upon. The increase of industry and thrift of the freed men was illustrated by their conduct in South Carolina before the organization of the Freedmen's Bureau by the decreasing government expenditure for their support. The expense in the department of the south was $41,544, but the monthly expense of that year was steadily reduced,

until in December it was less than $1,100, and this has always, I believe, been the case since the close of the war.

To back up his statement, Saxton informed the committee that he had established a savings bank for the freedmen in Beaufort: "More than $240,000 has been deposited in this bank by the freedmen since its establishment. I consider that the industrial problem has been satisfactorily solved at Port Royal, and that, in common with other races, the negro has industry, prudence, forethought, and ability to calculate results."

Saxton believed that African Americans, once given the rights of any citizens, would rapidly advance. He stated that "there are numerous intelligent leaders among the freedmen, who fully understand the meaning of suffrage" to guide the former slaves and "far from there being any danger to the peace of the country and to our institutions ... I believe it to be the only means of avoiding great and eminent dangers."[31]

Although Saxton's testimony may have helped enlighten members of the Congressional Joint Committee on Reconstruction about affairs in Beaufort County, he never again found himself in a position to officially assist the freedmen. After a brief assignment to general inspection duty for the bureau and a short leave of absence, Saxton mustered out of the volunteer army and returned to duty in the regular army, posted in the Quartermaster Bureau with the rank of major. He retired as a colonel in 1888 and lived in Washington until his death in 1908. He is buried in Arlington National Cemetery along with his wife, Matilda "Tilly" Saxton, and his brother Samuel Willard and his wife, Mary. The inscription on General Saxton's grave reads, "Be not afraid ye wailing ones who weep. For God still giveth his beloved sleep. And in an endless sleep—so best."[32]

Saxon's departure was keenly felt among the missionary community in Beaufort County. He had been their friend and protector during the war years. They shared equally idealistic hopes for the establishment of a federally protected enclave of self-sufficient freedmen in the South Carolina and Georgia lowcountry. As Elizabeth Hyde Botume noted, "When the order came that the lands should be restored, General Saxton decided that the government had failed in its promises to him. Hence his removal."

On St. Helena Island the church congregation "set up a testimonial to General Saxton" and raised one hundred dollars from the white and black people of the island. Laura Towne noted, "The children of our school wanted to show General Saxton that they were sorry he was going away and they have subscribed five and ten cents each, so we have ... about ten dollars." Laura Towne, who visited Rufus Saxton in February 1866, commented, "He is so pleasant and friendly—as gentlemanly and quiet in his troubles and reverses as he can be. It shows the nobleness of his nature."[33]

During his tenure in the Beaufort District, Saxton had accomplished much. He arrived with the expedition that captured Port Royal Sound on November 7, 1861, and as the army's original chief quartermaster, he initiated programs that eventually culminated in the Port Royal Experiment. After a brief absence, he returned and took charge of the movement that forever altered life on the sea islands, ending the prewar slaveholding aristocracy and replacing it with a community of freedmen and northern immigrants. However, Saxton's reach did not extend to the mainland, where leadership was still retained by former Confederates and prewar secessionists.

The upheaval of the Civil War created two distinct civilizations in Beaufort County, one on the sea islands and the other on the mainland. Both viewed the future differently. On the islands the freedmen and the northern immigrants wanted to continue the momentum toward a fresh order based on expanded commercial activities and increased social, political, and economic opportunities for the freed slaves. On the "main," white southerners hoped for a return to the old order with commercial and political power held by the prewar leaders and freedmen's rights severely restricted. The two distinct factions soon entered into a conflict that would eventually reshape Beaufort County and the lives of its inhabitants.

Chapter 19

The District Divided

"End the confusion and help all"

The Civil War forever changed Beaufort County. Not since 1715, when the Yemassee Indians controlled the mainland and British citizens the sea islands, had the region been so divided. At the conflict's end, white citizens moved to reclaim dominance over the mainland, while on the sea islands a coalition of freedmen and northern immigrants held sway. Much of the change had occurred because of the social, economic, and political policies implemented by representatives from the United States Treasury and War Department. Tax commissioners, enforcing the Direct Tax Act of 1862, had foreclosed and auctioned off the property of absentee proprietors, forever changing land-ownership patterns. At the same time that property changed hands, General Rufus Saxton, the region's military governor, oversaw a total transformation of the islands' economic, social, and educational systems. Though thwarted from expanding his great experiment to the mainland and eventually removed from his post, the West Point–trained reformer had set in place the dynamics that would set the county's future.

The removal of General Saxton as the Freedmen's Bureau assistant commissioner for South Carolina in January 1866 was only part of a conflict being waged by powerful forces vying for control of the reconstructed South. Initially President Johnson and his allies—conservative Republicans, northern Democrats, and southern whites—seemed to hold sway, but soon the pendulum began to swing. Violence against freedmen, Black Codes, and state governments formed by prewar secessionists that gave no civil rights to the former slaves began to change the opinion of moderate Republicans, who soon began to ally themselves with radical Republicans. A major turning point occurred when the southern states sent delegations to the Thirty-Ninth U.S. Congress. The majority of the representatives were former prewar secessionists and Confederates officers and officials. From the South Carolina Second District, which contained Beaufort County, came former governor William Aiken, who had defeated Stephen Elliott Jr. for the seat. The reaction of the Republican-dominated Congress was to refuse to seat the southern delegates.

With violence continuing throughout South Carolina and the rest of the old Confederacy, Congress began challenging President Johnson's Reconstruction policy. The president attempted to keep control. He vetoed the Civil Rights Act, which prohibited states from discriminating against citizens on the basis of color. He also hoped to close the issue of Reconstruction by declaring on April 2, 1866 that the insurrection of the southern states had ended. But Congress and public opinion in the North had turned against him. Congress overrode his veto of the Civil Rights Act and passed a bill over Johnson's veto extending the life of the Freedmen's Bureau.

Three months later Congress passed the Fourteenth Amendment and sent it to state legislatures for approval. The reaction by southern states was to rebuff the amendment. In South Carolina both chambers rejected it, the house opposing the measure ninety-five to one. Such obstinacy to the protection of the freedmen resulted in the radical Republicans' receiving an overwhelming and veto-proof majority in the congressional elections in November 1866. When the new Congress convened in 1867, it passed the First and Second Reconstruction Acts. Reactionary behavior on the part of the South Carolina General Assembly of 1865 and 1866 begot a stronger reactionary response from the U.S. Congress. The period of "Congressional Reconstruction" was underway by the spring of 1867. In South Carolina years of Republican rule would follow. The freedmen and reformers in the sea islands were delighted, and many took leading roles in the political and social revolution that followed.[1]

While the new Reconstruction Acts were being implemented, law enforcement in the South, including South Carolina and Beaufort County, remained under the jurisdiction of military courts that had to deal with a wide variety of situations involving both whites and freedmen. One particular case centered on the August 17, 1866, activities of two freedmen named Coaxum and Sambo Richardson, who attempted to murder Colonel William T. Bennett, whose Civil War career included service as the colonel of the 33rd USCT (the former 1st South Carolina), General John P. Hatch's chief of staff at Honey Hill, and commander of the Charleston garrison. Colonel Bennett, who had rarely served with the 1st South Carolina, being assigned primarily to staff positions for most of his service, had been mustered out in late January 1866, and by that summer was living at Coffin Point Plantation on St. Helena Island. The crime was particularly troubling because it was directed against an officer of the Provost Court on St. Helena Island and was a direct affront to the legal authority of the United States occupation troops. Bennett was at the time chief judge of the Provost's Circuit Court, which had been established in June 1866 specifically to bring law and order to St.

Helena Island. Coaxum's arrest had been ordered by the Provost's Circuit Court with Bennett presiding. Both Coaxum and Richardson were known for "being in league with other rogues for stealing cotton."

On August 17, 1866, Coaxum and Richardson armed themselves with shotguns and boldly walked onto the grounds of the Coffin Point plantation house asking for General Bennett. The general recognized Coaxum from a window and noticed that the men's shotguns were cocked and ready to fire. As a precaution Bennett put a loaded revolver in his pocket. When he met Coaxum and Richardson in the yard, both men fired at Bennett but missed. Bennett drew his pistol and shot Coaxum in the hand as the men fled. They were later captured and lodged in the Charleston jail. Bennett was not alone. Some of the constables appointed by the court "have encountered persecution from their friends because of their zeal in support of justice." On August 20, 1866, Constable March Aikin was struck unconscious with an axe handle by "a man named Rivers," who was lodged in jail in Beaufort.

The *New South* explained these and other serious breaches of law and order on the sea islands as follows: "There has been so little of law and authority on these islands for the last four or five years, that among the baser portion of the Negroes there seems to have raised an entire disregard of justice." The Provost's Circuit Court, however, proved to be popular with the great majority of law-abiding freedmen on St. Helena Island and was supported by General Dan Sickles, commander of the United States forces occupying North and South Carolina. The military courts and the military occupation were, of course, only temporary. The permanent solution for restoring civil order in South Carolina was to reestablish the state government and the state and local courts. That too was very uncertain in the months following the Civil War.[2]

Besides the question of local courts, questions concerning the restoration of land retained by the government still haunted the sea islands. Considered legal was property transferred under legal provisions of the U.S. Direct Tax Act of 1861 and under the direction of duly appointed commissioners. The U.S. direct tax commissioners were under the jurisdiction of the civilian U.S. Treasury Department. They did not "seize" or "confiscate" any land. Instead they "foreclosed" on the sea island plantation lands for nonpayment of the U.S. Direct Tax. Foreclosure is a long established and legally recognized form of land transfer for nonpayment of debts, whether mortgages or taxes, and in the sea islands the government recognized no claim from former owners to properties foreclosed upon under the U.S. Direct Tax Act of 1861. However, foreclosed property still retained but not yet sold by the government could be redeemed by its former owners by paying the back taxes and penalties. In some cases the transfer was done quickly, but where property was still being used by the military, the restoration could be delayed. In Beaufort County the military kept possession of large tracts of land well after the war before releasing it for redemption or sale at public auctions. On Hilton Head the Pope, Drayton, and Rivers families eventually reacquired the sites of the quartermaster freedmen's village of Mitchelville and nearby Fish Haul Plantation in the 1870s.[3]

Though some were able to redeem their land, the sea islands of Beaufort County, by and large, remained in the hands of the new owners. However, this did not prevent the old plantation owners of the occupied sea islands from bringing a cascade of lawsuits to recover their Beaufort County land. The close of the war and the vacillating policy of the U.S. government led several of the old planter families to raise legal challenges against the foreclosures and sale of their prewar property. By 1873 twenty-two white Beaufort County families brought lawsuits resulting in forty-four cases. Seven of those lawsuits were appealed to Federal District Court in Charleston. Two of those cases reached the U.S. Supreme Court. These lawsuits pitted the old owners against the new, the southerners against the northerners and, in many cases, whites against blacks. As a consequence, they perpetrated the animosities of the Civil War and threatened to provoke riots. When John Jenkins returned to try to reclaim his ancestral land at the north end of St. Helena Island in 1867, he found his former slaves claiming possession by "right of popular assembly." He contested these rights and found himself confronted by an armed band, or "marching company," of his "employees." He left St. Helena Island and never recovered his property. The principal Jenkins plantation house, the "Mary Jenkins Place," on the big bend of Jenkins' Creek, did not survive the Reconstruction years. In 1875, fearing that the courts would return the land to the planters, blacks on St. Helena Island threatened to resist by force. Laura Towne, the principal of the Penn School, stated, "I believe they would have a war if this thing should be done." The decisive case in these disputes over land titles was *DeTreville v. Smalls*, which was finally settled by the U.S. Supreme Court in 1878. This case upheld ex-slave and war hero Robert Smalls's title to a Beaufort home formerly owned by South Carolina lieutenant governor Richard DeTreville. In the end, the courts confirmed the vast majority of sea island wartime sales, and the social and economic revolution caused by war, conquest, foreclosure and land redistribution became a permanent part of Beaufort County history.

The effect of the tax sales and establishment of school farms in the sea islands was to form a permanent community of independent black landowners in Beaufort County that persists to this day. At the close of the war, up to two thousand freedmen owned land in Beaufort County. By 1870 this number was closer to one thousand black landowners. By 1880 black land ownership had increased to twelve hundred and increased again by 1900 to twenty-three hundred. The size of these small farms ranged from five to twenty acres on average and was estimated to be worth approximately ten dollars per acre, according to the U.S. Agricultural Census. These small farms, owned by freedmen, dominated most of St. Helena Island, all of Warsaw Island, and parts of Port Royal Island, Lady's Island, Parris Island, and Hilton Head Island. There were also some outstanding exceptions to the general pattern of small black land ownership. William H. Smalls owned a 500-acre plantation. Toney Talbird owned a 160-acre farm, and sea island political leader, Robert Smalls, owned a farm worth five thousand dollars. In all there were twenty-nine black landowners in Beaufort County who owned farms worth several thousand dollars.

By far the largest black landowner in Beaufort County was Christopher "Kit" Green of Lady's Island. Kit Green began acquiring sea island land at the first U.S. Direct Tax Commission Auction in 1863. At that time he bought the four-hundred-acre Oakland Plantation for one dollar per acre. He paid cash. This was the beginning of a business and farming empire that was to survive for three generations, well into the twentieth century. The Reynolds family, who had owned the property before the war, made no attempt to recover it, and Kit Green's title remained unmolested. In 1864 he planted cotton at Oakland using local labor and reaped a profit of four thousand dollars, as productive and profitable as any antebellum planter could have been. Green used these profits to purchase Ashdale (two hundred acres), the John Johnson place (three hundred acres), Brickyard (fifty acres), and several tracts on Coosaw Island. In 1869 Green's income from cotton planting was two thousand dollars. Green's plantations also produced vegetables and livestock in large quantities. Kit Green remained one of the richest men in Beaufort County until his death in 1883. Thereafter, his numerous descendants divided up and sold off his scattered holdings. The last of Kit Green's empire was finally disbursed after the death of his son Samuel Green in 1940.[4]

DIASPORA OF THE PLANTER CLASS

The historical consequence of this foreclosure and redistribution of sea island land was that few of the antebellum planter families ever returned to their ancestral lands. When the war concluded, several of the old planters returned to Beaufort to reclaim whatever family property they could. These visits coincided with the confusion of President Johnson's nonenforcement of the Freedmen's Bureau land clause and the challenges to the wartime sales of the U.S. Direct Tax Commission. The consequence was that the return of the "secesh," as the freedmen and their northern patrons called them, was seen as a threat to the new order.

An established Beaufortonian, Elizabeth Baker, had fled to Columbia with the occupation of Beaufort in 1861 and then was evacuated to Charlotte, North Carolina, when Sherman burned Columbia in February 1865. In September 1865 she returned to Beaufort with two aunts by taking a steamboat from Wilmington, North Carolina, to Norfolk, Virginia, and from there finding a vessel bound for Port Royal. When the three women finally arrived on Bay Street, they encountered two former acquaintances who warned, "You cannot stay here. This is no place for ladies; the Negroes are occupying the houses. . . . there are no white people here, except the Yankee garrison." These two men offered the women a ride in their carriage to Allendale. On the ride through the country that was to become Hampton County, they were relieved to encounter a mounted, armed Confederate veteran, Frank Fickling Davant of Gillisonville, who escorted them into Allendale. Elizabeth Baker of Beaufort and Frank Davant of Gillisonville were married a year later. They never returned to Beaufort.

Likewise, Sarah Barnwell Stuart, wife of Dr. Henry Middleton "Hal" Stuart (1835–1915), one of the few old Beaufortonians to return and remain in Reconstruction Beaufort, wrote to her aunt Sarah Bull Barnwell in February 1866 that "things in Beaufort still seem very trying . . . life is horrid there . . . she had but one servant to cook and wash for her . . . she had a little girl to mind little Allan, but . . . the girl went to school everyday from eight o'clock to one o'clock . . . she had to give her up." Sarah Stuart reported that seventy-five of the former inhabitants had returned, "but no one seems to be in their own homes . . . our dear old home is desolated and desecrated . . . the negroes are now cutting our window sills for fire wood . . . as our island homes and property are all given to our former slaves for three years and at the end of that time, our ruin will be complete."

Major John Gibbes Barnwell II (1816–1905), one of the grandees of antebellum Beaufort, returned only long enough to determine that he would never regain any of his five plantations. He commented that "no more complete ruin was ever visited by heathen conquerors on a defeated people than that which the people of Beaufort have suffered." John Gibbes Barnwell moved to Athens, Georgia, where he worked in the university library. He then bought a small farm near Rome, Georgia, where his son Stephen was the Episcopal rector. John Gibbes Barnwell traveled to visit his children in Alabama, Kentucky, and California. He died in Stateburg, South Carolina, and is buried in the Holy Cross churchyard.[5]

Reverend Edward T. Walker, brother of St. Helena's longtime rector, Dr. Joseph Walker, had fled to Edgefield, South Carolina, and reported from Beaufort in 1865 that the planters "returned here from suffering and poverty in exile" to find that their houses had been occupied by blacks, and they had lost hope of regaining any plantations. The resentment of the "secesh" was apparent, and Reverend Walker reported that "no white man can safely live in . . . Beaufort." Walker further commented on the work of the northern missionaries at Port Royal. They hoped to create an "American Liberia" among the sea islands. "And what is the result?" he asked rhetorically. "I will not say another Liberia. I would rather say another . . . Hayti!"[6]

Old Richard DeTreville lost his Prince Street home to Robert Smalls and pursued his legal challenges from the safety of Charleston. He died there in 1876, two years before his son argued the case before the Supreme Court, and never returned to the home of his ancestors. It was not until 1908 that the DeTreville family was able to resettle in old Beaufort.[7]

Laura Towne reflected on the resentment of the freedmen and northern missionaries to the return of the "secesh." The freedmen were polite and cordial to their old masters but firm in their resolution not to tolerate the return of any vestige of the old order. When one of the "best and most powerful of the old rebels" reoccupied his plantation, he was tolerated by the ex-slaves occupying the land. When he asked whether they would work for him for wages, they replied firmly, "No sir. Even if you pay as well, sir, we had rather work for the Yankees who have been our friends."[8]

Charles Nordhoff, wartime correspondent for *Harper's New Monthly Magazine,* expressed the particular resentment and vengefulness of some northerners to the old Beaufort families: "Here beneath these live oaks ... the Rhetts, the Barnwells, the Trescotts ... leading traitors conferred together.... here they planned in sober councils, the ruin of their country; here was nurtured the gigantic ... inexcusable crime which has made so many children fatherless." Nordhoff's bitterness toward the "few unscrupulous aristocrats" led him to conclude that the whole town was to blame: "The whole place is accursed." His recommendation to the Federal authorities was extreme: "It is a pleasant spot, this Beaufort; but I hope that whenever the soldiers leave it, they will raze it to the ground."[9]

The hostility between new northerners and old southerners lingered for a decade after the war, exacerbated by the continuing lawsuits over sea island land titles. The *Beaufort Republican,* the only local newspaper in Beaufort County during Reconstruction, regularly covered the progress of the lawsuits and published lively editorial opinions reflecting the anger and anxiety on both sides of the land dispute. In 1872 the northern editor of the newspaper, William Richardson, criticized the particular resentment of the old Beaufortonians: "However much poetic justice there may be in the fact that the hotbed of rebellion received the worst punishment, history will not bear them out in the assumption that the punishment was intended specifically against dwellers of the sea islands." The Direct Tax Law applied to all captured property equally. Beaufort, by the fortunes of war, just happened to be the first place where it was enforced. The "Tax Title Suits," in which the old planters persisted, were resented by the freedmen and the new northern merchants and "not approved by most southerners. Only small, innocent landowners were harmed by the lawsuits. The old planter's real dispute is with the U.S. government." Editor Richardson suggested restoration to private ownership of the land the government still owned to "end the confusion and help all."[10]

A year later, the *Beaufort Republican* published the other side of the dispute when it printed the letter of "An Old Citizen," who pointed out that his own real estate was valued before the war at twenty-five thousand dollars but sold by the government during the war for six thousand dollars. He felt this loss and his former neighbor's similar losses, were clearly government "takings" and deserved compensation. His suggested resolution was for the government to appoint a board of commissioners and to "let them value the property as nearly as possible to its worth before the war" and use the money from the sale of government property to indemnify the losses of the prewar land owners. This proposal, published in 1873, was likely the work of Colonel William Elliott (1838–1907), a Confederate veteran and Beaufort attorney, who was elected to Congress fifteen years later and there managed the legislative settlement that finally resolved these claims in 1892.[11]

Despite the lingering animosities over Civil War property transfers, northern newcomers and old Beaufortonians sometimes found common ground. And the humanitarian impulses that the northern missionaries and merchants brought with them occasionally even extended to the resentful and destitute "secesh." When Confederate veteran Colonel Paul Hamilton returned to Beaufort to reclaim his family's home, the Oaks, he found he was without sufficient funds to even pay the taxes and fines. When the house was auctioned off in 1866, several northern merchants, led by George Holmes, purchased it in Colonel Hamilton's name. Mary Stuart Hamilton, his daughter, recalled the moment and immediately overcame her animosity to the newcomers: "I had sworn never to shake hands with a Yankee, but that night I went to Mr. Holmes' store and thanked him from the bottom of my heart." Mary Stuart Hamilton opened a school in the servant's quarters, and for the next thirty-five years, she taught the children of Confederate veterans, Union veterans, wartime missionaries, and immigrant merchants alike. She became, as a consequence, one of the town's most beloved characters in the Reconstruction era. Acts of kindness like these were the beginning of the true Reconstruction of old Beaufort. By the end of the century, northern and southern families were intermarrying, and old Confederate veterans were promoting the son of a Union army officer and a wartime missionary as Beaufort County's representative in the state senate.[12]

The reality of Reconstruction Beaufort was that most of the sea island land was lost by its former owners, and with nothing to return to, few did. The old planter families resettled across North America. Many of those who prospered did so because they were particularly well educated, as was expected in antebellum Beaufort. They became authors in New York and New Orleans, ministers in Baltimore and Chicago, businessmen in Birmingham, Memphis, and New York, and artists and farmers in Texas, California, and Florida.

The most prominent of the antebellum leaders of Beaufort never returned. As a refugee in Greenville, South Carolina, Senator Robert W.

Barnwell was almost hanged by a troop of General Stoneman's Union cavalry, who mistook him for the great secessionist Robert Barnwell Rhett, his cousin. Robert W. Barnwell moved to Columbia and eked out a living as chairman of the faculty (essentially acting president) at the reorganized University of South Carolina. He worked to maintain the high standards of the antebellum college but was dismissed in 1873. He died in Columbia in 1882.[13] Senator Robert Barnwell Rhett, the "father of secession," had not lived in Beaufort for many years before the war but had visited his extended family there often. He never returned either. After the war he moved to New Orleans with his oldest daughter, Sallie Rhett Roman, and her ten children. There he settled in to write his memoirs. He died in New Orleans in 1886.[14] William Elliott III, William J. Grayson, and Edmund Rhett all died in the same year, 1863, as wartime refugees. Almost all the old Beaufort families had similar, poignant stories of their wartime flight and permanent postwar exile.

Some of Beaufort's exiles became pioneers all over again. On Merritt Island, Florida, in the shadow of the NASA launch pads at the Kennedy Space Center, a small Episcopal Church still stands among some of the last old citrus plantations that survive along the banks of the busy Indian River. Old Saint Luke's Church was built in 1888 by the first planters of Indian River fruit, refugees from the sea islands of Beaufort County. Their patriarch was Stanhope Sams, Confederate veteran and descendant of the Sams family of Dathaw Island. He and his numerous progeny and related families are buried in the old graveyard next to the original church, which bears a striking resemblance to the Church of the Cross in Bluffton. They were the pioneers of Merritt Island, Florida, the founders of Indian River fruit, and among the founders of the Florida citrus industry. Other old Beaufortonians settled on the Florida frontier. A colony of Fripps settled in Marion County, Florida, and much of the Baker family ended up in Jacksonville. Several family groups from Beaufort found their future on the Texas frontier. A colony of Sams family members settled in Williamson County, Texas, and several of the Stoney descendants staked their claim in Guadalupe County, Texas.

Some of the old Beaufortonians became standout citizens in their new communities. Robert Habersham Elliott became a civil engineer in Birmingham, Alabama, and laid out the route of the railroad line from Kansas City to Birmingham. His daughter, "Miss Hannah" Elliott, became an internationally recognized artist and a great southern belle of Birmingham, noted as "a lady of fine family and vivacious beauty ... with the posture of a queen in plumed hat."

Robert Habersham Elliott's sister was equally notable. Sara Barnwell Elliott (1848–1928) was raised and educated in Beaufort as a child and had no more formal education than that received at home. She became a bestselling author, publishing her first novel, *The Felmeres,* in 1879. She published five more novels and a biography of Sam Houston before 1901. From 1895 to

1902 she lived in New York, where she was a regular contributor to *Scribner's Magazine*. In 1902 she returned to Sewanee, Tennessee, where her father, Bishop Stephen Elliott of Georgia, founded the University of the South the year before the war and where her mother had died in 1895. There, in a log cabin study behind her family's home, she continued to write and hold "Monday salons" that became a tradition in Sewanee. Her most famous novel was *Jerry*, about a Tennessee mountain boy. Sarah Barnwell Elliott was an early suffragette and president of the Tennessee State Equal Suffrage Association. She died in Tennessee in 1928. Sewanee, Tennessee, became a center for the extended Elliott and Barnwell families for generations after the war.[15]

The last chapter of the Civil War land dispute in Beaufort County was written in 1892 when Congressman William Elliott authored legislation that finally compensated the descendants of antebellum owners of sea island plantations for their losses as a consequence of the U.S. Direct Tax Act foreclosures. To settle these obligations, the U.S. Court of Claims had to track down the heirs across the country. The settlements were substantial and the following list of claimants is testimony to the diaspora of the sea island planters.

U.S. Court of Claims

	Name of Claimant	Location	Amount of Settlement	Plantation
1.	Eliza and Charlotte Barnwell			"Old Fort"
	Elizabeth and Helen Smith		$14,019.02	"Otaheita"
2.	Jonathan Barnwell	Floyd Co., Georgia		?
	Joseph W. Barnwell	Charleston, S.C.	$6,510.11	?
3.	Caroline T. Baynard	Barnwell, S.C.		"Tom Baynard Place"
	Celia M. Rhodes	Barnwell, S.C.	$2,259.07	Lot C Block 44, Beaufort
	George Rhodes	Barnwell, S.C.		
4.	Edward M. Capers	Beaufort, S.C.	$990.00	"Edward Capers Place"
5.	Ann Chaplin	Fairfield Co. S.C.		?
	Frank Chaplin	Fairfield Co. S.C.	$5,139.00	
	Sarah O.B. Chaplin	Fairfield Co. S.C.		
6.	Rev. Thomas Cook	Talledega, Alabama	$1,150.00	Lot C, Block 71, Beaufort

	Name of Claimant	Location	Amount of Settlement	Plantation
7.	Ann Julianna Prioleau	Ellenton, S.C.		?
	A.P. Fripp	Block Mountain, N.C.	$2,768.00	?
	Charles DeSaussure	Shelby Co., Tennessee		?
	Thomas H. DeSaussure	Shelby Co., Tennessee		?
8.	Julia Fripp	Fairfield Co. S.C.		
	John Fripp	Fairfield Co. S.C.		
	R. Fuller Fripp	Fairfield Co. S.C.	$1,020.00	"Morgan Island"
	McNair Fripp	Fairfield Co. S.C.		
	Marion Fripp	Fairfield Co. S.C.		
	Ann Chaplin	Fairfield Co. S.C.		
9.	M.S. Fripp	Marion Co. Florida		?
	Ann H. Fripp	Marion Co. Florida	$6,661.25	
	M.A. Fripp	Marion Co. Florida		
	Melvin E. Fripp	Marion Co. Florida		
10.	Nathanial B. Fuller	Guadalupe Co., Texas	$6,020.27	?
11.	Ann Hankel	Charleston, S.C.		
	Thomas Heyward	Charleston, S.C.	$3,465.37	?
	Benjamin Heyward	Charleston, S.C.		
	Thomas Rhett	Charleston, S.C.		
	Mary Rhett	Charleston, S.C.		
	Albert Rhett	Charleston, S.C.		
12.	Mary W. Kidder	Maryland		
	Annie J. Elliott	Maryland	$12,755.90	?
	T.M. Stuart Rhett	Maryland		
13.	Anne S. Means	Charleston, S.C.	$6,437.66	?
14.	Clifford Oakman	Charleston, S.C.	$2,984.98	Town Lots, Beaufort
15.	Juliana M. Prioleau	Aiken, S.C.	$8,536.00	?
16.	H.P. Fripp	Spartanburg, S.C.		
	Hattie McWhirter	Spartanburg, S.C.	$3,427.17	?
	Annie Williams	Spartanburg, S.C.		
	E. Nora Fripp	Spartanburg, S.C.		
	Julia M. Boozer	Spartanburg, S.C.		
17.	Eliza M. Rhett	Charleston, S.C.	$3,675.00	?

	Name of Claimant	Location	Amount of Settlement	Plantation
18.	William B. Seabrook Martha Walpole Elias Rivers J. McL. Seabrook F.B. Seabrook Jane O. Rivers George R. Seabrook E.M. Seabrook	Charleston, S.C. Charleston, S.C. Charleston, S.C. Charleston, S.C. Charleston, S.C. Charleston, S.C. Charleston, S.C. Charleston, S.C.	$976.71	?
19.	Stanhope Sams	Merritt Island, Florida	$1,670.00	?
20.	Middleton Stuart Sarah Stuart James R. Stuart	Beaufort, S.C. Beaufort, S.C. Beaufort, S.C.	$3,278.05	"Rooplemonde" "Middleton Stuart Place"
21.	Dr. H.M. Stuart	Beaufort, S.C.	$512.73	Bought back family property and signed release to U.S. govt.
22.	Robert M. Fuller	Bexar Co., Texas	$6,938.75	?
23.	Matilda Morgan Henry G. Morgan	Chatham Co., Ga. Chatham Co., Ga.	$2,082.78	?
24.	S.H. Cunningham Julia Fripp John H. Fripp R. Fuller Fripp McNair Fripp Ann E. Fripp Marion Fripp James Walton	Fairfield Co., S.C. Fairfield Co., S.C. Fairfield Co., S.C. Fairfield Co., S.C. Fairfield Co., S.C. Fairfield Co., S.C. Fairfield Co., S.C. Fairfield Co., S.C.	$462.30	?
25.	Oliver Pritchard	Charleston, S.C.	$1,081.44	?
26.	Emma Julia Riggs Agnes Smoke	Orangeburg, S.C. Orangeburg, S.C.	$2,008.14	?
27.	Julianna M. Prioleau	Aiken, S.C.	$3,750.00	"Fripp Point Place"
28.	R.A. Ellis, et.al.	Barnwell, S.C.	$2,328.62	"Jericho Plantation"

	Name of Claimant	Location	Amount of Settlement	Plantation
	R.A. Ellis, et.al.	Barnwell, S.C.	$2,465.44	"Cherry Hill Plantation"
29.	Miles Brewton Sams	Spartanburg, S.C.	$3,233.58	Town lots, Beaufort
30.	Charles Cotesworth Pinckney	Charleston, S.C.	$3,537.50	"Rest Park"
31.	Emma Stuart	Kaufman Co., Texas	$995.00	"Otterburn" Hilton Head
	Middleton Stuart	Kaufman Co., Texas		"Otterhole"
32.	"Heirs of George Mosse Stoney" (Stoney, Graham, Fuller, Richardson, LeHardy, Jordan, Deas, Lawrence, Stuart, Gibson, et.al).	(Scattered)	$3,577.50	"Fairfield Plantation" Hilton Head
33.	Ellen Atkinson	Morgan Co., Ga.	$2,082.90	"Burton Hill Plantation"
	Catherine Fletcher	Morgan Co., Ga.		
	E.W. Morcock	Morgan Co., Ga.		
	Charles Morcock	Morgan Co., Ga.		
	Cooper Morcock	Morgan Co., Ga.		
	Susan Strobhart	Morgan Co., Ga.		
	William Garvin	Morgan Co., Ga.		
34.	Ann B. Elliott	Washington, D.C.	$575.00	Lot A, Block 81, Beaufort
35.	Ann B. Elliott	Washington, D.C.	$956.47	"Cedar Grove"
	Emily Elliott	Colleton Co., S.C.		"Shell Point"
	by the will of William Elliott III, dated February 3, 1863)			"The Ellis Place
36.	Mary A. Perryclear	Orangeburg, S.C.	$3,311.33	"Wm. Perryclear Place"
	Henria Perryclear	Orangeburg, S.C.		
	James S. Perryclear	Orangeburg, S.C.		"Wm. Perryclear Place"
	William T. Knotts	Orangeburg, S.C.		"Jack Island" Town Lots Beaufort
	Francis L. Knotts	Orangeburg, S.C.		
	Annie E. Scanlan	Orangeburg, S.C.		

	Name of Claimant	Location	Amount of Settlement	Plantation
37.	Elizabeth Sams Sarah Sams Adelaide Hallouquiser	Brevard Co., Florida (Merritt Island) (Merritt Island)	$1,238.25	"Loton Blacks Plantation" Block 5 and Lot B, Book 10, Beaufort
38.	Sarah G. Sams Calhoun Sams	Williamson Co., Texas Williamson Co., Texas	$3,118.39	"Hermitage" Port Royal Island
	Sarah J. Sams J. Graham Sams Mary E. Swan Elizabeth H. Noyes Eugenia Sams Lewis R. Sams	Williamson Co., Texas Williamson Co., Texas Williamson Co., Texas Williamson Co., Texas Williamson Co., Texas Williamson Co., Texas		"Oakland" St. Helena Island "Polawana Island" Town Lots, Beaufort
39.	Adeline Stoney Charlotte Fuller Anna B. Graham Emma Stuart (Heirs of George M. Stoney)	Guadalupe Co, Texas Guadalupe Co, Texas Guadalupe Co, Texas Guadalupe Co, Texas	$1,563.00	"Gardner's Plantation" Hilton Head
40.	Sallie B. Aiken	Escambia Co., Florida	$470.00	Town Lot, Beaufort
41.	Charles E. Coffin Francis W. Coffin Jessie C. Lamb Amory Coffin Elizabeth Coffin Mary Edmonston Henry P. Coffin	Richmond Co., Ga Richmond Co., Ga ? ? ? ? ?	$343.63 $343.63 $343.63 $343.63 $343.63 $343.63 $343.63	"Coffin Point" "McTureous" "Cherry Hill" St. Helena Island "Harbor Island"
42.	James McPherson Coffin Alice Church Coffin Elizabeth McP. Creighton (heirs of Thomas A. Coffin)	? Livingston Co., N.Y. ?	$10,124.91	"Coffin Point" "McTureous" "Cherry Hill," "Harbor Island" "Frog more," St. Helena Island
43.	John Elliott, et.al. (Elliott heirs & Benj. Edinas heirs)	Washington, D.C.	$1,036.40	450 acres on Parris Island

	Name of Claimant	Location	Amount of Settlement	Plantation
44.	Alfred Elliott	Washington, D.C./	$5,066.58	?
45.	Martha H. Moffett (sole heir of Richard W. Habersham, d. 1889)	?	$2,590.79	"Habersham Plantation" "Corn Island," "Walnut Hill," in family possession since 1834)
46.	Caroline Sams Richard F. Sams Robert W. Sams Nellie Worthy	Savannah, Georgia	$6,571.32	"Dathaw Pineland" Ladies Island "Dathaw Point Plantation" Dathaw Island Town Lots 17, 18, 48, Beaufort
47.	Elizabeth F. Nash (heir to Thomas F. Sams d. 1881	Fulton Co., Ga	$2,233.80	"The Cottage" Port Royal Island
48.	Edgar Fripp	?	$3,537.69	"Palmetto Hills" "Seaside," St. Helena Island "Flag Pond," next to Pritchard's Island
49.	Thomas M. McTureous et.al.	Charleston, S.C.	?	"Homestead" St. Helena Island
50.	John H. Rhodes, et.al.	Hampton Co., S.C.	$492.00	

With the old planters gone, the land titles secured and claims settled by the U.S. Government, the Civil War was finally over.[16] Beaufort County experienced entirely new and radically different political and economic reality. Political power was transferred from white planters to black freedmen, and economic activity shifted from the pastoral rhythms of the old plantations to the busy clatter of Yankee commerce. In Beaufort County the old South was gone forever.

YEARS OF BLACK REPUBLICAN POLITICAL RULE

The institution that the federal government established to ease and assist the transition from slavery to freedom was the U.S. War Department's Bureau of Refugees, Freedmen and Abandoned Lands. This agency had been established to provide for citizens displaced by the war and to provide services that would ease the transition of the new black citizens. Initially the Assistant Commissioner for The District Director of the Freedmen's Bureau for South Carolina, Georgia and Florida was Brigadier General Rufus Saxton. The Freedman's bureau agent for Beaufort County was H. G. Judd.

With the largest number of freedmen in the state, refugees from Sherman's march through Georgia and upcountry blacks still arriving in the lowcountry to escape violence and hoping to possibly gain land, H. G. Judd had his hands full in Beaufort County. Resources were scarce and support from the military limited.

The Freedmen's Bureau was intended to be financed by proceeds from the sale of cotton grown on U.S. government–controlled land, mostly in Beaufort County, and from the sale and rental of confiscated property. Both sources of income were quickly removed. The three hundred thousand dollars realized from the sale of cotton in 1865 was directed back to the Treasury Department, and most of the confiscated land in South Carolina was returned to its former owners by President Johnson's order of September 1865. General Saxton, as head of the bureau for the state, reported that of the three hundred thousand acres and twelve hundred homes controlled by the Freedmen's Bureau at the end of the war, the vast majority had been returned to their prewar owners by 1866. The bureau's rental income in South Carolina dropped from six thousand dollars per month in 1865 to fifty dollars per month in 1866.

With diminishing resources, Saxton had to rely on the occupation army to carry out the work of the bureau. Often the results were unsatisfactory. In Beaufort the local commander, Colonel Charles H. Howard, required all applicants for assistance to meet with a board in Beaufort once a month. This was impossible for those people living on isolated islands, as evidenced by the widespread suffering in the sea islands. Eventually Saxton had to dismiss the civilian agents because he could not meet the payroll. By 1870 Judd had a new job as clerk of court and registrar of deeds for the newly reconstituted Beaufort County Court.[17]

With the land distribution work undermined by President Johnson's order and the relief work greatly curtailed by lack of revenue, the most lasting contribution of the Freedmen's Bureau in South Carolina was in the field of education. By and large, the bureau's most effective contribution to the education of the freed slaves was by supporting the private charitable schools that had sprung up across the state in the years before the establishment of public schools. In 1865 Saxton appointed Pennsylvania native Reuben Tomlinson as superintendent of education for the Freedmen's Bureau in South Carolina.

The model for the bureau's support of private educational efforts had begun during the wartime occupation of the Port Royal area. The Port

Royal Experiment had spawned several successful schools in the Beaufort area. As one of the original members of "Gideon's Band" from Philadelphia, Superintendent Tomlinson was well aware of the success of these private, charitable schools and was determined that the Freedmen's Bureau would assist them and not compete with them. As Tomlinson put it, "The purpose of this branch ... is neither to destroy nor unnecessarily to interfere, but simply to assist ... in laying sure the foundations of future happiness and greatness of the people." The education policy of the Freedmen's Bureau was to form a productive partnership with the private schools that had already been established by charitable or religious organizations. The cooperative partnership was so successful that by 1866, Tomlinson could report 54 schools with 130 teachers and nearly 8,000 students enrolled.[18] These schools were the forerunners of the South Carolina public education system.

A unique feature of the education system in the sea islands was the government's use of "school farms" to support freedmen schools. The school farms were established on property gained by the government through foreclosures and auctions. Retained and rented to individuals who farmed the land, the resulting revenue was used to operate educational activities, continuing an important element of the Port Royal Experiment. School farms dotted the countryside of the sea islands and still appear on Beaufort County deeds. In later years some school farms were used to house and support paupers.[19]

The majority of the schools started during the Civil War were supported by northern freedmen associations, though some were operated by religious groups such as the Catholic and Baptist Churches. At the end of the war, the majority of the schools were consolidated into the Freedmen's Bureau operations, though a few retained their financial connections to the freedmen associations. One of the oldest of these schools was the Penn School, begun on St. Helena Island in 1862. The Port Royal Relief Commission, established in Philadelphia on March 3, 1862, had initially supported the Penn School. Among its teachers were Laura Towne, Ellen Murray, and Charlotte Forten. The school moved from its original home at the Oaks Plantation to the Brick Church and eventually to a permanent location at "Frogmore Corner." The "Corner" was the geographic center and crossroads of St. Helena Island, and under the leadership of Towne and Murray, the school soon became the focus of island activity. Towne and Murray's partnership at Penn would last until the twentieth century. By 1865 Penn School, with the support of the Pennsylvania Society, developed a graded curriculum with classes in primary, intermediate, and higher instruction. Each level of education had a separate teacher who taught in a separate room.

Throughout Towne and Murray's four decades of management of the Penn School, the subjects of instruction remained unchanged: reading, writing, spelling, geography, and arithmetic. Penn School survived the Reconstruction years because of the selfless dedication of Towne and Murray. It was the forerunner of many similar freedmen's schools across South Carolina and was one of the formative institutions in Reconstruction Beaufort. Penn School remains today an icon of the freedmen's struggle for equality as American citizens and as a monument to two remarkable women who founded and sustained the first freedmen's school in America.

Another important school was established on the grounds of John Joyner Smith's Old Fort Plantation on Port Royal Island. Operated by Elizabeth Hyde Botume, assisted by her nieces Frances "Fanny" Sophia Langford and Elizabeth "Lizzie" Botume Langford, it was sponsored by the New England Freedmen's Aid Society and soon garnered the support of the wealthy Winthrop family of Massachusetts. Botume described it as "a place of historic renown and great beauty." It was located on the site of Camp Saxton, bivouac of the 1st South Carolina Regiment (USCT). It was where the reading of the Emancipation Proclamation took place and the site of the great "jubilee" that followed on January 1, 1863. It is arguably the place where the reconstruction of the old South began. The United States Naval Hospital Beaufort occupies the site today. Botume and Langford's contributions to the education of the freedmen were to introduce industrial training—a method of schooling that met with great success and great enthusiasm among their students. They particularly concentrated on teaching sewing to the young girls, a skill to which the girls readily and eagerly adapted. Botume noted, "Sewing had a great fascination for all. They learned readily and soon developed much skill and ingenuity."

In 1867 Robert Smalls, Richard H. Gleaves, William J. Whipper, and Jonathan J. Wright, all black immigrants to the sea islands, formed a local Board of Education, purchased a block of land on Carteret, Washington, and Green Streets and sought the help of the Presbyterian Church Board of Missions for funds to start a school for freedmen.

In 1868 another school was opened on Port Royal Island. Rachel Crane Mather came to Beaufort from Boston with the backing of the American Home Baptist Mission Society. She started a school for homeless girls, where they would receive instruction in the Bible and in common household duties. For many years this instruction was called "home economics." This became the Mather Industrial School of Beaufort, and it survived as a private institution for nearly a century, finally closing in the 1960s. Its buildings are now incorporated into the campus of the Technical College of the Lowcountry.

These successful private institutions in Beaufort County set the early standard for similar institutions across the state during the Reconstruction years. In 1865 the Avery Normal Institute was founded in Charleston under the sponsorship of the American Missionary Association of the

Congregational Church and was named for its benefactor, Charles Avery of Pittsburgh. Also founded in Charleston in 1865 was the Shaw Memorial Institute named in honor of Colonel Robert Gould Shaw, who died in the assault on Battery Wagner. Shaw's wealthy Boston family supported the school until it was merged with the city's common schools in 1874. In Columbia the Howard School was erected in 1867 under the auspices of the Freedmen's Bureau and the New York Freedmen's Aid Society. Also in Columbia the Benedict Institute was established in 1870 by the philanthropy of Mrs. Bethsheba A. Benedict of Pawtucket, Rhode Island. It survives today as Benedict College.[20]

Some of these pioneer institutions continue today as important educational and cultural institutions for black South Carolinians. The movement, which began in Beaufort County, spread throughout the state during Reconstruction, with the assistance of the Freedmen's Bureau. The private schools began the education of the freedmen and laid the foundations of the public education system in South Carolina.

Another institution begun under the auspices of the Reconstruction Freedmen's Bureau was the Freedmen's Savings and Trust Company, commonly referred to as the "Freedmen's Bank." The U.S. Congress chartered the Freedmen's Savings and Trust Company in March 1865. It operated in all southern states as well as in Washington and New York. Its purpose was to encourage habits of thrift and independence among the freedmen. Though the freedmen's Savings and Trust Company was legally independent of the Freedmen's Bureau, General Oliver O. Howard, national head of the bureau, was a great champion, and each savings passbook contained his printed endorsement. In South Carolina the bureau and the bank were closely interlocked. The bank often operated out of bureau buildings, rent free, and bureau directors and agents often held positions with the bank. Rufus Saxton was on the bank's statewide advisory board.

Like much of the social experimentation of the Reconstruction era, the idea of a Freedmen's Savings and Trust Company grew out of the necessities of occupied Beaufort during the Civil War. When the Union Army began enlisting its first African American regiments, Military Governor Rufus Saxton wanted a secure depository for the soldier's pay and bonuses. Accordingly, on August 27, 1864, under the auspices of the U.S. Army, he established the South Carolina Savings Bank at Beaufort to encourage "the habits of carefulness and prudence" among the new recruits. This institution, originally the Military Bank of Beaufort, came to be known as the South Carolina Freedmen's Savings Bank. By the end of 1864, the Military Bank of Beaufort held more than sixty-five thousand dollars of soldier's deposits. Similar institutions were later established by General Nathaniel P. Banks in occupied New Orleans and by General Benjamin F. Butler in occupied

Norfolk, Virginia. When the privately chartered Freedmen's Savings and Trust Company opened its first South Carolina branch in Beaufort, the deposits of Saxton's earlier institution were transferred into it.

The first branch of the Freedmen's Savings and Trust Company in South Carolina opened in Beaufort in October 1865 in a building on Bay Street controlled by the Freedmen's Bureau. The cashier and chief operating officer was N. R. Scovill, said to be "an admirable gentleman and efficient officer." The chairman of the local advisory board was bureau agent H. G. Judd. The close association of the Freedmen's Bank with the federal agency and its published endorsements by General O. O. Howard, and even the martyred President Abraham Lincoln, gave the impression of financial backing from the U.S. Treasury. But the bank was chartered as a legally separate, nonprofit institution. The charter required the Freedmen's Bank to keep two-thirds of its deposits in government securities and pay interest up to a maximum of 7 percent on deposits exceeding five dollars. Additionally, any surplus funds were to be used for the purpose of educating the freedmen. The Freedmen's Bank was an integral part of Beaufort's business community from 1865 to 1874.

By 1871 the Beaufort branch of the National Freedmen's Savings and Trust Company was described as "exceedingly prosperous," with upwards of twelve hundred individual depositors. But like many businesses of the Reconstruction era, the Freedmen's Bank had fallen victim to fraud and mismanagement. In November 1871 the *Beaufort Republican* had to publish an emphatic denial of locally circulated rumors that the parent bank in Washington, D.C., was in trouble. "In fact," the newspaper noted, "it is probable that no more thriving institution exists in the United States." With total assets exceeding $3,000,000 and U.S. bonds worth $1,167,126, the parent bank seemed solid to local depositors. But mismanagement had weakened the bank, and when the financial crash of 1873 occurred, the Freedmen's Savings and Trust Company went under.

The financial crash of September 1873 was a severe blow to the national economy. The stock market suspended trading, several northern banks failed, and depositors made runs on banks in New York and Washington, D.C., including the Freedmen's Savings and Trust Company. In Beaufort the local branch suspended business and demanded sixty days' notice to cash checks. Weakened by mismanagement at the national level, the Freedmen's Bank could not withstand the financial collapse and ensuing recession of 1873. By 1874 the institution was bankrupt. In Beaufort the Freedmen's Bank closed, and its many depositors were never repaid. Twelve hundred struggling sea island farmers and fishermen lost $77,216.79. It was a lesson in "thrift and economy" and in reliance on the U.S. government that was not forgotten by a generation of freedmen. The Panic of 1873 was a serious setback for a state just recovering from the Civil War and uniquely dependent on northern capital for its economic recovery. It was one of several blows that weakened the Reconstruction regime in South Carolina.

Despite the revenue problems and President Johnson's veto, in 1867 Congress extended the life of the Freedmen's Bureau by two years. In 1869 Congress authorized a further continuation of the bureau in the states where it was most needed, including South Carolina. Some functions of the agency continued until Congress formally abolished the Freedmen's Bureau on June 30, 1872. By that time, the Reconstruction regime was firmly in control of the state government and would presumably look after the welfare of its own people.[21]

One of the other goals of the Freedmen's Bureau was political education, and the freedmen responded to their new privileges and responsibilities as citizens with gusto. Even before the Fifteenth Amendment was ratified, the freedmen of Beaufort County were participating in their own political future. The Reconstruction Act of 1867, passed by the U.S. Congress, required that all the rebellious southern states rewrite their state constitutions and include the freedmen in the process. The military governors of the occupied southern states were directed to conduct the selection of delegates to those constitutional conventions. The Federal military authorities were to be in charge of registering the new voters and even counting the ballots in the selection of delegates. All of this was prescribed to ensure that the freedmen would be allowed to vote.

During 1867 U.S. Army occupation forces registered 80,832 new black voters in South Carolina. The same registration counted only 46,929 white voters in the state. Many white voters had been disqualified by the Congressional Reconstruction Act of 1867 because of their participation in "the rebellion."[22] In the census of 1870, Beaufort County's total population of 34,359 comprised 29,050 black citizens and only 5,309 white—a ratio of five and a half to one. For many years after the Civil War, Beaufort County had the largest black majority in South Carolina.

Political education for the freedmen of the sea islands began when the Union League of northern Republican activists began educating the sea island blacks for political participation as early as 1866. This organized effort bore fruit when ex-slave and Civil War hero Robert Smalls held a meeting at the Stevens House in downtown Beaufort on March 26, 1867. Smalls and Richard H. Gleaves, along with thirty-six other black leaders and three whites, formed the Beaufort Republican Club, the first organization of the Republican Party in South Carolina. This was also the beginning of Robert Smalls's political career. He was to be the dominant figure in Beaufort County politics for the next twenty-one years and the first man to benefit from the new voting power of Beaufort's black majority.[23]

The first organized elections of Beaufort County's black majority took place in October and November 1867 for the purpose of selecting delegates to the South Carolina Constitutional Convention of 1868. Across Beaufort County political caucuses were held in the various neighborhoods to select delegates to the county convention to be held in Beaufort on November 6, 1867. Among those observing the elections was the Reverend George Newcomb, the Dedham, Massachusetts, schoolteacher who joined the Port Royal Experiment in 1864. Newcomb had been named by Saxton as head of the freedmen schools in South Carolina, but in 1866 he left the state for a teaching post at Elizabeth City, North Carolina. Forced to leave North Carolina because of ill health, he became a minister in the Methodist Episcopal Church and had returned to Beaufort in 1867 as a member of the church's Missionary Society. He was ordained as both deacon and elder and given authority to expand the Beaufort circuit using the Methodist Mission Chapel on West Street as his headquarters. He attended the caucuses in Beaufort and Gray's Hill. Of the Beaufort caucus he noted, "Captain Smalls presided with dignity and credit and all proceedings were conducted very orderly. The work done, speeches were called for, remarks were made by Messers Gage, Millett, Conant and myself."

Reverend Newcomb accompanied Captain Smalls to the meeting at Grays Hill, "about five miles out on the Shell Road." Smalls also presided over that meeting, a noon caucus "composed entirely of the colored population." Five delegates were chosen for the county convention, and both Smalls and George Newcomb gave speeches. These local elections in 1867 were the beginning of the political life of the ex-slaves as free citizens of the United States.

Reverend Newcomb returned from Hilton Head on November 6 to witness the county convention in Beaufort. Sixty delegates from across Beaufort County assembled in the town to nominate delegates to be elected on November 19 and 20, 1867. The Republican ticket nominated at the November 6 convention consisted of Robert Smalls, W. J. Whipper, J. J. Wright, and Landon S. Langley, all of whom were black, and Reuben G. Holmes, James O. Bell, and Dr. Francis E. Wilder, who were white. All resided in Beaufort except Dr. Wilder, Hilton Head's longtime country doctor.

Much activity accompanied these first elections. The regular Republican ticket had opposition, and heated arguments ensued. Robert Smalls got into a dispute with Peter Burns, a black man, and knocked him down. Friends of both men suppressed the fight. It was the beginning of a spirited political era in Beaufort County.

These first elections also displayed the first exercise of black voter intimidation, which would be a feature of Beaufort County elections throughout the Reconstruction years. The *Charleston Daily Courier* reported that many of the new African American voters arrived at the polls in military uniform to discourage any opposition: "The object was often to occupy the polls early and thereby impede the opposition's access to the polls. The four hundred men—some wearing their old Army uniforms who took possession of the Grey's Hill polls in Beaufort, or the eight hundred men who similarly occupied the polling place on St. Helena Island during the November 1867 election, had clearly mastered the strategy." The Charleston newspaper identified Robert Smalls as the architect of this election-day tactic. He had urged his followers "to shoot, knock the brains out or kill any man who attempted to vote any other ticket than the so called red [Republican] ticket."

Reverend Newcomb witnessed the first elections, and he saw it very differently: "Tuesday, November 19. The election was passed quietly.... Perfect order prevailed and the people enjoyed their new privilege with interest. Everybody was good natured." Newcomb also noted the reaction of the few white southerners in Beaufort: "Saw ... some two or three of the most prominent chivalry in town, stop as they were passing and look for a moment ... and with downcast eyes, passed on."

The powerful significance of the moment was not lost on Reverend Newcomb, who commented, "How changed from a few short years ago! Then the very building in which they met to vote [the arsenal] was used as the hall of justice as administered by the master to the slave and a few rods from it the slave pen and the jail. The colored people reminded me of it and rejoiced in the new use to which the building was put." Of the 518 votes cast in town, Robert Smalls led the ticket with 496 votes.[24]

The Constitutional Convention, which met in Charleston on January 14, 1868, was one of the most historic events in South Carolina's long history. Despite the best efforts of white Democrats to erase the influence of the constitution of 1868 in later years, it remains the foundation of most of the public life of South Carolina to this day. The most important aspects of the South Carolina Constitution of 1868 were the voting rights provisions.

There were no property qualifications, which was a feature of every antebellum state constitution before 1868. There was no literacy requirement or any requirement for "understanding the constitution" as was later imposed by the Constitution of 1895. Voter disqualifications for felony offences omitted most petty crimes, which could be used to exclude black voters. Most important, the Constitution of 1868 eliminated all racial barriers to voting in South Carolina, a circumstance that was bolstered two years later by the ratification of the Fifteenth Amendment.[25]

Beaufort County's delegate, William J. Whipper, even introduced a measure at the convention allowing women's suffrage. Whipper argued that democratic stability could only be achieved if "all human beings—not just all men—were considered equal." Whipper attempted to remove the word "male" from the voter registration requirements. His speech to the convention stated, "Governments will continue to fall until the rights of all parties are respected—womankind as well as mankind.... The systems of legislation have been laid on insecure foundations, and they will never be permanent until women are recognized as the equal of men, and with him permitted to enjoy the privileges which appertain to the citizen."[26] Women's suffrage was too radical even for the delegates of 1868, and Whipper's remarkably progressive proposal was voted down. Beaufort, however, was to become one of the wellsprings of the women's suffrage movement in South Carolina at the end of the century.

Another of the most significant stipulations of the Constitution of 1868 was the provision for establishing a statewide public school system. This was the one area of constitutional debate where Robert Smalls made lasting contributions. Like many of the ex-slaves at the Charleston Convention in 1868, Smalls kept a low profile, leaving much of the debate to white delegates and out-of-state black delegates who had a more formal education. But on the issue of public education, Robert Smalls stepped to the front and led the convention. He offered a resolution that inserted an article in the constitution providing for "a system" of common schools "to be open without charge to all classes of persons." Smalls wished to provide six months of free public education per year for all children from ages seven to fourteen. Smalls proposed that public schooling be compulsory. Though the proposal was modified in the final draft of the constitution of 1868, it was, nonetheless, the constitutional foundation of the public school system of South Carolina.

The constitutional efforts of Robert Smalls bore fruit in Beaufort County. By 1872 Beaufort School District Number 1 was formed with R. H. Gleaves as chairman and H. G. Judd as secretary. At the end of the 1872–73 school year, the district reported successfully operating fifteen schools with nineteen teachers and 1,643 students enrolled. The total cost of operating Beaufort School District Number 1 for the year was $4,702.98. Of that sum $4,145 went to teacher pay and $557.98 went toward rent. The district received a state appropriation of $2,017.08, obtained $538.55 from the county school tax, and received $319 from the poll tax. That year the district ran a deficit of $1,828.35. While that amount may seem insignificant, it was 39 percent of the total budget, and it was the kind of local public management that alarmed critics of the Reconstruction regime. The largest school was the Beaufort Town School with six teachers: Mrs. W. W. Fripp, Miss S. J. Keith, Miss Hannah Hunn, Mrs. Georgianna Gleaves, Mrs. Clara Haines, and Silas Taylor. Outside Beaufort there were several small one- or two-room country schools. The only teacher at the Laurel Bay School was George Curtis. J. C. Rivers and Mrs. Charlotte Jackson conducted the Oakland School. Francis Bowen and Joshua Dennis taught the Walker School. The Gray's Hill School was taught by Israel W. Brown, and the Parris Island School was managed by M. Simmons. Reverend George W. Harris, and William Middletown Brown conducted the Stuart Point School. The only teacher at the Perryclear School was Daniel Jenkins, while the only teacher at the Old Fort School was Miss Lizzie Hunn. The Higginsonville School was conducted by Tamar Williams and the Garden's (Corner) School by Sidney Benton.

At a school commissioners meeting in Columbia in 1873, Thomas E. Miller, the representative from Beaufort, recommended integrating the new public schools, contending that "both races should be educated together." His proposal was not popular. A large majority of even the black school commissioners was opposed, and the subject was dropped. Judge Jonathan J. Wright of the South Carolina Supreme Court, another of Beaufort's black political leaders, spoke for the majority when he "warmly condemned the gentleman from Beaufort." The Beaufort newspaper reported that "while he claimed for his race perfect equality and equal privileges with the white race ... he did not desire social equality nor the mixing of races in the common schools of the country."[27] South Carolina's public schools remained segregated for the next century. Though Robert Smalls was to make many lasting contributions to the history of Beaufort County over the next forty-seven years, his contribution as a principal founder of South Carolina's public schools was probably his most influential.

Another provision of the Constitution of 1868 of great historical importance to Beaufort County was the elimination of the old lowcountry parish system. The colonial Commons House of Assembly had created that system of political divisions in the lowcountry in 1706. In 1769 the four colonial parishes of St. Helena (1712), Prince William (1745), St. Peter (1747), and St. Luke (1767) were incorporated into the Beaufort Judicial District. The parish system hung on through the turmoil of the Revolution and was preserved by the antebellum South Carolina Constitution of 1790. It even survived the bitter sectional disputes that were resolved by the Compromise of 1808. Throughout the antebellum era, the upcountry grew while the lowcountry did not, and by the time of the Civil War, the old parishes had become relics of the colonial past. The upheaval of the Civil War ended them.

The postwar Constitution of 1865 formally abolished the four parishes, and the old Beaufort Judicial District was reconstituted as Beaufort County. The county system was reconfirmed by the constitution of 1868. Beaufort County then consisted of all of what are today Beaufort, Jasper, and Hampton Counties, as well as a small part of Allendale County. Beaufort County was, therefore, one of the largest and most populous counties in the state during the Reconstruction years.

Almost immediately upon creating Beaufort County in 1868, a controversy arose over the location of the county seat. When the Beaufort Judicial

District was created in 1769, the judicial capital was placed in old Beaufort, and a courthouse was built on the site of the arsenal. During the Revolution, mainlanders complained about the isolation of the district capital, and in 1783 the judicial seat was moved to Coosawhatchie, the geographical center of the Beaufort District. In 1836 the South Carolina Legislature removed the courthouse again, this time to Gillisonville, a higher, healthier, and less swampy location, where it stood until destroyed in January 1865 by Federal forces. With the creation of Beaufort County by the Constitution of 1868, Robert Smalls, then serving in the South Carolina House of Representatives, introduced legislation to move the county seat back to Beaufort, the economic and cultural center of his sea island black constituents. For many years after the Civil War, the sea islands remained the most densely populated district in the large county, but the removal of the county seat to Beaufort separated the mainlanders from the county government once again, leading to local disputes and eventually the division of the county.

The Constitution of 1868 also gave the new county governments in South Carolina greatly expanded constitutional authority over roads, highways, bridges, ferries, and "all matters relating to taxes and disbursements of money for county purposes." This was one of the most radical departures from the antebellum constitutions, which had reserved almost all authority for the state legislature; it was also the beginning of "home rule" in South Carolina.[28]

To administer this new local authority, each county was to elect three persons for two-year terms that would constitute the County Board of Commissioners. The first Beaufort County Board of Commissioners from 1868 to 1870 comprised John Hunn (chairman), Moritz Pollitzer, and J. H. Tonking; all were white, all new immigrants to Beaufort, all Republicans, and all residing in the city of Beaufort. The Board of Commissioners appointed E. S. Kuh as county treasurer, and he reported monthly revenues of $2,352 (approximately $28,224 annually) and monthly expenses of $1,842 (approximately $22,104 annually). This was the beginning of local government in Beaufort County.[29]

BEAUFORT'S AFRICAN AMERICAN POLITICAL LEADERS

With the application of the Constitution of 1868, the political revolution in South Carolina was complete. The new black majority asserted its voting power across the state, and the state house of representatives had a strong black majority for the next eight years. Beaufort County sent one of the most influential delegations to the state legislature, and the county produced some of the most influential African American politicians during Reconstruction years. Between 1867 and 1890, Beaufort County sent six African American state senators to Columbia and only two whites. During the same period, twenty-four different African American men and only three white men represented Beaufort County in the South Carolina house. African Americans served as sheriff, clerk of court, coroner, probate judge, treasurer, and county commissioners in the new Beaufort County government. African Americans also served as intendant(mayor), city constable, and public school trustees in the city of Beaufort. From 1868 to 1902, most of city wardens for the city of Beaufort were black, and until 1913 the city electorate returned at least two African Americans to the municipal council, the last black elected officials in South Carolina until the 1960s. Reconstruction Beaufort clearly was for many years what its political rivals dubbed it, the "Black Republic of Beaufort."[30]

Among the many black political leaders Beaufort County produced during Reconstruction, four stand out. The first and by far the most important was Robert Smalls (1839–1915). Next was Smalls's eventual rival, William J. Whipper. The highest-ranking black in the Reconstruction state government was Lieutenant Governor Richard Howell Gleaves from Beaufort. And finally, the man who followed Robert Smalls as the political leader of sea island blacks and who assumed many of Smalls's former offices was Thomas Ezekiel Miller.

Smalls, who had been born a slave in the servant's quarters behind the McKee family townhouse at 501 Prince Street in Beaufort, had through his wartime exploits become a national hero and heavily involved with the Reconstruction movement in the Beaufort District. Though many local men served heroically with the Union army during the war, Smalls was the most famous. When the war ended, he was the natural leader of the freedmen's community, and he did not shirk from the task. Though Smalls was never formally educated and remained only semiliterate throughout his career, he was nonetheless a skilled and effective orator. He was also described as a convivial man, who like many of his sea island constituents possessed a ready and engaging sense of humor. All of this made him the overwhelming popular choice of the Beaufort County electorate for the next twenty years.

Though named to the delegation sent to the Union Party 1864 convention, Smalls had been unable to attend. Duties with the Quartermaster Bureau and personal commercial activities in Beaufort kept him busy until 1867, when he organized the Beaufort Republican Club, the first Republican political organization in South Carolina and the core of the political machine that served Smalls for three decades.

After his historic service as a delegate to the South Carolina Constitutional Convention of 1868, Smalls was elected to the state house of representatives, where he served one term (1868–1870), and then was elected as Beaufort County's state senator, an office in which he served for three terms, from 1870 to 1875. During these years of state service, Smalls was chairman of the Beaufort County Republican Party, vice-chairman of the South Carolina Republican Conventions of 1868, 1872, and 1874, and Republican executive committeeman in 1868. While in the state legislature, Smalls consistently supported internal improvement and industrial development, especially for Beaufort County.

In 1874 Robert Smalls was elected to the U.S. Congress and served five terms, 1875–77, 1877–79, 1881–83, 1883–85, and 1885–87. His most important contribution to Beaufort County while in Congress was to promote the establishment of the U.S. Naval Station at Port Royal and the purchase of Parris Island as a naval shipyard. This, of course, had a greater long-term effect on the economy of Beaufort County than anything else that occurred in the late nineteenth century. At the height of Smalls's political influence, his political enemies in Charleston dubbed him "the King of Beaufort County," and like many political warriors before him, he wore the intended insult as a badge of honor.

Locally, Smalls was always a moderate politician and was often called upon to bring calm to potentially violent situations. His stature with all citizens of Beaufort County made him the indispensable man during the turbulent Reconstruction years. By the end of the century, with the ascendancy of the white Democratic Party in South Carolina, Smalls settled into a federal patronage job as U.S. Customs port collector for the Port of Beaufort. Even then he continued to be an honored symbol of the freedmen's struggle and a powerful influence on Beaufort County politics. As the white Democratic Party began to lock in its control of the state government in the 1880s, Smalls sought ways to protect what he could for his African American constituents. It was this motive that led him to become the architect of a local black-white power-sharing arrangement known as fusion politics.[31] So successful was fusion politics in Beaufort County that it protected the interests of Beaufort's black citizens until 1913, deep into the Jim Crow years. It was the last legacy of Beaufort County's most important Reconstruction politician.

The next most influential of Beaufort's Reconstruction political leaders was William J. Whipper. Born free in Philadelphia, Whipper was the son of a prominent lumber merchant, who was also an active Pennsylvania abolitionist. In March 1864 he joined the 30th Connecticut Regiment, which was merged into the 31st USCT. Whipper saw service around Petersburg, participated in the Battle of the Crater and the Appomattox Campaign, and ended the war doing occupation duty in Texas. He was mustered out in November 1865. He came to Charleston in February 1866, where he read the law and passed the South Carolina Bar. In October 1866 he moved his law practice to Beaufort and became the town's most prominent Reconstruction lawyer. He was elected as a delegate to the Constitutional Convention of 1868, where he became one of the most able and influential members of that historic assembly.

He returned to Beaufort and was elected to the South Carolina house for two terms, 1870–72 and 1872–74. While in Columbia, his talent and intellect made him one of the most influential members of the Reconstruction legislature. When the legislature elected him a circuit judge, he had fallen victim to the corruption scandals of the state government, and Governor Daniel Chamberlain refused to appoint him. Whipper returned to Beaufort and served for several years as Beaufort County probate judge. During the 1880s, he moved his family to Washington but was back in Beaufort by 1888.

Part of W. J. Whipper's special influence in the Reconstruction state government was due to his marriage to Francis Ann Rollin of Charleston on September 17, 1868. Rollin was the daughter of a wealthy and prominent free-black family of Charleston. During Reconstruction, her three sisters, Catherine de Medici Rollin, Charlotte Corday Rollin, and Louise Muhlbach Rollin, moved to Columbia. There they filled a large house with elegant furnishings and maintained a salon that became the center of the capital's social life. This was where Whipper gained his notably progressive views about women's suffrage.

Whipper was undoubtedly the intellectual leader of Beaufort's black community during the Reconstruction years. He published one newspaper, the *Beaufort Tribune,* in the 1870s and was a partner with S. J. Bampfield in publishing a second newspaper, the *New South,* in the 1890s. Whipper maintained a large and busy legal practice in Beaufort for thirty years. His last political duty was as a delegate to the state Constitutional Convention of 1895, where, along with Robert Smalls, he tried to head off the white Democrats' moves to disfranchise black voters. Unsuccessful in their effort, Whipper, Smalls, and the other black delegates from Beaufort refused to sign the Constitution of 1895.

W. J. Whipper would have been much more successful politically had he not fallen out with Robert Smalls in 1872. The two men exchanged charges of corruption, supported opposing factions of the Republican Party, and ran against each other for state senate in the election of 1872. They remained political rivals thereafter. It was a tragedy for Beaufort County because the men had complementary talents. Whipper's political enemy Governor Benjamin R. "Pitchfork Ben" Tillman called Whipper "the ablest colored man I ever met." But for all his intellectual ability, W. J. Whipper was no match for Robert Smalls in the electoral politics of Beaufort County, and the rivalry between Whipper and Smalls stunted Whipper's political career.[32]

The highest-ranking African American politician in the South Carolina Reconstruction government was Richard Howell Gleaves of Beaufort. Like most of Beaufort's postwar business and professional leadership, Gleaves was not a Beaufort native. He was born on July 4, 1819, in Philadelphia, the son of a Haitian father and an English mother. Educated in Philadelphia and New

Orleans, he worked before the war as a trader and steward on Mississippi River steamboats. He also lived in Ohio and Pennsylvania, where he rose to leadership positions in the York Rite Masonic Order.

Gleaves came to Beaufort in 1866 as a business partner of Robert Smalls. Twenty years his senior and a worldly, sophisticated urbanite, Gleaves was probably somewhat of a mentor as well as a partner of Smalls. Gleaves's experience leading Masonic lodges made him a natural leader of Beaufort's Reconstruction civic organizations. He helped organize the Republican Party in Beaufort and was president of the 1867 Republican state convention. Locally, Gleaves served in the 1870s as a trial justice, probate judge, and commissioner of elections. In 1872 he was elected lieutenant governor of South Carolina in the administration of Governor Franklin Moses. In 1874 he was reelected as lieutenant governor in the administration of Governor Daniel H. Chamberlain. To date, Gleaves remains the highest-ranking black elected official in South Carolina history.

Gleaves was elected for a third term as lieutenant governor in the disputed election of 1876. He protested the decision to seat the administration of Governor Wade Hampton, believing that it was a consequence of election fraud, but peacefully stepped aside in favor of his opponent, W. D. Simpson. Governor Hampton appointed Gleaves trial justice for Beaufort County. But in 1877 he left South Carolina in the face of one of the many scandals of South Carolina Reconstruction government. He worked as a clerk in the U.S. Treasury Department, as the steward of the Jefferson Club, and died in Washington, D.C., in 1907.[33]

The last of the major political leaders of Beaufort County during Reconstruction was Thomas Ezekiel Miller, who was born a free black in Ferebeeville, now in Jasper County, in 1849. If Richard Howell Gleaves was something of a mentor to Robert Smalls, then Miller, ten years Smalls's junior, was certainly Smalls's protégé. Like Smalls, and unlike much of the black political leadership during Reconstruction, Miller was a Beaufort County native. But Miller was a freeman and had the benefit of a formal education in Charleston and in Hudson, New York. He graduated from Lincoln University in Philadelphia in 1872. He returned to South Carolina, read the law, and was admitted to the state bar in 1875. He opened his practice in Beaufort and was elected to the state house of representatives. Between 1874 and 1882, Miller served three terms as a state representative and one term as a state senator.

With the retirement of Robert Smalls from Congress, Miller ran for his seat in 1888, was defeated by William Elliott, challenged the election results, and was seated by the U.S. Congress in 1890. He was defeated for reelection to Congress by William Elliott but was returned to the South Carolina house for the 1894–96 session. Miller, along with Smalls and Whipper, was a member of Beaufort County's famous black delegation to the South Carolina Constitutional Convention of 1895.

In his last session in the South Carolina house, Miller introduced the legislation establishing the Colored Normal, Industrial, Agricultural and Mechanical College of South Carolina in Orangeburg, founded in 1896. This is now South Carolina State University. Miller resigned from the state house in 1896 to accept the appointment as the first president of the college by Governor John Gary Evans. In 1911 he retired from the college and settled in Charleston, where he died in 1938.

Though Beaufort County voters regularly returned Thomas E. Miller to office, he was somewhat hampered by his racial identity. Miller was nearly white and often "passed" for white. His political opponents made much of this, claiming he was only "one sixty-fourth" black and often referring to him as the "canary bird." Miller bore his burden politely, always worked for the cause of blacks in South Carolina, and remained a constant champion of Beaufort County. His lifelong sensitivity to the issue is apparent on his tombstone in Brotherly Cemetery in Charleston; the inscription reads, "Not having loved the white man less, but having felt the Negro needed me more."[34]

Many other African American politicians represented Beaufort County during Reconstruction. Beaufort farmer Philip Ezekiel and Beaufort tinsmith William C. Morrison both served in the South Carolina House of Representatives in the first session following the Constitution of 1868. Samuel Jones Bampfield, Robert Smalls's son-in-law, served one term (1874–76) in the South Carolina house before settling in as Beaufort County clerk of court for nineteen years. Thomas Hamilton, a prosperous farmer from Pocotaligo, served three terms in the state house from 1872 to 1878. Hamilton Robinson, a Beaufort native and wounded Civil War veteran of the 33rd USCT, served one term as a South Carolina Senator (1882–84). He was the father of Stepney Robinson, St. Helena Island's famous root doctor "Dr. Buzzard." Thomas J. Reynolds, a St. Helena Island native and law partner of William J. Whipper, served one term in the South Carolina Senate (1884–86). Samuel Green, Kit Green's son, served three terms in the state house (1870–76) and two terms in the state senate (1875–77). Hasting Gantt served six terms in the house (1870–83) from Beaufort County. Julius Irwin Washington, who read the law with William J. Whipper and was admitted to the state bar in 1887, served two terms in the state house of representatives (1886–90). Julius I. Washington returned to Beaufort and practiced law there continuously from 1893 to 1938. He was Beaufort's most prominent and respected African American lawyer for forty-five years.[35]

The Reconstruction years were among the most politically active and patriotic years in Beaufort's long history. Any event from a solemn commemoration to a political rally was reason to launch a colorful celebration.

And the freedmen of Beaufort County had much to celebrate: freedom from slavery, victory in the great war, citizenship in the republic, power in state and local government, and hope for the prosperity of future generations.

One of the largest regular celebrations in Reconstruction Beaufort was Emancipation Day. This annually commemorated the announcement of Abraham Lincoln's Emancipation Proclamation on January 1, 1863. When the Emancipation Day celebration was held in 1872, notice went out for the entire 2nd and 3rd Regiments of the South Carolina National Guard to muster in front of the arsenal. On New Years Day 1872, nineteen officers and 367 guardsmen formed up in six companies on Craven Street. They marched up Carteret Street to the parade ground on Boundary Street. There they stood for review and then marched down Carteret Street, accompanied by patriotic band music, to the Stevens House on Bay Street, where political speeches were delivered. Most of the leading politicians were awarded commissions in the South Carolina National Guard during Reconstruction. Brigadier General Robert Smalls, Brigadier General W. J. Whipper, Colonel P. L. Wiggin, and Major E. F. English of the 3rd Regiment conducted the review. Surgeon Francis Wilder, Adjutant Joe Richardson, and Chaplain York Polite formed the rest of the regimental staff.

Company A, with fifty men, was commanded by Captain W. C. Morrison, First Lieutenant Joe Richardson, and Second Lieutenant Capers Harper. Captain E. M. Smith and First Lieutenant Glover commanded Company B with sixty men. Captain Geddes and First Lieutenant Joe Simmons commanded Company C with seventy men. Captain James Brown commanded Company D with sixty men. Company E, with fifty-two men, was commanded by Captain Mitchell, and Company G, with seventy-five men, was commanded by Captain V. S. Scott, First Lieutenant Albright, and Second Lieutenant T. H. Garner. The *Beaufort Republican* noted that "it was a gala day among the colored fraternity ... which brought hundreds of people into town and the display was very creditable."

During the speeches at the Stevens House, a letter from Brigadier General Robert Smalls to General Rufus Saxton was read, reminding the crowd that many of these South Carolina guardsmen were veterans of the 1st South Carolina Volunteers during the Civil War. According to the *Republican,* they "were present under the giant oaks and rejoiced that the year of the jubilee had come." Colonel Wiggins's speech noted that January 1 "is the anniversary of that great ... day that gave your race freedom ... human slavery shall no longer exist on American soil." Colonel Wiggin also asked the crowd to remember the fallen comrades of the regiments assembled there—"the dead heroes of Honey Hill, Wagner and Olustee."[36]

Throughout Reconstruction, the Fourth of July was a major celebration with parades, speeches, balls, and music. In 1872 the highlight of the occasion came when Robert Smalls's little daughter Lizzie, then thirteen years old, read the Declaration of Independence from the second story verandah of James M. Crofut's store on Bay Street. It was a remarkable and encouraging event because most of the adults in the audience could not read but they could see the possibilities for their children. Lizzie Smalls Bampfield would later go to Congress, where she served as her father's secretary. In 1876, in addition to the regular festivities, "the Union Band led by Mr. Macon Allen, Jr. serenaded Lt. Governor Richard Gleaves at his residence in Beaufort." It was the first notice of Beaufort's famous Allen Brass Band, which was to be a favorite feature of most lowcountry celebrations for generations and the constant herald for Robert Smalls on his many campaigns. In 1877 a notice for the July 4 celebration included a Grand Parade led by the Beaufort (Allen) Brass Band, a dress ball accompanied by the "string band from Savannah," and a demonstration by the Union Star Engine Company of Charleston. The visiting firemen were hosted by Beaufort's venerable black Union Number 1 Fire Engine Company, formed by Richard H. Gleaves in 1866 and composed of many of the African American civic leaders of Beaufort. Large crowds from the other islands were encouraged to attend the July 4 celebrations in Beaufort by the offer of half fares on the river ferries that were now operated under the jurisdiction of the Board of County Commissioners.[37]

During Reconstruction also, Beaufort began its famous Memorial Day celebrations for the Civil War dead. The focus of these ceremonies became the new Beaufort National Cemetery, where so many of the Union army's fallen were buried. It is the oldest national cemetery in South Carolina, and its dedication on May 31, 1877, inaugurated Memorial Day as a primarily African American celebration. It remains that to this day. In 1877 the highest-ranking officer in Beaufort was Rear Admiral Steven D. Trenchard, commanding the U.S. Navy Squadron in Port Royal Sound. Admiral Trenchard complimented Captain Niels Christenson, the designer and superintendent of the National Cemetery, for "his untiring, care in transforming the barren field of a few years ago into a most attractive spot lined with flourishing shade trees and choice and beautiful flowers."[38] During the Jim Crow years in the late nineteenth and early twentieth centuries, African American celebrations were notably constrained in many southern cities, and Memorial Day in Beaufort became a mecca for blacks from a large area of the South. Many of the traditional activities of Emancipation Day and the Fourth of July were later incorporated into it.

In Reconstruction Beaufort even impromptu political rallies attracted large crowds and were accompanied by boisterous festivities. In August 1874, during a busy campaign year, U.S. Senator J. J. Patterson visited Beaufort, seeking votes for the Republican Party. Robert Smalls and newspaper publisher A. G. Thomas hastily arranged a public meeting. The Beaufort Brass

Band provided entertainment, and abundant liquor provided enticement. A large crowd assembled, and Senator Patterson knew that the way to get votes in Beaufort County was to curry favor with sea island hero Robert Smalls. Patterson asserted that "when General Smalls was chattel, he was worth $500. When he ran the *Planter* into federal lines, they put a price of $4,000 on him. They never realized that he was worth his weight in *Gold!*" And the crowd, as they say, went wild. Bob Bythewood, a well-known ruffian in town, started a fight, as he often did at political rallies. And three men named Cohen, Morris, and Richards got drunk and ran their horse and buggy into a lamppost at high speed. Cohen was knocked unconscious and lost one eye.[39]

In the election of 1876, the state rejected Reconstruction and elected Confederate hero Wade Hampton as governor. While this had historic consequences for South Carolina, Beaufort and the sea islands remained apart as they had been since 1861. For another generation, Beaufort County remained a Republican stronghold in politics, a Yankee colony in economic terms, and with the U.S. Naval Station at Port Royal, a permanent beachhead for the Federal military establishment. One of the great, symbolic political celebrations of the era was the visit of the former president and Union commander Ulysses S. Grant to Beaufort on Emancipation Day 1880. President Grant was making a tour of the South on his way to visit Cuba. Throughout the South he was welcomed, even by former Confederate commanders, as the "American Caesar." For Beaufort on Emancipation Day, it was time for a great celebration.

Grant came directly from Augusta on the "down Train" of the new Port Royal and Augusta Railroad. In the railroad's 150-year history, Grant was its most famous passenger. Beaufort was alerted to the former president's arrival by a telegram from his son, Colonel Fred Grant, to Congressman Robert Smalls. A committee of local citizens was hastily arranged. They were the leaders of Reconstruction Beaufort. A Confederate veteran, Colonel William Elliott, headed the committee with another former Confederate, Colonel James M. Verdier, and Republican state senator J. W. Collins, a Union veteran, as escorts. Black postmaster P. E. Ezekiel, U.S. Customs Collector George Holmes, and Bay Street merchants George Waterhouse, Moritz Pollitzer, and George Gage completed the committee. The committee reflected Reconstruction Beaufort in that blacks and whites, Union and Confederate veterans, northern merchants and southern professionals, came together for the good of the community.

When President Grant arrived at the Beaufort depot, a crowd of nearly three thousand Beaufortonians greeted him. Virtually the whole town turned out. Two companies of Beaufort's famous Black National Guard formed the escort. General Robert Smalls led the Beaufort Light Infantry and Captain Joe Richardson led the Sumner Guards. A train of elegant carriages transported President Grant and his entourage, which included his wife, his son and aide, his Japanese valet, and General and Mrs. Philip Sheridan from the depot to the Sea Island Hotel. At the entrance to Beaufort, the committee had erected an evergreen arch for the party to pass under. Along the Bay Street bluff was stationed the venerable Beaufort Volunteer Artillery, commanded by Dr. Henry A. M. Stuart, a Confederate veteran, who welcomed the former president with a thirteen-gun salute. At the Sea Island Hotel, Beaufort's black intendant (mayor), Alfred Williams, offered "the hospitalities of the town." Commodore Thomas Pattison, commander of the naval station at Port Royal, and officers from the station's warships, in full-dress uniforms, formed a receiving line. General Grant then delivered the longest speech on his tour. It was five sentences: "It affords me great pleasure to be allowed the opportunity to visit Beaufort, though only for an hour. This locality occupies a conspicuous place in history. For the last twenty years it certainly has. The best qualities of the newly emancipated race developed here. I thank you for your hospitality and warm welcome." After pleasantries, the cavalcade of carriages returned to the railroad depot to see the former president off. It was a brief but auspicious occasion and one of the high points of Reconstruction Beaufort.[40]

Beaufort had much to celebrate during the Reconstruction years. The old town had been spared by the war. New citizens and new political leaders were providing regular deliveries of public largesse. New property owners and new merchants were transforming the local economy. Soon jobs and opportunity were abundant, and hope for the future seemed high. While much of the rest of South Carolina plotted and seethed under the yoke of Yankee occupation, Beaufort County celebrated one of the most prosperous times in its long history.

Chapter 20

Decades of Enterprise, 1873–1893

"The industries . . . have furnished the men with . . . higher wages"

One of the most beneficial and overlooked achievements of Reconstruction in South Carolina was the rapid growth of industry and commerce to complement the agricultural economy of the Old South. Railroads, textiles, mining, and shipping flourished following the Civil War. And surprisingly, Beaufort County was a leader in this kind of development. It was surprising because the old Beaufort District had been one of the most thoroughly rural and complacently agricultural districts in the state before the war. Surprising, too, because in the early decades of the twentieth century, Beaufort County reverted to an impoverished rural backwater. But for three decades following the Civil War, Beaufort County was one of the leading mining, timbering, and maritime centers in South Carolina.

The sea islands of Beaufort County had undergone a total political and economic revolution during the Civil War and Reconstruction. The old regime was almost totally replaced, and for three decades after the war, the county bore many characteristics of a colony—or, in modern language, an "enterprise zone"—for northern and foreign capitalists. Many capitalists stayed as long as profits were possible but drifted away when business slowed or greater profits beckoned elsewhere. Others, however, made their homes in Beaufort and remained through good times and bad to become the region's economic, civic, and, eventually, political leaders. Their descendants are the "old families" of modern Beaufort.

During these prosperous decades, the old cotton economy continued to flourish, benefiting farmers and merchants alike as it had before the war with predictably fluctuating good and bad years. Added to the old economy were several new and transforming enterprises. The greatest of these changes was the completion of the Port Royal and Augusta Railroad, the first permanent link between the sea islands and the mainland. The railroad opened up timber harvesting throughout the southernmost corner of the state. While the railroad was under construction, phosphate rock was discovered in local riverbeds, giving rise to the largest industry that Beaufort County has experienced in five centuries. Cotton, timber, phosphates, and the railroad combined to make Port Royal Sound the busiest deep-water port in South Carolina during the last decades of the nineteenth century.

A stroll down Beaufort's Bay Street in 1870 would have revealed the bustling optimism of Yankee commerce. The noise and clatter of twenty cotton-ginning machines, the shouts of ferrymen, draymen, jitney-cab men, and street vendors all fell silent as the shriek of the steam whistle signaled that the *Pilot Boy* from Charleston was rounding the Point. To the south the sky over Port Royal Sound was regularly punctuated by the black smoke of the steamer *Water Lily* coming straight up the Beaufort River from Savannah.

By 1870 several new merchants had established themselves on Bay Street. Many of these businesses lasted for generations. Moritz Pollitzer, an immigrant from Moravia in the old Austrian Empire, had established himself as a "factor, shipping and commission merchant" with a warehouse on Bay Street. In 1871 he owned the largest cotton-ginning house in Beaufort. Pollitzer probably accumulated the town's first great postwar fortune. George Waterhouse, a grocery and dry-goods merchant from Kennebunkport, Maine, started a store at the west end of Bay Street, where he sold "molasses, sugar, tobacco, tea, nails, dry goods, boots, shoes and wooden ware." At his mill behind the store he "manufactured hominy and meal." In 1866 Waterhouse married a Gideonite missionary teacher from upstate New York named Harriett Parmalee. By 1871 Waterhouse had built a dock and ginning house over the water behind his store. His partner in the cotton gin was George F. Ricker of Poland Springs, Maine. Both Pollitzer and Waterhouse had arrived before 1866 to seek their fortunes in the so-called New South. Pollitzer had financial backing from New York, and Waterhouse had commercial support from Boston. Before they died at the end of the century, both had established sizable business and real estate dynasties in Beaufort County.

Out on Pigeon Point, the whine of saws, the smell of resinous southern yellow pine, and steam-whistle screams could be heard from Colonel Duncan C. Wilson's Port Royal Sawmill, the largest business in Beaufort in 1870. Wilson was a native of Greenock, Scotland, who had come to Beaufort during the Civil War as chief carpenter for the military governor, General Rufus Saxton. He made Beaufort his home for forty years and became one of the town's most revered and civic-minded citizens.

Many other businesses lined Bay and Port Republic Streets. James and Alice O'Dell, bakers and confectioners, ran the bakery at "the free landing" at the head of Carteret Street. H. G. Ely sold marine, fire, and life insurance, while James Boyce ran the liquor store in the middle block of Bay Street. K. Hall was the town's watchmaker and jeweler. John Conant was the town butcher; later he operated a dairy between Beaufort and the new seaport town of Port Royal. In 1873 a photo gallery opened on Bay Street. The largest real estate agent was A. S. Davenport and the land surveyor, Edgar Nichols, was next door. The highest premium for real estate in 1870 was for land on or near the line of the Port Royal Railroad. Miss J. M. Lynch, the only female proprietor on Bay Street, ran a fancy goods store.

The professional community was the domain of a few prewar natives who had remained in Beaufort. Dr. Henry Middleton Stuart was the most prominent of this group. He was the town's chief physician, de facto coroner, and owner of the Bay Street apothecary. Colonel William Elliott, who advertised as an "Attorney-at-Law, and Solicitor in Equity," represented many old land claimants in Beaufort County Court before being elected to Congress and legislatively resolving the land issue in 1892. Dr. R. R. Sams, son of Dr. Berners Barnwell Sams of Datha Island, was the town dentist.

At the head of Bay Street, the old Barnwell Castle was the courthouse and office of George Gage, one of the Gideonites from Ohio. He was the son of the famous abolitionist Frances "Aunt Fanny" Gage. In 1870 Gage was Beaufort County surveyor. Later he operated a sawmill, Gage's Mill, on the site of the present Beaufort Memorial Hospital. Also at the courthouse was H. G. Judd, former Freedmen's Bureau agent and by 1870 Beaufort County clerk of court, registrar of deeds, and U.S. commissioner of conveyance.[1]

One of the busiest places in downtown Beaufort was the Sea Island Hotel, the former mansion of Nathaniel Heyward Jr. During the war it was owned by General Saxton, who used it as his residence and the headquarters. The mansion was the epicenter for all official visits and the meeting place for all the famous Union brass who passed through Beaufort. The building was converted to a commercial hotel in the late 1860s with M. M. Kingman and his wife as proprietors. Described as a "first class hotel," it offered all conveniences for business travelers. The Western Union telegraph office on the first floor offered instant communication to the mainland through wires strung along the new railroad right-of-way. The hotel boasted a livery stable, a bowling alley, and "an elegant billiard hall." Travelers described it as "the best kept hotel in South Carolina."

The hotel remained a central feature of town life well into the twentieth century. In 1873 a group of businessmen, led by designer and architect Paul Brodie, built a long pier with a pavilion and bathhouse on the river opposite the hotel; operated by the hotel, these facilities were a busy recreation site for three generations of Beaufortonians. In 1874 the hotel was closed, renovated, and expanded to include a large rear wing, dining hall, and ballroom. It reopened in 1876, owned by James and Alice O'Dell, who operated it for the next forty-three years. One New England guest described the Sea Island Hotel as "handsomely furnished and well kept. The rooms are large and airy, beds are clean. . . . the table is supplied by all the local markets . . . the waiters are attentive. It is, on the whole, a model hotel."[2] The local newspaper bragged that "the guest who cannot be satisfied at our hotel must be a misanthropical, dyspeptic, rheumatic wretch who had better stay home!"

By 1877 prosperity brought new and important businesses to Beaufort. Two German immigrants from Hanover, F. W. and E. A. Scheper, opened stores on Bay Street. F. W. Scheper opened a ship chandlery, a grocery store, and warehouse next to the ferry landing at the east end of Bay Street. E. A. Scheper operated the clothing and dry goods store next door. The property remained in the Scheper family until the 1970s. When the Freedmen's Savings Bank collapsed in scandal in 1873, William H. Lockwood opened a "Banking House" and gold exchange in the Freedmen's Bank building. Jacob Apple, an immigrant from Prussia, opened a clothing business on Bay Street. George Gage took over the insurance agency from Henry Ely, and John Franz took over the bakery from James and Alice O'Dell. S. Mayo's store sold "liquors, wines, fishline, cordage and net yarn." John Conant and J. A. Emmons opened an ice house and cold storage locker at the west end of Bay Street and delivered ice about the town. J. A. Whitman, "mechanical engineer," opened the Beaufort Machine Shop on Port Republic Street, and W. H. Calvert offered "tin, sheet iron, copper work and cooking ware" at his Bay Street store.[3]

By the end of the decade, more new businesses opened, and several established merchants expanded into new enterprises. The most important new businesses were those of Danish immigrant Captain Niels Christensen, who had come to Beaufort as an engineer and officer in the Union army. He was appointed the designer, architect, and superintendent of the Beaufort National Cemetery from 1870 to 1876. In 1876 he opened a lumber and hardware business at the corner of Bay and Carteret Streets, where he sold "doors, sashes, blinds, flooring, nails, bricks, palmetto logs and cypress shingles." In 1876 he opened the Christensen Real Estate agency to develop the rising real estate market. The Christensen lumber, hardware, and real estate businesses eventually became the most substantial enterprises in Beaufort. By 1900 Captain Christensen was the largest taxpayer in Beaufort County. In 1875 Christensen, like George Waterhouse, married a Gideonite missionary teacher, Abigail "Abby" Mandana Holmes of Massachusetts. His business success, combined with Abby Holmes Christensen's creative talent and high expectations for their children, produced Beaufort's most influential family of the next generation. Christensen Hardware operated on Bay Street until 1948, when it was sold to Angus Fordham. Another enduring establishment begun in 1873 was John Wallace and Charles E. Danner's clothing store on Bay Street. In 1879 Wallace and Danner advertised "shirts for $1.00" and other clothes and dry goods. Wallace and Danner remained in business on Bay Street until the 1970s.

While new enterprises began, established businesses added new stores and new lines of merchandise. By 1879 F. W. Scheper had opened a second grocery store, the new store at Tenth and Eighth Avenues in the new town of Port Royal. Scheper's store sold groceries, tobacco, meat, and canned goods. And George Waterhouse expanded his dry goods and grocery store to include a line of furniture, crockery, lamps, and glassware. In 1877 Waterhouse and Frank Ricker enlarged their wharf to "be the most commodious in town." Waterhouse was also half-owner of the Charleston packet, *Pilot Boy*. As a sign of the town's prosperity, expensive luxury items began to appear on Bay Street. In 1879 J. Baruch announced the "grand opening" of a store selling "pianos and organs" and other musical instruments, and Moritz Pollitzer advertised "a fine seven octave Steinway and Sons piano in perfect order."

Pianos were not the only luxury item that Moritz Pollitzer introduced to Beaufort. In 1872 he had delivered, direct from a New York boatyard, the "handsome yacht *Anna*," named for his wife. The *Anna* was the first true yacht in Beaufort. It was a thirty-two-foot gaff-rigged sloop with a thirteen-and-a-half-foot beam, and three feet of draft, perfect for the shallow waters of the sea islands. The *Anna* crowded on much canvas with a main sail, topsail, jib, and jib topsail. It had standing rigging of wire rope (new technology in the 1870s), a carved wooden steering wheel, a cabin "furnished in walnut and pine," and six skylights. The expensive yacht was "evidence of taste and liberality on the part of Mr. Pollitzer." Pollitzer was also generous. For years he entertained the extended families of Beaufort with picnics and moonlight excursions to Bay Point aboard the *Anna*. Thereafter, yachting became a regular recreation for Beaufort's commercial elite.[4]

The prosperity of the 1870s was so apparent that the *Beaufort Tribune and Port Royal Commercial* exclaimed, "We doubt there is a town in the state where ... so much building is going on as in Beaufort." In 1877 Dr. Hal Stuart, Colonel D. C. Wilson, John Wallace, and W.H. Lockwood were "all repairing or rebuilding large homes or stores." F. W. Scheper had almost completed his home next to the courthouse, described as "formerly an eyesore, now an ornamental residence divided into apartments for two families." Not only the white commercial elite but also black workers, artisans, merchants, and professionals were enlarging or building new homes all over town. Homes in the black community appeared "neat and tasteful with paint and blinds ... sure evidence of prosperity."

The building boom was so energetic that it appeared "the whole town is undergoing renovation ... the spirit of repair seems to be an epidemic." In 1877 the newspaper listed the building projects in just a few months of that year. The Schepers put a new addition on their store on Bay Street and built two new houses on Craven Street. D. C. Wilson converted the old Sams house on the Point into "an elegant mansion." George Holmes restored the George Parsons Elliott house and made "a fine residence." The Fuller mansion on the bay was "elegantly fitted and artistically painted" by John Wallace, while "Dr. Stuart, Mr. Pollitzer and Mr. Verdier all newly painted their homes." On Bay Street, Robert Smalls restored several buildings on the waterside opposite the post office. The Law Building was renovated and occupied by several lawyers, and the old Freedmen's Bank building was renovated and occupied by W. H. Lockwood's Bank.[5] Beaufort's prosperity was a consequence of industries that were transforming the county. For three decades, Beaufort was a model of New South economy.

COTTON

The late 1860s and the 1870s were good years for cotton producers. The Civil War had hampered the normal supply of fiber to the textile industries and pent-up industrial demand led to a minor boomlet in cotton. Not until the 1880s did the worldwide supply of cotton catch up with industrial demand. Thereafter, global stagnation and decline of cotton prices for the next half century had a profound effect on the history of Beaufort County. But for two decades following the war, cotton retained its position as the county's premier agricultural product. Many new black yeoman farmers made decent cash income producing a few bales of cotton each year, and some of Beaufort's new merchant elite grew rich on the cotton trade.

The economic reconstruction of Beaufort County after the Civil War saw energetic efforts to rebuild the agricultural enterprises that had made the Beaufort District rich and famous in the antebellum era. The radically altered social and economic realities of Reconstruction hampered the large-scale production of rice on the mainland, though a few Combahee River planters struggled to plant rice until shortly after the turn of the century. The social revolution also altered the production of sea island cotton. Cotton particularly lent itself to small-scale production, providing modest cash income for the black farmers on the sea islands to supplement their provisioning crops of corn and sweet potatoes. With long experience growing cotton, corn, and sweet potatoes, the freedmen continued to produce these crops and thereby dominated Beaufort County agriculture throughout the 1870s. The census of 1870 revealed that Beaufort County (Beaufort, St. Helena, St. Luke's, and Sheldon Townships) produced 1,258,650 pounds (2,700 bales) of cotton and 3,919,800 pounds (78,396 bushels) of sweet potatoes.

The agricultural base of Beaufort County's sea islands was dramatically altered by the revolutionary changes of the Civil War and Reconstruction. Most notably, the land was distributed much more widely. In 1860 the 209 individual planters who owned the land held an average of $9,223 worth of real estate per owner. By 1870 the number of individual landowners had increased to 1,233, and their individual real estate holdings were worth an average of $829. Most of these small landowners were freedmen. The social revolution saw Beaufort County shift, in the words of historian Hermine Munz Baumhofer, "from an aristocratic agrarian culture to a lower middle class culture."[6]

These black yeoman farmers produced a high volume of cotton throughout the 1870s. The quality of the once famous, long-staple sea island product, however, diminished in the freedmen's hands. The 1880 census recorded that the sea island section of Beaufort County produced slightly more cotton in 1880 than in 1870. In 1880 the district produced 2,740 bales (1,276,840 pounds) of cotton on 11,570 acres of cotton fields; in other words, it took 4.2 acres of sandy sea island soil to produce one bale (466 pounds) of cotton.

Overall, in 1880 Beaufort County contained 3,736 farms comprising 49,022 tilled acres with an average of 13.12 tilled acres per farm. The county's agricultural economy had been transformed into a society of small farmers. As the State Board of Agriculture reported in 1883, "Nowhere in the state, not even among the gardens on Charleston Neck, is the system of small culture so strikingly illustrated. The farmers usually own a cow, a mule or a horse, and the work stock is sufficiently numerous, though of very inferior quality. Farm fixtures are of the simplest and cheapest description. There is seldom any shelter for the stock, the cabin of the proprietor being generally the only house on the premises. The stock is fed on marsh grass, and is ... picketed out when not at work, to graze on such weeds as the fallow spontaneously produces. Plows are numerous enough, but the chief reliance is on the hoe, which for several generations was the only implement known to agriculturalists on this coast."[7]

These new independent farmers, however, had reaped several economic advantages during Reconstruction, according to the agriculture board. They had purchased their small farms on very favorable terms, often at "one-thirtieth or one-fiftieth of their value." They also benefited from high cotton prices during the Civil War and for several years thereafter: "They had the benefit of the famine prices of cotton during the war for their staple product." The biggest economic advantage for the new freedmen was the diversification of the Beaufort County economy: "Since the war, the industries connected with the working of phosphate rock ... have furnished the men with employment at higher wages than could be obtained elsewhere in the state." Sea islanders could also supplement their income by working as stevedores at the new seaport town of Port Royal: "The opening of the railway to Port Royal harbor [1873] has also made a demand for labor in loading and unloading vessels, at a better per diem than was obtainable."

With ownership of their own small farms, cotton prices still profitable, good wage-paying jobs in the phosphate and maritime industries, and the traditional natural bounty of the sea islands always available, the 1870s and

1880s represented the best of times for the black yeomanry of Beaufort County: "Fish, oysters and game abound, and poultry . . . chickens, ducks and turkeys do particularly well. This adds largely to the ease with which these people subsist. They live comfortably, happily and peacefully." In another sign of the radical transformation of the sea islands from the Old to the New South, the state survey noted the deliberate destruction of the old plantation houses on the sea islands: "All the larger houses and buildings about the old farmsteads have rotted down or been burned down and have been replaced by small cabins." The new yeoman farmers of the sea islands wanted as few reminders as possible of the old plantation regime.[7]

Many northern entrepreneurs settled in Beaufort County after the war specifically to pursue opportunities in the famous sea island cotton business. Some did very well. In 1871 ex–Union army cavalryman J.W. Collins sold forty thousand pounds of seed cotton to Moritz Pollitzer for ten thousand dollars, a small fortune in 1871. Pollitzer ginned the cotton at his Bay Street gin and sold it through New York brokers for more than thirty cents per pound, making a handsome profit for himself. Collins lived comfortably in Beaufort from his subsequent investments in local real estate and business ventures. Pollitzer made several such profitable transactions over the next twenty years and amassed a fortune. Likewise, George Waterhouse began as a grocer, bought a small, old cotton gin, and started to assemble a sizeable business conglomerate based on the cotton business.

In 1873 it was noted that Beaufort's increased ginning capacity and the great increase in shipping from the new seaport town of Port Royal had caused much more cotton to be processed, brokered and shipped from Beaufort and Port Royal than before the war. In 1870 four steam cotton gins, listed below by owner, were at work in downtown Beaufort.

Owner	Value/Horsepower	Vol. Cotton Ginned/ Value	Profit	Number Emp.
Moritz Pollitzer	$12,000/8hp	100,000 lbs./$8,500	$4,000	8
Silas Wallace	$8,000/8hp	90,000 lbs./$7,650	$3,600	4
H. M. Stuart	$4,300/10hp	100,000 lbs./$8,500	$4,000	6
George Waterhouse	$2,000/10hp	40,000 lbs./$3,400	$1,500	8

South Carolina State Archives, Ninth Census (1870); Beaufort County, Agricultural Schedule; *Beaufort Republican,* November 2, 1871, September 19, 1872, November 28, 1872, January 16, 1873.

In antebellum days, nearly the whole sea island cotton crop had been brokered and shipped through Charleston or Savannah. When the Port

Royal Railroad was completed in 1873, the cotton production of the whole southeastern corner of the state and even some of the Georgia crop passed through Beaufort and Port Royal. The cotton business was so brisk in Beaufort County in the 1870s that J. Rich and Company built the largest steam cotton press in the South at Port Royal in 1879.

All was not permanently rosy. During the 1870s the sea islands began to lose their monopoly on the production of long-staple cotton. A Beaufort newspaper in 1873 listed the new regions of the world where long-staple cotton was being grown. Algeria produced more long-staple cotton in that year than South Carolina, and as a colony of France, it became the favored fiber source for that nation's textile industry. William Elliott had opened the French market for sea island cotton at the Paris Exposition in 1855 when his cotton won a gold medal. Tahiti became a source for long-staple cotton when the British planted it there to replace the sea island source interrupted by the Civil War. Likewise, Fiji began growing long-staple cotton during the war from seeds transported from South Carolina. Fiji produced four thousand bales a year during the 1860s. In 1873 seven thousand bales of long-staple cotton were grown on the coast of Peru. The quality was so superior that British buyers paid the world's top price for Peruvian long-staple cotton that year.

The greatest competition came from Egypt. In 1873 Egyptians harvested fifteen thousand bales of "Galene" cotton in the Nile River delta. This new product (probably a very ancient one) only equaled the "medium and common" grades of sea island cotton quality, but its possibilities for expansion were enormous. As this global competition was increasing, British spinners began to complain about the uneven quality of sea island cotton produced after the war.[8] This was likely the consequence of many small producers replacing the large prewar plantations. Global competition and declining quality meant that the price of sea island cotton stagnated during the 1880s and began to decline in the 1890s.

THE PORT ROYAL RAILROAD

The major stimulus to the new prosperity of old Beaufort was the completion of the Port Royal Railroad on February 28, 1873. This was one of the most historic days in Beaufort County's long history. For the previous three centuries of settlement, the sea islands had been physically separated and isolated from the mainland. The Port Royal Railroad ended that isolation. The history of attempts to build a permanent link to the mainland goes far back into the antebellum era. In 1795, during the first sea island cotton boom, a group of Beaufort men formed the Port Republic Bridge Company to build a bridge across the Whale Branch River to the mainland. This had been the site of the crossing of the Port Royal Ferry since 1733. One hundred subscribers supported the project, but the bridge was never built. In 1805 the Bridge Company leased its rights to William Elliott and Francis Saltus. The following year Elliott became the sole proprietor with a fifty-year lease on the project. Elliott built causeways across the marshes at both ends of the crossing and maintained a rope ferry across the river. This was the only regular crossing to Port Royal Island for the rest of the antebellum era. In 1853 Beaufort's enterprising mayor, Edmund Rhett, paved all the streets in Beaufort with oyster shell and formed the Port Royal Road Company to pave the road to the Port Royal Ferry with shell. He then acquired the ferry rights from Elliott. For many years, before and after the Civil War, the Port Royal Road was known as the Shell Road.

In the 1850s railroad construction began to cross Beaufort District. The Charleston and Savannah Railroad was built between 1856 and 1860. In 1857 George Parsons Elliott of Beaufort and Richard J. Davant of Coosawhatchie incorporated the Port Royal Railroad. They held public meetings, sold company stock, and laid out a route. They had in fact graded part of the route and laid some rails before the war halted the project. But no trestles to Port Royal Island had been constructed and most of the route to Augusta remained forest.[9]

After the war commercial interests in Beaufort and Augusta grew interested in the project. D. C. Wilson led the Beaufort group. The real inspiration for the revival of the Port Royal Railroad project came from the northern businessman Stephen C. Millett, who had purchased property and started commercial activities in Beaufort during the war. At the first meeting in Beaufort in 1868, several participants recalled the "doubtful prospects." To many in Beaufort, the "proceedings were looked upon as almost farcical." But Millett would not be deterred; it was said that "his energy never tired, his hope never faltered." He personally surveyed the route and planned the railroad line after the war. When capital was obtained and construction began, Millett was the general superintendent. When the railroad opened in 1873, Millett was its first president.

The first obstacle for the railroad was to amass enough capital. War-ravaged South Carolina could barely feed itself, let alone risk capital on so expensive a project, but Stephen Millett had connections to the watchmaking firm of Robbins and Appleton of New York and Boston. The firm's principal partner, Daniel F. Appleton, was his uncle, his mother's brother. Family money and Stephen C. Millett's energy built the Port Royal Railroad.[10]

For the next five years, from 1868 to 1873, as work progressed along the line, excitement began to build. While the railroad was under construction, there were hundreds of good-paying jobs for local laborers. Millett paid fifteen dollars per month in wages and provided meals and camp accommodations for the workers. By 1871 the trestle connecting Port Royal Island to the mainland was completed, and the rails extended into the upper part of Beaufort, now Hampton County. On November 9, 1871, the railroad announced a "grand opening excursion" with "forty miles open for business." The special train left Port Royal at 9:30 A.M. and stopped at the new Beaufort depot at 10:00 A.M. With a few stops along the way, it arrived at the Yemassee Junction with the Charleston and Savannah Railroad at 12:10 P.M. From Yemassee, the train stopped at Ridge, Searsons, and Altmanus before arriving at the terminus fourteen miles north of Yemassee. The excursion was described as "a very pleasant affair ... with quite a number of ladies and gentlemen present" and marked by "good humor and good company." The rail line soon prompted connectors. In 1872 a new depot was erected at the Beaufort stop, two miles west of town, and a new Shell Road linked the depot to Bay Street. The new road was laid out and constructed with three thousand bushels of oyster shells under the supervision of Hermann Von Harten, R. S. Bennett, and George Waterhouse.

Hermann Von Harten was another recent immigrant from Germany, having come to Beaufort on the eve of the Civil War. His wife was E. A. Scheper's sister. H. H. Von Harten and his descendants were prominent in all aspects of Beaufort's maritime industries for many generations. When the shell road to the depot was constructed, the railroad opened a stage line that ran regularly from the depot to the Saxton House Hotel. In 1872 a group of Beaufort businessmen incorporated the Bull River Railroad, a spur of the Port Royal Railroad that connected the mainline to the new phosphate mining operations on Chisholm Island.

In March 1872 the Port Royal Railroad received an enormous capital boost when the Georgia Railroad endorsed Port Royal Railroad bonds for one million dollars. This allowed construction to progress rapidly and ensured profitable rail connections through Georgia into the Midwest. Rumors circulated of a connection to the Cincinnati Southern Railroad that would make Port Royal "the port of Ohio." The merger with the Georgia Railroad attracted the attention of the *New York Times,* which wondered about the future of Charleston once the shorter route to the superior harbor at Port Royal was complete. The *Times* predicted that Port Royal, not Charleston, would soon become "the chief cotton port."

In 1872 Stephen Millett was construction superintendent and president of the railroad and George Gage was the chief engineer. During 1872 the tracks were rapidly laid "with large gangs of men at work along the whole line of the road." When the rails arrived at "Dixie Station," the modern town of Varnville, the whole countryside turned out with "loud hurrahs" for the progress. The country crossroad, McBride's Store, became a large two-story brick building called the McBride-Peeples Building. Varnville town lots laid out along the railroad track rose 50 percent in value when the railroad arrived. By May fifty-one miles of track were finished, and the crews were laying ten miles of track per week. All along the route "great enthusiasm, optimism and rising prices " were apparent. In Beaufort the Sea Island Hotel was doubled in size, and "a buoyant, hopeful expression was seen on every face."

Progress on the railroad was so rapid that in May 1872, the crews ran out of iron rails and work had to stop briefly. During June 1872 eight ships arrived at Port Royal Harbor with thousands of tons of iron rails from New York, Norfolk, and Elizabeth, New Jersey. Work commenced at a rapid pace. By the end of that month, the railroad had passed out of Beaufort County and reached the country crossroads of Allendale in what was then Barnwell County.[11]

The story told in Allendale about the arrival of the railroad was that the rail line was to pass sixteen miles to the west of the old crossroads. But on a trip to visit her husband at the head of the line, Mrs. Millett's infant daughter became deathly ill with diphtheria. Major H. W. Richardson, a local landowner, carried the sick child to Allendale, where the skill of a country doctor, John W. Ogilvie, saved her life. In gratitude Stephen Millett rerouted the rail line eastward to pass through the present town of Allendale. On the Fourth of July 1872, the railroad reached Allendale with great patriotic fanfare. Hundreds of Beaufort citizens celebrated the Fourth by taking a train excursion to Allendale.[12] The town flourished and eventually became the seat of a new South Carolina county.

In November 1872 Daniel Appleton came to South Carolina to take a ride on his railroad. By then the lines had nearly reached the Savannah River at Beech Island, one hundred miles from its Atlantic terminus at Port Royal. Appleton and a large number of stockholders traveled the route at an average speed of thirty miles per hour. Observers commented on the effect of the railroad on the countryside: "The life infused into this country by the railroad is really wonderful. We saw more signs of energy and improvement in our three hour run from Yemassee than going from Charleston to Greenville." The investors were pleased. Receipts on the railroad had already reached twelve thousand dollars per month, and the line was not yet complete to Augusta. In December 1872 the last link in the Port Royal Railroad was nearly finished. The large masonry bridge across the Savannah River at Beech Island opened on January 10, 1873. On February 28, 1873, the last railroad spike was driven at the four-mile post south of Augusta.[13]

Great celebrations marked completion of the Port Royal Railroad. In Augusta a large crowd turned out for speeches and congratulations. A cannon boomed a salute of 110 rounds, one for each mile of track laid. The commentary in the *Augusta Chronicle and Sentinel* lamented only that George P. Elliott of Beaufort and R. J. Davant of Coosawhatchie, who had begun the project before the war, did not live to see it completed. Stephen C. Millet was recognized as the man most responsible for the railroad's success. On March 16, 1873, an "inspection train" full of excursionists from Beaufort led by Millett arrived in Augusta's Union Depot. All the locomotives at Augusta blew their whistles in an "engineers salute" to the opening of the new line. The salute was returned by the engineer of the first train, W. W. Lockwood. The first conductor was M. M. Hutson.

A regular passenger and freight schedule was immediately established. Each morning a locomotive with a train of passenger and freight cars left Port Royal headed for Augusta, and another train left Augusta headed for Port Royal. The trains passed at the halfway point near the present town of Brunson, where a siding and roundhouse were built. The 110-mile trip took most of the day as the trains arrived at their destinations by late afternoon. Two express freight trains ran at night. For the next fifty years, the trains of the Port Royal Railroad were a familiar sight to people along the line and the link of their rural neighborhoods to the outside world. Locals knew these trains simply as the "Up Train" and the "Down Train."[14]

The Port Royal Railroad had a profound effect on the whole southeast corner of the state. All the old towns in that region grew up along the railroad line; the economy was transformed; and two new counties were formed as a consequence. The towns along the railroad line were Port Royal, Burton, Seabrook, Sheldon, Yemassee, Early Branch, Almeda, Varnville, Hampton (originally Hoover's Station), Brunson, Fairfax, Allendale, Beldoc, Martin, Ellenton, Jackson, and Beech Island. The two new counties were Hampton and Allendale, and their county seats were on the Port Royal line. In northern Allendale County, two whistle-stop communities named Appleton and Millet honor the men who financed and built the railroad.[15]

As soon as the railroad was underway, grand dreams and ambitious schemes began to circulate around Beaufort County. Since the days of Pedro Menendez de Aviles in the sixteenth century, visionaries had imagined linking Port Royal Sound to the heart of the continent. To the enterprising Beaufort men of the 1870s, completion of the Port Royal Railroad offered the possibility of realizing those dreams. They could see the rail lines from Cincinnati and Knoxville opening the Ohio Valley to the Southeast, "stretching their iron arms to Port Royal." At the new town of Port Royal, they foresaw "a grand transportation depot . . . shipping iron, grain, lumber, cotton and etc." to Europe and South America. The railroad announced plans to build a steam cotton press at Port Royal to pack Georgia cotton and a grain elevator to store grain from Cincinnati and St. Louis. Port Royal, it was noted, was 280 miles closer to St. Louis than New York. Giving encouragement to the plan was the arrival at Port Royal of the first through shipment of grain from St. Louis on June 19, 1873. It was a carload of white corn consigned by St. Louis grain brokers, Marmaduke and Brown, to the Port Royal shipping firm of J. Rich, and Company. It was anticipated that European goods and European immigrants would use Port Royal as a gateway to the Midwest. Excitement grew when the new town became the corporate headquarters of the Port Royal Railroad. A railroad turntable and extensive machine shops for the locomotives and the rolling stock were built at Port Royal. M. G. W. Faber from Augusta was the master machinist of the local facilities. The *Beaufort Republican* predicted that "the Port Royal Railroad will become one of the most important in the South."[16]

In the fall of 1873, officials of the Port Royal Railroad attended the Chicago Railroad Convention. They met with the governors of Kentucky and North Carolina and the famous inventor and agricultural entrepreneur Cyrus McCormick of Illinois. Several delegates floated the idea of forming a Chicago and South Atlantic Railroad to end at Port Royal. The idea was much alive throughout the 1870s. In the spring of 1876, probably the largest business delegation ever to visit Beaufort County traveled to Port Royal by rail. Six hundred businessmen from fifteen cities and towns, including fifty members of the Chicago Board of Trade, traveled the rail lines from the Midwest to Port Royal. The group called itself the Port Royal Committee. A huge gala was planned at Port Royal with a sumptuous banquet at the Mansion House Hotel and rosette silk badges for all the participants. The Forrest City Brass Band was sent up from Savannah aboard the paddle wheeler *General Sedgwick*. The participants were to take the Port Royal pilot boat out into the sound to see the magnificent harbor. Unfortunately for the local planners, a railroad accident in Brunson delayed the delegation for ten hours, and the participants did not arrive until nearly midnight. In addition, the *General Sedgwick* ran aground in Calibogue Sound and the musicians never arrived. Many travelers switched at Yemassee and took trains to Savannah or Charleston. The local boosters were discouraged but not deterred.

In 1873 there was even talk of making Port Royal the eastern terminus of the Southern Pacific Railroad. The line was planned to run from California to Texas through Shreveport, Louisiana, Vicksburg, Jackson, and Meridian, Mississippi, Montgomery, Alabama, and Columbus, Macon, and Augusta, Georgia to Port Royal Harbor. The route was touted as the most direct overland route from the Pacific to the Atlantic, and Port Royal boosters claimed, "Foreign capitalists are standing ready to make Port Royal the Atlantic port of this great enterprise." In 1877 Colonel Tom Scott, known as the "Railroad King" and president of the Pennsylvania Railroad, and Philadelphia banker A. J. Drexel visited Port Royal to see what all the excitement was about.[17]

Throughout the 1870s business on the Port Royal Railroad was brisk, shipping cotton, timber, and occasionally grain to Europe and coal, iron, and guano from South America to southern and midwestern states. Passenger traffic was also growing. In 1877 the Port Royal Railroad began marketing its passenger line as the "Magnolia Route." Beginning in January 1877, the railroad planted magnolia trees at every mile marker along the line. Sleeping cars were added to the night trains at the request of businessmen. All the coaches were reupholstered and repainted to promote the Magnolia Route.[18]

At the terminus a brand new port city was laid out and developed. This was the origin of the town of Port Royal. Daniel F. Appleton bought up much of the real estate at the end of the railroad line. He had it surveyed and divided into town lots for resale. A month after train traffic commenced, the first auction of town lots occurred. The auctioneer for the occasion was James M. Croft, another new Bay Street merchant, whose family remained in Beaufort for generations. The lots sold rapidly at twenty dollars per front foot for lots twenty-five by one hundred feet in size. Forty lots sold the first day to business interests in Beaufort, Augusta, and all points in between. It was expected that "guano warehouses, wharves, coal depots, stores, storage houses and dwelling houses" would arise where cotton fields and oak groves had once stood. By the fall of 1873, the Bennett and McFall Company had built their steam-powered cotton press alongside the railroad line. Cotton brokers built a tramway so that cotton bales could be transported directly from press to the ships at the docks. The Bennett and McFall Company and Daniel Appleton both built brick office buildings at Port Royal. The largest building in the new town was the railroad machine shop managed by M. C. W. Faber. The *Augusta Chronicle and Sentinel* and nearly everyone in Beaufort County fully expected this all to be the start of a great enterprise and a grand new city. This would happen as soon as "the steam donkey lifts from the hold of the steamship to the boxcar the first cargo, or swings cotton bales from a railroad train to a ship's hold, or pours a continuous stream of western grain into the swept hull which rests upon the saltwater basin twenty-two feet deep."[19]

For all its promise and all the grand plans, the Port Royal Railroad never lived up to its potential. Bad luck struck the railroad in its first year of operation. The railroad had borrowed $2.5 million over the previous five years to build the line and had no income to make payments and the interest that was building daily to New York bankers. Six months after the railroad opened, New York financial markets collapsed in the Panic of 1873, which was caused by the Crédit Mobilier scandal of the Grant Administration, too-loose credit, and overspeculation in railroad construction. Eighty-nine railroads declared bankruptcy over the next year. One of them was the Port Royal Railroad. Saddled with a mountain of debt, the new line did not have a chance. The railroad could not pay the notes that were called in by their desperate financiers in New York and had to declare bankruptcy. In 1875 the railroad was placed in receivership. By 1877 Port Royal Railroad bonds were worth only thirty cents on the dollar.

The second blow to the railroad was the death of Stephen C. Millett in 1874. Millett had gone from Beaufort to the Taxpayers Convention in Columbia in February. There he contracted a "malarial poison," and despite receiving the best medical care in the capital, he died in forty-eight hours. He was only thirty-three years old. A draped car of the Port Royal Railroad returned his body to a somber Beaufort. Millett's funeral at St. Helena's Church brought out the whole town's business leadership as pallbearers. D. C. Wilson, Dr. H. M. Stuart, J. C. Mayo, George Waterhouse, George Gage, H. C. Judd, W. C. Bellows, and P. M. Whitman carried the casket while Reverend Dr. Joseph W. Walker read the eulogy. Across town flags flew at half-mast, the locomotives on the railroad were draped in mourning, and the whole community showed "a universal expression of sorrow."

D. C. Wilson was appointed receiver and president of the railroad by the bankruptcy court. Under his steady leadership, the trains kept running while the lawyers argued in court. In 1878, the company was reorganized under the Georgia Railroad and Banking Company. Thereafter, the company was known as the Port Royal and Augusta Railroad. For the next decade, suspicions lingered in Beaufort County that the railroad's controlling Georgia interests were diverting business and traffic to the Port of Savannah via the Central of Georgia Railroad. The South Carolinians exerted political pressure in the General Assembly, and in 1893 the legislature revoked the charter of the Port Royal and Augusta Railroad. In 1896 the railroad was reorganized again under South Carolina ownership. It merged with the old Charleston and Savannah Railroad and was renamed the Charleston and Western Carolina Line. The old Charleston and Western Carolina Line was a familiar institution to generations of Beaufortonians in the first half of the twentieth century.[20]

With financial troubles and unhappy investors, the new city of Port Royal never fulfilled early expectations. By 1877 Daniel F. Appleton publicly expressed annoyance at the lack of local support for his enterprises. One Port Royal Island property owner had sued the railroad for running the rail line across one-fourth of an acre of his ten-acre parcel without getting a right-of-way agreement. He brought suit despite the fact that the value of his property had increased substantially from its proximity to the railroad. The local newspaper complained of lack of development in the town of Port Royal: "Through bad management ... Port Royal has no charter ... and is still but a village" with only forty or fifty residents instead of four thousand or five thousand inhabitants. The paper claimed that landowners were overcharging for real estate and discouraging business development. This was too much for Appleton, who had already lost a bundle in his lowcountry enterprises. In a testy letter to the paper, he noted that despite never making a profit, he had built something in Port Royal every year while others had left their lots vacant. He was "now building cottages for the mechanics and their families who were employed at the machine shop of the railroad." He bristled at criticism from locals and reminded them that it was his public-spirited investments in building the railroad "which opened up Beaufort and Port Royal to the world." He wondered, "How large a reserve of enterprise and public spirit is required?" Appleton was particularly annoyed by the lawsuits. Perhaps, if the rail lines were taken up, the locals could "establish a line of stages to Yemassee." Appleton still owned most of the lots in Port Royal in 1885 when he sold all his property there to Edmund Flynn of New York for an $800 down payment on a $140,000 mortgage.[21]

TIMBER INDUSTRY

Despite the financial difficulties of the railroad company, the continued operation of the line encouraged new business across Beaufort County. The first business to expand rapidly along the railroad line was timber harvesting and lumber production. From 1865 to 1878 Beaufort County was one of the largest counties in South Carolina, and most of the mainland remained untapped forest. A few small sawmills had operated in the Beaufort District before the war, the largest being A. M. Speight's sawmill on the Coosawhatchie River. After the Civil War, timber harvesting and lumber production became one of the largest industries in the county.

Colonel Duncan C. Wilson was the first entrepreneur to capitalize on this opportunity. The lumber demands of the Union occupation army during the war and Wilson's regular contact with New York suppliers convinced him to stay in South Carolina to develop this untapped resource. After the war he constructed his Port Royal Sawmill on Pigeon Point. By 1870 it was the largest business in Beaufort. By 1871 Wilson had two three-masted lumber schooners making regular runs between Port Royal, New York, and Boston. Before the railroad opened the hinterland, logs were dragged out of the Coosawhatchie and Salkehatchie swamps and rafted down the rivers to the Port Royal Sawmill. Even after the railroad was completed, rafting remained the cheapest method of moving timber. Sometimes both transportation methods were used. In December 1871 a log train on the unfinished Port Royal Railroad dumped 4 million board feet of timber off the new railroad trestle and into the Whale Branch River. From there it was rafted to Savannah.

Business at Wilson's sawmill was brisk. In November 1871 the schooner *Farragut* sailed from Beaufort with 200,000 board feet of lumber for building cotton factories "down east," and the schooner *Altoona* took a cargo of lumber to Boston and returned with one hundred tons of iron rails for the railroad. In 1872 Wilson expanded the Port Royal Sawmill. The marsh in front of the mill was filled in, and the "made land" gave easy access to the water for timber carts. Today the city street heading from the Pidgeon Point Landing to the residential neighborhood nearby is called "Wilson Drive." New fences and new buildings to cover the machinery were constructed. A new planing machine and new shingle machine were added to the operation. All were driven by steam power. In September 1872 William Mason, superintendent of the mill, sawed 24,230 board feet of lumber in ten hours with a circular saw on yellow pine. In November 1872 John Rich and C. H. Wright formed a new company whose main business was to ship timber out of Port Royal. For many years J. Rich and Company was one of the principal shippers from the Port of Port Royal. In addition, John Rich married D. C. Wilson's eldest daughter.

With the profits from Beaufort's first big industry, D. C. Wilson bought the B. B. Sams mansion on Laurens Street. After extensive renovations he sold the house to James M. Crofut. In 1883 Wilson bought the old Cuthbert mansion on Bay Street. With its prominent location a block from the Sea Island Hotel and its grand view down the Beaufort River, Wilson's home became a necessary stop for all the business and political dignitaries who passed through Beaufort. When he died in 1903, a small park overlooking the Beaufort River, on land donated by George Waterhouse Jr., was named Wilson Park in his honor.[22]

When the Port Royal Railroad was completed, twenty sawmills started up along the rail line in upper Beaufort County within the year. Reuben G. Holmes of Massachusetts built a sawmill and planned a town on the railroad between Early Branch and Varnville. He named the new town after his little daughter Almeda. Holmes was a New England abolitionist missionary and father of Abby Holmes Christensen. Other sawmills included the Steinmeyer and Stokes mill at Early Branch and the Varn and Ward mill at Dixie Station, soon to be renamed Varnville.

The largest of these sawmills was the one begun at Hoover Station by Major William H. Mauldin. A Confederate veteran of Hampton's Legion, he had moved to the lowcountry from his home county of Pickens after the war. Mauldin's oldest daughter, Lillie, married J. C. Lightsey, one of the largest landowners in the district. To move timber from the Salkehatchie swamp to his sawmill, William Mauldin built the Hampton and Branchville Railroad and Lumber Company, the most important spur of the Port Royal Railroad. By 1891 there were twenty-five miles of track on the Hampton and Branchville line. W. H. Mauldin and Sons became the principal business in the region, and when the new county of Hampton was formed in 1878, Hoover Station became the county seat and was renamed Hampton. Mauldin was also the founder of the Bank of Hampton and the Hampton Cotton

Mill. Mauldin was a state senator and a founding trustee of Clemson College. When he died in 1900, he had carved a business empire from the forest of old Beaufort County.[23]

Mauldin's success with his branch line encouraged others in the region. In 1877 landowners to the west of the railroad line, in the old village of Lawtonville, planned to build a narrow-gauge railway to connect with the Port Royal Railroad. They called it the Lawtonville Narrow Gauge Railroad. Narrow-gauge railways were much cheaper to build and operate than standard railroads. The Lawtonville Narrow Gauge Railroad was intended to "open markets to vast forests" on the west side of the Coosawhatchie River.

From April 1872 to April 1873, eight sawmills along the Port Royal Railroad line shipped 12 million board feet of lumber on the railroad. In 1873 Mauldin's sawmill cut 250,000 board feet per month, and in June his mill received an order for 500,000 board feet of lumber for the "Spanish West Indies." On May 1, 1873, D.C. Wilson received an order from New York for 1 million railroad ties cut eight feet by seven inches by eight inches. As a consequence the Port Royal Railroad ordered new locomotives and new freight cars to handle the traffic, all reconditioned in the railroad machine shop at Port Royal. New wharves were built at Port Royal to handle the huge three- and four-masted lumber schooners. All of this prompted the *New York Times* to comment that Port Royal "has already become a great timber port."

The burgeoning timber industry encouraged further expansion. By 1877 a new sawmill was opened on Spanish Point just south of Beaufort. Atlantic Sawmills could load lumber onto oceangoing vessels directly from its own deepwater docks. Atlantic Sawmills soon became "the busiest place in the neighborhood," according to the local newspaper, which noted, "Three or four large vessels are constantly loading and the morning steam whistle gets us all up." In addition, George Gage built a sawmill on the bluff on the westside of the bay of the Beaufort River. Gage's Mill was on the current site of the Beaufort Memorial Hospital.

Many of the lumber shipments from Port Royal were for foreign markets. In January 1877, 300,000 board feet of lumber lay in the railroad yard at Port Royal awaiting transshipment to Great Britain. In April, W. H. Mauldin received an order for 1 million board feet of lumber for a European market. The same month, the Steinmeyer and Stokes' Sawmill at Early Branch was loading 450,000 board feet of lumber onto the bark *Moonbeam* bound for Amsterdam. It was the first shipment of lumber from Port Royal to Holland, and locals hoped it would "open a new market for our mills."[24]

Foreign capitalists began to look at Beaufort County timberlands as profitable investments. The largest of these purchases was that of H. B. Boddington and Company of Liverpool, England. In 1873 Boddington and Company bought up fifteen thousand acres between Grahamville and the Colleton

River on the south side of Beaufort County. They had huge plans. They wanted to build a canal from the Savannah River through the Great Swamp to the Colleton River. They expected a two-mile-per-hour downstream current in the canal and planned to use the Savannah River to tap the forests of north Georgia. They planned to build a lumber mill at Foote Point on the Colleton River with a production capacity of thirty thousand board feet per day. The site had deepwater access to Port Royal Sound and the Atlantic Ocean. The local agent for Boddington and Company was O. P. Law in Grahamville. The company employed local landowner W. J. Kirk to survey the canal.[25] This was the beginning of large-scale real estate purchases by major timber companies of the thinly inhabited Beaufort County lands between the Broad and Savannah Rivers. It was the beginning of a historical phenomenon that strongly affects the economies of Beaufort and Jasper Counties to this day.

PHOSPHATES, 1868–1890

The other major industry that contributed to the prosperity of Beaufort County in the decades following the Civil War was phosphate mining. From 1868 to 1890, South Carolina was the major source of phosphate rock in the United States. Of approximately 8 million tons of phosphate extracted from the South Carolina lowcountry in those two decades, 5 to 5.5 million tons were gathered from the river bottoms of Beaufort County. To this day it remains the largest mining industry in South Carolina history and the largest single industry that Beaufort County has experienced.

The existence of phosphate rock in the lowcountry had been known about as early as 1843, when Edmund Ruffin of Virginia made a geological survey of the state and reported on the phosphate deposits. After the war, the richness of the deposits was determined to be profitable, and the mining boom began. At first the mining companies were land-mining operations, which required buying or leasing real estate with marl beds beneath.

The phosphate boom in South Carolina began in 1867 when Dr. St. Julien Ravenel and Professor Francis S. Holmes of Charleston and Dr. N. A. Pratt of Georgia chemically tested a nodule of rock from the marl beds near the Ashley River in Charleston. The rock turned out to be 60 percent phosphate. Within a year, Holmes and Pratt had raised capital to begin a land-mining operation, and Ravenel had begun the Wando Fertilizer Company with some Charleston associates.

By 1870 it was discovered that huge deposits of phosphate rock lay exposed at the bottom of the tidal estuaries of the sea islands. With this discovery the state government stepped in to regulate and tax the riverbed deposits over which they had jurisdiction. This led to the act of March 1, 1870, whereby the Marine River Mining Company, an enterprise of Charleston entrepreneur George Walton Williams, was given exclusive rights to mine South Carolina rivers for a surety bond of fifty thousand dollars. He also agreed to pay the state a royalty of one dollar for every ton of rock extracted and offered liberal bribes to legislators who had to pass the act over Governor Scott's veto.[26]

The richest deposits of river rock in South Carolina were discovered in the Coosaw River in Beaufort County. In 1870 the Marine River Mining Company transferred its rights to mine the Coosaw riverbeds to the Coosaw Mining Company, which soon became the largest river phosphate mining company in the United States for twenty years. Robert Adger of Charleston, who obtained his principal financing from the old investment-banking firm of Alex Brown and Sons, Incorporated, of Baltimore, organized the Coosaw Mining Company.

The success of the Coosaw Mining Company spawned several more companies in Beaufort County. By 1878 there were nine separate river phosphate mining companies operating in the rivers and islands of Beaufort County: Coosaw Mining Company, South Carolina Phosphate and Phosphatic River Mining Company, Boatman's Mining Company, Beaufort Mining Company, Oak Point Company, Farmers Phosphate Company, Beaufort and Port Royal Phosphate Company, Sea Island (Chemical) Phosphate Company, and Port Royal Phosphate Company.

The ubiquitous D. C. Wilson, in addition to his lumber and railroad interests, founded the Sea Island Chemical Company. He and his son D. C. Wilson Jr. operated the Sea Island Chemical Company for more than a decade until it merged with the Coosaw Mining Company. Two sizeable land-mining companies operated in Beaufort County. The Pacific Guano Company purchased all of Chisholm Island and adjoining Palmetto Hall Plantation from Robert Chisholm, Edward Chisholm, Maxwell Chisholm, Louisa Chisholm, and Alice Chisholm Prioleau for seventy thousand dollars. This tract of approximately thirty-five hundred acres lay between the Coosaw and Bull Rivers in northern Beaufort County. It was adjacent to George S. Brown's land, where the Coosaw Mining Company had its processing factory, or "phosphate works." The Oak Point Mining Company also worked on the Bull River. The Williman Island Company was across the Bull River on Williman Island. The long, shallow trenches that scar Chisholm and Williman Islands to this day are still called "phosphate cuts" by local hunters.

When the phosphate boom in Beaufort County began in 1870, the method of mining was quite primitive, required little capital investment, and was easily conducted by unlicensed operators. Initially, individual divers would descend to the river bottoms with an iron basket on a rope without any diving equipment. The divers would load as much loose rock into the basket as possible before surfacing to catch their breath. This early method of "mining" was exhausting, sometimes dangerous, and inefficient, but it provided a ready source of cash income for thousands of black sea islanders for twenty years. Diving for rock also limited the depth from which river rock could be extracted to less than twenty feet.

The large mining companies soon began to invest in huge steam-powered floating dredges that could reach the richest deposits in the deepest rivers and extract phosphate rock by the ton. The first steam dredge in Beaufort County was operated by the Oak Point Mining Company on the Bull River. Campbell and Wylie, the British company that owned the Oak Point Mines, ordered the barge from Pregnal and Brothers of Brooklyn in 1872 and the iron machinery from Starbuck and Brothers foundry of Troy, New York. The "double timbered" barge measured eighty feet by twenty-eight feet. The crane weighed thirty-two thousand pounds. The rig employed four steam engines, two for hoisting the "dipper" and two for rotating and hoisting the crane. This leviathan was thought at the time to be "one of the largest dredging machines in the United States." By 1873 the dredge was lifting two hundred tons of crude rock per day from the river bottoms. The Coosaw Mining Company, with similar equipment, extracted three thousand tons of rock from Parrot Creek in less than a month.[27]

This was just the beginning. By the 1880s even the smaller operators were amassing enough capital to invest in steam-powered dredges. In 1886 the Farmers Phosphate Company, which had been "handpicking" phosphate from fifty small flats for a decade, ordered two floating steam dredges, the *Delaware* and the *Cresfield*. From the Farmers Company's phosphate works on Lucy Point Creek, workers hauled these barges into position with the steam tug *Stono*. The captain of the *Stono* and superintendent of the Farmers marine operations was George A. Crofut, son of Bay Street merchant James M. Crofut. By far the largest phosphate dredge ever to operate in Beaufort County waters was the *John Kennedy*, owned by the Phosphate Mining Company, Limited. The *John Kennedy* was 140 feet long, 38 feet in beam, and had a draft of 8 feet. It operated a "continuous chain" conveyor. It was so large that it required two large steam tugs to maneuver it, the 106-foot *Bristol* and the 70-foot *Kinkora*. These floating behemoths were surrounded by "lighters" and "flats" and often a steam-powered "washer barge" that used high-pressure hoses to clean the phosphate rock as it emerged from the briny rivers.[28]

With so many different companies in business, it was inevitable that disputes arose regarding river territories. In 1878, to resolve these disputes, the General Assembly revoked the charters of all the river mining companies in Beaufort County except the Coosaw Mining Company. To recover their charters, the other companies had to submit to tighter state regulations, put up surety bonds of fifty thousand dollars, and pay all back royalties owed to the state. This forced the elimination or consolidation of many small operators. By 1880 only four large phosphate mining companies were operating in Beaufort County: South Carolina Phosphate Company (Oak Point Mines), Pacific Guano Company, Coosaw Mining Company, and Farmers Phosphate Company.

Consolidation did not reduce production. In fact, the 1880s were the heyday of phosphate mining. Between 1880 and 1889, river phosphate rock production increased by 280 percent. In 1889 South Carolina mined 542,000 long tons of phosphate rock, fully 95 percent of the United States' domestic production. Eighty percent was extracted from the tidal rivers of northern Beaufort County and more than one half by the Coosaw Mining Company.[29] During the decade of the 1880s, the Coosaw Mining Company was the largest phosphate mining and production company in America.

At the peak of the phosphate boom in Beaufort County in 1886, J. A. Murray, the superintendent of the Farmers mines on Lady's Island, invited S. H. Rodgers, the editor and owner of the *Palmetto Post,* to tour the company's new works on Lucy Point Creek. Rodgers was impressed by the collection of large, busy, whitewashed buildings. The industrial complex was neatly kept, and the whole factory was surrounded by a white picket fence. Along Lucy Point Creek were three large wharves. Two wharves received the rock from the fleet of over fifty small flats and lighters that gathered around the steam dredges *Delaware* and *Cresfield,* which operated a few miles off Sam's Point in the Coosaw River. The third wharf loaded the processed phosphate onto oceangoing vessels to be shipped to markets around the world.

When the rock reached the works, it was off-loaded from the lighters, flats, and barges by a steam-powered conveyor and pumped onto cars on an elevated track. The cars then carried the rock to the massive brick drying kiln. The kiln was the heart of the works. It dried, or "burned," four hundred tons of rock on each charge, or "fire," and each charge took approximately eighteen hours to complete. The rock was top-loaded into the dome-shaped kiln from the elevated track. The kiln and track were housed in a gigantic wooden drying shed. Tons of firewood were placed on the floor of the kiln for each charge. When the fire burned out, relatively pure, clean phosphate was the residue. This dried phosphate was then transported by tram railway to a huge covered storage shed. There it awaited loading aboard cargo ships at the loading wharf. All the mechanical devices and tramways were driven by steam power. The storage shed held thirty-five hundred tons of phosphate. The phosphate was moved from the storage shed to the loading wharf on an iron rail tramway. At the time of Rodgers's visit in May 1886, "four vessels of 800 tons each" were loaded for overseas shipment. The Farmers phosphate works had cost more than seventy-five thousand dollars to construct.

The principal use of the processed phosphates was to make fertilizer. As a consequence, Charleston became the site of most of the nation's fertilizer production in the late nineteenth century. During the 1880s twelve fertilizer companies near Charleston utilized lowcountry phosphates. As more phosphate ore came from Beaufort County, it was natural that the fertilizer works would move there, too. In 1887 the Baldwin Fertilizer Company of Georgia built a large factory on Port Royal Island, halfway between Beaufort and Port Royal. The Baldwin Fertilizer plant had deepwater docks and ocean access. There were three large building complexes, a tall stack breaking the skyline, and an elevated railway to deliver the fertilizer directly to the ships' holds. The fertilizer plant was south of the Atlantic Sawmills on land purchased from William T. Seward and others in 1887. Unfortunately, the timing of the company's investment was poor, as the Beaufort County phosphate industry peaked in 1889 and declined thereafter.[30] Piles of old rock on the west shore of the Beaufort River are all that remain of one of the largest industrial sites ever built in Beaufort County.

The phosphate boom in Beaufort County had a huge effect on employment in the sea islands. For more than twenty years, the mining industry was the largest source of wage-earning jobs in the region, and by the standards of the time, they were good-paying jobs. Workers earned an average of one dollar per day. Virtually all these jobs went to the freedmen of the sea islands. When the mining companies began operating in Beaufort County, the local newspaper happily commented that "our colored friends will . . . not have to roam over the country next summer to look for work." The mining companies employed local labor not only to dive for rock but also to operate the dredges and washers, maneuver the flats and lighters, and crew on the tugs. The land-mining companies on Chisholm and Williman Islands employed hundreds of men in digging the shallow trenches or "cuts" to expose the marl beds below. Each of the phosphate works employed hundreds of men to operate the machinery and transport the rock. In addition, hundreds more men worked in the forests, cutting thousands of cords of firewood consumed each year by the drying kilns. For the twenty years of the phosphate boom in Beaufort County, there were wage-paying jobs for almost anyone willing to do the work. At the peak of its production in the 1880s, the Beaufort County phosphate industry employed between two thousand and thirty-five hundred men annually.[31]

The investors and managers of the mining companies had much to learn about the idiosyncrasies of sea island labor. In Beaufort County, virtually the entire workforce was African American, most of whom had grown up in slavery. Many laborers owned their own land, and therefore their mining jobs were not their only, or even their primary, interest. The sea islanders resisted the customary management of labor in industry. Most industries organized labor in gangs and geared wages to time worked. This did not suit the sea island labor force, which was accustomed to working the familiar plantation tasks. Eventually, phosphate managers adopted the "task system" for their mining operations in Beaufort County. In land mining a daily task was to dig a fifteen-by-six-foot pit and the worker was paid twenty-five cents to thirty five-cents per vertical foot excavated. Under this task system, it was the amount of work a man did that determined his pay, not the time spent or the volume of rock produced. To the sea islanders, the principal advantage of the "task system" in the phosphate industry was the same as it had been on the plantation. It allowed the laborer to control his time. He could work faster and complete his task earlier, leaving the remainder of the day for his other chores, responsibilities, or pleasures. Sometimes, the laborers would complete multiple tasks in a day and not show up for work for several days in a row. In addition, phosphate operators faced high absenteeism during the hunting, fishing, planting, and harvesting seasons. These unique sea island labor habits made it difficult for the managers to control the pace of production, but it was the only way that local labor would work. An 1883 U.S. Geological Survey report on the industry complained that the work habits of the sea islanders "prevent his co-operating in working gangs under contract which would tend to improve his condition."[32]

Beaufort County freedmen knew very well what would improve their condition. It was not wage dependency on fickle employers but the personal freedom and independence of controlling their own time. The wisdom of their communities taught them that time was more valuable than money. Money could be earned and wealth could be measured in many ways, but each man's time was a finite commodity and therefore of value that could not be calculated in economic terms. To the ex-slaves of the sea islands, their most treasured value was personal freedom for which generations had prayed, fought, and died. And at its most basic definition, personal freedom required that a man be master of his own time. Hence, sea island freedmen willingly sacrificed the little additional wages that might result from "co-operating in working gangs under a contract" for the far more important value of personal freedom and independence.

In 1963 the *Charleston News and Courier* visited Chisholm Island, site of the Pacific Guano Company's mining operations, and interviewed the landowners, Daniel and Margaret Witsell Lesesne. Margaret Lesesne had grown up on Chisholm Island surrounded by the vestiges of the phosphate industry. The old company store stood overgrown with wisteria. The foundations of the kiln and drying shed were covered by brush and weeds. The farm-to-county road was built on the cinder bed of the narrow-gauge railway that hauled the rock, and the banks of Bull River were still strewn with pilings from the old docks. Dan and Margaret's home had been the headquarters of the phosphate company. The phosphate cuts had filled with fresh water, returned to the jungle, and become infested with snakes and alligators.

One of the phosphate workers, Ed "Dog" Heyward, was nearly ninety years old and living near the cuts. He remembered vividly working for the Pacific Guano Company: "I got a $1 a day working on the dredge ... but them boys that work in the cut, they had the hard work. They get in with the pick and cut and cut and sometimes them boys fill that thing so fast it scares you. They get ten cents a bucket. Man, some of them boys make $3, $4, a day."[33] Fast work earned those men more than money; it earned them time.

The phosphate-mining boom in Beaufort County peaked in 1889. Thereafter, politics, economics, and natural disasters combined to send the industry into rapid decline. The last Beaufort County phosphate company, the Virginia-Carolina Chemical Company, ceased operations in 1914.

BEAUFORT'S NOTORIOUS SPECULATOR

Every community with a rapidly expanding economy will attract its share of hucksters, schemers, and frauds, and Beaufort in the 1870s and 1880s was no different. The most spectacular business fraud of the time was the scheme of a mysterious Frenchman named Peter Papin, who appeared in Beaufort in 1873 shortly after the completion of the railroad. His first scheme was to make Port Royal a major port for European immigration. He formed the "Co-operative Colonization Society of Port Royal" and enlisted the partnership of Rueben G. Holmes. Holmes laid out the town of Almeda on the railroad line between Early Branch and Varnville. The two proposed to sell lots to the immigrants while Holmes's lumber business would build small frame houses for them. The immigrants would provide labor for Holmes's lumber operations. It was hoped that Papin and Holmes's immigrant scheme at Almeda would be the phalanx of "an extensive movement of southern Europeans to the South."[34]

In September 1873 Papin and Holmes expanded their ambitions and changed the name of their enterprise to the Port Royal Direct Trade and Colonization Society. They also took in a high-profile partner from the antebellum lowcountry, General Ambrosio Gonzales, a Confederate veteran and son-in-law of William Elliott III. Gonzales traveled to Liverpool, England, where he arranged passage for fifteen Italian families. By November these immigrants had been bilked of their meager savings by Papin and cast adrift in the pine forests of Beaufort (now Hampton) County by Reuben Holmes. There were no homes, no jobs, and no money. By December they were starving. The plight of these immigrants was well known in Beaufort and reached the ears of the Italian consul in New York, Segnior Grandi, who traveled to Port Royal at Christmas to check on his countrymen and found twenty-three immigrants without food, shelter, or tools. Papin had taken fifteen dollars from each of them, most of what they had, and although he offered to repay it, never did. Holmes was bankrupt and failed to build even one house at Almeda. The fraud ruined the reputations of Holmes and Gonzales but only seemed to enlarge the ambitions of Peter Papin.[35]

Papin next tried to claim all the marshland in front of Port Royal by "adverse possession." He planned to pay the state fifty cents per acre for the marshland and then fill it in to build docks and warehouses. Papin's scheme gave rise to lawsuits from adjoining property owners. These suits went all the way to the South Carolina Supreme Court, which declared Papin's deeds to the marsh "trespass" and established the right of the adjoining property owners to the waterfront.[36] Undeterred, Papin's next scheme was the grandest of all. He returned from Europe claiming to have convinced a group of English investors to put up the astonishing sum of $10 million to build a grand new port city at Foot Point on the Colleton River. To advance his plan, he incorporated the South Carolina Land and Improvement Company. Representative Leroy W. Youmans of Barnwell County, champion of the landowners of the upper district, introduced the legislation to incorporate Papin's companies. Papin also formed the Port Royal Real Estate and Improvement Company and the Port Royal Harbor and General Shipping Company. The South Carolina Land and Improvement Company bought up vast tracts of land in Beaufort County, including Spring Island, Oak Forest, Camp Forest, and Trembledon Plantations on the Colleton River.

Papin aimed to build a "City of the Future" at Foot Point, connect it by rail to the Savannah and Charleston Railroad, and extend the rails west through Millen and Macon, Georgia. He claimed to have a charter to build the South Atlantic Railroad, the last leg of the Southern Pacific Railroad. The Colleton River site had twenty-one feet of water at low tide and direct access to the ocean. Charleston and Savannah could boast only thirteen and seventeen feet in their harbor channels. The "City of the Future" was closer to Europe than the Gulf of Mexico ports and warmer than the northeastern ports. Papin pointed out that Port Royal Sound was the deepest harbor in the one thousand miles of coastline between the Chesapeake Bay and Key West.[37]

Papin convinced some very influential businessmen to join his scheme. Colonel William Johnson of Charlotte, Atlanta railroad financier J. P. Southern, and General Richard Anderson, the highest-ranking Confederate veteran in South Carolina, were on the board of directors of Papin's corporation. To curry favor with the new Democratic power structure in South Carolina, Papin named his "new metropolis of the South" Hampton City after the state's new governor.

This was too much for the Beaufort business community, where Papin had been well known for several years as a "notorious speculator." The local community dispatched a delegation of its most influential and persuasive citizens to Columbia to "look after the interests of the people regarding the schemes of the infamous Papin." Industrialist Duncan C. Wilson, merchant George Waterhouse, and lawyer William Elliott rode the train to the capital and enlightened the new Democratic administration about Papin. By the end of May 1877, Papin was securely lodged in a Columbia jail for attempting to bribe the legislators.[38] The Beaufort delegation to Columbia in 1877 was significant because it united immigrants, northerners, and southerners for the greater good of the whole community.

But the memory of Peter Papin's grand deceits lingered for many years to plague the reputation of Port Royal. The *Charleston News and Courier* brought it up in 1885 to remind its smaller rival not to let its ambitious plans get out of control.[39] Yet, despite occasional setbacks, disappointments, and scoundrels, the period from 1873 to 1893 was one of the most enterprising and prosperous eras in Beaufort's five-hundred-year history.

Chapter 21

Beaufort County's Maritime Golden Age

"Vessels of all nations may repair to Port Royal without fear!"

The economic boom of the 1870s and 1880s, brought on by cotton, timber, phosphates, and the Port Royal Railroad, created the busiest period of maritime activity in Beaufort County's long history. A visitor to the rivers, bays, and docks of Beaufort County in the 1870s would have been astonished at the volume of shipping activity in any given week.

The second week of September 1873 was typical. Three large coasting schooners lay at the docks at Port Royal with a fourth due in during the week. The schooner *H. G. Ireland* arrived from New York with a mixed cargo for rail shipment across the South. A cotton press manufactured in New York, along with 5 bales of bagging, was to be shipped on the Port Royal Railroad to Atlanta. Fifty bales of cotton bagging were destined for Macon and 20 bales for Augusta. Twenty barrels of crackers were for George Waterhouse's Bay Street grocery store and 3 crates of furniture were for J. Brodie's Bay Street furniture store. J. Rich and Company at Port Royal ordered 102 bales of hay to pack ice. In addition, the *H. G. Ireland* delivered 120 kegs of nails for Augusta, 45 barrels of sugar for Macon, and 5 barrels of oil for the Georgia Railroad. The schooner *Fannie Keating* from New York had docked with 1,300 sacks of salt for Miller, Bysell, and Burnum of Augusta and 2,000 sacks of salt for Walton and Clark in Atlanta. At the next pier lay the schooner *Jennie Murphy* loaded with 145,000 board feet of lumber from Mauldin's Mill in Hampton for shipment to New York. The schooner *Montana* had cleared Boston for Port Royal and was due in a few days with 5,500 bags of fertilizer for Augusta.

At the north end of the county, three more large sailing vessels lay in the Bull River waiting to load with phosphate from the Pacific Guano Company works on Summerhouse Point. The *Isabella Jewett* was loading phosphate for Woods Hole, Massachusetts, as was the Brig *George Harris* for the same port. Woods Hole on Cape Cod was the headquarters of the Pacific Guano Company. The three-masted schooner *J. J. More* was loading phosphate for Green Point, Long Island. Word had just reached the St. Helena pilot station on Buzzard Island that the large British bark *Trident* was forty-six days out of Rio de Janeiro headed for St. Helena Sound to load with phosphate for England.

The pace of shipping at Port Royal Sound quickened throughout the 1870s. During the first week of January 1877, nine large sailing vessels passed through the port. The *A. G. Bentley* and *Daniel Britain* were both at the Port Royal docks loading with lumber for Baltimore. The *C. F. Hyer* was at the same dock loading lumber for New York. The large British bark *Kate* was unloading machinery manufactured in Middleborough, England, to be shipped via the Port Royal Railroad to South Pittsburgh, Tennessee.

During the 1870s Port Royal Harbor became a major transshipment point for guano, the fertilizer made from the droppings of sea birds, high in nitrogen, and helpful to the leached-out cotton fields of the American South. During 1876 alone, twelve thousand tons of guano, most of it collected from South America and the North Atlantic, were shipped through the Port of Port Royal. The railroad company constructed several more sheds to store the guano. Large amounts of guano in hot weather produce a foul odor, of which residents and visitors to Port Royal often complained; but guano fertilizer was big business in the nineteenth century, and Port Royal remained one of its chief entry ports for twenty years. In 1877 the railroad company added two new steam cranes to the docks and extended the pier up Battery River to accommodate the increase in guano importation. The local newspaper noted, "Port Royal might properly be called the 'Guano Port!'" In January four ships were unloading guano for southeastern agricultural markets: the *Edward Doran* from South America; the *Olive Crosby* from Nevassa, West Indies; the *Mair and Cranmer* from Philadelphia; and the *J. H. Wolf* from Boston. The long-shore routine of loading and unloading at the Port Royal docks was broken when the large ship *Harvey Mills* caught on fire at the dock. It was cut loose and anchored away from the wharf; the fire smoldered in the hold for several days before dying out.

The busiest time of the year for port activity was the late fall. By the end of the year, the cotton crop had been harvested and processed for shipment. Loose bags of sea island cotton and thousands of bales of upcountry short-staple cotton gathered at the Port Royal docks awaited shipment to northern or European mills. During the 1870s Port Royal became one of the leading ports on the Atlantic seaboard for the export of "seed cotton," or raw, unginned cotton. To enhance Port Royal's utility as a cotton port, the railroad company built one of the largest steam cotton presses in the United States at the docks in 1876. By December 1877 the cotton press, the railroad, and the docks were all working overtime.

During the last week of December 1877, nine large sailing vessels and three steamships were at the Port Royal docks loading with cotton and lumber. The Port Royal Railroad delivered 1,462 bales of upland cotton in that week alone. The full-rigged ship *Alexander* lay at the dock with 1,300 bales already loaded while the ship *Marcia Greenup*, of 1,250 tons displacement, awaited her berth. Five more schooners lay in the sound awaiting their cargoes. In addition, the *Katie L. Gifford* and *Elizabeth McCabe* from Baltimore lay at the next dock unloading 12,100 sacks of guano for railroad shipment. By 1877 new oceangoing steamships were making Port Royal a regular stop. In December 1877 the SS *City of Austin* left for New York with 642 bales of cotton, leaving 1,800 bales on the dock. The SS *City of Dallas* arrived from New York and unloaded ten railroad cars full of jute for shipment to St. Louis, Missouri. At the adjoining guano dock, the steamer SS *Calvert* was unloading 5,500 bags of "very odorous guano." The local newspaper exulted at the bustling commerce at the Port Royal docks: "The wharves are crowded with cotton and naval stores. . . . the Port Royal Railroad needs another wharf for deliveries."[1]

In addition to oceanic maritime shipping, the rivers and estuaries of the inland waterway were busy highways of commerce. Throughout the nineteenth century, Beaufort and the sea islands had been regularly served by steam paddle-wheelers plying the inland waterways. The first steamship to appear in Beaufort had been the SS *Charleston* on December 13, 1817. Thereafter, paddle-wheel steamers were the principal connection of the sea islands to the mainland until the completion of the Port Royal Railroad in 1873. Even after the railroad completed the first bridge to the mainland, steamboats provided regular service to Charleston and Savannah well into the twentieth century. Following the Civil War, two paddle wheelers became regular visitors to Beaufort and Port Royal. For thirty years the *Pilot Boy* served the sea islands. It ran through the sea islands twice a week from Charleston to Savannah with Beaufort as its midway stop. The vessel left Charleston at 8:00 A.M. every Sunday and Thursday morning and left Savannah every Monday and Friday at 2:00 P.M. Most Sunday, Monday, Thursday, and Friday nights, the *Pilot Boy* was laid over in Beaufort, usually at George Waterhouse's dock. Waterhouse owned 50 percent of the stock in the Charleston steamboat company that owned the *Pilot Boy*. In 1870 Allard Barnwell was the Beaufort agent for the *Pilot Boy*, a position held by William Harrison in 1872. The ship's Charleston agent was the firm of Ravenel and Holmes, and in Savannah, the agent was Jonathan Robinson. The *Pilot Boy* had some overnight accommodations but mostly carried freight and walk-on passengers. During the fall the decks were piled high with bags and bales of sea island cotton. Regular stops for the *Pilot Boy* were John's Island, Edisto Island, Sams Point on Lady's Island, Beaufort, Port Royal, Hilton Head, Daufuskie, and Savannah.

The other paddle wheeler that regularly served Beaufort and Port Royal was the *Water Lily*, which ran from Savannah to Bluffton, Hilton Head, Port

Royal, and Beaufort and back. It left Beaufort every Tuesday morning at 10:30 A.M. and made the round trip twice per week. Captain James Ferguson was master, and Erastus Hubbard was the ship's agent in Beaufort.[2] In 1871 a third steamer began regular runs from Savannah to Charleston with Beaufort as the midway stop. The *San Antonio* was commanded by Captain W. H. Lee. The agent in Savannah was F. M. Myrell and in Charleston was Ravenel and Company. The Beaufort agent for the *San Antonio* was Moritz Pollitzer. Passage to Savannah was one dollar per person.[3]

Throughout the late nineteenth century, river steamboats competed successfully with the railroad because of lower operating costs and cheaper freight rates. In 1877 a steamboat line opened that ran almost parallel to the line of the Port Royal Railroad. The *Howard Drake* ran once a week down the Broad River from Coosawhatchie to Beaufort and Charleston and then returned. In 1889, 598,000 tons of cargo worth $2,950,000 was transported on the inland waterways of Beaufort County.[4]

By the 1880s local pressure began to build on the U.S. Army Corps of Engineers, the agency responsible for inland and river navigation, to dredge and deepen the rivers, creeks, and "cuts" of Beaufort County to facilitate this traffic. This was the beginning of the Atlantic Intracoastal Waterway through the sea islands. The paddle-wheel steamboats were excellent craft for the shallow inland waterways. They were mostly large, flat-bottomed barges driven by large stern or side paddle wheels that barely dipped the water to propel the vessels. The *Pilot Boy* was a 329-ton ship that required little more than five feet of water to float it. Even with that draft, there were mud bars the *Pilot Boy* could not pass at low tide. The most troublesome inland waterway obstruction in Beaufort County was Brickyard Creek, which connected the Coosaw River and St. Helena Sound with the Beaufort River and Port Royal Sound. In the 1880s Brickyard Creek went practically dry at low tide, and even the shallowest-draft paddle wheelers had to wait for the tide to get through. The much deeper phosphate dredges and tugs could only get through Brickyard Creek at the top of the tide a few hours each day. In 1889 Beaufort's new Democratic congressman, William Elliott, began to lobby the Corps of Engineers to dredge the creek. To bolster his case, Congressman Elliott asked all the principal users of the waterway to describe the tonnage and type of vessels they employed and the number of trips they made through Brickyard Creek each year. Their reports constitute a fair summary of Beaufort County inland waterway traffic in 1889.

D. C. Wilson Jr. reported that the Sea Island Chemical Company employed the 62-ton steam tug *Reliance* to tow two 90-ton lighters, five 200-ton washer barges, and one 466-ton dredge through the creek daily. According to Francis Brotherhood, the Phosphate Mining Company Limited employed the 106-foot tug *Bristol* and the 70-foot tug *Kinkora* to tow the massive dredge *John Kennedy* around the rivers of Beaufort County. The *Bristol* drew ten feet six inches of water, and the *Kinkora* drew nine feet six inches of water. These vessels could only pass Brickyard Creek at high water. George Waterhouse estimated that the *Pilot Boy* would make 120 trips through the waterway each year. The cumulative tonnage was 39,480 tons, and the cargo was worth approximately $120,000 per year. A St. Helena Island planter, J. J. Dale, reported that his 31-ton cargo schooner, *C. A. Raymond,* made approximately one hundred trips annually, transporting cotton and produce worth about $100,000. And F. W. Scheper, who owned the property adjacent to Brickyard Creek, estimated the total tonnage passing Brickyard Creek to be 325,000 tons per year, carrying cargo valued at approximately $2,250,000.[5]

From the end of the Civil War to the mid-1920s, the paddle-wheel steamboats were regular sights on the bays and rivers of the sea islands. With throbbing steam pistons, clanking iron drive rods, and paddle wheels thrashing the water into white foam, the riverboats were welcome interruptions to the pastoral monotony of the islands. When the steam whistles announced the arrival of one of the regular packet boats, young boys from all over Beaufort, Port Royal, Bluffton, or any of the other landings along the route scrambled down to the docks to see what passengers and freight were arriving.

Another popular entertainment of the era was chartered "excursions," or floating parties. When the riverboats became too old or too slow for the regular packet runs, they were often employed for private parties. By 1877 a new model had replaced the original *Pilot Boy,* and the old boat was used for charter service. On July 5, 1877, the old *Pilot Boy* took a large group of Beaufort people on an evening excursion to Forrest City, Georgia. The moonlight cruise left Beaufort before dark and arrived at Forrest City at 1:00 A.M. Beaufort entrepreneurs Matt Clancy and Silas Wallace arranged the party, chartered the vessel, and made a handsome profit "on their first attempt at excursions." Two weeks later the Beaufort black community chartered the *Allison* and the *Cumberland* to take a large party to Savannah for the evening; it returned the next day with a large party of Savannah folks to spend the day in Beaufort. By 1877 the railroad had teamed up with the steamboat companies to offer combined excursions to upcountry people. On August 16, 1877, a large party from Augusta came down the railroad to Port Royal and embarked for "a trip down the Bay on the steamer *Allison.*" The success of these ventures prompted some Beaufort businessmen to plan an ocean excursion to New York City aboard the *City of Dallas.*[6]

Not just inland waterway commerce filled the rivers and bays of Beaufort County. Port Royal also became a regular stop for the coastal commerce of the Atlantic seaboard. Even before the railroad was completed, several shipping companies that employed sailing vessels began regular service between Port Royal Sound and the northeastern ports. In 1871 D. C. Wilson had two three-masted schooners making regular runs between Port Royal and New York; the *Farragut* and the *Altoona* were regular sights in the Beaufort River. On trips north they carried lumber from Wilson's Port Royal sawmill. On the voyages south, they delivered mixed cargoes for Beaufort or the railroad. In 1873 the Phoenix Line began running regular schooners between Port Royal and Philadelphia. The first Phoenix Line ship to appear in Port Royal was the schooner *Lena Reed,* which delivered a mixed cargo for the railroad and returned to Philadelphia loaded with lumber from Reuben Holmes's sawmill at Almeda. Well into the twentieth century, large sailing schooners were the primary means of transporting lumber out of Port Royal Harbor. In 1873 the Port Royal Railroad built a separate dock on Battery Creek especially for the lumber schooners. In November 1877 the three-masted schooner *Lucy Wheatly* cleared Port Royal for New York with 16,159 cubic feet of uncut timber and 195,000 board feet of lumber from Reuben Holmes's mill. Square-rigged ships were still most common for the transatlantic trade. In August 1877 the British bark *Gordon* took on a load of lumber from the Atlantic sawmills for the return trip to England. Occasional curiosities accompanied the sailing lumber trade from Port Royal Sound. In October 1877 the "oldest ship afloat . . . arrived at the lumber dock of Boddington and Company on the Colleton River." The brig *Derwent,* believed to have been built in 1776, had been in service for a century and was sound enough for ocean passages. The captain, Robert Wilkerson, was proud of his floating museum.[7]

What made the decades at the end of the nineteenth century unique in Port Royal Sound was the addition to the busy sailing trade of deep-draft oceangoing steamships. This new technology appeared before the Civil War. During the 1850s the United States Navy constructed a number of screw-propelled warships, including the massive steam frigate *Wabash,* which served as the South Atlantic Squadron's flagship. Port Royal Sound was the only anchorage south of Hampton Roads that the deep-drafted *Wabash* could enter.

After the war the screw propeller transformed ocean steamships, and by the 1870s they soon dominated the merchant fleets of the world. Screw propellers were entirely submerged and therefore a much more efficient means of propulsion than paddle wheels, which lifted out of the water in ocean swells and were easily damaged in storms at sea.

In September 1872 the screw-propelled steamship SS *Lady Dufferien* steamed directly to Port Royal from Cardiff, Wales, with thirteen hundred tons of railroad iron for the Port Royal Railroad. Captain Evans and the eighteen-man crew took the one-thousand-ton vessel directly up to the

Port Royal docks "neat as a pin" with no help from harbor tugs. It returned to England loaded with phosphate and cotton.

What was significant about the arrival of the SS *Lady Dufferien* was that it drew twenty feet of water, and Port Royal Sound was the only harbor on the southern coast it could enter. The early screw-propeller ships were powered by slow-turning, reciprocating steam engines and required very large, slow-turning propellers to move them. To keep the large, slow-turning propellers submerged, the ship's hull had to draw twenty or more feet of water. This deep draft hull made the ships more seaworthy during ocean voyages but greatly limited the number of coastal ports available to them. In fact, until the turn of the twentieth century, Port Royal channel, with twenty-six to thirty feet of water at low tide, was the only southern port on the Atlantic seaboard that could accommodate the new deep-draft oceangoing steamships on all tides.

The SS *Lady Dufferien* returned the following year, on August 21, 1873, after a passage of fifty-four days direct from Liverpool, England. The ship was loaded with cotton ties and drew nineteen feet of water. She could not get into Charleston harbor and could not get closer than fifteen miles downriver from Savannah. But it could steam right into the Port Royal docks. On his second visit to Port Royal, Captain Evans said, "For ships of deep draft, I consider Port Royal the best port on the South Atlantic coast."[8]

When the Port Royal Railroad was completed in February 1873, grand plans began to circulate regarding the future of Port Royal Harbor. In May 1873 D. C. Wilson and Judge John K. King of Augusta announced that they expected a steamship line to be established between Liverpool and Port Royal within thirty days. D. F. Appleton pledged some of the stock of the Port Royal Railroad toward the formation of the steamship line, and Judge King pledged much of the stock controlled by the Georgia Railroad "to induce a regular steamship line to Europe." Appleton addressed the Atlanta Grange about a new European steamer line to Port Royal, and the Grange members pledged to send three thousand bales of cotton to Liverpool via the Port Royal Railroad. Wilson pointed out that steamship companies operating screw-propelled ships of deeper draft could access southern markets only through Port Royal Harbor.

To promote Port Royal Harbor, some local businessmen suggested having the *Great Eastern,* the largest ship in the world and one of the first with screw-propeller engineering, make a voyage from Liverpool to Port Royal, fill up with midwestern grain, and invite the leaders of the *London Times* on the voyage. The *Great Eastern* had been built specifically to lay the transatlantic cable, one of the great engineering achievements of the nineteenth century, and was probably the most famous ship in the world at that time. As it turned out, the *Great Eastern* was not necessary to attract the interest of

British newspapers. In October 1873 the *London Cosmopolitan* reported that Port Royal was one of three "first class ports" on the Atlantic coast south of Newport, Rhode Island, the others being New York and Chesapeake Bay. In words reminiscent of Captain Jean Ribault in 1562, the *London Cosmopolitan* exclaimed that "vessels of all nations may repair to Port Royal without fear!" The same notice appeared in the *Liverpool Shipping and Telegraph,* which added that Port Royal was two hundred miles closer by rail to midwestern markets than New York.[9]

The first steamship company to open a regular route from Liverpool to Port Royal was the British Dominion Line, which began operating in the fall of 1873. The Dominion Line ran between Liverpool and New Orleans and made Port Royal its intermediate stop. By the end of October, the SS *Mississippi* had stopped at Port Royal on its way to New Orleans, and the SS *Nashville* had put in at Port Royal before crossing the Atlantic to Liverpool. In December 1873 the SS *Texas* arrived at Port Royal. The *Texas* was 359 feet long and drew 19 feet of water. When it docked at Port Royal, its bow hawser broke, and the ship did a 360 degree turn with the tide in the Port Royal channel. It never touched bottom all the way around, and the skipper, Captain Lawrence, was "very impressed" with the harbor at Port Royal. On Christmas Eve 1873, the SS *Mississippi* returned from New Orleans and stopped at Port Royal on its way to Liverpool carrying thirty-three hundred bales of cotton and other cargo weighing thirteen hundred tons. The *Mississippi* had no trouble with Port Royal but had been delayed by low water at the pass of the Mississippi River.

The success of the Dominion Line encouraged others. During the fall of 1873, a regular steamer line from New York to Port Royal was planned. Captain Evans of the SS *Lady Dufferien* brought word of a regular steamship line between London and Port Royal. In addition, a German steamship line from Bremen to New Orleans was considering Port Royal as its Atlantic port of call. The excitement these developments caused in Beaufort and Port Royal was evident on the streets of both towns.[10]

The New York and Port Royal Steamship Line was organized in 1876. The next year it was operating three ships between New Orleans, Galveston, Port Royal, and New York. The regular steamships on this route were the SS *City of Dallas,* the SS *City of Austin,* and the SS *Carondolet.* The Port Royal agent for the new line was R. P. Rundle. If the shipping schedules went as planned, the SS *City of Austin* was to leave Port Royal every Friday after the arrival of the "down train" from Augusta.

During 1877 rumors began to circulate of a regular steamship line from Port Royal to South America. Some Galveston, Texas, businessmen were considering extending their trade with Mexico and Brazil to the southeastern states through Port Royal. Word reached Beaufort that the U.S. Congress was ready to subsidize a regular line of U.S. Mail steamships to South America, and Port Royal was a likely entry point. Sensing the competition from upstart Port Royal and the loss of prestige to the old Port of Charleston, the powerful Charleston legislative delegation forced a resolution through the South Carolina General Assembly calling on Congress to send all U.S. Mail ships through the Port of Charleston.[11] Politics intervened and the U.S. Mail never came through Port Royal.

In addition to the deep water of Port Royal Sound, the other necessity that made Port Royal harbor attractive to maritime steamships was the availability of coal, the standard fuel of steam engines of the day. It is a heavy and bulky form of fuel. Often transatlantic steamships would consume all the coal they could carry in the ocean crossing and had to refuel with coal on the eastern seaboard in order to return or proceed. The completion of the Port Royal Railroad made possible the delivery of the tons of coal needed by the oceanic steamships.

When D. C. Wilson and Judge King announced the arrival of the Dominion Line from Liverpool in May 1873, they also reported that the Port Royal Railroad would commence regular deliveries of coal from Chattanooga, Tennessee. By October 1873 the local papers announced that coal would soon be available "at Port Royal for steamships that previously had to stop at Norfolk or New Orleans." In November 1873 the first coal train arrived at Port Royal to supply the Dominion Line, and by December the railroad was delivering two hundred tons of coal per day. By 1876 the railroad company had constructed a separate coaling dock at Port Royal to service the steamship fleet. The availability of coal at Port Royal not only attracted the merchant shipping companies but also attracted the United States Navy, a situation that soon had a profound influence on the future of Beaufort County.[12]

Port Royal was not the only busy harbor in Beaufort County during the 1870s and 1880s. Most of the phosphate exports left from St. Helena Sound north of Port Royal Sound. Like most inlets on the southeastern Atlantic seaboard, St. Helena Sound was wide, shallow, and dotted with treacherous sandbars. Spanish explorers, who first discovered and named St. Helena Sound in 1525, described the coast as looking as if a huge sea serpent had risen from the ocean and torn a ragged chunk of land from the continent. Spanish seamen called St. Helena Sound the "Bay of shoals," and the British general Augustine Prevost, evacuating his troops from near Charleston in 1779 during the Revolutionary War, described St. Helena Sound as "a Sound eight miles over with strong tides and shoals." St. Helena Sound had a terrible reputation with seamen through the centuries, but in the 1870s and 1880s, it was the source of most of the phosphate in the state and nation.

The principal loading facilities for the phosphate ships were along the Bull River, a northern tributary of St. Helena Sound. The Bull River is deep and wide, and along its banks were the Pacific Guano Company on Chisholm Island and Summerhouse Point, the Oak Point Mines on Oak Point, and the Williman Island Phosphate Company on Williman Island. The first full year of phosphate operations on the Bull River was 1871. In December 1871 the bark *Isabella Hartnett* left St. Helena Sound with 612 tons of phosphate bound for Cork, Ireland. In January 1872, the *County of Picton* left St. Helena Sound with 1,080 tons of phosphate bound for London and the *Danic* left with 1,050 tons of phosphate also bound for London. As these vessels left, the bark *Lizzie Marrow* from Demerara, Ireland, and the bark *Peter Crerar* from Charleston arrived to load with phosphates.[13]

By the middle of 1872, the growth of phosphate production in Beaufort County was so rapid that not enough ships were available to transport the mineral. George Wells, superintendent of the Marine River Phosphate Company (Coosaw Mines), said "a shortage of vessels in the Bull River is holding up production." One solution was larger vessels with greater capacity to carry away the phosphate. In August 1873 the largest ship ever to enter St. Helena Sound up to that time lay in the Bull River. The full-rigged ship *Calhoun* displaced 1,865 tons. It loaded at the Williman Island Phosphate Works with 1,900 tons of phosphate bound for the Scilly Islands in the English Channel. The *Calhoun* drew twenty-one and a half feet of water fully loaded and was towed across the St. Helena bar at high tide by the steam tug *Christiana*.[14]

By 1873 the "phosphate fleet" in St. Helena Sound was the largest international merchant fleet in South Carolina. During the second week in January 1873, ten ships lay in the Bull River waiting to transport thirty thousand dollars' worth of phosphate to foreign ports. The name, type, tonnage, and national registry of the 1873 "phosphate fleet" is listed below.

Name	*Ship Type*	*Tonnage*	*National Register*
Terentia	Bark	345	British
Pepita	Bark	291	Spanish
Ino	Brig	278	British
Mountain Ash	Bark	428	British
Ceasarea	Bark	344	British
Ana	Bark	536	Italian
Ferocepora	Bark	475	British
Webster	Ship	1,717	American
Ancilla	Ship	714	British
G. Lawrence	Schooner	309	American

Beaufort Republican, January 16, 1873.

St. Helena Sound became a regular stop for merchantmen in the Atlantic trade. In July 1873 Captain Sundstrom commanded the Danish bark *Rutines,* which sailed from the Bull River with 967 tons of phosphate from the Coosaw Mining Company bound for Copenhagen. The British brig *Ino* arrived from Dakar, West Africa. At the same time, the schooner *Eva May* was loading phosphate for Wood's Hole, Massachusetts. The following week, the British bark *St. Lawrence* arrived in St. Helena Sound from Buenos Aires, Argentina. Also sailing that week was the Russian bark *Kaleva* with 617 tons of phosphate bound for Copenhagen. The first steamship to carry phosphate out of St. Helena Sound was the SS *Carroll,* which took 700 tons of phosphate to Woods Hole in May 1873.

After a decade of growth in the phosphate, lumber, and maritime industries, the Port of Beaufort, whose U.S. Customs office served both Port Royal and St. Helena Sounds, had become one of the ten largest export ports on the Atlantic seaboard. Custom records for 1879–80 revealed that fifty-nine foreign vessels totaling 29,135 tons entered the Port of Beaufort, and seventy-two foreign vessels totaling 36,966 tons departed (or "cleared") the Port of Beaufort between July 1879 and July 1880. These vessels came from all over the Atlantic world: Brazil (19), Britain (10), British African colonies (7), Portugal (5), French West Indies (4), Germany (4), Azores, Madiera, and Cape Verde Islands (3), and the British West Indies, British Guiana, the Canary Islands, and Puerto Rico (1 ship each). Foreign vessels left the Port of Beaufort for equally exotic locations: England (55), Ireland (8), Scotland (5), Denmark (3), and Spain (1).

Custom statistics also revealed the nature of this trade. The Port of Beaufort exported $257,921 worth of phosphates to foreign ports (mostly in England, Scotland, and Ireland), making Beaufort County the largest phosphate port in the United States in 1880. New York ($174,811) and Charleston ($94,898) were second and third in value of phosphate exports. Inasmuch as the price of phosphate was approximately four dollars per ton in 1880, these figures indicate approximately 64,480 tons of phosphate were exported from Beaufort County to foreign ports in 1879–80. The Port of Beaufort was also second in the United States in volume of seed cotton exported to foreign ports. In 1879–80, 2,351,820 pounds of seed cotton was exported from Beaufort County, mostly to mills in Great Britain. Only Fernandina, Florida, exported more seed cotton in 1879–80. Total exports from the Port of Beaufort in 1879–80 were worth $1,927,644, making it the tenth largest export port on the Atlantic seaboard.

Imports through the Port of Beaufort, on the other hand, were negligible, representing only a fraction of the imports through Savannah or Charleston. Most foreign vessels entered Port Royal or St. Helena Sound "in ballast" (empty) to load with phosphate, cotton, or lumber. The exceptions were the numerous vessels from Brazil. No doubt they were delivering South American guano destined for cotton fields throughout the South.

Beaufort County also hosted a brisk coastwise domestic trade. In 1879–80 thirty-five cargo vessels, including twenty steamships, totaling 20,178 tons entered the Port of Beaufort and twenty-two cargo vessels, including nine steamships, totaling 13,947 tons cleared the Port of Beaufort.[15]

The rapid increase in maritime traffic from Port Royal and St. Helena Sound led to an increase in shipwrecks off the Beaufort County coast. Most of the shipwrecks were caused by Atlantic storms, but many were a consequence of the shifting sandbars and strong currents of St. Helena Sound. In April 1872 the bark *Bebington* ran aground off St. Helena Sound with 1,118 tons of phosphate aboard while under the direction of St. Helena harbor pilot A. H. Alston. The week before, the bark *Ebenezer* ran aground off Port Royal Sound under pilot Alston's direction. The following week Captain Rhodes and Captain Waters replaced Alston and pilot James Dupong as St. Helena Sound harbor pilots. In October 1872 the ship *Energy* wrecked on a bar ten miles off Hunting Island and was abandoned by its crew. Captain Dupong took Port Royal pilot boat number 2 out to the wreck of the *Energy*. While he was on board, alone, to claim the salvage rights, a gale-force wind struck, drove the *Energy* into St. Helena Sound, and broke the boat in half on the sand banks. Pilot Dupong lashed himself to the wreckage and floated at sea for three days without food or water before he was finally rescued. Wreckers got 100 tons of cargo, including 41 tons of railroad iron, off the *Energy* and burned what was left. In January 1873 the British ship *Ancilla* ran aground on the St. Helena sandbanks with 716 tons of phosphate aboard. The ship and cargo were lost. It was but one of many accidents and groundings suffered by the phosphate fleet, and it highlighted the treacherous nature of St. Helena Sound. The *Beaufort Republican* commented that "no port in the South now has a worse reputation than St. Helena Sound. . . . within a year there have been a half a dozen accidents." The editor suggested that the solution to the maritime hazards of St. Helena Sound was to build a railroad from the Bull River phosphate works to the Port Royal Railroad line and ship the phosphate out of Port Royal Sound. The Bull River and Port Royal Railroad was incorporated in 1873 but was never constructed.[16]

In February 1873 the schooner *Skylark* successfully departed St. Helena Sound loaded with phosphate for New England but was struck by a gale off Cape Hatteras. The survivors described the tempest: "the vessel scudding under double reefed foresail . . . sprung a leak in high seas . . . increasing gale winds, high seas and snow . . . (Feb. 22) fore top mast and gaff carried away . . . water increasing in the hold despite constant pumping . . . (Feb. 25) raised ensign to half mast, upside-down." The packet steamer SS *Montgomery* saw this international distress signal. The steamship rescued the crew and towed the battered schooner back to Savannah.

Without modern weather forecasting, coastal mariners—in fact all the sea island inhabitants—were at the mercy of violent Atlantic storms. On September 21, 1873, the sea islands were struck by a major hurricane. The eye of the hurricane passed somewhere close to Savannah, bringing the maximum winds in the northeast quadrant of the cyclone directly down on the sea islands. The *Beaufort Republican* reported, "Torrents of water fell . . . some in waterspouts . . . broke the railroad line in six or eight places. . . . it was the worst storm since 1854." Offshore, three schooners were abandoned at the mouth of Port Royal Sound. A steamship sank at the dock at Bull River, and dozens of phosphate flats and barges were scattered across the marshes. On St. Helena Island, "several houses were blown down. . . . the cotton crop was injured. . . . Mr. Burton's house was overturned." The flooding of the Salkehatchie River was "the worst since 1841." The swamps were so full of water that the deer were forced out "and the hunters are having a field day."[17]

In October 1873 the bark *T. J. Jeff Southward* made a navigational error entering Port Royal Sound and went north of the Port Royal bar. Unable to enter the harbor, it ran aground off Trenchard's Inlet. The ship would have broken up in the surf but for the masterful seamanship of Captain Early of the pilot boat *Keystone*. Early and a crew of local sailors boarded the abandoned vessel, backed the sails to the wind, and worked the ship into a safe anchorage in eight fathoms of water with little damage to the vessel. The next morning the steam tug *Forrest City* towed the *T. J. Jeff Southward* into Port Royal.

Not all maritime accidents had such a happy ending. In January 1874 twenty-nine people drowned off Hilton Head Island while traveling from Hilton Head to Savannah aboard the forty-foot sloop *Elizabeth Miller*. The sloop was "owned by a colored society," and the captain, George Bramad, was known as a capable seaman and "an honest man." The vessel got caught in a storm off Tybee Island, had its jib torn away, and drifted onto the sandbars off Hilton Head. The sloop capsized in the surf, and after several hours, the entire crew and passengers dropped into the sea and drowned. The sole survivor was Moses Polite, who clung to the mast until help arrived.

On March 23, 1876, word reached Port Royal that the large British ship *Emminidas,* loaded with lumber from the Port Royal Sawmill and headed for Greenock, Scotland, company owner D. C. Wilson's birthplace, capsized in a storm off Queenstown, Ireland. Seven crewmen survived, but the captain and thirteen crewmen died.[18] And in October 1877, the schooner *Ben,* carrying twenty-two tons of phosphate from Charleston to Philadelphia, sprang a leak, crossed the St. Helena bar, and came to rest on the Combahee bank. The steam tug *Ivanhoe* came from the Bull River phosphate works to tow the schooner off the bank and into the anchorage in Bull River.

Captain Craig of the *Ivanhoe* received nearly twelve thousand dollars in salvage money.

The worst maritime disaster of the era occurred during a tropical storm on August 25, 1885. That day a near hurricane brushed the coast. Five pilot boats were caught offshore in the storm and all were sunk. Fourteen crewmen were drowned. It was the worst loss for the local pilot service during the three decades of Beaufort County's "maritime golden age." The loss of life in 1885 would have been greater but for the heroism of the pilot captain, W. H. Von Harten, who swam through the raging surf off Bay Point to bring a life line to the stricken pilot boat of Captain John O'Brien. The lives of O'Brien and his crew were saved, and Von Harten was given a gold medal for lifesaving by the U.S. government.

Another act of heroism occurred during the winter of 1889 when a blizzard and northeast gale struck the coast. During the storm, the steamship *William Lawrence* "went ashore in the Port Royal north breaker." Pilot captains W. D. Schwartz and Robert Jenkins took the pilot boat *Addie* into the roaring surf and rescued the entire crew of the steamship. Schwartz, Jenkins, and the pilot crew nearly froze during the rescue.[19]

The increased maritime traffic and maritime accidents necessitated the improvement of the system of harbor pilots for Beaufort County as well as the addition of navigational aids. The Reconstruction legislature passed an act in 1871 establishing a three-man Board of Pilot Commissioners for the coastal counties: Charleston, Georgetown, and Beaufort. The Board of Pilot Commissioners for each county was to comprise one pilot and two present or past seafaring men. For a while the Board of Pilot Commissioners became another engine of Reconstruction political patronage. There was good money in the pilot service for a busy harbor such as Port Royal and a steady stream of applicants for the jobs. But it soon became apparent in Beaufort County that putting friends and political favorites in charge of expensive ships and cargoes in dangerous waters was a prescription for disaster. Some of Beaufort County's shipwrecks were due to the incompetence of politically appointed harbor pilots. The two accidents in a single week in 1872 caused by pilot A. H. Alston and another caused by pilot James Dupong cost them part of their responsibilities and commissions. But because Alston was also on the Board of Pilot Commissioners for Beaufort County, he was soon back at work, as was Dupong. In 1876 pilot William Samuels was accused of gross carelessness in the wreck of the Russian bark *Ruthinas*. He was also soon back at work. By 1877 Port Royal had fifteen active harbor pilots, only one half to one third of whom were regularly employed. In addition, several independent seamen were operating as unlicensed harbor pilots. The local businesses that depended on the maritime industries appealed to Captain William Samuels, then secretary of the Port Royal Pilots Association, to ask the Board of Pilot Commissioners to stop issuing any more licenses, to limit the number of pilot apprentices at any one time to four, and to prosecute anyone operating without a license.[20]

The pilot station for Port Royal Sound was located on the south end of Parris Island looking directly out the mouth of Port Royal Sound. The pilot station had a house and a lookout tower with a signal staff. In the days before wireless communication, ships would lie offshore and raise a signal flag requesting a harbor pilot. If the signal was not observed, then the ship would fire a cannon to signal for a pilot. Sometimes pilot boats stood offshore to be the first to meet incoming vessels. Pilot commissions were based on tonnage and were generally lucrative. There was also a pilot station for St. Helena Sound. It was located on the east end of Buzzard Island. Some of the harbor pilots known to have operated in the 1870s and 1880s were A. H. Alston, William Samuels, James Dupong, Antone Santos, George Harmes, W. D. Schwartz, Robert Jenkins, Early, Rhodes, Waters, Buckley, and John Kessler. By the 1890s one of the best-known local pilots was William H. Von Harten, who in 1893 was described as "one of the most skillful pilots of this bar."[21]

Each pilot station was adjacent to a quarantine station, which was required for any port serving international vessels. The quarantine station on Parris Island was well equipped and included a six-bed hospital. Dr. Hal Stuart was for many years assigned to the Port Royal quarantine station. He had to be periodically transported out from Beaufort on one of the pilot boats. The quarantine station for St. Helena Sound was next to the pilot station on Buzzard Island. There the phosphate companies provided doctors.

The pilot boats were regular sights on the offshore and inshore waters of Beaufort County. Mostly these vessels were thirty- to fifty-foot sloops or schooners sometimes built under contract specifically for the pilot association. In 1873 the phosphate companies on the Bull River bought the sloop *Louly* as the pilot boat for St. Helena Sound. The *Louly* had been originally built as a yacht for Colonel William DeSaussure. It cost five thousand dollars to construct and had its bottom sheathed in copper. The *Louly* was a centerboard sloop and thus particularly useful for the shallow waters of St. Helena Sound. In 1877 pilot boat *Bertha* was delivered. It was a large, thirty-one-ton, deep-draft schooner. The *Bertha* was built in Charleston specifically for the pilot trade. It cost six thousand dollars and was heavily built to allow it to stand offshore for days at a time.[22]

Navigational aids were also improved for the busy Beaufort County shipping trade. In 1872 the state of South Carolina ceded some public land to the U.S. government for navigational aids. They were "one acre of land on Otter Island for a lighthouse, one acre on the north side of Station Creek, St. Helena Island, for a beacon light and one acre of land on Bob Island,

Skull Creek, for a beacon light." Buoys marked the river channels, and in 1877 range lights were erected on Hilton Head and Parris Islands to mark the entrance to Port Royal Sound. In 1873 the first lighthouse on Daufuskie Island was constructed at Haig Point. The most permanent and most expensive navigational aid built at the time was the Hunting Island lighthouse.[23]

The first lighthouse on Hunting Island was built in 1859, shortly before the Civil War. The U.S. Lighthouse Service had purchased fifty acres on the north end of Hunting Island and erected a ninety-five-foot brick tower. The principal purpose of the first Hunting Island lighthouse was to warn coastal shipping away from the dangerous shoals that extend far offshore at the mouth of St. Helena Sound. When the Civil War began, the Confederate government had no desire to operate coastal navigational aids for the benefit of the Union blockading fleet, so they blew up the lighthouse. The Hunting Island lighthouse of 1859 had been constructed a quarter mile offshore and probably would not have survived erosion for very long. With the rise of the phosphate industry during Reconstruction and particularly with the large number of shipwrecks near St. Helena Sound, demands increased for a new Hunting Island lighthouse.

In January 1873 the *Beaufort Republican* echoed the demands of the phosphate operators: "The phosphate shipments ... need a lighthouse near St. Helena." Accordingly, Colonel Haines of the Sixth Lighthouse District reported that arrangements were being made to replace the old lighthouse. During the U.S. Direct Tax Commission wartime land sale in 1863, the U.S. government had purchased 315 acres on the north end of Hunting Island. The new lighthouse was to be 120 feet high, visible from seventeen miles out at sea, and built of iron caissons bolted together. The Corps of Engineers had appropriated twenty-five thousand dollars for the project. The lighthouse construction continued over the next two years. Each iron caisson weighed twelve hundred pounds. The cast-iron tower was lined with brick on the inside. The final cost of the project was over one hundred thousand dollars. The Hunting Island lighthouse began operating on July 1, 1875.

The lighthouse was said to be "the perfection of mechanical and engineering skill." It had a thirty-inch flash beacon visible for thirty miles at sea. Each coastal lighthouse had an individually distinctive flash so that ships could identify it at sea. The Hunting Island light flashed once every thirty seconds. Each lighthouse also had distinctive coloration for daylight identification. The Hunting Island lighthouse was black and white with the top third painted black.

As soon as the lighthouse was operating, local seamen complained that it had been built in the wrong place. They claimed it would have been more useful for St. Helena Sound if it had been built on Harbor Island to the west. Furthermore, they noted, it was only 450 feet from the breakers, and 150 feet of shoreline had been lost to erosion since construction began. Local critics estimated that the whole structure would have to be moved within three years. The locals were not just alarmists. In 1889 the government dismantled the caissons and moved the lighthouse to its present location closer to the middle of the island. The Hunting Island lighthouse stands to this day as the most prominent attraction of Hunting Island State Park and the most durable monument to Beaufort County's maritime golden age.[24]

The most enduring consequence of the maritime boom in Beaufort County during the 1870s and 1880s was the arrival of the United States Navy. The same circumstances that had attracted Atlantic merchant fleets to Port Royal also attracted the navy. The deep entrance and protected anchorage at Port Royal, the proximity of Port Royal Sound to the West Indies, and the availability of coal delivered by the newly completed Port Royal Railroad all made Port Royal Sound an ideal site for the navy's new steamer fleet.

The truth is that the U.S. Navy never really abandoned Port Royal after the Civil War. During the war Port Royal had been the headquarters and supply base of the South Atlantic Blockading Squadron and a beehive of merchant and naval shipping from 1861 to 1865. As the war ended, Beaufort's wartime newspaper, the *New South*, predicted that Port Royal would soon be "a place of some importance" to the navy. It noted in 1865 that "arrangements have already been made to erect a U.S. navy yard and arsenal on one of the islands in the Bay" and that there was a plan to connect the islands to the mainland by rail. A U.S. congressional committee had already recommended Port Royal for a military hospital, it being the "most healthy location on the coast." The paper also noted the promising commercial future of Beaufort and Port Royal at the close of the Civil War: "This whole section is rapidly coming under the influence and control of northern men and will ultimately be made to flourish like the West."[25]

Naval vessels visited Port Royal throughout the late 1860s, and when the railroad was completed in 1873, comments began to be heard across South Carolina and in Washington, D.C., about a future naval station at Port Royal. In October 1873 the *Washington Chronicle* recommended Port Royal as the "best site on the Atlantic coast for a U.S. navy yard." The *Columbia Union Herald* agreed, noting that Port Royal was "plainly the best place south of Norfolk for such an establishment." In November 1873 Robert Smalls introduced a resolution in the South Carolina Senate recommending Port Royal as the site of a naval station. The local newspaper suggested that a U.S. naval station could make productive use of some of the idle government-owned lands left over from the wartime foreclosures on the sea islands. In December 1873 the City of Beaufort and the Town of Port Royal sent petitions to the U.S. Congress requesting a naval station at Port Royal.[26]

The navy's North Atlantic Squadron continued to use Port Royal Sound as its regular anchorage, particularly during the winter months. Warships regularly mingled with the merchant sailing vessels in Port Royal Sound and with steamships at the Port Royal coaling dock. In December 1875 the local paper reported that Port Royal "has been used as a rendezvous for the North Atlantic Squadron for several months and we have no doubt . . . a navy yard will be established here." In January 1876, as if to confirm local expectations, the "largest fleet since the war was sent to Port Royal to prevent being frozen in Northern ports." The entire North Atlantic squadron was anchored in Port Royal Sound during the winter of 1876. The arrival of the Atlantic fleet was good news for local business. Local "bum boats" plied the fleet anchorage hawking fresh fish, tobacco, and other products to the sailors. The fleet bought coal from the Port Royal Railroad and lumber supplies from D. C. Wilson, Niels Christensen, and George Gage. It was reported that "Mr. O'Dell, the baker, was given the contract for bread for the fleet." Occasionally the sailors were permitted shore liberty, usually only twenty at a time, where they spent every dime of their pay in local bars and returned to the fleet roaring drunk. Sometimes the fleet activities were healthy. In April 1876 the sailors of the USS *Congress* and the USS *Brooklyn* entertained the local population with a colorful and boisterous longboat race. The *Congress's* crew won. Fourteen navy ships were in the Port Royal Sound during the winter months of 1876.[27]

This was the largest fleet in Port Royal Sound since the Civil War. The U.S. Navy wasn't the only navy to visit the Port Royal anchorage. In January 1877 a Russian naval corvette put in at Port Royal. Since the Russians lacked local currency, the crew was paid in gold and turned loose on the town. "The officers and men were paid off on Saturday and Port Royal reaped a harvest of gold from them," according to one news report.

In January 1877 the USS *Tallapoosa* was dispatched to Port Royal with "a board of Naval officers to survey Port Royal Sound." At the same time, a bill was introduced in Congress establishing Port Royal as a "Naval Station of the 4th class . . . commanded by a commodore . . . the same as New London, Newport, Key West and New Orleans."[28] Captain Stephen Bleeker Luce led the board of naval officers that surveyed Port Royal Sound in January 1877. Stephen Luce was one of the navy's senior captains, and he was intimately acquainted with Beaufort, having spent most of his Civil War duty on the South Carolina coast. He was an officer aboard the USS *Wabash* during the Battle of Port Royal Sound on November 7, 1861. Luce subsequently commanded warships during the Siege of Charleston (1863–64) and protected General Slocum's crossing of the Savannah River in January 1865. It was most likely his opinion that the survey board reflected.

The survey board reported what was already common knowledge to Atlantic sailors. Port Royal was the only harbor between Norfolk and Key West that could take the largest naval vessels. It had easy access to the ocean. It was equal distance by rail between Norfolk and Pensacola. It was near the Windward Islands and thus strategically located to command the seaward approaches to the Caribbean and Gulf of Mexico. It was only 480 nautical miles from the Bahamas. The naval yard could be built out of range of enemy guns and protected by coastal shore batteries at the mouth of Port Royal Sound. As if to confirm the superior circumstances of Port Royal Sound, the USS *Tallapoosa* went down to examine the Savannah River and Calibogue Sound and ran aground on the banks in Tybee Roads.[29]

In February 1877 a second party of naval officers and civilian officials traveled to Beaufort by rail. They stayed at the Sea Island Hotel and chartered the local paddle wheeler SS *Sea Weed* to examine Foot Point on the Colleton River as a possible site for a navy yard. During the spring of 1877, the naval board pondered the reports and recommendations of the survey parties. At the same time, naval activity in Port Royal Sound continued apace. Throughout the winter and spring of 1877, fifteen to twenty naval vessels were at anchor in Port Royal Sound. One hundred fifty officers and more than eight hundred sailors and marines were regularly stationed there. In April, Commodore Hughes replaced Commodore Clitz as commander of the Port Royal Station, and when the USS *Hartford* was in port, "an Admiral's flag flying from the mizzen," Port Royal was effectively the headquarters of the Atlantic fleet. When the fleet was in, Port Royal Sound was abuzz with naval activity, with "constant displays of bunting in the form of signal flags . . . boats under steam, boats under sail, boats under oars, plying from one ship to another." The whole of Port Royal harbor had "an air of bustling activity."

In April 1877 word reached Port Royal that the fleet was to swell with the arrival of the USS *Hartford* from the West Indies, the USS *Ossippee* from Havana, the USS *Swatara* from Jamaica, and the USS *Essex* from Vera Cruz. The 2,182-ton sloop-of-war USS *Powhatan* limped into Port Royal after encountering a storm at sea, and in May the USS *Catskill* and the USS *New Hampshire* arrived at the anchorage. The USS *New Hampshire,* an old wooden sailing ship, was later dismasted and anchored in Port Royal Sound as a stationary supply vessel. The USS *Pawnee* was converted to a coal barge and also permanently stationed at Port Royal.

When the fleet was in, local businesses flourished. The fleet needed coal, lumber, food, fresh water, and many sundry supplies. The steamboat *Hattie* was specifically designed and built to supply the fleet with fresh water from Beaufort's wells. Bum boats did brisk business with the shipboard crews. The local paper estimated that the business and labor necessary to supply one ship could support eight to ten sea island black families.[30]

In May 1877 the secretary of the navy officially established Port Royal Sound as a United States naval station. Soon thereafter, W. L. Mintoye was dispatched from Boston to Port Royal. Mintoye was inspector of the navy's Bureau of Yards and Docks. He made plans to construct a navy pier into forty feet of water in Port Royal Sound. He chartered the local steamer SS *Agnes* to take thorough soundings of the harbor, and he began to designate land for shoreside support facilities: machine shops, warehouses, and eventually a dry dock. In July a storm blew down the old, wooden, Civil War–era machine shop on Land's End, and the navy turned its attention to Parris Island. Bay Point was set aside as a quarantine station. In September 1877 the secretary of the navy visited Port Royal to determine its suitability as a dry dock to service the anticipated new fleet of iron-clad, deep-draft, screw-propeller battleships, the most advanced military technology of the age. By 1881 the U.S. government began purchasing large parcels of Parris Island as the support base for the Port Royal Naval Station.[31]

Naval activity remained brisk for the rest of 1877 and continued for the next twenty years. In November, Admiral Stephen Decatur Trenchard returned to Port Royal aboard his new flagship, the USS *Powhatan*. He designated the USS *New Hampshire* as the permanent supply ship for Port Royal Naval Station. In December the USS *Enterprise* entered Port Royal after a cruise to New Orleans and Key West, and a few weeks later the training ship USS *Saratoga* arrived. On Christmas weekend the seventy-nine crewmen of the USS *New Hampshire* were paid eleven thousand dollars from the navy paymaster. They were allowed ashore twenty at a time "and generally returned to the ship without a cent." The payroll added significantly to local commerce, but the sailors "usually returned broke and drunk."[32]

Throughout the 1880s, activity at the Port Royal Naval Station remained one of the economic mainstays of Beaufort County. While naval vessels arrived and departed, they needed constant support, supply, and repair. Throughout the 1880s the permanent support facilities on Parris Island grew. By 1893 the navy had laid out twelve streets, built two shoreside piers, and constructed eighteen temporary buildings, including a dispensary, kitchen, mess hall, canteen, barracks, privy, petty officers quarters, blacksmith shop, wood house, hose house, oil house, and lime house. During the 1890s the commandant's house and quarters for the executive officer, the civil engineer, the surgeon, and paymaster were erected. The largest buildings at the navy yard were the coal shed, the machine shop, and the pump and power house. One of the largest buildings at the Port Royal Naval Station was the marine barracks, a harbinger of the future use of Parris Island. In 1890 the navy unveiled plans to build the largest dry dock in the United States.[33] From 1877 to 1901, the Port Royal Naval Station was a mainstay of the local economy and the apogee of Beaufort County's maritime era.

From 1870 to 1900, Beaufort County was one of the busiest maritime centers in the South. With phosphates, lumber, and cotton for export and an accessible port and railroad to import the various necessities of the southeastern markets, the last three decades of the nineteenth century were heady times. However, the maritime golden age was not to last. The decline of cotton in the 1880s, the end of phosphates in the 1890s, the terrible storm of 1893, and the politically engineered demise of the naval station in 1901, brought the busy shipping activity in Beaufort County to an end. But for three decades, Port Royal Sound lived up to the grand expectations of Atlantic sailors through the centuries. From Captain Jean Ribault, who named the Sound in 1562, to Commodore Samuel Francis Du Pont, who conquered it in 1861, from Adelentado Pedro Menendez de Aviles, who founded La Ciudad de Santa Elena and made it Florida's first capital in 1566, to Admiral Stephen Decatur Trenchard and Admiral Stephen B. Luce, Port Royal Sound was a world-class maritime center.

Chapter 22

The Counterrevolution of 1876 and the Secession of Hampton County

"Wresting the county from the rule of ignorance and plunder"

The progressive achievements of the Reconstruction regime in South Carolina were remarkable. The black majority and the fledgling Republican Party had transformed the politics and economy of South Carolina, rewritten the state's constitution, and introduced citizenship, democratic politics, public education, and local "home rule" to the freedmen. With solid black voting majorities across the state, they might have ruled South Carolina for a generation. But they did not. The Republican Party controlled South Carolina for only eight years, from 1868 to 1876. The unraveling of the Republican regime had many causes. Mismanagement, political venality, and outright corruption were the principal objections of the growing Democratic opposition. But the larger causes were political rivalries among the Republicans themselves and their unfortunate habit of overtaxing all the people of South Carolina.

Beaufort County was a stronghold of the Republican regime. The influence of the new order and the black majority survived in Beaufort County thirty years after Reconstruction ended in the rest of the state. But all of the inherent weaknesses of the Reconstruction regime were apparent in Beaufort County.

The Constitution of 1868 had given the local public school districts and the local county governments wide latitude in levying taxes and managing their own finances. This was the state's first experiment in "home rule." In Beaufort County they did not handle their new responsibilities well. In its first full year of operation, the Beaufort School District Number 1 overspent its budget by 39 percent. In 1872 the school district acknowledged an accumulated debt of twenty-eight thousand dollars.

The state and county governments were worse. By the end of 1871, South Carolina state bonds had fallen to thirty-eight cents on the dollar and the *Beaufort Republican,* a newspaper founded by northerners sympathetic to the Reconstruction regime, asked, "Where are we headed . . . to the shores of bankruptcy and ruin?" The *Charleston News* reported in 1871 that many counties were bankrupt. Specifically highlighted were Charleston, Beaufort, and Colleton Counties, where the public treasuries were "wasted, given away, and stolen."

By 1872 the new Beaufort County government was so far in arrears that it was practically bankrupt. W. J. Whipper's *Beaufort Times* wrote a widely circulated article that claimed the county had an accumulated debt after four years of forty thousand dollars. This prompted a meeting of the county's leading citizens to ascertain the truth of the county's finances and "to consider what course was best to relieve Beaufort County of its embarrassments."

The meeting was well attended. Bay Street merchant J. C. Mayo was chairman and R. K. Carlton, another Bay Street merchant, was secretary. Senator Robert Smalls and Representative W. J. Whipper attended from the General Assembly. The principal spokesman for the citizens' group was James M. Crofut. All of these men, except Robert Smalls, were northern transplants, and all were inclined to be sympathetic to the Republican regime. But the mismanagement of the new county government alarmed them.

The man on the hot seat at the meeting of January 3, 1872, was the first and only chairman of the County Board of Commissioners, John Hunn. A Quaker from Delaware and a noted activist in the Underground Railroad, Hunn had been arrested and fined into destitution by Judge Roger Taney for his illegal activities in helping slaves escape their masters. Despite his heavy losses, he defiantly pledged to continue helping runaway slaves, whatever the cost. He came to the sea islands in the wake of the Union army to help manage the contrabands and assist their transition to freedom. Among the black population he was known affectionately as "Father Hunn." When the war ended, Hunn remained to seek opportunities with the Reconstruction regime. In 1868 he became chairman of the new County Board of Commissioners and thus the first practitioner of "home rule" in Beaufort County.

The meeting of January 3, 1872, was very animated. James Crofut demanded an accurate report of the county finances, and when John Hunn produced it, Robert Smalls noted that it differed significantly from the report submitted to the legislature. Hunn blamed the discrepancies on the clerk of the County Commission. Crofut noted that the same clerk had served since the county was organized: "[Had] . . . no one noticed his errors?" The itemized expenses for the county government for 1871 were as follows:

Public Buildings and Salaries	$13,093.83
Support for the poor	7,526.63
Jail Expenses	3,162.48
Trial Justices	574.03
Constables	609.87
Ferries	535.95

Bridges	1,927.95
Highways	300.75
Contingencies	1,180.42

Unpaid bills of the county that had already been "audited for" were:

Jail Expense	$2,166.85
Trial Justices	188.72
Constables	289.80
Poor	95.80
Ferries	75.79
Bridges	593.00
Highways	103.75
Contingencies	178.60

The debt amounted to $32,604.20, and there was no money left to pay it. Representative Whipper suggested a one-mill tax increase, but tax collections had already proven to be an unreliable source of revenue in the county. James Crofut suggested that the county should issue bonds to cover the debt. The bonds should be offered "to those who would sell their credits cheap . . . as there had been much speculation and discounts in claims." "Discounts in claims" meant that creditors of the county government were willing to accept partial payments for fear of never getting anything at all. Crofut's plan prevailed and a crisis was temporarily averted, but the new county government never regained the confidence of the electorate.

The large amount of the county budget expended for "salaries and public buildings" indicated that home rule had become just another patronage machine for the Reconstruction government. Among the salaries, John Hunn paid himself the exorbitant salary of $540 per year, more than lawyers, doctors, or other professional men customarily made.[1] Adding to the air of suspicion in 1872 was the fact that the first county treasurer, E. S. Kuh, was the brother of Anna Kuh, wife of Bay Street entrepreneur, cotton factor, and county commissioner Moritz Pollitzer. E. S. Kuh died in office in 1871.

When elections were held in 1872, the Board of County Commissioners was significantly changed. Bay Street merchant George Waterhouse, old Bluffton planter Dr. Paul Pritchard, and freedman Seaborn Drayton formed the new commission. With one northern merchant, one southern planter, and one freedman, this second County Commission could be considered Beaufort County's first experiment with "fusion" politics. Bay Street merchant George Holmes was made county treasurer, replacing E. S. Kuh. Waterhouse, Pritchard, Drayton, and Holmes worked to limit taxation and patronage and to balance the books. J. C. Mayo received a franchise to operate the Whitehall Ferry, which connected Lady's Island to Beaufort. Well-known ferrymen Bacchus Mitchell and Moses Scott continued to work the boats but were employed by J. C. Mayo, not by the county government. It was one of home rule's first experiments in privatization.[2] The county books were eventually balanced, but the confidence of the business community and the electorate in the local government was irreparably harmed. Rivalries among the leading Republican politicians were equally harmful.

In the early 1870s the two foremost political leaders in Beaufort County were Senator Robert Smalls and Representative W. J. Whipper. The two men were quite different in background and, evidently, in personality. Smalls was born and raised in Beaufort, was never formally educated and remained semiliterate throughout his life. By 1872 Smalls was relatively well to do with real estate and business interests in Beaufort and Charleston. What Smalls had he earned through his own hard work, courage, and resourcefulness. Whipper was well educated, from a well-to-do northern background, and had married into one of the wealthiest and most prominent families in Reconstruction South Carolina. Whipper considered himself socially and intellectually a cut above Robert Smalls. Most of the white community agreed. But the sea island freedmen identified with Robert Smalls and had little more in common with W. J. Whipper, other than the color of his skin, than they had with northern missionaries or southern planters. Smalls and Whipper had complementary strengths and talents. Had they worked together, as they did as delegates to the Constitutional Convention of 1868, they would have made a formidable political team. Instead, they fell out with one another in 1872 and remained bitter political rivals for twenty years.

The rivalry between Whipper and Smalls began with the General Assembly election of 1872. Robert Smalls was completing his first term as state senator for Beaufort County and Representative W. J. Whipper decided to challenge him for the position. Large corruption scandals were enveloping the Reconstruction regime throughout the State. A spirited party of reformers calling themselves the "True Republicans" put up school superintendent and former Beaufort Gideonite Reuben Tomlinson to challenge gubernatorial nominee Franklin J. Moses and the "Regular Republicans." The True Republicans embarrassed the party by revealing several financial scandals to the public. This split the electorate across the state and encouraged the demoralized and outnumbered Democrats. Many northern businessmen were still friends with Tomlinson, who had been the founder and publisher of the *Beaufort Republican*. W. J. Whipper was encouraged to challenge Robert Smalls because Smalls was associated with the corrupt Regular Republican regime in Columbia.

The campaign of 1872 began with the Emancipation Day ceremonies on January 1, 1872, when W. J. Whipper attacked Governor Scott for the corruption scandals in Columbia and attacked Robert Smalls for not voting to impeach the governor. Whipper claimed that "corruption is ruining the

Republican Party." Smalls defended himself by reminding Whipper that, as a senator, he was not constitutionally authorized to vote on an impeachment resolution but would have a role in a senatorial impeachment trial should the state house of representatives vote to impeach the governor. Representative Samuel Green, son of wealthy entrepreneur Kit Green, and a native sea islander, defended Robert Smalls. The senator, he asserted, was also anxious to root out corruption but "not to ruin the Republican Party."[3] This incident was the opening salvo of the divisive campaign of 1872 and the beginning of the rivalry between Whipper and Smalls. The dispute captured the news coverage and marred the otherwise festive Emancipation Day celebrations.

The campaign and the rivalry heated up through the year. In May, Smalls held a big rally in Beaufort, where he criticized the Republican leadership in Columbia "who had duped an infant party, made themselves millionaires and made the electorate mad at the Republican Party." He vowed to clean up the state government in Columbia but noted that these corrupt, self-enriching politicians "also exist in the Beaufort Party." It was a well-understood reference to Whipper that brought cheers from the crowd and loud calls for Whipper to respond, which he declined to do. Later that month Smalls spoke to a large crowd at the Brick Church on St. Helena Island, where he was "received with great enthusiasm."

On the Fourth of July, Smalls addressed a large rally at Coosawhatchie and a week later attended an enthusiastic meeting in the new railroad junction of Yemassee. At all of these meetings, Smalls was accompanied by the patriotic tones of the Allen Brass Band. By midsummer Robert Smalls's energetic campaign had solidified his political base among the freedmen of Beaufort County, and he was well on his way to a resounding victory. But that did not halt the attacks from Whipper.[4]

The *Beaufort Times,* edited by Whipper's wife, Frances Ann Rollin Whipper, kept up a steady drumbeat of attack. In August, Whipper printed a charge that haunted Smalls for the rest of his political career; namely that he had stolen a five-hundred-dollar appropriation intended for "that mythical armed force," the South Carolina National Guard, of which Smalls was brigadier general. Confident of victory in the October primary, Smalls fired back with a letter to the *Beaufort Republican* in which he asserted that on October 16 "the great Whipper will then be the great *Whipped!*"

Charge and countercharge continued. In August 1872 Smalls attended the "Regular Republican" convention and nominated his old friend and business partner, Richard Howell Gleaves of Beaufort, for lieutenant governor on the ticket with Franklin J. Moses. Whipper attended the "True Republican Convention," which nominated a former Beaufortonian, Reuben Tomlinson, for governor.[5]

During September the *Beaufort Republican* editor, J. G. Thompson, supported the reformers and Tomlinson, who had earlier edited the *Republican*. Thompson formed a new political party in Beaufort County, the Liberal Party, with himself as cochair. At the same time, the county Republican Party split into two conventions with Robert Smalls as chairman of the Regular Republicans and W. C. Morrison as chairman of the True Republicans. This factionalism encouraged the few white Democrats left in Beaufort County to rally for the first time since the war's end behind the Beaufort lawyer, Colonel William Elliott. Thus, four different political parties were at work in Beaufort County during the 1872 campaign.

It was a heated campaign. The Liberal Party endorsed Tomlinson for governor, calling the Moses-Gleaves ticket "a mingled mass of rascality, ignorance and stupidity." Two leading statewide Republicans, Martin R. Delany and Lieutenant Governor Alonzo Ransier, made campaign swings through Beaufort in support of Franklin Moses and Gleaves. Whipper accused Smalls of an altercation with a Whipper supporter and local thug, Bob Bythewood, which Smalls denied. Whipper also claimed that a large crowd at the phosphate works at Chisholm's Landing had turned against Smalls. Smalls replied that Whipper's paid agents were run off by a large crowd of phosphate workers supporting Smalls. On October 10 the offices of the *Beaufort Republican* were broken into and campaign material stolen. All of this proved to be thoroughly entertaining to the local electorate, with music, colorful speeches, and occasional fistfights throughout the campaign. In late October the *Beaufort Republican* commented, "Political songs are all the rage in Beaufort. Smalls and Whipper are belabored in doggerel verse and howled at in every key. Discord reigns supreme."[6]

The campaign climaxed in the October 16 Republican primary election. Across the county, 6,665 votes were cast. Robert Smalls and the Regular Republican ticket won a resounding victory. Smalls garnered 3,953 votes to Whipper's 1,047. Smalls carried all but five precincts in the county by large margins. The precincts Whipper carried were in the upper district on the mainland, where the largest number of white voters was concentrated: Brunson, Black Creek, Hickory Hill, Varnville, and Whippy Swamp. The Moses and Gleaves ticket also won by a wide margin.

The 1872 election was over but animosities arising from it lasted many years. In 1875, after Robert Smalls had gone to Congress, Governor Daniel H. Chamberlain refused to sign W. J. Whipper's commission as circuit judge. A story was printed in Washington and circulated locally that Congressman Smalls stated that the election of Whipper as circuit judge by the South Carolina legislature was a mistake "which jeopardizes the Republican ascendancy in South Carolina." Smalls was further quoted as saying that Whipper "is no lawyer and is unfit for the job." Smalls denied the story but it further divided the Beaufort County Republicans. Senator Samuel Green and Representative S. J. Bampfield, Smalls's son-in-law, supported Whipper, and Representative N. B. Myers supported Chamberlain.[7] This rift in Beaufort's Republican Party ended Whipper's political ambitions and helped set the stage for the Democratic counterrevolution of 1876.

Another issue arising from the campaign of 1872 was that of taxes. From the beginning of the Reconstruction regime, taxes had been rising at an alarming rate. Most of these were property taxes, so they fell most heavily on white landowners. However, in Beaufort County a large percentage of property owners were freedmen with small incomes, who could least afford the taxes. In addition, many white taxpayers in Beaufort were northern businessmen loyal to the Republican Reconstruction regime. Rising taxes and growing financial scandals soon disenchanted them. At the height of the 1872 campaign, during a series of Fourth of July speeches, an unidentified speaker made the startling admission that the tax increase of the previous legislative session was intended "to take the land out of the possession of the white people and place it in the hands of the colored people." In 1873 and 1874, 770,000 acres across the state were seized for nonpayment of taxes. The vast majority of these landowners were white. But in Beaufort County this land "redistribution" scheme backfired. In 1868, 14,316 acres in Beaufort County land, most of it owned by freedmen, were confiscated for a mere $756.80 in unpaid taxes. Between 1870 and 1872, two-thirds of the land sold at tax sales in Beaufort County belonged to freedmen.[8] The *Beaufort Republican* listed fourteen columns of delinquent tax sales for 1871 alone. In May 1876 the *Port Royal Standard and Commercial* listed 650 different parcels of land up for auction at the Beaufort County delinquent-tax sale.

As black landowners lost their land to high taxes, local reformers seized the issue in the 1872 campaign. In September the *Beaufort Republican* stated that both the land seizures and the fiscal scandals in Columbia were weakening the Regular Republicans: "If you want to pay a three mill Blue Ridge Tax this fall, vote for Frank Moses. He will see that you do it or lose your land."[9] The tax issue had a powerful impact on Beaufort's commercial class, which was mostly northerners and mostly Republicans. M. M. Kingman, proprietor of the Sea Island Hotel, published an angry letter complaining of exorbitant state, county, and city taxes. Kingman's property taxes, liquor license, and billiard license cost him $450 per year, a very large sum in 1872. "If the city wants a hotel," Kingman threatened, "they had better limit taxes."[10]

Taxation was the issue around which outnumbered Democrats rallied disaffected voters to oppose the Reconstruction regime. The first statewide tax convention was held in Columbia in 1871 and the second in 1874. These conventions were the beginning of the reorganized state Democratic Party. "Tax unions" became the opposition's grassroots organizations. By 1874 the political leaders of the Reconstruction regime were forced to answer the "tax unions." In August 1874 U.S. Senator John J. Patterson, a Pennsylvanian and a leader of the Reconstruction government in South Carolina, visited Beaufort to campaign for Daniel H. Chamberlain. Realizing the local sensitivity on the tax issue, Senator Patterson countered tax protesters' assertions and appealed to Beaufort County freedmen, stating, "They say there are taxes ... that there was misappropriation of the funds ... that the state was ruined. Now who ruined it? *They* went to war. *They* rebelled ... when you were slaves were you ever consulted about dissolving the Union? ... was that not taxation without representation?"[11]

By 1874 tax unions had been formed in twenty-one South Carolina counties. On August 14, 1874, the Beaufort County Tax Union was organized at Gillisonville, the old county seat, with branch organizations at Robertville and McPhersonville. The officers of the Beaufort County union were B. F. Buckner, president; A. G. Gill, vice president; Joseph O. H. Sanders, secretary; and Thomas S. Taylor, treasurer. Dr. Henry Goethe, William F. Colcock Jr., J. R. Youmans, and C. R. Fitts represented their respective neighborhoods. All were white Confederate veterans and all lived in the upper (mainland) districts.[12] Both the cast of characters and the setting were reminiscent of the "Southern Rights" association meeting at Gillisonville in 1850. Formation of the Beaufort County Tax Union was not only the start of the Democratic opposition to Reconstruction in Beaufort County, but it was also the beginning of the "secession" of Hampton County.

By 1874 the Reconstruction regime had observed the "suspicious" formation of "rifle clubs" across South Carolina. Throughout Reconstruction, lawlessness and violence were endemic. Much of this violence was politically motivated and represented the raw edge of the social revolution underway in the state. The Beaufort community followed closely the rise and fall of the Ku Klux Klan in upstate York and Chester Counties and generally approved the federal occupation and prosecutions in those counties. The *Beaufort Republican* labeled "KuKluxism" as "not honorable vigilantism but simply the banding together of cowardly, murdering assassins." What South Carolina needed was "Republican institutions over a people of common school and free press enlightenment."[13] The huge black majority in Beaufort County and a well-organized body of armed National Guardsmen, many of whom were Civil War veterans of the 33rd Regiment of United States Colored Troops, effectively deterred this type of political violence. The first Ku Klux Klan chapter in Beaufort County was not formed until 1921.

But Beaufort County was not immune to violence and lawlessness, political or otherwise, which undermined the Republican regime. Just after the Civil War ended, a gang of "murderers and incendiaries" committed a series of crimes on the mainland of Beaufort and Colleton Counties. Three white landowners named Henderson, White, and Grant were murdered. The criminals were not apprehended for more than a decade. The crimes were committed by a band of thieves and killers said to be "residents of the Sea Islands" who regularly raided plantations on the mainland. The last four outlaws of this gang were not finally arrested until 1877. They were Robert Washington and Ben Smalls of Coosaw Island, Paddy Grant of Walterboro, and Cypher "Double Quick" Ladson of Savannah, who was arrested only after "a desperate struggle."[14] Some of the violence occurred when white property owners attempted to reclaim their plantation lands. In 1871 Louis Montmollin and a Mr. Schley of Savannah ventured out of the city to reclaim Mrs. Montmollin's Savannah River rice plantation in Beaufort County. Both were shot dead by a black posse led by Constable Cumberland Middleton and dispatched to the scene by Trial Justice Robertson of Hardeeville, a black judge. Several Beaufort County witnesses swore that the white men fired the first shots and the matter was dropped.[15]

There were those in Savannah who thought that some parts of Beaufort County were dangerous places for white people to venture into, but, in fact, violence in Savannah spilled over into Beaufort County. In 1871 the "street car riots" touched off two days of racial violence and anarchy in downtown Savannah. The riots were begun in July 1871 when a group of black men, some from Beaufort County, entered an all-white streetcar. A gang of white men expelled them, and shots were exchanged between the two gangs. Five or six whites were shot and twelve blacks were wounded, though no one was killed. The municipal police lost control of the streets, and hostile crowds roamed through the city for two days.[16] In Beaufort County in 1872, a crowd of "unruly Negroes" sacked two stores in Varnville owned by McBride Peeples and Isaac Altman. Reports indicated that the crowd "had come up the railroad from Beaufort." Only twenty-six dollars was taken from Peeples's store and only ten dollars from Altman's store, but the incident upset the quiet village of Varnville and increased animosity between white landowners on the mainland and the black freedmen on the sea islands.[17]

One form of violence, perhaps unique to Beaufort County in the 1870s, was labor unrest. The busy seaport at Port Royal and the booming phosphate mining industry of the 1870s provided good-paying jobs for the sea islanders. But the work was very different and often more demanding than what they had been accustomed to during slavery. The first labor unrest in Beaufort County occurred at the Port Royal docks on September 16, 1872. Dockworkers walked off the job, demanding two dollars per day to return. When other men lined up to work, fifty striking dockworkers attacked them. "Fifty turbulent ones," it was reported, "armed themselves with sticks and threatened beatings to anyone who would go to work." A few days later, the docks were calm, and most of the men had returned to work. At the same time, the entire crew of the Charleston bark *Henrietta,* which was lying at the Coosaw Mines phosphate works on the Bull River, mutinied against their officers, jumped overboard, and swam to shore.[18] These were both minor incidents, but they were also a new and alarming kind of civil disorder for old Beaufort.

A far more serious incident occurred on May 20, 1877. Workers at the Pacific Guano Company at Chisholm's Landing refused to work under a new wage arrangement that paid the workers in the "cuts," or open pit mines, one dollar per day rather than one dollar per ton of rock excavated. For the efficient workers, day wages cut their pay almost in half and occupied more of their time. When the company employed new workers, the old hands "formed a Union . . . armed themselves and fired on the palmetto huts where the new workers were sleeping." Four of the new workers were ambushed and severely wounded by "Union men." The sheriff and deputies restored order and arrested five of the leading troublemakers. Four were local freedmen: Dick Young, Daniel Singleton, Francis Gibbons, and Prince Young. The local paper commented that "the practice of the Molly MaGuire's will not be tolerated here."[19] The incident clearly revealed that Beaufort County freedmen would not tolerate customary forms of industrial labor management.

The most serious labor unrest in Beaufort County's history was the summer 1876 strike among the Combahee River rice workers. Eighteen seventy-six was one of the most critical political years in South Carolina's long history, and racial tensions were high across the state. The Combahee River strikes, therefore, took on political overtones. But the root cause of the disturbance was purely economic. On the mainland, the old planter families along the Combahee River had generally retained ownership of their prewar plantations. For most of the war, the Union Army occupied only the sea islands, so the mainland plantations were not foreclosed and resold under the Direct Tax Act. After the war, the rice planters returned to the Combahee River and sought to produce rice by means of labor contracts with their former slaves. This innovation was at best a mixed success. The vagaries of the economy and the commodities market meant that the rice planters were often short of cash to pay their workers. Owners and plantation managers adopted the habit of paying their workers in certificates, or "scrip," redeemable only at the country stores of cooperating merchants. The planters themselves owned many of these stores. They then raised the prices on goods, increasing their profits, and effectively diminishing the wages of the workers.

In May 1876 six hundred to seven hundred rice workers in Colleton County walked off the job, demanding an increase in wages of forty cents to fifty cents per day and payment in cash, not scrip. Most of the workers returned to their jobs with a promise of wages paid in cash at the rate of "50 cents per task." Once again, receiving payment based on the familiar task system gave energetic workers the ability to increase their incomes and gave all the free laborers more control of their time. On the rice plantations, as opposed to the phosphate works, the managers were also accustomed to the task system of labor management.

The real issue in the rice fields, however, was payment in cash, and this was hard for the planters to do. In August 1876, at the peak of the rice harvest, three hundred Beaufort County rice workers walked off the job, demanding a cash advance of half their wages. Workers who refused to cooperate with the strikers were seized, whipped, and imprisoned in outhouses. The sheriff and a posse were outnumbered by the strikers, and in many mainland neighborhoods, whites armed themselves and gathered for safety.[20] Much of rural Beaufort County was in rebellion; regular law enforcement was overpowered by the strikers; and blacks and whites were arming for protection. It was the most serious law-enforcement crisis in Beaufort County's long history.

Congressman Robert Smalls strode into the midst of the crisis. Governor Chamberlain, hesitant to call out the militia, sent Smalls, a militia major general, to assess the situation for him. Without militia support and without an armed escort, Smalls confronted the strikers, convinced the leaders against whom warrants had been issued to turn themselves in, and defused the powder keg of rural unrest. Next to seizing the SS *Planter* in 1862, Smalls's ending of the Combahee "riots" was his greatest act of personal courage.

In his report to Governor Chamberlain, Smalls noted that the root of the problem was the payment of wages in scrip and the near-universal opinion among the rice workers that they were being cheated. "I am free to say," Smalls reported, "that had the laborers been paid in money, the rice fields would have been the most peaceful and orderly portion of the state." The solution to the disorder of the rice district, Smalls noted, was simple: "good money for honest labor." Smalls further reported "no lawless disposition among the strikers." Many of the strikers were National Guardsmen who had weapons at home, but knew that it was against the law to use them. They appeared armed only with clubs and sticks. They became alarmed, however, when forty to sixty white men appeared on horseback "armed with Spencer rifles, sixteen shooters and double barreled shotguns." Trial Justice Fuller at Garden's Corner had issued warrants for seven strikers on charges of assault. Smalls convinced these men to surrender, whereupon they "walked into Beaufort, fourteen miles distant, without a guard of any kind" and turned themselves in to the sheriff.

Thanks to Robert Smalls, the Combahee riots ended peacefully, but tension in the county remained high. Smalls recommended the removal of Trial Justice Fuller from the bench "as he is a large planter and one who issues checks [scrip] to his laborers; therefore, there must be, naturally, dissatisfaction on the part of laborers when brought before him." On the other hand, Smalls highly complimented the performance of Deputy Sheriff Sams, another white planter, who was "entitled to much credit for his coolness and bravery and the good judgment he exercised in the discharge of his duties." It was exactly the judgment that history should apply to Robert Smalls himself.[21]

This incident illustrated why Robert Smalls was the "indispensable man" in Reconstruction Beaufort. No white missionary, no northern black lawyer or politician, and no Federal army officer commanded the instant respect of the freedmen necessary to defuse such a dangerous situation. Despite the political invective hurled at Robert Smalls by his white opponents across the state, Beaufort County whites who knew him best always respected the man for his dignity, his political acumen, his strength of character, and most important, his personal courage.

The Combahee riots, however, had a lingering effect in the community. The *Charleston News and Courier,* the state's largest Democratic newspaper, claimed that "the riots and whippings in the rice fields have been instituted by Republicans" for political advantage. In Republican Beaufort, however, the *Port Royal Standard and Commercial* made a more accurate assessment, "We say there is nothing political in these riots." They were caused by purely "economic grievances."[22] The breakdown in civil order during the rice riots was blamed for continuing crime in the countryside. A string of burglaries in Beaufort and Colleton Counties was blamed on some of the leading strike organizers: "The men who organized the Combahee Riots have now organized themselves into a band of burglars and are preying on the country stores." The Colleton County stores of B. C. Adams and Bowman and Nehemias, as well as Henry Fuller's store in Beaufort County, were victimized. Adams's watchman exchanged gunfire with the leader of the gang, Peter Holmes of Beaufort County. Holmes was also suspected of the murder of a Mr. Mathews on Coosaw Island in 1876. Sheriff Wilson captured three brothers and two cousins of Holmes in Colleton County in January 1877, but the ringleader escaped. Governor Wade Hampton offered a reward for Peter Holmes's capture, and he was later arrested in Charleston in June 1877.[23]

When Wade Hampton was finally inaugurated governor in April 1877, he briefly stopped the rice field unrest by making a large amount of money available to the Combahee and Savannah River planters to pay their workers in cash and complete the spring planting. Hampton's decision was lauded even in staunchly Republican Beaufort: "Rice planters of the Combahee and Savannah Rivers most welcome Hampton's victory . . . a large amount of money will now be paid out to laborers . . . and just in time for the rice planting." The local newspaper expressed the relief of the whole community: "The Combahee and Ashepoo riots of last summer caused serious loss to the rice planters and no little suffering to the Negroes." The final chapter of the Combahee riots was written in June 1877, when fifteen strike leaders were convicted of riot in Walterboro and given light sentences.[24]

During the election year of 1876, with racial tension at its height in Beaufort County, there were several violent confrontations between blacks and whites, including the murders of two white planters by black men. On Saturday night, April 17, 1876, Fred Bright and John Snipe ambushed and murdered seventy-six-year-old General John H. Howard by shooting him in the back of the head. Howard was one of the leading citizens of the Grahamville district. The local paper noted that "General Howard was one of our oldest, most useful and most honored citizens.... his death is a public calamity ... a deed like this sends a thrill of sickening horror through every heart." Evidently there had been bad blood between Howard and some of the freedmen in the community. Some months before his murder, unknown parties had set fire to his plantation house and burned it to the ground. The perpetrators were never found, but arson was a signature crime, before and after the war, of disaffected blacks against white property owners. When General Howard was murdered, the assailants were soon arrested and brought to trial in Beaufort. The prosecutors were prominent white citizens of the mainland, William E. Bell and William Ferguson Colcock Jr. The defense attorneys were leading black lawyers in Beaufort, Samuel J. Bampfield and Thomas Wheeler. The *Charleston News* cried foul: "General Howard will not get justice.... juries in Beaufort County are notoriously untrustworthy." This assessment was wrong, however. A Beaufort jury convicted Snipe and Bright and condemned them to death.[25] During the spring of 1877, the son of another prominent Beaufort planter family, Joseph Edings Jr., was murdered on Parris Island by two black men, George Stevens and David Pearce. The murderers were arrested, tried, convicted, and sentenced to hang in Beaufort on July 13, 1877.[26]

Racial tensions during 1876 often led to gunfights and general rioting. The small railroad town of Brunson was the sight of several altercations. In April 1876 an argument between a local white landowner, Hardy Harrison, and a black man named Thomas Myers turned into a fight and then "a general riot" when their friends joined in: "Pistols were discharged and Thomas Myers was shot twice." A few days later, B. M. Riley, a white man, got drunk and shot a black man named Handy Gadsden. The incident was blamed on liquor and no riot ensued. These incidents were "too bad for Brunson, otherwise a sober place and with the railroad, great possibilities." A month later a murder in Allendale took on more specific political overtones. A white man named John Hutto was accused of shooting the black town marshal of Allendale. When Hutto came to trial in the Barnwell Courthouse, it was noted that "the counsel for the defense is paid by a local Democratic Club."[27]

With the completion of the Port Royal Railroad in 1873, the town of Yemassee became both the most important railroad junction in the southeast corner of the state and the crossroads of Beaufort County. On a daily basis white landowners from the upcountry mingled with black sea islanders; white Confederate veterans encountered black Union veterans; and travelers from the North, South, and West mixed with both. Restaurants and boarding houses opened in the village to serve railroad passengers. Yemassee also became the site of several racial confrontations, some of which turned violent.

In November 1873 Senator Robert Smalls, Representative Samuel Green, and Representative Thomas Hamilton were refused service at A. E. Owens's restaurant in Yemassee because they were black. This violated the Public Accommodations Act passed by the South Carolina General Assembly in 1870 and introduced by Robert Smalls himself. The three local leaders were not about to let the slight pass. Owens was arrested, taken to trial, and fined the hefty sum of five hundred dollars. Owens was represented in court by C. J. C. Hutson and J. C. Davant, two lawyers from old white planter families, while Smalls, Hamilton, and Green were represented by Beaufort black attorney J. M. Williams. Despite the heavy fine, Owens did not appeal the verdict, and the Yemassee case demonstrated the power of such progressive civil rights measures as the Public Accommodations Act.[28]

A more violent encounter occurred in April 1876, when Thomas Jones, a white clerk in the depot restaurant, asked a black railroad employee to deliver an umbrella to a passenger. When the railroad hand refused to comply, an argument ensued. Jones pulled a pistol, shooting and killing the black man. Many travelers at the busy railroad junction witnessed the murder and the incident aroused "strong public sentiment" divided along racial lines. Jones hired W. J. Whipper of Beaufort to defend him. Whipper immediately asked for a change of venue as local public opinion "would prejudice his case." One of the Beaufort County jury commissioners had publicly stated that he "would see Jones hang." The trial was moved to Walterboro, where Jones was convicted and sentenced to prison.[29] It was not surprising that a white man would hire Beaufort's most prominent black lawyer to defend him in a constituency where the juries were overwhelmingly black. Farther upcountry at Stafford's Crossroads, however, it was often dangerous for black attorneys to venture. In July 1876 State Representative Thomas E. Miller was "severely beaten" when he secured the conviction of a white man and was attacked by the losing side.[30]

Violence even intruded on isolated, pastoral Hilton Head Island. In January 1877 Robert McIntire, the postmaster, was murdered in his store by a shotgun blast from outside. McIntire was one of the few white men living on the island at the time. He had come from New York during the war and remained to open a dry goods and grocery store. The post office was in his store. Robert McIntire was planning to leave Hilton Head because of an earlier attempt on his life. Although no evidence was discovered of a political motive, it was noted that the postmaster was "a lifelong Democrat, but not active ... he paid the Hampton tax on the day he was murdered." Three Hilton Head blacks were arrested: Jim Giles, David Grant, and a young boy used as a lookout, Morris White. Although it was common knowledge who the murderers were, no one was willing to testify. Two months later there was still "not enough evidence to convict the three arrested."[31]

In April 1877 Brunson was the scene of a racial confrontation between Dick Eley, a local black man who "was implicated in several stealing scrapes" in 1876, and a group of five or six "disguised, armed men ... who said they were Barnwell men." The gang of white men broke into Eley's house, seized him, beat him, bagged his head, carried him into the woods, and stripped and whipped him. A local white landowner, Captain Williams, helped Eley recover from his wounds. While the Beaufort paper concluded that "the affair was non-political in nature," it bore all the signs of vigilante justice against local blacks perceived as undesirable.[32]

The most deadly confrontation of the era occurred in June 1877 at Stafford's Crossroads in the upper district of Beaufort County. The location is near the present town of Furman in Hampton County. The incident was the culmination of bad blood between a white landowner, W. B. Shuman, and black tenant families. A rumor circulated among the blacks that Shuman was determined to run off or kill all the blacks on the property. When the trouble began, Deputy J. D. Johnson arrested one of the black leaders, Frank Grant, and placed him in jail. The black community became aroused, and an armed mob led by Edward Cheney attempted to break Grant out of jail. Failing in that attempt and anticipating a reaction, the blacks gathered at Edward Cheney's house for protection. Soon an armed white posse arrived, led by J. D. Johnson and D. H. Ellis. The attempt to arrest Cheney led to a general riot. Both sides were well armed and a sharp gunfight ensued, with firing from both sides continuing for several minutes. When the smoke cleared, three men lay dead: W. B. Shuman and a Mr. Deloach, both white, and Cheney, the leader of the blacks. Cheney's wife was also wounded. Twenty-four black men were arrested and jailed for the murder of Shuman and Deloach. Two leaders of the white posse, Johnson and Ellis, were indicted for Cheney's murder.

Two trials rose from the incident at Stafford's Crossroads, the outcome of which only added to the breakdown of civil order. When the twenty-four blacks came to trial they were represented by W. J. Whipper. He challenged all the white men off the jury and stacked the jury with sympathetic blacks. Even the Republican-leaning Beaufort newspaper commented that because "the jury being comprised of as black and ignorant material as possible to find," the verdict was predictable. The case became a local political issue, and the all-black jury acquitted the black defendants of murder and riot. In the second trial, a jury of eleven whites and one black acquitted Johnson and Ellis of Cheney's murder. The Stafford's Crossroads gunfight revealed not only overt racism but also the political character of crime and justice in Reconstruction Beaufort County.[33]

Crime, social order, and political power were the chief reasons for the creation of the Varnville Mounted Rifle Club during the tense election season of 1876. No such organization was formed in the sea island portion of Beaufort County. It would have been pointless. With an overwhelmingly black population (a nine-to-one ratio) several companies of veteran armed National Guard and an entrenched and popular black political establishment, any white vigilante organization would have been both unsuccessful and possibly in great danger. In addition, most of the white industrial and commercial establishment of Beaufort and Port Royal were northerners or immigrants whose political allegiances were generally Republican. The few old Confederates left in Beaufort had long since adopted a conciliatory or cooperative attitude. But in the upper section of Beaufort County, on the mainland, the races were more evenly divided with an approximate two-to-one ratio of blacks over whites. That ratio diminished markedly above the rice districts along the Combahee, Pocotaligo, Coosawhatchie, and Savannah Rivers. That portion of Beaufort County had been upper St. Peters and upper Prince William Parishes in the antebellum era. The white property owners had not lost their land, and ex-Confederates had returned to their ancestral homes to rebuild their lives. There, resentment toward the Reconstruction regime was strongest; resistance to the social revolution in Beaufort County was greatest; and the white population believed in 1876 that they had the best chance of recovering social and political control of their neighborhoods.

One extralegal agency whites used to regain control of upper Beaufort County was the Varnville Mounted Rifle Club. Similar organizations had been formed across the state, such as the Allendale Rifle Club, the Colleton Hunt Club, and the Columbia Flying Artillery. The minutes of the Colleton Hunt Club in next-door Colleton County left no doubt of their political purpose. These organizations were thinly veiled methods to create armed, organized resistance to Reconstruction. Membership in the Varnville Mounted Rifle Club required that each club member be suitably mounted and armed with a Winchester or Spencer repeating rifle, the most advanced firearm technology of the day. The organization was strictly military. The commander was Colonel William Stokes. Second in command was Lieutenant Colonel J. T. Morrison. Third was Major W.A Riley. The civilian chairman was Confederate veteran Colonel J. W. Moore, and George Hoover was secretary.[34]

Colonel James Washington Moore was the political and military force behind the Varnville Mounted Rifle Club. Born in Coosawhatchie and educated in Gillisonville, he was a graduate of the University of Georgia. At the outbreak of the Civil War, he joined Hampton's Legion. He was soon promoted to first lieutenant in the 2nd South Carolina Cavalry. He fought at Seven Days, Antietam, Gettysburg, and Brandy Station, where he was wounded and sent home to defend the lowcountry. After the war he returned to Gillisonville, resumed his law practice with Leroy Franklin Youmans, and married Cornelia Tillinghast, daughter of R. L. Tillinghast. During the 1876 election year, he helped organize both the Varnville Mounted Rifle Club and the Gillisonville Rifle Club. James W. Moore was the leader of "Hampton's Red Shirts" in the upper part of Beaufort County in 1876. After Hampton's election Moore was elected to the state senate and held office for sixteen years.[35]

It grew common for white families to arm themselves with repeating rifles for protection during those violent times. In July 1877 a shooting contest with a sizable prize was held in the town of Beaufort. Thomas Farr, a Bluffton storeowner and Confederate veteran, won first place, and W. H. Lockwood, the Beaufort banker, placed second. Most of the white men in town turned out, and almost all were armed with the newest-model Winchester repeating rifles. The local paper was surprised by the firepower displayed: "It was astonishing to see what a large number of these celebrated guns were hidden away in the residences of our people and could but think that their presence betokened a determination to make good use of them . . . if necessary . . . during the late political excitement." Clearly, the white population of the county was well armed and anticipating trouble during the 1876 election campaign and the dispute that followed. Will Elliott, in his memoir of growing up in Beaufort during Reconstruction, reflected on the anxious, armed preparedness of the white minority. He recalled that during the 1878 election campaign, Beaufort blacks had threatened to instigate a race riot. They attacked a Democratic speaker's stand, destroyed the podium, and roamed the streets in armed gangs issuing "vociferous threats." Whites feared to venture outside but were prepared for just this circumstance. The few white families in Beaufort had concealed a small arsenal of repeating rifles in a locked closet in Colonel William Elliott's prominent mansion, now called the Anchorage. In case of riot, all the white families were to retreat to Elliott's large tabby house and defend it like a fortress until help arrived from the mainland. It seems clear that the white population had no confidence in local authorities to maintain civil order.[36]

Lingering violence during the fall of 1877 seemed to confirm their suspicion. In Brunson a small argument over a store bill led to a gunfight between B. J. Martin and T. T. Gill. Martin was killed but the jury ruled self-defense. At Port Royal a gang of burglars raided all the abandoned houses in town and broke into Ward's cotton house on the docks. As the tumultuous year closed, two hunters in the Savannah River swamp near Hardeeville found the body of a black man floating in a "lonely and desolate bayou of the Savannah River" called Coleman's Lake. The man's arms were bound behind him. He had been shot in the head, and his stomach had been slashed.[37] It was a gruesome reminder of one of the most violent periods in Beaufort County history.

During the 1876 campaign, General Wade Hampton toured the state and was greeted almost everywhere by the white population as a hero and savior. Sensing the divisions within the Republican regime, the Democrats were energized, organized, and confident. Across the state hardened Confederate veterans led by General Martin W. Gary of Edgefield formed rifle clubs, sabre clubs, and artillery clubs and dedicated them to the overthrow of the black Republican Reconstruction regime. Alarmed, Governor Daniel H. Chamberlain alerted President Ulysses S. Grant, who outlawed all rifle clubs in South Carolina and dispatched more federal troops to the state. Rather than disband, the clubs reorganized under new names, such as the First Baptist Sewing Club and Mother's Little Helpers. The Allendale Mounted Rifle Club became the Allendale Mounted Baseball Club, and the Columbia Flying Artillery became the Columbia Music Club with four "twelve-pounder flutes." The humor and irony masked a deadly earnest purpose—the return of white power. Across the state, these clubs donned the trademark Red Shirts and formed paramilitary escorts for Wade Hampton in nearly every community.[38]

Beaufort County's reaction to the rise of the white Democratic Party in the 1870s was to wave its own version of the bloody shirt of rebellion and civil war. In 1870 the local Beaufort newspaper observed that "the Democratic Party of South Carolina has a long black record ... all bloodstained and sickening ... they brought us the madness and wickedness of secession and rebellion ... a long line of as prejudiced aristocrats as ever shackled men and cursed the state with the meanest and most scornful pride. We cannot forget the old treacherous, purjured, bloodstained character of democracy in South Carolina."[39] But six years later, the bloody shirt had a different meaning when it rallied white Democrats instead of black Republicans.

The 1876 campaign opened in March with a bad omen for Beaufort Republicans. Charleston papers reported the sinking of the steamer *Planter* off Cape Romaine on March 23, 1876. The Beaufort paper acknowledged the significance of the event and regretted the loss of the "historic boat ... that a slave of the Negro race, Robert Smalls, at present a representative of this district to Congress, made a determined and successful effort to freedom."[40]

When the Republican Party held its convention at the Beaufort arsenal on April 6, Congressman Smalls sent a message warning local Republicans of the high stakes in the 1876 election. Republicans had lost control of the

United States House of Representatives and needed to work doubly hard to retain control of the state and county governments. Democratic victory "would imperil all that has been gained by the late war and the subsequent legislation on behalf of human rights." The Beaufort County Republican Convention selected Thomas Hamilton, Samuel Green, Robert Smalls, Samuel J. Bampfield, Hastings Gant, Richard H. Gleaves, and William Wilson as delegates to the state convention. Thomas E. Miller and George Holmes were alternates. These men were the established Republican leaders of Beaufort County; only Holmes was white.

In 1876 the county Democrats were sufficiently reorganized to send fourteen delegates to its state convention. All were white men and all but two represented the mainland townships. They were Colonel James W. Moore, Charles Bell, and Joseph Glover from Coosawhatchie; John G. Barnwell and William J. Verdier from Beaufort; Charles J. C. Hutson and Jesse Deloach from Pocotaligo; Stephen E. Whitehead from Yemassee; Alfred M. Martin and Dr. Rudell from Lawtonville; William J. Gooding and Jeffrey Warren from Peeples; Dr. Henry Goethe from Goethe; and Henry M. Fuller from Sheldon. These men formed the core of the Democratic leadership for a generation.[41]

In July, Republican Governor Chamberlain made a campaign visit. This was the first time since the war's end that a Republican candidate felt it necessary to seek votes in heavily black, Republican Beaufort, and his visit only served to highlight the disintegration of the Republican Party. Chamberlain was welcomed to town by Moritz Pollitzer. He reviewed the navy's South Atlantic Squadron anchored in Port Royal Sound and then held a public meeting with black political leaders Langdon Langley, Representative Thomas Hamilton, and Senator Samuel Green. Langley resolved to support Chamberlain for governor, but Samuel Green objected strenuously because Chamberlain had refused to appoint W. J. Whipper to a circuit judgeship. An argument ensued and Governor Chamberlain departed the stage, left the county, and did not return to Beaufort. That public embarrassment demonstrated the weakening of the Republican Party.[42]

During the last week of October, General Wade Hampton made a campaign visit to Beaufort County hoping to rally his base of white voters on the mainland and siphon off some black votes from the bickering Republicans on the sea islands. He rode the Port Royal and Augusta Railroad through Allendale, Brunson, Hoover Station, and Varnville. At each stop enthusiastic crowds of white farmers showed up to encourage him. At Early Branch, Hampton reviewed the Varnville Mounted Rifles and gave a rousing speech promising to clean up the corruption in Columbia, lower taxes, recover the state's lost credit, and restore the social fabric of South Carolina. The Red Shirts at Early Branch offered to provide an armed escort as the candidate proceeded into hostile territory in the sea islands. Hampton, however, urged caution. He knew that the Red Shirts were spoiling for a fight and that lower Beaufort County was the home of thousands of armed, black national guardsmen equally ready for a confrontation. Any outburst of political violence in Beaufort would place the Red Shirts in great danger and attract the attention of the U.S. Navy warships with their thousands of sailors anchored in Port Royal Sound. In 1876 Beaufort was still Union country and General Hampton knew it.

Hampton was rudely received in Beaufort. He held a public meeting at the William Elliott III mansion overlooking the Beaufort River. Another Confederate veteran, local attorney Colonel William Elliott, introduced him. The crowd was overwhelmingly black. During Hampton's speech, listeners shouted comments "filled with more profanity than any other political meeting." Representative Edmund W. M. Mackey of Charleston, a white Republican, asked Hampton a question calculated to embarrass him. He dared Hampton to admit that he was neither a property owner nor a taxpayer in South Carolina. This was a particularly telling question for a man who had been one of the richest men in America before the war but had lost all of his property after the war. Mackey hoped to point out the hypocrisy of Hampton's complaining of high Reconstruction taxes while paying none himself. Hampton refused to reply, "too high toned to admit that he was not a property owner or a taxpayer." Hampton's campaign stop in Beaufort was "a labored attempt to gain the Negro vote," but it failed. In fact, toward the end of the speech, the crowd became unruly and hostile. Just when it appeared that a riot might break out, Congressman Robert Smalls, the indispensable man, quieted the crowd, urged them to peaceful behavior, and personally escorted Hampton back to the railroad depot.[43]

When the election was held and the vote finally tabulated in Beaufort County, the result was predictable. Chamberlain received 6,986 votes to Hampton's 2,321. Robert Smalls was easily reelected to the U.S. House of Representatives. The only precincts Hampton won were in the upper portion of the mainland.[44] The vote totals were as follows:

Beaufort County Vote Totals by Precinct, 1876 Election

Precinct	Chamberlain	Hampton
SEA ISLAND PRECINCTS		
Beaufort	562	115
Grays Hill	476	9

(continued)

Precinct	Chamberlain	Hampton
Myrtle Bush	261	5
Port Royal	123	50
Parris Island	141	12
Lady's Island	312	8
Brick Church (St. Helena Is.)	719	6
Coffin Point	148	22

MAINLAND PRECINCTS, LOWER DISTRICT

Precinct	Chamberlain	Hampton
Chisholm's Landing	267	39
Garden's Corners	537	75
Pocotaligo	210	90
Grahamville	232	108
Bluffton	423	98
Bellinger Hill	412	28
Brighton	186	101
Levy's Crossroads	447	65

MAINLAND PRECINCTS, UPPER DISTRICT

Precinct	Chamberlain	Hampton
Gillisonville	223	178
Lawtonville	313	230
Lawton Church	210	40
Nixville	36	112
Gene's Crossroad	142	11
Henes' Crossroad	60	94
Matthew's Bluff	178	43
Varnville	66	271
Peeples	69	189
Brunson	310	230
Beech Branch	22	72
Black Creek	6	0

This list is a fair reflection of the distribution of the voting population of Beaufort County during the Reconstruction years. It displays the overwhelming dominance of the black vote on the sea islands, the majority black votes in the lower district near the old rice plantations, and the nearly even split of black and white votes in old St. Peters and Prince William Parishes. The political geography of Beaufort County was important in explaining the next event of Reconstruction Beaufort: the secession of Hampton County.

Wade Hampton won a narrow statewide victory, which was vigorously challenged. Republicans refused to vacate the state house, and U.S. troops, black state militia. and well-armed Red Shirts faced off in Columbia. The resolution of the issue went all the way to the White House. There, General Rutherford B. Hayes parlayed just enough electoral votes from South Carolina, Louisiana, and Florida to become president. In exchange for South Carolina's votes, Hayes's former battlefield foe, General Hampton, extracted a promise to remove federal troops and end Reconstruction in the state. In April 1877 Wade Hampton became governor, and Reconstruction in South Carolina ended. The sea island community was resentful and suspicious of Hampton's victory, believing the charges of fraud and intimidation in the upcountry. They had supported Governor Chamberlain, who they believed "beat a combination of violence and fraud" to win the election. They bemoaned the divided state government where "the situation in Columbia is humiliating to thoughtful men." A divided legislature and armed confrontation in the capital were "another dark page to the history of the state." In January 1877 Congressman Robert Smalls left Beaufort for Washington "to testify before Congress about fraud and intimidation in the election."[45]

Confusion reigned from October 1876 to April 1877 while the election outcome was disputed. In Columbia, Chamberlain refused to turn over the governor's office to Hampton and two rival house speakers, Republican Edmund M. W. Mackey and Democrat William H. Wallace, sat side by side and jointly—or, rather, in competition—presided in the house chamber. Uncertainty and hostility prevailed in each county as well. In Beaufort the school commissioner's office was turned over to the black attorney Thomas Wheeler, but H. G. Judd refused to surrender the clerk of court's office to Samuel J. Bampfield, who had won the local election. Governor Chamberlain attempted a "tombstone" appointment of two local supporters as trial justices, Ben Simmons at Bluffton and Macon Allen, founder of the Allen Brass Band, at Beaufort. The local paper thought neither man qualified for the job and noted that "such appointments make no friends for Chamberlain except the appointees." Beaufort Democrats met Hampton at Early Branch to plan their local strategy. The Democratic executive committee, chaired by Colonel James W. Moore, recommended appointing W. J. Gooding as county treasurer and J. A. Johnson as county auditor. Both were Red Shirts and members of the Varnville Mounted Rifle Club.[46]

The Republicans met at the Arsenal in Beaufort to support Chamberlain and "oppose by every legitimate means ... the efforts of the Democrats to install General Hampton." Senator Samuel Green described the scene in Columbia: "Riflemen came by train from all over South Carolina to fill the capital" and intimidate the opposition. The greatest condemnation was reserved for two state representatives, Thomas Hamilton and Nathaniel Myers. Both were black Republicans who had abandoned the Republican-controlled "Mackey House" and went over to the rival Democratic-controlled "William H. Wallace House." According to Green, their action had "done more to hurt the party than the actions of any other men." He claimed that Hamilton and Myers were bribed. Green said he had been offered ten thousand dollars to switch sides but had refused. The most extreme local reaction came from an unidentified white Republican in Port Royal. As a Beaufort newspaper reported, "Port Royal was much exercised by ... speeches of a white man who advised the colored people to arise and exterminate the whites and take possession of the town. The belligerent fellow was locked up."[47]

As desperate and violent as was the election of 1876, it did not lack for humor. In one house race, Representative Joseph Robinson, a black Republican, was pitted against A. P. Jenkins, a black Democrat. The two politicians made a wager and converted it to a written contract. If Chamberlain was elected governor, Jenkins would be the "servant" of Robinson. If Hampton was elected, Robinson would be the "servant" of Jenkins. When Hampton was confirmed as governor, Jenkins "hired out" Robinson to the Waterhouse and Ricker Company, stating "he had no use for him."[48]

Beaufort's highest-ranking black incumbent, Lieutenant Governor Richard H. Gleaves, acted with remarkable prudence and moderation in the volatile atmosphere of Columbia. When the transfer of power to the Hampton Democrats finally took place in April 1877, Gleaves was the president of the state senate. On April 24, 1877, Gleaves graciously turned the gavel of the Senate over to the incoming lieutenant governor, William D. Simpson, vacating his seat and the office he had held for two terms. In his farewell address to the senate, Gleaves stated that further opposition "cannot advance the interest of the Constitution." He departed with "the personal friendship of the Senators." The senate in return accorded Gleaves a "respectful and friendly farewell." His departure was a rare moment of civility in the rancorous transition. Gleaves's civility and moderation did him little good. In July 1877 he was indicted for conspiracy and fraud in office. On July 26, 1877, two men from Columbia arrived in Beaufort with a warrant to arrest Gleaves, who left the state and never returned. In August his household goods were sold at auction by James M. Crofut.[49]

Once in control of the state government, the Democrats took steps to reduce taxes, reduce the cost of government, and reform the Republican patronage machine or replace it with their own. In May 1877 the General Assembly passed an act to reduce the salaries of county treasurers and auditors and another one to reduce the pay of county commissioners. On St. Helena Island, Governor Hampton appointed former planter and Confederate veteran Thomas B. Chaplin of Tombee Plantation the trial justice. Like most sea island planters, Chaplin had fallen on hard times after the war. Unlike most sea island planters, he stayed in Beaufort County. The Datha Island planter, R. R. Sams, was appointed county auditor, and W. J. Gooding of Varnville became county treasurer. In June the General Assembly abolished the District School Tax on property, and Superintendent H. S. Thompson notified all the school trustees in the county that there was no money to pay them or the teachers. The new regime, however, did not abolish the poll tax of one dollar per voter. The local newspaper observed that the county poll tax revenue of $9,878 per year would be sufficient to keep the schools open if everyone paid the tax.[50]

Not everyone in Beaufort County was accustomed to paying the poll tax during Reconstruction, and local reformers took some satisfaction from the new regime's determination to collect from everyone. In the words of a Beaufort paper, "For the first time in their lives . . . the loud mouthed political strikers hereabouts will have the pleasure of paying the poll tax this year or going to jail. It is well known that a large number of turbulent politicians pay no taxes, their names not even appearing in the tax books. Treasurer Gooding is now in possession of the poll list . . . all who voted will now pay the school tax." In December 1877 the foreman of the Beaufort County Grand Jury, William Chauncey Bellows, a white northerner, Bay Street merchant, and prominent reformer, revealed that the records and accounts of most county offices were in total disarray. The judge ordered an immediate audit of the offices of treasurer, auditor, sheriff, coroner, and clerk of the county commission.[51]

Treasurer W. J. Gooding, quickly assembled $2,900 in county funds to settle some unpaid debts. In no time "a crowd of claimants assembled at the room of the county commissioners." William Wilson, the black sheriff, was disbursed $1,000. R. R. Sams, the new county auditor, was disbursed $400 "for assessments." W. H. Lockwood was disbursed $450. County Commissioners Vincent Scott, Renty Greaves, and the clerk of the county commission divided $571. Clerk of Court Samuel J. Bampfield received $100. All other claimants were paid thirty-three cents on the dollar. Payments went on until midnight. The crowd "ate sardines, fried sheepshead and crackers. . . . a youth struck up a fiddle but was silenced by the chairman." The fiddler retreated to an adjoining room and entertained the crowd until midnight. Gooding claimed that there was not enough county money to pay all the creditors because the previous county commissioners, B. J. Martin, Renty Greaves, Vincent Scott, and Dr. Paul Pritchard, had "paid their own salaries first." On August 30, 1877, Treasurer Gooding paid most of the teachers' back pay with a $6,000 appropriation from the state.[52]

One of the most sensitive, potentially dangerous elements in the shift of power from black Republicans to white Democrats was the disbandment of the Reconstruction National Guard and reorganization of the state militia under Hampton's command. In Beaufort County this meant disarming black Union veterans and transferring both command and access to state armories to white Confederate veterans. In August, John Porteous arrived to "collect the state arms scattered over the islands in the hands of the now disbanded militia regiments that once figured so prominently about election times." Porteous had little success. All he collected were "some old muskets." On November 29, 1877, Adjutant General Marion Moise came to Beaufort County to inspect the militia units and muster them into the state organization. Any units that passed inspection were to retain their weapons. Any units that failed to pass inspection were to turn in their weapons and submit to retraining before they would be reissued firearms. General Moise inspected "the white militia and one colored company at Early Branch." Then he came down the railroad to Beaufort "to see what was left of the once famous National Guard of Beaufort." When several companies of the local National Guard mustered at the arsenal, General Moise told them that they would have to retrain and reorganize in order to be part of the new state militia. He also ordered them to stack their state-issued weapons at the arsenal. The black militiamen quietly but firmly disobeyed this last order. The majority of the men were "in no doubt as to what to do fearing that the stacking of the arms in the arsenal was a trick of the Democrats to get the guns ... the majority kept them." Fearing the same violence that whites had faced a few years earlier, sea island blacks defied General Moise's orders, kept their firearms, and walked home. The presence of a large number of weapons in the homes of sea island freedmen, legally held or not, was a moderating factor in the conservative reaction to Reconstruction in Beaufort County. That night General Moise gave a speech to a mixed crowd in Beaufort. The audience was quiet and polite. It was said to be the "first time in years a Democrat has been able to speak in Beaufort without subjecting himself to every form of insult," although the local Republicans "did put forward a few drunken Negroes to annoy him."[53]

As Hampton's conservative Democratic regime closed in on Beaufort County's Reconstruction politicians, the black majority had one remaining government body that they could control, the town of Beaufort. The intendant (mayor) of Beaufort was Alfred Williams, a black Republican. He was roundly criticized by the local paper for high taxes and expensive and inefficient government. White commercial leaders in Beaufort began talk of an opposition reform ticket to take over the town council. This criticism provoked a response from Williams. He pointed out that "hundreds of new houses had been built in the last few years ... the town has the best equipped fire department outside of Charleston or Columbia," and that 181 cases brought before the municipal court had resulted in fines paid off by labor on the city streets, making the streets neat and tidy to the satisfaction of "most of our citizens." In July 1877 the annual town meeting was held at the arsenal. Alfred Williams and John P. Boyce were nominated for intendant. The speeches were interrupted by shooting, fights broke out in the audience, a rush was made to the stand, the speaker's table was upset, and a general brawl ensued. The paper called it a "repetition of the annual disgraceful exhibitions." As confusion reigned, Robert Smalls stepped to the front, took over the meeting, and brought order to the crowd. In the end, an opposition slate of candidates for intendant and six wardens was fielded. William Chauncey Bellows for intendant headed that slate with F. W. Scheper, George Waterhouse, W. H. Lockwood, W. M. Mitchell, Z. McGill, and Reverend J. B. Middleton for town wardens. Most of the town warden aspirants were recent immigrants and leading Bay Street merchants. The reform ticket was thoroughly trounced in the city election by the overwhelming black majority. Alfred Williams outpolled William C. Bellows 315 votes to 87. The Republican slate of G. F. Ricker, George Holmes, Samuel J. Bampfield, Cato Perry, R. Washington, and John P. Boyce all won by similar margins.[54] The black Republican regime retained a firm hold on town government. Beaufort, formerly the citadel and refuge of the sea island planter class, became one of the last refuges of the black Reconstruction regime in South Carolina.

Another example of the remaining power of the black Reconstruction regime was the special election for the state senate seat vacated by Samuel Green. The special election was held in early December 1877, and the white Democrats, buoyed by Hampton's victory, thought they had a chance to snatch another seat from the black Republicans. The Democrats quickly organized and nominated attorney William Elliott for the post. Elliott was the most prominent member of the old sea island planter aristocracy still in Beaufort. The third son of Reverend Stephen Elliott, he was born, raised, and educated in wealth and privilege in antebellum Beaufort. Like most of his generation, Elliott eagerly went off to fight in the Civil War. He probably saw more combat action than any other Beaufort Confederate officer. He was at Cummings Point during the bombardment of Fort Sumter. Transferred to the Army of Northern Virginia, he fought at the First Battle of Bull Run, Williamsburg, Seven Days, Second Bull Run, Antietam, and Fredericksburg. Elliott was promoted to captain and transferred to the western command, where he fought at the battles of Vicksburg, Hattiesburg, Atlanta, Jonesboro, Florence, Franklin, and Nashville. Retreating to North Carolina with General John Bell Hood, Lieutenant Colonel Elliott was in the Battles of Kingston and Bentonville, where he was wounded. Elliott was one of the bravest and luckiest of Confederate officers. He was a quintessential Hampton Democrat.

In any other South Carolina county but Beaufort, he would have been a shoo-in for elective office.

The Beaufort Republicans were still demoralized and disorganized in late 1877. At a hurried and confused county convention a few days before the election, W. J. Whipper was nominated but declined the offer. Needing a name on the ballot, someone in the crowd nominated the white Bay Street merchant and entrepreneur, Joseph W. Collins. Collins accepted the nomination and was unanimously approved. Collins had been born in Massachusetts. A trooper with the First Massachusetts Cavalry, he was transferred from Virginia to Hilton Head Island in 1863. After the war, he settled in Beaufort and opened a Bay Street dry goods and grocery store. The local paper noted that Collins "derives his income from judicial investments . . . he was always considered too liberal for the party but there is no other choice." In the short campaign, Elliott worked hard to get out the Democratic vote, and Collins, nominated a few days before the election, did not campaign at all. Nevertheless, the black voters of Beaufort County carried Collins to an overwhelming three-to-one victory. He received 4,329 votes across the county, and Elliott received 1,534 votes, almost all from the mainland precincts.[55]

The most serious blow of the Democratic regime in Columbia against the Republicans of Beaufort County was the arrest of Congressman Robert Smalls in October 1877 on charges of bribery. The sudden, unexpected arrest of Smalls "caused quite a commotion in town." A deputy sent from Columbia tapped Smalls on the shoulder while he was "quietly conversing" on Bay Street. The deputy said he must take Smalls to Columbia. Smalls offered bond of forty thousand dollars, but the deputy refused. Many black and white Beaufort friends rallied around him and offered help, but Smalls demurred. He would go to Columbia peacefully and face the charges. Smalls's old friend Laura Towne commented that the charges were entirely political and only "revealed the cunning of the examiners."

The charge was that while a state senator, Smalls had taken a five-thousand-dollar bribe from Josephus Woodruff of the Republican Printing Company to help Woodruff secure state printing contracts. The prosecutor, Leroy W. Youmans of Gillisonville, was the law partner of Colonel James Washington Moore. Youmans was a Confederate veteran and a leading Democrat of Beaufort County's upper district. He had amassed some powerful evidence, and Smalls had to expend some of his own fortune to defend himself. He sold his commercial building on Bay Street, which housed the newspaper offices, to E. A. Scheper for thirty-five hundred dollars and his "fine carriage and horses" were converted to a "hack" charging twenty-five cents per ride. On November 10, 1877, a court that was "prejudiced against his race, his color and his previous condition of servitude" convicted him. In

December, Smalls made bail of ten thousand dollars. His bail was guaranteed by F. W. and E. A. Scheper while he was out on appeal. George Waterhouse provided cash for his legal defense in exchange for a mortgage on some of Smalls's Bay Street property. Within a week, the rumor circulated in Beaufort that Smalls would receive "executive clemency from Governor Hampton within three months." Smalls's case remained on appeal for nearly a year, but on April 23, 1879, Smalls finally received a pardon from Hampton's successor, William D. Simpson.[56]

The Democrats were never able to shake the faith of the sea island freedmen in Robert Smalls, no matter what charges and threats they brought against him. This was never better illustrated than by the incident at Gillisonville in October 1878 during Smalls's third run for Congress. Smalls was to speak at a rally in the town square. While a crowd of black supporters was gathered, a large body of mounted Red Shirts came galloping into town, "whooping like Indians . . . giving the real rebel yell" and breaking up the crowd. Smalls and forty armed followers barricaded themselves in a store building. Some blacks from the crowd alerted the countryside that "their truly beloved leader was trapped in a house surrounded by 'Red Shirts' and that his life was in danger." Blacks from all over the county converged on Gillisonville bearing "guns, axes, and hoes." By six o'clock "a thousand negroes were approaching the town and the Red Shirts thought it best to gallop away." Smalls made it to the railroad and safely back to Beaufort. At every station he met "troops of negroes, one and two hundred together, all on their way to Gillisonville to the rescue."[57] Clearly, the new black voters of Beaufort County were not going to be easily intimidated by the white Democrats' method of electioneering. Black Republicans may have lost control of the state in 1877, but they still controlled Beaufort County and they still had Robert Smalls.

THE SECESSION OF HAMPTON COUNTY

Long before the 1876 election, it was apparent to the white landowners in the upper districts that they would never regain political and civil control of their neighborhoods as long as they remained part of Beaufort County. When, as a state representative, Robert Smalls introduced legislation in 1868 to move the county seat from Gillisonville back to Beaufort, he annoyed and inconvenienced the white landowners. Not since 1783 had mainland property owners been forced to travel to the sea islands to conduct public or court business. The movement to divide Beaufort County and create a new county in the lowcountry began almost immediately. A bill to create "Coosawhatchie County" was introduced in 1869 but failed its second reading in the Republican-controlled house. Over the next four years, momentum began to build on the mainland for a new county. Petitions from the property owners flooded the legislature. The earliest petition, in 1869, suggested separating the mainland from the islands, rebuilding the courthouse at Gillisonville, and naming the new county "Washington County." It was signed by eighteen local landowners: Charles E. Bell, H. M. Zahler, F. F. Smart, W. J. Lance, R. Sauls, A. C. Loper, William P. Zealy, E. P. Henderson, James Strobhart, Joshua Woods, Joseph M. Farr, Abram Huguenin, John Bessillieu, M. S. Fennell, W. M. Tison, H. W. Bellillieu, J. M. Loper, and John Alexander.

These were all white landowners, most of them with property near Gillisonville and Coosawhatchie. By 1872 the momentum for a new mainland county had spread and dozens of petitions had been filed with the legislature. One petition noted that "in 1868 the county seat... was removed from the village of Gillisonville which is located in the center of the said county" and that traveling sixty miles to Beaufort would expose the petitioners to disease, expense, and "denial of justice." Thirty-four landowners from the far western corner of the county signed it. Among them were four Deloaches, four Johnstons, three Warnocks, two Mearses, two Fitts, two Joneses, a Bostick, a Lawton, a Morrison, and a Hiers, all descendants of the pioneer families that had settled upper St. Peter's Parish in the eighteenth century. This petition suggested dividing Beaufort County along the line of the Charleston and Savannah Railroad, which separated the county "in two parts of nearly equal area." Palmetto County was offered as the name of the new county.

One objection to dividing Beaufort County was the cost of erecting a new courthouse. In 1872 eight large landowners offered to raise the "amount sufficient to defray the expense of erecting a courthouse." They were H. J. Smart, J. M. Moore, Charles E. Bell, J. Waddell, H. R. Box, A. M. Martin, Benjamin Martin, and J. C. Davant. Eleven more men signed later, including A. M. Youmans, J. B. Tuten, B. F. Buckner, and L. Mixson. One petition contained 240 signatures. By 1872 nearly every mainland property owner had expressed his desire to divide Beaufort County.[58]

The Beaufort community took notice of the growing demand to divide the county. "The desire for a division of the county," noted the *Beaufort Republican,* "is quite general in the upper part of the county and there is very little opposition to it on the islands." Beaufort County, it was acknowledged, was a large county in size and population and "deserves more representation in the Senate." A public meeting was held in Brunson on November 28, 1872, to support the formation of "Coosawhatchie County." Thomas Youmans led the meeting with W. J. Causey as secretary. H. C. Smart and James Aires were sent to Columbia to lobby the General Assembly. As political momentum grew, new towns along the Port Royal Railroad began to promote themselves as the most favorable sites of a new county seat. A writer calling himself "Phoenix" published a letter urging the advantages of Brunson as "high, elevated with pure, cold water, the cool air of the up-country... free of mosquitoes and malarial fevers so common in the lowcountry." "Spectave" promoted the incipient town of Varnville at Dixie Station. It was the "most prominent point on the railroad" and Colonel A. McBride Peeple's "Big Dixie Store... serves all the area."[59]

As long as Republicans controlled the state legislature, they found reasons to defeat or delay attempts to divide Beaufort County. After the 1876 election, it soon became apparent that the new Democratic regime was sympathetic to the idea. Opposition to dividing Beaufort County coalesced in the sea island district. In January 1877 the Beaufort paper noted with sarcasm that the "champions of the disunion of the county" would drop the matter quickly "if the change would not increase the number of public offices." The paper noted that the petitioners from the upper district complained of geographic isolation but contended that the real reason was political: "A change by many is desired to cut them off from the islands on account of the heavy Republican vote." Beaufortonians noted that the country lawyers were most ardent in promoting a new county, wanting a more convenient court "for more lawsuits." The sea islanders pointed to the unifying effect of the new railroad and suggested that both the mainland and sea island districts should "unite for progress." Too late, they suggested a compromise site for the courthouse. But they also acknowledged that this was unlikely because the "real object... is a political one." It was simply black Republicans on the sea islands versus white Democrats on the mainland.[60]

In fact, the differences between the two sections were quite profound. The sea islands were heavily populated and 90 percent black. They almost all voted Republican. The few white families who remained in Beaufort and the sea islands were mostly northerners who remained after the war or were recent immigrants from Europe. Many were Union army veterans. The economy of the sea islands in the 1870s was rapidly shifting from an agricultural to an industrial and commercial economy based on phosphates, timber, the railroad, and the maritime industries. The white people who inhabited Beaufort were mostly merchants and professional men, and in the 1870s many were becoming wealthy. Most of these Beaufortonians, black or white, had little sympathy for the Confederacy and no desire to re-create the antebellum past. Beaufort and the sea islands were prospering in the 1870s, and they saw themselves as the vanguard of the New South.

The mainland section of Beaufort County, on the other hand, was populated by old southerners. Much of the upper district was sparsely settled, rural, and nearly 50 percent white. The economy was almost entirely agricultural.

The antebellum families had not been dispossessed of their plantations, and the Confederate veterans had returned to their ancestral lands to rebuild their lives and repair their broken fortunes. They resented the Union occupation, the social and political revolution, and the black Republican regime that engulfed the state during Reconstruction. They saw themselves as a bulwark on the "black border" and the resolute defenders of the "Old South." By 1876 they saw only one way to preserve their cherished way of life: to secede from Beaufort County.

Leaders of the upper district of Beaufort County were among the state's most ardent Red Shirts. When their hero, Wade Hampton, was elected governor they immediately set out to chart their own political future. In May 1877 the Democrats who controlled the General Assembly introduced "a Bill to establish a new judicial and election county from a portion of Beaufort County." The bill specified that the county would be divided along the line of the Charleston and Savannah Railroad and that the new county would have three state representatives and one state senator, that the precincts would be those previously set for that district of Beaufort County, and that elections for new county offices and General Assembly seats would be held the second Tuesday in November 1878. After December 1878, all lawsuits were to be transferred to the new courthouse. Governor Hampton was to appoint the new county treasurer and auditor. Five men were named commissioners to survey the new county lines: C. J. C. Hutson, J. H. Rudell, Z. T. Morrison, O. P. Law, and George Hoover. Five others were to select a site for the new county courthouse: John Tison, John Gunter, William C. Johnston, Jeffrey D. Warren, and I. J. Nelson.[61]

Passage of the county bill in the next legislative session was a certainty, and festivities were held throughout the upper district for the rest of the year. These celebrations took on a distinctly military air. On July 4, 1877, three militia companies mustered at Brunson: the Brunson Company commanded by Captain J.A. Lightsey, the Allendale Company commanded by Captain George O. Riley, and the Prince William Company commanded by Captain A. A. Browning. The whole battalion marched to Brunson "all mounted and in full uniform. It reminded the spectators of the late war and the officers and privates showed that they had not forgotten the drill." Speeches by W. S. Tillinghast, Captain Davant, and Representative Lawrence Youmans of Barnwell were all met with "deafening cheers." Afterward, a huge outdoor picnic was held with ice cream and lemonade to break the heat. A stringed orchestra entertained the crowd. At Hoover Station the Prince William Company mustered to receive the azure blue palmetto flag presented by "three little maidens": Lillie Mauldin, Olivia Porcher, and Mattie Porcher. The girls read a poem dedicated to "the noble heart of Hampton."[62]

The largest celebration occurred on September 18, 1877, at Varnville when ten companies of the 3rd Regiment, Mounted Rifles, South Carolina Volunteers, mustered for a parade in review by Governor Hampton. This body of men, whose officers are listed below, represented nearly the entire political and military leadership of the new county.

3rd Regiment, Mounted Rifles, South Carolina Volunteers
Commander: Colonel William Stokes
Regimental Staff: Lt. Colonel John T. Morrison
Major George H. Hoover
Adjutant: Captain C.J. C. Colcock
Quartermaster: Captain W.H. Mauldin
Engineer: Captain Oliver P. Law
Paymaster: Captain Abram Martin
Surgeons: Major J. M. P. Gregorie
Asst. Surgeon: Captain B. F. Wyman

Company A, Brunson (60 men)
Captain Ben S. Williams
First Lieutenant E. B. Richardson
Second Lieutenant B. C. Reid

Company B, Early Branch (103 men)
Captain John H. Steinmeyer
First Lieutenant Wiley W. McTeer
Second Lieutenant Sanders Glover
Third Lieutenant Peter Appleby

Company C, Hoovers Station (96 men)
Captain A. A. Browning
First Lieutenant S. J. Lewis
Second Lieutenant J. B. Binneker
Third Lieutenant D. G. Simmons

Company D, Camp Branch (86 men)
Captain J. J. Gooding
First Lieutenant Walter McNiel
Second Lieutenant A. J. Tuten
Third Lieutenant C. W. Tuten

Company E, Brunson (35 men)
Captain John A. Lightsey
First Lieutenant W. E. Brunson
Second Lieutenant W. J. Causey

Company F, Whippy Swamp (72 men)
>   Captain B. W. Davis
>   First Lieutenant E. H. Wyman
>   Second Lieutenant C. F. Davis

Company G, Lawtonville (47 men)
>   Captain T. A. Causey
>   First Lieutenant T. A. Lawton
>   Second Lieutenant W. W. Smith

Company H, Nixville (67 men)
>   Captain A. S. Youmans
>   First Lieutenant T. S. Tuten
>   Second Lieutenant D. B. Gohegan
>   Third Lieutenant J. O. H. Sanders

Company I, Matthews Bluff (99 men)
>   Captain W. G. Roberts
>   First Lieutenant D. G. Peeples
>   Second Lieutenant John F. Morrison
>   Third Lieutenant B. E. Stokes

Forty-one officers and 647 men, mounted, in uniform, and well armed, represented every neighborhood and nearly every white family in the new county. They were the white property owners of the upper district and were determined to control the political and civil life of their neighborhoods. They greeted Governor Hampton as a hero and cheered the rise of the new Democratic regime in South Carolina.[63]

As the bill to divide Beaufort County approached passage, some half-hearted objections were voiced in the lower district. To divide the county became the single issue in the state senate race between Colonel Elliott and upstart J. W. Collins, who supported a compromise site for the courthouse to keep the county intact. Collins's white supporters noted that "such a division would leave the whites on the coast in ... such a fearful minority as to destroy all hope" of ever gaining control of the county. Or, as Elliott's supporters put it, they were "wresting the county from the rule of ignorance and plunder." Locals observed that large capitalists in Charleston and Savannah opposed the division of Beaufort County because "their interest in the rice fields would be endangered and their rights put in jeopardy." An editorial in the *Beaufort Tribune and Port Royal Commercial* suggested, ironically, that the new county should be named "Yemassee" as a "monument to a powerful tribe of Indians, now extinct, whose exploits burn the pages of the early history of Carolina." With even greater sarcasm, the *Tribune* suggested that if the reactionaries of the upper district "desired to have a modern name, one connected with the present history of the state, what better name than Hampton! . . . a name dearer to Carolina than ever were the Colletons, the Berkeleys or the Ashleys of our provincial history." It was the first published suggestion of the name adopted for the new county, and it was meant as a jest.

The movement to create a new county had gone too far, and the bill's passage was all but certain. As the end of the legislative session approached and the division of Beaufort County seemed inevitable, the *Tribune* finally editorialized: "We are finally in favor of the division of the county." It gave these reasons: the county was very large, with diverse interests; the lowcountry deserved more representation; and Beaufort County was commercial, while "Palmetto County" was agricultural. The paper concluded, "Let them depart in peace." The bill passed the General Assembly on December 20, 1877, the seventeenth anniversary of the signing of the Ordinance of Secession.

Governor Hampton waited until February 28, 1878, to sign the bill into law. In the two months between the General Assembly vote and the governor's signature, the opposition's ironic suggestion had been inserted into the bill. When Hampton finally signed the law, he created Hampton County.[64] The act and name were filled with symbolism, wildly popular with the new citizens and reflective of the political realities of the time. It was truly the "secession" of Hampton County.

BLACK MIGRATION

Another issue that arose from the Democratic counterrevolution of 1876 was a historic era of black migration. Black families in many upstate regions found local circumstances after 1876 difficult and even dangerous. The political climate had turned decidedly against them, and as tenant farmers, they had few economic ties to their communities. Some began to look elsewhere for better opportunities. Almost immediately after the October 1876 election, many upcountry families began arriving in Beaufort County, and their immigration was encouraged by local authorities. On January 9, 1877, twelve families arrived in one day. All were placed on the "school farms," where they could support themselves until they could find land of their own. At the time there were eighteen school farms on Port Royal Island, Lady's Island, and St. Helena Island. Each school farm consisted of 160 acres. By 1877 several were vacant because the previous tenants had "purchased small tracts of land of their own" and moved off the school farms. Settling these refugees on the school farms would add to the productivity and commerce of the county. "If these almost abandoned places could be populated by a thrifty set of laborers it would be desirable and add to the trade and wealth of the county," the *Tribune* asserted. The refugees left no doubt as to why they abandoned the upcountry and came to Beaufort County: "These people say they have been driven off for political reasons."[65]

Beaufort County not only welcomed the refugees but also provided places of shelter and opportunities for self-support. In addition, local businessmen made laudable efforts to provide land ownership for these newcomers. A former Freedman's Bureau agent, H. G. Judd, was a real estate broker who advertised "lands for sale ... for the landless people who are coming into the county to reside." He kept his office in the *Tribune* Building, owned by Robert Smalls at the time, and he advertised "land on the islands or mainland, one acre to 400 acres." Judd offered favorable terms to poor refugees. His terms "were desirable for those having small means, as they can have immediate possession by paying a very small sum of money." Captain Neils Christensen's new venture, the Christensen Lumber Company, offered to build small frame cottages for fifty dollars per room and finance the construction over many years.[66]

Some less scrupulous businessmen sought to capitalize on the state's racial unrest. In July 1877 George Curtis came to Beaufort to recruit blacks for a "Liberia scheme." Liberia had been an African refuge for freed American slaves since the 1820s. It was largely a product of the philanthropic efforts of the old American Colonization Society. Curtis found few takers in Beaufort and was soon run out of the county. Reverend James B. Middleton warned Charlestonians of "the unsavory record of George Curtis" and added that Beaufort County was the least likely place in the state to seek recruits for Liberia: "The colored people are too prosperous and content on the islands to go to the wilds of Africa." The *Tribune* reported that "The white people of South Carolina look with no favor upon an effort now being made to induce Negroes to emigrate to ... Liberia. The Negroes are Americans and have as much right to be here as anyone. This is their native land and they should remain."[67]

In spite of efforts by enlightened Beaufort businessmen and commercial boosters, attempts to settle blacks in other parts of America continued. In 1879 Robert Smalls planned a trip to Arizona Territory to look at the land situation with an eye to settling South Carolina blacks on Arizona lands. In 1881, when a group of Edgefield County blacks were preparing to move to Arkansas, Robert Smalls tried to divert them to Beaufort County to keep them in his constituency.[68] From the Civil War to the end of the nineteenth century, Beaufort County was a refuge for black Carolinians seeking to escape economic hardship and political persecution.

FUSION POLITICS

One truism of South Carolina politics was the fact that the black majority of Beaufort County would not be intimidated, no matter what the white

Democratic regime attempted. Laura Towne described the general election of November 1878 on St. Helena Island. The Democratic commissioners of elections for the county came to the island to conduct and control the election. All were white men well known to the black sea islanders. Towne recalled that one of the election commissioners was "the drunken 'C' who used to be so cruel and burn the people with pine tar droppings blazing on their backs." Island blacks formed their own committee, which stayed all day to oversee the proceedings and ensure fairness. Consequently, hundreds of blacks voted without incident or opposition. The local committee stayed late into the night to make sure that the vote count was as fair as the balloting.[69] Despite the fact that all the state-appointed local offices had gone to Democrats, the sea island communities of Beaufort County were not going to allow their hard-won Fifteenth Amendment rights be easily purloined. The result was that the white Democratic machine was forced to make political accommodations with the black majority. That political compromise came to be called "fusion politics" and resulted in "the People's Ticket" of 1888.

An early glimmer of this accommodation was published in the *Beaufort Crescent,* a newspaper begun in 1879 as the first Democratic-leaning paper in Beaufort since before the Civil War. Its publisher and editor, Samuel Henry Rodgers, had come to Beaufort through his marriage to Martha Ann Legare, daughter of an old lowcountry family. The *Crescent* office was across the street from the Republican paper, the *Beaufort Tribune and Port Royal Commercial*. Rodgers forthrightly pointed out that his newspaper was Democratic "but not straight-out." His inaugural editorial described the political reality of Beaufort County and the local Democrats' willingness to compromise: "We have always maintained that this county, though overwhelmingly Negro and Republican, possessed a more liberal ... spirited population in politics than any other section of the country ... it was here that the first experiences of emancipation were felt ... there is more freedom and unrestrained license of political opinion in this one black county" than in the whole rest of the state. Rodgers noted that despite their political differences, none of the "colored chiefs" had withdrawn his advertising or his subscription from the *Crescent*. "Even on the islands," the editorialist wrote, "opposing opinions are respectfully tolerated [and the] bitterest radicals complimented the *Crescent* on its honesty and pluck."[70]

Robert Smalls was reelected to Congress in 1880, but the old "Regular Republican" machine that he had commanded for twelve years had begun to break up. In 1882 young Thomas Ezekiel Miller forged an alliance between the Republicans and the new Greenback-Labor Party, which had some southern populist support. In June 1882 a group of ambitious young black politicians formed the Young Men's Republican Club of Beaufort to seek reform and influence in the party. Its leaders were Julius I.

Washington, Thomas J. Reynolds, A. C. Maxwell and H. G. Grant. Miller, Reynolds, and Washington were all elected to the General Assembly during the 1880s.

A new election law of 1882 mandated a complicated, cumbersome system of registration to vote and required that all voters, regardless of previous status, to reregister. Democratic election commissioners controlled the time and place of reregistration and were not bound by law to advertise these. Most famously, the Democratic legislature passed the "eight box rule," requiring separate ballots for each election to be placed in their corresponding box or be invalidated. Poll managers shifted the boxes around to confuse black voters, many of whom could not read the box labels.[71] Such election chicanery successfully disfranchised many black voters across the state, but not in Beaufort County. During the election of 1884, the "Straight-out" Democrats put up a ticket of old planter descendants to challenge the Regular Republican ticket. The results (listed below) were, once again, a crushing defeat for the Democrats and an overwhelming victory for the Republicans, who won by a margin of nearly six to one.

Republicans	*Votes*	*Democratic*	*Votes*
STATE REPRESENTATIVES			
Joseph Robinson	1,729	James M. Rhett	302
F. S. Mitchell	1,718	Joseph Glover	303
W. H. Sheppard	1,717	W. N. Heyward	302
STATE SENATOR			
Thomas J. Reynolds	1,884	W. J Verdier	307

Similar results were recorded for all the local offices elected in 1884 as well:

Republican	*Votes*	*Democratic*	*Votes*
SCHOOL COMMISSIONER			
Thomas H. Wheeler	2,033	Paul Hamilton	281
COUNTY COMMISSIONERS (3)			
George Reid	2,012	S. H. Rodgers	294
F. E. Wilder	2,012	William H. Lockwood	277
F. C. Brown	2,012	T. H. Martin	283
SHERIFF			
John P. Boyce	2,289	Henry D. Elliott	282

(continued)

Republican	Votes	Democratic	Votes
CLERK OF COURT			
S. J. Bampfield	2,033	H. D. Burnett	282
CORONER			
W. P. Graham	2,033	H. M. Fuller	283
PROBATE JUDGE			
W. J. Whipper	2,012	C. E. Bell	234

South Carolina State Archives, South Carolina Legislature, Reports and Resolutions, 1884, 791.

These 1884 results revealed that eight years and several election cycles after the Democrats seized power, they could not make a dent in the Republican stronghold of Beaufort County.

Despite their power, the Republican Party machine fell to infighting, and in 1886, Robert Smalls was defeated for Congress by a Democrat, William Elliott. It was a disputed election in which every trick the Democrats could marshal was employed to knock Smalls out of office. The worst fraud was on St. Helena Island, where a false claim of riot and intimidation gave the Democratic election managers the excuse to throw out the entire vote in the most populous Republican precinct in the district.[72] There was also evidence that some sea islanders had abandoned Smalls out of envy or what the Charleston newspapers claimed was a campaign of "Black vs. Tan." This kind of report asserted that the black Republican leadership in South Carolina was actually mulatto. Class and race distinctions within the black community supposedly permitted the mulatto leaders to exploit the Gullah blacks to their advantage. The *News and Courier* observed that Smalls had angered many blacks by refusing to appoint St. Helena men to county office and had foreclosed the mortgage he held on the First African Baptist Church across from his home. This was a clever divide-and-conquer tactic of the Democrats, but it carried just enough truth to be believable. In any case, it worked. The "Black and Tan" election of 1886 was the end of Robert Smalls's political career but far from the end of his political influence. During the 1888 election, Smalls helped craft a compromise with white Democrats to create a "fusion ticket" of both black Republicans and white Democrats. Promoted as the "People's Ticket," it was a classic power-sharing arrangement.

The Beaufort County house seats were divided among two black Republicans, A. C. Reynolds and Julius I. Washington, and one white Democrat,

William Nathaniel Heyward. The senate seat went to William Joyner Verdier, the first white Democrat to hold the seat since the Civil War. George Reed, a black Republican, was sheriff; Samuel J. Bampfield, a black Republican and Smalls's son-in-law, was the recording clerk of court; and A. S. Bascomb, another black Republican, was school commissioner. Thomas Talbird, a white Democrat replaced W. J. Whipper as probate judge. Nursing his longtime feud with Robert Smalls, Whipper had refused to endorse the compromise. Renty Greaves, a black Republican, was picked for coroner. The County Commission was divided between two black Republicans, W. H. Gregory and Solomon Deas, and one white Democrat, Heyward Lynch.[73]

The great advantage of the "fusion ticket" was that it promoted peace and racial harmony in the politics of Beaufort County. Blacks and whites could avoid trickery, intimidation, and violence at election time, and the social warfare of the previous twenty years could be resolved in the council chambers. In large measure fusion politics became the regular order of political business in Beaufort County for the next decade. It was the last great gift of Robert Smalls to his sea island constituents.

The People's Ticket would not have succeeded if Robert Smalls had not endorsed it. Fusion politics helped abate the racial animosity that surfaced every election year. Until 1895 the fusionist Republicans shared at least an equal number of political offices with the white Democrats. But the People's Ticket did not succeed without heated controversy. Regular Republicans fielded their own set of candidates, many of whom openly attacked Robert Smalls as a traitor and threatened violence if they did not win office. Republican state senator Thomas J. Reynolds asserted that "if the regular Republican ticket is not elected ... the streets of this town will run red with blood and many houses will be laid in ashes." Reynolds lost his state senate seat to fusion leader William J. Verdier, the first white Democrat elected to the General Assembly from Beaufort since Reconstruction. The election aftermath did not fulfill Reynold's violent prediction.

Thomas J. Reynolds was the law partner of W. J. Whipper, and Whipper was the biggest loser in the election of 1888. The People's Ticket promoted a white Democrat, Thomas Talbird, for Beaufort County probate judge. This judgeship was a fulltime paid position, and Whipper had regularly been reelected to the post for many years. Thomas Talbird (1855–1928) was an old Beaufortonian and a descendant of the hated "secesh." When the election returns demonstrated Talbird's victory, Whipper refused to turn over his office, claiming election fraud. Three other Republican officeholders also refused to relinquish their positions: County Coroner W. P. Graham and County Commissioners F. C. Brown and F. E. Wilder. When the four defied a judge's order to relinquish their offices to the fusionist victors, they were thrown in jail for contempt of court. From his jail cell Whipper published a broadside that attacked Robert Smalls as the architect of the fusion compromise.

Thomas E. Miller and Julius I. Washington also blamed Smalls for the defeat of the party regulars. Miller noted the week after the election, "There was an intense feeling against General Smalls, because he had been the most blatant of radical Republicans.... when it was found out that he, above all others, was striving to destroy the party unity, the men whom he had taught to despise all that was Democratic were astonished. Smalls has killed himself in Beaufort and he will not rise again soon." While it was true that Smalls was never again elected to office, neither were Washington nor Reynolds. Miller, on the other hand, successfully challenged his defeat for U.S. Congress in 1888 by Colonel William Elliott based on the familiar charge of electoral fraud. The Republican-controlled House of Representatives agreed, and Miller served in Congress from 1889 to 1891.[74]

Even out of office, Robert Smalls's influence remained a large part of the success of fusion politics for several years. Will Elliott, the son of Congressman William Elliott, reflected on the cordial relationship between Robert Smalls and the Elliotts despite their intense political rivalries. Robert Smalls retained William Elliott Sr. as his attorney even when they were running against each other for Congress. After the Elliotts moved to Columbia in 1902, Smalls always greeted them as valued old friends when they visited Beaufort. Indeed, they were old friends. Colonel Elliott and General Smalls shared a childhood in antebellum Beaufort. They shared combat experience in the Civil War, where both had displayed personal courage under fire. Together, in postbellum Beaufort, they had survived a profound, often violent, social revolution. Such experiences bound people across racial, class, and ideological lines. Thousands of similar interracial business and personal relationships marked turn-of-the century Beaufort as a distinctive southern society. Will Elliott always respected Smalls's moderation during tense political moments. In Elliott's words, Smalls "never stirred the Negroes to violence and on the contrary was always conservative and worthy of respect." That respect for Smalls from "conservative" blacks and even southern whites was a key to the success of fusion politics.

One beneficiary of fusion politics was Robert Smalls's son-in-law, Samuel J. Bampfield, who was elected clerk of court on the 1888 Peoples Ticket. Bampfield, too, earned and held the respect of white Beaufortonians. Will Elliott was a young lawyer when Bampfield was the fusionist clerk of court. Elliott left a personal assessment of Bampfield: "S. J. Bampfield was clerk-of-court practically the whole time I practiced in Beaufort, from 1893 to 1900. He was a remarkable Negro. His people in Charleston had been free Negroes. He was well educated and ... while I was in Beaufort he took up the study of Spanish. Many circuit judges said he was one of the best clerks-of-court in the state. Furthermore, he had the manners of a gentleman. He never let his color cause the slightest embarrassment."

One unspoken understanding of the power-sharing arrangement was that white Democrats would hold all the positions responsible for handling public money. Black Republicans were given other management responsibilities. Thus, the People's Ticket of 1888, listed below, revealed this "private" agreement.

White Democrats	
County Treasurer:	Joseph S. Reed
County Probate Judge:	Thomas Talbird
County Supervisor:	Joseph Glover
Black Republicans	
County Sheriff:	George A. Reed
School Commissioner:	James Wigg
Clerk of Court:	S. J. Bampfield

Will Elliott Memoir, 8, 38–39.

The watershed year in Beaufort County politics was 1892. It was the last presidential election year before enactment of the state Constitution of 1895 and thus the last "Reconstruction" election in the state and Beaufort County. "Pitchfork Ben" Tillman was running for a second term as governor, and that alone made for colorful electioneering. Tillman was not generally supported in the lowcountry, and he was not shy about his racial prejudices. Beaufort County had other specific reasons to dislike Tillman. In 1890 he had campaigned against the phosphate companies that provided the majority of Beaufort County's jobs. In the 1892 campaign, Tillman was opposed in the Democratic primary by the conservative former governor John C. Sheppard. It was a bitter campaign across the state and centered upon Tilllman's controversial personality. Although Tillman was unpopular in Beaufort County, he had a few supporters among the white Democrats, notably the county Democratic chairman, Thomas Talbird.

The governor's race was only one of many contests in 1892. The fusionist coalition nominated a full slate of candidates for local offices. Lawyer and conservative Democrat William Joyner Verdier led the "fusionist" ticket in his bid for reelection to the state senate. Other "fusionist" candidates in 1892 divided between white Democrats and black Republicans:

White Democrats	
House of Representatives	Sanders Glover
	F.T. Hardee
Solicitor	B. D. Bellinger
Probate Judge	Thomas Talbird

(continued)

	Black Republicans
House of Representatives	January Rivers
	Maurice Hamilton
Sheriff	George A. Reed
Clerk of Court	S. J. Bampfield

Will Elliott Memoir, 8, 38–39.

The Regular Republicans offered opponents to the fusionist ticket for several offices. James Wigg ran for sheriff as a Regular Republican, and former Representative A. C. Reynolds, another Regular Republican, challenged William J. Verdier for the Senate seat. Julius I. Washington ran against the fusionist S. J. Bampfield for clerk of court.

Eighteen ninety-two was a presidential and congressional election year, so both parties were very active. The Democratic county convention was held in Beaufort on May 5, 1892. It was expected that Beaufort County's white Democrats would support John C. Sheppard against Tillman, but the chairman, Thomas Talbird, was an ardent Tillmanite. Tillman also had support in the sparsely settled areas around Bluffton and Barrell Landing. On a motion by Captain W. N. Barnes of Barrell Landing, the executive committee voted seventeen to five to support Tillman for governor and the "Fusion ticket" for all local offices. The *Palmetto Post* admitted that it had misread Beaufort County's opposition to Tillman, and the Columbia *State* took note of Beaufort County's surprise conversion to Tillmanism: "Presto! Beaufort County suddenly converts to Tillmanism."[75]

Their predictions were premature. Tillman and Sheppard both campaigned in Beaufort in June. When the Beaufort Democratic Club met at the arsenal on July 28, 1892, one hundred members attended and voted overwhelmingly to support Sheppard over Tillman. County chairman Thomas Talbird walked out in a huff. Among those supporting Sheppard were Senator William J. Verdier, Mayor W. H. Townsend, and phosphate superintendents Julian Lopez and W. C. Vincent. When the primary election was held on August 30, 1892, Sheppard outpolled Tillman 322 to 203. The Democratic precinct vote revealed Tillman's popularity in some of the mainland precincts and his immense unpopularity among the white voters on the sea islands. In the phosphate community of Coosaw Mines, not a single voter supported Tillman. The totals by precinct were as follows:

	Sheppard	*Tillman*
Beaufort	94	62
Coosaw Mines	73	0

(continued)

	Sheppard	Tillman
Port Royal	46	22
Sheldon	24	0
Grahamville	31	14
Barrell Landing	4	55
Bluffton	16	28
Hardeeville	34	22
Total	322	203

Palmetto Post, June 9, 1892; July 28, 1892; September 8, 1892.

Among the black Republicans, 1892 was also a busy, eventful year. Fusion Republicans fought bitter, rancorous campaigns against the Regular Republicans. Robert Smalls spoke at a large Republican rally in Port Royal in July 1892. He defended the "fusion" movement along with George A. Reed, the fusionist black sheriff. Former state senator Thomas J. Reynolds shouted at Smalls and called him a "dirty damned liar." Smalls maintained his composure and made a "statesmanlike" defense of the fusion ticket. The *Palmetto Post* dismissed Reynolds as a "ranting hothead." The perspective of conservative blacks toward the fusion movement was expressed in an unsigned letter to the *Palmetto Post* during the summer of 1892:

> Ever since ... Lincoln issued the Emancipation Proclamation, I have been a staunch and uncompromising Republican up to four years ago when the Fusion Movement was started in this county. I worked for the Fusion Party believing it was for the good of my people, promoted friendliness between the two races with all differences amicably adjusted. The black and white fusion ticket was elected and blacks held two-thirds of the offices. They were re-elected two years ago. Now the elections are approaching and the Fusionists are divided by greed for the spoils. If they don't stop squabbling, I will work for the straight-out Democratic ticket![76]

One of the most revealing races of the 1892 election season was the race for the congressional seat formerly held by Robert Smalls, William Elliott, and Thomas E. Miller. Until 1892 the seat was held by Colonel William Elliott (1891–1893), but reapportionment favored the midland counties and Elliott did not run for reelection. Instead, General Edwin W. Moise of Sumter County represented the Democrats while George Washington Murray represented the Republican Party. Robert Smalls and Miller had briefly entered the Republican primary against Murray. Both were soundly defeated. It was

Robert Smalls's last campaign, and he did not try too hard. The *Palmetto Post* commented, "Smalls is practically out of politics.... he talks but he has lost his fervor." After Murray outpolled Smalls and Miller in the primary, Smalls campaigned for him in the general election. Thus, Smalls, like the white Democrats on the other side, supported traditional Republican candidates in the statewide and national elections but locally backed the fusion ticket.

Murray's opponent for Congress was Edwin W. Moise of Sumter. Moise had been adjutant general of the South Carolina militia under Governor Wade Hampton. A practicing Jew, he was moderate in racial matters and was one of the few Red Shirts who tried to attract blacks to the Democratic Party. In 1877 he had politely, but unsuccessfully, tried to disarm "Beaufort's famous National Guard." He took no offense and no action against the armed veterans who disobeyed his orders. In Greenville, Moise had prominently led a parade of white and black state troops. He was well thought of by the county's moderate black voters. The *Palmetto Post,* whose politics were anti-Tillmanite and fusionist, promoted Moise's moderate racial views in 1892: "General Moise is universally popular with the colored people in this county ... a faithful advocate for the rights of *all* his constituents, black as well as white." Besides, the paper noted, "He will help develop the Port Royal Naval Station. We need him in Washington."

When G. W. Murray came to campaign in Beaufort, he was introduced by Robert Smalls and entertained by the Allen Brass Band. In his speech Murray played the race card, making "a long bitter race harangue, appealing altogether to color prejudices and antagonizing the lighter color Negroes, some of whom vote the Republican ticket. Fortunately the blacks in Beaufort County are so conservative and unimpressionable to such violent appeals to race prejudice that there was little enthusiasm for any of the outbursts."

Shades of brown were important in Beaufort County politics. Black prejudice against mulattos had contributed to Robert Smalls's defeat for Congress in the famous "black and tan" election of 1886, and Smalls's successor, Thomas Ezekiel Miller, was so "high yellow" that his opponents tagged him the "canary bird." In the election of 1892, George W. Murray used the color prejudice of South Carolina black Republicans to displace both the mulatto Robert Smalls and the "canary bird" Thomas E. Miller. During this primary campaign, Miller "found it necessary to exculpate himself from the odium of his light skin." George Washington Murray was known as the "Republican Black Eagle." He was entirely black "with not a drop of white blood running in his veins." A contemporary interviewer described Murray as "by no means a bad-looking colored man." He had a "cannonball head" and a complexion as black as "the Ace of Spades," but "his voice did not show his African origin."

To influence the Beaufort County electorate in favor of Moise, the Democratic *Palmetto Post* also played the race card. They described the Republican candidate for county commissioner, January Rivers, a supporter of Murray, as having "a continence extremely Gullah in its contours." When Murray spoke to a rally in Port Royal, the *Palmetto Post* described another speaker named Bingham as a "a canary colored postal agent on the Charleston and Savannah Railway." James Wigg was dismissed as "a very uninfluential yellow man."

George Washington Murray handily defeated General Moise. In the byzantine politics of post-Reconstruction South Carolina, Murray's surprising rise to power was due to a remarkable confluence of political opportunism. Murray had risen from rural Sumter County on the strength of the Colored Farmers' Alliance, the black Republican counterpart to Tillman's populist Farmers' Movement. Thus, he opposed the hard-money Republican position of the 1890s and favored the "free silver" populist position championed by the Tillmanites. Tillman's followers in Murray's congressional district were instructed to oppose Moise or not to vote at all. The Tillmanites' betrayal of the white Democratic candidate insured Murray's victory in 1892, and the Tillman-controlled Board of State Canvassers certified Murray's election.

Murray served one full term in Congress (1893–1895). In 1894 he was defeated for reelection by Colonel William Elliott of Beaufort. This time Smalls and Miller conspired with their Beaufort County constituents to oust Murray and elect their friend and neighbor, the Democrat William Elliott. Murray challenged Elliott's victory based on charges of Democratic electoral fraud and was finally seated in Congress for its last session in 1896. Murray thus had the distinction of being the last African American congressman from South Carolina during the nineteenth century.[77]

When the general election concluded in November 1892, Democrat Grover Cleveland won the presidency. Tillman won his second term as governor, and the "fusion ticket" won a narrow majority in local elections. The local elections were a "desperate contest" between the "Fusion Party" and the "straight-out Republicans." The 1892 vote totals were as follows:

	Fusion Party	(votes)	Straight-out Republican	(votes)
Sheriff:	G. A. Reed	(985)	James Wigg	(878)
Clerk of Court:	S. J. Bampfield	(986)	Julius I. Washington	(881)
S.C. Senate:	W. J. Verdier	(947)	A. C. Reynolds	(690)
S.C. House:	Samuel Glover	(911) white	Whole "fusion" slate elected.	
	F. T. Hardee	(911) white		
	J. R. Rivers	(906) black		
	Maurice Hamilton	(906) black		

When the 1892 election was over and the fusion victory was confirmed, a torchlight parade was held on Bay Street. Black and white fusion officeholders marched together. The all-black Allen Brass Band led the parade. The all-white Beaufort Volunteer Artillery provided the military escort and a booming artillery salute. Black and white elected officials together spoke to a large illuminated crowd from the piazza of the Sea Island Hotel. It was the high point of fusion politics in Beaufort County.[78]

The 1892 election of the People's Ticket" may have been the pinnacle of fusion politics in local elections, but it was also the end of the direct influence of the Reconstruction regime in Beaufort County. Before the next presidential election year, South Carolina Democrats led by Senator Tillman assembled a constitutional convention and passed the South Carolina Constitution of 1895. This document enshrined the Jim Crow era in state law and effectively disfranchised African American voters for the next sixty years. But even before the political milestone of 1895, Beaufort County was struck by a natural disaster that ended the prosperity of the Reconstruction era and altered the history of the county for half a century.

Notes

CHAPTER 1: THE CONFEDERATES EVACUATE THE SEA ISLANDS

1. Here and throughout the text, when a particular source is cited over several paragraphs, the citation will appear at the end of the final paragraph. "Permanent Fortifications and Sea Coast Defenses," 116, 135–39, 146–51, 194, 204, 334, 389–92, 405; Bache, "Notes on the Coast of the United States

2. Barnwell, *History of an American Family,* 68–71; Stockton, *Beaufort Arsenal,* 50–53; Spieler and Rowland, *Brief History of the Beaufort Arsenal,* 5–7.

3. *The War of the Rebellion: The Official Records of the Union and Confederate Armies,* ser. 1, 1: 167–68, 171 (hereinafter cited as *ORA,* with all citations to series 1 unless otherwise noted); De La Cova, "Ambrosio Jose Gonzales," 270.

4. Viele, "Port Royal Expedition," 329–40; Ammen, "Du Pont and the Port Royal Expedition," 671–77; Hayes, *Samuel Francis Du Pont,* 171, 179, 181, 201, 217–19, 224–25; *Official Records of the Union and Confederate Navies,* ser. 1, 12: 214–15, 261–319 (hereinafter cited as *ORN,* with all citations to series 1 unless otherwise noted); *ORA,* 6: 6–27; Wise, "To Capture an Island," 1–8; Beecher, *First Light Battery,* 95–96.

5. Freeman, *R. E. Lee,* 1: 606–8; Dowdey, *Wartime Papers of R. E. Lee,* 81–84; *ORA,* 6: 309, 313–14.

6. *ORA,* 6: 309.

7. *ORA,* 6: 312–13.

8. Wise, *Gate of Hell,* 10–11; Freeman, *R. E. Lee,* 1: 613–14.

9. De La Cova, "Ambrosio Jose Gonzales," 270–73; *ORA,* 6: 278–83.

10. *ORA,* 6: 323, 327; Dowdey, *Wartime Papers of R. E. Lee,* 95–97; Freeman, *R. E. Lee,* 1: 608–14.

11. *ORA,* 6: 323–24, 326; De La Cova, "Ambrosio Jose Gonzales," 278–81.

12. *ORA,* 6: 366; Freeman, *R. E. Lee,* 1: 612, 617, 629–30; Wise, *Gate of Hell,* 8, 12.

13. Dowdey, *Wartime Papers of R. E. Lee,* 90.

14. *ORA,* 6: 312; Freeman, *R. E. Lee,* 1: 612, 640–41.

15. Barnwell, *History of an American Family,* 145, 150; Young, *Robert E. Lee and Fort Pulaski,* 13; Dowdey, *Wartime Papers of R. E. Lee,* 88–91.

16. *ORA,* 6: 324, 326.

17. *Charleston Daily Courier,* December 9, 1861.

18. *ORA,* 6: 33–36.

19. *ORA,* 6: 38; Freeman, *R. E. Lee,* 1: 607–8, 613–15, 623; Connelly, *Marble Man,* 16–18.

20. *ORA,* 6: 329–31, 338.

21. *ORA,* 5: 100, 996, 6: 338, 345–49; Freeman, *R. E. Lee,* 1: 617.

22. *ORA,* 6: 344–45; Wise, *Gate of Hell,* 11–12.

23. *ORA,* 6: 344–46, 349.

24. *ORA,* 6: 85–87, 344; *ORN,* 12: 500–506.

25. Freeman, *R. E. Lee,* 1: 615–16, 644–47; Sears, "Getting Right with Robert E. Lee," 70; personal correspondence between Stephen R. Wise and R. E. L. Krick, October 20, 1997.
26. Dowdey, *Wartime Papers of R. E. Lee,* 95–97.
27. *ORA,* 6: 44–75, 337; *ORN,* 12: 413, 446–53.
28. *ORA,* 6: 367–68, 373–76.
29. *ORA,* 6: 375, 380, 382–84; Freeman, *R. E. Lee,* 1: 623.
30. *ORA,* 6: 35, 392, 395, 398; Dowdey, *Wartime Papers of R. E. Lee,* 121–23.
31. *ORA,* 6: 400, 402; Freeman, *R. E. Lee,* 1: 627–30, 2: 1–8.
32. *ORA,* 6: 407–19.
33. *ORA,* 6: 103.
34. *ORA,* 6: 101–11.
35. *ORA,* 6: 428, 432–34.

CHAPTER 2: FEDERAL OCCUPATION BEGINS

1. Johnson, *Rear Admiral John Rodgers,* 176–79; Hayes, *Samuel Francis Du Pont,* 1: 224–25; *ORA,* 6: 3–4; Ammen, "Du Pont and the Port Royal Expedition," 677–86.
2. Walkley, *History of the Seventh Connecticut,* 28; Caldwell, *Old Sixth Regiment,* 26; Toutelloutte, *History of Company K,* 16–17; *ORA,* 6: 185.
3. *New York Tribune,* November 12, 21, December 7, 1861.
4. Tafft, "Reminiscences of the Signal Service" 1–4; Eldridge, *Third New Hampshire Regiment,* 73–74; *New York Tribune,* November 12, December 7, 1861.
5. Walkley, *History of the Seventh Connecticut,* 34; Eldridge, *Third New Hampshire,* 67; Stevens, *Isaac Ingalls Stevens,* 2: 49.
6. *ORA,* 6: 186–87; Caldwell, *Old Sixth Regiment,* 30.
7. Caldwell, *Old Sixth Regiment,* 28–29; Walkley, *History of the Seventh Connecticut,* 30–31.
8. The 3rd Rhode Island was redesignated from infantry to artillery Dec. 19, 1861. Todd, *Seventy-Ninth Highlanders,* 98–100; Denison, *Shot and Shell,* 25–26, 50; Ammen, "Du Pont and the Port Royal Expedition," 686–87.
9. West Point graduated two classes in 1861: one in May, which had a course of five years, and one in June, which had a course of four years. Cullum, *Officers and Graduates of West Point,* 1: 642–44, 2: 227–28, 239–40, 494–96, 498–99, 520, 548–49; Longacre, *From Union Stars to Top Hat,* 48.
10. Todd, *Seventy-Ninth Highlanders,* 56–67, 85–88; Stevens, *Isaac Ingalls Stevens,* 2: 342–49; *ORA,* 7: 178–79; Cullum, *Officers and Graduates of West Point,* 1: 729–33, 2: 5–6, 202–3; Longacre, *From Union Stars to Top Hat,* 48.
11. *ORA,* 6: 186–87; Stevens, *Isaac Ingalls Stevens,* 2: 349–50.
12. *ORA,* 6: 4–5; Ammen, "Du Pont and the Port Royal Expedition," 689.
13. *New York Tribune,* November 2, 20, 1861.
14. *ORA,* ser. 3, 1: 243–44.
15. *ORA,* 6: 176–77.
16. *ORA,* 6: 204, 187; Denison, *Shot and Shell,* 52.
17. Daniel Drew Barrows Papers, letter of December 12, 1861; *ORA,* 6: 187–88; Hayes, *Samuel Francis Du Pont,* 1: 247; Toutelloutte, *History of Company K,* 17.
18. Hayes, *Samuel Francis Du Pont,* 1: 247–48; *ORA,* 6: 187–88.
19. Eldridge, *Third New Hampshire,* 273; Hayes, *Samuel Francis Du Pont,* 1: 174, 235, 255–57, 275; *ORN,* 12: 341–42, 348, 359, 438.

20. *ORN*, 12: 335.
21. Boyle, *Reminiscences of the Civil War*, 3–6.
22. *ORN*, 12: 336–38; Hayes, *Samuel Francis Du Pont*, 1: 231; Ammen, "Du Pont and the Port Royal Expedition," 687–89.
23. *ORN*, 12: 338–39; Hayes, *Samuel Francis Du Pont*, 1: 236–37.
24. Jesse J. Comstock and Eldridge were civilian captains of transports who had gained Du Pont's respect. *ORN*, 12: 349–50; Hayes, *Samuel Francis Du Pont*, 1: 235–37.
25. Hayes, *Samuel Francis Du Pont*, 1: 321.
26. Hayes, *Samuel Francis Du Pont*, 1: 237–38.
27. Hayes, *Samuel Francis Du Pont*, 1: 281, 294, 337, 411–13.
28. *ORN*, 12: 353.
29. *ORN*, 12: 320–23.
30. Hayes, *Samuel Francis Du Pont*, 1: 71, 182, 184–88, 212; Stapleton, "Assistant Charles O. Boutelle," 252–60.
31. *ORN*, 12: 320–23.
32. *ORN*, 12: 273, 388–90.
33. Hayes, *Samuel Francis Du Pont*, 1: 254.

CHAPTER 3: THE NORTHERN FOOTHOLD EXPANDS

1. *ORA*, 6: 200–201, 224, 240; Eldridge, *Third New Hampshire*, 120; *New York Tribune*, November 12, 1862.
2. *ORA*, 6: 218.
3. *ORA*, 6: 222–23.
4. *ORA*, 6: 188–89.
5. Reed, *Combined Operations in the Civil War*, 9–10, 44–46, 50; *ORA*, 6: 207–8, 211–12.
6. Reed, *Combined Operations in the Civil War*, 9–10, 44–46, 50; *ORA*, 6: 207–8, 211–12, 224–25.
7. Haydon, *Military Ballooning during the Early Civil War*, 376–83; *ORA*, ser. 3, 3: 123–24; Bryant, *Diary of Charles A. Bryant*, 41.
8. *ORA*, 6: 211–22.
9. *ORA*, 6: 188–89, 221.
10. *ORN*, 12: 363–65, 324–27, 378; Schiller, *Sumter Is Avenged*, 15.
11. *ORA*, 6: 192; Gillmore, "Siege and Capture of Fort Pulaski," 1–12.
12. *ORA*, 6: 193–96; Bryant, *Diary of Elias A. Bryant*, 26–30.
13. Albert, *Forty-Fifth Pennsylvania*, 22–29, 37–39; *ORA*, 6: 198; Hayes, *Samuel Francis Du Pont*, 1: 275, 336, 402; *ORN*, 12: 322–23, 387–8, 392–93; Denison, *Shot and Shell*, 59–60; *ORA*, 6: 89.
14. *ORA*, 6: 197–200; *ORN* 12: 386–87, 390; Stevens, *Isaac Ingalls Stevens*, 2: 349–50, 357–58, 353–55.
15. Stevens, *Isaac Ingalls Stevens*, 2: 353–56; Todd, *Seventy-Ninth Highlanders*, 108; *ORA*, 6: 201–3.
16. Denison, *Shot and Shell*, 51, 54–55; Stevens, *Isaac Ingalls Stevens*, 2: 353.
17. Todd, *Seventy-Ninth Highlanders*, 197; Petrie, *Civil War Surgeon*, 102–3; Beecher, *First Light Battery*, 1: 94.
18. Gavin, *Campaigning with the Roundheads*, 62–64; *New York Tribune*, January 24, 1862.
19. Boyle, *Reminiscences of the Civil War*, 7.

20. Boyle, *Reminiscences of the Civil War*, 7–10; Todd, *Seventy-Ninth Highlanders*, 108.

21. Todd, *Seventy-Ninth Highlanders*, 108; *ORA*, 6: 199–200, 207–8; *ORN*, 12: 412.

22. Although contemporary useage prefers "it" when referring to ships, the authors have used the sentimental "she" throughout this work with deliberate intent in an effort to more fully draw the reader into the scene of the narrative and to stay consistent with the ship references found in the period quotes.

23. Denison, *Shot and Shell*, 56; *ORA*, 6: 45–46; *ORN*, 12: 412–13.

24. Hayes, *Samuel Francis Du Pont*, 1: 296.

25. *ORA*, 6: 47–53; Gavin, *Campaigning with the Roundheads*, 64–56; Stevens, *Isaac Ingalls Stevens*, 2: 357–59.

26. *ORN*, 12: 446–51; Stevens, *Isaac Ingalls Stevens*, 2: 357–58; *ORA*, 6: 47–61; Todd, *Seventy-Ninth Highlanders*, 109–14; Nichols, *Perry's Saints*, 73–75.

27. *ORA*, 6: 47–53, 61–63; Tafft, "Reminiscences of the Signal Service," 3–9.

28. *ORA*, 6: 66–75; Tafft, "Reminiscences of the Signal Service," 8–9.

29. *ORA*, 6: 56–57; *ORN*, 12: 450–51; Boyle, *Reminiscences of the Civil War*, 7–10.

30. Todd, *Seventy-Ninth Highlanders*, 109–14; *ORA*, 6: 44–75.

31. *ORA*, 6: 66, 75.

32. Schiller, *Sumter Is Avenged*, 52–54.

33. *ORA*, 6: 215–16; Longacre, *From Union Stars to Top Hat*, 46–48.

34. Denison, *Shot and Shell*, 69; *ORA*, 6: 147; *ORN*, 12: 478.

35. *ORN*, 12: 491–98.

36. Schiller, *Sumter Is Avenged*, 44; Longacre, *From Union Stars to Top Hat*, 48; Gillmore, *Reduction of Fort Pulaski*, 12–15; *ORA*, 6: 148–52.

37. Nichols, *Perry's Saints*, 77–80.

38. *ORN*, 12: 491–98; *ORA*, 6: 142–43, 151–52; Denison, *Shot and Shell*, 69–74; Caldwell, *Old Sixth Regiment*, 34–35; Palmer, *History of the Forty-eighth Regiment*, 30–35; Nichols, *Perry's Saints*, 80–82; Gillmore, *Reduction of Fort Pulaski*, 16–21.

39. *ORN*, 12: 491–98; *ORA*, 6: 143, 151–52; Denison, *Shot and Shell*, 69–74; Caldwell, *Old Sixth Regiment*, 34–35; Palmer, *History of the Forty-eighth Regiment*, 30–35; Gillmore, *Reduction of Fort Pulaski*, 15–19.

40. Denison, *Shot and Shell*, 71; Gillmore, *Reduction of Fort Pulaski*, 20–21; *ORA*, 6: 143–44.

41. Denison, *Shot and Shell*, 72–73; Gillmore, *Reduction of Fort Pulaski*, 20–21; *ORA*, 6: 143–44.

42. *ORN*, 12: 502–3.

43. Palmer, *History of the Forty-eighth Regiment*, 32–35; Denison, *Shot and Shell*, 72–73.

44. Denison, *Shot and Shell*, 72–73; Palmer, *History of the Forty-eighth Regiment*, 32–33; Caldwell, *Old Sixth Regiment*, 34–35.

45. Eldridge, *Third New Hampshire*, 132–34.

46. Hayes, *Samuel Francis Du Pont*, 1: 272, 275; *ORN*, 12: 325–26, 416, 419–20, 422–23; Browning, *Success Is All*, 52–56, 70–74.

47. *ORA*, 6: 236, 238–39, 242–43, 248–52, 255; Browning, *Success Is All*, 65–73; Hayes, *Samuel Francis Du Pont*, 1: 372–77; *ORN*, 12: 577, 584, 595–99, 604, 607, 638–39, 657–58.

48. *ORA*, 6: 699–702; West, *Lincoln's Scapegoat General*, 120–22; Butler, *Autobiography and Personal Reminiscences*, 92, 348–35; *New South*, March 15, 1862.

49. *ORA*, 6: 248.

50. *ORA*, 6: 245–47, 254; Eldridge, *Third New Hampshire*, 126–27; Schiller, *Sumter Is Avenged*, 70–71; Hayes, *Samuel Francis Du Pont*, 1: 397–98.

51. After his recall Sherman would go on to command a division in the Army of the Tennessee and later the Army of the Mississippi during Halleck's Corinth Campaign. Assigned to the Department of the Gulf in September 1862, Sherman held various commands around New Orleans until May 1863, when he again commanded a division during Banks's Port Hudson Campaign. On May 27, 1863, while leading his division on horseback against the Confederate defenses, Sherman was badly wounded in the right leg, which was amputated. After recovering, Sherman returned to duty in the Department of the Gulf in March 1864, where he held various commands until the end of the war. He later served as colonel of the 3rd Regiment of Artillery until he retired because of disability in 1870. He died on March 16, 1879 in Newport, Rhode Island. Hayes, *Samuel Francis Du Pont*, 1: 399–400; Cullum, *Officers and Graduates of West Point*, 1: 642–43.

52. Gillmore, *Reduction of Fort Pulaski*, 38; *ORA*, 6: 156–59, 259–62; Longacre, *From Union Stars to Top Hat*, 51.

53. *ORA*, 6: 148, 157–65.

54. *ORA*, 6: 134.

55. Haydon, *Military Ballooning during the Early Civil War*, 383–84.

CHAPTER 4: THE PORT ROYAL EXPERIMENT BEGINS

1. *ORA*, 6: 192, 205; Todd, *Seventy-Ninth Highlanders*, 106; Hendricks, "Union Army Occupation," 19–20.

2. *ORA*, 6: 200–201; Todd, *Seventy-Ninth Highlanders*, 106; Hendricks, "Union Army Occupation," 19–20; Niven, *Salmon P. Chase Papers*, 3: xxi.

3. Niven, *Salmon P. Chase Papers*, 1: xi–xxiii, 3: 237; Lamphier, *Kate Chase and William Sprague*, 11–12, 21–22.

4. Lamphier, *Kate Chase and William Sprague*, 27–35, 39.

5. McGuire, "Hands on the Land," 3; Johnson, *Social History of the Sea Islands*, 108; *ORA*, 6: 208; Rowland, Moore, and Rogers, *History of Beaufort County*, 369.

6. Rose, *Rehearsal for Reconstruction*, 19; Niven, *Salmon P. Chase Papers*, 3: 116; *ORA*, 6: 208.

7. Niven, *Salmon P. Chase Papers*, 3: 116–17; Holland, *Letters and Diary of Laura M. Towne*, 16; Hendricks, "Union Army Occupation," 22.

8. Niven, *Salmon P. Chase Papers*, 3: 117–18.

9. Stevens, *Isaac Ingalls Stevens*, 2: 356, 367–68; Rowland, Moore, and Rogers, *History of Beaufort County*, 286–87; *Frank Leslie's Illustrated Weekly*, November 29, 1862; U.S. Congress, House, Transfer of Duplicates, 1940, H.R. 1284, 1–12; U.S. Congress, House, Beaufort Library Society, Beaufort, S.C., H.R. 1284, 1894, 1–2.

10. The *Flora* would later be renamed the *Nemaha* and serve as a revenue cutter and sometimes a transport along the southeastern coast. Niven, *Salmon P. Chase Papers*, 3: 117, 385; Hendricks, "Union Army Occupation," 20; Hayes, *Samuel Francis Du Pont*, 2: 29; Mitchell, *Merchant Steam Vessels*, 73; Hendricks, "Union Army Occupation," 25–26, 49.

11. Basler, *Works of Abraham Lincoln*, 5: 446; Elizabeth Stranger Diary and Scrapbook; *Baptist Home Missions*, 396–99; Cathcart, *Baptist Encyclopedia*, 893; Barnwell, *History of an American Family*, 133–34.

12. French, *Ancestors*, 72–82; Niven, *Salmon P. Chase Papers*, 1: 268; *Dictionary of American Biography*, 8: 253–54.

13. French, *Ancestors,* 81–83; Richardson, *Christian Reconstruction,* 1–5; Swint, *Northern Teacher in the South,* 11–15.

14. French, *Ancestors,* 83; McGuire, "Hands on the Land," 31, 33; Niven, *Salmon P. Chase Papers,* 1: 268.

15. McGuire, "Hands on the Land," 31–33; Niven, *Salmon P. Chase Papers,* 1: 238, 265, 277–28, 295, 3: 17, 27, 115–16, 121; Hayes, *Samuel Francis Du Pont,* 1: 412.

16. Niven, *Salmon P. Chase Papers,* 3: 115–16, 123.

17. Niven, *Salmon P. Chase Papers,* 3: 115–16, 120–24.

18. Pierce, "Negroes at Port Royal," 302–15; Rowland, Moore, and Rogers, *History of Beaufort County,* 416; *New York Tribune,* December 7, 30, 1861, February 14, 1862.

19. Hayes, *Samuel Francis Du Pont,* 1: 412; Pierce, "Negroes at Port Royal," 314–15; Niven, *Salmon P. Chase Papers,* 3: 123.

20. Niven, *Salmon P. Chase Papers,* 3: 123; *ORN,* 12: 540–42.

21. *ORA,* 6: 218, 222–23.

22. At this time Lincoln was still mourning the loss of his son Willie. Basler, *Works of Abraham Lincoln,* 5: 132; Hendricks, "Union Army Occupation," 46–47; McGuire, "Hands on the Land," 35.

23. *ORA,* 6: 227; Niven, *Salmon P. Chase Papers,* 3: 133–34, 137–38.

24. Niven, *Salmon P. Chase Papers,* 3: 136–37; Hendricks, "Union Army Occupation," 19–20.

25. Professor Lindsay may well have been the Reverend Dr. John Wesley Lindsay, a clergyman in New York City from 1860 to 1865. Correspondence by Stephen R. Wise with Carol Salomon, archives librarian, Cooper Union Library, New York, August 16, 2006; McGuire "Hands on the Land," 35–36; Swint, *Northern Teacher in the South,* 15; Niven, *Salmon P. Chase Papers,* 3: 136–38; Hendricks, "Union Army Occupation," 12–13; Sherwood, "Journal of Miss Susan Walker," 9; French, *Ancestors,* 85–88; Richardson, *Christian Reconstruction,* 17–18.

26. Rybczynski, *Clearing in the Distance,* 197, 205–7.

27. Reverend Henry W. Bellows, a major backer of the New York National Commission for Freedmen's Relief Association and the organizer of the Sanitary Commission, convinced Olmsted to become its director. Niven, *Salmon P. Chase Papers,* 3: 140–41; Rybczynski, *Clearing in the Distance,* 197, 205–7.

28. Niven, *Salmon P. Chase Papers,* 3: 145–46; 116, 139–40.

29. Sherwood, "Journal of Miss Susan Walker," 12; Niven, *Salmon P. Chase Papers,* 3: 138–39; Swint, *Northern Teacher in the South,* 17.

30. Niven, *Gideon Welles,* 362–63; Hughes, *John Murray Forbes,* 1: 293–96.

31. Niven, *Salmon P. Chase Papers,* 3: 143–44; Sherwood, "Journal of Miss Susan Walker," 12–14.

32. Sherwood, "Journal of Miss Susan Walker," 13–15.

33. "Persons Recommended by the Educational Commission" and "Persons Approved by the National Freedmen's Relief Association"; Wolf, "Laura Towne and the Freed People," 396; Smith, *Nation Comes of Age,* 729; "John Celivergos Zachos" (website).

34. The Port Royal Relief Committee would later become the Pennsylvania Freedmen's Relief Association. Wolf, "Laura Towne and the Freed People," 378–79; Rose, *Rehearsal for Reconstruction,* 75–76; McKim, *Address Delivered by J. Miller M'Kim,* 1–3.

35. Hughes, *John Murray Forbes,* 1: 300–304; Holland, *Letters and Diary of Laura M. Towne,* 3–10.

36. Hayes, *Samuel Francis Du Pont*, 1: 412; Hughes, *John Murray Forbes*, 1: 300–302; Niven, *Salmon P. Chase Papers*, 3: 144; Hendricks, "Union Army Occupation," 48; Stevens, *Isaac Ingalls Stevens*, 2: 369–70.

37. Niven, *Salmon P. Chase Papers*, 3: 144, 146–47, 157–58.

38. Hayes, *Samuel Francis Du Pont*, 2: 44; Sherwood, "Journal of Miss Susan Walker," 22, 35; Niven, *Salmon P. Chase Papers*, 3: 154–56; 181–82; 198–99; Hughes, *John Murray Forbes*, 1: 300–302.

39. Niven, *Salmon P. Chase Papers*, 1: 331, 3: 150–51, 182.

40. Schwartz, *Woman Doctor's Civil War*, 33–34; Ford, *Cycle of Adams Letters*, 1: 117–19; Holland, *Letters and Diary of Laura M. Towne*, 3–7; 10–16, 80–81; Todd, *Seventy-Ninth Highlanders*, 104, 118; Hughes, *John Murray Forbes*, 1: 300–302.

41. Basler, *Works of Abraham Lincoln*, 4: 445–46; Niven, *Salmon P. Chase Papers*, 1: 333; Sherwood, "Journal of Miss Susan Walker," 18; *Baptist Home Missions*, 400; Holland, *Letters and Diary of Laura M. Towne*, 92.

42. Sherwood, "Journal of Miss Susan Walker," 29–30; Palmer, *History of the Forty-eighth Regiment*, 36; Holland, *Letters and Diary of Laura M. Towne*, 16, 25, 27–32; Niven, *Salmon P. Chase Papers*, 3: 163.

43. Beecher, *First Light Battery*, 1: 102; Todd, *Seventy-Ninth Highlanders*, 100–102.

44. McGuire, "Hands on the Land," 36–38; Sherwood, "Journal of Miss Susan Walker," 33; Pearson, *Letters from Port Royal*, 1, 11; McPherson, *Struggle for Equality*, 163–65; Foner, *Reconstruction*, 52–53.

45. Niven, *Salmon P. Chase Papers*, 1: 334, 3: 148–50; Todd, *Seventy-Ninth Highlanders*, 118.

46. McPherson, *Struggle for Equality*, 161; Niven, *Salmon P. Chase Papers*, 3: 140–41, 181, 183, 200–201, Rybczynski, *Clearing in the Distance*, 206–7.

47. Holland, *Letters and Diary of Laura M. Towne*, 61–62; Sherwood, "Journal of Miss Susan Walker," 44–45; Niven, *Salmon P. Chase Papers*, 3: 19, 199.

CHAPTER 5: THE CONFEDERATE BEAUFORT DISTRICT

1. Davis, *Rhett*, 519–523; Edgar, Bailey, and Moore, *South Carolina House of Representatives*, 1: 358, 362, 5: 12–15.

2. Bailey, Morgan, and Taylor, *South Carolina Senate*, 1: 362–63, 375, 472–73, 506–7, 2: 898–99, 1291–92, 1355–56, 1383; Rowland, Moore, and Rogers, *History of Beaufort County*, 1: 428–29, 439.

3. Edgar, Bailey, and Alexander, *South Carolina House of Representatives*, 1: 384–85, 388–89, 391–92, 397; Rowland, Moore, and Rogers, *History of Beaufort County*, 1: 428–29, 438–39.

4. Barnwell, *History of an American Family*, 194–95, 203–4; Taylor, Mathews, and Powers, *Leverett Letters*, 139–42, 144–45, 164–67, 315–17, 357–59; Sifakis, *Who Was Who*, 203; Warner, *Generals in Gray*, 81–82; Edgar, Bailey, and Moore, *South Carolina House of Representatives*, 1: 384–85, 388–89, 391–92, 397; *ORN*, 14: 114–21; Wise, "The U.S.S. George Washington," *Beaufort Low Country Ledger*, January 5, 1989.

5. Cullum, *Officers and Graduates of West Point*, 1: 747; Sifakis, *Who Was Who*, 376–77; Warner, *Generals in Gray*, 175–76.

6. Johnson had narrowly lost to Francis Pickens for governor of South Carolina in 1860. Spieler, "Johnson Memoirs Reveal an Interesting Family Life"; McArthur and Burton, *Gentleman and an Officer*, 50, 53, 85; Tancig, *Confederate Military Land Units*, 81.

7. *New York Times,* April 10, 1865; Barnwell, *History of an American Family,* 164–76, 210–11; letters to authors from Rick Hatcher, historian, Fort Sumter National Monument, September 25, 26, 2007; Cullum, *Officers and Graduates of West Point,* 2: 117, 215; Sifakis, *Who Was Who,* 541–22.

8. Barnwell, *History of an American Family,* 212–14

9. Cullum, *Officers and Graduates of West Point,* 306; Compiled Confederate Service Records for Richard DeTreville Sr., Robert DeTreville, Richard DeTreville Jr., John DeTreville and Edward DeTreville; Richard DeTreville letter of March 11, 1867.

10. Huguenin, "Journal of Thomas Abram Huguenin" (website).

11. Cullum, *Officers and Graduates of West Point,* 1: 579; Barnwell, *History of an American Family,* 85, 209.

12. Barnwell, *History of an American Family,* 80.

13. Barnwell, *History of an American Family,* 151–52, 203.

14. Barnwell, *History of an American Family,* 204–6; Compiled Confederate Service Record for William Elliott.

15. Barnwell, *History of an American Family,* 199–200.

16. Barnwell, *History of an American Family,* 116–25, 151–52, 214–17.

17. Rowland, Moore, and Rogers, *History of Beaufort County,* 1: 415–17; U.S. Census, Population Schedules, Beaufort District, 8th Census; U. S. Census, Slave Schedules, Beaufort District, 8th Census; Spieler, "Many Died in Area for Confederacy."

18. Stone, *Vital Rails,* 7–8; 25, 27; Myers, *Children of Pride,* 1495; Tancig, *Confederate Military Land Units,* 80; Sifakis, *Compendium of the Confederate Armies,* 41–42, 46–47; Hewett, *South Carolina Confederate Soldiers,* 2: 8–13, 19–28; Emerson, *Sons of Privilege,* 22.

19. Hewett, *South Carolina Confederate Soldiers,* 2: 19–28.

20. Taylor, Mathews, and Powers, *Leverett Letters,* 92–93; Hewett, *South Carolina Confederate Soldiers,* 2: 387; Barnwell, *History of an American Family,* 194–95; Baxley, *No Prouder Fate,* 3–9; Tancig, *Confederate Military Land Units,* 77.

21. Barnwell, *History of an American Family,* 189–90; Hewett, *South Carolina Confederate Soldiers,* 2: 389–90; Baxley, *No Prouder Fate,* 3–9.

22. Barnwell, *History of an American Family*; *South Carolina Confederate Soldiers,* 2: 390–91; Baxley, *No Prouder Fate,* 3–9.

23. Bailey, *Biographical Directory,* 7; Barnwell, *History of an American Family,* 155; Hewett, *South Carolina Confederate Soldiers,* 2: 387, 391; *ORA,* 6: 13, 29; Baxley, *No Prouder Fate,* 3–9.

24. *South Carolina Genealogies,* 2: 352–64; Cullum, *Officers and Graduates of West Point,* 460; Linder, *Atlas of the Rice Plantations,* 159.

25. Hewett, *South Carolina Confederate Soldiers,* 2: 387–89; Sifakis, *Compendium of the Confederate Armies,* 83–85; Taylor, Mathews, and Powers, *Leverett Letters,* 92–93; *ORA,* 6: 6–7, 11, 13, 24; Baxley, *No Prouder Fate,* 3–9.

26. Taylor, Mathews, and Powers, *Leverett Papers,* 121–22; Baxley, *No Prouder Fate,* 3–9; Sifakis, *Compendium of the Confederate Armies,* 83–85.

27. *ORA,* 14: 480.

28. *ORA,* 14: 471–80, 483, 505, 509.

29. *ORA,* 14: 483, 493, 509, 523, 525.

30. *Beaufort Gazette,* February 5, 1931.

31. McPherson, *Negro's Civil War,* 58–59; Taylor, Mathews, and Powers, *Leverett Letters,* 171–72; Barnwell, *History of an American Family,* 179, 180, 212; *New York Tribune,* December 12, 1861.

32. *ORA*, 489, 491–93; Taylor, Mathews, and Powers, *Leverett Letters*, 171, 190, 200–201.

33. *ORN*, ser. 2, 1: 180; ser. 1, 12: 820–26; Miller, *Gullah Statesman*, 1–12.

34. The Fuller House may at one time been the Thomas Fuller House. Miller, *Gullah Statesman*, 7–9; Billingsley, *Yearning to Breathe Free*, 24–27, 34–35, 44–47; Bailey, Morgan, and Taylor, *South Carolina Senate*, 3: 1482–85; Pearson, *Letters from Port Royal*, 268.

35. Miller, *Gullah Statesman*, 11–12; *ORN*, 12: 821–22; Billingsley, *Yearning*, 54–57.

36. Miller, *Gullah Statesman*, 1; *ORN*, 12: 821–22; Billingsley, *Yearning to Breathe Free*, 58–60.

37. *ORN*, 12: 821–22; Beecher, *First Light Battery*, 96.

38. Hayes, *Samuel Francis Du Pont*, 2: 49–51.

39. *ORN*, 12: 824–25; 12: 28, 52–24, 102–3, 125–26; Miller, *Gullah Statesman*, 11–12; Hayes, *Samuel Francis Du Pont*, 2: 49–50, 60, 91, 93.

CHAPTER 6: ARMING THE SLAVES AND THE BATTLE OF POCOTALIGO

1. *New South*, March 15, 1862; McCracken and McCracken, *Forgotten History*, 31–42; Denison, *Shot and Shell*, 138; *ORA*, 6: 245–47.

2. Albert, *Forty-Fifth Pennsylvania*, 26–26; Eldridge, *Third New Hampshire*, 190; Price, *History of the Ninety-Seventh Regiment*, 132–33.

3. *New South*, March 15, 1862; McCracken, *Forgotten History*, 31–42.

4. Beecher, *Light Battery*, 1: 90–94.

5. Tubman pension records, National Archives; Conrad, *Harriet Tubman*, 158–65; Sternett, *Harriet Tubman*, 84–87, 95; Wood, Pension Files.

6. Numerous vessels operated between New York and Port Royal, including the *Ericson, Empire City, Massachusetts, S. R. Spaulding*, and the *General McClellan* (formerly the *Joseph Whitney*). Besides the *Atlantic* the most prominent were the *Arago*, which replaced the Atlantic in January 1865, and the *Fulton*. Dana and Gibson, *Dictionary of Transports and Combatant Vessels*, 20, 24, 121; Heyl, *Early American Steamers*, 1: 39–40; Hayes, *Samuel Francis Du Pont*, 1: 204, 210, 236, 241–42.

7. Browning, *Success Is All*, 75–85; Hayes, *Samuel Francis Du Pont*, 2: 53, 257; Eldridge, *Third New Hampshire*, 273; *ORN*, 12: 558.

8. Miller, *Lincoln's Abolitionist General*, 1–15, 28–31; Cullum, *Officers and Graduates of West Point*, 1: 290–93.

9. Thomas and Hyman, *Stanton*, 235–36; Cullum, *Officers and Graduates of West Point*, 1: 290–93; Miller, *Lincoln's Abolitionist General*, 73–85;

10. Cullum, *Officers and Graduates of West Point*, 1: 290–93, 733–40; Miller, *Lincoln's Abolitionist General*, 86–87, 96; *ORA*, 6: 248; Thomas and Hyman, *Stanton*, 132–34, 230, 234, 237.

11. Stockton was the son of Hunter's sister Mary, while Kinzie was the son of John H. Kinzie, brother of Hunter's wife. "Private Miles O'Reilly" (website); Miller, *Lincoln's Abolitionist General*, 66–67; *ORA*, 6: 257–58.

12. *ORA*, 6: 257–58.

13. Hayes, *Samuel Francis Du Pont*, 1: 396–97, 2: 45, 75, 99.

14. *ORA*, 6: 254, 263, 14: 338, 362–63; *ORA*, ser. 3, 2: 27–28; *New York Tribune*, April 7, 1863.

15. *ORA*, 6: 263–64; Hendricks, "Union Army Occupation," 63–64; Niven, *Chase Papers*, 3: 333–34; *New York Times*, April 7, 19, May 1, 1862; Sherwood, "Journal of Miss Susan Walker," 36–37.

16. *ORA*, 14: 333; Sherwood, "Journal of Miss Susan Walker," 36–37.

17. *ORA*, 6: 176–77; *ORA*, 14: 341; *ORA*, ser. 3, 2: 29–31; Hendricks, "Union Army Occupation," 62–65; Miller, *Lincoln's Abolitionist General*, 97–100.

18. *ORA*, ser. 3, 2: 42.

19. Hayes, *Samuel Francis Du Pont*, 2: 44–46; Miller, *Lincoln's Abolitionist General*, 99–100.

20. Miller, *Lincoln's Abolitionist General*, 100–101; Sherwood, "Journal of Miss Susan Walker," 37–40; Holland, *Letters and Diary of Laura M. Towne*, 34–44, 48–54; *ORA*, ser. 3, 2: 50–60.

21. *ORA*, ser. 3, 2: 50–60.

22. Miller, *Lincoln's Abolitionist General*, 100–105; Holland, *Letters and Diary of Laura M. Towne*, 48–54.

23. A case for the war's first black regiment can also be made for a New Orleans militia unit raised in May 1861 made up of free men of mixed blood. The unit participated in parades but was never mustered into Confederate service and disbanded in February 1862. Higginson, *Army Life in a Black Regiment*, 272–73; *Washington National Tribune*, October 27, 1892; "1st Louisiana Native Guard" (website).

24. Freeman, *R. E. Lee*, 2: 38; Cullum, *Officers and Graduates of West Point*, 2: 239–40.

25. Basler, *Works of Abraham Lincoln*, 5: 222–23.

26. Hayes, *Samuel Francis Du Pont*, 2: 80; Miller, *Lincoln's Abolitionist General*, 102–3.

27. Miller, *Lincoln's Abolitionist General*, 103; Basler, *Works of Abraham Lincoln*, 5: 317–19.

28. Miller, *Lincoln's Abolitionist General*, 105; Taylor, *Reminiscences of My Life in Camp*, 41–42; *Washington National Tribune*, October 27, 1892; Higginson, *Army Life in a Black Regiment*, 272–73.

29. Miller, *Lincoln's Abolitionist General*, 105; *Washington National Tribune*, October 27, 1892; *New York Tribune*, May 12, 1862.

30. Miller, *Lincoln's Abolitionist General*, 105; *Washington National Tribune*, October 27, 1892; *New York Tribune*, May 12, 1862.

31. Hayes, *Samuel Francis Du Pont*, 2: 80–81.

32. Thomas and Hyman, *Stanton*, 234–39; Pearson, *Life of John A. Andrew*, 2: 2–3, 9–12; Niven, *Chase Papers*, 3: 344.

33. Todd, *Seventy-Ninth Highlanders*, 170; *New York Tribune*, July 29, 1862; Schmidt, *History of the 47th Regiment*, 170, 177–78.

34. Hayes, *Samuel Francis Du Pont*, 2: 65–66, 142–43, 156–57.

35. Miller, *Lincoln's Abolitionist General*, 104–6; 110–12; O'Reilly, *Baked Meats of the Funeral*, 178–89, 206–7; Rawley, *Politics of Union*, 78–79; Miller, *Lincoln's Abolitionist General*, 110–12; Pearson, *Life of John A. Andrew*, 2: 71–73; McPherson, *Struggle for Equality*, 110–16.

36. *ORA*, ser. 3, 2: 152–53.

37. Hayes, *Samuel Francis Du Pont*, 2: 143; Hendricks, "Union Army Occupation," 40, 55–56, 59; Miller, *Lincoln's Abolitionist General*, 112–13.

38. Holland, *Letters and Diary of Laura M. Towne*, 72–73.

39. Holland, *Letters and Diary of Laura M. Towne*, 71–76; *ORA*, 14: 363–64, 367. 374–76.

40. Nordhoff, *Freedmen of South Carolina*, 13; Hendricks, "Union Army Occupation," 58.

41. *New York Tribune*, July 31, 1862; Miller, *Lincoln's Abolitionist General*, 105.

42. Also included in General Order Number 60 was General John W. Phelps, who was outfitting black troops under General Benjamin Butler at New Orleans. *ORA*, 14: 599, ser. 2, 4: 835, 328–39; Miller, *Lincoln's Abolitionist General*, 122–24.

43. *New York Tribune*, August 19, 1862; Miller, *Lincoln's Abolitionist General*, 108–13.

44. Miller, *Lincoln's Abolitionist General*, 110; *New York Tribune*, August 22, 1862; Looby, *Thomas Wentworth Higginson*, 55.

45. Ford, *Cycle of Adams Letters*, 1: 174–75.

46. Taylor, *Reminiscences of My Life in Camp*, 111; *New York Tribune*, August 9, 1862; Schwartz, *Woman Doctor's Civil War*, 40; Rogers, "Surgeon's War Letters," 394.

47. Miller, *Lincoln's Abolitionist General*, 112; *ORA*, 14: 374.

48. *ORA*, 14: 374–76.

49. Billingsley, *Yearning to Breathe Free*, 70–71; Miller, *Lincoln's Abolitionist General*, 112–13; Miller, *Gullah Statesman*, 14–16; *ORA*, 14: 377–78.

50. *ORA*, 14: 377–78

51. *ORA*, 14: 377–78.

52. Niven, *Chase Papers*, 3: 391, 404, 416, 418; *ORA*, 14: 380, 387. Cullum, *Officers and Graduates of West Point*, 2: 19–20.

53. Du Pont had been promoted to Rear Admiral July 16, 1862. Hayes, *Samuel Francis Du Pont*, 2: 216–17; *ORN*, 13: 312–13.

54. Niven, *Chase Papers*, 3: 382; Looby, *Higginson Journal*, 41; Hendricks, "Union Army Occupation," 34.

55. Hayes, *Samuel Francis Du Pont*, 2: 216–18, 263–64; *ORA*, 14: 376, Miller, *Lincoln's Abolitionist General*, 112–14.

56. Brennan, *Secessionville*, 3–6.

57. Brennan, *Secessionville*, 45; *ORA*, 14: 20–23; Todd, *Seventy-Ninth Highlanders*, 130–31.

58. Brennan, *Secessionville*, 45; *ORA*, 14: 20–24; Beecher, *First Light Battery*, 1: 117–18, 125–26; Todd, *Seventy-Ninth Highlanders*, 130–31;

59. Halliburton, *Saddle Soldiers*, 30.

60. Halliburton, *Saddle Soldiers*, 31; Beecher, *First Light Battery*, 1: 124–30; James Burst Letter, June 12, 1863.

61. Taylor, Mathews, and Powers, *Leverett Letters*, 136.

62. Beecher, *First Light Battery*, 123.

63. Halliburton, *Saddle Soldiers*, 31; *ORA*, 14: 20–27.

64. *ORA*, 14: 21, 26; Beecher, *First Light Battery*, 1: 123.

65. Beecher, *First Light Battery*, 1: 124.

66. *ORA*, 14: 31–32.

67. Hayes, *Samuel Francis Du Pont*, 2: 107–10; Sherwood, "Journal of Miss Susan Walker," 46–47; Holland, *Letters and Diary of Laura M. Towne*, 62–65; Hayes, *Samuel Francis Du Pont*, 106–8; *ORA*, 14: 31–32; Taylor, Mathews, and Powers, *Leverett Letters*, 150–51.

68. *ORA*, 14: 51–53, 86–88, 347–48, 353–54.

69. Miller, *Lincoln's Abolitionist General*, 111–13; Todd, *Seventy-Ninth Highlanders*, 169–70; Caldwell, *Old Sixth Regiment*, 44; Hayes, *Samuel Francis Du Pont*, 2: 161–62; *ORA*, 14: 363–66, 374.

70. Denison, *Shot and Shell*, 128; Little, *Seventh Regiment*, 57–58; Beecher, *First Light Battery*, 1: 101, 186; National Archives, Beaufort SC National Cemetery, Consolidated

Correspondence File, Hilton Head, Record Group 92; Caldwell, *Old Sixth Regiment*, 44; Schmidt, *History of the 47th Regiment*, 167, 190; Price, *History of the Ninety-Seventh Regiment*, 136.

71. Hurst Papers, Letter of June 12, 1862; Beecher, *First Light Battery*, 1: 231–32; Schmidt, *History of the 47th Regiment*, 167.

72. Beecher, *First Light Battery*, 1: 183, 189; *Third Rhode Island*, 150; Hurst Papers, Letter of June 12, 1863.

73. Price, *History of the Ninety-Seventh Regiment*, 130–36; Denison, *Shot and Shell*, 150; Consolidated Correspondence for the Quartermaster, General Quartermaster Records for the Department of the South, National Archives Record Group 92; *New York Tribune*, August 9, 1862; Eldridge, *Third New Hampshire*, 195–97.

74. *ORA*, 14: 20–27, 505, 539, 584–86; Robinson, "Defense of the Charleston and Savannah Railroad," 16–21.

75. *ORA*, 14: 112; Taylor, Mathews, and Powers, *Leverett Letters*, 152; Little, *Seventh Regiment*, 59.

76. *ORA*, 14: 586–88, 604.

77. Some reports list the three captured Federals as deserters. *ORA*, 14: 115–20; Halliburton, *Saddle Soldiers*, 44–47; Baxley, *No Prouder Fate*, 51–54; Taylor, Mathews, and Powers, *Leverett Letters*, 165–67.

78. *ORA*, 14: 601, 625–26, 632–33, 537, 640–41.

79. Mitchel, *Ormsby MacKnight Mitchel*, 358–60; Cullum, *Officers and Graduates of West Point*, 1: 429–31.

80. Mitchel, *Ormsby MacKnight Mitchel*, 369–70; *New South*, September 20, 1862; *ORA*, 14: 383; Schmidt, *History of the 47th Regiment*, 193–94; Niven, *Chase Papers*, 3: 404, 416–17.

81. Mitchel, *Ormsby MacKnight Mitchel*, 350–69; Niven, *Chase Papers*, 3: 382; *ORA*, 14: 384–85; *New York Times*, September 10, 1862.

82. *New York Times*, October 8, 1862.

83. The church is Hilton Head's only surviving government-built Civil War–era building. Eldridge, *Third New Hampshire*, 219–20; *New South*, October 18, 1862; Schmidt, *History of the 47th Regiment*, 66; Mitchel, *Ormsby MacKnight Mitchel*, 365–68; *New York Times*, October 19, 1862.

84. Hayes, *Samuel Francis Du Pont*, 2: 224, 234; *ORA*, 14: 383.

85. Nichols, *Perry's Saints*, 118, 121–22; Halliburton, *Saddle Soldiers*, 54; Mitchel, *Ormsby MacKnight Mitchel*, 355–71; Denison, *Shot and Shell*, 113; *ORA*, 14: 127–44; *ORN*, 13: 355–71.

86. Caldwell, *Old Sixth Regiment*, 46; Mitchel, *Ormsby MacKnight Mitchel*, 372–73.

87. Schmidt, *Battle of Pocotaligo*, 4.

88. *ORN*, 13: 399; *ORA*, 14: 144–47.

89. *Hartford Courant*, October 31, 1862.

90. Lloyd Phoenix Journal; Schmidt, *History of the 47th Regiment*, 138; *Philadelphia Inquirer*, October 30, 1862; *ORN*, 13: 400, 402; *ORA*, 14: 144–47.

91. Jenkins, *Abstract of the Cruise of the U.S. Steam Frigate* Wabash, 26; *ORA*, 14: 164–69; Eldridge, *Third New Hampshire*, 222; Lloyd Phoenix Journal.

92. *New York Times*, October 29, 1862; Brown, *Battle of Pocotaligo, South Carolina*; *New South*, October 25, 1862; Schmidt, *History of the 47th Regiment*, 227–30; *Philadelphia Inquirer* October 30, 1862.

93. *New South,* October 25, 1862; *Philadelphia Inquirer,* October 30, 1862; *ORN,* 13: 400–401.

94. Eldridge, *Third New Hampshire,* 222–23; *New York Times,* October 29, 1863; Schmidt, *Battle of Pocotaligo,* 41–46; *ORA,* 14: 169–70; *Abstract of the Cruise of U.S. Steam Frigate Wabash,* 26; *New South,* October 25, 1863; Eldridge, *Third New Hampshire,* 222–23; *ORN,* 13: 400; Lloyd Phoenix Journal.

95. *ORN,* 13: 400–401; *ORA,* 14: 150–51, 175–76, 178.

96. Denison, *Shot and Shell,* 116–17; *ORA,* 14: 150–51, 160–61, 164–66; Schmidt, *Battle of Pocotaligo,* 80–96; *New South,* October 25, 1862; Lloyd Phoenix Journal.

97. *ORA,* 14: 180–81, 185–86.

98. *ORA,* 14: 160–62, 166, 181; Stephen Elliott Papers, South Caroliniana Library.

99. Emerson, *Sons of Privilege,* 47; *ORA,* 14: 151, 157, 181.

100. *ORA,* 14: 150–51, 158–59, 161, 163; Bryant, *Diary of Charles A. Bryant,* 70–71; Toutelloutte, *History of Company K,* 54; *Hartford Weekly,* November 15, 1862; *Philadelphia Inquirer,* October 30, 1862.

101. Emerson, *Sons of Privilege,* 47; *Cruise of the Wabash,* 26; *ORN,* 13: 402–3; *New York Times,* October 29, 1862; *ORA,* 14: 151, 161; Schmidt, *Battle of Pocotaligo,* 127; Lloyd Phoenix Journal.

102. *ORA,* 14: 151, 155, 159–63, 166, 181; Stephen Elliott Papers.

103. Bryant, *Diary of Charles A. Bryant,* 73; *ORA,* 14: 151, 157–60, 163, 167–67.

104. Schmidt, *History of the 47th Regiment,* 264–69; *ORA,* 14: 175–79, 185–87, *Philadelphia Inquirer,* October 30, 1862; Lloyd Phoenix Journal.

105. *ORA,* 14: 173.

106. Schmidt, *History of the 47th Regiment,* 264–69; *ORA,* 14: 175–79, 185–87; *Philadelphia Inquirer,* October 30, 1862.

107. *ORA,* 14: 185.

108. Other reports have the train consisting of three platform and two box cars. Schmidt, *Battle of Pocotaligo,* 60–64; *Philadelphia Inquirer,* October 30, 1862; *ORA,* 14: 175–79, 185–87.

109. Schmidt, *Battle of Pocotaligo,* 60–64; *Philadelphia Inquirer,* October 30, 1862; *ORA,* 14: 175–79, 185–87.

110. Schmidt, *Battle of Pocotaligo,* 60–64; *Philadelphia Inquirer,* October 30, 1862; *ORA,* 14: 175–79, 185–87.

111. *ORA,* 14: 158, 160, 170.

112. Bryant, *Diary of Charles A. Bryant,* 73–74; Schmidt, *History of the 47th Regiment,* 247–50; *ORN,* 13: 403; *ORA,* 14: 151–52, 155, 158, 160–63, 166–67, *Philadelphia Inquirer,* October 30, 1862.

113. Emerson, *Sons of Privilege,* 48–49; Schmidt, *History of the 47th Regiment,* 251–52; *ORA,* 14: 159–60, 171–72; Stephen Elliott Papers; Lloyd Phoenix Journal.

114. *ORA,* 14: 166–67, 171–72; Toutelloutte, *History of Company K,* 59–60; Lloyd Phoenix Journal.

115. Toutelloutte, *History of Company K,* 59–60; *ORA,* 14: 168, 181–82.

116. Bryant, *Diary of Charles A. Bryant,* 75; Denison, *Shot and Shell,* 118–19; Schmidt, *History of the 47th Regiment,* 256–57; *Philadelphia Inquirer,* October 30, 1862; *ORA,* 14: 160, 162, 168.

117. *ORA,* 14: 167–68; *Philadelphia Inquirer,* October 30, 1862; Lloyd Phoenix Journal.

118. *ORA,* 14: 182, 187–88.

119. *ORA*, 14: 152, 155, 158, 160, 164, 167–68, 172, 175, 182; *ORN*, 13: 401; *Philadelphia Inquirer*, October 30, 1862; Schmidt, *History of the 47th Regiment*, 256–57; Bryant, *Diary of Charles A. Bryant*, 76.

120. *ORN*, 13: 403–4; *ORA*, 14: 148, 180; Schmidt, *History of the 47th Regiment*, 256–57; Stephen Elliott Papers.

121. Hayes, *Samuel Francis Du Pont*, 2: 262–63.

122. *ORA*, 13: 408–9.

123. *Philadelphia Inquirer*, November 7, 1862; Mitchel, *Ormsby MacKnight Mitchel*, 378–79; Price, *History of the Ninety-Seventh Regiment*, 139–40; Nichols, *Perry's Saints*, 50; *New South*, November 1, 1862; Hayes, *Samuel Francis Du Pont*, 2: 268–69; Caldwell, *Old Sixth Regiment*, 50.

124. At the time of Mitchel's death, the officer's hospital was located in the Senator Robert Barnwell House at the junction of North and Hamilton streets. *Philadelphia Inquirer*, November 7, 1862; Hayes, *Samuel Francis Du Pont*, 2: 268–69; *New South*, November 1, 1862.

125. Wise, *Gate of Hell*, 25–29.

126. Hayes, *Samuel Francis Du Pont*, 2: 27.

CHAPTER 7: EMANCIPATION

1. The *Galena* had its armor removed and was recommissioned in February 1864. Hayes, *Samuel Francis Du Pont*, 2: 91–92, 96–97.

2. Hayes, *Samuel Francis Du Pont*, 2: 236–37, 241–49; Johnson, *Rear Admiral John Rodgers*, 238; Thompson and Wainwright, *Confidential Correspondence of Gustavus Fox*, 1: 173; Drayton, *Naval Letters from Percival Drayton*, 29.

3. *ORA*, 6: 228–35; *ORA*, 14: 396–428; *ORA*, 28: 2; Hayes, *Samuel Francis Du Pont*, 2: 443–44.

4. Hunter was unable to return immediately to Port Royal because of his assignment to the court-martial board trying Brigadier General Fritz John Porter. Also serving on the board was Brigadier General John A. Garfield. Hunter had encouraged Garfield to join him at Port Royal, but the future president was eventually assigned to the Army of the Tennessee as Major General William S. Rosecrans's chief of staff. Miller, *Lincoln's Abolitionist General*, 126–31; *ORA*, 14: 387–89; *New York Tribune*, January 28, 1863; Looby, *Higginson Journal*, 41; Niven, *Chase Papers*, Vol. 1, 382.

5. Cullum, *Officers and Graduates of West Point*, 2: 257; Hayes, *Samuel Francis Du Pont*, 2: 226; *Beaufort Free South*, June 13, 1863.

6. Basler, *Works of Abraham Lincoln*, 5: 336–38, 433–36; McPherson, *Struggle for Equality*, 111; *Philadelphia Inquirer*, October 31, 1862.

7. *ORA*, 14: 189–94; *New York Times*, September 24, 1862; *New York Tribune*, November 17, 1862; Denison, *Shot and Shell*, 114–15.

8. Harris, "Higginson, Thomas Wentworth," 244–45; Looby, *Higginson Journal*, 13–16.

9. Looby, *Higginson Journal*, 44–46, 70; Higginson, *Army Life in a Black Regiment*, 2–8, 38; "Lem Coley's words" (website).

10. Higginson, *Army Life in a Black Regiment*, 4.

11. Rogers, "Surgeon's War Letters," 357.

12. Higginson, *Army Life in a Black Regiment*, 4, 10–11, 17–22; Looby, *Higginson Journal*, 58–60; 62, 65.

13. Higginson, *Army Life in a Black Regiment*, 18, 113.

14. McGuire, "Hands on the Land," 22–25; Davis, "South's First City," 460–61; Schuckers, *Salmon Portland Chase*, 314–15; Richardson, *Messages and Papers of the Presidents*, 8: 837–38; McLaughlin, *Cyclopedia of American Government*, 837.

15. Rowland, Moore, and Rogers, *History of Beaufort County*, 1: 415–17; Alcorn, "William Henry Brisbane Project" (website).

16. "Hon. William E. Wording (website).

17. Smith; Dunley, "In Search of A. D. Smith," 16–27.

18. McGuire, "Hands on the Land," 66–68; Davis, *The New South's First City*, 300.

19. Schwartz, *Woman Doctor's Civil War*, 1–20, 33, 38.

20. Schwartz, *Woman Doctor's Civil War*, 39.

21. Laura Towne wrote that the school became known as Penn School when it moved from the Oaks to the Brick Church on September 22, 1862. Ellen Murray puts the name change shortly after her arrival in June 1862. Wolf, "Laura Towne and the Freed People," 390; Stevenson, *Journals of Charlotte Forten Grimké*, 382–90.

22. McPherson, *Struggle for Equality*, 117–22.

23. McPherson, *Struggle for Equality*, 20–22; Cooper, *Jefferson Davis*, 439.

24. Within ten days of the ceremony, Reverend Phillips, the nephew of Wendell Phillips, would die. Stevenson, *Journals of Charlotte Forten Grimké*, 405–6; Looby, *Higginson Journal*, 46; Beecher, *First Light Battery*, 1: 220–21; Schmidt, *History of the 47th Regiment*, 287.

25. Taylor, *Reminiscences of My Life in Camp*, 11–17; Higginson, *Army Life in a Black Regiment*, 8.

26. Denison, *Shot and Shell*, 133.

27. Looby, *Higginson Journal*, 72.

28. Holland, *Letters and Diary of Laura M. Towne*, 96–97.

29. The account of the celebration was compiled from Pearson, *Letters from Port Royal*, 128–35; Looby, *Higginson Journal*, 78–79, 255–56; Holland, *Letters and Diary of Laura M. Towne*, 98–99; Stevenson, *Journals of Charlotte Forten Grimké*, 428–35; Schwartz, *Woman Doctor's Civil War*, 40–42; *Beaufort Free South*, January 25, 1863; Franklin, "Emancipation Proclamation" (website).

30. Basler, *Works of Abraham Lincoln*, 5: 433–36; "Preliminary Emancipation Proclamation" (website).

31. Description of the day's events can be found in Pearson, *Letters from Port Royal*, 128–35; Looby, *Higginson Journal*, 78–79, 255–56; Holland, *Letters and Diary of Laura M. Towne*, 98–99; Stevenson, *Journals of Charlotte Forten Grimké*, 428–35; Schwartz, *Woman Doctor's Civil War*, 40–42; *Beaufort Free South*, January 17, 25, 1863, *New York Tribune*, January 14, 1863. See also Ash, *Firebrand of Liberty*, 22–27.

32. Hayes, *Samuel Francis Du Pont*, 2: 332–33; Bryant, *Diary of Charles A. Bryant*.

33. Basler, *Works of Abraham Lincoln*, 6: 28–31.

34. Looby, *Higginson Journal*, 83–84.

35. McPherson, *Struggle for Equality*, 125–26; Rogers, "Surgeon's War Letters," 341–44.

36. *Beaufort Free South*, January 17, 1863.

37. *New York Tribune*, February 13, 1863.

38. Looby, *Higginson Journal*, 88–90; Denison, *Shot and Shell*, 31–33.

39. Looby, *Higginson Journal*, 91–92, *New York Tribune*, January 28, 1863.

40. Looby, *Higginson Journal*, 99; Higginson, *Army Life in a Black Regiment*, 64–65; *New York Tribune*, January 28, 1863.

CHAPTER 8: INITIAL TAX SALES AND THE *GEORGE WASHINGTON*

1. Hayes, *Samuel Francis Du Pont,* 2: 366–73.
2. Hayes, *Samuel Francis Du Pont,* 2: 366–73; *New York Tribune,* January 28, 1863.
3. *New York Tribune,* Feb 11, 1863; Browning, *Success Is All,* 138–44; *ORN,* 13: 623.
4. Edward L. Cook Papers, E. L. Cook to parents, January 31, 1863.
5. Alfred Marple Diary and Letters, letters of February 8, February 2, 1863; Edward L. Cook Papers, Letters of February 2, 3, 1863.
6. Eldridge, *Third New Hampshire,* 252; Hayes, *Samuel Francis Du Pont,* 2: 418, 443–44; *ORA,* 14: 394–400; Committee of the Regimental Association, *Maine Regiment,* 111–12; Hall and Hall, *Cayuga in the Field,* 172–75.
7. *ORA,* 14: 394–420
8. Thompson and Wainwright, *Correspondence of Gustavus Fox,* 1: 119, 122–23, 160–61, 173; Johnson, *Rear Admiral John Rodgers,* 225–26, 238; Hayes, *Samuel Francis Du Pont,* 2: 452; Secretary of the Navy, *In Relation to Armored Vessels,* 51.
9. Secretary of the Navy, *In Relation to Armored Vessels,* 16, 33, 53–55; Johnson, *Rear Admiral John Rodgers,* 238; Hayes, *Samuel Francis Du Pont,* 3: 128; Drayton, *Naval Letters,* 29.
10. Stowits, *One-hundredth New York Volunteers,* 128–30, 137; Dickey, *Eighty-fifth Regiment Pennsylvania Volunteer Infantry,* 238–40; Committee of the Regimental Association, *Story of One Regiment,* 110.
11. Committee of the Regimental Association, *Story of One Regiment,* 110, 111–13; Eldridge, *Third New Hampshire,* 287; Stowits, *One Hundredth New York Volunteers,* 128–29; *Eighty-fifth Pennsylvania,* 238–40; Roe, *Civil War Soldier's Diary,* 140–41; Hall and Hall, *Cayuga in the Field,* 172–75; Holland, *Letters and Diary of Laura M. Towne,* 102–3; John Guest Papers, February 18, 1863, United States Military History Institute, Carlise Army Barracks; *New York Tribune,* March 24, 1863.
12. Price, *History of the Ninety-Seventh Regiment,* 148–50; Roe, *Civil War Soldier's Diary,* 107–8.
13. Price, *History of the Ninety-Seventh Regiment,* 148–50; Roe, *Civil War Soldier's Diary,* 107–8
14. After making penance, both Generals Heckman and Stevenson were returned to duty for the April movement against Charleston. *New York Tribune,* March 9, 1863; *ORA,* 14: 429; Hayes, *Samuel Francis Du Pont,* 2: 441–42.
15. Committee of the Regimental Association, *Story of One Regiment,* 110, 110, 112; Dickey, *Eighty-fifth Regiment Pennsylvania Volunteer Infantry,* 242; Clark, *Thirty-ninth Regiment Illinois Volunteer Infantry,* 108; Hayes, *Samuel Francis Du Pont,* 2: 441–42; *ORA,* 14: 428–31.
16. Eldridge, *Third New Hampshire,* 249–50; *New York Herald,* February 9, 1863; Edward L. Cook Papers, letter of February 15, 1863.
17. Eldridge, *Third New Hampshire,* 244–45, 252, 258.
18. Denison, *Shot and Shell,* 112.
19. Eldridge, *Third New Hampshire,* 993–94.
20. Eldridge, *Third New Hampshire,* 994–97; "Bands and Musicians of the Civil War" (website).
21. Committee of the Regimental Association, *Story of One Regiment,* 110, 121; Schmidt, *History of the 47th Regiment,* 163.
22. *Beaufort Free South,* January 17, 1863; *Third Rhode Island,* 130–31; Davis, "South's First City," 119.

23. Davis "South's First City," 298–302; McGuire, "Hands on the Land," 44–48, 66; Dunley, "In Search of A. D. Smith," 162, 180–82.

24. *ORA*, 14: 394–95; Ochiai, "Port Royal Experiment Revisited," 94–99; Holland, *Letters and Diary of Laura M. Towne*, 100–101; *New York Tribune*, February 13 and 27, 1863; Dunley, "In Search of A. D. Smith," 178–80.

25. Basler, *Works of Abraham Lincoln*, 6: 98–99.

26. Holland, *Letters and Diary of Laura M. Towne*, 106–7; McGuire, "Getting their Hands," 66–70; Hughes, *John Murray Forbes*, 2: 70–71; *Beaufort Free South*, March 26, 1863.

27. Holland, *Letters and Diary of Laura M. Towne*, 101; Davis "South's First City," 479–80; Ochiai, "Port Royal Experiment Revisited," 98–100; McGuire, "Hands on the Land," 69–70; Foner, *Reconstruction*, 50–53.

28. Looby, *Thomas Wentworth Higginson*, 92–104; *New York Tribune*, February 11, 1863; *ORA*, 14: 194–98; Apthorp, "Montgomery's Raids" (website).

29. Rogers, "Surgeon's War Letters," 359; Looby, *Thomas Wentworth Higginson*, 97, 103–4.

30. Holland, *Letters and Diary of Laura M. Towne*, 103–4; *New York Tribune*, February 27, 1863.

31. Higginson, *Army Life in a Black Regiment*, 99–100; *New York Tribune*, March 16, 1863; *ORA*, 14: 423.

32. Part of the town was burned by the white regiments when it was evacuated. Higginson, *Army Life in a Black Regiment*, 99–129; *ORA*, 14: 226, 850; Looby, *Thomas Wentworth Higginson*, 109–23; Rogers, "Surgeon's War Letters," 391.

33. *New York Tribune*, March 8, 16, 24, 1863; Eldridge, *Third New Hampshire*, 261.

34. *New York Tribune*, May 16, 1863.

35. *ORA*, 14: 435–36; Daniel Barrows Papers, March 29, 1863.

36. Edward L. Cook Papers, letter of May 7, 1863; Alfred Marple Diary and Letters, letters of April 19 and May 8, 1863.

37. The air for the poem was the "Low Backed Chair." O'Reilly, *Baked Meats of the Funeral*, 205–6; O'Reilly, *Life and Adventures*, 52–58.

38. Johnson, *Rear Admiral John Rodgers*, 243–46; Rodgers, "Du Pont's Attack on Charleston," 4: 32–47; *ORN*, 14: 3–36; Looby, *Thomas Wentworth Higginson*, 129; Browning, *Success Is All*, 178–79; Miller, *Lincoln's Abolitionist General*, 139–40; Wise, *Gate of Hell*, 29–31.

39. Davis, *History of the 104th Pennsylvania*, 57–58; Stowits, *One-hundredth New York Volunteers*, 160–65; Copp, *Reminiscences of the War*, 208; Hayes, *Samuel Francis Du Pont*, 3: 41, 111; Wise, *Gate of Hell*, 31–32.

40. Johnson, *Rear Admiral John Rodgers*, 250; Hayes, *Samuel Francis Du Pont*, 3: 40, 50–88; Welles, *Diary of Gideon Welles*, 1: 288; Wise, *Gate of Hell*, 32.

41. *ORN*, 14: 455–70.

42. *ORA*, 14: 779–80, 783, 787, 791–95; Denison, *Shot and Shell*, 140–41.

43. *ORA*, 14: 791–95, 813–14.

44. *ORA*, 14: 799, 801–2, 809–11; Taylor, Mathews, and Powers, *Leverett Letters*, 204, 206.

45. *ORA*, 14: 862–63.

46. Price, *History of the Ninety-Seventh Regiment*, 150; Denison, *Shot and Shell*, 140; *ORA*, 14: 427–28; Taylor, Mathews, and Powers, *Leverett Letters*, 203.

47. Taylor, Mathews, and Powers, *Leverett Letters*, 200.

48. Mitchell, *Merchant Steam Vessels*, 60, 84; *ORN,* ser. 2, 1: 76.

49. Stephen Elliott Papers; Dennison, *Third Rhode Island,* 147–50; *ORA,* 14: 280–84; *ORN,* 14: 114–17; 127–28.

50. Looby, *Thomas Wentworth Higginson,* 125–27; Higginson, *Army Life in a Black Regiment,* 141–43.

51. One of the *George Washington*'s 24-pound howitzers was later recovered in the mid-twentieth century by a fisherman and placed on display at the Beaufort arsenal. Stephen Elliott Papers; Denison, *Shot and Shell,* 147–50; *ORA,* 14: 280–84; *ORN,* 14: 114–17, 127–28; Looby, *Thomas Wentworth Higginson,* 125–27; Higginson, *Army Life in a Black Regiment,* 141–43; Rogers, "Surgeon's War Letters," 389; *New York Tribune,* April 28, 1863.

52. *ORN,* 14: 115–17.

53. *ORN,* 14: 114–21, 127–28; *ORA,* 14: 281–84, 906.

54. Looby, *Thomas Wentworth Higginson,* 126–36; Higginson, *Army Life in a Black Regiment,* 143–45; Beecher, *First Light Battery,* 1: 226.

55. Rogers, "Surgeon's War Letters," 389; *New York Tribune,* April 28, 1863.

56. *ORA,* 14: 903; Looby, *Thomas Wentworth Higginson,* 132–33; *New York Tribune,* April 28, 1863.

57. Looby, *Thomas Wentworth Higginson,* 132–33; *ORA,* 14: 903; *New York Tribune,* April 28, 1863.

58. O'Reilly, *Baked Meats of the Funeral,* 192–201.

59. Miller, *Lincoln's Abolitionist General,* 131–32; *ORA,* 14: 448–49; *ORA,* ser. 2, 5: 795–97, 867; 940–41; *New York Times,* June 2, 1863; *Philadelphia Inquirer,* June 10, 1863; O'Reilly, *Baked Meats of the Funeral,* 192–93.

60. Looby, *Thomas Wentworth Higginson,* 134.

61. *ORA,* 14: 889, 906, 924, 930, 932, 934, 937, 944.

CHAPTER 9: REVIVAL AND THE COMBAHEE AND BLUFFTON RAIDS

1. Edward L. Cook Papers, April 12, 1863.

2. Committee of the Regimental Association, *Story of One Regiment,* 110, 118–19; Edward L. Cook Papers, April 11, 1863.

3. Alfred Marple Diary and Letters, letter of April 13, 1862.

4. Alfred Marple Diary and Letters, letter of May 31, 1863.

5. Alfred Marple Diary and Letters, letters of April 13, 25, 1863.

6. Beecher, *First Light Battery,* 1: 313–19.

7. Horan, *Timothy O'Sullivan,* 34–35; Teal, *Partners with the Sun,* 106–7.

8. Teal, *Partners with the Sun,* 114–16; Hayes, *Samuel Francis Du Pont,* 2: 226–28; "Guide to the Civil War Photograph File" (website).

9. Bolster and Anderson, *Soldiers, Sailors, Slaves, and Ships,* 21–26.

10. *Beaufort Free South,* June 13, 1863; Graydon, *Tales of Beaufort,* 81.

11. Teal, *Partners with the Sun,* 107–13.

12. *ORA,* 14: 361.

13. Looby, *Thomas Wentworth Higginson,* 281.

14. Hayes, *Samuel Francis Du Pont,* 2: 359–61; Winter, *Shadows of the Stage,* 151–55; Roe, *Civil War Soldier's Diary,* 47–48, 52, 148, 250; Ecelbarger, *Frederick W. Lander,* 62–64, 81–89, 137–38, 274–78; Professor Sheila Tombe to Stephen R. Wise, e-mail, June 23, 2009.

15. *Beaufort Free South*, March 26, 1863; Roe, *Civil War Soldier's Diary*, 110–11; Hayes, *Samuel Francis Du Pont*, 2: 224, 359–61; Petrie, *Civil War Journal*, 91–92; Denison, *Shot and Shell*, 150; *New York Tribune*, February 27, 1863; Winter, *Shadows of the Stage*, 155.

16. Roe, *Civil War Soldier's Diary*, 109–10; Rogers, "Surgeon's War Letters," 392; Thayer, *Life and Letters of John Hay*, 1: 150–56; Looby, *Thomas Wentworth Higginson*, 146–47.

17. *New York Tribune*, June 5, 1863.

18. Schwartz, *Woman Doctor's Civil War*, 47–50.

19. Rogers, "Surgeon's War Letters," 367; *University of the State of New York: Eighty-Second Annual Report*, 812–13.

20. The endorsement came from Major Edward V. Preston, who began the war as quartermaster for the 5th Connecticut and advanced to brigade quartermaster and assistant division quartermaster before being appointed a paymaster with the rank of major. Oates, *Woman of Valor*, 133; "Edward V. Preston" (website).

21. Oates, *Woman of Valor*, 146–53; Wise, *Gate of Hell*, 64–65; Barton Papers, Journal April 2–6, 1863, and C. Barton to Cousin Vira, June 26, 1863, July 11, 1863; Voris, "Charleston in the Rebellion," 334–35; Craven, "Report Extract," 1, pt. 1: 241; Ross, *Angel of the Battlefield*; Epler, *Life of Clara Barton*, 76–77.

22. Looby, *Thomas Wentworth Higginson*, 128; "Scoundrel or Scapegoat?" (website); Daniels, *Prince of Carpetbaggers*, 62–66, 70, 75, 77–78.

23. *New York Tribune*, May 28, June 2, 1863; *ORA*, 14: 462–63.

24. Rogers, "Surgeon's War Letters," 367; John W. M. Appleton Letterbook and Journal, July 10, 1863; Denison, *Shot and Shell*, 156.

25. Looby, *Thomas Wentworth Higginson*, 152, 154, 158–89.

26. *New York Tribune*, June 5, 1863.

27. Cullum, *Officers and Graduates of West Point*, 2: 227, 239–40; Looby, *Thomas Wentworth Higginson*, 152, 154, 284, 287–88; *New York Tribune*, June 2, 1863.

28. *ORA*, 14: 290–308, 983, 945, 962–63.

29. *ORA*, 14: 290–93, 299, 307.

30. *ORA*, 14: 290–93, 299, 307; *ORA* 35, pt. 2, 463; Dedmondt, *Flags of Civil War South Carolina*, 35.

31. Special Orders Department of the South; Denison, *Shot and Shell*, 155; *Boston Commonwealth*, July 17, 1863; *New York Times*, June 19, 1863; *New York Tribune*, June 19, 1863; *Philadelphia Enquirer*, June 19, 1863; Bradford, *Harriet*, 99.

32. Apthorp, "Montgomery's Raids" (website); Denison, *Third Rhode Island*, 155–57.

33. Linder, *Atlas of the Rice Plantations*, 514.

34. Apthorp, "Montgomery's Raids" (website); Denison, *Third Rhode Island*, 155–57; *Philadelphia Inquirer*, June 19, 1863.

35. *ORA*, 14: 293, 297, 299–302.

36. *ORA*, 14: 293–96.

37. *ORA*, 14: 290–91, 297–98.

38. Apthorp, "Montgomery's Raids" (website).

39. Apthorp, "Montgomery's Raids" (website); Denison, *Third Rhode Island*, 155–57; Linder, *Atlas of the Rice Plantations*, 158–60, 167, 371–74, 433, 514, 644.

40. Denison, *Third Rhode Island*, 155–57; *ORA*, 14: 301; Beecher, *First Light Battery*, 1: 224.

41. *ORA*, 14: 307–8; Denison, *Third Rhode Island*, 155–57; *Philadelphia Inquirer*, June 19, 1863.

42. *Philadelphia Inquirer,* June 19, 1863; *Boston Commonwealth,* July 17, 1863; Denison, *Third Rhode Island,* 155–57; *ORA,* 14: 295–96, 300–303; Bradford, *Harriet,* 101–2.

43. Apthorp, "Montgomery's Raids" (website); Denison, *Shot and Shell,* 155–57.

44. Apthorp, "Montgomery's Raids" (website); Dennison, *Shot and Shell,* 155–57; *ORA,* 14: 293–97, 303–6; *Philadelphia Inquirer,* June 19, 1863.

45. *ORA,* 14: 290–308, 983, 945, 962–63; *New York Tribune,* June 19, 1863.

46. *New South,* June 6, 1863; *Boston Commonwealth,* June 10, July 17, 1863; *Beaufort Free South,* June 6, 1863; Apthorp, "Montgomery's Raids" (website); Alfred Marple Diary and Letters, letter of June 6, 1863.

47. Botume, *Amongst the Contrabands,* 50–54.

48. Oates, *Woman of Valor,* 154–55; Barton Papers, Journal, June 3, 1863, and C. Barton to Cousin Vira, June 26, 1863, July 11, 1863.

49. Poole, "Memory and the Abolitionist Heritage," 449–58; Looby, *Thomas Wentworth Higginson,* 280, 285.

50. John W. M. Appleton Letterbook and Journal, June 5, 1863; Emilio, *Brave Black Regiment,* 1–25; Wise, *Gate of Hell,* 48–50; Cornish, *Sable Arm,* 105–6; Quarles, *Negro in the Civil War,* 8–10; *Xenia Torchlight,* June 6, 1863; Pearson, *Life of John A. Andrew,* 2: 74–76.

51. Wise, *Gate of Hell,* 48–50; Quarles, *Negro in the Civil War,* 11–13; Cornish, *Sable Arm,* 148; Emilio, *Brave Black Regiment,* 24–35; Pearson, *Life of John A. Andrew,* 2: 74–76.

52. Duncan, *Blue-Eyed Child of Fortune,* 338–39; Alfred Marple Diary and Letters, letter of June 6, 1863; *ORA,* 14: 290–308, 462; *Beaufort Free South,* June 6, 1863; John W. M. Appleton Letterbook and Journal, June 8, 1863.

53. *ORA,* 14: 463.

54. *ORN,* 14: 236–39.

55. *Philadelphia Inquirer,* June 19, 1863; *ORN,* 14: 238–39.

56. Halliburton, *Saddle Soldiers,* 84–85; *ORA,* 14: 309–12.

57. Baxley, *No Prouder Fate,* 85–88; *ORA,* 14: 309–13.

58. *ORA,* 14: 309–14; *ORN,* 14: 236–39.

59. Baxley, *No Prouder Fate,* 339; *Charleston Mercury,* June 13, 1863; *ORA,* 14: 314.

60. *ORN,* 14: 236–39; *ORA,* 14: 314.

61. Bowditch, "War Letters of Charles P. Bowditch," 436; *Beaufort Free South,* June 20, 1863; Emilio, *Brave Black Regiment,* 39–44; Robert Gould Shaw Papers, R. Shaw to wife, June 9, 1863, R. Shaw to Gov. Andrew, June 14, 1863; *ORA,* 14: 426, 463–67.

62. *ORA,* 14: 466–68; Looby, *Thomas Wentworth Higginson,* 286–88; Alfred Marple Diary and Letters, letter of June 18, 1863.

CHAPTER 10: THE ATTACK ON CHARLESTON, 1863

1. Wise, *Gate of Hell,* 33–34.

2. *ORN,* 14: 241; Wise, *Gate of Hell,* 34–36; Welles, *Diary of Gideon Welles,* 1: 312–14.

3. Welles, *Diary of Gideon Welles,* 1: 312–14; Foote, "Notes on the Life of Admiral Foote," 347.

4. Welles, *Diary of Gideon Welles,* 1: 317; Dahlgren, *Memoirs of John A. Dahlgren,* 391–95; Farenholt, *Monitor Catskill,* 16; Browning, *Success Is All,* 215–18, Symonds, *Lincoln and His Admirals,* 138, 191, 238–39, 242–44.

5. Hayes, *Samuel Francis Du Pont,* 3: 180; Farenholt, *Monitor Catskill,* 12–13; Gleaves, *Life and Letters of Rear Admiral Stephen B. Luce,* 91; Thompson and Wainwright, *Correspondence of Gustavus Fox,* 1: 160–61.

6. Welles, *Diary of Gideon Welles,* 1: 325–26, 335, 337; Dahlgren, *Memoirs of John A. Dahlgren,* 395; *ORN,* 14: 465; Denison, *Shot and Shell,* 163.

7. Hayes, *Samuel Francis Du Pont,* 3: 173–74; *Philadelphia Inquirer,* June 19, 1863; *New York Times,* June 18, 1863; *ORA,* 28, pt. 2: 4; Eldridge, *Third New Hampshire,* 289.

8. The *Atlanta* remained at Port Royal as a guard ship at Port Royal until September 1863. Looby, *Thomas Wentworth Higginson,* 288; Hayes, *Samuel Francis Du Pont,* 3: 178; *ORN,* 14: 249–51, 281–82; 263–96.

9. Hayes, *Samuel Francis Du Pont,* 3: 194–96; Browning, *Success Is All,* 215.

10. *ORA,* 28, pt. 2: 4; Looby, *Thomas Wentworth Higginson,* 157, 286–87.

11. McPherson, *Struggle for Equality,* 75–81, 178–80.

12. Rose, *Rehearsal for Reconstruction,* 206–10, 236–41; McPherson, *Struggle for Equality,* 182–87; *New York Times,* June 19, 1863; *ORA,* ser. 3, 3: 430–54; *Port Royal Free South,* April 9, 1864.

13. Eldridge, *Third New Hampshire,* 288–91, Wise, *Gate of Hell,* 121.

14. Cullum, *Register,* 2: 449; *ORA,* 28, pt. 2: 7, 9, 13.

15. Shaw Papers, Letters of June 6 and 14, 1863, and July 6, 1863; Duncan, *Blue-Eyed Child of Fortune,* 341–52; Bowditch, "War Letters of Charles P. Bowditch," 436; Emilio, *Brave Black Regiment,* 39–44; Wise, *Gate of Hell,* 51–53; *Boston Evening Post,* May 3, 1916; *ORA,* 28, pt. 2: 15.

16. Wise, *Gate of Hell,* 51–55; Shaw, "Letters," 226–31; *Boston Evening Post,* May 3, 1916; Emilio, *Brave Black Regiment,* 47–49; Cornish, *Sable Arm,* 150; Stevenson, *Journals of Charlotte Forten Grimké,* 493–94; *Memorial: RGS (Robert Gould Shaw),* 35.

17. MacDonald, *Selected Statutes and other Documents Illustrative of the History of the United States 1861–1898,* 48–53, 54–56.

18. Duncan, *Blue-Eyed Child of Fortune,* 365–70; Shaw, "Letters," 226–31; Pearson, *Life of John A. Andrew,* 2: 98–106; *Boston Evening Post,* May 3, 1916; Emilio, *Brave Black Regiment,* 47–48; Westwood, *Black Troops, White Commanders,* 126–27.

19. Emilio, *Brave Black Regiment,* 48; Shaw Papers, Letter of July 7, 1863; Eldridge, *Third New Hampshire,* 291; Duncan, *Blue-Eyed Child of Fortune,* 378; Looby, *Thomas Wentworth Higginson,* 158–59.

20. Eldridge, *Third New Hampshire,* 285–92; Emilio, *Brave Black Regiment,* 46–47.

21. Beaufort, *Free South,* June 27, 1863.

22. Eldridge, *Third New Hampshire,* 295–96.

23. Shaw, "Letters," 226–31; Duncan, *Blue-Eyed Child of Fortune,* 372–79; Emilio, *Brave Black Regiment,* 49.

24. Duncan, *Blue-Eyed Child of Fortune,* 372–73; Stevenson, *Journals of Charlotte Forten Grimké,* 490–91.

25. Stevenson, *Journals of Charlotte Forten Grimké* 493–94; Holland, *Letters and Diary of Laura M. Towne,* 113–14, Emilio, *Brave Black Regiment,* 49–51; Shaw, "Letters," 226–31; Gaustad and Noll, *Documentary History of Religion,* 596; Butt, *History of African Methodism in Virginia* (website).

26. Stevenson, *Journals of Charlotte Forten Grimké,* 491–92.

27. Looby, *Thomas Wentworth Higginson,* 292–93.

28. Duncan, *Blue-Eyed Child of Fortune,* 373–74, 377–78.

29. Stevenson, *Journals of Charlotte Forten Grimké,* 492–94; Duncan, *Blue-Eyed Child of Fortune,* 374.

30. Wise, *Gate of Hell,* 64–65; Oates, *Woman of Valor,* 153, 160–61.

31. *ORA*, 28, pt. 2: 15.

32. Mitchell, *Merchant Steam Vessels*, 65, 84, supplement 2; *ORA*, 29, pt. 1: 194–95; Higginson, *Army Life in a Black Regiment*, 167–84; Beecher, *First Light Battery*, 236–50.

33. *ORA*, 28, pt. 1: 194–95; Higginson, *Army Life in a Black Regiment*, 167–84; Beecher, *First Light Battery*, 236–50.

34. Beecher, *First Light Battery*, 249–50; *ORA*, 28, pt. 1: 194–95; Looby, *Thomas Wentworth Higginson*, 294–95.

35. Looby, *Thomas Wentworth Higginson*, 296.

36. Wise, *Gate of Hell*, 99–101, 113–15, 233–34; *New York National Anti-Slavery Standard*, August 8, 1863; *Beaufort Free South*, July 25, 1863; Oates, *Woman of Valor*, 172–75.

37. Holland, *Letters and Diary of Laura M. Towne*, 114–16; *Beaufort Free South*, July 25, 1863.

38. *Beaufort Free South*, July 25, 1863.

39. Schwartz, *Woman Doctor's Civil War*, 51–53.

40. Schwartz, *Woman Doctor's Civil War*, 52–55; *Beaufort Free South*, July 25, 1863.

41. Stevenson, *Journals of Charlotte Forten Grimké*, 496–97; Holland, *Letters and Diary of Laura M. Towne*, 114–15.

42. Stevenson, *Journals of Charlotte Forten Grimké*, 499–501; Pearson, *Letters from Port Royal*, 196.

43. *Beaufort Free South*, August 1, 8, 1863; Holland, *Letters and Diary of Laura M. Towne*, 116; *New York Tribune*, September 30, 1863.

44. Wise, *Gate of Hell*, 142–43, 150–55; Davis, *History of the 104th Pennsylvania*, 251; Fox, *Fifty-fifth Regiment of Massachusetts*, 11–12; *ORA*, 28, pt. 1: 279, 313, 316–17.

45. Also mustered into service in July at Fernandina Florida was a company of the 4th South Carolina. The 3rd and 4th South Carolina Regiments never reached full strength and were eventually merged, forming the 3rd South Carolina. Wise, *Gate of Hell*, 121; Westwood, *Black Troops, White Commanders*, 128–29; *New York Tribune*, November 14, 1863.

46. *ORA*, 6: 196–97; *ORA*, 28, pt. 1: 74, 124; *ORA*, 28, pt. 2: 212, 246, 261–62, 326, 333.

47. Looby, *Thomas Wentworth Higginson*, 338; Wise, *Gate of Hell*, 138.

48. Pearson, *Letters from Port Royal*, 201, 210, 220, 237.

49. Pierce, "Freedmen at Port Royal," 310; *New York Tribune*, September 17, 1863.

50. Pierce, "Freedmen at Port Royal," 312–15; *New York Tribune*, September 15, 1863.

51. Davis, "South's First City," 247; *ORA*, 28, pt. 2: 74–77; Spieler, "Old Deeds Clear up Early History."

52. Looby, *Thomas Wentworth Higginson*, 159–62.

53. Pearson, *Life of John A. Andrew*, 2: 98–121; Higginson, *Army Life in a Black Regiment*, 280–92.

54. Higginson, *Army Life in a Black Regiment*, 280; Westwood, *Black Troops, White Commanders*, 125–38.

55. Westwood, *Black Troops, White Commanders*, 125–38; Higginson, *Army Life in a Black Regiment*, 280–92; Pearson, *Life of John A. Andrew*, 2: 98–121.

56. *ORA*, 28, pt. 2: 127–29; *New York Tribune*, November 28, December 2, 9, 1863; Wise, *Gate of Hell*, 216.

57. *Beaufort Free South*, October 21, 1863.

58. *ORA*, 28, pt. 2: 346, 367–68, 375, 444, 467, 602.

59. Looby, *Thomas Wentworth Higginson*, 309–10, 324; Higginson, *Army Life in a Black Regiment*, 231–33; *New York Herald*, September 19, 1863; Halliburton, *Saddle Soldiers*, 111–12; Rogers, "Surgeon's War Letters," 394–96; Taylor, *Reminiscences of My Life in Camp*, 63.

60. Taylor, Mathews, and Powers, *Leverett Papers*, 250–52.

61. Roman, *Military Operations of General Beauregard*, 2: 167; Halliburton, *Saddle Soldiers*, 115–16; Stone, *Vital Rails*, 160–61; *Charleston Mercury*, November 3, 1863; *Charleston Courier*, November 3, 1863.

62. *ORA*, 28, pt. 1: 745–46; Halliburton, *Saddle Soldiers*, 119–20; *New York Tribune*, December 2, 1863; Rogers, "Surgeon's War Letters," 396–97; Taylor, *Reminiscences of My Life in Camp*, 71–72.

63. Higginson, *Army Life in a Black Regiment*, 230–31; Looby, *Thomas Wentworth Higginson*, 332; *New York Tribune*, December 2, 1863.

64. *ORA*, 28, pt. 2: 544, 547.

65. *ORA*, 28, pt. 2: 506, 568, 577–78, 601.

66. *ORA*, 28, pt. 2: 602.

67. *New York Tribune*, November 24, December 30, 1863.

68. Walkley, *History of the Seventh Connecticut*, 112–16; Little, *Seventh Regiment*, 208.

69. Wise, *Gate of Hell*, 124–27, Caldwell, *Old Sixth Regiment*, 81–82.

70. Clark, *Thirty-Ninth Illinois Volunteer Infantry*, 155–56; Dickey, *Eighty-fifth Regiment Pennsylvania Volunteer Infantry*, 297; Chisman, *76th Regiment Pennsylvania Volunteer Infantry*, 40–41; Roe, *Civil War Soldier's Diary*.

71. Fisk, *56th New York*, 49–50.

72. Fisk, *56th New York*, 49–51; Looby, *Thomas Wentworth Higginson*, 182; Guterman, "Doing 'Good Brave Work,'" 154, 158–60.

73. *Port Royal Free South*, December 12, 1863.

74. Though some historians place the meeting between Susie Baker King Taylor and Clara Barton in early June 1863, such a timeline does not match King's account. In June the 1st South Carolina was on picket duty along the northern end of Port Royal Island, and the encampment outside Beaufort had not yet been named Camp Shaw. Taylor, *Reminiscences of My Life in Camp*, 29–30; Oates, *Valor*, 155–56, 186–88; *Barton Journal*, December 25–30, 1863; Ross, *Angel of the Battlefield*, 65.

75. *New York Tribune*, December 23, 1863.

76. Looby, *Thomas Wentworth Higginson*, 179–80, 334, 339.

77. *New York Tribune*, January 4, 1863; Looby, *Thomas Wentworth Higginson*, 181–82; Mushkay, *Citizen-Soldier's Civil War*, 153.

78. Looby, *Higginson Journal*, 180; Stevenson, *Journals of Charlotte Forten Grimké*, 511.

79. Looby, *Thomas Wentworth Higginson*, 180–82.

80. Looby, *Thomas Wentworth Higginson*, 181.

81. *Beaufort Free South*, January 9, 1864; Holland, *Letters and Diary of Laura M. Towne*, 122; *New York Tribune*, September 10, 1863; "Gilbert Pillsbury" (website).

CHAPTER 11: TAX SALES AND PREEMPTION

1. Dunley, "In Search of A. D. Smith," 162, 180–82.

2. McPherson, *Negro's Civil War*, 298; Saville, *Work of Reconstruction*, 40–42; Berlin, Miller, Reidy, and Rowland, *Freedom*, 59–60; Ochiai, "Port Royal Experiment Revisited," 100–104; Foner, "Meaning of Freedom," 438–47.

3. Basler, *Works of Abraham Lincoln*, 6: 453–59.

4. Hendricks, "Union Army Occupation," 127.

5. *New York Daily Tribune,* November 9, 14, 1863; Smith and Payne, *History of the African Episcopal Church,* 52.

6. Though the reporter wrote that the church was in the center of Port Royal Island, the description more properly fits the Brick Church in the center of St. Helena Island. *New York Daily Tribune,* November 9, 14, 1863.

7. Ochiai, "Port Royal Experiment Revisited," 101; Pearson, *Letters from Port Royal,* 243.

8. Pearson, *Letters from Port Royal,* 229–31.

9. Dunley, "In Search of A. D. Smith," 184–85; William Henry Brisbane Diary, January 15, 1864.

10. Basler, *Works of Abraham Lincoln,* 7: 98–99; Niven, *Salmon P. Chase Papers,* 4: 236–37; *New York Tribune,* January 27, 1864.

11. William Henry Brisbane Diary, January 16, 1864; Dunley, "In Search of A. D. Smith," 185–87.

12. Dunley, "In Search of A. D. Smith," 186–87; William Henry Brisbane Diary, January 16, 1864; *New York Tribune,* January 27, 1864.

13. *New York Tribune,* January 27, 1864.

14. *New York Tribune,* January 27, 1864.

15. *Letters from Port Royal,* 243–47, Ochiai, "Port Royal Experiment Revisited," 101; *New York Tribune,* January 27, 1864; Laura M. Towne Diary, January 17, 1864; William F. Allen Diary, January 17, 1864.

16. Berlin, Miller, Reidy, and Rowland, *Freedom,* 287; *ORA,* ser. 3, 4: 118–19; *New York Tribune,* January 27, 1864.

17. Dunley, "In Search of A. D. Smith," 188–90; Berlin, Miller, Reidy, and Rowland, *Freedom,* 3: 283–87.

18. Niven, *Salmon P. Chase Papers,* 4: 259–60.

19. Dunley, *A. D. Smith,* 188–90; Hendricks, "Union Army Occupation," 131; *New York Tribune,* Jan 27, 1864.

20. Niven, *Salmon P. Chase Papers,* 4: 266–69.

21. Niven, *Salmon P. Chase Papers,* 4: 266–69.

22. *New York Times,* January 25, 1864.

23. *Beaufort Free South,* January 30, 1864; phone conversation between Colin Brooker and Stephen R. Wise, February 6, 2010; *History of Rock County,* 618, 644, 758–59; Cutter, *New England Families,* 1: 179; Davis, *The New South's First City; National Cyclopedia of American Biography,* Appendix I, 11: 417.

24. Berlin, Miller, Reidy, and Rowland, *Freedom,* 287–88; Quincy Gillmore to Salmon P. Chase, January 31, 1863, Niven, *Salmon P. Chase Papers,* Library of Congress.

25. Dunley, "In Search of A. D. Smith," 192–93, 195–96.

26. William Henry Brisbane Diary, February 12, 1864; Hendricks, "Union Army Occupation," 132; Niven, *Salmon P. Chase Papers,* 4: 293; Saville, *Work of Reconstruction,* 43–45.

27. Berlin, Miller, Reidy, and Rowland, *Freedom,* 289–91; William Henry Brisbane Diary, February 13, 1864.

28. Berlin, Miller, Reidy, and Rowland, *Freedom,* 293–94; Hendricks, "Union Army Occupation," 132–33.

29. William Henry Brisbane Diary, February 18, 19, 1864.

30. *New York Tribune,* May 14, 1864; Hendricks, "Union Army Occupation," 133–36; McGuire, "Hands on the Land," 83–86.

31. Niven, *Salmon P. Chase Papers,* 4: 292–93.
32. Laura M. Towne Diary, March 3, 8, 1864; *Beaufort Free South,* April 2, 1864; *Salmon P. Chase Papers,* 4: 292–93.
33. Berlin, Miller, Reidy, and Rowland, *Freedom,* 291–96; Dunley, "In Search of A. D. Smith," 196.
34. Dunley, "In Search of A. D. Smith," 194–95.
35. Niven, *Salmon P. Chase Papers,* 4: 310–11; *United States Biographical Dictionary,* 34–36.
36. William Henry Brisbane Diary, March 5, 1864; Dunley, "In Search of A. D. Smith," 197–98.
37. Dunley, "In Search of A. D. Smith," 198–200.
38. Hendricks, "Union Army Occupation," 133.
39. Sifakis, *Who Was Who,* 56.
40. McGuire, "Hands on the Land," 85–86; Hendricks, "Union Army Occupation," 133–35; *New York Tribune,* April 16, 1864.
41. McGuire, "Hands on the Land," 85–86; Hendricks, "Union Army Occupation," 133–35.
42. McGuire, "Hands on the Land," 85.
43. McGuire, "Hands on the Land," 82–83; Berlin, Miller, Reidy, and Rowland, *Freedom,* 299–303; Pearson, *Letters from Port Royal,* 254–55.
44. Pearson, *Letters from Port Royal,* 254–55.
45. Berlin, Miller, Reidy, and Rowland, *Freedom,* 308–9.
46. Hendricks, "Union Army Occupation," 133–36; McGuire, "Hands on the Land," 83–85; Schedule of Direct Tax, Beaufort District. The Beaufort District comprised present-day Beaufort, Jasper, and Hampton Counties. Present-day Beaufort County was St. Helena Parish, the Sea Islands of St. Luke's Parish, and the adjacent mainland portions of lower St. Luke's and lower Prince William Parishes. "Beaufort County" was not formed until 1868.
47. William Henry Brisbane Diary, June 1–5, 1865; Dunley, "In Search of A. D. Smith," 207–9.
48. Pearson, *Letters from Port Royal,* 249, 254.

CHAPTER 12: SEA ISLAND TRANSFORMATION AND MILITARY STALEMATE

1. *Beaufort Free South,* January 9, 1864; Holland, *Letters and Diary of Laura M. Towne,* 122; *New York Tribune,* September 10, 1863, December 4, 1863; *New York Times,* September 20, 1863; Hendricks, "Union Army Occupation," 136–37.
2. *New York Times,* September 20, 1863.
3. Holland, *Letters and Diary of Laura M. Towne,* 104–5; Laura M. Towne Diary, 7, 13, 25, 26, 27, 1863.
4. Laura M. Towne Diary, October 26, 27, 1863.
5. Laura M. Towne Diary, March 18, 1864; Berlin, Miller, Reidy, and Rowland, *Freedom,* 308; *Baptist Home Missions,* 397–98.
6. Laura M. Towne Diary, March 25, 1864.
7. Wolf, "Laura Towne and the Freed People," 390, 402–4; Holland, *Letters and Diary of Laura M. Towne,* 141.
8. Hendricks, "Union Army Occupation," 136–37; Basler, *Works of Abraham Lincoln,* 6: 455–56.

9. Hendricks, "Union Army Occupation," 136–37; Laura M. Towne Diary, January 10, March 14, 1864.

10. The lot in Beaufort for the Free Will Baptist Church, donated by Captain Springer of Massachusetts, was redeemed by its former owners and the congregation broke up. Brewster, *Centennial Record of Freewill Baptists 1780–1880*, 147–48; "Knowlton, Ebenezer" (website); Coffin, *The Boys of 1861 or Four Years of Fighting*, 176–80; *Baptist Home Mission*, 606; Berlin, Miller, Reidy, and Rowland, *Freedom*, 315–16.

11. *New York Tribune*, September 17, 1863; Lynch, *A Few Things about the Educational Work Among the Freedmen of South Carolina and Georgia*, 32–35.

12. Laura M. Towne Diary, February 5, 1864; Holland, *Letters and Diary of Laura M. Towne*, 127–28.

13. Lynch, *Freedmen*, 35–37.

14. Lynch, *Freedmen*, 36; *Beaufort Free South*, December 12, 1863.

15. Langley's military records list his first name as Landon instead of Loudon and sometimes the name appears as Langdon. Landon S. Langley Pension records; Emilio, *Brave Black Regiment*, 347; Spieler, "Langdon S. Langley"; Elise Guyette, e-mail to Stephen R. Wise, September 7, 2010; Langley, "Letters of Louden S. Langley" (website).

16. *Boston Commonwealth*, December 18, 1863; Miller, *Gullah Statesman*, 22–23.

17. *Beaufort Free South*, May 21, 1864.

18. *New York Tribune*, May 12, 18, 26, 1864; *Beaufort Free South*, May 21, 1864; Pearson, *Letters from Port Royal*, 267–68; William F. Allen Diary, May 21, 1863; *Port Royal Palmetto Post*, March 31, 1864.

19. Miller, *Gullah Statesman*, 22.

20. Hendricks, "Union Army Occupation," 80–82.

21. Laura M. Towne Diary, March 25, 30, April 14, 20, 26, May 18, September 21, 22, 1863.

22. *New York Tribune*, January 20, 1864; Hendricks, "Union Army Occupation," 97–98; Eldridge, *Third New Hampshire*, 420, 439; *Beaufort Free South*, April 9, 1864; *ORA*, 28, pt. 2: 135.

23. Hendricks, "Union Army Occupation," 98–102; Pearson, *Life of John A. Andrew*, 2: 142–45; McKee, *Back in War Times*, 180–81.

24. Pearson, *Letters from Port Royal*, 249; Hendricks, "Union Army Occupation," 38–39; Warner, *Generals in Blue*, 157–58.

25. Hendricks, "Union Army Occupation," 102–6; Pearson, *Letters from Port Royal*, 282–85; *Beaufort Free South*, August 13, 1864.

26. Berlin, *Freedom*, 327–29.

27. *ORA*, 28, pt. 2: 116–17; 129–30, 136–39; *ORA*, 25, pt. 1: 276, 463–66; Dyer, *Compendium of the War*, 1724.

28. *ORA*, 28, pt. 2: 601–4; *ORA*, 35, pt. 1: 321, 327, 321, 557–60.

29. *ORA*, 25, pt. 1: 275–77; *Hilton Head New South*, February 20, 1864.

30. Looby, *Thomas Wentworth Higginson*, 194–97.

31. Looby, *Thomas Wentworth Higginson*, 197–98.

32. Looby, *Thomas Wentworth Higginson*, 197–98.

33. Looby, *Thomas Wentworth Higginson*, 197–98.

34. Looby, *Thomas Wentworth Higginson*, 198–200; *New York Tribune*, March 1 and May 2, 1864.

35. Taylor, Mathews, and Powers, *Leverett Letters*, 286; Baxley, *No Prouder Fate*, 112–13; *ORA*, 25, pt. 1: 372, 622.

36. *ORN*, 15: 93–94; *ORN*, ser. 2, 1: 122; Holland, *Letters and Diary of Laura M. Towne*, 108–10.

37. *ORA*, 25, pt. 1: 597, 621; *New York Tribune*, March 25, 1864; *ORA*, 35, pt. 2: 357; Taylor, Mathews, and Powers, *Leverett Letters*, 286, 289.

38. *New York Tribune*, March 30, 1864.

39. *ORA*, 35, pt. 2: 357, 359, 460, 648.

40. *ORA*, 35, pt. 2: 357, 359, 460, 648. *ORN*, 15: 383–88; Holland, *Letters and Diary of Laura M. Towne*, 137; Laura M. Towne Diary, May 22, 1864; Pearson, *Letters from Port Royal*, 94.

41. Dickey, *Eighty-fifth Regiment Pennsylvania Volunteer Infantry*, 311, 378; *New York Tribune*, April 19, May 18, 1864; *ORN*, 15: 388–89, 394.

42. *ORA*, 25, pt. 1: 463–66, 493; *ORA*, 25, pt. 2: 73–80; Palmer, *History of the Forty-eighth Regiment*, 139.

43. *ORA*, 35, pt. 2: 362, 364–65, 368–70, 375, 402, 457, 463–64, 487, 531.

44. *ORA*, 35, pt. 2: 398, 408, 423, 436, 441–61, 452–53, 456, 518; Baxley, *No Prouder Fate*, 117–18.

45. *ORA*, 25, pt. 2: 441–61, 463–64, 487, 531; Taylor, Mathews, and Powers, *Leverett Letters*, 296.

46. Taylor, Mathews, and Powers, *Leverett Letters*, 296–97, 301.

47. *ORA*, 35, pt. 2: 444, 486, 490, 513, 516–18, 524–26, 543–44, 591, 599.

48. *ORA*, 35, pt. 2: 463–64.

49. *ORA*, 35, pt. 2: 444, 486, 490, 513, 516–18, 524–26, 543–44, 591, 599.

50. *ORA*, 35, pt. 2: 630, 635, 637, 643–44, 648; Hughes, *General William J. Hardee*, 248–55.

51. Cullum, *Officers and Graduates of West Point*, 2: 124; *New York Tribune*, May 11, 1864; *ORA*, 35, pt. 2: 27, 48, 80.

52. *ORA*, 25, pt. 2: 84–85, 92; *ORN*, 15: 458–63.

53. *ORN*, 15: 461–62; *New York Tribune*, June 3 and 11, 1864; *New York Times*, June 3, 1864; *Port Royal (Hilton Head) Herald*, June 2, 1864; Ripley, *Chapman's Fort*, 37–43.

54. *ORN*, 15: 461–62; *New York Tribune*, June 3 and 11, 1864; *New York Times*, June 3, 1864; *Port Royal (Hilton Head) Herald*, June 2, 1864; Ripley, *Chapman's Fort*, 43–45.

55. *New York Tribune*, June 3 and 11, 1864; *New York Times*, June 3, 1864; *Port Royal (Hilton Head) Herald*, June 2, 1864; Ripley, *Chapman's Fort*, 45–47.

56. Ripley, *Chapman's Fort*, 49–51, 57–61; *ORA*, 35, pt. 1: 400.

57. "Medal of Honor Recipients, A-L" (website); Medal of Honor Recipients, M–Z" (website); *New York Tribune*, June 3 and 11, 1864; *New York Times*, June 3, 1864; *Port Royal (Hilton Head) Herald*, June 2, 1864; Ripley, *Chapman's Fort*, 46–50.

58. *ORN*, 15: 461–62; *New York Tribune*, June 3 and 11, 1864; *New York Times*, June 3, 1864; *Port Royal (Hilton Head) Herald*, June 2, 1864; Ripley, *Chapman's Fort*, 49–50; *ORA*, 35, pt. 1: 400.

59. *ORN*, 15: 461–62; *New York Tribune*, June 3 and 11, 1864; *New York Times*, June 3, 1864; *Port Royal (Hilton Head) Herald*, June 2, 1864; Ripley, *Chapman's Fort*, 49–51.

60. *ORN*, 15: 458–61.

61. *ORA*, 35, pt. 1: 7–8; *ORA*, 35, pt. 2: 104–6.

62. *ORA*, 35, pt. 1: 8–11.

63. Civil Works Map File, Record Group 77, Map of Beaufort and its Defenses.
64. *ORA,* 35, pt. 2: 106, 122, 130.
65. *ORA,* 35, pt. 1: 118.
66. *ORA,* 35, pt. 2: 106, 122, 130.
67. *ORA,* 35, pt. 1: 14–17; 79–86; *ORA,* 35, pt. 2: 225.
68. ORA, 35, pt. 2: 212, 244–46, 259–60.
69. *ORA,* 35, pt. 2: 245; Annual Report of Brevet Major Charles R. Suter, September 11, 1865, Record Group 393, National Archives, Washington, D.C., 2–3, 10–14.
70. Suter, *Annual Report,* 2–3, 10–14; Legg, et al., "Camp Baird," 28–34; Stephen R. Wise, phone conversation with James Legg, April 13, 2011; *Supplement to the Official Records,* pt. 2, vol. 51: 686–721; *ORA,* 77: 719–31.
71. *ORN,* 15: 584; Suter, *Annual Report,* September 11, 1865, 2–3; 10–14.
72. Civil Works Map File, Record Group 77, Map of Mitchelville.
73. Suter, *Annual Report,* September 11, 1865, 12–13; Special Orders, September 14 and 19, 1864.
74. Civil Works Map File, Record Group 77, Map of Beaufort and its Defenses.
75. *Beaufort Free South,* July 28, April 9, 13, 28, May 21, July 28, August 13, 1864; Denison, *Shot and Shell,* 264.
76. McCracken and McCracken, *Forgotten History,* 73–80; *New York Tribune,* September 10, 1863, April 8, 1864.
77. *New York Tribune,* April 8, 1864.
78. Berlin, Miller, Reidy, and Rowland, *Freedom,* 315–16; Hendricks, "Union Army Occupation," 174–75.
79. Botume, *Amongst the Contrabands,* 78.
80. Berlin, Miller, Reidy, and Rowland, *Freedom,* 316–19; *ORA,* 35, pt. 2: 273–74; Hendricks, "Union Army Occupation," 174–75.
81. Berlin, Miller, Reidy, and Rowland, *Freedom,* 316–19; *ORA,* 35, pt. 2: 273–74; Hendricks, "Union Army Occupation," 174–75.
82. *ORN,* 15: 262–63, 327–38, 429–30, 472, 562, 564, 573.
83. Browning, *Success Is All,* 297–98; *ORA,* 15: 592; National Archives, Charles O. Boutelle to William Reynolds, February 4, 1865, Record Group 19.
84. *ORN,* 15: 506–7, 525, 584, 622–24; Browning, *Success Is All,* 305, 307, 316, 327–29; Schneller, *Quest for Glory,* 297–99.
85. *ORN,* 15: 622–24.

CHAPTER 13: BATTLE OF HONEY HILL

1. Sherman, *Memoirs of William T. Sherman,* 2: 178–79.
2. *ORA,* 39, pt. 3: 740.
3. *ORA,* 39, pt. 3: 750.
4. *ORA,* 35, pt. 2: 328.
5. *ORA,* 64: 543, 547.
6. McKee, *Back in War Times,* 177–78; Special Orders—Post of Beaufort.
7. McGrath, *127th New York "Monitors,"* 118–19; "Abraham Lincoln, From His Own Words" (website).
8. Pearson, *Letters from Port Royal,* 287–88; Holland, *Letters and Diary of Laura M. Towne,* 143.
9. McGrath, *127th New York "Monitors,"* 118–19; *ORA,* 44: 420–21.

10. *ORA*, 44: 547, 591; *ORA*, 81: 52; Dyer, *Compendium of the War*, 1240, 1393–94, 1730; Hewett, *Supplement to the Official Records*, pt. 2, 77: 752–78; Marple Family in the American Civil War (website).

11. Dyer, *Compendium of the War*, 1266–67, 1425, 1730; Hewett, *Supplement to Official Records*, pt. 2, 44: 295–313, 78: 230–305, 77: 719–32.

12. Barlow, *Company G*, 200; Dyer, *Compendium of the War*, 1392–93, 1464, 1459–69, 1508, Hewett, *Supplement to the Official Records*, pt. 2, 44: 55–64, 373–82, 51: 686–721; "Union Regimental Histories: New York" (website); Davis, *Dear Wife*, 44, 84, 87–88.

13. "127th Infantry Regiment" (website); Dyer, *Compendium of the War*, 1454–55, 1628–30, 1738; Hewett, *Supplement to the Official Records*, pt. 2, 44: 638–49, 79: 115–47; "26th U.S.C.T. Commanding Officer Killed" (website).

14. "Lt. Col. Henry L. Chipman" (website); "102nd United States Colored Troops" (website); Dyer, *Compendium of the War*, 1738; Hewett, *Supplement to the Official Records*, pt. 2, 79: 115–47.

15. Press Reference Library, *Notables of the Southwest, Los Angeles Examiner*, 1912, 290; Denison, *Shot and Shell*, 35–36, 134, 138, 147, 206, 244, 284, 338.

16. Barlow, *Company G*, 200; Emilio, *Brave Black Regiment*, 234–37; Fox, *Fifty-Fifth Regiment of Massachusetts*, 40–41; Hall and Hall, *Cayuga in the Field*, 207–9; McGrath, *127th New York "Monitors,"* 119; Fisk, *56th New York*, 61; Charles Fox Letterbooks, Papers, Extracts, 2: 90–94.

17. *ORA*, 25, pt. 2: 86; Warner, *Generals in Gray*, 380–81; Sifakis, *Who Was Who*, 518.

18. Emilio, *Brave Black Regiment*, 24; Wise, *Gate of Hell*, 138–39.

19. Denison, *Shot and Shell*, 281.

20. Denison, *Shot and Shell*, 284–85.

21. Schneller, *Quest for Glory*, 300; Browning, *Success Is All*, 329–30; *ORN*, 16: 57, 61–66.

22. Sullivan, *United States Marine Corps in the Civil War*, 74–77; *ORN*, 16: 72, 99–100, 110–11.

23. *ORN*, 16: 68.

24. *ORN*, 16: 40, 45, 55, 57–58, 61.

25. *ORN*, 16: 104.

26. *ORN*, 16: 69–70, 72–74; Emilio, *Brave Black Regiment*, 238.

27. Wildman Family Papers, Letter of Samuel Wildman, December 5, 1864; *New York Tribune*, December 9, 1864; McKee, *Back in War Times*, 185; *Charleston Sunday News*, November 8, 1898; Soule, "Annals of the War: Battle of Honey Hill"; Sullivan, *United States Marine Corps in the Civil War*, 79; Reid, *Practicing Medicine in a Black Regiment*, 198.

28. *ORA*, 44: 421–22; *ORN*, 16: 73, 76; Emilio, *Brave Black Regiment*, 238; Soule, "Annals of the War: Battle of Honey Hill."

29. *ORN*, 16: 73–74.

30. *ORN*, 16: 76; Emilio, *Brave Black Regiment*, 239; Soule, "Annals of the War: Battle of Honey Hill"; Wildman Family Papers, Letter of Samuel Wildman, December 5, 1864; McKee, *Back in War Times*, 185; McGrath, *127th New York "Monitors,"* 121; Barlow, *Company G*, 157th, 200; *ORA*, 44: 431.

31. Barlow, *Company G*, 185–86; *ORA*, 44: 422, 431; Bodine, "The Battle of Honey Hill."

32. *ORA*, 44: 871–77; Williams, *P. G. T. Beauregard*, 240–47; Hughes, *General William J. Hardee*, 250–55; McWhiney and Hallock, *Braxton Bragg and Confederate Defeat*, 2: 226–27.

33. Clement, Wise, Smith, and Grunden, *Mapping the Defense,* 16, 87–89.
34. John Jenkins Papers, C. G. Henderson to J. Jenkins, July 8, 1896; *Charleston Sunday News,* November 8, 13, 1898.
35. *Charleston Sunday News,* November 8, 13, 1898.
36. *Charleston Sunday News,* November 20, 1898; Courtenay, "Heroes of Honey Hill," 232–41.
37. McKee, *Back in War Times,* 192; *Charleston Sunday News,* November 8, 13, 1898.
38. *Charleston Sunday News,* November 8, 13, 1898; "South Carolina Cavalry Units in the War of the Rebellion" (website).
39. John Jenkins Papers, Jenkins's Battle Narrative, n.d.; Colcock, "Battle of Honey Hill."
40. *ORA,* 44: 904–9.
41. *ORA,* 44: 909; John Jenkins Papers, Jenkins's Battle Narrative, n.d.; De La Cova, *Cuban Confederate General,* 235.
42. Hughes, *General William J. Hardee,* 254–56; Bragg and Scaife, *Joe Brown's Pets,* 116–18; *ORA,* 44: 902–9.
43. Bragg and Scaife, *Joe Brown's Pets,* 4–6, 115–19, 204; Smith, "Georgia Militia during Sherman's March," 668–69; Bragg, "The Fight at Honey Hill," 14–15.
44. Currant, *Encyclopedia of the Confederacy,* 4: 1474–75; Warner, *Generals in Gray,* 280–81; Cullum, *Officers and Graduates of West Point,* 1: 1118.
45. *ORA,* 44: 906.
46. Smith, "Georgia Militia During Sherman's March," 667–69; *ORA,* 44: 906; William H. Bragg, e-mail to Stephen R. Wise, May 21, 2011.
47. Hughes, *General William J. Hardee,* 256; Smith, "Georgia Militia During Sherman's March," 668; *ORA,* 44: 906.
48. *ORA,* 44: 913; Hughes, *General William J. Hardee,* 256; Smith, "Georgia Militia during Sherman's March," 668; De La Cova, *Cuban Confederate General,* 236.
49. John Jenkins Papers, Lt. Zealy's account of battle, n.d., Jenkins's Battle Narrative, n.d.
50. *Charleston Sunday News,* November 8, 1898; John Jenkins Papers, Jenkins's Battle Narrative, n.d.
51. John Jenkins Papers, H. M. Stuart to C. Colcock, April 18, 1896, H. D. Burnett to J. Jenkins, June 1, 1896, Edward Fraser to J. Jenkins, July 19, 1896, Jenkins's Battle Narrative, n.d.; Colcock, "The Battle of Honey Hill"; Charles C. Jones Papers, C. J. Colcock to Charles C. Jones Jr., November 5, 1867.
52. *ORA,* 44: 422, 426, 431; McKee, *Back in War Times,* 185–86.
53. *ORA,* 44: 422, 426, 431; McKee, *Back in War Times,* 186–87; Emilio, *Brave Black Regiment,* 241; *ORN,* 16: 79; McGrath, *127th New York "Monitors,"* 122–23.
54. *ORA,* 44: 428, 435.
55. *ORA,* 44: 425–26, 428–29; McKee, *Back in War Times,* 185–86; McGrath, *127th New York "Monitors,"* 122–23; Hall and Hall, *Cayuga in the Field,* 211; Baird, *32nd Regiment, U.S.C.T.* 1–4; Colcock, "Battle of Honey Hill"; Charles C. Jones Papers, C. J. Colcock to Charles C. Jones Jr., November 5, 1867.
56. Colcock, "Battle of Honey Hill"; John Jenkins Papers, Edward W. Fraser to J. Jenkins, July 19, 1896; Hall and Hall, *Cayuga in the Field,* 211; McGrath, *127th New York "Monitors,"* 123; McKee, *Back in War Times,* 187; *ORA,* 44: 426, 429.
57. John Jenkins Papers, Jenkins's Battle Narrative, n.d.; Colcock, "Battle of Honey Hill"; Charles C. Jones Papers, C. J. Colcock to Charles C. Jones Jr., November 5, 1867.

58. Bragg and Scaife, *Joe Brown's Pets*, 120–21, 126; Smith, "Georgia Militia during Sherman's March," 668–69.

59. Soule, "Annals of the War: Battle of Honey Hill"; *ORA*, 44: 435; Hall and Hall, *Cayuga in the Field*, 211; McKee, *Back in War Times*, 186; Henry Orlando Marcy Diary, November 30, 1864.

60. Colcock, "Battle of Honey Hill"; John Jenkins Papers, Report of H. M. Stuart, n.d., C. G. Henderson to J. Jenkins, July 8, 1896, Jenkins's Battle Narrative, n.d.; W. A. Courtenay to John Jenkins, June 19, 1897.

61. McKee, *Back in War Times*, 188–89.

62. *ORA*, 44: 426; 428–29; Baird, *32nd Regiment, U.S.C.T.* 1–4; Barlow, *Company G*, 202.

63. McKee, *Back in War Times*, 188; *ORA*, 44: 426, 428, 430.

64. Soule, "Annals of the War: Battle of Honey Hill"; *ORA*, 44: 435; Hall and Hall, *Cayuga in the Field*, 213–14.

65. *ORA*, 44: 426; Soule, "Annals of the War: Battle of Honey Hill"; Dhalle, "Battle of Honey Hill (website); Charles C. Jones Papers, C. J. Colcock to Charles C. Jones Jr., November 5, 1867, George T. Jackson to Charles C. Jones, Jr., n.d.; Henry Orlando Marcy Diary, November 30, 1864.

66. Baird, *32nd Regiment, U.S.C.T.* 1–4; *ORA*, 44: 429–30; Culp, *Twenty-fifth Ohio Veteran Volunteer Regiment*, 104–5; *Savannah Republican*, December 3, 1864.

67. *ORN*, 16: 77.

68. John Jenkins Papers, Jenkins's Battle Narrative; De La Cova, *Cuban Confederate General*, 238–39; *Savannah Republican*, December 3, 1864.

69. Emilio, *Brave Black Regiment*, 243–44; *ORA*, 44: 426, 430–32; Hall and Hall, *Cayuga in the Field*, 212–13; MacDonald and Beckman, "Heroism at Honey Hill," 20–43, 28–36; Wildman Family Papers, Letter of Samuel Wildman, December 5, 1864

70. John Jenkins Papers, Report of H. M. Stuart, n.d.

71. Emilio, *Brave Black Regiment*, 243–44; *ORA*, 44: 426, 430–32; Hall and Hall, *Cayuga in the Field*, 212–13; MacDonald and Beckman, "Heroism at Honey Hill," 28–36; Luck, *Journey to Honey Hill*, 83–85; Trudeau, *Voices of the 55th*, 165–66; 190–91; Hall and Hall, *Cayuga in the Field*, 212–13; Reid, *Practicing Medicine in a Black Regiment*, 199–201.

72. John Jenkins Papers, Jenkins's Battle Narrative, n.d.: Williams, "Battle of Honey Hill," 46–48; McGrath, *127th New York "Monitors,"* 126; *ORA*, 44: 423, 428–29.

73. *ORN*, 16: 79; Emilio, *Brave Black Regiment*, 246–47; *ORA*, 44: 431; "Letter from William Warren Marple" (website).

74. *ORN*, 16: 79; Emilio, *Brave Black Regiment*, 246–47; *ORA*, 44: 431; "Letter from William Warren Marple" (website).

75. *ORA*, 44: 423–23.

76. *ORA*, 44: 433–35; McKee, *Back in War Times*, 191; Hall and Hall, *Cayuga in the Field*, 215–16.

77. Emilio, *Brave Back Regiment*, 246–47; Hall and Hall, *Cayuga in the Field*, 215–16.

78. Emilio, *Brave Black Regiment*, 248; Hall and Hall, *Cayuga in the Field*, 214–15.

79. Barlow, *Company G*, 204–5; *ORA*, 41: 423.

80. Ryan, "To the Shores of Carolina," 194–211; 208; *ORA*, 44: 430; Sullivan, *United States Marine Corps in the Civil War*, 88; *ORN*, 16: 77, 80, 100.

81. Ryan, "To the Shores of Carolina," 208; Emilio, *Brave Black Regiment*, 249–50.

82. John Jenkins Papers, Jenkins's Battle Narrative, n.d., J. Jenkins to C. G. Henderson, April 1898; Colcock, "Battle of Honey Hill"; Correspondence of James Legg to author, January 14, 2011.

83. *ORN,* 16: 100; *ORA,* 44: 430, 416, 423–24, 426–27.

84. Charles's company was also known as the Inglis Artillery and Charles' Independent Artillery Company. *ORA,* 28 pt. 2: 612, 616; Colcock, "Battle of Honey Hill"; Jenkins' Papers, Jenkins' Battle Narrative, n.d.; *ORA,* 44: 416, 423–24, 426–27, 914.

85. *ORA,* 44: 426–27, 429, 434; McKee, *Back in War Times,* 192; Reid, *Practicing Medicine in a Black Regiment,* 200.

86. Bodine, "The Battle of Honey Hill"; Soule, "Annals of the War: Battle of Honey Hill"; Emilio, *Brave Black Regiment,* 250–51; Reid, *Practicing Medicine in a Black Regiment,* 200–201; Henry Orlando Marcy Diary, November 30, 1864.

87. Holland, *Letters and Diary of Laura M. Towne,* 143; *Port Royal (Hilton Head) Palmetto Herald,* December 8, 1864; Trudeau, *Voices of the 55th,* 167–68, 228; Schwartz, *Woman Doctor's Civil War,* 95–96; Burt Wilder Papers, letter of December 7, 1864.

88. McGrath, *127th New York "Monitors,"* 131; *ORN,* 16: 106.

89. Williams, "Battle of Honey Hill," 46–48; *ORA,* 44: 416; Colcock, "Battle of Honey Hill"; Bragg, "The Fight at Honey Hill," 19; Charles C. Jones Papers, C. J. Colcock to Charles C. Jones Jr., November 5, 1867.

90. Warner, *Generals in Gray,* 48–49; Currant, *Encyclopedia of the Confederacy,* 1: 298–99;

91. *ORA,* 44: 416, 908, 417; Warner, *Generals in Gray,* 48–49; Currant, *Encyclopedia of the Confederacy,* Vol. I, 289–99; Cullum, *Officers and Graduates of West Point,* 2: 304; *ORA,* 44: 416, 908, 417.

92. *ORA,* 44: 417, 917, 919, 930; Hughes, *General William J. Hardee,* 256–57; Salley, "Captain John Colcock," 232.

93. Bragg and Scaife, *Joe Brown's Pets,* 128; John Jenkins Papers, Lt. Zealy's account of battle, n.d.; *Savannah Republican,* December 3, 1864; Soule, "Annals of the War: Battle of Honey Hill."

94. John Jenkins Papers, Report of H. M. Stuart, n.d.; Bragg and Scaife, *Joe Brown's Pets,* 128–29; *Savannah Republican,* December 3, 1864.

95. Porter, *One of the People,* 202–4; MacDonald and Beckman, "Heroism at Honey Hill," 35; Bragg and Scaife, *Joe Brown's Pets,* 128.

CHAPTER 14: BATTLES OF TULLIFINNY

1. *ORA,* 44: 911, 918; Conrad, *Young Lions,* 118–19; Baker, *Cadets in Gray,* 135–37; Still, *Confederate Navy,* 45, 68, 92–94.

2. *ORA,* 44: 443.

3. *ORA,* 44: 443; Warner, *Generals in Gray,* 101–2; Sifakis, *Who Was Who,* 241.

4. Young was promoted to Major General on December 30, 1864. *ORA,* 44: 443, 902, 933; Warner, *Generals in Gray,* 348; Sifakis, *Who Was Who,* 737.

5. It has been suggested that the Federals were using Coston Lights instead of Calcium Lights. The latter, unless mounted on ships, would have been very difficult to operate in the field. Conversation between Willis J. Keith and Stephen R. Wise, October 18, 2012; Hall and Hall, *Cayuga in the Field,* 215; Emilio, *Brave Black Regiment,* 254–55.

6. *ORN,* 16: 75, 82–83; Emilio, *Brave Black Regiment,* 255; Fox Journal, 93; McGrath, *127th New York "Monitors,"* 131; Hall and Hall, *Cayuga in the Field,* 215; Denison, *Shot and Shell,* 286.

7. The 25th Ohio's expedition had been originally scheduled for December 3, but bad weather delayed the movement one day. Later the Federals would refer to the landing as Blair's Landing when it became the primarily supply point for General Frank Blair's Seventeenth Corps after they occupied the area around Pocotaligo. Culp, *Twenty-fifth Ohio Veteran Volunteer Regiment*, 108–9; Wildman Family Papers, Letter of Samuel Wildman, December 5, 1864; Emilio, *Brave Black Regiment*, 255; *ORA*, 44: 438–48; Robinson, "Defense of the Charleston and Savannah Railroad," 51–57; Hughes, *General William J. Hardee*, 256–58.

8. Barlow, *Company G*, 208–11; Reid, *Practicing Medicine in a Black Regiment*, 202.

9. Hall and Hall, *Cayuga in the Field*, 215; Emilio, *Brave Black Regiment*, 255–56.

10. DeVeaux's Neck is also referred to as DeVeaux Neck, Gregorie's Neck, or Gregorie's Point. *ORN*, 16: 83.

11. Sullivan, *United States Marine Corps in the Civil War*, 92–93; Fisk, *56th New York*, 62; McGrath, *127th New York "Monitors,"* 132; *ORN*, 16: 81–87; Fox, *Fifty-fifth Regiment of Massachusetts*, 44–45; Reid, *Practicing Medicine in a Black Regiment*, 202–3.

12. Though claimed by the 127th New York, a commission awarded the flag as a trophy to the 56th New York. In 1885 the flag was returned to surviving veterans of the 5th Georgia. *ORA*, 44: 438–39, 443–44; *ORN*, 16: 82–87, 106–7; Sullivan, *United States Marine Corps in the Civil War*, 92–94; McGrath, *127th New York "Monitors,"* 132–13; McKee, *Back in War Times*, 201–3; Barlow, *Company G*, 210–11; Wildman Family Papers, Letter of Samuel Wildman, December 5, 1864; Conrad, *Young Lions*, 119; Baker, *Cadets in Gray*, 139–40.

13. McKee, *Back in War Times*, 203.

14. *ORN*, 16: 99; Sullivan, *United States Marine Corps in the Civil War*, 95–96; Hall, *Cayuga in the Field*, 216.

15. Hall, *Cayuga in the Field*, 216.

16. Mitchell King's artillery company had been initially designated Company A, First South Carolina Infantry. *ORA*, 44: 4474–78.

17. *ORA*, 44: 443–44, 447–48; Hall and Hall, *Cayuga in the Field*, 216.

18. *ORA*, 44: 438–48; *ORN*, 16: 88–89; Robinson, "Defense of the Charleston and Savannah Railroad," 51–54; Emilio, *Brave Black Regiment*, 254–58.

19. *Charleston Sunday News*, September 2, 1897; *ORA*, 44: 444, 448; Baker, *Cadets in Gray*, 140–42.

20. Wildman Family Papers, Letter of Samuel Wildman, December 5, 1864; Hall and Hall, *Cayuga in the Field*, 216; McGrath, *127th New York "Monitors,"* 135; Barlow, *Company G*, 211; Ryan, "To the Shores of Carolina," 208; *ORN*, 16: 88–89, 100–101.

21. Emilio, *Brave Black Regiment*, 256, 258; Baker, *Cadets in Gray*, 147–48; *ORA*, 44: 439–40, 447; *ORN*, 16: 96–97, 102–3; Barnwell, *History of an American Family*, 217, 272–75.

22. Emilio, *Brave Black Regiment*, 256–57; McGrath, *127th New York "Monitors,"* 135–36.

23. *ORN*, 16: 88.

24. Fox, *Fifty-fifth Regiment of Massachusetts*, 44–46; Fox, Letterbook, Papers, 94–95.

25. *ORA*, 44: 446, 943.

26. *ORA*, 44: 942; Stone, *Vital Rails*, 237; Sherman, *Memoirs of William T. Sherman*, 2: 194–95; Roman, *Military Operations of General Beauregard*, 2: 312.

27. Roman, *Military Operations of General Beauregard*, 2: 312.

28. Wooster, "124th New York Volunteer Infantry" (website); "Colonel William C. Silliman" (website); "26th Infantry, US Colored Troops" (website).

29. Lord, *Civil War Collector's Encyclopedia*, 2: 49–50; *ORN*, 16: 89–90; McKee, *Back in War Times*, 205; Fisk, *56th New York*, 62; Denison, *Shot and Shell*, 287; Saxton Papers, Willard Saxton Diary, December 16, 1865.

30. *ORN*, 16: 88–89; *ORA*, 54: 438–42; McGrath, *127th New York "Monitors,"* 136–41; McKee, *Back in War Times*, 205–8; Barlow, *Company G*, 212.

31. *ORA*, 44: 446.

32. *ORN*, 16: 101; Ryan, "To the Shores of Carolina," 209; Sullivan, *United States Marine Corps in the Civil War*, 98–99.

33. McGrath, *127th New York "Monitors,"* 139–41; *ORA*, 44: McKee, *Back in War Times*, 205–8; *ORN*, 16: 88–89.

34. Culp, *Twenty-fifth Ohio Veteran Volunteer Regiment*, 111–12; McKee, *Back in War Times*, 205–8; Barlow, *Company G*, 212; *ORN*, 16: 88–89.

35. *ORA*, 44: 446–47; Emilio, *Brave Black Regiment*, 260.

36. Porter, *One of the People*, 205–6; Smith, *107th Regiment Ohio Volunteer Infantry*, 180–82; Stone, *Vital Rails*, 246–47.

37. Emilio, *Brave Black Regiment*, 260–61; *ORA*, 44: 765, 771.

38. McGrath, *127th New York "Monitors,"* 142; Smith, *107th Regiment Ohio Volunteer Infantry*, 181.

39. McGrath, *127th New York "Monitors,"* 142; Smith, *107th Regiment Ohio Volunteer Infantry*, 181; *ORA*, 44: 11.

40. *ORN*, 16: 470, 473.

41. *ORA*, 44: 235, 238, 250–52, 328, 694, 727.

42. Emilio, *Brave Black Regiment*, 260–62; Sherman, *Memoirs of William T. Sherman*, 2: 202–3; *ORA*, 44: 11, 729.

43. The Izard and Smith Plantations were owned by Joseph Allen Smith Izard (1810–1879), grandson of Ralph Izard (1742—1804) and son of Charlotte Georgina Izard (1792–1832) and Joseph Allen Smith (1769–1828). Although Izard was a graduate of the U.S. Military Academy in the same class as Robert E. Lee, he did not participate in the Civil War and resided in the North during the conflict. Sherman, *Memoirs of William T. Sherman*, 2: 216–17; *ORA*, 44: 723–24, 737–38, 749–50; Smith, "Baronies of South Carolina," 156; Cullum, *Officers and Graduates of West Point*, 1: 421; McInnis, *In Pursuit of Refinement*, 42.

44. Sherman, *Memoirs of William T. Sherman*, 2: 216–17; *ORA*, 44: 723–24, 737–38, 749–50.

45. *ORA*, 44: 450–51; Emilio, *Brave Black Regiment*, 262–63.

46. *ORA*, 44: 949–50, 952, 954.

47. Bearss, "Joseph Wheeler"; *ORA*, 44: 998–99.

48. *ORA*, 44: 949, 955, 958, 960–62.

49. *ORA*, 44: 966, 974; Roman, *Military Operations of General Beauregard*, 2: 315–19.

50. Habersham-Elliott Papers, John B. Elliott letter, January 10, 1865; Hughes, *General William J. Hardee*, 266–68; *ORA*, 44: 237, 786; McGrath, *127th New York "Monitors,"* 143; Fisk, *56th New York*, 63–66.

51. Roman, *Military Operations of General Beauregard*, 2: 323–24; *ORA*, 44: 975; Hollis and Stokes, *South Carolina Rice Fields*, 161, 173, 178–81, 187–88, 194; De La Cova, *Cuban Confederate General*, 241–43.

52. *ORA*, 44: 992–93.

53. Warner, *Generals in Gray*, 204–5; Sifakis, *Who Was Who*, 420; Piston, *Lee's Tarnished Lieutenant*, 78–81.

54. *ORA*, 44: 974–76, 985, 997–1000, 1009.

55. *ORA*, 44: 991–92, 998–99, 1002–3; Hollis and Stokes, *South Carolina Rice Fields*, 165.

56. *ORA*, 44: 1009–11.

57. Sherman, *Memoirs of William T. Sherman*, 2: 221–28, 237–40; *ORA*, 44: 820–21.

58. Marszalek, *Sherman*, 288–89; Sherman, *Memoirs of William T. Sherman*, 2: 239–40.

59. Culp, *Twenty-fifth Ohio Veteran Volunteer Regiment*, 114; Emilio, *Brave Black Regiment*, 264; Hall and Hall, *Cayuga in the Field*, 217–18.

60. *ORN*, 16: 93, 101, 108; Dennison, *Shot and Shell*, 287; Fisk, *56th New York*, 144; Smith, *107th Regiment Ohio Volunteer Infantry*, 182–83, 184–85.

61. *ORN*, 16: 90–98; 108; *ORA*, 44: 787, 819, 855–56.

62. Hollis and Stokes, *South Carolina Rice Fields*, 14, 160–61, 168, 170, 172–74, 176–77, 185, 193.

63. Schwartz, *Woman Doctor's Civil War*, 96–97; Saxton Papers, Willard Saxton Diary, December 16–18, 1864.

64. Botume, *Amongst the Contrabands*, 73–74.

65. Holland, *Letters and Diary of Laura M. Towne*, 144–46; Saxton Papers, Willard Saxton Diary, December 25, 1864.

66. Saxton Papers, Willard Saxton Diary, December 30–31, January 1, 1865.

67. Botume, *Amongst the Contrabands*, 75–76; Saxton Papers, Willard Saxton Diary, January 1–2, 1865; *Special Orders*, September 14 and 19, 1864; Special Orders—Post of Beaufort, September 14 and 19, 1864; "New Castle Courthouse" (website); McPherson, *Struggle for Equality*, 162; Newcomb, *Genealogical Memoir of the Newcomb Family* (website).

CHAPTER 15: SHERMAN INVADES THE BEAUFORT DISTRICT

1. Warner, *Generals in Blue*, 538–39; Sifakis, *Who Was Who*, 691.

2. Colonel Case was in charge of a brigade formerly commanded by Colonel Benjamin Harrison, who had been furloughed to take part in the fall 1864 elections. Harrison had intended to rejoin his brigade at Savannah, but illness delayed his return. *ORA*, 47, pt. 1: 581, 782, 787, 792, 802; Miller, *Gullah Statesman*, 23; Cuthbert and Hoffius, *Northern Money, Southern Land*, 140.

3. *ORA*, 47, pt. 1: 17–18, 191.

4. *ORA*, 47, pt. 1: 191, 374; Anders, *Eighteenth Missouri*, 287–88; Rose, *Rehearsal for Reconstruction*, 323–25.

5. Botume, *Amongst the Contrabands*, 133–36; Rose, *Rehearsal for Reconstruction*, 323–25; Glatthaar, *March to the Sea*, 52–56, 59–60.

6. Saxton Papers, Willard Saxton Diary, January 4, 5, 1865.

7. Botume, *Amongst the Contrabands*, 133–36; Rose, *Rehearsal for Reconstruction*, 323–25; Howard, *Autobiography of Oliver Otis Howard*, 97–100; Saxton Papers, Willard Saxton Diary, January 4, 1865; Reed Photograph Album, photograph of General Blair's Headquarters.

8. Cullum, *Officers and Graduates of West Point*, 2: 369–70.

9. Howard, *Autobiography of Oliver Otis Howard*, 2: 98; MOLLUS Photograph Collection, photographs of the Stevens House.

10. Howard, *Autobiography of Oliver Otis Howard*, 2: 98–99; McFeely, *Yankee Stepfather*, 46–47; Saxton Papers, Willard Saxton Diary, January 3, 4, 10, 11, 1865.

11. Sherman, *Memoirs of William T. Sherman*, 2: 246–49; *ORA*, 44: 836; *ORA*, 47, pt. 1: 36–37.

12. Sherman, *Memoirs of William T. Sherman*, 2: 244–45; *ORA*, ser. 3, 4: 1022–31; Holland, *Letters and Diary of Laura M. Towne*, 150–51.

13. Sherman, *Memoirs of William T. Sherman*, 2: 248–50.

14. *ORA*, 44: 787.

15. Saxton Papers, Willard Saxton Diary, January 11–12, 1865.

16. Sherman, *Memoirs of William T. Sherman*, 2: 253–47; Marszalek, *Sherman*, 514–15; Thomas and Hyman, *Stanton*, 344–45.

17. *ORA*, 47, pt. 2: 60–63.

18. Though the order has become known as "forty acres and a mule," no mule was mentioned in the order. Sherman, *Memoirs of William T. Sherman*, 2: 249–52; Lewis, *Sherman*, 480; *ORA*, 47, pt. 2: 60–62.

19. Saxton Papers, Willard Saxton Diary, January 15, 1865.

20. Holland, *Letters and Diary of Laura M. Towne*, 148–49

21. Botume, *Amongst the Contrabands*, 120–24; Johnson Family Papers, Letter of Martha Johnson, January 12, 1865.

22. The *Nemaha* had been originally purchased and operated as the *Flora* for use at Port Royal by the Treasury Department. The band from Hilton Head, the former regimental band of the Third New Hampshire, served as the department's headquarters band. Saxton Papers, Willard Saxton Diary, January 14, 15, 1865; Thomas and Hyman, *Stanton*, 346; Cullum, *Officers and Graduates of West Point*, 2: 240; Holland, *Letters and Diary of Laura M. Towne*, 150–51; Rose, *Rehearsal for Reconstruction*, 328–29; Sherman, *Memoirs of William T. Sherman*, 2: 252.

23. Saxton Papers, Willard Saxton Diary, January 15, 1865; "Langford-L Archives" (website); "Martha S. Winters–Genealogy" (website).

24. Saxton Papers, Willard Saxton Diary, January 15, 1865.

25. *ORA*, 44: 986–88; 1000, 1004, 1011–12.

26. Richard Burnham (1711–1752) was an Englishman who collected the dying sayings of more than one hundred pious persons with accounts of their lives and last hours. Stephen, *Dictionary of National Biography*, 7: 421; *Charleston Mercury*, January 12, 1865.

27. *Charleston Mercury*, January 12, 13, 16, 19, 26, February 3, 1865.

28. Sherman, *Memoirs of William T. Sherman*, 2: 254; Hazen, *Narrative of Military Service*, 336.

29. Fox, *Fifty-fifth Regiment of Massachusetts*, 47–48; Dhalle, "History of the 55th Massachusetts Volunteer Infantry" (website); Emilio, *Brave Black Regiment*, 270.

30. *ORN*, 16: 168, 182, 185–88.

31. *ORA*, 47, pt. 1: 192, 374.

32. Sherman, *Memoirs of William T. Sherman*, 2: 270; *ORA*, 47, pt. 1: 374; *ORA*, 47, pt. 2: 1010–12.

33. *ORA*, 47, pt. 1: 374; *ORA*, 47, pt. 2, 1010–12.

34. Saxton Papers, Willard Saxton Diary, January 15, 1865; Hitchcock, *Marching with Sherman*, 219, 224–25; Map of Pocotaligo and Vicinity Record Group 77; Sherman, *Memoirs of William T. Sherman*, 2: 254–57; *ORA*, 47, pt. 2: 1045.

35. *ORA*, 47, pt. 2: 1012–18, 1022, 1033, 1036, 1041, 1049.

36. Emilio, *Brave Black Regiment*, 265–67; McGrath, *127th New York "Monitors,"* 146–48; Fisk, *56th New York*, 66–67; Denison, *Shot and Shell*, 287–88;

37. *ORA*, 44: 841; *ORA*, 47, pt. 1: 18, 81, 782, 597–98, 680–81; Sherman, *Memoirs of William T. Sherman*, 2: 236, 253, 264–65; Quaife, *From the Cannon's Mouth*, 366; Warner, *Generals in Blue*, 248–49.

38. *ORA*, 47, pt. 1: 314–15; "Galena Generals" (website).

39. *ORA*, 47, pt. 1: 314–15;

40. *ORA*, 47, pt. 1: 315; Quaife, *From the Cannon's Mouth*, 367.

41. Quaife, *From the Cannon's Mouth*, 367–68; Hight and Stormont, *Fifty-eighth Regiment of Indiana*, 452–53; *New York Daily Tribune*, January 30, 1865.

42. Quaife, *From the Cannon's Mouth*, 370–72

43. Cullum, *Officers and Graduates of West Point*, 2: 307–8; Warner, *Generals in Blue*, 4451–53; Tagg, "Major General Henry Warner Slocum" (accessed 28 April 2013).

44. Girardi, *Campaigning with Uncle Billy*, 324–25.

45. Hight and Stormont, *Fifty-eighth Regiment of Indiana*, 460–66; Girardi, *Campaigning with Uncle Billy*, 324–25; *ORA*, 47, pt. 1: 419, 426, 429, 444, 465, 481, 530, 549, 572, 578; Gibson, *Those 163 Days*, 135–36.

46. *ORA*, 47, pt. 2: 104.

47. Sherman, *Memoirs of William T. Sherman*, 2: 253; *ORA*, 47, pt. 1: 18.

48. *ORA*, 47, pt. 2: 52, 108–15.

49. Hitchcock, *Marching with Sherman*, 228.

50. Hitchcock, *Marching with Sherman*, 225–28, 234–35.

51. Sherman, *Memoirs of William T. Sherman*, 2: 253; *ORA*, 47, pt. I, 18; *ORA*, 47, pt. 2: 116–21; Saxton Papers, Willard Saxton Diary, January 22–24, 1865.

52. Sherman, *Memoirs of William T. Sherman*, 2: 255–56; Linder, *Atlas of the Rice Plantations*, 505; *ORA*, 47, pt. 2: 125; Todd and Hutson, *Prince William's Parish and Plantations*, 257, 259.

53. Nichols, *Story of the Great March*, 117–22, 131–32, 138–49; Lewis, *Sherman*, 477, 483–85; Sherman, *Memoirs of William T. Sherman*, 2: 261–67; *ORN*, 16: 181.

54. Cisco, *Wade Hampton*, 149; Martin, *Matthew Calbraith Butler*, 133–38; *ORA*, 47, pt. 2: 997, 999, 1009, 1014, 1016, 1018.

55. Hollis and Stokes, *South Carolina Rice Fields*, 193; *ORA*, 47, pt. 2: 984, 1011, 1015, 1022, 1029, 1032, 1034, 1041, 1047, 1067; Sifakis, *Who Was Who*, 7–8, 420–21, 324–25, 732; Warner, *Generals in Gray*, 5, 144–45, 204–5, 345–46; De La Cova, *Cuban Confederate General*, 242–43.

56. Nichols, *Story of the Great March*, 131–32, 138–49; Lewis, *Sherman*, 483–85; Sherman, *Memoirs of William T. Sherman*, 2: 261–67; *ORN*, 16: 181, 185–88.

57. *ORN*, 16: 192–202.

58. *ORN*, 16: 190–202; *ORN*, ser. 2, 1: 60, 70; Browning, *Success Is All*, 340–41; Hollis and Stokes, *South Carolina Rice Fields*, 180–81, 199–200.

59. Sullivan, *United States Marine Corps in the Civil War*, 204; *ORN*, 16: 189.

60. Warner, *Generals in Blue*, 115–16; Sherman, *Memoirs of William T. Sherman*, 2: 244; Miles, *To the Sea*, 117–20.

61. *ORA*, 47, pt. 1: 419, 426, 429.

62. Kaminsky, *War to Petrify the Heart*, 309.

63. *ORA*, 44: pt. I, 420, 582, 598; Howard, *Autobiography of Oliver Otis Howard*, 2: 113–14; Kaminsky, *War to Petrify the Heart*, 309.

64. *ORN,* 16: 208.

65. *ORA,* 47, pt. 1: 419, 426, 429, 479; 581–82, 598; Crabb, *Facing Sherman in South Carolina,* 97.

66. *ORA,* 47, pt. 2: 63, 70–71, 106, 138.

67. *ORA,* 47, pt. 2: 86, 100, 124, 991.

68. *ORA,* 47, pt. 2: 85, 99, 120, 122, 129, 131–33, 137, 1044, 1049.

69. *ORA,* 47, pt. 2: 180; Hitchcock, *Marching with Sherman,* 217–18. 230, 233–35.

70. For the Carolina Campaign the Seventeenth Corps contained three divisions: the First, Third, and Fourth. *ORA,* 47, pt. 1: 48–50; *ORA,* 47, pt. 2: 182–83; Anders, *Eighteenth Missouri,* 294.

71. Warner, *Generals in Blue,* 338–39; *ORA,* 47, pt. 1: 193, 375, 387.

72. Anders, *Eighteenth Missouri,* 294–95; *ORA,* 47, pt. 1: 193, 375, 387; Howard, *Autobiography of Oliver Otis Howard,* 2: 105; Harwell and Racine, *Fiery Trail,* 92–94.

73. Howard, *Autobiography of Oliver Otis Howard,* 2: 105; Harwell and Racine, *Fiery Trail,* 93–94; *ORA,* 47, pt. 1: 193.

74. Warner, *Generals in Blue,* 155; *ORA,* 47, pt. 1: 405.

75. *ORA,* 47, pt. 1: 405–6.

76. *ORA,* 47, pt. 1: 375–76, 387, 400; Harwell and Racine, *Fiery Trail,* 93–94; Powell, "Additional Sketch, Tenth Battalion," 4: 335; Power, "This Indescribably Ugly Salkehatchie," 13–14.

77. Harwell and Racine, *Fiery Trail,* 94; Howard, *Autobiography of Oliver Otis Howard,* 2: 106–7; *ORA,* 47, pt. 1: 375–76, 387, 400.

78. Power, "This Indescribably Ugly Salkehatchie," 14; *ORA,* 47, pt. 1: 376–77, 387–88; Harwell and Racine, *Fiery Trail,* 94–95.

79. Howard, *Autobiography of Oliver Otis Howard,* 2: 107; *ORA,* 47, pt. 1: 387, 398; Henry Orlando Marcy Diary, February 5, 1865.

80. Glatthaar, *March to the Sea,* 24; *ORA,* 47, pt. 1: 376–77, 387–88; Harwell and Racine, *Fiery Trail,* 94–97; Anders, *Eighteenth Missouri,* 297–99.

81. Power, "This Indescribably Ugly Salkehatchie," 5–6; Bell, "Strongest Position I Ever Saw," 8–9.

82. *ORA,* 47, pt. 1: 376–77, 387–88, 393, 397–98, 400–401; Harwell and Racine, *Fiery Trail,* 94–97.

83. Warner, *Generals in Blue,* 456–57; Nichols, *Story of the Great March,* 137; *ORA,* 47, pt. 1: 411–12.

84. Howard, *Autobiography of Oliver Otis Howard,* 2: 107–8; *ORA,* 47, pt. 1: 411–12; Harwell and Racine, *Fiery Trail,* 97; Bell, "Strongest Position I Ever Saw," 195–96.

85. Hitchcock, *Marching with Sherman,* 236–38; *ORA,* 47, pt. 1: 194, 222–23, 245, 278, 316.

86. *ORA,* 47, pt. 1: 194, 222–23, 245, 278, 316; Nichols, *Story of the Great March,* 132–38; Jones, *Black Jack,* 246–48; Hazen, *Narrative of Military Service,* 340–43; Hitchcock, *Marching with Sherman,* 236–50.

87. *ORA,* 47, pt. 1: 582, 803, 814, 821, 831; *Atlas to Accompany the Official Records,* plate LXXX.

88. Martin, *Kill-Cavalry,* 189–90, 208–9; Parrish, *Frank Blair,* 212; *ORA,* 47, pt. 1: 857; Todd, "First Alabama Cavalry U.S.A." (website).

89. Girardi, *Campaigning with Uncle Billy,* 326; Warner, *Generals in Blue,* 266–67; Martin, *Kill-Cavalry,* 209.

90. *ORA,* 47, pt. 1: 857, 876, 881, 891; Starr, *Union Cavalry in the Civil War,* 3: 568–70, 580–81.
91. Warner, *Generals in Blue,* 169–70; Sifakis, *Who Was Who,* 243–44.
92. *ORA,* 47, pt. 1: 681–83; *Official Atlas of the Civil War,* plates 80 and 86.
93. Warner, *Generals in Blue,* 94–95; Sifakis, *Who Was Who,* 144–45.
94. *ORA,* 47, pt. 1: 337–38.
95. *ORA,* 47, pt. 1: 444–45; Warner, *Generals in Blue,* 69–70.
96. Warner, *Generals in Blue,* 15; *ORA,* 47, pt. 1: 549–50.
97. Warner, *Generals in Blue,* 334–35; *ORA,* 47, pt. 1: 482.
98. Girardi, *Campaigning with Uncle Billy,* 326–27; *ORA,* 47, pt. 1: 482.
99. *ORA,* 47, pt. 1: 482; Campbell, *When Sherman Marched North,* 44–45.

CHAPTER 16: THE WAR LEDGER

1. Sherman, *Memoirs of William T. Sherman,* 2: 174–76.
2. Harwell and Racine, *Fiery Trail,* 91, 109; "Bummer," definition (website).
3. Sherman, *Memoirs of William T. Sherman,* 2: 254; James W. Kirk, letter, December 8, 1864, transcript in possession of the author.
4. Sherman, *Memoirs of William T. Sherman,* 2: 254; Nichols, *Story of the Great March,* 131.
5. *ORA,* 47, pt. 1: 194–98; Pt. 2, 171; Howard, *Autobiography of Oliver Otis Howard,* 2: 106; Harwell and Racine, *Fiery Trail,* 108; Bradley, *Star Corps,* 275–76.
6. *ORA,* 47, pt. 1: 222; Jones, *Black Jack,* 246; Todd and Hutson, *Prince William's Parish and Plantations,* 76–78.
7. Hazen, *Narrative of Military Service,* 337–338; Warner, *Generals in Blue,* 225–26.
8. *ORA,* 47, pt. 2: 184–85; Williams, *From the Cannon's Mouth,* 373–74.
9. Though records are silent as to Trowell's immediate fate at the hands of the Federals he did not seem to suffer any physical harm, and died in October, 1865. He is buried in Lebanon Methodist Church Cemetery near his plantation in Hampton County, S.C. "Thomas Jefferson Trowell, Find a Grave," (website); *ORA,* 47, pt. 1: 683, 813–14; Boyle, *Soldiers True,* 277.
10. Girardi, *Campaigning with Uncle Billy,* 328; Todd and Hutson, *Prince William's Parish and Plantations,* 76–78; Wilmesherr, "Independent Church of Indian Land," 4; "Stony Creek Independent Presbyterian Chapel" (website); Rowland, Moore, and Rogers, *History of Beaufort County,* 1: 386.
11. Harwell and Racine, *Fiery Trail,* 92–93; Nichols, *Story of the Great March,* 132–33; Conversation between Stephen R. Wise and Ms. Betty Jane Miller, October 19, 1996.
12. Taylor, Mathews, and Powers, *Leverett Letters,* 403, 405; Todd and Hutson, *Prince William's Parish Plantations,* 81.
13. Henry Orlando Marcy Diary, Jan 17–Feb 12, 1865; Wynn, "Gillisonville Baptist Church," (website); "Church of the Holy Trinity" (website).
14. Henry Orlando Marcy Diary, January 19, 1865.
15. Baxley, "200 Years Of History" (website); Henry Orlando Marcy Diary, January 19–23, 1865; *New York Tribune,* February 16, 1865.
16. Todd and Hutson, *Prince William's Parish Plantations,* 76–78, 81, 103–4, 257.
17. Emilio, *Brave Black Regiment,* 269–71; *ORA,* 47, pt. 2: 109, 134, 141.
18. Culp, *Twenty-fifth Ohio Veteran Volunteer Regiment,* 115–16; *ORA,* 47, pt. 2: 314.
19. Barnwell, *History of an American Family,* 151; Smith, *107th Regiment Ohio Volunteer Infantry,* 185–87.

20. Smith, *107th Regiment Ohio Volunteer Infantry*, 185–87; *ORA*, 47, pt. 2: 314, 324.

21. Emilio, *Brave Black Regiment*, 273; *ORA*, 47, pt. 2: 82, 324–25, 339; Culp, *Twenty-fifth Ohio Veteran Volunteer Regiment*, 117; Smith, *107th Regiment Ohio Volunteer Infantry*, 188; McGrath, *127th New York "Monitors,"* 147.

22. Emilio, *Brave Black Regiment*, 273; *ORA*, 47, pt. 2: 82, 324–25, 339; Culp, *Twenty-fifth Ohio Veteran Volunteer Regiment*, 117; Smith, *107th Regiment Ohio Volunteer Infantry*, 188, McGrath, *127th New York "Monitors,"* 147; Henry Orlando Marcy Diary, February 12, 1865; Linder, *Atlas of the Rice Plantations*, 521–25.

23. Smith, *107th Regiment Ohio Volunteer Infantry*, 187; *ORA*, 47, pt. 2: 402; Emilio, *Brave Black Regiment*, 275–79

24. Emilio, *Brave Black Regiment*, 275–80.

25. Warner, *Generals in Blue*, 386–87; *ORA*, 47, pt. 2: 300, 312, 314, 324, 367, 585; Sievers, *Benjamin Harrison*, 290.

26. Sifakis, *Who Was Who*, 286–87.

27. Sievers, *Benjamin Harrison*, 290–91

28. Sievers, *Benjamin Harrison*, 290–92.

29. Sievers, *Benjamin Harrison*, 295–96.

30. Saxton Papers, Willard Saxton Diary, January 30, 1865; Madden, "Catholics in South Carolina."

31. Hendricks, "Department of the South," 109–11; Saxton Papers, Willard Saxton Diary, January 26, 1865; *ORA*, 47, pt. 2: 186–87.

32. *ORA*, 35, pt. 2: 219; *ORA*, 47, pt. 2: 186–87.

33. *ORA*, 47, pt. 2: 201.

34. *ORA*, 47, pt. 2: 209.

35. *ORA*, 47, pt. 2: 210.

36. *ORA*, 47, pt. 2: 211; Hendricks, "Department of the South," 111–13.

37. Saxton Papers, Willard Saxton Diary, February 2, 1865; *New York Tribune*, April 4, 1865.

38. Saxton Papers, Willard Saxton Diary February 3, 1865; *ORA*, 47, pt. 2: 313.

39. *ORA*, 47, pt. 2: 367, 338.

40. *ORA*, 47, pt. 2: 367.

41. *ORA*, 47, pt. 2: 368–69.

42. *ORA*, 47, pt. 2: 424–25, 465; Hendricks, "Union Army Occupation," 111–13.

43. *ORN*, 16: 220–21; Emilio, *Brave Black Regiment*, 270–75; Schneller, *Quest for Glory*, 307–9.

44. *New York Times*, January 13, 1865; Saxton Papers, Willard Saxton Diary, January 16, 21, 1865.

45. *New South*, May 6, 1865.

46. Daniel, *Prince of Carpetbaggers*, 110–12.

47. *New South*, May 6, 1865; Reid, *After the War*, 89–91; Daniel, *Prince of Carpetbaggers*, 110–12; Trinkley, *Indian and Freedmen Occupation at Fish Haul Site*, 81–83.

48. Saxton Papers, Willard Saxton Diary, February 25–27, 1865.

49. Saxton Papers, Willard Saxton Diary, February 25–27, 1865.

50. Saxton Papers, Willard Saxton Diary, February 27–28, 1865.

51. The home purchased by Rufus Saxton on March 25, 1865, may have been the Cuthbert home, which he later sold to Duncan Wilson. Saxton Papers, Willard Saxton Diary, March 2–17, 1865; Holland, *Letters and Diary of Laura M. Towne*, 158.

52. Saxton Papers, Willard Saxton Diary, March 19, 1865; Schwartz, *Woman Doctor's Civil War*, 125–26; *New South*, April 22, 1865.

53. *New York Tribune*, April 4, 1865; *New York Times*, April 4, 1865.

54. Rollin, *Martin R. Delany*, 79–94; "Time Line of Martin R. Delany's Life" (website).

55. *ORA*, 47, pt. 2: 581, 979; *ORA*, 47, pt. 3: 34; Saxton Papers, Willard Saxton Diary, March 24, 1865.

56. Saxton Papers, Willard Saxton Diary April 1, 8, 14, 1865; Holland, *Letters and Diary of Laura M. Towne*, 160.

57. Saxton Papers, Willard Saxton Diary, April 24, 1865; *New York Times*, April 18, 1865; French and Cary, *Trip of the Steamer Oceanus*, 43; Rollin, *Martin R. Delany*, 93–94.

58. *New York Times*, April 18, 1865; *Port Royal Free South*, April 22, 1865; Billingsley, *Yearning to Breathe Free*, 90–92; Miller, *Gullah Statesman*, 24–25; Schwartz, *Woman Doctor's Civil War*, 130–32; Holland, *Letters and Diary of Laura M. Towne*, 159–61; French and Cary, *Trip of the Steamer Oceanus*, 82–84; Schneller, *Quest for Glory*, 317–18.

59. *New York Times*, April 8, 1865.

60. Billingsley, *Yearning to Breathe Free*, 90–92; Miller, *Gullah Statesman*, 24–25; Schwartz, *Woman Doctor's Civil War*, 130–32; Holland, *Letters and Diary of Laura M. Towne*, 159–61; French and Cary, *Trip of the Steamer Oceanus*, 82–84; Schneller, *Quest for Glory*, 317–18.

61. Schwartz, *Woman Doctor's Civil War*, 132; Holland, *Letters and Diary of Laura M. Towne*, 161; Saxton Papers, Willard Saxton Diary, April 15, 1865; Rollin, *Martin R. Delany*, 94–95.

62. Saxton Papers, Willard Saxton Diary, April 16–19, 1865.

63. *New South*, April 22, June 3, 1865; *New South*, May 6, 1865.

64. *New South*. May 6, 1865.

65. Holland, *Letters and Diary of Laura M. Towne*, 162.

66. Holland, *Letters and Diary of Laura M. Towne*, 162.

67. Botume, *Amongst the Contrabands*, 173–75.

68. *New South*, June 3, 1865

69. Botume, *Amongst the Contrabands*, 176–77; *New South*, May 6, 20, 1865.

70. Saxton Papers, Willard Saxton Diary, May 2, 1865.

CHAPTER 17: THE BEGINNING OF THE NEW SOUTH

1. Seigler, *South Carolina's Military Organizations*, 119–20, 215–16, 269; *ORA*, 47, pt. 3: 312, 362; Saxton Papers, Willard Saxton Diary, April 21, 1865; *New South*, May 13, 1865.

2. *ORA*, 47, pt. 3: 312, 337, 358; *New South*, May 6, 1865.

3. *ORA*, 47, pt. 3: 312–13, 473–74, 498, 560, 565, 579, 579, 588; *New South*, May 20, 1865.

4. Cullum, *Officers and Graduates of West Point*, 2: 240, 369–71; Warner, *Generals in Blue*, 237–39; McFeely, *Yankee Stepfather*, 61–66; McPherson, *Struggle for Equality*, 178–79, 181, 190–91; *ORA*, 47, pt. 3: 477.

5. Niven, *Salmon P. Chase Papers*, 1: 525–26.

6. Niven, *Salmon P. Chase Papers*, 1: 526.

7. Niven, *Salmon P. Chase Papers*, 1: 535–41, 5: 37–45; Reid, *After the War*, 31–33.

8. Reid, *After the War*, 82–83; 581–86; Niven, *Salmon P. Chase Papers*, 1: 544–48.

9. Reid, *After the War*, 92–93; Niven, *Salmon P. Chase Papers*, 1: 548–49.

10. Reid, *After the War*, 100–102.

11. Reid, *After the War*, 103–6.
12. Reid, *After the War*, 107.
13. Reid, *After the War*, 109–12.
14. Reid, *After the War*, 112.
15. Reid, *After the War*, 118–20, Niven, *Salmon P. Chase Papers*, 1: 549, 5: 48; Saxton Papers, Willard Saxton Diary, May 14, 1865.
16. Reid, *After the War*, 119–22; Niven, *Salmon P. Chase Papers*, 1: 549, 5: 48; Saxton Papers, Willard Saxton Diary, May 14, 1865.
17. Reid, *After the War*, 107.
18. Saxton Papers, Willard Saxton Diary May 15, 1865; Niven, *Salmon P. Chase Papers*, 1: 549–50, 5: 48.
19. The *Emilie* was formerly the *William Seabrook*, a prewar, Charleston-based, thirty-four-year-old wooden side-wheeler. The *Emilie* was used as a blockade runner. Captured June 3, 1862, it was chartered and later purchased by the Quartermaster Bureau. Reid, *After the War*, 134; Niven, *Salmon P. Chase Papers*, 1: 550, 5: 49; Wise, *Lifeline of the Confederacy*, 327; Gibson, *Dictionary of Transports and Combat Vessels*, 102; *New South*, April 22, May 6, May 20, 1865.
20. Niven, *Salmon P. Salmon P. Chase Papers*, 1: 551.
21. Wheeler had been promoted by the Confederate Congress to lieutenant general on February 28, 1865. Schott, *Alexander H. Stephens*, 450–52; *New South*, April 22, May 6, May 20, 1865; Saxton Papers, Willard Saxton Diary, May 16, 1865; Dyer, *From Shiloh to San Juan*, 183–87.
22. Saxton Papers, Willard Saxton Diary, May 17, 1865; "Jim Limber" (website).
23. Botume, *Amongst the Contrabands*, 181–90.
24. Saxton Papers, Willard Saxton Diary, May 29, 1865; "Law Creating the Freedmen's Bureau" (website); Newcomb, *Genealogical Memoir of the Newcomb Family* (website).
25. Reid, *After the War*, 117; Saxton Papers, Willard Saxton Diary, May 29, 1865.
26. Saxton Papers, Willard Saxton Diary, May 30, 1865; Welles, *Diary of Gideon Welles*, 2: 310–13.
27. *ORA*, 47, pt. 3: 514, 525, 560–61.
28. Hendricks, "Union Army Occupation,"170; Rollin, *Martin R. Delany*, 109–13, 133–37.
29. Hayes, *Samuel Francis Du Pont*, 1: xc–xciv, 3: 479–82.
30. Hayes, *Samuel Francis Du Pont*, 3: 482.

CHAPTER 18: AN UNCERTAIN FUTURE

1. Edgar, *South Carolina*, 383–84; Bailey, Morgan, and Taylor, *South Carolina Senate*, 1: 363–64; 2: 1061; Edgar, Bailey, and Moore, *South Carolina House of Representatives*, 1: 597; Rowland, Moore, and Rogers, *History of Beaufort County*, 1: 309; *New South*, May 13, 1865.
2. McKitrick, *Andrew Johnson and Reconstruction*, 111–12; McGuire, "Hands on the Land," 102.
3. *New South*, May 13, 1865.
4. McFeely, *Yankee Stepfather*, 98–102, 103–5; McGuire, "Hands on the Land," 102–3.
5. McFeely, *Yankee Stepfather*, 98; Saxton Papers, Willard Saxton Diary, July 16, 1865.
6. Rosengarten, *Tombee*, 701, 703; Holland, *Letters and Diary of Laura M. Towne*, 163–4.

7. Joseph Daniel Pope to Major General Q. A. Gillmore, June 29, 1865; Bailey, Morgan, and Taylor, *South Carolina Senate*, 1: 362–63, 375, 472–73, 506–7, 2: 898–99, 1291–92, 1355–56, 1383; Rowland, Moore, and Rogers, *History of Beaufort County*, 1: 428–29, 439; Rosengarden, *Tombee*, 679.

8. Hendrick, "Union Army Occupation," 35; *New South*, July 22, 1865; *ORA*, 47, pt. 3: 679, 681.

9. Reverend Stephen Elliott's home had been the home of his father, William Elliott II. Rose, *Rehearsal for Reconstruction*, 78; *Journal of the Convention*, representatives listed in appendix to the volume; Edgar, *South Carolina*, 382–83; Zuczek, *State of Rebellion*, 12–13; *New South*, August 5, 1865.

10. Edgar, *South Carolina*, 383–84; Bailey, Morgan, and Taylor, *South Carolina Senate*, 1: 363–64, 2: 1061; Edgar, Bailey, and Moore, *South Carolina House of Representatives*, 1: 597; Rowland, Moore, and Rogers, *History of Beaufort County*, 1: 309; *New South*, May 13, 1865; Zuczek, *State of Rebellion*, 11–14; Edgar, *South Carolina*, 383; Andrews, *South since the War*, 67, 80, 85.

11. *New South*, May 6, 1865; Botume, *Amongst the Contrabands*, 191.

12. Joseph Daniel Pope to Major General Q. A. Gillmore, June 29, 1865; Rollin, *Martin R. Delany*, 110; Holland, *Letters and Diary of Laura M. Towne*, 166–68; Botume, *Amongst the Contrabands*, 201.

13. *New South*, May 13, 1865; *Charleston News*, October 19, 1865; Botume, *Amongst the Contrabands*, 196.

14. Westwood, "Sherman Marched—and Proclaimed," 42; McFeely, *Yankee Stepfather*, 96–100, 130–33; Howard, *Autobiography of Oliver Otis Howard*, 2: 230–31; McGuire, "Hands on the Land," 102.

15. McFeely, *Yankee Stepfather*, 128–29, 133; Saxton Papers, Willard Saxton Diary, September 26, 1865.

16. Warner, *Generals in Blue*, 446–47; Safaris, *Who Was Who*, 594–55; Cullum, *Officers and Graduates of West Point*, 2: 227–28; Keneally, *American Scoundrel*, 317; Trinckley, "Indian and Freedmen Occupation," 99–104; McGuire, "Hands on the Land," 101.

17. Saxton Papers, Willard Saxton Diary, December 1–3, 1865; *New York Times*, December 11, 1865; Simon, *Papers of Ulysses S. Grant*, 15: 434–37.

18. Leroy Youmans was appointed solicitor of the Southern Circuit by Governor James L. Orr on March 2, 1866 and was replaced by James A. Moore. Stephen Elliott Jr. died from his war wounds on February 21, 1866 and was replaced by his brother William Elliott. Edgar, Bailey, and Moore, *South Carolina House of Representatives*, 1: 397, 597; Bailey, Morgan, and Taylor, *South Carolina Senate*, 1: 363–64; Barnwell, *History of an American Family*, 219; Woodward, *Mary Chesnut's Civil War*, 827; Rowland, Moore, and Rogers, *History of Beaufort County*, 1: 309; *New South*, May 13, 1865; Zuczek, *State of Rebellion*, 11–14; Edgar, *South Carolina*, 383.

19. Edgar, *South Carolina*, 379; *New South*, May 20, 1865; June 3, 1865; Andrews, *South since the War*, 56–57; Holland, *Letters and Diary of Laura M. Towne*, 167.

20. *Charleston Courier*, October 19, 1865; Saville, *Work of Reconstruction*, 149–50.

21. *New South*, June 3, August 25, 1865; Davis, "South's First City," 318–20. The authors thank John Martin Davis for making his prepublication manuscript available.

22. Holland, *Letters and Diary of Laura M. Towne*, 166–68; Botume, *Amongst the Contrabands*, 201.

23. *New South*, June 3, 1865; August 25, 1865; Davis, "New South's First City," 318–20.

24. Zuczek, *State of Rebellion*, 15; Edgar, *South Carolina*, 384; Barnwell, *History of an American Family*, 172; Keneally, *American Scoundrel*, 321.

25. Zuczek, *State of Rebellion*, 15; Edgar, *South Carolina* 377–406; Barnwell, *History of an American Family*, 172; Keneally, *American Scoundrel*, 321; Botume, *Amongst the Contrabands*, 204–6.

26. McFeely, *Yankee Stepfather*, 96–100, 130–33; Howard, *Autobiography of Oliver Otis Howard*, 2: 230–31; McGuire, "Hands on the Land," 102.

27. Barnwell, *History of an American Family*, 71–72; McFeely, *Yankee Stepfather*, 96–100, 130–34, 147; Howard, *Autobiography of Oliver Otis Howard*, 2: 230–31; Westwood, "Sherman Marched—and Proclaimed," 44–46; McGuire, "Hands on the Land," 107; *New York Daily Tribune*, December 21, 1865

28. Westwood, "Sherman Marched—and Proclaimed," 46–48; McFeely, *Yankee Stepfather*, 226–27; Saxton Papers, Willard Saxton Diary, January 9, 1866; McGuire, "Hands on the Land," 107–16; *New York Daily Tribune*, December 21, 1865; Davis, "New South's First City," 298–305; Rose, *Rehearsal for Reconstruction*, 350–57

29. Taylor, *Reminiscences of My Life in Camp*, 115–18.

30. Holland, *Letters and Diary of Laura M. Towne*, 169; McFeely, *Yankee Stepfather*, 227–28; Saxton Papers, Willard Saxton Diary, January, 14, 17, 18, 22, 23, 1866.

31. Saxton, "Report of the Joint Committee" (website).

32. Cullum, *Officers and Graduates of West Point*, 2: 239–40; "Rufus Saxton" (website).

33. Edgar, *South Carolina*, 379; *New South*, May 20, 1865; June 3, 1865; Andrews, *South since the War*, 56–57; Holland, *Letters and Diary of Laura M. Towne*, 167.

CHAPTER 19: THE DISTRICT DIVIDED

1. Zuczek, *State of Rebellion*, 21, 32–38; Edgar, *South Carolina*, 384–86.

2. Bennett is sometimes referred to as a brigadier general, but this was his brevet rank. His actual rank was colonel. Holland, *Letters and Diary of Laura M. Towne*, 173; *New South*, August 25, 1866. By 1866 the only newspaper in Beaufort County had moved from Hilton Head Island to Beaufort, which was the headquarters of the occupation garrison and was rapidly reestablishing itself as the center of commerce for the Sea Islands. The *New South* also acquired a new editor and proprietor, James Thompson, who was to remain Beaufort's principal journalist for more than a decade. He had operated the newspaper the *Free South* in Beaufort during the war. Thompson was an early member of "Gideon's Band" as was his sister, Matilda (Tilly), who married General Rufus Saxton. Rose, *Rehearsal for Reconstruction*, 78.

3. Trinckley, "Indian and Freedmen Occupation," 99–104; McGuire, "Hands on the Land, 132–33.

4. McGuire, "Hands on the Land," 23–23; Saville, *Work of Reconstruction*, 191; "Mary Jenkins Place" picture in Rowland, Moore, and Rogers, *History of Beaufort County*, 1: following p. 288.

5. McGuire, "Hands on the Land," 237–41.

6. Taylor, Mathews, and Powers, *Leverett Letters*, 408; Barnwell, *History of an American Family*, 76–77, 220–21; Spieler, "Travel Was Difficult."

7. William Nelson Pendleton Memoirs, 443.

8. Spieler, "Hamilton's Post War Return."

9. Holland, *Letters and Diary of Laura M. Towne*, 167.

10. Spieler, "Sea Island Families Suffered Tragedies."

11. *Beaufort Republican,* January 11, 1872.
12. *Beaufort Republican,* May 1, 1873.
13. Spieler, "Hamilton's Post War Return."
14. Barnwell, *History of an American Family,* 263–65.
15. Davis, *Rhett,* 570–73.
16. Barnwell, *History of an American Family,* 2356–56.
17. U.S. Direct Tax Cases.
18. *New South,* April 22, 1865; Holland, *Letters and Diary of Laura M. Towne,* 159, 162, 167.
19. Abbott, *Freedmen's Bureau in South Carolina,* 12–15; *Beaufort Republican,* October 12, 1871; Taylor, *Negro in South Carolina,* 85–90; Abbott, *Reconstruction in South Carolina,* 84–86; Rose, *Rehearsal for Reconstruction,* 78.
20. Abbott, *Freedmen's Bureau in South Carolina,* 87–93; Taylor, *Negro in South Carolina,* 84–90; Rose, *Rehearsal for Reconstruction,* 372–73; Miller, *Gullah Statesman,* 44.
21. Davis, "Bankless in Beaufort," 25–45; Simkins and Woody, *South Carolina during Reconstruction,* 270–72; Abbott, *Freedmen's Bureau,* 22, 109–11; Taylor, *Negro in South Carolina,* 68–69; *Beaufort Republican,* October 12, November 2, 1871; September 25, 1873.
22. Underwood, *Constitution of South Carolina,* 4: 9–11.
23. Petty, *Growth and Distribution of Population,* 228; Miller, *Gullah Statesman,* 44–45.
24. As a minister for the Missionary Society of the Methodist Episcopal Church, Reverend Newcomb had returned to Beaufort in 1867 and took over the mission church at Prince and West Streets. In charge of the Beaufort Methodist Circuit, he upped membership from 159 to 739 and established three churches and six preaching places. After a brief time ministering in Florida he was named customs collector for the port of Beaufort, where he died of yellow fever on October, 12, 1871, and was buried in the graveyard of the Wesley Methodist Episcopal Church on West Street. Newcomb, *Genealogical Memoir of the Newcomb Family* (website); Saville, *Work of Reconstruction,* 175: "Journal of Reverend George Newcomb in Beaufort, South Carolina, October 11, 1867–March 30, 1868," copy in possession of Mr. Gerhard Spieler.
25. Simkins and Woody, *South Carolina during Reconstruction,* 90–95; Underwood, *Constitution of South Carolina,* 4: 10–14.
26. Underwood, *Constitution of South Carolina,* 4: 18.
27. Miller, *Gullah Statesman,* 49; *Beaufort Republican,* July 3, 1873; *Port Royal Commercial and Beaufort Republican,* October 30, 1873.
28. Underwood, *Constitution of South Carolina,* 2: 48.
29. *Beaufort Republican and Sea Island Chronicle,* May 21, 1870.
30. Bailey, Morgan, and Taylor, *South Carolina Senate,* 3: 1894–1915; Edgar, Bailey, and Moore, *South Carolina House of Representatives,* 1: 408, 450.
31. Bailey, *Biographical Directory,* 3: 1482–85; Pearson, *Letters from Port Royal,* 268; Miller, *Gullah Statesman,* 7–9, 164–66, 188;
32. Tindall, *South Carolina Negroes,* 11, 60, 81, 145–46; Gatewood, "Remarkable Misses Rollin"; Rose, *Rehearsal for Reconstruction,* 390–404; Miller, *Gullah Statesman,* 44, 133–35, 151–52, 206–10; Taylor, *Negro in South Carolina,* 127, 141–42, 155, 294, 303–4; Simkins and Woody, *South Carolina during Reconstruction,* 368; Whipper, Civil War Pension Records and Compiled Military Records.
33. Bailey, Morgan, and Taylor, *South Carolina Senate,* 1: 574–75; Tindall, *South Carolina Negroes,* 17; Miller, *Gullah Statesman,* 44, 87, 105.

34. Bailey, Morgan, and Taylor, *South Carolina Senate*, 2: 1114–16; Tindall, *South Carolina Negroes*, 48, Miller, *Gullah Statesman*, 165, 206–14.

35. Bryant, *Negro Lawmakers in the South Carolina Legislature*, 15–17, 19, 21–22, 38, 68; Bailey, Morgan, and Taylor, *South Carolina Senate*, 2: 1353–85; Edgar, Bailey, and Moore, *South Carolina House of Representatives*, 1: 412–16; 424–37.

36. *Beaufort Republican*, November 2, December 7, 1871, January 4, 1872.

37. *Beaufort Republican*, July 11, 1872, August 14, 1873; *Port Royal Standard and Commercial*, July 6, 1876; *Beaufort Tribune and Port Royal Commercial*, June 21, 1877.

38. *Beaufort Tribune and Port Royal Commercial*, May 31, 1877.

39. *Beaufort Republican and Sea Island Chronicle*, August 20, 1874.

40. *Charleston News and Courier*, January 2, 1880; Simon, *Papers of Ulysses S. Grant*, 30: 345. The authors are grateful to Stephen G. Hoffius for drawing their attention to the *News and Courier* article.

CHAPTER 20: DECADES OF ENTERPRISE, 1873–1893

1. *New South*, June 16, August 11, 1866; *Beaufort Republican and Sea Island Chronicle*, May 21, 1870; *Beaufort Republican*, October 12, 1871; *Beaufort Tribune and Port Royal Commercial*, January 4, 1877; *Port Royal Commercial*, October 30, 1873.

2. *Beaufort Republican*, September 5, 1872, June 26, September 4, 1873; *Beaufort Tribune and Port Royal Commercial*, July 12, 1877.

3. *Beaufort Tribune and Port Royal Commercial*, January 4, 1877.

4. *Beaufort Crescent*, September 11, 1879; *Port Royal Standard and Commercial*, April 20, 1876; *Beaufort Republican*, September 17, 1872; *Beaufort Tribune and Port Royal Commercial*, April 19, 1877; Tetzlaff, *Cultivating a New South*, 115.

5. *Beaufort Tribune and Port Royal Commercial*, August 9, September 20, 1877.

6. Baumhofer, "Economic Changes in St. Helena's Parish," 1–13.

7. State Board of Agriculture, *South Carolina*, 31, 663–68.

8. *Port Royal Commercial*, October 30, 1873.

9. Johnson, "Beaufort and the Sea Islands," *Beaufort Republican*, March 6, 1873; Williams, *Railroads and Sawmills*, 20–21.

10. *Beaufort Republican*, March 6, 1873; Williams, *Varnville*, 22; Wilson and Fiske, *Appleton's Cyclopedia of American Biography*, 1: 83–84; *History of Rock County*, 618, 644, 758–59; Cutter, *New England Families*, 1: 179; Davis, "South's First City," Appendix I; *National Encyclopedia of American Biography*, 11: 417.

11. *Beaufort Republican*, March 21, April 4, April 18, April 25, May 9, May 23, June 6, June 27, 1872.

12. Williams, *Varnville*, 25. This story was verified in 1922 by Mrs. Sallie Richardson of Allendale, wife of Major Richardson and one of the first passengers on the railroad in 1872. She gave a speech in Allendale on the fiftieth anniversary of the arrival of the railroad line. *Beaufort Republican*, July 4, 1872.

13. *Beaufort Republican*, November 21, December 19, 1872, January 16, 1873.

14. *Beaufort Republican*, March 6, 1873; Williams, *Varnville*, 25–29.

15. *Beaufort Republican*, April 17, 1873; Williams, *Varnville*, 31.

16. *Beaufort Republican*, April 24, May 1, June 19, 1873.

17. *Port Royal Commercial*, October 23, 1873; *Port Royal Standard and Commercial*, March 23, 1876; *Beaufort Republican*, April 17, 1873; *Beaufort Tribune and Port Royal Commercial*, January 18, 1877.

18. *Beaufort Tribune and Port Royal Commercial,* January 18, January 25, September 6, 1877.

19. *Beaufort Republican,* April 17, September 18, 1873; Williams, *Varnville,* 27.

20. *Port Royal Commercial,* Feburary 26, 1874; *Beaufort Tribune and Port Royal Commercial,* August 9, October 18, 1877; Williams, *Varnville,* 30–32.

21. *Port Royal Standard and Commercial,* April 6, 1876; *Beaufort Tribune and Port Royal Commercial,* August 9, 1877; Moore, *South Carolina in the 1880s,* 212.

22. *Beaufort Republican,* November 30, December 28, 1871, March 21, April 4, September 5, September 19, November 7, 1872, February 6, 1873. Information on D. C. Wilson was also supplied by Mr. And Mrs. Gary Groves, owners of the Cuthbert Inn, and by Mr. And Mrs. Robert Mc C. Wilson of Cedar Grove, New Jersey, great grandson of Duncan C. Wilson.

23. *Beaufort Republican,* April 24, 1873; Bailey, Morgan, and Taylor, *South Carolina Senate,* 2: 1076–77.

24. *Beaufort Republican,* March 21, 1872; *Beaufort Tribune and Port Royal Commercial,* January 11, April 5, May 10, June 28, October 18, 1877.

25. *Beaufort Republican,* July 17, August 7, 1873.

26. Shick and Doyle, "South Carolina Phosphate Boom," 4–6; Simkins and Woody, *South Carolina during Reconstruction,* 305–7.

27. Whitney, "The History of Phosphate Mining in Beaufort County, 1870–1914," 873; *Charleston News and Courier,* September 10, 1903.

28. *Congressional Record,* F. Brotherhood to Colonel William Elliott, October 24, 1888.

29. Shick and Doyle, "South Carolina Phosphate Boom," 20; Whitney, "Phosphate Mining in Beaufort County," 10.

30. *Beaufort Gazette* ; Baldwin Fertilizer Company Conveyance.

31. *Beaufort Republican,* November 16, 1871; Whitney, "Phosphate Mining in Beaufort County," 10.

32. Shick and Doyle, "South Carolina Phosphate Boom," 11–12.

33. *Charleston News and Courier,* October 6, 1963.

34. *Beaufort Republican,* August 7, 1873.

35. *Beaufort Republican,* September 4, November 6, 1873; *Port Royal Commercial,* December 25, 1873.

36. *Beaufort Tribune and Port Royal Commercial,* April 19, 1877.

37. *Beaufort Tribune and Port Royal Commercial,* June 28, 1877.

38. *Beaufort Tribune and Port Royal Commercial,* May 17, May 21, May 31, 1877.

39. Moore, *South Carolina in the 1880s,* 212.

CHAPTER 21: BEAUFORT COUNTY'S MARITIME GOLDEN AGE

1. *Beaufort Republican,* September 18, 1873; *Beaufort Tribune and Port Royal Commercial,* January 4, 1877; December 20, 1877.

2. *Beaufort Republican and Sea Island Chronicle,* May 21, 1870; *Beaufort Republican,* January 4, 1872.

3. *Beaufort Republican,* December 7, 1871, January 4, 1872.

4. *Beaufort Tribune and Port Royal Commercial,* July 26, 1877.

5. *Congressional Record,* Executive Document No. 42, 5–7.

6. *Beaufort Tribune and Port Royal Commercial,* June 14, July 5, August 2, August 16, 1877.

7. *Beaufort Republican,* November 30, 1871, July 5, September 4, 1873; *Beaufort Tribune and Port Royal Commercial,* October 25, November 8, 1877.

8. *Beaufort Republican,* September 19, 1872, August 28, September 4, 1873.

9. *Beaufort Republican,* October 16, October 23, October 30, 1873, May 1, June 20, 1873; *Port Royal Commercial,* November 6, 1873.

10. *Beaufort Republican,* September 4, October 16, 1873; *Port Royal Commercial,* November 30, 1873 ; December 11, December 25, 1873.

11. *Beaufort Tribune and Port Royal Commercial,* August 9, December 20, December 27, 1877.

12. *Beaufort Republican,* May 1, 1873; *Port Royal Commercial and Beaufort Republican,* October 30, 1873; *Port Royal Commercial,* November 20, 1873; *Port Royal Standard and Commercial,* April 6, 1876.

13. *Beaufort Republican,* November 16, 1871, January 25, February 1, 1872.

14. *Beaufort Republican,* August 22, 1872.

15. *Beaufort Republican,* May 15, July 24, July 31, 1873; U.S. Treasury Department, *Annual Statements of the Bureau of Statistics,* 234–35, 248, 262, 682, 805, 834.

16. *Beaufort Republican,* April 4, April 25, October 31, November 21, 1872, January 16, 1873.

17. *Beaufort Republican,* March 6, September 25, October 9, 1873.

18. *Port Royal Commercial,* October 30, 1873; January 1, 1874; *Port Royal Standard and Commercial,* March 23, 1876.

19. *Beaufort Tribune and Port Royal Commercial,* March 1, October 11, 1877; *Beaufort Gazette,* January 27, 1911.

20. Whitney, " History of Phosphates in Beaufort County"; *Beaufort Republican,* April 4, April 25, October 31, 1872; *Beaufort Tribune and Port Royal Commercial,* September 6, 1877; *Port Royal Standard and Commercial,* March 25, 1876.

21. *Palmetto Post,* January 5, 1893.

22. *Beaufort Republican,* February 13, 1873; *Beaufort Tribune and Port Royal Commercial,* September 6, 1877.

23. Burn, *An Island Named Daufuskie,* 187–91; *Beaufort Republican,* February 13, 1873; *Statutes of South Carolina, 1872,* 5.

24. *Beaufort Republican,* January 2, 1873; *Beaufort Tribune and Port Royal Commercial,* September 13, 1877; Cole, *Road to Hunting Island,* 83–90; "Hunting Island High House Project," WJWJ-TV, January 2000. The authors are indebted to Ms. Suzanne Larson, Mr. Paul Keyserling, and WJWJ-TV Beaufort, for their research notes on the history of the Hunting Island Lighthouse.

25. *New South,* May 13, 1865.

26. *Port Royal Commercial,* November 13, November 27, December 18, 1873.

27. *Port Royal Standard and Commercial,* January 13, April 6, April 13, May 11, 1876.

28. *Beaufort Tribune and Port Royal Commercial,* January 4, January 25, 1877.

29. Wilson and Fiske, *Appleton's Cyclopaedia of American Biography,* 4: 49–50; *Beaufort Tribune and Port Royal Commercial,* January 11, 1877.

30. *Beaufort Tribune and Port Royal Commercial,* February 8, April 12, April 19, May 3, 1877.

31. *Beaufort Tribune and Port Royal Commercial,* May 21, July 12, September 5, 1877.

32. *Beaufort Tribune and Port Royal Commercial,* November 15, November 29, December 27, 1877.

33. *Congressional Record,* "Removal of Naval Station," 56–57.

CHAPTER 22: THE COUNTER REVOLUTION OF 1876 AND THE SECESSION OF HAMPTON COUNTY

1. *Beaufort Republican and Sea Island Chronicle,* May 21, 1870; *Beaufort Republican,* November 16, 1871; January 11, 1872; Rose, *Rehearsal for Reconstruction,* 78, 366–67.

2. *Beaufort Republican,* November 9, 1871; June 26, 1873.

3. *Beaufort Republican,* January 4, 1872.

4. *Beaufort Republican,* May 28, May 30, July 4, 1872.

5. *Beaufort Republican,* August 22, 1872.

6. *Beaufort Republican,* September 5, September 12, September 19, October 3, October 10, October 12, 1872.

7. *Beaufort Republican,* October 18, October 24, 1872; *Port Royal Standard and Commercial,* December 23, December 28, December 30, 1875, April 6, 1876.

8. *Beaufort Republican,* July 11, 1872; Edgar, *South Carolina,* 394; Simkins and Woody, *South Carolina during Reconstruction,* 180; Miller, *Gullah Statesman,* 53.

9. *Beaufort Republican,* September 5, 1872; *Port Royal Standard and Commercial,* May 18, 1876.

10. *Beaufort Republican,* February 20, 1873.

11. Simkins and Woody, *South Carolina during Reconstruction,* 157, 178–82; *Beaufort Republican and Sea Island Chronicle,* August 20, 1874.

12. *Port Royal Standard and Commercial,* August 20, 1874.

13. *Beaufort Republican and Sea Island Chronicle,* November 16, 1871, August 20, 1874; *Beaufort Republican,* November 16, 1871.

14. *Beaufort Tribune and Port Royal Commercial,* August 16, 1877.

15. *Beaufort Republican,* November 2, 1871.

16. *Beaufort Republican,* August 1, 1871.

17. *Beaufort Republican,* September 19, 1872.

18. *Beaufort Republican,* September 19, 1872.

19. *Beaufort Tribune and Port Royal Commercial,* May 21, 1877.

20. *Port Royal Standard and Commercial,* May 28, 1876; Simkins and Woody, *South Carolina during Reconstruction,* 504.

21. Chamberlain Papers, Report of Robert Smalls to Governor Daniel H. Chamberlain; Miller, *Gullah Statesman,* 104–6.

22. *Port Royal Standard and Commercial,* September 28, 1876.

23. *Beaufort Tribune and Port Royal Commercial,* January 4, June 28, 1877.

24. *Beaufort Tribune and Port Royal Commercial,* April 19, June 28, 1877.

25. *Port Royal Standard and Commercial,* April 27, May 4, 1876.

26. *Beaufort Tribune and Port Royal Commercial,* June 28, 1877.

27. *Port Royal Standard and Commercial,* April 27, May 18, 1876.

28. Powers, "Community Evolution and Race Relations," 221–22; *Port Royal Commercial,* November 6, 1873.

29. *Port Royal Standard and Commercial,* May 4, June 15, 1876.

30. *Port Royal Standard and Commercial,* July 27, 1876.

31. *Beaufort Tribune and Port Royal Commercial,* February 8, February 15, March 22, 1877.

32. *Beaufort Tribune and Port Royal Commercial,* April 19, 1877.

33. *Beaufort Tribune and Port Royal Commercial,* June 14, 1877.

34. *Beaufort Tribune and Port Royal Commercial,* June 28, 1877; Minutes of the Colleton Hunt Club; Edgar, *South Carolina,* 403.

35. Perry, *Moving Finger of Jasper,* 125–26; Bailey, Morgan, and Taylor, *South Carolina Senate,* 2: 1135–36.

36. *Beaufort Tribune and Port Royal Commercial,* July 19, 1877; Will Elliott Memoir, 4.

37. *Beaufort Tribune and Port Royal Commercial,* November 15, December 6, 1877.

38. Miller, *Gullah Statesman,* 107; Edgar, *South Carolina,* 403.

39. *Beaufort Republican and Sea Island Chronicle,* May 21, 1870.

40. *Port Royal Standard and Commercial,* April 6, 1876.

41. *Port Royal Standard and Commercial,* May 4, 1876.

42. *Port Royal Standard and Commercial,* July 20, 1876.

43. *Port Royal Standard and Commercial,* November 2, 1876; Williams, *Hampton and His Red Shirts,* 325–27.

44. *Port Royal Standard and Commercial,* November 9, 1876.

45. *Port Royal Standard and Commercial,* December 7, 1876; *Beaufort Tribune and Port Royal Commercial,* January 4, March 29, 1877; Edgar, *South Carolina,* 406.

46. *Beaufort Tribune and Port Royal Commercial,* January 11, 1877, 48.

47. *Beaufort Tribune and Port Royal Commercial,* January 18, January 25, March 1, 1877.

48. *Beaufort Tribune and Port Royal Commercial,* April 19, 1877.

49. *Beaufort Tribune and Port Royal Commercial,* April 26, July 26, 1877; Bailey, Morgan, and Taylor, *South Carolina Senate,* 1: 575.

50. *Beaufort Tribune and Port Royal Commercial,* May 10, May 21, June 21, June 21, June 28, 1877.

51. *Beaufort Tribune and Port Royal Commercial,* August 9, 1877.

52. *Beaufort Tribune and Port Royal Commercial,* August 20, September 6, December 13, 1877.

53. *Beaufort Tribune and Port Royal Commercial,* August 30, November 29, 1877.

54. *Beaufort Tribune and Port Royal Commercial,* June 21, June 28, July 12, July 26, August 2, August 9, 1877.

55. *Beaufort Tribune and Port Royal Commercial,* December 13, December 20, 1877; Barnwell, *History of an American Family,* 204–6; Bailey, Morgan, and Taylor, *South Carolina Senate,* 1: 321.

56. *Beaufort Tribune and Port Royal Commercial,* October 4, 1877; October 18, 1877; November 15, 1877; November 28, 1877; December 6, 1877; Miller, *Gullah Statesman,* 116–18, 131–32.

57. Miller, *Gullah Statesman,* 125; Rupert Holland, *Letters and Diary of Laura M. Towne,* 289.

58. Legislative Petitions, 1872. These petitions are all filed under 1872 although some were obviously received in earlier years. They are not otherwise dated.

59. *Beaufort Republican,* August 29, September 19, October 31, November 28, 1872.

60. *Beaufort Tribune and Port Royal Commercial,* January 18, March 29, 1877.

61. *Beaufort Tribune and Port Royal Commercial,* May 10, May 17, 1877.

62. *Beaufort Tribune and Port Royal Commercial,* July 12, 1877.

63. *Beaufort Tribune and Port Royal Commercial,* September 20, 1877.

64. *Beaufort Tribune and Port Royal Commercial,* March 1, October 25, December 6, December 20, 1877; Williams, *Varnville,* 52.

65. *Beaufort Tribune and Port Royal Commercial,* January 11, 1877.

66. Lawrence S. Rowland, *Beaufort Tribune and Port Royal Commercial,* April 5, 1877; interview with Niels Christenson III, October 3, 2000.

67. *Beaufort Tribune and Port Royal Commercial,* July 19, August 9, August 23, 1877.

68. Miller, *Gullah Statesman,* 133, 141; Holland, *Letters and Diary of Laura M. Towne,* 294.

69. Holland, *Letters and Diary of Laura M. Towne,* 289.

70. *The Crescent,* September 11, 1879.

71. Gelston, "Radical vs. Straight Out," 232.

72. Gelston, "Radical vs. Straight Out," 233.

73. Miller, *Gullah Statesman,* 164–66; Gelston, "Radical vs. Straight Out," 235.

74. Miller, *Gullah Statesman,* 182–83; Bailey, Morgan, and Taylor, *South Carolina Senate,* 2: 1114–16, 13.

75. *Palmetto Post,* May 5, 1892; *The State,* November 24, 1892.

76. *Palmetto Post,* July 21, June 9, 1892. This letter might have been written by Robert Smalls.

77. Tindall, *South Carolina Negroes,* 49, 56–58, 286; *Palmetto Post,* September 8, October 6, November 10, 1892; Miller, *Gullah Statesman,* 202–3.

78. *Palmetto Post,* November 10, 1892; November 24, 1892.

Bibliography

MANUSCRIPTS

American Baptist–Samuel Colgate Library, Rochester, N.Y.
Peck Winans Family Collection. Record Group 1483.
Stranger, Elizabeth. Diary and Scrapbook.

Beaufort County Library, Beaufort District Collection, Beaufort, S.C.
Beaufort County Historical Society Papers and Photographs.
Reed Photograph Album.

Boston Public Library, Boston, Mass.
Shaw, Robert Gould. Papers.

Catholic Diocese Of Charleston, Office of the Archives, Charleston, South Carolina.
Madden, Richard. Catholics in South Carolina. Manuscript.

Cornell University Library, Department of Manuscripts and University Archives, Ithaca, New York.
Wilder, Burt. Papers.

Library of Congress, Washington, D.C.
Barton, Clara. Papers.
Chase, Salmon P. Papers.

Massachusetts Historical Society, Boston, Mass.
Fox, Charles. Letterbooks, Papers, Extracts From Letters to My Wife During My Connection with the 55th Mass. 2 vols.

National Archives, Washington, D.C.
Beaufort, S.C., National Cemetery. Consolidated Correspondence File. Hilton Head. Record Group 92.
Chares O. Boutelle to William Reynolds, February 4, 1865. Record Group 19.
Civil Works Map File. Record Group 77.
Consolidated Correspondence for the Quartermaster General. Quartermaster Records for the Department of the South. Record Group 92.
Langley, Landon S. Pension Records. Record Group 137.
"Persons Recommended by the Educational Commission of Boston & Accepted by Edward L. Pierce to aid in the Superintendence & Instruction of Persons of Color at Port Royal" and "Persons Approved by the National Freedmen's Relief Association of New

York, and Accepted by Edward L. Pierce, Special Agent of the Treasury Department." Record Group 366, Port Royal Correspondence.
Pope, Joseph Daniel, to Major General Q. A. Gillmore, June 29, 1865. Miscellaneous Records, Department of the South. Record Group 393, Part 1, Entry 4171.
Records of the Office of the Chief of Engineers. Record Group 77.
Special Orders—Post of Beaufort, September 14 and 19, 1864. Record Group 39.
Special Orders, Department of the South. Record Group 393, Part 1, Entry 4128, Vol. 2/5.
Tubman, Harriet. Pension Records. Record Group 233.
Whipper, William J. Civil War Pension Records. Record Group 137.
———. Compiled Military Records of Volunteer Union Soldiers. Record Group 94.
Wood, Charles P. Manuscript. Pension Files, Washington D.C.

Ohio Historical Society, Columbus, Ohio

Wildman, Samuel. Letter of December 5, 1864. Wildman Family Papers.

Perkins Library, Duke University, Durham, N.C.

Jones, Charles C., Jr. Papers

South Carolina Historical Society, Charleston, S.C.

Compiled Confederate Service Records.
Marcy, Henry Orlando. Diary.
Minutes of the Colleton Hunt Club.

South Carolina State Archives, Columbia, S.C.

Chamberlain, Governor Daniel H. Papers. Report of Robert Smalls to Governor Daniel H. Chamberlain, August 24, 1876.
Jenkins, John. Papers
Legislative Petitions, 1872. Citizens of Beaufort County to the Senate and House for the formation of a new County.
Ninth Census (1870), Beaufort County, Agricultural Schedule
Schedule of Direct Tax, Beaufort District, true copy of U.S. Treasury Record, March 4, 1892
South Carolina Legislature, Reports and Resolutions, 1884
Tillman, Governor Benjamin. Papers. Report of Dr. J.W. Babcock to Governor Benjamin R. Tillman," September 4, 1893.
U.S. Census. Population Schedules, Beaufort District, 8th Census. Microfilm.
U.S. Census. Slave Schedules, Beaufort District, 8th Census. Microfilm.

South Caroliniana Library, University of South Carolina, Columbia, S.C.

Bodine, Lt. A. S. "The Battle of Honey Hill."
Christensen, Frederick. Diary.
Marple, Alfred. Diary and Letters.
DeTreville, Richard. Letter of March 11, 1867.
Elliott, Stephen. Papers.
Elliott, Will. Memoir.
U.S. Direct Tax Cases. Vols. I, II and III, cases numbers 17,206–17,612.

Southern Historical Collection, University of North Carolina Chapel Hill, N.C.

Habersham-Elliott Papers.
Laura M. Towne Diary.

Spieler, Gerhard, Private Collection, Beaufort, S.C.

Baldwin Fertilizer Company Conveyance to Charles F. Borden, July 3, 1899. Register of Mesne Conveyance, Beaufort County.
Pendleton, William Nelson, D.D. Memoirs.
Journal of Reverend George Newcomb in Beaufort, South Carolina, October 11, 1867–March 30, 1868.

United States Military History Institute, Carlisle Army Barracks, Carlisle, Pa.

Barrows, Daniel. Papers.
Burst, James. Letter, June 12, 1863.
Guest, John. Papers.
Hurst Letters. Letter of June 12, 1862
MOLLUS Photograph Collection.

United States Naval Academy Archives, Special Collections and Archives Division, Nimitz Library, Annapolis, Md.

Phoenix, Lieutenant Lloyd. Journal.

University of California Santa Barbara, Special Collections and Archives, Santa Barbara, Calif.

Cook, Edward L. Papers.

Vermont Historical Society, Montpelier, Vt.

Johnson Family of Peacham, Vermont Papers.

West Virginia University Library, Morgantown, W.V.

Appleton, John W. M. Letterbook and Journal.

Wisconsin Historical Society, Madison, Wisc.

Allen, William F. Diary.
Brisbane, William Henry. Diary.

Yale University Library, Manuscripts and Archives, New Haven, Conn.

Saxton, Rufus, and S. Willard. Papers.

NEWSPAPERS

Beaufort Crescent
Beaufort Free South
Beaufort Gazette
Beaufort Low Country Ledger
Beaufort Republican and Sea Island Chronicle
Beaufort Tribune and Port Royal Commercial

Boston Commonwealth
Charleston Daily Courier
Charleston New and Courier
Charleston Sunday News
Frank Leslie's Illustrated Newspaper
Hartford Courant
Hartford Weekly
Hilton Head New South
New York Herald
New York National Anti-Slavery Standard
New York Times
New York Tribune
Philadelphia Commonwealth
Philadelphia Inquirer
Philadelphia Weekly Times
Port Royal (Hilton Head) *New South*
Port Royal (Hilton Head) *Palmetto Herald*
Port Royal Palmetto Post
Port Royal Standard and Commercial
Savannah Republican
Washington National Tribune
Xenia Torchlight

INTERNET SOURCES

"Abraham Lincoln, From His Own Words and Contemporary Accounts." ParkNet, National Park Service. http://www.nps.gov/history/history/online_books/source/sb2/sb2w.htm (accessed April 28, 2013).

Alcorn, Wallace. "William Henry Brisbane Project." http://www.wallacealcorn.org/wallacealcorn.org/William_Henry_Brisbane_Project.html (accessed June 20, 2014).

Apthorp, Lt. Col. William Lee, 34th USCT. "Montgomery's Raids in Florida, Georgia, and South Carolina." *Florida History Online.* University of North Florida. http://www.unf.edu/floridahistoryonline/montgomery/ (accessed Dec. 6, 2012).

"Bands and Musicians of the Civil War." http://americanrevwar.homestead.com/files/civwar/bands.html (accessed September 26. 2009).

Baxley, Lt. Col. Neil. "200 Years of History." Beaufort County Sheriff's Office. http://www.bcso.net/history.htm (accessed April 28, 2013).

"Bummer." Definition in *Wiktionary: A Wiki-Based Open Content Dictionary.* A Wikipedia Project. http://en.wiktionary.org/wiki/bummer (accessed Dec. 12, 2013).

Butt, Israel L. *History of African Methodism in Virginia.* Norfolk, Va.: 1908. Documenting the American South, University of North Carolina. http://docsouth.unc.edu/church/butt/butt.html.

"Church of the Holy Trinity, Jasper County (S.C. Sec. Rds. 13 & 29, Ridgeland vicinity)." National Register Properties in South Carolina. National Register Properties in South Carolina. South Carolina Department of Archives and History. http://www.nationalregister.sc.gov/jasper/S10817727004/index.htm (accessed April 28, 2013).

"Colonel William C. Silliman." GenForum.Genealogy.com. http://genforum.genealogy.com/silliman/messages/614.html (accessed April 28, 2013).

Dhalle, Katherine. "The Battle of Honey Hill." Bits of Blue and Gray: An American Civil War Notebook. http://www.bitsofblueandgray.com/Feb2002.htm (accessed 28 April 2013).

———. "History of the 55th Massachusetts Volunteer Infantry." Lest We Forget website. http://people.coax.net/lwf/55HIST.HTM (accessed April 28, 2013).

"Edward V. Preston." Genealogyfinds.com. http://genealogyfinds.com/cgi-bin/data.cgi?prestonedward (accessed September 27, 2009).

"1st Louisiana Native Guard." *Wikipedia*. http://en.wikipedia.org/wiki/1st_Louisiana_Native_Guard (accessed April 27, 2013).

Franklin, John Hope. "The Emancipation Proclamation: An Act of Justice." *Prologue Magazine* 25, no. 2 (1993), National Archives website, http://www.archives.gov/publications/prologue/1993/summer/emancipation-proclamation.html (accessed April 28, 2013).

"The Galena Generals." East Dubuque Local Area History Project. http://www.eastdbqschools.org/archive/District/LocalAreaHistory/GalenaGeneralslah.htm (accessed June 18, 2014).

"Gilbert Pillsbury." Ancestry.com. http://www.rootsweb.ancestry.com/~nhchs/Preservation/People/Gilbert_Pillsbury.html (accessed April 28, 2013).

"Gillisonville Baptist Church, Jasper County (U.S. Hwy. 278, Gillisonville)." National Register Properties in South Carolina. National Register Properties in South Carolina. South Carolina Department of Archives and History. http://www.nationalregister.sc.gov/jasper/S10817727001/index.htm (accessed April 28, 2013).

"Guide to the Civil War Photograph File 1861–1865 [1880–1889], PR 164." New York Historical Society Museum and Library website. http://dlib.nyu.edu/eadapp/transform?source=nyhs/civilwar.xml&style=nyhs/nyhs.xsl&part=body (accessed 28 April 2013).

"Hon. William E. Wording." Biographical article from unidentified book. University of Wisconsin Library. http://images.library.wisc.edu/WI/EFacs/USAIN/IRW/IRW1872/reference/wi.irw1872.i0010.pdf (accessed February 2, 2009).

Huguenin, Thomas H. "The Journal of Thomas Abram Huguenin: Last Confederate Commander of Fort Sumter." Huguenin-family.com. http://huguenin-family.com/tah.html (accessed Nov. 28, 2012).

"Jim Limber." *Encyclopedia of Virginia*. Virginia Foundation for the Humanities. http://encyclopediavirginia.org/Limber_Jim (accessed April 28, 2013).

"John Celivergos Zachos." Virtual American Biographies. tp://www.famousamericans.net/johncelivergoszachos/ (Accessed Sept. 18, 2006).

"Knowlton, Ebenezer." Biographical Directory of the United States Congress, 1774–Present. http://bioguide.congress.gov/scripts/biodisplay.pl?index=K000294 (accessed Dec. 28, 2013).

"Langford-L Archives." Ancestry.com. http://archiver.rootsweb.ancestry.com/th/read/LANGFORD/1999-09/0937451991 (accessed April 28, 2013).

Langley, Louden S. "Letters of Louden S. Langley before and during the Civil War." Vermont African Americans Correspondence. Vermont in the Civil War. http://vermontcivilwar.org/units/afam/ll.php (accessed April 28, 2013).

"Law Creating the Freedmen's Bureau." Freedmen & Southern Society Project, University of Maryland. http://www.history.umd.edu/freedmen/fbact.htm (accessed April 28, 2013).

"Lem Coley's words from the December 30, 2001, Sunday Service at the UU Fellowship at Stony Brook." Long Island Area Council of U.U. Congregations website. http://www.liacuu.org/SocialJustice/higginsonService.htm (accessed Dec. 4, 2012).

"Letter from William Warren Marple, Lt. Col. 34th USCT, to his brother Alfred Marple in Langhorne, Pennsylvania, describing action during the Battle of Honey Hill, South Carolina, U.S. Civil War." The Marple Website. http://www.marple.com/usctletter.html (accessed April 28, 2013).

Lt. Col. Chipman, Henry L. http://www.geocities.ws/pvtchurch61/2inf/HQ/bio/ChipmanHL.html (accessed Aug. 9, 2014).

The Marple Family in the American Civil War. http://marplecivilwar.troosevelt1904.com/ (accessed 28 April 2013).

"Martha S. Winters—Genealogy." Ancestry.com. http://wc.rootsweb.ancestry.com/cgi-bin/igm.cgi?op=GET&db=mswinters&id=I2254 (accessed April 28, 2013).

"Medal of Honor Recipients, A-L." U.S. Army Center of Military History. http://www.history.army.mil/html/moh/civwaral.html (accessed April 28, 2013).

"Medal of Honor Recipients, M–Z." U.S. Army Center of Military History. http://www.history.army.mil/html/moh/civwarmz.html (accessed April 28, 2013).

"New Castle Courthouse." Living Places website. http://www.livingplaces.com/DE/New_Castle_County/New_Castle_City/New_Castle_Courthouse.html (accessed 28 April 2013).

Newcomb, John Bearse. *Genealogical Memoir of the Newcomb Family.* Chicago: Knight and Leonard, 1874 (text version). Internet Archive. http://www.archive.org/stream/genealogicalmemo00newc/genealogicalmemo00newc_djvu.txt (accessed April 28, 2013).

"127th Infantry Regiment Civil War National Volunteers; Monitors." New York State Military Museum. http://dmna.state.ny.us/historic/reghist/civil/infantry/127thInf/127thInfMain.htm (accessed April 28, 2013).

"102nd United States Colored Troops." Everything2 website. http://everything2.com/title/102nd+United+States+Colored+Troops (accessed April 28, 2013)

"The Preliminary Emancipation Proclamation (issued September 22, 1862)," New York State Library. http://www.nysl.nysed.gov/library/features/ep/ (accessed Jan. 21, 2009).

"Private Miles O'Reilly." Poetry and Music of the War Between the States. http://www.civilwarpoetry.org/authors/oreilly.htm (accessed April 27, 2013).

"Rufus Saxton." Find a Grave, http://www.findagrave.com/cgi-bin/fg.cgi?page=gr&GRid=5885503

Saxton, Rufus. "Report of the Joint Committee on Reconstruction (Washington, 1866)." http://www.drbronsontours.com/bronsongeneralrufussaxtontestimonyreportofjointcommitteeonreconstruction.html ((accessed April 28, 2013).

"Scoundrel or Scapegoat?" Review of *Prince of Carpetbaggers* by Jonathan Daniels. *Time* (online), July 14, 1958. http://www.time.com/time/magazine/article/0,9171,868621,00.html (accessed April 28, 2013).

Smith, A. B. Wisconsin Historical Society website. http://www.wisconsinhistory.org/wmh/pdf/winter05_dunley.pdf (accessed January 15, 2009).

"South Carolina Cavalry Units in the War of the Rebellion." http://corktree.tripod.com/South_Carolina_Cavalry_Units_in_the_War_of_the_Rebellion (accessed April 28, 2013).

"Stony Creek Independent Presbyterian Chapel of Prince William Parish, Hampton County (McPhersonville)." National Register Properties in South Carolina. National Register Properties in South Carolina. South Carolina Department of Archives and

History. http://www.nationalregister.sc.gov/hampton/S10817725009/index.htm (accessed April 28, 2013).

Tagg, Larry. "Major General Henry Warner Slocum." Excerpt from *The Generals of Gettysburg: The Leaders of America's Greatest Battle*. 1998. Reprint, Boston: DaCapo Press, 2003. http://www.rocemabra.com/~roger/tagg/generals/general30.html.

"Thomas Jefferson Trowell." Find a Grave. http://www.findafrave.com/cgi-bin/fg.cgi?page=gr&Grid=119372478 (accessed Aug. 11, 2014).

"Time Line of Martin R. Delany's Life 1812–1885." West Virginia University Libraries. http://www.libraries.wvu.edu/delany/earlyage.htm (accessed Dec. 12, 2012).

Todd, Glenda McWhirter. "First Alabama Cavalry U.S.A.: Homage to Patriotism." http://www.lwfaam.net/todd/1stalacav.htm (accessed April 28, 2013).

"26th Infantry, US Colored Troops." New York State Military Museum. http://dmna.state.ny.us/historic/reghist/civil/other/coloredTroops/coloredTroopsMain.htm#26thInf (accessed April 28, 2013).

"26th USCT Commanding Officer Killed." New York Correction History Society. http://www.correctionhistory.org/html/chronicl/cw-usct/26th-usct-on-parade.html (accessed April 28, 2013).

"Union Regimental Histories, New York: 144th Regiment Infantry." The Civil War Archive. http://www.civilwararchive.com/Unreghst/unnyin10.htm#1

Wooster, Kenneth Jennings. "124th New York Volunteer Infantry: American Guard; Orange Blossoms." http://skaneateles.org/124_inf/124_inf.html (accessed April 28, 2013).

PRINTED SOURCES

Abbott, Martin. *The Freedmen's Bureau in South Carolina, 1865–1872*. Chapel Hill: University of North Carolina Press, 1967.

Abstract of the Cruise of U.S. Steam Frigate Wabash Bearing the Flag of Rear Admiral S. F. Du Pont 1861, '62 & '63. New York: Edward D. Jenkins, 1863.

Albert, Allen D., comp. *History of the Forty-Fifth Regiment Pennsylvania Veteran Volunteer Infantry, 1861–1865*. Williamsport, Pa.: Grit Publishing Company, 1912.

Ammen, Daniel. "Du Pont and the Port Royal Expedition." In *Battles and Leaders of the Civil War*, 1: 671–91. 4 vols. 1887; reprint, New York: Thomas Yoseloff, 1956.

Anders, Leslie. *The Eighteenth Missouri*. Indianapolis: Bobbs-Merrill, 1968.

Andrews, Sidney. *The South since the War*. 1866; reprint, Boston: Houghton Mifflin, 1971.

Ash, Stephen V. *Firebrand of Liberty*. New York: W. W. Norton, 2008.

Atlas to Accompany the Official Records of the Union and Confederate Armies. Washington, D.C.: U.S. Government Printing Office, 1891–95.

Bache, A. D. "Notes on the Coast of the United States." Section V, Coast of Carolina, June 1861, pp. 15–32. Record Group 45, National Archives, Washington, D.C.

Bailey, N. Louise, Mary L. Morgan, and Carolyn R. Taylor, eds. *Biographical Directory of the South Carolina Senate, 1776–1986*. 3 vols. Columbia: University of South Carolina Press, 1986.

Baird, George W. *The 32nd Regiment, U.S.C.T. at the Battle of Honey Hill*. Boston: n.p., 1889.

Baker, Gary R. *Cadets in Gray*. Columbia, S.C.: Palmetto Bookworks, 1989.

Baptist Home Missions in North America. New York: Baptist Home Mission Rooms, 1883.

Barlow, Albert Rowe. *Company G: A Record of One Company of the 157th N.Y. Vols. in the War of the Rebellion*. Syracuse, N.Y.: A. W. Hall, 1899.

Barnwell, Stephen B. *A History of an America Family*. Marquette, Mich.: privately printed, 1969.

Barrows, Daniel Drew. Papers. *Pamphlet 1673*. Parris Island Museum, Parris Island, S.C.

Basler, Roy P., ed. *Collected Works of Abraham Lincoln*. 8 vols. New Brunswick, N.J.: Rutgers University Press, 1953–1955.

Baxley, Neil. *No Prouder Fate: The Story of the 11th South Carolina Volunteer Infantry*. Bloomington, Ind.: Author House, 2005.

Baumhofer, Hermine Munz. "Economic Changes in St. Helena's Parish, 1860–1870." *South Carolina Historical and Genealogical Magazine* 50, no. 1 (1949): 1–13.

Bearss, Edwin C. "Joseph Wheeler." In *The Confederate General*, edited by William C. Davis and Julie Hoffman, 6: 124–29. Harrisburg, Pa.: National Historical Society, 1991.

Beecher, Herbert W. *History of the First Light Battery Connecticut Volunteers, 1861–1865*. 2 vols. New York: A. T. De La Mare, 1901.

Bell, Daniel J. *The Strongest Position I Ever Saw in My Life: Mapping and Site Study of the Rivers Bridge Battlefield*. A Project Report for the American Battleground Protection Program Draft—December 16, 2004, South Carolina Park Service, South Carolina Department of Parks, Recreation and Tourism.

Berlin, Ira, Steven F. Miller, Joseph P. Reidy, and Leslie S. Rowland, eds. *Documentary History of Emancipation*. Series 1, Vol. 2, *The Wartime Genesis of Free Labor: The Lower South*. New York: Cambridge University Press, 1993.

Billingsley, Andrew. *Yearning to Breathe Free: Robert Smalls of South Carolina and His Families*. Columbia: University of South Carolina Press, 2007.

Bolster, W. Jeffrey, and Hilary Anderson. *Soldiers, Sailors, Slaves, and Ships: The Civil War Photographs of Henry P. Moore*. Concord: New Hampshire Historical Society, 1999.

Botume, Elizabeth Hyde. *First Days Amongst the Contrabands*. 1893; reprint, New York: Arno Press, 1968.

Bowditch, Charles P. "War Letters of Charles P. Bowditch." *Massachusetts Historical Society Proceedings* 57 (February–April 1924): 412–73.

Boyle, John R. *Soldiers True: The Story of the One hundred and eleventh Regiment Pennsylvania Veteran Volunteers, and of its Campaigns in the War for the Union 1861–1865*. New York: Eaton and Mains, 1903.

Boyle, J. R. *Reminiscences of the Civil War*. Columbia, S.C.: Bryan Printing, 1890.

Bradford, Sarah H. *Harriet: The Moses of Her People*. 1869; reprint, New York: Citadel Press, 2000.

Bradley, George S. *The Star Corps; or, Notes of an Army Chaplain, During Sherman's Famous "March to the Sea."* Milwaukee: Jermain and Brighton, 1865.

Bragg, William Harris. "The Fight at Honey Hill." *Civil War Times Illustrated* 22 (January 1984): 12–19.

Bragg, William Harris, and William R. Scaife. *Joe Brown's Pets: The Georgia Militia, 1861–1865*. Macon, Ga.: Mercer University Press, 2004.

Brennan, Patrick. *Secessionville: Assault on Charleston*. Campbell, Calif.: Savas Publishing, 1996.

Brewster, Jonathan McDuffie. *Centennial Record of Freewill Baptists 1780–1880*. Dover: The Printing Establishment, 1881.

Brown, Robert. *Battle of Pocotaligo, South Carolina*. Sumter, S.C.: n.p., n.d.

Browning, Robert M., Jr. *Success Is All That Was Expected: The South Atlantic Blockading Squadron during the Civil War*. Washington, D.C.: Brassey, 2002.

Burn, Billie. *An Island Named Daufuskie.* Spartanburg, S.C.: Reprint Company, 1991.
Butler, Benjamin F. *Autobiography and Personal Reminiscences of Major General Benjamin F. Butler: Butler's Book.* Boston: A. M. Thayer, 1892.
Bryant, Elias A. *The Diary of Elias A. Bryant.* Concord, N.H.: Rumford Press, n.d.
Bryant, Lawrence C. *Negro Lawmakers in the South Carolina Legislature,* 1868–1902. Orangeburg, S.C.: Orangeburg School of Graduate Studies, South Carolina State College, 1968.
Caldwell, Charles K. *The Old Sixth Regiment, Its War Record 1861–65.* New Haven, Conn.: Tittle, Morehouse and Taylor, 1875.
Campbell, Jacqueline Glass. *When Sherman Marched North from the Sea: Resistance on the Confederate Home Front.* Chapel Hill: University of North Carolina Press, 2003.
Cathcart, William, ed. *Baptist Encyclopedia.* Philadelphia: Louis H. Everts, 1881.
Chisman, James A., ed. *76th Regiment Pennsylvania Volunteer Infantry Keystone Zouaves: The Personal Recollections 1861–1865 of Sergeant John A. Porter Company "B."* Wilmington: Broadfoot Publishing, 1988.
Cisco, Walter Brian. *Wade Hampton: Confederate Warrior, Conservative Statesman.* Washington, D.C.: Brassey's Inc., 2004.
The Civil War: Its Music and Its Sounds. Liner notes. 2 vols. Mercury Records. 33 1/3 rpm, 1960.
Clark, Charles M. *The History of the Thirty-ninth Regiment Illinois Volunteer Infantry (Yates Phalanx).* Chicago: Veteran Association of the Regiment, 1889.
Clement, Christopher O., Stephen R. Wise, Steven D. Smith, and Ramona M. Grunden. "Mapping the Defense of the Charleston to Savannah Railroad Civil War Earthworks in Beaufort and Jasper Counties, South Carolina." Report Prepared for the American Battlefields Protection Program, Grant #GA-2255–98–016, February 2000.
Coffin, Charles Carleton. *The Boys of 1861 or Four Years of Fighting.* Boston: Dana Estes and Company, 1896.
Coffman, Richard M., Kurt D. Graham. *To Honor These Men: A History of the Phillips Georgia Legion Infantry Battalion.* Macon, Ga.: Mercer University Press, 2007.
Colcock, Charles J., Jr. "The Battle of Honey Hill." *Charleston Sunday News,* December 10, 1899.
Cole, Nathan. *The Road to Hunting Island.* Dover, N.H.: Arcadia Publishing, 1997.
Committee of the Regimental Association, comp. *The Story of One Regiment: The Eleventh Maine Infantry Volunteers in the War of the Rebellion.* New York: J. J. Little, 1896.
Congressional Record. 51st Cong., Executive Document No. 42, December 7, 1889.
———. 51st Cong., 1st sess., House of Representatives, Executive Document No. 42, Ltr. F. Brotherhood to Colonel William Elliott, U.S. Congress, October 24, 1888.
———. 56th Cong., 2nd sess., Senate Document No. 188, "Removal of Naval Station, Port Royal, S.C."
Connelly, Thomas L. *The Marble Man: Robert E. Lee and His Image in American Society.* New York: Alfred A. Knopf, 1977.
Conrad, Earl. *Harriet Tubman.* New York: Paul S. Eriksson, 1943.
Conrad, James L. *The Young Lions: Confederate Cadets at War.* Columbia: University of South Carolina Press, 2004.
Cooper, William J., Jr. *Jefferson Davis, American.* New York: Vintage, 2000.
Copp, Eldridge, *Reminiscences of the War.* Nashua, N.H.: Telegraph Publishing, 1911.
Cornish, Dudley. *The Sable Arm.* New York: W. W. Norton, 1966.

Courtenay, William A. "Heroes of Honey Hill." *Southern Historical Society Papers* 26 (1898): 232–41.
Crabb, Christopher G. *Facing Sherman in South Carolina: March through the Swamp.* Charleston: History Press, 2010.
Craven, J. J. "Report Extract." In *Medical and Surgical History of the War of the Rebellion.* Vol. 1, 334–39. Washington, D.C.: U.S. Government Printing Office, 1870.
Crowninshield, Benjamin W. *A History of the First Regiment of Massachusetts Cavalry Volunteers.* Boston: Houghton, Mifflin and Compnay, 1891.
Cullum, George Washington. *Biographical Register of the Officers and Graduates of West Point.* 2 vols. Boston: Houghton Mifflin, 1891.
Culp, Edward C. *The 25th Ohio Veteran Volunteer Regiment.* Topeka, Kans.: George W. Crane, 1885.
Cuthbert, Robert B., and Stephen G. Hoffius, eds. *Northern Money, Southern Land: The Lowcountry Plantation Sketches of Chlotilde R. Martin.* Columbia: University of South Carolina Press, 2009.
Cutter, William Richard. *New England Families, Genealogical and Memorial.* Vol. 1. New York: Lewis Historical Publishing, 1914.
Currant, Richard N., ed. *Encyclopedia of the Confederacy.* 4 vols. New York: Simon and Schuster, 1993.
Dahlgren, Madeline V. *Memoirs of John A. Dahlgren.* Boston: Osgood, 1882.
Daniels, Jonathan. *Prince of Carpetbaggers.* Philadelphia: J. B. Lippincott, 1958.
Davis, John Martin. "Bankless in Beaufort: A Reexamination of the 1873 Failure of the Freedmen's Savings Branch at Beaufort, South Carolina." *South Carolina Historical Magazine* 104 (2003): 25–45.
———. "The New South's First City: Occupied Beaufort, South Carolina 1861 to 1865." Manuscript in possession of authors.
Davis, William C. *Rhett: The Turbulent Times of a Fire-Eater.* Columbia. University of South Carolina Press, 2001.
———, ed. *Dear Wife: Letters of a Civil War Soldier.* Louisville, Ky.: Sulgrave Press, n.d.
Davis, W. W. H. *History of the 104th Pennsylvania.* Philadelphia: Rodgers, 1866.
Dedmondt, Glenn. *The Flags of Civil War South Carolina.* Gretna, La.: Pelican, 2000.
De La Cova, Antonio Rafael. "Ambrosio Jose Gonzales: A Cuban Confederate Colonel." Ph.D. diss., West Virginia University, 1994.
———. *Cuban Confederate General. The Life of Ambrosio Jose' Gonzales.* Columbia: University of South Carolina Press, 2003.
Denison, Frederick. *Shot and Shell: The Third Rhode Island Heavy Artillery Regiment in the Rebellion 1861–1865.* Providence, R.I.: J. A. and R. A. Reid, 1879.
Dictionary of American Biography. New York, Charles Scribner's Sons, 1935.
Dickey, Luther S. *History of the Eighty-fifth Regiment Pennsylvania Volunteer Infantry 1861–1865.* New York: J. C. and W. E. Powers, 1915.
Dowdey, Clifford, ed. *Wartime Papers of R. E. Lee.* New York: Bramhall House, 1961.
Drayton, Percival. *Naval Letters from Percival Drayton: 1861–1865.* Presented to the New York Public Library in 1906 by Gertrude Hoyte.
Duncan, Russell, ed. *Blue-Eyed Child of Fortune: The Civil War Letters of Robert Gould Shaw.* Athens: University of Georgia Press, 1992.
Dunley, Ruth. "A. D. Smith: Knight Errant of Radical Democracy." Ph.D. diss., University of Ottawa, 2008.

———. "In Search of A. D. Smith." *Wisconsin Magazine of History* 89, no. 2 (2005–06): 16–27.
Dyer, Frederick H. *A Compendium of the War of the Rebellion*. Dayton, Ohio: Morningside, 1978.
Dyer, John P. *From Shiloh to San Juan: The Life of Fightin' Joe Wheeler*. Baton Rouge: Louisiana State University Press, 1961.
Ecelbarger, Gary L. *Frederick W. Lander: The Great American Soldier*. Baton Rouge: Louisiana State University Press, 2000.
Edgar, Walter B., N. Louise Bailey, and Alexander Moore, eds. *Biographical Directory of the South Carolina House of Representatives*. 5 vols. Columbia: University of South Carolina Press, 1974–1993.
Edgar, Walter. *South Carolina: A History*. Columbia: University of South Carolina Press, 1998.
Eldridge, Daniel. *The Third New Hampshire Regiment*. Boston: E. B. Stillings, 1893.
Emerson, W. Eric. *Sons of Privilege: The Charleston Light Dragoons in the Civil War*. Columbia: University of South Carolina Press, 2005.
Emilio, Luis F. *A Brave Black Regiment: History of the Fifty-Fourth Massachusetts Volunteer Infantry, 1863–1865*. 1894; reprint, New York: Arno Press, 1969.
Epler, Percy H. *The Life of Clara Barton*. New York: Macmillan, 1927.
Farenholt, Oscar. *The Monitor Catskill: A Year's Reminiscences*. San Francisco: Shannon, 1912.
Fisk, Joel C., and William H. D. Blake. *A Condensed History of the 56th New York Veteran Volunteer Infantry*. Newburgh, N.Y.: Journal Printing House, 1906.
Foner, Eric. "The Meaning of Freedom in the Age of Emancipation." *Journal of American History* 81, no. 2 (1994): 438–47.
———. *Reconstruction: America's Unfinished Revolution, 1863–1877*. New York: Harper and Row, 1988.
Foote, John A. "Notes on the Life of Admiral Foote." In *Battles and Leaders of the Civil War*, 1: 347. 4 vols. 1887; reprint, New York: Thomas Yoseloff, 1956.
Ford, Worthington Chauncey, ed. *A Cycle of Adams Letters 1861–1862*. 2 vols. Boston: Houghton Mifflin, 1920.
Fox, Charles Bernard. *Record of the Service of the Fifty-fifth Regiment of Massachusetts Volunteer Infantry*. Cambridge, Mass.: John Wilson and Son, 1868.
Freeman, Douglas Southall. *R. E. Lee*. 4 vols. New York: Charles Scribner's Sons, 1951.
French, J. Clement, and Edward Cary. *The Trip of the Steamer Oceanus to Fort Sumter and Charleston, S.C.* Brooklyn, N.Y.: Union Steam Printing Office, 1865.
French, Mansfield Joseph. *Ancestors and Descendants of Samuel French, the Joiner, of Stratford, Connecticut*. Ann Arbor: Edwards Brothers Inc., 1940.
Gatewood, Willard B., Jr. "The Remarkable Misses Rollin: Black Women in Reconstruction South Carolina." *South Carolina Historical Magazine* 92, no. 3 (1991): 172–88.
Gaustad, Edwin S., and Mark A. Noll, eds. *A Documentary History of Religion in America to 1877*. Grand Rapids, Mich.: Wm. B. Eerdmans, 2003.
Gavin, William Gilfillan. *Campaigning with the Roundheads: The History of the Hundredth Pennsylvania Veteran Volunteer Infantry Regiment in the American Civil War 1861–1865. The Roundhead Regiment*. Dayton, Ohio: Morningside, 1989.
Gelston, Arthur Lewis. "Radical vs. Straight Out in Post-Reconstruction Beaufort County." *South Carolina Historical Magazine* 75, no. 4 (1974): 225–37.
Gibson, Charles Dana and E. Kay Gibson, compilers. *Dictionary of Transports and Combatant Vessels Steam and Sail Employed by the Union Army 1861–1868*. Camden, Me.: Ensign Press, 1995.

Gibson, John M. *Those 163 Days: A Southern Account of Sherman's March from Atlanta to Raleigh.* New York: Bramhall House, 1961.

Gillmore, Quincy A. "The Siege and Capture of Fort Pulaski." In *Battles and Leaders of the Civil War,* 2: 1–12. 4 vols. 1887; reprint, New York: Thomas Yoseloff, 1956.

———. *Siege and Reduction of Fort Pulaski, Georgia, February, March, and April, 1862.* New York: D. Van Nostrand, 1862.

Girardi, Robert I., ed., *Campaigning With Uncle Billy: The Civil War Memoirs of Sgt. Lyman S. Widney Infantry.* Victoria, British Columbia: Trafford Publishing, 2008.

Glatthaar, Joseph T. *The March to the Sea and Beyond: Sherman's Troops in the Savannah and Carolinas Campaigns.* New York: New York University Press, 1985.

Gleaves, Albert. *Life and Letters of Rear Admiral Stephen B. Luce.* New York: Putnam, 1925.

Graydon, Nell S. *Tales of Beaufort.* Orangeburg: Sandlapper, 1997.

Guterman, Benjamin. "Doing 'Good Brave Work': Harriet Tubman's Testimony at Beaufort, South Carolina." *Prologue* 32, no. 3 (2000): 154–65.

Hall, Henry, and James Hall. *Cayuga in the Field.* Syracuse, N.Y.: Truair, Smith and Company, 1873.

Halliburton, Lloyd, ed. *Saddle Soldiers: The Civil War Correspondence of General William Stokes of the 4th South Carolina Cavalry.* Orangeburg, S.C.: Sandlapper, 1993.

Harris, Mark W. "Higginson, Thomas Wentworth." In *Historical Dictionary of Unitarian Universalism,* 243–45. Lanham, Md.: Scarecrow Press, 2004.

Harwell, Richard, and Philip N. Racine, eds. *The Fiery Trail: A Union Officer's Account of Sherman's Last Campaign.* Knoxville: University of Tennessee Press, 1986.

Haydon, F. Stansburg. *Military Ballooning during the Early Civil War.* Baltimore: Johns Hopkins University Press, 2000.

Hayes, John D., ed. *Samuel Francis Du Pont: A Selection from His Civil War Letters.* 3 vols. Ithaca, N.Y.: Cornell University Press, 1969.

Hazen, William B. *A Narrative of Military Service.* Boston: Ticknor and Company, 1885.

Hendricks, George Linton. "Union Army Occupation of the Southern Seaboard 1861–1865." Ph.D. diss., Columbia University, 1954.

Hewett, Janet B., ed. *South Carolina Confederate Soldiers 1861–1865, Unit Roster.* 2 vols. Wilmington, N.C.: Broadfoot Publishing, 1998.

———, ed. *Supplement to the Official Records of the Union and Confederate Armies.* Wilmington, N.C.: Broadfoot Publishing, 1997.

Heyl, Eric. *Early American Steamers.* 6 vols. Buffalo: Eric Heyl, 1953–1969.

Higginson, Thomas W. *Army Life in a Black Regiment.* Williamstown, Mass.: Corner House, 1964.

Hight, John J., and Stormont, Gilbert R. *History of the Fifty-eighth Regiment of Indiana Volunteer Infantry.* Princeton, Ind.: Press of the Clarion, 1895.

The History of Rock County, Wisconsin. Chicago: Western Historical Company, 1929.

Hitchcock, Henry. *Marching with Sherman.* New Haven, Conn.: Yale University Press, 1927.

Holland, Rupert Sargeant, ed. *Letters and Diary of Laura M. Towne.* New York: Negro Universities Press, 1969.

Hollis, Belser, and Allen H. Stokes, eds. *Twilight on the South Carolina Rice Fields: Letters of the Heyward Family, 1862–1871.* Columbia: University of South Carolina Press, 2010.

Horan, James D. *Timothy O'Sullivan: America's Forgotten Photographer.* New York: Bonanza Books, 1966.

Howard, Oliver O. *Autobiography of Oliver Otis Howard: Major General United States Army.* 2 vols. New York: Baker and Taylor, 1907
Hughes, Nathaniel Cheairs, Jr. *General William J. Hardee: Old Reliable.* Baton Rouge: Louisiana State University Press, 1965.
Hughes, Sarah Forbes. *Letters and Recollections of John Murray Forbes.* 2 vols. Boston: Houghton Mifflin, 1899.
Hunting Island High House Project. WJWJ-TV, January 2000.
In Memoriam: George Waterhouse, Born in Lyman, Maine, May 16, 1839. Died in Saluda, North Carolina, August 17, 1894. Booklet in possession of the authors.
Johnson, Guin Griffis. *Social History of the Sea Islands.* Chapel Hill: University of North Carolina Press, 1930.
Johnson, John H. "Beaufort and the Sea Islands." *Beaufort Republican,* March 6, 1873
Johnson, Robert Erwin. *Rear Admiral John Rodgers.* Annapolis, Md.: United States Naval Institute Press, 1967.
Jones, James Pickett. *"Black Jack": John A. Logan and Southern Illinois in the Civil War Era.* Carbondale: Southern Illinois University Press, 1995.
Journal of the Convention of the People of South Carolina, Held in Columbia, S.C., September, 1865. Columbia, S.C.: J. A. Selby, 1865.
Kaminsky, Virginia Hughes. *A War to Petrify the Heart: The Civil War Letters of a Dutchess County N.Y. Volunteer, Richard T. Van Wyck.* Hensonville, N.Y.: Black Dome Press, 1997.
Keneally, Thomas. *American Scoundrel: The Life of the Notorious Civil War General Dan Sickles.* New York: Random House, 2002.
Lamphier, Peg A. *Kate Chase and William Sprague: Politics and Gender in a Civil War Marriage.* Lincoln: University of Nebraska Press, 2003.
Legg, James, Christopher T. Espenshade, and Lynn M. Snyder. *Camp Baird: Archaeological and Historical Investigation of the Autumn 1864 Camp of the 32nd U.S. Colored Infantry Hilton Head Island, South Carolina.* Atlanta: Brockington and Associates, 1991.
Lewis, Lloyd. *Sherman: Fighting Prophet.* New York: Harcourt, Brace, 1932.
Linder, Suzanne C. *Historical Atlas of the Rice Plantations of the ACE Basin—1860.* Columbia: South Carolina Department of Archives and History, 1995.
Little, Henry F. *The Seventh Regiment.* Concord, N.H.: J. Evan, 1896.
Longacre, Edward G. *From Union Stars to Top Hat: A Biography of the Extraordinary General James Harrison Wilson.* Harrisburg, Pa.: Stackpole Books, 1972.
Looby, Christopher, ed. *The Complete Journal and Selected Letters of Thomas Wentworth Higginson.* Chicago: University of Chicago Press, 2000.
Lord, Francis A. *Civil War Collector's Encyclopedia: Military Materiel, Both American and Foreign Used by the Union and Confederacy.* Vol. 2. West Columbia, S.C.: Lord Americana and Research, 1975.
Luck, Wilbert H. *Journey to Honey Hill.* Washington, D.C.: Wiluk Press, 1976.
Lynch, James. *A Few Things about the Educational Work Among the Freedmen of South Carolina and Georgia.* Baltimore: William K. Boyle, 1865.
MacDonald, Sharon S., and W. Robert Beckman. "Heroism at Honey Hill." *North and South* 12, no. 1 (2010): 20–43
MacDonald, William. *Selected Statues and Other Documents Illustrative of the History of the United States 1861–1898.* New York: MacMillan Company, 1903.
Marscher, William, and Fran Marscher. *The Great Sea Island Storm of 1893.* Macon, Ga.: Mercer University Press, 2003.

Marszalek, John F. *Sherman: A Soldier's Passion for Order.* New York: Free Press, 1993.
Martin, Samuel J. *"Kill-Cavalry": Sherman's Merchant of Terror; The Life of Union General Hugh Judson Kilpatrick.* Madison, N.J.: Fairleigh Dickinson University Press, 1996.
———. *Southern Hero Matthew Calbraith Butler: Confederate General, Hampton Red Shirt, and U.S. Senator.* Mechanicsburg, Pa.: Stackpole Books, 2001.
McArthur, Judith N., and Orville Vernon Burton. *A Gentleman and an Officer: A Military and Social History of James B. Griffin's Civil War.* New York: Oxford University Press, 1996.
McCracken, Charles C., and Faith M. McCracken, eds. *The Forgotten History: A Photographic Essay on Civil War Hilton Head Island.* Hilton Head Island, S.C.: Time Again Publications, 1993.
McFeely, William S. *Yankee Stepfather: General O. O. Howard and the Freedmen.* New York: W. W. Norton, 1994.
McGrath, Franklin. *The History of the 127th New York "Monitors."* N.p., 1898.
McGuire, Mary Jennie. "Getting Their Hands on the Land: The Revolution in St. Helena Parish, 1861–1900." Ph.D. diss., University of South Carolina, 1985.
McInnis, Maurie D. *In Pursuit of Refinement: Charlestonians Abroad, 1740–1860.* Charleston: Historic Charleston Foundation, 1999.
McKee, James Harvey. *Back in War Times: History of the 144th Regiment New York Volunteer Infantry.* Unadilla, N.Y.: Lieut. Horace E. Bailey, 1903.
McKim, J. Miller. *An Address Delivered by J. Miller M'Kim in Sansom Hall, July 9th, 1862 Together with a Letter From the Same to Stephen Colwell, Esq., Chairman of the Port Royal Relief Committee.* Philadelphia: Willis P. Hazard, 1862.
McKitrick, Erik L. *Andrew Johnson and Reconstruction.* Chicago: University of Chicago Press, 1960.
McLaughlin, Andrew C., ed. *The Cyclopedia of American Government.* New York: Appleton, 1914.
McPherson, James M. *The Negro's Civil War: How America's Negroes Felt and Acted during the War for the Union.* Urbana: University of Illinois Press, 1962.
———. *The Struggle for Equality: Abolitionists and the Negro in the Civil War and Reconstruction.* Princeton, N.J.: Princeton University Press, 1964.
McTeer, J. E. *Adventures in the Woods and Waters of the Lowcountry.* Beaufort, S.C.: JEMCO Publishing, 1972.
McWhiney, Grady, and Judith Lee Hallock. *Braxton Bragg and Confederate Defeat.* 2 vols. Tuscaloosa: University of Alabama Press, 1991.
Memorial: RGS (Robert G. Shaw). Cambridge (Mass.): University Press, 1864.
Miles, Jim. *To the Sea.* Nashville: Rutledge Hill Press, 1989.
Miller, Edward A., Jr. *Gullah Statesman: Robert Smalls from Slavery to Congress, 1839–1915.* Columbia: University of South Carolina Press, 1995.
———. *Lincoln's Abolitionist General: The Biography of David Hunter.* Columbia: University of South Carolina Press, 1997.
Mitchel, Frederick A. *Ormsby MacKnight Mitchel: Astronomer and General.* Boston: Houghton Mifflin, 1887.
Mitchell, C. Bradford, ed. *Merchant Steam Vessels of the United States 1780–1868: The Lytle-Holdcamper List.* Staten Island, N.Y.: Steamship Society of America, 1975.
Moore, John Hammon, ed. *South Carolina in the 1880s: A Gazetteer.* Orangeburg, S.C.: Sandlapper, 1989.

Mushkay, Jerome, ed. *A Citizen-Soldier's Civil War: The Letters of Brevet Major General Alvin Voris.* DeKalb: Northern Illinois University Press, 2002.

Myers, Robert Manson, ed. *The Children of Pride.* New Haven, Conn.: Yale University Press, 1972.

National Cyclopedia of American Biography. 63 Volumes. New York: J. T. White and Compnay, 1893.

Nichols, George Ward. *The Story of the Great March from the Diary of a Staff Officer.* New York: Harper and Brothers, 1865.

Nichols, James Moses. *Perry's Saints.* Boston: D. Lothrop, 1886.

Niven, John. *Gideon Welles: Lincoln's Secretary of the Navy.* New York: Oxford University Press, 1973.

———, ed. *The Salmon P. Chase Papers.* 5 vols. Kent, Ohio: Kent State University Press, 1993–1998.

Nordhoff, Charles. *The Freedmen of South Carolina.* New York: Charles T. Evans, 1863.

Oates, Stephen B. *A Woman of Valor: Clara Barton and the Civil War.* New York: Free Press, 1994.

Ochiai, Akiko. "The Port Royal Experiment Revisited: Northern Visions of Reconstruction and the Land Question." *New England Quarterly* 74 (March 2001): 94–117.

Official Records of the Union and Confederate Navies in the War of the Rebellion. 32 vols. Washington, D.C.: U.S. Government Printing Office, 1901.

Official Atlas of the Civil War. New York: Thomas Yoseloff, 1956.

O'Reilly, Miles [Charles Halpine]. *Baked Meats of the Funeral: A Collection of Essays, Poems, Speeches, Histories and Banquets.* New York: Carleton, 1866.

———. *The Life and Adventures, Songs, Services, and Speeches of Private Miles O' Reilly.* New York: Carleton, 1866

Palmer, Abraham John. *The History of the Forty-eighth Regiment New York State Volunteers.* Brooklyn, N.Y.: Veteran Association of the Regiment, 1885.

Parrish, William E. *Frank Blair: Lincoln's Conservative.* Columbia: University of Missouri Press, 1998.

Pearson, Elizabeth Ware, ed. *Letters from Port Royal.* New York: Arno, 1969.

Pearson, Henry Greenleaf. *The Life of John Andrew: Governor of Massachusetts 1861–1865.* 2 vols. Boston: Houghton Mifflin, 1904.

"Permanent Fortifications and Sea Coast Defenses." House of Representatives Report No. 86, 37th Cong., 2nd Sess., April 23, 1862.

Perry, Grace Fox. *Moving Finger of Jasper.* Ridgeland, S.C.: Jasper Confederate Centennial Commission, 1962.

Petrie, Stewart J. *Letters and Journal of a Civil War Surgeon.* Raleigh, N.C.: Pentland Press, 1998.

Petty, Julian J. *The Growth and Distribution of Population in South Carolina.* Columbia, S.C.: State Council for the Defense Industrial Development Committee, 1943.

Pierce, Edward. "The Freedmen at Port Royal." *Atlantic Monthly* 12 (September 1863): 291–315.

Pierce, Edward L. "The Negroes at Port Royal, S.C.: Report of the Government Agent." In *The Rebellion Record,* edited by Frank Moore, vol. 12, doc. 51: pp. 302–15. 12 vols. New York: D. Van Nostrand, 1864.

Piston, William G. *Lee's Tarnished Lieutenant: James Longstreet and His Place in Southern History.* Athens: University of Georgia Press, 1987.

Poole, W. Scott. "Memory and the Abolitionist Heritage: Thomas Wentworth Higginson and the Uncertain Meaning of the Civil War." *Civil War History* 51 (2005): 449–58.
Porter, Burton B. *One of the People*. Colton, Calif.: privately published, 1907.
Powell, C. S. "Additional Sketch, Tenth Battalion (Second Battalion Heavy Artillery)." In *Histories of the Several Regiments and Battalions from North Carolina in the Great War 1861–1865, Written by Members of the Respective Commands,* edited by Walter Clark. Vol. 5, 329–37. Goldsboro, N.C.: Nash Brothers, 1901.
Power, J. Tracy. "'This Indescribably Ugly Salkehatchie': The Battle of Rivers' Bridge, 2–3 February." South Carolina State Historic Preservation Office, South Carolina Department of History, Columbia, S.C.: July 22, 1991.
Powers, Bernard E. "Community Evolution and Race Relations in Reconstruction Charleston, South Carolina." *South Carolina Historical Magazine* 95, no. 1 (1994): 27–46.
Press Reference Library. *Notables of the Southwest*. Los Angles: Los Angles Examiner, 1912.
Price, Isaiah. *History of the Ninety-Seventh Regiment Pennsylvania Volunteer Infantry*. Philadelphia: privately printed, 1875.
Quaife, Milo M., ed. *From the Cannon's Mouth: The Civil War Letters of General Alpheus S. Williams*. Detroit: Wayne State University Press and the Detroit Historical Society, 1959.
Quarles, Benjamin. *The Negro in the Civil War*. Boston: Little, Brown, 1953.
Rawley, James A. *The Politics of Union: Northern Politics during the Civil War*. Lincoln: University of Nebraska Press, 1980.
Reed, Rowena. *Combined Operations in the Civil War*. Annapolis, Md.: Naval Institute Press, 1978.
Reid, Richard M., ed. *Practicing Medicine in a Black Regiment: The Civil War Diary of Burt G. Wilder*. Amherst: University of Massachusetts Press, 2010.
Reid, Whitelaw. *After the War: A Southern Tour, May 1, 1865 to May 1, 1866*. London: Sampson Low, Son and Marston, 1866.
Reports and Resolutions of the General Assembly of the State of South Carolina 1893. Columbia, S.C.: R. L. Bryan, 1894.
Richardson, James D. *A Compilation of the Messages and Papers of the Presidents, 1789–1897*. Washington, D.C.: U.S. Government Printing Office, 1898.
Richardson, Joe M. *Christian Reconstruction: The American Missionary Association and Southern Blacks, 1861–1870*. Athens: University of Georgia Press, 1986.
Ripley, Warren. *The Battle of Chapman's Fort: May 26, 1864*. Green Pond: Privately Printed, 1978.
Robinson, Joseph M. "The Defense of the Charleston and Savannah Railroad 1861–1865." Master's thesis, University of South Carolina, 1950.
Rodgers, Christopher R. P. "Du Pont's Attack on Charleston." In *Battles and Leaders of the Civil War,* 4: 32–47. 4 vols. 1887; reprint, New York: Thomas Yoseloff, 1956.
Rogers, Seth. "A Surgeon's War Letters." *Proceedings of the Massachusetts Historical Society* 43 (October 1909–June 1910): 337–98.
Roe, David D., ed. *A Civil War Soldier's Diary: Valentine C. Randolph, 39th Illinois Regiment*. DeKalb: University of Northern Illinois Press, 2006.
Roll of the Dead: South Carolina Troops Confederate States Service. Columbia: South Carolina Department of Archives and History, 1994.
Rollin, Frank (Frances Rollin Whipper). *Life and Public Services of Martin R. Delany, Sub-Assistant Commissioner, Bureau Relief of Refugees, Freedmen, and of Abandoned Lands, and Late Major 104th U.S. Colored Troops*. Boston: Lee and Shepard, 1883.

Roman, Alfred. *The Military Operations of General Beauregard.* 2 vols. New York: Harper and Brothers, 1884.

Rose, Willie Lee. *Rehearsal for Reconstruction: The Port Royal Experiment.* 1964; reprint, New York: Oxford University Press, 1976.

Ross, Isabel. *Angel of the Battlefield.* New York: Harper and Brothers, 1956.

Rowland, Lawrence S., Alexander Moore, and George C. Rogers Jr. *The History of Beaufort County, South Carolina.* Vol. 1, *1514–1861.* Columbia: University of South Carolina Press, 1996.

Ryan, Jeffrey T. "To the Shores of Carolina: Dahlgren's Marine Battalions." *Civil War Regiments* 2, no. 3 (1992): 194–211.

Rybczynski, Witold. *A Clearing in the Distance: Frederick Law Olmsted, an America in the Nineteenth Century.* New York: Scribner, 1999.

Salley, A. S., Jr. "Captain John Colcock and Some of His Descendants." *South Carolina Historical Magazine* 3 (January 1902): 216–41.

Saville, Julie. *The Work of Reconstruction: From Slave to Wage Laborer in South Carolina, 1860–1870.* New York: Cambridge University Press, 1994.

Schiller, Herbert M. *Sumter Is Avenged! The Siege and Reduction of Fort Pulaski.* Shippensburg, Pa.: White Mane, 1995.

Schmidt, Lewis G. *A Civil War History of the 47th Regiment of Pennsylvania Veteran Volunteers.* Allentown, PA: Lewis G. Schmidt, 1986.

———. *The Battle of Pocotaligo.* Allentown, Pa.: Lewis G. Schmidt, 1993.

Schneller, Robert J., Jr. *A Quest for Glory: A Biography of Rear Admiral John A. Dahlgren.* Annapolis, Md.: Naval Institute Press, 1996.

Schott, Thomas E. *Alexander H. Stephens of Georgia: A Biography.* Baton Rouge: Louisiana State University Press, 1988.

Schuckers, J. W. *Life and Public Service of Salmon Portland Chase.* New York: D. Appleton, 1874.

Schwartz, Gerald, ed. *A Woman Doctor's Civil War: Esther Hill Hawks' Diary.* Columbia: University of South Carolina Press, 1984.

Sears, Stephen W. "Getting Right with Robert E. Lee." *American Heritage* 42, no. 3 (1991): 58–72.

Secretary of the Navy. *Report of the Secretary of the Navy in Relation to Armored Vessels.* Washington, D.C.: U.S. Government Printing Office, 1864.

Seigler, Robert S. *South Carolina's Military Organizations during the War Between the States: The Lowcountry and Peedee.* Charleston: History Press, 2008.

Shaw, Robert G. "Letters." *Magazine of History* 18 (1914): 226–31.

Sherman, William T. *Memoirs of William T. Sherman.* 2 vols. New York: Charles L. Webster, 1892.

Sherwood, Henry Noble. "Journal of Miss Susan Walker." *Quarterly Publication of the Historical and Philosophical Society of Ohio* 7 (January–March 1912): 3–48.

Shick, Tom W., and Don H. Doyle. "The South Carolina Phosphate Boom and the Stillbirth of the New South." *South Carolina Historical Magazine* 86, no. 1 (1985): 1–12, 14–15, 17–31.

Sievers, Harry J. *Benjamin Harrison: Hoosier Warrior.* New York: University Publishers, 1960.

Sifakis, Stewart. *Compendium of the Confederate Armies, South Carolina and Georgia.* New York: Facts on File, 1992.

———. *Who Was Who in the Civil War.* New York: Facts on File, 1988.

Simkins, Francis Butler, and Robert Hilliard Woody. *South Carolina during Reconstruction.* Chapel Hill: University of North Carolina Press, 1932.

Simon, John Y., ed. *The Papers of Ulysses S. Grant.* 31 vols. Carbondale: Southern Illinois University Press, 1967–2008.

Smith, Charles S. and Daniel A. Payne. *A History of the African Episcopal Church.* Philadelphia: Book Concern of the A.M.E. Church, 1922.

Smith, Gustavus W. "The Georgia Militia during Sherman's March to the Sea." In *Battles and Leaders of the Civil War,* 4: 667–69. 4 vols. 1887; reprint, New York: Thomas Yoseloff, 1956.

Smith, Jacob. *Camps and Campaigns of the 107th Regiment Ohio Volunteer Infantry, from August 1862, to July, 1865.* N.p., n.d.

Smith, Henry A. M. "The Baronies of South Carolina." *South Carolina Historical and Genealogical Magazine* 15 (October 1914): 149–65.

Smith, Page. *The Nation Comes of Age.* New York: McGraw-Hill, 1981.

Soule, Charles C. "Annals of the War: Battle of Honey Hill." *Philadelphia Weekly Times,* May 10, 1884.

South Carolina: Resources and Population, Institutions and Industries. Charleston, S.C.: Walker, Evans and Cogswell and the State Board of Agriculture, 1883.

South Carolina Genealogies. 5 vols. Spartanburg, S.C.: Reprint Company, 1983.

Spieler, Gerhard. "Hamilton's Post War Return Denied Former Lifestyle." *Beaufort Gazette,* May 16, 2000.

———. "Johnson Memoirs Reveal an Interesting Family Life." *Beaufort Gazette,* May 2, 2000.

———. "Langdon S. Langley." *Beaufort Gazette,* August 20, 2006.

———. "Many Died in Area for Confederacy." *Beaufort Gazette,* June 9, 1992.

———. "Old Deeds Clear up Early History of First African Baptist Church." *Beaufort Gazette,* October 31, 1995.

———. "Sea Island Families Suffered Tragedies After the War." *Beaufort Gazette,* January 18, 2000.

———. "Travel Was Difficult in the Aftermath of the South's Defeat." *Beaufort Gazette,* July 27, 1982.

Stapleton, Darwin H. "Assistant Charles H. Boutelle of the United States Coast Survey, with the South Atlantic Blockading Squadron, 1861–1863." *American Neptune* 31 (October 1971): 252–67.

Starr, Stephen Z. *The Union Cavalry in the Civil War.* 3 vols. Baton Rouge: Louisiana State University Press, 1985.

Statutes of South Carolina, 1872. Columbia, S.C.: Republican Printing Company, 1873.

Sternett, Milton C. *Harriet Tubman: Myth, Memory, and History.* Durham, N.C.: Duke University Press, 2007.

Stevens, Hazard. *The Life of Isaac Ingalls Stevens.* 2 vols. Boston: Houghton Mifflin, 1900.

Stephen, Leslie, ed. *Dictionary of National Biography.* 63 vols. London: Smith, Elder and Company, 1886.

Stevenson, Brenda, ed. *The Journals of Charlotte Forten Grimké.* New York: Oxford University Press, 1988.

Still, William N., ed. *The Confederate Navy: The Ships, Men and Organization, 1861–65.* Annapolis, Md.: Naval Institute Press, 1997.

Stockton, Robert P. *The Beaufort Arsenal: An Architectural History.* Charleston: n.p., 1992.

Stone, H. David, Jr. *Vital Rails: The Charleston & Savannah Railroad and the Civil War in Coastal South Carolina*. Columbia, S.C.: University of South Carolina Press, 2007.

Stowits, Smith B. *History of the One-hundredth New York Volunteers*. Buffalo, N.Y.: Matthews and Warren, 1870.

Sullivan, David M. *The United States Marine Corps in the Civil War—The Final Year*. Shippensburg, Pa.: White Mane, 2001.

Sumner, Merlin E., comp. and ed. *The Diary of Cyrus B. Comstock*. Dayton, Ohio: Morningside, 1987.

Swint, Henry Lee. *The Northern Teacher in the South*. Nashville: Vanderbilt University Press, 1941.

Symonds, Craig L. *Lincoln and His Admirals*. New York: Oxford University Press, 2008.

Tafft, Henry S. *Reminiscences of the Signal Service in the Civil War*. Providence: Published by the Society, 1899.

Tancig, W. J. *Confederate Military Land Units*. New York: Thomas Yoseloff, 1967.

Taylor, Rances Wallace, Catherine Taylor Matthews, and J. Tracy Powers, eds. *The Leverett Letters: Correspondence of a South Carolina Family, 1851–1868*. Columbia: University of South Carolina Press, 2000.

Taylor, Alrutheus Ambush. *The Negro in South Carolina during Reconstruction*. New York: AMS Press, 1924.

Taylor, Susie King. *Reminiscences of My Life in Camp*. New York: Arno Press, 1968.

Teal, Harvey S. *Partners with the Sun: South Carolina Photographers, 1840–1940*. Columbia: University of South Carolina Press, 2001.

Tetzlaff, Monica. *Cultivating a New South: Abby Holmes Christensen and the Politics of Race and Gender in a Southern Region*. Columbia: University of South Carolina Press, 2002.

Thayer, William Roscoe. *The Life and Letters of John Hay*. 2 vols. Boston: Houghton Mifflin, 1915.

Thomas, Benjamin P., and Harold M. Hyman. *Stanton: The Life and Times of Lincoln's Secretary of War*. New York: Alfred Knopf, 1962.

Thompson, Robert Means, and Richard Wainwright. *Confidential Correspondence of Gustavus Fox: Assistant Secretary of the Navy, 1861–1865*. 2 vols. New York: DeVinne Press, 1918.

Tindall, George Brown. *South Carolina Negroes, 1877–1900*. Columbia: University of South Carolina Press, 1952.

Todd, John R., and Francis M. Hutson. *Prince William's Parish and Plantations*. Richmond, Va.: Garrett and Massie, 1935.

Todd, William. *The Seventy-Ninth Highlanders New York Volunteers in the War of the Rebellion*. Albany, N.Y.: Brandau and Boston, 1886.

Touteloutte, Jerome. *A History of Company K of the Seventh Connecticut Volunteer Infantry in the Civil War*. n.p., 1910.

Trinkley, Michael, ed. *Indian and Freedmen Occupation at Fish Haul Site (38BU805), Beaufort County, South Carolina*. Research Series 7. Columbia, S.C.: Chicora Foundation, 1986.

Trudeau, Noah Andre, ed. and annotator. *Voices of the 55th: Letters from the 55th Massachusetts Volunteers 1861–1865*. Dayton, Ohio: Morningside, 1996.

Turner, Norman Vincent. *A List of the Confederate Soldiers Killed or Wounded in the Battle of Honey Hill or Grahamville, South Carolina, on November 30, 1864*. Springfield, Ga.: n.p., 2011.

———. *Torpedoes Buried in the Union Army's Path*. Springfield, Ga.: n.p., 2011.

"Under the Red Cross: The Work of Relief on the Storm Stricken Coats." *News and Courier,* January 9, 1894.

Underwood, James Lowell. *The Constitution of South Carolina.* Vol. 4. Columbia: University of South Carolina Press, 1994.

The United States Biographical Dictionary and Portrait Gallery of Eminent and Self Made Men. Iowa volume. Chicago: American Biographical Company, 1878.

United States Congress, House. Beaufort Library Society, Beaufort, S.C. H.R. 1284, 53d Cong., 2d sess., 1894.

———. Transfer of Duplicates of Certain Books in the Library of Congress to Beaufort Library. H.R. 2829, 76th Cong., 3d sess., 1940.

United States Treasury Department. *Annual statements of the Bureau of Statistics on the Commerce and Navigation of the United States for the year ended June 30, 1880.* Washington, D.C.: U.S. Government Printing Office, 1880.

University of the State of New York: Eighty-Second Annual Report of the Regents and the University made to the Legislature, February 26, 1869. Albany, N.Y.: Argus Company, 1869.

Viele, Egbert L. "The Port Royal Expedition, 1861: The First Union Victory of the Civil War." *Magazine of American History* 14 (October 1885): 329–40.

Voris, Alvin C. "Charleston in the Rebellion." In *Sketches of War History, 1861–1865.* 293–341. Cincinnati: Robert Clarke, 1888.

Walkley, Stephen W., Jr. *History of the Seventh Connecticut Volunteer Infantry, Hawley's Brigade, Terry's Division, Tenth Army Corps, 1861–1865.* Hartford, Conn.: n.p., 1905.

The War of the Rebellion: The Official Records of the Union and Confederate Armies. 128 vols. Washington, D.C.: U.S. Government Printing Office, 1889–1901

Warner, Ezra J. *Generals in Gray.* Baton Rouge: Louisiana State University Press, 1964.

———. *Generals in Blue.* Baton Rouge: Louisiana State University Press, 1959.

Welles, Gideon. *Diary of Gideon Welles.* 3 vols. Boston: Houghton Mifflin, 1911.

West, Richard Sedgewick, Jr. *Lincoln's Scapegoat General: A Life of Benjamin F. Butler, 1818 1893.* Boston: Houghton Mifflin, 1965.

Westwood, Howard C. *Black Troops, White Commanders, and Freedmen during the Civil War.* Carbondale: Southern Illinois University Press, 1992.

———. "Sherman Marched—and Proclaimed Land for the Landless." *South Carolina Historical Magazine* 85, no. 1 (1984): 33–50.

Whitney, Richard A. "The History of Phosphate Mining in Beaufort County, 1870 1914." Paper presented to the Beaufort County Historical Society, November 14, 1985.

Williams, T. Harry. *P. G. T. Beauregard: Napoleon in Gray.* Baton Rouge: Louisiana State University Press, 1955.

Williams, Alfred B. *Hampton and His Red Shirts: South Carolina's Deliverance in 1876.* Charleston, S.C.: Walker, Evans, and Cogswell, 1935.

Williams, Ben S. "Battle of Honey Hill." In *Recollections an Reminiscences, 1861–1865 through World War I.* Columbia: South Carolina Division, United Daughters of the Confederacy, 1990.

Williams, Rose-Marie Eltzroth, ed. *Railroads and Sawmills: Varnville, South Carolina; 1872–1997; The Making of a Low Country Town in the New South.* Varnville, S.C.: Varnville Community Council, 1998.

Wilmesherr, Milton. "Independent Church of Indian Land." *Sandlapper,* April 2009, 4.

Wilson, James Grant, and John Fiske, eds. *Appleton's Cyclopaedia of American Biography.* 6 vols. New York: D. Appleton, 1886–1888.

Winter, William. *Shadows of the Stage.* New York: Macmillan, 1893.
Wise, Stephen R. *Gate of Hell: Campaign for Charleston Harbor, 1863.* Columbia: University of South Carolina Press, 1994.
———. *Lifeline of the Confederacy: Blockade Running during the Civil War.* Columbia: University of South Carolina Press, 1988.
———. "To Capture an Island: Amphibious Operations in the Department of the South, 1861–1863." *Civil War Regiments* 5, no. 2 (1996): 1–8.
Wolf, Kurt J. "Laura Towne and the Freed People of South Carolina, 1862–1901." *South Carolina Historical Magazine* 98 (October 1997): 375–405.
Woodward, C. Vann, ed. *Mary Chesnut's Civil War.* New Haven, Conn.: Yale University Press, 1981.
Wynn, Jessie Mae. "Gillisonville Baptist Church, Gillisonville Baptist Church, Gillisonville." Brochure, n.d.
Young, Robert W. *Robert E. Lee and Fort Pulaski.* Washington, D.C.: Eastern National Parks and Monument Service, 1970.
Zuczek, Richard. *State of Rebellion: Reconstruction in South Carolina.* Columbia: University of South Carolina Press, 1996.

Index

A. G. Bentley (sailing ship), 521
Abraham (1st S.C. Private), 113
Adams, B. C., 552
Adams, Charles Francis, Jr., 120
Adams, Jo, 113
Addie (pilot boat), 533
Adelaide, SS, 106
Adger, Robert, 512
African Methodist Episcopal, 231, 277–79
Agnes, SS, 539
Aiken, Sallie B., 470
Aiken, S.C., 467–68
Aiken, William, 294, 457
Aikin, March, 459
Aires, James, 569
Alabama troops (U.S.A.):
  Cavalry-Regiment: *1st,* 401
Albright,—Lieutenant, 488
Alex Brown and Sons, 512
Alexander (ship), 522
Alexander, Edward P., 44
Alexander, John, 569
Alexander, Jonathan C., 281
Alice Price, USQM, 235
Allen,—Mr., 26, 39, 176
Allen family, 92
Allen, G., 220
Allen, George, 220
Allen, Macon, 489, 562
Allen, T. G., 212
Allen, William W., 389
Allen Brass Band, 489, 545, 562, 584, 586
Allendale, S.C., 92, 401, 462, 503–4, 533, 559, 632
Allendale Company, 571
Allendale County, 481, 504
Allendale Mounted Baseball Club, 558
Allendale Mounted Guard, 8

Allendale Mounted Rifle Club, 556, 558
Allison, SS, 524
Allston, Joseph B., 139, 140, 144
Almeda, S.C., 504, 517–18, 525
Alston, A. H., 531, 533–34
Altman, Isaac, 549
Altman's Store, 549
Altoona (schooner), 508, 525
American Freedmen's Inquiry Commission, 226–27
American Missionary Association, 66, 73, 474
American Waltham Watch Company, 268
Ames, William, 307
Ammen, Daniel, 18, 26–27, 43, 46
Ana (bark), 529
Ancilla (ship), 529, 531
Anderson, Richard H., 423–24
Anderson, Robert H., 87, 518
Anderson, Ruel W., 361
Andersonville, 290, 343, 434
Andrew, John A., 73, 75, 102, 114, 216–17, 226, 228–29, 240–41, 242, 307
Angley Post Office, 396–97
Ann, SS, 417
Anna (yacht), 596
Anthony (1st S.C. Private), 113
Apple, Jacob, 495
Appleby, Peter, 572
Appleton, Daniel Fuller, 267, 501, 503, 506–8, 526
Appleton, James, 267
Appleton, John W.M., 216–17
Appleton, Sarah Fuller, 267
Appleton, S.C., 504
Apthorp, William Lee, 209
Arago, USQM, 115, 132, 173, 176, 205, 224, 260–61, 274, 277, 434
Argyle Island, 355–56, 358

Army of Georgia, 354, 368, 385, 394, 400, 407
Army of Mississippi, 89
Army of Northern Virginia, 87, 89, 282, 314, 337, 341, 360, 388–89, 411, 424, 566
Army of Tennessee (C.S.A.), 244, 312, 340, 377, 389
Army of the Cumberland, 403
Army of the James, 282, 287
Army of the Potomac, 21, 107, 177, 201, 217, 271, 291, 304, 370, 385, 446
Army of the Tennessee (U.S.A.), 354, 368–70, 382, 396, 399, 406, 591
Arnold, Lewis G., 107
Arsenal Cadets, 340
Ashley, John T., 74
Ashley Dragoons, 92
Atkinson, Edward, 184
Atkinson, Ellen, 469
Atlanta, CSS, 224, 225, 230
Atlanta, Ga., 89, 288, 290, 301–2, 312, 318–19, 362, 370, 385, 396, 403, 405, 413, 447, 518, 520, 526, 566
Atlantic, USQM, 27, 58, 74–75, 102–3, 595
Atlantic Sawmills, 510, 515, 525
Augusta, Ga., 11, 34, 95, 290, 301, 312, 316–20, 337–38, 341, 357–58, 362–63, 389, 343, 401, 403–404, 434, 437, 445, 447, 490, 501, 503–506, 520, 524, 526, 527, 559
Augusta, USS, 99
Augusta Dinsmore, USS, 225
Averasboro, Battle of, 85–86, 88
Avery, Charles, 475
Avery Normal Institute, 474
Ayer, Lewis Malone, Jr., 83
Azalea (yacht), 77

Babcock, Orville E., 447
Bache, Alexander Dallas, 29, 81
Bachman, William K., 286, 290, 314, 316, 320, 351, 360
Bacon, Edwin H., Jr., 346, 360, 398
Bacon, Francis, 22–23
Bacon, George, 218–20

Badeau, Adam, 20, 51, 58–59, 101, 447
Baird, Absalom, 403–4
Baird, George W., 297, 305, 311, 327, 334
Bailey family, 92
Baker, Elizabeth, 461–62
Baker, John Morgandollar, 268
Baker, Laurence S., 337–38
Baker, Susie, 163 *See also* King, Susie Baker
Baker family, 465
Balch, George, 391
Baldwin, Augustus S., 103
Baldwin Fertilizer Company, 515
Ballad of Paris Island, 178
Baltic, USQM (transport), 27, 67
Bampfield, Elizabeth Smalls, 489
Bampfield, Samuel Jones, 485, 487, 547, 553, 559, 562, 564, 566, 578–79, 581, 582, 585
Bank of Hampton, 509
Banks, Nathaniel P., 475, 591
Bankhead, John, 26
Bannister, Dwight, 186
Baptist Church Praise House, 65, 182
Baptist Church Tabernacle, 240
Baptist Home Mission, 275–77, 474
Baptists, 65–66, 69, 77, 80, 165, 182, 200, 277, 412, 432, 473
Barker's Mill, 396–97, 399–400
Barnard, Francis E., 74
Barnes, W. N., 482
Barney, Hiram, 60–62, 64, 74, 370
Barnwell, Allard, 90, 522
Barnwell, Catherine Osborn, 90
Barnwell, Charlotte, 466
Barnwell, Edward, 88
Barnwell, Edward H. "Teddy," 89
Barnwell, Eliza, 466
Barnwell family, xiv, 8, 90, 92, 186, 463, 466
Barnwell, Frank, 239
Barnwell, John G., 559
Barnwell, John Gibbs, 87, 462
Barnwell, Jonathan, 466
Barnwell, Joseph Walker, 90, 348, 466
Barnwell, Mary, 90
Barnwell, Nathaniel, 87
Barnwell, Oscar, 8
Barnwell, Robert Hayne, 87

Barnwell, Robert W., 465
Barnwell, Robert W. (Reverend), 88, 90
Barnwell, Robert Woodward (Senator), 83, 87
Barnwell, Sarah Bull, 462
Barnwell, Stephen, 244
Barnwell, Stephen Elliott, 90
Barnwell, Stuart, 87
Barnwell, Thomas Osborn, 23, 88
Barnwell, William, 89
Barnwell, William Hazard Wigg, 89–90, 348
Barnwell Artillery, 361
Barnwell District, 91–93, 396, 397, 400, 403
Barnwell Dragoons, 92
Barnwell Island, 244, 451
Barnwell (Woodward) Oak, 204
Barrell Landing, 582–83
Barton, Clarissa "Clara" Harlowe, 205–6, 215, 232, 235, 248–49
Barton, David, 205
Barton, William B., 137, 141–43, 218–20, 224
Baruch, J., 496
Bascomb, A. S., 579
Bates, Edward, 241–42
Battery Brayton, 296
Battery Burnet, 391
Battery Burnside, 295
Battery Damnation, 363
Battery Hamilton, 54
Battery Hell, 363
Battery Holbrook, 297
Battery Plantation, 8, 207, 215
Battery Saxton, 296
Battery Seymour, 296
Battery Taylor, 296
Battery Vulcan, 51, 52, 53, 54
Battery Wagner, 87–88, 235–38, 304–5, 452, 475
Battery Williams, 297
Baumhofer, Hermine Munz, 498
Bayard, Profit, 113
Bayard, Stephen, 113
Bayley, Thomas, 291–93, 295
Baynard, Caroline T., 466

Baynard, Joseph, 220
Bear Island, 130
Beard, Oliver T., 50–51, 53–54, 59, 153–54
Beaufort, S.C.: pre-war, 1–3; Confederate raids, 7–8, 127–28, 348; U.S. occupies, 22–30, 37–42; federal troops in, 57, 63, 102, 128–29, 134, 176, 226; library, 63–64; missionaries in, 64–66, 76–80, 117, 160, 227; refugee camps, 68, 185, 215, 239, 299; medical and hospital, 159, 195, 203–5, 234, 237, 240, 241, 285, 336, 396, 398, 414; schools, 159, 182, 275, 414, 474, 480, 541; religious revival in, 200–201; businesses, 181, 201–2, 417–18, 493–97, 509, 510, 511, 518; Emancipation Day celebrations, 251–52, 365–66, 489; auction, town lots, 253, 257, 261, 265, 267–68; churches, 277; National Convention Union Party, 280; Sherman's troops, 363–64, 368–370, 379, 381; Stanton visits, 372, 376–77; Chase-Fuller visit, 431–34; Welles visit, 436–37; diaspora of Beaufort families, 461–71; post-war businesses, 475–76, Grant visit, 490–91; railroad, 500–508
Beaufort and Port Royal Phosphate Company, 512
Beaufort Arsenal, 2, 27, 29, 128, 182, 479, 482, 488, 557–58, 562, 565–66, 582
Beaufort Baptist Church, 65, 80, 165, 200, 215, 237, 240, 432
Beaufort Bridge. *See* Buford Bridge
Beaufort College, 63, 240, 365, 414, 434, 436
Beaufort County, S.C.: creation of, 444, 449; black Republican rule in, 471–88, 541, 546, 558, 561, 576, 568; county schools, 481, 541; county seat moved, 481–82; industry and enterprise, 492–519; maritime activity, 521–40; Ku Klux Klan, 548; violence, 551–55; rise of Democratic Party, 558, 561, 568, 576; secession of Hampton County, 568–74; black migration, 574–78; fusion politics, 578–86

Beaufort County Board of Commissioners, 464, 482, 489, 542, 554
Beaufort County School District, 480–81, 483, 541
Beaufort Democratic Club, 582
Beaufort District: Confederate defense, 4–14, 96–97, 190–91, 208–10, 245–46, 288–91, 312–14, 349, 357, 362; Confederate government, 83–85; tax sales, 157–58, 183–84, 253–81, 375, 437, 460–71; Jefferson Davis visits, 244–45; Sherman invades, 367–413; sea island vs. mainland, 437–39; post-war government, 443–44; end of Beaufort District, 444, 481
Beaufort Judicial District, 444, 481–82
Beaufort Library, 39, 63, 64
Beaufort Light Infantry, 490
Beaufort Machine Shop, 495
Beaufort Mining Company, 512
Beaufort National Cemetery, 129, 489, 495
Beaufort Republican, 463–64, 476, 488, 499, 505, 529, 531–32, 535, 541, 544–47
Beaufort Republican Club, 477, 483
Beaufort Tax Union, 547–48
Beaufort Times, 542, 545
Beaufort Tribune and Port Royal Commercial, 496, 573, 576
Beaufort Troop, 92
Beaufort Volunteer Artillery, 7, 84, 85, 87–89, 92–94, 96, 128, 130–31, 138–39, 143, 145, 191–92, 244, 285, 288–89, 314, 320, 359–61, 389, 428, 491, 586
Beauregard, Pierce G.T., xiv, 2–3, 14, 84, 131, 156, 189–90, 196, 208, 245–46, 284, 288–89, 302, 312, 337, 340, 349, 350, 357–58, 362, 431
Bebington (bark), 531
Bee, Robert, 96
Bee's Hill Battery, 190–91, 313–15, 320, 324, 332, 343–44, 359
Beech Hill House, 356
Beech Branch Church, 403,
Beech Branch Post Office, 402, 443, 561

Beech Island, 503–4
Beecher, Frances, 336
Beecher, Henry Ward, 201, 278, 304, 423–26
Beecher, James C., 304, 326–27, 333, 364
Beecher, Lyman, 304
Beldoc, 504
Bell, Charles E., 559, 567, 569, 578
Bell, James O., 478
Bell, John, 266–67
Bell, Louis, 147
Bell, Mary, 266–67
Bell, William E., 553
Bellamy, Albert, 74
Bellillieu, H. W., 569
Bellinger, B. D., 581
Bellows, E. P., 417
Bellows, Henry Whitney, 73, 81, 592
Bellows, M.A., 417
Bellows, William Chauncey, 507, 564, 566
Ben (schooner), 532
Ben Deford, USQM, 38, 224
Benedict, Bethsheba A., 475
Benedict College, 475
Benham, Henry W., 58–59, 78, 107–109, 123–24, 127–28, 132
Benjamin, Judah P., 4, 9
Bennett, Augustus G., 241–42
Bennett family, 92
Bennett, Orson W., 333
Bennett, S.W., 281
Bennett, William True, 307, 447, 458–59, 630
Bennett and McFall Company, 506
Bennett's Point, 286, 289, 291–94
Benton, Sidney, 481
Bentonville, Battle of, 85, 89, 481
Bertha (pilot boat), 534
Bessillieu, John, 569
Bethel Episcopal Chapel, 311
Bethel United Methodist Church, 412
Bienville, USS, 15
Big Barnwell Island, 244
Billinghurst-Requa Battery, 227
Billy (horse), 384
Binneker, J. B., 572

Binyard, Andre, 113
Binyard, Frank, 113
Birney, David D., 271
Birney, James, 61, 271
Birney, William, 271–72, 291–95, 416
Black Codes, 450, 457
Black Migration, 574
Black Republic of Beaufort, 483
Black troops: viii, 75, 82, 106–8, 110–11, 115–17, 119–20, 123–24, 128, 133, 152–53, 155, 174, 185–86, 188, 200, 206–7, 210, 213, 216–17, 227–29, 231–32, 235, 238, 240, 243, 250, 258, 271, 280–83, 296–97, 299, 335, 338, 349, 369, 371, 381–82, 411, 414, 431, 442–43, 447, 449, 548; Pay issue, 153, 186, 229–31, 240–43
Black vs. Tan, 578
Blair, Francis P., Jr., 362, 368–70, 379, 381, 387, 394–95, 397, 399–400, 410, 619
Blair, Montgomery, 369
Blair's Landing, 394, 398, 402, 412–13, 619
Blake, George H., 74
Blake, Walter, 212
Blanchard, Albert G., 359
Blanding, Jabez B., 143
Blauvelt, A. J., 202
Bleeker, Stephen, 537
Bliss, John F., 234
Blocker family, 92
Blountville, 192
Bluffton, S.C., 4, 6, 13–14, 30, 55, 93, 134, 138, 180, 190–92, 217–21, 287, 314, 356, 358, 465, 522, 524, 561–62, 582–83; March 22, 1862 Expedition, 55; Sept. 30, 1862 Expedition, 134; June 3–4, 1863 Expedition, 218–221
Boatman's Mining Company, 512
Boddington and Company, 510–11, 525
Boineau, Stephen H., 364
Bolan, James, 312
Bolan Church, 311–13, 317, 320–22, 332, 334, 336, 342–43
Bold, Charles, 267
Bomar, Thomas, 209, 211, 213–14

Bonham, Milledge L., 357
Booth, Sherman, 158
Boozer, Julia M., 467
Bostic, Agnes M., 313, 338, 569
Bostick family, 92
Boston, USQM, 292–95
Boston Education Commission, 73, 74, 160
Boston Emancipation League, 226
Botume, Elizabeth Hyde, 299, 364–65, 370, 376–77, 427, 434–35, 444, 449, 451, 455, 474
Boutelle, Charles O., 29–30, 57, 294, 418
Bowe, Daniel, 74
Bowen, Francis, 480
Bowers family, 92
Bowles, Loby, 113
Bowman and Nehemias, 552
Box, H. R., 569
Boyce, James, 493
Boyce, John P., 566, 577
Boyd's Landing, 6, 304, 309–11, 314–16, 321, 331–32, 335–37, 340, 342–44, 348–49, 354, 379, 383
Brabham family, 92
Braddock's Point, 17, 44, 93, 101, 297, 317, 338, 340–41, 357
Bradford, Joseph M., 424
Brady, Mathew, 201
Bragg, Braxton, 18, 89, 312, 316
Bramad, George, 532
Brannan, Eliza Crane, 152
Brannan, John M., 107, 122, 132, 134–37, 140–41, 143, 145–46, 148–49, 152–53, 174, 357
Bray's Island, 132, 342, 394
Brayton, Charles, 209–10, 212, 394
Breckinridge, John C., 21, 78
Breeden, Peter Lindsey, 211–14
Brenholts, Thomas S., 43
Brick Baptist Church, 65, 69, 82, 165, 230–32, 263–64, 269, 275–76, 278, 365, 432, 473
Briggs, Thomas B., 193–96
Bright, Fred, 553
Brighton, 401, 403–4, 561
Brinkerhoff, Isaac W., 74

Brisbane, William Henry, 69, 157–58, 165–66, 168, 182, 184, 252–54, 260, 262–64, 268–71, 273–74, 276–77, 387, 445
Bristol (tug), 523–24
Bristol (dredge), 513
Broad River, 2, 4, 5–6, 10–11, 14, 31, 41–43, 46, 104, 130, 135–36, 176, 193, 204, 238, 287, 304, 306–7, 309, 316, 344, 363, 383, 511, 523
Brodhead, Edgar, 193–96
Brodie, J., 520
Brodie, Paul, 494
Brooker family, 92
Brooklyn, USS, 537
Brooks, James Henry, 435. *See also* Limber, Jim
Brotherhood, Francis, 523
Broun, Joseph, 10
Broun, Thomas L., 10
Brown, Angus P., 360
Brown, Charles H., 74
Brown, F. C., 577, 579
Brown, George S., 512
Brown, Israel W., 481
Brown, James, 488
Brown, John (abolitionist), 75, 120, 155, 174, 197, 207, 216
Brown, John (1st S.C. soldier), 120
Brown, John H., 74
Brown, Joseph, 85, 318–19
Brown, Nathaniel, 149
Brown, William, 113
Brown, William Middleton, 481
Browne, Albert G., 248
Browne, R. Audley, 40
Browning, A. D., 571, 572
Broxton Bridge, 396–97, 399
Brunson,—(Lieutenant), 212
Brunson, S.C., 347, 504–5, 533, 555, 557, 559, 561, 569, 570–72
Brunson, W. E., 572
Brunson family, 92–93
Brush, George Washington, 293
Bryan, John E., 244–45
Bryan, George, 113
Bryan, Mayer, 113

Bryant, William Cullen, 73
Buckhalter, J. H., 142
Buckley,—(pilot), 534
Buckner, B. F., 548
Buckner, Thaddeus G., 92, 410
Buckingham Ferry, 55, 130
Buell, Don Carlos, 132
Buford Bridge, 400
Buist, Henry, 141–42
Bull River, 502, 513, 516, 520, 529–31, 534, 550
Bull River Railroad, 502
Bullchen, J. G., 220
Bummers, 405–406, 408
Bunting family, 92
Bureau of Colored Troops, 229
Bureau of Emancipation, 226–27
Bureau of Refugees, Freedmen, and Abandoned Lands, 429, 472. *See also* Freedmen's Bureau
Burnet, Andrew, 211, 284, 359
Burnet Point, 390–91
Burnett, H. D., 578
Burnham, Richard, 622
Burroughs, John E., 110
Butler, Benjamin, 23, 57, 67, 110, 228, 287, 475
Butler, Matthew, 388
Butler, William Allen, 73
Buncombeville, 192
Burns, Peter, 478
Buzzard Island, 521, 534
Bythewood, Bob, 490, 546

C. A. Raymond (schooner), 524
C. F. Hyer (sailing ship), 521
Cain (1st S.C. Private), 113
Calcium Lights, 342
Caldwell, John W., 362
Calhoun (ship), 529
Calhoun, William R., 86
Calhoun Mounted Men, 92
Calvert (steamship), 522
Calvert, W.H., 495
Cameron, Simon, 23, 106, 116, 421–22
Camp Allen, 192
Camp Baird, 297

Camp Branch, 572
Camp DeSaussure, 192
Camp Saxton, 153, 155–56, 161, 163, 165, 169–70, 172–74, 184–85, 215, 239, 299, 474
Camp Stevens, 185–86
Campbell, Archibald L., 313, 320, 324–25, 328, 334, 359
Campbell, C.H. (owner of *George Washington*), 193, 194
Campbell, Smart, 278
Campbell, W.L., 138
Campbell and Wylie, 513
Cannon, John S., 125
Canter, D., 220
Canter, J., 220
Capers, Edward M., 466
Capers, Will, 108
Capers, William Gabriel, 441
Captured and Abandoned Property Act, 375
Carlton, R. K., 542
Carman, Ezra A., 355–56
Carmichael, James C., 304, 343
Carondolet, SS, 527
Carroll, SS, 530
Carter, Woodward, 308, 345
Carver, James M., 209, 211, 213–14
Case, Henry, 367–68
Cashman, James, 108
Cat Island, 60, 65, 79, 118
Catskill, USS, 188, 538
Causey family, 92
Causey, T.A., 573
Causey, W. J. , 569, 572
Ceasarea (bark), 529
Chalmers, 220
Chalmers, J., 220
Chamberlain, Daniel H., 486, 546–48, 551, 558–62
Chapel of Ease (McPhersonville), 408
Chapel of Ease (St. Helena), 118, 230, 232
Chaplin, Ann, 466, 467
Chaplin, Benjamin, 255, 261
Chaplin family, viii, 90, 92
Chaplin, Frank, 466
Chaplin, James C., 256, 292, 294, 390–91

Chaplin, John F., 256, 266
Chaplin, Sarah O. B., 466
Chaplin, Saxby, 256
Chaplin, Thomas B., 255, 563–64
Chapman's Fort, 290, 292–95
Charles (Daniel Heyward's slave), 126
Charles, William E., 334, 361
Charleston, S.C., 2–3, 5–6, 18, 24, 34–35, 38, 56–57, 60, 65, 70, 79, 84–91, 95, 97–99, 104, 123–124, 127–28, 132, 135, 138, 142, 149, 152, 158, 174–77, 181, 185, 188–89, 193, 196, 199–200, 202, 204, 206, 211, 221, 243–45, 247, 279–80, 282–83, 285–86, 288, 290–91, 293, 296, 299, 302, 304–5, 307, 312, 315–18, 338, 340, 347, 357–58, 362, 373, 377, 385, 390, 410, 412, 414, 417–18, 420–25, 428, 430–31, 434, 436, 443, 446–47, 450–51, 453, 458–59, 463, 475, 479–80, 484–87, 493, 496, 499, 511–12, 515, 522–23, 526, 528–29, 530, 534, 544, 552, 573, 578, 580; Summer 1863 attack, 221–37
Charleston, SS, 522
Charleston and Savannah Railroad, 2, 3, 4, 5, 11–12, 14–15, 24, 33, 36, 38, 41, 48, 55, 87, 91, 95, 132, 134, 146, 151, 189, 190, 211, 214, 302, 304, 307, 309, 313, 319–20, 337, 349–50, 354, 394, 437, 501, 502, 507, 518, 569, 571
Charleston and Western Carolina Railroad, 507
Chase, Janet "Nettie" Ralston, 431, 433
Chase, Katherine "Katie" J., 62. *See also* Sprague, Katherine J. Chase
Chase, Philander, 61
Chase, Salmon P., 61–67, 69, 71–74, 78–79, 81–82, 108, 114, 117, 121–22, 132, 152, 157–58, 183, 253, 257, 259–61, 264–65, 268–71, 429–35
Chatfield, John L., 136–40
Cheever, George B., 168
Cheney, Edward, 555–56
Chesnut, James, 90, 337–38, 341, 349, 359, 361
Chesnut, Mary Boykin, 337
Cheves, Battery, 190

Index

Cheves, Charles, 358
Chipman, Henry Laurens, 305, 332–33
Chippewa, USS, 286–87
Chisholm, Alice, 512
Chisholm, Edward, 512
Chisholm family, 92
Chisholm, Louisa, 512
Chisholm, Maxwell, 512
Chisholm Island, 41, 43, 44–47, 135, 192–96, 502, 512, 515–16, 529, 546, 550, 561
Chisolm family. *See* Chisholm family
Chisolm, Robert, 141, 142
Chisolmville, 210
Christ Church of the Combahee, 411, 412
Christ, Benjamin, 124
Christensen, Abigail "Abby" Holmes, 495, 509
Christensen, Niels, 495, 537, 575
Christensen Hardware, 495
Christensen Lumber Company, 495, 575
Christensen Real Estate, 495
Christiana (tug), 529
Circular 13, 441, 446, 451
Citadel Cadets, 340, 346–48, 360
City of Austin, SS, 522, 527
City of Dallas, SS, 522, 527
Civil Rights Act, 458
Clancy and Wallace, 524
Clark, William S., 74
Cleland family, 92
Cleveland, Grover, 585
Clinch, Duncan Lamont Jr., 355
Clingman, Thomas Lanier, 313
Clitz, John M. B., 538
Clover, USS, 390, 391
Clyde, William P., 435
Coaxum, 458, 459
Cockrell family, 92
Coffin, Alice Church, 470
Coffin, Amory, 470
Coffin, Charles E., 470
Coffin, Elizabeth, 470
Coffin, Francis W., 470
Coffin, Henry P., 470
Coffin, James McPherson, 470

Coffin, Thomas A., 470
Coffin Point, viii, 30, 68, 77, 78, 184, 272, 303, 307, 330, 458–59, 470, 561
Cogley, Jeremiah, 334
Cogswell, William B., 103
Cogswell, William S., 44, 45
Cohen, 490
Cohen, Israel, 266
Cohen, Samuel, 266, 267
Colcock, C.J.C., 572
Colcock, Charles J., xiv, 6, 91, 138, 141, 190, 245–46, 288–89, 313–15, 320, 323–25, 328, 338, 340, 358, 380, 389–90, 395, 397
Colcock family, 92
Colcock, Richard H., 145
Colcock, Thomas H., 320
Colcok, William Ferguson Jr., 548, 553
Cold-Chisel Brigade, 55
Cole, Isaac W., 74
Colfax, Schuyler, 117
Colleton County, S.C., 444, 469, 542, 548, 550, 552, 556
Colleton District, 91, 92, 94, 210, 359, 399, 411, 444
Colleton Hunt Club, 556
Colleton River, 10, 287, 510, 511, 518, 525, 538
Collins, Joseph B., 73
Collins, Joseph W., 470, 499, 569, 573
Collins, Napoleon, 27
Colored Farmers Alliance, 585
Colored Normal, Industrial, Agricultural and Mechanical College of South Carolina, 487
Colquitt, Peyton H., 14
Columbia Flying Artillery, 556
Combahee Raid, 208–17
Combahee Riots, 551, 552
Combahee River, 2, 5, 6, 10, 36, 92, 94, 123, 127, 130–31, 190–91, 244–45, 283–84, 292–93, 298, 312–13, 320, 358–59, 362, 380, 387–91, 394, 410–12, 415, 497, 531, 550, 552, 556
Commodore McDonough, USS, 218–20, 294
Comstock, Cyrus B., 447
Comstock, Jesse J., 27, 589

Conant, John, 478, 493, 495
Conemaugh, USS, 136
Congregationalists, 67, 75, 77, 80, 304, 475
Congress, USS, 537
Connecticut troops: Artillery, Light – Batteries: *1st,* 124, 126, 128, 196, 201, 234–35; Infantry, Regiments: *6th,* 16, 135–38, 140, 144, 185, 202, 218, 238; *7th,* 16, 22, 59, 136–38, 145–47, 218, 247; *9th,* 443; *30th,* 484
Contrabands, 23, 32–33, 40, 55, 58, 60, 63, 67–69, 71–73, 76, 79–80, 97, 100, 102, 104, 108–10, 114, 117–18, 124, 129, 133, 142, 153, 161–62, 165, 181–82, 186, 203, 215, 235, 265, 542
Cook, F. W. C., 324, 330
Cook family, 90–91
Cook, Thomas, 466
Cooke, John Rogers, 190–91
Cooley, Dennis N., 271, 276, 455
Cooley, Emily, 202
Cooley, Samuel, 147, 201–2, 248, 281, 418, 436
Cooper, Drury, 74
Cooper, Raleigh L., 191–92
Cooper, Samuel, 11
Cooper Union Institute, 73, 114
Co-operative Colonization Society, 517
Coosaw Island, 2, 37, 68, 110, 118, 255–56, 276, 461, 549, 552
Coosaw Mining Company, 512–14, 529–30, 550, 582
Coosaw River, 2, 30, 36, 38, 41–43, 45, 104, 127–28, 130, 135, 196, 199, 209, 247, 421, 511, 514, 523
Coosawhatchie, S.C., 2, 4, 5–7, 9–11, 13–14, 88, 95, 127, 134, 137–38, 141–43, 151, 190–91, 208, 304, 310, 313–15, 319, 341, 343–48, 351–53, 357–61, 363, 380–82, 389, 394, 482, 501, 503, 523, 545, 556, 559
Coosawhatchie River, 2, 4, 6, 130, 135, 137–38, 141–43, 147–48, 347, 350, 408, 410, 508, 510
Coquette, CS, 390
Corbin family, 90
Corn Island, 256

Corse, John M., 384, 394, 401–3
Cosmopolitan, USQM, 76, 236, 285, 335, 447
Cossack, USQM, 218
Coston Lights, 618
Cotton, Sea Island, 6, 8, 9, 32, 62–64, 70–72, 74, 78, 81, 110, 118, 121, 161, 172, 183, 238, 239
County of Picton, 529
Cowderry, Henry A., 74
Cowley, Charles, 524
Crabbe, William, 146
Craig,—Captain, 533
Crane, Charles H., 133, 149, 152, 203
Crane, Ichabod, 152
Crane, William D., 303, 307, 329–30
Creighton, Elizabeth McP., 470
Creighton, J. Blakely, 311
Cresfield (dredge), 513–14
Crews family, 93
Crocker, George H., 326, 328–29, 332
Croft, Edward, 45, 46
Crofut, George A., 513
Crofut, James M., 484, 506, 509, 513, 542–43, 563
Crosby, 220
Crosby, A., 220
Crosby family, 90
Crossman, Alexander, 310
Croton, USQM, 286, 287
Cruger, Sarah, 94
Cruz, Vincent, 278
Cummings, John B., 361
Cunningham, S. H., 468
Curlew, USS, 26, 27
Curtis, George, 480, 575
Curtis, Hannah, 74
Cuthbert, Eliza Natalia, 451
Cuthbert, Edward Barnwell Jr., 96
Cuthbert family, 90

Daffodil, USS, 309, 342, 390–91
Dahlgren, John A. B., 223–25, 237–38, 246, 284, 291, 299–300, 302, 307–11, 343, 345, 348–49, 354–56, 364, 379, 386, 390, 417, 424, 431, 436
Dai Ching, USS, 242, 294, 390–91

Dale, J. J., 524
Dale, USS, 36
Danby, Robert, 424
Danic (sailing ship), 529
Daniel, Charles P., 344, 347, 360
Daniel Britain (sailing ship), 521
Danielson, William H., 113
Danner, Charles E., 495
Darien, Georgia, 221, 228
Darlington, USQM, 136, 153, 154
Dataw Island. *See* Dathaw Island
Dathaw Island, 68, 118 , 465, 471
Daufuskie Island, 35, 50–52, 68, 76, 120, 287, 522, 535
Davant, Frank Fickling, 462, 571
Davant, J. C., 554, 569
Davant, Richard James, 83, 448, 501, 503
Davenport, A. S., 494
David (torpedo boats), 286
Davis, B.W., 473
Davis, C.F., 573
Davis, Charles H., 49, 56
Davis family, 92
Davis, Henry C., 25, 49
Davis, Jefferson, 4–5, 12, 14, 83, 85, 87, 90, 95, 105, 119, 130, 162, 196, 197, 244–45, 290, 312, 337, 340–41, 357–58, 377–78, 388, 434–35
Davis, Jefferson C., 371, 384, 392, 394, 403, 408
Davis, Jim, 113
Davis, John, 113
Davis, John Martin, 9
Davis, Varina, 435
Davis, William W. H., 208, 226, 232
Dawson Bluff, 190, 289, 359, 363
Dawson Bluff Battery, 364
Deas, Lawrence, 469
Deas, Solomon, 579
Deering, Rufus, 277
Delany, Martin, 422–25, 431, 437, 445, 546
Delaware (dredge), 513, 514
Delaware, USQM, 43
DeLoach,—Mr., 555
DeLoach, James Edward, 83
Deloach, Jesse, 559
Deloach family, 469

Democratic Party, 484, 541, 547, 558–59, 563, 567, 576, 578, 580, 583, 585
De Molay, USQM, 216
Dennis, Gorman, 280
Dennis, Joshua, 480
Dennison, William, 436
Department of the South, 57, 78, 104, 106–7, 109–10, 131–32, 152, 162–63, 186, 188, 202, 203, 205, 208, 222, 240, 282, 288, 291, 295, 306, 307, 312, 375, 386, 409, 412, 414–17, 447; established, 57
Department of South Carolina, Georgia and East Florida, 4, 5, 9, 11–13
DePass, William L., 246, 359, 360–61
Derwent (brig), 525
DeSaussure, Charles, 467
DeSaussure, Daniel, 267
DeSaussure, Louis D., 315, 325
DeSaussure, Thomas H., 467
DeSaussure, William D., 6, 534
DeTreville, Edward White, 87
DeTreville family, xiii, 90
de Treville, John de La Boularderie, 87
DeTreville, John L., 289
DeTreville, John La Boularderie, 87
DeTreville, Richard Jr., 87
DeTreville, Richard Sr., 87, 98, 267, 460, 463
DeTreville, Robert, 87–88
DeTreville vs. Smalls, 460, 463
Devens, Charles, 447
Diamond, SS, 423
Dickinson, Emily, 154
Direct Tax Act, 157–59, 253–54, 264–65, 386, 457, 459, 461, 463, 466, 550
Dix, Dorthea, 203–204, 206, 249
Dix, John A., 423–24
Dixie Station, 502, 509, 570
Dobson family, 93
Dominion Line, 527–28
Donaldson, Mary A., 74
Donelson, Daniel Smith, 9, 11, 13–14, 46, 48
Doolittle, James R., 159, 183, 253, 268, 421–22
Doubleday, Abner, 424

Downey, William, 293
Doyle family, 92
Dr. Buzzard, 487. *See also* Robinson, Stepney
Draper, Simon, 370
Drayton, Percival, 15, 29, 30, 36, 151, 175, 437, 438
Drayton, Seaborn, 543
Drayton, Thomas Fenwick, xiv, 3, 4, 6, 10–11, 13–14, 16, 95, 220, 438
Drayton family, 460
Drexel, A. J., 505
Duffy, John, 293
Dunbar family, 92
Dunbar, P., 281
Duncan, William H., 359
Dunovant, Richard G. M., 6
Dupong, James, 531, 533, 534
Du Pont, Samuel Francis, 3, 15–16, 24–25, 27- 30, 32, 33, 35, 38, 42, 49, 55–58, 71, 73, 77, 99–100, 103–104, 107, 109, 112, 114–15, 121–24, 128, 132–33, 148–52, 170, 174–75, 177, 179, 181, 189, 196, 202, 203, 217–18, 222–25, 431, 437–38, 540
DuPont family, 406
Durant, Henry K., 159–60, 420
Dustin, Daniel, 367–68
Dutch, John C., 285–87

E.B. Hale, USS, 43, 45, 47, 193–96, 294
Earle, William, 219, 238, 245, 290, 293–94, 314–15, 317, 320, 325, 361, 398
Early,—(Captain Pilot), 532
Early Branch, S.C., 504, 509–10, 517, 561–62, 565, 572
Eaton, Samuel E., 141, 143
Eaton, William F., 277
Ebenezer (bark), 531
Ebenezer Creek, 371, 392
Eddings Point, 255, 256
Edings family, 90
Edings, Joseph Jr., 553
Edisto Island, 37, 76, 92, 108, 118, 120–21, 159, 180, 202, 239, 286, 298, 314, 372, 375, 421, 436, 445, 446, 451, 452, 552

Edisto River, 2, 94, 123, 233–35, 285, 291, 294, 296, 390
Edmonds, John, 73
Edmonston, Mary, 470
Edmund B. Hale, 193. *See also* E.B. Hale
Educational Commission for Freedmen, 73, 74
Edward, USS (USN workshop), 103, 300
Edward Doran (vessel), 521
Edwards, Aaron C., 351, 360
Edwards, George, 195
Edwards, Oliver E., 6
Edwin Lewis, USQM, 292–94
Eldridge, Oliver M. (*Atlantic*), 103
Election of 1876, 486, 490, 553, 556–58, 560, 562–63, 568, 570–71
Eley, Dick, 555
Elizabeth McCabe (sailing ship), 522
Elizabeth Miller (sloop), 532
Ellen, USS, 43, 46–47, 300
Ellenton, S.C., 467, 504
Elliott, Alfred, 471
Elliott, Ann B., 469
Elliott, Annie J., 467
Elliott, Emily, 469
Elliott family, 8, 92
Elliott, George, 46
Elliott, George P., 2, 139, 497, 501, 503
Elliott, Hannah, 465
Elliott, Henry, 289
Elliott, Henry D., 577
Elliott, John, 358, 470
Elliott, Robert Habersham, 465
Elliott, Middleton, 88
Elliott, Ralph Ems, 7, 88
Elliott, Sara Barnwell, 465, 466
Elliott, Stephen (Bishop), 89, 358, 466
Elliott, Stephen, Jr., 8, 84, 85, 88, 90, 92–94, 127–28, 130, 138–40, 144–45, 191–95, 448–49, 457
Elliott, Stephen, Sr. (Rev.), 89–90, 181, 266–67, 411, 443
Elliott, Thomas, 146, 190
Elliott, William, 88–89, 464, 466, 486, 490, 494, 519, 523, 546, 557, 560, 566–67, 573, 578, 580, 583, 585

Elliott, William "Will" Jr., 557, 580–82
Elliott, William S., 124
Elliott, William, II, 501
Elliott, William, III, 5, 7, 316, 465, 469, 500, 517
Elliott, William St. George, 46
Elliott, William Waight, 93, 94
Ellis, Daniel Hix, 83, 93, 94, 555–56
Ellis, R. A., 468, 469
Ellsworth, Thomas F., 331
Elwell, John J., 206, 215, 232, 235, 249, 252, 263, 279–80
Ely, Henry G., 495
emancipation, 62, 72, 111, 114, 117, 226–27, 251, 365, 430, 437, 583
Emancipation Day Celebrations, 165–70, 251, 263, 365, 367, 450, 474, 488–90, 544–45
Emancipation Proclamation: Fremont's, 105; Hunter's, 106, 109, 111, 114, 127; preliminary, 133, 153, 161, 165; final, 170–72
Emanuel, William P., 209–11, 213–14
Emerson, George B., 73
Emerson, Ralph Waldo, 154, 185
Emilie, USQM, 434, 628
Emminidas (ship), 532
Emmons, J. A., 495
Empire (brig), 34
Empire City, USQM, 595
Energy (ship), 531
English, E.F., 488
Enterprise, USS, 539
Episcopalians, 278
Ericsson, USQM, 595
Esau (1st S.C. private), 113
Essex, USS, 538
Etowah, CS, 98
Eustis, Frederick A., 70, 74–75, 78–79, 159, 182
Eustis, Patience Izard, 70, 190
Eustis, William, E.C., 75
Eva May (schooner), 530
Evans,—Captain, 525–27
Evans, John Gary, 487
Evans, Nathan S., 84, 288
Ezekiel, Philip, 487, 490

Faber, M.G.W., 505, 506
Faircloth, F.M., 292
Fairfax, S.C., 504
Fannie Keating (schooner), 520
Farenholt, Oscar, 145
Farmers Phosphate Company, 512–14
Farr family, 92
Farr, Joseph M., 569
Farr, Thomas, 557
Farragut (schooner), 508, 525
Fellows, Enoch Q., 180
Fennell family, 90
Fennell, M.S., 569
Fenwick Island, 37, 68
Ferebee family, 406
Ferebeeville, 10, 13
Ferguson, Charles, 113
Ferguson, John, 113
Fernandina, Fla., 33–34, 37, 56, 154, 185, 281, 373, 530, 608
Ferocepora (bark), 529
Fessenden, James Deering, 119
Fessenden, William Pitt, 119
Fickling, Francis Wellman, 83
Field's Point, 209–11, 213–14, 290
Fingal, CSS, 224
First African Baptist Church, 578
First Confiscation Act, 108, 119
Fiser, John C., 361
Fisk, Lyman, 113
Fitts, C.R., 548
Fitts family, 91–92, 569
Fletcher, Catherine, 469
Flora (Treasury Department Vessel), 64, 136, 165, 169, 204, 376, 591, 622. See also *Nemaha*
Florida, CSS, 309
Florida troops: Artillery–Light, companies: *Abell's,* 361
Flyer, John S., 78, 159, 182
Flynn, Edmund, 508
Folsom, Charles Follen, 231, 437, 438
Foot Point, 91, 238, 284, 287, 418, 511, 518, 538
Foote, Andrew H., 222–24
Forbes, John Murray, 75, 77, 183–84

Force, Manning Ferguson, 395–97, 399–400
Forrest City (tug), 532
Forrest City Brass Band, 505
Fort Beauregard, 2–3, 15, 18, 25, 33, 44, 84, 93–94, 201, 431
Fort Drayton, 37
Fort Duane, 295, 443
Fort Hardee, 360
Fort Howell, 297, 305
Fort Marion, 93
Fort McAllister, 177, 354–55
Fort Mitchel, 180, 297
Fort Monroe, 19, 44, 66–67, 111, 167, 287, 430, 434
Fort Moultrie, 86, 88, 188, 385
Fort Prince Frederick, 28, 153, 165, 215
Fort Pulaski, 7, 13–14, 17, 33–37, 48–51, 54–55, 57–59, 85, 107–8, 123, 132, 134, 148–49, 202, 208, 212, 222, 224, 304, 307, 354, 429, 434
Fort Sherman, 297
Fort Stevens, 297
Fort Sumter, 2, 84, 86, 88, 98–99, 106, 152, 181, 188, 233, 237–38, 247, 280, 282, 295, 300, 306, 318, 378, 392, 416, 418, 421, 423–26, 447, 566
Fort Walker, 3, 9, 15–17, 25, 29, 33, 44, 93, 129, 179, 201
Forten, Charlotte, xiv, 160–61, 164–65, 169, 231–32, 236–37, 251–52, 473
Forty Acres and a Mule, 386, 622
Foster, John G., xiv, 152, 174–77, 179, 188–89, 282–83, 291, 295–300, 302, 304, 306–311, 329, 332, 336, 342–43, 348–50, 354–56, 363, 371–72, 376–77, 379, 386, 390, 409, 412, 414–17
Fourteenth Amendment, xv, 458
Fowler, James H., 156, 163, 165, 169, 172, 194, 244
Fox, Charles B., 328–29, 349
Fox, George C., 74
Fox, Gustavus, 24–25, 151, 424
Franz, John, 495
Fraser, Edward W., 314–15
Fraser, USQM, 310

Free South (newspaper), 181, 184, 267, 440, 443
Freedmen, 81, 169, 173, 183, 184, 186, 204, 206, 225–26, 238, 243–44, 248–50, 252, 257, 260, 263, 265, 271, 279–82, 285, 297–98, 304, 336, 364, 369–73, 375–77, 386, 395, 414–18, 422, 425, 427–28, 430–37, 439–42, 444–46, 449–51, 453–57, 459–60, 463, 471–74, 483–84, 488, 515, 541, 544–45, 553
Freedmen's Association, 420
Freedmen's Bureau, 429, 436–37, 440–41, 445–46, 448, 452–53, 455, 457–58, 461, 472–73, 475–77, 483, 494
Freedmen's Relief Association, 73–74
Freedmen's Saving and Trust Company, 475–76, 495, 497
Freewill Baptist Church, 66
Fremont, John C., 105–106
French, Austa M., 66, 74, 76
French, Mansfield, 65, 71–78, 80–81, 108, 113–15, 119–22, 153–54, 160, 163, 168, 170, 182–83, 185, 237, 253–54, 257–60, 263, 267–71, 273, 278, 365, 386–87, 414–16, 422, 431, 450–51
Friday, Jacob, 113
Fripp, A. P., 467
Fripp, Alvira, 70
Fripp, Ann E., 468
Fripp, Ann H., 467
Fripp, Clarence, 70
Fripp, E. Nora, 467
Fripp, Edgar, 76, 237, 336, 364, 471
Fripp family, 8, 90, 92, 465
Fripp, H.P., 467
Fripp, Hamilton, 256, 287
Fripp, John, 467
Fripp, John H., 468
Fripp, Julia, 467, 468
Fripp, M.A., 467
Fripp, M.S., 467
Fripp, Marion, 467, 468
Fripp, McNair, 467, 468
Fripp, Melvin E., 467
Fripp, Oliver, 255, 256
Fripp, R. Fuller, 467, 468

674 Index

Fripp, Thomas James, 255–56
Fripp, W.W., Mrs., 480
Fripp, William, 70, 77, 266–67
Frogmore Corner, 473
Fry, William H., 64
Fuller,—Trial Justice, 551
Fuller, Charles E., 68
Fuller, Charlotte, 470
Fuller family, 8, 92, 469
Fuller, Henry, Dr., 190
Fuller, Henry M., 240, 552, 559, 578
Fuller, John W., 397, 399
Fuller, Nathaniel B., 467
Fuller, Richard, 65, 79, 159, 182, 264, 265, 426, 429–34
Fuller, Robert B., 145
Fuller, Robert M., 468
Fuller, Thomas, 65, 76, 160, 267, 278
Fuller, Thomas, Dr., 8, 181
Fulton,—(Captain of *Mississippi*), 57
Fulton, USQM, 237, 249, 421, 595
fusion politics, xii, 484, 543, 575–76, 578, 580–81, 583, 586
fusion ticket, 579, 582–84

G. Lawrence (schooner), 529
Gabriel,—Sgt., 113
Gage, Frances Dana Barker, xiv, 149, 154, 160, 162, 169, 179, 204, 206, 232, 236, 278, 336, 494
Gage, George, 179, 478, 490, 494–95, 502, 507, 510, 537
Gage, Mary, 206, 232, 235
Gadsden, Handy, 533
Galena, USS, 151, 600
Galvanized Yankee, 343, 363
Gannet, William C., 184, 272, 274, 303
Gantt, Frederick H., 94
Gantt, Hasting, 487, 559
Garden's Corner, 46, 127, 410, 481, 551, 561
Gardner, Alexander, 201
Garfield, John A., 600
Garner, T.H., 488
Garrison, William Lloyd, 66, 160, 423–26
Gartrell, Lucius J., 341, 344, 346–47, 349, 351–52, 357

Garvin, William, 469
Gary, Martin W., 558
Geary, Edward C., 323
Geary, John W., 382, 384, 401–402, 408
Geddes,—Captain, 488
General Order Number 60 (C.S.A.), 119, 597
General McClellan, USQM, 117, 122
General Sedgwick, SS, 505
George Harris (brig), 520
George M. Bird, 234. *See* also *Governor Milton,* USQM
Georgetown, S.C., 119, 154, 209, 533
George Washington, USQM, 84, 134, 136, 141, 143, 193–96
Georgia Railroad and Banking Company, 507
Georgia troops: Artillery, Light-Battalions: *14th,* 361; Artillery, Light-Batteries: *Anderson's* (Co. B, 14th Battalion), 361; *Barnwell's,* 361; *Brooks',* 86, 89, 361; *Chestatee,* 209, 211, 213–14; Infantry-Battalions: *12th,* 246; *27th,* 361; Regiments: *5th,* 344–47, 351, 360–61, 398; *32nd,* 246, 317, 334, 346, 351, 360–61, 398; *46th,* 14; *47th,* 317, 328, 331, 336, 341, 343, 346–47, 351, 360–61, 398; *54th,* 246; Legions: *Holcombe's,* 84, 87; *Phillips',* 9, 13, 127; Reserves-Battalions: *Athens,* 317–19, 324, 330, 361; *Augusta,* 317–19, 324, 346; Reserve Regiments: *1st,* 347, 351, 360, 361; *2nd,* 347, 361; *3rd,* 351, 359, 361; *5th,* 361; Militia-Divisions: *1st,* 318; Militia Brigades: *1st,* 317; State Line, 316–19, 324
Geranium, USS, 364
Gerrard, H., 220
Gettings, E. (3rd U.S. Art.), 136, 140, 144
Gibbes, H.S., 370
Gibbes, Robert M., 462
Gibbons, Francis, 550
Gifford, David L., 293
Gilchrist, A.E., 211, 213–14
Giles, Jim, 555
Gill, A.G., 548
Gill, T. T. , 557

Gillis, Jonathan, 29
Gillisonville Baptist Church, 409
Gillisonville, S.C., 83, 91, 92, 389, 410, 448, 462, 482, 548, 556–57, 561, 567–69
Gillmore, Quincy Adams, 17–19, 34, 52–54, 57–59, 208, 222–26, 228, 230, 232–33, 235, 238, 240–41, 243, 247–48, 250, 252, 268–69, 271, 280–285, 287, 291, 416–17, 420, 423–24, 428–29, 431–32, 434, 436–37, 440–43, 446
Gilmer, Jeremy, 245–46, 288–89
Giradeau, Thomas J., 330
Girardey, Camille E., 360, 361, 480, 483, 485–86, 489, 545–46, 559, 563
Gleaves, Georgianna, 480
Gleaves, Richard Howell, 474, 477
Glover,—Lieutenant, 488
Glover family, 406
Glover, Joseph, 559, 577, 581
Glover, Joshua, 158
Glover, Samuel, 585
Glover, Sanders, 572
Godbold, Huger, 211, 213, 217
Godon, Sylvanus W., 135
Goethe family, 92
Goethe, Henry, 548, 559
Goethe, S.C., 559
Gohegan, D.B., 573
Golden Gate, SS, 425
Gonzales, Ambrosio J., 2, 5, 6, 316–17, 319–20, 324, 328, 359, 388, 517
Good, Tilghman, 137, 139–40, 144, 146
Gooding family, 90
Gooding, J.J., 93
Gooding, William J., 83, 93, 559, 562, 564, 572
Goodwin, Julius, 113
Gopher Hill, 2, 141, 244, 304, 313, 317, 320, 326, 381
Gordon (bark), 525
Gould, Charles, 73
Gould, John, 141
Gouraud, George E., 329
Governor Milton, USQM, 233–35
Graham, Alexander, 60

Graham, Anna B., 470
Graham, E.H., 320, 322–23, 325
Graham family, 469
Graham, Henry, 113
Graham, Stephen, 113
Graham's Neck, 137, 138, 141, 315, 344, 348, 356, 381
Grahamville, 2, 6, 14, 125, 141–42, 190–91, 246, 304, 310, 313–17, 319–20, 326, 332, 337–38, 340–41, 343, 348, 359, 361, 380, 409, 510, 561, 582
Graham, W. P., 578–79
Grandi, Segnior, 517
Grant,—Mr., 549
Grant, David, 555
Grant, Frank, 555
Grant, H.G., 577
Grant, Jim, 113
Grant, Paddy, 549
Grant, Ulysses S., 19–20, 222, 296, 302, 362, 382, 385, 388, 415, 447, 448, 490–91, 506, 558
Gray, Sylvester F., 137
Grays Hill, 38, 42, 186, 194, 256, 478, 480
Grayson family, 186
Grayson, January, 113
Grayson, William J., 465
Great Eastern, SS, 526
Greaves, Renty, 564, 579
Greeley, Horace, 114
Green,—Sgt., 113
Green, Charles, 372
Green, Kit, 184, 461, 487, 545, 547
Green, Prince, 113
Green, Samuel, 487, 545, 547, 554, 559, 562–63, 566
Green, William, 113
Green Pond, S.C., 138, 209–13, 244–45, 291, 411
Greenback-Labor Party, 576
Greenbrier (horse), 10
Greene, James Durell, 443
Greenleaf, Arthur W., 205
Gregg, Maxey, 10, 13, 14
Gregorie family, 406
Gregorie, J. M. P., 572
Gregorie, James, 313

Gregorie, John White, 387
Gregory, W. H., 579
Gregory's Landing, Battle of, 347
Greves, James P., 74
Gries, William R., 200, 230
Grimes, James W., 421
Grover, Cuvier, 382
Guano, 505–6, 521, 522, 531
Gullah, 25, 84, 102, 128, 433, 478, 485
Gunter, John, 571
Gurney, William, 323, 329, 331, 344–45
Guss, Francis M., 179

H.B. Boddington and Company, 510–11
H.G. Ireland (schooner), 520
H. L. Hunley, CS, 299
Haas, Philip, 201
Habersham, Maria Elliott, 88, 90
Habersham, Richard W., 471
Habersham, Robert W., 449
Hagood, Johnson, 288
Haines,—Colonel, 535
Haines, Mrs. Clara, 480
Hale, Elizabeth B., 74
Hale, Mena, 74
Hall, James D.S., 231, 252, 277–78
Hall, K., 493
Halleck, Henry, 21, 85, 106, 132, 148, 176, 291, 296, 301–2, 371, 415, 591
Hallouquiser, Adelaide, 470
Hallowell, Edward N., 231, 237, 354, 356, 381, 410, 411
Halpine, Charles G., 106–7, 115, 172–73, 178, 187–88, 197, 224, 653.
Hamilton family, 90
Hamilton, John, 50
Hamilton, Gavin, 60
Hamilton, Mary Stuart, 464
Hamilton, Maurice, 582, 585
Hamilton, Paul, 76, 91, 181, 236, 464
Hamilton, Paul, 577
Hamilton, Thomas, 287, 554, 559, 563
Hamilton Guards, 93
Hamner, William Henry, 305–7, 336
Hampton, S.C., 504, 509, 520
Hampton, V.A., 66
Hampton, Wade, 388, 486, 490, 552, 558–62

Hampton and Branchville Railroad and Lumber Company, 509
Hampton City, 518
Hampton County, xii, xv, 462, 471, 481, 502, 504, 509, 517, 548, 555
Hampton Cotton Mill, 510
Hankel, Ann, 467
Harbor Island, 470
Hardee,—Mrs., 220
Hardee, F.T., 581, 585
Hardee family, 92
Hardee, William, 89
Hardee, William J., 290, 312, 315–20, 338, 340–41, 349–50, 355–58, 362, 380, 388, 389–90
Hardeeville, S.C., 2, 6, 11, 94, 95, 127, 130, 138, 142, 190–92, 218–20, 238, 244, 246, 341, 354, 358, 363, 368, 381–84
Harding, William, 68
Hardy, Washington M., 361
Harlan, James (Mrs.), 74
Harmes, George, 534
Harold, James H., 113
Harper, Capers, 488
Harriett A. Weed, USQM, 209–11, 213–14
Harrington, John W., 359
Harris, George W., 481
Harrison, Benjamin, 362, 412–13
Harrison, Carrie, 413
Harrison family, 90
Harrison, Hardy, 553
Harrison, John J., 93, 142
Harrison, George P., 361
Harrison, Samuel, 241
Harrison, Thomas, 398
Harrison, William, 522
Hartford, USS, 538
Hartwell, Alfred S., 306–7, 311, 321–22, 329–32, 338, 364
Harvest Moon, USS, 309
Harvey family, 92–93
Harvey Mills (ship), 521
Hasell, Dr., 8
Hatch, John Porter, 291, 295, 306–7, 312, 332, 336, 379, 409–10, 421, 424, 458
Hastings, 441

Index   677

Hattie, SS, 538
Hawks, Esther Hill, 159–60, 169, 205, 236, 425
Hawks, John Milton, 159, 169, 204–5, 216
Hawley, Joseph R., 145, 247, 249
Hawley, William, 145, 247, 249, 355–56
Hay, Charles E., 106
Hay, John, 106, 204, 284
Hayes, Rutherford B., 562
Haynes, Henry, 281
Hazen, William B., 379, 381, 384, 407
Henderson,—Mr., 549
Henderson, E.P., 569
Heape family, 93
Heasey, Alexander W., 245
Heckman, Charles A., 179
Helper, Hinton R., 29
Henrietta (bark), 590
Henry, A. G., 267
Henry, Guy V., 136, 140, 144–46
Henry Andrew, USS, 51
Heyward, Benjamin, 467
Heyward, Charles, 364, 411
Heyward, Daniel, 126, 410
Heyward, Daniel Blake, 125, 138
Heyward, Ed "Dog," 517
Heyward family, xiv, 40, 92
Heyward, George C., 92
Heyward, Nathaniel, 149, 181, 267, 370, 387, 494
Heyward, Thomas (signer), 94
Heyward, Thomas, 467
Heyward, William of (Old House), 93
Heyward, William, 190
Heyward, William Cruger, 6, 93–94, 210, 212–13
Heyward, William Nathaniel, 577, 579, 315
Hickory Hill, S.C., 190, 389, 399–400, 402–403, 546
Hiers family, 569
Higginson, Francis "Frank," 231
Higginson, Thomas Wentworth, 163, 203–204, 206–207, 215, 217, 221, 225–27, 229–30, 232, 240, 242, 244–45, 248, 272, 284, 452; takes command, 154, 156; Emancipation Day celebration, 164–174; Jacksonville occupation, 185–88; sinking of George Washington, 194–99; Edisto River Raid, 233–35; Emancipation Day (1864), 250–52
Higginsonville, 299, 418, 481
Hill, Daniel H., 357
Hill, Edwin R., 329
Hilton Head Island, 24, 32, 35, 37–38, 41, 43–44, 50, 55, 76, 94–94, 107–108, 117–18, 132, 149, 188, 204–205, 215, 217–18, 224, 232, 236, 247–49, 251, 254, 285, 295, 303–6, 364, 373, 417–20, 422–23, 426, 428, 433, 435–37, 439, 443, 446, 450, 460–61, 469–70, 555, 567; November 1861 attack, 13–18; federal encampments, 30–38, 69, 101, 128–29, 170, 179–81, 202, 237–38, 296–98, 300; Jubilee of Freedom, 40; plantations, 68; 1st South Carolina formed, 109–12, 120; refugee camp, 68, 70, 133, 239, 258, 275, 298
Hiott, Malichi, 334
Hitchcock,—Mrs., 232
Hitchcock, Henry, 386–87
Holmes, Abby, 495
Holmes, Almeda, 509
Holmes, Francis S., 511
Holmes, George, 464, 490, 496, 543, 559, 566
Holmes, Peter, 522
Holmes, Reuben G., 478, 509, 517–18, 525
Holt, Joseph, 114, 242, 424
Holy Trinity Episcopal Church (Grahamville), 409
Homans, William H., 333
Home Rule, 482, 541–44
Honey Hill, 6, 190, 348–50, 359–60, 381, 458, 488; Battle of, 301–40
Hood, John B., 312, 340, 362
Hooper, Edward W., 74, 77, 117, 186, 227, 259, 334
Hooper, Henry N., 310, 329
Hoover, George, 571–72
Hoover's Station, 504, 509, 559, 571

Horton family, 90
Hospitals: B.B. Sams I (contraband), 159, 209; B.B. Sams II (#3), 236; Baptist Church (#14), 240; Barnwell Castle (#5), 182, 286; Barnwell-Gough (#10), 204–5, 236, 240, 249, 414; Beaufort College, 240, 414, 434; Bolan Church, 334–35; Boyd Mansion, 349; Edgar Fripp house (#7), 237, 336, 364; Edward Means (#2), 181, 236; George Parsons Elliott (#15), 497; H.M. Fuller (#10), 240; Hilton Head Hospital, 129, 180–81, 204; Honey Horn, 129; John Johnson (#8), 181–82, 236; John Joyner Smith (#9), 236; Joseph Johnson (#6), 236–37; Lewis Reeve Sams (#13), 117, 181, 232; Naval Hospital (Land's End), 300; Paul Hamilton (#1), 181, 236; Robert W. Barnwell house (officer's hospital), 181, 236; St. Helena Church (#12), 240, 279; William Elliott, III (#11), 557, 560; William Wigg Barnwell (#4) 182, 236
Houghton, Nathaniel, 305
Hotchkiss, Cyrus C., 352
Housatonic, USS, 299
Houses: A.G. Verdier, 220; Adams House, 43, 45–47; Andrew Burnet, 211; Baker House, 266; Barnwell Castle, 236, 494; Beech Hill, 356; Berners B. Sams I, 182; Berners B. Sams II, 236; Chalmers, 220; Chaplin House, 47–48; Charles Cheves, 358, 367–68, 383, 384; Charles E. Leverett, 40; Charles Green, 372; Club House, 39; Cockroft, 181; Crofut, 509; Crosby, 220; D. Freeman, 220; D. and J. Canter, 220; Daniel Heyward, 126, 410; David L. Thompson, 202; Dr. A. G. Verdier, 220; Dr. F.H. Pope, 220; Dr. Fickling, 395; Dr. J.W. Kirk, 220; Dr. Mellichamp, 220; Dr. Paul Pritchard, 220; Dr. Thomas Fuller, 181; Duncan C. Wilson, 509; Edgar Fripp, 237, 336; Edmund Rhett, 159; Edward Barnwell, 44, 182; Elizabeth Hext Sams, 266; Estate Norton, 220; Ferguson Hutson, 289; Fuller-McKee House (Bay and Carteret), 98, 117, 181; G. Allen, 220; G. W. Lawton, 220; George Allen, 220; George Chisolm Mackay, 7; George Parsons Elliott, 497; Gregory, 410; H. Gerrard, 220; H.F. Train, 220; H.M. Fuller, 240; H.R. Pope, 220; H.S. Gibbes, 379; Halfway House, 256; Henry G. Judd, 227; Henry Verdier, 220; J. Bullchen, 220; J. Chalmers, 220; J. McKenzie, 220; J.G. Bullchen, 220; J.J. Pope, 220; J.J. Stoney, 220; James Crofut, 509; James Gregory, 344; James L. Paul, 211; James Robert Verdier, 205; James Seabrook, 220; John A. Cuthbert, 410; John F. Chaplin, 266; John J. Smith, 236, 369; John Bell house, 266; John Jeremiah Theus Pope, 76; John Johnson, 236; John Joyner Smith, 236, 369; John McKee, 97–98, 267; Joseph Baynard, 220; Joshua Nicholls, 209, 211; Langballe, 220; Ledbetter, 159; Lewis Reeves Sams, 117, 181, 232; M.J. Kirk, 220; Maner, 389; Martin, 220; Mary Jenkins, 460; McKee House/DeTreville/Smalls House, 97, 483; Mission House, 277, 278; Morris, 235; Mr. Strobhart, 220; Mrs. Hardee, 220; Mrs. McBribe, 400; Mrs. Pinckney, 220; Mrs. Winingham, 220; Nathaniel Heyward, 181, 267, 387; Old House, 93; Pope House (Fort Walker), 44, 179; Porteus, 181; Rev. Stephen Elliott (William Elliott II), 266, 443; Richard DeTreville, 7; Squire Pope, 220; Stewart, 46; Stuart House, 227, 267; Talbird House, 347; Thomas Drayton, 220; Thomas Fuller, 238; Thomas Fuller House (Fuller-French), 238; Thomas Hazel, 266; Thomas Ledbetter, 266, 159; W. Pope, 220; W. Winn, 220; W.J. Jenkins (Saxton House), 280; Whitehall, 238; Wiggins, 220; William Elliott (Ralph Ems Elliott/Anchorage), 557, 560; William Fripp, 266–67; William Kirkland, 211; William W. Barnwell, 182; Chisholm,

181; Daniel Heyward House, 126, 410; David L. Thompson House, 202; Dr. Charles Cheves House, 358, 367–68, 383–84; Dr. Ficklin House, 395; Dr. Thomas Fuller House (Fuller-McKee), 97, 117; Edgar Fripp House (Hospital #7), 237; Edmund Rhett House, 157; Edward Means House (Hospital #8), 181, 236; Ferguson Hutson House, 289; Fish Haul Plantation, 40, 101, 112, 115, 460; Fuller-McKee House (Bay and Carteret), 97, 117, 181; George Parsons Elliott House, 497; H.M. Fuller House, 240; James Gregory House, 344; James Robert Verdier House, 205; John A. Cuthbert House, 410; John Johnson House (Hospital #3), 182, 236; John Joyner Smith House (Hospital #9), 236, 369; Joseph Johnson House (Hospital #6), 236; Lewis Reeves Sams House, 117, 181, 232; Maner House, 389; McKee House/DeTreville House/Smalls House, 97, 267; Nathaniel Heyward House, 149, 267, 376; Paul Hamilton House (Hospital #1), 181, 236; Robert Smalls, 267, 460–61, 463; Senator Robert Barnwell House, 182; Talbird House, 347; Thomas Fuller House (Fuller-French), 65, 76, 160, 238; W.J. Jenkins House, 280; William W. Barnwell House (Hospital #4), 182, 236
Howard, Charles H., 420–21, 431, 442, 445–46, 472
Howard, James M. F., 74
Howard, John H., Sr., 314, 553
Howard, Oliver O., 354, 356, 372, 377, 379–80, 394, 429, 435, 445–46, 451–52, 475
Howard, Thomas Heyward, 314
Howard Drake, SS, 423
Howard School, 475
Howe, Samuel Gridley, 76, 81, 168, 226
Howell, Joshua, 287
Hoyt, Edmund (Capt. 2nd S.C.), 210, 212
Hubbard, Erastus, 202, 523
Hudson family, 92

Hughes, Aaron Konkle, 538
Huguenin, Abram, 569
Huguenin, Thomas A., 88
Humes, William Y. C., 390, 395, 589
Hunn, Elizabeth, 160, 165, 169, 232, 481
Hunn, Hannah Miss, 480
Hunn, John, 365, 482, 542–43
Hunter, David, 107, 133, 150, 173–74, 180–81, 189, 196, 201–2, 205, 258, 277, 281–82, 409, 422, 452, 595, 600; takes command, 57–59, 78, 104–6; raises 1st S.C., 108–20, 154; and Jefferson Davis, 119, 197–98; Emancipation Proclamation, 108–12; returns to command, 150, 152; and N.C. troops, 175–79; tax sales, 183–84, 253; use of black troops, 185–88, 190, 206–9, 215–17, 221, 228; relieved, 222, 224–25
Hunter, William W., 354–55
Hunting Island, 27, 30, 37, 98, 255, 287, 531, 535–36
Hunting Island (Kirk's), 218, 220
Hurlbut, George R., 304
Hutson,—Dr., 138
Hutson, Charles J. C., 554, 559, 571
Hutson family, 93
Hutson, M. M., 504
Hutson, William Ferguson, 83, 289, 448
Hutto, John, 553

Ida, CSS, 54, 355
Illinois troops: Mounted Infantry – Regiments: *9th,* 395–97, 402; *20th,* 396; Infantry-Regiments: *34th,* 403, 408
India (USN workshop), 103, 300
Indiana troops: Infantry-Regiments: *25th,* 397; *33rd,* 408
Ingalls, Gustavus W., 180–81, 202, 230
Ino (brig), 529–30
Isaac (1st S.C. Private), 113
Isaac Smith, USS, 36
Isabella Hartnett (bark), 529
Isabella Jewett (schooner), 520
Island City, USQM, 218
Ismael, Tom, 113

Isondiga, CSS, 356
Isundiga (locomotive), 353
Ivanhoe (tug), 532–33
Izard, Charlotte Georgina, 620
Izard, Joseph Allen Smith, 620
Izard, Ralph, 356, 358, 362, 620

J. H. Wolf (vessel), 521
J. J. More (schooner), 569
J. Rich and Company, 500, 505, 509
Jackson,—Cpl., 113
Jackson, Andrew, 16, 21
Jackson, Charlotte, 480
Jackson, John H., 55–56, 146
Jackson, George T., 324, 327, 400, 402
Jackson, Nathaniel James, 381–82, 393
Jackson, S.C., 504
Jackson, Thomas "Stonewall" J., 85, 111, 223
Jacksonboro, 233–34
Jacksonville, Fla., 134, 185–86, 242, 283–85, 304–306, 336, 354, 373, 465
James Adger, USS or USQM, 175
James, LaRue P., 135
James, William, 120
Jamison, David F., 83
Jasper County, xii, 481, 486, 511, 611
Jaundon family, 92
Jeffords, R. J., 138
Jeffry (1st S.C. Private), 113
Jenkins, A. P., 563
Jenkins, Daniel, 481
Jenkins, John, 314–17, 320, 342, 328, 330, 334–35, 344, 360, 460
Jenkins, Joseph, 274
Jenkins, Mary, 460
Jenkins, Micah, 314
Jenkins, Michael, 348, 356–57, 381
Jenkins, Robert, 533–34
Jenkins, William, 193
Jenkins, William J., Dr. 25, 60, 68, 280
Jenkins Island, 101, 286, 297
Jenks, 309
Jennie Murphy (schooner), 520
Jerry (book), 466
Jerry (1st S.C. Private), 113
Joe (1st S.C. Private), 113

John Adams, USQM, 209–10, 212–14, 233–34, 251
John Kennedy (dredge), 513, 524
Johnson, Andrew, 427, 430, 440, 443–44, 446–47, 449, 451, 453, 457–58, 461, 472, 477
Johnson, Benjamin Jenkins, 85
Johnson family, 90, 92
Johnson, J. A., 562
Johnson, J. D., 555
Johnson, John A., 358, 461
Johnson, Nathan R., 74
Johnson, R., 290
Johnson, Richard (Lt.), 359–60
Johnson, Thomas H., 91, 141–43, 218–20, 246
Johnson, Mrs. Walter R., 74
Johnson, William, 518
Johnston family, 569
Johnston, Joseph E., 89, 318, 428–29
Johnston, William C., 571
Jones family, 569
Jones, Hannah, 98
Jones, J. S., 218
Jones, James, 6, 8, 45, 47–48
Jones, Samuel, 289–90, 312, 315–17, 320, 340–41, 344, 346–47, 349, 357, 360
Jones, Thomas, 554
Jones Island, 51–53, 55
Joseph Whitney, SS, 595
Jubilee of Freedom, 17, 33, 133, 162, 166, 422
Judd, Henry G., 169, 227, 252, 281, 472, 476, 480, 494, 507, 562, 575
Julian, George W., 259

Kadesh Church, 380
Kanapaux, John Theodore (Capt. Lafayette), 191, 290, 314, 320, 361
Kansas troops: Infantry-Regiment: *3rd,* 174
Katahdin, USS, 309
Kate (bark), 521
Katie L. Gifford (sailing ship), 522
Keith, S. J. Miss, 480
Kennedy, John Doby, 377, 388, 411
Keokuk, USS, 150, 188–89

Kessler, John, 534
Ketchum, Alexander P., 259, 269
Ketchum, Edgar, 73
Key, Francis Scott, 446
Key, Philip Barton, II, 446
Keystone (pilot boat), 532
Kidder, Mary W., 467
Killingsworth family, 92
Kilpatrick, Judson, 363, 384, 387, 401, 408
Kinard family, 92
King, Edward, 163
King, John K., 526, 528
King, Mitchell, Jr., 346, 619
King, Robert, 330
King, Susie Baker, 120, 249, 609
Kingfisher, USS, 233–34, 285–87
Kingman, M. M., 494, 547
Kingman, Samuel, 98
Kings Creek Post Office, 404
Kinkora (dredge), 513, 523
Kinzie, Arthur M., 106, 113, 119
Kinzie, John H., 595
Kinzie, Maria Indiana, 105, 595
Kirby, Dennis T., 379, 397
Kirk, James W., Dr., 55, 220, 287
Kirk, John W., 406
Kirk, Manning J., 135, 138, 144, 147, 191, 196, 288, 317, 334–35, 341, 360–61
Kirk, W. J., 246, 511
Kirkland, G. H., 92
Kirkland, William, 211
Knotts, Francis L., 469
Knotts, William T., 469
Knowlton, Ebenezer, 277
Knowlton, Lyman, 74
Ku Klux Klan, 548
Kuh, Anna, 543
Kuh, E. S., 482, 543

Ladson, Cypher "Double Quick," 549
Lady Dufferien, SS, 525–27
Lady's (Ladies) Island, 25, 68, 76, 79, 96, 110, 124, 128, 135, 165, 184, 255–56, 426, 432, 454, 461, 514, 561
Lamb, Jessie C., 470
Lamkin, Jameo N., 192
Lance, W. J., 569

Lander, Frederick West, 21, 203
Lander, Jean Davenport, 203–5, 207, 215, 231–32, 234–36, 238, 248–52
Langballe, 220
Langford, Elizabeth "Lizzie" Botume, 377, 434, 474
Langford, Frances "Fanny" Sophia, 377, 434, 474
Langley, Square, 279
Langley, Loudon S. (Langley, Landon), 279, 478, 559, 612
Lathrop, John D., 74
Law, Oliver P., 571–72
Lawton, Alexander J., 83
Lawton, Alexander R., 85
Lawton family, 569
Lawton, G. W., 220
Lawton, Joseph M., 83
Lawton, T. A., 573
Lawton Church, 561
Lawtonville, 389, 395, 400–403, 406, 510, 559
Lawtonville Narrow Gauge Railroad, 510
Lay, John F., 220
Leach, Franklin S., 390–91
Leasure, Daniel, 40, 47–48
Leavitt, Joshua, 424
LeBleux, Louis F., 138, 143
Ledbetter, Thomas D., 159, 219, 266
Lee, Agnes, 7
Lee, Annie, 7, 12
Lee, Barnard K., Jr., 68, 70, 281, 417
Lee, Francis D., 3, 4
Lee, Robert E. (Commander of S.C., Ga. and Fla.), 3–14, 35, 38, 41, 95, 111, 119, 130, 288, 318, 377–78, 388, 423
Lee, Stephen D., 89
Lee, W. H., 523
Legare, Martha Ann, 576
Leggett, Mortimer Dormer, 380
Leigh, Charles C., 73
Lena Reed (schooner), 525
Lesesne, Daniel, 516
Lesesne, Margaret Witsell, 516
Leverett, Charles E., 40, 93
Leverett, Frederic P., 94
Leverett, Milton Maxcy, 92, 409

Lewis, James, 305, 352
Lewis, Joseph Jackson, 257, 260, 262, 264, 268–70
Lewis, S. J., 572
Lewis, T. W., 266, 278–79
Liberal "Republican" Party, 546
Liberia Scheme, 462, 575
Lighthouses, 25, 27, 30, 36–37, 98, 418, 534–36
Lightsey, J. C., 509
Lightsey, John A., 571–72
Lightsey family, 92
Ligon, Robert B., 359
Lilley, William, 68
Limber, Jim, 435. *See also* Brooks, James Henry
Lincoln, Abraham, 17, 21, 29, 34, 50, 64, 82, 106, 121, 132, 183, 189, 203–4, 206, 229, 237, 252, 284, 303, 318, 362, 369, 422, 430, 435, 476, 488, 583; reconstruction, 61–62, 66, 69, 72, 436, 440; emancipation, 111–17, 153, 161–63, 166–68, 171–72; churches in Beaufort, 80; and Hunter, 105, 111–14, 186, 197; pay for black troops, 241–42; tax sales, 253–62, 268, 270, 273; death, 425–427
Lindsay, Arod E., 333
Lindsay, John, 73, 592
Little Barnwell Island, 244
Littlefield, Milton S., 206, 241, 243, 281–83, 414–17, 419–21, 426
Lizzie Marrow (bark), 529
Lockwood, W. W., 504
Lockwood, William H., 495–97, 557, 564, 566, 577
Logan, John A., 362, 370, 379, 381–82, 387, 394–95, 399–400, 402, 407
Longbrow Plantation, 211
Longstreet, James, 89, 360–61
Loper, A. C., 569
Loper, J. M., 569
Loper's Crossroads, S.C., 400
Lopez, Julian, 582
Louly (sloop), 534
Low, Elizabeth C., 207
Lowe, Thaddeus S.C., 34

Lowndes, Charles T., 210
Lowndes, James, 196
Lowrey, A. M., 213
Lowrey, A. W., 92
Lowthar family, 92
Lubbock, Francis Richard, 434
Luce, Stephen B., 43, 309, 344, 349, 390–93, 537, 540
Lucy Wheatly (schooner), 525
Lynch, Heyward, 579
Lynch, J. M., 494
Lynch, James T., 231, 251, 277–79, 372

Macaulay, Thomas Babbington, 376
Macbeth, John R., 247
Mack, David, 74
Mackey, Edmund W. M., 560, 562–63
Mackey, George Chisolm, 7
Mackey, John, 7
Mackey, Margaret, 7
Mackey's Neck, 134, 139, 315
Mackey's Point, 47, 136–37, 141, 143, 147, 149
Macon, CSS, 340, 355
Macon, Ga., 318, 340, 505, 518, 520
Maffitt, John Newland, 7–8
Magee, J. J., 286
Magnolia Route, 506
Magrath, Andrew Gordon, 377, 429
Mahan, Alfred Thayer, 308–309
Mahan, Dennis Hart, 423
Maine troops: Infantry-Regiments: *8th*, 45, 149, 165, 173, 181, 185, 244, 251; *9th*, 192, 228; *13th*, 57
Mair and Cranmer (ship), 521
Malphrus family, 92
Mandel, William C., 292
Manning, Jacob, 67
Marblehead, USS, 136, 147
March (1st S.C. Private), 74
Marcia Greenup (ship), 522
Marcy, Henry Orlando, 324, 327, 398, 409–11
Marine River Mining Company. 511–12, 529
Marines, U.S., 16, 29, 31, 36, 225, 294, 307–10, 314, 328, 334, 344–45,

347–48, 351–52, 363–64, 392, 424, 538
Marion Men of Combahee, 91
Marple, William W., 304, 331–32
Marsh, Marvin Manville, 205
Martin, 220
Martin, A. M., 569
Martin, Abram, 572
Martin, Alfred M., 83, 92, 448, 559
Martin, B. J., 557, 564
Martin, Benjamin, 569
Martin, Edmund, 448
Martin, William E., 6–9, 91
Martin, William Edward, 91
Martin, S.C., 504
Martin, T.H., 577
Mary A. Boardman, USQM, 292
Mary Ann, SS, 428
Mason, William, 509
Massachusetts, USQM, 121
Massachusetts troops: Cavalry-Regiments: *1st,* 75, 120, 124, 128, 136, 149, 567; *4th,* 292–93, 304, 311, 321–22, 336, 349, 410–11; Infantry-Regiments: *2nd,* 217, 356; *3rd,* 67; *16th,* 153; *31st,* 37; *51st,* 154–55; *54th,* 216–17, 221, 228–29, 231–33, 235–37, 241, 250, 279, 304, 307, 310, 329, 331–32, 339, 347, 354, 356, 381, 410–12, 424, 454; *55th,* 303–4, 307, 321, 324, 328–31, 342, 349, 379
Matanzas, USQM, 57
Mather Industrial School, 474
Mather, Rachel Crane, 474
Mattano, USQM, 110
Matthew's Bluff, 361, 573
Matthews, Orville E., 308, 424
Mauldin, Lillie, 509, 511
Mauldin, W. H., 509–10, 520, 572
Mauldin, William H., 509
Maxwell, A.C., 577
May River, 13, 55, 134, 218, 287, 314–15, 317
Mayflower, USQM, 41–42, 52–53, 59, 218–20
Mayo, J. C., 507, 542–44
Mayo, S., 495

Mayo, Sylvanus, 267
McBride,—Mrs., 400
McBride Store, 502
McClellan, SS, 117, 122
McClellan, George B., 19–21, 33–34, 41, 50, 111, 201
McGill, Z., 566
McGowan, Samuel, 45, 47
McIntire, Robert, 544
McKaye, James, 226–27
McKee, Henry, 23, 98, 268
McKee, John, 97–98
McKenzie family, 406
McKenzie, J., 220
McKim, James, 77, 81, 226
McLaws, Lafayette, 289–90, 312–13, 360–62, 380, 389–90
McNath, J. D., 68
McNiel, Walter, 572
McPhersonville, S.C., 130, 211, 238, 289, 314, 390, 394–95, 399, 407–8, 548
McPhersonville Chapel of Ease, 408
McPhersonville Hospital, 192
McPhersonville Road, 126, 145, 399
McTeer, Wiley W., 572
McTier's Mill, 380, 390
McTureous, Thomas M., 470–71
McWhirter, Hattie, 467
Means, Anne S., 467
Mearses family, 569
Meigs, Montgomery, 18, 296, 370
Mellichamp, Dr., 220
Melville, SS, 417
Memorial Day, 489
Mercury, USS, 128
Merriam, Francis, 216
Mersereau, Thomas J., 304, 307, 335
Methodists, 66, 75, 77, 80, 156, 220, 278, 412, 478
Methodist Church (Wesley), 66, 182, 200, 275, 278, 478
Michigan troops: Infantry-Regiments: *1st (colored),* 296–97; *2nd,* 305; *8th,* 41–43, 45, 47, 124, 127; *19th,* 36
Mickler, John H., 93, 130, 218, 220
Middleton, Cumberland, 549
Middleton, Edward, 212

Middleton family, 211, 213–14
Middleton, James B., Rev., 566, 575
Midddleton, John Izard, 212
Middleton, Williams, 212
Military Bank of Beaufort, 298, 475
Militia Act of 1792, 229
Militia Act of 1862, 117, 229
Miller, Bysell and Burnum, 520
Miller, Caesar, 278
Miller, Thomas Ezekiel, 481, 483, 486–87, 554, 559, 576–77, 580, 583–84
Miller, William A., 314
Millett, Stephen Caldwell, Jr., 267–68, 281, 478, 501–504, 507
Millett, Stephen Caldwell, Sr., 267
Milton, John, 70
Mingle,—(1st S.C. Private), 113
Mingoe, USS, 309, 311, 344
Mintoye, W. L., 539
Mission House, 277–78
Mississippi, SS, 527
Mississippi, USQM, 56–58
Missouri troops: Infantry-Regiments: *11th,* 395; *18th,* 396; *29th,* 399
Mitchel,—Captain, 488
Mitchel, Charles L., 330
Mitchel, Julian, 451
Mitchel, Ormsby McKnight, 122, 131–35, 148–52, 600
Mitchel, W. M., 566
Mitchell, Bacchus, 543
Mitchell, F. S., 577
Mitchell, Joseph Davis, 149
Mitchelville, 129, 249, 258, 275, 278, 297–99, 419–20, 431, 460
Mixson family, 90, 93
Mixson, L., 569
Missroon, John S., 35
Moffett, Martha H., 471
Mohican, USS, 15
Moise, Edwin W., 583–85
Moise, Marion, 565
Monitor, USS, 59, 150–52, 157, 175
Montana (schooner), 520
Montauk, USS, 175, 247
Montgomery, SS, 531
Montgomery Hill, 215, 298, 376

Montgomery, James, 155, 174, 184–85, 188, 201, 207–10, 213–17, 221, 228–30, 232, 292–94, 298, 304, 376
Montgomery, Milton, 397, 399
Montmollin, Louis, 549
Moonbeam (bark), 570
Moore, Henry P., 202
Moore, James Washington, 556–57, 559, 562, 567, 569
Moore, John L., 359
Moore, Joseph, 394
Morcock, Charles, 4
Morcock, Cooper, 4
Morcock, E. W., 4
Morgan,—Sgt. (54th Mass.), 236
Morgan, George D., 75
Morgan, Henry G., 468
Morgan, James Dada, 403–4
Morgan, Joseph H., 139
Morgan, Matilda, 468
Morgan Island, 68, 118, 467
Morgan Landing, 358
Morgan River, 30, 36
Morrall family, 92
Morrill, Justin, 421
Morris, 490
Morris family, 92, 234
Morris Island, 88, 188, 233, 235, 237–38, 249, 280, 304–7, 354, 452
Morris Rice Mill, 234
Morrison family, 569
Morrison, John F., 573
Morrison, John T., 556, 572
Morrison, William C., 487, 546
Morrison, Z. T., 571
Morton, Oliver P., 392
Moses, Franklin J., 486, 544–47
Mountain Ash (bark), 529
Mower, Joseph A., 368, 395–400
Murchison, Abraham, 108, 277, 279, 299
Murray, Ellen, 118, 161, 164, 207, 231, 275–76, 278–79, 286, 365, 370, 375, 453, 473–74
Murray, George Washington, 583–85
Murray, J. A., 514
Myer, Albert J., 44, 48
Myers, N. B., 547

Myers, Nathaniel, 563
Myers, Thomas, 553
Myrell, F.M., 523

Naglee, Henry M., 176
Nahant, USS, 188, 224
Nantucket, USS, 188
Nash, Elizabeth F., 471
Nashville, SS, 527
National Commission for Freedmen's Relief Association, 73–74
National Freedmen's Relief Association, 73–74, 159
Nelson, I. J., 571
Nelson, William (USN), 292
Nelson, William (U.S.A.), 392
Nemaha, USQM, 310, 342, 346, 377, 431, 591, 622
Nesbitt, Miles, 346
Nettles family, 90
Nevada, USQM, 370, 376–77
New England Freedmen's Aid Society, 102
New Hampshire troops: Infantry-Regiments: *3rd,* 55, 84, 130, 136–38, 144, 146, 176, 180, 202, 228, 230; *4th,* 41, 136, 138, 141, 144, 146–47; *7th,* 133
New Hampshire, USS, 299, 538–39
New Ironsides, USS, 150–51, 155, 188–89, 300
New Jersey troops: Infantry-Regiments: *13th,* 356
New River, 6, 10–11, 13, 30, 41, 50–51, 190, 192, 246, 314, 358, 368, 382–83; fortifications, 6, 10, 246, 290, 314, 361
New South (newspaper), 101, 181, 427, 439–40, 450, 459–60, 485, 536
New York and Port Royal Steamship Line, 527
New York Herald, 106, 179
New York Times, 106, 129, 265, 500, 502, 510
New York Tribune, 154, 215, 231, 263, 298, 337, 419
New York troops: Artillery, Light-Regiments: *3rd ,* 304, 307, 321, 326–27, 329, 332–33, 343–45, 349, 351; Batteries: *B,* 304, 307, 326–27, 329, 332–33, 335, 349; *E (Hamilton),* 38, 42; *F,* 304, 307, 327, 329, 333, 335, 343–45, 351; Engineer-Regiments: *1st,* 18, 49, 108, 113, 133–34, 136–38, 141, 201–2, 218, 297; Infantry-Battalions: *Enfans Perdus,* 52, 177; Infantry-Regiments: *31st,* 268; *46th,* 36; *47th,* 37, 42–43, 47, 107; *48th,* 42, 43, 47, 50–52, 80, 113, 134, 136–37, 141, 143, 149, 153, 218, 228, 251, 288; *56th,* 169, 247, 258, 304, 306, 321, 323, 326, 333, 335–36, 344–45, 350, 381; *69th (militia),* 106; *79th,* 18, 21, 32, 38, 42, 43, 46, 60, 109, 114, 124, 127; *115th,* 356; *127th,* 169, 228, 303, 305, 306, 311, 321–23, 326–27, 329, 331, 335–36, 344–45, 350, 352, 354, 381; *140th,* 20; *144th,* 282, 297, 303, 305, 306, 311, 321–23, 325–26, 329, 335, 337, 342, 345, 350, 352; *150th,* 354, 393; *157th,* 304, 306, 311, 321, 326, 333, 337, 343–45, 350, 352; National Guard-Regiments: *71st,* 268
Newcomb, George, 365, 436, 478–79, 631
Newton, H. H., 210
Nichols, Edgar, 494
Nichols, George Ward, 406
Nicholson, James William Augustus, 36–37
Nicholson, Mary, 74
Nicholls, Joshua, 211, 213
Nickels, J. Frederick, 98–99
Niven, Ninian, 74
Nixville, S.C., 402, 561, 573
Nobles, William H., 32, 60–61, 63, 78
Nordhoff, Charles, 463
North Carolina troops (C.S.A.): Artillery-Battery, light: *Anderson's,* 361; Cavalry-Regiment: *1st,* 337; Infantry-Battalions: *10th,* 361, 397; Infantry-Regiments: *8th,* 6; *25th,* 6; *27th,* 191; *47th,* 191; *48th,* 191; *50th,* 191; Reserves-Regiments: *1st,* 360; *7th,* 361

North Carolina troops (U.S.A.): Infantry-Regiments: *1st (colored),* 304; *1st,* 306
Northerner, USRC, 430
Norton, Estate, 220
Noyes, Elizabeth H., 470

O.M. Pettit, USS, 128, 309
Oak Point Company (Mines), 512–14, 529
Oakman, Clifford, 467
Ocean Queen, USQM, 68
Oceanus, SS, 425
O'Brien, John, 533
O'Dell, Alice, 493–95
O'Dell, James, 493–95
Oglesby family, 92
Ohio troops: Infantry-Regiments: *25th,* 297, 305, 306, 310, 311, 321–23, 325, 326, 328, 329, 333–36, 342, 345, 350, 352, 381, 410, 619; *67th,* 250; *75th,* 354; *107th,* 354, 363, 410
O'Kane, James, 308, 363
Old Fort Schoolhouse, 299, 364–65, 370, 376–77, 427, 434–35, 444, 449, 451, 474
Old Rina, 426, 441
Old Sam (horse), 388
Olive Crosby (vessel), 521
Olmstead, Charles H., 58–59
Olmstead, Frederick Law, 20
Olustee, Battle of, 285, 287, 304, 488
Onward, USS, 98
O'Reilly, Miles, 107, 187. *See also* Halpine, Charles G.
Oriental, USQM, 77
O'Rorke, Patrick H., 20, 30, 51–54, 59
Osage, USQM, 174
Ossippee, USS, 538
O'Sullivan, Timothy, 201
Oswald, George Washington, 8, 9, 48
Ottawa, USS, 43–45, 128
Otter Island, 30, 36–37, 159, 534
Owen, Robert Dale, 226
Owens, A. E., 554

Pacific Guano Company, 512, 514, 516–17, 520, 529, 550

Page, Charles A., 215
Page, Nathaniel, 231–32
Page Point, 8–10, 14, 40–41, 46, 130
Palmer, James H., 74
Palmetto Post, 298, 514, 582, 584–85
Panic of 1873, 476, 506
Papin, Peter, 517, 519
Park, William E., 74
Parker, Charles H., 125
Parker, J. W., 276
Parker, Theodore, 154
Parmalee, Harriett, 493
Parris Island, 8, 22, 24, 68, 76, 79, 96, 118, 128, 168, 172, 178–79, 183, 204, 206, 232, 249, 255–56, 276, 278, 306, 442, 449, 461, 470, 481, 484, 534–35, 539, 553, 561
Parrott, Enoch G., 99
Parrott, Robert, 243
Passaic, USS, 150–51, 175, 188
Passaic Class Monitors, 150–51, 175
Patapsco, USS, 176, 188
Patroon, USS, 136–37, 141
Patterson, John H., 331
Patterson, John J., 489–90, 548
Patterson, William Bailey, 348
Pattison, Thomas Harmon, 491
Paul, James L., 211
Paul Jones, USS, 135–37, 147
Pawnee, USS, 29, 309, 311, 342, 390–91, 538
Peale, Washington, 202
Pearce, David, 553
Pearson, Frederick, 135, 137
Peck, Ellen H., 74, 128
Peck, George B., 74
Peck, Solomon, 65, 70, 76, 79–80, 128, 159, 165, 182, 240, 269, 277–78
Peeples, S.C., 559, 561
Peeples, D. G., 573
Peeples, McBride, 502, 549
Peeples, William B., 92, 313, 315, 317, 320, 322, 324
Pemberton, John C., 9–14, 45–46, 95, 97, 130, 190
Pembina, USS, 26–28, 43, 45, 47, 51
Penn School, 164, 275, 473

Pennsylvania Freedmen's Commission, 276
Pennsylvania Freedmen's Relief Association, 592
Pennsylvania troops: Infantry-Regiments: *45th,* 37; *47th,* 114, 136–40, 144, 146, 149, 447; *50th,* 38, 42–43, 45, 47, 124–25, 128–29; *52nd,* 230, 232; *55th,* 136–38, 140, 144–45, 148–49; *76th,* 136, 138, 144–46, 228, 287; *97th,* 169; *100th,* 40, 42, 47; *104th,* 186, 200, 208, 215, 226, 230, 304
Pennyworth Island, 358
People's Ticket, 576–81, 586
Pepita (bark), 529
Perritt, J. A., 92
Perry, Benjamin Frankin, 443
Perry, Cato, 556
Perry, Edward S., 146
Perry, James H., 52
Perryclear, Henria, 469
Perryclear, James S., 469
Perryclear, Mary A., 469
Perryclear School, 481
Peter Crerar (bark), 529
Philbrick, Edward S., 74, 77–78, 81, 118, 183–84, 239, 253–54, 260, 263, 272, 275, 303
Phillips, Samuel D., 162, 601
Phillips, Wendell, 114, 160, 250, 278, 601
Phillips, William S., 263–64, 267
Phoenix (writer), 570
Phoenix, Lloyd, 135, 137–38, 140, 145, 147
Phoenix Line, 252
Phosphate Industry, 535, 540, 546, 549–51, 570, 581–82
Phosphate Mining Company, 513–15
Pickens, Francis W., 6, 9
Pierce, Edward Lille, 66–81, 108–10, 117–18, 161, 226–27, 231, 235–37, 239–40, 437, 443
Pillsbury, Ann, 251
Pillsbury, Gilbert, 251
Pillsbury, Parker, 251
Pilot Boy (1), SS, 493, 496, 522–24
Pilot Boy (2), SS, 524

Pinckney,—Mrs., 220
Pinckney, Abraham, 113
Pinckney, August, 113
Pinckney, Charles Cotesworth, 464
Pinckney family, 90
Pinckney Island, 17, 68, 76, 84, 101, 118, 130–31, 180, 217–18, 247, 286
Plantations: Abigail Jenkins Mackey Plantation, 137, 147; Ashdale Plantation, 97, 269, 461; Battery Plantation, 8, 207, 215; Baynard Plantation, 55, 218; Benjamin Chaplin Plantation, 255; Bluff Farm Plantation, 269; Bonnie Doon, 91; Bonny Hall Plantation, 212; Bostick Plantation, 403; Box Plantation, 11; Boyd Plantation, 310, 349; Braddock's Point Plantation, 101; Brickyard Plantation, 461; Bull's Point Plantation, 89; Burton Hill Plantation, 469; Camp Forest Plantation, 518; Castle Hill Plantation, 125, 144; Cedar Grove Plantation, 255–56, 469; Chapman Bluff Plantation, 292; Charles Heyward Plantation (Rose Hill), 411; Cherry Hill Plantation, 272, 469–70; Coffin Point Plantation, 30, 68, 77–78, 184, 272, 303, 458–59, 470, 561; Coggins Point Plantation, 17, 179; Cuthbert Point, 96; Cypress Plantation, 94, 210, 212–13; Dalton Plantation, 211; Daniel Heyward Plantation, 126, 410; Dathaw Pineland Plantation, 471; Dathaw Point Plantation, 471; Dr. Hutson, 138; Dr. James Kirk, 55, 287; Dr. Joseph Jenkins (Land's End), 274; Dr. William J. Jenkins 25, 60, 78; Drayton Plantation (Fish Haul), 112, 112, 115, 129, 460; Dudley Plantation, 285; Dunn Plantation, 51; Edward Capers Place, 466; Ellis Place, 469; Eustis Plantation, 69–70, 78–79, 161, 182, 190; Fairfield Plantation, 469; Fish Haul Plantation, 112, 112, 115, 129, 460; Flag Pond Plantation, 471; Foot Point, 91; Fripp Point Place, 468; Frogmore, 255–56, 426; Gardner's Plantation, 470; George Chisholm

Plantations (*continued*)
Mackay Plantation, 137; Gregory Plantation, 348; Habersham Plantation, 471; Hardee Plantation, 368; Harrison Plantation, 396; Hermitage Plantation, 255, 470; Homestead Plantation, 471; Honey Horn Plantation, 101, 129; Jack Island, 469; James Kirk Plantation, 55, 287; Jenkins Plantation, 25, 60, 68, 78, 460; Jericho Plantation, 256, 468; John Jeremiah Theus Pope Plantation (Oaks), 76; John Johnson Plantation, 256; John Joyner Smith Plantation (Old Fort), 28; Joseph Allen Smith Plantation, 356; Land's End Plantation, 255, 261, 274; Laurel Bay Plantation, 255–56; Lawton Plantation, 11; Longbrow Plantation, 211; Lowndes Plantation (Oakland), 210, 213, 214; Loton Blacks Plantation, 470; Mackay Plantation, 137, 139, 147; Mary Jenkins Plantation, 460; McTureous Plantation, 470; Means Plantation (Parris Island), Michael Jenkins Plantation, 348, 356, 357, 381; Middleton Stuart Place (Rooplemonde), 468; Milne Plantation, 185–86, 194, 215; Morgan Island, 461; Munger Plantation, 52; Newport Plantation, 212; Nicholls Plantation, 209–11, 213; Oak Forest Plantation, 418; Oakland Plantation, 184, 210, 213, 256, 461, 470; Oaklands Plantation (St. Helena Island), 161, 184, 461; Oaks Plantation (John Jeremiah Theus Pope House), 76–78, 117–18, 160, 255–56, 270, 277, 473; Old Fort Plantation, 28, 110, 153–55, 166, 185, 201, 216, 255–56, 376, 427, 434–35, 444, 449, 466, 474; Otaheita Plantation, 466; Otterburn Plantation (Otterhole), 469; Otterhole Plantation (Otterburn), 469; Palmetto Hall Plantation, 512; Palmetto Hills, 471; Paul Plantation, 211; Perryclear Place, 469; Polawana Island, 470; Pope Plantation (Coggins Point), 17, 44, 179; Proctor Plantation, 11; Ralph Izard Plantation, 356; Rest Park Plantation, 469; Retreat Plantation, 22; Richfield Plantation, 387, 410; Rivers Plantation, 460; Rooplemonde Plantation, 468; Rose Hill Plantation, 411; Rose Hill Plantation (Joshua Nicholls), 211; Roseland Plantation, 88, 383; Seabrook Plantation, 287; Seaside Plantation, 365, 471; Shell Point Plantation, 469; Smith Plantation, *See* John Joyner Smith Plantation; Spanish Wells Plantation, 44, 101, 192, 286, 297, 300; Stoddard Plantation, 52; Stuart Plantation, 356; The Cottage Plantation, 255–56, 471; Thomas A. Huguenin (Roseland), 88, 383; Thomas Elliott Plantation, 146; Tom Baynard Place, 466; Tombee Plantation, 563; Trembledon Plantation, 518; Upper Delta Plantation, 358, 367; Walnut Hill Plantation, 471; Whitehall Plantation (Euhaw Creek), 238, 314, 336, 383; William Aiken Plantation , 294; William C. Heyward, 210, 212; William Hazard Wigg Barnwell Plantation (Laurel Bay), 89, 256, 286, 480; William Pope (Coggins) Plantation, 17, 44; Wm. Perryclear Place, 469, 481; Woodburne Plantation, 211; Woodward Plantation, 204

Planter, USQM, USS and CS, 97–101, 114, 121–22, 124, 134, 136–37, 141–43, 176, 279, 281, 293, 355, 368, 420–21, 424–25, 433, 490, 551, 558

Plaskett, William, 352

Plato, USQM, 292, 294, 342

Pocahontas, USS, 15, 29

Pocotaligo, S.C., 2, 6, 13, 26, 40, 46, 70, 79, 90, 92, 95–96, 190–92, 238, 245–46, 289, 313–16, 320, 342, 344, 348–49, 356, 358–61, 363–64, 377, 379–81, 383, 387, 389, 394, 399, 402, 407, 409–10, 413, 443, 487, 556, 561

Pocotaligo, First Battle of, 123–28

Pocotaligo, Second Battle of, 134–51

Pocotaligo River, 2, 4, 13, 363, 394

Pocotaligo Station, 2, 14, 45, 130, 211, 238, 315, 395, 413, 556

Polite, Frank, 113

Polite, Marcus, 113
Polite, Moses, 532
Polite, York, 488
Polk, Leonidas, 89
Pollitzer, Moritz, 482, 493, 496–97, 499, 543, 559
Pontiac, USS, 309, 311, 344, 349, 390, 392–93, 404
Pope, Daniel, 83
Pope, F. H., Dr., 220
Pope family, 92, 460
Pope, George, 331–33
Pope, H. R., 220
Pope, Harry, 113
Pope, J. J. T., 76, 220
Pope, Joseph Daniel, 441–43
Pope, Sam, 142
Pope, Squire, 220
Pope, Tom, 113
Pope, W., 220
Porcher, Mattie, 571
Porcher, Olivia, 571
Port of Beaufort, 499, 530–31
Port Royal, Battle of, 3, 32
Port Royal (town on Hilton Head), 101–103, 243, 297–99
Port Royal (town on Port Royal Island), 498–502, 504–8, 510, 517–19, 521–22, 524, 527, 530–32, 536–39, 549, 556–57, 561, 563, 583, 585
Port Royal and Augusta Railroad, 490, 492, 499–508, 510–11, 520, 522–25, 531, 553, 559, 569
Port Royal Direct Trade and Colonization Society, 517
Port Royal Expedition, 19–23, 33
Port Royal Experiment, 19, 60–82, 122, 161, 226, 228, 238–40, 248, 252–74, 282, 365–66, 454–56, 473–78
Port Royal Ferry, 6, 8–10, 22–23, 25, 38–39, 41–42, 44, 46, 130, 186, 190, 193–94, 224, 286, 342, 363, 379
Port Royal Ferry, Battle of, 38–49
Port Royal Harbor and General Shipping Company, 518
Port Royal Island, 8, 22, 37–38, 42, 60, 92, 118, 128, 169, 181, 185, 196, 208, 215, 232–33, 271–73, 300, 305, 376–77, 418, 444, 450, 461, 515, 575
Port Royal Naval Station (1861–1865), 103–104, 151–52, 175, 225, 237, 246, 300
Port Royal Naval Station (1877–1901), 484, 489–91, 537–40, 584
Port Royal Pilots Association, 533–34
Port Royal Phosphate Company, 512
Port Royal Real Estate and Improvement Company, 518
Port Royal Relief Committee (Philadelphia), 114
Port Royal Sawmill, 493, 509, 532
Port Royal Sound, 1, 2, 4, 11, 15, 28, 35–36, 43, 56–57, 62, 84, 132, 188, 225, 283–84, 300, 310, 418, 434–35, 442, 446, 493, 521, 525–28, 530–39, 549, 560
Port Royal Standard and Commercial, 547, 552
Porter, Horace, 19, 51, 53–54, 58–59
Porteous, John, 565
Potomac, USQM, 128
Potter, Edward A., 297, 306, 311, 321–23, 325–27, 329, 335, 343–46, 348, 350, 386, 416, 421
Powhattan, USS, 538–39
Pratt, N. A., 511
Preble, George Henry, 308–12, 314, 327, 348, 351–52, 363–64
Preemption, 182–83, 252–74, 278–79
Preston, Edward V., 605
Price, Edmund, 74, 77
Price, Philip Smith, 292
Priester family, 92
Prince, Colonel (1st S.C. Private), 113
Prince, Henry, 412–13
Prince William Company, 571
Prince William Parish, 83, 90, 93, 97, 127, 418, 445, 481, 556, 561
Prince William Parish Church (Sheldon), 93, 409
Prioleau, Alice Chisholm, 512
Prioleau, Ann Julianna, 467
Prioleau, Julianna M., 467–68
Pritchard, Edward, 159, 182

Pritchard, Oliver, 468
Pritchard, Paul, Dr., 220, 543, 564
Provost Circuit Court, 548–49
Public Accommodations Act, 554

Quad (1st S.C. Private), 113
Quakers, 77, 365, 542
quarantine stations, 133, 534, 539

R.R. Spaulding, USQM, 176
Radcliffe, James D., Colonel, 6
Rains, Gabriel J., 246
Rains, George W., 11
Ramsey, Alexander, 421
Randolph, William J., 216
Ransier, Alonzo, 546
Ravenel, St. Julien, 511
Ravenel and Holmes, 522–23
Raysor, Henry C., 92, 313, 315, 324
Read, Buchanan, 232
Rebel Troop, 92
Red Shirts, ix, 557–60, 562, 568, 571, 584
Reed, Joseph S., 581
Reed, George, 579, 581–83, 585
Reed, William B., 266–67
Reconstruction, 60–62, 225, 227, 254, 430, 437, 439–40, 445, 452–53, 455, 458, 460, 462–64, 474–75, 478–78, 480–92, 497–98, 533, 535, 541–44, 547–48, 552, 556–58, 561–62, 564, 566, 571, 579, 581, 585–86
Reconstruction Acts, 440, 458, 464
Red Bank, 10
Regular Republicans, 544, 546–47, 576, 579–80, 582–83
Reid, B. C., 572
Reid, David, 333
Reid, George, 577
Reid, Whitelaw, 419, 430–33, 436
Reliance (tug), 523
Relief, USQM, 136
Republican Blues, 93
Republican Party, 61–62, 67, 74–75, 105, 159, 241, 271, 477, 483–86, 489, 541, 544–47, 558–59, 563, 567, 576, 578, 580, 583–85
Republican Printing Company, 567

Resolute, CSS, 354–55
Reynolds, A.C., 578, 582, 585
Reynolds family, 461
Reynolds, John F., 103
Reynolds, Thomas J., 487, 577, 579–80, 583
Reynolds, William, 103–104
Reynolds, William H., 61–64, 67–68, 70, 78
Rhett, Alfred, 84, 86, 88
Rhett, Andrew Burnett, 86, 89
Rhett, Albert, 467
Rhett, Benjamin Smith, Sr., 86
Rhett, Edmund, xiv, 7, 28, 83, 159, 182, 386, 441, 465
Rhett, Edmund Smith, 86, 450
Rhett, Eliza M., 467
Rhett family, xiii, 463
Rhett, James, 86
Rhett, James M., 577
Rhett, John Grimké, 86
Rhett, Julius Moore, 86
Rhett, Mary, 467
Rhett, Robert Barnwell, Sr., 83, 85–86, 289, 377–78, 448, 465, 501
Rhett, Robert Woodward (son of R.B. Rhett, Sr.), 87
Rhett, Sallie, 465
Rhett, Thomas Grimke, 86
Rhett, T. M. Stuart, 467
Rhett, Thomas, 289
Rhett, Thomas Moore, 85
Rhett, Thomas Smith, Jr., 85, 467
Rhett, Thomas Smith, Sr., 85
Rhett, William Haskel, 86
Rhode Island troops:
    Artillery-Regiments: *2nd,* 62; *3rd,* 18, 39, 41, 50, 53, 110, 134, 136, 137, 140, 142, 143, 147, 149, 180, 193, 195, 209, 210, 212, 213, 218, 294, 305–307, 321, 342, 351; Companies: *A,* 193, 305, 306; *C,* 41; *G,* 141; *H,* 110; *I,* 37
Rhodes,—(Captain Pilot), 531, 534
Rhodes and Bold, 267
Rhodes, Celia M., 466
Rhodes, George, 466
Rhodes, John H., 471

rice, xiii, 72, 172, 190, 208–9, 211, 214, 354, 373, 497, 549–52, 556, 561, 573
Rice, Calvin A., 352
Rich, John, 509
Richards, 490
Richardson, E. B., 572
Richardson family, 469
Richardson, H. W., 503
Richardson, James G., 280
Richardson, Joe, 488, 490
Richardson, Sambo, 458–59
Richardson, William, 463
Richmond, L. (1st Mass.), 136
Ricker, Frank, 496
Ricker, George F., 493, 566
Rifle Clubs, 548, 558
Riley, B. M., 553
Riggs, Emma Julia, 468
Riggs, Luther G., 120
Riley, George O., 571
Riley, Owen, 323
Riley, W. A., 556
Ripley, Roswell Sabine, 3–7, 9, 12–13, 97, 99
Ritter, Abram, 113
Rivers, 459
Rivers, Elias, 468
Rivers family, 91, 460
Rivers, J. C., 480
Rivers, Jane O., 468
Rivers, January, 582, 585
Rivers, Prince, 114, 119, 155, 169, 173, 258–59, 266–67, 279, 281
Rivers Bridge, 389, 396, 399–400, 424
Robbers Row, 101, 180, 298
Robbins and Appleton Company, 267, 418
Roberds, William George, 83
Robert, Henry Martyn, 393
Robert's Rules of Order, 393
Roberts, W. G., 573
Robertson, Beverly, 245, 289, 334–35, 349, 351–52, 357
Robertson, Judge, 549
Robertville, 313, 320, 338, 362–63, 368, 381, 393–94, 400–403, 406–8, 548

Robinson,—Sgt. (Rutledge Mounted Rifle), 148
Robinson, Hamilton, 487
Robinson, Jacob, 251
Robinson, Jonathan, 522
Robinson, Joseph, 563, 577
Robinson, Stepney (Dr. Buzzard), 487
Rodgers, Christopher Raymond Perry, 16, 42–47, 58, 109, 149–50
Rodgers, John, 16, 49, 51, 53, 173, 224, 230
Rodgers, S. H., 514
Rodgers, Samuel Henry, 576–77
Rogers, James, 155, 198, 245
Rogers, Seth, 155, 160, 165, 172, 184–85, 196, 204–5, 215, 230, 232, 234, 237
Rollin, Catherine de Medici, 485
Rollin, Charlotte Corday, 485
Rollin, Francis Ann, 485, 545
Rollin, Louise Muhlbach, 485
Rosecrans, William S., 600
Ross, Samuel, 368
Rowan, Stephen, 424
Rowse family, 92
Rudell,—Dr., 559
Rudell, J. H., 571
Ruffles, T. Edwin, 74
Rundle, R. P., 527
Russell, Ruth, 204
Rushing family, 91
Russia, USQM, 428, 430
Rust, John D., 149
Ruth, Grafton Geddes, 142
Ruthinas (bark), 533
Rutledge, B. Huger, 245
Rutledge, Benjamin H., 138

St. Augustine, 56, 107, 281, 375
St. Helena Episcopal Church, 22, 90, 92, 134, 149, 170, 200, 240, 278–79, 462, 507
St. Helena Island, 7, 25, 37, 63, 65, 68, 70, 76, 78, 96, 109–10, 117–18, 128, 160, 176, 179, 183–84, 192, 221, 227–28, 230–31, 233, 247, 249, 251, 255–56, 258, 261, 263, 269, 273, 275–76, 278, 295, 300, 303, 330, 370, 375, 417–18,

St. Helena Island (*continued*)
    426, 432, 437, 441, 445, 449, 454–55, 458, 460–61, 470–71, 473, 479, 487, 497, 524, 532, 545–46, 563, 574, 576, 578, 610
St. Helena Parish, 62, 83–85, 157, 254–55, 257, 273, 441, 481, 611
St. Helenaville, 83, 118, 239, 255, 278, 298, 375, 418
St. Lawrence (bark), 530
St. Louis, USS, 309
St. Luke's Church (Fla.), 465
St. Luke's Parish, 88, 97, 157, 441, 444–45, 448, 481, 497, 611
St. Peters Guard, 92
St. Peters Parish, 83, 89, 91–92, 97, 157, 313, 403, 408, 441, 448, 481, 556, 561, 569
St. Simons Island, 153, 163, 174, 217, 221, 372
Salisbury, Alfred, 78
Salisbury, Edward, 78
Salkehatchie, S.C., 2, 130, 138, 190–91, 211, 359, 388–89, 394, 397, 411–12
Sam (1st S.C. Private), 113
Sampson,—Sgt., 113
"Sambo's Right to be Kilt" (poem), 187
Sampson, CSS, 354–55
Sams,—Deputy Sheriff, 551
Sams,—Major, 8
Sams, B. B., 182, 236, 494, 496, 509
Sams, Calhoun, 470
Sams, Caroline, 471
Sams, Elizabeth, 266–67, 470
Sams, Eugenia, 470
Sams family, 90, 92, 465
Sams, J. Graham, 470
Sams, Lewis R., 117, 181, 232, 470
Sams, Miles Brewton, 469
Sams, R. R., 494, 564
Sams, Richard F., 471
Sams, Robert W., 471
Sams, Sarah, 470
Sams, Sarah G., 470
Sams, Sarah J., 470
Sams, Stanhope, 465, 468
Sams, Thomas F., 471
Sams Point, 2, 522

Samuels, William, 533–34
San Antonio, SS, 523
Sanders family, 92
Sanders, J. O. H., 548, 573
Santos, Antone, 534
Saratoga, USS, 539
Sauls family, 92–93
Sauls, R., 569
Savage, A. L., 218–19
Savage Islands, 55
Savannah, Ga., 4–6, 11, 85, 91, 95, 129, 131, 142–43, 177, 190, 244, 246, 251, 283, 290–91, 315–17, 320, 338, 367–68, 387, 392–94, 402, 404, 415, 434, 489, 493, 508, 522–24, 532, 549; and Fort Pulaski, 7, 13, 31–37, 48–59; capture and occupation by Sherman, 312–13, 340–41, 349–63, 370, 372–85
Savannah River, 2, 5–6, 10, 13, 17, 35, 49–56, 59, 85, 92, 97, 130, 138, 190–91, 208, 283, 288, 312–13, 338, 340–41, 349, 355, 357, 359, 361, 367, 381, 383–85, 387–90, 392–95, 401–403, 434, 503, 511, 536, 538, 552, 556–58
Sawyer (1st S.C. Private), 113
Saxton, Edward "Eddie," 435
Saxton, Elizabeth "Tilly" Thompson, 201, 204, 250, 377, 387, 422, 426
Saxton, Mary, 387
Saxton, Rufus, 110–11, 113, 142, 156, 159–60, 174, 194–96, 201–2, 204, 207–8, 221, 227, 232–33, 236–37, 248–52, 275, 387, 422–26, 431–34, 443, 451, 456, 475, 488, 493–94; with expeditionary force, 18–21, 60, 62, 64, 66, 68, 78, 82; takes command of experiment, 107–108; as military governor, 108, 117–19, 161–70, 224, 226, 280, 369, 386, 428–29; black troops, 121–22, 132, 153–56, 161–73, 198, 216, 221, 281, 283–84, 414–18; cemetery, 129; conflict with Brannan, 132, 149, 152; conflict with Gillmore, 208, 226, 232, 233; tax sales, 181–86, 243, 253–73; reconstruction activities, 225,

298, 421; and Sherman, 365, 370–72, 374, 387; and Howard, 370, 420; implements field orders #15, 374–75, 386, 414–18, 421; and Stanton, 376–77; and Foster, 414–18; Freedmen's Bureau, 429, 436–37, 441, 445–47, 450, 457, 472; and Jefferson Davis, 435–36
Saxton, Willard, 377, 414, 416–17, 421–23, 426–27, 435–36, 447
Saxton House, 280, 502
Saxton's Dock, 129
Saxtonville, 418, 426, 432
Scanlan, Annie E., 469
Scanlan, Patrick, 493
Scheper, E. A., 495, 502, 567–68
Scheper, F. W., 495–96, 524, 566, 568
Schley,—Mr., 549
Schools: Beaufort Town School, 182, 275, 434, 474, 480–81; Garden's Corner School, 481; Gray's Hill School, 480; Higginsonville School, 481; Laurel Bay School, 480; Mather Industrial School, 474; Oakland School, 480; Old Fort School, 370, 377, 449, 481; Parris Island School, 481; Penn School, 160, 164, 275–76, 370, 426, 455, 460, 473–74; Perryclear School, 481; Stuart Point School, 481; Walker School, 480
School Farms, 255, 257, 276–77, 460, 473
Schwartz, W. D., 533–34
Scott, Moses, 543
Scott, Robert K., 452, 512, 544
Scott, Tom, 505
Scott, V. S., 488
Scott, Vincent, 564
Scott, Winfield, 33
Scovill, N. R., 476
Screven, Henry, 83
Screven, John, 144
Screven's Ferry Road, 190, 192, 367–68
Screven's Rice Canal, 125–26
Sea Island Hotel, 267, 491, 494, 503, 509, 538, 547, 586
Sea Island (Chemical) Phosphate Company, 512, 523
Sea Weed, SS, 538
Seabrook, E. M., 468

Seabrook, F. B., 468
Seabrook family, xiii, 90, 186, 286
Seabrook, George R., 468
Seabrook, J. McL., 468
Seabrook, James, 220
Seabrook, John L., 313
Seabrook, Prince, 113
Seabrook, S.C., 504
Seabrook, Thomas L., 92
Seabrook, William B., 368
Seabrook Ferry, 41–42, 46, 130
Seabrook Landing, 17, 51, 57, 101, 297
Sears, Joseph H., 101, 440
Searson, S.C., 502
Secessionville, Battle of, 128, 180
Second Baptist Church (Savannah), 416
Second Confiscation Act, 117, 122, 153, 229
Selfridge, James L., 393–94, 402
Seneca, USS, 18, 22–23, 25, 27–28, 43, 46–47
Sentinel, USQM, 209
Serrell, Edward Wellman, 18, 49–50
Seventh Baptist Church (Baltimore), 65, 79, 426
Seward, William (Minister), 278
Seward, William (Secretary of State), 153, 166, 172, 426
Seward, William T., 515
Seymour, Truman, 152, 170, 173, 177, 181, 189, 235, 284, 291
Shaw, Francis G., 73, 250
Shaw Memorial Institute, 475
Shaw, Robert Gould, 217, 221, 228–32, 235–37, 241, 421, 475
Sheldon, S.C., 497, 504, 559, 583
Sheldon Church, 93, 409. *See also* Prince William Parish Church
Sheppard, John C., 581–83
Sheppard, W. H., 577
Sheridan, Irene Rucker, 451
Sheridan, Philip, 451
Sherman, John, 421
Sherman, Thomas West, 17–24, 27–28, 30, 32–33, 35–38, 41–42, 44, 48–50, 52, 56–61, 63–64, 71–73, 77–78, 101, 104, 106, 108, 116, 122–23, 201, 208, 491

Sherman, William Tecumseh, 17, 85, 88–91, 301–3, 307–8, 312–13, 318–19, 321, 338, 340–42, 349, 353–57, 362, 365–66, 421, 428–31, 436–37, 440, 448, 451, 461, 472, 491; invades Beaufort District, 367–415
Shorter, John F., 330
Shoup, Francis A., 89
Shuman, W. B., 555
Sickles, Daniel E., 446–47, 450, 459
Silliman, Anna, 350
Silliman, Jonathan, 350
Silliman, William, 305, 344, 348, 350–51, 354, 364
Sillimansville, 418, 476
Simmons, Ben, 562
Simmons, D. G., 572
Simmons, Joe, 488
Simmons, M., 481
Simpson, William D., 486, 563, 568
Sinclair, Edward, 202
Singleton, Daniel, 550
Singleton, Henry, 113
Sisson, James F., 74
Sizer, Merritt, 266–67
Skinner, R. M., 125
Skull Creek, 15–16, 31, 57, 93, 180, 218, 310, 535
Skylark (schooner), 531
slaves, 3, 6–9, 11, 16–17, 22–30, 32–33, 36–40, 42, 59, 101–102, 117–18, 122–23, 126–27, 134, 154, 158, 162, 166–68, 170–72, 183–85, 197, 207–9, 211–16, 221, 227, 234, 236, 245, 248, 254, 298–99, 338, 371–72, 374–76, 378, 382, 384, 392, 406, 408, 414, 422, 429–30, 432; Freedom Jubilee, 40; Port Royal Experiment and, 60–82; disloyalty to masters, 84, 96–97, 359, 364; arming of, 108–17, 120–21
Sligh, W. H., 146
Slocum, Henry W., 354, 356, 363, 381, 384–85, 387, 390, 392–94, 400–401, 403, 407, 537
Small, I., 113
Small, Stephen, 390–91
Smalls, Ben, 549

Smalls, Elizabeth "Lizzie." *See* Bampfield, Elizabeth Smalls.
Smalls, Elizabeth "Lizzie," 98, 489. *See also* Bampfield, Elizabeth Smalls
Smalls, Hannah, 98
Smalls, Lydia, 90, 98
Smalls, Robert, 90, 114, 124, 149–50, 162, 176, 178, 293, 497, 562; escapes in Planter, 97–101; visits Washington, 119–23; ironclad attack on Charleston, 188–89; purchases house, 267; Captain of the *Planter,* 279–81, 355, 368, 420–21, 424–25, 433; court case over home, 460, 463; schools, 474; political leader and career, 477–91, 542–47, 554, 558–60, 566–68, 575–76, 578–80, 583–85; and naval station, 536; Combahee riots, 551–52
Smalls, Robert, Jr., 98
Smalls, William H., 461
Smart, F. F., 569
Smart family, 92
Smart, H. J., 569
Smart, Henry C., 92, 219, 443, 569
Smart, Uncle, 254
Smith, Abram D., 157–59, 182–83, 227, 253–54, 257, 260, 262–64, 268, 69, 271, 273–74, 280–81
Smith, Andrew, 330–31
Smith, E. M., 488
Smith, Elizabeth, 466
Smith family, 91, 93
Smith, Giles Alexander, 395, 399
Smith, Gustavus, 5, 316–20, 323–25, 328, 330, 336, 338
Smith, Helen, 466
Smith, John E., 382–84, 387
Smith, John Joyner, 28, 76, 110, 153–55, 184–85, 201, 215, 369
Smith, Joseph Allen, 356
Smith, Robert N., 74
Smith, Samuel M., 137
Smith, W. W., 573
Smith, Wilson M., 218–19
Smithsonian Institution, 64
Smoke, Agnes, 468
Snelling family, 92

Snipe, John, 553
Sonoma, USS, 309, 311, 342, 344, 390
Soule, Charles C., 303, 330
Soule, Richard, Sr., 34
South Carolina Constitution of 1865, 443–44, 448, 450
South Carolina Constitution of 1868, 477–82, 484–85, 541, 544
South Carolina Constitution of 1895, 487, 586
South Carolina Military Academy, 340
South Carolina National Guard, 488, 490, 545, 548, 560, 584
South Carolina Phosphate and Phosphatic River Mining Company, 512, 514
South Carolina Savings Bank, 475
South Carolina State University, 487
South Carolina troops (C.S.A.): Heavy Artillery- Regiments: *1st (regulars)*, 88; *1st (artillery)*, 84, 86; Battalions: *18th (Siege Train)*, 4, 5; *Co. A*, 346, 360; Light Artillery-Battalions: *3rd (Palmetto)*, 192, 290; *Co. A (Furman)*, 192, 219, 238, 245, 290, 293–94, 314–15, 317, 320, 325, 359, 361, 398; *Co. F (Chesnut)*, 233–34; *Co. G (DePass/DeSaussure)*, 290, 246, 359–61; Light Artillery-Companies: *Beaufort Volunteer*, 2, 8, 84, 87–89, 92–97, 122–31, 138, 144, 145, 191, 192–96, 244, 285, 288, 290, 314–17, 320, 324, 359–61, 389, 428, 491; *Colcock*, 246, 290, 313; *Girardey*, 360, 361; *Johnson*, 359, 360; *Lafayette*, 138, 143, 246, 290, 314, 316, 317, 359–61; *Preston*, 191; *German (Bachman)*, 246, 286, 290, 314, 320, 360; *Inglis (Charles)*, 334, 361, 618; *Rutledge Mounted Rifles (horse artillery)*, 211, 246, 346, 618; *Washington*, 290; Infantry-Regiments: *1st*, 89; *2nd*, 87, 88; *9th*, 6, 92, 94; *11th*, Companies: *A (See* Beaufort Volunteer Artillery); *B (St. Paul's Rifles)*, 92–93; *C (Summerville Rifles)*; 92–93; *D (Whippy Swamp Guards)*, 94, 143; *E (Hamilton Guards)*, 91–92; *F (Republican Blues)*, 92–93; *G (Butler Guards)*, 92–93; *H (St. George Volunteers)*, 92–93; *I (Colleton Guards)*, 92–93; *K (Round O Guards)*, 92–93; *12th*, 6; *13th*, 6; *14th*, 6; *15th*, 6; *17th*, 127; 24th, 189, 191; 25th, 87; Battalions: *1st (Charleston)*, 84; *1st (sharpshooters)*, 87, 139, 189–91; Reserves: *1st*, 359–61; *2nd*, 359–361; *3rd*, 359–61; *6th*, 361; *8th*, 361; Militia-Regiments: *1st*, 359, 360; *2nd*, 359–361; *3rd*, 359–61; *4th*, 359–361; *17th*, 87; *South Carolina State Cadets*, 346, 347, 360; *State troops: 2nd*, 346; Cavalry- Regiments: *1st*, 293, 346, 360–61; *2nd*, 91, 141, 218, 246, 317, 322, 324, 328, 344, 346, 351, 354, 360, 361, 380, 389, 390, 395, 397, 398; *4th*, 218, 245, 246; *5th*, 191, 246; *7th*, 87; Battalions: *1st*, 125, 138; *2nd*, 125, 139; *8th*, 361; *17th*, 138; *Reserve Cavalry*, 361; Companies: *Charleston Light Dragoons*, 91, 138, 140, 144, 145; *Kirk (Partisan Rangers)*, 144, 246, 334, 361; *Rutledge Mountain Rifles (Trenholm)*, 144; *Trezevant*, 6; Militia: *1st S.C. Mounted Militia*, 6–9, 91; Troops-South Carolina State Troops: *National Guard (black militia)*, *2nd Regiment*, 488; *3rd Regiment*, 488, 490, 545, 548, 551, 556, 560, 562, 565, 584; 3rd Regiment, Mounted Rifles (white militia), 572; *Co. A Brunson*, 572; *Co. B Early Branch*, 572; *Co. C Hoover's Station*, 572; *Co. D Branch Camp*, 572; *Co. E Brunson*, 571, 572; *Co. F Whippy Swamp*, 573; *Co. G Lawtonville*, 573; *Co. H Nixville*, 573; *Co. I Matthew's Bluff*, 573; Companies: *Allendale*, 571; *Prince William*, 571
South Carolina troops (U.S.A.): Infantry-Regiments: *1st (See: 33rd USCT)*, 108–17, 132, 153–56, 159, 161, 163, 169, 172–73, 184, 194–96, 204–205, 215, 229, 234, 238, 243–45, 249–51, 259, 266, 267, 279, 281, 284, 293, 354, 381, 417, 452–53, 458, 474, 488 ; *2nd (See: 34th USCT)*, 174, 184, 186, 201, 205, 207, 215, 228–29, 233, 235, 243, 292, 304, 331, 334, 443; *3rd (See: 21st USCT)*, 206, 216, 218, 229, 238, 241, 243, 245, 281, 420, 422;

South Carolina troops (U.S.A.) (*continued*)
    4th (See: 21st USCT), 243; 5th (21st USCT), 243
Southern, J. P., 518
Special Field Orders Number 15, 372, 375–76, 405, 414–15, 421, 440–41, 451
Special Field Orders Number 120, 405
Speidel, John, 140
Speight, A. M., 508
Sprague, Katherine J. Chase, 62
Sprague, William, 62, 64
Spring Island, 287, 518
Springer,—Captain, 612
Sproston, J. Glendy, 26
S.R. Spaulding, USQM, 176, 595
Stadelbauer, Joseph, 393
Standley family, 93
Stanton, Edwin, 64, 72, 81, 106–8, 111, 114–15, 117, 119–21, 132, 198, 217, 227, 229, 241, 370–72, 375–77, 392, 414–15, 417, 422, 429, 446
Stafford's Crossroads, 554–56
Star of the South, USQM, 181
Starkweather, John B., 34, 59
Starlight, USQM, 134
Steedman, Charles, 135–37, 148
Steinmeyer, John H., 572
Steinmeyer and Stokes Mill, 509–10
Stephen (1st S.C. Private), 113
Stephens, Alexander, 434
Stettin, USS, 391
Stevens, Clement H., 191
Stevens, George, 553
Stevens, Hazard, 77, 109
Stevens House, 370, 477, 488
Stevens, Isaac Ingalls, 18, 20, 21, 37–39, 41–48, 60, 63–64, 76–78, 85, 102, 108–9, 124–24, 127–28, 297
Stevens, Sam, 113
Stevens, Thaddeus, 429
Stevenson, Thomas G., 179
Stewart, Christopher, 392
Stickney, Lyman, 169
Stockton, Samuel W., 106
Stoddard, George G., 308, 328, 345, 352
Stokes, B. E., 573

Stokes family, 92
Stokes, William, 127, 244–45, 556, 572
Stone, Edward E., 294
Stone family, 92
Stone, Henry, 113
Stone Fleet, 24–25, 55–56
Stoney, Adeline, 470
Stoney family, 92, 465, 469
Stoney, George Mosse, 469–70
Stoney, J. J., 220
Stoney Creek Battery, 190
Stoney Creek Presbyterian Church, 408
Stono (tug), 513
Stono River, 86, 97, 99, 124, 127, 279
Stowe, Harriet Beecher, 304
Strange family, 92
Strawbridge, De Witt C., 146
Strickland, William P., 149
Strobhan,—Mrs., 406
Strobhart,—Mr., 220
Strobhart, James, 579
Strobhart, Susan, 469
Strong, George C., 228
Strong, John D., 234
Stuart, Emma, 469–70
Stuart family, 8, 114, 469
Stuart, Henry "Hal" Middleton, Jr., 92–93, 96, 130, 138, 143, 192, 288, 290, 314, 320, 323–25, 328, 330, 338, 361, 468, 491, 494, 496–97, 499, 507
Stuart, James R., 468
Stuart, Middleton "Minny," 94, 468–69
Stuart, Robert, 126
Stuart, Sarah, 468
Stuart, Sarah Barnwell, 462
Sumner, Charles, 67, 74, 183, 429
Sumner Guards, 490
Sundstorm,—Captain, 530
Supreme Court (U.S.), 271, 398, 424, 429, 460, 463
Susquehanna, USS, 15–16
Suter, Charles E., 297
Sutton, Robert, 155, 169, 185, 216, 244
Suydam, James A., 32
Swamp Battery, 353, 363
Swan, Mary E., 470
Swatara, USS, 538

Swayne, Noah, 424
Swayne, Wager, 394, 398

T.J. Jeff Southward (bark), 532
Taftt, Henry S., 43–45
Talbird family, 92
Talbird, Thomas, 579, 581–82
Talbird, Toney, 461
Talbird House, 347
Taliaferro, William B., 357, 359
Tallapoosa, USS, 537–38
Tappan, Lewis, 66
Tar Bluff, 10, 209, 211, 213–14, 390
Tardy, John A., 19
Tattnall, John R. F., 7
Tattnall, Josiah, 35, 54
Tax Sales (1862), 175, 183–84, 238, 253, 259–60, 272–74, 434, 451, 460, 547
Taylor, Silas, 480
Taylor, James E., 74
Taylor, Richard, 312
Taylor, Thomas S., 548
Taylor, William N., 396
Tennessee troops: Infantry-Regiments: *8th,* 9, 14, 48; *16th,* 9, 14, 48
Terentia (bark), 529
Terry, Alfred Howe, 17, 135–36, 138, 141, 144–48, 173, 180, 232–33, 235
Texas, SS, 527
Thirteenth Amendment, 172, 450–51
Thompson, David L., 159, 182, 202
Thomas, Elijah, 331
Thomas family, 93
Thomas Foulkes, USQM, 286–87
Thompson, Elizabeth "Tilly," 170. *See also* Saxton, Elizabeth "Tilly" Thompson
Thompson, George, 424–25
Thompson, H. S., 564
Thompson, J. C., 346
Thompson, James G., 181, 281, 433, 443, 546
Thompson, John G., 267
Thompson, Thomas N., 209, 211, 213–14
Thompson House, 202, 256
Thorpe, David F., 74
Tillinghast, Cornelia, 557
Tillinghast family, 92

Tillinghast, R. L., 557
Tillinghast, W. S., 571
Tillman, Benjamin R., 485, 581–86
Tillson, John, 397, 399
Tilton, Theodore, 424, 426
Timber Industry, 492, 508–71
Tison, John, 571
Tison, W. M., 569
Tison, William McKenzie, 83
Titus, Edgar H., 304, 307, 329, 333–35, 345–46
Tomlinson, Reuben, 160, 251, 365, 472–73, 544–46
Tonking, J. H., 482
Toombs, Robert, 357
Totten, Joseph G., 5, 50
Towne, Laura, 77, 79, 82, 109–10, 118, 160–62, 169–70, 183, 185, 227, 231, 236–37, 275–79, 286, 303, 336, 365, 370, 375, 423, 425–26, 441, 445, 449, 453, 455, 460, 463, 473–74, 567, 576
Townsend, Edward D., 370, 372, 377, 417, 424
Townsend, James, 278
Townsend, W. H., 582
Train, H. F., 220
Transcendentalists, 75, 154–55
Traveller (horse), 10
Trenchard, Stephen Decatur, 489, 539, 540
Trenholm, William L., 125, 138, 144, 211, 288, 290
Trescott family, 463
Trescott, William Henry, 451
Trezevant, James D., 6, 360
Trident (bark), 521
Trotter, James M., 330
Trowbridge, Charles Tyler, 108, 110, 120, 154, 233–34, 356–57, 452–53
Trowell, Thomas J., 408, 625
True Republicans, 544, 546
Trumbull, Lyman, 421
Tubman, Harriet, 102, 209, 213, 215, 236, 248, 252
Tullifinny, Battle of, 344–45
Tullifinny Crossroads, Battle of, 346–48
Tullifinny Hill, 345, 347

Tullifinny River, 2, 4, 6, 134, 190, 343–54, 356, 357, 359–60, 381
Tunbridge Landing, 190, 246, 358
Turner, Gabriel, 293
Tuten, A. J., 572
Tuten, C. W., 572
Tuten family, 91–92
Tuten, J. B., 569
Tuten, T. S., 573
Twiggs, John D., 293–94
Two Sisters Ferry, 340, 355, 357, 368, 381, 384–85, 387, 390, 392–94, 402–3, 408
Tybee Island, 35–37, 49, 54, 56, 58, 295, 532
Tybee Roads, 538
Tyng, Stephen Higginson, 73

Ulmer family, 92
Unadilla, USS, 27–28, 51
Uncas, USS, 136–37, 140
Uncle Smart (freedman), 254
Union Causeway, 355, 358, 367, 382–83
Union Number 1 Fire Engine Company, 489
Union Star Engine Company, 489
Unitarians, 73, 75, 77, 79–80, 149, 154, 156, 168, 244, 276, 278
United Sanitary Commission, 73
United States, USQM, 160
United States Colored (USCT) troops: Artillery-Regiments: *2nd,* 443; Companies *C,* 443; Infantry-Regiments: *9th,* 292; *21st,* 243, 281, 420, 422, 443; *26th,* 295, 305, 307, 321, 329, 335–36, 348, 356, 376, 443; *32nd,* 297, 304–306, 311, 321–23, 326–28, 334–35, 337, 342, 346, 351–52, 443; *33rd,* 243, 279, 354, 356, 381, 450, 452, 458, 487; *34th,* 243, 292–93, 304, 306, 321, 329, 331, 336, 342, 351, 411–12; *35th,* 304, 306, 311, 321, 324, 326–27, 329, 333, 337, 343, 351, 409; *103rd,* 415; *104th,* 415, 443; *105th,* 415; *128th,* 415, 421, 431, 443
United States Sanitary Commission, 205–206, 235–36, 245
United States troops: Corps: *Tenth (X),* 132, 179, 181, 205, 287; *Fourteenth (XIV),* 301, 368, 381, 384, 392, 403, 408; *Fifteenth (XV),* 368, 370, 379, 381–82, 384, 394, 396, 400, 402; *Seventeenth (XVII),* 368, 370, 379, 381, 394–96, 400; *Eighteenth (XVIII),* 176; *Twentieth (XX),* 355, 367–68, 381–82, 384, 393, 401–402, 407, 412; Artillery-Regiments: 1st , 85, 392; Companies *M,* 136, 138; 3rd , Companies *E,* 136, 138; Infantry-Regiments: 3rd, 88; 6th, 443; 11th, 305
Universalists, 149
Upshur, John H., 43

Vaigneur family, 92
Vanderveer, Thorn and Bellows, 417
Van Wyck, Charles H., 248, 252, 258, 304
Van Wyck, Richard T., 393
Varn and Ward Mill, 509
Varnadore family, 92
Varnville, S.C., 502, 504, 509, 517, 546, 549, 559, 561, 564, 570, 572
Varnville Mounted Rifle Club, 556–57, 559, 562
Venus Point, 51–54
Verdier, A. G., 220
Verdier, A. G., Dr., 220
Verdier family, 90
Verdier, Henry, 220
Verdier, James M., 490
Verdier, William Joyner, 497, 559, 577, 579, 581–82, 585
Verdier House, 205
Vermont, 65, 279, 395, 407, 421
Vermont, USS, 103–4, 135
Viele, Egbert Ludovicus, 20, 21, 38, 42, 54
Vincent, W. C., 582
Virginia, 3, 4, 6, 9–10, 22–23, 44, 64, 66–67, 82, 87, 88–90, 11, 117–20, 128, 161, 171, 176, 203, 205–6, 228, 282, 287–89, 291, 296, 304–5, 307, 312, 314, 318, 337, 341, 357, 360, 362, 367, 377–78, 382, 388–89, 411, 422, 424, 430, 434, 436, 461, 476, 511, 517, 566–67
Virginia, CSS, 54, 175

Index 699

Virginia-Carolina Chemical Company, 517
Virginia troops: Artillery-Battalions: *Nelson (Leake's),* 131, 138, 191–92; Artillery-Companies: Cooper's, 191; *Leake's,* 9, 131, 138, 191–92; *Thornton's,* 9; Infantry-Regiments: *3rd (local defense),* 87; *60th,* 9–10
Vixen, USS, 136, 137, 141, 294
Von Harten, H., 63
Von Harten, Herman, 502
Von Harten, William H. 533–34
Voris, Alvin C., 250

W.W. Coit, USQM, 385–86
Wabash, USS, 15–16, 31, 42–43, 58, 99, 107, 122, 132, 135–37
Waddell, J., 569
Wade, Benjamin, 421–22
Wagner, Gus, 22–23
Wakefield, A. Judson, 74
Waldock, James, 74
Waldock, Mary, 74
Walker, Edward T., 462
Walker, George D., 113
Walker, Joseph R., 22, 462
Walker, Joseph W., Rev., 507
Walker, L. J. (Rutledge Mounted Rifles), 147, 290
Walker, Robert J., 95
Walker, Susan, 74–76, 80, 110, 128
Walker, William, 241
Walker, William S., xiv, 90, 95–97, 125–27, 129–31, 138–41, 143–48, 190–93, 196, 199, 208–209, 211–12, 215, 238, 244–46, 283–86, 288
Wall, W. D., 210
Wallace, James, 135
Wallace, John, 495–97
Wallace, Silas, 499, 524
Wallace, William H., 562–63
Walpole, Martha, 468
Walter, G. H., 290
Walton, James, 468
Walton Cornet Band, 303
Wando Fertilizer Company, 511
War Department (Confederate), 5, 12, 119, 196, 288, 377

War Department (U.S.), 19, 23, 32–33, 60, 64, 74, 80–81, 106, 108, 111, 115, 132, 150, 180, 226–27, 229, 241, 243, 281, 295, 374, 377, 392, 415–16, 423, 428–29, 443, 447, 457, 471
Ward, George C., 73
Ward, Julia, 76
Ward, William T., 367–68, 382, 384, 393, 400, 408
Ward's Cotton House, 557
Ware, Charles P., 184, 303
Ware, Harriet, 303
Waring, Andrew P., 113
Warnocks family, 569
Warren, Jeffrey D., 559, 571
Washington (balloon), 34, 59
Washington, D.C., 20, 34, 64, 66–67, 72, 74, 95, 105–6, 108, 111, 119, 121–22, 128, 132–33, 135, 151, 168, 172, 183, 201, 203, 206, 223, 228–29, 240, 257, 259–60, 262, 264, 295, 414, 416, 441, 446–47, 453, 455, 469–71, 475–76, 485–86, 536, 546, 562, 584
Washington, George, 104, 186, 284
Washington, Julius I., 487, 576–78, 580, 582, 585
Washington, R., 566
Washington, Robert, 549, 522
Washington Light Infantry, 85, 290
Washington Navy Yard, 430
Washington Race Track, 450
Water Lily, SS, 493
Water Witch, USS, 136
Waterhouse, Edward A., 195
Waterhouse, George, 490, 493, 495–96, 502, 507, 519–20, 522, 524, 543, 563, 566, 568
Waterhouse, George, Jr., 509
Waters,—(Captain Pilot), 531
Watson, William, 99
Wayanda, U.S.R.C. (revenue cutter), 430–34
Wayland, Frances, 158
Webb, Benjamin C., 360
Webb family, 90
Webster, Daniel, 378
Webster (ship), 529

Weehawken, USS, 188, 224
Weekley family, 92
Welles, Gideon, 100, 151, 222–24, 307, 436
Welles, Mary Jane Hale, 436
Wells, George, 76, 529
Wells, George M., Mrs., 287
Welsh, Thomas, 37
Werden, Reed, 136
Wescoat, J. J., 211
Wesson, Leonard, 74
West, James B., 233
Wever, Clark R., 382
Whale Branch River, 10, 37–38, 41–43, 46–48, 84, 104, 185, 192–94, 196, 199, 316, 379, 500, 508
Whaley, William, 451
Wheeler, Joseph, 357–58, 361–62, 380, 389–90, 401, 408, 434
Wheeler, Thomas, 553, 562
Wheeler, Thomas H., 577
Whipper, Frances Ann Rollin, 485
Whipper, William J., 474, 478–80, 483–88, 542–47, 554–55, 567, 578–79
Whippy Swamp, 94, 395–96, 403, 546
Whippy Swamp Crossroads, 395–97
Whippy Swamp Guards, 93, 143, 573
White, James B., 340
White, Morris, 555
White, Richard, 149
Whitehead, Stephen E., 559
Whiting, William, 229
Whitman, J. A., 495
Whitman, P. M., 507
Whitney, Henry A., 245
Whittier, John Greenleaf, 160–61, 164–65, 169, 364
Wickliffe, Charles, 115–17
Wiggins, Colonel, 488
Wiggins family, 220
Wilcox,—Mr., 25–26
Wilder, Francis E., 478–79, 488, 577
Wildt, Edward A., 322–26
Wilkes, John, 103, 267
Wilkes and Thompson, 266
Willcoxon, John B., 13–14
William Lawrence, SS, 533

William P. Clyde, USQM, 434–35
William Seabrook (Emilie), SS, 628
Williams,—Captain, 555
Williams,—(pilot), 43
Williams, Alfred, 491, 565–66
Williams, Alpheus S., 355, 367, 382–84, 387, 393, 400–401, 407
Williams, Annie, 467
Williams, Benjamin S., 336, 347, 572
Williams, Charles, 113
Williams family, 92, 256
Williams, George Walton, 512
Williams, Harry, 245
Williams, J. C., 149
Williams, J. M., 554
Williams, Jerry, 113
Williams, Paddy, 113
Williams, Sam, 113
Williams, Tamar, 481
Williman Island, 512, 515, 529
Williman Island Company, 512, 529
Willis, James, 324
Willis, Samuel B., 303
Willtown Bluff, 233–34, 291, 294
Wilmington, De., 437
Wilmington, Ma., 74
Wilmington, N.C., 151–52, 300, 312, 338, 357, 431, 447, 461
Wilson, Duncan C., Sr., 68, 258–59, 276, 420–21, 493, 496, 501, 507–10, 512, 519, 525–26, 528, 532, 537
Wilson, Duncan C., Jr., 512, 523
Wilson family, 92
Wilson, Henry, 423–26
Wilson, James, Lt. Col. (C.S.A.), 324
Wilson, James Harrison, 19–20, 50–51, 53–54, 58–59
Wilson, William (Sheriff), 552, 559, 564
Wilson Park, 509
Winfield Scott, SS, 16, 51–52
Winingham,—Mrs., 220
Winn, W., 220
Winona, USS, 309, 311
Winsor,—Mr., 118
Winsor, Ellen "Nelly," 74, 118, 160–61, 169–70, 286
Wisconsin, 105, 158–59, 253, 270, 421

Wisconsin troops: Infantry-Regiments: *2nd,* 158; *3rd,* 355–56; *25th,* 398; *32nd,* 397
Wise family, 92
Wissahickon, USS, 136, 309–310
Wood, William J., 186
Woodford, Stewart L., 329, 331, 344–45, 351
Woodruff, Josephus, 567
Woods, Charles R., 400
Woods, Joshua, 569
Worden, John, 175
Wording, William E., 157–58, 182, 253–54, 260–64, 268, 270–71, 273–74, 386, 445
Worthington, George S., 196
Worthy, Nellie, 471
Wright, Ambrose R., 389
Wright, C. H., 509
Wright, Horace Gouverneur, 16–17, 20–21, 38, 56, 128
Wright, Jonathan J., 474, 478, 481
Wright River, 13, 50–51, 54, 246
Wright's Cut, 11
Wyman, B. F., 138, 143, 572
Wyman, E. H., 573
Wyman family, 93
Wyman, Powell T., 152–53

Xenia, Ohio, 66

Yemassee, S.C., 504, 553–54, 559
Yemassee Station, 2, 502–5, 508, 545
York (1st S.C. Private), 113
Youmans, A. M., 569
Youmans, A. S., 573
Youmans family, 92
Youmans, J. R., 548
Youmans, Lawrence, 571
Youmans, Leroy Franklin, 7, 83, 443–44, 448, 557
Youmans, Leroy W., 518, 567
Youmans, Thomas, 569
Young, Dick, 550
Young, Prince, 550
Young Men's Republican Club, 576
Young, Pierce Manning Butler, 341

Zachos, John C., 74, 76, 168, 172, 204
Zahler, H. M., 569
Zealy, Charles J. "Kit," 317, 320, 322–23, 325, 338
Zealy, William P., 569
Zeppelin, Count Ferdinand Adolf Heinrich August Graf von, 243
Zion Presbyterian Church (Charleston), 425, 431, 453

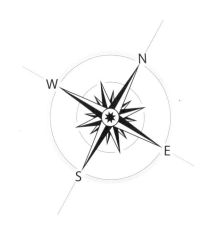